WALKER & WALKER'S
English Legal System

Eleventh Edition

RICHARD WARD

Emeritus Professor of Public Law,
De Montfort University, Leicester

AMANDA AKHTAR

Senior Lecturer in Law,
De Montfort University, Leicester

OXFORD

UNIVERSITY PRESS

OXFORD
UNIVERSITY PRESS

Great Clarendon Street, Oxford OX2 6DP

Oxford University Press is a department of the University of Oxford.
It furthers the University's objective of excellence in research, scholarship,
and education by publishing worldwide in

Oxford New York

Auckland Cape Town Dar es Salaam Hong Kong Karachi
Kuala Lumpur Madrid Melbourne Mexico City Nairobi
New Delhi Shanghai Taipei Toronto

With offices in

Argentina Austria Brazil Chile Czech Republic France Greece
Guatemala Hungary Italy Japan Poland Portugal Singapore
South Korea Switzerland Thailand Turkey Ukraine Vietnam

Oxford is a registered trade mark of Oxford University Press
in the UK and in certain other countries

Published in the United States
by Oxford University Press Inc., New York

© Oxford University Press 2011

The moral rights of the authors have been asserted
Database right Oxford University Press (maker)

Eighth edition 1998
Ninth edition 2005
Tenth edition 2008

Contains public sector information licensed under the Open Government
Licence v1.0 (http://www.nationalarchives.gov.uk/doc/open-government-licence/
open-government-licence.htm)

Crown Copyright material reproduced with the permission of the
Controller, HMSO (under the terms of the Click Use licence)

British Library Cataloguing in Publication Data
Data available

Library of Congress Cataloging in Publication Data
Library of Congress Control Number: 2011922680

Typeset by Newgen Imaging Systems (P) Ltd, Chennai, India
Printed in Great Britain
on acid-free paper by
CPI Antony Rowe, Chippenham, Wiltshire

ISBN 978–0–19–958810–7

1 3 5 7 9 10 8 6 4 2

Preface

This new edition aims, like its predecessors, to provide an accessible and relatively concise exposition of the main principles, rules and issues of the English legal system.

The pace of change within the legal system has not diminished since the last edition three years ago; if anything it has increased. There have been major changes (both actual and proposed) to legal services, the legal profession and civil procedure, the reforms introduced by the Tribunals Courts and Enforcement Act 2007 are now in operation, and the criminal justice system is the subject of ongoing debate. Meanwhile, the Human Rights Act 1998 and the European Convention on Human Rights continue to raise issues of fundamental importance for our legal system and constitution, and the rights given effect through those instruments are now all pervading. Yet in an era of change a text can only ever be a snapshot of the legal landscape at any particular time, and to this end the availability of an Online Resource Centre enables ongoing treatment of changes as they happen.

We have been greatly informed by comments on the last edition from students, colleagues and reviewers, and some of the changes that follow result from this feedback: the chapters on Judicial Review and Costs (as separate issues) have been removed, for example. Other changes have been driven by the sheer complexity of the law involved—sentencing law is now so horribly complicated that it is both impossible and unwise to attempt even a broad-brush overview—whilst constraints of length mean that the separate treatment of youth justice and summary trial have also gone (though key material is dealt with as appropriate in other parts of the text). We have, at the same time, sought to increase accessibility by highlighting the key issues arising in each chapter and posing questions which might encourage further research and help students to identify important themes.

The preparation of the new edition has been greatly assisted by input and comments from a wide range of colleagues and students, and particularly by the great editorial support that we have had from Helen Swann, Heather Smyth and other staff at OUP, and from Julian Roskams (our copyeditor). Responsibility for any errors or omissions is ours. Richard would also like to thank Sarah Ward, whose support has been crucial in the completion of this edition. Amanda would like to thank her husband Jang, and their two beautiful girls Laylah and Samirah, for providing a never-ending supply of love and patience.

The law is stated as we believe it to be at 1 December 2010.

Richard Ward
Amanda Akhtar

Leicester

Outline Contents

Part I Sources of English Law

Part II The Administration of Justice

Part III Civil Proceedings

Detailed Contents

Part II The Administration of Justice

Part III Civil Proceedings

Part IV Criminal Proceedings

Table of Cases

Table of Statutes

Table of Statutory Instruments

Table of EU Legislation

Table of Treaties and Conventions

The English Legal System—An Overview

1

INTRODUCTION

This chapter is designed to give a brief and general overview of the English legal system. The detail is discussed further in the main body of the text.

The principal sources of law

Legislation

The emergence of Parliament as the dominant force within the United Kingdom constitution[1] led to the growth of legislation as a major source of law, transcending both common law and equity in its importance. Its role today is unquestioned. Common law and equity are nowadays concerned essentially with the application and development of existing principles, and whilst this does involve the making of law,[2] courts generally take the view that the development of entirely new principles should be left to Parliament. Legislation can also change or abolish existing common law principles, and amend or repeal earlier statutes.

The nature, creation, and interpretation of legislation are the subject of detailed consideration in Chapter 2 of this book.

Common law and equity

Despite the significance of legislation in modern times, common law, developed through judicial decisions, is still one of the most important sources of legal rules, both civil and criminal. The role of judges in developing the law is discussed at Chapter 9 and the impact of the doctrine of judicial precedent is the subject of detailed consideration in Chapter 3.

The basic principle underpinning the early development of the common law was that a right only existed if there was a procedure for enforcing it *(ubi remedium ibi ius)*,

---

[1] Through the development of the doctrine of the legislative supremacy of Parliament. Under this, no court can question the validity of an Act of Parliament: see *British Railways Board* v *Pickin* [1974] AC 765, [1974] 1 All ER 609.

[2] See further, p 72.

and for this reason substantive law became inextricably bound up with procedure. The need to mitigate some of the effects of such a system, with its technical restrictions, led, in part, to the development of principles of *equity*.[3] Equity developed primarily to correct deficiencies in the common law, and this inevitably meant that the two systems were frequently in conflict. Although the conflict was ultimately resolved in favour of equity,[4] the existence of two systems of law and two sets of courts, each with their own procedures, remedies, and routes of appeal, continued to cause problems of jurisdiction. The Judicature Acts 1873–75 were intended to bring about fundamental reform, and their immediate effect was to create a unified system of courts and procedure. The Acts did not merge the substantive rules and it is still correct to talk about 'principles of equity' or 'equitable remedies', but the unification of the courts did lead to considerable fusion between the two sets of rules. Courts can now apply both rules of common law and equity, irrespective of their origins, and it is often unclear to which of the two historical systems a rule owes its parentage.

The European Union

The European Union is a fundamentally important source of law. The basis of the EU was the European Economic Community, created by the Treaty of Rome in 1957, which later expanded in membership and role to become the European Community. The Union is a supranational body with its own legal personality, institutions, and the capacity to make and enforce laws. The United Kingdom joined the European Community in 1972, and by virtue of the European Communities Act 1972, what is now called EU law takes effect in English law. This often happens automatically, with no further implementation required, and EU law should therefore be regarded as a direct source of English law. The EU, and the nature of EU law, is discussed further at Chapter 4.

The European Convention on Human Rights

The United Kingdom was one of the first signatories to the Convention for the Protection of Human Rights and Fundamental Freedoms in 1950.[5] This Convention, usually referred to as the European Convention on Human Rights (or ECHR), is a treaty of the Council of Europe. A treaty does not have direct legal effect in English law until incorporated into English law by Act of Parliament, and the ECHR was not incorporated directly into English law until the passage of the Human Rights Act 1998. This Act obliges public authorities to act compatibly with Convention rights,[6] and in the event of a breach of those rights, it enables victims to seek a direct remedy in the domestic courts.[7] It also requires courts to interpret legislation in a manner compatible with Convention rights as far as it is possible to do so,[8] although it stops short of allowing the courts to disapply Acts of Parliament that cannot be interpreted

---

[3] See further p 229.   [4] *Earl of Oxford's case* (1615) 1 Rep Ch 1.
[5] The Convention came into effect in 1953.   [6] Section 6.
[7] Section 7.   [8] Section 3; see p 152.

in this way. Both the Human Rights Act and the Convention itself are the subject of more detailed discussion in Chapters 5 and 6.

Other sources

A variety of other sources exist, but these are mainly, although not exclusively, of historic interest. These include *custom* (discussed below), and *textbooks* (which are dealt with in Chapter 3).

Custom

Custom is no longer an important source of law in its own right, although much of the early common law developed through the application by the courts of existing English customs, for example in the area of criminal law. 'Custom' can refer also to conventional trade or business practice, relevant mainly in the law of contract. A third meaning is in respect of local custom, rules of law that apply only in a definite locality. This type of custom *is* a separate source of law, and it has two elementary and unvarying characteristics. First, it must be an exception to the common law, and second, it must be confined in its application to a particular locality or a class of persons within a locality, such as fishermen. Examples of the type of local customary right still existing include rights of way, rights to indulge in sports and pastimes on a village green,[9] and rights to dry fishing nets on land within a parish.[10]

Local customary rights only exist in law when recognized by judicial decision and this means satisfying certain tests.[11] Firstly, the custom must have existed 'from time whereof the memory of man runneth not to the contrary' (time immemorial) and this has been fixed by statute at 1189.[12] In practice, proof of existence in 1189 is rarely available, and the courts are usually satisfied by evidence that the custom has existed for a long time. It must have existed uninterrupted, however, and any interruption of the custom since 1189 defeats its existence. In addition, a custom can only exist by common consent. This means that it must not have been exercised by the use of force, nor secretly, nor under a revocable licence. Thus, where the right to fish depended upon the grant of a licence by the owners of an oyster fishery, it was held that there was no custom since enjoyment had never been as of right.[13] Other requirements are that the custom is certain, that it is consistent with other local customs, and that any duty imposed by the custom is obligatory. Finally, the most important test is that of reasonableness. A custom that is repugnant to the common law cannot be reasonable, and for this reason the House of Lords in one case rejected a custom that enabled a lord to undermine his tenant's land without compensating him for the resulting damage.[14]

[9] *New Windsor Corporation* v *Mellor* [1975] Ch 380, [1975] 3 All ER 44.
[10] *Mercer* v *Denne* [1905] 2 Ch 538.   [11] These tests owe their origins to the work of Blackstone.
[12] Statute of Westminster I 1275.
[13] *Mills* v *Colchester Corporation* (1867) LR 2 CP 476; see also *Alfred F Beckett Ltd* v *Lyons* [1967] Ch 449, [1967] 1 All ER 833.
[14] *Wolstanton Ltd and Duchy of Lancaster* v *Newcastle-under-Lyme Corporation* [1940] AC 860, [1940] 3 All ER 101.

Canon law

Canon law, which is the law of the Western or Catholic Church, has influenced the growth of English law in two ways. First, it was the basis of many concepts formulated in the law courts, and as such it is an original source of other, more modern sources. Examples include the nature of criminal law and its close association with moral fault, the use of imprisonment as a punishment for crime, and, of course, the nature of Christian marriage and family rights. Canon law also influenced the nature of equity, the strong moral content of which is attributable to the fact that the early Chancellors were clerics.

The second way in which canon law became a source of English law was by its application in the ecclesiastical courts. In this context, it was a system of law wholly independent of the common law, and during the Middle Ages the ecclesiastical courts were completely outside the control of the King. Their jurisdiction remained separate from the common law except in the areas of probate and matrimonial jurisdiction, but since 1857 it has been confined to matters affecting members of the Church.[15]

The distinction between civil and criminal matters

The importance of the distinction

Before we look at the court structure itself, it is important to understand the broad difference between civil and criminal matters. It is important for several reasons. First, the terminology used is different. In civil proceedings a *claimant* (formerly called a plaintiff) sues a *defendant* or makes an application for a civil order, while in a criminal case a *prosecutor* prosecutes the *accused*.

Second, the burden and standard of proof differ. In a civil case the party asserting a particular matter bears the burden of proving it, usually to the civil standard of the balance of probabilities. In contrast, the burden of proof in a criminal case normally rests with the prosecution,[16] and the standard is that of proof beyond reasonable doubt. However, this statement disguises the fact that even in a civil case the standard of proof may be high.

The decision as to whether a matter is civil or criminal

This decision is not always easy to make, and it cannot be made simply by asking whether the court that deals with the matter is a civil or a criminal court. It is increasingly possible to identify areas in which the boundary between criminal and civil proceedings has become blurred. For example, the same acts or omissions may give rise to both civil and criminal proceedings. Thus, while a motorist who causes

---

[15] See p 282.   [16] See *Woolmington* v *DPP* [1935] AC 462.

damage, injury or loss of life may well be prosecuted for a motoring offence, that same motorist will almost certainly be liable in damages if sued by the aggrieved party. The relatives of a person who has been unlawfully killed, but in respect of whose death no prosecution has been brought, may sue in tort; ostensibly for compensation, but in reality to provide a forum in which the culpability of the defendant can be established. Similarly, if a rape victim sues his or her assailant, the assailant is liable irrespective of whether he has been successfully prosecuted. Another example is contempt of court, which can be both civil and criminal in nature.

The courts

This text deals with the court system in England and Wales. Scotland and Northern Ireland are separate jurisdictions with their own courts and laws.

The classification of courts

Civil and criminal
It is often convenient to classify courts as *civil courts* and *criminal courts*. Civil jurisdiction is predominantly concerned with compensation or regulation. Criminal jurisdiction is principally penal in nature. This statement is itself an oversimplification, because civil and criminal matters overlap, and often have a wide variety of purposes. To classify courts in terms of their principal jurisdiction is useful for the purposes of exposition, but potentially inaccurate: examples can be found of courts with a predominantly criminal jurisdiction also having some civil jurisdiction (magistrates' courts are an example).

Courts of original jurisdiction and appellate courts
An alternative method of classification is to distinguish between appellate courts and courts of original jurisdiction. Again, however, it is not possible to place all courts into one category or the other. While courts such as the Court of Appeal exercise a purely appellate jurisdiction, and those such as magistrates' courts have no appellate role, many other courts have both original and appellate functions. Indeed, the Queen's Bench Divisional Court is neither a court of first instance nor a court of appeal; it is primarily a court of review. In addition, although the Court of Justice of the European Communities (the European Court of Justice) is not technically a court of appeal, its decisions are binding on all domestic courts.

Courts and tribunals
Strictly speaking, the term 'tribunal' is an umbrella term capable of encompassing not only the bodies that generally use this name, but also those that are usually labelled 'courts'. It also has a narrower meaning, however, and when used in this sense it

refers only to those tribunals that cannot be described as courts. Tribunals currently perform an extremely important role in what can now be described as a system of administrative justice, and are discussed further at Chapter 8.

Courts of record

Historically, the distinction between courts of record and other courts depended upon whether the court maintained records of its proceedings and preserved them in the Public Record Office. The central characteristic of a court of record now is that it has the power to punish for contempt. However, it should be noted that magistrates' courts, which are not courts of record, have a statutory power to punish contempts committed in the face of the court.[17] In addition, the High Court has a common law jurisdiction to punish contempts committed before courts that are not courts of record.[18]

Superior and inferior courts

Traditionally, the most significant division has been between superior and inferior courts.[19] The fact that a court is presided over by judges of the level of High Court does not mean that a court is a 'superior court'. Nor does the fact that a statute describes a court as a 'superior court', although that will be important. It is the nature and function of the body that matters.[20]

The jurisdiction of superior courts is limited neither by geography nor by the value of the cases that they can hear. The Supreme Court, Court of Appeal, High Court, Crown Court, Privy Council, and Employment Appeal Tribunal are all superior courts. The most important of the inferior courts are the county courts and magistrates' courts. One of the distinctive features of inferior courts is that they are amenable to the supervisory jurisdiction of the High Court.[21] However, the Crown Court is also subject to this jurisdiction in the exercise of its appellate functions, even though it is a superior court.[22] The distinction is also important in relation to contempt of court, as the superior courts are able to inflict more stringent penalties than those available to the inferior courts.[23]

---

[17] Contempt of Court Act 1981, s 12: see p 243.   [18] *R v Davies* [1906] 1 KB 32.

[19] Whether a court is an inferior or a superior court can usually be ascertained by reference to its historical origins or, where applicable, to the terms of the statute creating it. If this does not settle the matter it is necessary to look at the nature and powers of the court to see whether they are analogous to those of a superior or an inferior court. See, e.g., *R v Cripps, ex parte Muldoon* [1984] QB 68, [1983] 3 All ER 72, in which the Queen's Bench Divisional Court held an election court (under the Representation of the People Act) to be an inferior court.

[20] See *R v Cripps, ex parte Muldoon* [1984] QB 68, [1983] 3 All ER 72; *R v (Woolas) The Speaker of the House of Commons* [2010] EWHC 3169; *R (Cart) v The Upper Tribunal* [2010] EWCA Civ 859.

[21] See p 256.

[22] The Crown Court is only open to the supervisory jurisdiction of the Divisional Court where jurisdiction is expressly granted by the Supreme Court Act 1981, ss 28 and 29(1). Matters relating to 'trial on indictment' are not within that jurisdiction.

[23] See p 244.

The hierarchy

The court system is hierarchical in nature. At the top of the hierarchy are the *Senior Courts of England Wales*,[24] comprising the Supreme Court (which replaced the judicial function of the House of Lords), the Court of Appeal, and the High Court. The hierarchical nature is reflected in the system of judicial precedent, which stated simply, means that courts lower in the hierarchy are usually bound by the decisions on matters of law by the courts higher in the hierarchy. The hierarchy is shown in Figures 1.1 and 1.2 below in the context of civil and criminal process.

Civil jurisdiction

The main courts dealing with civil disputes are the county court and the High Court. They have an overlapping jurisdiction (see Chapter 7), often, although not always, defined by financial value of the matter being litigated or the allocation to a particular type of court by statute. Wide powers of transfer between the county court and High Court exist.

The High Court comprises three Divisions. The Queen's Bench Division deals typically with a wide range of civil matters, including all matters in contract or tort. It also has a supervisory function, exercised by the Divisional Court of the Queen's Bench Division (now known as the Administrative Court). The Chancery Division typically deals with matters relating to land, trusts, insolvency, and matters of corporate law. The Family Division deals with matters relating to marriage, children, and other family law matters. The Queen's Bench Divisional Court and the Family Division have limited roles as courts of appeal from magistrates' courts and from family courts respectively.[25]

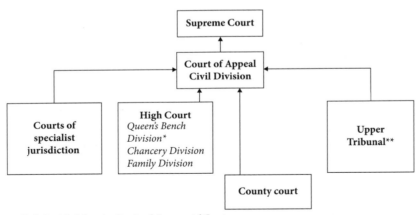

*Includes Administrative Court and Commercial Court

** This structure does not deal with the complete structure of administrative justice created by the Tribunals, Courts and Enforcement Act 2007.

Fig. 1.1 Civil hierarchy

[24] Formerly known as the Supreme Court of England and Wales. [25] See p 256 and p 258.

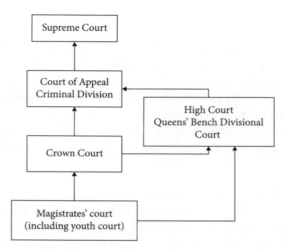

Fig. 1.2 Criminal court hierarchy

Appeals from both these courts lie, generally, to the Court of Appeal (Civil Division) and, on matters of points of public importance, to the Supreme Court.

In addition to theses courts a number of courts of specialist jurisdiction exist. The Patents Court is part of the Chancery Division. The Commercial Court, the Admiralty Court, and the Technology and Competition Court are each part of the Queen's Bench Division.

Criminal jurisdiction

Criminal offences fall into one of three categories: summary-only offences; indictable-only offences; and either-way offences that may be tried either summarily or on indictment. The vast majority of offences are tried summarily in the *magistrates' court* (or, in the case of children or young persons, the *youth court*). Offences that are tried on indictment are tried before a jury in the Crown Court.

Appeals from the magistrates' court lie, on matters of law, to the Divisional Court of the Queen's Bench Division and, in the case of appeals by way of retrial on the facts, to the Crown Court. Appeals from the Divisional Court and the Crown Court lie to the Court of Appeal (Criminal Division). A final appeal on points of law of public importance lie from the Court of Appeal (Criminal Division) to the Supreme Court.

The administration of the English legal system

Because of the piecemeal way in which the English legal system has developed, no single institution has had overall responsibility for its administration. The creation of the Ministry of Justice in 2007 went some way towards addressing this, but other government departments and a growing number of executive agencies and other bodies continue to play a role. For example, the police,[26] Crown Prosecution Service,[27] National Offender Management Service,[28] Youth Justice Board,[29] and Parole Board[30] all perform important functions with regard to the criminal justice system. In addition, Her Majesty's Courts Service provides administrative support for the major courts,[31] while the Legal Services Commission plays a central role in the funding of legal actions.[32] Some of these bodies may not survive the review of non-governmental bodies announced in 2010.[33] The Public Bodies Bill, currently before Parliament, will, if enacted, give Ministers unprecedented powers to abolish a wide range of bodies or offices. Amongst those identified in Schedule 1 to that Bill include the Administrative Justice and Tribunals Council, the Chief Coroner, the Crown Court Rule Committee, Her Majesty's Inspectorate of Court Administration, the Victim Advisory Council, and the Youth Justice Board. It is not yet clear how organizational structures within the English legal system will change, if at all.

---

[26] See Chapter 12.   [27] See p 389.   [28] See 568.   [29] See p 573.
[30] An executive non-departmental public body sponsored by the Ministry of Justice: see Criminal Justice Act 2003, s 239.
[31] See p 232.   [32] See Chapter 11.   [33] *Solicitors Journal*, 28 September 2010.

PART I

Sources of English Law

Legislation

2

INTRODUCTION

This chapter focuses on legislation as one of the two main sources of law within the domestic legal system. Under the United Kingdom constitution Parliament is recognized as being legislatively supreme, and for centuries this has meant that the validity of an Act of Parliament cannot be challenged in any court. When interpreting an Act a court therefore has a duty to seek to give effect to Parliament's intentions, although there are different approaches to this task and the duty has been modified somewhat by developments in European law and human rights. Secondary legislation, by contrast, does not have the same 'supreme' status as Acts of Parliament, and it may therefore be subject to a greater level of judicial scrutiny. This chapter will look at the characteristics of both types of legislation, in addition to examining the principles governing their interpretation by the courts. In particular, it will address the following:

- the distinction between primary and secondary legislation, and the different purposes for which legislation may be made;
- the law-making process;
- the impact of EC law and the Human Rights Act 1998 on the legislative supremacy of Parliament;
- the geographical and temporal operation of statutes;
- approaches to statutory interpretation and the impact of the Human Rights Act 1998;
- specific presumptions and other aids that may influence statutory interpretation.

Legislation and law reform

The broad function of all legislation is to create, alter, or revoke law to give effect to the intention of the legislative body. The functions of Acts of Parliament, which are by far the most important form of legislation, may be classified as follows.

Law reform

Although all statutes are concerned with law revision in the broadest sense, relatively few are concerned with altering or revising substantive rules of law. When statutes are passed to revise existing legal rules, it is usually because these rules have become stale and incapable of adaptation. A statute may also be passed to alter the law following an unpopular decision of a court, and there are many examples of Acts passed with the apparent intention of overruling a House of Lords decision.[1] However, the process of law reform is often more haphazard and piecemeal, and sometimes the impetus for change comes from ad hoc committees, departmental working groups, or Royal Commissions. The Police and Criminal Evidence Act 1984 is one such example, having been enacted following the report of the Royal Commission on Criminal Procedure.[2] More recently, major changes to the civil justice system were implemented following the report of a committee chaired by Lord Woolf.[3] Reviews of the criminal justice and tribunal systems by other committees have prompted similar reforms.[4]

An example of what can happen if law reform is not carefully considered is provided by attempts to reform the system of committal proceedings in criminal cases. Committals for trial were 'abolished' in 1994, to be replaced by a new system of transfers for trial. However, the government soon recognized the force of objections put by those who would have to operate the new system, and the transfer for trial provisions were repealed in 1996 without ever having been introduced. Further changes were included in a 1998 Act, and in 2003 Parliament once again changed the procedures for allocating criminal cases and sending them to the Crown Court.[5]

The Law Commission

A major addition to the machinery of law reform was made by the Law Commissions Act 1965, which established the Law Commissions.[6] Section 3(1) of the Act defines the duty of the Commissions thus:

> [I]t shall be the duty of each of the Commissions to take and keep under review all the law with which they are respectively concerned with a view to its systematic development and reform, including in particular the codification of such law, the elimination of anomalies, the repeal of obsolete and unnecessary enactments, the reduction of the number of separate enactments and generally the simplification and modernisation of the law.

The mission of the Law Commission is to make the law simpler, fairer, and cheaper to use. Reform projects may be included in a programme of work submitted by the Commission to the Minister of Justice, or they may be referred to the Commission by government departments. The process begins with a period of research and analysis of the relevant area of law, and the opinions of academics and professionals will often be

---

[1] Examples are: Parliamentary Papers Act 1840; Limitation Act 1963; War Damage Act 1965; Criminal Evidence Act 1979.   [2] Cmnd 8092 (1981).

[3] Lord Woolf, *Final Report on Access to Justice* (HMSO, 1996): see Part III of this book for a detailed discussion.

[4] Lord Justice Auld, *Review of the Criminal Courts* (HMSO, 2001), discussed further in Part IV of this book; Leggatt, *Tribunals for Users: One System, One Service* (HMSO, 2001), discussed in Chapter 8.

[5] See p 606.

[6] Prior to 1965, the machinery for generating law reform consisted mainly of the Law Revision Committee and the Law Reform Committee, which considered, on their own initiative or at the invitation of the Lord Chancellor, branches of the law requiring change.

canvassed. This is generally followed by the publication of a consultation paper, which will describe the existing problems with the law and suggest possible solutions and reform options. Following a consultation period, a final report is published, and this may include a draft Bill.

The creation of the Law Commissions was an important step forward in law reform. The Law Commission for England and Wales[7] has five full-time Commissioners and a full-time administrative staff, and it has produced a steady flow of reports, recommendations, and draft Bills, many of which have been implemented by Acts of Parliament.[8]

KEY ISSUE

How effective is the Law Commission? By the time of its 43rd Annual Report in 2009, the Law Commission had published 180 law reform reports.[9] The range of these reports is wide, including matters of direct interest to the public, such as reports on consumer and landlord and tenant law, but also reports dealing with highly technical areas of law. In the year 2007–08 covered by the 43rd Annual Report, the reports issued included proposals on proportionate dispute resolution, reform of the law of bribery, intoxication and criminal liability, and the admissibility of expert evidence. Of the 180 reports published, around 135 had been implemented in full or in part, with a further twelve awaiting decision from the government as to implementation. Reports are often cited by appellate courts.[10] However, the success of the Commission's role depends on timely implementation of recommendations for reform. The Law Commission has indicated 'real concern' about the speed of implementation.[11] This is due the acute pressures on parliamentary time.

❓ Questions

1. How might the concerns of the Law Commission be met?
2. Look carefully at the process of legislation.[12] How might technical law reform be speeded up?
3. Is there too much legislation?

Consolidation of enactments

Where a branch of the law has evolved piecemeal, the existing law may effectively be re-enacted in a consolidating statute for the purpose of clarification. There are three sorts of consolidating Acts: (1) 'pure' consolidation (simple re-enactment); (2) consolidation under the Consolidation of Enactments (Procedure) Act 1949, which allows

---

[7] There is a separate Commission for Scotland.

[8] See, e.g.: Landlord and Tenant Act 1988; Law of Property (Miscellaneous Provisions) Act 1989; Children Act 1989; Civil Evidence Act 1995; Contracts (Rights of Third Parties) Act 1999.

[9] Law Commission, *Annual Report 2007–08* (Law Com No 280), Appendix B, p 59.

[10] Fifty-nine citations in the United Kingdom during 2007/08: 43rd Annual Report, *op cit,* at p 12.

[11] 43rd Annual Report, Introduction.   [12] See p 21, and **www.parliament.uk**

'corrections and minor improvements';[13] and (3) consolidation with amendments recommended by the Law Commission. Many of the major consolidating Acts in recent years have fallen into the third category.[14]

Consolidation Acts are not subject to parliamentary debate, but there are special procedures designed to ensure that they do not depart from the provisions that are to be consolidated. The type of consolidation effected appears from the long title of the Act in question.[15] Substantive changes in the law will often be made before the process of consolidation is undertaken. Thus, for example, section 106 of the Crime and Disorder Act 1998 has the side heading 'pre-consolidation amendments'.

Codification

Codification differs from consolidation in that an Act may only be said to consolidate statute law, whereas it may codify both statute law *and* case law. The processes are similar in function, however, in that the object is to simplify and clarify the existing law rather than to effect substantial alterations to it. Notable examples of major codifying statutes include the Sale of Goods Act 1893 (which was later consolidated in the Sale of Goods Act 1979) and the Marine Insurance Act 1906. Since then there has been very little codification, although one notable exception is the Police and Criminal Evidence Act 1984 (PACE). This statute radically altered and codified the existing common law and statutory rules relating to police powers of search, entry to premises, the treatment and questioning of suspects, and the admissibility of confession evidence.

There is a pressing need for codification in many areas of the law, and this is largely due to the manner in which Parliament approaches the task of amending statutes. Rather than producing a comprehensive re-enactment that would enable the law on a topic to be set out in a single Act, piecemeal amendments have often been made, with one statute dealing with a large number of different topics and amending an equally large number of earlier statutes. Subsequently the amending provision may itself be repealed, so that in order to discover what the law is, it becomes necessary to pick one's way through a maze of separate statutory provisions. This situation, in the field of industrial relations legislation, led Sir John Donaldson MR to make the following observation:[16]

---

[13] These are defined by s 2 as amendments that have the effect of resolving ambiguities, removing doubts, bringing obsolete provisions into conformity with modern practice or removing unnecessary provisions or anomalies that are not of substantial importance, and amendments designed to facilitate improvement in the form or manner in which the law is stated. This category also covers any transitional provisions that may be necessary in consequence of such amendments.

[14] Examples are Water Industry Act 1991, Water Resources Act 1991, Social Security Contributions and Benefits Act 1992, Taxation of Chargeable Gains Act 1992.

[15] See, e.g.: Employment Protection (Consolidation) Act 1978 (pure consolidation) (see, now, Employment Rights Act 1996); Road Traffic Act 1988 (Law Commission amendments); Juries Act 1974 (1949 Act 'corrections and improvements').

[16] *Merkur Island Shipping Corporation* v *Laughton* [1983] 2 AC 570 at 594–5, [1982] 1 All ER 334 at 351.

My plea is that Parliament, when legislating in respect of circumstances which directly affect the 'man or woman in the street' or the 'man or woman on the shop floor', should give as high a priority to clarity and simplicity of expression as to refinements of policy. Where possible, statutes, or complete parts of statutes, should not be amended but re-enacted in an amended form so that those concerned can read the rules in a single document. When formulating policy, ministers, of whatever political persuasion, should at all times be asking themselves and asking parliamentary counsel; 'Is this concept too refined to be capable of expression in basic English?' Having to ask such questions would no doubt be frustrating for ministers and the legislature generally, but in my judgment this is part of the price which has to be paid if the rule of law is to be maintained.

Lord Diplock expressly adopted these remarks when the case reached the House of Lords.[17] However the problem continues to bedevil many areas of law. One area that vividly demonstrates this is sentencing in criminal cases, in which legislation, despite attempts at consolidation, remains at times over-complex, and at times incomprehensible.[18] In particular, sentencing law is almost an impossible and complex mess in terms of the clarity and accessibility of the law.

KEY ISSUE

Some believe that the idea of consolidation should be taken to the point of producing a consolidated statute book, in which the whole of our statute law would be arranged under titles and kept up to date by textual amendments. This is not a reform likely to be implemented in the foreseeable future. In May 1973 the government set up the Renton Committee to review the form in which public Bills are drafted, 'with a view to achieving greater simplicity and clarity in statute law'. The Committee reported in 1975[19] and concluded that it would not be practical to consolidate the whole statute book within a limited number of years, nor to do so on the principle of 'one Act, one subject'.

❓ Questions

1. What causes the problem of legislative schemes that are difficult to comprehend?
2. How could this problem be resolved?

Collection and disbursement of revenue

The annual Finance Act implementing the Budget proposals is concerned primarily with the collection of revenue by the Crown. Other Acts, notably the Income and Corporation Taxes Act 1988, fulfil the same function. Conversely, public expenditure is authorized by Parliament annually through Consolidated Fund Acts (which authorize payments out of the Consolidated Fund), and the Appropriation Act (which appropriates public expenditure to specific purposes).

---

[17] [1983] 2 AC 570 at 662, [1983] 2 All ER 189 at 198–9.   [18] See p 683.
[19] *The Preparation of Legislation*, Cmnd 6053 (HMSO, 1975).

Implementation of treaties

Treaties do not form part of English law until they are incorporated into law by Act of Parliament.[20] The United Kingdom, by entering into treaties, undertakes to implement the laws that form the subject matter of those treaties. For example, the directives and decisions of the European Union usually require implementation by statute or statutory instrument,[21] and the United Kingdom may also be obliged to legislate in order to give effect to decisions on the European Convention on Human Rights.[22] Examples of domestic legislation intended to implement other treaties and conventions include the Taking of Hostages Act 1982, the Employment Act 1989, and the Companies Act 1989.

Social legislation

These Acts are varied in their scope and functions but may be classified together as social legislation. Such Acts are concerned with regulating the day-to-day running of the social system rather than with creating criminal offences or rights and duties between individuals, although there is an increasing tendency for Parliament to delegate the power to make regulations of this nature to subordinate bodies.[23]

Forms of legislation[24]

Early legislation in England took several different forms, such as charters, provisions, ordinances, and statutes. At the present day, however, United Kingdom legislation may take one of three forms: Acts of Parliament; delegated legislation; and autonomic legislation.

Acts of Parliament

Legislative supremacy

Parliament is legislatively supreme. By that we mean that there are no limits in law on what Parliament can do. Our membership of the European Union raises important issues but does not affect the theoretical position. Parliament is recognized as sovereign and as possessing unlimited legislative power. This has not always been so,[25] but in modern times it had not been seriously contended that the courts have any power to override the intention of the legislature until *British Railways Board* v *Pickin*.[26] In

---

[20] *Blackburn* v *Attorney-General* [1971] 1 WLR 1037.   [21] See p 124.

[22] See p 143.   [23] See p 26.

[24] This chapter is confined to United Kingdom legislation. For EC legislation, see Chapter 4.

[25] See, e.g., dicta of Coke CJ in *Bonham's case* (1609) 8 Co Rep 113 and of Holt CJ in *City of London* v *Wood* (1701) 12 Mod Rep 669.

[26] [1974] AC 765, [1974] 1 All ER 609.

this case, an attempt was made to impugn the validity of the British Railways Act 1968, on the ground that the British Railway Board had fraudulently concealed certain matters from Parliament and had misled Parliament into an enactment that deprived the plaintiff of his land. If it was surprising that such a point should be pleaded, it was perhaps more surprising that the Court of Appeal should have held that it raised a triable issue.[27] The House of Lords, however, allowed the Board's appeal and restored the judge's order that the pleading be struck out as frivolous, vexatious, and an abuse of process. Accordingly, it is now clear that no court is entitled to go behind that which Parliament has enacted, and this rule is equally applicable to both public and private Acts.

The decision in *R (on the application of Jackson)* v *A-G* suggests that there may be a limited exception to this rule, in that the House of Lords was prepared to consider the validity of an Act made using the modified procedure set out in the Parliament Acts.[28] However, the issue in *Jackson* was whether the terms of the Parliament Act 1911 permitted the use of the procedures set out in that Act to pass further laws (in the form of the Parliament Act 1949). It was not a question of the court investigating how an Act of Parliament had been passed.

The European dimension

In addition, where there is a potential conflict between a UK Act and legislation of the European Union, the courts have power to restrain enforcement of the former. This occurred in *R* v *Secretary of State for Transport, ex parte Factortame (No 2)*.[29] The applicants, who were companies controlled by Spanish nationals, sought to challenge the validity of the Merchant Shipping Act 1988 on the basis that it contravened the EC Treaty and deprived them of their European Community law rights. Since determination of this issue by the European Court of Justice was likely to take some time, the applicants applied for an interim injunction to restrain the Secretary of State from enforcing the Act. The House of Lords initially decided that they had no power to make such an order,[30] but following a reference to the European Court of Justice[31] they granted the applicants the interim relief sought. The effect of this unprecedented decision was to 'disapply' Part II of the Merchant Shipping Act. The decision was taken a stage further in *Equal Opportunities Commission* v *Secretary of State for Employment*,[32] in which the House of Lords held that it was entitled to judicially review legislation to ensure that it complied with European law. On the facts,

---

[27] [1973] QB 219, [1972] 3 All ER 923. For another unsuccessful attempt to have a statute declared ultra vires, see *Manuel* v *A-G* [1983] Ch 77, [1982] 3 All ER 822.

[28] [2005] UKHL 56, [2006] 1 AC 262, [2005] 4 All ER 1253. See further, p 23.

[29] [1991] 1 AC 603, [1991] 1 All ER 70. For the subsequent litigation, see *R* v *Secretary of State for Transport, ex parte Factortame (No 3)* [1992] QB 680, [1991] 3 All ER 769; *R* v *Secretary of State for Transport, ex parte Factortame (No 4)* Case 48/93 [1996] QB 404, [1996] All ER (EC) 301; *R* v *Secretary of State for Transport, ex parte Factortame (No 5)* [2000] 1 AC 524, [1999] 4 All ER 906.

[30] *R* v *Secretary of State for Transport, ex parte Factortame (No 1)* [1990] 2 AC 85, [1989] 2 All ER 692.

[31] Case C-213/89 [1990] ECR I-2433, [1990] 3 CMLR 1.

[32] [1995] 1 AC 1, [1994] 1 All ER 910.

provisions in the Employment Protection (Consolidation) Act 1978 were held to be contrary to European law, and a declaration to this effect was issued.

The impact of EU law on the legislative supremacy of Parliament was considered further in *Thoburn* v *Sunderland City Council*.[33] The appellants had been convicted for selling produce in imperial measurements, contrary to delegated legislation implementing a European directive on the use of metric weights. The appeal by way of case stated centred on the claim that the Weights and Measures Act 1985 (which permitted the use of imperial weights) had, by implication, partially repealed section 2 of the European Communities Act 1972 (which authorizes the implementation of Community obligations by delegated legislation). The Divisional Court rejected this argument and, in doing so, Laws LJ sought to distinguish between 'constitutional statutes', such as the European Communities Act, and 'ordinary' Acts of Parliament:[34]

> There are now classes or types of legislative provision which cannot be repealed by mere implication. These instances are given and can only be given, by our own courts, to which the scope and nature of Parliamentary sovereignty are ultimately confided.

He continued:[35]

> In my opinion, a constitutional statute is one which (a) conditions the legal relationship between citizen and State in some general overarching manner, or (b) enlarges or diminishes the scope of what we would now regard as fundamental constitutional rights.

Other statutes said by Laws LJ to be immune from implied repeal include Magna Carta, the Human Rights Act 1998, and the Scotland Act 1998.

In an earlier decision, Lord Hoffmann had made similar observations about Parliament's ability to legislate contrary to fundamental human rights principles:[36]

> The principle of legality means that Parliament must squarely confront what it is doing and accept the political cost. Fundamental rights cannot be overridden by general or ambiguous words...In the absence of express language or necessary implication to the contrary, the courts therefore presume that even the most general words were intended to be subject to the basic rights of the individual.[37]

KEY ISSUE

The question remains: is it still accurate to say that there are no legal limits on what Parliament may do by Act of Parliament? It is true that the *Factortame* litigation shows that a court must give effect to European law, even to the extent of disapplying an Act of Parliament. The reality is that Parliament cannot legislate contrary to European law, and that the latter must take precedence. Theoretically, this is because Parliament has required

[33] [2002] EWHC 195 (Admin), [2003] QB 151, [2002] 4 All ER 156.
[34] Ibid at [60].   [35] Ibid at [62].
[36] *R* v *Secretary of State for the Home Department, ex parte Simms* [2000] 2 AC 115 at 131, [1999] 3 All ER 400 at 412; see also Lord Steyn, 'Democracy through Law' [2002] EHRLR 723.
[37] See also the discussion at p 333.

this, in the European Communities Act 1972. That Act is the legal cornerstone for the status of European Union law, as the European Union Bill currently before Parliament attempts to make clear. It is therefore still open to Parliament (in law, if not internationally) to repeal the European Communities Act 1972.

? Questions

1. What do you think are the real limits on what Parliament can do?
2. Why is it important to draw a distinction between 'constitutional statutes' and other legislation?

Public and private Acts

Most Acts of Parliament are what are known as 'public general Acts',[38] and the impetus for the vast majority of these comes from the government. Some may be based on specific manifesto pledges but many originate within government departments. They are drafted by the Office of Parliamentary Counsel to the Treasury, in liaison with relevant Ministers. Occasionally, however, a public general Act may begin life as a private member's Bill. As the name indicates, such Bills are introduced by individual MPs rather than by Ministers acting on behalf of the government, and they rarely become law unless the government can be persuaded to lend its time and support. Examples of private member's Bills that have been enacted with government support include the Obscene Publications Act 1959 (introduced by Roy Jenkins), the Abortion Act 1967 (David Steel), and the Public Interest Disclosure Act 1998 (Richard Shepherd).

Alongside public general Acts there are also private Acts, which are usually proposed by either local authorities (local Acts) or large public companies and corporations (personal Acts). Such Acts tend to affect only the interests of those who originally proposed them.

Acts of Parliament are published in Queens' Printers' Copy form by Her Majesty's Stationery Office (HMSO) and they are also made available electronically on the Office of Public Sector Information (OPSI) website.[39] The Stationery Office publishes these statutes in annual volumes and also publishes an annual Index to the Statutes in Force, for reference purposes.

The legislative process

Before a Bill is drafted, the government may outline its intentions in a consultation paper, inviting feedback from interested parties on the range of options that is being considered. This consultation period will usually be followed by a White Paper setting

---

[38] By virtue of the Interpretation Act 1978, s 3, every Act passed since 1850 is presumed to be a public Act in the absence of a contrary provision.

[39] **www.opsi.gov.uk**

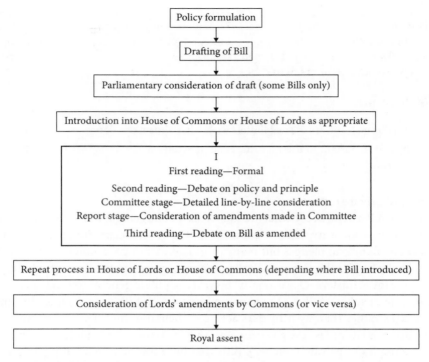

Fig. 2.1 The legislative process—a government Public Bill

out the government's revised proposals in detail. It is also becoming more common for Bills to be published in draft, providing an early opportunity for scrutiny and revision by the parliamentary select committees.

Once the government is satisfied with a Bill it will be introduced in Parliament. Money Bills and Bills dealing with politically contentious matters are usually presented to the House of Commons first, but less controversial Bills may begin life in the House of Lords. The title of the Bill will be read out in what is known as the first reading, and a date will be set for the second reading and a full debate on the Bill's merits.[40] At the end of this debate, the Bill and any amendments that have been proposed will be put to the vote. It is unlikely that any government-sponsored Bill will be defeated at this stage, although on 17 January 2004 the government's Higher Education Bill survived its second reading in the Commons by a margin of just five votes. Assuming that a Bill does get this far, it will be referred to a committee[41] for

---

[40] Section 19 of the Human Rights Act 1998 requires the Minister sponsoring a Bill to make a written statement before the second reading as to whether, in his view, its provisions are compatible with the rights specified in Sch 1 to the 1998 Act: see p 160.

[41] In the House of Commons the committees involved in this stage of the legislative process have been known since 2006 as public Bill committees. In the House of Lords Bills are usually dealt with by either a Grand Committee or a Committee of the Whole House.

more detailed consideration. On occasion the committee may receive evidence from experts and organizations. The committee will then report back to the House in the report stage, before the Bill proceeds to the third reading and a final vote. If a simple majority of the House votes in favour of enacting the Bill, it will be sent to the other House and the process is repeated.[42] Only when it has received the approval of both Houses can a Bill be presented for the royal assent and become an Act of Parliament.[43]

The Parliament Acts procedure

The Parliament Acts of 1911 and 1949 modify the principle that a Bill cannot be enacted without the approval of both the Commons and the Lords. Under the provisions of these Acts, the House of Lords no longer has the power of veto and can only delay Bills that have Commons support for a period of up to one year,[44] or in the case of money Bills, for up to one month.[45] If, at the end of this period the House of Lords rejects a Bill for a second time, the Commons can then invoke the Parliament Acts procedure and present the Bill for the royal assent. There is, however, no power enabling the House of Lords to legislate without the consent of the Commons. The Parliament Acts procedure has only been invoked on seven occasions, most recently to enact the Hunting Act 2004,[46] although on occasion the threat of its use has led to compromise and the passage of contentious legislation.

In the case of *R (on the application of Jackson) v A-G*,[47] which concerned a challenge to the validity of the Hunting Act, it was argued that statutes made using the Parliament Acts procedure are in fact a form of delegated legislation. When the Parliament Act 1911 removed the Lords' power to veto legislation, it replaced it with the power to delay Public Bills for up to two years. The 1911 Act was then itself used to pass the Parliament Act 1949, which reduced this delaying period to one year. The argument advanced in *Jackson* was that the 1911 Act was an enabling Act that delegated law-making powers to the House of Commons and the monarch.[48] It followed that the 1949 Act was a subordinate instrument made pursuant to the 1911 Act, and to the extent that it sought to amend its own 'parent Act', it was ultra vires: a subordinate body could not give itself greater powers than those originally conferred by Parliament. The applicant therefore sought a declaration that both the 1949 Act and the Hunting Act 2004 (which was made under it) were invalid. However, the House of

---

[42] If any further amendments are proposed at this stage, the Bill must go back to the first House so that it can have the opportunity to vote on them.

[43] The usual procedure for this is set out in the Royal Assent Act 1967.

[44] Parliament Act 1911, s 2(1), as amended.

[45] Ibid, s 1.

[46] The Welsh Church Act 1914, the Government of Ireland Act 1920, the Parliament Act 1949, the War Crimes Act 1991, the European Parliamentary Elections Act 1999, and the Sexual Offences (Amendment) Act 2000 were also passed in this way.

[47] [2005] UKHL 56, [2006] 1 AC 262, [2005] 4 All ER 1253.

[48] Delegated legislation is discussed at p 26.

Lords refused to grant the declaration and ruled that the effect of the Parliament Acts was to create an alternative way of enacting primary legislation:[49]

> To describe an Act of Parliament made by this procedure as 'delegated' or 'subordinate' legislation...would be an absurd and confusing mischaracterization. It would be equally inappropriate to liken the House of Commons to a 'delegate' or 'agent' when applying the 1911 Act procedure. The appropriate approach, rather, is to recognize that in enacting section 2 the intention of Parliament was to create a second, parallel route by which...any public Bill introduced in the Commons could become law as an Act of Parliament. It would be inconsistent with this intention to interpret section 2 as subject to an inherent, over-arching limitation comparable to that applicable to delegated legislation.

Section 2 of the 1911 Act specifies a limited number of exclusions to the use of this modified procedure, most notably in respect of Bills purporting to extend the maximum duration of a Parliament. Their Lordships agreed in *Jackson* that a Bill passed in contravention of section 2 would not be an Act of Parliament, and that the courts would have the jurisdiction to declare such an 'Act' invalid. However, the question of whether there might be any *implied* exclusions to section 2, in addition to those expressly mentioned, was left unresolved.[50]

In most cases of disagreement between the two Houses a compromise can be reached without the need for the Parliament Acts to be invoked. Usually this involves the House of Lords voting in favour of a Bill in return for the House of Commons accepting certain amendments. Indeed, in one of the most extraordinary episodes in British political history Parliament sat through the night to debate what became the Prevention of Terrorism Act 2005. The Bill 'ping-ponged' between the two Houses four times before a compromise was finally reached. The deadlock was only broken when the government reluctantly agreed to give Parliament the opportunity to amend the Act at a later date.

Citation

The mode of citation of statutes has undergone change. Early statutes were cited by the name of the place where Parliament met.[51] Subsequently statutes were cited by reference to their regnal year and chapter. Thus, for example, the Criminal Justice Act 1948 would be cited as 11 & 12 Geo 6, c 58 indicating that the Act was the fifty-eighth passed in the parliamentary session extending over the eleventh and twelfth years of the reign of George VI. This exceedingly cumbersome method of citation was not abolished until 1962.[52] Although Acts still have chapter numbers (a legacy of the fiction that only one Act was passed in a parliamentary session), reference is now to the calendar year

---

[49] [2005] UKHL 56 at [64], [2006] 1 AC 262 at [64], *per* Lord Nicholls.

[50] Their Lordships were divided on this point. For further discussion see McHarg, 'What Is Delegated Legislation?' [2006] PL 539. As to the question of whether there might be any limits to parliamentary supremacy itself, see the discussion at p 129.

[51] For example, Statute of Gloucester 1278; Provisions of Oxford 1258.

[52] Acts of Parliament Numbering and Citation Act 1962 (10 & 11 Eliz 2, c 34).

rather than to the regnal year. Acts are usually cited by reference to their short title, and this is permissible by section 2 of the Short Titles Act 1896.

Enforcement of statutory duties

The creation of new rights and causes of action is virtually the prerogative of Parliament, and where a statute imposes a duty the question often arises whether a breach of that duty is actionable in tort. The issue in such cases is whether the legislature intended to confer a cause of action on the claimant, not whether the claimant belongs to a class that the provision was intended to protect. It might be thought that where a statute creates rules but provides no criminal penalty for their breach, Parliament must have intended to create a right of civil action to a person who suffers as a result of a breach, 'for, if it were not so, the statute would be but a pious aspiration'.[53] This is not, however, invariably the case. Thus in *R* v *Deputy Governor of Parkhurst Prison, ex parte Hague*,[54] the House of Lords held that the Prison Rules 1964 (made under the Prison Act 1952) conferred no right to sue for damages upon a prisoner who had been restrained in a manner not permitted by those Rules. The prisoner's remedies were to complain to the governor or board of visitors. He might also challenge any administrative decision of the Secretary of State or the governor by judicial review proceedings.

A similar approach was taken in *O'Rourke* v *Camden LBC*, in which the House of Lords held that provisions in Part 3 of the Housing (Homeless Persons) Act 1977 did not confer private rights. The public duties imposed by the Act could be enforced through judicial review proceedings, but the Act did not suggest a legislative intention to create an additional remedy in private law:[55]

> Public money is spent on housing the homeless not merely for the private benefit of people who find themselves homeless but on grounds of general public interest: because, for example, proper housing means that people will be less likely to suffer illness, turn to crime or require the attention of other social services...It is not simply a private matter between the claimant and the housing authority. Accordingly, the fact that Parliament has provided for the expenditure of public money on benefits in kind such as housing the homeless does not necessarily mean that it intended cash payments to be made by way of damages to persons who, in breach of the housing authority's statutory duty, have unfortunately not received the benefits which they should have done...

Ultimately the matter depends on the construction of each individual statute, but if the duty is of a general administrative or regulatory nature, a right in tort is unlikely to be implied.[56]

[53] *Cutler* v *Wandsworth Stadium Ltd* [1949] AC 398 at 407, [1949] 1 All ER 544 at 548, *per* Lord Simonds.
[54] [1992] 1 AC 58, [1991] 3 All ER 733.
[55] [1998] AC 188 at 193, [1997] 3 All ER 23 at 26, *per* Lord Hoffmann. A power to make delegated legislation will not necessarily include a power to create new enforceable rights: *Olutu* v *Home Office* [1997] 1 All ER 385, [1987] 1 WLR 328.
[56] *Capital and Counties plc* v *Hampshire County Council and others* [1997] QB 1004, [1997] 2 All ER 865 (duty to ensure a water supply under Fire Services Act 1947 did not confer enforceable right).

KEY ISSUE

The question as to the role of the court in scrutinizing how an Act of Parliament has been passed is important. The ability to 'entrench' fundamental legislation—to make it more difficult to repeal or amend through procedural devices—depends on whether a court has the right to uphold specific statutory rules as to the way in which legislation is passed. The decision in *Jackson* is some recognition that, whilst a court cannot challenge the validity of an Act passed by a particular procedure, it is entitled to be satisfied that the procedure laid down by Parliament has been followed. In the case of the Parliament Acts 1911 and 1949, that is achieved by the Speaker of the House of Commons giving an appropriate certificate that the procedure has been followed. The fact that government proposals in the European Union Bill, currently before Parliament, require certain procedures to be followed before some new European Union treaties can be ratified makes this a live issue.

 Question

How can we reconcile the enforcement of procedural requirements with the theoretical power of Parliament?

Delegated legislation

'Delegated legislation' is the term used to describe the vast body of rules, orders, regulations, and byelaws, created by subordinate bodies under powers delegated through Acts of Parliament. Parliament has neither the time nor the expertise to enact all of the legislation needed in a modern, complex society, and the use of delegated legislation enables legal rules to be made and altered quickly without taking up valuable parliamentary time.[57]

Orders in Council are the highest form of delegated legislation.[58] They are nominally made by the Privy Council, although in most cases the Privy Council merely sanctions Orders that have in practice been made by the government. Orders in Council made pursuant to statutory powers are published in statutory instruments,[59] as are the various regulations, orders, directions, and rules made by Ministers of the Crown and other subordinate bodies.[60] Statutory instruments are published by Her

[57] In 2002, for example, a total of 2,959 statutory instruments applicable to the United Kingdom were made, compared with just 44 public Acts of Parliament. In 2009 the number of statutory instruments issued that year had risen to almost 3,500. Exceptionally, as many as 3,806 statutory instruments were made in 2001, but 597 of these related directly to the outbreak of foot and mouth disease in that year.

[58] Note that Orders in Council can also amount to primary legislation pursuant to the royal prerogative: *Council of Civil Service Unions* v *Minister for the Civil Service* [1985] AC 374, [1984] 3 All ER 935.

[59] See the Statutory Instruments Act 1946. Statutes conferring subordinate legislative powers frequently provide that the statutory instrument made thereunder shall be laid before Parliament. In this event a copy of the instrument must be so laid before it comes into operation: s 4. Some statutory instruments cannot take effect until expressly approved by resolution, while others take effect immediately subject to cancellation by negative resolution within forty 'sitting' days.

[60] Not all statutory instruments are made by Ministers. The Courts Act 2003, for example, empowers the Criminal Procedure Rule Committee to make rules of practice and procedure for the criminal courts

Majesty's Stationery Office and are cited by calendar year and number: for example, SI 2003/1660. They also have a short title. Failure to publish does not affect the validity of a statutory instrument, but it may provide a defence to any prosecution brought in respect of it.[61]

Local authority byelaws are another form of delegated legislation.[62] Alongside numerous powers to make byelaws on specific matters, local authorities also have a general power under the Local Government Act 1972 to make byelaws 'for good rule and government and suppression of nuisances'.[63]

As noted previously,[64] it has been suggested that legislation enacted using the Parliament Acts procedure is also a form of delegated legislation, but this view was rejected by the House of Lords in *R (on the application of Jackson) v A-G*.[65]

Use of Henry VIII clauses and other wide-ranging powers

Delegated legislation is not a new phenomenon, and where it is concerned solely with implementing the detail of a general policy contained in an Act of Parliament it is useful and unexceptionable.[66] However, it is increasingly common for delegated powers to be defined in extremely wide terms,[67] with the effect of conferring extensive legislative power upon government departments. One example of this is section 2(2) of the European Communities Act 1972, which confers a wide power on Ministers or Her Majesty in Council to make delegated legislation giving effect to Community obligations.[68] The potential scope of this power is vast. In 2003, for example, the government introduced a series of regulations designed to give effect to two EC directives on discrimination.[69] Entirely new grounds for challenging discrimination in employment were created,[70] and existing Acts of Parliament dealing with 'race',

(s 69), and gives equivalent powers to a new Family Procedure Rule Committee (s 75). See also the Civil Procedure Act 1997, s 1, for the powers of the Civil Procedure Rule Committee.

[61] Statutory Instruments Act 1946, s 3; *R v Sheer Metalcraft* [1954] 1 QB 586, [1954] 1 All ER 542.

[62] Certain other bodies are also empowered to make byelaws. For example, s 210(1) of and Sch 25 to the Water Resources Act 1991 empower the Environment Agency to make byelaws for purposes connected with the carrying out of its functions.

[63] Section 235(1). Such byelaws only take effect when they are confirmed by the Secretary of State.

[64] See p 23.   [65] [2005] UKHL 56, [2006] 1 AC 262, [2005] 4 All ER 1253.

[66] For example, many Acts of Parliament are brought into operation by Order in Council. An Act may be brought into force in this way, even though the power to make the Order derives from the Act itself; Interpretation Act 1978, s 13.

[67] Such powers tend to be very widely defined in time of war. See, e.g., the extraordinarily wide powers conferred by the Supplies and Services (Transitional Powers) Act 1945 (now repealed).

[68] See p 124. The scope of s 2(2) is limited by Sch 2, which excludes the power to make any provision imposing or increasing taxation, any retrospective provision or any criminal offence punishable with imprisonment for more than two years, or, on summary conviction with imprisonment for more than three months. Even with these limitations the power is far-reaching, and in 2003, 138 statutory instruments affecting England and Wales were made pursuant to s 2(2) of this Act.

[69] EC Employment Directive (2000/78/EC); EC Race Directive (2000/43/EC).

[70] Employment Equality (Religion or Belief) Regulations 2003, SI 2003/1660; Employment Equality (Sexual Orientation) Regulations 2003, SI 2003/1661.

gender, and disability discrimination were substantially amended.[71] These reforms have had a significant impact on the entire field of anti-discrimination law; yet by relying on the enabling power in section 2(2) of the European Communities Act 1972, the government was able to bring about these changes without asking Parliament to enact further primary legislation.

There are numerous other examples of so-called 'Henry VIII clauses' that allow delegated legislation to amend Acts of Parliament. For instance, the Legislative and Regulatory Reform Act 2006 empowers Ministers to amend or repeal legislation in order to remove or reduce burdens resulting from it.[72] Another example can be found in the Human Rights Act 1998. Where a court has declared that a legislative provision is incompatible with a Convention right,[73] section 10 empowers a Minister to make such amendments to the legislation as he or she considers necessary to remove the incompatibility. In *R (on the application of H)* v *North and East London Regional Mental Health Tribunal*, the Court of Appeal declared provisions of the Mental Health Act 1983 to be incompatible with the right to liberty under Article 5, ECHR.[74] The offending provisions were amended by the Mental Health Act 1983 (Remedial) Order 2001,[75] and because the Secretary of State considered that there were 'compelling reasons' for acting quickly he was able to make this Order without waiting for further parliamentary approval.[76]

Widely drawn powers to amend legislation can extend as far as altering the basic structures of government and the legal system. The provisions of the Public Bodies Bill, currently before Parliament, are an example: the Bill will, if enacted, permit the abolition or amendment of a wide range of statutory bodies and offices, such as the Youth Justice Board, the Victims Advisory Panel, the Administrative Justice and Tribunals Council, and the office of Chief Coroner.

Scrutiny of delegated legislation

The vital feature that distinguishes Parliament from any other person or body with legislative powers is that only Parliament is sovereign. This means that delegated legislation is valid only if it is within the legislative powers conferred by Parliament (intra

---

[71] Race Relations Act 1976 (Amendment) Regulations 2003, SI 2003/1626; Sex Discrimination Act 1975 (Amendment) Regulations 2003, SI 2003/1657; Disability Discrimination Act 1995 (Amendment) Regulations 2003, SI 2003/1673.

[72] Section 1. This replaces and extends the power previously contained in the Regulatory Reform Act 2001, although the power is still subject to certain limitations.

[73] A 'Convention right' means any of the rights contained in Articles 2–12 and 14 of the ECHR, Articles 1–3 of the First Protocol and Article 1 of the Thirteenth Protocol (Human Rights Act, s 1). Not all courts have the power to make such a declaration: see p 155.

[74] [2001] EWCA Civ 415, [2002] QB 1, [2002] 3 WLR 512. The provisions concerned the test to be applied when determining a restricted patient's entitlement to release from a secure hospital. The provision was held to be incompatible with Article 5 as the patient bore the burden of proving that his continued detention under the Act was no longer warranted.

[75] SI 2001/3712. See also the Naval Discipline Act 1957 (Remedial Order) 2004, SI 2004/66, and the Marriage Act 1949 (Remedial) Order 2007, SI 2007/438.

[76] Human Rights Act 1998, s 10(2); Sch 2, para 2(b).

vires). Thus, while the courts have no power to declare Acts of Parliament invalid, delegated legislation *can* be declared invalid if it is ultra vires (outside the power). The scope of the courts' jurisdiction in such cases was considered in *R v Secretary of State for the Home Department, ex parte Javed*.[77] The case centred on an Order designating Pakistan as a country where there was 'no serious risk of persecution'.[78] The applicants were Pakistani asylum seekers who had been subjected to a fast-track procedure on the basis of this Order. The Court of Appeal confirmed that delegated legislation could be judicially reviewed on the grounds identified in the *GCHQ* case,[79] namely illegality, procedural impropriety, and *Wednesbury* unreasonableness.[80] The courts can also strike down subordinate legislation that is incompatible with the rights protected by the Human Rights Act,[81] unless the terms of the enabling Act make the incompatibility inevitable.[82] However, unless and until declared ultra vires by a final judgment in the courts, a statutory instrument must be treated as part of the law and enforced accordingly.[83]

Although any challenge to delegated legislation is usually made in an application for judicial review, it is also possible to raise the question of validity as a defence to a civil action[84] or a prosecution[85] in what is known as a 'collateral challenge'. However, the fact that part of delegated legislation is ultra vires does not necessarily invalidate the whole of that legislation. The valid part may be severable, meaning that the invalid part may be severed whilst the valid part remains intact and enforceable.[86]

KEY ISSUE

Despite the possibility of judicial review, the role of the court is limited to ensuring that the delegated legislation is authorized by the enabling Act. Where that Act has been drafted so

[77] [2001] EWCA Civ 789, [2002] QB 129.

[78] Asylum (Designated Countries of Destination and Designated Safe Third Countries) Order 1996, SI 1996/2671. The Order was purportedly made under powers conferred by the Asylum and Immigration Appeals Act 1993.

[79] *Council of Civil Service Unions v Minister for the Civil Services* [1985] AC 374, [1984] 3 All ER 935.

[80] *Associated Provincial Picture Houses Ltd v Wednesbury Corpn* [1948] 1 KB 223, [1947] 2 All ER 680. The Court of Appeal in *Javed* held that the 1996 Order was void for unreasonableness. Delegated legislation may also be declared ultra vires where it breaches a fundamental right, such as the right of access to a court—see *R (on the application of Anufrijeva) v Secretary of State for the Home Department* [2003] UKHL 36, [2004] 1 AC 604, [2003] 3 All ER 827.

[81] A Minister or other body exercising a power to make delegated legislation is subject to s 6(1) of the Act, which makes it unlawful for a public authority to act incompatibly with Convention rights.

[82] Section 6(2).

[83] Compare *Hoffmann-La Roche & Co AG v Secretary of State for Trade and Industry* [1975] AC 295 at 329, [1974] 2 All ER 1128; *Percy v Hall* [1997] QB 924, [1996] 4 All ER 523.

[84] *R v Reading Crown Court, ex parte Hutchinson* [1988] QB 384, [1988] 1 All ER 333.

[85] *Boddington v British Transport Police* [1999] 2 AC 143, [1998] 2 All ER 203. The House of Lords confirmed in *Boddington* that a collateral challenge could be based on either substantive or procedural ultra vires.

[86] *DPP v Hutchinson* [1990] 2 AC 783, [1990] 2 All ER 836.

as to confer very wide powers, the scope for judicial scrutiny of their exercise is necessarily limited. Such powers are always subject to control by Parliament, and the Joint Committee on Statutory Instruments is able to consider the technical aspects of individual instruments and draw them to the attention of Parliament. In addition, most, although not all, statutory instruments must be laid before Parliament for a period of forty days before they can take effect, and some require an affirmative resolution of both Houses.[87] There is generally no power to amend statutory instruments—they must be approved or not approved. The sheer volume of delegated legislation that is now being made and the inability of the Joint Committee to review its merits, does raise doubts about the effectiveness of parliamentary scrutiny. However, the ultimate form of parliamentary control is that without the authority of an Act of Parliament there would be no power to make delegated legislation.

? Questions

1. How could parliamentary control of delegated legislation be improved?
2. What issues are raised by the wide authority powers sometimes granted to Ministers?

Autonomic legislation

This differs from delegated legislation in that an autonomous body has an independent power to legislate for its own members, and in some cases, for members of the general public. Although this power is usually conferred by Parliament, this is not always so. However, in all cases the power is sanctioned by Parliament. Examples of autonomous legislative bodies are public undertakings such as transport authorities, and bodies created by royal charter. The Church of England, the General Medical Council, the Law Society, trade unions, and even limited companies are also autonomous in the sense that they have power to control their own internal structures and to legislate for their members.

In almost all cases autonomic legislation is confined in its extent by Act of Parliament and is therefore subject to the doctrine of ultra vires. An important exception, however, is the prerogative jurisdiction of the Privy Council. This jurisdiction is principally concerned with legislating by Order in Council for Crown colonies. The power is subject to the ordinary rules of English law, although not to the doctrine of ultra vires.[88] It will thus be apparent that an Order in Council may be passed either under powers conferred by individual Acts or under a general prerogative power independent of statute. Both are subject to the power of the law to determine the existence and extent of the power to make the Order.[89]

---

[87] For example, certain orders made under the Legislative and Regulatory Reform Act 2006 will be subject to an affirmative resolution procedure, while others may be subject to a *super-affirmative* resolution procedure involving a sixty-day waiting period: see ss 12–18; cf. Human Rights Act 1998, Sch 2, para 2(b).

[88] *The Zamora* [1916] 2 AC 77.   [89] See p 28.

Codes of practice

Before leaving the topic of forms of legislation it is necessary to refer to codes of practice, which are of considerable significance in certain legislative contexts. A number of Acts of Parliament specifically require or authorize the preparation of accompanying codes of practice, usually for the purpose of providing further guidance, instructions, or rules governing matters of practice and procedure. Whether such codes are classifiable as 'legislation' is a moot point. In one sense they have the characteristic of delegated legislation in that the power to issue them is conferred by statute,[90] and presumably a code of practice could be declared ultra vires. Certain codes must be laid before Parliament before they can come into operation, and some are even subject to an affirmative resolution procedure.[91] On the other hand, the very nature of codes of practice means that they do not have the force of law. As discussed below, however, this does not mean that they are without legal effect.

Examples of particular codes

In the context of the enforcement of the criminal law, several codes are of particular importance. Section 66 of the Police and Criminal Evidence Act 1984 (PACE) authorizes the Home Secretary to make codes of practice dealing with the different stages of police investigations. Codes dealing with the exercise of stop-and-search powers (Code A), the execution of search powers (Code B), the treatment and questioning of suspects (Code C), the identification of suspects (Code D), and the tape-recording of police interviews (Code E) have been in operation for some time. More recently, codes dealing with the visual recording of interviews (Code F),[92] statutory powers of arrest (Code G), and the detention, treatment, and questioning of terror suspects (Code H) have also been introduced.[93] The PACE codes are important to both the practitioner and the police, and if there is a 'significant and substantial' breach of the codes,[94] evidence obtained as a result of that breach may be excluded from consideration by the courts. The status of one of the PACE codes was discussed by Lord Woolf CJ:[95] 'The Code has statutory backing under the Police and Criminal Evidence Act 1984. However, it remains a code and it does not have the status of subordinate legislation.'

---

[90] Not all codes of practice are issued pursuant to statutory powers. Numerous voluntary codes exist in both the private and public sectors, but these do not raise the same legal issues as those backed by a statutory framework.

[91] Codes of practice made under s 66 of the Police and Criminal Evidence Act 1984 (PACE) can only be brought into force by a statutory instrument that has been approved by both Houses of Parliament (s 67(7)). However, revisions to existing codes are not subject to affirmative resolution (s 67(7A)).

[92] Made pursuant to s 60A of the Act.

[93] New Codes A–E have effect from 1 February 2008.

[94] *R v Walsh* (1990) 91 Cr App R 161, [1989] Crim LR 822; *R v Aspinall* [1999] 2 Cr App R 115, (1999) 96(7) LSG 35. See further, p 440.

[95] *R v Sanghera (Rashpal)* [2001] 1 Cr App R 20 at 6, [2000] All ER (D) 1415. The Court of Appeal upheld the trial judge's decision not to exclude evidence obtained in breach of Code B because there was no doubt as to its reliability.

Another example is the code of practice on the preservation and disclosure of evidence, made under section 23 of the Criminal Procedure and Investigations Act 1996. This code is intended to ensure that important material is made available to the prosecutor and disclosed to the defence if it may assist them.[96] In the context of the civil law, perhaps the most important example of a code of practice is that issued by the Advisory Conciliation and Arbitration Service (ACAS) under the Trade Union and Labour Relations (Consolidation) Act 1992. ACAS may issue codes of practice containing 'such practical guidance as the Service thinks fit for the purpose of promoting the improvement of industrial relations or for purposes connected with trade union learning representatives'.[97]

The status of codes of practice

As already indicated, although codes of practice cannot be directly enforced through the courts, they are not without legal effect. For example, codes issued under the Trade Union and Labour Relations (Consolidation) Act 1992 are specifically admissible in any proceedings before a court, employment tribunal, or the Central Arbitration Committee.[98] Similarly, by section 67(11) of the Police and Criminal Evidence Act, any code under the Act is admissible in evidence, and if appearing to be relevant to any question arising in the proceedings, 'it shall be taken into account in determining that question'.

Codes of practice approved or issued by the Health and Safety Commission have even greater force, since a failure to comply with such a code amounts to prima facie proof of a breach of the Act's provisions for the purposes of any criminal proceedings.[99] Reference may also be made to the Highway Code, first issued pursuant to the Road Traffic Act 1930. Failure to comply with its provisions is not an offence in itself, but it may be relied upon by any party in civil or criminal proceedings.[100]

Probably one of the important effects of a code is to require administrative decision-makers to have regard to the contents of the code. A decision-maker who failed to have regard to a relevant code might well face successful challenge by way of judicial review. Judicial review is the process by which the legality of executive actions is challenged.

The operation of statutes

In defining the scope of a statute it is necessary to advert both to its geographical area of operation and to the time during which it is operative.

---

[96] See p 635.   [97] Section 199, as amended by the Employment Act 2002, s 43(1).
[98] Section 207(2), (3).   [99] Health and Safety at Work etc. Act 1974, ss 16 and 17(2).
[100] Road Traffic Act 1988, s 38(7).

Geographical operation

There is a presumption that an Act of Parliament is operative throughout the United Kingdom but not elsewhere unless a contrary intention appears in the Act itself.[101] The contrary intention may either limit or extend the geographical operation of the Act, and statutes frequently contain a section restricting their operation to exclude Scotland or Northern Ireland. A similar reduction in geographical operation occurs with Acts that are expressed to apply only to a limited locality. Such Acts are described as 'local Acts'.

Conversely, an Act may expressly or by necessary implication extend outside the United Kingdom, although there is a presumption against this.[102] For example, section 57 of the Offences Against the Person Act 1861 provides that the crime of bigamy is committed 'whether the second marriage shall have taken place in England or Ireland, or elsewhere'. Another example is section 72 of the Sexual Offences Act 2003, which extends the jurisdiction of United Kingdom courts to allow trial in the United Kingdom of British citizens who commit sex offences abroad. However, an Act with extraterritorial operation will usually (but not always) apply only to British subjects or persons owing allegiance to the Crown.[103]

Temporal operation

When a statute begins to be operative

Until 1793[104] a statute came into force on the first day of the parliamentary session in which it was passed. Consequently virtually all legislation was retrospective. The present law is that a statute comes into force on the day on which it receives the royal assent, unless some other date is specified in the Act itself. Increasingly, however, an Act may provide that it is to come into force on a 'day to be appointed' by statutory instrument, and different sections within an Act may be brought into force at different times. For example, most of the provisions of the Human Rights Act 1998 were brought into force in England and Wales approximately two years after the Act was passed, the commencement date having been effected by statutory instrument.[105]

---

[101] Since it lies within the prerogative power of the Crown to extend its sovereignty and jurisdiction across both land and sea, the words 'United Kingdom' incorporate such area of land or sea as may be formally declared by the Crown to be subject to its sovereignty and jurisdiction: see *Post Office* v *Estuary Radio Ltd* [1968] 2 QB 740, at 748, [1967] 3 All ER 663 at 680, *per* Diplock LJ.

[102] The presumption is particularly strong in criminal cases: see *Air-India* v *Wiggins* [1980] 2 All ER 593, [1980] 1 WLR 815.

[103] *Joyce* v *DPP* [1946] AC 347, [1946] 1 All ER 186; cf. the Internationally Protected Persons Act 1978, under which attacks upon the person or property of protected persons (such as heads of state and their families) are offences justiciable in the United Kingdom, even though committed outside the United Kingdom by a person 'whether a citizen of the United Kingdom and Colonies or not' (s 1). See also the Suppression of Terrorism Act 1978, s 4, and the War Crimes Act 1991.

[104] Acts of Parliament (Commencement) Act 1793.

[105] For England and Wales—see s 22(3); Human Rights Act 1998 (Commencement No 2) Order 2000, SI 2000/1851.

Certain provisions, however, came into effect as soon as the Act received the royal assent.[106]

There are portions of Acts in existence that have never been brought into force, and sometimes the decision not to implement is taken quite soon after the Act is passed. Thus, for example, sections 8–27 of the Crime (Sentences) Act 1997 introduced a new scheme for the early release of prisoners. Within months, and after a change of government, it was announced that the new scheme would not be implemented.[107]

Sometimes the failure to bring a statutory provision into force may give rise to problems, as was vividly demonstrated in *R* v *Secretary of State for the Home Department, ex parte Fire Brigades' Union.*[108] The Criminal Justice Act 1988 provided for a statutory compensation scheme for victims of violent crime, this being intended to replace the *ex gratia* Criminal Injuries Compensation Scheme established under the royal prerogative.[109] The statutory provisions were not brought into force and in 1994 the Home Secretary purported to introduce a new scheme pursuant to the royal prerogative. The House of Lords held, by a majority, that the Home Secretary had acted unlawfully. Although he was not obliged to bring the statutory scheme into effect at any given time, he was under a duty to keep the matter under review. It was an abuse of prerogative power to exercise it in a manner inconsistent with bringing the statute into force. Lord Browne-Wilkinson observed that if the Home Secretary wanted to introduce a scheme inconsistent with that in the 1988 Act, he should have first asked Parliament to repeal the statutory provisions.

Retrospective operation

As a general rule a statute only affects factual situations that arise during the period of its operation. There is a presumption against the statute being retroactive, although the courts have been keen to point out that it is in each case a question of ascertaining the intentions of Parliament.[110] The presumption is particularly strong where a statute creates criminal penalties or would operate to deprive a person of a vested right in property.[111] In the case of the former, the presumption can only have been strengthened by section 3 of the Human Rights Act 1998, under which the courts must try to interpret legislation in a manner compatible with the prohibition on

---

[106] Sections 18 (appointment of judges to the European Court of Human Rights), 20 (the power to make supplementary orders) and 21(5) (abolition of the death penalty for certain military offences).

[107] See 299 HC Official Report (6th series) cols 342–350, 30 July 1997.

[108] [1995] 2 AC 513, [1995] 2 All ER 244.

[109] Sections 108–117 and Schs 6 and 7.

[110] *L'Office Cherifien des Phosphates* v *Yamashita-Shinnihon Steamship Co Ltd* [1994] 1 AC 486, [1994] 1 All ER 20; *Wilson* v *First County Trust (No 2)* [2003] UKHL 40, [2004] 1 AC 816, [2003] 4 All ER 97.

[111] *Yew Bon Tew* v *Kenderaan Bas Mara* [1983] 1 AC 553, [1982] 3 All ER 833. In *R* v *Fisher* [1969] 1 All ER 100, [1969] 1 WLR 8, the rule against retrospective operation operated *against* the accused, as he was convicted of an offence that had been abolished at some point between the commission of the offence and the date of his trial.

retrospective criminal offences in Article 7, ECHR.[112] Parliament is sovereign, however, and statutes are occasionally expressed to be retrospective even where this operates to deprive a person of a vested right in property. A modern illustration was the War Damage Act 1965, which operated to remove rights to compensation from the Crown, and which was expressed to apply to proceedings commenced before the Act came into force.[113] A more recent example is provided by the provisions in Part 10 of the Criminal Justice Act 2003. These provisions bought about changes to the double jeopardy rule and are expressed to apply 'whether the acquittal was before or after the passing of this Act'.[114]

An Act of indemnity, the purpose of which is to validate or legalize that which was initially invalid or illegal, must by its nature be retroactive.[115] Similarly, a statute that alters rules of evidence or procedure is always retroactive in the absence of a contrary intention, since the rules of evidence and procedure that a court is bound to observe are those in existence at the time of the hearing.[116] On the other hand, sentencing provisions usually apply only in respect of offences committed after the provisions were introduced.

Even if the statutory provision does not take effect retrospectively, it may nevertheless be held to entitle a court to have regard to what has occurred prior to its passage. Thus in *L'Office Cherifien des Phosphates* v *Yamashita-Shinnihon Steamship Co Ltd*,[117] the House of Lords held that an 'inordinate and inexcusable delay', which had occurred *before* section 13A of the Arbitration Act 1950 came into force, entitled an arbitrator to dismiss a claim.

When a statute ceases to be operative

No statute becomes obsolete by the passing of time. Nevertheless there are many ancient statutes more honoured in the breach than in the observance. At one time the approach of the legislature was to do nothing until the need for repeal manifested itself. Thus, the plaintiff in a nineteenth-century case was no doubt disturbed to discover that his opponent had a right to claim trial by battle,[118] while resort to the Bill of Rights 1688 is by no means uncommon.[119] The present position is that the Law Commissions are expressly required to review 'obsolete and unnecessary enactments' with a view

---

[112] See p 196. The Human Rights Act itself is presumed not to be retrospective, except to the extent that it can be relied upon in proceedings instigated by public authorities that concern events occurring before the Act came into force. See s 22(4); *R* v *Lambert* [2001] UKHL 37, [2002] 2 AC 545, [2001] 3 All ER 577.

[113] Section 1(2). The action affected was *Burmah Oil Co Ltd* v *Lord Advocate* [1965] AC 75, [1964] 2 All ER 348.

[114] Section 75(6).

[115] Examples of Acts of indemnity are: Indemnity Act 1920; Indian Divorces (Validity) Act 1921.

[116] See *Blyth* v *Blyth* [1966] AC 643, [1966] 1 All ER 524; *R* v *Cruttenden* [1991] 2 QB 66, [1991] 3 All ER 242 (evidence); cf. *Yew Bon Tew* v *Kenderaan Bas Mara* [1983] 1 AC 553, [1982] 3 All ER 833 (limitation statute in Malaysia held not to revive statute-barred cause of action).

[117] [1994] 1 AC 486, [1994] 1 All ER 20.   [118] *Ashford* v *Thornton* (1818) 1 & Ald 405.

[119] See, e.g., *Rost* v *Edwards* [1990] 2 QB 460, [1990] 2 All ER 641; *R* v *Parliamentary Commissioner for Standards, ex parte Al-Fayed* [1998] 1 WLR 669, [1998] 1 All ER 93.

to repeal.[120] In consequence there are now regular Statute Law (Repeals) Acts, each of which repeals hundreds of obsolete enactments following recommendations of the Law Commissions.

Certain statutes are expressed to be operative only for a limited period, usually because they are experimental or transitional. However, temporary statutes may acquire a new lease of life by the passing of an Expiring Laws Continuance Act, which is effected solely for the purpose of renewing statutes that would otherwise expire. Thus Part I of the Commonwealth Immigrants Act 1962, an experimental measure expressed to last for only one year, was renewed annually until 1971 when the Immigration Act 1971 was passed to supersede it.

Unless it is expressed to be operative for a limited period, a statute ceases to have effect only when this is provided for by another statute, since only Parliament is competent to repeal (or authorize the repeal of) its own enactments.[121] Repeal of one statute does not have the effect of reviving any earlier legislative provision, statutory or otherwise, unless the contrary intention is expressed by Parliament.[122]

Repeal may be express or implied. In modern times almost all repeal is express and it is common for a schedule of repeals to be incorporated into the body of an Act. Implied repeal is possible, however, and occurs where two statutory provisions are inconsistent with one another. In this situation the later provision impliedly repeals the earlier to the extent of the inconsistency.[123] The courts generally lean against implied repeal and will attempt to reconcile seemingly conflicting provisions wherever possible. Moreover, the recent decision of the Divisional Court in *Thoburn v Sunderland City Council and others* suggests that there is a certain class of legislation, labelled 'constitutional statutes', which can only be repealed expressly.[124] The European Communities Act 1972, the Human Rights Act 1998, and the Scotland Act 1998 are said to be examples of such legislation.[125]

The interpretation and construction of statutes[126]

The need for interpretation and construction

Where the words of a statute are clear and unambiguous, persons affected by its provisions will be able to regulate their conduct according to its terms and the need for

---

[120] Law Commissions Act 1965, s 3(1).

[121] An enactment may be impliedly repealed by EC legislation: *Amministrazione delle Finanze dello Stato v Simmenthal SpA* [1978] ECR 629, [1978] 3 CMLR 263; see p 120. In addition, Parliament may confer power on a Minister to amend or repeal statutory provisions: see p 28.

[122] Interpretation Act 1978, ss 15, 16(1).

[123] See, e.g., *Smith v Benabo* [1937] 1 KB 518, [1937] 1 All ER 523; *Ellen Street Estates Ltd v Minister of Health* [1934] 1 KB 590; *Dryden v Dryden* [1973] Fam 217, [1973] 3 All ER 526.

[124] [2002] EWHC 195 (Admin) at [60], [2003] QB 151 at [60], [2002] 4 All ER 156, *per* Laws LJ.

[125] Ibid. See further, p 20.

[126] See e.g., Cross, Bell and Engle, *Statutory Interpretation* (Butterworths: 3rd edn, 1995); Bennion and Goodall, *Bennion on Statutory Interpretation* (LexisNexis Butterworths: 5th edn, 2007).

judicial interpretation will not arise. However, if the meaning or extent of a statute is uncertain or ambiguous, the statute will fall to be interpreted. There is a technical distinction between interpretation and construction. 'Interpretation' is simply the process whereby a meaning is assigned to the words in a statute. 'Construction', on the other hand, is the process whereby uncertainties or ambiguities are resolved. It follows that every statute that comes before a court is interpreted, whereas only uncertain or ambiguous provisions require construction.

The words of the statute

The need for interpretation or construction may arise for a variety of reasons. One may be careless drafting, or the form and content of the Act having been the subject of hasty or ill-thought-out amendments during the parliamentary process. However, many issues of construction arise simply because of the very uncertainty of words themselves. In the drink-driving case of *DPP* v *Johnson*,[127] for example, the Divisional Court had to consider the meaning of the word 'consume' in section 5 of the Road Traffic Act 1988. As Schiemann LJ put it:

> It is not unusual to speak of a house being consumed by fire and it would not be strange to speak of a bottle of medical alcohol having been consumed by rubbing its contents into skin prior to administering an injection...One can also talk of consuming snuff by sniffing.

The meaning of a word depends on the context in which it is used. It was the context of section 5, together with the marginal note, that persuaded the court to reject the submission that 'consume' in section 5 meant 'consume by mouth'. It therefore held that a drink-drive offence could be committed even if the alcohol had, in part, been ingested by injection.

Ambiguity

Ambiguity arises when words used in a statute are found to be capable of bearing two or more literal meanings. Language is an imprecise tool and even parliamentary draftsmen, in using words intended to convey one meaning, occasionally contrive to give rise to an alternative meaning that neither they nor the legislature envisaged. Thus the Restriction of Offensive Weapons Act 1959 made it an offence to 'offer for sale' certain offensive weapons, including 'flick knives'. A shopkeeper who displayed weapons of this type in his window was held not to be guilty of an offence under the Act, because the exhibition of goods in a shop window does not constitute an offer.[128]

Where a statute concerns an intrinsically complex area of law, such as landlord and tenant or income tax, it seems to be virtually impossible to choose language that

---

[127] [1995] 4 All ER 53, [1995] 1 WLR 728.
[128] *Fisher* v *Bell* [1961] 1 QB 394, [1960] 3 All ER 731. In reaching this decision, the Divisional Court relied heavily upon established common law principles of contract law: see also *Partridge* v *Crittenden* [1968] 2 All ER 421, [1968] 1 WLR 1204.

is entirely free from ambiguity. Nevertheless the judiciary has on occasion been less than sympathetic to the draftsman's plight. Thus, in *R v Royle*,[129] section 16 of the Theft Act 1968 was described as being so obscure as to have 'created a judicial nightmare', while in *Central Asbestos Co Ltd v Dodd*, Lord Reid said that the Limitation Act 1963 had 'a strong claim to the distinction of being the worst drafted Act on the statute book'.[130]

Uncertainty

Uncertainty is far more common than ambiguity. Uncertainty occurs where the words of a statute are intended to apply to various factual situations and the courts are called upon to decide whether the set of facts before them was envisaged by the Act. For example, the words 'an accident arising out of and in the course of his employment' in the Workmen's Compensation Acts were the source of innumerable cases, not because they were in any way ambiguous, but because their scope was adaptable to endless permutations of facts and was therefore uncertain.[131]

The use of general and ostensibly straightforward words, such as 'road',[132] 'premises',[133] and 'board'[134] has created problems of construction that the legislature could not have envisaged. More recently, the courts have had to resolve such conundrums as whether the cremation of humans is 'the subjection of goods or materials to any process',[135] whether an orange squeezed by hand is a 'manufactured beverage',[136] whether a partner in a long-term homosexual relationship is a member of the other partner's 'family',[137] and whether a male-to-female transsexual is a 'female'.[138] Lord Denning once expressed the difficulty as follows:[139]

> It must be remembered that it is not within human powers to foresee the manifold sets of facts which may arise, and, even if it were, it is not possible to provide for them in terms free from all ambiguity.

---

[129] [1971] 3 All ER 1359 at 1363, [1971] 1 WLR 1764 at 1767, *per* Edmund Davies LJ. The offending part of the section (s 16(2)(a)) was eventually repealed and replaced by the Theft Act 1978.

[130] [1973] AC 518 at 529, [1972] 2 All ER 1135 at 113; the Limitation Act 1975 (replacing that part of the 1963 Act) seemed to aim at similar distinction. The Acts concerned are now consolidated in the Limitation Act 1980.

[131] The words are still used in social security legislation (currently the Social Security Contributions and Benefits Act 1992, s 94) where they continue to cause trouble; see *Chief Adjudication Officer v Rhodes* [1999] ICR 178, [1999] IRLR 103.

[132] *Cutter v Eagle Star Insurance Co Ltd* [1998] 4 All ER 417, [1998] 1 WLR 1647.

[133] *Whitley v Stumbles* [1930] AC 544; *Maunsell v Olins* [1975] AC 373, [1975] 1 All ER 16.

[134] *Otter v Norman* [1989] AC 129, [1988] 2 All ER 897.

[135] *Bourne (Inspector of Taxes) v Norwich Crematorium Ltd* [1967] 2 All ER 576, [1967] 1 WLR 691.

[136] *Customs and Excise Commissioners v Savoy Hotel Ltd* [1966] 2 All ER 299, [1966] 1 WLR 948. For a delightfully sardonic exposition of the difficulty of ascertaining the 'right' meaning of words, see the judgment of Diplock LJ in *Slim v Daily Telegraph Ltd* [1968] 2 QB 157 at 171–2, [1968] 1 All ER 497 at 504.

[137] *Fitzpatrick v Sterling Housing Association Ltd* [2001] 1 AC 27, [1999] 4 All ER 705.

[138] *Bellinger v Bellinger* [2003] UKHL 21, [2003] 2 AC 467, [2003] 2 All ER 593.

[139] *Asher v Seaford Court Estates Ltd* [1949] 2 KB 481 at 499, [1949] 2 All ER 155 at 164.

Judicial approaches to interpretation

The basic task of the judge is to ascertain the intention of Parliament. Nevertheless there are alternative approaches to this task. These approaches, which differ radically, are commonly known as the 'literal' approach and the 'purposive' approach. It is never possible to know in advance which approach any particular court will favour, and it may be that a court will adopt the approach that best enables it to reach the conclusion considered just in all of the circumstances. In *Re M (A Minor) (Care Order: Threshold Conditions)*,[140] Lord Templeman spoke of 'ascertaining and giving effect to the intention of Parliament by construing a statute in accordance with the spirit rather than the letter of the Act'.

Both of these approaches to interpretation are discussed below, although they must now be considered in the light of the obligation arising from section 3 of the Human Rights Act 1998.[141]

The literal approach

The basic approach to statutory interpretation, as already stated, is to ascertain the intention of the legislature. The literal approach to this task is that this intention must be found in the ordinary and natural meaning of the language used in the statute. In other words, the focus is on the 'objective' meaning of the words, not on the subjective intention that might lie behind their use. While this approach may be defended as respecting the proper boundaries between the judicial and legislative functions,[142] it does have certain obvious shortcomings. Firstly, it relies on an assumption that the 'ordinary and natural meaning' of a word or phrase can always be ascertained. Yet as discussed previously, this is not always the case and the courts have often had considerable difficulty in interpreting seemingly straightforward words.[143] Secondly, if the words used in a provision are capable of *alternative* ordinary and natural meanings, the court still needs to find a mechanism for choosing between these alternatives.

Despite these shortcomings, the literal approach will, in most cases, produce a reasonable interpretation of the statute. Difficulty arises, however, where a literal interpretation produces either an improbable result or a manifest absurdity. Where the result is merely less plausible than that which Parliament might be assumed to have intended, a strict application of the literal approach means that this interpretation ought nevertheless to be given. Thus in *Inland Revenue Commissioners* v *Hinchy*,[144] the House of Lords was called upon to construe section 25(3) of the Income Tax Act 1952, which provided that any person delivering an incorrect tax return should forfeit 'treble the tax which he ought to be charged under this Act'. Although Parliament

---

[140] [1994] 2 AC 424, [1994] 3 All ER 298.

[141] The impact of the Human Rights Act on statutory interpretation is discussed at pp 45 and 152. As to the interpretation of European Union legislation, see Chapter 4.

[142] See, e.g., the judgment of Viscount Dilhorne in *Kammins Ballrooms Co Ltd* v *Zenith Investments (Torquay) Ltd* [1971] AC 850, [1970] 2 All ER 871.

[143] See p 38.   [144] [1960] AC 748, [1960] 1 All ER 505.

presumably intended a penalty of treble the *unpaid* tax,[145] the House of Lords took a literal approach to the subsection, and held that the respondent was liable to pay treble the *whole* amount of tax payable by him for the year. *Fisher v Bell*, cited earlier,[146] is a further example of the application of the literal rule producing a result that appeared contrary to the intention of the legislature.

The golden rule

The strict application of the literal approach may be modified by the use of 'the golden rule'. This means that where the literal approach would produce a manifestly absurd outcome, judges may depart from the ordinary meaning of the word(s), in favour of an interpretation that avoids the absurdity. Lord Blackburn explained this approach as follows:[147]

> [W]e are to take the whole statute and construe it all together, giving the words their ordinary signification, unless when so applied they produce an inconsistency or absurdity or inconvenience so great as to convince the Court that the intention could not have been to use them in their ordinary signification, and to justify the court in putting them in some other signification, which, though less proper, is one which the Court thinks the words will bear.

The use of the golden rule is well illustrated by the unanimous decision of the House of Lords in *McMonagle v Westminster City Council*.[148] The appellant was charged with using premises as a 'sex encounter establishment' without a licence. The statutory definition of these words was 'premises at which performances which are not unlawful are given, which wholly or mainly comprise the sexual stimulation of persons admitted to the premises'. The appellant's defence was that the prosecution had failed to prove that the performances were not unlawful, and that if they were, according to the plain words of the statute, a licence was not required. The House of Lords rejected this interpretation as manifestly absurd. Lord Bridge explained his reasoning:[149]

> I am satisfied that the main object of paragraph 3A(c) of Schedule 3 is to require any premises, not falling within the proviso, where live nude entertainment is provided to be licensed and that in order to avoid the substantial frustration of that object it is both necessary and legitimate that the words 'which are not unlawful' should be treated as surplusage and as having been introduced by incompetent draftsmanship for no other purpose than to emphasise that a licence confers no immunity from the ordinary criminal law.

---

[145] The law was in fact changed shortly after this decision by the Finance Act 1960, s 44.

[146] [1961] 1 QB 394, [1960] 3 All ER 731; see p 37. The Law Commission report, *The Interpretation of Statutes* (Law Com No 21, 1969) recommended a statutory provision to the effect that a construction that would promote the general legislative purpose underlying the provision in question 'is to be preferred to a construction which would not'.

[147] *River Wear Commissioners v Adamson* (1877) 2 App Cas 743 at 764–5.

[148] [1990] 2 AC 716, [1990] 1 All ER 993.

[149] [1990] 2 AC 716 at 727, [1990] 1 All ER 993 at 998.

Another example is provided by *Adler* v *George*.[150] In this case, a conviction for caus-ing an obstruction *'in the vicinity of'* a prohibited place was upheld by the Divisional Court even though the incident had occurred *inside* the place in question. Similarly, in *R* v *Allen*,[151] the court applied the golden rule to the statutory definition of bigamy in order to avoid a manifestly absurd outcome. Section 57 of the Offences Against the Person Act 1861 stated that 'whosoever being married shall marry another per-son . . . shall be guilty of bigamy'. A literal interpretation of these words would have ren-dered it impossible to commit the offence, since any attempt to 'marry' whilst already being married to someone else would be ineffective. The court therefore interpreted the phrase 'shall marry' to mean 'shall go through a marriage ceremony'.[152]

The difficulty, of course, lies in drawing the line between a literal interpretation that appears to produce a 'manifest absurdity', and one that merely appears to be improba-ble. For those who advocate a literal approach to statutory interpretation, the adoption of a different meaning in the former case may be accepted as a legitimate extension of this approach. To depart from the ordinary meaning of words in the latter case, how-ever, might be seen as unacceptable judicial activism. Lord Bridge is amongst those to have warned against the judiciary substituting its own judgment for that of the legislature:[153]

> It is one thing to abstain from giving to the language of a statute the full effect of its ordinary grammatical meaning in order to avoid some positively harmful or manifestly unjust consequence. This I would describe as a legitimate process of construction to avoid a positive absurdity. But it is quite another thing to read into a statute a meaning which the language used will not bear in order to remedy a supposed defect or shortcoming which, if not made good, will make the statutory machinery less effective than the court believes it ought to be in order to achieve its proper purpose.

A case that arguably stretches the limits of the golden rule is *DPP* v *McKeown*.[154] The House of Lords had to consider the meaning of section 69 of the Police and Criminal Evidence Act 1984, which allowed computer-generated documents to be admitted as evidence if the court was satisfied that any fault in the computer had not affected the production of the document or the accuracy of its contents. Because the computer's clock had been set inaccurately, the time stated on a document produced by the com-puter was wrong. On a literal interpretation, it was thus inadmissible: the contents were inaccurate. However, the House of Lords avoided this conclusion because it con-sidered that Parliament could not have intended it—the inaccurate time shown on the document did not affect its reliability as proof of what was being disputed.

---

[150] [1964] 2 QB 7, [1964] 1 All ER 628.   [151] (1872) LR 1 CCR 367.

[152] This reasoning should be compared with that applied in *Whiston* v *Whiston* [1995] Fam 198, [1998] 1 All ER 423, to prevent a bigamist from claiming financial relief under the Matrimonial Causes Act 1973 (cf. *Rampal* v *Rampal (No 2)* [2001] EWCA Civ 989, [2002] Fam 85, [2001] 3 WLR 795.)

[153] *R* v *Central Criminal Court, ex parte Francis & Francis* [1989] AC 346 at 375, [1988] 3 All ER 775 at 783.

[154] [1997] 1 All ER 737, [1997] 1 WLR 295. The provision in question has now been repealed.

Finally, it should be noted that there is a residual category of cases in which a literal interpretation of a statute is rejected in order to avoid an outcome that would clearly be contrary to public policy. Thus, in *Re Sigsworth*,[155] the golden rule was applied to prevent a murderer from inheriting the estate of his victim, although he was, as her son, the 'sole issue' on a literal interpretation of the Administration of Estates Act 1925. In a later case, the Court of Appeal took a similar approach in rejecting the judicial review application of a double killer. The applicant had a psychotic illness that was known to involve extreme hatred of his adoptive parents. His application for a copy of his birth certificate was turned down by the Registrar General out of concern that he might use the information to find and harm his natural mother. Despite the fact that the ordinary words in the Adoption Act 1976 did not give the Registrar General any discretion to refuse the applicant's request, the Court of Appeal upheld his decision on the basis that Parliament could not have intended to facilitate the commission of a crime.[156]

The purposive approach

The 'mischief rule', or rule in *Heydon's case*,[157] is a form of purposive interpretation with a relatively long history. It means that where a statute was passed to remedy a mischief the court will, if possible, adopt the interpretation of the statute that will have the effect of correcting that mischief. In *Heydon's case* itself, the rule was defined thus:

> four things are to be discussed and considered; (1) what was the common law before the making of the Act; (2) what was the mischief and defect for which the common law did not provide; (3) what remedy the Parliament hath resolved and appointed to cure the disease of the commonwealth; and (4) the true reason of the remedy.

In order to ascertain the mischief that the statute was passed to correct, the judge may legitimately have regard to the preamble of the statute, the long title, headings, and extrinsic sources that may indicate the state of the law before the passing of the Act.[158]

The rule has often been used to resolve ambiguities in cases in which the literal rule would produce an unsatisfactory outcome. For example, a 'single woman' for the purposes of affiliation proceedings was held to be a woman with no husband to support her, not necessarily an unmarried woman—the relevant Acts were passed to remedy the mischief of women having illegitimate children without the means of supporting them.[159] Similarly, medically induced abortions brought about by nurses acting under the instruction of doctors constituted lawful 'termination by a registered medical practitioner'. This was because the statute in question was intended to correct the mischief of legal uncertainty and to ensure that abortions were carried out safely.[160]

---

[155] [1935] Ch 89.   [156] *R v Registrar General, ex parte Smith* [1991] 2 QB 393, [1991] 2 All ER 88.
[157] (1584) 3 Co Rep 7a.
[158] For further discussion of the use of both internal and external aids, see pp 57–67.
[159] *Kruhlak v Kruhlak* [1958] 2 QB 32, [1958] 1 All ER 154.
[160] *Royal College of Nursing v Department of Health and Social Security* [1981] AC 800, [1981] 1 All ER 545.

Unlike in Heydon's day, most modern legislation is not specifically concerned with rectifying mischief but with the fulfilment of some more general policy objective:[161]

> Even for the lawyer, the expression [the mischief rule] is unsatisfactory. It tends to suggest that legislation is only designed to deal with an evil, and not to further a positive social approach.

The 'mischief rule' has therefore given way to the slightly broader notion of 'purposive' interpretation. This emphasizes the need to construe the wording of a statute in its wider context, so as to give effect to its underlying purpose. One criticism that could be made of the wide application of this purposive approach is that it is inherently subjective. The judge who decides that a literal interpretation is contrary to the intention of the legislature is, *ipso facto*, ascertaining its intention from some source other than the statute, and this might be regarded as going beyond the judicial function. Moreover, the judge may expose himself to the criticism that he is giving effect to his own views of what the policy of Parliament *ought* to be.[162] The contrary view, however, is that a consideration of the context in which Parliament has used particular words can only enhance a judge's ability to ascertain their intended meaning:[163]

> The starting point is that language in all legal texts conveys meaning according to the circumstances in which it was used. It follows that the context must always be identified and considered before the process of construction or during it. It is therefore wrong to say that the court may only resort to evidence of the contextual scene when an ambiguity has arisen.

In *Shah v Barnet London Borough Council*,[164] the House of Lords offered *some* guidance as to when a purposive interpretation of a provision could be adopted in preference to its literal meaning. It concluded that this would only be legitimate where a clear expression of the legislative intention could be found in either the Act or permissible extrinsic sources.

Supplying omissions

The legitimacy of going beyond a literal interpretation of a statute is often called into question when a court is faced with a factual situation for which the statute does not provide. Such a situation is termed a *casus omissus*, and it can only be remedied by attributing to Parliament an intention that it never had. This amounts to a legislative act on the part of the judiciary, and it is a function that the more conservative judges

---

[161] Law Commission, *The Interpretation of Statutes* (Law Com No 21, 1969).

[162] See *Duport Steels Ltd v Sirs* [1980] 1 All ER 529, [1980] 1 WLR 142; *Shah v Barnet London Borough Council* [1983] 2 AC 309, [1983] 1 All ER 226.

[163] *Westminster City Council v National Asylum Support Service* [2002] UKHL 38 at [5], [2002] 4 All ER 654 at [5], [2002] 1 WLR 2956, *per* Lord Steyn.

[164] [1983] 2 AC 309, [1983] 1 All ER 226.

are slow to adopt. Denning LJ, in the Court of Appeal, expressed his personal view of the judicial function as follows:[165]

> We sit here to find out the intention of Parliament and of Ministers and carry it out, and we do this better by filling in the gaps and making sense of the enactment than by opening it up to destructive analysis.

On appeal Lord Simonds condemned this approach, describing it as a 'naked usurpation of the legislative function under the thin disguise of interpretation'.[166] 'If a gap is disclosed,' Lord Simonds explained, 'the remedy lies in an amending Act'. However, in *Inco Europe Ltd v First Choice Distribution*, the House of Lords was unanimous in confirming that the courts do have the power to correct obvious drafting errors:[167]

> Before interpreting a statute in this way the court must be abundantly sure of three matters: (1) the intended purpose of the statute or provision in question; (2) that by inadvertence the draftsman and Parliament failed to give effect to that purpose in the provision in question; and (3) the substance of the provision Parliament would have made, although not necessarily the precise words Parliament would have used, had the error in the Bill been noticed.

The trend towards purposive interpretation

While the literal and purposive approaches to statutory interpretation may be alternative models, it would be wrong to treat them as mutually exclusive. Firstly, a literal reading of a provision will not always be able to resolve an ambiguity, and, secondly, even under a purposive approach the court's primary obligation is to interpret the words of the Act. As Lord Hoffmann explained in one case:[168] 'There is ultimately only one principle of construction, namely to ascertain what Parliament meant by using the language of the statute.' Moreover, since these are merely approaches rather than strict rules, judges can, and do, adopt whichever method of interpretation they consider appropriate, and it is common to find elements of both approaches influencing the same decision. Thus, as Laws LJ observed, 'the difference in purposive and literal construction is in truth one of degree only,'[169] and the cases do not always fall neatly into distinct categories.

For some judges, the choice of approach is a matter of principle, and it is inextricably linked with ideas about the role of the courts within the framework of the constitution and the separation of powers.[170]

> [I]t cannot be too strongly emphasised that the British Constitution, though largely unwritten, is firmly based on the separation of powers. Parliament makes the laws, the

---

[165] *Magor and St Mellons Rural District Council v Newport Corporation* [1950] 2 All ER 1226 at 1236.
[166] [1952] AC 189 at 191, [1951] 2 All ER 839 at 841.
[167] [2000] 2 All ER 109 at 115, [2000] 1 WLR 586 at 592, *per* Lord Nicholls. See also *Kammins Ballrooms Co Ltd v Zenith Investments (Torquay) Ltd* [1971] AC 850, [1970] 2 All ER 871.
[168] *MacNiven v Westmoreland Investments* [2001] UKHL 6, [2003] 1 AC 311, [2001] 1 All ER 865.
[169] *Oliver Ashworth (Holdings) Ltd v Ballard (Kent) Ltd* [2000] Ch 12 at 34, [1999] 2 All ER 791 at 805.
[170] *Duport Steels v Sirs* [1980] 1 All ER 529 at 541, [1980] 1 WLR 142 at 157, *per* Lord Diplock.

judiciary interprets them. When Parliament legislates to remedy what the majority of its members at the time perceive to be a defect or lacuna in the existing law…the role of the judiciary is confined to ascertaining from the words that Parliament has approved as expressing its intention what that intention was, and giving effect to it. Where the meaning of statutory words is plain and unambiguous it is not for judges to invent fancied ambiguities as an excuse for failing to give effect to its plain meaning…Under our constitution it is Parliament's opinion on these matters that is paramount.

Increasingly, however, many judges take the view that the approach to interpretation must be determined on an individual basis, taking into account all of the circumstances of a case.

KEY ISSUE

It is clear that the willingness to look beyond a strict literal approach is commonplace and the decision to permit limited use of Hansard as an extrinsic aid is evidence of this. It is equally beyond doubt that the particular approach adopted by the court will turn not only on the inclinations of the individual judge, but also upon the context in which the matter is being decided. As will be seen later, the courts are always anxious to adopt a purposive approach to statutes in order to give effect to international obligations, and in the context of EU law they are under a legal obligation to do so. In addition, the Human Rights Act 1998 obliges the courts to take a more creative approach to statutory interpretation in all cases that could impact on the protection of ECHR rights.

❓ Questions

1. Is there a right approach to the interpretation of statutes?

2. Is it the intention of Parliament at the time of passage of an Act that matters or the view of the court interpreting the statute?

Statutory interpretation under the Human Rights Act 1998[171]

The Human Rights Act 1998 adds a new dimension to the task of statutory interpretation.[172] The long title describes it as 'an Act to give further effect to rights and freedoms guaranteed under the European Convention on Human Rights', and one of the principal mechanisms by which it seeks to do this is contained in section 3(1). This provides that: 'So far as it is possible to do so, primary legislation and subordinate legislation must be read and given effect in a way which is compatible

---

[171] Much has been written about statutory interpretation under the Human Rights Act 1998. See e.g., Clayton, 'The Limits of What's "Possible": Statutory Construction Under the Human Rights Act' [2002] EHRLR 559; Kavanagh, 'The Role of Parliamentary Intention in Adjudication under the Human Rights Act 1998' (2006) 26(1) OJLS 179; Lord Lester, 'The Art of the Possible: Interpreting Statutes under the Human Rights Act' [1998] EHRLR 665; Marshall, 'The Lynchpin of Parliamentary Intention: Lost, Stolen or Strained?' [2003] PL 236; Van Zyl Smit, 'The New Purposive Interpretation of Statutes: HRA Section 3 after *Ghaidan* v *Godin-Mendoza*' (2007) 70(2) MLR 294.

[172] The overall significance of this major piece of legislation is discussed in Chapter 5.

with the Convention rights.'[173] Section 3 applies to *all* legislation, whether enacted before or after the Human Rights Act,[174] and it significantly enhances the courts' powers of interpretation. However, it stops short of enabling them to disapply Acts of Parliament[175] and it does not affect the validity, continuing operation, or enforcement of any incompatible primary legislation. Nor does it affect the validity of incompatible subordinate legislation where primary legislation prevents removal of the incompatibility.[176] If a Convention-compliant interpretation of an Act is not possible, a court[177] may issue a declaration of incompatibility but it must still give effect to the legislation as Parliament intended.[178] Thus, as Lord Steyn explained:[179]

> It is crystal clear that the carefully and subtly drafted Human Rights Act 1998 preserves the principle of Parliamentary sovereignty. In a case of incompatibility which cannot be avoided by interpretation under section 3(1), the courts may not disapply the legislation. The court may merely issue a declaration of incompatibility which then gives rise to a power to take remedial action.

Section 3 is more than just a 'tool' that judges may consider in the event of an ambiguity, and its effect is not simply to add yet another approach to existing canons of interpretation. Instead, it imposes an *obligation* on judges to seek a Convention-compatible interpretation, regardless of whether the provision in question is ambiguous. Once it is established that Convention rights are engaged, courts are permitted to go far beyond previously accepted limits in seeking 'possible' meanings of words:[180]

> [Section 3] will require a very different approach to interpretation from that to which the English courts are accustomed. Traditionally, the search has been for the true meaning: now it will be for a possible meaning that would prevent the making of a declaration of incompatibility.

---

[173] Section 1(1) provides that 'Convention rights' are those ECHR rights contained in Articles 2–12 and 14, Articles 1–3 of the First Protocol and Article 1 Thirteenth Protocol. The text of these Articles is set out in Sch 1 to the Act.

[174] Section 3(2).

[175] Compare the European Communities Act 1972, s 2(4); discussed further in Chapter 4.

[176] Section 3(2).

[177] For these purposes, the term 'court' means the House of Lords, the Judicial Committee of the Privy Council, the Court Martial Appeal Court, the Court of Appeal, the High Court, the Court of Protection, and the Scottish High Court of Justiciary (except when sitting as a trial court or Court of Session): s 4(5).

[178] Section 4. The effect of such a declaration is simply to bring the incompatibility to the attention of Parliament, and, where appropriate, to allow Ministers to take remedial action under s 10. Incompatible *subordinate* legislation may be declared invalid unless primary legislation prevents removal of the incompatibility. In the latter case a declaration of incompatibility may be issued.

[179] *R v DPP, ex parte Kebilene* [2000] 2 AC 326 at 333, [1999] 4 All ER 801 at 831.

[180] Lord Cooke, 582 HL Official Report (5th series) col 1272, 3 November 1997. (Even before the Human Rights Act, there is evidence that some judges were prepared to take a more teleological approach to the interpretation of human rights provisions. See, e.g., the Privy Council's experience of interpreting written constitutions and bills of rights from other jurisdictions: *Huntley* v *Attorney-General for Jamaica* [1995] 2 AC 1, [1995] 1 All ER 308; *Attorney-General of Hong-Kong* v *Lee Kwong-kut* [1993] AC 951, [1993] 3 All ER 939.)

On the other hand, section 3 need not be considered at all unless an 'ordinary' reading of the disputed legislation would give rise to a Convention breach:[181]

> [U]nless the legislation would otherwise be in breach of the Convention section 3 can be ignored; so courts should always first ascertain whether, absent section 3, there would be any breach of the Convention...

Several cases decided since the Act came into force have considered the permissible boundaries of interpretation under section 3. In *Poplar Housing and Regeneration Community Association* v *Donoghue*, the Court of Appeal sought to distinguish between the tasks of legislation and interpretation:[182] '[I]f it is necessary in order to obtain compliance to radically alter the effect of the legislation this will be an indication that more than interpretation is involved.' It is clear that 'reading down' legislation to narrow the effect of a provision, and reading additional words *in*, are both legitimate techniques in Human Rights Act cases. Thus, in *R* v *Lambert*,[183] the House of Lords read down a provision of the Misuse of Drugs Act 1971, so as to impose an evidential rather than a legal burden on the accused and thereby avoid a breach of the presumption of innocence. Similarly, in *Ghaidan* v *Godin-Mendoza*,[184] the phrase 'as his or her wife or husband' was construed to mean '*as if they were* his or her wife or husband', in order to avoid a conclusion that the Rent Act 1977 discriminated against same-sex partners.

The leading case on section 3 is *R* v *A (No 2)*.[185] The defendant was prosecuted for rape and sought to rely on the defence of consent. He wanted to adduce evidence of the complainant's sexual history in support of this defence, but the use of such evidence appeared to be precluded by section 41 of the Youth Justice and Criminal Evidence Act 1999. Defence counsel contended that a refusal to admit the evidence would breach the right of the accused to a fair trial under Article 6 of the Convention: the issue for the court was whether it was 'possible' to interpret section 41 in a manner compatible with that right. The House of Lords held that it was, interpreting it as being subject to an implied discretion to permit evidence of sexual history in order to ensure a fair trial. Lord Steyn explained the effect of section 3 as follows:[186]

> [T]he interpretive obligation under s 3 of the 1998 Act is a strong one. It applies even if there is no ambiguity in the language in the sense of the language being capable of two different meanings... Under ordinary methods of interpretation a court may depart from the language of the statute to avoid absurd consequences: s 3 goes much further. Undoubtedly, a court must always look for a contextual and purposive interpretation: s 3 is more radical in its effect. It is a general principle of the interpretation of legal instruments that the text is the primary source of interpretation: other sources are subordinate to it... Section 3

---

[181] *Poplar Housing and Regeneration Community Association Ltd* v *Donoghue* [2001] EWCA Civ 595 at [75], [2002] QB 48 at [75], [2001] 4 All ER 604, *per* Lord Woolf CJ. This approach was endorsed by Lord Hope in *R* v *A (No 2)* [2001] UKHL 25 at [58], [2002] 1 AC 45 at [58], [2001] 3 All ER 1.
[182] [2001] EWCA Civ 595 at [76], [2002] QB 48 at [76], [2001] 4 All ER 604, *per* Lord Woolf CJ.
[183] [2001] UKHL 37, [2002] 2 AC 545, [2001] 3 All ER 577.
[184] [2004] UKHL 30, [2004] 2 AC 557, [2004] 3 All ER 411.
[185] [2001] UKHL 25, [2002] 1 AC 45, [2001] 3 All ER 1.   [186] Ibid at [40].

qualifies this general principle because it requires a court to find an interpretation compatible with Convention rights if it is possible to do so…In accordance with the will of Parliament as reflected in s 3 it will sometimes be necessary to adopt an interpretation, which linguistically may appear strained. The techniques to be used will not only involve the reading down of express language in a statute but also the implication of provisions.

Thus far, *R v A (No 2)* probably constitutes the 'high-water mark' of judicial creativity under the Human Rights Act, and in subsequent decisions the courts have not always been willing to go quite this far. In *Re S (Children) (Care Order: Implementation of Care Plan)*,[187] the Court of Appeal read words into the Children Act 1989 to give the courts increased discretionary powers concerning children taken into care. On appeal to the House of Lords, however, this use of section 3 was rejected, and their Lordships cautioned against reading words into an Act to the point of making it unintelligible or unworkable:[188]

> [Section] 3(2)(b) presupposes that not all provisions in primary legislation can be rendered convention compliant by the application of section 3(1)…For present purposes, it is sufficient to say that a meaning which departs substantially from a fundamental feature of an Act of Parliament is likely to have crossed the boundary between interpretation and amendment.

In *Ghaidan v Godin-Mendoza*,[189] the House of Lords enthusiastically returned to the creative approach adopted in *R v A (No 2)*. More recently, in *Secretary of State for the Home Department v MB*,[190] a majority of the House of Lords held that provisions in the Prevention of Terrorism Act 2005 could be read down so as to ensure compatibility with the right to a fair trial. The applicant was subject to a control order made on the basis of undisclosed material, and he challenged the order on the grounds that he did not know the case against him. The House of Lords agreed that the rights of an individual could be limited on grounds of national security, and that any potential injustice might be mitigated by the use of special advocates or other procedural devices. However, such devices might not always be sufficient to ensure compliance with the right to a fair trial under Article 6 of the Convention and in such circumstances the provisions could be read down to ensure that they only took effect where that would be consistent with fair procedure for the individual.

To date, relatively few cases have resulted in a declaration of incompatibility.[191] In *R (on the application of H) v North and East London Regional Mental Health Tribunal*, the Court of Appeal declared sections 72(1) and 73(1) of the Mental Health Act 1983

---

[187] [2001] EWCA Civ 757, [2002] 2 FLR 582, [2002] HRLR 50.

[188] [2002] UKHL 10 at [38]–[43], [2002] 2 AC 291 at [38]–[43], [2002] 2 All ER 192, *per* Lord Nicholls. See also *International Transport Roth GmbH v Secretary of State for the Home Department* [2002] EWCA Civ 158, [2003] QB 728, [2002] HRLR 31. In this case the Court of Appeal was unable to find a compatible interpretation of provisions in the Immigration and Asylum Act 1999 without crossing the boundaries of legitimate interpretation. A declaration of incompatibility was issued.

[189] [2004] UKHL 30, [2004] 2 AC 557, [2004] 3 All ER 411.   [190] [2007] UKHL 46.

[191] Of these, a number have been overturned on appeal. See, e.g., *R (on the Application of Alconbury) v Secretary of State for the Environment, Transport and the Regions* [2001] UKHL 23, [2003] 2 AC 295, [2001] 2

to be incompatible with the right to liberty under Article 5.[192] The offending provisions were subsequently amended by the Mental Health Act 1983 (Remedial) Order 2001.[193] In another case, the Court of Appeal issued a declaration of incompatibility in relation to provisions of the Immigration and Asylum Act 1999. The provisions imposed a fixed penalty of £2,000 per entrant on hauliers responsible for bringing illegal entrants into the United Kingdom.[194] The legislative response to this decision was to amend the offending provisions by Act of Parliament.[195] In *Bellinger* v *Bellinger*,[196] a provision stating that a marriage shall be void if 'the parties are not respectively male and female'[197] was held to be incompatible with the rights of the transsexual applicant under Articles 8 and 12. Parliament's response was to enact the Gender Recognition Act 2004. Declarations of incompatibility have also been made in relation to provisions denying the possibility of review by the Parole Board to prisoners subject to deportation orders,[198] and provisions allowing the detention without trial of foreign nationals suspected of involvement in terrorism.[199]

KEY ISSUE

How sections 3 and s 4 of the Human Rights Act 1998 are used has proved one of the most contentious of legal issues. Critics of some of the decisions of the courts under section 3 argue that judges are going beyond the legitimate interpretive role of the courts.[200] It was clearly the intention of Parliament that judges should give the words of a statute a modified meaning in at least some circumstances, but the very fact that section 4 was passed also is a recognition that in some circumstances it would not be possible or appropriate to give the words a modified meaning. The preference by the courts for the use of section 3 rather than section 4 may also reflect the fact that a declaration of incompatibility does not affect the result of the particular case. The real difficulty for the courts is in deciding where to draw the line. If they go too far, judges are in danger of stepping outside their proper role under the separation of powers

All ER 929, reversing [2002] HRLR 2; *Matthews* v *Ministry of Defence* [2002] EWCA Civ 773, [2002] 3 All ER 513, [2002] 1 WLR 2621, reversing [2002] EWHC 13.

[192] [2001] EWCA Civ 415, [2002] QB 1, [2002] 3 WLR 512. Section 73 of the Mental Health Act 1983 concerns the test to be applied when determining a restricted patient's entitlement to release from a secure hospital. The provision was held to be incompatible with Article 5 as the burden of proof rested on the patient to show that his continued detention under the Act was no longer warranted.

[193] SI 2001/3712.

[194] *International Transport Roth GmbH* v *Secretary of State for the Home Department* [2002] EWCA Civ 158, [2003] QB 728, [2002] HRLR 31.

[195] Nationality, Asylum and Immigration Act 2002.

[196] [2003] UKHL 21, [2003] 2 AC 467, [2003] 2 All ER 593. Their Lordships noted that the government had already indicated its acceptance of the decision in *Goodwin* v *UK* (2002) 35 EHRR 18, in which the European Court of Human Rights had concluded that UK law was in breach of the Convention.

[197] Matrimonial Causes Act 1973, s 11.

[198] *R (on the application of Clift and others)* v *Secretary of State for the Home Department* [2006] UKHL 54, [2007] 1 AC 484, [2007] 2 All ER 1.

[199] *A* v *Secretary of State for the Home Department* [2004] UKHL 56, [2005] 2 WLR 87: see p 159.

[200] See p 153.

> **? Questions**
>
> 1. What criteria might a court use to determine whether the use of section 3 is preferable to the making of a declaration of incompatibility?
> 2. Have the courts struck the balance between the use of sections 3 and 4 correctly?

Rules of interpretation and language

The statute must be read as a whole

The meaning suggested by a word when used in isolation might be different from that suggested when used in conjunction with other words. A statute must therefore be read as a whole, and every section must be interpreted in the light of other sections. The decision of the House of Lords in *Beswick* v *Beswick* provides an interesting illustration of this.[201] The case concerned the interpretation of section 56(1) of the Law of Property Act 1925, which states that 'a person may take an interest in land or other property...although he may not be named as a party to the conveyance or other instrument'. The interpretation section of the same Act states that 'in this Act unless the context otherwise requires "property" includes "any thing in action"'.[202] It was argued that the combined effect of these provisions was to enable a stranger to a contract to enforce it, but the House of Lords rejected this argument. Their Lordships pointed out that section 56 is one of twenty-five sections in the Act grouped under the heading 'conveyances and other instruments', and in the context of the Act as a whole it was held that the word 'property' must be interpreted to mean 'real property'.

The general principle that a statute must be read as a whole has given rise to three specific presumptions concerning the use of language, each of which is known by a Latin title.

Noscitur a sociis

This translates as 'a thing is known by its associates', and in practical terms it means that where a provision contains a list of items, the meaning of each individual word in the list is coloured by the meaning of the others. In *Foster* v *Diphwys Casson Slate Co*,[203] the court had to consider whether a statute prohibited the taking of explosives into a mine when carried in a cloth bag. The relevant statute stated that explosives could only be taken into a mine when carried in a 'case or canister'. Although in one sense a cloth bag might be thought of as a 'case', when interpreted in the context of the surrounding words it was held that the word only referred to containers of the same strength and solidity as a 'canister'.

---

[201] [1968] AC 58, [1967] 2 All ER 1197. Note that the law on privity of contract has now been substantially altered by the Contract (Rights of Third Parties) Act 1999.

[202] Section 205(1).   [203] (1887) LR 18 QBD 428.

Ejusdem generis

This rule means that general words that follow two or more particular words in an Act must be confined to a meaning of the same kind as the particular words. When the intention is to cover a wide range of similar circumstances, it is common drafting practice to use two or three particular examples, followed by a general expression such as 'or other place'. The effect of this is to extend the operation of the enactment to all circumstances within the same genus.

The operation of the rule can best be illustrated by two examples. Section 1 of the Betting Act 1853 prohibited the keeping of a 'house, office, room *or other place*' for the purposes of betting. In *Powell* v *Kempton Park Racecourse Co*,[204] the issue was whether Tattersalls' ring at a racecourse was an 'other place' within the meaning of the Act. The House of Lords held that it was not, since the words 'house, office, room' created a genus of indoor places within which an outdoor place did not fall. *Brownsea Haven Properties Ltd* v *Poole Corporation*[205] concerned a power to make traffic orders 'in all times of public processions, rejoicings, or illuminations, *and in any case when the streets are thronged or liable to be obstructed*'. It was held that this did not confer power to create a one-way traffic system for the six months of the summer holiday season.

It should be noted that there must be at least two specific words to create a genus. Thus where an Act referred to 'theatres and other places of amusement', it was held that a funfair was within the Act even though not *ejusdem generis* with the word 'theatres'.[206] Similarly, the *ejusdem generis* rule does not apply where the particular words in a statute are sufficiently different that they do not create a genus at all.[207]

Expressio unius est exclusio alterius

This translates as 'to express one thing is to exclude another'. It means simply that where a provision includes an item or list that is *not* followed by general words such as 'or other place', it is presumed that Parliament did not intend any unspecified items to be included. Thus, in *R* v *Cuthbertson*,[208] a power to order forfeiture of property following a conviction for 'an offence under *this* Act' did not authorize forfeiture for *conspiracy* to commit an offence: the offence of conspiracy was not created by that Act.[209]

---

[204] [1899] AC 143; cf. *Culley* v *Harrison* [1956] 2 QB 71, [1956] 2 All ER 254.

[205] [1958] Ch 574, [1958] 1 All ER 205; see also *DPP* v *Jordan* [1977] AC 699, [1976] 3 All ER 775. Section 4(1) of the Obscene Publications Act 1959 provides a public good defence in the case of articles considered to be 'in the interests of science, literature, art or learning, or of other objects of general concern'. The House of Lords held that when construed *ejusdem generis* with the preceding words, the phrase 'other objects of general concern' did not include the psychotherapeutic value of pornography to sexual deviants.

[206] *Allen* v *Emmerson* [1944] KB 362, [1944] 1 All ER 344.

[207] For an illustration of this, see *Re C (A Minor) (Interim Care Order: Residential Assessment)* [1997] AC 489, [1996] 4 All ER 871.

[208] [1981] AC 470, [1980] 2 All ER 401.

[209] The statute in question was the Misuse of Drugs Act 1971.

Interpretation Act 1978

This Act, which consolidated and amended the Interpretation Act 1889, prescribes definitions of certain words and phrases that are commonly encountered in Acts of Parliament. Thus, for example:

> unless the contrary intention appears: (a) words importing the masculine gender include the feminine; (b) words importing the feminine gender include the masculine; (c) words in the singular include the plural and words in the plural include the singular.[210]
>
> 'month' means calendar month.[211]

However, these and other definitions are only presumptive and they yield to a contrary intention in the Act being interpreted. Thus, although the Interpretation Act defines the word 'person' to include a body corporate, a corporation carrying out legal work was not held to be not guilty of acting as an unqualified 'person': the statute concerned could only apply to persons who could qualify as solicitors.[212]

Presumptions of substance

It is possible to express almost any rule of statutory interpretation in the form of a presumption. The rules against retrospective and extraterritorial operation are often expressed as presumptions, and the 'rules' concerning the interpretation of language can also be thought of as presumptions since their operation can be displaced by an express provision to the contrary. Nevertheless, although it is probably a mere matter of terminology, the following are always described as presumptions rather than rules.[213] Recent decisions indicate that these presumptions may simply be facets of the wider principle of legality:[214]

> Parliament does not legislate in a vacuum. Parliament legislates for a European liberal democracy founded on the principles and traditions of the common law. And the courts may approach legislation on this initial assumption. But this assumption only has prima facie force. It can be displaced by a clear and specific provision to the contrary.

Penal provisions are construed narrowly

Where a statute imposes criminal liability or tax obligations (which are treated as penal) and the statute is ambiguous or uncertain, it should be construed in favour of

---

[210] Section 6. For an illustration of this rule, see *Floor* v *Davis* [1980] AC 695, [1979] 2 All ER 677.

[211] Section 5 and Sch 1.

[212] *Law Society* v *United Service Bureau Ltd* [1934] 1 KB 343. This lacuna was filled by the Solicitors Act 1957 (now Solicitors Act 1974, s 20).

[213] For a useful discussion of several presumptions, see *Wilson* v *First County Trust (No 2)* [2003] UKHL 40 at [186]–[201], [2004] 1 AC 816 at [186]–[201], [2003] 4 All ER 97, *per* Lord Rodger.

[214] *R* v *Secretary of State for the Home Department, ex parte Pierson* [1998] AC 539 at 587, [1997] 3 All ER 577 at 603, *per* Lord Steyn. In *Wilson* v *First County Trust (No 2)* [2003] UKHL 40 at [153], [2004] 1 AC 816 at [153], [2003] 4 All ER 97, Lord Scott described the presumption against giving retrospective effect to legislation as 'part of a broader presumption that Parliament does not intend a statute to have an unfair or unjust effect.'

the individual.[215] Thus it has been held that the offence of 'knowingly possessing an explosive' requires knowledge on the part of the accused that the substance possessed is explosive, not merely that he possesses the substance.[216] One aspect of this general rule is the presumption against the imposition of liability without fault.

However, this rule of interpretation is not strong enough to displace the literal rule. Consequently, where a statute unambiguously creates a criminal offence or a tax, the court is bound to give effect to it. The provision will be regarded as unambiguous if the court considers the intention of Parliament to be clear, notwithstanding that the words are capable of bearing more than one meaning.[217]

Presumption against the imposition of criminal liability without fault

At common law, *mens rea* (intent) is an element in all crimes,[218] and although the legislature can, and does, create strict liability offences, the intention so to do must be clear and unambiguous. In *Sweet* v *Parsley*,[219] the House of Lords quashed a conviction for managing premises used for the smoking of cannabis, on the basis that the accused rented out the premises and did not know that her tenants were using drugs. Lord Reid explained the judicial approach as follows:[220]

> [O]ur first duty is to consider the words of the Act; if they show a clear intention to create an absolute offence, that is an end of the matter. But such cases are very rare. Sometimes the words of the section which creates a particular offence make it clear that mens rea is required in one form or another. Such cases are quite frequent. But in a very large number of cases there is no clear indication either way. In such cases there has for centuries been a presumption that Parliament did not intend to make criminals of persons who were in no way blameworthy in what they did. That means that, whenever a section is silent as to mens rea, there is a presumption that, in order to give effect to the will of Parliament, we must read in words appropriate to require mens rea.

The more serious the alleged offence, the more difficult it will be to rebut the presumption of the need for *mens rea*. Thus, in *B* v *DPP*,[221] the House of Lords allowed the appeal of a 15-year-old boy who had pleaded guilty to inciting a child under the age of 14 to commit an act of gross indecency: the boy had honestly believed that the girl was over 14.[222] In contrast, where a statute is silent on the question of *mens rea*,

---

[215] *Kingston-upon-Hull Dock Co* v *Browne* (1831) 2 B & Ad 43; *D'Avigdor-Goldsmid* v *Inland Revenue Commissioners* [1953] AC 347, [1953] 1 All ER 403.

[216] *R* v *Hallam* [1957] 1 QB 569, [1957] 1 All ER 665.

[217] See, e.g., *Attorney-General's Reference (No 1 of 1988)* [1989] AC 971, [1989] 2 All ER 1; *Inland Revenue Commissioners* v *Hinchy* [1960] AC 748, [1960] 1 All ER 505. See also pp 37 and 39.

[218] See *R* v *Tolson* (1889) LR 23 QBD 168; *Younghusband* v *Luftig* [1949] 2 KB 354, [1949] 2 All ER 72.

[219] [1970] AC 132, [1969] 1 All ER 347.   [220] [1970] AC 132 at 148, [1969] 1 All ER 347 at 349.

[221] [2000] 2 AC 428, 1 All ER 833.

[222] See also, *R* v *K (Age of Consent: Reasonable Belief)* [2001] UKHL 41, [2002] 1 AC 462, [2001] 3 All ER 897, where the same reasoning was applied to a charge of indecent assault under the Sexual Offences Act 1956, s 14(1). The 14-year-old alleged victim had in fact consented to the act and the defendant had a genuine belief that she was over the age of 16. The House of Lords reversed the Court of Appeal's finding and held that the prosecution was required to prove *mens rea* in respect of the girl's age. Interestingly, the Court of Appeal seems to have based its reasoning on an application of *expressio unius est exclusio alterius*: the

a court *may* be prepared to treat an offence as one of strict liability if this would help to further some general social objective and if the offence is not 'truly criminal' in character.[223]

An analogous presumption is that Parliament does not intend to create new criminal offences. In *R v Horseferry Road Justices, ex parte Independent Broadcasting Authority*,[224] the Queen's Bench Divisional Court held that 'the inference that Parliament did not intend to create an offence in the absence of an express provision to that effect is, nowadays, almost irresistible'. This is of very limited application, however, since when Parliament does intend to create a new criminal offence this is usually made clear by the fact that penalties for the offence are specified.

Presumption against alteration of the law

Parliament, like the judiciary, is presumed to know the law. Consequently if an Act does not *expressly* alter the law, it will be presumed that Parliament did not intend it to have that effect. In the words of Devlin J,[225] 'a statute is not to be taken as effecting a fundamental alteration in the general law unless it uses words which point unmistakably to that conclusion'. It is important to remember, however, that Parliament can and does make fundamental alterations to the common law, and if such a change appears from a literal interpretation of the words used, the use of any presumption to the contrary is out of place.

The presumption against fundamental change also applies in relation to statute law. One aspect of this is the presumption that where a provision is re-enacted in a consolidating statute, a modest change in the wording does not necessarily introduce a fundamental change in meaning. Conversely, the mere fact that a provision *is* re-enacted cannot be assumed to mean that Parliament is endorsing judicial interpretations of the earlier enactment. The court must interpret the enactment as it stands, although if the scales are equally balanced, the fact that Parliament has re-enacted a provision that has been the subject of judicial interpretation might tip the balance in favour of that interpretation.[226]

Presumptions against deprivation of liberty and property

There is a well-established presumption that, in the absence of express provision, the courts will not construe a statute as depriving a person of any property right vested in him before the statute came into operation. For example, every person has a right to the use and enjoyment of his own land. The remedy for infringement of this right

---

Act expressly required *mens rea* in relation to other offences but was silent with regard to indecent assault: [2001] 1 Cr App R 35, [2001] Crim LR 134.

[223] See, e.g., *R v Bezzina* [1994] 3 All ER 964, [1994] WLR 1057 (owning or handling a dog that is dangerously out of control in a public place); and *Harrow LBC v Shah* [1999] 3 All ER 302, [2000] 1 WLR 83 (selling a National Lottery ticket to a child under the age of 16).

[224] [1987] QB 54 at 72, [1986] 2 All ER 666 at 674, *per* Lloyd LJ.

[225] *National Assistance Board v Wilkinson* [1952] 2 QB 648 at 661, [1952] 2 All ER 255 at 260.

[226] See p 66.

is an action in trespass or nuisance, depending on the character of the interference. Consequently where a statute authorizes the performance of an act that constitutes a nuisance to the claimant, the statute will not be construed as removing the claimant's right unless it is clearly intended to have that effect.[227] There is an even stronger presumption against the deprivation of a person's liberty. Thus, in a case concerning detention under the Mental Health Act 1983, it was said that[228] 'Parliament is presumed not to enact legislation which interferes with the liberty of a subject without making it clear that this was its intention'. Both presumptions must now be considered in the context of the Human Rights Act 1998, which requires legislation to be interpreted as far as possible in a manner compatible with the rights to liberty and to peaceful enjoyment of possessions.[229] Even in the Human Rights Act era, however, liberty and proprietary rights may be taken away by express words. In *R (on the application of H) v North and East London Regional Mental Health Tribunal*,[230] the Court of Appeal found it impossible to interpret provisions of the Mental Health Act 1983 in a manner compatible with the right to liberty. A declaration of incompatibility was issued, but this did not, of course, alter the validity of the legislation.[231]

Presumption against ousting the jurisdiction of the courts

Individuals cannot, by contract, exclude the jurisdiction of the courts. Although Parliament may exclude an individual's recourse to the courts, any provision purporting so to do must be absolutely clear and unambiguous since the courts are extremely wary about permitting interference with their jurisdiction.[232] So reluctant are the courts to see their jurisdiction ousted that even seemingly clear words may not suffice. Thus, in *Anisminic v Foreign Compensation Commission*,[233] a provision stating that any 'determination' of the Commission 'shall not be called into question in any court of law' did not prevent a court declaring that the Commission had made a fundamental error of law that deprived it of power to act. Because it had no power, no *valid* 'determination' was being called into question. Such legal sophistry can only be prevented by the clearest of words. An example of such words is the amended wording introduced following the *Anisminic* decision: section 3 of the Foreign Compensation Act 1969 prevents judicial review even of a 'purported determination'.

---

[227] *Metropolitan Asylum District Managers v Hill* (1881) 6 App Cas 193.

[228] *R v Hallstrom, ex parte W* [1986] QB 1090 at 1104, [1986] 2 All ER 306, *per* McCullough J.

[229] Section 3: see p 55. The rights to liberty (Article 5, ECHR) and the peaceful enjoyment of possessions (Article 1, Protocol 1, ECHR) are protected Convention rights under s 1 of the 1998 Act.

[230] [2001] EWCA Civ 415, [2002] QB 1, [2001] 3 WLR 512.

[231] The offending provisions were subsequently amended by the Mental Health Act 1983 (Remedial) Order 2001, SI 2001/3712. See further p 159.

[232] See, e.g., *Ealing London Borough v Race Relations Board* [1972] AC 342 at 353, [1972] 1 All ER 105 at 108. In this case the House of Lords held that the machinery established under the Race Relations Act 1968 for referring disputes to county courts did not exclude the inherent supervisory jurisdiction of the High Court.

[233] [1969] 2 AC 147, [1969] 1 All ER 208.

On the basis of this presumption, a provision stating that the decision of an inferior court, tribunal, or administrative body shall be 'final' will be held not to exclude the prerogative jurisdiction of the High Court to review the decision:

> if a tribunal goes wrong in law and the error appears on the face of the record, the High Court will interfere…to quash the decision. It is not to be deterred by the enactment that the decision is 'final'. The decision may be final on the facts but it is not final on the law.[234]

In contrast, a statute permitting challenge within a limited period is likely to be effective in preventing any review after that period. In *R v Cornwall County Council, ex parte Huntington*,[235] a Divisional Court held that the terms of the Wildlife and Countryside Act 1981, which excluded judicial challenge after a forty-two-day period, prevented the court from engaging in judicial review of an order made under the Act.

Presumption that a statute does not bind the Crown

One of the few relics of the prerogative of the Crown is the rule that the Crown is not bound by a statute unless expressly named in it. The rule extends to the Crown and to its servants and agents, although not to nationalized industries.[236] The Crown Proceedings Act 1947 placed the Crown, with certain exceptions, in the same position as a private person in the law of torts. Consequently, statutes that affect common law rights and duties are usually expressed to bind the Crown. Examples are the Limitation Act 1980 and the Occupiers' Liability Act 1957. In practice, the general trend of modern legislation is towards the removal of the Crown's privileges and immunities.

Presumption that Parliament does not intend to violate international law

There is a presumption that Parliament does not intend to legislate in a manner incompatible with international law. The courts generally take a purposive approach when interpreting statutes designed to give effect to treaty obligations, the presumption being that Parliament intends such legislation to achieve its objectives.[237] Similarly, where a provision is genuinely ambiguous, the courts may take account of a treaty when choosing between two equally reasonable interpretations, regardless of whether the statute was enacted for the purpose of giving effect to that treaty.[238]

---

[234] *Tehrani v Rostron* [1972] 1 QB 182 at 187, [1971] 3 All ER 790 at 793, *per* Lord Denning MR: see also *R v Medical Appeal Tribunal, ex parte Gilmore* [1957] 1 QB 574, [1957] 1 All ER 796, where the earlier authorities are reviewed.

[235] [1992] 3 All ER 566. The decision was upheld on appeal: see [1994] 1 All ER 694.

[236] *Tamlin v Hannaford* [1950] 1 KB 18, [1949] 2 All ER 327; for an account of the history of this presumption and a recent illustration of its operation, see *Lord Advocate v Dumbarton District Council* [1990] 2 AC 580, [1990] 1 All ER 1.

[237] *Salomon v Commissioners of Customs and Excise* [1967] 2 QB 116, [1966] 3 WLR 1223. The interpretation of legislation designed to give effect to obligations of EU law is discussed in Chapter 4.

[238] *R v Chief Immigration Officer, ex parte Salamat Bibi* [1976] 3 All ER 843, [1976] 1 WLR 979. It was held that where such an ambiguity arose, the courts had a discretion to take into account the United Kingdom's obligations under the European Convention on Human Rights. Since the introduction of the Human Rights Act 1998, however, courts have had a *statutory obligation* to seek an ECHR-compatible interpretation of all legislation, whether it is ambiguous or not. See further, p 152.

Of course, as with other presumptions, this is subject to the overriding principle that Parliament is legislatively supreme: clear and unambiguous words in the main body of an Act will take precedence over any inconsistent treaty obligations:[239] 'International obligations cannot alter the clear meaning of statutes. They may, however, be permitted to make clear which of more than one reasonable meaning was intended by Parliament.'

Material aids to construction

Alongside the various approaches and presumptions that are applied in the process of statutory interpretation, there are also several aids to construction that may be considered in the event of ambiguity. There are two classes of aids to construction; internal aids and external aids. The extent to which these are used varies from case to case, but those who advocate a strict literal approach would generally regard the use of *external* aids as illegitimate.

Internal aids

An internal (or intrinsic) aid is an aid that is to be found within the Queen's Printer's copy of the statute itself. The principle that a statute must be read as a whole means that those parts of the statute that form part of the enactment should always be consulted as part of the general process of interpretation. Certain other parts of the statute, such as punctuation, headings, and marginal notes, may also be used in cases of ambiguity, even though they are not strictly part of the enactment.

'Notes' of the type found in section 118 of the Criminal Justice Act 2003 fall into a different category. The Act makes significant changes to the rules governing the admissibility of hearsay evidence in criminal cases, and section 118 expressly preserves certain categories of evidence that were already admissible at common law. Thus section 118(2) preserves 'any rule of law under which in criminal proceedings evidence of a person's reputation is admissible for the purpose of proving his good or bad character'. This is qualified by a 'note', which states that the rule is 'preserved only so far as it allows the court to treat such evidence as proving the matter concerned'. Despite the label, this note is an integral part of the provision, and, as such, it is likely to be crucial to its interpretation.[240]

Long title

The long title of an Act begins with the words 'an Act' and goes on to describe the general effect of the legislation. Thus the Law of Property Act 1925 has the long title 'An Act to consolidate the enactments relating to Conveyancing and the Law of Property in England and Wales'. The long title is usually succinct rather than explanatory and it is unlikely to do more than identify the subject matter of the Act. However, as it forms

---

[239] *J. H. Rayner Ltd* v *Department of Trade and Industry* [1989] Ch 72 at 231, [1988] 3 All ER 257 at 342, *per* Ralph Gibson LJ (affirmed [1990] 2 AC 418, [1989] 3 All ER 523, HL).

[240] See also, s 118(3).

part of the enactment and may be debated or amended by Parliament, it is regarded as a legitimate aid to interpretation and construction.[241] It is, though, a minor aid: there have been conspicuously few cases in which it has been consulted and it certainly cannot prevail over an express provision in the body of the Act. Thus an Act to 'amend the law with respect to wills of personal estate made by British subjects' (Wills Act 1861) was held to apply to the will of an alien.[242] The long title should not be confused with the preamble, although preambles are rare in modern statutes and judges occasionally use the terms interchangeably.[243]

Short title

This is the title by which Acts are commonly, and properly, cited. In theory, the short title is a valid aid to both interpretation and construction, but there appears to be no reported case in which the short title has been used to determine a point of construction. The short title could certainly not be used to introduce ambiguity into the body of the Act: indeed, the short titles of certain Acts do not reflect their content accurately. The Criminal Procedure Act 1865, for example, applies to both civil and criminal proceedings.

Preamble

The preamble is that part of the statute which precedes the enacting words and sets out the reason for the statute being passed. In old cases great weight was attached to the preamble as an aid to construction,[244] and important Acts such as the Statute of Frauds 1677 and the Parliament Act 1911 have long and instructive preambles. Probably the best-known preamble is that of the Charitable Uses Act 1601, which, until recently, was regarded as containing the criteria to be adopted when considering whether a particular object is a 'charitable' one.[245] Modern statutes, however, rarely contain a preamble, and where one is included it is generally too brief to be of assistance. Moreover, as Lord Steyn made clear in *R (on the application of Jackson) v A-G*, arguments based on a preamble 'cannot possibly prevail against the clear language of the substantive provisions'.[246]

Headings

A section or group of sections in an Act may be preceded by a heading. Such headings are not part of the enactment and for that reason logic would suggest their exclusion. In fact, however, headings are often consulted as an aid to construction where the

[241] See *Fielding* v *Morley Corporation* [1899] 1 Ch 1 at 3, *per* Lindley MR. Before the nineteenth century the long title did not form part of the enactment and therefore could not be used in this way.

[242] *Re Groos* [1904] P 269; see also *R v Bates* [1952] 2 All ER 842, [1953] 1 WLR 77; *R v Galvin* [1987] QB 862, [1987] 2 All ER 851.

[243] For example, Winn LJ in *Crook* v *Edmondson* [1966] 2 QB 81 at 89, [1966] 1 All ER 833 at 835.

[244] *Belasco* v *Hannant* (1862) 3 B & S 13; *Sussex Peerage Case* (1844) 11 Cl & Fin 85.

[245] See, e.g., *McGovern v A-G* [1982] Ch 321, [1981] 3 All ER 493; *R v Radio Authority, ex parte Bull* [1996] QB 169, [1995] 4 All ER 481.

[246] [2005] UKHL 56 at [89], [2006] 1 AC 262 at [89], [2005] 4 All ER 1253. The preamble in question was that contained in the Parliament Act 1911.

enactment is uncertain or ambiguous.[247] The modern judicial tendency appears to be to treat a heading as if it were a preamble.[248] In *DPP* v *Schildkamp*,[249] Lord Upjohn was in favour of according greater weight to headings than were the other Law Lords. He observed:[250]

> In my opinion, it is wrong to confine their role to the resolution of ambiguities in the body of the Act. When the court construing the Act is reading it through to understand it, it must read the cross-headings as well as the body of the Act and that will always be a useful pointer as to the intention of Parliament in enacting the immediately following sections.

Marginal notes

Marginal notes or 'clause titles' are not part of an Act and are inserted by the draftsman purely for ease of reference. Sometimes a marginal note bears no relation to the content of a section that has been altered during the passage of the Bill, and sometimes it may simply be misleading. For example, the marginal note to section 143 of the Criminal Justice and Public Order Act 1994 referred to 'male rape and buggery', yet the provision itself only related to the latter.[251]

For this reason, the old rule was that marginal notes were not regarded as a legitimate aid to construction, even in the event of ambiguity. In *Re Woking Urban District Council (Basingstoke Canal) Act 1911*, Philimore LJ explained that this was because they were not inserted into legislation by Parliament but by 'irresponsible persons'.[252] Now, however, it is clear that marginal notes can be taken into account, as explained by Lord Hope in *R* v *Montila*:[253]

> The question then is whether headings and sidenotes, although unamendable, can be considered in construing a provision in an Act of Parliament. Account must, of course, be taken of the fact that these components were included in the Bill not for debate but for ease of reference. This indicates that less weight can be attached to them than to the parts of the Act that are open for consideration and debate in Parliament. But it is another matter to be required by a rule of law to disregard them altogether... Subject, of course, to the fact that they are unamendable, they ought to be open to consideration as part of the enactment when it reaches the statute book.

The defendants in this case were being prosecuted for converting the proceeds of drug trafficking and criminal conduct, contrary to section 49 of the Drug Trafficking

---

[247] For an instructive case see *Crook* v *Edmondson* [1966] 2 QB 81, [1966] 1 All ER 833, in which the words 'immoral purposes' were construed in the light of the group of sections of the Sexual Offences Act 1956 in which those words occurred.

[248] *Martins* v *Fowler* [1926] AC 746; *Qualter, Hall & Co Ltd* v *Board of Trade* [1962] Ch 273, [1961] 3 All ER 389.

[249] [1971] AC 1, [1969] 3 All ER 1640.

[250] [1971] AC at 28, [1969] 3 All ER at 1656. See also *R* v *Montila* [2004] UKHL 50, [2004] 1 WLR 3141, [2005] 1 All ER 113, discussed below.

[251] The provision was eventually repealed by the Sexual Offences Act 2003.

[252] [1914] 1 Ch 300 at 322. See also *Chandler* v *DPP* [1964] AC 763, [1962] 3 All ER 142.

[253] [2004] UKHL 50 at [34], [2004] 1 WLR 3141 at [34], [2005] 1 All ER 113. See also the dicta of Upjohn LJ in *Stephens* v *Cuckfield Rural District Council* [1960] 2 QB 373 at 383, [1960] 2 All ER 716 at 720.

Act 1994 and section 93C of the Criminal Justice Act 1988.[254] The issue was whether the prosecution needed to *prove* that the property in question had its origins in drug trafficking and criminal conduct, or whether it was sufficient to show that the defendants knew or suspected that it did. The fact that the sidenotes accompanying the provisions referred to 'concealing or transferring proceeds' was one of several factors leading to the conclusion that the prosecution had to prove the illegal origins of the property. Similarly, in *DPP* v *Johnson*,[255] it was held that the note accompanying section 8 of the Road Traffic Act 1988 provided evidence that Parliament's intention was to reduce the number of people driving with alcohol in their bodies. The note referred to 'driving or being in charge of a motor vehicle with alcohol consumption above the prescribed limit', and on this basis the court construed the word 'consuming' widely to embrace the ingestion of alcohol by any method. The appellant had had alcohol injected into his body as a part of a pain killing drug, and he was therefore guilty of an offence.

Punctuation

Acts of Parliament were not punctuated before 1850, and as punctuation tends to be left to the draftsman and is not scrutinized by Parliament, there is some old authority for the proposition that punctuation cannot be taken into account as an aid to construction. Modern courts take a more realistic attitude, however, and following the observations of Lord Reid in *DPP* v *Schildkamp*,[256] the House of Lords has held that punctuation can and should be taken into account.[257]

Interpretation sections

Most modern statutes include at least one interpretation section indicating the meaning that Parliament intended to be given to particular words. The context in which a word is used is still important, however, and where there is an inconsistency between the meaning given in an interpretation section and that suggested by the context, the latter prevails. This is especially so when the interpretation section uses the word 'includes'. In this case it will be regarded as extending rather than restricting the normal meaning of the words in question. Thus, in *R* v *Fulling*,[258] the court defined the term 'oppression' in section 76 of the Police and Criminal Evidence Act 1984 by reference to its ordinary, natural meaning, as stated in the *Oxford English Dictionary*. It did not even cite the content of section 76(8) of that statute, which provides that oppression 'includes' inhuman or degrading treatment, torture, violence, or the threat of violence.

Another example is *Shimizu (UK) Ltd* v *Westminster City Council*.[259] In that case, the House of Lords had to consider the meaning of the term 'listed building' in the Planning (Listed Buildings and Conservation Areas) Act 1990. Section 336 of the Town and Country Planning Act 1990 defined a 'building' as including 'part of a building',

---

[254] Both provisions have since been repealed by the Proceeds of Crime Act 2002.
[255] [1995] 4 All ER 53, [1995] 1 WLR 728.   [256] [1971] AC 1 at 28, [1969] 3 All ER 1640 at 1654.
[257] *Hanlon* v *The Law Society* [1981] AC 124, [1980] 2 All ER 199; see also *Bodden* v *Commissioner of Police of the Metropolis* [1990] 2 QB 397, [1989] 3 All ER 833.
[258] [1987] QB 426, [1987] 2 All ER 65.   [259] [1997] 1 All ER 481, [1997] 1 WLR 716.

unless the context otherwise requires. That definition was incorporated into the Listed Buildings Act by section 91 of the Act. Despite that, Lord Hope was able to conclude that the expression 'listed building' included *part* of a listed building for the purposes of section 1 of the Act, but did not do so in respect of virtually all other provisions of that Act.

Schedules

Acts of Parliament often contain one or more schedules. They are always placed at the end of the Act and are usually used for prescribing forms, furnishing illustrations, listing repeals effected by the Act, and setting out transitional provisions. They cannot be regarded as altering the ordinary meaning of words used in the Act, but it is probable that they can be considered in cases of ambiguity.

The Consumer Credit Act 1974 utilized a novel concept in parliamentary drafting—the use of examples. Section 188(1) provides that 'Schedule 2 shall have effect for illustrating the use of terminology employed in this Act'. The Schedule contains twenty-four examples, each expressed in the form of a set of facts and an analysis of the application of the new terminology to those facts. The examples are expressed not to be exhaustive and section 188(3) provides that, in the case of conflict between Schedule 2 and any other provision of the Act, the latter shall prevail.

When an Act of Parliament is passed to implement an international treaty, the text of that treaty will normally be included in a schedule to the Act. This may give rise to difficulties in interpretation if the treaty is in a foreign language or is set out in more than one language. A purposive approach will usually be adopted in such cases,[260] and the court may consult extrinsic sources such as dictionaries, *travaux préparatoires*, and the decisions of foreign courts. The words used in the treaty will be construed so as to conform to the generally accepted meaning of the provision. As Lord Browne-Wilkinson put it in *Re H and others (Minors) (Abduction: Acquiescence)*:[261] 'An international convention, expressed in different languages and intended to apply to a wide range of differing legal systems, cannot be construed differently in different jurisdictions.' In *Fothergill v Monarch Airlines Ltd*,[262] the House of Lords had to consider a provision of the Warsaw Convention contained in Schedule 1 to the Carriage by Air Act 1961. Reversing the decision of the Court of Appeal, it held that the loss of articles from a suitcase constituted 'damage' to baggage. It reached this conclusion by taking a purposive approach, and by looking at extrinsic sources to ascertain that the word '*avarie*' (used in the French text) has a slightly wider meaning than the term 'damage' (used in the English): it is also capable of meaning 'loss'.

---

[260] In one case involving a statute designed to give effect to a treaty, the Court of Appeal adopted the text of the treaty even though its meaning differed from the text used in the main body of the Act: *Corocraft Ltd v Pan American Airways Inc* [1969] 1 QB 616, [1969] 1 All ER 82.

[261] [1998] AC 72, [1997] 2 All ER 225.

[262] [1981] AC 251, [1980] 2 All ER 696. Section 1(2) of the 1961 Act expressly provides that in the event of inconsistency between the English and French texts, the latter is to prevail.

External aids

An external (or extrinsic) aid to construction is an aid that is not to be found in the Queen's Printer's copy of the Act. The use of such aids is restricted and has always been controversial: those who favour a literal approach would generally reject their use on the basis that the courts should be concerned with what Parliament *actually* said, not what it *intended* to say. Even for advocates of a more purposive approach, the use of external aids is only legitimate to the extent that they can shed light on the intentions of Parliament:[263]

> '[T]he intention of Parliament' is an objective concept, not subjective. The phrase is a shorthand reference to the intention which the court reasonably imputes to Parliament in respect of the language used. It is not the subjective intention of the Minister or other persons who promoted the legislation. Nor is it the subjective intention of the draftsman, or of individual members of…either House.

Reports of parliamentary debates[264]

Since the function of the courts is to ascertain the intention of the legislature, it might be thought that they would readily refer to statements made in Parliament as to the intention of the member or party introducing the Bill. In fact, until recently, the reports of debates on the Bill during its passage through Parliament were rigidly excluded.[265] However, in 1993 the House of Lords in *Pepper* v *Hart*[266] reconsidered the position, and held (Lord Mackay LC dissenting) that in certain circumstances a court should be entitled to refer to parliamentary materials. The objection that by so doing the courts would be calling proceedings in Parliament into question, contrary to the Bill of Rights 1688, was rejected. The preconditions for the exercise of the power were stated by Lord Browne-Wilkinson:

> the exclusionary rule should be relaxed so as to permit reference to parliamentary materials where: (a) legislation is ambiguous or obscure, or leads to an absurdity; (b) the material relied upon consists of one or more statements by a Minister or other promoter of the Bill together if necessary with such other parliamentary material as is necessary to understand such statements, and their effect; (c) the statements relied upon are clear.

Only statements made in respect of a Bill passing through Parliament can be considered under this rule. The rule does not permit the use of statements to indicate a Minister's understanding of the law at the time;[267] nor does it permit the use of statements that are not concerned with the point at issue in the litigation.[268] Lord Mackay's dissenting

---

[263] *R* v *Secretary of State for the Environment, Transport and the Regions, ex parte Spath Holme Ltd* [2001] 2 AC 349 at 387, [2001]1 All ER 195 at 206, *per* Lord Nicholls.

[264] For discussion see Kavanagh, '*Pepper* v *Hart* and Matters of Constitutional Principle' (2005) 121 LQR 98; Klug, 'The Human Rights Act 1998, *Pepper* v *Hart* and All That' [1999] PL 246; Lord Steyn, '*Pepper* v *Hart*: A Re-examination' (2001) 21 OJLS 59.

[265] *Assam Railways and Trading Co Ltd* v *Inland Revenue Commissioners* [1935] AC 445.

[266] [1993] AC 593, [1993] 1 All ER 42.

[267] *Hillsdown Holdings plc* v *Pensions Ombudsman* [1997] 1 All ER 862.

[268] *Pepper (Inspector of Taxes)* v *Hart* [1993] AC 593, [1993] 1 All ER 42; *Melluish (Inspector of Taxes)* v *BMI (No 3) Ltd* [1996] AC 454, [1995] 4 All ER 453; *Three Rivers District Council* v *Bank of England (No 2)* [1996] 2 All ER 363.

speech expressed concern that the costs of litigation would be immensely increased by the onerous task of searching through Hansard, and the frequency with which the courts have been asked to apply *Pepper* v *Hart* lends support to these concerns.[269] The House of Lords recently endorsed the *Pepper* v *Hart* rule, but it also expressed scepticism as to its value, cautioning that recourse to Hansard should be permitted only exceptionally.[270] On a related matter, it has held that a court *is* entitled to have regard to ministerial statements and explanatory notes when determining the compatibility of legislation with the Human Rights Act 1998. A court should not, however, use extrinsic aids in a manner that amounts to questioning proceedings in Parliament:[271]

> The courts are now required to evaluate the effect of primary legislation in terms of Convention rights and, where appropriate, make a formal declaration of incompatibility...Sometimes the court may need additional background information tending to show, for instance, the likely practical impact of the statutory measure and why the course adopted by the legislature is or is not appropriate...Beyond this use of Hansard as a source of background information, the content of parliamentary debates has no direct relevance...The proportionality of a statutory measure is not to be judged by the quality of the reasons advanced in support of it in the course of parliamentary debate, or by the subjective state of mind of an individual Minister or other member.

The courts tend to take a more flexible approach to the use of Hansard and other external aids when interpreting legislation designed to implement international or European obligations.[272] It may also be noted that most continental countries take a very positive view of extrinsic materials or *travaux préparatoires*, and they encourage consultation of the parliamentary and political history of the statute.

Explanatory notes

'Explanatory notes' are now published to accompany all Bills presented to Parliament.[273] These notes set out the purposes and key provisions of the Bill in clear and simple terms, and they may be revised as and when the Bill is amended during the legislative process. However, they do not form part of the enactment and Parliament

---

[269] See, e.g., *R* v *Warwickshire County Council, ex parte Johnson* [1993] AC 583, [1993] 1 All ER 299 (reference made to Minister's speech in debate on a proposed amendment to Consumer Protection Act 1987, s 20); *Stubbings* v *Webb* [1993] AC 498, [1993] 1 All ER 322 (reference made to the speech of the chairman of the Committee upon whose report s 11 of the Limitation Act 1980 was based); *Mirvahedy* v *Henley* [2001] EWCA Civ 1749, [2002] QB 769, [2002] 2 WLR 566 (reference to ministerial statements to ascertain the scope of s 2(2) of the Animals Act 1971.)

[270] *R* v *Secretary of State for the Environment, Transport and the Regions, ex parte Spath Holme Ltd* [2001] 2 AC 349, [2001] 1 All ER 195. By a majority of four to one, the House of Lords held that the *Pepper* v *Hart* conditions were not satisfied.

[271] *Wilson* v *First County Trust (No 2)* [2003] UKHL 40 at [61]–[67], [2004] 1 AC 816 at [61]–[67], [2003] 4 All ER, *per* Lord Nicholls. Their Lordships permitted the Speaker of the House of Commons and the Clerk of Parliaments to make submissions expressing their concern about any expansion in the use of Hansard.

[272] *Three Rivers District Council* v *Bank of England (No 2)* [1996] 2 All ER 363; *Pickstone* v *Freemans plc* [1989] AC 66, [1988] 2 All ER 803; *Fothergill* v *Monarch Airlines Ltd* [1981] AC 251, [1980] 2 All ER 696.

[273] See Select Committee on Modernisation of HC, 2nd Report: Explanatory Material for Bills, 1997–1998, HC 389, pp 1–2. Before 1998, the practice was for a Bill to be accompanied by an explanatory document prepared by the sponsoring department and indicating its broad provisions and likely financial impact.

has left it to the courts to determine what use, if any, can be made of them when construing legislation. Their status was considered by Lord Steyn in *Westminster City Council* v *National Asylum Support Service*.[274] Despite having made some rather sceptical extra-judicial comments about the merits of using Hansard,[275] he was more enthusiastic about the use of explanatory notes:[276]

> Insofar as the Explanatory Notes cast light on the objective setting or contextual scene of the statute, and the mischief at which it is aimed, such materials are…always admissible aids to construction. They may be admitted for what logical value they have…After all, the connection of Explanatory Notes with the shape of the proposed legislation is closer than pre-parliamentary aids which in principle are already treated as admissible.

Subsequently, Lord Hope has observed that 'it has become common practice for their Lordships to ask to be shown the Explanatory Notes when issues are raised about the meaning of words used in an enactment'.[277] It is recognized, however, that the distinction between legitimate and illegitimate uses of explanatory notes is a fine one:[278]

> If exceptionally there is found in Explanatory Notes a clear assurance by the executive to Parliament about the meaning of a clause, or the circumstances in which a power will or will not be used, that assurance may in principle be admitted against the executive in proceedings in which the executive places a contrary contention before the court…What is impermissible is to treat the wishes and desires of the government about the scope of the statutory language as reflecting the will of Parliament. The aims of the government…cannot be attributed to Parliament. The object is to see what is the intention expressed by the words enacted.

Ministerial statements of compatibility

Section 19 of the Human Rights Act 1998 provides that before the second reading of a Bill, the Minister in charge of it must either: (a) make a statement that in his view the provisions of the Bill are compatible with Convention rights;[279] or (b) make a statement that although the Bill is *not* compatible, the government nevertheless wishes to proceed. Section 19 statements do not normally include an explanation as to *why* the Minister thinks that an Act is compatible or not, and for this reason their probative value is limited. Nevertheless, when a court is considering whether it is possible to interpret an Act in a Convention-compliant manner,[280] a section 19 statement may have some value as a general indication of Parliament's intention.

---

[274] [2002] UKHL 38, [2002] 4 All ER 654, [2002] 1 WLR 2956.

[275] '*Pepper* v *Hart*: A Re-examination' (2001) 21 OJLS 59.

[276] [2002] UKHL 38 at [5], [2002] 4 All ER 654 at [5].

[277] *R* v *Montila* [2004] UKHL 50 at [35], [2004] 1 WLR 3141 at [35], [2005] 1 All ER 113.

[278] [2002] UKHL 38 at [6], [2002] 4 All ER 654 at [6]. See also *Wilson* v *First County Trust (No 2)* [2003] UKHL 40, [2004] 1 AC 816, [2003] 4 All ER 97; Munday, 'Explanatory Notes and Statutory Interpretation' (2006) 170(8) JP 124.

[279] By s 1, 'Convention rights' are those ECHR rights contained in Articles 2–12 and 14, Articles 1–3 of the First Protocol and Article 1 of the Thirteenth Protocol.

[280] Under s 3 of the 1998 Act: see further, pp 152–161.

Section 19 came into effect on 24 November 1998, and it is perhaps unsurprising that virtually all of the statements made under it have been to the effect that legislation is compatible. The exception is the Communications Act 2003. The Minister responsible for introducing the Bill felt unable to make a statement of compatibility because it included provisions prohibiting political advertising in broadcasting. The advertising ban was at odds with a decision of the European Court of Human Rights,[281] although the Minister made it clear that she did not consider an incompatible interpretation inevitable:[282]

> [G]iven the existence of the Swiss precedent, I must ask the House to consider this Bill with a section 19(l)(b) of the Human Rights Act 1998 statement attached to it. That does not mean that we believe the Bill to be incompatible with the ECHR, and we would mount a robust defence if it were legally challenged.

When the provisions in question were challenged, the Administrative Court refused to make a declaration of incompatibility, holding that the restriction on freedom of expression fell within the United Kingdom's margin of appreciation.[283] In reaching this decision the court did not appear to give any direct weight to the Minister's statement, but Ousley J attached 'great weight' to the fact that Parliament had 'expressed a considered view, having grappled with the human rights implications' of the provisions.[284]

Dictionaries

Words in statutes are presumed to bear their ordinary and natural meaning, and it is legitimate to consult a dictionary when interpreting words with no particular legal meaning. Dictionaries bear only slight weight, however, and in context the dictionary meaning may not be the one that Parliament intended. In a Court of Appeal case concerning the interpretation of the word 'ethnic' in the Race Relations Act 1976, Lord Denning MR rejected a 1972 dictionary definition in favour of one from 1934.[285] The House of Lords in the same case rejected both definitions and came to its own conclusions about the meaning of the word.[286] Words and phrases with a particular legal meaning are described as 'terms of art', and they do not necessarily bear the meaning that laymen would attribute to them.[287] In interpreting the foreign text of a convention, a court is entitled to consult foreign dictionaries, textbooks, and articles, and even to receive expert evidence.[288]

---

[281] *VgT Verein gegen Tierfabriken* v *Switzerland* (2002) 34 EHRR 4.

[282] Tessa Jowell, MP (Secretary of State for Culture, Media and Sport), 395 HC Official Report (6th series) col 789, 3 December 2002.

[283] *R (on the application of Animal Defenders International)* v *Secretary of State for Culture, Media and Sport* [2006] EWHC 3069 (Admin), [2007] HRLR 9. For a discussion of the concept of 'margin of appreciation', see p 176.

[284] Ibid, at [114].   [285] *Mandla* v *Dowell Lee* [1983] QB 1 at 12.

[286] [1983] 2 AC 548, [1983] 1 All ER 1062, HL.

[287] See *Barclays Bank Ltd* v *Cole* [1967] 2 QB 738, [1966] 3 All ER 948 on the meaning of the word 'fraud'; cf. *Lloyds Bank Ltd* v *Marcan* [1973] 2 All ER 359, [1973] 1 WLR 339.

[288] *Fothergill* v *Monarch Airlines Ltd* [1981] AC 251, [1980] 2 All ER 696.

Reports of committees

Reports of the Law Commissions, Law Reform Committees, and similar bodies are legitimate aids to discovering the state of the pre-existing law and the mischief that a statute was passed to remedy.[289] Once again, however, if the words of a statute are unambiguous, it is not legitimate to interpret them otherwise in order to accord with the recommendations of a Committee. Thus, in *Letang v Cooper*,[290] the Court of Appeal held that the words 'negligence, nuisance or breach of duty' in the Law Reform (Limitation of Actions) Act 1954 were wide enough to embrace the tort of trespass to the person. This was despite the fact that the Tucker Committee report,[291] which preceded the 1954 Act, expressed an intention to exclude this form of action from the shorter limitation period recommended in that report.

Other statutes

Where the words of one statute are ambiguous or uncertain, assistance as to their meaning may be gained from considering the way in which similar words have been used in statutes dealing with the same subject matter. Thus, in *R v Wheatley*,[292] the question before the Court of Appeal was whether a pipe bomb filled with a mix-ture of sodium chlorate and sugar was an 'explosive' substance within the meaning of section 4 of the Explosive Substances Act 1883. The defendant's expert evidence was to the effect that the materials would produce only a pyrotechnic effect, and not an explosive one. The judge directed the jury that this was no defence, having regard to the definition of 'explosive' in section 3(1) of the Explosives Act 1875, which included a substance used to produce a 'pyrotechnic effect'. It was held that this direction was correct, since the long title of the 1883 Act indicated that it was intended to amend the 1875 Act and both Acts dealt with the same subject matter. It followed that what was an explosive substance for the purposes of the 1883 Act was to be determined by applying the definition used in its 1875 equivalent.

Judicial precedents

Where a superior court has already interpreted words in an Act, an inferior court is bound to adopt that interpretation if faced with the same words in the same Act. Similarly, the Court of Appeal and Divisional Courts are bound to follow their own previous decisions on the interpretation of statutes to the same extent as they are bound to follow any of their other previous decisions. In addition, if an Act employs words or phrases that have been the subject of interpretation in an earlier statute dealing with the same subject matter, it may be inferred that they are intended to bear the same meaning. For example, the House of Lords, in assigning a meaning

---

[289] See, e.g., *Rookes v Barnard* [1964] AC 1129, [1964] 1 All ER 367; *Black-Clawson International Ltd* v *Papierwerke Waldhof-Aschaffenburg AG* [1975] AC 591, [1975] 1 All ER 810.

[290] [1965] 1 QB 232, [1964] 2 All ER 929.

[291] Cmnd 7740. See also *Sagnata Investments v Norwich Corporation* [1971] 2 QB 614, [1971] 2 All ER 1441, in which the report of the Royal Commission on Betting, Lotteries and Gaming (Cmnd 8190, 1951) was used as an aid to the construction of the Betting, Gaming and Lotteries Act 1963.

[292] [1979] 1 All ER 954, [1979] 1 WLR 144.

to the word 'wreck' in the Merchant Shipping Act 1925, adopted the interpretation of that word that had been given in a case decided on the Merchant Shipping Act 1894.[293]

This is, however, no more than a possible inference, and it must not be supposed that by re-enacting a provision that has been the subject of judicial interpretation Parliament is necessarily giving statutory force to that interpretation. If it is a wrong interpretation, then provided that it is not binding on the court in accordance with the doctrine of precedent, the court is perfectly free to disregard it.[294] Moreover, where the earlier decision is upon similar words in a statute that does not deal with the same subject matter, or where the words are used in a different context, that decision is of little, if any, value.[295] Finally, where the earlier case was decided before the Human Rights Act 1998 came into effect, a court should not follow that decision if doing so would result in a finding that the legislation is in breach of Convention rights.[296]

Interpretation of European Union legislation

The techniques of interpretation that English courts have developed over the centuries have been described above. As already noted, approaches to interpretation have influenced approaches to legislative drafting, and vice versa. EU legislation is drafted in a different mould. It is expressed in terms of broad principle, leaving the courts to supply the detail by giving effect, in particular cases, to the general intention of the body that enacted the instrument in question. Thus regulations, directives, and decisions of the Council and Commission have to state the reasons on which they have been based. They must also refer to any proposals or opinions that were required to be obtained pursuant to the treaties. These reasons are normally set out in the preamble to the instrument in question. Accordingly, English judges are required to take a purposive approach to the interpretation of EU legislation, referring points of law to the Court of Justice when necessary or required. The 'literal' approach plays little or no part in this process.[297]

---

[293] *Barras* v *Aberdeen Steam Trawling and Fishing Co Ltd* [1933] AC 402. See also *R* v *Freeman* [1970] 2 All ER 413, [1970] 1 WLR 788: in this case the Court of Appeal held that since there was no relevant distinction between the definition of 'firearm' in s 57(1) of the Firearms Act 1968 and the definitions in earlier Firearms Acts, Parliament must be taken to have adopted the interpretation of the earlier Acts when enacting the 1968 statute.

[294] See *Dun* v *Dun* [1959] AC 272, [1959] 2 All ER 134; *R* v *Chard* [1984] AC 279, [1983] 3 All ER 637 (in which the House of Lords expressly disapproved dicta to the contrary in *Barras* v *Aberdeen Steam Trawling and Fishing Co Ltd* [1933] AC 402).

[295] *London Corporation* v *Cusack-Smith* [1955] AC 337, [1955] 1 All ER 302; *Brown* v *Bennett (No 1)* [2002] 2 All ER 273, [2002] 1 WLR 713.

[296] See *Ghaidan* v *Godin-Mendoza* [2002] EWCA Civ 1533, [2003] Ch 380, [2002] 4 All ER 1162, in which the Court of Appeal declined to follow the House of Lords' interpretation of a provision in the Rent Act 1977 (*Fitzpatrick* v *Sterling Housing Association Ltd* [2001] 1 AC 27, [1999] 4 All ER 705). For a discussion of the impact of the Human Rights Act on the doctrine of judicial precedent, see Chapter 3.

[297] The interpretation of EU law is discussed in more detail in Chapter 4.

Further reading

CLAYTON, 'The Limits of What's "Possible": Statutory Construction under the Human Rights Act' [2002] EHRLR 559

KAVANAGH, '*Pepper* v *Hart* and Matters of Constitutional Principle' (2005) 121 LQR 98

KAVANAGH, 'The Role of Parliamentary Intention in Adjudication under the Human Rights Act 1998' (2006) 26(1) OJLS 179

KLUG, 'The Human Rights Act 1998, *Pepper* v *Hart* and All That' [1999] PL 246

LESTER, 'The Art of the Possible: Interpreting Statutes under the Human Rights Act' [1998] EHRLR 665

MARSHALL, 'The Lynchpin of Parliamentary Intention: Lost, Stolen or Strained?' [2003] PL 236

STEYN, 'Democracy through Law' [2002] EHRLR 723

3

Case Law, Precedents, and Law Reports

INTRODUCTION

This chapter considers the operation of the doctrine of precedent within the English legal system. The notion that judges should look to earlier cases when making decisions is established throughout the legal world, but the idea that a court might be *bound* to follow an earlier precedent is a particular feature of common law systems. In England and Wales, the principles derived from earlier cases constitute one of the two main sources of law—the common law—and this means that the rules of precedent are themselves of great significance. It also means that a system of reliable and comprehensive law reporting is a necessity. This chapter will therefore examine both the rules of judicial precedent and the law reports upon which those rules depend. The specific areas addressed will include:

- the historical development of the doctrine of precedent and its place in the modern legal system;
- the impact of the Human Rights Act 1998 on the doctrine;
- the different elements of a judicial decision, and the distinction between the *ratio decidendi* and *obiter dicta*;
- binding and persuasive precedents;
- what it means to 'reverse', 'overrule' or 'distinguish' an earlier case;
- the relationship between the doctrine of precedent and the hierarchy of the courts;
- the modern system of law reporting and the rules governing the citation of cases in court.

The relationship between law reports and the doctrine of precedent

The operation of the doctrine of precedent is inextricably bound up with law reporting. Precedents are almost always contained in law reports, and the modern doctrine of binding precedent did not develop until an integrated system of law reporting evolved in the nineteenth century. Nevertheless, until recently, any decision could be cited in court provided that it was vouched for by a barrister, solicitor, or other qualified person[1] who was present when the judgment was delivered, and decisions did not need to be reported in order to be relied upon in court. However, in the face of concern about the over-citation of cases, particularly those that are unreported, the judiciary is now seeking to limit the use of unreported decisions. In *Roberts Petroleum Ltd* v *Bernard Kenny*, Lord Diplock caused considerable consternation among some sections of the profession by stating that:[2]

> [T]he time has come when your Lordships should adopt the practice of declining to allow transcripts of unreported judgments of the Civil Division of the Court of Appeal to be cited on the hearing of appeals to this House unless leave is given to do so...such leave should only be granted on counsel's giving an assurance that the transcript contains a statement of some principle of law, relevant to an issue in the appeal to this House, that is binding on the Court of Appeal and of which the substance, as distinct from the mere choice, of phraseology, is not to be found in one of the generalised or specialised series of reports.

The Court of Appeal has since adopted much the same approach[3] and in 2000 it issued a Practice Direction restricting the range of cases that can be cited in the civil courts.[4] The effect of this is that (a) applications attended by one party only, (b) applications for permission to appeal, (c) decisions that an application is arguable, and (d) decisions of the county court[5] cannot be cited unless there is a clear indication that the decision in question purports to establish a new principle or extend the present law.[6] The Practice Direction also discouraged reliance on cases from foreign jurisdictions other than those of the European Court of Human Rights and European Court of Justice. Lord Woolf CJ explained the reasons for these changes:[7]

> The current weight of available material causes problems both for advocates and for courts in properly limiting the nature and amount of material that is used in the preparation and argument of subsequent cases. Recent and continuing efforts to increase the efficiency, and thus reduce the cost, of litigation, whilst maintaining the interests of justice, will be threatened if courts are burdened with a weight of inappropriate and unnecessary authority.

The problem though remains. A recent example is the over-citation of authority in the Court of Appeal (Criminal Division). In *R* v *Erskine*,[8] Lord Judge CJ, having reviewed the authorities dealing with over-citation, observed:

> We must do more than complain...there can be little doubt that firm measures are immediately required, at least in this court, to ensure that appeals can be heard without

---

[1] Courts and Legal Services Act 1990, s 115. See pp 132 and 380.

[2] [1983] 2 AC 192 at 200–2, [1983] 1 All ER 564 at 566–8.

[3] *Practice Statement (Court of Appeal: Authorities)* [1996] 3 All ER 382, [1996] 1 WLR 854.

[4] *Practice Direction (Citation of Authorities)* [2001] 2 All ER 510, [2001] 1 WLR 1001.

[5] A county court decision may be cited if it deals with a point of law in respect of which no higher authority is available, or in order to illustrate the measure of damages in a personal injury case.

[6] Since the Practice Direction, if a decision falling into one of these categories does extend the law or establish a new principle, it must include an express statement to this effect in the judgment.

[7] [2001] 2 All ER 510 at [1]–[2], [2001] 1 WLR 1001 at [1]–[2].   [8] [2009] EWCA Crim 1425.

excessive citation of or reference to many of its earlier, largely factual decisions. The essential starting point, relevant to an appeal or sentence, is that...if it is not necessary to refer to a previous decision of this court, it is necessary not to refer to it. Similarly if it is not necessary to include a previous decision in the bundle of authorities, it is necessary to exclude it. That approach will be rigidly enforced...It follows that when the advocate is considering what authority, if any, to cite for a proposition, only an authority which establishes the principle should be cited. Reference should not be made to authorities which do no more than either (a) illustrate the principle or (b) restate it.

It is important to distinguish a law report from a court record. A court record consists of the names of the parties, the pleadings, and the decision or order of the court. A law report contains most of these, along with the judgment of the court setting out the reasoning upon which the decision was based. It is this reasoning that is important for the purposes of the doctrine of precedent, and court records are therefore of little value in this context.

KEY ISSUE

It used to be argued that an obvious criticism that could be made of the present system of law reporting in England is that it remains informal and the selection of cases for reporting is entirely at the discretion of the law reporters.[9] While there cannot be many important cases that have escaped the elaborate net of the law reporters, there are undoubtedly some: the Court of Appeal, for example, decides about 3,000 cases every year, of which only a small proportion are reported in traditional sets of reports. Yet the electronic era has made these arguments redundant. The difficulty today is that there is too much law in the sense that virtually every decision of the higher courts is available online, irrespective of whether the decision is important in creating or developing principle, or is merely illustrative or fact-specific. The courts have increasingly complained about the quantity of authority cited, often to little effect.

This is not a new problem. The court in *Erskine* identified that complaints about the proliferation of reported cases were made as long ago as 1863, with guidelines issued for the control of citations that could easily pass muster in 2010. However, the availability of virtually all cases online has exacerbated the problem. As noted above, exhortations and warnings[10] have been issued. Yet for the advocate there is, perhaps, the danger that over-selectivity in the choice of authorities might mean the court is not aware of an authority that it might find persuasive or useful. For that reason the continued exhortations to concentrate on fewer volumes of case law may not always be heeded.

❓ Questions

1. How rigidly should courts restrict the use and citation of authority?

2. How does an advocate clearly identify what authorities are essential?

---

[9] See p 101.

[10] *Roberts Petroleum Ltd v Bernard Kenny* [1983] 2 AC 192, [1983] 1 All ER 564; *Practice Direction (Citation of Authorities)* [2001] 2 All ER 510, [2001] 1 WLR 1001. See p 70.

3. Are illustrative authorities of no value?

4. Is the amount of case law available today helpful?

The operation of the doctrine of precedent

The doctrine of binding precedent

The traditional view of the function of an English judge has been that it is not to make law but to decide cases in accordance with existing legal rules. The doctrine of binding precedent (or *stare decisis*), whereby the judge is not merely referred to earlier decisions for guidance but is also bound to apply rules of law decided by those cases, was founded on this 'declaratory' view of the judicial process. However, few would now deny that judges have a powerful law-making function.

> The theoretical position has been that judges do not make or change law: they discover and declare the law which is throughout the same. According to this theory, when an earlier decision is overruled the law is not changed: its true nature is disclosed, having existed in that form all along. This theoretical position is, as Lord Reid said in the article 'The Judge As Law Maker' (1972–1973) 12 J.S.P.T.L. (N.S.) 22, a fairy tale in which no-one any longer believes. In truth, judges make and change the law. The whole of the common law is judge-made and only by judicial change in the law is the common law kept relevant in a changing world.[11]

The operation of the doctrine depends upon the hierarchy of the courts. All courts stand in a definite relationship to one another. A court is bound by decisions of courts above itself in the hierarchy and, usually, by courts of equivalent standing. Given that the doctrine of precedent has binding force within this framework, the question naturally arises of how the law may develop if cases are always to be determined according to ageless principles. In practice there are several ways in which the doctrine retains its flexibility. These are dealt with in detail below, but two basic principles should be noted: first, that superior courts have power to overrule decisions of inferior courts and, in certain cases, to overrule their own earlier decisions; and, second, that any rule of law may be changed by statute. Consequently every rule of law is subject to change, either by the judges themselves or by Parliament.

The advantages of the precedent system are said to be certainty, precision, and flexibility.[12] Legal certainty is achieved, at least in theory, because judges are bound to deal with like situations in a consistent way. Precision is achieved by the sheer volume of reported cases that provide specific solutions to innumerable factual problems.

---

[11] *Kleinwort Benson* v *Lincoln City Council* [1999] 2 AC 349 at 358, [1998] 4 All ER 513 at 518, *per* Lord Browne-Wilkinson.

[12] See the observations of Russell LJ in *Gallie* v *Lee* [1969] 2 Ch 17 at 41, [1969] 1 All ER 1062 at 1076, and of Lord Hailsham in *Cassell & Co Ltd* v *Broome* [1972] AC 1027 at 1054, [1972] 1 All ER 801 at 809 ('in legal matters, some degree of certainty is at least as valuable a part of justice as perfection').

Finally, flexibility is achieved by the possibility of decisions being overruled or distinguished, thus allowing the law to adapt to new or previously unforeseen circumstances. The obvious disadvantages of the system are its inherent rigidity, which can occasionally cause hardship, and the vast and ever-increasing bulk of cases to which courts must refer in order to determine what the law is. Indeed, it is this latter concern that has led the courts to impose restrictions on the citing of certain types of case as precedents.[13]

Finally, it is self-evident that there cannot be an infinite regression. Every rule of law must have its origin, and if it was not created by statute then it must have been created by a court. Even in modern times cases arise for which there is no precedent, and the court's decision in such a case must inevitably be based on general principles. These cases are described as cases of first impression and they require the judge to make law rather than to simply apply it.[14] Although he or she will do this by reference to analogous principles, even legal principles must have their origin. The failure to account properly for this is an inherent weakness of the declaratory theory.[15]

The impact of the Human Rights Act 1998 on the doctrine of precedent

Under the Human Rights Act 1998,[16] courts and tribunals are obliged to perform their functions in accordance with Convention rights,[17] and they must interpret legislation in a manner compatible with these rights so far as it is possible to do so.[18] Not only does this sanction the appellate courts to overrule incompatible precedents in the ordinary way, but it also permits, and requires, a court to interpret statute in a Convention-compliant way. One commentator described this as a 'year zero' approach to *stare decisis*.[19] This is because a court's obligations under the Act must prevail over any duty to obey the normal rules of precedent. In other words, a pre-Human Rights Act decision of a higher court cannot stand in the way of a lower court performing its duty as set out by the 1998 Act. For example, the Court of Appeal has already declined to follow a previous decision of the House of Lords, in order to avoid the conclusion that a provision of the Rent Act 1977 was in breach of Article 14 of the Convention.[20] Similarly,

---

[13] See p 70.

[14] For example, *Philips v Brooks Ltd* [1919] 2 KB 243; *Malone v Metropolitan Police Commissioner (No 2)* [1979] Ch 344, [1979] 2 All ER 620; *Midland Bank Trust Co Ltd v Green (No 3)* [1982] Ch 529, [1981] 3 All ER 744; *Parker v British Airways Board* [1982] QB 1004, [1982] 1 All ER 834.

[15] See Lord Simon's observations on the declaratory theory of common law in *Jones v Secretary of State for Social Services* [1972] AC 944 at 1026, [1972] 1 All ER 145 at 198, quoted at p 320.

[16] The overall significance of this major piece of legislation is discussed in Chapter 5.

[17] Section 6. Convention rights are defined in s 1.

[18] Section 3(1). The effect of the Act on statutory interpretation is discussed further in Chapter 2.

[19] See Mead, 'Swallowing the Camel, Straining at the Gnat: The Implications of *Mendoza v Ghaidan*' [2003] 5 EHRLR 501 at 509.

[20] *Ghaidan v Godin-Mendoza* [2002] EWCA Civ 1533, [2003] Ch 380, [2002] 4 All ER 1162 (affirmed: [2004] UKHL 30, [2004] 2 AC 557, [2004] 3 All ER 411). The House of Lords decision in question was *Fitzpatrick v Sterling Housing Association Ltd* [2001] 1 AC 27, [1999] 4 All ER 705.

in order to comply with Article 6, the same court[21] made a 'modest adjustment' to the test for bias established by the House of Lords in *R v Gough*.[22] The modified approach adopted in this case was later approved by the House of Lords in *Porter v Magill*.[23]

This does not mean, however, that a court can decline to follow a precedent on the grounds that it conflicts with a decision of the European Court of Human Rights. Domestic courts and tribunals must take *account* of the Strasbourg court's decisions when determining Convention cases,[24] but they are not required to treat those decisions as binding precedents.[25] Thus the Court of Appeal is normally bound by a decision of the Supreme Court even if that is contradicted by a subsequent decision of the Court of Human Rights.[26]

The binding element in precedents

The *ratio decidendi*

Strictly speaking, it is a misstatement to say that a 'decision' is binding on anyone other than the parties to the case in question. Similarly, it is not technically correct to regard a 'decision' as having been overruled. It is not the decision that binds (or is overruled); it is the rule of law contained within the decision. This element of the decision is termed the *ratio decidendi*, and not every statement of law made by a judge in the case forms part of this *ratio*.

Every decision contains the following basic ingredients:

(1) findings of material facts, both direct and inferential;[27]

(2) statements of the principles of law applicable to the legal problems disclosed by the facts; and

(3) a judgment (or judgments) based on the combined effect of (1) and (2).

For the purposes of the parties themselves, (3) is the material element in the decision, for it is what ultimately determines their rights and liabilities in relation to the subject matter of the case. However, for the purpose of the doctrine of precedent, (2) is the vital element in the decision, and it is this that is termed the *ratio decidendi*. Thus the

---

[21] *Director General of Fair Trading v Proprietary Association of Great Britain* [2001] 1 WLR 700, [2001] HRLR 17; *sub nom Re Medicaments and Related Classes of Goods (No 2)*.

[22] [1993] AC 646, [1993] 2 All ER 724.

[23] [2001] UKHL 67, [2002] 2 AC 357, [2002] 1 All ER 465; see, in the context of criminal appeals, *R v Dunn* [2010] EWCA Crim 1823.

[24] Human Rights Act 1998, s 2.

[25] *Kay v Lambeth LBC*; *Leeds City Council v Price* [2006] UKHL 10, [2006] 2 AC 465, [2006] 4 All ER 128. See now, *Manchester City Council v Pinnock* [2010] UKSC 45. See further, pp 143 and 147.

[26] See *R (on the application of M) v Secretary of State for Work & Pensions* [2008] UKHL 63.

[27] An inferential finding of fact is the inference that the judge (or jury) draws from the direct or perceptible facts. For example, negligence may be inferred from the direct facts of the speed of a vehicle, the length of skid marks, and the state of the road. Negligence is thus an inferential finding of fact.

ratio decidendi may be defined as the statement of law applied to the legal problems raised by the facts, upon which the decision is based.

The two other elements in the decision are not precedents at all: the findings of fact are not binding on anyone, and the judgment is only binding on the parties to the case in question.[28] This means that even where the direct facts of a case appear to be identical to those before the court in an earlier decision, the judge or jury is not bound to draw the same inferences. *Qualcast (Wolverhampton) Ltd* v *Haynes*[29] is a good example of this point. In that case, an employee sued his employers for negligence in failing to provide a safe system of work. At first instance the county court judge held himself bound to follow earlier cases in which employers who had acted in a similar manner had been held liable. The House of Lords held that this was not the correct approach, since the cases relied upon by the judge were based upon inferences of fact that were not binding. Otherwise, as Lord Somervell observed,[30] 'the precedent system will die from a surfeit of authorities'. Not every statement of law in a judgment is binding; only those statements that are based upon the facts and upon which the decision is based are binding. Any other statement of law is, strictly speaking, superfluous and is described as an *obiter dictum* (something said 'by the way'). It should not, however, be concluded from this that *obiter dicta* are of little or no weight or importance.

Obiter dicta

There are two types of *obiter dicta*. Firstly, a statement of law is regarded as *obiter* if it is based upon facts that either were not found to be material or were not found to exist at all. For example, the famous statement of equitable estoppel contained in the judgment of Denning J in *Central London Property Trust Ltd* v *High Trees House Ltd*[31] is clearly *obiter* since it applied to a set of facts that were not found to be present in the case. Similarly, in *Rondel* v *Worsley*,[32] the House of Lords expressed opinions to the effect that a barrister might be held liable in tort when acting outside the province of litigation, and that a solicitor acting as an advocate might enjoy immunity from action. Since the case concerned only the liability of a barrister when acting as an advocate, these opinions were necessarily *obiter*.

Secondly, even where a statement of law *is* based on the facts as found, it will be regarded as *obiter* if it does not form the basis of the decision. A statement of law made in support of a dissenting judgment is an obvious example. Similarly, where a court makes statements of law leading to one conclusion but then comes to a contrary conclusion for a different reason, those statements are necessarily *obiter* since they do not support the decision. An example is provided by the seminal case of *Hedley Byrne &*

---

[28] See *R* v *Secretary of State for the Home Department, ex parte Ku* [1995] QB 364, [1995] 2 All ER 891.

[29] [1959] AC 743, [1959] 2 All ER 38.

[30] [1959] AC 743 at 758, [1959] 2 All ER 38 at 43. In the tort of negligence, only the existence of a duty of care is a question of law; whether or not the defendant has broken this duty is a question of fact.

[31] [1947] KB 130, [1956] 1 All ER 256n.

[32] [1969] 1 AC 191, [1967] 3 All ER 993. The House of Lords has since overruled its decision in this case in *Arthur J S Hall* v *Simons and others* [2002] 1 AC 615, [2000] 3 All ER 673; see p 405.

Co Ltd v *Heller & Partners*.[33] The central proposition of law in that case was that the maker of a statement owes a duty of care, in certain circumstances, to persons whom he may expect to rely upon that statement. Strictly speaking, however, this statement was *obiter*, because on the facts of the case it was found that the bank that had given the disputed advice was protected by a disclaimer of responsibility. That being so, the further statement as to what rule of law *would* have been applied but for the disclaimer cannot be regarded as essential to the decision. Nevertheless, *Hedley Byrne* illustrates that the strict rules for isolating the *ratio* of a case are sometimes of limited value, since the reasoning of the House of Lords undoubtedly represents the present state of the law:[34]

> When five members of the House of Lords have all said, after close examination of the authorities, that a certain type of tort exists, I think that a judge of first instance should proceed on the basis that it does exist without pausing to embark on an investigation whether what was said was necessary to the ultimate decision.

Hedley Byrne has since been expressly applied by the Court of Appeal and approved by the House of Lords.[35] It seems reasonable to conclude that where the House of Lords states a rule of law and expressly rejects earlier contrary decisions, that statement will be treated as binding even though not strictly essential to the decision.

Ascertaining the *ratio decidendi*

Although the distinction between *obiter dicta* and the *ratio* of a case is clear enough in theory, drawing this distinction in practice is often fraught with difficulty. First of all, a case may be argued on more than one ground. If the court is willing to decide the case on one ground, it will usually refrain from expressing an opinion on any other point of law, but sometimes a court may feel compelled to deal with every point of law raised. Isolating the *ratio decidendi* in such a case may be extremely difficult. The problem is often particularly acute in the case of appellate decisions, since different members of the court may arrive at the same conclusion for different reasons. The starting point in this situation is that a reason adopted by a majority of the court is presumed to be *ratio*, whereas a reason adopted only by a minority is usually regarded as non-essential to the decision and therefore not binding. The position becomes complicated where no one reason is favoured by a majority, yet every case must be assumed to have a *ratio decidendi*. The answer seems to be that it depends upon which of the alternative reasons subsequent courts are prepared to accept as *rationes*. One classic example is the decision of the House of Lords in *Sinclair* v *Brougham*.[36] It was held in this case that, once the creditors of a society had been paid in full by agreement, the assets remaining were to be divided between depositors and members of the society in accordance with the proportion of new payments to the society. The reasons for this

---

[33] [1964] AC 465, [1963] 2 All ER 575.
[34] *W B Anderson and Sons Ltd* v *Rhodes* [1967] 2 All ER 850 at 857, *per* Cairns J.
[35] *Arenson* v *Casson, Beckman, Rutley & Co* [1977] AC 405, [1975] 3 All ER 901.
[36] [1914] AC 398, [1914–15] All ER Rep 622.

conclusion were far from clear, with one member of the court concurring with a judgment based on reasons that were at odds with his own.[37] The multiplicity of opinion and reasoning was sufficient to provoke Lord Browne-Wilkinson to observe in a later case that it was:[38]

> a bewildering authority: no single *ratio* can be detected; all the reasoning is open to serious objection, it was only intended to deal with cases where there were no trade creditors in competition and the reasoning is incapable of application where there are such creditors.

In so far as the decision of the court in *Sinclair* v *Brougham* was discernible at all, it was overruled.

A further difficulty is that what may initially be considered to be *obiter dicta*, even by the court itself, may subsequently be viewed differently. Thus, in *Luc Thiet Thuan* v *R*,[39] the court considered that what may have been an *obiter dictum* in *R* v *Ahluwalia*[40] 'certainly ripened' into *ratio decidendi* in *R* v *Dryden*.[41]

It is certainly possible for a case to have two or more *rationes decidendi*. The case of *Fairman* v *Perpetual Investment Building Society*[42] is an example. The House of Lords in that case gave two reasons for its decision, both of which were accepted as binding by the House in *Jacobs* v *London County Council*.[43] On the other hand, in *Read* v *J Lyons & Co Ltd*,[44] the House of Lords advanced two reasons for its decision that the defendants were not liable under the rule in *Rylands* v *Fletcher*:[45] (1) that the rule did not apply in the absence of an escape of the dangerous substance from the defendant's occupation or control; and (2) that the rule did not apply unless the plaintiff had an interest in land affected by the escape. The second reason, which is principally contained in the speech of Lord Macmillan, was, in a later case,[46] treated by the Court of Appeal as *obiter*, on the basis that it was not essential to the decision. The position is further complicated by the fact that the Court of Appeal's statement on this point was itself *obiter*, because the plaintiff's action failed for another reason. The question of whether the second reason in *Read* v *J Lyons & Co Ltd* is *ratio* or *obiter* was therefore left unresolved.[47]

---

[37] Lord Dunedin.

[38] *Westdeutsche Handesbank Girozentrale* v *Islington LBC* [1996] AC 669 at 713, [1996] 2 All ER 961 at 996.

[39] [1997] AC 131, [1996] 2 All ER 1033. See also, *St John the Evangelist, Chopwel* [1995] Fam 254, [1996] 1 All ER 275. In this case, the judge said that statements made in *Re St Thomas, Pennywell* [1995] Fam 50, [1995] 4 All ER 167, 'were not strictly necessary to that decision but now I adopt them as part of the *ratio decidendi* of the present case.'

[40] [1992] 4 All ER 889, (1993) 96 Cr App R 133.   [41] [1995] 4 All ER 987.

[42] [1923] AC 74.

[43] [1950] AC 361, [1950] 1 All ER 737. The case is particularly notable in that one of the two reasons given in *Fairman*'s *case* was clearly not essential to the decision.

[44] [1947] AC 156, [1946] 2 All ER 471.   [45] (1868) LR 3 HL 330.

[46] *Perry* v *Kendricks Transport Ltd* [1956] 1 All ER 154, [1956] 1 WLR 85.

[47] The Court of Appeal in *Dunne* v *North-Western Gas Board* [1964] 2 QB 806, [1963] 3 All ER 916, expressly left the point open.

A variation of this problem can arise if a majority of the judges in a case favour a reason that does not actually support the court's decision. The reason cannot be a *ratio* because it does not support the decision, yet on the other hand it seems logically odd to conclude that the *ratio* can be found in the contrary reasoning of the minority. The occasions on which such a dilemma will arise are likely to be very rare, but the decision of the House of Lords in *Central Asbestos Co Ltd* v *Dodd*[48] was such an occasion. The question before the House turned on the construction of the ill-drafted provisions of section 7(3) of the Limitation Act 1963. Lords Reid and Morris took one view of the law, Lords Simon and Salmon a different view. The fifth member of the court, Lord Pearson, was in favour of deciding the appeal in the same way as Lords Reid and Morris, but his view on the point of law substantially supported that of Lords Simon and Salmon. It was not long before the Court of Appeal was called upon to decide the point of law that had arisen in *Dodd's case*, and it concluded that since the case had no discernible *ratio* at all, it would go back to the law contained in the earlier cases.[49]

Precedents that are not binding

Persuasive authorities

Obiter dicta

Although *obiter dicta* lack binding authority, they may nevertheless have a strong persuasive influence. This is particularly so where the statement in question has come from a court of high authority and is a deliberate statement of law as opposed to a casual expression of opinion. Such a dictum will usually be followed in the absence of any binding authority to the contrary. In the case of *Adams* v *Naylor*,[50] for example, the House of Lords disapproved the practice of government departments setting up a nominal defendant to avoid the Crown's immunity from actions in tort. Although this disapproval was *obiter*, the Court of Appeal in *Royster* v *Cavey*[51] adopted it and refused to sanction this long-standing practice. *Hedley Byrne & Co Ltd* v *Heller & Partners*[52] provides another example of *obiter dicta* that has subsequently had considerable influence, but perhaps the most striking example of all is the 'neighbour principle' propounded by Lord Atkin in *Donoghue (or M'Alister)* v *Stevenson*.[53] This statement of law has become the basis of the modern tort of negligence, and has been cited and applied on occasions too numerous to mention, yet the statement was far wider than the case itself required and strictly therefore it was *obiter*.

---

[48] [1973] AC 518, [1972] 2 All ER 1135.
[49] *Harper* v *National Coal Board* [1974] QB 614, [1974] 2 All ER 441.
[50] [1946] AC 543, [1946] 2 All ER 241.
[51] [1947] KB 204, [1946] 2 All ER 642. This decision precipitated the passing of the Crown Proceedings Act 1947, which enabled the Crown to be sued in tort.
[52] [1964] AC 465, [1963] 2 All ER 575; see p 75.   [53] [1932] AC 562.

Decisions of inferior courts

Decisions of courts lower in the hierarchy may have some persuasive authority for those courts above them. Court of Appeal decisions, for example, are generally regarded as having persuasive authority in the House of Lords.

Decisions of the Judicial Committee of the Privy Council

'Decisions' of the Judicial Committee of the Privy Council are not strictly binding on any English court,[54] and in theory, even a first-instance judge may legitimately decline to follow a Privy Council decision.[55] In practice, however, such decisions are of very great persuasive authority for the obvious reason that the Judicial Committee is composed of the same persons who usually sit in the House of Lords (now the Supreme Court). There had not been any suggestion that Privy Council authorities were of equivalent weight to House of Lords cases until the decision in *Doughty* v *Turner Manufacturing*.[56] In this case, the Court of Appeal expressed the view that its own decision in *Re Polemis*[57] was no longer good law in the light of the subsequent Privy Council decision in *The Wagon Mound*.[58] Similarly, when the Court of Appeal in *Worcester Works Finance Ltd* v *Cooden Engineering Co Ltd*[59] was faced with a conflict between one of its own decisions and a later decision of the Privy Council, it had no hesitation in preferring the latter.

Since Privy Council decisions are merely persuasive, it cannot be assumed that they will always be followed, and in *R* v *Smith*[60] both the Court of Appeal and the House of Lords declined to follow a Privy Council decision concerning the defence of provocation to murder.[61] However, in the truly exceptional case of *R* v *James (Leslie)*,[62] the Court of Appeal declined to follow the House of Lords decision in *Smith*, preferring instead to follow a later decision of the Privy Council.[63] Although this was a very unusual and radical step, it should not be taken to signal a more general departure from the established rules of precedent. The decision in *Smith* had been widely criticized, and the nine Law Lords who were party to the Privy Council's decision made it clear that they intended it to resolve a question of English law. The Privy Council normally follows House of Lords (and now Supreme Court) decisions when deciding

[54] Privy Council decisions on 'devolution questions' affecting Wales, Scotland and Northern Ireland *were* binding, even on the House of Lords. However, now that such matters are part of the jurisdiction of the Supreme Court, these decisions will be binding in the same way. See pp 248 and 276.
[55] Diplock J did so in *Port Line Ltd* v *Ben Line Steamers Ltd* [1958] 2 QB 146, [1958] 1 All ER 787; see also *Dulieu* v *White* [1901] 2 KB 669.
[56] [1964] 1 QB 518, [1964] 1 All ER 98. [57] [1921] 3 KB 560.
[58] *Overseas Tankship (UK) Ltd* v *Morts Dock and Engineering Co Ltd* [1961] AC 388, [1961] 1 All ER 404.
[59] [1972] 1 QB 210, [1971] 3 All ER 708.
[60] *R* v *Smith* [1999] QB 1079, [1998] 4 All ER 387, CA; [2001] 1 AC 146, [2000] 4 All ER 289, HL.
[61] The decision in question was *Luc Thiet Thuan* v *R* [1997] AC 131, [1996] 2 All ER 1033.
[62] [2006] EWCA Crim 14, [2006] QB 588, [2006] 1 All ER 759; cf. *Re Spectrum Plus Ltd. (In Liquidation)* [2004] EWCA Civ 670, [2004] Ch 337, [2004] 4 All ER 995 (affirmed [2005] UKHL 41, [2005] 2 AC 680, [2005] 4 All ER 209).
[63] *Attorney General for Jersey* v *Holley* [2005] UKPC 23, [2005] 2 AC 580, [2005] 3 All ER 371.

cases in which the applicable law is English,[64] but this was clearly a case in which their Lordships felt that an exception should be made:[65]

> This appeal, being heard by an enlarged board of nine members, is concerned to resolve this conflict and clarify definitively the present state of English law, and hence Jersey law, on this important subject.

The Court of Appeal in *James* had no doubt what the outcome would be if the case were to end up in the House of Lords, and this was, after all, a homicide case in which the liberty of the subject was at stake:[66]

> What are the exceptional features in this case which justify our preferring the decision in Holley's case to that in the Morgan Smith case? We identify the following. (i) All nine of the Lords of Appeal in Ordinary sitting in Holley's case agreed in the course of their judgments that the result reached by the majority clarified definitively English law on the issue in question. (ii) The majority in Holley's case constituted half the Appellate Committee of the House of Lords... (iii) In the circumstances, the result of any appeal on the issue to the House of Lords is a foregone conclusion.
>
> We doubt whether this court will often, if ever again, be presented with the circumstances that we have described above. It is those circumstances which we consider justify the course that we have decided to take, and our decision should not be taken as a licence to decline to follow a decision of the House of Lords in any other circumstances.

Decisions of the European Court of Human Rights

Section 2 of the Human Rights Act 1998 requires any court or tribunal determining a matter involving a Convention right to take into account any judgment, decision, or advisory opinion of the European Court of Human Rights, along with certain decisions of the Commission and Committee of Ministers, in so far as they may be relevant. Decisions of the European Court of Human Rights and the other institutions are thus given the status of persuasive precedents, and it is left to individual courts and tribunals to decide whether they should be followed in any particular case. The suggestion that courts ought to be bound by the Strasbourg jurisprudence was rejected by the government during the passage of the Human Rights Bill through Parliament. The Lord Chancellor explained that to make the Strasbourg jurisprudence binding on domestic courts would be inconsistent with the spirit of the Convention itself:[67]

> We must remember that Clause 2 requires the courts to take account of all the judgments of the European Court of Human Rights, regardless of whether they have been given in a case involving the United Kingdom... the United Kingdom is not bound in international law to follow that Court's judgments in cases to which the United Kingdom

---

[64] *Tai Hing Cotton Mill Ltd* v *Liu Chong Hing Bank Ltd* [1986] AC 80, [1985] 2 All ER 947.

[65] [2005] UKPC 23 at [1], [2005] 2 AC 580 at [1], *per* Lord Nicholls.

[66] [2006] EWCA Crim 14 at [43]–[44], [2006] QB 588 at [43]–[44], *per* Lord Phillips of Worth Matravers CJ. For further discussion, see Conaglen and Nolan, 'Precedent from the Privy Council' (2006) 122 LQR 349.

[67] Lord Irvine of Lairg, 583 HL Official Report (5th series) col 511, 18 November 1997.

had not been a party, and it would be strange to require courts in the United Kingdom to be bound by such cases.

The precise effect of section 2 was subsequently considered by Lord Slynn in the leading case of *R (on the Application of Alconbury)* v *Secretary of State for the Environment, Transport and the Regions*:[68]

> In the absence of some special circumstances it seems to me that the court should follow any clear and constant jurisprudence of the European Court of Human Rights. If it does not do so there is at least a possibility that the case will go to that court which is likely in the ordinary case to follow its own constant jurisprudence.

Occasionally, this causes real problems. In *R* v *Horncastle (Michael Christopher)*,[69] the Supreme Court concluded that the Court of Human Rights had not sufficiently understood the English law relating to hearsay (and contained in the Criminal Justice Act 2003) and for that reason it held that two previous decisions of the Strasbourg court should not be followed. By contrast the Court of Human Rights in *Kay* v *United Kingdom*[70] concluded that the House of Lords in *Doherty* v *Birmingham City Council*[71] failed to pay proper regard to an earlier decision of the Court of Human Rights in *Connors* v *United Kingdom*.[72]

As stated previously, however, taking account of Strasbourg case law does not mean disregarding binding decisions of the domestic courts. The House of Lords recently confirmed that in the event of a conflict between a domestic decision and a decision of the Court of Human Rights, the normal rules of precedent will still apply.[73] This means that a court cannot decline to follow the binding precedent of a court higher in the legal hierarchy, even where that precedent is inconsistent with a more recent decision of the Strasbourg court. There may, however, be cases in which the facts are of such an 'extreme character' that a departure from an otherwise binding precedent is justified.[74] *D* v *East Berkshire Community Health NHS Trust* is an example of such a case.[75] Here, the Court of Appeal declined to follow a pre-1998 House of Lords decision[76] on the basis that the policy considerations underlying that decision had been largely eroded by the introduction of the Human Rights Act. An additional factor was that the claimants whose case had been rejected as unarguable by the House

---

[68] [2001] UKHL 23 at [26], [2003] 2 AC 295 at [26], [2001] 2 All ER 929. For an example of a case in which the Strasbourg jurisprudence was *not* followed, see *R* v *Spear and others; R* v *Saunby and others* [2002] UKHL 31, [2003] 1 AC 734, [2002] 3 All ER 1074.

[69] [2009] UKSC 14 ; *R (on the application of Purdy)* v *Director of Public Prosecutions* [2009] EWCA Civ 624; *Kay* v *Lambeth LBC* [2006] AC 465. See p 148.

[70] [2010] ECHR 322.   [71] [2008] UKHL 57.   [72] 2005) 40 EHRR 9.

[73] *Kay* v *Lambeth LBC*; *Leeds City Council* v *Price* [2006] UKHL 10 at [40]–[44], [2006] 2 AC 465 [40]–[44], [2006] 4 All ER 128, *per* Lord Bingham. *R (on application of Purdy)* v *Director of Public Prosecutions* [2009] EWCA 648; *R (on application of M)* v *Secretary of State for Work and Pensions* [2008] UKHL 63.

[74] Ibid, at [45].

[75] [2003] EWCA Civ 1151, [2004] QB 558, [2003] 4 All ER 796 (affirmed [2005] UKHL 23, [2005] 2 AC 373, [2005] 2 All ER 443).

[76] *X (Minors)* v *Bedfordshire CC* [1995] 2 AC 633, [1995] 3 All ER 353.

of Lords had later succeeded in establishing a breach of the Convention before the Court of Human Rights.[77]

KEY ISSUE

The short discussion above highlights an extremely important point. The Court of Human Rights is not a court of appeal, nor is it a court that is in any sense higher than the other courts within the system on which the doctrine of precedent operates. Its decisions do not *bind* United Kingdom courts: the Human Rights Act 1998 simply requires that the court *has regard* to the decisions of the Court of Human Rights. Yet the clear attitude of the courts is that such decisions should normally be followed.[78] It therefore follows that in reality the Court of Human Rights has a status more fundamental than its formal position might suggest. It is thus right that it is the Supreme Court (or, before it, the House of Lords) that should resolve any conflict.

? Questions

1. Why do you think this is so?
2. What would be the effect of the courts taking a different approach?

Decisions from other jurisdictions

A third class of persuasive authorities consists of the decisions of Scottish, Irish, Commonwealth, and foreign courts. There is an increasing tendency on the part of English lawyers and judges to draw analogies from other legal systems, and decisions from other jurisdictions—particularly Scotland, Ireland, the USA, Australia, Canada, and New Zealand—are frequently cited. In an effort to reduce the sheer volume of cases being used in this way, the Court of Appeal felt compelled to take steps discouraging reliance on foreign cases except where they genuinely have something to add to existing domestic law.[79] At the same time, however, the Lord Chief Justice acknowledged that 'cases decided in other jurisdictions can, if properly used, be a valuable source of law'.[80]

Statements of law made *per incuriam*

The Court of Appeal in the leading case of *Young* v *Bristol Aeroplane Co Ltd*[81] established that it was entitled to depart from one of its previous decisions if satisfied that the decision in question was reached *per incuriam* (through lack of care). When a decision is described as having been made *per incuriam*, this usually, although not

---

[77] *Z* v *United Kingdom* (2002) 34 EHRR 3.

[78] *Kay* v *Lambeth BC* [2006] UKHL 10; *R (on the application of Animal Defenders International)* v *Secretary of State for Culture, Media and Sport* [2008] UKHL 15. See p 147.

[79] *Practice Direction (Citation of Authorities)* [2001] 2 All ER 510 at [9.1], [2001] 1 WLR 1001 at [9.1], *per* Lord Woolf CJ.

[80] Ibid.

[81] [1944] KB 718, [1944] 2 All ER 293 (affirmed [1946] AC 163, [1946] 1 All ER 98); see p 95.

always, means that some relevant statutory provision or precedent that would have led the court to a different conclusion was not brought to the court's attention.[82] Although the principle in *Young's case* was expressed to apply only to the Court of Appeal, it has since been applied in other courts. Thus, in *R v Northumberland Compensation Appeal Tribunal, ex parte Shaw*,[83] a Divisional Court of the King's Bench Division declined to follow a Court of Appeal decision on the ground that the latter had been reached *per incuriam*, a relevant House of Lords decision not having been cited to the Court of Appeal. However, when the Court of Appeal refused to follow a House of Lords decision on exemplary damages[84] that it considered to have been made *per incuriam*, it was roundly condemned by the House of Lords for having done so.[85] Lord Hailsham LC, in the course of the leading speech for the majority, asserted that:[86]

> it is not open to the Court of Appeal to give gratuitous advice to judges of first instance to ignore decisions of the House of Lords in this way. The course taken would have put judges of first instance in an embarrassing position, as driving them to take sides in an unedifying dispute between the Court of Appeal and the House of Lords.

These words proved to be prophetic because, in *Miliangos v George Frank (Textiles) Ltd*,[87] Bristow J found himself in the embarrassing position foreseen by Lord Hailsham. This was because the Court of Appeal in *Schorsch Meier GmbH v Hennin*[88] had held that the rule of law whereby money judgments could only be expressed in sterling had ceased to exist, notwithstanding clear House of Lords authority for the existence of the rule. Bristow J preferred to follow the House of Lords authority, but the Court of Appeal later stated that he was wrong to do so because *Schorsch Meier* was binding upon him. On appeal,[89] the House of Lords decision in question[90] was overruled, although not on any of the grounds cited by the Court of Appeal.

The *per incuriam* principle is of limited application, and few decisions have subsequently been regarded as having been reached in this way.[91] The mere fact that a case was not fully or expertly argued,[92] or that it was argued on one side only (as *Schorsch Meier* was), does not entitle a court to disregard it as having been made *per incuriam*.

[82] *Duke* v *Reliance Systems Ltd* [1988] QB 108, [1987] 2 All ER 858 (affirmed [1988] AC 618, [1988] 1 All ER 626).

[83] [1951] 1 KB 711, [1951] 1 All ER 268. See also *Hughes* v *Kingston upon Hull City Council* [1999] QB 1193, [1999] 2 All ER 49.

[84] *Rookes* v *Barnard* [1964] AC 1129, [1964] 1 All ER 367. This decision had already been subjected to devastating criticism in the courts of the Commonwealth and had been repudiated by the Privy Council; see *Australian Consolidated Press Ltd* v *Uren* [1969] 1 AC 590, [1967] 3 All ER 523.

[85] *Cassell & Co Ltd* v *Broome* [1972] AC 1027, [1972] 1 All ER 801.

[86] [1972] AC 1027 at 1054, [1972] 1 All ER 801 at 809.   [87] [1975] QB 487, [1975] 1 All ER 1076.

[88] [1975] QB 416, [1975] 1 All ER 152.   [89] [1976] AC 443, [1975] 3 All ER 801.

[90] *Re United Railways of the Havana and Ragla Warehouses Ltd* [1961] AC 1007, [1960] 2 All ER 332 (a decision to which Lord Denning himself had been a party).

[91] For two examples, see *Royal Bank of Scotland* v *Etridge (No 2)* [1998] 4 All ER 705 and *R (on the application of W)* v *Lambeth LBC* [2002] EWCA Civ 613, [2002] 2 All ER 901.

[92] *Joscelyne* v *Nissen* [1970] 2 QB 86, [1970] 1 All ER 1213; *Morelle Ltd* v *Wakeling* [1955] 2 QB 379, [1955] 1 All ER 708.

Similarly, a case cannot be considered *per incuriam* solely because the court appeared to misunderstand the law or was not aware of the policy considerations behind a statute.[93] However, if it appears to a court that a previous interpretation of a statute was clearly wrong, then it would seem that the duty of the later court is to apply a correct interpretation.[94] Whether this is an example of the *per incuriam* doctrine or simply an illustration of a judge's general obligations concerning the interpretation of statutes is a moot point. In *IM Properties* v *Cape & Dalgleish*,[95] the Court of Appeal was referred to an earlier House of Lords decision[96] that it considered to be based on an incorrect interpretation of section 35A of the Supreme Court Act 1981. The Court of Appeal held that in these circumstances it had no option but to depart from the earlier decision, and it is clear that it regarded this as an application of the *per incuriam* doctrine:[97]

> [U]nder these circumstances we are not bound by this aspect of the *Westdeutsche* decision and... we are entitled to determine this appeal upon what we consider is the correct construction of s 35A.

Precedents embodying former rules of international law

The decision in *Trendtex Trading Corporation Ltd* v *Central Bank of Nigeria*[98] indicates that there may be a further limited exception to the doctrine of binding precedent in respect of that part of English law that embodies current international law. In this case, the Court of Appeal held that the defendant bank could not claim sovereign immunity from action because, inter alia, as a matter of international law the doctrine of state immunity was not applicable to ordinary commercial transactions. In reaching this decision the court declined to follow an earlier Court of Appeal decision that would otherwise have been considered binding, the majority holding that the rule of *stare decisis* could not stand in the way of giving effect to changes in international law. The point does not appear to have been judicially considered since this case, and the decision must therefore be taken as an accurate statement of the current law.

---

[93] *Farrell* v *Alexander* [1976] QB 345, [1976] 1 All ER 129 (reversed [1977] AC 59, [1976] 2 All ER 721); but see *Industrial Properties (Barton Hill) Ltd* v *Associated Electrical Industries Ltd* [1977] QB 580, [1977] 2 All ER 293. In the latter case, the Court of Appeal declared one of its previous decisions *per incuriam* where the court had misunderstood an earlier case because of deficiencies in the law report to which it had been referred. See also *Dixon* v *BBC* [1979] QB 546, [1979] 2 All ER 112 in which one *ratio* of an earlier case was treated as *per incuriam* on the ground that the statutory provision under construction had been considered in isolation rather than in context. See also, *R (on the application of W)* v *Lambeth LBC* [2002] EWCA Civ 613, [2002] 2 All ER 901.

[94] Ibid.   [95] [1999] QB 297, [1998] 3 All ER 203.

[96] *Westdeutsche Handesbank Girozentrale* v *Islington LBC* [1996] AC 669 at 713, [1996] 2 All ER 961 at 996.

[97] [1999] QB 297 at 308–9, [1998] 3 All ER 203 at 212, *per* Hobhouse LJ.

[98] [1977] QB 529, [1977] 1 All ER 881. The question at issue in the case has now been resolved by the State Immunity Act 1978, s 3(1).

Reversing, overruling, and distinguishing

Reversing

Reversing occurs when one of the parties to a case appeals against the decision of a lower court and the appellate court then reaches a different conclusion. The effect of this is literally to 'reverse' the lower court's decision in the case and to alter the outcome for the parties concerned. The process of reversing a decision must be carefully distinguished from that of 'overruling', since the latter does not change the outcome in the case that is overruled.

Overruling

Overruling occurs when a court in one case makes a decision affecting the rule of law upon which the decision in a *different* case was based. This means that, semantically, it is not correct to describe a decision as having been 'overruled' since it is only the rule of law contained in the decision that is affected, and not the decision itself.

A decision may be overruled either by statute or by a higher court. If overruled by a court, the earlier decision is deemed to have been based on a misunderstanding of the law, and on a strict application of the declaratory theory, the earlier rule is deemed never to have existed. On this view the common law is never changed; it is merely restated correctly. However, such a rationalization ignores the reality that judges do make law, and often change the law because of changing circumstances or attitudes. An example of such a decision is that of *R* v *R*,[99] in which the House of Lords held that the long-established rule that a husband cannot be criminally liable for raping his wife no longer formed part of English law.

Whatever the theoretical basis, judicial overruling operates retrospectively, and this is one important respect in which it differs from most instances of overruling by statute.[100] Another difference between overruling by the courts and overruling by statute is that statutes do not expressly name the decisions that they overrule. Nevertheless it is not usually difficult to identify the cases that are overruled by a statute, particularly where the statute follows closely upon an unpopular decision of a superior court.[101]

The United States Supreme Court has the power to overrule decisions prospectively. This means that it may overrule an existing legal rule for the benefit of future decisions, yet still apply it to the particular case before it.[102] This power is said to be based on the common law, but until recently it had never been recognized in this country. In *Jones* v *Secretary of State for Social Services*,[103] Lord Simon suggested that the most satisfactory method of dealing with the case would have been to allow the

---

[99] *R* v *R (Rape: Marital Exemption)* [1992] 1 AC 599, [1991] 4 All ER 481; see p 322.

[100] The War Damage Act 1965 is a rare example of an Act that was expressly stated to be retrospective, and that was passed with the apparent intention of overruling a House of Lords decision (*Burmah Oil Co Ltd* v *Lord Advocate* [1965] AC 75, [1964] 2 All ER 348). The presumption against the retrospective operation of statutes is discussed further in Chapter 2.

[101] Ibid.　　　[102] *Linkletter* v *Walker* 381 US 618 (1965).

[103] [1972] AC 944, [1972] 1 All ER 145; see pp 88 and 320.

appeal on the basis that it was covered by an existing precedent, but then to overrule that precedent prospectively. In the event, he simply concurred with the majority of the House of Lords and decided to allow the appeal, observing that any extension of judicial power to include prospective overruling should preferably be left to Parliament.[104] However, the House of Lords has revisited the question of whether there is a power to prospectively overrule in a handful of recent cases,[105] and in *Re Spectrum Plus Ltd (In Liquidation)*, their Lordships were unanimous in holding that such a power existed:[106]

> There could be cases where a decision on an issue of law, whether common law or statute law, was unavoidable but the decision would have such gravely unfair and disruptive consequences for past transactions or happenings that this House would be compelled to depart from the normal principles relating to the retrospective and prospective effect of court decisions…If, altogether exceptionally, the House as the country's supreme court were to follow this course I would not regard it as trespassing outside the functions properly to be discharged by the judiciary…Rigidity in the operation of a legal system is a sign of weakness, not strength…'Never say never' is a wise judicial precept…

On the facts of the case, however, their Lordships held that there were no grounds for postponing the effect of their ruling.

A precedent does not lose its authority with the passing of time. Indeed the strength of a precedent arguably increases with age, and courts tend to be reluctant to overrule long-standing authorities unless they are clearly wrong. Apart from the desirability of attaining certainty, the main reason for the reluctance of judges to overrule old decisions is the fact that this might have the effect of disturbing existing financial arrangements, depriving persons of vested proprietary rights, or even imposing criminal liability retrospectively. In *Re Compton*,[107] for example, the Court of Appeal was unwilling to overrule a long line of old authorities concerning charitable trusts, even though it considered these cases to be anomalous. Similarly, although the rule in *Pinnel's case*[108] is plainly anomalous, even the House of Lords has refused to overrule it. Thus, in *Foakes* v *Beer*,[109] Lord Fitzgerald expressed doubt about the merits of the rule but felt that, because of its longevity, the House would not be justified in overruling it.[110]

---

[104] [1972] AC 944 at 1026–7, [1972] 1 All ER 145 at 198; Lord Simon advanced similar suggestions in *Miliangos* v *George Frank (Textiles) Ltd* [1976] AC 443 at 490, [1975] 3 All ER 801 at 832.

[105] Including *Kleinwort Benson Ltd* v *Lincoln City Council* [1999] 2 AC 349, [1998] 4 All ER 513; and *R* v *Governor of Brockhill Prison, ex parte Evans (No 2)* [2001] 2 AC 19 at 26, [2000] 4 All ER 15 at 19. In the latter case Lord Slynn stated that, in his view, 'there may be situations in which it would be desirable, and in no way unjust, that the effect of judicial rulings should be prospective or limited to certain claimants'.

[106] [2005] UKHL 41 at [40]–[41], [2005] 2 AC 680 at [40]–[41], [2005] 4 All ER 209, *per* Lord Nicholls.

[107] [1945] Ch 123, [1945] 1 All ER 198.   [108] (1602) 5 Co Rep 117a.

[109] (1883–84) LR 9 App Cas 605.

[110] Ibid at 630. The rule has, of course, been undermined by the doctrine of equitable estoppel; see *D & C Builders Ltd* v *Rees* [1966] 2 QB 617, [1965] 3 All ER 837. See also *Re Selectmove* [1995] 1 WLR 474, [1995] 2 All ER 531.

On the other hand, the courts generally have little hesitation in overruling decisions that they consider to be clearly wrong. Thus, in *Bourne* v *Keane*,[111] the House of Lords overruled a series of long-standing decisions on the law of trusts, even though this had the effect of disturbing many existing trusts and settlements. In *Button* v *DPP*,[112] it held that the common law offence of affray could be committed in a private place, and thus overruled a line of authority to the effect that the offence could occur only in a public place. Similarly, in the leading case of *Miliangos* v *George Frank (Textiles) Ltd*,[113] the House of Lords effectively overruled a decision that embodied one of the clearest and most firmly entrenched rules of English law, namely that judgment must be given in sterling.[114]

Distinguishing

The process of 'distinguishing' is probably the major factor in enabling the doctrine of precedent to remain flexible and adaptable. Cases are distinguished on their facts. The *ratio decidendi* of a case is, by definition, based upon the material facts of that case, and courts are only bound to apply precedents that share the same material facts. Consequently, if a court is willing to regard as material any fact that is not common to both the case before it and the precedent cited, the two cases can be distinguished. The law reports are full of strained distinctions in which the court was evidently anxious not to follow an apparently binding precedent. In theory, it is possible to distinguish virtually any precedent, since factual situations will almost never precisely duplicate themselves. Nevertheless there are practical limits beyond which the court will be unlikely to go. Cases that are indistinguishable are described as being 'on all fours' with one another.

To illustrate how fine a distinction may be drawn between ostensibly parallel factual situations, reference may be made to two cases concerning the tort of conversion. In *England* v *Cowley*,[115] the defendant refused to allow the claimant to remove goods from his, the defendant's, premises. This was held not to be conversion since there was no absolute denial of title. This case was distinguished by the Court of Appeal in *Oakley* v *Lyster*,[116] in which the defendant refused to allow the claimant to remove material from his (the defendant's) land, and in addition asserted his own title to the material. This was held to be an act of conversion, the assertion of title apparently making the denial of title absolute.

---

[111] [1919] AC 815. On the other hand, in *Prudential Assurance Co Ltd* v *London Residuary Body* [1992] 2 AC 386, [1992] 3 All ER 504, the House of Lords felt unable to overrule ancient authorities requiring the maximum duration of a term of years to be determinable at the outset. This conclusion was reached on the ground that overruling the earlier authorities might upset long-established titles, yet the House itself acknowledged that it led to a 'bizarre outcome' in the instant case.

[112] [1966] AC 591, [1965] 3 All ER 587.　　　[113] [1976] AC 443, [1975] 3 All ER 801.

[114] *Re United Railways of the Havana and Regla Warehouses Ltd* [1961] AC 1007, [1960] 2 All ER 332.

[115] (1873) LR 8 Exch 126.　　　[116] [1931] 1 KB 148.

The hierarchy of the courts

It has already been noted that the doctrine of binding precedent rests upon the under-lying principle that the courts form a hierarchy, with each court standing in a definite position in relation to every other court. The structure of this hierarchy must now be considered for the purposes of the doctrine of precedent.

European Court of Justice[117]

In matters concerning (1) the interpretation of the Treaties, (2) the validity and interpretation of acts of the EU institutions, and (3) the interpretation of the statutes of bodies established by an act of the Council, the Court of Justice of the European Union is the supreme tribunal. Accordingly, its decisions in these areas of jurisdiction will be binding on all English courts. Indeed section 3(1) of the European Communities Act 1972 expressly provides that:

> for the purpose of all legal proceedings any question as to the meaning or effect of any of the Treaties, or as to the validity, meaning or effect of any Community instrument, shall be treated as a question of law (and, if not referred to the European Court, be for determi-nation as such in accordance with the principles laid down by and any relevant decision of the European Court or any court attached thereto).

The European Court of Justice does not observe a doctrine of binding precedent and does not regard itself as bound by its previous decisions. This does not, however, mean that its previous decisions have no influence upon it.

Supreme Court

The Supreme Court (and the House of Lords before it) stands at the summit of the English hierarchy of courts, and decisions of the Supreme Court are binding upon all other courts trying civil or criminal cases.

Formerly, the House of Lords regarded itself as strictly bound by its own earlier decisions, which were thus immutable except by legislation.[118] However, in 1966 Lord Gardiner LC issued a Practice Statement to the effect that their Lordships would in future be willing to depart from their earlier decisions 'when it appears right to do so'.[119] They would, however, bear in mind the danger of disturbing financial arrange-ments and proprietary rights retrospectively, and the especial need for certainty as to the criminal law. The Lord Chancellor made it clear, moreover, that this statement was not intended to affect other courts.

The practical consequences of this change in the law were, at first, slight. In the five years following Lord Gardiner's statement the House of Lords did not overrule any of its previous decisions. This reticence is aptly demonstrated by *Jones* v *Secretary of State*

---

[117] See Chapter 4.
[118] This principle was established in *London Tramways Co* v *London County Council* [1898] AC 375.
[119] [1966] 3 All ER 77, [1966] 1 WLR 1234.

for Social Services.[120] In this case, a seven-member House declined to overrule one of its previous decisions[121] even though a majority of their Lordships were of opinion that the earlier decision was wrong. Since there was no suggestion that the earlier authority could be distinguished, it might appear that there was no alternative but to overrule it, and three members of the House were prepared to do this. Lord Simon, however, gave several reasons why he thought that it would be wrong to depart from the earlier case, even though he agreed that it had been wrongly decided. In particular, he emphasized that the power to depart from a previous decision 'is one to be most sparingly exercised', and he concluded that a variation of view on a matter of statutory construction would rarely provide a suitable occasion. The wait for a suitable occasion was not a long one, however, and in *British Railways Board* v *Herrington*[122] the House refused to follow a precedent that had stood for over forty years,[123] concerning the duty of care owed by an occupier of land to trespassers.

In *R* v *Secretary of State for the Home Department, ex parte Khawaja*,[124] the House of Lords rejected a previous decision that had unduly restricted the power of the courts to review the detention and removal of suspected illegal immigrants.[125] Lord Scarman stated that the House must be satisfied of two things before it was entitled to take such a step:[126]

> [T]he House must be satisfied not only that adherence to the precedent would involve the risk of injustice and obstruct the proper development of the law, but also that a judicial departure by the House from the precedent is the safe and appropriate way of remedying the injustice and developing the law. The possibility that legislation may be the better course is one which, though not mentioned in the [Practice] Statement, the House will not overlook.

Both conditions were clearly satisfied on the facts of the case because the liberty of the subject was at stake and the decision raised fundamental issues about the ability of the courts to review executive decisions.

A more recent example is provided by the case of *Arthur JS Hall & Co* v *Simons*,[127] in which the House of Lords departed from the precedent set in *Rondel* v *Worsley*[128] and removed the immunity of advocates from liability in tort. While their Lordships did not doubt that *Rondel* v *Worsley* had been correctly decided at the time, it was felt that the original justifications for the immunity no longer applied and that it was therefore in the interests of public policy for the immunity to be removed.[129]

[120] [1972] AC 944, [1972] 1 All ER 145.
[121] *Minister of Social Security* v *Amalgamated Engineering Union* [1967] 1 AC 725, [1967] 1 All ER 210.
[122] [1972] AC 877, [1972] 1 All ER 749.
[123] *Robert Addie & Sons (Collieries) Ltd* v *Dumbreck* [1929] AC 358.
[124] [1984] AC 74, [1983] 1 All ER 765.
[125] *R* v *Secretary of State for the Home Department, ex parte Zamir* [1980] AC 930, [1980] 2 All ER 768.
[126] [1984] AC 74 at 106, [1983] 1 All ER 765 at 778.   [127] [2002] 1 AC 615, [2000] 3 All ER 673.
[128] [1969] 1 AC 191, [1967] 3 All ER 993.   [129] This is discussed further in Chapter 11.

Notwithstanding the especial need for certainty as to the criminal law, the House in *R* v *Shivpuri*[130] departed from its own previous decision in *Anderton* v *Ryan*[131] on the law of criminal attempts. *Anderton* had been decided less than a year earlier but had meanwhile been the subject of devastating academic criticism. Lord Bridge (who had also been a party to the earlier decision) gave the following reasons:[132]

> Firstly, I am undeterred by the consideration that the decision in *Anderton* v *Ryan* was so recent. The 1966 Practice Statement is an effective abandonment of our pretention to infallibility. If a serious error embodied in a decision of this House had distorted the law, the sooner it is corrected the better. Secondly, I cannot see how, in the very nature of the case, anyone could have acted in reliance on the law as propounded in *Anderton* v *Ryan* in the belief that he was acting innocently and now find that, after all, he is to be held to have committed a criminal offence.

Despite these and other examples,[133] the House of Lords' power to depart from its previous decisions was exercised sparingly. As Lord Reid observed in one case:[134]

> our change of practice in no longer regarding previous decisions of this House as absolutely binding does not mean that whenever we think a previous decision was wrong we should reverse it. In the general interest of certainty in the law we must be sure that there is some very good reason before we so act.

As *R* v *Kansal*[135] confirms, the House would not overrule its own decisions lightly, and a belief that an earlier case was wrongly decided was not necessarily a sufficient justification. In *Kansal*, the House declined to overrule a decision that it had reached only four months earlier,[136] despite a majority of the House agreeing that the earlier case had been wrongly decided. The unwillingness of their Lordships to invoke the Practice Statement on this occasion was largely because the cases concerned the status of the Human Rights Act 1998 during the transitional period before it came into force. The decisions were therefore unlikely to have any long-term significance.

Apart from the possibility of the Supreme Court being prepared to depart from its own earlier decisions, there are now four other means by which a Supreme Court (or House of Lords) decision may lose its authority. Firstly, and most obviously, it may be overruled by statute or as a result of a decision of the European Court of Justice. Secondly, the potential scope of a decision may be lessened if it can be distinguished. The process of distinguishing applies in the Supreme Court as in other courts. Indeed,

---

[130] [1987] AC 1, [1986] 2 All ER 334.   [131] [1985] AC 560, [1985] 2 All ER 355.

[132] [1987] AC 560 at 23, [1986] 2 All ER 355 at 345.

[133] See *The Johanna Oldendorff* [1974] AC 479, [1973] 3 All ER 148; *Vestey* v *Inland Revenue Commissioners* [1980] AC 1148, [1979] 3 All ER 976; *Murphy* v *Brentwood District Council* [1991] 1 AC 398, [1990] 2 All ER 908.

[134] *Knuller (Publishing, Printing and Promotions) Ltd* v *Director of Public Prosecutions* [1973] AC 435 at 455, [1972] 2 All ER 898 at 903; see also, *Fitzleet Estates Ltd* v *Cherry* [1977] 3 All ER 996, [1977] 1 WLR 1345.

[135] *R* v *Kansal (No 2)* [2001] UKHL 62, [2002] AC 69, [2002] 1 All ER 257.

[136] *R* v *Lambert* [2001] UKHL 37, [2002] 2 AC 545, [2001] 3 All ER 577. *Kansal* has since been applied in *R* v *Benjafield* [2002] UKHL 2, [2003] 1 AC 1099, [2002] 1 All ER 815.

before the 1966 Practice Statement it was applied with more force in the House of Lords than elsewhere because there was no other judicial means of avoiding a precedent that the House felt to be wrong. Thirdly, the Supreme Court may reject one of its own previous decisions (or a decision of the House of Lords) if it was made *per incuriam*. This is, however, of limited application, since it would be virtually inconceivable in modern times for a case to progress through to the Supreme Court (or, before it, the House of Lords) with a crucial authority being overlooked. Moreover, it is doubtful whether this option is open to other courts. As noted earlier, the Court of Appeal in *Broome* v *Cassell & Co Ltd*[137] regarded a House of Lords decision as being given *per incuriam* on the basis that two House of Lords authorities were not cited to the House. Not only did the House of Lords disapprove the Court of Appeal's application of the *per incuriam* doctrine, but Lord Diplock also stated clearly that the Court of Appeal had no power to treat a House of Lords decision in this way:[138]

> The Court of Appeal found themselves able to disregard the decision of this House in *Rookes* v *Barnard* by applying to it the label *per incuriam*. That label is relevant only to the right of an appellate court to decline to follow one of its own previous decisions, not to its right to disregard a decision of a higher appellate court or to the right of a judge of the High Court to disregard a decision of the Court of Appeal.

This dictum has been approved in subsequent cases[139] and it may therefore be assumed to be authoritative.

Finally, the status of certain House of Lords or Supreme Court decisions may be undermined by the application of the Human Rights Act 1998. As discussed earlier in this chapter, the Human Rights Act obliges courts to act consistently with the ECHR, and to interpret legislation in a Convention-compatible way wherever it is possible to do so. Thus, a court may have no option but to depart from a precedent that would otherwise be binding upon it, in order to reach a decision that is consistent with its obligations under the Human Rights Act. This is so, even if the precedent concerned was established by the Supreme Court or House of Lords.[140]

Court of Appeal

Civil Division

Decisions of the Court of Appeal are binding on all inferior courts trying civil or criminal cases, including Divisional Courts.[141] The Court of Appeal itself is bound

---

[137] [1971] 2 QB 354, [1971] 2 All ER 187; see p 83.

[138] *Cassell & Co Ltd* v *Broome* [1972] AC 1027 at 1131, [1972] 1 All ER 801 at 874.

[139] See *Baker* v *R* [1975] AC 774, [1975] 3 All ER 55; *Miliangos* v *George Frank (Textiles) Ltd* [1976] AC 443 at 479, [1975] 3 All ER 801 at 822–3, *per* Lord Simon; cf. *Hughes* v *Kingston upon Hull City Council* [1999] QB 1193, [1999] 2 All ER 49, in which the Divisional Court of the Queen's Bench Division rejected a *per incuriam* decision of the Court of Appeal.

[140] See, e.g., the decision of the Court of Appeal in *Ghaidan* v *Godin-Mendoza* [2002] EWCA Civ 1533, [2003] Ch 380, [2002] 4 All ER 1162, discussed further at pp 48 and 73.

[141] *Brownsea Haven Properties Ltd* v *Poole Corporation* [1958] Ch 574, [1958] 1 All ER 205.

by decisions of the European Court, the House of Lords (now the Supreme Court),[142] and by its own earlier decisions.[143] The last principle was established in *Young* v *Bristol Aeroplane Co Ltd*.[144] In delivering the judgment in this case, Lord Greene MR cited three exceptional circumstances in which an earlier decision of the Court of Appeal would not be regarded as binding, as follows.

(1) **Where there are two conflicting decisions, the court may choose which it will follow and the decision not followed will be deemed to have been overruled**. Thus, in *Fisher* v *Ruislip-Northwood Urban District Council*,[145] the court had to choose between conflicting decisions on the liability of local authorities to motorists who collided with unlit air-raid shelters. Similarly, in *Tiverton Estates Ltd* v *Wearwell Ltd*,[146] the Court of Appeal was able to avoid following its decision in *Law* v *Jones*[147] because it conflicted with earlier decisions of the court.

(2) **The court is bound to refuse to follow a decision of its own that, although not expressly overruled, cannot stand with a later House of Lords (or Supreme Court) decision**. It is notable that in *Young* this exception was said to apply to cases in which a Court of Appeal decision was inconsistent with a *later* House of Lords (now Supreme Court) decision. There was no mention of what should happen in the event of a conflict with an earlier decision of that House. It may be that Lord Greene did not envisage that such a situation would ever arise, or, alternatively, he may have assumed that any such situation would be covered by the third of his exceptions. In the recent case of *Iqbal* v *Whipps Cross University Hospital NHS Trust*,[148] the Court of Appeal held that it was bound to follow its own decision in *Croke (A Minor)* v *Wiseman*,[149] even though that decision was inconsistent with *two* earlier decisions of the House of Lords.[150] The situation was not covered by the *per incuriam* exception as the court in *Croke* had been referred to the earlier decisions, but in the Court of Appeal's view any error in its reasoning could only be corrected by the House of Lords:[151]

> If the first Court of Appeal has considered the decision of the House of Lords and either wrongly distinguished it or misinterpreted its effect the second Court of Appeal would be simply disagreeing with the reasoning of the first Court of Appeal; something which the doctrine of *stare decisis* forbids.

---

[142] Subject to such decisions being compatible with EU law and with the Human Rights Act 1998; see p 94.

[143] The Court of Appeal is also bound by the decisions of courts that exercised equivalent jurisdiction prior to 1875: the Court of Exchequer Chamber and the Chancery Court of Appeal; see *Re Stevens, ex parte M'George* (1882) 20 Ch D 697.

[144] [1944] KB 718, [1944] 2 All ER 293 (affirmed [1946] AC 163, [1946] 1 All ER 98).

[145] [1945] KB 584, [1945] 2 All ER 458.   [146] [1975] Ch 146, [1974] 1 All ER 209.

[147] [1974] Ch 112, [1973] 2 All ER 437.   [148] [2007] EWCA Civ 1190.

[149] [1982] 1 WLR 71, [1981] 3 All ER 852.

[150] *Pickett* v *British Rail Engineering Ltd* [1980] AC 136, [1979] 1 All ER 774; *Gammell* v *Wilson* [1982] AC 27, [1981] 1 All ER 578.

[151] [2007] EWCA Civ 1190 at [57], *per* Gage LJ. See also *Miliangos* v *George Frank (Textiles) Ltd* [1976] AC 443 at 479, [1975] 3 All ER 801 at 823, *per* Lord Simon; cf. *Turton* v *Turton* [1988] Ch 542, [1987] 2 All ER 641.

(3) **The court is not bound to follow a decision of its own if that decision was given** *per incuriam*. Thus, in *Royal Bank of Scotland v Etridge (No 2)*[152] the court refused to follow its own decision in *Royal Bank of Scotland v Etridge (No 1)*[153] because it had not, in the earlier case, been referred to two previous decisions by which it ought to have been bound.

If a decision is described as having been given *per incuriam* this usually means that the court has overlooked a relevant statutory provision or a binding precedent,[154] but there is a residual category of other cases in which the principle may be invoked. Thus, in *Williams v Fawcett*,[155] the Court of Appeal rejected a number of earlier authorities on the grounds that there had been a 'manifest slip or error' affecting the liberty of the subject, and it was unlikely that the House of Lords would have the opportunity to correct this error. The court applied the same test in *Rickards v Rickards*[156] and refused to follow an earlier decision involving a wrongful rejection of jurisdiction by the court. In the circumstances of the case there was no possibility of an appeal to the House of Lords.

While he was Master of the Rolls, Lord Denning engaged in a tireless but ultimately unsuccessful campaign to give the Court of Appeal the freedom to depart from its previous decisions at will. In *Gallie v Lee*,[157] he made the following assertion:

> We are, of course, bound by the decisions of the House [of Lords], but I do not think we are bound by prior decisions of our own, or at any rate, not absolutely bound. We are not fettered as it was once thought. It was a self-imposed limitation; and we who imposed it can also remove it. The House of Lords have done it. So why should not we do likewise?

This was, however, a minority opinion. Russell LJ saw the position of the House of Lords in quite a different light, saying of the Master of the Rolls:[158]

> I think that in one respect he has sought to wield a broom labelled 'for the use of the House of Lords only'. I do not support the suggestion that this court is free to override its own decisions...the availability of the House of Lords to correct error in the Court of Appeal makes it in my view unnecessary for this court to depart from its existing discipline.

In *Barrington v Lee*,[159] a case concerned with liability in respect of an estate agent's default over a deposit, Lord Denning again made the bold statement that the Court of Appeal was not bound by a previous decision on similar facts. Again, however, he found himself in the minority: while Edmund Davies and Stephenson LJJ felt able

---

[152] [1998] 4 All ER 705.   [153] [1997] 3 All ER 628.   [154] See p 82.
[155] [1986] QB 604, [1985] 1 All ER 787.   [156] [1990] Fam 194, [1989] 3 All ER 193.
[157] [1969] 2 Ch 17 at 37, [1969] 1 All ER 1062 at 1072 (affirmed *sub nom Saunders* v *Anglia Building Society* [1971] AC 1004, [1970] 3 All ER 961).
[158] [1969] 2 Ch 17 at 41, [1969] 1 All ER 1062 at 1082. The third member of the court, Salmon LJ, took a middle view and stated that any change in policy would require a pronouncement of the whole Court of Appeal. Nevertheless, in *Davis v Johnson* [1979] AC 264, [1978] 1 All ER 1132, Lord Salmon and other members of the House of Lords expressly reaffirmed *Young's case*.
[159] [1972] 1 QB 326 at 338, [1971] 3 All ER 1231 at 1238; see also *Hanning v Maitland (No 2)* [1970] 1 QB 580 at 587, [1970] 1 All ER 812 at 815.

to distinguish the earlier case and to concur with Lord Denning on the result of the appeal, they both reaffirmed the principles set out in *Young* v *Bristol Aeroplane*. Faced with such opposition, Lord Denning was constrained to resile from the statements he had made in this case and *Gallie* v *Lee*, and in *Miliangos* v *George Frank (Textiles) Ltd*[160] he expressly applied the principles in *Young* v *Bristol Aeroplane Co Ltd*. Nevertheless, in *Davis* v *Johnson*,[161] a controversial case dealing with the power of the courts to protect battered wives, Lord Denning led the full Court of Appeal in yet another attack on *Young*. This attack was repulsed when the case reached the House of Lords,[162] and the rule in *Young* was, in Lord Diplock's words, 'expressly, unequivocally and unanimously' reaffirmed.

The general rule that the Court of Appeal is bound to follow its previous decisions is now well settled, and in the light of the unequivocal House of Lords decision in *Davis* v *Johnson* it is difficult to envisage the Court making any further attempt to free itself from this position. This does not, however, preclude the possibility of adding to the list of recognized exceptions, and the Court of Appeal's willingness to depart from a previous decision in order to give effect to changes in international law may be regarded as one such example.[163] The Court of Appeal has also held that it is not bound by its previous decisions on applications for permission to appeal,[164] although an earlier finding that it was not obliged to follow interlocutory decisions made by only two judges[165] has now been rejected.[166]

Two further exceptions to the rule that the Court of Appeal is obliged to follow its previous decisions have arisen as a result of statutory intervention. Firstly, as already noted,[167] the Human Rights Act 1998 has important implications for the doctrine of precedent. Given that the Court of Appeal has already refused to follow an earlier House of Lords decision in order to give effect to Convention rights,[168] it seems certain that the Court will not hesitate to depart from its own previous decisions in similar circumstances. Secondly, when faced with a conflict between one of its own decisions (or a decision of the House of Lords) and a decision of the European Court of Justice, section 3 of the European Communities Act 1972 obliges the Court of Appeal to follow the latter.

---

[160] [1975] QB 487, [1975] 1 All ER 1076.   [161] [1978] 2 WLR 182, [1978] 1 All ER 841.
[162] [1979] AC 264, [1978] 1 All ER 1132.
[163] *Trendtex Trading Corporation Ltd* v *Central Bank of Nigeria* [1977] QB 529, [1977] 1 All ER 881; see p 84.
[164] *Clark* v *University of Lincolnshire and Humberside* [2000] 3 All ER 752, [2000] 1 WLR 1988. This is, of course, consistent with the current rule of practice that decisions on applications for permission to appeal cannot normally be cited as precedents in the civil courts; *Practice Direction (Citation of Authorities)* [2001] 2 All ER 510, [2001] 1 WLR 1001.
[165] *Boys* v *Chaplin* [1968] 2 QB 1, [1968] 1 All ER 283; *Welsh Development Agency* v *Redpath Dorman Long* [1994] 1 WLR 1409, [1994] 4 All ER 10.
[166] *Cave* v *Robinson Jarvis and Rolfe* [2001] EWCA Civ 245, [2002] 1 WLR 581.
[167] See p 73.
[168] *Ghaidan* v *Godin-Mendoza* [2002] EWCA Civ 1533, [2003] Ch 380, [2002] 4 All ER 1162, discussed further at pp 48 and 73.

It may be noted finally that a 'full court' of five or more judges of the Civil Division is sometimes convened to hear cases involving particularly important or difficult points of law. The full court has, however, no greater authority than the normal court and its decisions carry no more weight as precedents.[169]

Criminal Division

Decisions of the Criminal Division of the Court of Appeal are binding on all inferior courts, including the Divisional Court of the Queen's Bench Division. The Division regards itself as bound by decisions of its predecessor, the Court of Criminal Appeal, and also by decisions of the Civil Division of the Court of Appeal, subject to the exceptions contained in *Young v Bristol Aeroplane Co Ltd*. Thus, in *DPP v Merriman*,[170] the Criminal Division reluctantly allowed an appeal that was totally lacking in merit, because of the existence of a direct authority of the Court of Criminal Appeal in favour of the appellant. However, the court certified a point of law of general public importance and granted leave to appeal to the House of Lords. The appeal was subsequently allowed and the earlier authority was overruled.[171]

The Court of Criminal Appeal formulated the principle that it would not be bound by its own previous decisions where this would cause injustice to an appellant, the rationale being that the desire for justice transcends the desirability of certainty. In *R v Taylor*, Lord Goddard CJ explained the rule as follows:[172]

> This court... has to deal with questions involving the liberty of the subject, and if it finds, on reconsideration, that, in the opinion of a full court assembled for that purpose, the law has been either misapplied or misunderstood in a decision which it has previously given, and that, on the strength of that decision, an accused person has been sentenced and imprisoned, it is the bounden duty of the court to reconsider the earlier decision with a view to seeing whether that person had been properly convicted. The exceptions which apply in civil cases ought not to be the only ones applied in such a case as the present.

This rule was adopted by the Criminal Division of the Court of Appeal in *R v Gould*.[173] A recent example of the application of the rule is the case of *R v Simpson*,[174] in which the Criminal Division declined to follow its previous decision in *R v Palmer (John)*

---

[169] *Young v Bristol Aeroplane Co Ltd* [1944] KB 718, [1944] 2 All ER 293. Likewise the authority of a two-judge court is no less than that of a three-judge court: *Langley v North West Water Authority* [1991] 3 All ER 610, [1991] 1 WLR 697.

[170] [1971] 2 QB 310, [1971] 2 All ER 1424.   [171] [1973] AC 584, [1972] 3 All ER 42.

[172] [1950] 2 KB 368, [1950] 2 All ER 170. See also *DPP v Merriman* [1973] AC 584 at 605, [1972] 3 All ER 42 at 58, *per* Lord Diplock; *R v Howe* [1986] QB 626, [1986] 1 All ER 833 (affirmed [1987] AC 417, [1987] 1 All ER 771); cf. *R v Charles* [1976] 1 All ER 659, [1976] 1 WLR 248 (affirmed *sub nom Metropolitan Police Commissioner v Charles* [1977] AC 177, [1976] 3 All ER 112).

[173] [1968] 2 QB 65, [1968] 1 All ER 849. The necessity for a 'full court' of five or more judges seems to have been tacitly abolished, although *R v Newsome* [1970] 2 QB 711, [1970] 3 All ER 455 suggests that a court of five has a greater power to depart from earlier decisions. On occasions when the need to choose between conflicting decisions arises, a full court is sometimes convened; see, e.g., *R v Jackson* [1974] QB 802, [1974] 1 All ER 640. See also, Zellick, 'Precedent in the Court of Appeal, Criminal Division' [1974] Crim LR 222.

[174] [2003] EWCA Crim 1499, [2004] QB 118, [2003] 3 All ER 531. See also *R v Rowe* [2007] EWCA Crim 635, [2007] 3 WLR 177, [2007] 3 All ER 36.

because it considered that the law in the earlier case had been misunderstood and mis-applied.[175] The exceptional case of *R* v *James (Leslie)*, in which the Criminal Division followed a Privy Council decision instead of an earlier House of Lords ruling, can also be considered in this context.[176]

However, as the court made clear in *Simpson*, the power to depart from its own previous decisions is limited to where the departure is in favour of the accused. That is not the same as permitting an accused a defence to a charge based on an erroneous statement of law in an earlier case. In such circumstances the Court of Appeal is entitled to depart from that decision.

The Court of Appeal (Criminal Division) sits in five or six panels, and consistency is important. For that reason departure from a previous decision is usually by a court sitting with a five-judge panel instead of the normal three-judge panel. In *R* v *Mago*,[177]the court considered that a five-judge court had a discretion to decide that a previous decision was wrong, under the *Young* v *Bristol Aeroplane* principle, but it was a discretion to be used circumspectly. A five-judge court was not entitled to disregard or deprive of authority the only previous decision on a clear and fully argued point of law, particularly when the consequence would be to the detriment of the accused.

High Court

Divisional Courts

In civil matters, Divisional Courts are bound by decisions of the House of Lords (now Supreme Court) and Court of Appeal. They are also bound by their own previous decisions to the same extent as the Court of Appeal, and this means that they are entitled to rely on the exceptions established in *Young* v *Bristol Aeroplane* and elsewhere.[178] Thus, when faced with a conflict between two of their previous decisions, Divisional Courts can choose which one to follow, and they need not follow previous decisions that are incompatible with EC law, the Human Rights Act 1998, or any decision of the Court of Appeal, House of Lords (now Supreme Court), or European Court of Justice. Divisional Courts can also depart from their own previous decisions if they are regarded as having been made *per incuriam*, and, occasionally, they have even rejected Court of Appeal decisions on this basis.[179] Divisional Court decisions in civil cases are binding on judges of the same division of the High Court sitting alone, and possibly on judges of other divisions.[180]

---

[175] [2002] EWCA Crim 2202, [2003] 1 Cr App R (S) 12.

[176] [2006] EWCA Crim 14, [2006] QB 588, [2006] 1 All ER 759; see p 79.   [177] [2010] EWCA Crim 1575.

[178] See p 92; *Huddersfield Police Authority* v *Watson* [1947] KB 842, [1947] 2 All ER 193.

[179] *R* v *Northumberland Compensation Tribunal, ex parte Shaw* [1952] 1 KB 338, [1952] 1 All ER 122; *Hughes* v *Kingston upon Hull City Council* [1999] QB 1193, [1999] 2 All ER 49; cf. *Cassell & Co Ltd* v *Broome* [1972] AC 1027 at 1131, [1972] 1 All ER 801 at 874, in which Lord Diplock asserted that the *per incuriam* doctrine did not entitle either the Court of Appeal or the High Court to disregard any decision of a higher appellate court.

[180] *Re Seaford, Seaford* v *Seifert* [1967] P 325, [1967] 2 All ER 458 (reversed [1968] P 53, [1968] 1 All ER 482) in which a judge of the Probate, Divorce and Admiralty Division regarded himself as bound by a decision

In criminal cases, the position of the Divisional Court of the Queen's Bench Division is analogous to that of the Criminal Division of the Court of Appeal. Thus it is free to depart from its own decisions in the same circumstances as in that court.

Finally, when exercising its supervisory jurisdiction, a Divisional Court is in the same position as a High Court judge sitting alone, and it may depart from one of its own previous decisions if convinced that the decision is wrong. The above principles appear from the judgment of the Queen's Bench Divisional Court, delivered by Goff LJ in *R* v *Greater Manchester Coroner, ex parte Tal*.[181]

Judges at first instance

Decisions of High Court judges sitting alone at first instance are binding on inferior courts but not on other High Court judges. For this reason, principles of law contained only in first-instance decisions should not be relied upon too heavily. Naturally, however, they are of persuasive authority and a High Court judge will hesitate before 'not following' the decision of one of his brethren, if only for reasons of comity. Nevertheless, where a first-instance judge is clearly convinced that an earlier decision at first instance is wrong, he will be free to refuse to follow that decision.

There have been several direct clashes between judges deciding cases at first instance. A notable example concerned the question of whether a failure to wear a seat belt in a motor vehicle should be treated as contributory negligence in the event of an accident in which injury is sustained. This question divided the judges of the Queen's Bench Division in some fourteen reported cases between 1970 and 1975, before the Court of Appeal finally resolved the conflict in *Froom* v *Butcher*.[182]

It is sometimes said that Chancery Division judges are less willing than judges of other divisions to depart from decisions of their brethren. However, this is only true in the sense that there is often a greater risk in Chancery Division cases that departing from an earlier decision might disturb financial arrangements or deprive a person of a proprietary right.

High Court judges are bound by the decisions of Divisional Courts, the Court of Appeal, and the House of Lords (now Supreme Court). However, as with the appellate courts, the strict application of the *stare decisis* doctrine must be considered in the light of the High Court's statutory obligations to give effect to EU law and to decide cases in accordance with the Human Rights Act 1998.[183]

---

of the Divisional Court of the Queen's Bench Division; cf. *Elderton* v *United Kingdom Totalisator Co Ltd* (1945) 61 TLR 529 (affirmed [1946] Ch 57, [1945] 2 All ER 624).

[181] [1985] QB 67, [1984] 3 All ER 240. A 'full' Divisional Court of five or more judges has no greater authority than a court of two or three: *Younghusband* v *Luftig* [1949] 2 KB 354, [1949] 2 All ER 72.

[182] [1976] QB 286, [1975] 3 All ER 520; all of the reported cases on the subject are reviewed in the judgment of Lord Denning MR in this case. The Court of Appeal concluded that failure to wear a seat belt *did* amount to contributory negligence. For another illustration of clashes between judges at first instance, see *Esso Petroleum Co Ltd* v *Harper's Garage (Stourport) Ltd* [1965] 3 WLR 469, [1965] 2 All ER 933 and *Petrofina Ltd* v *Martin* [1965] Ch 1073, [1965] 2 All ER 176.

[183] See pp 73 and 94.

County courts, magistrates' courts, and the Crown Court

Magistrates' courts and county courts are bound by the decisions of all superior courts, including first-instance decisions of the High Court. Judges deciding cases in the Crown Court are also bound by these decisions, despite the bold assertion of one circuit judge that he was not bound by decisions of the Divisional Court.[184] The decisions of one inferior court do not bind other inferior courts, chiefly because they are unlikely to address new legal principles and are rarely reported. Decisions made by Crown Court judges *are* occasionally reported, however, and they may have persuasive authority for other inferior courts, especially when the Crown Court is presided over by a High Court judge.

Tribunals

Lower tribunals do not set binding precedents for themselves or for any other court, and they are bound by the decisions of the appellate tribunals and superior courts. The Employment Appeal Tribunal and other appellate tribunals are bound by decisions of the Court of Appeal and Supreme Court, but they do not generally regard themselves as being bound by their own decisions.

KEY ISSUE

It would be optimistic to state categorically that the doctrine of binding precedent achieves certainty while retaining flexibility. Its operation depends, as with the interpretation of statutes, on each judge or court's conception of the judicial function. The hierarchy of the courts is clear. The principles for the ascertainment of the *ratio decidendi* of a case are clear enough, although sometimes troublesome in their application. The *ratio* of a case is not set in stone. It can be explained, narrowed and restated in subsequent cases. *Rationes decidendi* of cases may be followed even if subsequent judges consider them wrong. Dissenting judgements may over a period of time become more important and influential than those of the majority. The *per incuriam* doctrine, the process of distinguishing, the capacity of superior courts to overrule decisions, and the absolute power of Parliament to change the law all serve to keep the doctrine flexible. So, too, the rare occasions of bold judicial innovation, such as that of Lord Denning in *Nagle* v *Fielden*.[185] The doctrine of precedent is usually seen to operate fairly, although how far this is attributable to the inherent qualities of the doctrine and how far to the good sense of English judges is a matter of debate.

❓ Questions

1. Do you agree with the above conclusion?
2. Does the doctrine of judicial precedent operate too rigidly?
3. What might the consequences be of a more liberal approach to the doctrine of precedent?

---

[184] *R* v *Colyer* [1974] Crim LR 24. The judge's refusal to follow a decision of the Queen's Bench Divisional Court must surely have been incorrect, given that decisions of the divisional courts are even binding upon themselves.

[185] [1966] 2 QB 633.

Law reporting

As stated at the beginning of this chapter, the doctrine of binding precedent became a part of English law only when the system of law reporting had become comprehensive. The doctrine of precedent, as such, is of far greater antiquity but it was only in the nineteenth century that precedents became binding rather than merely persuasive. If it were possible to mark the turning point, the decision in *Mirehouse v Rennell*[186] in 1833 would appear to herald the evolution of the modern system. One might suppose that, because the doctrine of precedent is the cornerstone of the English legal system, the courts would have created a methodical system of producing law reports. In fact, however, this has never been done and law reporting has been left entirely to private enterprise. There is still an element of chance in the matter of whether or not a case is reported, although the growth of electronic legal databases means that few cases decided by the superior courts[187] (other than the Crown Court) escape the scrutiny of researchers. In addition, certain key tribunal decisions and Crown Court rulings become known to practitioners and academics through specialist journals and encyclopaedias.

The history of law reporting can be roughly divided into three periods: the period of the Year Books extending approximately from 1272 to 1535; the period of the private named reporters extending from 1535 to 1865; and the modern, semi-official system of reporting that began in 1865.

The Year Books

The Year Books are the first available law reports. They were first compiled during the reign of Edward I and their exact purpose is uncertain. They were certainly not intended for use by the judges as precedents, and were probably just notes compiled by students and junior advocates as guides to pleading and procedure. However, there are indications that they may have been used by some judges as a direct source of precedent. Thus in 1310 Stanton J referred to a case decided at least ten years earlier,[188] while Bereford CJ in 1312 cited a decision some twenty-five years old.[189] By the fifteenth century there are many examples of Year Book cases in which the judge is reported as having relied upon a number of old authorities, and there is ample evidence that judges were conscious of their decisions being recorded for use as precedents.[190] Compilation of printed Year Books ceased in about 1535.[191] With the introduction of printing in the

---

[186] (1833) 1 Cl & Fin 527.　　[187] See Chapter 7.

[188] *Kembeare v K* YB 4 Edw 2 (SS iv), 153. Note the method of citation by regnal year.

[189] *Anon* YB 6 Edw 2 (SS xiii), 43.

[190] For examples, see Allen, *Law in the Making* (Clarendon Press: 7th edn, 1964), p 190 *et seq*.

[191] Although manuscript Year Books continued to be produced into the seventeenth century.

fifteenth century, many Year Book manuscripts were printed in the so-called 'Black Letter' editions. The most widely used modern versions of the Year Books are the Rolls Series (RS) and the Selden Society Series (SS), both of which date from the early twentieth century. They contain the original text of the Year Book manuscripts, which are in 'law French', a peculiar combination of Norman French, English, and Latin, together with an English translation.

The private reports

As soon as the compilation of the Year Books ceased, private sets of reports began to be produced and published under the name of the law reporter. These reports proliferated in the period from 1535 to 1865, and the citation of precedents became progressively more common as the reports became more comprehensive.

The standard of reporting varied greatly. At one end of the scale were those whose reports contain what are still regarded as classic expositions of the common law, with Coke being the most notable example. Coke's Reports (Co Rep) are so well known as to be citable merely as 'reports' (Rep), and they contain comprehensive expositions of virtually every aspect of the common law. Published between 1600 and 1658, Coke's Reports contain many of the great constitutional cases of the seventeenth century, such as *Prohibitions del Roy*,[192] *Proclamations*,[193] and *Magdalen College*.[194] Alongside Coke, other highly regarded law reporters include Dyer, Plowden, and Burrow. Burrow's Reports of cases in the Court of King's Bench are widely regarded as the first set of law reports produced in the modern pattern, since they contain headnotes and the argument of counsel is carefully separated from the judgment.

It must not be thought that every one of the private law reporters was a Plowden or a Coke. At the other end of the scale were reporters such as Barnardiston, Atkyns, and Espinasse, whose reports became virtually uncitable so low were they held in judicial esteem.[195] Indeed, Lord Mansfield would not permit certain series of reports to be cited to him, while Holt CJ famously complained that 'these scrambling reports will make us appear to posterity for a parcel of blockheads'.[196]

The private reports are cited by the name of the reporter (usually abbreviated) and a volume and page number. The date of the report is not part of the reference but is usually inserted in ordinary round brackets. Thus the reference to the case of *Pillans* v *Van Mierop* (1765) 3 Burr 1664 indicates that the case can be found in the third volume of Burrow's Reports at page 1664. In practice, most law libraries have the reports of the private reporters in the reprinted edition known as 'the English Reports' (ER or Eng Rep).

---

[192] (1607) 12 Co Rep 63. [193] (1610) 12 Co Rep 74.
[194] (1615) 11 Co Rep 66b. [195] See Allen, *op cit*, p 221 *et seq*.
[196] *Slater* v *May* (1704) 2 Ld Raym 1071.

The present system of law reporting

The Law Reports

In 1865 the system of private reporting gave way to the current system. A Council was established to publish reports of superior court decisions as cheaply as possible, and it was, from its inception, under professional control. The Council was incorporated in 1870 as the Incorporated Council of Law Reporting for England and Wales.[197] It now produces the Law Reports, the Weekly Law Reports (WLR), the Industrial Cases Reports (ICR), and the Law Reports Statutes. The Law Reports are not an official publication, but judges are given the opportunity to revise reports of their own judgments and they are the series of reports to which counsel should refer when citing a case that is reported in them.[198] One advantage of these reports over other series is that legal argument, as well as the judgments, is published. Where the court has adjourned to take time to consider its decision, judgment is said to be 'reserved'. This fact is indicated in the reports by the words *curia advisari vult, cur ad vult,* or *cav,* and reserved judgments are generally accorded greater weight than *ex tempore* judgments.

Before 1875, cases published in the Law Reports were cited by reference to the court in which they were decided and a serial number dating from 1865, prefixed by the letters 'LR'. The date was not part of the reference and was therefore inserted in ordinary round brackets. Thus *Irving* v *Askew* (1870) LR 5 QB 208 was reported in the fifth volume of reports of cases in the Court of Queen's Bench, at page 208. Between 1875 and 1890 citation was by an abbreviation of the appropriate division of the High Court (Ch D; QBD; PD; CPD; Ex D[199]) or App Cas for an appeal case. The prefix LR was dropped but the date was still not part of the reference and the serial number dated from 1875. An example of citation during this period is *Symons* v *Rees* (1876) 1 Ex D 416.

In 1891 the date was made part of the reference in place of a serial number and the letter 'D' (for Division) was dropped. The fact that the date is part of the reference is signified by its inclusion in square brackets. There is a separate volume of Reports for each division of the High Court (QB; Ch; Fam),[200] and a separate volume for House of Lords (now Supreme Court) and Privy Council cases (AC).[201] Court of Appeal decisions are reported in the volume for the division of the High Court from which the

---

[197] The Council is a charity: *Incorporated Council of Law Reporting for England and Wales* v *A-G* [1972] Ch 73, [1971] 3 All ER 1029.

[198] *Practice Note (CA: Reports: Citations)* [1991] 1 All ER 352; *Practice Direction (Citation of Authorities)* [2001] 2 All ER 510, [2001] 1 WLR 1001. The House of Lords has stated that counsel may refer to a report in Tax Cases, rather than the Law Reports: *Bray* v *Best* [1989] 1 All ER 969, [1989] 1 WLR 167.

[199] The last two were abolished in 1880; see p 227.

[200] When the Family Division was named the Probate, Divorce and Admiralty Division, this volume of Reports was cited by the letter 'P'.

[201] Before 1974, when a case reached the House of Lords, the Privy Council, or a Divisional Court on appeal, the appellant's name used to be cited first. Thus, for example, the case known in the Court of Appeal as *Lever Brothers Ltd* v *Bell* [1931] 1 KB 557 became *Bell* v *Lever Brothers Ltd* [1932] AC 161 in the House of Lords. This practice was altered in 1974, and petitions for leave to appeal and appeals to the House of Lords carry the same title that they had at first instance; [1974] 1 All ER 752, [1974] 1 WLR 305. In criminal cases

appeal came. County court appeals and appeals to the Criminal Division of the Court of Appeal are usually reported in the volume for the Queen's Bench Division. There is thus nothing in the reference to distinguish a Court of Appeal decision from a decision at first instance.

The Weekly Law Reports

The Weekly Law Reports have been published since 1953 and they include a report of every decision that will ultimately appear in the Law Reports proper.[202] The cases are reported in full, but legal argument is omitted because of the restriction on space. In addition, many cases are published in the Weekly Law Reports that are not subsequently included in the Law Reports. These cases make up Volume 1, whereas cases destined to reach the Law Reports can be found in Volumes 2 and 3.

The year is part of the reference for cases published in the Weekly Law Reports, and it therefore appears in square brackets. There is, however, no attempt to classify cases by the court in which they were decided. All cases appear in 1 WLR, 2 WLR, or 3 WLR irrespective of whether they are House of Lords (now Supreme Court) or first-instance decisions.

Other series of reports

The All England Reports

Perhaps the most important of the commercially published reports are the All England Law Reports.[203] These are published on a weekly basis by LexisNexis-Butterworths, and are eventually collated in annual volumes. Their virtue lies principally in the speed with which they follow decisions and the fact that they include many cases that do not find their way into the Law Reports. The All England Law Reports are cited by the year in square brackets, followed a volume number,[204] the abbreviation 'All ER' and a page number.

'Official' reports

Several series of reports are published under government authority and they concentrate on reporting cases in certain specialized areas. These series include Reports of Tax Cases, Reports of Patent, Design and Trade Mark Cases, and Immigration Appeal Reports.

Specialist reports published commercially

There are many series of specialist reports published commercially. For example, the Criminal Appeal Reports (CAR or Cr App R), first published shortly after the creation

---

this had the effect of terminating the practice whereby the Director of Public Prosecutions was substituted for *Rex* (or *Regina*).

[202] These replaced the 'Weekly Notes' (WN), which were published in the form of a current précis and were not strictly citeable as reports; see *Re Loveridge* [1902] 2 Ch 859 at 865, *per* Buckley J.

[203] The Law Journal Reports (LJ) and Law Times Reports (LT) have been incorporated in the All England Law Reports.

[204] There are usually three or four volumes published each year.

of the Court of Criminal Appeal, are still produced and include a number of criminal cases not reported elsewhere. Similarly Lloyd's List Law Reports (Lloyd's Rep) contain a number of commercial cases not reported elsewhere, while the Road Traffic Reports (RTR) contain, as the title would suggest, reports of road traffic cases. Other specialist series in general use are Local Government Reports (LGR), Building Law Reports (BLR), Simon's Tax Cases (STC), Property and Compensation Reports (PCR), Industrial Relations Law Reports (IRLR), Housing Law Reports (HLR), Fleet Street Patent Law Reports (FSR), and Human Rights Law Reports (HRLR).

European cases

European Community law decisions are to be found principally in the European Court Reports (ECR) published by the European Court of Justice, and the Common Market Law Reports (CMLR), which are an unofficial source. The main source of decisions of the European Court of Human Rights is the European Human Rights Reports series (EHRR).

Newspapers and periodicals

A number of legal periodicals such as the Solicitors Journal, Justice of the Peace, Estates Gazette, Criminal Law Review, New Law Journal, and Current Law include notes of cases to which reference may be made in the absence of a full report in a recognized series. In addition, *The Times, The Guardian*, and *The Independent* also publish reports of decided cases, and while these are inevitably brief, they may be cited in court in the absence of an alternative source.

Electronic sources

Many of the different series of law reports are now available electronically, either on CD ROM or on the Internet, either from commercial sites or non-commercial sites such as BAILI, and the use of this technology allows lawyers to access an increasingly large volume of case law, often within a relatively short time of the decisions being made. Important examples of commercially produced online databases include LexisNexis, Westlaw, Lawtel, and Casetrack. In addition, the decisions of several courts, including the House of Lords (now Supreme Court)[205] and Privy Council,[206] can be accessed through official websites,[207] as can cases decided by the European Court of Justice[208] and the European Court of Human Rights.[209]

Neutral citation of judgments

With effect from 11 January 2001, the Lord Chief Justice issued a Practice Direction[210] establishing a new system of neutral citation for cases decided by the Administrative Court and Court of Appeal. Under this system an official number is assigned to each

---

[205] **www.supremecourt.gov.uk**   [206] **www.privy-council.org.uk**

[207] See also: **www.courtservice.gov.uk**   [208] **http://curia.europa.eu/**

[209] **www.echr.coe.int**

[210] *Practice Direction (Sup Ct: Form of Judgments)* [2001] 1 All ER 193, [2001] 1 WLR 194.

new decision, and when used in conjunction with the year and the abbreviation for the court issuing the decision, this gives each case a unique reference. In addition, judgments of the courts concerned are now issued with numbered paragraphs instead of page numbers. Thus, to adopt the example used in the Practice Direction, paragraph 30 of the tenth case decided by the Civil Division of the Court of Appeal in 2001 would be cited as [2001] EWCA Civ 10 at [30]. The Practice Direction further provides that, when used in court, the neutral citation of a judgment should be given before the citation from the law report series. Lord Woolf CJ explained the reasons for this new system as follows:[211]

> The main reason of these changes is to facilitate the publication of judgments on the World Wide Web and their subsequent use by the increasing numbers of those who have access to the Web. The changes should also assist those who use and wish to search judgments stored on electronic databases.

Although not covered by the Practice Direction, the House of Lords, the Privy Council, and even the Immigration Appeals Tribunal adopted the same approach, and the system of neutral citation has now been extended to all divisions of the High Court.[212] The correct form of citation for these courts is illustrated in the examples below.

R v Lambert [2001] UKHL 37	(House of Lords)
Progress Property Co Ltd v Moore [2010] UKSC 55	(Supreme Court)
A v B [2002] EWCA Civ 337	(Court of Appeal, Civil Division)
R v Barker [2002] EWCA Crim 1508	(Court of Appeal, Criminal Division)
Percy v DPP [2001] EWHC 1125 (Admin)	(Administrative Court)
Douglas v Hello! [2003] EWHC 786 (QB)	(High Court, Queen's Bench Division)
Re B [2002] EWHC 429 (Fam)	(High Court, Family Division)[213]
B v Auckland District Law Society [2003] UKPC 38	(Privy Council)
S v Secretary of State for the Home Dept [2003] UKIAT 3	(Immigration Appeals Tribunal)

Further reading

CROSS and HARRIS, *Precedent in English Law* (Clarendon Press: 4th edn, 1991)

MEAD, 'Swallowing the Camel, Straining at the Gnat: The Implications of *Mendoza v Ghaidan*' [2003] 5 EHRLR 501

---

[211] Ibid at [3].

[212] *Practice Direction (Sup Ct: Judgments: Neutral Citations)* [2002] 1 All ER 351, [2002] 1 WLR 346.

[213] Other categories of High Court decision use the following abbreviations in place of (Fam): Chancery Division (CH); Patent's Court (Pat); Commercial Court (Comm); Admiralty Court (Admlty); Technology and Construction Court (TCC).

European Law[1]

4

INTRODUCTION

This chapter looks at the role of European Union law within the English legal system. Since the United Kingdom joined what is now the European Union in 1970, it has become an increasingly important source of domestic legal rules. In addition, the doctrine of the supremacy of European over national law has significant implications for the United Kingdom's established constitutional orthodoxy. Any work on the English legal system would therefore be incomplete without some discussion of the role of European law within it. The specific areas addressed by this chapter will include:

- the history and development of the European Community and European Union;
- the general scope of European law and the principles of subsidiarity and proportionality;
- the structure and functions of the main European institutions;
- the different types of European law and the concepts of direct and indirect effect;
- the relationship between European and domestic law;
- the role of the European Court of Justice and the Article 267 procedure.

A brief history

On 1 January 1973 the United Kingdom became a member state of the European Communities. There were originally three communities: the European Coal and Steel Community (ECSC); the European Atomic Energy Community (Euratom); and the European Economic Community (EEC). The EEC, which was by far the most ambitious and significant of the three projects, was officially renamed 'the European Community' (EC) by the Treaty on European Union (TEU) in 1992. The ECSC expired on 23 July 2002, leaving Euratom and the EC as the two remaining elements of the European Communities. Further changes took effect once the process of ratifying the Treaty of

---

[1] See generally, Steiner, Woods and Twigg-Flesner, *EU Law* (OUP: 10th edn, 2009); Hartley, *The Foundations of European Community Law* (OUP: 7th edn, 2010); Wyatt and Dashwood, *European Union Law* (Sweet & Maxwell: 11th edn, 2011); Craig and De Búrca, *EU Law: Text, Cases and Materials* (OUP: 4th edn, 2007).

Lisbon was completed.[2] References to the Treaty provisions are, unless otherwise stated, to provisions as they are following ratification of the Lisbon Treaty. From this point onwards the European Community has been replaced and succeeded by the European Union, and the Treaty establishing the European Community—the Treaty of Rome—is renamed 'the Treaty on the Functioning of the European Union' (TFEU).

Created in 1957 by the Treaty of Rome, the European Community (or the EEC as it then was) initially comprised six members,[3] but has since expanded to its current composition of twenty-seven Member States.[4] The Treaty reflected a post-war desire to achieve stability through European unity, and the aim set out in the Preamble was to create an 'ever closer union' amongst the peoples of Europe. This was to be achieved through common action in the economic field. The Community was to have its own institutions, along with laws that could regulate the powers and obligations of Member States in economic matters.

The Single European Act and the Treaty on European Union

The Community has now developed far beyond the original aims set by the Treaty of Rome. In 1987 the Single European Act was adopted,[5] which amended the Treaty and established the objective of making 'concrete progress towards European unity'. The process of amendment and reform was continued by the Treaty on European Union (TEU), which is more commonly referred to as the Maastricht Treaty. The United Kingdom ratified this Treaty in 1993 after considerable political controversy,[6] and it was given effect in law by the European Communities (Amendment) Act 1993. Not only did the Maastricht Treaty formally rename the EEC as the 'European Community', but it also radically amended the Treaty of Rome in order to achieve its aims. These aims are stated in the Preamble to be a continuation of the process of 'ever closer union', economic and monetary union, the development of a single currency,[7] common citizenship, common foreign and defence policies, and the enhancement of the democratic functions of EU institutions.

The effects of the Maastricht Treaty were significant. Firstly, it extended the area of legal competence of the Union: it created a common citizenship, expanded existing

---

[2] 1 January 2009: see p 108.

[3] Belgium, France, Germany, Italy, Luxembourg, and the Netherlands.

[4] Denmark, Ireland and the United Kingdom became members in 1973; Greece in 1981; Portugal and Spain in 1986; Finland, Austria and Sweden in 1995; Cyprus, the Czech Republic, Estonia, Hungary, Latvia, Lithuania, Malta, Poland, the Slovak Republic, and Slovenia in 2004; and Bulgaria and Romania in 2007. The number of Member States could rise to thirty if negotiations with Croatia, Turkey, and Macedonia come to fruition.

[5] Despite the name, this is a Treaty and should not be confused with an Act of the United Kingdom Parliament.

[6] For an unsuccessful challenge to the incorporation of the Treaty, see *R v Secretary of State for Foreign Affairs, ex parte Lord Rees-Mogg* [1994] QB 552, [1994] 1 All ER 457.

[7] The United Kingdom and Denmark reserved their positions on aspects of economic and monetary union, as did Sweden when it joined in 1995. The other twelve states adopted the euro in 1999, and their national currencies ceased to be legal tender three years later.

rights of movement and voting, increased coordination of general economic policy, established a central bank, and increased the rights of workers. Secondly, the Treaty established a European Union (EU), founded on the existing Member States of the European Communities. The EC and its body of laws formed one of the three pillars of the European Union, the other two being concerned with (a) establishing a common foreign and security policy, and (b) achieving cooperation in justice and home affairs. These other two pillars did not form part of the EC framework, with the result that decisions made under them have thus far been made at a political level and have not been subject to the jurisdiction of the European Court of Justice. More recent reforms mean that this position is now changing.

The Treaty of Amsterdam[8]

The next significant step was the signing of the Treaty of Amsterdam in 1997. The Treaty came into force on 1 May 1999 and made substantive amendments to both the EC Treaty and the TEU. It also made specific commitments to a number of important non-economic goals, including human rights, environmental protection, and equality. Another important objective was to simplify the existing treaties by removing obsolete provisions, and most of the provisions in the earlier treaties were renumbered as a result.[9] The position of the European Parliament was also strengthened.[10] Economic cooperation still lay at the heart of the 'closer Europe' objective, but this was now balanced against other important aims.

From a legal perspective, one of the most important changes brought about by the Treaty of Amsterdam was the redrawing of the boundaries between the EC and the EU. The justice and home affairs pillar of the EU was retitled 'police and judicial cooperation in criminal matters', and a large part of it was brought within the framework of the EC pillar, making it susceptible to the jurisdiction of the European Court of Justice. Article 6(2) is another EU provision that was expressly made justiciable by the Treaty of Amsterdam. This provides that: 'The Union shall respect fundamental rights as guaranteed by the European Convention on Human Rights and Fundamental Freedoms... as general principles of Community law.' However, the second EU pillar—the common foreign and security policy—still lies beyond the jurisdiction of the Court of Justice.

The Treaty of Nice and the Charter of Fundamental Rights

The Treaty of Nice was signed by the Member States on 26 February 2001 but it did not come into force until 1 February 2003.[11] Unlike its predecessors this Treaty was

---

[8] Given effect in the United Kingdom by the European Communities (Amendment) Act 1998.

[9] Unless otherwise stated, references in this book are to the new numbers.

[10] See p 113.

[11] The process of ratification was initially delayed when the Irish rejected the Treaty in a referendum in June 2001. The Irish government was eventually able to proceed with ratification following a

primarily concerned with institutional reform, and it paved the way for the number of Member States to be increased from fifteen. In anticipation of the likelihood that achieving unanimity would become more difficult as the EU expanded, it also provided for more measures to be adopted by qualified majority.[12]

Another important document to be agreed when the European Council met in Nice was the Charter of Fundamental Rights of the European Union. The Charter sets out a number of economic and social rights of the kind that one might expect from an organization founded on an economic agenda. Thus it includes the right to education, the right to engage in work, the right not to be dismissed unjustifiably, and the right to collective bargaining. However, it also includes many of the civil and political rights found in most other international human rights agreements,[13] along with more novel ones such as the right to protection of family data. The civil and political rights correspond closely with those found in the ECHR,[14] and to avoid any inconsistency the Charter states that:[15]

> In so far as this Charter contains rights which correspond to rights guaranteed by the Convention for the Protection of Human Rights and Fundamental Freedoms, the meaning and scope of those rights shall be the same as those laid down by the said Convention. This provision shall not prevent Union law providing more extensive protection.

The Charter was signed in December 2000. At that time it was not expressed to be legally binding, but the Treaty of Lisbon has since provided for a new Article 6(1) to be added to the Treaty on European Union. This will give the rights, freedoms and principles set out in the Charter the same legal value as the treaties, meaning that they will be binding on EU institutions as well as on the Member States when they are implementing EU law. The United Kingdom and Poland, however, have both negotiated exemptions.

The Treaty of Lisbon: A constitution in all but name?

In 2004, almost three years after the idea was first accepted in principle, the heads of state and government formally signed the EU Constitutional Treaty. The intention was that this document should replace the four major treaties on which the Union is founded, and that the EU should be given a distinct legal personality. The idea was to formally merge the EU with the EC and abolish its pillar structure, in addition to incorporating the Charter of Fundamental Rights into the main body of European Law. The Constitutional Treaty was also intended to make the EU more democratic, and to this end many of its provisions were concerned with institutional reform.

second referendum in October 2002. The Treaty was given effect in the United Kingdom by the European Communities (Amendment) Act 2002.

[12] See p 112.

[13] For example, it includes provisions on equality, freedom of expression, and privacy.

[14] See Chapter 5.   [15] Article 52(3).

The Constitutional Treaty was an ambitious and controversial project, and despite being ratified by several Member States, it was effectively derailed by rejection in national referenda in both France and the Netherlands. The United Kingdom's referendum plans were postponed indefinitely, and the President of the European Commission acknowledged that the Treaty had probably been dealt a fatal blow:[16]

> It is difficult to see what a renegotiation would achieve. It is highly unlikely it would produce a radically different or better document. The Constitution is already the best possible compromise. It represents a delicate balance of competing views, which contains many improvements to the way in which the EU carries out its business. That is why there is no plan B.

A 'plan B' eventually did emerge in the shape of the Treaty of Lisbon, and although billed as an 'amending' treaty it brings about many of the changes intended by the ill-fated Constitutional Treaty. It significantly amends both the Treaty on European Union and the Treaty of Rome (to be known in future as the Treaty on the Functioning of the European Union), and, as stated previously, it will give legal effect to the Charter of Fundamental Rights. It provides for the EU to formally replace and succeed the EC, and gives the EU a distinct legal personality. It also incorporates many of the institutional and democratic changes originally set out in the Constitution: for example, it reduces the size of the European Commission, redistributes the seats within the European Parliament, and gives the Parliament an enhanced role. National parliaments also have a greater role, as they have the opportunity to consider proposals for new EU legislation directly. The EU will be forced to reconsider any proposed laws that are deemed by at least a third of national parliaments to infringe the principle of subsidiarity,[17] and if a majority of national parliaments oppose a proposal, it may be struck down altogether.

The Treaty was signed by representatives from each member state in December 2007, and following ratification is now in force.

The scope of European law

European law is a significant source of English law, although that statement should be read in the context of the practical as well as the theoretical position. European law is technically part of English law because Parliament, in the European Communities Act 1972, has said that that should be so, but in the early days it was seen merely as an adjunct that would only apply in certain situations. In *Bulmer Ltd* v *Bollinger SA*, Lord Denning MR states:[18]

> The treaty does not touch any of the matters which concern solely the mainland of England and the people in it. These are still governed by English law. They are not affected

---

[16] Jose Manuel Barroso, speaking at the National Forum on Europe, Dublin, 30 June 2005.
[17] 'Subsidiarity' means that decisions must be taken at a level that is as close as possible to the citizens of the Union.   [18] [1974] Ch 401 at 418, [1974] 2 All ER at 1231; see p 137.

by the treaty. But when we come to matters with a European element, the treaty is like an incoming tide. It flows into the estuaries and up the rivers. It cannot be held back. In future, in transactions which cross the frontiers we must no longer speak or think of English law as something on its own. We must speak or think of Community law, of Community rights and obligations, and we must give effect to them.

This statement might have been true in 1974, but today grossly underestimates the involvement of EU law beyond matters that 'cross frontiers'. Many areas of law and of domestic life that 'solely concern the mainland of England and the people in it' may nevertheless be affected by EU provisions. A major proportion of the law in the United Kingdom is in fact made by or through the EU. Some aspects of EU law concern obligations of an economic character, which are imposed on Member States rather than on individuals. Others, however, create individually enforceable rights, even within litigation that appears on its face to have no European context. Article 157, for example, concerns equality of treatment between male and female employees, while Article 191 provides for the regulation of environmental matters. Even where the implementation of EU obligations is achieved by domestic legislation, it is clear that the influence of European law is significant.

The scope of the EU's legal competence is subject only to the limits imposed by the EC Treaty, and many of its provisions are drafted in very wide terms. For example, legitimate areas of EU activity under Articles 3–5 include the elimination of restrictions on the free movement of goods and services, a common commercial policy, the creation of an internal market, free movement of persons, common agricultural, fisheries, and transport policies, competition policy, social and environmental policies, consumer protection, and measures in the spheres of energy, civil protection, and tourism. In addition, Article 94 empowers the Council to issue directives for the approximation of laws, regulations, or administrative provisions directly affecting the common market, and the European Union may enter into treaties and international agreements in order to fulfil its objectives.[19]

The principle of subsidiarity

Article 3B of the Treaty outlines the EU's relationship with its Member States by reference to the principle of subsidiarity:

> In areas which do not fall within its exclusive competence, the EU shall take action, in accordance with the principle of subsidiarity, only if and in so far as the objectives of the proposed action cannot be sufficiently achieved by the Member States and can therefore, by reason of the scale or effects of the proposed action, be better achieved by the Community.

The wording of this provision is arguably inconsistent with the principle that EU law is supreme, since this principle suggests that the Union should have the final word on

---

[19] Article 207, Treaty of Lisbon.

any matter within its competence, regardless of whether this competence is 'exclusive' or not. Moreover, there is no agreed method for determining whether the Union's competence in a particular matter *is* exclusive. In *UK* v *EU Council*,[20] the United Kingdom challenged the Working Time Directive made under Article 118a (now 138) of the Treaty, arguing that it conflicted with the principle of subsidiarity. In the United Kingdom's view there was no evidence that the aims of the Directive could not instead be achieved by action at a domestic level. However, the Court of Justice rejected this argument on the basis that health and safety issues fell within the Council's competence and the Council had an obligation to adopt minimum standards.[21]

The Member States sought to clarify the subsidiarity principle in a Protocol to the Treaty of Amsterdam. This provides that:[22]

> Subsidiarity is a dynamic concept and should be applied in the light of the objectives set out in the Treaty. It allows Community action within the limits of its powers to be expanded where circumstances so require, and conversely, to be restricted or discontinued where it is no longer required.

The Protocol also introduced a requirement for new legislative proposals to include statements detailing their compliance with the principles of subsidiarity and proportionality. The Treaty of Lisbon built on these changes by enabling national parliaments to call for a review of any draft legislation that is thought to contravene the principle of subsidiarity.[23]

KEY ISSUE

It should be clear from the history set out above that the treaties governing the European Union are in reality no ordinary treaties. They create a supranational body with its own legal powers, courts, and authorities. It has law-making powers, which, as we will see, bind Member States. In many ways it has the structures and trappings of a state, and has its own legal personality. To speak, as we do above, of European law as being a significant source of English law disguises the fact that its laws take effect directly as a result of its own law-making powers and that the EU has competence to act on its own in many areas.

? Questions

1. Is it accurate today to describe EU law as a source of English law?

2. Is EU law a source in its own right?

3. Who do you think decides the question whether the EU has competence to act?

---

[20] Case C-84/94, [1996] All ER (EC) 877.

[21] The Court also rejected an argument that the Directive should have been made under a different provision that would have given the United Kingdom a power of veto.

[22] The Protocol on the Application of the Principles of Subsidiarity and Proportionality.

[23] See Article 6 of the new Protocol on the Application of the Principles of Subsidiarity and Proportionality.

The institutions

The EU operates through four main institutions, although these institutions have only a limited role with regard to foreign and security policy and certain other aspects of EU business. These institutions are the Council, the Commission, the Court of Justice, and the European Parliament.

The Council

The Council of the European Union, formerly known as the Council of Ministers,[24] is the EU's main legislative and decision-making body. Article 202 of the EU Treaty states that its task is to ensure that the Treaty's objectives are obtained, and that the general economic policies of the Member States are coordinated. It also empowers the Council to 'take decisions', which primarily means approving legislation proposed by the Commission.[25] The Council is also responsible for negotiating with non-EU states, approving the EU budget, and making decisions under the second and third pillars.[26]

The Council is composed of the ministers from each Member State,[27] with the precise composition at any given time being determined by the matter under discussion. For example, a Council meeting to discuss environmental issues would be attended by the environment Minister from each state and it would be referred to as 'the Environment Council'. For the purposes of continuity, a permanent committee of officials (COREPAR)[28] conducts much of the Council's routine work for later ratification. In addition, the Treaty of Lisbon provides that the Council is assisted by a High Representative of the Union for Foreign Affairs and Security Policy.[29] The presidency of the Council is held by each state in turn for a period of six months. The main functions of the presidency are to convene and chair meetings of the Council, and also to determine the agendas.

The Treaty requires decisions on certain matters to be unanimous, but in most areas the Council operates on the basis of qualified majority voting (QMV).[30] Each Member State is entitled to cast a certain number of votes, with the numbers being weighted to give the most votes to the most populous countries. The current QMV rules date from 2004, when the EU was expanded from fifteen states. The United Kingdom, France, Germany, and Italy now have twenty-nine votes each, followed

---

[24] It was renamed in 1993: Council Decision 93/592. It should not be confused with the European Council, which consists of the heads of state and foreign ministers of the EU countries, together with the President and the President of the Commission. Under the Treaty of Lisbon the European Council will become a full EU institution with a permanent President.

[25] Under Article 208 TEU the Council may also initiate legislation by asking the Commission to examine a particular issue and submit its proposals.

[26] See p 107.   [27] Article 9B TEU.

[28] Article 240.   [29] Article 9B(2) TEU.

[30] Article 238. The Council can make certain decisions by a simple majority on the basis of one vote per state, but this is generally limited to decisions about procedural matters.

by Spain and Poland with twenty-seven. The least populous state, Malta, has just three. A qualified majority requires at least 72 per cent of the available votes and the approval of a majority (or sometimes a two-thirds majority) of the Member States.[31] In addition, a Member State can ask for confirmation that the votes cast in favour represent at least 62 per cent of the EU's population. This means that if a handful of large countries act together, they will be able to veto measures that have the support of the remaining states.

The Treaty of Lisbon provides for QMV to become the default method of decision-making within the Council,[32] and this means that it is extended to a whole new range of policy areas. From 2014 a new system of 'double majority voting' will be phased in. Under this system, a qualified majority will require at least 55 per cent of the members of the Council (that is, fifteen out of the twenty-seven states) to vote in favour of a measure. Those voting in favour will also have to represent at least 65 per cent of the EU's population.

The Commission

The powers of the Commission are set out in Article 9D of the EU Treaty. They principally concern the formulation of legislative proposals and the implementation and enforcement of measures adopted by the institutions. The Commission can investigate potential breaches of EU law and may refer them to the European Court of Justice,[33] although frequently it is able to resolve such issues through political negotiations. The Commission can even impose its own sanctions where it finds breaches of competition law, fining states and large companies that are found to have engaged in anti-competitive behaviour.[34] Finally, the Commission is also responsible for managing the EU budget, and acting together with the Council it is able to represent the EU at an international level.

The Commissioners hold office for a renewable term of five years,[35] with each one being responsible for a particular policy area. There is currently one Commissioner per country,[36] but the Treaty of Lisbon provides for this number to be reduced from 2014 onwards. In future only two-thirds of Member States will have a Commissioner at any given time, based on a system of equal rotation.[37]

The Parliament

Although originally comprising members nominated by Member States, the European Parliament has been directly elected since 1979.[38] Elections are held every five years,

---

[31] See Article 3 of the Protocol on EU Enlargement, attached to the Treaty of Nice.
[32] Article 9C TEU.   [33] Article 258 TEU.   [34] Articles 101–103 TEU.
[35] Article 9D TEU.   [36] Article 4 of the Protocol on EU Enlargement.
[37] As provided by the new Article 9D(5) of the TEU.
[38] In 1999 a system of proportional representation was introduced in the UK for the election of MEPs: European Parliamentary Elections Act 1999 (replaced by the European Parliamentary Elections Act 2002).

with the total number of MEPs now standing at 785. The UK currently contributes seventy-two MEPs. The Treaty of Lisbon provides for the total number of MEPs to be capped at 751 (including the President): each state will be represented by between six and ninety-six MEPs.[39] The Parliament holds plenary sessions in both Strasbourg and Brussels, although much of the preparatory work is done in committees. The General Secretariat and its departments are based in Luxembourg.

In the original Article 137 of the EC Treaty , the role of the Parliament was stated to be 'advisory and supervisory'. Its position has since been considerably strengthened and it now has much greater involvement in the legislative process. It also has important roles in approving the EU budget and scrutinizing the other institutions. There are different legislative procedures for different areas of EU law, and many of them now require the approval or involvement of the Parliament. The most significant of these is the co-decision procedure, established under Article 251 EC Treaty, which, although rather complicated, effectively gives the Parliament a power of veto in a wide range of matters. The range of measures made by this procedure increases considerably under the Treaty of Lisbon, so much so that it is to be known in future as 'the ordinary legislative procedure'.[40] Despite this welcome development, however, the Parliament will still lack the power to legislate independently.

In addition to its legislative role, the Parliament can ask questions of the Commission and Council, and it can even censure the Commission and remove it on a motion passed by a two-thirds majority.[41] Although the power of censure was once regarded as a largely theoretical sanction, a significant milestone was reached in 1999 when the *threat* of a vote of no confidence forced the entire Commission to resign. This action followed a damning report into accusations of maladministration and fraud in matters for which the Commission was responsible. Had the Commission not resigned of its own accord the Parliament would undoubtedly have forced it to do so by passing a motion of no confidence.[42]

The Court of Justice

The Court of Justice consists of one judge from each member state, assisted by eight Advocates-General. It can sit either in chambers of three or five judges, in a Grand Chamber of thirteen judges, or exceptionally, in plenary session.[43] It has a crucial role in enforcing EU obligations and in ensuring the uniform interpretation of European law throughout the Union.[44] Cases reach the Court either through direct actions

---

[39] See Article 9A(2) TEU.   [40] Article 2(2)(c), TEU

[41] Article 234.

[42] See Craig, 'The Fall and Renewal of the Commission: Accountability, Contract and Administrative Organisation' (2000) 6 ELJ 98.

[43] Article 251 TEU. See also Article 9F TEU.

[44] *Van Gend en Loos* v *Nederlandse Administratie de Belastingen* Case 26/62 [1963] ECR 1, [1963] CMLR 105; *R* v *Secretary of State for Transport, ex parte Factortame* Case C-213/89 [1990] ECR I-2433, [1990] 3 CMLR 1.

or through references from national courts on points of EU law. Member States are obliged to apply its principles within their own jurisdictions, and the United Kingdom gives effect to this obligation by virtue of the European Communities Act 1972.

A Court of First Instance was created in 1988 to ease the problems of workload and delay that had bedevilled the Court of Justice.[45] Renamed the 'General Court' under the Lisbon Treaty, the court deals with disputes between the EU and its servants, along with actions for judicial review brought by natural or other legal persons. Since the Treaty of Nice came into force on 1 February 2003, it has also been able to deal with some references from national courts under the Article 234 procedure. The work of both the General Court and the Court of Justice is considered in more detail later in this chapter.[46]

KEY ISSUE

The role of the EU Parliament may be contrasted with that of the Westminster Parliament in the United Kingdom. It has in the past been argued that there is a 'democratic deficit' in the EU. Much has been done to try to address that, with the European Parliament now being directly elected, and with significantly enhanced powers, particularly following the Lisbon Treaty.

 Questions

1. Do you think the role of the EU Parliament could be strengthened further?

2. If so, in what ways?

3. In what ways does the European Parliament differ from the Westminster Parliament?

The sources of EU law

Legislation

The treaties are the primary source of European law, and create a wide framework of powers, duties, and individual rights. Their provisions are framed in broad terms, requiring further legislative action and subsequent interpretation by the Court of Justice. By Article 263 the EU institutions are empowered to issue regulations, directives, decisions, recommendations, and opinions. These are the instruments through which the policies inherent in the treaties are achieved. Regulations, directives, and decisions may be classed as 'secondary' or 'delegated' EU legislation, and their legality may be challenged in the Court of Justice. However, national courts have no power to declare EU measures invalid unless they have already been declared as such by the Court of Justice.[47] If the legality of an EU measure is raised

---

[45] Article 251 TEU.   [46] See p 133.

[47] *Firma Foto-Frost v Hauptzollamt Lübeck-Ost* Case 314/85 [1987] ECR 4199, [1988] 3 CMLR 57.

as an issue in a domestic case, the national court may make a reference to the Court of Justice for a ruling on the matter. In some circumstances it will be under a duty to do so.[48]

The differences between the types of instrument set out in Article 263 are as follows:

> A regulation shall have general application. It shall be binding in its entirety and directly applicable in all Member States.
>
> A Decision shall be binding in its entirety. A decision which specifies those to whom it is addressed shall be binding only on them.
>
> Recommendations and opinions shall have no binding force.

There is thus a distinction between regulations and decisions on the one hand, and directives, recommendations, and opinions on the other. Only the former are immediately binding, although the doctrine of direct effects may confer a similar status on directives in practice. Where a measure is not immediately binding the task of implementation is left to the Member States. It should also be noted that only regulations and decisions may be challenged directly by individuals under Article 230:[49]

> Any natural or legal person may ... institute proceedings against an act addressed to that person or which is against a regulatory act which is of direct concern to them and does not entail implementing measures.

Case law

The other important source of EU law is the case law of the Court of Justice. The doctrine establishing the supremacy of EU law owes its origins to the court's creativity, as does the concept of direct effect. In addition, the treaties are framed in broad terms and it is the duty of the court to interpret and apply EU law in ways that fulfil their underlying spirit and policy. Besides this interpretative role, the court has developed a number of general principles:

Legal certainty and legitimate expectations

The principle of legal certainty applies in various ways: a measure may not be altered once it has been adopted and it will be presumed that provisions do not operate retrospectively. In *Officier van Justitie* v *Kolpinghuis Nijmegen BV*,[50] the Dutch authorities sought to rely in criminal proceedings on a directive that had not been implemented. The Court of Justice held that criminal liability could not be imposed

---

[48] Article 267; see p 136.

[49] As reworded by the Treaty of Lisbon. Note that, in applying this provision, the Court of Justice has regard to the substance rather than the form of the measure; see, e.g., *Confédération Nationale des Producteurs de Fruits et Légumes* v *Commission* Case 16/62 [1962] ECR 471; *Salamander AG* v *Parliament and Council* Cases T-172 and 175–77/98 [2000] 2 CMLR 1099.

[50] Case 80/86 [1987] ECR 3969, [1989] 2 CMLR 18.

in this way. The legitimate expectations[51] of individuals who are affected by EU measures will also be protected, although not to the point of fettering the Union's freedom of action.[52]

Natural justice

EU bodies are required to give reasons for their actions, and not to act arbitrarily.[53]

Equality of treatment in comparable situations[54]

Until recently, European legislation did not set out any general principle of equality, although there were specific provisions on gender discrimination in employment and on the free movement of workers regardless of EU nationality.[55] A wider principle was established by the Court of Justice, however, to the effect that comparable situations should be treated in the same way and different situations should be treated differently.[56] This principle has now been reinforced by Article 19 TEU. The Article does not in itself prohibit discrimination, but instead empowers the EU institutions to 'take appropriate action to combat discrimination based on sex, racial or ethnic origin, religion or belief, disability, age or sexual orientation'. The Article has already generated two major directives.[57]

Proportionality

Obligations may not be imposed on an individual except to the extent necessary to achieve the purpose of the measure.[58] This concept applies not only in respect of EU measures, but also in determining the legality of the actions of Member States. Thus Hoffman J in *Stoke-on-Trent City Council* v *B & Q plc* had to determine whether the restrictions on Sunday trading in the Shops Act 1950 were proportionate to those permitted by Article 30.[59] The question was ultimately decided in the affirmative by the House of Lords. The concept of proportionality may apply equally to the remedy

---

[51] The phrase is borrowed from English law. See Usher, 'The Influence of National Concepts on Decisions of the European Court' [1976] 1 EL Rev 359. For an example, see *EC Commission* v *EC Council* Case 81/72 [1973] ECR 575.

[52] *ATB* v *Ministero per le Politiche Agricole* Case C-402/98 [2000] ECR I-5501. For a domestic example, see *R* v *Ministry of Agriculture and Fisheries, ex parte Hamble Fisheries* [1995] 2 All ER 714, [1995] 1 CMLR 533.

[53] *Transocean Marine Paint Association* v *EC Commission* Case 17/74 [1974] ECR 1063.

[54] See generally, Bell, *Anti-Discrimination Law and the European Union* (2002).

[55] Articles 2 and 12 EC Treaty; Equal Treatment Directive 76/207; Regulation 1612/68.

[56] *Sabbatini* v *European Parliament* Case 20/71 [1972] ECR 345; *Graff* v *Hauptzollamt Köln-Rheinau* Case C-351/92 [1994] ECR-I-3361.

[57] EC Employment Directive 2000/78; EC Race Directive 2000/43. Statutory instruments to implement these measures in UK law have now been introduced: SI 2003/1626 (race); SI 2003/1657 (sex); SI 2003/1660 (religion or belief); SI 2003/1661 (sexual orientation); SI 2003/1673 (disability); SI 2006/1031 (age).

[58] *Internationale Handelsgesellschaft GmbH* v *Einfuhr- und Vorratsstelle für Getreide* Case 11/70 [1970] ECR 1125, [1972] CMLR 255; *Johnston* v *Chief Constable of the RUC* Case 222/84 [1987] QB 129, [1986] 3 All ER 135.

[59] [1991] Ch 48, [1991] 4 All ER 221. Article 30 is renumbered Article 36 TEU.

that the court is being asked to grant. In *Taittinger* v *Allbev*,[60] the court granted an injunction restraining the use of the expression 'Elderflower Champagne' on the basis that it infringed a Community directive. The Court of Appeal rejected a submission that the remedy was disproportionate to the infringement.

Fundamental rights[61]

The original treaties of the European Communities did not include specific human rights provisions, but the protection of fundamental rights was nevertheless considered important. A Joint Declaration in 1977[62] stressed the role of the European Convention on Human Rights (ECHR), and in *Nold* v *Commission* the Court of Justice stated that:[63]

> [T]he Court is bound to draw inspiration from constitutional traditions common to the Member States, and it cannot therefore uphold measures which are incompatible with fundamental rights recognised and protected by the Constitutions of those States. Similarly, international treaties for the protection of human rights on which the Member States have collaborated or of which they are signatories, can supply guidelines which should be followed within the framework of Community law.

In respect of national legislation that falls outside the scope of EU law, the court does not have any general power to examine its compatibility with the ECHR.[64] However, the court is increasingly prepared to take a generous approach to the question of whether EU law is engaged. Thus, in the *Familiapress*[65] case, the court ruled that since a ban on the distribution of a magazine obstructed the free movement of goods, any justification for the ban would need to be compatible with the right to freedom of expression under Article 10 of the ECHR.

Following the lead of the Court of Justice, the Member States included a provision in the Treaty on European Union stating that the ECHR 'shall be respected by Member States'.[66] Although the provision was initially not justiciable, it was expressly brought within the court's jurisdiction by the Treaty of Amsterdam. The wording was also strengthened, and Article 7 made it possible for the voting rights of Member States to be suspended in the event of a 'serious and persistent' breach of human rights principles. The suggestion that the EU might itself become a signatory to the

---

[60] [1994] 4 All ER 75, [1993] 2 CMLR 741.

[61] See Alston, Heenan and Bustelo, *The EU and Human Rights* (OUP, 1999).

[62] Joint Declaration by the European Parliament, Council and Commission ([1977] OJ C103/1). See also *Prais* v *Council* Case C-130/75 [1976] ECR 1589.

[63] Case 4/73 [1974] ECR 491 at [13]; see Drzemczewski, 'The Domestic Application of the European Human Rights Convention as European Community Law' (1981) 30 ICLQ 118.

[64] *Demirel* v *Stadt Schwabisch Gmund* Case 12/86 [1987] ECR 3719, [1989] 1 CMLR 421; *Kremzow* v *Austria* Case C-299/95 [1997] ECR I-2629.

[65] *Vereingte Familiapress Zeitungsverlags- und Vertriebs GmbH* v *Heinrich Bauer Verlag* Case C-368/95 [1997] ECR-I-3689, [1997] 3 CMLR 1329.

[66] Article 6.

ECHR was mooted,[67] but in 1994 the Court of Justice advised that any move in this direction would require amendments to the Treaty.[68] Such amendments have now been included in the Treaty of Lisbon. Article 6(2) of the TEU provides for the Union to accede to the ECHR, while Article 6(3) gives Convention rights the status of 'general principles of the Union's law'. In a corresponding move, the Council of Europe agreed an amendment to the ECHR paving the way for the EU's accession.[69]

Quite apart from the developments outlined above, each EU Member State is already a Convention signatory in its own right, and a number of states have been challenged under the Convention in relation to aspects of EU law and procedure.[70] A German company fined by the EU Commission for a breach of competition laws recently challenged *all* of the EU Member States before the Court of Human Rights. The essence of the claim was that by refusing to suspend the fine pending the outcome of a hearing, the Commission had violated the presumption of innocence and the right to a fair trial under Article 6 of the ECHR.[71] The Court of Human Rights declared the claim inadmissible because by this stage the Court of First Instance had quashed the fines: the company was not a 'victim' of anything.[72] The rather more difficult question of whether the states *could* be collectively liable in this way was neatly side-stepped, but it is notable that the Strasbourg court did not rule out this possibility. From the other side, the European Court of Justice recently directed its attentions to the compatibility of its own institutions with Article 6, concluding that the involvement of the Advocate-General in cases before the court did not give rise to any breach of this provision.[73]

Finally, in December 2000 the Member States signed the Charter of Fundamental Rights of the European Union. Although the Charter was not initially expressed to be legally binding,[74] the Treaty of Lisbon provides for a new Article 6(1) to be added to the Treaty on European Union, and, once in force, this will give the rights, freedoms and principles set out in the Charter the same legal value as the treaties. It should be noted, however, that the United Kingdom and Poland have both negotiated exemptions.

[67] See Harmsen, 'National Responsibility for EC Acts under the ECHR: Recasting the Accession Debate' (2001) 7 EPL 625.
[68] *Re Accession of the Community to the European Human Rights Convention (Opinion 2/94)* [1996] 2 CMLR 265.
[69] An amendment to Article 59 ECHR will be made by the new Protocol 14: see p 218.
[70] *Matthews* v *UK* (1999) 28 EHRR 361; *JS* v *Netherlands* (1995) 20 EHRR CD 41; *Pafitis* v *Greece* (1999) 27 EHRR 566; see Canor, *'Primus Inter Pares*: Who is the Ultimate Guardian of Fundamental Rights in Europe?' (2000) 25(1) EL Rev 3.
[71] *Senator Lines* v *15 EU Member States* (2004) 39 EHRR SE3; see also *Senator Lines GmbH* v *Commission* Case C-364/99 [1999] ECR I-8733, [2000] 5 CMLR 600.
[72] Whether there had been a breach initially was irrelevant, because until the company's case had been considered by the CFI its legal remedies had not been exhausted: see p 220.
[73] *Emesa Sugar* v *Aruba* Case C-17/98 [2000] ECR I-665. The role of Advocates-General is discussed at p 134.
[74] See p 108; Arnull, 'From Charter to Constitution and Beyond: Fundamental Rights in the New European Union' [2003] PL 774.

KEY ISSUE

The interrelationship between the EU law and European Convention on Human Rights is important. Although the United Kingdom is not bound by the Charter of Fundamental Rights, it is bound by the Convention on Human Rights (and the Court of Human Rights) both because it is part of domestic law following the passage of the Human Rights Act 1998[75] and because its principles will be upheld by the Court of Justice when that court is deciding the meaning and effect of European Union law. There is thus an important interrelationship between domestic law and the two European jurisdictions. A ruling as to the Convention in the context of an EU matter may have different consequences depending on how the matter arises, because of the different status in English law of the two systems of law

Interesting issues may arise when there are conflicts concerning the interpretation and application of the European Convention, and its application: the primary role of determining the meaning and application of the Convention is, and should be continue to be, the Court of Human Rights

❓ Questions

1. How far, now, is the European Convention on Human Rights directly enforceable via EU law?
2. Does the Convention provide an additional route for legal accountability of EU actions or legislation?

The relationship between EU and national law

The general approach of the Court of Justice

In a series of important decisions, the Court of Justice has developed the doctrine of supremacy of EU over national law. In *Van Gend en Loos* v *Nederlandse Administratie der Berlastingen*,[76] it stated that Member States had 'limited their sovereign rights, albeit within limited fields'. Then, in *Costa* v *ENEL*,[77] it held that:

> The transfer by the states from their domestic legal system to the Community legal system of the rights and obligations arising under the Treaty carries with it a permanent limitation of their sovereign rights, against which a subsequent unilateral act incompatible with the concept of the Community cannot prevail.

The supremacy of EU law means that national courts must enforce Community rights even if this involves overriding national legislation.[78] Thus, in the event of a

---

[75] See p 146.   [76] Case 26/62 [1963] ECR 1, [1963] CMLR 105.
[77] Case 6/64 [1964] ECR 585, [1964] CMLR 425.
[78] *Amministrazione delle Finanze dello Stato* v *Simmenthal* Case 106/77 [1978] ECR 629, [1978] 3 CMLR 263.

conflict, directly applicable EU law prevails. In addition, Member States have a duty to take any action necessary to implement EU law. Article 3A TEU states:[79]

> Member States shall take all appropriate measures, whether general or particular, to ensure fulfilment of the obligations arising out of this Treaty or resulting from actions taken by the institutions of the Union. They shall facilitate the achievement of the Union's tasks. They shall abstain from any measure which could jeopardise the attainment of the objectives of this Treaty.

In *R v Secretary of State for Transport, ex parte Factortame*,[80] the Court of Justice held that national courts must ensure the legal protection of rights derived from directly applicable EU law—that is, those arising from the treaty, regulations, or rulings of the Court of Justice. Where rules of national law prevent this, they must be set aside. In cases in which the EU and national authorities share jurisdiction, national courts must avoid reaching conclusions at variance with EU institutions. They must also avoid the adoption of national procedural rules that render the exercise of EU rights virtually impossible or extremely difficult.[81]

Direct applicability and direct effect

Identifying the concepts

Direct applicability

The treaties, regulations, and some decisions of European law are said to be directly applicable. This means that they are automatically incorporated into domestic legal systems and come into force without the need for any further action on the part of Member States. Achieving direct applicability in the United Kingdom initially required an Act of Parliament: the United Kingdom is a dualist state and treaties do not become part of domestic law without specific legislation to implement them. Thus the European Communities Act 1972 was enacted, section 2(1) of which states that:

> All such rights, powers, liabilities, obligations and restrictions from time to time created or arising by or under the Treaties, and all such remedies and procedures from time to time provided for by or under the Treaties, as in accordance with the Treaties are without further enactment to be given legal effect or used in the United Kingdom shall be recognised and available in law, and shall be enforced, allowed and followed accordingly; and the expression 'enforceable EU right'[82] and similar expressions shall be read as referring to one to which this subsection applies.

---

[79] Article 3a TEU.

[80] Case C-213/89 [1990] ECR I-2433, [1990] 3 CMLR 1. For the *Factortame* litigation generally, see p 129.

[81] *SCS Peterbroeck van Compeenhout and Cie v Belgium* Case 312/93 [1996] All ER (EC) 242. In deciding this, the basic principles of the domestic judicial system must be considered: *Van Schijndel v Stichling Pensioenfonds* [1996] All ER (EC) 259; *Van der Weerd v Minister van Landbouw, Natuur en Voedselkwaliteit* Case C-222/05 [2007] 3 CMLR 7.

[82] As amended by The European Union (Amendment) Act 2008.

The wording of this provision is cumbersome and does not fully convey its immense significance, but since it came into force all directly applicable European laws have automatically formed part of United Kingdom law without any further legislation to incorporate them being needed.

Not all European laws are directly applicable: directives and most decisions usually require an act of implementation by the Member State before they can take effect. In the United Kingdom, the power to implement such provisions by statutory instrument is contained in section 2(2) of the 1972 Act. The scope of this section is limited by Schedule 2, which excludes the power to do any of the following:

(a) make any provision imposing or increasing taxation; or

(b) make any provision taking effect from a date earlier than that of the making of the instrument containing the provision; or

(c) confer any powers to legislate by means of orders, rules, regulations or other subordinate instrument, other than rules of procedure for any court or tribunal; or

(d) create any new criminal offence punishable with imprisonment for more than two years or punishable on summary conviction with a fine or imprisonment for more than three months.[83]

Even with these limitations the power is far-reaching.

Direct effect

In the context of European law, a provision is said to have 'direct effect' if it creates rights that an individual can rely upon in court. The courts have sometimes used the terms 'directly applicable' and 'direct effect' interchangeably,[84] but they are not, strictly speaking, synonymous.[85] Many directly applicable provisions can be described as having 'direct effect' because they are capable of creating rights enforceable by individuals. It does not necessarily follow, however, that *all* directly applicable provisions will have such an effect. In order for a provision to have direct effect, certain criteria must be satisfied. These were set out in the important case of *Van Gend en Loos*:[86]

(a) it must not relate to inter-state relations alone;

(b) it must be clear and precise;

(c) no further action by the state for implementation must be necessary; and

(d) it must not be conditional at the time of enforcement.

---

[83] Obligations in these areas can only be implemented by Act of Parliament or through some other enabling provision.

[84] See, e.g., *Johnston* v *Chief Constable of the RUC* Case 222/84 [1987] QB 129, [1986] 3 All ER 135; *Van Duyn* v *Home Office* Case 41/74 [1975] Ch 358, [1975] 3 All ER 190.

[85] See Winter, 'Direct Applicability and Direct Effects' (1972) 9 CML Rev 425; Hilson and Downes, 'Making Sense of Rights: Community Rights in EC Law' (1999) 24 EL Rev 121.

[86] *Van Gend en Loos* v *Nederlandse Administratie der Belastingen* Case 26/62 [1963] ECR 1, [1963] CMLR 105; see further, Lenaerts and Corthaut, 'Of Birds and Hedges: The Role of Primacy in Invoking Norms of EU Law' (2006) 31(3) EL Rev 287.

Whether a particular provision fulfils these criteria is a question of interpretation, to be determined as a question of European law.

The treaties

Treaty provisions are directly applicable and therefore require no further implementation. However, in order for a Treaty provision to have direct effect and give rise to individual rights, the *Van Gend en Loos* criteria must be satisfied.

A number of Articles of the Treaty of Rome have been held by the Court of Justice to be directly effective, and they must therefore be taken to create rights and obligations within English law. These include: Article 25,[87] which prohibits the introduction of new customs duties; Article 90, which prevents Member States from imposing discriminatory taxes on the products of other Member States;[88] Article 141, which states that men and women should receive equal pay for equal work;[89] and Article 39, which is concerned with the free movement of workers.[90]

These cases should be compared with the decision in *Zaera* v *Institutio Nacionale de la Seguriad Social*.[91] In this case, the Court ruled that the commitment in Article 2 to 'raising the standard of living' was simply an aim of the Union and was insufficiently precise to confer enforceable rights.

Regulations

Article 228 of the EU Treaty provides that regulations are to be directly applicable and binding in their entirety. They automatically form part of UK law by virtue of section 2(1) of the European Communities Act 1972, and by their very nature they are likely to have the characteristics needed for direct effect.[92] There are, however, exceptions. In a case challenging the labelling of supermarket produce as 'Parma ham', the House of Lords held that the applicable regulation was intended to establish rights over brand marks that could be relied upon in Member States and was therefore directly effective.[93] However, the Court of Justice ruled that 'notwithstanding the principle of the direct effect of regulations...a Community measure is capable of creating individual rights only if it is sufficiently clear, precise and unconditional'.[94] As the regulation in question sought to impose conditions derived from another instrument that had not been properly publicized, those conditions could *not* be directly enforced by the applicants.

---

[87] Now Article 30 TEU.
[88] Now Article 110 TEU; *Alfons Lütticke GmbH* v *Hauptzollamt Saarlouis* Case 57/65 [1966] ECR 205.
[89] Now Article 157 TEU; *Defrenne* v *Sabena* Case 43/75 [1976] ECR 455, [1976] 2 CMLR 98.
[90] Now Article 45 TEU; *Van Duyn* v *Home Office* Case 41/74 [1975] Ch 358, [1975] 3 All ER 190.
[91] Case 126/86 [1987] ECR 3697.
[92] *Commission* v *Italy* Case 39/72 [1973] ECR 101; *Antonio Muñoz* v *Frumar Ltd* Case C-253/00 [2003] Ch 328, [2003] All ER (EC) 56.
[93] *Consorzio del Prosciutto di Parma* v *Asda Stores Ltd* [2001] UKHL 7, [2001] CMLR 43.
[94] Case 108/01 [2003] ECR I-5121, at [85].

Directives

Unlike regulations, directives do not necessarily have immediate binding force. They are addressed to Member States but it is left to individual national authorities to implement them, and in the United Kingdom this is normally done by an Order in Council or statutory instrument under section 2(2) of the European Communities Act 1972. This means that although directives are binding on Member States as to the result to be achieved, they are not directly applicable, and for this reason it was initially assumed that they could not have direct effect. However, in *Grad v Finanzampt Traunstein*,[95] the Court of Justice ruled that a directive *could* create rights that would be enforceable by individuals. This was confirmed in *Van Duyn v Home Office*:[96]

> [W]here the Community authorities have, by directive, imposed on Member States the obligation to pursue a particular course of conduct, the useful effect of such an act would be weakened if individuals were prevented from relying on it before their national courts and if the latter were prevented from taking it into consideration as an element of Community law.

There are, however, various limitations to the doctrine. Firstly, the conditions for direct effect must be fulfilled, and this means that the directive must be precise and unconditional as set out in *Van Gend en Loos*.[97] In addition, a directive cannot have direct effect until the deadline for implementation has expired. In *Publico Ministero v Ratti*,[98] the Court of Justice held that whilst one directive could have direct effect and prevent the Italian authorities from relying on domestic laws relating to solvents, another could *not* have this effect because the date for implementation had not yet passed.

Even where these conditions are satisfied, directives only have 'vertical' direct effect: in other words, they can only be enforced against the state.[99] They do not have 'horizontal' direct effect and therefore cannot be enforced against private individuals. This was confirmed in *Marshall v Southampton and South West Hampshire Area Health Authority*, in which it was stated that:[100]

> [T]he binding nature of a directive, which constitutes the basis for the possibility of relying on the directive before a national court, exists only in relation to 'each Member State to which it is addressed.' It follows that a directive may not of itself impose obligations on an individual...

---

[95] Case 9/70 [1970] ECR 825, [1971] CMLR 1.

[96] Case 41/74 [1975] Ch 358 at 376–7, [1975] 3 All ER 190 at 205.

[97] Case 26/62 [1963] ECR 1, [1963] CMLR 105: see p 122. See also, *Becker v Finanzamt Münster-Innenstadt* Case 8/81 [1982] ECR 53, [1982] 1 CMLR 499.

[98] Case 148/78 [1979] ECR 1629, [1980] 1 CMLR 96.

[99] Note that the doctrine does not operate the other way round and a state cannot enforce an unimplemented directive against an individual; see *Officier van Justitie v Kolpinghuis* Case 80/86 [1987] ECR 3969, [1989] 2 CMLR 18.

[100] Case 152/84 [1986] QB 401 at 422, [1986] 2 All ER 584, at 600. For the subsequent litigation, see *Marshall v Southampton and South West Hampshire Area Health Authority (No 2)* [1994] 1 AC 530, [1994] 1 All ER 736.

Marshall itself concerned a challenge to an employer's policy of operating different retirement ages for men and women. Female employees were normally required to retire at the age of 60, whereas their male colleagues were able to continue working until they reached the age of 65. This policy potentially violated the Equal Treatment Directive,[101] and since Miss Marshall's employer happened to be a state body, it was held that she was entitled to rely upon the Directive as having direct effect. Yet if Miss Marshall were to have been employed by a private company, she would have had no remedy.

The meaning of 'the state' for these purposes was considered in *Foster* v *British Gas*,[102] which, like *Marshall*, was a case concerning discriminatory retirement ages. On a reference under Article 234 of the EC Treaty, the Court of Justice ruled that the Equal Treatment Directive could be relied upon against a body if it provided a public service under the control of the state and exercised special powers for that purpose. In applying this guidance to the facts, the House of Lords held[103] that British Gas (at a time when it was a public corporation) was provided by statute with the duty of performing a public service. It had a monopoly power and it was also under the control of the state, since the state could dictate its policies and reclaim revenue. The Directive was therefore directly effective.

Although not definitive, *Foster* is the leading case in this area and is the starting point for any consideration of whether a body is 'an emanation of the state'. On the basis of the *Foster* test, the governing body of a voluntary-aided school in receipt of state funding has been held to be an emanation of the state,[104] as has a privatized water company.[105] On the other hand, in *Doughty* v *Rolls-Royce*,[106] it was held that Rolls Royce was *not* a state body, even though the Crown owned 100 per cent of the company's shares at the time. More recently, the approach of the Court of Justice in *Kampelmann*[107] seems to suggest that the criteria set out in *Foster* are alternative rather than cumulative, and that a body may be regarded as an emanation of the state as long as *some* of these criteria can be satisfied.

This distinction between vertical and horizontal direct effect causes difficulties, not only in determining when a body is under the control of the state, but also in applying the rules evenly. For example, it has already been noted that rights in employment law may depend upon whether the employer is within the public or private sector, and the fact that cases can hinge on such matters has led to considerable criticism.[108] However, in the light of case law establishing that directives can also have '*indirect* effect', this distinction between vertical and horizontal effect has lost some of its significance.

---

[101] Directive 76/207.   [102] Case C-188/89 [1991] 1 QB 405, [1990] 3 All ER 897.

[103] [1991] 2 AC 306, [1991] 2 All ER 705.

[104] *National Union of Teachers* v *Governing Body of St Mary's Church of England (Aided) Junior School* [1997] 3 CMLR 630, [1997] IRLR 242.

[105] *Griffin* v *South-West Water Services Ltd* [1995] IRLR 15.

[106] [1992] 1 CMLR 1045, [1992] ICR 538.

[107] *Kampelmann* v *Landschaftsverband Westfalen-Lippe* Cases C 253–258/96 [1997] ECR I-6907 at [46].

[108] See, e.g., Lenz A-G *in Faccini Dori* v *Recrab Srl* Case C-91/92 [1994] ECR I-3325, [1995] All ER (EC) 1; Arnull, 'The Direct Effect of Directives: Grasping the Nettle' (1986) 35 ICLQ 939.

Indirect effect

In *von Colson* v *Land Nordrhein-Westfalen*,[109] the Court of Justice stated:

> [I]n applying the national law and in particular the provisions of a national law specifically introduced in order to implement [a directive], national courts are required to interpret their national laws in the light of the wording and the purpose of the directive in order to achieve the result referred to in the third paragraph of Article 189.

This approach was strengthened by the decision in *Marleasing SA* v *La Comercial Internacional de Alimentación SA*:[110]

> [I]n applying national law, whether the provisions concerned pre-date or post-date the directive, the national court asked to interpret national law is bound to do so in every way possible in the light of the text and the aims of the directive to achieve the results envisaged by it and thus comply with Article 189(3) of the Treaty.

The Court of Justice has since endorsed this strong interpretive obligation in a number of other cases,[111] and, as far as possible, national courts must now interpret all legislation in a manner consistent with the provisions of directives. In adopting this approach the Court of Justice has undoubtedly reduced the significance of the direct effect doctrine,[112] but it should be remembered that the obligation described in *Marleasing* is merely one of interpretation. Its application depends upon whether a compatible interpretation of national law is 'possible', and the Court of Justice has generally left it to the domestic courts to answer this question.[113]

Damages

In some circumstances the failure of a member state to implement a directive may give rise to an action for damages. There is a general obligation to make good damage caused by an infringement of European Union law.[114] In *Francovich* v *Italian Republic*,[115] the Court of Justice ruled that an individual could claim for financial loss resulting from the non-implementation of a directive if three conditions were satisfied, as follows.

(1) The directive must have been intended to confer individual rights.

---

[109] Case 14/83 [1984] ECR 1891, [1986] 2 CMLR 430. The Article 189 in question is now Article 288 TEU.

[110] Case C-106/89 [1990] ECR I-4135, [1992] 1 CMLR 305; ibid.

[111] See *Centrosteel* v *Adipol* Case C-456/98 [2000] ECR I-6007.

[112] See Craig, 'Directives: Direct Effect, Indirect Effect and the Construction of National Legislation' (1997) 22 EL Rev 519; Drake, 'Twenty Years after *Von Colson*: The Impact of "Indirect Effect" on the Protection of the Individual's Community Rights' (2005) 30 EL Rev 329.

[113] *Faccini Dori* v *Recrab Srl* Case C-91/92 [1994] ECR I-3325, [1995] All ER (EC) 1; *Alcatel Austria* v *Bundesministerium für Wissenschaft und Verkehr* Case C-81/98 [1999] ECR I-7671. For the approach of the English courts, see p 131.

[114] *Cooper* v *Attorney General* [2008] EWHC 2285, [2010] EWCA Civ 464.

[115] Case C-6, 9/90 [1991] ECR I-5357, [1993] 2 CMLR 66. Note that in *Emmott* v *Minister for Social Welfare* Case C-208/90 [1993] ICR 8 the Court of Justice ruled that where a state fails to implement a directive properly, the individual may sue the state in reliance on that directive (if directly effective) until proper implementation occurs.

(2) It must be possible to identify the content of those rights on the basis of the provisions of the directive.

(3) There must be a causal link between the breach of the state's obligation and the damage suffered.

English law was slow to accept the right to seek damages in such cases,[116] but the decision in *R v Secretary of State for Transport, ex parte Factortame*[117] made it clear that domestic courts have a duty to confer effective protection for EU rights. The position was put beyond doubt by the decisions in *Brasserie du Pêcheur SA v Germany* and *R v Secretary of State for Transport ex parte Factortame (No 4)*.[118] In the first of these two companion cases, it was alleged that a German law relating to the purity of beer contravened European law, whilst in the second, the breach of Community law had already been established.[119] The Court of Justice confirmed the approach in *Francovich* and ruled that even where the infringement of Community law had resulted from the legislation of a national parliament, liability for damages could still arise. The general principle to emerge from these cases is that if a state is responsible for a breach of EU obligations—even if those obligations derive from a measure that does not have direct effect—the state may be liable in damages for any losses that result. In determining whether a breach of EU law is sufficient to warrant compensation, the decisive test is whether the state manifestly and gravely disregarded the limits of its discretion. The House of Lords in *Factortame (No 5)* accepted the duty to provide a remedy for breaches of Community obligations and entered judgment for the claimant.[120] Such an action is an action in tort.[121]

Factors to be considered by the court include: (a) the clarity and precision of the rule breached; (b) the measure of discretion left to the authorities; (c) whether the infringement and the damage caused was intentional; (d) whether any error of law was excusable; and (e) whether the position taken by an EU institution may have contributed to the omission.

In *R v HM Treasury, ex parte British Telecommunications plc*,[122] the Court of Justice stated that in order for a Member State to be liable in damages:

> [T]he rule of law infringed must be intended to confer rights on individuals; the breach must be sufficiently serious; and there must be a direct causal link between the breach of the obligation resting on the state and the damage sustained by the injured parties.

On the facts of the case, which concerned the incorrect implementation of a directive, it was held that the breach was not sufficiently serious to give rise to damages: the United Kingdom had acted in good faith and the wording of the directive was imprecise. By

---

[116] *Bourgoin SA v Ministry of Agriculture Fisheries & Food* [1986] QB 716, [1985] 3 All ER 585.
[117] Case C-213/89 [1990] ECR I-2433, [1990] 3 CMLR 1.
[118] Cases C-46/93 and 48/93 [1996] QB 404, [1996] All ER (EC) 301.
[119] See p 129.   [120] [2000] 1 AC 524, [1999] 4 All ER 906.
[121] See *Spencer v Secretary of State for Work & Pensions* [2008] EWCA Civ 750.
[122] Case C-392/93 [1996] QB 615 at 655, [1996] All ER (EC) 411 at [39].

contrast, in *R v Ministry of Agriculture, Fisheries and Food, ex parte Hedley Lomas*,[123] the breach was blatant. The United Kingdom had refused to grant a licence for the export of sheep for slaughter in Spain, without any legal justification for doing so. The fact that the United Kingdom believed the Spanish abattoir to be operating in breach of Community law was irrelevant. More recently, it was held that a breach of a directly effective Treaty Article concerning anti-competitive agreements could give rise to an action for compensation to cover damage caused by a non-state party.[124] So, too, in *Cooper v Attorney General*,[125] the factors said to be relevant were: (a) whether the rule of law infringed was introduced to confer rights on individuals; (b) whether the breach is sufficiently serious , although that does not confine state liability to cases involving intentional fault or serious misconduct; and (c) whether there is a causal link between the breach of the obligation and the loss and damage suffered. On the facts the breach of a directive was not held to be sufficiently serious.

Decisions

Decisions may be made by the Council and Commission as a formal method of enunciating policies or initiating actions. They are binding upon those to whom they are addressed, and, like directives, they are capable of having direct effect.

KEY ISSUE

Article 263 draws a clear distinction between Treaty provisions, regulations and decisions—all of which are directly applicable—and directives—which are not? Yet we see that through the doctrines of direct effect and indirect effect, and through the availability of damages for failure to implement EU obligations, real legal consequences can flow from the failure to implement a directive or to do so properly. The Court of Justice has created, through judicial law-making, a body of law that might at first sight appear to be at odds with the Treaty, in order to give full effect to the supremacy of EU law over national law. It is fundamentally based on the concept that under the treaties Member States are bound to take all steps necessary to fulfil their Treaty obligations, and should not be allowed to escape from that. The doctrine of direct effect also allows domestic courts to enforce EU obligations in individual cases, rather than rely on enforcement action by the EU against the United Kingdom in the Court of Justice.

 Question

Has the Court of Justice made the distinction between regulations and directives redundant?

---

[123] Case C-5/94 [1996] ECR I-2553, [1996] All ER (EC) 493.

[124] *Courage v Crehan* Case C-453/99 [2002] QB 507, [2001] All ER (EC) 886; see also *Manfredi v Lloyd Adriatico Assicurazioni SpA* Case C-295/04 [2006] ECR I-6619, [2006] 5 CMLR 17. Both cases concerned Article 81 of the EC Treaty.

[125] [2010] EWCA Civ 464.

The impact upon English courts

The question of supremacy

The insistence of EU law that it shall prevail over conflicting national law presents distinct challenges to the United Kingdom's constitutional orthodoxy. It was this potential conflict that led to the unsuccessful attempt in *Blackburn* v *AG*[126] to challenge the United Kingdom's accession to the Treaty of Rome and the passage of the 1972 Act, which is the statute that gives European Union law legal status in the United Kingdom. The Court of Appeal ruled that the treaty-making power of the Crown was beyond challenge, although it also confirmed that Parliament retained the theoretical power to legislate in any way that it saw fit: if it chose to do so, it could repeal the 1972 Act. The fact that the 1972 Act is, and remains, the legal basis for EU law, has not gone without criticism or challenge,[127] but is reaffirmed by the declaratory statements contained in clause 18 of the European Union Bill currently before Parliament.

Implementation of the Treaty in English law was achieved by the passage of section 2(1) of the Act. In addition, section 2(4) states that: '[A]ny enactment passed or to be passed, other than one contained in this part of this Act, shall be construed and have effect subject to the foregoing provisions of this section.' Directly applicable EU obligations therefore take precedence over conflicting national law. By these means Parliament has ensured that most conflicts between English law and European law are resolved in favour of the latter. The constitutional challenge can be avoided by relying on the will of Parliament itself. In *Macarthys Ltd* v *Smith*,[128] the majority of the court held that the individual rights arising under what was then Article 119[129] should prevail over the clear and unambiguous words of the Equal Pay Act 1970. By contrast Lord Denning used the Article as an aid to construction, concluding that the terms of the 1970 Act were capable of bearing a meaning that would allow compliance with Community obligations. Alternatively he considered that if Parliament had intended to derogate from its obligations under the Treaty, it would (and could) do so by express words: in the absence of such words, an intention to comply with Treaty obligations would be presumed.

The authority conferred by the 1972 Act has enabled courts both to quash executive actions and to declare delegated legislation invalid. More fundamentally, the courts have now accepted that it may even require them to declare the provisions of a subsequent Act of Parliament to be inoperative. This occurred in *Factortame* v *Secretary of State for Transport (No 2)*.[130] The applicants, who were companies controlled by Spanish nationals, sought to challenge the validity of the Merchant

---

[126] [1971] 2 All ER 1380, [1971] 1 WLR 1037.

[127] See *R (on the application of Jackson)* v *A-G* [2005] UKHL 56, [2006] 1 AC 262, [2005] 4 All ER 125, and p 23.

[128] [1979] 3 All ER 325, [1979] 1 WLR 1189.   [129] Now Article 157 TEU.

[130] [1991] 1 AC 603, [1991] 1 All ER 70.

Shipping Act 1988 on the basis that it contravened the EC Treaty and deprived them of their Community law rights. The Divisional Court had made a reference to the Court of Justice under what is now Article 267 (then 177), but since determination of the issues was likely to take some time, the applicants applied for an interim injunction to restrain the Secretary of State from enforcing the Act. The House of Lords initially held that it had no power to make such an order,[131] but following a further reference to the Court of Justice,[132] it granted an interim injunction to suspend the operation of the 1988 Act. Lord Bridge stated:[133]

> Whatever limitation of its sovereignty Parliament accepted when it enacted the European Communities Act 1972 was entirely voluntary. Under the terms of the 1972 Act it has always been clear that it was the duty of a United Kingdom court, when delivering final judgment, to override any rule of national law found to be in conflict with any directly enforceable rule of Community law... [T]here is nothing in any way novel in according supremacy to rules of Community law in those areas to which they apply, and to insist that, in the protection of rights under Community law, national courts must not be inhibited by rules of national law from granting interim relief in appropriate cases is no more than a logical recognition of that supremacy.

Whether such an injunction will be granted depends upon the merits of the particular case, and it is certainly not automatic. A significant factor will be the likelihood of the Court of Justice giving a ruling that favours one party or the other. If a trial judge considers that this likelihood is evenly balanced, he is entitled to decide that the applicant's interest in having the Act of Parliament struck down is outweighed by the public interest in enforcing it.[134]

The impact of European law on the legislative supremacy of Parliament was revisited in the case of *Thoburn* v *Sunderland City Council and others*.[135] The appellants had been prosecuted for selling produce in imperial measurements, contrary to delegated legislation implementing a directive on the use of metric weights. The appeal by way of case stated centred on the claim that the Weights and Measures Act 1985 (which permitted the use of imperial weights) had, by implication, partially repealed section 2 of the European Communities Act 1972. The Divisional Court rejected this argument, and, in doing so, Laws LJ stated expressly what many had assumed for some time:[136]

> There are now classes or types of legislative provision which cannot be repealed by mere implication. These instances are given and can only be given, by our own courts, to which the scope and nature of Parliamentary sovereignty are ultimately confided.

In the view of Laws LJ, the European Communities Act forms part of this special class of legislative provisions, which he collectively termed 'constitutional statutes', and it

---

[131] [1990] 2 AC 85, [1989] 2 All ER 692.   [132] Case C-213/89 [1990] ECR I-2433, [1990] 3 CMLR 1.
[133] [1991] 1 AC 603 at 659, [1991] 1 All ER 70 at 107.
[134] Ibid; see also *R* v *Secretary of State for the National Heritage, ex parte Continental Television BV* [1993] 3 CMLR 387.
[135] [2002] EWHC 195 (Admin), [2003] QB 151, [2002] 4 All ER 156.   [136] Ibid at [60].

is therefore immune from implied repeal.[137] Although not a decision of the House of Lords, *Thoburn* is the strongest indication yet that, as far as the national courts are concerned, the supreme status of European law is still dependent on the authority of the 1972 Act. However, unless and until Parliament chooses to expressly repeal that Act, it seems that any conflict between domestic and European law will be resolved in favour of the latter.

The supremacy of EU law has thus been achieved, and in appropriate cases the courts will be prepared to disapply Acts of Parliament in order to give it proper effect. In an action for judicial review, a court may also consider a declaration to the effect that the United Kingdom is in breach of its EU obligations.[138]

Interpretation

In most of the cases to come before the domestic courts, judges have been able to avoid confronting the issue of supremacy. The approach of Lord Denning in *Macarthys Ltd* v *Smith* was to use European law as an aid to construction, and it is this interpretative approach that has generally found favour with English judges. In *Garland* v *British Rail Engineering,* Lord Diplock stated:[139]

> [I]n the instant case the words of section 6(4) of the Sex Discrimination Act 1975 that fall to be construed, 'provision in relation to retirement', without any undue straining of the ordinary meaning of the language used, are capable of bearing either the narrow meaning accepted by the Employment Appeal Tribunal or the wider meaning preferred by the Court of Appeal but acknowledged by that court to be largely a matter of first impression. Had the attention of the court been drawn to Article 119 of the EEC Treaty and the judgment of the European Court of Justice in *Defrenne* v *Sabena* I have no doubt that, consistently with statements made by Lord Denning MR in previous cases, they would have construed section 6(4) so as not to make it inconsistent with Article 119.

The same approach was adopted in *Pickstone* v *Freeman's plc,*[140] in which the House of Lords considered that an amendment to the Equal Pay Act 1970, which was intended to give effect to the ruling of the Court of Justice in *Marshall,*[141] was capable of being so construed. Although on a literal reading the amendment did not achieve its objective, the House of Lords felt able to read words into the legislation to give effect to the clear intention of Parliament. In *Litster* v *Forth Dry Dock and Engineering Co Ltd,*[142] regulations were made to give effect to a directive. The claimant could not rely on the directive itself because the defendant company was not an organ of the state and there was

---

[137] See p 36.

[138] *Equal Opportunities Commission* v *Secretary of State for Employment* [1995] 1 AC 1, [1994] 1 All ER 910. On the facts, provisions in the Employment Protection (Consolidation) Act 1978 were declared to be contrary to the Equal Pay Directive (57/117) and Article 141 (then 119) of the Treaty.

[139] [1983] 2 AC 751 at 771. What was Article 119 is now Article 157 TEU.

[140] [1989] AC 66, [1988] 2 All ER 803.

[141] Case 152/84 [1986] QB 401, [1986] 2 All ER 584. See p 124.

[142] [1990] 1 AC 546, [1989] 1 All ER 1134.

thus no direct effect. Nevertheless, in a clear application of the *von Colson* principle, the House of Lords accepted that it had a duty to interpret the regulation in a manner consistent with the directive.

In both *Pickstone* and *Litster*, the courts were concerned with the interpretation of laws that had been made or amended to give effect to European law. This was not the case in *Duke* v *GEC Reliance,* however,[143] and the House of Lords refused to distort the meaning of a statute to give effect to a Community provision that was not directly effective. The House held that in such circumstances it was required by English law to give the words of the statute their ordinary and natural meaning, and that the *von Colson* ruling[144] was not applicable because the court had no discretion as to the approach to interpretation. The reasoning in this case is unconvincing, and in *Marleasing,*[145] the Court of Justice confirmed that the duty to interpret national law in the light of European law is not confined to measures passed with the intention of implementing European provisions.

The House of Lords returned to this issue in *Webb* v *EMO Air Cargo (UK) Ltd.* The claimant in this case had been hired to cover for another employee who was on maternity leave, but she was dismissed when she too became pregnant. Her situation did not appear to fall within the scope of the Sex Discrimination Act 1975, but she argued that it *was* covered by the Equal Treatment Directive and that the 1975 Act should be interpreted in the light of the latter instrument. The House of Lords accepted the principle expressed in *Marleasing*, but emphasized that the obligation to interpret statutes in a manner compatible with European law applied only to the extent that a compatible interpretation was 'possible':[146]

> It is for a United Kingdom court to construe domestic legislation in any field covered by a Community directive so as to accord with the interpretation of the directive as laid down by the European Court, *if that can be done without distorting the meaning of the domestic legislation.* [emphasis added]

The House of Lords initially took the view that a compatible interpretation was *not* possible in this case. However, following a reference to the Court of Justice,[147] it accepted that the provision could be interpreted so as to comply with the directive without distorting the meaning of the Act.[148]

KEY ISSUE

There is an unreality about the theoretical position that exists. EU law takes precedence over national law, because, the court in *Factortame* confirmed, Parliament has said so. This

---

[143] [1988] AC 618, [1988] 1 All ER 626.

[144] Case 14/83 [1984] ECR 1891, [1986] 2 CMLR 430; see p 126.

[145] Case C-106/89 [1990] ECR I-4135, [1992] 1 CMLR 305; see p 126. For criticism of the *Duke* decision, see Foster, 'The Effect of the European Communities Act 1972, s 2(4)' (1988) 51 MLR 775.

[146] [1992] 4 All ER 929 at 939, [1993] 1 CMLR 259 at 270, *per* Lord Keith of Kinkel.

[147] Case C-32/93 [1994] QB 718, [1994] 4 All ER 115.

[148] *Webb* v *EMO Air Cargo (UK) Ltd (No 2)* [1995] 1 WLR 1454, [1996] 4 All ER 577.

maintains the theoretical constitutional position that ultimate authority rests with the United Kingdom. And it does in some sense continue to do so, in that the UK Parliament may repeal the 1972 Act that creates the legal underpinning for the authority of EU law. This is confirmed by the terms of the European Union Bill, which, if passed into law in 2011, will enshrine this principle into statute. However, repeal of the 1972 Act is not likely and would be contrary to the UK's treaty obligations. The reality is that courts have to give precedence to EU law even if that means the disapplication of an Act of Parliament. They also have to interpret statutes in a way that conforms with EU law, even in the face of seemingly clear and unambiguous words.

❓ Questions

1. Where does authority now lie within the English legal system?
2. What purpose does clause 18 of the European Union Bill serve?
3. Should we simply accept that we now have a superior body of law, and jettison the belief that this turns on parliamentary authority?

The European Court of Justice

Composition and procedure

The Court of Justice comprises one judge for each member state, assisted by eight Advocates-General.[149] Both the judges and the Advocates-General are appointed for a renewable period of six years, and appointments are staggered so that a proportion of the court is replaced or reappointed every three years. Article 253 of the TFEU[150] provides that members of the court shall:

> be chosen from persons whose independence is beyond doubt and who possess the qualifications required for appointment to the highest judicial offices in their respective countries or who are jurisconsults of recognised competence.

Article 253 further stipulates that the judges must nominate one of their number as President of the court. The President holds office for a renewable term of three years, and is responsible for directing the judicial business of the court and for overseeing its administration. The court also appoints its own registrar and lays down rules governing his service.

The court may sit either in chambers of three or five judges, in a Grand Chamber of thirteen judges, or exceptionally, in plenary session.[151] Its organization and procedures are set out in the Statute of the Court (annexed to the TFEU) and in the Rules of Procedure adopted by the court itself.

---

[149] Articles 251 and 252 TEU. The nationality of the judges is not specified at present, but it is assumed that each state will be represented. The new Article 9F of the TEU makes this explicit, by providing that 'the Court of Justice shall consist of one judge from each Member State'.

[150] Formerly Article 223 EC.   [151] Article 221.

Advocates-General

The role of Advocate-General has no direct parallel within the English legal system. Comparisons with counsel acting as *amicus curiae* are inexact, because, despite the name, an Advocate-General does not act on anyone's behalf. Instead his role is to present independent, reasoned conclusions on cases submitted to the court, in order to assist the court in performing its duties.[152] The opinion of the Advocate-General is not binding but it is clearly of persuasive value. It will be reported with the judgment of the court and may therefore be important in assisting in the development of legal doctrine.

The General Court

The Court of First Instance was created in 1988 in an attempt to ease the workload of the Court of Justice.[153] It deals mainly with disputes between the Union and its servants and with actions for judicial review brought under Article 263 TEU. Since the Treaty of Nice came into force in February 2003, it has also been able to deal with some references from national courts under what is now the Article 267 procedure. The jurisdiction of the Court of First Instance was further expanded under the Treaty of Lisbon, and it is now known as 'the General Court'.[154]

The court has one judge for each member state but there are no separate Advocates-General. In most other respects, the structure of the court is very similar to that of the Court of Justice: judges are appointed for six years, they nominate a President who holds office for three years, and they normally sit in chambers of three or five. There is a right of appeal to the Court of Justice on a point of law.

Jurisdiction

The main jurisdiction of the Court of Justice is as follows:

Judicial review of EU institutions

Under Article 263 the court can review the legality of an act of the Council or the Commission. Under Article 265 failures to act can also be challenged.

Member States, the Council and the Commission have the status of privileged applicants, and may bring an action under these provisions on the grounds of lack of competence, infringement of an essential procedural requirement, infringement of EU law, or misuse of power.[155] An individual or 'non-privileged applicant' can only challenge (a) decisions addressed to him, and (b) decisions or regulations

---

[152] Article 222. The compatibility of the Advocate-General's role with the right to a fair trial was considered in *Emesa Sugar* v *Aruba* Case C-17/98 [2000] ECR I-665.

[153] Article 225; see Brown, 'The First Five Years of the Court of First Instance and Appeals to the Court of Justice' (1995) 32(3) CML Rev 743.

[154] Article 2(2)(n), Treaty of Lisbon.

[155] See, e.g. the challenge to the Working Time Directive in *UK* v *EU Council* Case C-84/94 [1996] All ER (EC) 877.

that are of direct and individual concern. The requirement for standing has been restrictively interpreted, and matters cannot be of direct concern to an individual if there is a discretion as to their implementation.[156] Where no real discretion exists, or where implementation is automatic, then the 'direct concern' test is satisfied.[157]

The established approach is typified by the decision in *Plaumann & Co v EEC Commission*.[158] Even though the applicants in this case imported clementines, they did not have standing to challenge a decision on the import duties on clementines, since any person could potentially be a clementine importer. Despite the restrictive effect of this ruling, it has been followed in numerous subsequent cases.[159] In *Jégo-Quéré at Cie SA v Commission*, the Court of First Instance adopted a more relaxed approach, citing the importance of providing an effective remedy for those affected by Community law.[160] However, the Court of Justice overturned this decision[161] and confirmed the *Plaumann* approach as correct.

Since the Treaty of Lisbon, Article 263 allows natural or legal persons to challenge any 'regulatory act which is of direct concern to them and does not entail implementing measures'. The absence of any reference to *individual* concern should make it easier to challenge certain EU acts.

Direct actions against Member States

A Member State may be challenged directly in the Court of Justice for a failure to fulfil its EU obligations. Actions against Member States may be brought either by the Commission[162] or by other Member States.[163] Proceedings by the latter are extremely rare,[164] although the *threat* of a challenge from a Member State can sometimes lead the Commission to take action under what is now Article 258. In 1999 for example, France refused to allow the importation of UK beef even though the Community had lifted a worldwide ban imposed in response to a health scare. The United Kingdom notified the Commission of its intention to bring an action against France, and the Commission responded by successfully challenging the ban itself under Article 226.[165]

Cases concerning the liability in damages of the EU and its servants

Under Articles 268 and 272 the Court of Justice has jurisdiction over disputes concerning damage caused by the EU institutions and their servants in the performance

---

[156] *Alcan v EC Commission* Case 69/69 [1970] ECR 385.

[157] *International Fruit Co v NV Commission* Case 41–44/70 [1971] ECR 411.

[158] Case 25/62 [1963] ECR 95, [1964] CMLR 29.

[159] See, e.g. *Piraiki-Patraiki v Commission* Case 11/82 [1985] ECR 207. The approach to standing in such cases can be compared with that of the domestic courts on applications for judicial review.

[160] Case T-177/01 [2002] All ER (EC) 932 at [51], [2002] 2 CMLR 44.

[161] Case C-263/02 [2005] QB 237, [2004] All ER (EC); see also *Unión de Pequeños Agricultores v Council* Case C-50/00 [2002] All ER (EC) 893, [2002] 3 CMLR 1.

[162] Article 258 TEU.   [163] Article 263 TEU.

[164] See *France v UK* Case 141/78 [1979] ECR 2923; *Belgium v Spain* Case C-388/95 [2000] ECR I-3121.

[165] *Commission v France*; *sub nom Re Ban on British Beef* Case C-1/00 [2001] ECR I-9989, [2002] 1 CMLR 22.

of their duties. The General Court can also hear disputes between the EU and its servants.[166]

References from national courts requesting a preliminary ruling

This is a major source of work for the Court, and has important consequences for the courts of Member States. The jurisdiction is governed by Article 267 TEU and is considered in more detail below.

References for a preliminary ruling under Article 267

Article 267 creates a power, and in some circumstances imposes a duty, to refer questions concerning the interpretation of European law to the Court of Justice. This plays a key role in ensuring that the treaties and other instruments are applied consistently. This is not an appellate role: the Court of Justice is not a superior appellate court, but, rather, it deals with the meaning of EU law. Article 267 states:

(1) The Court of Justice shall have jurisdiction to give preliminary rulings concerning:

    (a) the interpretation of this Treaty;

    (b) the validity and interpretation of acts of the institutions of the EU.

(2) Where such a question is raised before any court or tribunal of a Member State, that court or tribunal may, if it considers that a decision on the question is necessary to enable it to give judgment, request the Court of Justice to give a ruling thereon.

(3) Where any such question is raised in a case pending before a court or tribunal of a Member State, against whose decisions there is no judicial remedy under national law, that court or tribunal shall bring the matter before the Court of Justice.

If such a question is raised in a case pending before a court or tribunal of a Member State with regard to a person in custody, the Court of Justice of the European Union shall act with the minimum of delay.

The power to refer

This power to refer matters under Article 267 is conferred upon courts and tribunals. It is for the Court of Justice to decide whether a body constitutes a 'court or tribunal', and the term has been held to include state bodies exercising judicial or quasi-judicial functions.[167]

When is a reference mandatory?

If the interpretation of European law is raised as an issue in a case, the domestic court or tribunal involved in that case must decide whether to refer the matter to the Court of Justice. If the domestic court is one 'against whose decisions there is

---

[166] Article 270 TEU.

[167] *Broekmeulen* v *Huisarts Registratie Commissie* Case 246/80 [1981] ECR 2311; *De Coster* v *Collège des Bourgmestre et Échevins de Watermael-Boitsfort* Case C-17/00 [2001] ECR I-9445.

no judicial remedy', a reference to the Court of Justice will be mandatory. Thus if a matter falling within the scope of Article 267 is raised in a case before the Supreme Court, that matter *must* be referred to the Court of Justice since there is no possibility of a further appeal. A reference is not only mandatory for courts the decisions of which can *never* be challenged;[168] what matters is whether an appeal is possible in the particular case in question. On this basis, it could be suggested that the Court of Appeal would often be obliged to make a reference, since an appeal from a decision of this court is only possible with leave and leave may not be granted. However, if leave is not granted by the Court of Appeal it may still be requested from the Supreme Court, and this means that the Court of Appeal usually has a discretion as to whether to seek a ruling:[169]

> Except...where the Court of Appeal is the court of last resort, the Court of Appeal is not *obliged* to make a reference to the ECJ...If the Court of Appeal does not make a reference to the ECJ, and gives its final judgment on the appeal, then the House of Lords becomes the court of last resort.

It should also be noted that the concept of a judicial remedy under Article 267 is wide enough to encompass judicial review. Since inferior courts and tribunals are under the supervisory jurisdiction of the High Court, it would appear that such bodies will never be caught by the mandatory reference requirement, even if no right of appeal exists.[170]

When is a decision on a point of European law 'necessary'?

Unless a decision on a point of European law is 'necessary' for the determination of a case, there is neither a duty nor a discretion to make a reference to the Court of Justice: necessity is a precondition to the use of the preliminary ruling procedure. In *HP Bulmer Ltd* v *J Bollinger SA*, Lord Denning stressed that a decision on a matter is not 'necessary' if substantially the same point has already been decided by the Court of Justice or if the point is 'reasonably free from doubt'.[171] In the *CILFIT case*,[172] the Court of Justice stated that there is no need to refer a question if the answer to it 'can in no way affect the outcome of the case'. Other English courts have interpreted the phrase as meaning 'reasonably necessary' or 'substantially determinative' of the litigation.[173]

---

[168] Compare Lord Denning in *HP Bulmer Ltd* v *J Bollinger SA* [1974] Ch 401, [1974] 2 All ER 1226, who suggested that only the House of Lords could be under an obligation to make a reference.

[169] *Chiron Corporation* v *Murex Diagnostics* [1995] All ER (EC) 88 at 93, *per* Balcombe LJ. See also *Lyckeskog* Case C-99/00 [2002] ECR I-4839, [2003] 1 WLR 9. The position is arguably different in the case of a Divisional Court that refuses to certify a point of law on appeal from a decision of a magistrates' court, since this extinguishes any possibility of taking the case further; see *SA Magnavision MN* v *General Optical Council (No 2)* [1987] 2 CMLR 262.

[170] See *Re a Holiday in Italy* [1975] 1 CMLR 184.

[171] [1974] Ch 401, [1974] 2 All ER 1226. He also suggested that the point of law must be conclusive of the case, but this goes too far and is inconsistent with the approach of the Court of Justice.

[172] *CILFIT Srl* v *Ministro della Sanita* Case 283/81 [1982] ECR 3415, [1983] 1 CMLR 472.

[173] *Customs and Excise Commissioners* v *Aps Samex* [1983] 1 All ER 1042.

The doctrine of acte clair

Lord Denning's suggestion, that a matter need not be referred if it is already reasonably free from doubt, mirrors the European law doctrine of *acte clair*. In *CILFIT*, the Court of Justice stated:[174]

> [T]he correct application of Community law may be so obvious as to leave no scope for any reasonable doubt as to the manner in which the question raised is to be resolved. Before it comes to the conclusion that such is the case, the national court or tribunal must be convinced that the matter was equally obvious to the courts of the other Member States and to the Court of Justice.

The court also stated that in determining whether a point is *acte clair* regard should be had to the fact that EU law is drafted in different languages and may not always translate easily. In addition, it emphasized that EU concepts may bear different meanings from similar concepts in domestic law, and that such points need to be considered in the context of EU law as a whole. In *R v Pharmaceutical Society of Great Britain, ex parte the Association of Pharmaceutical Importers*,[175] Kerr LJ observed that an English court should 'hesitate long' before concluding that a point of European law was so obvious as to leave no room for reasonable doubt. Note also that since a national court has no power to declare actions of the EU invalid, a reference under Article 267 may sometimes be necessary even where the point of law is clear.[176]

The existence of a 'precedent'

Although the Court of Justice does not operate a rigid doctrine of precedent, it does tend to follow its previous decisions in the interests of legal certainty. A national court may therefore consider it unnecessary to refer a point that has been answered by the Court of Justice in a previous case,[177] although much will depend on the national court's view of whether the earlier decision was correct. In *Da Costa*,[178] the Court of Justice suggested that an obligation to make a reference will not arise where a 'precedent' exists, although there will still be a discretion to ask for a preliminary ruling.

The discretion to refer

The discretion to refer is ultimately that of the national court or tribunal, and its decision will not be reviewable by the Court of Justice unless the reference is spurious or an abuse of process.[179] The Court of Justice will not, however, deliver advisory opinions or opinions on hypothetical questions.[180]

---

[174] Case 283/81 [1982] ECR 3415 at [16], [1983] 1 CMLR 472.

[175] [1987] 3 CMLR 951. See also the judgment of Bingham J in *Customs and Excise Commissioners v ApS Samex* [1983] 1 All ER 1042.

[176] *Firma Foto-Frost v Hauptzollamt Lubeck-Ost* Case 314/85 [1987] ECR 4199, [1988] 3 CMLR 57.

[177] *R v Secretary of State for the Home Department, ex parte A* [2002] EWCA Civ 1008, [2002] 3 CMLR 14; *Parfums Christian Dior v Evora BV* Case C-337/95, ECR I-6013, [1998] 1 CMLR 737.

[178] *Da Costa v Nederlandse Belastringadministratie* Cases 28–30/62 [1963] ECR 31, [1962] CMLR 224.

[179] *ICI Chemical Industries v Colmer (HM Inspector of Taxes)* Case C-264/96 [1998] ECR I-4695; *Foglia v Novello (No 2)* Case 244/80 [1981] ECR 3045.

[180] *Zabala Erasu v Instituto National de Empleo* Cases C-422–424/93 [1995] All ER (EC) 758.

It will be for the national court to formulate the question to be answered, and it should also define the factual and legislative context. In one case,[181] the Court of Justice held that it could not rule on the questions posed by the national court because it had not been provided with sufficient information. In *Bulmer v Bollinger*,[182] Lord Denning set out some guidelines for the exercise of the discretion by English courts, although these guidelines are not binding and the decision to make a reference must rest with the court or tribunal concerned:

(a) the time needed to obtain a ruling;

(b) the importance of not overloading the European Court with references;

(c) the difficulty and importance of the point;

(d) the expense involved; and

(e) the wishes of the parties.

He also stated that the facts should be established first: an 'injunction of obvious merit'.[183] The importance of deciding the facts first is that they provide the legal context for the point at issue, and indeed may determine whether or not a reference is in fact necessary. However, as the Court of Justice stated in *Irish Creamery Milk Suppliers Association v Ireland*,[184] the national court has responsibility for giving judgment in the case and it is therefore in the best position to judge when a reference is required. There is nothing to prevent a reference being made at an interlocutory stage, and important issues were raised and resolved in this way in the *Factortame* litigation.[185] In each case, however, it is a matter for the discretion of the trial court. In *Henn and Darby v DPP*,[186] Lord Diplock indicated that a reference in a criminal case should be dealt with if necessary *after* the trial, at the appellate stage. By contrast, in *R v Goldstein*, it was said that in a criminal case the best time to deal with such a matter would be on a motion to quash the indictment.[187] It would seem that the real issue in all cases is whether the interests of justice provide a compelling reason for going ahead with the trial, pending determination of the reference.

Notwithstanding Lord Denning's guidelines, the workload of the Court of Justice appears not to be a relevant factor when deciding whether to make a reference. By contrast, expense *is* an important consideration. In *R v Pharmaceutical Society of Great Britain, ex parte Association of Pharmaceutical Importers*,[188] Kerr LJ expected the case to reach the House of Lords, at which point a reference would become mandatory. He considered that an immediate reference would therefore save considerable

---

[181] *Telemarsicabruzzo SpA v Circostel and others* Cases C-320–322/90 [1993] ECR I-393.

[182] [1974] Ch 401, [1974] 2 All ER 1226.

[183] *Customs and Excise Commissioners v ApS Samex* [1983] 1 All ER 1042 at 1055, *per* Bingham J.

[184] Case 36/80 [1981] ECR 735, [1981] 2 CMLR 455.

[185] *R v Secretary of State for Transport, ex parte Factortame* Case C-213/89 [1990] ECR I-2433, [1990] 3 CMLR 1.

[186] [1981] AC 850, [1980] 2 All ER 166.   [187] [1983] 1 All ER 434, [1983] 1 WLR 151.

[188] [1987] 3 CMLR 951.

time and costs. As Hodgson J observed in the *Factortame* case, if a reference is going to be made, 'the sooner it is done the better'.[189]

The wishes of the parties will be a relevant but not decisive factor, for it is the court's judgment as to the need for a reference that is important. However, where only one party wishes a reference to be made there is no inevitability: it will usually be the case that a reference will assist one party only. A reference may be appropriate even against the wishes of both parties. The court may also take into account the fact that the matter is one upon which the European Commission has strong views. Once a decision to make a reference is taken, however, the domestic court is not at liberty to disregard the outcome, and it must apply the ruling of the Court of Justice to the facts before it.[190]

Further reading

Website of the European Union: **http://europa.eu**

ARNULL, 'The Direct Effect of Directives: Grasping the Nettle' (1986) 35 ICLQ 939

ARNULL, 'The Use and Abuse of Article 177, EEC' (1989) 52(5) MLR 622

ARNULL, 'From Charter to Constitution and Beyond: Fundamental Rights in the New European Union' [2003] PL 774

CRAIG, 'Directives: Direct Effect, Indirect Effect and the Construction of National Legislation' (1997) 22 EL Rev 519

DRAKE, 'Twenty Years after *Von Colson*: The Impact of "Indirect Effect" on the Protection of the Individual's Community Rights' (2005) 30 EL Rev 329

DRZEMCZEWSKI, 'The Domestic Application of the European Human Rights Convention as European Community Law' (1981) 30 ICLQ 118

FOSTER, 'The Effect of the European Communities Act 1972, s 2(4)' (1988) 51 MLR 775

HARMSEN, 'National Responsibility for EC Acts under the ECHR: Recasting the Accession Debate' (2001) 7 EPL 625

WINTER, 'Direct Applicability and Direct Effects' (1972) 9 CML Rev 425

---

[189] *R v Secretary of State for Transport, ex parte Factortame (No 1)* [1989] 2 CMLR 353 at 380.

[190] See *Arsenal v Reed* [2003] EWCA Civ 696, [2003] 3 All ER 865, which raises some interesting questions about the extent to which courts should follow any views expressed by the Court of Justice about the application of the law to the facts.

5 The Human Rights Act 1998 and the European Convention on Human Rights

INTRODUCTION

This chapter focuses on the Human Rights Act 1998 and its impact on the English legal system.

It was not until October 2000, exactly half a century after the United Kingdom became a signatory to the European Convention on Human Rights, that its provisions were explicitly given effect in domestic law by the Human Rights Act. Yet the Act has already left an indelible impression on the legal landscape, and its impact has been described as 'irreversible'. The specific issues addressed in this chapter will include:

- the history of the ECHR and its impact on the English legal system before 1998;
- the arguments in favour of incorporation, and the aims and objectives of the 1998 Act;
- the Act's key provisions and their impact on the role of the courts and other public authorities;
- the impact of the Act on disputes between private individuals—the issue of horizontal effect;
- the future of the Act and the current campaign for a 'British bill of rights'.

The context

The Convention and its history[1]

The United Kingdom is a signatory to the Convention for the Protection of Human Rights and Fundamental Freedoms, usually referred to as the European Convention on Human Rights (ECHR). It is an instrument of the Council of Europe, which, like the European Community,[2] is an intergovernmental body formed in the aftermath of the Second World War. Since it was established in 1949 the membership of the Council

---

[1] For a comprehensive account, see Simpson, *Human Rights and the End of Empire: Britain and the Genesis of the European Convention* (OUP, 2001).
[2] See Chapter 4.

of Europe has steadily increased from ten to forty-six states,[3] and it includes all of the current member states of the EU. As already noted in Chapter 4, there are now plans for the EU itself to accede to the Convention,[4] but it is important to remember that the Council of Europe and the EU are separate bodies with their own separate treaties and institutions. Whereas what is now the EU was initially established as a vehicle for greater economic cooperation, human rights were at the centre of the Council of Europe's agenda from the outset. The ECHR was the Council's first major project and is undoubtedly its single most important achievement. The United Kingdom played a significant role in the drafting process and was one of the first countries to sign the Convention in November 1950. It entered into force in the United Kingdom on 3 September 1953.

The emphasis of the Convention is on protecting basic 'human rights', along with what might be termed civil and political rights, and its text is closely modelled on the UN's Universal Declaration on Human Rights 1948. The key rights are the right to life (Article 2), freedom from torture (Article 3), freedom from slavery (Article 4), the right to liberty and security of the person (Article 5), the right to a fair trial (Article 6), the right not to be subject to retrospective criminal liability or penalties (Article 7), respect for private and family life (Article 8), freedom of thought, conscience, and religion (Article 9), freedom of expression (Article 10), freedom of assembly and association (Article 11), and the right to marry and found a family (Article 12). These rights are considered in more detail in Chapter 6.

One other provision should be noted: Article 13 guarantees the availability of a remedy at national level to enforce the substance of Convention rights in whatever form they are secured in domestic law.

> [T]he remedy required by Article 13 must be 'effective' in practice as well as in law. In particular its exercise must not be unjustifiably hindered by the acts or omissions of the...respondent State.[5]

The list of Convention rights has been enhanced over the years by a number of additional protocols. Although acceptance of the Convention is now a prerequisite for Council of Europe membership, most of the protocols are optional,[6] and this has enabled the Convention to address issues that probably would not have been brought within its framework at all if unanimity had been required. To date, fourteen protocols have been added to the Convention. Some of these have been concerned solely with institutional reform, but others have added new substantive rights. Protocol 1 includes the right to peaceful enjoyment of possessions, to education, and to free elections,

---

[3] Albania, Andorra, Armenia, Austria, Azerbaijan, Belgium, Bosnia and Herzegovina, Bulgaria, Croatia, Cyprus, the Czech Republic, Denmark, Estonia, Finland, France, Georgia, Germany, Greece, Hungary, Iceland, Ireland, Italy, Latvia, Liechtenstein, Lithuania, Luxembourg, Malta, Moldova, Monaco, the Netherlands, Norway, Poland, Portugal, Romania, Russia, San Marino, Serbia and Montenegro, Slovenia, the Slovak Republic, Spain, Sweden, Switzerland, Turkey, the former Yugoslav Republic of Macedonia, the Ukraine, and the UK.

[4] See p 118.   [5] *Keenan* v *UK* (2001) 33 EHRR 38 at [122].

[6] Acceptance of Protocol 6 is now mandatory: see p 179.

while Protocol 6 is concerned with the abolition of the death penalty in peace time. Both of these protocols have been signed and ratified by the United Kingdom, as has Protocol 13, which strengthens Protocol 6 by banning the use of the death penalty in *any* circumstances. However, the United Kingdom has thus far not accepted Protocol 4 (which prohibits the imprisonment of debtors, the expulsion of nationals, and the collective expulsion of aliens), Protocol 7 (which, inter alia, guarantees equality between spouses and the right not to be tried more than once for the same offence), or Protocol 12 (which prohibits discrimination on a range of grounds).

What distinguishes the ECHR from most other international human rights treaties is not the catalogue of rights that it protects, but its machinery for enforcement. It established both a Commission and a Court of Human Rights, which together were given the task of ensuring that the Convention was observed. The Commission was abolished in 1998, but the court, based in Strasbourg, has gone from strength to strength. It received around 57,000 individual complaints in 2009 alone.[7]

The status of the ECHR before the Human Rights Act 1998

Unlike the European Communities, the Council of Europe did not set out to establish a superior legal order, and the ECHR does not oblige member states to directly incorporate its provisions into their national legal systems. The United Kingdom's constitutional arrangements mean that international treaties are not binding in domestic law unless accompanied by an Act of Parliament,[8] and it was not until the implementation of the Human Rights Act 1998 that it was possible for Convention rights to form the basis of a domestic legal challenge. Even before this Act, however, decisions of the Court of Human Rights provided the impetus for several pieces of legislation and Convention rights were occasionally taken into account by the national courts. In addition, the Convention was able to have a subtle and indirect influence through the decisions of the European Court of Justice.

The impact of findings of the European Court of Human Rights

Since the United Kingdom accepted the jurisdiction of the European Court of Human Rights and the right of individuals to petition that court,[9] it has been found to be in breach of Convention rights on numerous occasions. States are obliged to give effect to any decision of the Court in cases to which they are parties, and several Acts of Parliament have been enacted in response to adverse findings in Strasbourg. For example, the Contempt of Court Act 1981 followed the decision in *Sunday Times* v *UK*[10] that the common law approach to contempt was incompatible with freedom

---

[7] European Court of Human Rights, *Annual Report 2009*. The majority of applications are declared inadmissible or otherwise resolved: 2395 judgments were delivered in 2009, eighteen of which concerned the UK. See p 218.

[8] *R* v *Chief Immigration Officer, Heathrow Airport, ex parte Bibi (Salamat)* [1976] 3 All ER 843, [1976] 1 WLR 979.

[9] On 14 January 1966.   [10] (1979–1980) 2 EHRR 245; see p 207.

of expression. Similarly, the finding in *Malone* v *UK*[11] that there was insufficient legal regulation of telephone tapping led to the enactment of the Interception of Communications Act 1985. Decisions in Strasbourg have also triggered changes in the procedures for dealing with life prisoners[12] and the abandonment of the policy preventing homosexuals from serving in the military.[13] Following the decision in *Hirst* v *UK*,[14] the government recently announced plans to extend voting rights to some prisoners, although Ministers are clearly less than enthusiastic about the prospect. When announcing the government's intention in Parliament, the Parliamentary Secretary to the Cabinet Office stressed: '[T]his is not a choice; it is a legal obligation...I suspect that every Member of the House is exasperated about this but we have no choice about complying with the law.'[15] Occasionally, the mere *likelihood* of an adverse finding has been enough to bring about legislative reform. Thus in anticipation that aspects of the courts-martial system would be found to breach the fair trial provisions in Article 6, the government introduced the Armed Forces Act 1996. This Act made a number of changes to the courts-martial system, although it did not, of course, prevent the Strasbourg court from finding a breach of Article 6 in the case in question.[16]

An indirect influence on the domestic courts[17]

There is a presumption that Parliament does not intend to legislate in a manner incompatible with international law,[18] and where a statutory provision is genuinely ambiguous it is legitimate to take account of an international treaty when choosing between two equally reasonable interpretations. Thus even before the passage of the Human Rights Act, the ECHR could be taken into account as an aid to statutory interpretation.[19] The position was considered by the House of Lords in *R* v *Secretary of State for Home Affairs, ex parte Brind*.[20] The Home Secretary had made a directive prohibiting the broadcasting of statements by representatives of proscribed organizations, and the applicant argued that this contravened the right to freedom of expression under Article 10. In dismissing the applications, the House recognized that the Convention *could* be used for the resolution of a legislative ambiguity. However, it held that it did not require an administrative body such as the Home Office to exercise its discretion within the terms of the Convention. To conclude otherwise would

---

[11] (1985) 7 EHRR 14. The 1985 Act was replaced by the Regulation of Investigatory Powers Act 2000 following further criticism in *Halford* v *UK* (1997) 24 EHRR 523.

[12] See p 187.

[13] *Smith and Grady* v *UK* (2000) 29 EHRR 493; *Lustig-Prean and Beckett* v *UK* (2000) 29 EHRR 548.

[14] (2006) 42 EHRR 41.

[15] Mark Harper, MP, 517 HC Official Report (6th series) cols 771–772, 2 November 2010.

[16] *Findlay* v *UK* (1997) 24 EHRR 221; see p 279.

[17] See Beloff and Mountfield, 'Unconventional Behaviour? Judicial Uses of the European Convention in England and Wales' [1996] EHRLR 467.

[18] See p 56.

[19] See the dictum of Lord Denning in *R* v *Chief Immigration Officer of Heathrow Airport, ex parte Bibi (Salamat)* [1976] 3 All ER 843 at 847, [1976] 1 WLR 979 at 984.

[20] [1991] 1 AC 696, [1991] 1 All ER 720.

amount to incorporation of the Convention by the judiciary, and this would be a usurpation of the legislative function.

The courts were more willing to use the Convention when interpreting statutes enacted to give effect to decisions of the Court of Human Rights,[21] or when considering the scope of the common law, but for the most part its effect was limited to reinforcing a conclusion that would have been reached in any event.[22] Indeed, in the vast majority of domestic cases the Convention had no decisive effect at all, and on a number of occasions the courts made it clear that they felt unable to use it to develop the common law. Thus, in *Malone v Metropolitan Police Commissioner (No 2)*,[23] Sir Robert Megarry considered the legality of the police interception of telephone calls. Even though not bound by any authority, and despite considering that the practice could breach Article 8 of the Convention,[24] he declined to develop the law in a way that would ensure compliance, suggesting that any reform in this area would be best left to Parliament.[25]

An influence through the EU

All of the EU's member states are signatories to the ECHR, and amendments made to the Treaty on European Union by the Treaty of Lisbon provide for the EU itself to accede to the Convention.[26] The European Court of Justice has frequently asserted that Convention rights form part of its legal order, and, as already noted,[27] Article 6(3) of the amended Treaty gives Convention rights the status of 'general principles of the Union's law'. In addition, where national legislation falls within the scope of European law, the Court of Justice will examine its compatibility with the ECHR.[28] In the *Familiapress*[29] case, for example, the Court ruled that any justification for a ban on the distribution of a magazine would need to be compatible with the right to freedom of expression under Article 10 ECHR. This led some to conclude that a measure of indirect incorporation was being achieved through the influence of what was then EC law:[30]

> There is no case in which the European Court [of Justice] has upheld the validity of actions which conflicted with the European Convention on Human Rights. It seems therefore,

---

[21] *R v Secretary of State for the Home Department, ex parte Norney* (1995) 7 Admin LR 861.

[22] See, e.g., *R v Secretary of State for the Home Department, ex parte Leech (No 2)* [1994] QB 198, [1993] 4 All ER 539.

[23] [1979] Ch 344, [1979] 2 All ER 620.

[24] In that it was not prescribed by law. The Strasbourg court later agreed with this assessment: *Malone v UK* (1985) 7 EHRR 14. Parliament responded by enacting the Interception of Communications Act 1985.

[25] [1979] Ch 344 at 380, [1979] 2 All ER 620 at 649.

[26] Article 6(2) of the amended Treaty provides that 'the Union shall accede to the European Convention for the Protection of Human Rights and Fundamental Freedoms' (in force since December 2009).

[27] See p 118.

[28] *Johnston v Chief Constable of the RUC* Case C-222/84 [1987] QB 129, [1986] 3 All ER 135; *Prais v Council* Case C-130/75 [1976] ECR 1589; *Rutili v Minister of the Interior* Case C-36/75 [1975] ECR 1219.

[29] *Vereingte Familiapress Zeitungsverlags und Vertriebs GmbH v Heinrich Bauer Verlag* Case C-368/95 [1997] ECR-I-3689, [1997] 3 CMLR 1329.

[30] Browne-Wilkinson, 'The Infiltration of a Bill of Rights' [1992] PL 397 at 401. See also Grief, 'The Domestic Impact of the European Convention on Human Rights as Mediated through Community Law' [1991] PL 555.

that in those areas affected by the EEC Treaties, the ECHR is already indirectly incorporated into English domestic law.

The remainder of this chapter explores the content and structure of the Human Rights Act itself, while the interpretation of specific Convention rights will be considered in Chapter 6.

KEY ISSUE

The history of the application of the Convention prior to the implementation of the Human Rights Act 1998 demonstrates the impact a treaty can have even without incorporation, but it also reveals the limitations. The impact of the Convention prior to 1998 was inevitably limited by the fact that it could not be directly enforced in the national courts. This meant that a 'victim' of a Convention breach had to go to the Court of Human Rights in Strasbourg. The fact that the government might choose to bring the law into line with the rulings of the court did not provide an automatic remedy for such a victim. The argument that the United Kingdom had an exemplary human rights record and that incorporation was unnecessary did not stand up to scrutiny. By 1997 the United Kingdom had lost more cases in Strasbourg than any other state except Italy.[31]

? Questions

1. To what extent did the Convention have an impact on domestic law prior to the Human Rights Act?

2. Do you think that a more formal status for the ECHR in EU law has practical effects for the UK?

The Human Rights Act 1998

The Human Rights Act 1998, which came fully into force on 2 October 2000,[32] is described in its long title as 'an Act to give further effect to rights and freedoms guaranteed under the European Convention on Human Rights'. The United Kingdom's constitutional framework means that the Act is not 'entrenched' in the same manner as the human rights documents adopted by many other states, but it is presumed that any attempt to repeal or amend its provisions would require the clearest possible words.[33]

The scheme of the Act is complex: it obliges public authorities to perform their functions in a manner compatible with Convention rights, and it gives the Convention and its jurisprudence a significant influence over the interpretation of domestic law.

---

[31] Lord Irvine (Lord Chancellor), 582 HL Official Report (5th series) col 1227, 3 November 1997.

[32] For England and Wales—s 22(3); SI 2000/1851. Sections 18, 20 and 21(5) came into force on the date of royal assent.

[33] *Thoburn v Sunderland City Council and others* [2002] EWHC 195 (Admin), [2003] QB 151, [2002] 4 All ER 156. The Act was described in this case as a 'constitutional statute'. See p 20.

However, it stops short of allowing the courts to 'disapply' or invalidate incompatible Acts of Parliament, and in this crucial respect it does not give the Convention primacy over domestic law.[34]

The status of Convention rights and jurisprudence

Section 1: The rights protected

Section 1 provides that the 'Convention rights' given effect shall be those contained in Articles 2–12 and 14 of the Convention, in Articles 1–3 of the First Protocol, and in Article 1 of the Thirteenth Protocol. These rights are reproduced in Schedule 1 of the Act. The 'missing' right, Article 13, is the right to a remedy for an infringement of the Convention. The government took the view that the very existence of the Human Rights Act was sufficient to give effect to Article 13, and that to expressly incorporate it would involve unnecessary duplication.[35]

Section 2: The Strasbourg case law[36]

Section 2 requires any court or tribunal determining a matter involving a Convention right, to take into account any judgment, decision, or advisory opinion of the European Court of Human Rights, along with certain decisions of the Commission and Committee of Ministers, *in so far as they may be relevant*. It is clear from this wording that Strasbourg decisions do not formally bind the national courts, and they thus have the status of persuasive precedents. The fact that Parliament chose not to *oblige* the courts to follow the Strasbourg case law is entirely consistent with the Convention itself, as states are afforded a margin of appreciation in the application of its provisions (although that may vary depending on the nature of the right involved). Moreover, domestic courts will frequently be required to decide human rights cases in which the only relevant case law concerns other jurisdictions, and it would be illogical to prevent them from reaching their own conclusions in such cases.

The domestic courts have made it clear that in the absence of exceptional circumstances they are unlikely to depart from any 'clear and constant jurisprudence of the European Court of Human Rights',[37] and, so far, most judges have adhered fairly closely to Strasbourg decisions. For example, despite considering that mandatory and discretionary life sentences raised similar issues, the Court of Appeal in *R (on the application of Anderson)* v *Secretary of State for the Home Department*[38] followed the Strasbourg line and ruled that mandatory sentences were not subject to the same requirements as those that were discretionary. Their Lordships were clearly influenced

[34] Compare the status given to EU law by the European Communities Act 1972: see Chapter 4 for a discussion.

[35] Jack Straw MP (Home Secretary), 312 HC Official Report (6th series) col 975, 20 May 1998.

[36] See also p 80.

[37] *R (on the Application of Alconbury)* v *Secretary of State for the Environment, Transport and the Regions*: [2001] UKHL 23 at [26], [2003] 2 AC 295 at [26], [2001] 2 All ER 929, *per* Lord Slynn.

[38] [2001] EWCA Civ 1698, [2002] 2 WLR 1143.

by the knowledge that another case on this point was already pending before the Court of Human Rights:[39]

> In the end there are two factors which have persuaded me to regard the Strasbourg case law as for the present determinative. First, that whatever advantage we might enjoy through our domestic knowledge and experience of the mandatory life sentence regime could perhaps be thought balanced (or even conceivably outweighed) by the Court of Human Rights' deeper appreciation of the true ambit and reach of Articles 5(4) and 6(1) of the Convention... The second factor which weighs with me is that of comity... I shall be surprised if the present regime for implementing mandatory life sentences survives the Court of Human Rights' re-examination of the issue in *Stafford*. The final decision, however, I am persuaded should be theirs.

As predicted, when the Strasbourg court did have the opportunity to revisit the issue in *Stafford v UK*,[40] it departed from its previous jurisprudence and agreed that the regime for implementing mandatory life sentences infringed the Convention. Consequently, when the House of Lords heard the appeal in *Anderson*,[41] it felt able to declare that the Home Secretary's power to determine the tariff for mandatory life prisoners was incompatible with the Convention. What is notable is that, in reaching its conclusions in *Stafford*, the Court of Human Rights drew heavily on the opinions expressed by the domestic courts in both *Stafford*[42] and *Anderson*. Thus, although the Court of Appeal thought it appropriate to leave the final decision to Strasbourg, it was able to influence that decision through its own jurisprudence.

On occasions, the national courts have felt less constrained by the Strasbourg case law. For example, in dismissing a claim that the courts-martial system was incompatible with Article 6, the House of Lords in *R v Spear* politely suggested that a recent Strasbourg case[43] on the point had been wrongly decided.[44] At the next opportunity a unanimous Grand Chamber took account of the judgments in *Spear* and again departed from previous Strasbourg case law, declaring that there was, after all, no incompatibility with the Convention.[45] Similarly, in *Al-Khawaji and Tahery v UK*, the Court of Human Rights held that allowing hearsay evidence from absent witnesses to form the 'sole or decisive basis' of a conviction was a violation of Article 6,[46] but in a unanimous judgment clearly aimed at influencing the decision of the Grand Chamber in that case, the Supreme Court in *R v Horncastle (Michael Christopher)* rejected the Strasbourg analysis:[47]

> The requirement to 'take into account' the Strasbourg jurisprudence will normally result in this court applying principles that are clearly established by the Strasbourg Court.

---

[39] Ibid at [65]–[66], *per* Simon Brown LJ.   [40] (2002) 35 EHRR 32.

[41] [2002] UKHL 46, [2003] 1 AC 837, [2002] 4 All ER 1089.

[42] *R v Secretary of State for the Home Department, ex parte Stafford* [1999] 2 AC 38, [1998] 4 All ER 7, HL.

[43] *Morris v UK* (2002) 34 EHRR 52.

[44] *R v Spear and others; R v Saunby and others* [2002] UKHL 31 at [12], [2003] 1 AC 734 at [12].

[45] *Cooper v UK* (2004) 39 EHRR 8.   [46] (2009) 49 EHRR 1.

[47] [2009] UKSC 14 at [11], [2010] 2 WLR 47 at [11], [2010] 2 All ER 359, *per* Lord Phillips: see Requa, 'Absent Witnesses and the UK Supreme Court: Judicial Deference as Judicial Dialogue' (2010) 14(3) *International Journal of Evidence and Proof* 208.

There will, however, be rare occasions where this court has concerns as to whether a decision of the Strasbourg Court sufficiently appreciates or accommodates particular aspects of our domestic process. In such circumstances it is open to this court to decline to follow the Strasbourg decision, giving reasons for adopting this course. This is likely to give the Strasbourg Court the opportunity to reconsider the particular aspect of the decision that is in issue, so that there takes place what may prove to be a valuable dialogue between this court and the Strasbourg Court.

As the above decisions demonstrate, the obligation to *consider* rather than to *follow* Strasbourg case law means that there is at least the potential for the national courts to develop a human rights jurisprudence of their own. Moreover, the flexibility inherent in section 2 means that 'domestic courts are perfectly entitled to accord *greater* rights than those guaranteed by the Convention'.[48] The majority of decisions, however, have emphasized the importance of following the Strasbourg line. For example, in *Secretary of State for the Home Department* v *F*, Lord Carswell took the view that 'the authority of a considered statement of the Grand Chamber is such that our courts have no option but to accept and apply it',[49] and in a recent case concerning the right of access to a lawyer in Scotland, the Supreme Court held that it was compelled to follow a Grand Chamber decision. Contrasting the position in *Spear* and *Horncastle*, Lord Hope observed that:[50]

> In this case the court is faced with a unanimous decision of the Grand Chamber. This, in itself, is a formidable reason for thinking that we should follow it...As for the question whether *Salduz* has given rise to a clear and constant jurisprudence, the case law shows that it has been followed repeatedly in subsequent cases.

KEY ISSUE

Cases such as *Spear* and *Horncastle* remain the exception rather than the rule, and, given that in both cases the effect of rejecting the Strasbourg approach was to conclude that there had been no breach of the Convention, it is questionable whether the domestic courts were really asserting their freedom to develop their own line of jurisprudence, or whether they were simply deferring to Parliament. In the leading case of *R (on the application of Ullah)* v *Special Adjudicator*, Lord Bingham stated that 'the duty of national courts is to keep pace with the Strasbourg jurisprudence as it evolves over time: no more, but certainly no less', and this is the approach that the majority of domestic cases have followed.[51] Lord Brown has since observed that this last sentence could just as easily have ended 'no less, but certainly no more',[52] and it is perhaps regrettable that this should be the case.

[48] *Begum (Runa)* v *Tower Hamlets* [2003] UKHL 5 at [69], [2003] 2 AC 430 at [69], [2003] 1 All ER 731, *per* Lord Hoffmann. See also, Lewis, 'The European Ceiling on Human Rights' [2007] PL 720.

[49] [2009] UKHL 28 at [108], [2009] 3 WLR 74 at [108], [2009] 3 All ER 643.

[50] *Cadder* v *HM Advocate* [2010] UKSC 43 at [46]–[47]: see *Salduz* v *Turkey* (2009) 49 EHRR 19.

[51] [2004] UKHL 26 at [20], [2004] 2 AC 323 at [20], [2004] 3 All ER 785. See also, his judgment in *Kay* v *Lambeth LBC* [2006] UKHL 10 at [28], [2006] 2 AC 465 at [28], [2006] 4 All ER 128.

[52] *R (on the application of Al-Skeini)* v *Secretary of State for Defence* [2007] UKHL 26 at [106], [2007] 3 WLR 33 at [106], [2007] 3 All ER 685.

> **? Questions**
>
> 1. What is the effect of the attitude of the United Kingdom courts to section 2?
> 2. If there is a general practice of following ECHR decisions, does that negate the terms of section 2 itself?
> 3. Does the fact that Strasbourg decisions are not binding on domestic courts weaken the level of protection afforded by the Human Rights Act?
> 4. Does the decision in *R v Horncastle (Michael Christopher)* indicate a greater willingness on the part of the domestic courts to develop their own human rights jurisprudence, or is it merely example of the courts deferring to Parliament rather than the Court of Human Rights?

Sections 12 and 13: The special status of freedom of religion and freedom of expression

Section 12

Section 12 applies when a court is considering whether to grant relief that could affect the right to freedom of expression. Section 12(2) provides that relief should not be granted against a party who is neither present nor represented unless the court is satisfied that all reasonable attempts to notify him have been made, or that there are compelling reasons for not notifying him. Section 12(3) adds that the publication of disputed material should not be restrained before trial unless the applicant is 'likely to establish that publication should not be allowed'. Finally, section 12(4) requires the court to have particular regard to the importance of freedom of expression. It states that when considering granting relief in relation to material that is 'journalistic, literary or artistic', it must take into account: (a) the extent to which the material is (or is about to become) available to the public; (b) whether publication would be in the public interest; and (c) any relevant privacy code.

Section 12 was included in the Act in response to strong lobbying from sections of the media who were concerned that incorporation might be the catalyst for new rights of privacy. In fact, however, the provision has not been interpreted to give freedom of expression priority over other rights. In *Douglas v Hello! Ltd (No 1)*, for example, Sedley LJ stated that:[53]

> That Convention right, when one turns to it, is qualified in favour of the reputation and rights of others and the protection of information received in confidence. In other words, you cannot have particular regard to Article 10 without having equally particular regard at the very least to Article 8.

The irony here is that not only was section 12 assumed to make Article 10 directly applicable between private parties, but it was also assumed that it indirectly did the

---

[53] [2001] QB 967 at 1003, [2001] 2 All ER 289 at 322.

same for the right to respect for private life in Article 8. This led one commentator to observe that section 12 was proving to be 'largely irrelevant' in practice.[54]

In a breach-of-confidence case, the Court of Appeal confirmed that section 12 does not require freedom of expression to take priority over other Convention rights: it simply means that any attempt to restrict free speech must be clearly justified.[55] This point was not challenged when the case went to the House of Lords, but it was held that section 12 nevertheless required a new approach to the granting of pre-trial injunctions.[56] Lord Nicholls concluded that in the light of section 12 it would not necessarily be sufficient for the party seeking an injunction to establish 'a real prospect of succeeding'[57] at trial. Instead, he stated that the courts should be 'exceedingly slow to make interim restraint orders where the applicant has not satisfied the court that he will *probably* ("more likely than not") succeed at the trial'.[58]

Section 13

The other Convention right given a special status under the Human Rights Act is freedom of religion. Section 13(1) provides that if the determination of an issue under the Act could affect the exercise by a religious organization or its members of the right to freedom of thought, conscience, and religion, a court must have particular regard to the importance of that right.[59] This provision was included in response to lobbying from church leaders, who were concerned that they may find themselves compelled to conduct gay marriages or to employ those whose lifestyles or beliefs were incompatible with their doctrines.[60] In fact, the churches probably overestimated the extent to which they would be affected by the Act. The guarantees under Article 9 are already sufficient to ensure that a minister of religion could not be compelled to perform a marriage ceremony against his conscience, and most of the functions of a church would not be caught by section 6 in any event.[61] Moreover, the interpretation given to section 12 makes it unlikely that section 13 will allow freedom of religion to trump other Convention rights. Having 'particular regard' to the right will therefore mean paying equal regard to the grounds upon which religious freedom can be restricted in Article 9(2).

---

[54] Amos, 'Can We Speak Freely Now? Freedom of Expression under the Human Rights Act' [2002] 6 EHRLR 750 at 755.

[55] *Cream Holdings* v *Banerjee* [2003] EWCA Civ 103 at [54], [2003] Ch 650 at [54], [2003] 2 All ER 318, *per* Simon Brown LJ.

[56] [2004] UKHL 44, [2004] 4 All ER 617, [2004] 3 WLR 918.

[57] This is the test established in *American Cyanamid Co* v *Ethicon Ltd* [1975] AC 396, [1975] 1 All ER 504.

[58] [2004] UKHL 44 at [22], [2004] 4 All ER 617 at [22] (emphasis added). Their Lordships overturned the Court of Appeal's decision on the facts and discharged the injunction that had been granted. For a novel application of this decision, see *Browne* v *Associated Newspapers Ltd* [2007] EWCA Civ 295, [2007] 3 WLR 289; *Boehringer Ingelheim* v *Vetplus* [2007] EWCA Civ 583, [2007] HRLR 33.

[59] For a discussion, see Cumper, 'The Protection of Religious Rights under s 13 of the Human Rights Act' [2000] PL 254.

[60] A House of Lords amendment that would have allowed Article 9 to prevail over other Convention rights was removed in the Commons: what is now s 13 was inserted in its place.

[61] See *Aston-Cantlow and Wilcote with Billesley Parochial Church Council* v *Wallbank* [2003] UKHL 37 at [63], [2004] 1 AC 546 at [63], [2003] 3 All ER 1213. Lord Hope confirmed that a church council was not a 'core' public authority for the purposes of the Human Rights Act: see p 163.

The impact on legislation

The courts must interpret legislation in accordance with the principles contained in section 3 of the Human Rights Act. If it is possible for a court to give effect to a legislative provision in accordance with convention rights, it *must* do so. If it is not, then a court *may* make a declaration of incompatibility under section 4. The approach can be stated simply as in Figure 5.1.

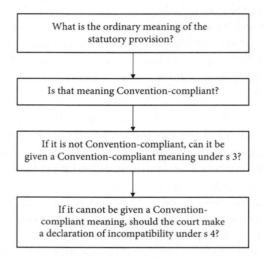

Fig. 5.1 Interpretation of legislation and the ECHR

Section 3: The interpretative obligation

One of the principal mechanisms by which the Act seeks to give effect to Convention rights is set out in section 3(1). This provides that:

> So far as it is possible to do so, primary legislation and subordinate legislation must be read and given effect in a way which is compatible with the Convention rights.

This interpretive obligation applies to *all* legislation, whether enacted before or after the Human Rights Act,[62] and it permits the courts to go far beyond previously accepted limits in seeking 'possible' meanings of words. Once it is established that a provision engages a Convention right, the court must then consider whether it appears on its face to be compatible with that right. Most Convention rights are not absolute and the interference with the right may be a legitimate one: if this is the case the court need do nothing except give effect to the provision in the ordinary way. If, however, the provision appears to be inconsistent with the Convention, section 3 obliges the court to seek a different interpretation.

---

[62] Section 3(2). The impact of the Act on statutory interpretation is discussed further at p 45.

It is important to note that section 3 does not authorize the courts to disapply Acts of Parliament,[63] and it does not affect the validity, continuing operation, or enforcement of any incompatible primary legislation.[64] Nevertheless, it is clear that the interpretive obligation under section 3 is a strong one. In the leading case of *R v A (No 2)*, Lord Steyn explained that:[65]

> It applies even if there is no ambiguity in the language...In accordance with the will of Parliament as reflected in s 3 it will sometimes be necessary to adopt an interpretation, which linguistically may appear strained. The techniques to be used will not only involve the reading down of express language in a statute but also the implication of provisions.

The implications of this approach are potentially dramatic. In *R v A* itself, the disputed provision[66] had been specifically enacted to prevent defendants in sex offence cases from adducing evidence of a complainant's sexual history. Yet in reliance on section 3, the House of Lords interpreted the provision as being subject to an implied discretion to *allow* such evidence in the interests of a defendant's right to a fair trial. Section 3 does have its limits, however, and in other cases the courts have cautioned against reading words into an Act to the point of making it unworkable:[67] '[I]f it is necessary in order to obtain compliance to radically alter the effect of the legislation this will be an indication that more than interpretation is involved.' In *Re S (Children) (Care Order: Implementation of Care Plan)*,[68] the Court of Appeal read words into the Children Act 1989 to create new discretionary powers for the courts to supervise local authority care orders. On appeal, however, the House of Lords rejected this use of section 3 on the basis that it would have undermined a fundamental feature of the 1989 Act: namely, that 'the courts are not empowered to intervene in the way local authorities discharge their parental responsibilities under final care orders'.[69] Their Lordships also noted that the Court of Appeal had failed to identify any specific provision of the Children Act that was capable of being interpreted in the manner suggested.[70] Similarly, in *Bellinger v Bellinger*,[71] the House of Lords held that section 11 of the Matrimonial Causes Act 1973 could not be interpreted so as to allow a male-to-female transsexual to marry a man. Such an interpretation would have represented a major change in the law and would have had far-reaching ramifications that were best left to Parliament to determine.[72]

---

[63] Compare the European Communities Act 1972, s 2(4); discussed further in Chapter 4.

[64] Nor does it affect the validity of incompatible subordinate legislation where primary legislation prevents removal of the incompatibility: s 3(2).

[65] [2001] UKHL 25 at [40], [2002] 1 AC 45 at [40], [2001] 3 All ER 1.

[66] Youth Justice and Criminal Evidence Act 1999, s 41.

[67] *Poplar Housing and Regeneration Community Association Ltd* v *Donoghue* [2001] EWCA Civ 595 at [76], [2002] QB 48 at [76], [2001] 4 All ER 604, *per* Lord Woolf CJ.

[68] [2001] EWCA Civ 757, [2002] 2 FLR 582, [2001] HRLR 50: *sub nom Re W and B (Children) (Care Plan)*.

[69] [2002] UKHL 10 at [42], [2002] 2 AC 291 at [42], [2002] 2 All ER 192, *per* Lord Nicholls.

[70] Ibid, at [43].   [71] [2003] UKHL 21, [2003] 2 AC 467, [2003] 2 All ER 593.

[72] At the time the House of Lords was aware that legislation to remedy the defect was imminent: the government had already accepted that United Kingdom law was in breach of the Convention following the decision in *Goodwin* v *UK* (2002) 35 EHRR 18.

Re S and *Bellinger* v *Bellinger* were initially seen as evidence of a shift away from the 'high-water mark' of *R* v *A* towards a more restrictive approach,[73] but the subsequent decision in *Ghaidan* v *Godin-Mendoza*[74] confirmed that this was not the case. By a majority of four to one, the House of Lords construed provisions in the Rent Act 1977 so as to confer the tenancy rights of spouses on same-sex partners, thus avoiding the conclusion that the Act was incompatible with the non-discrimination requirements in Article 14. Lord Nicholls confirmed that section 3 required a radical approach:[75]

> Section 3 enables language to be interpreted restrictively or expansively...It is also apt to require a court to read in words which change the meaning of the enacted legislation, so as to make it Convention-compliant. In other words, the intention of Parliament in enacting section 3 was that, to an extent bounded only by what is 'possible', a court can modify the meaning, and hence the effect, of primary and secondary legislation.

Lord Nicholls acknowledged that there would inevitably be cases in which a Convention-compliant interpretation was not possible, and both *Re S* and *Bellinger* v *Bellinger* were said to be examples:[76]

> Parliament...cannot have intended that in the discharge of this extended interpretative function the courts should adopt a meaning inconsistent with a fundamental feature of legislation. That would be to cross the constitutional boundary section 3 seeks to demarcate and preserve.

Nevertheless, the majority of the House felt that the Rent Act could be given a Convention-compliant interpretation without crossing this constitutional boundary, and all five Law Lords endorsed the decision in the earlier case of *R* v *A (No 2)*.

By contrast, in *R (on the application of Wilkinson)* v *Inland Revenue Commissioners*, the House of Lords held that a provision of the Income and Corporation Taxes Act 1988 could not be interpreted as applying to 'widowers' as well as 'widows'.[77] Section 262 of the Act stated that 'where a married man whose wife is living with him dies, his widow shall be entitled...to an income tax reduction'. The applicant argued that, as a widower, he should be entitled to the same reduction, but despite endorsing *Ghaidan* v *Godin-Mendoza*, the House of Lords held that it was not possible to interpret the provision in this way:[78]

> [T]here is no way in which any reasonable reader could understand the word 'widow' to refer to the more general concept of a surviving spouse. The contrary indications in the...Act are too strong.

---

[73] Nicol, 'Statutory Interpretation and Human Rights after *Anderson*' [2004] PL 274; cf. Kavanagh, 'Statutory Interpretation and Human Rights after *Anderson*: A More Contextual Approach' [2004] PL 537.

[74] [2004] UKHL 30, [2004] 2 AC 557, [2004] 3 All ER 411: see Van Zyl Smit, 'The New Purposive Interpretation of Statutes: HRA Section 3 after *Ghaidan* v *Godin-Mendoza*' (2007) 70(2) MLR 294.

[75] Ibid at [32].   [76] Ibid at [33].

[77] [2005] UKHL 30, [2005] 1 WLR 1718, [2006] 1 All ER 529.

[78] Ibid at [19], *per* Lord Hoffmann.

It should be noted that extending widow's bereavement allowance to widowers would not, in their Lordship's view, have been sufficient to achieve compliance with the Convention,[79] and their approach to section 3 must be considered in this context. Nevertheless, the decision serves as a reminder that although the interpretative obligation decreed by section 3 is of an 'unusual and far-reaching character',[80] there will always be cases in which a compatible interpretation of legislation is not 'possible'.

More recently, in an approach reminiscent of that taken in *R v A (No 2)*, a majority of the House of Lords held that provisions in the Prevention of Terrorism Act 2005 could be read down so as to ensure compatibility with the right to a fair trial.[81] AF was subject to a control order made on the basis of undisclosed material, and he challenged the order on the grounds that he did not know the nature of the case against him. Their Lordships agreed that the right of a person to be informed of the case against him could be limited in the interests of national security, and that any potential injustice might be mitigated by the use of special advocates or other procedural devices. However, the majority accepted that such devices might not always be sufficient to comply with Article 6, and on this basis they held that that the provisions could, if necessary, be read down so as so take effect only where this would be consistent with fairness.

Sections 4, 5, and 10: Declarations of incompatibility and remedial orders

If a court[82] concludes that a compatible interpretation of a provision is not possible, it may issue a declaration of incompatibility under section 4 of the Act. The effect of a declaration is to bring the matter to the attention of the government so that a change in the law can be considered. It does not affect the validity, continuing operation, or enforcement of the statute, and the court must give effect to the incompatible provision as Parliament intended.[83] Nevertheless, where a court is contemplating such a step, the Crown is entitled to be given notice and the relevant Minister or his nominee is entitled to be joined as a party to the proceedings.[84]

Where a declaration of incompatibility has been made, or where the Strasbourg court has made an equivalent finding, section 10 empowers a Minister to make such

---

[79] The allowance had been abolished altogether before the case even came to court.

[80] *Ghaidan v Godin-Mendoza* [2004] UKHL 30 at [30], [2004] 2 AC 557 at [30], [2004] 3 All ER 411, *per* Lord Nicholls.

[81] *Secretary of State for the Home Department v MB* [2007] UKHL 46, [2007] 3 WLR 681. See also *R v Holding (Terence Anthony)* [2005] EWCA Crim 315, [2006] 1 WLR 1040: provisions on election expenses in the Representation of the People Act 1983 read down so as to comply with Article 10.

[82] For these purposes, the term 'court' covers the Supreme Court, the Judicial Committee of the Privy Council, the Courts-Martial Appeal Court, the Court of Appeal, the High Court, the Court of Protection and the Scottish High Court of Justiciary (except when sitting as a trial court or Court of Session): s 4(5). Even the lower courts are bound by s 3 and may occasionally need to decide that a compatible interpretation of legislation is impossible. However, as they have no power to make formal declarations of incompatibility, such decisions cannot trigger the power to make a remedial order under s 10.

[83] Incompatible *subordinate* legislation may be declared invalid unless primary legislation prevents removal of the incompatibility: s 3(2). In the latter case a declaration of incompatibility may be issued.

[84] Section 5.

amendments to the legislation as he considers necessary to remove the incompatibility. It is important to note that this is a power, not an obligation, and it only arises where the Minister considers that there are 'compelling reasons' for proceeding under this section. The requirement for compelling reasons was inserted during the committee stage in the House of Lords, the idea being to limit this potentially far-reaching power.[85] Ironically, however, it has been argued that the amendment may be to the detriment of human rights if it means that a breach of the Convention goes uncorrected for want of parliamentary time.[86]

So far, relatively few declarations have been made, and some have been overturned on appeal.[87] In *R (on the application of Nasseri) v Secretary of State for the Home Department*, for example, the House of Lords confirmed the Court of Appeal's decision to discharge a declaration of incompatibility made by the High Court.[88] Provisions in the Asylum and Immigration (Treatment of Claimants, etc.) Act 2004 established an irrebuttable presumption that the removal of asylum seekers to countries listed as safe would be lawful. The claimant argued that returning him to Greece would put him at risk of being deported to his native Afghanistan, where he would face inhuman and degrading treatment, and that this was contrary to Article 3. However, the House of Lords declined to reinstate the declaration of incompatibility because there was no evidence that the particular claimant in this case would be at any real risk if deported. Whilst this conclusion may be sound as a finding of fact, it is easy to conceive of a situation in which removal to a 'safe' country *could* put an individual at risk, and given the irrebuttable nature of the presumption it would surely have been open to the House to declare the provision in question incompatible. As Buxton points out, if this approach is followed in other contexts, it will 'limit the use of section 4 as a valuable means of identifying ways in which the domestic law does not meet the requirements of the Convention',[89] and, viewed in this light, the *Nasseri* decision is regrettable.

In *Secretary of State for the Home Department v MB*, Baroness Hale had no doubt that the House of Lords had a duty to avoid making a declaration of incompatibility if at all possible. Having concluded that provisions governing the imposition of control orders could be interpreted in a Convention-compliant manner, she explained why this was desirable:[90]

> [W]hen Parliament passed the [Prevention of Terrorism Act 2005], it must have thought
> that the provisions with which we are concerned were compatible with the Convention

---

[85] Remedial orders are normally subject to affirmative resolution, but this may be avoided if the Minister certifies that a more urgent response is necessary. In the latter case, the remedial order will expire after 120 days unless it has been approved by an affirmative resolution of both Houses: Sch 2.

[86] Wadham and Mountfield, *Blackstone's Guide to the Human Rights Act 1998* (OUP: 2nd edn, 1999), p 49.

[87] See, e.g., *R (on the Application of Alconbury) v Secretary of State for the Environment, Transport and the Regions* [2001] UKHL 23, [2003] 2 AC 295, [2001] 2 All ER 929 (reversing [2001] HRLR 2); *R (on the application of Black) v Secretary of State for Justice* [2009] UKHL 1, [2009] 1 AC 949, [2009] 4 All ER 1 (reversing [2008] EWCA Civ 359, [2008] 3 WLR 845).

[88] [2009] UKHL 23, [2010] 1 AC 1, [2009] 3 All ER 774; [2008] EWCA Civ 464, [2008] 3 WLR 1386.

[89] Buxton, 'The Future of Declarations of Incompatibility' [2010] PL 213, at 221–2.

[90] [2007] UKHL 46 at [73], [2008] 1 AC 440 at [73], [2008] 1 All ER 657.

rights. In interpreting the Act compatibly we are doing our best to make it work. This gives the greatest possible incentive to all parties to the case, and to the judge, to conduct the proceedings in such a way as to afford a sufficient and substantial measure of procedural justice. This includes the Secretary of State, who will, of course, be anxious that the control order be upheld. A declaration of incompatibility, on the other hand, would allow all of them to conduct the proceedings in a way which they knew to be incompatible.

Although critics argue that the courts have sometimes exceeded the permissible bounds of 'interpretation',[91] ministerial comments made during the debates on the Human Rights Bill support the idea that declarations of incompatibility should only be made in exceptional cases:[92]

> [W]e want the courts to strive to find an interpretation of legislation that is consistent with Convention rights, so far as the plain words of the legislation allow, and only in the last resort to conclude that the legislation is simply incompatible with them.

On the other hand, the very existence of section 4 means that Parliament must have envisaged that a compatible interpretation would not always be 'possible'. The danger in placing so much emphasis on section 3 is that the courts may interpret Convention rights quite narrowly, in order to make a finding of compatibility easier. More generally, there is concern that some judges may be too ready to accept that an interference with a right is justifiable, thus avoiding the need to fully engage with either section.

KEY ISSUE

How should section 4 be used, and what is its relationship with section 3? What the limited use of section 4 tells us about the level of human rights protection has been the subject of considerable debate, and much has been written about the extent to which deference plays a part in the courts' decisions.[93] A detailed examination of these issues is beyond the scope of this work, but it is worth remembering that a declaration of incompatibility does not oblige Parliament or the government to take remedial action. If there is a reluctance to use section 4 because of a concern that elected bodies should have the final word on policy matters, it is therefore unwarranted. On the other hand, the desire to avoid declarations is not always due to excessive deference. From a human rights perspective, a declaration of incompatibility may be the least desirable outcome: it will not affect the validity of the legislation and there is no guarantee of remedial action. Even if remedial action is taken, it will not assist those involved in the original case. A compatible interpretation under section 3 is potentially far more powerful because it means *giving effect* to the provision in a Convention-compliant way.

---

[91] See, e.g., Nicol [2004] PL 274; Ekins, 'A Critique of Radical Approaches to Rights Consistent Statutory Interpretation' [2003] EHRLR 641.

[92] Jack Straw MP (Home Secretary), 313 HC Official Report (6th series) cols 421–2, 3 June 1998. In *Ghaidan v Godin-Mendoza* [2004] UKHL 30 at [39], [2004] 2 AC 557 at [39], [2004] 3 All ER 411, Lord Steyn observed that in the first three-and-a-half years of the Human Rights Act there had been at least as many declarations of incompatibility as there had been uses of s 3. On the basis of these statistics, he suggested that the law may have taken 'a wrong turning'.

[93] See p 165.

? Questions

1. What dangers are there if the courts use their section 3 powers widely?

2. Should the courts show 'deference' to elected bodies on human rights matters?

3. Do you think the courts have on occasion exceeded their permissible role?

4. What (if anything) do sections 12 and 13 of the 1998 Act add to the protection already afforded by Articles 10 and 9 of the Convention? Why were they included in the Act?

5. Did the House of Lords in *R v A (No 2)* really adopt a 'possible' interpretation of the disputed provision?

6. Is the fact that there have been so few declarations of incompatibility under section 4 evidence of the success of the Human Rights Act?

7. Does the ministerial obligation to make statements of compatibility under section 19 of the Human Rights Act serve any useful purpose?

Responding to declarations of incompatibility

In respect of the few declarations that have not been successfully challenged, the government has yet to refuse to take remedial action.[94] Thus, provisions of the Immigration and Asylum Act 1999 that were found to be incompatible with the Convention[95] were amended by the Nationality, Immigration and Asylum Act 2002, while laws that breached the Convention rights of transsexuals[96] were amended by the Gender Recognition Act 2004. In some cases, the offending legislation had already been repealed or amended by the time that the matter came to court. Widow's bereavement allowance, for example, was abolished several years before the Court of Appeal declared the relevant provisions incompatible with Article 14.[97] Similarly, provisions denying the possibility of parole to prisoners subject to deportation orders had already been repealed when they were declared incompatible with Articles 5 and 14,[98] although they continue to apply to offences committed before 4 April 2005.[99]

---

[94] The response to such declarations has tended to be very slow, however, and the Strasbourg bodies do not consider a declaration of incompatibility to be an effective remedy for the purposes of Article 13. This may change if evidence of a long-standing and established practice of giving effect to them emerges: *Burden v UK* (2008) 47 EHRR 38, at [42].

[95] *International Transport Roth GmbH* v *Secretary of State for the Home Department* [2002] EWCA Civ 158, [2003] QB 728, [2002] HRLR 31. The provisions imposed a fixed penalty on hauliers responsible for bringing illegal entrants into the United Kingdom and were found to be incompatible with Article 6 and with Article 1 of the First Protocol.

[96] The inability of transsexuals to marry in accordance with their new gender was found to be incompatible with Articles 8 and 12 in *Goodwin* v *UK* (2002) 35 EHRR 18 and *Bellinger* v *Bellinger* [2003] UKHL 21, [2003] 2 AC 467, [2003] 2 All ER 593.

[97] *R (on the application of Wilkinson)* v *Inland Revenue Commissioners* [2003] EWCA Civ 814, [2003] 1 WLR 2683, [2003] 3 All ER 719. Section 262 of the Income and Corporation Taxes Act 1988 was repealed with effect from 2000.

[98] *R (on the application of Clift and others)* v *Secretary of State for the Home Department* [2006] UKHL 54, [2007] 1 AC 484, [2007] 2 All ER 1. The provisions in question were ss 46(1) and 50(2) of the Criminal Justice Act 1991.

[99] Criminal Justice Act 2003 (Commencement No 8 and Transitional and Saving Provisions) Order 2005, SI 2005/950.

A v Secretary of State for the Home Department

The government was presented with perhaps its most difficult Human Rights Act challenge to date by the decision of the House of Lords in *A* v *Secretary of State for the Home Department*.[100] The case was brought by a number of foreign nationals who had been detained without trial for almost three years under powers in the Anti-Terrorism, Crime and Security Act 2001.[101] The purpose of these powers was to enable the government to deal with those foreign nationals who were suspected of involvement in terrorism, but who could not be put on trial and who could not be deported for humanitarian reasons. The government had sought to pre-empt any legal challenge to these powers by derogating from the Article 5 right to liberty and security of the person.[102] However, by a majority of eight to one their Lordships held that by singling out non-nationals for detention, the Act was interfering with the right to liberty in a discriminatory manner and was therefore in breach of both Article 5 and Article 14. The Court of Appeal had taken the view that the difference in treatment was justifiable because foreign nationals, unlike British nationals, had no right to remain in the United Kingdom.[103] In the House of Lords' view, however, the logic of this argument was flawed. Once it was accepted that the threat of terrorism was not confined to non-nationals, the different legal status of such persons could not provide an objective basis for the difference in treatment. A declaration of incompatibility was therefore granted, and the Order dealing with the derogation from Article 5 was quashed. The government did not release the detainees immediately, but it did agree to seek alternative ways of dealing with them. Within three months the internment powers in the 2001 Act had been replaced with a system of 'control orders'. These control orders may involve restricting the movement or communications of suspected terrorists, but crucially they can be used in respect of both nationals and non-nationals.[104] The Home Office also agreed to seek assurances about human rights from other states, so that more suspected foreign terrorists could be deported.[105]

Remedial orders

To date there have been only three occasions on which Ministers have considered it appropriate to make a remedial order under section 10, and only one of these resulted from a decision of a domestic court. The decision in question was a Court of Appeal case in which provisions of the Mental Health Act 1983 were found to be incompatible with the right to liberty under Article 5.[106] The Secretary of State was satisfied in this case that there were compelling reasons for acting quickly, and the offending

---

[100] [2004] UKHL 56, [2005] 2 AC 68, [2005] 3 All ER 169.   [101] Section 23.

[102] The concept of derogation is discussed at p 177. The derogation in question was registered by the Secretariat General on 18 December 2001; SI 2001/4032.

[103] [2002] EWCA Civ 1502, [2004] QB 335, [2003] 1 All ER 816.

[104] Prevention of Terrorism Act 2005.

[105] Charles Clarke MP (Home Secretary), 430 HC Official Report (6th series) col 307, 26 January 2005.

[106] *R (on the application of H)* v *North and East London Regional Mental Health Review Tribunal* [2001] EWCA Civ 415, [2002] QB 1, [2001] 3 WLR 512. The provisions had effectively required a restricted patient seeking release from a secure hospital to prove that his continued detention was no longer warranted.

provisions were amended by the Mental Health Act 1983 (Remedial) Order 2001.[107] The other two remedial orders made so far have followed decisions of the European Court of Human Rights.[108]

Section 19: Ministerial statements of compatibility[109]

The courts may be aided in their efforts under section 3 by ministerial statements made under section 19 of the Act. This provides that before the second reading of a Bill, the Minister in charge of it must either: (a) make a statement that in his view its provisions are compatible with Convention rights; or (b) make a statement that although it is *not* compatible, the government nevertheless wishes to proceed. The purpose of section 19 is presumably to aid the legislative process and to enable incompatible Bills to be subjected to heightened scrutiny. However, governments will inevitably be reluctant to declare that they are advocating Bills that infringe human rights. Indeed, virtually all of the statements made under section 19 have been to the effect that legislation is compatible,[110] and as the section does not require a Minister to explain *how* he arrived at his conclusion, the probative value of these statements is greatly limited. For this reason, they risk being seen as little more than labels of approval, giving no real indication as to the true human rights implications of the Bills concerned.

Much will depend in practice on the willingness of MPs to engage with human rights issues, and to subject ministerial statements to proper scrutiny. The Joint Committee on Human Rights has an important role to play here:[111]

> The Joint Committee ... is able to monitor the operation of section 19 of the HRA speedily and effectively, and reports to each House of Parliament its views as to the compatibility or lack of compatibility of legislative proposals.

The knowledge that a statement of compatibility must be made might also serve to concentrate the Minister's mind during the preparatory stages of a Bill. In addition, section 19 statements may be considered by the courts,[112] and it has been said that they will 'inevitably be a strong spur to the courts to find the means of construing statutes compatibly with the Convention'.[113] They are not, of course, binding, and a ministerial statement of compatibility does not prevent a court from making a declaration of *in*compatibility in the future. Indeed, the courts have so far made section 4 declarations

---

[107] SI 2001/3712.

[108] The Naval Discipline Act 1957 (Remedial) Order 2004, SI 2004/66, was introduced following the decision in *Grieves* v *UK* (2004) 39 EHRR 2. The Marriage Act 1949 (Remedial) Order 2007, SI 2007/438, followed the decision in *B and L* v *United Kingdom* (2006) 42 EHRR 11.

[109] See also, p 64.

[110] The knowledge that provisions of the Anti-Terrorism, Crime and Security Bill would almost certainly be *in*compatible led to a derogation from Article 5: see the discussion of *A* v *Secretary of State for the Home Department* [2004] UKHL 56, [2005] 2 AC 68, [2005] 3 All ER 169, above.

[111] Lester, 'Parliamentary Scrutiny under the Human Rights Act 1998' [2002] 4 EHRLR 432, at 437.

[112] *Wilson* v *First County Trust (No 2); sub nom Wilson* v *Secretary of State for Trade and Industry* [2003] UKHL 40 at [61]–[67], [2004] 1 AC 816 at [61]–[67], [2003] 4 All ER 97, *per* Lord Nicholls.

[113] Lord Irvine of Lairg, 'The Development of Human Rights in Britain under an Incorporated Convention on Human Rights' [1998] PL 221.

in respect of two statutes enacted since the Human Rights Act came into force,[114] both of which were judged to be compatible with human rights by the Ministers who introduced them. Nevertheless, the ministerial statement may give tacit encouragement to the judiciary to maximize the interpretive obligation under section 3. After all, if a Minister considers a Bill to be compatible, and Parliament enacts it on that basis, it might be suggested that Parliament must intend a compatible interpretation to be found. Baroness Hale may have been alluding to this when suggesting in *MB*[115] that Parliament must have thought the Prevention of Terrorism Act 2005 to be compatible with Convention rights, although she did not refer specifically to section 19.

Ironically, in the only case so far in which a Minister has felt unable to make a statement of compatibility, a court has subsequently found the statute concerned to be Convention-compliant. The Communications Act 2003 prohibits political advertising in broadcasting, and this is at odds with the decision of the Court of Human Rights in *VgT* v *Switzerland*.[116] On this basis, the Minister introducing the Bill felt unable to make a statement of compatibility, although she made it clear that she did not consider an incompatible interpretation to be inevitable.[117] In a subsequent challenge to the provisions, the House of Lords refused to make a declaration of incompatibility, holding that the restriction on freedom of expression fell within the United Kingdom's margin of appreciation. Lord Bingham attached 'great weight' to the fact that: [118]

> Parliament has resolved ... that the prohibition of political advertising on television and radio may possibly, although improbably, infringe article 10 but has none the less resolved to proceed under section 19(1)(b) of the Act. It has done so, while properly recognising the interpretative supremacy of the European court, because of the importance which it attaches to maintenance of this prohibition. The judgment of Parliament on such an issue should not be lightly overridden.

Direct enforcement of Convention rights

Section 6: The duty of public authorities to act compatibly with the ECHR

Section 6(1) of the Act makes it unlawful for a public authority to act in a way that is incompatible with a Convention right. However, the authority will have a defence under section 6(2) if it can be shown that:

(a) as the result of one or more provisions of primary legislation, the authority could not have acted differently; or

---

[114] Section 23 of the Anti-Terrorism, Crime and Security Act 2001 (*A* v *Secretary of State for the Home Department* [2004] UKHL 56, [2005] 2 AC 68, [2005] 3 All ER 169); and s 19(3) of the Asylum and Immigration (Treatment of Claimants etc.) Act 2004 (*R (on the application of Baiai)* v *Secretary of State for the Home Department* [2008] UKHL 53, [2009] 1 AC 287, [2008] 3 All ER 1094.

[115] *Secretary of State for the Home Department* v *MB* [2007] UKHL 46 at [73], [2007] 3 WLR 681 at [73].

[116] *VgT Verein gegen Tierfabriken* v *Switzerland* (2002) 34 EHRR 4.

[117] Tessa Jowell, MP (Secretary of State for Culture, Media and Sport), 395 HC Official Report (6th series) col 789, 3 December 2002. See further, p 65.

[118] *R (on the application of Animal Defenders International)* v *Secretary of State for Culture, Media and Sport* [2008] UKHL 15 at [33], [2008] 1 AC 1312 at [33], [2008] 3 All ER 193.

(b) in the case of one or more provisions of, or made under, primary legislation which cannot be read or given effect in a way which is compatible with the Convention rights, the authority was acting so as to give effect to or enforce those provisions.

Section 6(3) makes it clear that neither House of Parliament constitutes a public authority for these purposes, and persons exercising functions in connection with proceedings in Parliament are also excluded. However, courts and tribunals are expressly *in*cluded within the definition, and thus have an obligation to perform their functions in a manner compatible with Convention rights.

Identifying public authorities

The Act takes a functional approach to the meaning of 'public authority', and this means that even seemingly 'private' bodies may be subject to the Act if certain of their functions are public in nature.[119] A person or body may fall into one of three categories for these purposes: (1) 'standard' public authorities, that must act compatibly with the Convention at all times; (2) 'hybrid' or 'quasi-public' bodies, which are only caught by the Act when performing their public functions; and (3) private bodies, which are not subject to the duty under section 6(1) at all. The first category includes bodies such as government departments, the police, and local authorities, which are all self-evidently public in nature and present relatively few difficulties. The precise scope of the second category is rather more complex, and predictably the courts have drawn upon principles that were already established in the field of judicial review.[120] In one of its early Human Rights Act decisions, the Court of Appeal held that a registered social landlord was subject to section 6 in respect of its relationship with its tenants. The fact that the landlord performed functions that a public authority would otherwise have to carry out was relevant but not conclusive:[121]

> What can make an act, which would otherwise be private, public, is a feature or a combination of features which impose a public character or stamp on the act. Statutory authority for what is done can at least help to mark the act as being public; so can the extent of control over the function exercised by another body which is a public authority. The more closely the acts that could be of a private nature are enmeshed in the activities of a public body, the more likely they are to be public.

It was considered relevant that the housing association had been specifically created to take over a large proportion of residential council property.[122] It was also in receipt of state funding, had various statutory duties, and was supervised by a statutory body. However, in the subsequent *Aston-Cantlow* decision, the House of Lords held that

---

[119] Section 6(3)(b).

[120] See, e.g., *R v Panel on Takeovers and Mergers, ex parte Datafin* [1987] QB 815, [1987] 1 All ER 564.

[121] *Poplar Housing and Regeneration Community Association Ltd* v *Donoghue* [2001] EWCA Civ 595 at [65], [2002] QB 48 at [65], [2001] 4 All ER 604.

[122] See also *R (on the application of Beer (t/a Hammer Trout Farm))* v *Hampshire Farmers Markets Ltd* [2003] EWCA Civ 1056, [2004] 1 WLR 233: a company created by a local authority to manage a farmers' market was deemed to be exercising public functions when licensing stall-holders.

a parochial church council was not performing public functions when exercising a statutory power to compel a landowner to repair a church chancel:[123]

> It may be said that, as the church is a historic building which is open to the public, it is in the public interest that these repairs should be carried out. It is also true that the liability to repair the chancel rests on persons who need not be members of the church…But… [t]he nature of the act is to be found in the nature of the obligation which the PCC is seeking to enforce. It is seeking to enforce a civil debt. The function which it is performing has nothing to do with the responsibilities which are owed to the public by the State.

The decision in YL v Birmingham[124]

The *Aston-Cantlow* case was the House of Lords' first opportunity to comment on the meaning of 'public authority', and although the decision was welcomed by some[125] it was also criticized for failing to make any express reference to *Poplar*.[126] As a result, there is still some confusion as to where the line between hybrid and purely private bodies might be drawn, and the recent House of Lords decision in *YL* v *Birmingham* has done little to clarify matters.

The issue in *YL* was whether a private care home was subject to duties under section 6 when providing care and accommodation under a contract with a local authority. By a majority of three to two the House of Lords held that it was not.[127] All of the opinions emphasized the importance of a functional approach, and some expressly criticized the importance attached to institutional relationships in *Poplar*.[128] However, the conclusion of the majority was that the provision of care and accommodation in such cases is not an 'inherently governmental function',[129] and on this basis, the owners of the care home were held not to be exercising functions of a public nature.

KEY ISSUE

The decision in *YL* v *Birmingham* has only served to fuel the debate about the scope of section 6. Of the two dissenting judges, Baroness Hale had 'no doubt' that Parliament had

---

[123] *Aston-Cantlow and Wilcote with Billesley Parochial Church Council* v *Wallbank* [2003] UKHL 37 at [64], [2004] 1 AC 546 at [64], [2003] 3 All ER 1213, *per* Lord Hope. Other bodies deemed not to be public authorities include Network Rail (*Cameron* v *Network Rail Infrastructure Ltd (formerly Railtrack plc)* [2006] EWHC 1133 (QB), [2007] 1 WLR 163, [2007] 3 All ER 241), and Lloyd's (*R (on the application of West)* v *Lloyd's of London* [2004] EWCA Civ 506, [2004] 3 All ER 251).

[124] [2007] UKHL 27, [2008] 1 AC 95, [2007] 3 All ER 957.

[125] Meisel, 'The *Aston-Cantlow Case*: Blots on English Jurisprudence and the Public / Private Law Divide' [2004] PL 2.

[126] See Quane, 'The Strasbourg Jurisprudence and the Meaning of a '"Public Authority" Under the Human Rights Act' [2006] PL 106.

[127] In doing so their Lordships endorsed a similar decision made by the Court of Appeal in respect of a charitable foundation: *R (on the application of Heather)* v *Leonard Cheshire Foundation* [2002] EWCA Civ 366, [2002] 2 All ER 936.

[128] Baroness Hale, for example, stated at [61] that the Court of Appeal had 'relied too heavily upon the historical links between the local authority and the registered social landlord'.

[129] [2007] UKHL 27 at [115], [2007] 3 WLR 112 at [115], [2007] 3 All ER 957, *per* Lord Mance.

intended care homes to be subject to the Human Rights Act,[130] while Lord Bingham agreed that the position on this matter was 'clear'.[131] By contrast, two of the majority opinions gave weight to the contractual and commercial motives of the care providers,[132] apparently adding another factor to the equation. The decision was widely criticized for unduly restricting the potential reach of the Human Rights Act,[133] and following *YL*, Landau suggested that registered social landlords such as those in *Poplar* were unlikely to be treated as having public functions in future.[134] It is perhaps surprising then that the Court of Appeal subsequently deemed a housing trust to be a hybrid public authority that was performing an act of a public nature when terminating a tenancy agreement.[135] Elias LJ identified a range of factors that, 'when considered cumulatively … establish sufficient public flavour to bring the provision of social housing [within the concept of "public function"]'.[136] These included the fact that the housing trust operated in close harmony with local government, placed significant reliance on public finance, had charitable objectives, and performed the 'governmental' function of providing social housing:[137]

> In my judgement, the act of termination is so bound up with the provision of social housing that once the latter is seen…as the exercise of a public function, then acts which are necessarily involved in the regulation of the function must also be public acts. The grant of a tenancy and its subsequent termination are part and parcel of determining who should be allowed to take advantage of this public benefit. This is not an act which is purely incidental or supplementary to the principal function, such as contracting out the cleaning of the windows of the Trust's properties. That could readily be seen as a private function of a kind carried on by both public and private bodies.

The previous government considered that *YL* took a much narrower approach to 'public authority' than Parliament had originally intended, and sought to reverse the immediate impact of the case by legislating to bring the provision of publicly arranged care and accommodation within the scope of section 6(3)(b).[138] However, its commitment to looking at the problem of how 'public authority' should be defined more generally never came to fruition,[139] and a private member's Bill aimed at addressing the same issue was also unsuccessful.[140]

---

[130] Ibid, at [73].   [131] Ibid, at [2].

[132] Ibid, at [31] *per* Lord Scott, and at [116] *per* Lord Mance.

[133] See, e.g., Palmer, 'Public Functions and Private Services: A Gap in Human Rights Protection' (2008) 6 IJCL 585; Williams, '*YL* v *Birmingham City Council*: Contracting Out and "Functions of a Public Nature"' [2008] EHRLR 524.

[134] Landau, 'Functional Public Authorities after *YL*' [2007] PL 630, at 633.

[135] *R (on the application of Weaver)* v *London & Quadrant Housing Trust* [2009] EWCA Civ 587, [2010] 1 WLR 363, [2009] 4 All ER 962.

[136] Ibid, at [72].   [137] Ibid, at [77].

[138] Health and Social Care Act 2008, s 145(1).

[139] See Ministry of Justice, *The Human Rights Act 1998: The Definition of "Public Authority"—Government Response to the Joint Committee on Human Rights' Ninth Report of Session 2006–07*, Cm 7726 (HMSO, Oct 2009).

[140] The Human Rights Act 1998 (Meaning of Public Function) Bill, introduced by Andrew Dismore MP, had its first reading in the House of Commons on 18 December 2007.

> **?** **Questions**
>
> 1. How should the term 'public authority' be defined and applied?
> 2. What do you think the consequences of the *YL* decision might be?
> 3. Should those in receipt of publicly funded care and accommodation ever have been in a more advantageous position with regard to human rights than those cared for on a private basis?

Judicial deference and proportionality

In determining whether public authorities have acted in breach of Convention rights, the courts are required to assess the legitimacy of any interference with those rights and to measure the extent of the interference against the yardstick of proportionality. This concept is discussed further at p 176, but in essence it means that a balance must be struck between the general interests of the community and the rights of the individual,[141] and that any restriction on a right must be limited to the extent necessary to achieve a legitimate aim. The House of Lords confirmed at an early stage that the actions of public authorities in Human Rights Act cases must be measured against this principle of proportionality:[142]

> First, the doctrine of proportionality may require the reviewing court to assess the balance which the decision maker has struck, not merely whether it is within the range of rational or reasonable decisions. Secondly, the proportionality test may go further than the traditional grounds of review inasmuch as it may require attention to be directed to the relative weight accorded to interests and considerations. Thirdly...the intensity of the review...is guaranteed by the twin requirements that the limitation of the right was necessary in a democratic society, in the sense of meeting a pressing social need, and the question whether the interference was really proportionate to the legitimate aim being pursued.

These principles require a different level of scrutiny to that traditionally applied in judicial review cases, and the debate about how much judicial deference should be paid to the executive in human rights cases is ongoing.[143] In *R (on the application*

---

[141]   *Soering* v *UK* (1989) 11 EHRR 439.

[142]   *R (on the application of Daly)* v *Secretary of State for the Home Department* [2001] UKHL 26 at [27], [2001] 2 AC 532 at [27], [2001] 3 All ER 433, *per* Lord Steyn. A blanket policy authorizing searches of a prisoner's cell and requiring his correspondence with his lawyer to be examined in his absence was *not* a proportionate response to the legitimate objective of maintaining prison discipline. (Judicial review is discussed further in Chapter 7.)

[143]   See: Allan, 'Human Rights and Judicial Review: A Critique of Due Deference' (2006) 65(3) CLJ 671; Clayton, 'Judicial Deference and "Democratic Dialogue": The Legitimacy of Judicial Intervention under the Human Rights Act 1998' [2004] PL 33; Edwards, 'Judicial Deference under the Human Rights Act' (2002) 65 MLR 859; Jowell, 'Judicial Deference: Servility, Civility or Institutional Incapacity?' [2003] PL 592; Kavanagh, 'Judging the Judges under the Human Rights Act: Deference, Disillusionment and the "War on Terror"' [2009] PL 287; Morris, 'Separating Human Rights Adjudication from Judicial Review' [2007] EHRLR 679; and Steyn, 'Deference: A Tangled Story' [2005] PL 346. See also, p 327.

of ProLife Alliance) v *BBC*, Lord Walker endorsed an earlier attempt by Laws LJ to establish some general principles:[144]

(1) greater deference is to be paid to an Act of Parliament than to a decision of the executive or subordinate measure;

(2) there is more scope for deference where the Convention itself requires a balance to be struck, much less so where the right is stated in terms which are unqualified;

(3) greater deference will be due to the democratic powers where the subject-matter in hand is peculiarly within their constitutional responsibility, and less when it lies more particularly within the constitutional responsibility of the courts;

(4) greater or less deference will be due according to whether the subject matter lies more readily within the actual or potential expertise of the democratic powers or the courts.

The courts have certainly taken a more 'interventionist' stance under the 'due process' rights in Articles 5 and 6, which might be regarded as falling within their particular sphere of expertise. Thus, in *A* v *Secretary of State for the Home Department*,[145] which concerned the right to liberty under Article 5, Lord Bingham stated that the courts were not 'precluded by any doctrine of deference from scrutinising the issues raised', even though those issues included decisions about national security. On the other hand, the courts have tended to concede a wider margin of discretion under Articles such as 8 and 10, which require individual rights to be balanced against the public interest and which leave more scope for restrictions on policy grounds. In the light of these principles, Lord Hoffmann has taken exception to the word 'deference' being used at all:[146]

> I do not think that its overtones of servility, or perhaps gracious concession, are appropriate to describe what is happening... The principle that the independence of the courts is necessary for a proper decision of disputed legal rights or claims of violation of human rights is a legal principle. It is reflected in Article 6 of the Convention. On the other hand, the principle that majority approval is necessary for a proper decision on policy or allocation of resources is also a legal principle. Likewise, when a court decides that a decision is within the proper competence of the legislature or executive, it is not showing deference. It is deciding the law.

Horizontal effect

In keeping with the scheme of the Convention, the Act does not oblige private bodies and individuals to act compatibly with Convention rights, and it does not expressly

---

[144] [2003] UKHL 23 at [136], [2004] 1 AC 185 at [136], [2003] 2 All ER 977 (applying the judgment of Laws LJ in *International Transport Roth GmbH* v *Secretary of State for the Home Department* [2002] EWCA Civ 158, [2003] QB 728, [2002] HRLR 31).

[145] [2004] UKHL 56 at [29] and [42], [2005] 2 AC 68 at [29] and [42], [2005] 3 All ER 169; see further pp 159 and 189.

[146] *R (on the application of ProLife Alliance)* v *BBC* [2003] UKHL 23 at [75]–[76], [2004] 1 AC 185 at [75]–[76], [2003] 2 All ER 977. See also the comments of a unanimous House of Lords in *Huang* v *Secretary of State for the Home Department* [2007] UKHL 11 at [16], [2007] 2 AC 167 at [16], [2007] 4 All ER 15.

require the courts to give effect to the Convention in developing the common law. However, given that the courts are clearly under a general duty to perform their functions in accordance with the Convention, there was much academic speculation from the outset about whether the Human Rights Act would have 'indirect horizontal effect'.[147] In other words, would the courts be obliged to give effect to the Convention in developing the common law, and would this mean that Convention rights could be directly enforced against private individuals?

It soon became apparent that Convention rights and principles would have an influence on judicial reasoning in common law cases. For example:[148]

> If there is an intrusion in a situation in which a person can reasonably expect his privacy to be respected then that intrusion will be capable of giving rise to liability in an action for breach of confidence unless the intrusion can be justified.

Thus far, however, the courts have stopped short of recognizing any new common law torts, preferring instead to take the Convention into account when applying established torts such as breach of confidence and nuisance. Thus, in *Wainwright* v *Home Office*, the House of Lords held that a new tort of privacy could only be recognized by Parliament, but that the courts could develop existing torts and remedies in order to satisfy Article 8.[149]

Section 7: Challenging public authorities under the Act

Proceedings under the Act and the 'victim' test

Where a person claims that a public authority has acted (or is proposing to act) in breach of Convention rights, proceedings may be brought against that authority under section 7(1)(a) of the Act. However, such proceedings can only be brought by a person who is able to show that he is (or would be) 'a victim of the unlawful act'. This is consistent with the criteria for bringing a Strasbourg application under Article 34 of the Convention, but it is rather stricter than the 'sufficient interest' test applied in conventional judicial review cases.[150] Public interest groups with a particular interest and expertise may have standing to bring a judicial review action on conventional grounds, but they will not be considered 'victims' under the Human Rights Act

---

[147] Buxton, 'The Human Rights Act and Private Law' (2000) 116 LQR 48; Hunt, 'The "Horizontal Effect" of the Human Rights Act' [1998] PL 424; Phillipson, 'The Human Rights Act: "Horizontal Effect" and the Common Law: A Bang or a Whimper?' (1999) 62(2) MLR 825; Wade, 'Horizons of Horizontality' (2000) 116 LQR 217.

[148] *A* v *B; H* v *Associated Newspapers* [2002] EWCA Civ 337 at [11], [2003] QB 195 at [11], [2002] 2 All ER 545, *per* Lord Woolf CJ. See also *Douglas* v *Hello! Ltd (No 1)* [2001] QB 967, [2001] 2 All ER 289; *Venables and Thompson* v *News Group Newspapers* [2001] Fam 430, [2001] 1 All ER 908.

[149] [2003] UKHL 53, [2004] 2 AC 406, [2003] 4 All ER 969; cf. *Peck* v *UK* (2003) 36 EHRR 41, which revealed significant deficiencies in the ability of domestic law to safeguard the right to respect for private life: see p 201.

[150] See, e.g., *R* v *Inspectorate of Pollution, ex parte Greenpeace (No 2)* [1994] 4 All ER 329; *R* v *Secretary of State for Foreign and Commonwealth Affairs, ex parte World Development Movement* [1995] 1 WLR 386, [1995] 1 All ER 611. See also Marriott and Nicol, 'The Human Rights Act, Representative Standing and the Victim Culture' [1998] EHRLR 730.

unless they are actually affected by a Convention breach. The government considered that the Strasbourg approach would help to prevent the courts from becoming clogged up with test cases, and it rejected the suggestion that the 'victim' test could lead to injustice:[151]

> If there is an unlawful action or if unlawful action is threatened, then there will be victims or potential victims who will complain and who will in practice be supported by interest groups. If there are no victims, the issue is probably academic and the courts should not be troubled.

In addition to being able to bring a direct action under section 7(1)(a), whether in the form of judicial review proceedings or an action for breach of statutory duty under section 6(1), section 7(1)(b) also allows a victim (or potential victim) of a Convention breach to raise the issue in proceedings that have been commenced on some other basis. Thus, a Convention issue may be raised by a party to a civil action involving a public authority, by a defendant in a criminal case, or by an applicant in a judicial review action based on other grounds. However, a 'judicial act' of a court or tribunal may only be challenged in judicial review proceedings or during the course of an appeal.[152] In addition, section 7(3) states that:

> If the proceedings are brought on an application for judicial review, the applicant is to be taken to have a sufficient interest in relation to the unlawful act only if he is, or would be, a victim of that act.

This provision is designed to prevent public interest groups from circumventing the victim requirement by raising Convention issues in judicial review proceedings brought on other grounds. Nevertheless, a court conducting a judicial review of statutory powers will be obliged to seek a Convention-friendly interpretation of those powers, even if the applicant is not a 'victim'.[153] It would also appear that if a court accepts a judicial review application from a public interest group, it will be obliged to act compatibly with the Convention when conducting that review, in order to fulfil its own obligations under section 6.

KEY ISSUE

The scope of the Convention is affected not only by the definition of who may bring a claim against a public authority, but also whether horizontal effect is given to the Act.

---

[151] Lord Irvine (Lord Chancellor), 583 HL Official Report (5th series) col 832, 24 November 1997.
[152] Section 9(1).
[153] See, e.g., *R (on the application of Rusbridger)* v *Attorney-General* [2003] UKHL 38, [2004] 1 AC 357, [2003] 3 All ER 784. The House of Lords confirmed that the editor of *The Guardian* did not need to be a 'victim' in order to seek a declaration that s 3 of the Treason Felony Act 1848 was incompatible with the Convention. However, the action failed because the provision had not actually been applied and the issue was purely hypothetical: see p 206.

> **? Questions**
>
> 1. Has the Human Rights Act resulted in the creation of new private law rights?
> 2. Is the 'victim' test under section 7 of the Act an important mechanism for preventing frivolous claims or simply an unnecessary impediment to the development of human rights?

The Equality and Human Rights Commission

The Equality and Human Rights Commission was established under section 1 of the Equality Act 2006. Its statutory remit is to encourage and support the development of a society in which, amongst other things, there is respect for and protection of each individual's human rights, and respect for the dignity and worth of each individual.[154] More specifically, section 9(1) of the Equality Act provides that the Commission shall: (a) promote understanding of the importance of human rights; (b) encourage good practice in relation to human rights; (c) promote awareness, understanding and protection of human rights; and (d) encourage public authorities to comply with section 6 of the Human Rights Act. To this end it has been given a range of legal powers, including the power to intervene in litigation or to commence judicial review proceedings in its own name.[155] In exercising these powers the Commission is entitled to rely on section 7(1)(b) of the Human Rights Act, although it can only act if there is or would be one or more victims of the unlawful act complained of.[156]

Time limits

Actions for judicial review must normally be brought within three months,[157] whereas section 7(5) of the Human Rights Act specifies a one-year time limit for actions brought under section 7(1)(a).[158] In this respect, an applicant whose complaint is based solely on a breach of Convention rights appears to be in a better position than an applicant seeking review on both Convention and non-Convention grounds. In *A* v *Essex County Council*, the Supreme Court dismissed an application to extend the one-year time limit in respect of an autistic boy who claimed that his right to education under Article 2 of the First Protocol had been denied. In reaching this conclusion, the majority of the court took into account the fact that the claimant was highly unlikely to have been awarded any significant sum in damages, even if his case had been brought within time and had been successful.[159] Lady Hale, however, felt that the nine-month delay in this case was not long given that the claim related to the past (and was not

---

[154] Section 3.
[155] Section 30. The Commission can also provide legal assistance to individuals binging proceedings under equality legislation (s 28), but significantly there is no equivalent power in relation to human rights.
[156] Section 30(3).   [157] See p 511.
[158] The courts have a discretion to allow a longer period if it is considered equitable.
[159] [2010] UKSC 33 at [169], [2010] 3 WLR 509 at [169], [2010] 4 All ER 199, *per* Lord Kerr JSC.

seeking a remedy for the future), and that the delay was partly due to funding difficulties and did not appear to have prejudiced the defendant.[160]

Retrospective application

Section 7(6) confirms that Convention issues may be raised in proceedings brought by or at the instigation of a public authority, or in any appeal against the decision of a court or tribunal. Most of the Act's provisions did not come into force until 2 October 2000, and a section 7 claim may only be brought against a public authority in respect of acts occurring on or after this date. However, section 22(4) states that where proceedings are instigated or brought by a public authority, a breach of the Convention may be challenged under section 7(1)(b) whenever the act in question took place. In other words, a demonstrator arrested for a public order offence in September 2000 would have been entitled to raise issues based on Articles 10 or 11 in the course of his defence. In *R* v *Lambert*,[161] the House of Lords gave a restrictive interpretation to this provision and held that where a person had actually been tried and convicted before the commencement of the Act, pre-commencement breaches of the Convention could not be raised in a subsequent appeal. Within months a differently constituted House suggested that *Lambert* had been wrongly decided, but it was nevertheless unwilling to overrule the decision.[162]

Section 8: Remedies

Where a court or tribunal has found that a public authority has acted unlawfully under section 6(1), it may grant 'such relief or remedy, or make such order within its powers as it considers just and appropriate'.[163] An award of damages can only be made by a court that already has the power to award damages in civil proceedings,[164] and only where the court is satisfied that an award is necessary to afford 'just satisfaction'.[165] In exercising the power to award damages a court must take into account the principles applied by the European Court of Human Rights under Article 41 of the Convention,[166] which itself tends to adopt a fairly conservative approach. Having reviewed the Strasbourg authorities, the House of Lords in *R (on the application of Greenfield)* v *Secretary of State for the Home Department* indicated that, in an Article 6 case, the finding of a breach of Convention rights would often be an adequate remedy in itself:[167]

> [T]he Court [of Human Rights] has ordinarily been willing to depart from its practice of finding a violation of Art.6 to be, in itself, just satisfaction under Art.41 only where the Court finds a causal connection between the violation found and the loss for which an applicant claims to be compensated...and [it] has on the whole been slow to award such compensation.

---

[160] Ibid, at [113]–[117].   [161] [2001] UKHL 37, [2002] 2 AC 545, [2001] 3 All ER 577.

[162] *R* v *Kansal (No 2)* [2001] UKHL 62, [2002] AC 69, [2002] 1 All ER 257.

[163] Section 8(1). For a discussion see: Hartshorne, 'The Human Rights Act 1998 and Damages for Non-Pecuniary Loss' [2004] EHRLR 660; Clayton, 'Damage Limitation: the Courts and the Human Rights Act Damages' [2005] PL 429.

[164] Section 8(2).   [165] Section 8(3).   [166] Section 8(4).

[167] [2005] UKHL 14 at [11], [2005] 1 WLR 673 at [11], [2005] 2 All ER 240, *per* Lord Bingham (with whom the other Law Lords agreed).

Lord Bingham rejected the defendant's assertion that awards under section 8 should compare favourably with tortious awards, and he held that in normal circumstances the Strasbourg approach should be followed:[168]

> First, the 1998 Act is not a tort statute. Its objects are different and broader. Even in a case where a finding of violation is not judged to afford the applicant just satisfaction, such a finding will be an important part of his remedy and an important vindication of the right he has asserted... Secondly, the purpose of the 1998 Act was not to give victims better remedies at home than they could recover in Strasbourg, but to give them the same remedies without the delay and expense.

The discretionary nature of the power to award damages was emphasized in *R (on the application of Faulkner)* v *Secretary of State for Justice*, and it was pointed out in this case that there may be circumstances in which *any* award of damages would be inequitable.[169] The claimant in this case was a prisoner who had absconded whilst on bail, and it was held that even if his claim had been successful he would not have been entitled to damages. In *Dobson* v *Thames Water Utilities,* the Court of Appeal held that where an award of damages had been made at common law for the tort of nuisance, this would normally constitute just satisfaction for the purposes of Article 41, and no further award of damages for any human rights infringement should be necessary. This was so despite the fact that damages in nuisance were normally awarded as damages to 'land'.[170]

In its 2006 *Review of the Implementation of the Human Rights Act*, the Department for Constitutional Affairs noted that section 8 had been interpreted 'so strictly' that 'it is now very difficult to obtain damages under the HRA'.[171] Indeed, in the five-and-a-half-year period covered by the Review there were only three reported cases in which damages under section 8 were awarded, and in one of these the finding of liability has since been overturned.[172]

Section 9(3) of the Act states that courts and tribunals cannot be liable in damages for judicial acts done in good faith unless there has been a breach of Article 5(5). Where there has been such a breach, the award must be made against the Crown and the 'appropriate person'[173] must be joined to the proceedings.

---

[168] Ibid, at [19]; cf. *Anufrijeva* v *Southwark LBC* [2003] EWCA Civ 1406, [2004] QB 1124, [2004] 1 All ER 833.

[169] [2009] EWHC 1507 (Admin).   [170] [2009] EWCA Civ 28, [2009] 3 All ER 319.

[171] (HMSO, July 2006), at p 18.

[172] Ibid: *R (Bernard)* v *Enfield London Borough Council* [2002] EWHC 2282 (Admin), [2003] HRLR 4 (£8,000 awarded to a disabled claimant required to live in unsuitable accommodation for twenty months); *R (on the application of KB)* v *Mental Health Review Tribunal* [2003] EWHC 193 (Admin), [2004] QB 936, [2003] 2 All ER 209 (damages ranging from £750 to £4,000 awarded following delays to tribunal hearings); and *Van Colle* v *Chief Constable of Hertfordshire* [2006] EWHC 360 (QB), [2006] 3 All ER 963 (damages of £50,000 awarded to parents of a witness murdered following inadequate police protection—overturned on appeal [2008] UKHL 50, [2009] 1 AC 225, [2008] 3 All ER 977).

[173] The 'appropriate person' is defined by s 9(5) to mean 'the Minister responsible for the court concerned, or a person or government department nominated by him'.

A British bill of rights?

Four years before the 2010 election, the *Review of the Implementation of the Human Rights Act* by the Department for Constitutional Affairs concluded that the effect of the Act 'has been far from marginal, and has involved the courts in a much more active and intense scrutiny of the Executive' than had been required prior to October 2000.[174] As Klug explains, the Act has been 'rather too successful at challenging the executive for the government's comfort',[175] and decisions on human rights have been at the centre of much of the recent tension between the courts and the government. The Act has been widely misunderstood and misinterpreted by both public servants and the public in general,[176] and even politicians have occasionally succumbed to some of the urban myths surrounding its impact. For example, whilst still in opposition, David Cameron gave a speech to the Police Federation in which he made reference to 'a series of disgraceful incidents', including 'prisoners given access to pornography' and 'burglars given Kentucky Fried Chicken'.[177] In fact, a challenge to a decision to deny a prisoner access to pornography was thrown out at the application stage, while the decision to supply a burglar with fast food was part of a routine negotiating strategy designed to coax him down from the roof where he had taken refuge. It was, in any event, a decision taken by the police rather than the courts.[178]

Against this background it is perhaps not surprising that some have called for the Act to be amended or repealed, and in 2006 David Cameron announced that his party would, if elected to government, seek to replace it with a 'British' bill of rights more 'in tune with British traditions about liberty'.[179] At the time Labour Ministers were also hinting at the possibility of making changes to the Act—almost invariably when judicial decisions had gone against them[180]—but outright repeal was never suggested as official government policy. The DCA's Review restated the government's commitment to the ECHR and the Human Rights Act, and listed several reasons why repeal of the Act had been 'comprehensively and publicly ruled out':[181]

> [Any attempt at repeal] is likely at best to be fruitless and at worst to introduce a damaging conflict with a judiciary unwilling to see the common law divorced from the protection

---

[174] At p 35.

[175] 'A Bill of Rights: Do We Need One or Do We Already Have One?' [2007] PL 701 at 714. See also Amos, 'Problems with the Human Rights Act 1998, and How to Remedy Them: Is a Bill of Rights the Answer?' (2009) 72(6) MLR 883.

[176] DCA, *op cit*, at ch 4. An example cited at p 31 of the *Review* is the widespread, but false, assumption that the Act makes it unlawful to film school nativity plays.

[177] Cited in JUSTICE, *A British Bill of Rights: Informing the Debate* (2007) at p 14.

[178] DCA, *op cit*, at pp 30–1.

[179] Reported in *The Observer*, 4 November 2007.

[180] While still prime minister, for example, Tony Blair suggested that there was a case for reviewing the Act (reported in *The Guardian*, 15 May 2006). His comments followed a High Court ruling preventing nine Afghan hijackers from being deported: *R (on the application of S) v Secretary of State for the Home Department* [2006] EWHC 1111 (Admin), The Times, 14 June 2006. The decision was subsequently affirmed by the Court of Appeal: EWCA Civ 1157, The Times, 9 October 2006.

[181] DCA, *op cit*, at p 38.

of fundamental rights. It would also, probably, increase further the scrutiny received by the UK at Strasbourg.

However, the Review also suggested that 'in a number of key areas, and particularly when public safety is in issue, key decision takers may be getting the balance wrong by placing undue emphasis upon the entitlements of individuals'.[182] The then government subsequently decided to join the bill of rights bandwagon, but instead of calling for the Human Rights Act to be scrapped, it proposed that it should be supplemented by a 'British Bill of Rights and Responsibilities':[183]

> [Such a Bill] could provide explicit recognition that human rights come with responsibilities and must be exercised in a way that respects the human rights of others. It would build on the basic principles of the Human Rights Act, but make explicit the way in which a democratic society's rights have to be balanced by obligations.

KEY ISSUE

Not all of those who support the idea of a bill of rights are motivated by a desire to qualify the scope of existing protection. JUSTICE, for example, has added its voice to the campaign for such an instrument, suggesting that the government should consider: whether any rights not covered by the 1998 Act 'are now ripe for inclusion'; whether a different model of entrenchment could be adopted; and whether the existing mechanisms for enforcement are satisfactory.[184]

With the change of government following the 2010 elections, the future of the Human Rights Act itself may be in question. In June 2010 the newly formed Conservative–Liberal Democrat coalition government appeared to have reached a compromise position and announced plans to establish a Commission:[185]

> We will establish a Commission to investigate the creation of a British Bill of Rights that incorporates and builds on all our obligations under the ECHR, ensures that these rights continue to be enshrined in British law, and protects and extends British liberties. We will seek to promote a better understanding of the true scope of these obligations and liberties.

No specific time frame for this process has been given, and 'the Commission is widely viewed as a means of deferring indefinitely this contentious area of policy'.[186] The future of the Human Rights Act therefore remains uncertain, but whatever the outcome of the current debate it is likely that its impact will prove to be irreversible.

❓ Questions

1. Do we need a British bill of rights?
2. Should the Human Rights Act be 'scrapped'?

[182] Ibid, at p 39.
[183] *The Governance of Britain*, Cm 7170 (HMSO, 2007), at [210]; for discussion see Le Sueur, 'Gordon Brown's New Constitutional Settlement' [2008] PL 21.
[184] JUSTICE, *op cit*, at p 16.
[185] HM Government, *The Coalition: Our Programme for Government* (HMSO, 2010), at p 11.
[186] Donald, 'A Bill of Rights for the UK? Why the Process Matters' [2010] EHRLR 459 at 459.

Further reading

Beloff and Mountfield, 'Unconventional Behaviour? Judicial Uses of the European Convention in England and Wales' [1996] EHRLR 467

Clayton, 'Judicial Deference and "Democratic Dialogue": The Legitimacy of Judicial Intervention under the Human Rights Act 1998' [2004] PL 33

Department for Constitutional Affairs, *Review of the Implementation of the Human Rights Act* (HMSO, 2006)

Edwards, 'Judicial Deference under the Human Rights Act' (2002) 65 MLR 859

Hunt, 'The "Horizontal Effect" of the Human Rights Act' [1998] PL 424

Jowell, 'Judicial Deference: Servility, Civility or Institutional Incapacity?' [2003] PL 592

Landau, 'Functional Public Authorities after *YL*' [2007] PL 630

Morris, 'Separating Human Rights Adjudication from Judicial Review' [2007] EHRLR 679

Quane, 'The Strasbourg Jurisprudence and the Meaning of a "Public Authority" under the Human Rights Act' [2006] PL 106

Wade, 'Horizons of Horizontality' (2000) 116 LQR 217

Convention Rights[1]

INTRODUCTION

This chapter focuses on the rights protected by the European Convention on Human Rights and given effect in domestic law by the Human Rights Act 1998. The specific areas covered will include:

- the general characteristics of the rights protected;
- the concepts of proportionality and the margin of appreciation;
- derogation;
- the scope of specific rights and their impact at both Strasbourg and domestic level;
- the European Court of Human Rights and its role in enforcing the Convention.

The nature of the rights protected

The Convention only imposes obligations on states and it is not possible to bring an action against a private individual at Strasbourg level. However, where an individual interferes with a Convention right, the state may be liable if it has failed to take appropriate steps to protect that right or if it has failed to provide an adequate remedy. In *Earl Spencer* v *UK*,[2] for example, the European Court of Human Rights was prepared to consider a claim based on alleged breaches of privacy by several newspapers, because the applicant had made an arguable case that United Kingdom law did not protect individual rights of privacy.

Most Convention rights are not absolute. Although the rights to freedom from torture and slavery are unqualified and non-derogable,[3] the other rights are subject to

---

[1] See Harris, O'Boyle and Warbrick, *Law of the European Convention on Human Rights* (OUP: 2nd edn, 2009); Janis, Kay and Bradley, *European Human Rights Law: Text and Materials* (OUP: 3rd edn, 2008); Van Dijk et al, *The Theory and Practice of the European Convention on Human Rights* (Intersentia: 4th edn, 2006); Mowbray, *Cases and Materials on the European Convention on Human Rights* (OUP: 2nd edn, 2007); Ovey and White (eds), *Jacobs and White: European Convention on Human Rights* (OUP: 5th edn, 2010).

[2] (1998) 25 EHRR CD 105. The claim was ultimately unsuccessful because the applicants failed to demonstrate the inadequacy of domestic law. See also, *Halford* v *UK* (1997) 24 EHRR 523.

[3] See below.

certain limitations. The doctrines of proportionality and the margin of appreciation are both important in determining the permissible extent of these limitations.[4]

Proportionality[5]

Inherent in the Convention is the principle that a fair balance must be struck between the general interests of the community and the individual's fundamental rights.[6] Where limitations on specific rights are permitted, they are usually expressed to be subject to a requirement of necessity, and this is given effect in the courts' jurisprudence by the application of the principle of proportionality. For example, Article 10(2) states that any limitation on the right to freedom of expression must go no further than is 'necessary in a democratic society'. In other words, the restriction must conform to a 'pressing social need' and the interference must be proportionate to the legitimate aim pursued.[7]

This principle applies equally to the other qualified rights in the Convention. Thus, in *Dudgeon* v *UK*,[8] laws criminalizing homosexual acts between consenting adult males infringed the Article 8 right to respect for private life because they failed the test of proportionality. This was so notwithstanding the fact that the state was pursuing the 'legitimate aim' of protecting vulnerable young members of society. The House of Lords has confirmed that the actions of public authorities in Human Rights Act cases must be measured against the principle of proportionality, and this involves a different level of scrutiny to that traditionally applied in judicial review cases.[9]

The margin of appreciation

The 'margin of appreciation' describes the degree of deference shown to states in areas in which there is room for discretion in the interpretation of Convention provisions. It arises most often in the context of the 'personal freedom' provisions in Articles 8–11,[10] since these are subject to a range of possible exceptions and there is room for disagreement about their scope. The principle was clearly articulated in the *Handyside* case:[11]

> By reason of their direct and continuous contact with the vital forces of their countries, State authorities are in principle in a better position than the international judge to give

---

[4] For the application of the concept of proportionality in EU law, see p 117.

[5] See Blake, 'Importing Proportionality: Clarification or Confusion?' [2002] EHRLR 19; Hickman, 'The Substance and Structure of Proportionality' [2008] PL 694.

[6] *Soering* v *UK* (1989) 11 EHRR 439.

[7] See *Sunday Times* v *UK* (1979–1980) 2 EHRR 245; *Handyside* v *UK* (1979) 1 EHRR 737.

[8] (1982) 4 EHRR 149.

[9] *R (on the application of Daly)* v *Secretary of State for the Home Department* [2001] UKHL 26, [2001] 2 AC 532, [2001] 3 All ER 433: see the quotation from this decision at p 165.

[10] See Yourow, *The Margin of Appreciation Doctrine in the Dynamics of European Human Rights Jurisprudence* (1996).

[11] *Handyside* v *UK* (1979) 1 EHRR 737 at para [48].

an opinion on the exact content of these requirements as well as on the 'necessity' of a 'restriction' or 'penalty' intended to meet them.

The existence or non-existence of common ground between the states is an important factor in determining the extent of any national margin,[12] but not everyone sees the doctrine as an appropriate response to European diversity. Lewis, for example, warns that it is 'intellectually lazy' to rely on the doctrine as a way of avoiding difficult issues,[13] and Jones argues that its use 'can only...devalue Convention rights and freedoms at the expense of the limitations'.[14] In a partly dissenting judgment in *Z* v *Finland*, De Meyer J stated that:[15]

> [W]here human rights are concerned, there is no room for a margin of appreciation which would enable the states to decide what is acceptable and what is not. On that subject the boundary not to be overstepped must be as clear and precise as possible. It is for the Court, not each state individually to decide that issue.

Domestic courts are not required to apply Convention rights to a diverse group of states, and the margin of appreciation doctrine therefore has no application in Human Rights Act cases.[16] However, the role of the courts in reviewing public authority decisions is essentially a supervisory one, and even though decisions affecting human rights are subject to a heightened standard of judicial scrutiny, those charged with making those decisions are still afforded a measure of discretion. This is particularly relevant in cases that involve questions of proportionality or competing rights, and in such cases the decision-maker will be allowed 'an area of judgment comparable to the margin of appreciation'.[17]

Derogation

Most Convention rights are subject to the possibility of derogation in times of war or other public emergency.[18] The United Kingdom entered a derogation in respect of Article 5 following the decision[19] that provisions of the Prevention of Terrorism (Temporary Provisions) Act 1984 were in breach of the Convention. At the time, the United Kingdom deemed the situation in Northern Ireland to constitute an 'emergency threatening the life of the nation', and the European Court of Human Rights

---

[12] *Rasmussen* v *Denmark* (1984) 7 EHRR 371.

[13] Lewis, 'What Not to Wear: Religious Rights, the European Court, and the Margin of Appreciation' [2007] ICLQ 395, at 414; cf. Schokkenbroek, 'The Basis, Nature and Application of the Margin of Appreciation Doctrine in the Case Law of the European Court of Human Rights' (1998) 19(1) HRLJ 30; Letsas, 'Two Concepts of the Margin of Appreciation' (2006) 26(4) OJLS 705.

[14] 'The Devaluation of Human Rights Under the European Convention' [1995] PL 430, at 449.

[15] (1997) 25 EHRR 371 at 415.

[16] *R (on the application of Begum)* v *Denbigh High School* [2006] UKHL 15 at [63], [2007] 1 AC 100 at [63], [2006] 2 All ER 487, *per* Lord Hoffmann.

[17] Ibid at [64].

[18] Derogation from Articles 3, 4(1) and 7 is not possible, and Article 2 is only derogable in respect of 'deaths resulting from lawful acts of war'.

[19] *Brogan* v *UK* (1989) 11 EHRR 117.

was not prepared to disagree with this assessment.[20] The provisions were eventually replaced by more stringent measures in the Terrorism Act 2000 and the derogation was withdrawn in February 2001. However, in December of the same year, the United Kingdom once again derogated from Article 5 in respect of the newly enacted power[21] to detain suspected foreign terrorists without trial. The public emergency this time was said to stem from the heightened threat of terrorism in the wake of 9/11 and the presence of suspected international terrorists in the United Kingdom.[22] When this derogation was challenged, a majority of the House of Lords accepted the government's assertion that the United Kingdom was facing a public emergency, but in doing so they demonstrated far less deference than that previously exhibited by the Court of Human Rights:[23]

> The courts' power to rule on the validity of the derogation is another of the safeguards [contained in the Human Rights Act 1998]...It would be meaningless if we could only rubber-stamp what the Home Secretary and Parliament have done. But any sensible court, like any sensible person, recognises the limits of its expertise. Assessing the strength of a general threat to the life of the nation is, or should be, within the expertise of the Government and its advisers...Protecting the life of the nation is one of the first tasks of a Government in a world of nation states. That does not mean that the courts could never intervene. Unwarranted declarations of emergency are a familiar tool of tyranny. If a Government were to declare a public emergency where patently there was no such thing, it would be the duty of the court to say so. But we are here considering the immediate aftermath of the unforgettable events of 11 September 2001...

It was held that the government had failed to demonstrate the need to single out foreign nationals for detention in circumstances in which British nationals posed an equally serious threat. The derogation was thus incompatible with the Convention, and the government's derogation order[24] was quashed. The European Court of Human Rights has since confirmed that this case was correctly decided.[25]

KEY ISSUE

The extent to which the Court of Human Rights permits signatory states a margin of appreciation is crucial in the interrelationship between the Court of Human Rights and the United Kingdom courts. In Chapter 5 we saw the issues that arise in the context of how

[20] *Brannigan and McBride* v *UK* (1994) 17 EHRR 539.
[21] Anti-Terrorism, Crime and Security Act 2001, s 23. The power was limited to circumstances in which the suspect could not be deported because of the risk that he or she would face persecution or torture.
[22] Declaration registered by the Secretariat General on 18 December 2001.
[23] *A* v *Secretary of State for the Home Department* [2004] UKHL 56 at [226], [2005] 2 WLR 87 at [226], *per* Baroness Hale. Lord Hoffman dissented on this point, stating at [96] that 'terrorist violence, serious as it is, does not threaten our institutions of government or our existence as a civil community'. Judicial deference under the 1998 Act is discussed at p 165.
[24] Human Rights Act (Amendment No 2) Order 2001, SI 2001/4032. Further derogations are contemplated by the Prevention of Terrorism Act 2005, although none have been made to date. See further, p 189.
[25] *(A)* v *UK* (2009) EHRR 29.

section 2 of the Human Rights Act 1998 is to be used. A wide margin of appreciation may permit a United Kingdom court to put a distinctly British interpretation on Convention rights, and avoid conflict between the courts at Strasbourg and those in the United Kingdom. Conversely, narrow approaches to the concept may mean continuing stresses between Strasbourg and the United Kingdom. Cases such as *Marper* v *United Kingdom*[26] and *Connors* v *United Kingdom*[27] demonstrate this. More fundamentally, questions arise as to what extent signatory states should have a margin of appreciation at all?

❓ Questions

1. Why does the concept of margin of appreciation exist?
2. Given that most Convention rights may be subject to lawful restrictions on a wide range of different grounds, is the power of a state to derogate from Convention rights really necessary or desirable?

Specific rights

Article 2: The right to life

This states that 'everyone's right to life shall be protected by law' and that 'no-one shall be deprived of his life intentionally save in the execution of a sentence of a court following his conviction of a crime for which this penalty is provided by law'. This form of words originally allowed states to retain the use of capital punishment, but the possibility of imposing the death penalty in peace time has effectively been removed by Protocol 6. Acceptance of this Protocol is now mandatory,[28] and as of 1 August 2010, only Russia had still to ratify it. Forty-two states, including the United Kingdom, had also ratified the more extensive provisions in Protocol 13, which bans the use of the death penalty in *any* circumstances.

Lethal force

The remaining limitations on the right to life permit the use of force where this is necessary to defend a person from unlawful violence, to effect a lawful arrest, to prevent the escape of a lawfully detained person, or to quell a riot or insurrection. In *McCann* v *UK*,[29] the SAS shot and killed three members of the Provisional IRA who were suspected of planning a terrorist attack in Gibraltar. Although the court accepted that force had been used in pursuit of a legitimate aim, it found a violation of the Convention because it was not persuaded that the use of lethal force had been

---

[26] (2009) 48 EHRR 50. See p 203.   [27] (2005) 40 EHRR 9. See p 200.
[28] Parliamentary Assembly, Resolution 1044 (1994).
[29] (1996) 21 EHRR 97. See also *Kelly* v *UK* (1993) 74 D & R 139 (use of fatal force against a 'joyrider' at an army checkpoint).

absolutely necessary.[30] Where a state is mounting a legitimate security operation, a breach of Article 2 will be established if the state does not take all reasonable precautions to avoid or minimize loss of life.[31] However, no violation was found in *Stewart v UK*[32] when a teenager was killed by plastic baton rounds fired into a crowd during a riot. Similarly, no violation was found in *R (on the application of DaSilva)* v *DPP*, which concerned the decision not to prosecute firearms officers who fatally shot an innocent man in the mistaken belief that he was a suicide bomber.[33] The Code for Crown Prosecutors, which requires prosecutors to be satisfied that there is a 'realistic prospect of conviction' before commencing proceedings, was held to be compatible with Article 2, and it had been properly applied in this case.

A duty to investigate deaths

Article 2 imposes a procedural obligation to investigate deaths caused by state action or while the deceased was in the state's care. A duty to investigate will also arise where a death occurs in suspicious and unexplained circumstances, regardless of whether the state is implicated in actually causing that death.[34] In *Jordan* v *UK*,[35] the Court of Human Rights ruled that the holding of an inquest did not discharge this obligation because it was not a forum for determining the identity or culpability of those responsible for causing death. This decision triggered the government's *Review of Coroner Services*,[36] along with several domestic cases. In the leading case of *Middleton*, it was held that an inquest would be sufficient to meet the United Kingdom's obligations under Article 2 as long as the requirement to ascertain 'how' a person died[37] was interpreted to mean 'by what means *and in what circumstances*'. The issue in each case is whether the verdicts available to the jury and the questions put to them enable them to express their conclusions on all major factual issues.[38] Thus, in *R (on the application of Amin)* v *Secretary of State for the Home Department*,[39] an inquest was held to be an inadequate forum to investigate the death of a prisoner at the hands of his racist cellmate. An inquest into the death of a prisoner suffering from heroin withdrawal was also unsatisfactory, because the jury was not invited to consider a verdict of

---

[30] Compare *Brady* v *UK* (2001) ECHR 55151/00: the police shooting of an unarmed robbery suspect did not give rise to an admissible Article 2 claim because the officer had genuinely and reasonably believed that the suspect was reaching for a gun.

[31] *Ergi* v *Turkey* (2001) 32 EHRR 18.   [32] (1985) 7 EHRR CD 453.

[33] [2006] EWHC 3204 (Admin). The office of the Metropolitan Police Commissioner was prosecuted under health and safety legislation.

[34] *Rantsev* v *Cyprus and Russia* (2010) 51 EHRR 1.

[35] (2003) 37 EHRR 2 (an unarmed member of the Provisional IRA shot by RUC officers): see Ní Aoláin, 'Truth Telling, Accountability and the Right to Life in Northern Ireland' [2002] EHRLR 572.

[36] See p 272.   [37] Coroners' Rules 1984, r 36(1)(b).

[38] *R (on the application of Middleton)* v *HM Coroner for West Somerset* [2004] UKHL 10, [2004] 2 AC 183, [2004] 2 All ER 465.

[39] [2003] UKHL 51, [2004] 1 AC 653, [2003] 4 ALL ER 1264. See also *R on the application of Khan)* v *Secretary of State for Health* [2003] EWCA Civ 1129, [2004] 1 WLR 971, [2003] 4 All ER 1239 (Article 2 breached by failure to provide funds enabling Khan to be legally represented at his daughter's inquest). These decisions prompted an amendment to the exceptional funding provisions in the Access to Justice Act 1999.

systemic neglect.[40] Similarly, a breach of Article 2 was established in *Finucane* v *UK*, because allegations of RUC collusion in the murder of a solicitor were not properly investigated.[41]

Overseas conflicts

There is a growing body of case law examining the Article 2 implications of the United Kingdom's military operations in Iraq. The ECHR only obliges states to secure Convention rights and freedoms to those 'within their jurisdiction', and several recent cases have confirmed that British soldiers are only subject to ECHR protection whilst on territory over which the United Kingdom has effective control. Thus, in *R (on the application of Smith)* v *Oxfordshire Assistant Deputy Coroner*,[42] the Supreme Court held that although British soldiers serving overseas are subject to the control and authority of the United Kingdom wherever they might be, they are only protected by the Convention whilst they are on military bases or other places within the United Kingdom's territorial jurisdiction. Moreover, the investigative duty under Article 2 is not automatically engaged each time a soldier dies whilst on active service because such fatalities do not in themselves raise an inference of breach of duty on the part of the state. On the facts of the case in question however, a coroner had heard evidence suggesting that a soldier's death may be attributable to a failure to protect military personnel from the risks posed by the extreme temperatures in which they had to serve, and this necessitated an Article 2 investigation.

Jurisdictional issues were also central to the decision in *Al-Skeini*, which was a judicial review case brought by the relatives of six Iraqi civilians who lost their lives at the hands of British soldiers. One of those civilians, Mr Baha Mousa, had been beaten to death whilst in a military detention unit. The others were shot and killed during military operations in Basra. The House of Lords held that whilst Mr Mousa had been within United Kingdom jurisdiction at the relevant time, because he had died as the result of misconduct that took place within a British military base, the other five civilians were not subject to protection under the Convention.[43] The European Court of Human Rights has since confirmed that those detained in British military bases fall within United Kingdom jurisdiction by reason of the 'total and exclusive... control exercised by the United Kingdom authorities over the premises in question'.[44] Finally, in *R (on the application of Gentle)* v *Prime Minister*, the House of Lords held that there is no obligation under Article 2 for the government to satisfy itself as to the legality of overseas military operations. There was therefore no basis for granting judicial

---

[40] *R (on the application of Davies)* v *HM Deputy Coroner for Birmingham* [2003] EWCA Civ 1739, [2004] HRLR 13: a finding of accidental death had been reached.

[41] (2003) 37 EHRR 29.

[42] [2010] UKSC 29, [2010] 3 All ER 1067, [2010] 3 WLR 223. See also *Bankovic* v *Belgium* (2007) 44 ECHR SE5.

[43] *R (Al Skeini)* v *Secretary of State fot Defence (The Redress Trust Intervening)* [2007] UKHL 26, [2008] AC 153, [2007] 3 All ER 685.

[44] *Al Saadoon and Mufdhi* v *UK* (2009) 49 EHRR SE 95, at [88].

review of the government's decision not to order an independent inquiry into the circumstances leading up to the invasion of Iraq.[45]

Protecting life

In *Osman* v *UK*,[46] the Court of Human Rights confirmed that Article 2 may impose a positive duty on states to protect life. The case challenged the failure of the police to arrest a teacher who was known to have formed an obsessive attachment to a former pupil. The teacher later shot and killed the boy's father, and although the Court found no breach of Article 2 on the facts, it indicated that the United Kingdom *would* have been liable if the applicants had been able to establish that:[47]

> [T]he authorities knew or ought to have known at the time of the existence of a real and immediate risk to the life of an identified individual or individuals... and that they failed to take measures within the scope of their powers which, judged reasonably, might have been expected to avoid that risk.

The *Osman* ruling influenced the decision to grant injunctions to the killers of James Bulger upon their release from prison, as the court was satisfied that they would face a real threat of revenge attacks if details of their whereabouts and new identities were published.[48] On similar grounds the House of Lords has emphasized that the right to life must underpin any determination of asylum applications.[49] In general, however, a failure to *protect* life will only breach Article 2 if the authorities knew or should have known of an imminent and specific threat in circumstances in which they can be said to have assumed responsibility for protecting the person at risk. In *Mitchell* v *Glasgow City Council*, it was held that the defendants did not have a duty to warn a tenant that his neighbour may become violent after being threatened with eviction. Foreseeability was not the only issue, and given the nature of the relationship between the parties it would not be fair, just, or reasonable to hold the defendant liable for the deceased's death.[50] Similarly, in *Van Colle*, the House of Lords reversed an award of damages made to the parents of a man who was murdered for refusing to drop the charges against someone who had stolen from him.[51] In the view of their Lordships it could not be said that the police should have anticipated a 'real and imminent' threat to the man's life. In *Younger* v *UK*,[52] a failure to prevent a suicide in police custody did not violate the right to life because the police had no prior knowledge that the deceased was a suicide risk. In *Savage*, however, a failure to prevent the suicide of a paranoid schizophrenic detained under the Mental Health Act 1983 did give rise to a breach of Article 2.[53]

---

[45] [2008] UKHL 20, [2008] AC 1356, [2008] 3 All ER 1.   [46] (2000) 29 EHRR 245.

[47] Ibid at [116].

[48] *Venables and Thompson* v *News Group Newspapers* [2001] Fam 430, [2001] 1 All ER 908.

[49] *R (on the application of Sivakumar)* v *Home Secretary* [2003] UKHL 14, [2003] 2 All ER 1097, [2003] 1 WLR 840.   [50] [2009] UKHL 11, [2009] 1 AC 874, [2009] 3 All ER 205.

[51] *Van Colle* v *Chief Constable of Hertfordshire* [2008] UKHL 50, [2009] 1 AC 225, [2008] 3 All ER 977.

[52] (2003) 36 EHRR CD 252.

[53] *Savage* v *South Essex Partnership NHS Foundation Trust* [2008] UKHL 74, [2009] 1 AC 681, [2009] 1 All ER 1053. See also *Edwards* v *UK* (2002) 35 EHRR 19 (failure to protect a mentally ill prisoner from being kicked to death by his cellmate).

End-of-life decisions

Finally, the Court of Human Rights[54] has confirmed the decision in *R (on the application of Pretty) v DPP*[55] that Article 2 does not guarantee the right to end life. The applicant had motor neurone disease and wanted to end her life so as to avoid further suffering and loss of dignity. However, she was physically unable to commit suicide alone and the DPP refused to undertake not to prosecute her husband if he assisted. The DPP has since published a 'Policy for Prosecutors in respect of Cases of Encouraging or Assisting Suicide', after being ordered by the House of Lords to clarify his position.[56] Both the House of Lords and the Strasbourg court have stressed that Article 2 is concerned with the protection of life and does not confer a right to die It does not, however, prevent a state from permitting the carrying out of lawful abortions,[57] nor does it prevent surgery to separate conjoined twins that will inevitably result in the death of one of them, but which is necessary to preserve the life of the other.[58]

KEY ISSUE

The scope of the Convention is clearly crucial. Right-to-life issues raises profound social, moral and political dilemmas, as the debates about euthanasia or assisted suicide clearly demonstrate.

To extend the operation of the Convention generally to activities such as those conducted in Iraq raises major issues as to how far the military should, in a situation of armed conflict, be subject to judicial oversight on Human Rights Act grounds. The distinctions drawn by the cases discussed above strike a balance between loss of life in conflict and death of individuals in custody or whilst subject to the control of British forces. However, the decisions in *Smith* and *Gentle* go to the heart of what many would see to be a tension between judicial and political accountability—namely, how far decisions to go to war, and how war is conducted, are suitable for or subject to judicial oversight.

❓ Questions

1. To what extent should it be possible for Convention rights to be relied upon by soldiers and civilians affected by overseas conflicts?

2. Should the right to life in Article 2 of the ECHR include a right to end life?

---

[54] *Pretty v UK* (2002) 35 EHRR 1. Mrs Pretty died from her illness twelve days after this decision. For an extended analysis, see Morris, 'Assisted Suicide under the European Convention on Human Rights: A Critique' [2003] EHRLR 65.

[55] [2001] UKHL 61, [2002] 1 AC 800, [2002] 1 All ER 1.

[56] *R (on the application of Purdy) v DPP* [2009] UKHL 45, [2010] 1 AC 345, [2009] HRLR 32. The Policy was published in February 2010.

[57] *Open Door Counselling v Ireland* (1993) 15 EHRR 244.

[58] *Re A (Children) (Conjoined Twins: Surgical Separation)* [2001] Fam 147, [2000] 4 All ER 961.

Article 3: The prohibition of torture and inhuman or degrading treatment

Article 3 is concerned with different levels of ill treatment. 'Degrading treatment' is treatment that grossly humiliates a person beyond the level of humiliation inherent in any punishment, or which drives him to act against his own will or conscience. 'Inhuman treatment' involves causing physical or mental suffering, while 'torture' is an aggravated form of deliberate inhuman treatment causing 'very serious and cruel suffering'.[59] Article 3 has been used on several occasions to provide a standard against which the treatment of suspects and prisoners can be judged. In *Ireland* v *UK*, the use of certain interrogation techniques on suspected terrorists was found to constitute degrading treatment.[60] Article 3 was also breached in *Keenan* v *UK*,[61] when the authorities failed to provide adequate medical care to a mentally ill prisoner who eventually committed suicide. In another important decision, the House of Lords has held that a court must refuse to admit any evidence that it is satisfied was obtained under torture.[62]

As with the right to life there are some circumstances in which Article 3 imposes a positive obligation to investigate alleged breaches, and in *Mousa* v *Secretary of State for Defence*, 102 Iraqis were granted permission to seek judicial review of the government's failure to hold a public inquiry into allegations of systemic ill-treatment on the part of British soldiers.[63] The positive obligations imposed by Article 3 have also been addressed in several immigration and asylum cases. Thus, in *Chahal* v *UK*, it was held that to deport a Sikh separatist leader to India, in the face of a real risk that he would be ill-treated, would amount to a violation of Article 3.[64] In *R (on the application of Q)* v *Secretary of State for the Home Department*, it was held that certain procedural safeguards must be met before late asylum seekers could lawfully be deprived of state support,[65] and in *R (on the application of Limbuela)* v *Secretary of State for the Home Department*, it was held that the withdrawal of support would breach Article 3 if it

---

[59] *Ireland* v *UK* (1979) 2 EHRR 25.

[60] Ibid. Detainees were forced to wear hoods, to stand in stress positions, to go without food, drink and sleep for long periods, and to endure loud and continuous noise. In some cases the treatment of prisoners has been sufficiently cruel and severe to constitute torture: see *Aydin* v *Turkey* (1998) 25 EHRR 251 (the rape of a detainee by an official); *Aksoy* v *Turkey* (1997) 23 EHRR 553 (being stripped naked, hung by the arms, beaten and subjected to electric shocks).

[61] (2001) 33 EHRR 38 (an Article 2 claim failed); cf. *R* v *Drew* [2003] UKHL 25, [2003] 4 All ER 557, [2003] 1 WLR 1213.

[62] *A* v *Secretary of State for the Home Department (No 2)* [2005] UKHL 71, [2006] 2 AC 221, [2006] 1 All ER 575.

[63] [2010] EWHC 1823 (Admin). Two ongoing inquiries were not deemed to be sufficiently effective and independent.

[64] (1996) 23 EHRR 413. See also *Hilal* v *UK* (2001) 33 EHRR 2.

[65] [2003] EWCA Civ 364, [2004] QB 36, [2003] 2 All ER 905. Support was denied under the Nationality, Immigration and Asylum Act 2002 on the grounds that the applicants did not claim asylum as soon as reasonably practicable after arrival.

resulted in an asylum seeker being left destitute.[66] Article 3 was also the basis of a successful challenge to the designation of Pakistan as a safe third country.[67]

The Article has also been used in more novel ways. In has been held, for example, that it may be breached by deporting an AIDS sufferer to a country with inadequate medical facilities,[68] or by extraditing a man to a country where he could face the death penalty.[69] In *Ahmad, Ahsan and Mustafa v UK*, diplomatic assurances were sufficient to remove the risk that Abu Hamza and others would face the death penalty or be designated as enemy combatants if extradited to the USA to face terrorism charges. However, it was held that the possibility of the applicants being detained under very harsh conditions in a 'supermaximum prison' if convicted *did* give rise to an admissible complaint under Article 3.[70] Article 3 has even been considered in the context of a failure to protect an applicant from domestic violence,[71] and in relation to the use of corporal punishment in schools[72] and homes.[73] Finally, in *R (on the application of Foster) v Governor of Highdown Prison,* the High Court firmly rejected the idea that Article 3 had been breached by the short-term withdrawal of tobacco privileges from a detainee at a young offender institution.[74]

Article 4: The prohibition of slavery and forced labour

Few cases have arisen under Article 4 and until recently none had been successful. However, in *Siliadin v France*, a Togolese national established a breach of the Article after enduring four years of domestic slavery.[75] She was aged just 15 when she arrived in France, and having had her passport confiscated by her employer she was sent to work for a family who made her work fifteen-hour days with little rest and no pay. France was held to be in breach of Article 4 because of a failure adequately to safeguard her rights. In an earlier case a lawyer had unsuccessfully challenged an obligation to do pro bono work: his claim failed because he knew when he became a barrister that this would be expected.[76] A more novel use of Article 4 came in a recent case on compulsory jury service. Although it was not suggested that this amounted to a breach of Article 4 itself, the fact that the burden of jury service was inequitably distributed

---

[66] [2005] UKHL 66, [2006] 1 AC 396, [2007] 1 All ER 951.

[67] *R v Secretary of State for the Home Department, ex parte Javed* [2001] EWCA Civ 789, [2002] QB 129.

[68] *D v UK* (1997) 24 EHRR 423.   [69] *Soering v UK* (1989) 11 EHRR 439. C

[70] (2010) 51 EHRR SE6.

[71] *Z v UK* (2002) 34 EHRR 3 (failure to remove children from a home in which they were known to be neglected and abused).

[72] *Tyrer v UK* (1979–1980) 2 EHRR 1; *Costello-Roberts v UK* (1995) 19 EHRR 112.

[73] *A v UK* (1999) 27 EHRR 611; *R v H (Reasonable Chastisement)* [2001] EWCA Crim 1024, [2001] 2 FLR 431, [2002] 1 Cr App R 7; Rogers, 'A Criminal Lawyer's Response to Chastisement in the European Court of Human Rights' [2002] Crim LR 98.

[74] [2010] EWHC 2224 (Admin).

[75] (2006) 43 EHRR 16; see Mantouvalou, 'Servitude and Forced Labour in the 21st Century: the Human Rights of Domestic Workers (2006) 35(4) ILJ 395.

[76] *Van der Mussele v Belgium* (1984) 6 EHRR 163.

between the sexes meant that there had been a breach of Article 14 when read along-side the prohibition on forced labour.[77]

Following the important decision in *Rantsev* v *Cyprus* and *Russia*,[78] Article 4 may be used more widely in the future in the context of human trafficking. In this case the European Court of Human Rights ruled that states are obliged to have adequate criminal law measures in place to deal with the problem of trafficking. Cyprus was found to be in breach of Article 4 because its visa system was not robust enough to provide effective protection for women who, like the applicant's daughter, travelled to Cyprus on artiste visas. Significantly, the Court also ruled that where there is a specific, known risk of exploitation to a particular individual, Article 4 imposes a duty on states to take any necessary operational steps to protect that individual, as well as a procedural obligation to investigate a situation in which trafficking is thought to have occurred.

Article 5: The right to liberty and security of the person

Article 5 provides that no one shall be deprived of his liberty save in accordance with a procedure prescribed by law for one of the purposes specified in Article 5(1). The Article then lists a number of procedural safeguards for the benefit of those lawfully detained: an arrested person must be informed promptly of the reasons for his deten-tion in a language that he understands, and he must be brought promptly before a judge. A detainee is also entitled to trial within a reasonable time, or to release pending trial, and he must have the right to challenge his detention.

Policing decisions

The purposes for which a person can be legitimately deprived of his liberty under Article 5 include: (a) detention after conviction; (b) arrest or detention for failing to comply with a court order or legal obligation; and (c) arrest or detention for the pur-pose of bringing a person before a competent legal authority on reasonable suspicion of having committed an offence. With regard to the latter, the requirement for 'reason-able suspicion' is an essential safeguard against arbitrary detention. An 'honest belief' that an offence has been committed will not suffice,[79] and a police officer cannot sim-ply assume that his superiors must have had reasonable grounds for suspicion when acting on instructions to make an arrest.[80] On the other hand, the Strasbourg court has held the power to arrest for breach of the peace to be compatible with Article 5 even though breach of the peace is not 'an offence'.[81]

---

[77] *Adami* v *Malta* (2007) 44 EHRR 3.   [78] (2010) 51 EHRR 1.

[79] *Fox, Campbell and Hartley* v *UK* (1991) 13 EHRR 157; cf. *Murray* v *UK* (1995) 19 EHRR 193 (mere sus-picion sufficient in circumstances in which officers could demonstrate an objective basis).

[80] *Raissi* v *Commissioner of Police of the Metropolis* [2008] EWCA Civ 1237, [2009] QB 564, [2009] 3 All ER 14.

[81] *Steel* v *UK* (1999) 28 EHRR 603: see *Williamson* v *Chief Constable of West Midlands* [2003] EWCA Civ 337, [2004] 1 WLR 14. Detention for longer than necessary to prevent an imminent breach of the peace or to bring a person before magistrates will be unlawful: *R (on the application of Laporte)* v *Chief Constable of*

In *R (on the application of Gillan)* v *Commissioner of Police for the Metropolis*, the House of Lords held that stop-and-search powers do not normally engage Article 5 at all because the period of detention involved is so brief.[82] Similarly, in *Austin* v *Commissioner of Police of the Metropolis*, their Lordships found no breach of Article 5 when a demonstrator was detained within a police cordon for seven hours as part of a crowd control strategy.[83] When the *Gillan* decision was challenged in Strasbourg, however, the Court of Human Rights adopted a broader approach to the concept of 'detention'. Although it found it unnecessary to actually rule on the Article 5 issue, having already found a violation of the right to respect for private life under Article 8, the Court observed that:[84]

> [A]lthough the length of time during which each applicant was stopped and searched did not in either case exceed 30 minutes, during this period the applicants were entirely deprived of any freedom of movement. They were obliged to remain where they were and submit to the search and if they had refused they would have been liable to arrest, detention at a police station and criminal charges. This element of coercion is indicative of a deprivation of liberty within the meaning of Art.5(1).

Sentencing and life prisoners

The procedural requirements set out in Article 5 have had a significant impact on the arrangements for making decisions about life prisoners. In *Thynne, Wilson and Gunnell* v *UK*,[85] the Court of Human Rights ruled that those serving discretionary life sentences were entitled to periodic reviews to determine whether their continued detention could be justified. A similar conclusion was reached in respect of juveniles detained at Her Majesty's pleasure.[86] The Home Secretary's involvement in setting the minimum term that must be served in such cases was also contrary to Article 5(4), because it meant that the period of detention was not controlled by a court.[87] New arrangements have since been put in place for determining and reviewing such sentences.[88] Once the minimum term has been served, however, it is for the prisoner to show that his continued detention on public safety grounds is unnecessary and unlawful. The fact that there are not enough places available on programmes providing an opportunity to demonstrate rehabilitation does not in itself breach Article 5(4).[89]

Mandatory life sentences were thought to raise different issues because the Strasbourg court had previously found that they were not indeterminate and did not

---

Gloucester [2004] EWHC 253 (Admin), [2004] 2 All ER 874 (affirmed on appeal, although without reliance on Article 5: [2006] UKHL 55, [2007] 2 AC 105, [2007] 2 All ER 529).

[82] [2006] UKHL 12, [2006] 2 AC 307, [2006] 4 All ER 1041.

[83] [2009] UKHL 5, [2009] 1 AC 564, [2009] 3 All ER 455. For a critique of this decision see Mead, 'Of Kettles, Cordons and Crowd Control' [2009] EHRLR 376.

[84] *Gillan and Quinton* v *UK* (2010) 50 EHRR 45, at [56].

[85] (1991) 13 EHRR 666. [86] *Hussain and Singh* v *UK* (1996) 22 EHRR 1.

[87] *T and V* v *UK* (2000) 30 EHRR 121.

[88] Crime (Sentences) Act 1997, s 28; Powers of Criminal Courts (Sentencing) Act 2000, s 82A.

[89] *Wells* v *Parole Board*; *sub nom R (James)* v *Secretary of State for Justice* [2009] UKHL 22, [2010] 1 AC 553, [2009] 4 All ER 255.

need to be periodically reviewed.[90] However, in *Stafford* v *UK*,[91] the court concluded that there was no material difference between discretionary and mandatory life prisoners. In both cases the setting of the tariff was a sentencing exercise, and Articles 5 and 6 required that it should be performed by a court. Mr Stafford had in fact been released on life licence, but the Home Secretary had revoked the licence following his conviction for fraud. This also violated Article 5, because the original life sentence could not authorize a further period of detention for an unrelated, non-violent offence.[92] Shortly after this decision, the House of Lords concluded that it was impossible to interpret the mandatory life sentence powers in a manner compatible with Article 6 without doing 'judicial vandalism' to the legislation.[93] It therefore issued a declaration of incompatibility.[94] Provisions to bring the arrangements for mandatory life prisoners into line with these judgments were included in Part 12 of the Criminal Justice Act 2003. As far as determinate sentences are concerned, the House of Lords recently confirmed that the procedural safeguards set out in Article 5(4) apply only to the original sentencing decision: there is no requirement for any subsequent decision on early release to be subject to review by a court.[95]

Combating terrorism

Measures taken to combat terrorism have given rise to Article 5 issues on a number of occasions. In *Brogan* v *UK*,[96] laws allowing suspected terrorists to be detained for up to seven days without being brought before a judicial authority were found to breach Article 5. Instead of amending the offending legislation, the government derogated from Article 5,[97] and the derogation remained in force until February 2001. The withdrawal of the derogation followed the decision to replace the existing anti-terror laws with the Terrorism Act 2000. Following amendments made in 2006, this Act now permits detention without charge for up to twenty-eight days, but judicial authority must be obtained for detentions in excess of forty-eight hours.[98]

The United Kingdom entered a further derogation from Article 5 following the enactment of the Anti-Terrorism, Crime and Security Act 2001.[99] This Act provided that where a foreign national was suspected of terrorism but could not be deported

---

[90] *Wynne* v *UK* (1995) 19 EHRR 333.   [91] (2002) 35 EHRR 32.

[92] See also *Waite* v *UK* (2003) 36 EHRR 54 (revocation of licence following conviction for further offences); *R (on the application of Giles)* v *Parole Board* [2003] UKHL 42, [2004] 1 AC 1, [2003] 4 All ER 429 (no breach of Article 5(4) in respect of judicial powers to impose an extended determinate sentence on public safety grounds).

[93] *R (on the application of Anderson)* v *Secretary of State for the Home Department* [2002] UKHL 46 at [30], [2003] 1 AC 837 at [30], [2002] 4 All ER 1089, *per* Lord Bingham; Crime (Sentences) Act 1997, s 29. See Amos, '*R* v *Secretary of State for the Home Department, ex parte Anderson*: Ending the Home Secretary's Sentencing Role' (2004) 67(1) MLR 108.

[94] For declarations of incompatibility, see p 155.

[95] *R (Black)* v *Secretary of State for Justice* [2009] UKHL 1, [2009] 1 AC 949, [2009] 4 All ER 1.

[96] (1989) 11 EHRR 117; Prevention of Terrorism (Temporary Provisions) Act 1984, s 14.

[97] The derogation was unsuccessfully challenged in *Brannigan and McBride* v *UK* (1994) 17 EHRR 539.

[98] Terrorism Act 2000, s 41 and Sch 8; as amended by the Terrorism Act 2006.

[99] Declaration registered by the Secretariat General on 18 December 2001; SI 2001/4032.

on humanitarian grounds, the Secretary of State could certify that he was believed to present a threat to national security. The suspect could then be detained indefinitely, without trial. The government sought to pre-empt any legal challenge by derogating from Article 5 immediately, but in *A v Secretary of State for the Home Department*[100] the House of Lords nevertheless made a declaration of incompatibility. It held that by singling out non-nationals for detention the Act was interfering with the right to liberty in a discriminatory manner, and that it was therefore in breach of Articles 5 and 14.[101] The government's response was the Prevention of Terrorism Act 2005, which replaces the internment powers with a system of control orders. This Act avoids the element of discrimination inherent in the earlier legislation, by providing that the new powers may be exercised against any person suspected on reasonable grounds of involvement in terrorism-related activity. Nevertheless, the range of controls permitted can have serious consequences for individual liberties, and the Act contemplates the possibility that some control orders may require a further derogation. The only control orders made thus far have been 'non-derogating', and several attempts to challenge them through the courts have been unsuccessful.[102] However, the House of Lords recently upheld a decision to quash six control orders, having likened their effect to being in indefinite solitary confinement.[103] The applicants had been subject to eighteen-hour curfews and were forced to reside in one-bedroom flats in unfamiliar areas. They were electronically tagged, their use of communications equipment was restricted to a single, landline telephone, and they could not meet with anyone without Home Office clearance. By contrast, Article 5 was not infringed by an order involving a twelve-hour curfew, where the applicant was able to continue living in his family home and had fewer restrictions on his movements.[104]

Finally, Article 5(4) provides that a detainee must be able to challenge the legality of his detention, and this requirement has implications for the use of 'closed material' in anti-terror cases. The key issue here is whether the prosecution has disclosed sufficient evidence to the detainee to allow him the opportunity to challenge the case against him:[105]

> [Non-disclosure cannot go so far as to deny a party knowledge of the essence of the case against him, at least where he is at risk of [severe] consequences... [but] where the interests of national security are concerned in the context of combating terrorism, it may be acceptable not to disclose the source of evidence that founds the grounds of suspecting that a person has been involved in terrorism-related activities.

---

[100] *A v Secretary of State for the Home Department* [2004] UKHL 56, [2005] 2 AC 68, [2005] 3 All ER 169; see pp 159 and 166.

[101] The Grand Chamber of the European Court of Human Rights recently endorsed both the decision and the reasoning of the majority in this case: *A and others v UK* (2009) 49 EHRR 29.

[102] See, e.g. *Secretary of State for the Home Department v MB* [2007] UKHL 46, [2008] 1 AC 440, [2008] 1 All ER 657, discussed at p 156.

[103] *Secretary of State for the Home Department v JJ* [2007] UKHL 45, [2008] 1 AC 385, [2008] HRLR 5.

[104] *Secretary of State for the Home Department v E*, [2007] UKHL 47, [2008] 1 AC 499, [2008] HRLR 7.

[105] *Secretary of State for the Home Department v F* [2009] UKHL 28 at [65]–[66], [2009] 3 WLR 74, at [65]–[66], [2009] 3 All ER 643, *per* Lord Phillips; see also *A and others v UK* (2009) 49 EHRR 29.

Detention on medical grounds

Article 5(1)(e) expressly permits the lawful detention of persons of unsound mind, but the state must demonstrate an objective and reliable basis for the detention, and it must be subject to periodic review.[106] In a 2001 case,[107] the Court of Appeal declared provisions of the Mental Health Act 1983 to be incompatible with Article 5, because the patient bore the burden of proving that his continued detention was no longer necessary. The Act was subsequently amended by remedial order.[108] Following the decisions in *Stafford* and *Anderson*, a further declaration of incompatibility was made in *R (on the application of D) v Secretary of State for the Home Department*,[109] because the Act failed to provide an adequate right of review to restricted patients serving prison sentences.

Deportation and extradition

Article 5(1)(f) permits the detention of persons pending deportation or extradition, and for the purpose of preventing unauthorized entry into the country. In *R (on the application of Saadi) v Secretary of State for the Home Department*, the policy of detaining asylum seekers at 'reception centres' was challenged, on the basis that it affects those whose applications have yet to be determined, and in respect of whom no decision to deport has been taken.[110] However, the House of Lords held that because asylum applicants were only detained where there was a reasonable belief that they might abscond, the policy was a lawful and proportionate means of controlling entry.

KEY ISSUE

The control order decisions in *A* and other cases discussed above raise fundamental issues. They are vivid illustrations of the tensions between the judiciary and the courts in terms of the legitimate role of the courts in human rights cases.[111] They illustrate concepts of basic freedoms. Yet the distinctions being drawn by the House of Lords are not always easy to justify on a principled basis. The difficulties with control orders are as much matters of principle as they are matters of detail relating to the terms of the orders themselves. For that reason, the future of control orders is subject to a further review by the government, due in 2011.

 Question

When determining whether a person has been unlawfully deprived of his liberty in breach of Article 5 ECHR, are the domestic courts right to regard the length of the period of detention as significant?

---

[106] *Johnson v UK* (1997) 27 EHRR 296.
[107] *R (on the application of H) v North and East London Regional Mental Health Review Tribunal* [2001] EWCA Civ 415, [2002] QB 1, [2001] 3 WLR 512.
[108] Mental Health Act 1983 (Remedial) Order 2001, SI 2001/3712.
[109] [2002] EWHC 2805 (Admin), [2003] 1 WLR 1315. The Act has since been amended.
[110] [2002] UKHL 41, [2002] 4 All ER 785, [2002] 1 WLR 3131. The Grand Chamber of the European Court of Human Rights recently confirmed this decision: *Saadi v UK* (2008) 47 EHRR 17.
[111] See pp 157 and 327.

Article 6: The right to a fair trial

Article 6(1) concerns the right to a fair trial, the main elements of which are: (a) a fair and public hearing; (b) an independent and impartial tribunal; (c) a trial within a reasonable period of time; (d) a public judgment; and (e) a reasoned decision. It applies to all proceedings that involve a criminal charge or the determination of civil rights and obligations.

Civil rights and obligations

A broad view is taken of what constitutes 'civil rights and obligations', and it is not confined to matters regarded as 'civil' for other purposes. Administrative decisions affecting 'personal, economic and individual' rights are also covered,[112] and this means that decisions relating to planning,[113] care proceedings,[114] social security,[115] and welfare payments[116] have all been held to engage Article 6(1). Conventional wisdom suggests that the extent of any discretion in conferring a benefit is crucial to the question of whether a 'right' exists, but the jurisprudence in this area is not entirely consistent. For example, in *Begum (Runa)* v *Tower Hamlets*, the House of Lords had assumed that Article 6(1) was engaged by a decision concerning a homeless person's refusal of accommodation,[117] but the Supreme Court recently held that a duty to make accommodation available for homeless people did not give rise to any 'civil rights'.[118] The court in the latter case criticized the Strasbourg jurisprudence for failing to make clear where to draw the line between 'those rights in public law which are to be regarded as "civil rights" and those which are not to be so regarded',[119] and Lord Hope sought to clarify the position:[120]

> [C]ases where the award of services or benefits in kind is not an individual right of which the applicant can consider himself the holder, but is dependent upon a series of evaluative judgments by the provider as to whether the statutory criteria are satisfied and how the need for it ought to be met, do not engage art. 6(1).

Other matters held not to involve 'civil rights and obligations' include taxation decisions,[121] assessments as to the categorization of prisoners,[122] and school exclusions.[123]

---

[112] *Feldbrugge* v *Netherlands* (1986) 8 EHRR 425 at [37].
[113] *R (on the Application of Alconbury)* v *Secretary of State for the Environment, Transport and the Regions* [2001] UKHL 23, [2003] 2 AC 295, [2001] 2 All ER 929.
[114] *McMichael* v *UK* (1995) 20 EHRR 205.
[115] *Feldbrugge* v *Netherlands* (1986) 8 EHRR 425 at [37].
[116] *Mennitto* v *Italy* (2002) 34 EHRR 48.
[117] [2003] UKHL 5, [2003] 2 AC 430, [2003] 1 All ER 731. The point was left open for future consideration.
[118] *Ali* v *Birmingham City Council* [2010] UKSC 8, [2010] 2 WLR 471, [2010] 2 All ER 175.
[119] Ibid, *per* Lord Collins at [60]; see also *Stec* v *UK* (2006) 43 EHRR 1017.
[120] Ibid, *per* Lord Hope at [49]. See Elliott, 'Statutory Duties, Administrative Discretion and "Civil Rights"' (2010) 69(2) CLJ 215.
[121] *Ferrazzini* v *Italy* (2002) 34 EHRR 45.   [122] *Brady* v *UK* (1979) 3 EHRR 297.
[123] *R (on the application of V)* v *Independent Appeals Panel for Tom Hood School* [2010] EWCA Civ 142, [2010] HRLR 21.

Criminal charge

The term 'criminal' also has an autonomous meaning for Article 6 purposes, and the content of what is alleged and the nature of any penalty must be taken into account.[124] Proceedings for non-payment of council tax[125] and for binding over to keep the peace[126] are both considered to be 'criminal'. However, proceedings relating to anti-social behaviour orders,[127] control orders,[128] the revocation of a prisoner's release on licence,[129] the forfeiture of goods seized by customs and excise,[130] and the confiscation of the proceeds of criminal activity,[131] are not.

A fair hearing and equality of arms

Article 6 provides an important yardstick against which to measure any aspect of the trial process, and it has generated far more case law than any other Convention right. The idea that there should be equality of arms between the parties to an action is an important theme. Amongst other things, it entails an obligation to ensure the disclosure of relevant evidence,[132] the ability to challenge that evidence,[133] and the ability to participate effectively in the proceedings. The latter requirement may be breached where a child is tried in an adult court[134] or where language difficulties prevent a party to an action from fully understanding the proceedings.[135] Article 6 may also be breached by the operation of certain evidential rules,[136] or by the admission of unfairly or covertly obtained evidence.[137]

---

[124] *Engel* v *The Netherlands (No 1)* (1979–1980) 1 EHRR 647.

[125] *Benham* v *UK* (1996) 22 EHRR 293.

[126] *Steel* v *UK* (1999) 28 EHRR 603; *Hooper* v *UK* (2005) 41 EHRR 1; cf. *Williamson* v *Chief Constable of West Midlands* [2003] EWCA Civ 337, [2004] 1 WLR 14. The civil/criminal distinction is discussed at p 4.

[127] *R (on the application of McCann)* v *Manchester Crown Court and others* [2002] UKHL 39, [2003] 1 AC 787, [2002] 4 All ER 593.

[128] *Secretary of State for the Home Department* v *MB* [2007] UKHL 46, [2007] 3 WLR 681.

[129] *R (on the application of Smith)* v *Parole Board* [2005] UKHL 1, [2005] 1 WLR 350, [2005] 1 All ER 755.

[130] *R (on the application of Mudie)* v *Dover Magistrates Court* [2003] EWCA Civ 237, [2003] QB 1238, [2003] 2 All ER 631.

[131] *R* v *Briggs-Price* [2009] UKHL 19, [2009] 1 AC 1026, [2009] 4 All ER 594.

[132] *Edwards* v *UK* (1992) 15 EHRR 417; *Rowe and Davis* v *UK* (2000) 30 EHRR 1 (use of public interest immunity certificates); *A and others* v *UK* (2009) 49 EHRR 29 (use of closed material and special advocates).

[133] *R* v *A (No 2)* [2001] UKHL 25, [2002] 1 AC 45, [2001] 3 All ER 1; *Re W (Children) (Family Proceedings: evidence)* [2010] UKSC 142

[134] *T and V* v *UK* (2000) 30 EHRR 121.

[135] *Cuscani* v *UK* (2003) 36 EHRR 2; cf. *Williams* v *Cowell (t/a The Stables)* [2000] 1 WLR 187, [2000] ICR 85 (EAT's refusal to conduct its proceedings in Welsh did not deprive the applicant of a fair trial because he had perfectly good English.)

[136] *Trivedi* v *UK* (1997) ECHR 31700/96 (exceptions to hearsay rule); *Hoare* v *UK* (1997) ECHR 31211/96 (availability of expert evidence): both applications were found to be inadmissible on the facts.

[137] *R* v *Looseley; sub nom Attorney-General's Reference (No 3 of 2000)* [2001] UKHL 53, [2001] 4 All ER 897 (entrapment); *Khan* v *UK* (2001) 31 EHRR 45 (use of covert listening device breached Article 8 but not Article 6); *Allan* v *UK* (2003) 36 EHRR 12 (placing informant in cell to obtain confession infringed privilege against self-incrimination); *R* v *Nudds (Christopher Ronald)* [2008] EWCA Civ 148 (use of confession made to cellmate did *not* breach Article 6 because the two had shared a cell by chance and Nudds had not been repeatedly questioned by officers first); *R* v *Veneroso* [2002] Crim LR 306 (drugs found while officers on premises illegally were inadmissible under Article 8—outcome may have been different if semtex found.).

The right of unimpeded access to legal advice is also fundamental,[138] and the availability of legal aid is an important factor here. The requirement for legal aid to be available is more explicit where criminal charges are involved,[139] but the Court of Human Rights recently found a breach of Article 6(1) when legal aid was denied to the defendants in a complex libel action.[140] The 'McLibel Two' were sued for distributing leaflets containing allegations about the fast-food giant, McDonalds. Legal aid is generally unavailable in defamation cases, and although the defendants were helped by volunteer lawyers they represented themselves throughout the two-and-a-half-year trial. It was held that the complexity of the issues, the potential severity of the consequences,[141] and the applicants' capacity to defend themselves effectively against the resources of McDonalds had all contributed to an unacceptable inequality of arms.

An independent and impartial tribunal

Several cases have examined the requirement for an 'independent and impartial tribunal', and decisions on this aspect of Article 6 have had a considerable influence on the English legal system. The principle that decisions should be free from bias is well established in English law, but when the Human Rights Act came into force the Court of Appeal held that a 'modest adjustment' to the existing test was needed.[142] Article 6 was also instrumental in bringing about reforms to the procedures for dealing with life prisoners,[143] and the Armed Forces Act 1996 pre-empted a finding that the courts-martial system lacked sufficient guarantees of independence.[144] Following the decision in *Lawal* v *Northern Spirit*,[145] barristers ceased to be used as part-time Employment Appeal Tribunal judges, and the decision in *McGonnell* v *UK*[146] also proved to be highly significant. The facts of the latter case were that the Guernsey Royal Court Bailiff had adjudicated in a planning case, having also been involved in making the applicable legislation. The court concluded that this amounted to a breach of Article 6, and although the decision was not concerned with wider constitutional issues, it had clear implications for both the Appellate Committee of the House of Lords and the office of Lord Chancellor. It is partly because of this decision that the Constitutional Reform Act 2005 was introduced.[147]

---

[138] *Brennan* v *UK* (2002) 34 EHRR 18 (Article 6 breached by police presence at a meeting between defendant and solicitor); *P, C and S* v *UK* (2002) 35 EHRR 31 (refusal to adjourn care proceedings to allow a mother to obtain legal advice).

[139] See Article 6(3)(c); *Benham* v *UK* (1996) 22 EHRR 293.

[140] *Steel and Morris* v *UK* (2005) 41 EHRR 22.

[141] The defendants had been ordered to pay damages of £76,000, although McDonalds had not sought to enforce the award.

[142] *Director General of Fair Trading* v *Proprietary Association of Great Britain*; *sub nom Re Medicaments and Related Classes of Goods (No 2)* [2001] 1 WLR 700, [2001] HRLR 17. The modification was subsequently approved by the House of Lords in *Porter* v *Magill* [2001] UKHL 67, [2002] 2 AC 357, [2002] 1 All ER 465.

[143] See p 187.

[144] The Strasbourg court made such a ruling in *Findlay* v *UK* (1997) 24 EHRR 221: see p 279.

[145] [2003] UKHL 35, [2004] 1 All ER 187, [2003] ICR 856: see p 304.

[146] (2000) 30 EHRR 289. See also *Starrs* v *Ruxton*; *sub nom Starrs* v *Procurator Fiscal* 2000 JC 208, 2000 SLT 42; p 344.

[147] The reforms brought about by this Act are considered in more detail in Chapters 7 and 9.

A trial within a reasonable time

The question of whether a trial has taken place within a 'reasonable time' can only be resolved by reference to both the circumstances of the case and the complexity of the issues. Nine-year delays in resolving legal disputes have been held to breach Article 6,[148] although not in the criminal case of *Korbely v Hungary* because the events with which the case was concerned had happened over forty years earlier.[149] In *R v James (David John)*, a five-year delay in dealing with a complicated fraud case was not considered unreasonable.[150]

Open justice

The principle that justice should be seen to be done is also highly valued, but it is subject to the proviso that publicity may be restricted where the interests of justice demand it. Private hearings may be necessary in order to protect the identity of vulnerable witnesses,[151] and fairness may also require the imposition of reporting restrictions pending the outcome of proceedings. In *R (on the application of the Telegraph Group plc) v Sherwood*,[152] a decision to delay the reporting of one trial until a related trial had been concluded was held to be a justifiable and proportionate response to a substantial risk of prejudice.

Criminal offences: Additional safeguards

Whilst the elements of a fair trial enshrined in Article 6(1) are applicable to both civil and criminal proceedings, Article 6(2) and 6(3) list additional safeguards that apply only in criminal cases.

Article 6(2) expressly provides that anyone charged with a criminal offence has the right to be presumed innocent of that offence, and in several Human Rights Act cases it has been used as the basis for modifying the interpretation of burden of proof provisions.[153] In addition, although freedom from self-incrimination and the related idea of the right to silence are not specifically mentioned, both principles have been held to be covered by the fair trial concept in Article 6(1). In *Saunders v UK*, the Court of Human Rights considered the effect of provisions of the Companies Act 1985, under which Mr Saunders was compelled to answer questions put to him during a fraud

---

[148] *Darnall v UK* (1994) 18 EHRR 205; *Blake v UK* (2007) 44 EHRR 29.   [149] (2010) 50 EHRR 48.

[150] [2002] EWCA Crim 1119.

[151] See *X v UK* (1993) 15 EHRR CD 113 (witnesses testified from behind a screen where they could not even be seen by the defendant). See also *R v Lord Saville of Newdigate, ex parte A* [1999] 4 All ER 860, [2000] 1 WLR 1855.

[152] [2001] EWCA Crim 1075, [2001] 1 WLR 1983; cf. *R v B* [2006] EWCA Crim 2692, [2007] HRLR 1, discussed at p 239.

[153] *R v Lambert* [2001] UKHL 37, [2002] 2 AC 545, [2001] 3 All ER 577 (provisions of the Misuse of Drugs Act 1971 read down so as to impose an evidential rather than a legal burden); *Attorney-General's Reference (No 4 of 2002)* [2004] UKHL 43, [2005] 1 AC 264, [2005] 1 All ER 237 (provisions of the Terrorism Act 2000 read down so as to impose an evidential rather than a legal burden); *International Transport Roth GmbH v Secretary of State for the Home Department* [2002] EWCA Civ 158, [2003] QB 728, [2002] HRLR 31 (a compatible interpretation of provisions in the Immigration and Asylum Act 1999 could not be found and a declaration of incompatibility was issued).

investigation.[154] The use made of these answers at Mr Saunders' trial, and the fact that they had been obtained under compulsion, was held to infringe Article 6. The right to silence is not absolute, however, and allowing a court to draw adverse inferences from silence will not automatically involve a breach of the Convention. Thus, restrictions on the right to silence in *Murray* v *UK*[155] did not violate Article 6 because the weight of evidence meant that the drawing of inferences had not been unfair. Moreover, the case was tried by a single judge who was required to give a reasoned decision. The risk of unfairness is considered to be greater where a defendant is tried by jury: Article 6 may be breached if the judge does not ensure that appropriate weight is given to any explanation offered by the accused.[156]

Article 6(3) provides that everyone charged with a criminal offence has the right: (a) to be promptly and intelligibly informed of the nature of any charges; (b) to adequate time and facilities to prepare his defence; (c) to defend himself in person or through legal assistance (in some circumstances free); (d) to call and examine witnesses; and (e) to an interpreter where necessary.

KEY ISSUE

The standards upheld by the rights in Article 6 are key to the operation of the English legal system. Concepts relating to fair hearings, open justice, representation and a fair and independent tribunal are explored throughout this text. The concepts in Article 6 in many respects reflect traditional United Kingdom standards and judicial values, with Convention case law adding refinement of argument rather than fundamentally different approaches. The case law relating to reverse onus burdens of proof, where a defendant is made subject to a legal obligation to prove particular aspects of matters under consideration by a court, have been the subject of considerable domestic consideration in the light of Article 6, but the principle that reverse onus provisions may be permissible remains despite the seemingly broad statements of the presumption of innocence in Article 6. So, too, with case law relating to entrapment. The principles developed by the Court of Human Rights in large measure reflect the principles adopted by the United Kingdom courts.

❓ Questions

1. Where a person has been convicted on the strength of unfairly or covertly obtained evidence, can it really be said that they have had a fair trial for the purposes of Article 6 ECHR?

2. Do you think it is right that a burden of proof can be placed on a defendant in some circumstances in a criminal case?

---

[154] (1997) 23 EHRR 313. The Companies Act was later amended by the Youth Justice and Criminal Evidence Act 1999; cf. *Brown* v *Stott* [2003] 1 AC 681, [2001] 2 All ER 97 and *O'Halloran and Francis* v *UK* [2007] Crim LR 897 (requirement to answer potentially incriminating questions under the Road Traffic Act 1988 does not infringe the Convention); *R* v *K* [2009] EWCA Crim 1640, [2010] QB 343, [2010] 2 All ER 509 (party making financial disclosures in 'without prejudice' meetings during ancillary relief proceedings could not invoke the privilege against self-incrimination when prosecuted for tax evasion).

[155] (1996) 22 EHRR 29.   [156] *Condron* v *UK* (2001) 31 EHRR 1; *Beckles* v *UK* (2003) 36 EHRR 13.

Article 7: No punishment without law

Retrospective criminal liability

Article 7 prohibits the imposition of criminal liability for an act that was not an offence when it was carried out. Legislation imposing retrospective criminal liability is virtually unknown in modern times,[157] but issues may arise where offences are given a different interpretation to that which might have been expected. Article 7 may also be infringed if an offence is not sufficiently precise to enable an individual to regulate his conduct. In practice, however, it will be rare for this type of challenge to succeed. In *CR and SW v UK*, for example, the applicants claimed that the removal of the marital rape exemption in *R v R*[158] amounted to the creation of a retrospective offence, contrary to Article 7. However, the Strasbourg court ruled that the applicants should have foreseen that their conduct would be considered criminal, and there was therefore no breach of the Convention.[159]

In *O'Carroll v UK*, the court pointed out that it was 'not possible to attain absolute rigidity in the framing of laws', particularly where there was a need to keep pace with changing circumstances.[160] O'Carroll had argued that the law was not precise enough for him to know in advance that receiving photographs of a child playing naked on a beach might lead to a conviction for indecency, but his application was deemed to be manifestly ill-founded. The domestic courts have rejected similar arguments in relation to the offences of public nuisance[161] and gross negligence manslaughter.[162]

Penalties and sentencing

Article 7 also forbids the imposition of a heavier criminal penalty than that in force at the time of the offence. Most of the cases that arise in this context hinge on whether a particular requirement constitutes a penalty, and the purpose of the requirement is usually crucial to this determination. Compelling a person to register as a sex offender has been held not to constitute a penalty, even though non-compliance is a criminal offence, because the purpose of the requirement is not to punish.[163]

In *R (on the application of Uttley) v Secretary of State for the Home Department*, the defendant was sentenced to twelve years' imprisonment more than a decade after committing a series of sex offences. He argued that his release on licence after eight years amounted to a breach of Article 7, on the grounds that if he had been given

---

[157] See p 34. The War Crimes Act 1991 is a notable exception but it is the type of legislation envisaged by Article 7(2). This allows the retrospective criminalization of acts that would have been recognized as criminal when committed under general principles of international law. Compare *Kononov v Latvia* (2009) 25 BHRC 317 (Article 7 violated when applicant prosecuted for war crimes in respect of act committed in 1944).

[158] *R v R (Rape: Marital Exemption)* [1992] 1 AC 599, [1991] 4 All ER 481: see p 322.

[159] (1996) 21 EHRR 363. The Court of Appeal reached the same conclusion on similar facts in *R v C (Barry)* [2004] EWCA Crim 292, [2004] 1 WLR 2098, [2004] 3 All ER 1.

[160] (2005) 41 EHRR SE1.

[161] *R v Rimmington (Anthony)* [2005] UKHL 63, [2006] 1 AC 459, [2006] 2 All ER 257 (the defendants' convictions were quashed, however, as the ingredients of the offence had not been made out).

[162] *R v Misra (Amit)* [2004] EWCA Crim 2375, [2005] 1 Cr App R 21.

[163] *Adamson v UK* (1999) ECHR 42293/98.

the same sentence at the time of his offences, he would have been released after the same number of years but *without* licence. His argument was rejected by the House of Lords on the basis that Article 7 was only concerned with the maximum 'applicable' sentence, and not with the sentence that a particular offender was likely to receive.[164] In *Kafkaris* v *Cyprus*, Article 7 was breached by a change in the law that meant that a murderer was likely to serve the whole of his mandatory life sentence instead of being considered for release after twenty years. The Grand Chamber found that although this did not amount to the retrospective imposition of a heavier penalty, there was an issue as to 'quality of law': at the time of the offence the relevant law 'had not been formulated with sufficient precision,' and it would have been reasonable to assume that, in practice, a life sentence was tantamount to twenty years' imprisonment.[165]

Article 8: The right to respect for a person's private and family life, his home and correspondence

Article 8 establishes rights in relation to four key areas—private life, family life, home, and correspondence—although it is often unnecessary to distinguish clearly between them, and they can be 'read together as guaranteeing collectively more than the sum of their parts'.[166] The rights protected by Article 8 may be subject to limitations that are in accordance with law and that are necessary in a democratic society in the interests of national security, public safety, or the economic well-being of the country, for the prevention of disorder or crime, for the protection of health or morals, or for the protection of the rights and freedoms of others. The body of case law generated by this Article is vast, and numerous diverse rights have been recognized as flowing from it. It is impossible to give a comprehensive account of these rights here, but the pages that follow aim to give a flavour of the Article's scope.

Personal and family relationships

The right to respect for private life includes the right to develop personal relationships with others,[167] and relationships that do not establish a conventional 'family' may nevertheless fall within the scope of Article 8. Moreover, where national laws confer particular rights or benefits on family members, there may be a breach of Article 8 if the state's interpretation of what constitutes a family is too narrow. Thus, in *X, Y and X, Y and Z* v *UK*,[168] the relationship between a woman, a female-to-male transsexual, and a child that the woman had conceived through artificial insemination was held

---

[164] [2004] UKHL 38, [2004] 1 WLR 2278, [2004] 4 All ER 1. See also *Taylor* v *UK* (2003) 36 EHRR CD 104 (boy who committed a crime as a 14-year-old punished as a young offender because he was aged 15 when sentenced: Article 7 not engaged).

[165] (2009) 49 EHRR 35 at [151].

[166] Ovey and White (eds), *Jacobs and White: European Convention on Human Rights* (OUP: 3rd edn, 2002) at p 218.

[167] *Niemietz* v *Germany* (1993) 16 EHRR 97; *X and Y* v *Netherlands* (1986) 8 EHRR 235.

[168] (1997) 24 EHRR 143.

to constitute a family. Similarly, in *Ghaidan* v *Godin-Mendoza*,[169] the House of Lords upheld a ruling that the Rent Act 1977 should be interpreted to confer the rights of a 'spouse' on the surviving gay partner of a protected statutory tenant. However, the Strasbourg court is proving to be a little slower in recognizing same-sex relationships as falling within the scope of 'family life':[170]

> [I]in the present state of Strasbourg jurisprudence, contracting states are not required by the Convention to accord to the relationship between same-sex couples the respect for family life guaranteed by Article 8. For the time being the respect afforded to this relationship is a matter for contracting states.

The ability to maintain family ties is of fundamental importance, and any denial of parental rights of access to a child will be subject to strict scrutiny.[171] Indeed, a failure to involve a parent in otherwise justified decisions about care and custody may amount to a breach of Article 8.[172] Article 8 may also be violated by immigration and deportation decisions that have a disproportionate impact on the ability to maintain family relationships.[173] However, states are not obliged to respect the choice of married couples as to their country of residence,[174] and a key issue is whether the life of the family can reasonably be expected to be enjoyed elsewhere.[175]

The scope of the right to family life has also been considered in the context of adoption decisions[176] and the destruction of embryos following the withdrawal of consent to *in vitro* fertilization.[177]

Sexuality

Article 8 entails respect for personal identity and sexual preferences, and it has been used alongside Article 14 in several cases concerning discrimination against homosexuals and transsexuals. The decision in *Smith and Grady* v *UK*[178] forced the Ministry of Defence to abandon its ban on gays in the military, and judicial decisions in both the United Kingdom and Strasbourg provided the impetus for a new law conferring

---

[169] [2004] UKHL 30, [2004] 2 AC 557, [2004] 3 All ER 411.
[170] *M* v *Secretary of State for Work and Pensions* [2006] UKHL 30 at [26], [2006] 2 AC 91 at [26], [2006] 4 All ER 929, *per* Lord Nicholls; see also *Mata Estevez* v *Spain* [2001] ECHR 56501/00.
[171] *K and T* v *Finland* (2003) 36 EHRR 18.   [172] *TP and KM* v *UK* (2002) 34 EHRR 2.
[173] *Berrehab* v *Netherlands* (1989) 11 EHRR 322 (refusal of residence permit to Moroccan national who maintained regular contact with ex-wife and their child); *EM (Lebanon)* v *Secretary of State for Home Department* [2008] UKHL 64, [2009] 1 AC 1198, [2009] 1 All ER 559 (deportation of asylum seeker and child, which would result in violent ex-husband being given custody).
[174] *Abdulaziz, Cabales and Balkandali* v *UK* (1985) 7 EHRR 471.
[175] *EB (Kosovo)* v *Secretary of State for Home Department* [2008] UKHL 41 at [12], [2009] 1 AC 1159 at [12], [2008] HRLR 40, *per* Lord Bingham; see also *Huang* v *Secretary of State for the Home Department* [2007] UKHL 11, [2007] 2 AC 167, [2007] HRLR 22.
[176] *Re B (A Minor) (Adoption: Natural Parent)* [2001] UKHL 70, [2002] 1 All ER 641, [2002] 1 WLR 258; *Keegan* v *Ireland* (1994) 18 EHRR 342.
[177] *Evans* v *UK* (2008) 46 ECHR 34; see also *L* v *Human Fertilisation and Embryology Authority* [2008] EWHC 2149 (Fam), [2008] 2 FLR 1999 (Article 8 not breached by failure to store sperm taken from woman's deceased husband as he had not given effective consent).
[178] (2000) 29 EHRR 493; *Lustig-Prean and Beckett* v *UK* (2000) 29 EHRR 548.

legal rights on transsexuals.[179] The Strasbourg court also found breaches of Articles 8 and 14 in a case concerning the United Kingdom's age of consent laws, although the offending laws were amended before the case was decided.[180]

Article 8 was successfully relied upon by a gay man prosecuted for gross indecency after videotaping consensual sex acts for his own private use.[181] However, the prosecution of a group of men who recorded themselves engaging in sado-masochism did not involve a similar breach.[182] The Court accepted that the interference in the latter case was in the interests of public health. Similarly, the dismissal of a probation officer who published on the Internet photographs of himself engaging in acts of bondage and domination, and who maintained a website advertising the sale of sado-masochistic equipment, was not a violation of Article 8.[183] Although there had been an interference with the applicant's right to respect for private life, this interference was not disproportionate given that his job involved working with sex offenders.

Home life and the environment

The effectiveness of Article 8 in protecting environmental and housing rights has been rather more measured.[184] In *Hatton* v *UK*,[185] for example, the Grand Chamber overturned a finding that night flights from Heathrow Airport breached the Article 8 rights of local residents. In another case the House of Lords rejected a nuisance action brought by a householder whose property was flooded by water from the sewers.[186] In the latter case the defendant's activities were subject to scrutiny by an independent regulator, and the statutory regime was held to strike an appropriate balance between the rights of those such as the claimant and those who depended on the defendant for sewerage services. Nevertheless, it is clear that severe pollution affecting home and family life *is* capable of being addressed under Article 8,[187] and in certain circumstances the state may have a positive obligation to provide information about serious environmental hazards.[188]

Decisions concerning possession proceedings and eviction will also raise Article 8 issues, and although the courts have generally found any interference with the right to a home to be legitimate,[189] the Court of Human Rights took a different stance in

---

[179] The Gender Recognition Act 2004, introduced following *Goodwin* v *UK* (2002) 35 EHRR 18 and *Bellinger* v *Bellinger* [2003] UKHL 21, [2003] 2 AC 467, [2003] 2 All ER 593.

[180] *B* v *UK* (2004) 39 EHRR 30. The age of consent for male homosexuals was 18; it was 16 for heterosexuals. The age of consent was equalized at 16 by the Sexual Offences (Amendment) Act 2000. The relevant law is now contained in s 9 of the Sexual Offences Act 2003. See also *Dudgeon* v *UK* (1982) 4 EHRR 149, discussed at p 176.

[181] *ADT* v *UK* (2001) 31 EHRR 33.   [182] *Laskey* v *UK* (1997) 24 EHRR 39.

[183] *Pay* v *UK* (2009) 48 EHRR 362.

[184] See Cook, 'Environmental Rights as Human Rights' [2002] 2 EHRLR 196.

[185] (2003) 37 EHRR 28.

[186] *Marcic* v *Thames Water Utilities* [2003] UKHL 66, [2004] 2 AC 42, [2003] 1 All ER 135.

[187] *Lopez Ostra* v *Spain* (1995) 20 EHRR 277; *Vetterlein* v *Hampshire CC* [2001] EWHC 560 (Admin), [2002] Env LR 8.

[188] *Guerra* v *Italy* (1998) 26 EHRR 357.

[189] *Buckley* v *UK* (1997) 23 EHRR 101; *Chapman* v *UK* (2001) 33 EHRR 18; *South Buckinghamshire DC* v *Porter (No 1)*; *sub nom Wrexham CBC* v *Berry* [2003] UKHL 26, [2003] 2 AC 558, [2003] 3 All ER 1.

Connors v *UK*.[190] In this case a summary procedure used to evict a family from a local authority caravan site was found to be in breach of Article 8. In the view of the court, the serious consequences of eviction meant that 'particularly weighty reasons of public interest' were required by way of justification, and in this case the United Kingdom government had failed to provide any. The government had also failed to establish that there was any pressing social need to justify the summary nature of the rules, given that gypsies on privately owned sites enjoyed greater procedural safeguards. The House of Lords had previously taken a narrow approach to Article 8 in a case concerning a man whose ex-wife unilaterally gave notice on a house that they had shared. A majority of their Lordships held that the landlord had an unqualified statutory right to recover possession, and that it was unnecessary to establish a justification under Article 8(2).[191] The reasoning in *Connors* casts doubt on the correctness of this decision, and in *Kay* v *Lambeth* the House of Lords questioned whether *Connors* and *Qazi* were reconcilable.[192] Since then the European Court of Human Rights has effectively endorsed the reasoning of the minority in *Kay*,[193] and the House of Lords has conceded that the ratio of *Qazi* must be modified.[194]

Privacy and the media

Article 8 has, of course, been applied in cases involving more 'conventional' privacy claims, and in an important line of domestic jurisprudence the national courts have considered whether the Human Rights Act requires them to develop a common law tort of privacy. It is clear that no such tort existed before the Act,[195] although it was possible to bring some privacy claims within the scope of existing torts such as breach of confidence, nuisance and trespass. In the first post-Human Rights Act 'privacy' case to come before the national courts, Sedley LJ famously asserted that:[196] '[W]e have reached a point where it can be said with confidence that the law recognises and will appropriately protect a right of personal privacy.'

However, in subsequent decisions the courts have stopped short of recognizing the existence of a new tort. In the first such case to reach the House of Lords, it was held that the creation of new torts was a matter for Parliament, and that Article 8

---

[190] (2005) 40 EHRR 9.

[191] *Qazi* v *Harrow LBC* [2003] UKHL 43, [2004] 1 AC 983, [2003] 4 All ER 461.

[192] *Kay* v *Lambeth LBC*; *Leeds City Council* v *Price* [2006] UKHL 10, [2006] 2 AC 465, [2006] 4 All ER 128.

[193] *McCann* v *UK* (2008) 47 EHRR 40.

[194] *Doherty* v *Birmingham City Council* [2008] UKHL 57 at [20], [2009] 1 AC 367 at [20], [2009] 1 All ER 653, *per* Lord Hope. Note also *Manchester City Council* v *Pinnock* [2010] UKSC 45. See: Loveland, 'A Tale of Two Trespassers: Reconsidering the Impact of the Human Rights Act on Rights of Residence in Rented Housing: Part 1' [2009] EHRLR 148; Loveland, 'A Tale of Two Trespassers: Reconsidering the Impact of the Human Rights Act on Rights of Residence in Rented Housing: Part 2' [2009] EHRLR 495.

[195] *Kaye* v *Robertson* [1991] FSR 62.

[196] *Douglas* v *Hello! Ltd (No 1)* [2001] QB 967 at 997, [2001] 2 All ER 289 at 316. For the final chapter in this long-running legal battle, see *Douglas* v *Hello! Ltd (No 6)* [2005] EWCA Civ 595, [2006] QB 125, [2005] 4 All ER 128; [2007] UKHL 21, [2007] 2 WLR 920, [2007] 4 All ER 545.

could instead be given effect by developing established torts and remedies.[197] In cases concerning media intrusions and the publication of information, it is the tort of breach of confidence that has begun to develop in this way:[198]

> The essence of [breach of confidence] is better encapsulated now as misuse of private information. In the case of individuals this tort, however labelled, affords respect for one aspect of an individual's privacy.

In *Murray* v *Express Newspapers*, the Court of Appeal confirmed that in order to succeed in such cases a claimant must first establish a 'reasonable expectation of privacy'. Once this has been done, the court must then go on to consider how the balance should be struck between the privacy right and the competing right to publish derived from Article 10.[199] In *Murray* itself, it was held to be arguable that a child walking down a street with his parents had a reasonable expectation of privacy, notwithstanding the fact that his mother was a famous author (JK Rowling). An appeal against a decision to strike out his claim for infringement of privacy and data protection breaches was therefore allowed. In *A* v *B*, Lord Woolf set out a number of guidelines for use in cases in which media interference with the right to respect for private life is alleged. On the facts, it was held that a Premier League footballer was not entitled to an injunction preventing details of extramarital sexual relationships from being published.[200]

The Strasbourg court has rarely had to consider claims involving media intrusions,[201] and it rejected Earl Spencer's claim that the government had failed to protect him from such interference because it was not convinced that he lacked a remedy in domestic law.[202] In *Peck* v *UK*, however, the court found a breach of Article 8 when CCTV footage recorded shortly after the applicant's suicide attempt was broadcast on television.[203] The case highlighted significant weaknesses in the ability of domestic law to safeguard individual privacy, and further developments in this field now seem inevitable. The only question is whether Parliament will finally grasp the nettle before the judiciary's hand is forced:[204]

> The recent judgment in *Peck* v *United Kingdom*…shows that in circumstances where the law of confidence did not operate, our domestic law has already been held to be

---

[197] *Wainwright* v *Home Office* [2003] UKHL 53, [2004] 2 AC 406, [2003] 4 All ER 969.

[198] *Campbell* v *MGN* [2004] UKHL 22 at [14]–[15], [2004] 2 AC 457 at [14]–[15], [2004] 2 All ER 995, *per* Lord Nicholls.

[199] [2008] EWCA Civ 446, [2009] Ch 481.

[200] [2002] EWCA Civ 337, [2003] QB 195, [2002] 2 All ER 545. See also *Mosley* v *Newsgroup Newspapers Ltd.* [2008] EWHC 1777 (QB), [2008] EMLR 20 (president of Formula One's ruling body had reasonable expectation of privacy in respect of unconventional sexual activities carried on at his home).

[201] See *Von Hannover* v *Germany* (2006) 43 EHRR 7 for an example of a case in which a breach of Article 8 was established. See also Moreham, 'The Right to Respect for Private Life in the ECHR: A Re-examination' [2008] EHRLR 44.

[202] *Earl Spencer* v *UK* (1998) 25 EHRR CD 105.

[203] (2003) 36 EHRR 41. See also *Wainwright* v *UK* (2007) 44 EHRR 40, discussed at p 202.

[204] *Douglas* v *Hello! Ltd (No 6)* [2003] EWHC 786 (Ch) at [229], [2003] 3 All ER 996 at [229], *per* Lindsay J. See Aplin, 'The Development of the Action for Breach of Confidence in a Post-HRA Era' [2007] IPQ 19; Singh and Strachan, 'Privacy Postponed' [2003] EHRLR Special Issue 12.

inadequate. That inadequacy will have to be made good and if Parliament does not step in then the courts will be obliged to. Further development by the courts may merely be awaiting the first post-Human Rights Act case where neither the law of confidence nor any other domestic law protects an individual who deserves protection.

Correspondence, surveillance, and other aspects of private life

Police and prison searches and the use of covert surveillance techniques will obviously give rise to privacy issues, but they will generally be justifiable on one of the grounds set out in Article 8(2). However, in order to avoid a breach of the Convention, such actions must be in accordance with a lawful procedure and must satisfy the requirements of proportionality. Breaches of Article 8 have been established in several cases concerning the interception of prisoners' correspondence, on the basis that the authorities' objectives could have been achieved by less restrictive means.[205] Similarly, in *Wainwright* v *UK*, Article 8 was held to have been breached by intimate searches of two visitors to a prison. Although the searches had been conducted for the legitimate purpose of tackling a drug problem within the prison, the nature of the searches was wholly disproportionate and the prison officers had failed to comply with their own procedures.[206] In *Malone* v *UK*,[207] the finding that police telephone tapping was not properly regulated led to the enactment of the Interception of Communications Act 1985, and further criticism in *Halford* v *UK* prompted a more comprehensive piece of legislation.[208] More recently, breaches of the Convention have been established in respect of an employer's monitoring of email and Internet usage,[209] the use of covertly obtained footage in a video identification parade,[210] and the mass interception of telephone communications between the United Kingdom and an external receiver.[211]

Two separate Article 8 issues arose from the case of a defendant prosecuted for rape on the strength of DNA evidence. His DNA sample had been taken when he was arrested for an unrelated burglary offence, but the match linking him to the rape case was not made until after he had been acquitted of the burglary. Because his DNA record should have been destroyed after that acquittal in accordance with section 64 of PACE, the trial judge ruled that its use as the basis for his arrest was prohibited and he directed an acquittal. However, on a reference from the Attorney

---

[205] *R (on the application of Daly)* v *Secretary of State for the Home Department* [2001] UKHL 26, [2001] 2 AC 532, [2001] 3 All ER 433; *Campbell* v *UK* (1993) 15 EHRR 137.

[206] (2007) 44 EHRR 40. The House of Lords had rejected the Article 8 complaint, in part because the Human Rights Act was not in force at the time of the incident: *Wainwright* v *Home Office* [2003] UKHL 53, [2004] 2 AC 406, [2003] 4 All ER 969.

[207] (1985) 7 EHRR 14.

[208] (1997) 24 EHRR 523; Regulation of Investigatory Powers Act 2000. See also *Khan* v *UK* (2001) 31 EHRR 45.

[209] *Copland* v *UK* (2007) 45 EHRR 37 (interference not properly regulated by law).

[210] *Perry* v *UK* (2004) 39 EHRR 3 (interference not in accordance with law as contrary to PACE Codes of Practice).

[211] *Liberty* v *UK* (2009) 48 EHRR 1 (interference not properly regulated by law).

General, the House of Lords ruled that the judge had a discretion as to whether to allow the prosecution to proceed: although Article 8 rights were engaged in such a case, any interference with those rights under Article 8(2) could be fully justified.[212] At the beginning of the hearing the House of Lords had made an anonymity order to protect the defendant's identity, but a differently constituted House later discharged that order following an application from the BBC.[213] Their Lordships held that although the defendant could have no reasonable expectation of privacy concerning the fact of his prosecution and acquittal, the reporting of the existence of a DNA sample linking him to the rape offence would amount to a significant interference with his rights under Article 8. This interference could be justified, however, and any concerns about trial by media were outweighed by the right of freedom of expression on a matter of legitimate public interest. In another case the Grand Chamber found the long-term retention of DNA records and fingerprints taken in the course of criminal investigations to be a violation of Article 8.[214] The power to retain such data clearly engaged the right to respect for private life, and the impact on that right was disproportionate due to its blanket and indiscriminate nature. A breach of Article 8 was also established when a member of a group opposed to the arms trade was photographed in the street by the police after attending the annual general meeting of a company linked to the arms industry.[215]

Article 8 rights have also been considered in the context of the sale of electoral registers,[216] the hunting ban,[217] and the availability of therapeutic abortions.[218]

Article 9: The right to freedom of thought, conscience, and religion

This right includes the freedom to change religion or belief, and the freedom to manifest one's religion or belief in worship, teaching, practice, and observance. The bare right to freedom of thought, conscience, and religion is absolute, but the right to *manifest* a religion or belief is qualified by Article 9(2). This permits the right to be restricted on the grounds of public safety, public order, the protection of health or morals, and the protection of the rights and freedoms of others. To comply with Article 9(2), any such restriction must be prescribed by law and must be 'necessary in a democratic society'.

---

[212] *Attorney-General's Reference (No 3 of 1999)* [2001] 2 AC 91, [2001] 2 WLR 56.

[213] *Attorney-General's Reference (No 3 of 1999)* [2009] UKHL 34, [2010] 1 AC 145, [2010] 1 All ER 235.

[214] *S and Marper* v *UK* (2009) 48 EHRR 50.

[215] *R (on the application of Wood)* v *Metropolitan Police Commissioner* [2009] EWCA Civ 414, [2010] 1 WLR 123, [2009] 4 All ER 951.

[216] *R (on the application of Robertson)* v *Wakefield MDC* [2001] EWHC 915 (Admin), [2002] QB 1052, [2002] 2 WLR 889 (absence of right to opt out of commercial register did engage Article 8).

[217] *R (on the application of Countryside Alliance)* v *Attorney General* [2007] UKHL 52, [2008] 1 AC 719 (Article 8 not engaged due to public nature of hunting).

[218] *Tysiac* v *Poland* (2007) 45 EHRR 42 (no effective mechanism for determining availability of abortion on therapeuitic grounds; breach of Article 8 established).

Alongside major world faiths such as Islam[219] and Christianity,[220] pacifism,[221] Scientology,[222] atheism,[223] and Buddhism[224] have all been assumed to constitute protected beliefs. Moreover, the term 'religion or belief' has been interpreted widely to extend beyond purely theistic beliefs and beliefs with a metaphysical element:[225]

> [Article 9] is, in its religious dimension, one of the most vital elements that go to make up the identity of believers and of their conception of life, but it is also a precious asset for atheists, agnostics, sceptics and the unconcerned.

On the other hand, the manifestation of purely political views is *not* protected, and in a case under Article 2 of the First Protocol the Court stated that protected beliefs are those that 'attain a certain level of cogency, seriousness, cohesion and importance'.[226] In *R* v *Secretary of State for Education and Employment, ex parte Williamson*, the House of Lords was prepared to accept as 'religious' the belief that corporal punishment was a biblically mandated part of a Christian education.[227] By contrast, in *Friend* v *Lord Advocate*, the House of Lords rejected the idea that a strongly held belief in the right to hunt with hounds was comparable to a religious belief for Article 9 purposes.[228]

'Manifestations' of religion or belief

Thus far most Article 9 cases have been unsuccessful: the Court or former Commission has generally found either that there has been no interference with a protected 'manifestation', or that any interference was justified. 'Manifestations' covered by Article 9 include worship,[229] proselytism,[230] observing dietary restrictions,[231] and religious education.[232] In *Arrowsmith* v *UK*,[233] however, the distribution of leaflets urging troops not to serve in Northern Ireland was held not to be a manifestation of pacifism because the leaflets were not actually an expression of the applicant's pacifist views.[234] In addition, although there is a positive obligation for states to ensure the peaceful enjoyment of religious freedom, there is no requirement to guarantee equality between religions or to prohibit religious discrimination.[235] It seems that religious discrimination will only

---

[219] *Ahmad* v *UK* (1982) 4 EHRR 126.   [220] *Kokkinakis* v *Greece* (1994) 17 EHRR 397.
[221] *Arrowsmith* v *UK* (1978) 19 D&R 5.
[222] *X and Church of Scientology* v *Sweden* (1978) 16 D&R 68.
[223] *Angelini* v *Sweden* (1986) 51 D&R 41.   [224] *X* v *UK* (1974) 1 D&R 41.
[225] *Kokkinakis* v *Greece* (1994) 17 EHRR 397 at [31].
[226] *Campbell and Cosans* v *United Kingdom* (1982) 4 EHRR 293.
[227] [2005] UKHL 15, [2005] 2 All ER 1, [2005] HRLR 14. The ban on corporal punishment in schools was nevertheless held to be compatible with Article 9, as any interference with the claimants' freedom to manifest their beliefs was justifiable.
[228] [2007] UKHL 53, [2008] HRLR 11.   [229] *Holy Monasteries* v *Greece* (1995) 20 EHRR 1.
[230] *Kokkinakis* v *Greece* (1994) 17 EHRR 397.
[231] *Cha'are Shalom Ve Tsedek* v *France* (2000) 9 BHRC 27.
[232] *Kjeldsen, Busk Madsen and Pedersen* v *Denmark* (1979–1980) 1 EHRR 711.
[233] (1978) 19 D&R 5.
[234] See also *R (on the application of Playfoot (a child))* v *Millais School Governing Body* [2007] EWHC 1698 (Admin), [2007] HRLR 34: Article 9 not engaged by ban on the wearing of a chastity ring as not a manifestation of Christian beliefs.
[235] Except in states that have ratified Protocol 12: the United Kingdom is not one of those states. Note also that EU states, including the United Kingdom, are required by EU law to have legislation in place prohibiting religious discrimination.

violate Article 9 where there is an element of compulsion. Thus, where an individual has voluntarily put himself in a position in which his religious freedom is restricted, the courts have generally found either that there has been no interference with Convention rights, or that the interference is justified. In *X* v *UK*,[236] for example, the Commission agreed with the United Kingdom government that a law requiring Sikh motorcyclists to wear crash helmets was a 'necessary' restriction on religious freedom. However, the government subsequently changed its mind and turban-wearing Sikhs are now exempt from the law in question.[237] In another case,[238] the Commission rejected the claim of a Muslim teacher who was dismissed for missing forty-five minutes of classes each week in order to attend the mosque. The Commission concluded that the teacher had accepted restrictions on his religious freedom when taking up his post.

Turning to the domestic courts, the Court of Appeal recently found no breach of Article 9 when a Christian registrar was dismissed for refusing to perform civil partnerships,[239] and in *R (on the application of Swami Suryananda)* v *Welsh Ministers*, a refusal to exempt a Hindu community's temple bullock from a policy of slaughtering cattle testing positive for bovine tuberculosis was held to be justifiable and proportionate.[240]

Religious dress codes

Several recent decisions have dealt with restrictions on the freedom to observe a religious dress code. In *R (on the application of Begum)* v *Denbigh High School*, a 14-year-old Muslim girl challenged a decision to exclude her from the defendant school for refusing to comply with its uniform policy. The policy allowed girls to wear a form of dress—the *shalwar kameeze*—that was acceptable to the vast majority of its Muslim students, but the applicant believed that she was obliged by her religion to wear a more loose-fitting garment, the *jilbab*. The House of Lords found in favour of the school,[241] with the majority of the panel concluding that there had been no interference with the applicant's Article 9 rights: she and her family had chosen the school with full knowledge of its uniform policy, and other schools in the area would have accepted her as a pupil and allowed her to wear the *jilbab*. In partly dissenting judgments, Lord Nicholls and Baroness Hale held that the applicant's religious freedom had been restricted, but they agreed that her claim should be dismissed as they considered the restriction to be justifiable. In rejecting the idea that Ms Begum's Article 9 rights were even engaged in this case, the approach of the majority is arguably too narrow. The minority approach, however, would appear to be compatible with the Grand Chamber's decision in *Sahin* v *Turkey*.[242] In this case rules preventing university

---

[236] (1978) 14 D&R 234.   [237] Road Traffic Act 1988, s 16(2).

[238] *Ahmad* v *UK* (1982) 4 EHRR 126; see also *Copsey* v *WWB Devon Clays* [2005] EWCA Civ 932, [2005] ICR 1789.

[239] *Ladele* v *London Borough of Islington* [2009] EWCA Civ 1357, [2010] 1 WLR 955.

[240] [2007] EWCA Civ 893.

[241] [2006] UKHL 15, [2007] 1 AC 100, [2006] 2 All ER 487.

[242] (2007) 44 EHRR 5: see Hill and Sandberg, 'Is Nothing Sacred? Clashing Symbols in a Secular World' [2007] PL 488; Lewis, 'What Not to Wear: Religious Rights, the European Court, and the Margin of Appreciation' (2007) 56 ICLQ 395.

students from wearing headscarves were found to be compatible with Article 9 on the basis that they pursued the legitimate aim of protecting the rights and freedoms of others in a secular state.

A school that banned pupils from wearing the veil or *niqab* successfully defended its actions in *R (on the application of X) v Headteachers and Governors of Y School*,[243] but in *R (on the application of Watkins-Singh) v Governing Body of Aberdare Girls' School*, the High Court found a refusal to allow a Sikh pupil to wear a small religious bangle (*kara*) to be unlawful.[244]

Article 10: The right to freedom of expression

Article 10 covers the right to hold opinions and to receive and impart information and ideas. The right may be restricted in the interests of national security, territorial integrity or public safety, for the prevention of disorder or crime, for the protection of health, morals or the rights and freedoms of others, in order to prevent the disclosure of confidential information, or in order to maintain the authority and impartiality of the judiciary.[245] Freedom of expression lies at the heart of the Convention system, and its importance is expressly recognized by section 12 of the Human Rights Act.[246] It has also played a significant role in the jurisprudence on Article 8.[247]

Protected forms of expression can include words, pictures, dress, and even conduct,[248] although some types of expression are more highly valued than others. Commercial speech, for example, does not attract the same level of protection as political speech,[249] and as Lord Hoffmann observed in *Belfast City Council v Miss Behavin' Ltd*, 'the right to vend pornography is not the most important right of free expression in a democratic society'.[250]

When compared with some of the other Convention rights it could be said that Article 10(1) is easily engaged, and most of the case law under this Article focuses on whether an interference with freedom of expression is justifiable. However, *R (on the application of Rusbridger) v Attorney-General* is a rare example of a claim that failed because the court found that Article 10 was not even engaged. The House of Lords had been asked to declare that a treason provision was incompatible with freedom of expression, but it declined to grant the relief sought because the applicants had already published articles advocating the peaceful overthrow of the monarchy and no one had attempted to prosecute them. Their freedom of expression had therefore not been

---

[243] [2007] EWHC 298 (Admin), [2008] 1 All ER 249.

[244] [2008] EWHC 1865 (Admin), [2008] ELR 561. The case was brought under anti-discrimination legislation, but the court clearly took the view that Article 9 pointed to the same conclusion.

[245] Article 10(2).   [246] See p 150.   [247] See p 197.

[248] *Stevens v UK* (1986) D&R 245; *Steel v UK* (1999) 28 EHRR 603.

[249] *X and the Church of Scientology v Sweden* (1978) 16 D&R 68; *R (on the application of British American Tobacco UK Ltd) v Secretary of State for Health* [2004] EWHC 2493 (Admin).

[250] [2007] UKHL 19 at [16], [2007] 1 WLR 1420 at [16], [2007] 3 All ER 1007.

inhibited, and the question before the court was purely hypothetical. Nevertheless, Lord Scott did not refrain from expressing his opinion on the matter:[251]

> It is plain as a pike staff to the respondents and everyone else that no-one who advocates the peaceful abolition of the monarchy...is at any risk of prosecution. Whatever may be the correct construction of s 3, taken by itself, it is clear beyond any peradventure first, that the section would now be 'read down' as required by s 3 of the Human Rights Act 1998...and second, that no Attorney-General or Director of Public Prosecutions would or could authorise a prosecution for such advocacy without becoming a laughing stock. To do so would plainly be an unlawful act under s 6(1) of the 1998 Act.

Limitations under Article 10(2)

Freedom of expression is limited in numerous ways by domestic law, but most of the restrictions could be said to pursue one of the legitimate aims permitted under Article 10(2). The decision in most cases therefore turns on the issue of proportionality and whether the restriction in question could be considered 'necessary in a democratic society'. Thus, in *Handyside* v *UK*,[252] a prosecution under the Obscene Publications Act 1959 was held to be a legitimate and proportionate means of protecting public morals: the court was prepared to grant a wide margin of appreciation in the absence of a uniform conception of morality. In another case, the refusal to give a film certificate to an allegedly blasphemous video was found to be a legitimate way of protecting the rights and freedoms of others.[253] As the decision in the latter case indicates, the Strasbourg court does not consider restrictions on blasphemous speech to be inherently incompatible with Article 10,[254] but the government nevertheless legislated to abolish the offences of blasphemy and blasphemous libel in 2008.[255] These offences were widely perceived to be anachronistic, and, given that they protected only the Anglican faith, the extent to which they pursued a legitimate purpose was highly questionable. Prior to abolition there had been no public prosecution under the blasphemy laws since 1922,[256] and in 2007 the High Court held that a magistrate had correctly refused to allow a private prosecution following the BBC's screening of *Jerry Springer: The Opera*.[257]

Reporting restrictions pending the outcome of legal proceedings are permissible under the Convention, in the interests of protecting the rights and freedoms of others and maintaining the impartiality of the judiciary. However, any restrictions must be prescribed by law and proportionate to their objectives, and criticism that the common law contempt jurisdiction was too uncertain in scope[258] led to the

---

[251] [2003] UKHL 38 at [23], [2004] 1 AC 357 at [23], [2003] 3 All ER 784; Treason Felony Act 1848, s 3.

[252] (1979) 1 EHRR 737.   [253] *Wingrove* v *UK* (1997) 24 EHRR 1.

[254] *Otto-Preminger Institut* v *Austria* (1995) 19 EHRR 34.

[255] Criminal Justice and Immigration Act 2008, s 79.   [256] *R* v *Gott* (1922) 16 Cr App R 87.

[257] *R (on the application of Green)* v *City of Westminster Magistrates Court* [2007] EWHC 2785(Admin), (2007) 157 NLJ 1767.

[258] *Sunday Times* v *UK* (1979–1980) 2 EHRR 245.

enactment of the Contempt of Court Act 1981.[259] It has also been held that the law of defamation is compatible with freedom of expression, as long as the level of damages awarded in successful cases is not so high as to have a 'chilling effect' on the essence of the right.[260]

Advertising is a form of speech capable of protection under Article 10, and it follows that any restrictions on advertising must pursue a legitimate purpose in order to survive Convention scrutiny. A legal challenge to regulations restricting the advertising of tobacco failed in *R (on the application of British American Tobacco UK Ltd)* v *Secretary of State for Health*, because the impact on freedom of expression was proportionate to the legitimate aim of protecting public health.[261] The House of Lords has also upheld the United Kingdom's legislative ban on political advertising.[262]

Article 10 cases raising national security issues include the related cases of *R v Shayler*[263] and *Attorney-General v Punch*.[264] In the first case, David Shayler, a former MI5 officer, was prosecuted under the Official Secrets Act 1989 for disclosing information obtained during the course of his employment. In a ruling on a preliminary matter, the House of Lords held that the restrictions on free speech were a legitimate and proportionate response to the interests of national security, and it was not necessary to read a public interest defence into the Act. In the second case, a magazine published an article by David Shayler while proceedings against him were still ongoing. Injunctions had already been obtained to prevent Mr Shayler from publishing such information, and it was held that the publisher could be liable for contempt of court. The fact that it did not believe the material to be harmful to the national interest was no defence: the purpose of the injunction was to preserve the confidentiality of the information until its status had been determined, and the terms of the order were proportionate to this objective.

A right to cause offence?

Article 17 of the Convention states that it does not confer any right to engage in activities aimed at the destruction of protected rights and freedoms, and this provides a basis for denying protection to speech inciting racial or religious hatred.[265] In any

---

[259] A line of Human Rights Act cases is already developing concerning the circumstances in which reporting restrictions and injunctions should be imposed: see *Venables and Thompson* v *News Group Newspapers* [2001] Fam 430, [2001] 1 All ER 908. In *R (on the application of the Telegraph Group plc)* v *Sherwood* [2001] EWCA Crim 1075, [2001] 1 WLR 1983, the Court of Appeal suggested that the pre-Human Rights Act approach was already broadly compatible with the Convention.

[260] *Tolstoy Miloslavsky* v *UK* (1995) 20 EHRR 442. In *Steel and Morris* v *UK* (2005) 41 EHRR 22, it was held that Article 10 could also be infringed if the defendant in a defamation case had no access to legal aid and faced a significant inequality of arms: see p 193.

[261] [2004] EWHC 2493 (Admin), (2004) The Times, 11 November.

[262] *R (on the application of Animal Defenders International)* v *Secretary of State for Culture, Media and Sport* [2008] UKHL 15, [2008] 1 AC 1312, [2008] 3 All ER 193; see p 161.

[263] [2002] UKHL 11, [2003] 1 AC 247, [2002] 2 All ER 477.

[264] [2002] UKHL 50, [2003] 1 AC 1046, [2003] 1 All ER 289.

[265] *Norwood* v *UK* (2005) 40 EHRR SE11 (public display of an Islamophobic poster did not enjoy the protection of Article 10).

event, laws aimed at restricting hate speech will generally fall within the exceptions permitted under Article 10(2), subject to the principle of proportionality.

The fact that certain ideas are controversial, or may 'offend, shock or disturb',[266] is not a sufficient justification for preventing their expression, but in a recent case the BBC was held to have acted lawfully in refusing to broadcast an election video containing graphic images of aborted foetuses.[267] The House of Lords accepted that the video constituted a form of protected speech, but found the BBC's decision to be consistent with Article 10(2) and with its statutory duty not to offend against good taste and decency. Lord Walker explained that although material likely to cause 'a significant degree of revulsion' could potentially be justified by its purpose, the BBC had considerable experience in determining accepted standards of taste and decency and its decision was within the limits of its discretion.[268]

In another case a man was convicted of a public order offence[269] after preaching in a city centre whilst displaying a sign with the words: 'Stop Immorality. Stop Homosexuality. Stop Lesbianism.' The Administrative Court held that although the man had been motivated by sincerely held religious beliefs and had intended to preach rather than cause offence, his conviction was compatible with Article 10.[270] Article 10 was also considered in *R (on the application of Farrakhan)* v *Secretary of State for the Home Department*.[271] In this case the Home Office had refused to allow a controversial political figure to enter the United Kingdom on the basis that his radical views might inflame religious tensions and lead to disorder. The court accepted that Article 10 was engaged but held that the decision to refuse entry had been legitimate. By contrast, a refusal to allow a Dutch MP (Geert Wilders) to enter the country because of his controversial views about Islam was held to be a substantial interference with his Article 10 rights. The purpose of Mr Wilders's intended visit was to meet with MPs and other policymakers to seek to persuade them of his views. As this was just the sort of expression for which the Article 10 right existed, any decision to exclude him would require evidence of a threat that he would do something unlawful if admitted.[272]

KEY ISSUE

Is there a right to cause offence? If not, why not? A right of freedom of expression must surely include the right to shock or offend, and to allow the reader, viewer, or listener the chance to make up his or her own mind. The right of freedom of expression extends, as it

---

[266] *Handyside* v *UK* (1979) 1 EHRR 737 at 48; see also *Jersild* v *Denmark* (1995) 19 EHRR 1.

[267] *R (on the application of ProLife Alliance)* v *BBC* [2003] UKHL 23, [2004] 1 AC 185, [2003] 2 All ER 977.

[268] Ibid, at [122].

[269] The offence of causing harassment, alarm, or distress: Public Order Act 1986, s 5.

[270] *Hammond* v *DPP* [2004] EWHC 69 (Admin), (2004) 168 JP 601. (It was also compatible with Article 9.) See further, Turenne, 'The Compatibility of Criminal Liability with Freedom of Expression' [2007] Crim LR 866.

[271] [2002] EWCA Civ 606, [2002] QB 1391, [2002] 4 All ER 289.

[272] *Re GW (Netherlands) (EEA Reg 21: Fundamental Interests)* [2009] UKAIT 50.

must, to unpopular and uncomfortable facts and opinions. The degree of deference shown to the BBC in the *Pro-Life Alliance* case has been criticized,[273] and in a strong dissenting judgment Lord Scott concluded that the restriction was not 'necessary':[274]

> A broadcasters' mind-set that rejects a party election television programme dealing with an issue of undeniable public importance such as abortion, on the ground that large numbers of the voting public would find the programme 'offensive' denigrates the voting public, treats them like children who need to be protected from the unpleasant realities of life, seriously undervalues their political maturity and can only promote…voter-apathy.

A key question must be where the balance between the right and its limitation is to be struck, and the degree of deference to be shown by the court to individual publishers or broadcasters.

 Questions

1. Was too much deference shown to the views and judgements of the BBC?
2. Where should the limits of free speech be drawn?

Article 11: The right to freedom of peaceful assembly and freedom of association with others

Freedom of association

The right to freedom of association expressly includes the right to 'form and join a trade union', and states have a positive duty to create conditions in which the exercise of this right is possible.[275] The right not to join a union is also protected, although it may be that this right is only breached if the individual is opposed to union membership for reasons of conscience and principle.[276] Professional associations are not considered to be trade unions for these purposes, and requiring members of a profession to join a relevant association will not normally be contrary to Article 11.[277]

The rights set out in Article 11 may be subject to restrictions in the interests of national security or public safety, for the prevention of disorder or crime, for the protection of health or morals, or for the protection of the rights and freedoms of others.[278] Any such restrictions must be prescribed by law and necessary in a democratic society, and this means taking into account the rights of associations themselves. For example, a law preventing a union from expelling a member on the grounds of

---

[273] MacDonald, '*R (on the application of ProLife Alliance)* v *British Broadcasting Corporation*' [2003] 6 EHRLR 651; Barendt, 'Free Speech and Abortion' [2003] PL 580.

[274] [2003] UKHL 23 at [99], [2004] 1 AC 185 at [99], [2003] 2 All ER 977.

[275] *Swedish Engine Drivers Union* v *Sweden* (1979–80) 1 EHRR 617.

[276] *Young* v *UK* (1982) 4 EHRR 38; cf. *Sibson* v *UK* (1994) 17 EHRR 193 (no breach in respect of a worker who simply wanted to change from one union to another and who had been offered redeployment).

[277] *Le Compte* v *Belgium* (1982) 4 EHRR 1.   [278] Article 11(2).

his involvement with the BNP was recently found to be incompatible with Article 11 because, despite its legitimate aim, it had a disproportionate impact on the union's freedom to choose its own members.[279] Similarly, in *RSPCA v Attorney General*, it was held that Article 11 did not preclude the RSPCA from having a membership policy excluding those who wished to change its policy on hunting. This was because the Article 11 right 'embraces the freedom to exclude from association those whose membership [a society] honestly believes to be damaging to [its] interests'.[280]

Freedom of assembly

The 'assembly' limb of Article 11 has primarily been used in the context of the right to peaceful protest. It has been held, for example, that a decision to arrest demonstrators for breach of the peace must be measured against the yardstick of proportionality,[281] and at Strasbourg level the power to bind over to keep the peace has been criticized as too vague to constitute a limitation 'prescribed by law'.[282] However, in several domestic cases in which the police have taken action against demonstrators, it has been held that Article 11 rights are simply not engaged. In *Gillan*, for example, the House of Lords found no interference with Article 11 when random stop-and-search powers were used against a student participating in a protest against an arms fair.[283] When the case was heard in Strasbourg the Court of Human Rights found the use of these powers to be in breach of Article 8, and deemed it unnecessary to consider the 'intimidatory and chilling effect' that they might have on the right to peaceful protest.[284] This approach is not untypical, and the domestic courts have shown a tendency to gloss over any potential interference with the right to freedom of assembly where Article 11 is raised in conjunction with other rights. In *R (on the application of Wood) v Metropolitan Police Commissioner*, for example, the High Court dismissed the idea that being photographed by the police after leaving the annual general meeting of a company linked to the arms industry might have a chilling effect on the Article 11 rights of an anti-arms campaigner.[285] Instead the decision focused on the issues arising under Article 8,[286] and when the case was heard in the Court of Appeal Article 11 was not even raised.[287]

Recent challenges to legislation having a regulatory effect on demonstrations have met with mixed success. In *Blum v DPP*, the Divisional Court held that four protestors who had taken part in an unauthorized but peaceful demonstration in the designated

---

[279] *ASLEF v UK* (2007) 45 EHRR 34. See Ewing, 'The Implications of the *ASLEF* case' (2007) 36(4) ILJ 425.

[280] [2002] 1 WLR 448 at 466, [2001] 3 All ER 530 at 547, *per* Lightman J.

[281] *R (on the application of Laporte) v Chief Constable of Gloucester* [2006] UKHL 55, [2007] 2 AC 105, [2007] 2 WLR 46. See also: Smith, 'Protecting Protest: A Constitutional Shift' (2007) 66(2) CLJ 253.

[282] *Steel v United Kingdom* (1999) 28 EHRR 603.

[283] *R (on the application of Gillan) v Commissioner of Police for the Metropolis* [2006] UKHL 12, [2006] 2 AC 307, [2006] 4 All ER 1041.

[284] *Gillan and Quinton v UK* (2010) 50 EHRR 45, at [88].

[285] *R (on the application of Wood) v Metropolitan Police Commissioner* [20089] EWHC 1105 (Admin), [2008] HRLR 34.

[286] The claim under Article 8 was also rejected, although this was overturned by the Court of Appeal.

[287] [2009] EWCA Civ 414, [2010] 1 WLR 123, [2009] 4 All ER 951.

area around Parliament had been properly prosecuted and convicted, and the statutory provisions requiring authorization for such protests were deemed to be compatible with Article 11.[288] By contrast, in *R (on the application of Tabernacle) v Secretary of State for Defence*, byelaws prohibiting camps from being set up in the vicinity of atomic weapons establishments were held to constitute an unjustifiable limitation on the applicant's rights under Articles 10 and 11.[289]

Note, finally, that 'assemblies' will only be protected under Article 11 if they are of a type necessary to the proper functioning of a democracy, and gatherings for recreational or sporting purposes will not normally fall into this category. A recent challenge to the ban on hunting with dogs was rejected on this basis.[290]

Article 12: The right to marry and found a family

The right to marry

This Article provides that 'men and women of marriageable age have the right to marry and to found a family, according to the national laws governing the exercise of this right.' On its face the wording appears to restrict the right to marry to couples of the opposite sex, and it also gives states considerable scope to regulate the exercise of the right as they see fit. However, in *Goodwin v UK*, it was held that the refusal to recognize the change in gender of a post-operative transsexual, and the negative impact of this decision on the right to marry, was a violation of Articles 8 and 12.[291] In the view of the court, evidence of changing attitudes towards gender and marriage meant that there was less scope for affording a wide margin of appreciation, although states still have some discretion as to how the effects of a change in gender should be recognized.[292] Other relevant decisions include the ruling that laws prohibiting a man and his former daughter-in-law from marrying were incompatible with the Convention,[293] and the decision that laws designed to prevent certain classes of immigrant from entering into sham marriages had a disproportionate impact on Article 12 rights.[294]

---

[288] [2006] EWHC 3209 (Admin); see also *Ziliberberg v Moldova* (2005) ECHR (Admissibility) 61821/00.

[289] [2009] EWCA Civ 23.

[290] *R (on the application of Countryside Alliance) v Attorney-General* [2007] UKHL 52, [2007] 3 WLR 922.

[291] (2002) 35 EHRR 18; applied in *Bellinger v Bellinger* [2003] UKHL 21, [2003] 2 AC 467, [2003] 2 All ER 593. The Gender Recognition Act 2004 was introduced in response to these decisions.

[292] *R and F v UK* (2006) ECHR 35748/05 (no breach in respect of a male-to-female transsexual who could not obtain a full gender recognition certificate under the 2004 Act without first divorcing a woman to whom she wished to remain married.)

[293] *B and L v UK* (2006) 42 EHRR 11. The incompatibility identified was removed by the Marriage Act 1949 (Remedial) Order 2007, SI 2007/438.

[294] *R (on the application of Baiai) v Secretary of State for the Home Department* [2008] UKHL 53, [2009] 1 AC 287, [2008] 3 All ER 1094. At first instance the High Court also issued a declaration of incompatibility in respect of Article 14, because the law did not apply to marriages conducted by the Church of England: the government responded by announcing that it would extend the scheme to Church of England marriages as well, so as to remove the element of discrimination.

The right to found a family

There have been fewer cases concerning the 'right to found a family', although the courts have dealt with a handful of claims arising from restrictions on prisoners' access to facilities for artificial insemination. In *R (on the application of Mellor) v Secretary of State for the Home Department*, a refusal to provide such facilities was deemed to be lawful,[295] but in a more recent case the government's policy was found to be in breach of Article 8 because it failed to strike a fair balance between competing private and public interests.[296] On the other hand, Article 12 does not entitle a prisoner to receive conjugal visits.[297]

Article 14: The right not to be discriminated against with regard to other Convention rights

The substantive rights set out in the Convention must, by virtue of Article 14, be respected and protected in a non-discriminatory way:

> The enjoyment of the rights and freedoms set forth in this Convention shall be secured without discrimination on any grounds such as sex, race, colour, language, religion, political or other opinion, national or social origin, association with a national minority, property, birth or other status.

The list of prohibited grounds of discrimination is broad and non-exhaustive, and the reference to 'other status' has enabled additional grounds such as sexual orientation,[298] illegitimacy,[299] homelessness,[300] and place of residence[301] to be brought within its ambit. A class of persons will only enjoy a common 'status' if they share something akin to a personal characteristic—a mutual interest in hunting, for example, will not suffice[302]—but both the Strasbourg jurisprudence and recent House of Lords decisions suggest that the concept should be given a generous meaning.[303]

Article 14 does not create a free-standing right, and a breach of the non-discrimination principle can only be established in conjunction with another Convention right. However, although the link with another right must be more than merely tenuous,[304] it will be sufficient to demonstrate that an act or omission 'falls

---

[295] [2001] EWCA Civ 472, [2002] QB 13, [2001] 3 WLR 533.

[296] *Dickson v UK* [2007] 3 FCR 877. In the light of this, it was considered unnecessary to examine the claim under Article 12.

[297] *ELH v UK* (1998) 25 EHRR CD 158.   [298] *Smith and Grady v UK* (2000) 29 EHRR 493.

[299] *Marckx v Belgium* (1979–80) 2 EHRR 330.

[300] *R (on the application of M) v Secretary of State for Work and Pensions* [2008] UKHL 63, [2009] 1 AC 311, [2009] 2 All ER 556.

[301] *Carson v UK* (2009) 48 EHRR 41.

[302] *R (on the application of Countryside Alliance) v Attorney-General* [2007] UKHL 52, [2007] 3 WLR 922.

[303] *R (on the application of M) v Secretary of State for Work and Pensions* [2008] UKHL 63 at [42], [2009] 1 AC 311 at [42], [2009] 2 All ER 556, *per* Lord Neuberger. See also *Kjeldsen, Busk Madsen and Pederson v Denmark* (1979–80) 1 EHRR 711.

[304] *M v Secretary of State for Work and Pensions* [2006] UKHL 11, [2006] 2 AC 91, [2006] 4 All ER 929.

within its ambit'. This means that even where the Convention does not *require* a state to take positive steps to protect or enhance a particular freedom, if it *chooses* to do so in respect of *some* groups, Article 14 may demand that the benefit is extended to all. For example, *Abdulaziz, Cabales and Balkandali* v *UK*[305] concerned an immigration rule governing when spouses who were non-nationals would be granted indefinite leave to remain in the United Kingdom, which treated men and women differently. There was no breach of Article 8 but the rule fell 'within the ambit' of the right to family life, and as it discriminated on gender grounds it was held that there had been a breach of Article 14.

It is well settled that in order for an issue to arise under Article 14 there must be a difference in the treatment of persons in relevantly similar situations,[306] and in *Wandsworth LBC* v *Michalak*, Brooke LJ stated that Article 14 cases normally require a court to address four questions:[307]

> If the answer to any of the four questions is 'no', then the claim is likely to fail, and it is in general unnecessary to proceed to the next question. These questions are:
>
> (i)   Do the facts fall within the ambit of one or more of the substantive Convention provisions…?
>
> (ii) If so, was there different treatment as respects that right between the complainant on the one hand and other persons put forward for comparison ('the chosen comparators') on the other?
>
> (iii) Were the chosen comparators in an analogous situation to the complainant's situation?
>
> (iv) If so, did the difference in treatment have an objective and reasonable justification…?

However, in *Carson* v *Secretary of State for Work and Pensions*, it was held that this approach may not be appropriate in every case.[308]

Where breaches of substantive Convention rights have been established, the Strasbourg bodies have often deemed it unnecessary to determine whether there has also been a breach of Article 14,[309] and the Article 14 jurisprudence is significantly underdeveloped as a result. Nevertheless, it is clear that the provision is capable of addressing both direct and indirect discrimination,[310] and in *Thlimmenos* v *Greece*, the court ruled that 'the right not to be discriminated against … is violated when States without an objective and reasonable justification fail to treat differently persons whose situations are significantly different', as well as where 'they treat differently persons in

---

[305] (1985) 7 EHRR 471.   [306] *Carson* v *UK* (2010) 51 EHRR 13, at [83].

[307] [2002] EWCA Civ 271 at [20], [2003] 1 WLR 617 at [20], [2002] 4 All ER 1136.

[308] [2005] UKHL 37 at [28]–[33], [2006] 1 AC 173 at [28]–[33], [2005] 4 All ER 545, *per* Lord Hoffmann. See also: McColgan, 'Cracking the Comparator Problem: Discrimination, "Equal" Treatment and the Role of Comparisons' [2006] EHRLR 650.

[309] In *Chassagnou and others* v *France* (2000) 29 EHRR 615, at [89], the court expressed the view that an examination of Article 14 is not generally required when the court finds a violation of one of the other substantive Articles, unless a 'clear inequality of treatment' is fundamental to the case.

[310] *Belgian Linguistics Case (No 2)* (1979–1980) 1 EHRR 252.

analogous situations without providing an objective and reasonable justification'.[311] There is also an emerging line of jurisprudence suggesting that 'a failure to attempt to correct inequality though different treatment may in itself give rise to a breach of [Article 14]',[312] although it is not entirely clear when the need for such positive action will arise.

Examples of laws and policies challenged successfully under Article 14 include the criminalization of homosexual acts in Northern Ireland,[313] the denial of rights to same-sex partners that would be afforded to other unmarried couples,[314] and the ban on gays in the military.[315]

Protocol 1

Protocol 1 of the Convention is concerned with three distinct rights: the right to peaceful enjoyment of possessions; the right to education; and the right to participate in free and fair elections.

Peaceful enjoyment of possessions

The right to peaceful enjoyment of possessions is set out in Article 1 of the First Protocol. It may be restricted 'in the public interest' and is subject to the conditions provided for by domestic and international law. The term 'possessions' has been interpreted quite widely,[316] and includes entitlements to pensions, income support, and other welfare benefits.[317] On the other hand, the right is subject to a wide range of exceptions, and states are afforded considerable discretion in deciding when a restriction is in the public interest. For example, in *Wilson* v *First County Trust (No 2)*, a provision of the Consumer Credit Act 1974 that could render a credit agreement unenforceable if the amount of credit were calculated incorrectly was held to be a proportionate mechanism for achieving the legitimate objective of consumer protection.[318]

Claims under Article 1 of the Protocol are unlikely to succeed unless there is a clear lack of proportionality or a defective procedure. As a consequence, such claims

---

[311] *Thlimmenos* v *Greece* (2001) 31 EHRR 411.

[312] *DH* v *Czech Republic* (2008) 47 EHRR 3, at [175]; see also *Stec* v *UK* (2006) 43 EHRR 47.

[313] *Dudgeon* v *UK* (1982) 4 EHRR 149 (a breach of Articles 8 and 14 because of the disproportionate impact on private life).

[314] See, e.g. *Ghaidan* v *Godin-Mendoza* [2004] UKHL 30, [2004] 2 AC 557, [2004] 3 All ER 411.

[315] *Smith and Grady* v *UK* (2000) 29 EHRR 493.

[316] For example, it is capable of including licences, patents, planning permission, leasehold interests, and even goodwill in a business: see *Van Marle and others* v *Netherlands* (1986) 8 EHRR 483; *Mellacher* v *Austria* (1990) 12 EHRR 391.

[317] The Grand Chamber has since held that *all* entitlements to welfare payments fall within the ambit of the First Protocol, regardless of any link with personal contributions: *Stec* v *UK* (2005) 41 EHRR SE18. See also *R (on the application of RJM)* v *Secretary of State for Work and Pensions* [2008] UKHL 63, [2009] 1 AC 311, [2009] 2 All ER 556.

[318] [2003] UKHL 40, [2004] 1 AC 816, [2003] 4 All ER 97. As the credit company had never had a right to enforce the payments, 'proprietary rights' were not even engaged in this case. However, their Lordships did not need to decide this point because the agreement was made before the Human Rights Act came into force.

are often made in conjunction with a claim under Article 6 or 14 of the Convention. For example, differentials in welfare payments corresponding with differences in age or country of residence were recently challenged under Article 1 of the Protocol and Article 14 of the Convention. The differences were found to be justifiable, however, and the challenge failed on both grounds.[319] The right to peaceful enjoyment of possessions was also considered in *Aston Cantlow* v *Wallbank*.[320] The defendant owned the freehold over a plot of rectorial land, and the parish council sought to invoke section 2(1) of the Chancel Repairs Act 1932, under which the owners of such land could be obliged to repair the chancel of the parish church. The defendants claimed that this was a breach of both Article 14 of the Convention and Article 1 of the First Protocol: they argued that requiring them to pay for the repairs was an arbitrary deprivation of property that discriminated against them as owners of the land. The defendants ultimately lost their case because the House of Lords found that the parish council was not performing a public function.[321] However, it added that there would have been no interference with Convention rights in any event, because the defendant had acquired her property with full knowledge of the accompanying repair obligation. *International Transport Roth*[322] is an example of a challenged based on a procedural defect. The case centred on a penalty regime under which hauliers could be fined £2,000 for every clandestine immigrant brought into the country by their vehicles. The challenge was partly based on Article 6 because hauliers were required to prove that they had an effective scheme for preventing such incidents, and this amounted to a reversal of the burden of proof. However, there was also an issue under Article 1, Protocol 1, because officials were empowered to detain vehicles in order to ensure payment. The regime was found to be in breach of both provisions and a declaration of incompatibility was issued.

The second limb of Article 1 of the First Protocol states that the right to peaceful enjoyment of possessions does not 'in any way impair the right of a State to enforce such laws as it deems necessary to control the use of property in accordance with the general interest or to secure the payment of taxes or other contributions or penalties'. Although controls on the use of property are still subject to a 'fair balance' test in the same way as deprivations of property, controls do not normally attract any entitlement to compensation. This means that the effect of deciding that a measure is merely a control is often to preclude liability. In *Pye* v *UK*, for example, the legal rules on adverse possession were held to amount to a control on the use of land, even though the applicants had effectively lost their land because of them.[323] The Grand Chamber took the view that the fair balance required by the Convention had not been

[319] *Carson* v *Secretary of State for Work and Pensions* [2005] UKHL 37, [2006] 1 AC 173, [2005] 4 All ER 545; *Carson* v *UK* (2010) 51 EHRR 13.

[320] *Aston-Cantlow and Wilcote with Billesley Parochial Church Council* v *Wallbank* [2003] UKHL 37, [2004] 1 AC 546, [2003] 3 All ER 1213.

[321] See p 163.

[322] *International Transport Roth GmbH* v *Secretary of State for the Home Department* [2002] EWCA Civ 158, [2003] QB 728, [2002] HRLR 31.

[323] *JA Pye (Oxford) Ltd.* V *United Kingdom* (2008) 46 EHRR 45.

upset the application of these rules, and they were therefore deemed compatible with Protocol 1. In *R (on the application of Countryside Alliance) v Attorney General*, the hunting ban was also dealt with as a control on the use of land, and as such it was held not to be in breach of Convention rights.[324]

The right to education

Article 2 of the First Protocol states that 'no person shall be denied the right to education', and it imposes an obligation on states to 'respect the right of persons to ensure such education and teaching in conformity with their own religious and philosophical convictions'. Upon signing the Protocol, the United Kingdom entered a reservation in respect of this Article, which provides that it is accepted 'only so far as it is compatible with the provision of efficient instruction and training and the avoidance of unreasonable public expenditure'. The wording of the first part of the Article is deliberately restrictive, referring to the negative right not to be denied education rather than a positive right to receive it. This means that it is primarily concerned with ensuring that existing educational facilities are available on an equal basis: it does not, for example, confer any positive right to have children educated in a particular language;[325] nor does it compel states to provide special needs education for those who cannot benefit from mainstream schooling.[326] In *Campbell v UK*,[327] the use of corporal punishment in a school was successfully challenged under this provision, on the basis that it contravened the applicant's right to have her child educated in accordance with her religious and philosophical beliefs. This can be contrasted with the decision in *R (on the application of Williamson) v Secretary of State for Education and Employment*.[328] In this case a ban on the use of physical chastisement in schools was held to be justifiable, notwithstanding the applicant's belief that corporal punishment was integral to a Christian upbringing.

The holding of free elections

Article 3 of the First Protocol obliges states to hold 'free elections at reasonable intervals by secret ballot, under conditions which will ensure the free expression of the opinion of the people'. The Article does not expressly create any individual rights, but the right to participate in elections is implied. A breach of this implied right was established in *Hirst v UK*, which concerned the disenfranchisement of prisoners under section 3 of the Representation of the People Act 1983.[329] In a landmark ruling it was held that, although section 3 pursued a legitimate aim, its blanket application to all prisoners could not be justified and the interference with the right to vote was disproportionate. The government accepted the decision, but at the time of writing has yet to remedy this incompatibility. A prohibition on aliens

---

[324] [2007] UKHL 52, [2008] 1 AC 719.
[325] *Belgian Linguistics Case (No 2)* (1979–1980) 1 EHRR 252.
[326] *A v Essex County Council* [2010] UKSC 33, [2010] 3 WLR 509, [2010] 4 All ER 199.
[327] (1982) 4 EHRR 293. [328] [2005] UKHL 15, [2005] 2 AC 246, [2005] 2 All ER 1.
[329] (2006) 42 EHRR 41.

standing for election to the Sark legislature has also been held to be compatible with the Convention.[330]

The European Court of Human Rights

> With its highly legalistic character and its several decades of interpretive jurisprudence, the European Convention on Human Rights has engendered the most sophisticated jurisprudence of any of the international judicial instruments promulgated to protect human rights...in many respects, the theory and practice of the European Convention on Human Rights parallel the theory and practice of the United States Supreme Court more closely than any domestic system operating in Europe. The key to understanding the Convention lies in the case-law of the European Commission and Court, whose role it is to interpret the Convention...[331]

In its original form, the ECHR established both a Commission and a Court of Human Rights. The Commission's role was to examine applications under the Convention and to reject at an early stage those that were manifestly unfounded or otherwise inadmissible. Admissible claims were then subject to the Commission's attempts to negotiate a 'friendly settlement'. Only if a settlement could not be reached would the matter finally be referred to the court, but not before the Commission had examined the case and prepared a written opinion as to the merits. In the 1990s, the Committee of Ministers[332] decided to streamline the complaints procedure in order to cope with the growing number of applications that were being received each year. The reforms were set out in Protocol 11 and came into effect on 1 November 1998. After a brief transitional period to allow the resolution of cases that were already in the system, the Commission was abolished and a revamped, full-time court now deals with all stages of a complaint. Further changes have since been made by Protocol 14 (with effect from 1 June 2010), and although these changes are rather more modest it should be noted that they have resulted in several Convention Articles being amended or renumbered.[333]

The composition and procedure of the court

The number of judges of the court is equal to the number of parties to the Convention, although they are appointed to sit in an individual capacity and there are no

[330] *R (on the application of Barclay)* v *Secretary of State for Justice and the Lord Chancellor* [2009] UKSC 9, [2010] 1 AC 464.
[331] Gomien, Harris and Zwaak, *Law and Practice of the European Convention on Human Rights and the European Social Charter* (Council of Europe, 1996) at p 19.
[332] The Council of Europe's political and executive body.
[333] None of the provisions dealing with substantive rights have been affected. References in this chapter are to the new numbers. As an interim measure Protocol 14*bis* came into effect in 2009, and this allowed the Court to implement some of the new arrangements early for those states that had already ratified Protocol 14.

requirements as to nationality.[334] Judges are elected by the Parliamentary Assembly from a list of candidates supplied by each Member State,[335] and they serve for a single nine-year term.[336] The court is divided into four sections. Rule 25(2) of the Rules of Procedure provides that 'the composition of the Sections shall be geographically and gender balanced and shall reflect the different legal systems among the Contracting Parties'. The sections are headed by two Vice-Presidents and two Presidents of Section. The holders of these positions are elected by the judges from amongst their ranks, as is the court's President.[337]

Applications to the court may be made in any language used by the member states, although once a case reaches the merits stage proceedings are normally conducted in English or French.[338] Each application is assigned to a section, and a rapporteur decides whether to refer the case directly to a Chamber of seven judges, or whether to allocate it to a three-member committee or single-judge formation for a preliminary examination.[339] Committees perform a filtering role similar to that performed by the former Commission and may strike out inadmissible claims without a hearing.[340] In addition, claims that are clearly inadmissible or without merit may now be struck out by a single judge.[341]

Applications not struck out at a preliminary stage are normally referred to a Chamber for a full determination. However, since June 2010, 'if the underlying question in [a] case...is already the subject of well-established case law', it is possible for a committee of three judges to deal with both the admissibility and the merits claim in a single judgment.[342] In addition, under the amended and renumbered Article 39 the court can facilitate the negotiation of a friendly settlement between the parties at any stage in the proceedings.

Within three months of the judgment of a Chamber, any party may request that the case be referred to the Grand Chamber on the grounds that it raises a serious issue of interpretation or some other serious issue of general importance.[343] The Grand Chamber consists of seventeen judges, including the President, Vice-Presidents, and section Presidents.[344] Exceptionally, where a case raises sufficiently important issues, the Chamber may decline to deliver a judgment and may instead refer the case directly to the Grand Chamber for a ruling.[345]

---

[334] Articles 20 and 21 ECHR. The judge currently occupying Liechtenstein's seat in the court is Swiss.
[335] Article 22.
[336] Article 23. Prior to June 2010 they were appointed for a renewable term of six years.
[337] Rule 8, Rules of Procedure.   [338] Rule 34.
[339] Rule 49. Under r 48, all inter-state applications must be referred to a Chamber.
[340] Article 28.
[341] New Article 27, with effect from June 2010. Where a single judge is used, he or she cannot be the judge elected in respect of the state with which the case is concerned.
[342] Article 28.
[343] Article 43. See further, Mowbray, 'An Examination of the Work of the Grand Chamber of the European Court of Human Rights' [2007] PL 507.
[344] Article 26.   [345] Article 30.

By Article 41, if a violation of the Convention is established, the court can afford 'just satisfaction' to the injured party. This may involve an order for a state to pay compensation and costs. Final judgments of the court are binding on the Member States concerned, and the Committee of Ministers is responsible for overseeing their execution and for ensuring that any remedial action is taken. Failure to comply with a judgment might lead to the Committee of Ministers bringing proceedings in the court for persistent infringement, or to the state in question being suspended from the Council of Europe.[346]

The admissibility of complaints

Complaints may be brought either by other Convention states or by individual victims of a Convention breach.[347] Inter-state applications are rare, but this is perhaps inevitable given the likely diplomatic consequences of bringing such an action. Most inter-state cases have been brought by countries directly connected to the 'victims' of the complaints,[348] but the *Greek case* is a notable exception.[349] Several countries pursued this case when the 'regime of the colonels' seized power in Greece in a military coup. Specific complaints included the use of torture, the use of courts-martial to sentence political prisoners, the prohibition of political activity, censorship of the press, and suspension of the rule of law. In total, violations of ten different Convention rights were established, forcing Greece to withdraw from the Council of Europe. It did not return until democracy was restored in 1974.

The vast majority of complaints lodged with the court are from individual applicants. The basic admissibility criteria are set out in Article 35 of the Convention. This stipulates that the applicant must have already exhausted all effective remedies in his or her own country, and that he or she must have lodged his complaint within six months of a final decision by a national court or tribunal.[350] These criteria are applied fairly rigidly, although a journalist who was refused a job following a secret vetting process was able to make a later application because the alleged breach was not discovered until nine years later.[351] An additional admissibility criterion introduced by Protocol 14 empowers the court to declare an individual application inadmissible if the applicant 'has not suffered a significant disadvantage'. However, the case should still be examined on its merits if respect for human rights requires it.[352] The complainant

---

[346] Article 46.

[347] Recognition of the right of individual petition has been compulsory on Convention states since 1998: Article 34. The United Kingdom accepted this right on 14 January 1966.

[348] *Ireland* v *UK* (1979) 2 EHRR 25; see p 184. See also *Cyprus* v *Turkey* (2002) 35 EHRR 30.

[349] (1969) 12 YB ECHR 196.

[350] Article 35. There is no obligation to have recourse to remedies that are inadequate or ineffective: *Aksoy* v *Turkey* (1997) 23 EHRR 553.

[351] *Hilton* v *UK* (1988) 57 D&R 108.   [352] Article 35.

must also be a victim or potential victim of a Convention breach,[353] and a 'victim' for these purposes is a person directly affected by a violation of a right, or someone who runs the risk of being directly affected in the future. In *Norris v Ireland*,[354] for example, a gay man who risked prosecution under a law criminalizing homosexual acts was considered to be a 'victim' for Article 34 purposes.

Further reading

ASHWORTH and STRANGE, 'Criminal Law and Human Rights' [2004] EHRLR 121

BARENDT, 'Free Speech and Abortion' [2003] PL 580

HARRIS, O'BOYLE and WARBRICK, *Law of the European Convention on Human Rights* (Butterworths: 2nd edn, 2009)

HICKMAN, 'The Substance and Structure of Proportionality' [2008] PL 694

HILL and SANDBERG, 'Is Nothing Sacred? Clashing Symbols in a Secular World' [2007] PL 488

LETSAS, 'Two Concepts of the Margin of Appreciation' (2006) 26(4) OJLS 705

MOWBRAY, 'An Examination of the Work of the Grand Chamber of the European Court of Human Rights' [2007] PL 507

SCHOKKENBROEK, 'The Basis, Nature and Application of the Margin of Appreciation Doctrine in the Case Law of the European Court of Human Rights' (1998) 19(1) HRLJ 30

SINGH and STRACHAN, 'Privacy Postponed' [2003] EHRLR Special Issue 12

SMITH, 'Protecting Protest: A Constitutional Shift' (2007) 66(2) CLJ 253

VAN DIJK et al, *The Theory and Practice of the European Convention on Human Rights* (Intersentia: 4th edn, 2006)

---

[353] Article 34.   [354] (1991) 13 EHRR 186.

PART II

The Administration
of Justice

The Courts

INTRODUCTION

This chapter explores the role played by each of the major courts in the English legal system, and seeks to give an overview of the hierarchy within which they operate. In addition to affecting the general distribution of work within the system and determining the destination of appeals, this hierarchy also plays a crucial role in the doctrine of precedent. The chapter begins with an outline of some of the courts that have been important historically, before going on to examine the work of their modern counterparts in some depth. In particular, it will address the following:

- the distinctions to be made between different types of court—civil or criminal, first instance or appellate, court or tribunal, etc;
- the administration of the courts—the roles played by the Ministry of Justice, Her Majesty's Courts Service and other bodies;
- the importance of open justice, and the implications of this principle for the conduct of proceedings in court. The law governing contempt of court will also be considered;
- the constitution and jurisdiction of each of the major courts and the distribution of work between them;
- the unique roles of coroners' courts and the Judicial Committee of the Privy Council;
- the work of courts martial and ecclesiastical courts, as examples of courts with special jurisdiction.

Historical context

The Curia Regis

Any examination of the modern legal system would be incomplete without an awareness of its historical background. As already noted, the monarch had a pivotal role in the development of the early courts, and the exercise of regal power through the King's Council or Curia Regis is therefore a useful starting point for this analysis.

In medieval times the King's Council exercised legislative, executive, and judicial functions, and it is therefore the predecessor of both Parliament and the courts. Over a period of time the courts began to assume an independent jurisdiction, and the three main common law courts—the Court of Exchequer, the Court of Common Pleas, and the Court of King's Bench—split off from the Council. Their judges exercised jurisdiction over civil disputes and major criminal cases in London and on assize, and the King's justices assumed jurisdiction over other criminal offences. The residual jurisdiction of the King persisted, however, and it was not until the seventeenth century that the Council finally discontinued its judicial function.

The Court of Exchequer

This was the first of the three main common law courts to split off from the Curia Regis. Originally its jurisdiction was confined to disputes between subjects and the Crown concerning revenue, but it later acquired jurisdiction over disputes between subjects, such as writs of debt and covenant.[1] It also appears to have exercised an equity jurisdiction in its early days. When the Court of Exchequer was finally abolished in 1875, its common law jurisdiction was transferred to the newly formed High Court. Its equity jurisdiction had already been transferred by statute to the Chancery in 1841.[2]

The Court of Common Pleas

While the King was determining civil disputes in Council, suitors were obliged to follow the court wherever it travelled. Because of the inconvenience that this caused, it became the practice for some judges to remain permanently in Westminster Hall to try Common Pleas.[3] These judges were senior advocates who were highly paid and had an exclusive right of audience in the court. The court had jurisdiction over disputes between subjects in which the King's interest was not involved, and it therefore tried all real actions, the personal actions of debt, convenant, and *detinue*, and trespass actions in which the title to land was involved. When the court was abolished in 1875, its jurisdiction was transferred to the High Court.

The Court of King's Bench

This was the last of the three central courts to break away from the Council, and through its close association with the King it acquired jurisdiction to issue the prerogative writs of mandamus, prohibition, and certiorari,[4] and thus to restrain abuses of power by inferior courts and public officials. It is this supervisory role that has

---

[1] These were the earliest personal actions recognized by the common law. For more detailed discussion, see the 6th edition of this work, pp 22–9.

[2] 5 Vict, c 5.

[3] As opposed to Pleas of the Crown, which were based upon breaches of the King's peace and usually involved a fine or forfeiture.

[4] Now called mandatory orders, prohibiting orders, and quashing orders. This 'judicial review' jurisdiction is still exercised by the Queen's Bench Division of the High Court.

provided the foundation for the process of judicial review. It also had the power to issue the writ of habeas corpus, which was later of great constitutional importance in curbing the use of prerogative powers by the King. The court was presided over by the Chief Justice of England, and it had both original and appellate functions. The court's original jurisdiction was exercised principally in civil matters, covering most actions in tort and contract. Its appellate jurisdiction covered both civil and criminal cases, although the right of appeal was based on an error in procedure in the court below.[5]

The Courts of Exchequer Chamber

At different times there have been no fewer than four courts bearing the title 'Exchequer Chamber'.

(1) The oldest was established in 1357 and its jurisdiction was solely as a court of error from the Exchequer.

(2) Even before 1357 there was a practice of judges reserving difficult points of law for consideration by a bench of judges. The meetings were relatively informal and initially the opinions delivered were purely persuasive, but by the fifteenth century its judgments were regarded as binding.[6] The court was known as the Court of Exchequer Chamber because that was where it usually sat, and many of the leading common law cases were decided in this court. It continued to determine civil cases until the seventeenth century, and decided criminal matters until the nineteenth century.

(3) A third Court of Exchequer Chamber was created by statute in 1585[7] as a court of error from the King's Bench. Thus, in addition to the House of Lords there were at this time three courts of error, and this complex hierarchy prevailed until the creation of the last Court of Exchequer Chamber in 1830.

(4) The court created in 1830[8] was the court of error from all three common law courts, and any appeal from this court lay to the House of Lords. It existed until 1875 when its jurisdiction was transferred to the Court of Appeal.

Assizes

Even in the Middle Ages it was impossible to hold all criminal trials in London, and Norman and Plantagenet monarchs adopted the system of sending out royal justices to hold 'assizes' (or sittings) of the royal courts. The jurisdiction of these courts was at first purely criminal but was later extended to civil matters. Assize judges held office under royal commission, and while most were judges of the common law courts they

---

[5] 31 Edw 3, St 1, c 12.

[6] In 1483 the Chief Justice of the Common Pleas followed a decision of the Exchequer Chamber even though he thought it wrong (Y1 Ric 3, Michs, no 2).

[7] 31 Eliz 1, c 1.   [8] 11 Geo 4 & 1 Will 4, c 70.

could also be serjeants-at-law or even prominent laymen. The system was organized on the basis of circuits, with each circuit consisting of a group of counties visited three or four times a year. The statute of Nisi Prius 1285 extended the system to certain civil actions triable by jury, and the jurisdiction was further extended in the fourteenth and fifteenth centuries to cover all types of civil action.[9]

Justices of the peace

Justices of the peace[10] originate from a royal proclamation of 1195, which created the knights of the peace to assist the sheriff in enforcing the law. Initially the office was administrative in nature, but it assumed a judicial function in the fourteenth century because of the declining criminal jurisdiction of the local courts and the inability of the assizes to deal with the growing number of offenders. By 1330, the holders of the office had become so powerful that they were given statutory power to punish the sheriff if he abused his powers of granting bail to prisoners.

Statutes of Labourers were passed from 1351 in an attempt to regulate wages, and the enforcement of these statutes was placed in the hands of 'justices of labourers'. In 1361 these justices were included in the same commissions as the keepers of the peace, and it is from this date that the office of 'justice of the peace' in its modern sense originates. The criminal jurisdiction of the new justices was at first exercised solely in the quarter sessions that they were compelled by statute[11] to hold, but in 1496[12] they were given jurisdiction to try offences out of sessions. This summary jurisdiction was exercised without a jury by what is now termed a 'magistrates' court'.[13] In 1590 justices in quarter sessions were given jurisdiction over all criminal offences, including capital felonies, and it was not until the Quarter Sessions Act 1842 that their jurisdiction was limited to exclude treason, murder, and felonies punishable with life imprisonment.

The administrative functions of justices of the peace declined as their criminal jurisdiction grew, and most of these functions are now in the hands of local authorities. However, certain important functions remain, most notably the power to issue warrants of arrest and search. The task of conducting preliminary investigations into indictable offences was conferred on justices of the peace in 1554 but now largely no longer exists.[14]

The Star Chamber

The Star Chamber derived its jurisdiction from the King in the same way as the common law courts, but because it retained its links with the King in Council it administered the royal prerogative rather than the common law. It seems to have originated

---

[9] The assize system survived until 1 January 1972, when the Courts Act 1971 came into operation.

[10] The term dates from about 1327: Plucknett, *A Concise History of the Common Law* (Little, Brown & Co: 5th edn, 1956), p 168.

[11] 36 Edw 3, st 1, c 12.   [12] 11 Hen 7, c 3.

[13] See p 627.   [14] 1 & 2 P & M, c 13 and 2 & 3 P & M, c 10.

from sittings of the Council in a chamber in Westminster known as the Star Chamber, possibly on account of its interior decor. It consisted of members of the Council, the Chancellor, Treasurer, and Privy Seal, and common law judges, and it had jurisdiction over a range of civil matters. It is, however, the Star Chamber's criminal jurisdiction that is of the greatest interest, since it recognized and tried many new offences, including riot, unlawful assembly, conspiracy, criminal libel, perjury, and forgery.

Procedure differed radically from that in the common law courts. Criminal proceedings were commenced by the Attorney-General and the defendant was examined in an inquisitorial procedure, sometimes under torture. Evidence was frequently given by affidavit, thus denying the accused any opportunity to cross-examine witnesses, and guilt or innocence was determined by members of the court rather than by a jury. Despite this, even Coke, that most noted champion of the common law, described the court as 'the most honourable Court (our Parliament excepted) that is in the Christian world'.[15] Eventually the court came to be seen as a symbol of prerogative power, and one of the first legislative acts of the Long Parliament was the abolition of the Star Chamber in 1641.

The Court of Chancery

The Court of Chancery was the principal court of equity, and its most important jurisdiction was the recognition and enforcement of equitable principles. The office of Chancellor and the principles of equity are, historically, inexorably linked, and the nature and effectiveness of the court depended upon the characteristics of the particular Chancellor. The court was brought into disrepute in the seventeenth century by the sale of offices in the court,[16] and the scale of the corruption was so great that on the 'bursting' of the South Sea Bubble in 1725 (an eighteenth-century speculative venture) a deficiency of £100,000 in court funds was discovered.

A further defect in the court was its organization. It had an excess of court officials who attempted to extend their duties so as to increase their revenue, and this naturally made litigation extremely slow and expensive. The excess of court officers was equalled only by the paucity of judges. At first the Chancellor himself was the only judge, but by the sixteenth century he was accustomed to delegate his judicial functions to the Masters in Chancery. This did little to speed up the conduct of litigation, however, since the parties had a right to apply to the Chancellor for a rehearing. During Lord Eldon's time in office (1807–27) there are records of judgments being reserved for months and even years, and in 1813 he approved the appointment of a Vice-Chancellor. The Court of Chancery was eventually abolished by the Judicature Acts 1873–75, and most of its jurisdiction was transferred to the Chancery Division of the High Court.

---

[15] 4 Inst, p 65.

[16] The office of Master of the Rolls was apparently worth £6,000 in the eighteenth century. See *ex parte the Six Clerks* (1798) 3 Ves 589.

In addition to its equitable jurisdiction, the court acquired jurisdiction over other miscellaneous matters. For example, the Crown had protective custody of all infants within the realm, and this jurisdiction, comprising such matters as the power to appoint guardians, was assigned to the Court of Chancery.[17] A similar concept existed in relation to persons of unsound mind, and this jurisdiction continues to be exercised by the Court of Protection.[18]

The impact of the Judicature Acts 1873–75 in sweeping away many of the old courts has already been noted, and the modern system is very different from that which preceded it. The superior courts in England and Wales continue to derive their jurisdiction from the Crown, but they are now heavily regulated by statute and some courts and tribunals owe their origins entirely to statutory intervention.

The organization and administration of the courts

Leaving aside the work of tribunals,[19] the principal courts exercising jurisdiction in England and Wales are the Court of Appeal, the High Court, the Crown Court, the Supreme Court, county courts, and magistrates' courts. The first three courts in this list collectively comprise the Senior Courts of England and Wales.[20] The role of each of these courts was briefly described in Chapter 1, and considered in detail later in this chapter. Their roles can be summarized as follows.

(1) First-instance jurisdiction over civil matters is primarily shared between the county courts and the High Court. The Crown Court and magistrates' courts also have a limited civil jurisdiction.

(2) Jurisdiction over criminal cases at first instance is divided between magistrates' courts and the Crown Court.

(3) The Crown Court and High Court exercise certain appellate functions alongside their original jurisdiction.

(4) The Court of Appeal hears appeals from the decisions of courts lower down in the hierarchy, although not from the decisions of magistrates' courts.

(5) The Supreme Court is the final court of appeal for England and Wales, Scotland, and Northern Ireland.

As outlined in Chapter 1, the English legal system has evolved in a piecemeal way over many centuries, and although the Ministry of Justice has assumed responsibility for most of its components, its organizational structure remains complex.[21] The rules

---

[17] It is now exercised by the Family Division of the High Court: see p 257.
[18] See p 270.   [19] See Chapter 9.
[20] Formerly known as 'The Supreme Court', but which was replaced when the new Supreme Court replaced the House of Lords as the final court of appeal.
[21] See p 8.

governing the procedure and jurisdiction of the courts are contained in a multitude of statutes, practice directions, court rules, and other statutory instruments, all of which seem to be subject to constant revision and amendment. The distribution of business between the courts has been revised many times, and the legal system has been the focus of numerous reports and recommendations. In 1996, for example, the Woolf Report on *Access to Justice* led to a major restructuring of the civil justice system less than a decade after fundamental changes had been brought about by the Courts and Legal Services Act 1990.[22] Lord Justice Auld's review of the criminal justice system produced similarly far-reaching recommendations,[23] and although the government rejected his proposal to replace the Crown Court and magistrates' courts with a unified criminal court, a number of his other recommendations were given effect by the Courts Act 2003.

In 1998 the Civil Justice Council was established, with a remit of keeping the civil justice system under review and considering new ways of making it accessible, fair, and efficient.[24] A Family Justice Council and a Criminal Justice Council have since been created and, following the Auld Review,[25] a Criminal Justice Board with responsibility for direction and strategy at a national level was also set up. The criminal justice agencies are now supported by the Office for Criminal Justice Reform (OCJR), which is a cross-departmental team reporting to the Ministry of Justice, the Home Office, and the Office of the Attorney-General. In 2010 a review of many such bodies was announced.[26] It is not yet clear how organizational structures within the English legal system will change, if at all.

The absence of a truly national framework applicable to all courts has long been criticized, and the focus of many of the recent reforms has been on achieving greater harmonization and efficiency. The Auld Review had much to say on this subject, describing the criminal justice system as 'structurally inefficient, ineffective and wasteful'.[27] Prior to the Woolf reforms, the county courts and the High Court were subject to different procedural rules, despite the fact that their jurisdiction is largely concurrent. The Civil Procedure Act 1997 changed this by establishing a Civil Procedure Rule Committee with the authority to make rules for the High Court, the county courts, and the Civil Division of the Court of Appeal.[28] The Courts Act 2003 introduced a similar approach for the criminal justice system: instead of being subject to three different sets of rules, all criminal cases are now governed by new Criminal Procedure Rules regardless of in which court they are heard.[29] A Family Procedure Rule Committee has similar powers to make rules governing family proceedings.[30] All rule committees are subject to an overriding duty to ensure that the system is

---

[22] Most of Woolf's recommendations were adopted in the Access to Justice Act 1999 and the Civil Procedure Rules 1998, SI 1998/3132: see p 473.

[23] *Review of the Criminal Courts of England and Wales* (HMSO, 2001); see p 567.

[24] Civil Procedure Act 1997, s 6.   [25] See ch 8 of the Report.

[26] *Solicitors Journal*, 28 September 2010.   [27] At para 14.

[28] Civil Procedure Rules 1998, SI 1998/3132, or 'CPR'.

[29] 2003 Act, s 69; Criminal Procedure Rules 2005, SI 2005/384.   [30] 2003 Act, ss 75–77.

'accessible, fair and efficient', and that any rules made are both 'simple and simply expressed'.[31]

Under section 1(1) of the Courts Act 2003 the Lord Chancellor has a duty to ensure that there is an efficient and effective system to support the business of the Supreme Court, Court of Protection, county courts, and magistrates' courts. The Act also provides for England and Wales to be divided into separate local justice areas, with each area having its own Courts Board. Courts Boards are responsible for scrutinizing and reviewing the administration of the courts and for making recommendations to the Lord Chancellor.[32] The principal aim of the Courts Act is to provide a framework for a unified court structure, and to this end the Lord Chancellor has transferred administrative responsibility for all but one of the major courts to a single executive agency called 'Her Majesty's Court Service'.[33] This body administers all of the courts that were previously managed by the Courts Service—that is, the Crown Court, High Court, Court of Appeal, and county courts—and it has also assumed responsibility for managing the network of magistrates' courts.[34] This leaves the Supreme Court as the only major court not covered by the Courts Agency. However, it is considered appropriate for the latter court to be administered separately because of its unique position as an appellate court for all parts of the United Kingdom. These arrangements allow for greater sharing of resources, making it easier, for example, to use the same facilities as a venue for magistrates' and county court business, as well as for sittings of the Crown Court. It also opens up the possibility of creating specialist centres where magistrates, county courts, and High Court judges can exercise their family jurisdiction under one roof.

Despite the wholesale changes of recent years, it seems inevitable that there will be further reforms in the near future. Indeed, while the House of Commons was still debating legislation that led to the creation of a new Supreme Court,[35] the Department for Constitutional Affairs was already looking at the possibility of combining the existing civil courts.[36]

The principle of open justice[37]

'Open justice' is a key principle of the English legal system, and amongst other things it requires that the courts should sit in public. In the words of Lord Hewart CJ in *R v Sussex Justices, ex parte McCarthy*:[38]

---

[31] Ibid, ss 69(4); 75(5); Civil Procedure Act 1997, s 1(3), as amended.
[32] Sections 4 and 5.   [33] Formally launched on 1 April 2005.
[34] These were previously managed by forty-two separate Magistrates' Courts Committees: see p 263.
[35] Constitutional Reform Act 2005: see p 246.
[36] DCA, *A Single Civil Court? The Scope for Unifying the Civil Jurisdictions of the High Court, the County Courts and the Family Proceedings Courts* (HMSO, 2005) CP 06/05. Having considered the responses to this consultation document, the government announced that the creation of single Civil and Family Courts would be adopted as a 'long-term objective': *A Single Civil Court? Responses to the Consultation* (HMSO, 2005) CP(R) 06/05, at p 42.
[37] For a detailed analysis, see Jaconelli, *Open Justice: A Critique of the Public Trial* (OUP, 2002).
[38] [1924] 1 KB 256 at 259; see also *R v Denbigh Justices, ex parte Williams* [1974] QB 759, [1974] 2 All ER 1052; Supreme Court Act 1981, s 67.

a long line of cases shows that it is not merely of some importance but is of fundamental importance that justice should not only be done, but should manifestly and undoubtedly be seen to be done.

The principle, and the circumstances that may justify departure from it, were set out by the House of Lords in *Scott v Scott*[39] and later explained by Lord Diplock in *A-G v Leveller Magazine Ltd*:[40]

> As a general rule the English system of administering justice does require that it be done in public: *Scott v Scott*. If the way the courts behave cannot be hidden from the public ear and eye this provides a safeguard against judicial arbitrariness or idiosyncrasy and maintains the public confidence in the administration of justice.

More recently the principle was endorsed by Butler-Sloss P, quoting from the work of Jeremy Bentham:[41]

> Publicity is the very soul of justice. It is the keenest spur to exertion and the surest of all guards against improbity. It keeps the judge himself while trying under trial.

From this it follows that, if at all possible, proceedings should be held in open court, and fair and accurate reports of those proceedings should be permissible. In *Storer v British Gas*,[42] the Court of Appeal quashed the decision of an industrial tribunal because the hearing had taken place in an office that was kept locked and marked 'Private'. On the other hand, certain restrictions on the principle of open justice may be permitted where this is necessary to protect the administration of justice, or where Parliament has created a specific exception.

Article 6(1) of the European Convention on Human Rights is also relevant in this context, and has assumed added importance since the coming into force of the Human Rights Act 1998.[43]

Article 6(1)

> In the determination of his civil rights and obligations or of any criminal charge against him, everyone is entitled to a fair and public hearing...Judgment shall be pronounced publicly but the press and public may be excluded from all or part of the trial in the interests of morals, public order or national security in a democratic society, where the interests of juveniles or the protection of the private life of the parties so require, or to the extent strictly necessary in the opinion of the court in special circumstances where publicity would prejudice the interests of justice.

---

[39] [1913] AC 417.   [40] [1979] AC 440, [1979] 1 All ER 745.

[41] *Clibbery v Allan* [2002] EWCA Civ 45 at [16], [2002] Fam 261 at [16], [2002] 1 All ER 865.

[42] [2000] 2 All ER 440, [2000] 1 WLR 1237.

[43] See Chapter 5. For an illustration of the correct approach to this issue under Article 6(1), see *B v UK* [2001] 2 FLR 261, (2002) 34 EHRR 19. It was found in this case that a county court hearing to determine the residence of a child did not breach the Convention, even though it was held in private.

A hearing in open court

Statutory provisions

Parliament has granted a power to sit in private (in camera) in various types of proceedings. These include proceedings in the youth court, proceedings covered by the Children Act 1989,[44] and proceedings under the Official Secrets Acts.[45] In addition, provisions designed to assist vulnerable witnesses in criminal proceedings are contained in the Youth Justice and Criminal Evidence Act 1999.[46] Part II of this Act enables courts to take 'special measures' to assist certain categories of witness (although not, generally, defendants) who might have difficulty giving evidence or who might be reluctant to do so. These categories include those under the age of 17, alleged victims of sex offences, those suffering from a mental or physical impairment likely to affect the quality of evidence given, and those whose evidence is likely to be impaired by fear or distress.[47] One of the special measures available to the courts is the power to allow a vulnerable witness to give evidence in private,[48] subject to section 25(3), which states that one representative of the press must be allowed to stay. Other special measures include the possibility of screening the witness from the accused,[49] or allowing the witness to give evidence via a pre-recorded video or live video link.[50] In response to the decision of the European Court of Human Rights in *SC v UK*,[51] the government looked at whether child defendants, who are largely excluded from the regime created by the 1999 Act, should have access to the same special measures as child witnesses.[52] Amendments to the Act have been made to allow vulnerable child defendants to give evidence by live video link,[53] and, when fully in force, the 1999 Act will permit certain defendants to testify through an intermediary.[54]

Common law

In addition to these specific provisions, the courts also have a general jurisdiction to sit in private where the presence of the public would render the administration of

---

[44] Section 97.   [45] Official Secrets Act 1920, s 8(4).

[46] Most of the relevant provisions have been in force since 24 July 2002; see Youth Justice and Criminal Evidence Act 1999 (Commencement No 7) Order 2002, SI 2002/1739.

[47] Sections 16 and 17. These criteria will change when provisions in Coroners and Justice Act 2009 are brought into force.

[48] Section 25. This applies only to evidence given in relation to a sex offence, or where there are grounds for believing that the witness has been or may be intimidated. See also s 37 of the Children and Young Persons Act 1933. For an analysis of the 1999 Act, see Birch, 'A Better Deal for Vulnerable Witnesses?' [2000] Crim LR 223. The Home Office has produced its own guidelines on the new provisions: *Achieving Best Evidence in Criminal Proceedings: Guidance for Vulnerable and Intimidated Witnesses, including Children.*

[49] Section 23.

[50] Sections 24, 27, and 28. Note that the Criminal Justice Act 2003 makes provision for the use of both live and pre-recorded video evidence to be used in a wider range of circumstances. At the time of writing, however, these provisions had yet to be implemented.

[51] (2005) 40 EHRR 10.   [52] Chapter 5.

[53] Section 33A, 1999 Act. The court must be satisfied that the ability of the accused to participate effectively in the proceedings is compromised by his level of intellectual ability or social functioning.

[54] 1999 Act, s 33BA, inserted by Coroners and Justice Act 2009, s 104.

justice impracticable. This was confirmed in *R v Richards (Randall)*[55] when a judge decided to clear the court so that a witness to a murder could give evidence. The witness had refused to testify under any other circumstances, and in denying an application for leave to appeal, the Court of Appeal observed that courts have an inherent jurisdiction to do what is necessary for the proper administration of justice. In another case, the Court of Appeal upheld a decision to allow an in camera hearing concerning allegations that a defendant had been tortured whilst in detention in a foreign jurisdiction.[56] The defendant was on trial for conspiracy to cause terrorist explosions, and along with representatives of the media he argued that the evidence should be heard in open court. The Court of Appeal held, however, that the evidence could be heard in camera for reasons of national security and the avoidance of harm to the administration of justice. It also confirmed that the judge had been right to hear the defendant's application for leave to appeal *against* this ruling in private. The judge's reasons for granting the in camera hearing were cited with approval:[57]

> [G]eneral publication of the relevant parts of [the evidence] could give rise to a substantial risk to national security. Additionally it could obstruct the identification of, and cause the Crown to be deterred from prosecuting in this and other cases, those who it is in the public interest should be tried.

In *R v Malvern Justices, ex parte Evans*,[58] magistrates sat in private to hear a mitigation plea in respect of a driving offence. The mental health of the defendant was such that if the court had not sat in private, the defendant would have been inhibited in making her plea. An appeal against the making of the order was dismissed, but the Divisional Court observed that it would rarely be appropriate to make such an order, and doubted whether it had in fact been appropriate in this particular case.

However, the courts are not permitted to restrict open justice in circumstances in which the fair administration of justice is not threatened. There is certainly no jurisdiction to hear a case in private purely for the convenience of the parties.

Witness anonymity and other withholding of information: The common law

At common law the courts have had the power to allow a witness anonymity if the interests of the administration of justice required that. Thus, a court would usually permit a victim of blackmail to be identified during proceedings by a title such as 'Mr X', and to communicate his name and address to the court by writing it down.[59]

---

[55] [1999] Crim LR 764.

[56] *R (on the application of A) v Crown Court at the Central Criminal Court* [2006] EWCA Crim 4, [2006] 1 WLR 1361, [2006] HRLR 10. The judge's order did not prevent the defendant himself from giving evidence in open court of his alleged treatment.

[57] Ibid, at [7].

[58] [1988] QB 540, [1988] 1 All ER 371. *R v Evesham Justices, ex parte McDonagh* [1988] QB 540; [1988] 1 All ER 371; *R v Mayes (Jordan)* [2008] EWCA Crim 2989; *Times Newspapers v R* [2008] EWCA Civ 2559, in which case there was a real risk that the lives of two soldiers would be at risk if not granted anonymity

[59] *R v Socialist Worker Printer and Publishers Ltd, ex parte A-G* [1975] QB 637, [1975] 1 All ER 142.

There are also statutory provisions for preserving the anonymity of young witnesses,[60] complainants in sex offence cases,[61] and other vulnerable parties.[62] Exceptionally, the identity of witnesses may be protected even from other parties to the proceedings.[63]

Parties to proceedings will not normally be granted anonymity. The position was discussed by the Court of Appeal in *R* v *Legal Aid Board, ex parte Kaim Todner*,[64] in which a firm of solicitors sought anonymity in judicial review proceedings against the Legal Aid Board. In rejecting any special rule relating to the legal profession, Lord Woolf MR stressed that any exception to the general rule in *Scott* v *Scott* could only be justified if this was necessary in the interests of justice. This was a matter for the court and could not be determined by any agreement of the parties in the case. As had been noted in *ex parte P*,[65] 'when both sides agreed that information should be kept from the public, that was when the court had to be the most vigilant'. Public scrutiny was necessary in order to deter inappropriate behaviour by the courts, and to maintain confidence in the administration of justice. In addition, members of the public could not come forward with relevant evidence if they were unaware of its relevance to proceedings. In deciding whether to protect the anonymity of a party to an action, it was not unreasonable for a court to assume that a party who initiated proceedings had accepted the normal consequences of that action. On the other hand, a witness with no interest in the proceedings would have a stronger claim if he or she would be prejudiced by publicity, although even this would not attract automatic anonymity.[66]

In *R* v *Davis*,[67] the House of Lords held that the use of anonymity to protect witnesses who were in fear of their life contravened both common law and Article 6 of the European Convention on Human Rights.[68] The immediate response to deal with what is a serious problem was the passage of the Criminal Evidence (Witness Anonymity) Act 2008, which replaced the common law power in criminal proceedings. It permitted a court to make a witness anonymity order, subject to pre-conditions in that Act. The 2008 Act has now been repealed and replaced by the Coroners and Justice Act 2009.

[60] Youth Justice and Criminal Evidence Act 1999, s 45; see also the Children and Young Persons Act 1933, s 39. For the relevant principles, see *R* v *Leicester Crown Court, ex parte S* [1992] 2 All ER 659, [1993] 1 WLR 111; *Re S (A Child) (Identification: Restrictions on Publication)* [2004] UKHL 47, [2005] 1 AC 593, [2004] 4 All ER 683.

[61] Sexual Offences (Amendment) Act 1992, s 1 (as amended). Once an allegation of an offence has been made, it is an offence to publish information likely to lead members of the public to identify the complainant unless the judge has lifted these restrictions under s 3.

[62] Youth Justice and Criminal Evidence Act 1999, s 46.   [63] See p 194.

[64] [1999] QB 966, [1998] 3 All ER 541.   [65] (1998) The Times, 31 March.

[66] An exceptional case in which there were sound reasons for preserving the anonymity of witnesses is *R* v *Lord Saville of Newdigate, ex parte A* [1999] 4 All ER 860, [2000] 1 WLR 1855. The Court of Appeal agreed with the Divisional Court that it had been unreasonable to deny anonymity to seventeen members of the armed forces who were due to give evidence to the Bloody Sunday Inquiry. Although not strictly concerned with a trial, this decision indicates the principles to be applied when considering a restriction on open justice. On the facts, it was found that revealing the identity of the witnesses was not vital to the fairness of the inquiry, and in any event, the clear risk that the lives of the witnesses could be threatened if their identities were made public outweighed any other considerations.

[67] [2008] UKHL 36.   [68] See p 194.

The Coroners and Justice Act 2009

Section 86 of the 2009 Act empowers a court to make a witness anonymity order in the circumstances identified by section 88. Three conditions (A, B and C) each have to be met. Condition A is that the order is necessary in order to protect the safety of the witness or another person, to prevent serious damage to property, or to prevent real harm to the public interest in respect of activities being performed in the public interest, or to stop a person performing those activities. Condition B is that, having regard to all of the circumstances, the effect of the order is consistent with the defendant receiving a fair trial. Condition C is that the importance of the witness's testimony is such that it is in the public interest that the witness testifies, and the witness would not testify if an order were not made, or real harm would ensue if an order were not made. There is therefore a judgment to be made by the court. In deciding how to make that judgment the court must have regard to any reasonable fear on the part of the witness in respect of death or injury, or serious damage to property, that might occur if an order was not made.

The order will require steps to be taken in relation to a witness in criminal proceedings that are appropriate to ensure that the identity of the witness is not disclosed in or in connection with the proceedings. The kind of measures that may be required to be taken in relation to a witness include the withholding of the witness's name or other identifying details, the removal of such details from documents disclosed to other parties in the case, and allowing a witness to use a pseudonym. An order might restrict what questions can be asked of a witness, so that the witness is not required to disclose details that might identify him or her, might provide that the witness is screened (but there are limits: the witness must be visible to the judge or members of the court, and to the jury—if there is one). An order might permit the modulation of a witness's voice, again to protect identity—but, again, the members of the court and jury must be able to hear the witness's natural voice

Restricting material available to a defendant

Denying access of a defendant to information or evidence in relation to the matters in respect of which he being tried fundamentally strikes at concepts of a fair trial. There is no power for a court to deny a defendant access to evidence, and to adopt a 'closed procedure', unless statutory authority for that exists, and even then must be justified under the Human Rights Act 1998.[69] Yet in some cases of a terrorist nature, under the Prevention of Terrorism Act 2005, a defendant, and his lawyers, may be denied access to 'closed material', material that is of such nature in terms of its content that it cannot be disclosed even to the defence. In such circumstances a special advocate is appointed, from a panel of specially vetted and approved lawyers, to represent the interests of the defendant in respect of that material. Such an approach may be necessary, but is certainly controversial, with some concerns as to how effectively a special advocate can represent the interests of a defendant without fully being able to take

---

[69] *Al-Rawi* v *Security Service* [2010] EWCA Civ 482, reversing *Al Rawi* v *Security Service* (2009) EWHC 29597.

instructions from the defendant or his or her legal team. Clearly, major human right issues arise.[70] The reality of this was considered by the House of Lords in *Secretary of State for the Home Department* v *F*.[71] F was subject to a 'control order' significantly restricting his liberty in terms of place of residence, curfew and many other conditions. In the proceedings in which the order was being challenged he was subject to this 'special advocate' procedure. The Court of Appeal had held that there was no principle that a hearing would be unfair in the absence of open disclosure of a minimum level of allegation or evidence. Following an adverse ruling from the Court of Human Rights in *A* v *United Kingdom*,[72] the House of Lords ruled that it was possible to achieve a fair trial for a controlled person even if that person is not provided with the details of the evidence, or the sources of that evidence. However, in cases in which the 'open material' comprises general assertion, the requirements of a fair trial would not be satisfied. A trial is not fair if a party is kept in ignorance of the case against him.

KEY ISSUE

The concept of open justice is at the heart of fair proceedings. As already noted, justice must be seen to be done. Justice that is done behind closed doors should be exceptional and require justification. The youth court sits with limited rights of attendance and even more restricted reporting rights.[73] Family courts have been heavily restricted in terms of attendance and with no rights to publicize or report their decisions at all.[74] In fact, complaints about the lack of rights to report their decisions has led to ongoing complaints about injustices to individuals (often fathers of children) done with no publicity or public accountability.

But even more fundamental is the denial to some accused of the right for them, or even their lawyers, to know the specific evidence on which the actions or decisions that are being challenged are based. The idea of 'closed material' runs great risks of creating great injustice. The decision in *F* goes some way to ensuring the concept of 'fair trial' does have irreducible minima in terms of procedural standards.

❓ Questions

1. Can it ever be right that an individual should be denied access to evidence relevant to his or her case?

2. Do the interests of national security mean that in some cases fair procedures have to be modified?

3. Do the criteria for a witness anonymity order provide sufficient safeguards for an individual?

The reporting of proceedings in court

A final principle of open justice is that reports of judicial proceedings should not be prevented or discouraged, as long as they are fair, contemporaneous, and accurate.

---

[70] See p 192.   [71] [2009] UKHL 28.
[72] [2009] ECHR 301.   [73] See pp 234 and 269.   [74] See p 269.

The publication of such reports is expressly permitted by section 4 of the Contempt of Court Act 1981, but the law recognizes that there are circumstances in which a departure from the general rule may be justified. Section 11, for example, confers a power to prevent the reporting of details that have not been disclosed in open court. In addition, section 4(2) of the Act empowers a court to *postpone* reporting where this is necessary in the interests of justice.[75] If, however, those interests can be satisfied in less restrictive ways, the section 4(2) power should not be used. This was the approach before the Human Rights Act came into effect,[76] and the decision in *R (on the application of the Telegraph Group plc) v Sherwood* suggests that it is still correct.[77] The Court of Appeal in this case identified three key principles. Firstly, a judge has no discretion to restrict publication unless there is a substantial risk of prejudice to particular legal proceedings. Secondly, where such a risk exists, an order should not be made unless the judge is satisfied that it is the least restrictive means of avoiding that risk. Finally, any risk of prejudice must be balanced against the public interest in the proceedings being reported. On the facts of the case, a decision to delay the reporting of one trial until a second, related trial had been concluded was held to be a justifiable and proportionate response to a substantial risk of prejudice.[78] The decision in *Sherwood* should be compared with that in *R v B*.[79] In this case the defendant had pleaded guilty to conspiracy to commit murder, and the judge had made an order postponing the reporting of the sentencing hearing until the trial of his alleged co-conspirators had taken place. Applying the three-stage approach outlined in *Sherwood*, the Court of Appeal held that the order should be quashed: although the right to a fair trial had primacy over all other considerations, the duties imposed on publishers by the Contempt of Court Act were deemed to be a sufficient safeguard of fairness, and the court had confidence in the integrity of juries and in their ability to focus on the evidence presented in court:[80]

> [T]he responsibility for avoiding the publication of material which may prejudice the outcome of a trial rests fairly and squarely on those responsible for the publication. In our view, broadcasting authorities and newspaper editors should be trusted to fulfil their responsibilities accurately to inform the public of court proceedings, and to exercise sensible judgment about the publication of comment which may interfere with the administration of justice.

[75] Note that the latter provision is concerned with avoiding prejudice to specific proceedings, and it does not provide a basis for restrictions to be imposed indefinitely: *R v Times Newspapers Ltd.* [2007] EWCA Crim 1925, (2007) The Times, 31 July.

[76] In *Re Central Independent Television* [1991] 1 All ER 347, [1991] 1 WLR 4, an order prohibiting radio or television reporting whilst a jury was staying overnight at a hotel was held to be excessive. See also, *ex parte Telegraph plc* [1993] 2 All ER 971, [1993] 1 WLR 980.

[77] [2001] EWCA Crim 1075, [2001] 1 WLR 1983. For a discussion of the effect of reporting restrictions on the Convention right to freedom of expression, see Cram, 'Reporting Restrictions in Criminal Proceedings and Article 10 of the ECHR' [1998] EHRLR 742.

[78] Compare the earlier decision in *R v Beck, ex parte Daily Telegraph plc* [1993] 2 All ER 177, in which reporting restrictions were refused in similar circumstances. The court in the recent case felt able to distinguish *Beck* on the facts, however, and did not doubt that it was correctly decided.

[79] [2006] EWCA Crim 2692, [2007] HRLR 1.   [80] Ibid, *per* Sir Igor Judge at [25].

The rules governing the reporting of legal proceedings are considered in more detail below, in the context of the law of contempt.

KEY ISSUE

Given the high-tech age in which we now live, some would question whether allowing only printed reports of legal proceedings is still sufficient to ensure that justice is done in public. One practical problem that already faces the court is instant reporting by the use of the Internet, or by texting, or the use of Twitter or similar facilities. Following recent problems, the Lord Chief Justice has authorized the use of Twitter on a case-by-case basis.[81] The basic principle remains: nothing must interfere with the fairness of the administration of justice.

The government is currently considering whether there is a case for allowing the television cameras to have access to the courts, but a consultation exercise found only limited support for the idea.[82] Although some respondents felt that television coverage might be useful in helping to increase understanding of the justice system, most were concerned about the possible implications of widespread reporting for the fair administration of justice.[83] On this basis, it seems likely that if the government does decide to move in this direction, it will proceed with extreme caution.

? Questions

1. Should the law continue its general prohibition on the use of mobile phones in court? Should texting be permissible on a routine basis?

2. What are the advantages or dangers of permitting text-based applications as a form of communication of what courts are doing?

3. Should the proceedings of courts be televised?

4. What do you think the effects of televising proceedings might be?

Contempt of court[84]

Judges have an inherent jurisdiction to punish conduct calculated to prejudice or interfere with the process of the law. Such conduct is termed a contempt of court and may be either criminal or civil in nature.

---

[81] See *Interim Practice Guidance: The Use of Live Text Based Forms of Communication (Including Twitter) From Court For The Purposes Of Fair and Accurate Reporting*, issued by the Lord Chief Justice on 20 December 2010.

[82] DCA, *Broadcasting Courts* (HMSO, 2005) CP 28/04.

[83] DCA, *Broadcasting Courts: Responses to the Consultation* (HMSO, 2005) CP(R) 28/04, at p 42.

[84] See generally: Miller, *Contempt of Court* (OUP: 3rd edn, 2000); Eady and Smith, *Arlidge, Eady and Smith on Contempt* (Sweet & Maxwell: 3rd edn, 2005), Fenwick and Phillipson, *Media Freedom under the Human Rights Act* (OUP, 2006).

Criminal contempt

Criminal contempt is an offence at common law and comprises conduct that interferes with the administration of justice or that creates a substantial risk that the course of justice will be prejudiced.[85] Thus, it is a criminal contempt to interfere with a juror or witness,[86] or to prevent or unlawfully deter a party from pursuing a legal action.[87] A journalist who refuses to disclose his or her source of information when required to do so by a court may also be liable for contempt.[88] However, a court may only require disclosure if satisfied that this is necessary in the interests of justice, national security, or the prevention of crime or disorder.[89]

It is also a contempt to publish the name of a party or witness where publication is prohibited by statute or is contrary to a court order.[90] In *Attorney-General v Punch*,[91] the publishers and editor of a magazine were convicted of contempt after publishing an article by the former MI5 officer, David Shayler. Mr Shayler was being prosecuted for disclosing intelligence obtained while working for the security services, and he was the subject of an injunction preventing him from making further disclosures while his case was still pending. The injunction did not apply to the defendants directly, but on appeal to the House of Lords it was held that their publication nevertheless amounted to a contempt of court:[92]

> The primary effect of such an injunction is to regulate the conduct of the person against whom it is made. But it also has an indirect effect upon the conduct of third parties. In general, it is a contempt of court for anyone, whether party to the proceedings or not, deliberately to interfere with the due administration of justice. One species of such interference ... is the deliberate publication of information which the court has ordered someone else to keep confidential. Publication interferes with the administration of justice because it destroys the subject-matter of the proceedings. Once the information has been published, the court can no longer do justice between the parties by enforcing the obligation of confidentiality.

Their Lordships acknowledged that the injunction had implications for the right to freedom of expression, and that Article 10 of the ECHR was therefore engaged. Nevertheless, they emphasized that the Article 10 right could be lawfully restricted

---

[85] *A-G v Times Newspapers Ltd* [1992] 1 AC 191, [1991] 2 All ER 398.

[86] *Re Attorney-General's Application* [1963] 1 QB 696, [1962] 3 All ER 326.

[87] *Raymond v Honey* [1981] QB 874, [1981] 2 All ER 1084 (prisoner unlawfully prevented from making an application to the High Court); *A-G v Hislop and Pressdram* [1991] 1 QB 514, [1991] 1 All ER 911 (defendant in a libel case published further articles to deter the claimant from pursing the action).

[88] In *DPP v Channel 4 Television Co Ltd* [1993] 2 All ER 517, fines totalling £75,000 were imposed on the defendant for failure to comply with an order to produce documents.

[89] Contempt of Court Act 1981, s 10; *X Ltd v Morgan-Grampian (Publishers) Ltd* [1991] 1 AC 1, [1990] 2 All ER 1; *Ashworth Hospital Authority v MGN Ltd* [2002] UKHL 29, [2002] 1 WLR 2033, [2002] 4 All ER 193, *Interbrew SA v Financial Times Ltd* [2002] EWCA Civ 274, [2002] EMLR 24; cf. *Goodwin v UK* (1996) 22 EHRR 123. See also, the discussion of Article 10, ECHR, at p 208.

[90] *R v Socialist Worker Printers and Publishers Ltd, ex parte A-G* [1975] QB 637, [1975] 1 All ER 142. There must, however, be a clear direction and not merely a request: *A-G v Leveller Magazine Ltd* [1979] AC 440, [1979] 1 All ER 745.

[91] [2002] UKHL 50, [2003] 1 AC 1046, [2003] 1 All ER 289.   [92] Ibid at [66], *per* Lord Hoffmann.

on a number of grounds, and held that the injunction in this case had been proportionate to the legitimate objective of protecting national security.[93] The defendants'
motive was not important and the fact that they did not believe the material to be
harmful to national security was irrelevant: what mattered was that their conduct was
intentional.

In addition to the common law rule, contempt of court may also be committed
under certain statutory provisions. For example, it is a contempt to obtain, disclose or
solicit any particulars of statements made, opinions expressed, arguments advanced,
or votes cast by members of a jury in the course of their deliberations.[94] There is also a
strict liability rule covering publications that are seriously prejudicial to a fair trial.

Strict liability contempt

The strict liability rule is set out in sections 1 and 2 of the Contempt of Court Act 1981,
and it covers the publication of material that creates a substantial risk of impeding
or prejudicing 'active'[95] legal proceedings. In assessing whether a risk of prejudice is
substantial, it is relevant to take into account the lapse of time between the publication and the date of any trial, and the likelihood of the material being encountered
by potential jurors.[96] A publication creating such a risk will amount to a contempt of
court, regardless of whether there was any intention to interfere with the course of
justice.[97] However, publications *intended* to prejudice the course of justice can still be
dealt with at common law,[98] as can material published when proceedings are imminent but not active.[99]

There are three statutory defences to the strict liability rule: (a) innocent publication or distribution;[100] (b) fair and accurate reports of legal proceedings held in public,
which are published contemporaneously and in good faith;[101] and (c) discussion of
public affairs or other matters of general public interest, where the risk of prejudice
to particular legal proceedings is incidental.[102] An illustration of the defence of inci-

---

[93] Other legitimate grounds for restricting freedom of expression include maintaining judicial
independence and protecting the rights and freedoms of others. The right must also be balanced against
the right to a fair trial under Article 6.

[94] Contempt of Court Act 1981, s 8(1). Proposals to relax this rule to allow legitimate jury research are
discussed at p 371.

[95] In criminal cases, proceedings will be active from the time of an arrest, the issue of an arrest warrant,
or the issue of a summons. In civil proceedings, the relevant date will usually be the date of setting down for
trial: ibid, Sch 1. See also, *A-G v Hislop and Pressdram* [1991] 1 QB 514, [1991] 1 All ER 911.

[96] In *R v Taylor and Taylor* (1994) 98 Cr App R 361, it was held that the prejudicial impact of an article
could be heightened by the use of photographs.

[97] The position was previously governed by common law, which made it an offence to publish material
prejudging the issues to be determined in pending litigation: *A-G v Times Newspapers* [1974] AC 273, [1973]
3 All ER 54. The 1981 Act was passed following the ruling of the European Court of Human Rights in *Sunday
Times v UK* (1979–1980) 2 EHRR 245, which found that the common law rule was too vague and imprecise
and went further than was necessary in a democratic society.

[98] Contempt of Court Act 1981, s 6(c); *A-G v Punch* [2002] UKHL 50, [2003] 1 AC 1046, [2003] 1 All
ER 289.

[99] *A-G v Times Newspapers* [1992] 1 AC 191, [1991] 2 All ER 398.   [100] 1981 Act, s 3(1).

[101] Ibid, s 4. Note that the court may order publication to be postponed under s 4(2): see p 239.

[102] Ibid, s 5.

dental discussion is provided by the case of *Attorney-General* v *English*,[103] in which the House of Lords decided that an article discussing the merits of mercy killing did not amount to contempt, even though at the time of publication a doctor was on trial accused of the mercy killing of a disabled child.

Where a publication is sufficiently prejudicial to justify the quashing of a conviction or a stay of proceedings, a finding of contempt will usually be possible. However, the case of *Attorney-General* v *MGN*[104] illustrates some of the difficulties that may arise. Criminal proceedings against the partner of a well-known actress were abandoned when highly prejudicial reports appeared in five tabloid newspapers. The court found that there was a risk of prejudice stemming from the cumulative effect of these reports, but that when considered separately, none of them were sufficiently prejudicial to satisfy the test for contempt. Conversely, a finding of contempt may be made in circumstances in which a stay of proceedings is unnecessary, as in *Attorney-General* v *BBC and Hat Trick Productions*.[105] The case concerned satirical remarks about Robert Maxwell's sons, which were broadcast six months before the brothers stood trial on serious fraud charges. The judge in the fraud case refused to order a stay of proceedings, on the basis that the six-month gap and the likely length and complexity of the trial would concentrate the juror's minds on the evidence presented in court. Nevertheless, the broadcaster and producers of the programme were convicted of strict liability contempt.

Contempt in the face of the court

If judicial proceedings are actually disrupted, or a contempt is committed in the vicinity of the courtroom, this will constitute contempt in the face of the court. This offence may be committed by, for example, distributing leaflets and shouting during proceedings,[106] using a tape-recorder in court without leave,[107] taking a photograph or making an unauthorized sketch in court,[108] or refusing to give evidence when summoned as a witness.[109] In one case a man was sentenced to six months' imprisonment after attacking his wife and her solicitor during a child custody hearing.[110] In addition, disobeying a witness summons is punishable as a contempt in the same way as if it had been committed in the face of the court.[111]

---

[103] [1983] 1 AC 116, [1982] 2 All ER 903.   [104] [1997] 1 All ER 456.

[105] [1997] EMLR 76. See also *A-G* v *Birmingham Post and Mail Ltd* [1998] 4 All ER 49, [1999] 1 WLR 361, where it was suggested that strict liability contempt requires a lesser degree of prejudice than would be needed to stay proceedings or quash a conviction.

[106] *Morris* v *Crown Office* [1970] 2 QB 114, [1970] 1 All ER 1079.

[107] Contempt of Court Act 1981, s 9.

[108] Criminal Justice Act 1925, s 41(1), as amended; *R* v *D (Contempt of Court: Illegal Photography)* [2004] EWCA Crim 1271, (2004) The Times, 13 May—the defendant in this case was given an immediate twelve months' custodial sentence for using his mobile phone to take photographs during proceedings.

[109] *A-G* v *Mulholland* [1963] 2 QB 477, [1963] 1 All ER 767.

[110] *Wilkinson* v *Lord Chancellor's Department* [2003] EWCA Civ 95, [2003] 2 All ER 184, [2003] 1 WLR 1254.

[111] Criminal Procedure (Attendance of Witnesses) Act 1965, s 3, as amended.

Civil contempt

Civil contempt will occur where a party fails to comply with a court order. For example, a civil contempt may be committed by a failure to comply with an injunction, or by the failure of a solicitor to comply with an undertaking.[112] Mere failure to pay a judgment debt is not contempt, although wilful refusal to do so is.[113] In addition, if an alternative method of securing compliance with a court order is available, the Court of Appeal has stated that this method should be adopted rather than sending the contemnor to prison.[114]

The House of Lords made an important decision on civil contempt in *M v Home Office*.[115] M was seeking leave to apply for judicial review of the Home Secretary's decision to refuse his asylum application. At the end of the hearing the judge made it clear that he wished M to remain in the country until his application had been determined, and he understood the Home Secretary to have given an undertaking not to deport him. M was nevertheless flown out of the country, and the judge made an order obliging the Home Secretary to return him to the jurisdiction. When the Minister failed to comply, he was found to be in contempt of court.

Jurisdiction to punish contempt

The jurisdiction to punish for contempt is inherent in superior courts of record. Such courts may commit for contempt and can punish contempt in the face of the court by an immediate fine and a prison term of up to two years.[116] Although a county court is an inferior court, it is treated as a superior court for these purposes.[117] Most other contempts relating to inferior courts are dealt with by the Queen's Bench Division,[118] although inferior courts of record can punish contempt in the face of the court by an immediate fine and a prison term not exceeding one month.[119] In addition, although not courts of record, magistrates' courts have equivalent powers to punish the wilful interruption of magistrates' proceedings and other forms of misbehaviour in court.[120] Until 1960 there was no right of appeal against punishment for criminal contempt, but this position was altered by section 13 of the Administration of Justice Act 1960. Appeal lies to the Court of Appeal, Divisional Court, or Supreme Court, as the case may be.

---

[112] *Re Kerly* [1901] 1 Ch 467; *Re A Solicitor* [1966] 3 All ER 52, [1966] 1 WLR 1604.

[113] Debtors Act 1869, as amended by the Administration of Justice Act 1970, s 11.

[114] *Danchevsky v Danchevsky* [1975] Fam 17, [1974] 3 All ER 934; *Re G (Contempt: Committal)* [2003] EWCA Civ 489, [2003] 1 WLR 2051.

[115] *Re M* [1994] 1 AC 377; *sub nom M v Home Office* [1993] 3 All ER 537.

[116] Contempt of Court Act 1981, s 14(1).   [117] Ibid, s 14(4A).

[118] *R v Davies* [1906] 1 KB 32. Note that this jurisdiction is limited to 'courts' properly so-called, and it may therefore be important to ascertain whether a particular tribunal is a court: *A-G v BBC* [1981] AC 303, [1980] 3 All ER 161; see p 6.

[119] 1981 Act, s 14(1), (2).

[120] Ibid, s 12. Magistrates can also punish the making of insults against justices, witnesses, solicitors, barristers, and officers of the court.

Contempt may be punished by a summary procedure far removed from the ordinary processes of the law: no precise charges are put, the accused may have no opportunity to consult a lawyer, and the judge making the decision may have been the person insulted. Article 6 of the ECHR establishes certain safeguards for a person charged with a criminal offence, including the presumption of innocence, the right to be informed of the nature of any charges, the right to adequate time and legal assistance in preparing a defence, and the right to be dealt with by an independent and impartial tribunal. Doubts have been raised about the compatibility of the summary procedure with these requirements, and the Court of Appeal has indicated that it should not be used in the absence of a clear contempt that cannot wait to be dealt with:[121]

> Nearly all contempt proceedings require to be adjourned to a separate hearing, in many cases to a different judge, with the rest of the case continuing if possible. An adjournment will usually be necessary if the first judge has already heard evidence from the party alleged to be in contempt which he would not be obliged to give, for risk of self-incrimination, if he were faced with an allegation of contempt.

KEY ISSUE

Contempt of court is a wide concept capable of wide effects. The power to punish for contempt in the face of the court is the most obvious form of contempt but, with the procedural safeguards that the courts have built up, arguably of relatively little concern. More difficulty arises with the punishing of publications on the basis of strict liability. Strict liability contempt has the potential to have a 'chilling' effect: to create conditions of uncertainty that discourage publication of matters that it might well be in the public interest to have aired. The 1981 Act has removed some of the worst effects of the law, but there is a case for the law to be liberalized further.

 Questions

1. Should strict liability contempt exist at all?
2. Are trial courts ever likely to be influenced by what is published?
3. Should there be a wide 'public interest publication' defence?

The European Court of Justice and European Court of Human Rights

These courts play an increasingly important role in the English legal system, and their functions and powers have been considered in detail in Chapters 5 and 6.

---

[121] *Re G (Contempt: Committal)* [2003] EWCA Civ 489 at [21], [2003] 1 WLR 2051 at [21], *per* Butler Sloss P. See also, *Balogh* v *St Albans Crown Court* [1975] QB 73, [1974] 3 All ER 283.

The Supreme Court

The creation of the court

Historically, Parliament was the oldest common law court, its judicial functions being exercised by the House of Lords since the fifteenth century. In theory an appeal to the House of Lords was an appeal to the whole House, and until the nineteenth century this was literally true in that any member of the House could and did vote in judicial sessions. Even those peers who were lawyers were rarely the most senior and well-respected judges of their day, and puisne judges were frequently invited to advise their Lordships on the law.[122] The convention against lay peers participating in judicial sittings of the House was not firmly established until the Appellate Jurisdiction Act 1876, which provided for the creation of salaried life peers to hear appeals. The new life peers were called Lords of Appeal in Ordinary ('Law Lords'), and their number was subsequently fixed at between seven and twelve.[123]

In June 2003 the government unexpectedly announced that it planned to transfer the jurisdiction of the House of Lords' Appellate Committee to a new Supreme Court. This was to be part of a package of measures aimed at modernizing the constitution and ensuring a more formal separation of powers. This was particularly important in ensuring the formal independence of a court required under the European Convention on Human Rights. Other parts of the package included reforming the office of Lord Chancellor,[124] the creation of a government department with administrative responsibility for most major courts,[125] and the creation of an independent Judicial Appointments Commission.[126] A consultation paper explained that the idea behind the proposed new court was to separate formally the judiciary from Parliament and the executive. 'Transparency of independence' was cited as the key issue:[127]

> The considerable growth of judicial review in recent years has inevitably brought the judges more into the political eye. It is essential that our systems do all that they can to minimise the danger that judges' decisions could be perceived to be politically motivated. The Human Rights Act 1998, itself the product of a changing climate of opinion, has made people more sensitive to the issues and more aware of the anomaly of the position whereby the highest court of appeal is situated within one of the chambers of Parliament.

---

[122] The last case in which this appears to have happened was *Allen* v *Flood* [1898] AC 1.

[123] Appellate Jurisdiction Act 1947; Administration of Justice Act 1968, s 1(1)(a); Maximum Number of Judges Order 1994, SI 1994/3217. By custom, one or two Law Lords have always been from Scotland and one from Northern Ireland: these members have usually sat in appeals from the Court of Session and the Court of Appeal of Northern Ireland.

[124] DCA, *Constitutional Reform: Reforming the Office of the Lord Chancellor* (HMSO, 2003) CP 13/03. The original proposal was for abolition; see p 315.

[125] Ibid.

[126] DCA, *Constitutional Reform: A New Way of Appointing Judges* (HMSO, 2003) CP 10/03; see p 339.

[127] DCA, *Constitutional Reform: A Supreme Court for the United Kingdom* (HMSO, 2003) CP 11/03, at para 1.2. The proposed reforms were considered sufficiently fundamental for at least one journal to devote an entire edition to the issue: (2004) 24 Legal Studies.

In its published response to the consultation paper,[128] the Judges' Council broadly accepted the proposals, whilst making it clear that not all of its members were convinced of the need for change. The main area of disagreement concerned the proposal to remove the senior judges from the legislature entirely:[129]

> While the House of Lords remains wholly, or mainly, an appointed (rather than elected) body there is a strong case for the Lord Chief Justice of England and Wales, the Lord President of the Court of Session, the Lord Chief Justice of Northern Ireland and the President of the Supreme Court being members. It would not be sensible to exclude from a House of Lords those best placed to contribute to debates on the justice system and the judiciary. All other members of the Supreme Court should cease to exercise any rights they may have to speak or vote in the House while they serve as judges.

The final blueprint for the new Court was included in the Constitutional Reform Act 2005. The Act reflects most of the preferences expressed by the Judges' Council as to the court's membership, size, composition, and jurisdiction.[130] Crucially, however, the recommendation that some senior judges should continue to sit in the House of Lords has not been adopted.

The Supreme Court came into operation in December 2009.

Composition and jurisdiction

Section 23 of the 2005 Act provides that 'there is to be a Supreme Court of the United Kingdom', and that it shall consist of twelve judges.[131] The court will be properly constituted when an uneven number of not fewer than three judges is sitting, more than half of whom must be permanent members,[132] and in its first twelve months it sat in benches of five, seven, and nine members, the size of the bench reflecting the importance or difficulty of the issue before the court.

The pre-existing Lords of Appeal became the first members of the new court, and at this point ceased to be entitled to sit in Parliament.[133] They are known as 'Justices of the Supreme Court',[134] the court's two most senior members hold the offices of President and Deputy President.[135] The President is able to supplement the court's permanent membership by asking other senior judges to sit on a temporary basis. Former Law Lords and Supreme Court Justices are also eligible to sit.[136]

---

[128] Judges' Council Response to the Consultation Papers on Constitutional Reform (available online at **www.dca.gov.uk/judicial/pdfs/jcresp.pdf**). The Law Lords' response is discussed at p 331.

[129] Ibid, at para 17.

[130] Some of the Council's recommendations were *not* adopted. For example, the Act does not include provisions making the Lord Chief Justice, Master of the Rolls, Lord President of the Court of Session, and Lord Chief Justice of Northern Ireland *ex officio* members of the new court; nor does it prevent leapfrog appeals from the High Court in criminal cases.

[131] This number may be varied by Order in Council, subject to an affirmative resolution procedure.

[132] Section 42.   [133] Sections 24 and 137.   [134] Section 23(6).

[135] Sections 23(5) and 24.   [136] Sections 38 and 39.

The Supreme Court is not a constitutional court in the sense that it has no power to strike down legislation as unconstitutional or contrary to the ECHR, although the nature of the matters that come before the Supreme Court (and, before it, to the House of Lords) gives many of its deliberations and judgments major constitutional importance. Its jurisdiction is broadly the same as that formerly exercised by the House of Lords.[137] Its powers include an inherent jurisdiction to make such orders as are necessary for the purpose of the proceedings. It has, however, inherited jurisdiction over devolution matters from the Privy Council.[138] As it will hear appeals from all parts of the United Kingdom it remains legally separate from the existing courts of England and Wales. The court sits at Middlesex Guildhall in London's Parliament Square.

Civil cases

The Supreme Court hears appeals in civil cases from the Court of Appeal, but only with leave of either the Court of Appeal or the Supreme Court itself. Most cases that reached the House of Lords involved points of law of public importance, although this is not a prerequisite in civil cases.

The Administration of Justice Act 1969 introduced a 'leap-frog' procedure, allowing appeals to bypass the Court of Appeal and go directly from the trial court to the (then) House of Lords. This procedure continues to exist. A leapfrog appeal is only possible if two conditions are satisfied, as follows.

(1) The trial judge must grant a certificate (with the consent of all parties) that the case involves a point of law of general public importance. The point of law must either relate wholly or mainly to the construction of an enactment, or it must be one in respect of which the judge would be bound by a previous decision of the Court of Appeal or House of Lords or Supreme Court

(2) The Supreme Court must grant leave.

Criminal cases

The House of Lords' jurisdiction in criminal cases was of comparatively modern origin, and it was not until the Court of Criminal Appeal was created in 1907[139] that there was any general right to appeal to the Lords in a criminal case. The equivalent right of appeal to the Supreme Court now exists.[140] The right of appeal from the Queen's Bench Divisional Court was created in 1960, and appeal also lies from the High Court, the Court Martial Appeal Court, and the Court of Appeal of Northern Ireland.[141] There is no right of appeal to the Supreme Court from Scotland's highest criminal court, the High Court of Justiciary.

---

[137] Section 40.

[138] Section 40(4)(b); Sch 9. The Privy Council's jurisdiction is discussed at p 275.

[139] Criminal Appeal Act 1907. The jurisdiction of this court was transferred to the Criminal Division of the Court of Appeal by the Criminal Appeal Act 1966.

[140] For details, see p 708.   [141] The conditions required for an appeal are discussed at p 708.

The Court of Appeal

The English superior courts were completely reorganized by the Supreme Court of Judicature Acts 1873–75. The Acts created the Supreme Court of Judicature (subsequently renamed in 1981 and, now, again by the Constitutional Reform Act 2005, which confers the title 'The Senior Courts of England and Wales'). The Judicature Acts transferred to it the jurisdiction of the existing superior courts: the appellate jurisdiction was transferred to the Court of Appeal and the original jurisdiction was transferred to the High Court. The Crown Court was added to the list by the Courts Act 1971. The Senior Courts now consist of three courts: the Court of Appeal; the High Court; and the Crown Court. The relevant law is consolidated in the Supreme Court Act 1981.

Constitution

The Court of Appeal is split into Civil and Criminal Divisions, and is composed of a number of *ex officio* judges along with the Lord and Lady Justices of Appeal.[142] The *ex officio* judges comprise the Lord Chief Justice, the Master of the Rolls, the Presidents of the Queen's Bench and Family Divisions of the High Court, the Chancellor of the High Court, former Lord Chancellors,[143] and, now, the Justices of the Supreme Court.[144] Of these, only the Master of the Rolls (in civil cases) and the Lord Chief Justice (in criminal cases) usually sit, and they are, in fact, the Presidents of the Civil and Criminal Divisions, respectively. In addition to the regular judges of the Court, any High Court judge or circuit judge may be required to sit.[145] Former High Court and Court of Appeal judges may also be asked to sit, but they cannot be compelled to do so.

The Civil Division may be duly constituted with only one judge present, but most cases are heard by three judges sitting together.[146] As to the Criminal Division, at least two judges must be present to hear appeals against sentence,[147] and three or more judges are required for any of the following:[148]

(a) an appeal against conviction;

(b) an appeal against a verdict of not guilty by reason of insanity;

---

[142] Supreme Court Act 1981, s 2. Section 2(3) was amended by the Courts Act 2003 to permit the use of the title 'Lady Justice of Appeal' where appropriate. The maximum number of ordinary Court of Appeal judges is thirty-seven: Maximum Number of Judges Order 2002, SI 2002/2837.

[143] Only those who held this office before 12 June 2003.

[144] The Court has sometimes been composed of three Law Lords: see *Mallett* v *Restormel Borough Council* [1978] 2 All ER 1057.

[145] Supreme Court Act 1981, s 9: note that circuit judges can only sit in the Criminal Division.

[146] Ibid, s 54(2), as amended. The Master of the Rolls may give directions about the minimum number of judges needed for (a) any description of proceedings, or (b) any particular proceedings; s 54(3)–(4A).

[147] Ibid, s 55(4).   [148] Ibid; there must be an odd number. For details, see p 250.

(c) an appeal against a finding of unfitness to plead;

(d) an application for leave to appeal to the Supreme Court;

(e) a refusal of leave to appeal against conviction (or against any of the verdicts and findings referred to above), unless the application has already been refused by a single judge; or

(f) a review of a sentencing decision that has been referred by the Attorney-General under Part IV of the Criminal Justice Act 1988.

In addition, a single judge of the Criminal Division has jurisdiction under the Criminal Appeal Act 1968 to hear certain types of application: notably for leave to appeal.[149] Either division may occasionally convene a 'full court' of five or more members to hear appeals involving novel or difficult points of law. However, such a court has no wider powers than the normal court.

Jurisdiction

The Court of Appeal has consisted of a Civil and a Criminal Division since 1 October 1966, which is when the Criminal Appeal Act 1966 came into operation.

Civil Division

The Civil Division exercises:

(a) all jurisdiction conferred on it by the Supreme Court Act 1981 or any other Act; and

(b) all jurisdiction exercisable by it prior to the commencement of the 1981 Act.[150]

Its jurisdiction is entirely civil and entirely appellate. Until recently, appeals in civil cases from both the county court and the High Court were generally heard by the Court of Appeal, but in 1997 a review carried out by Sir Jeffrey Bowman concluded that the Civil Division's workload was unnecessarily high.[151] Two of the review's most important recommendations were that:

(a) any appeal against the first-instance decision of a civil court should normally require leave;[152] and

(b) more appeals should be dealt with at a lower level, the guiding principle being simply that the judge or court hearing an appeal should have a superior jurisdiction to the first-instance decision-maker.

---

[149] Section 31, as amended.   [150] Supreme Court Act 1981, s 15(2).

[151] *Report to the Lord Chancellor by the Review of the Court of Appeal* (Lord Chancellor's Department, 1997); see also Jacob J, 'Bowman Review of the Court of Appeal' (1998) 61(3) MLR 390. Similar recommendations were made in Woolf's *Final Report on Access to Justice* (1996).

[152] The Review recommended that an appeal should still be as of right in cases in which the liberty of the subject was at stake, and in certain cases involving children.

The main aim of these proposals was to reduce the workload of the Civil Division and to improve the speed and overall efficiency of the appeals process.

Reform under the Access to Justice Act 1999

The Bowman recommendations were broadly implemented by the Access to Justice Act 1999 and the Civil Procedure Rules, Part 52.[153] Under section 56 of the Act the Lord Chancellor is empowered to make more detailed rules for the allocation of civil appeals by way of statutory instrument.[154] Appeals against many county court decisions are now dealt with by High Court judges, whilst the Court of Appeal continues to hear appeals against final decisions in multi-track[155] and specialist proceedings cases.[156] In addition, there is a discretion to allow any civil appeal that would normally be heard by a lower court to be dealt with instead by the Court of Appeal.[157]

Any second appeal against the decision of a county court or High Court judge will also lie to the Court of Appeal, but second appeals can only be granted exceptionally and the Court of Appeal must be satisfied that either:

(a) the appeal would raise an important point of principle or practice; or

(b) there is some other compelling reason for hearing it.[158]

Finally, the Civil Division has jurisdiction to hear appeals on points of law from the Employment Appeal Tribunal and various other tribunals.

The appeal itself normally takes the form of a limited review unless the court considers that it would be in the interests of justice to hold a rehearing, or, exceptionally, to order a new trial.[159] The appeals system applicable to civil cases is discussed further in Chapter 18 of this book.

Criminal Division

The Criminal Division of the Court of Appeal was established by the Criminal Appeal Act 1966 as the successor to the Court of Criminal Appeal.[160] Its jurisdiction is entirely criminal and entirely appellate. Its principal function is to hear appeals against conviction and sentence from persons convicted in the Crown Court. It can also consider sentencing decisions referred by the Attorney-General on the grounds that they are

---

[153] SI 1998/3132, as inserted by SI 2000/221; in force since 2 May 2000. For a discussion of the key changes, see *Tanfern Ltd* v *Cameron-MacDonald* [2000] 2 All ER 801, [2000] 1 WLR 1311.

[154] An Order pursuant to this provision has been made: see the Access to Justice Act 1999 (Destination of Appeals) Order 2000, SI 2000/1071.

[155] Ibid, Article 4. Multi-track cases are discussed at p 524.

[156] Ibid. Specialist proceedings are those involving the Patents Court or Technology and Construction Court, commercial proceedings, admiralty matters, and proceedings under the Companies Acts.

[157] 1999 Act, s 57. This discretion may be exercised by either the Master of the Rolls or a court involved in the case.

[158] Ibid, s 55(1); SI 2000/1071, article 5.

[159] Civil Procedure Rules, Part 52. The difference between a review and a rehearing is considered in *Assicurazoni Generali Spa* v *Arab Insurance Group* [2002] EWCA Civ 1642, [2003] 1 WLR 577.

[160] Established by the Criminal Appeal Act 1907, to supersede the Court for Crown Cases Reserved.

unduly lenient.[161] The court also deals with applications from the Attorney-General on points of law following acquittal, and occasionally, applications for the retrial of an acquitted person.[162] In addition, where a trial on indictment has ended in a conviction, a finding of not guilty by reason of insanity, or a finding that a person did the act in question but is under a disability, the case can be referred by the Criminal Cases Review Commission for determination as an appeal.[163]

The High Court

Constitution

The High Court was established by the Supreme Court of Judicature Acts 1873–75 and to it was transferred the jurisdiction of several existing superior courts. These included the three superior common law courts of first instance, the Court of Chancery, and the Courts of Admiralty, Probate, and Divorce and Matrimonial Causes.[164] The constitution and jurisdiction of the High Court are now governed by the Supreme Court Act 1981. The court sits primarily in London, but, by virtue of section 71 of the Act, sittings may be conducted at any place in England or Wales.[165] Regional centres can, and have been created: thus the Commercial Court sits in various centres, as does the Administrative Court.[166] The centres at which sittings are actually held are determined in accordance with the Lord Chancellor's directions, and ad hoc directions may be given to enable the court to sit at a particular location. Thus, in a case concerning a disputed right of way in Iken, a small village in Suffolk,[167] the Lord Chancellor authorized the court to sit at Iken so that the evidence of an elderly witness could be taken. In 2007 the Administrative Court sat in Wales and now sits regionally.[168]

Jurisdiction

The jurisdiction of the High Court is both civil and criminal. In civil actions its jurisdiction is virtually unlimited and it is broadly concurrent with that of the county courts. However, there is a minimum financial limit for the value of claims that can be commenced in the High Court, and subject to any statutory exceptions this is currently £50,000 for personal injury actions, and £15,000 for other

[161] Criminal Justice Act 1988, s 36; see p 707.   [162] See p 699.
[163] Criminal Appeal Act 1995, s 9: see p 694. This power was formerly exercisable by the Home Secretary: Criminal Appeal Act 1968, s 17.
[164] The jurisdiction of the Chancery Courts of the Counties Palatine of Lancaster and Durham was *not* transferred, but these courts were merged with the High Court under s 41 of the Courts Act 1971.
[165] Evidence may be taken outside the jurisdiction. In *Tito* v *Waddell* [1975] 3 All ER 997, [1975] 1 WLR 1303 the judge visited two Pacific islands in order to view land at the centre of a legal dispute.
[166] See p 256.
[167] *St Edmundsbury and Ipswich Diocesan Board of Finance* v *Clark* [1973] Ch 323, [1973] 2 All ER 1155.
[168] See *T (on application of Deeplock) v Welsh Member* [2007] EWCA 3347 (Admin), and p 256.

cases.[169] For claims exceeding these limits proceedings can be commenced in either court, and there are provisions for transferring appropriate cases from one court to the other.[170] Following the Woolf reforms, the allocation of cases between the High Court and the county courts now depends not only on the sums involved, but also on whether they are designated as 'small claims', 'fast-track', or 'multi-track' cases.[171] These reforms are the subject of more detailed analysis in Chapter 13 but for present purposes it is sufficient to note that the majority of the High Court's workload now consists of multi-track cases, and most civil actions continue to be determined at county court level.

In addition to its original jurisdiction in civil cases, the High Court also has both appellate and supervisory functions. The historic role of the courts in supervising the actions of inferior bodies and tribunals has already been noted,[172] and this role is now performed mainly by a Divisional Court of the Queen's Bench Division. All three divisions of the High Court also have an appellate role, and this has increased since the restructuring of the civil appeals system in 1999.[173]

The divisions

The High Court initially consisted of five divisions, but these were reduced in 1880 to the three that currently exist:[174] the Chancery Division; the Queen's Bench Division; and the Family Division.[175] Each division handles a different type of subject matter, although it is important to note that the divisions are of equal competence and they are not separate courts. Indeed, the inherent jurisdiction of the High Court judge may be exercised by a judge of any division,[176] and the fact that a matter falls within a particular division's class of business does not necessarily mean that that the matter must be allocated accordingly.[177] Moreover, in certain cases the jurisdiction of the divisions overlaps, and this means that claimants sometimes have a choice about where to commence their actions. Many actions for professional negligence, for example, can be commenced in either the Queen's Bench Division or the Chancery Division.[178] Nevertheless, the overall effect of the relevant statutes and rules of procedure is to

[169] High Court and County Courts Jurisdiction Order 1991, SI 1991/724; High Court and County Courts Jurisdiction (Amendment) Order 1999, SI 1999/1014.

[170] CPR, Part 30.   [171] See p 521.   [172] See p 226.   [173] See p 552.

[174] See now, the Supreme Court Act 1981, s 5. Section 7 of the Act provides that the number of divisions may be increased or reduced on the recommendation of the senior judges specified in s 7(2).

[175] The Family Division was originally called the Probate, Divorce and Admiralty Division, but was renamed by the Administration of Justice Act 1970, s 1. Its Admiralty jurisdiction was reassigned to the Queen's Bench Division and contentious probate business was assigned to the Chancery Division.

[176] Supreme Court Act 1981, s 5(5): see *Re L* [1968] P 119, [1968] 1 All ER 20.   [177] Ibid.

[178] The contract disputes in *Petrofina (Great Britain) Ltd* v *Martin* [1965] Ch 1073, [1965] 2 All ER 176 and *Esso Petroleum Co Ltd* v *Harper's Garage (Stourport) Ltd* [1965] 3 WLR 469, [1965] 2 All ER 933 may also be considered in this context. The two cases concerned very similar issues, yet the former was tried in the Chancery Division and the latter in the Queen's Bench Division.

confer a distinct jurisdiction upon each division,[179] and suggestions that the divisions should be merged have thus far been rejected.[180]

Chancery Division

The business of the Chancery Division is carried out by the Chancellor of the High Court and seventeen puisne judges.[181] Before 1972, sittings of the Chancery Division were held only in the Royal Courts of Justice in London, and Chancery judges did not go on assize. The Supreme Court Act 1981 authorizes sittings of the High Court to be held anywhere in England and Wales,[182] but most Chancery business is still heard in London.[183]

Jurisdiction

Section 34 of the Supreme Court of Judicature Act 1873 gave the Chancery Division jurisdiction over matters that were previously heard in the Court of Chancery. The distribution of High Court business is now governed by section 61 and Schedule 1 of the Supreme Court Act 1981 and, under these provisions, the Chancery Division is assigned jurisdiction over all causes and matters concerning:

(a) the sale, exchange or partition of land, or the raising of charges on land;

(b) the redemption or foreclosure of mortgages;

(c) the execution of trusts;

(d) the administration of estates of deceased persons;

(e) bankruptcy;

(f) the dissolution of partnerships or the taking of partnership or other accounts;

(g) the rectification, setting aside or cancellation of deeds or other instruments in writing;

(h) probate business, other than non-contentious or common form business;

(i) patents, trade marks, registered designs or copyright;

(j) the appointment of a guardian of a minor's estate; and

(k) matters relating company law.

Various other statutes and rules of procedure give the Chancery Division jurisdiction over revenue matters, town and country planning, and landlord and tenant disputes.

---

[179] For the distribution of business between the divisions, see Supreme Court Act 1981, s 61 and Sch 1.

[180] See, e.g., Woolf, *Final Report on Access to Justice* (HMSO, 1996), at p 261.

[181] *Judicial Statistics 2005*, p 129. The Lord Chancellor has historically been head of the Division but modern Lord Chancellors have rarely sat at first instance. When Lord Falconer was appointed in 2003 he announced that he did not intend to sit at all, and Part 2 of the Constitutional Reform Act 2005 has formally stripped the Lord Chancellor of all judicial functions: see p 316. The Act also replaces the title Vice-Chancellor with that of 'Chancellor of the High Court'; Sch 4, para 115.

[182] Section 71(1).

[183] Cases are also heard in Birmingham, Bristol, Cardiff, Leeds, Liverpool, Manchester, Newcastle-upon-Tyne, and Preston.

The appellate jurisdiction of the Chancery Division has always been limited, and has primarily related to taxation, insolvency, and land registration. As stated previously, however, reforms since 1999 mean that many more appeals from county court decisions can now be determined at High Court level. The implications of these changes are discussed further in Chapter 18, but their overall effect is to extend the appellate jurisdiction of all three divisions of the High Court to cover a broader spectrum of cases.

Patents Court The Patents Court is part of the Chancery Division and is one of a number of 'specialist courts' within the High Court. It was established by the Patents Act 1977 and hears patent actions at first instance and on appeal from the Comptroller-General of Patents, Designs and Trademarks.

Queen's Bench Division

The Queen's Bench Division has seventy-two puisne judges and is headed by the President of the Queen's Bench Division.[184] It has both a civil and a criminal jurisdiction, and performs original, appellate, and supervisory functions.

Civil jurisdiction

The most important aspect of this Division's business is its first-instance jurisdiction over civil matters, and most of its workload consists of actions in contract and tort. Its role in the civil appeals system has always been very limited, although High Court judges of all divisions were given a greater appellate jurisdiction when the system was restructured in 1999.[185] In addition, a Divisional Court of the Queen's Bench Division, consisting of two or more judges, has a limited civil jurisdiction to hear appeals by way of case stated from the Crown Court and magistrates' courts.[186]

Commercial Court This court has jurisdiction over commercial matters and, like the Patents Court, it is a specialist court operating within a division of the High Court. It was officially designated as a court by the Administration of Justice Act 1970,[187] although a 'commercial list' of cases has been maintained since 1895. The court has its own rules of procedure[188] and is served by nominated puisne judges with particular expertise in this area of law.

Admiralty Court This is also a specialist court, and it has jurisdiction over matters assigned to the Queen's Bench Division by section 20 of the Supreme Court Act 1981. Its business includes actions to enforce claims for damages arising out of collisions between ships, claims to the possession or ownership of ships, claims for loss of or damage to goods carried in a ship, towage claims, and other specified proceedings. When trying admiralty actions the judge often sits with lay assessors.

---

[184] Supreme Court Act 1981, s 5. Prior to implementation of the Constitutional Reform Act 2005, the Lord Chief Justice was head of the Division.

[185] See p 251.   [186] Appeals from magistrates' courts in family cases lie to the Family Division.

[187] Section 3(1).   [188] See CPR, Parts 49 and 58, and the accompanying Practice Direction 58.

Technology and Construction Court Since 1998 this specialist court has been responsible for dealing with disputes involving construction, engineering, surveying, and similar matters, along with certain cases concerning information technology, the sale of goods, trespass, and nuisance.[189] However, a dispute will only warrant allocation to this court if it involves technically complex questions of fact.

As a final point, it should be noted that judges of the Queen's Bench Division also exercise many other functions. Not only do they handle most of the business of the Criminal Division of the Court of Appeal, they also sit in the Court Martial Appeal Court and determine disputed parliamentary elections when sitting as an election court.[190] In addition, the 'first-tier' jurisdiction of the Crown Court is exercised principally by judges from this Division.[191]

Criminal jurisdiction

The criminal jurisdiction of the High Court is exercised exclusively by the Queen's Bench Division and is entirely appellate. It comprises appeals by way of 'case stated'[192] from magistrates' courts, and also from the Crown Court when acting in its capacity as an appellate court. These appeals are heard by a Queen's Bench Divisional Court consisting of at least two but often three judges.

Supervisory jurisdiction and the Administrative Court

The supervisory jurisdiction of the Queen's Bench Division is also exercised by a Divisional Court. It includes the power to make mandatory orders, prohibition orders, and quashing orders,[193] which compel inferior courts and tribunals to exercise their powers properly and within the scope of their authority (intra vires). It also includes the power to issue the prerogative writ of habeas corpus. The Division's supervisory jurisdiction is exercised through the procedure known as 'judicial review', which is currently governed by Part 54 of the Civil Procedure Rules.[194] The Upper Tribunal, created by the Tribunals Courts and Enforcement Act 2007, and which is a superior court of record,[195] also has an important judicial review function.

These cases used to be dealt with as part of the Crown Office list, but the group of increasingly specialized judges who determine judicial review matters is now known as 'the Administrative Court'.[196] Since 2009 it sits in Birmingham, Cardiff, Leeds, Manchester, and (from 2010) Bristol. Whether sufficient judicial expertise in this area

---

[189] Supreme Court Act 1981, s 68 and Sch 2, as amended by the Civil Procedure Act 1997. The matters dealt with by the court were formally known as 'Official Referee's Business'.

[190] Representation of the People Act 1983, s 120. This is not actually part of the Queen's Bench Division: indeed, it is an inferior court and is therefore subject to judicial review (*R v Cripps, ex parte Muldoon* [1984] QB 68, [1984] 3 All ER 72).

[191] See pp 261 and 606.

[192] Magistrates' Courts Act 1980, s 111; Supreme Court Act 1981, ss 28 and 28A. For details of the procedure, see p 688.

[193] Formerly known as orders of mandamus, prohibition, and certiorari.

[194] This replaces RSC, Ord 53

[195] For discussion of the term 'superior court' see p 6, and *R (on application of Cart and others) v Special Immigration Appeals Commission and Upper tribunal and others* [2009] EWHC 3052 (Admin).

[196] *Practice Direction (Administrative Court: Establishment)* [2000] 4 All ER 1071, [2000] 1 WLR 1654.

exists remains to be seen, given ongoing concerns about the current levels of availability of judicial expertise to meet rising caseloads.[197]

Family Division

The Family Division[198] consists of the President and nineteen nominated puisne judges,[199] who are assisted in their work by a number of district judges. Its jurisdiction is set out in the Supreme Court Act 1981, and is both original and appellate. The following functions are assigned to it by Schedule 1 of the Act:

(a) all High Court matrimonial causes and matters (whether at first instance or on appeal);

(b) all causes and matters (whether at first instance or on appeal) relating to:

   (i) legitimacy;

   (ii) the exercise of the inherent jurisdiction of the High Court with respect to minors, the maintenance of minors and any proceedings under the Children Act 1989, except proceedings solely for the appointment of a guardian of a minor's estate;

   (iii) adoption;

   (iv) non-contentious or common-form probate business;

(c) applications for consent to the marriage of a minor;

(d) proceedings on appeal from an order or decision made under section 63(3) of the Magistrates' Courts Act 1980 to enforce an order of a magistrates' court made in matrimonial proceedings or with respect to the guardianship of a minor;

(e) certain proceedings under the Family Law Act 1986;

(f) proceedings under the Children Act 1989;

(g) certain proceedings under the Childcare Act 2006;

(h) certain proceedings under the Gender Recognition Act 2004;

(i) civil partnership causes and matters; and

(j) proceedings under various other statutory provisions.[200]

---

[197] See the comments of Nason, 'Rationalisation of Administrative Court and the Tribunalisation of Judicial Review' [2009] PL 440; Bondy and Sunkin, 'Accessing Judicial Review' [2008] PL 647.

[198] Prior to the Administration of Justice Act 1970, it was known as the Probate, Divorce and Admiralty Division. Sir Alan Herbert described the jurisdiction as 'wills, wives and wrecks': of these, 'wills' have gone to the Chancery Division, and 'wrecks' (other than the wrecks of marriages) to the Queen's Bench Division.

[199] Supreme Court Act 1981, s 5. The President of the Family Division also holds the title of Head of Family Justice: Constitutional Reform Act 2005, s 9.

[200] Family Law Acts 1986 and 1996; Child Abduction and Custody Act 1985; Human Fertilisation and Embryology Act 1990; Welfare Reform and Pensions Act 1999; Child Support Act 1991.

The effect of these provisions is to give the Division exclusive High Court jurisdiction over matrimonial disputes and children, thus avoiding the conflicts that used to arise between the Family and Chancery Divisions before 1970.[201]

For proceedings arising under the Children Act 1989, magistrates' courts, county courts, and the Family Division each have jurisdiction.[202] The distribution of work between the three courts is governed by an order made by the Lord Chancellor,[203] which also provides for the transfer of cases between the three courts. In addition, the Courts Act 2003 establishes a Family Procedure Rule Committee with the power to make Family Procedure Rules governing practice and procedure across all three courts.[204] The creation of a single Family Court has now been adopted as a long-term government objective.[205]

The appellate business of the Family Division consists largely of appeals from family courts concerning matrimonial causes and children.

County courts

Constitution

The county courts were established by the County Courts Act 1846 to meet the need for a system to deal with small claims. There are currently 218 county courts in England and Wales, each serving a particular district. Every county court district is assigned at least one circuit judge and one district judge, and deputy district judges may also be appointed.[206] In theory, even High Court and Court of Appeal judges may be asked to sit,[207] but it is rare for such senior judges to be used in this capacity.

Jurisdiction

The jurisdiction of the county courts is entirely civil, and in terms of subject matter it is broadly concurrent with the civil jurisdiction of the High Court. Thus the County Courts Act 1984 gives them jurisdiction over cases involving tort, contract, land, equity, family law, probate, and even admiralty, whilst other statutes confer jurisdiction in matters such as discrimination, divorce, landlord and tenant, and insolvency.[208] However, as county courts owe their origins entirely to statute, they only have jurisdiction in matters specifically assigned to them by legislation. They do not, for

---

[201] See, e.g., *Hall* v *Hall* [1963] P 378, [1963] 2 All ER 140.   [202] Children Act 1989, s 92.

[203] Children (Allocation of Proceedings) Order 1991, SI 1991/1677, as amended. See also, the Family Law Act 1996 (Part IV) (Allocation of Proceedings) Order 1997, SI 1997/1896.

[204] Sections 75–81.

[205] DCA, *A Single Civil Court? Responses to the Consultation* (HMSO, 2005) CP(R) 06/05, at p 42.

[206] County Courts Act 1984, ss 1, 5, 6, and 8.   [207] Ibid, s 5.

[208] See, e.g., Race Relations Act 1976, s 57; Sex Discrimination Act 1975, s 66; Matrimonial and Family Proceedings Act 1984, s 33; Rent Act 1977, s 141; Insolvency Act 1986, ss 117 and 373.

example, have any inherent jurisdiction to conduct judicial review proceedings, nor can they grant the associated prerogative remedies.[209]

Not all county courts deal with the full range of cases eligible for determination at this level: almost a quarter do not have jurisdiction to hear divorce petitions, and over a third do not deal with insolvency matters. In addition, some county courts have been designated as specialist centres for dealing with particular types of action. For example, whilst all county courts have jurisdiction to hear proceedings under the Children Act 1989, a number have been designated as specialist 'family hearing centres' to which difficult cases may be transferred.[210] One county court in London even specializes in patent cases. There is also a 'bulk centre' at Northampton County Court, which processes computer-generated debt recovery claims from major claimants such as public utilities and mail-order companies. The same court also processes a large volume of claims for unpaid car-parking charges.

There are two further limitations on the county courts' jurisdiction, the first of which is geographical. Unlike the High Court, which is a single court with the jurisdiction to sit anywhere in England and Wales, each county court is a separate entity serving a particular district. Although most claims can be commenced in any county court, a defended action to recover a sum of money will normally be transferred to the defendant's home district. Other claims may also be transferred at the court's discretion.[211]

The second limitation is a financial one. County courts were created primarily to handle minor civil actions such as the recovery of small debts, and until 1991 their jurisdiction in tort and contract was limited to claims involving £5,000 or less. Reforms under the Courts and Legal Services Act 1990 led to this upper ceiling being removed,[212] and the emphasis shifted to setting *minimum* financial limits for cases commenced in the High Court. Cases involving less than £25,000 generally had to be commenced at county court level. Further reforms since 1999 mean that the allocation of cases between the two courts now depends not only on the financial value of the claim, but also on whether it is designated as a 'small claims', 'fast-track', or 'multi-track' case.[213] The allocation and management of civil cases is discussed further in Chapters 14 and 15, but in essence, 'small claims' (involving less than £5,000) continue to be dealt with by the county courts, and other actions involving less than £15,000 (or £50,000 for personal injuries) must also begin life at this level. Most claims for higher amounts can be commenced in either court, and the decision about where a case is ultimately determined depends not only on the sums involved, but also on the importance and complexity of the issues. County courts now have unlimited jurisdiction in tort, contract, and land cases, but financial limits are still in place for certain

[209] See p 256.
[210] Children (Allocation of Proceedings) Order 1991, SI 1991/1677, as amended. The designated centres are listed in Sch 1 of the Order.
[211] CPR, rr 30.2 and 26.2.
[212] Section 1; High Court and County Courts Jurisdiction Order 1991, SI 1991/724.
[213] See p 521.

other types of action. For example, in equity matters and contentious probate cases, the upper limit is currently £30,000.[214]

Finally, it should be noted that although the jurisdiction of the county courts is largely original, circuit judges do have jurisdiction to hear appeals from the decisions of district judges.[215]

The Crown Court

Creation of the Crown Court

The Crown Court was created by the Courts Act 1971 and came into operation on 1 January 1972. Before this date trials on indictment took place at quarter sessions or assizes. Both quarter sessions and assizes had local jurisdiction and were generally confined to dealing with offences that had been committed locally.

The assize courts were grouped into circuits and did not sit continuously: judges were sent out on circuit by royal commission and sat at each assize town for the duration of the assize. Their jurisdiction was equivalent to that of the High Court and at least two Queen's Bench Division judges were usually named in the commissions. County court judges and Queen's Counsel were also included, and even the Master of the Rolls and Lord Justices of Appeal could theoretically be asked to sit. The assize courts generally dealt with the most serious criminal offences, although they also handled a certain amount of civil work. Less serious offences tried on indictment were dealt with at quarter sessions. These were held four times a year at almost 150 different courts, and like the assizes they dealt with both civil and criminal cases. Quarter sessions also had jurisdiction to hear appeals from the decisions of magistrates' courts, and to sentence persons committed for sentencing following summary conviction. The whole of this jurisdiction was subsequently transferred to the Crown Court.

Before leaving the pre-1972 system, three other courts should also be mentioned. The Central Criminal Court—popularly known as the 'Old Bailey'—was the assize court with jurisdiction over indictable offences committed in Greater London and on the high seas. In addition, the Criminal Justice Administration Act 1956 established Crown Courts in Liverpool and Manchester. These courts exercised a criminal jurisdiction equivalent to that of the assizes and quarter sessions in their respective areas.

This plethora of courts with workloads determined largely by historical factors led to the establishment of a Royal Commission chaired by Lord Beeching. The Commission's recommendations[216] formed the basis for the system introduced by the Courts Act 1971. The Act abolished all courts of assize and quarter sessions, including the Crown Courts of Liverpool and Manchester and the Central Criminal Court

---

[214] This is the effect of the County Courts Jurisdiction Order 1981, SI 1981/1123.
[215] See p 315.
[216] See *Report of the Royal Commission on Assizes and Quarter Sessions*, Cmnd 4153 (HMSO, 1969).

in London.[217] It replaced them with a single court, to be known as the Crown Court, which is one of the Senior Courts of England and Wales[218] and a superior court of record.[219] Its constitution and jurisdiction are now governed by the Supreme Court Act 1981.

Constitution

As already indicated, the essential feature of the Crown Court is that it has a national jurisdiction. There are not various Crown Courts throughout the country; there is only one Crown Court, sittings of which may be held anywhere, at any time.[220] There are currently seventy-eight permanent Crown Court centres in England and Wales,[221] and for administrative purposes they are grouped into six circuits. Each centre falls into one of three categories:

(1) 'first-tier' centres—these deal with the full range of Crown Court business and also provide a venue for High Court judges to handle some of their civil work;

(2) 'second-tier' centres—these deal with the full range of the Crown Court's criminal work; and

(3) 'third-tier' centres—High Court judges do not usually visit third-tier centres, which means that the workload of these venues is generally confined to less serious criminal cases.

The Supreme Court Act 1981 provides that the Crown Court's jurisdiction may be exercised by High Court judges, circuit judges, recorders, and district judges from magistrates' courts.[222] Deputy circuit judges may also be appointed.[223] The most serious or difficult cases are usually reserved for High Court judges, who, in practice, are almost invariably drawn from the Queen's Bench Division.[224] In addition to the regular judges of the Court, any judge of the Court of Appeal and any former Court of Appeal or puisne judge may also be asked to sit, although they cannot be compelled to do so.[225] Crown Court judges normally sit alone, but when hearing appeals from

---

[217] The latter has been retained in name, however, as s 8(3) of the Supreme Court Act 1981 provides for the Crown Court to be known as the Central Criminal Court when sitting in London. The same section preserves the right of the Lord Mayor and Aldermen of the City to sit as judges with any High Court judge, circuit judge, recorder or district judge (magistrates' courts). The reasons for this are unclear, but a seat in the Old Bailey is still traditionally left vacant for the Lord Mayor.

[218] See p 6.

[219] Supreme Court Act 1981, ss 1 and 45(1). When exercising its appellate jurisdiction the Crown Court is subject to the High Court's supervisory jurisdiction as if it were an inferior court: s 29(3) (see p 256). It is not, however, subject to this jurisdiction in matters relating to trial on indictment.

[220] Ibid, s 78.

[221] There are also several satellite centres, bringing the current number of locations to ninety-two: *Judicial Statistics 2005*, at p 80.

[222] Section 8.   [223] Courts Act 1971, s 24.

[224] As to the distribution of business, see pp 262 and 631.   [225] Supreme Court Act 1981, s 9.

magistrates' courts they must sit with between two and four justices of the peace.[226] A judge may also sit with justices of the peace when hearing a case on indictment, unless the case has been listed for a plea of not guilty.[227] Where justices do sit, they must play a full part in all decisions, and in the event of disagreement the decision of the majority prevails.[228]

Jurisdiction and procedure

The Crown Court has exclusive jurisdiction over all trials on indictment, including proceedings on indictment for offences within the jurisdiction of the Admiralty in England.[229] Before the Criminal Justice Act 2003 all trials on indictment were tried by a judge sitting with a jury, but it is now possible for cases in which there is a real risk of jury tampering to be tried by a judge sitting alone. A similar power has been introduced in relation to complex fraud cases, although this has yet to be implemented.[230] The jurisdiction formerly exercised by the quarter sessions is also vested in the Crown Court.[231] This includes hearing appeals against summary conviction from the magistrates' courts,[232] sentencing those committed for sentence following summary conviction,[233] and exercising a limited civil jurisdiction in relation to licensing appeals.

The Lord Chief Justice is empowered by section 75 of the Supreme Court Act to give directions for the distribution of Crown Court business. The current directions[234] establish three different classes of offence. Class 1 offences are the most serious, and must be tried by a High Court judge or specially authorized circuit judge. Class 2 offences must also be tried by a High Court judge unless a particular case is released by or on the authority of a presiding judge,[235] while all other offences fall into Class 3 and may be listed for trial by a High Court judge, circuit judge, or recorder.

Magistrates' courts

A magistrates' court is defined by section 148 of the Magistrates' Courts Act 1980 as 'any justice or justices of the peace[236] acting under any enactment or by virtue of his or their commission or under the common law'. Magistrates currently sit in over

---

[226] Ibid, ss 8 and 74(1).

[227] Ibid, s 75; *Practice Direction (Crown Court: Business)* [2001] 4 All ER 635 at 638, [2001] 1 WLR 1996 at 2000.

[228] If the court is evenly split, the regular judge has the casting vote: s 73(3).

[229] Supreme Court Act 1981, s 46.

[230] Criminal Justice Act 2003, ss 43–49: see pp 360 and 650. See also the discussion of the use of sample counts, at p 652.

[231] Courts Act 1971, s 8, Sch 1; although note that certain administrative functions were transferred to local authorities.

[232] See p 688.   [233] See p 687.

[234] *Consolidated Criminal Practice Direction*, Pt III, as amended: effective in this respect since 6 June 2005. For further details of the classification of offences, see p 606.

[235] A presiding judge is a High Court judge with special responsibility for a particular circuit.

[236] For the historical role of justices of the peace, see p 228.

1,000 courtrooms throughout England and Wales, although proposals have been announced by government to cut some 103 magistrates' courts in the interests of cost-efficiency.[237]

Constitution and organization

Before April 2005, each area of England and Wales had a separate commission of the peace,[238] and each commission area was divided into petty session areas. Magistrates' court committees (MCCs)[239] were responsible for the 'efficient and effective administration' of the courts in each commission area, and magistrates were appointed on a local basis to exercise a local jurisdiction. All of this has now changed as a result of the Courts Act 2003, which is the latest in a long line of reforms to affect the magistrates' courts. Executive responsibility for magistrates' courts was transferred from the Home Office to the Lord Chancellor's Department in 1992, and in 1993 the Magistrates' Court Service Inspectorate was established. This was followed by the Police and Magistrates' Courts Act 1994, which reduced the size of the MCCs and attempted to give them a more clearly defined management role. It also empowered the Lord Chancellor to reduce the number of commission areas in order to improve efficiency. Prior to the 1994 Act, it had been suggested that the local committees should be abolished and replaced with a national executive agency,[240] but this proposal was widely opposed by magistrates and the government did not pursue it.

The Justices of the Peace Act 1997 was primarily a consolidating Act, but the process of reform continued under the Access to Justice Act 1999. A unified Greater London Magistrates' Courts Authority replaced the twenty-two MCCs in London, and the Lord Chancellor was given greater powers to alter commission areas. In the explanatory notes accompanying the Act, the government set out the need to develop a 'coherent geographical structure' for the criminal justice system, by moving towards common boundaries for the various agencies involved.[241] This meant that not only should MCCs be able to reorganize the petty session areas within their commission boundaries, but also that there should be greater alignment between the commission boundaries, police force areas, and Crown Prosecution areas.

Reform under the Courts Act 2003

In his review of criminal justice,[242] Auld LJ made the radical recommendation that the Crown Court and magistrates' courts should be replaced with a single Criminal Court. The government rejected this particular proposal but accepted that the

---

[237] See (2020) 154 Sol Jo 3.

[238] In December 2003 there were forty-seven such areas in England and a further five in Wales: Justices of the Peace (Commission Areas) (Amendment) Order 2001, SI 2001/696, Schedule.

[239] Consisting of justices of the peace and other members co-opted by the committee or appointed by the Lord Chancellor: Justices of the Peace Act 1997, s 28.

[240] See the Home Office study, *Magistrates' Courts: Report of a Scrutiny* (HMSO, 1989).

[241] At paras 248–250.   [242] *Review of the Criminal Courts of England and Wales* (HMSO, 2001).

criminal courts should be more closely aligned. This provided the impetus for the White Paper *Justice for All*, and for the subsequent Courts Act 2003. The Act repeals the Justices of the Peace Act 1997, although many of its provisions are re-enacted.

The Courts Act establishes a single commission of the peace for England and Wales,[243] and gives magistrates a national jurisdiction. It also provides for magistrates to be assigned to local justice areas,[244] which means in practice that they will continue to sit locally. The MCCs and the Greater London Magistrates' Courts Authority have been abolished,[245] and the Lord Chancellor is now under a general duty to ensure that there is an efficient and effective system to support the Supreme Court, Court of Protection, county courts, and magistrates' courts.[246] Magistrates' courts, like most other major courts, are now administered by Her Majesty's Courts Service, which is an executive agency of the Ministry of Justice.[247] An element of local accountability has been retained through the creation of Local Courts Boards, which are established and appointed by the Lord Chancellor.[248] The membership of these Boards must include at least one judge, at least two local representatives, at least two other persons with 'appropriate knowledge or experience', and two or more justices of the peace.[249] They are concerned not only with magistrates' courts but also with the Crown Court and county courts in their areas,[250] and they are responsible for scrutinizing the management of the courts and making recommendations where appropriate.

Justices of the peace

The vast majority of justices of the peace are lay magistrates, who are currently appointed by the Lord Chancellor on the advice of local advisory committees.[251] They are unqualified and unpaid, but they are required to attend training courses[252] and may claim allowances for travel, subsistence, and loss of earnings.[253] They are expected to be available for at least twenty-six half-days each year, and normally sit in pairs or groups of three.[254] A single lay justice has a limited jurisdiction and cannot order a person to pay more than one pound or impose imprisonment for more than fourteen days.[255] However, a single justice can hear proceedings to determine the allocation of cases that are triable either way, and can also transfer cases to the Crown Court for trial on indictment.[256] Under amendments made by the Criminal

---

[243] Section 7.   [244] Sections 8 and 10(2); Local Justice Areas Order 2005, SI 2005/554, as amended.
[245] 2003 Act, s 6.   [246] Ibid, s 1.
[247] This was launched on 1 April 2005: see p 230.   [248] 2003 Act, s 4; Sch 1.
[249] Ibid, Sch 1.   [250] Ibid, s 5.
[251] The Constitutional Reform Act 2005 makes provision for justices of the peace to be selected by the Judicial Appointments Commission, but at the time of writing a timetable for transferring responsibility has not been agreed.
[252] Courts Act 2003, s 19 (replacing the Justices of the Peace Act 1997, s 64).
[253] Ibid, s 15 (replacing s 10 of the 1997 Act).   [254] Magistrates' Courts Act 1980, s 121(1).
[255] Ibid, s 121(5).   [256] Ibid, ss 17–18 (as amended).

Justice Act 2003,[257] a single justice may also accept a guilty plea in a case that is to be dealt with summarily.

Appointments to the lay magistracy are intended to reflect all sections of the community, but there is persistent criticism that the majority of justices tend to be white, middle class, conservative, and old.[258] In fact, research carried out by Morgan and Russell in 2000[259] found that around 4 per cent of lay magistrates were black or Asian, with a further 1 per cent coming from other ethnic minority backgrounds. Although this indicated that at a national level the magistracy was 'approaching ethnic representativeness',[260] in cities with large ethnic minority populations the bench was still disproportionately white. The same study found that around 94 per cent of lay justices were aged between 40 and 70, and that they were 'disproportionately middle class, and almost certainly financially well-off, compared to the population at large'.[261] For example, 69 per cent of lay magistrates in the survey described their current or former occupation as 'professional or managerial', while only 3 per cent described themselves as skilled manual workers. Given that lay magistrates are unpaid, it should come as no surprise that those who are retired or in well-paid employment are more likely to volunteer their services, and Morgan and Russell concluded that achieving greater diversity would inevitably be costly:[262]

> A more socially representative magistracy could almost certainly be recruited, but:
>
> - the members would be unlikely to be so willing or able to sit as often as many lay magistrates do today
> - we believe that more socially representative recruits would be more likely to claim loss of earnings and expenses.
>
> Which is to say that a more socially representative lay magistracy would be a more expensive one.

Upon reaching the age of 70, lay magistrates join the supplemental list and can no longer serve as justices of the peace.[263]

In 2010 there were 29,270 lay justices in England and Wales, but the magistracy is also served by 139 district judges (magistrates' courts) and around 169 deputy district judges (magistrates' courts).[264] These judges used to be called stipendiary magistrates, but they were renamed by section 78 of the Access to Justice Act 1999. The

---

[257] Ibid, ss 18 and 20(7) (as amended).

[258] See Darbyshire, 'For the New Lord Chancellor: Some Causes for Concern about Magistrates' [1997] Crim LR 861, at 862–6.

[259] Morgan and Russell, *The Judiciary in the Magistrates' Courts* (HMSO, 2000), ch 2. This study was jointly commissioned by the Home Office and the Lord Chancellor's Department.

[260] Ibid, at p 14. Figures published by the Ministry of Justice indicate that almost 7 per cent of lay magistrates were from minority ethnic backgrounds as of 31 March 2006: *Statistics on Race and the Criminal Justice System—2006* (HMSO, 2007), at p 110.

[261] Morgan and Russell, *op cit*, at p 16.   [262] Ibid, at p 108.

[263] Courts Act 2003, ss 12 and 13. A younger magistrate may have his name added to this list at his own request or on the grounds of incapacity.

[264] See **www.judiciary.gov.uk/publications-and-reports/statistics/magistrates-statistics**

same provision also merged the metropolitan and provincial benches.[265] Unlike lay magistrates, district judges (magistrates' courts) are legally qualified and serve on a full-time, professional basis. They have all of the powers of two lay justices and therefore sit alone.[266]

KEY ISSUE

The participation in the criminal justice trial process of a lay element has been an enduring characteristic since the earliest times.[267] As noted above the office of justice of the peace is ancient in origin, and provides that lay, non-legal element, mirrored in the Crown Court by the jury. In recent years we have seen the growth in numbers of district judges (qualified lawyers) sitting in magistrates' courts. The question remains: how important is this lay element in the magistrates' court? The advantages a district judge brings to the process are professional knowledge and training, and the ability quickly to assimilate relevant evidence and deal with proceedings expeditiously and fairly, perhaps at the risk of getting 'case-hardened' by sitting week in, week out. Yet the composition of the lay magistracy does not command confidence that it is truly representative of the public as a whole.

? Questions

1. Do you think that more district judges sitting in place of lay magistrates would be a good idea?
2. What qualities do you think a lay magistrate should bring to the magistrates' court?

Justices' clerks and justices' chief executives

Justices' clerks are responsible for advising magistrates on matters of law. They are appointed by the Lord Chancellor and must have either: (a) a five-year magistrates' court qualification;[268] (b) five years' experience as an assistant to a justices' clerk and a qualification as a solicitor or barrister; or (c) previous experience as a justices' clerk.[269] The functions of a justices' clerk include:[270]

> [G]iving advice to any or all of the justices of the peace to whom he is clerk about matters of law (including procedure and practice) on questions arising in connection with the discharge of their functions, including questions arising when the clerk is not personally attending on them.

Most justices' clerks cover more than one court and it is impossible for them to personally advise every courtroom for which they are responsible. As a result, many of

---

[265] The functions and terms of appointment of District Judges (Magistrates' Courts) are set out in the Courts Act 2003, ss 22–26 (replacing ss 10A–10E of the 1997 Act).

[266] Ibid, s 26 (replacing s 10D of the 1997 Act).   [267] See p 264.

[268] Within the meaning of the Courts and Legal Services Act 1990, s 71.

[269] Courts Act 2003, s 27.

[270] Ibid, s 28(4). This largely re-enacts s 45 of the Justices of the Peace Act 1997.

their functions are delegated to justices' clerks' assistants or 'court clerks', not all of whom are professionally qualified. Concerns have been raised in the past[271] about the number of lay magistrates being advised by unqualified clerks, and more stringent professional requirements have now been introduced. Since January 1999, all newly appointed court clerks must be qualified solicitors or barristers, and those in post before this date have until 2010 to reach the same standard.[272]

The primary function of a clerk is to provide legal advice, and he has a duty to offer such advice whenever he considers it appropriate, regardless of whether it has been specifically requested.[273] However, care must be taken to ensure that he does not appear to interfere with the magisterial function. This means that a clerk should not play any part in helping magistrates to make findings of fact, and that any legal advice given should normally be stated in open court.[274] In addition to his advisory functions, a justices' clerk may also perform many of the pre-trial functions otherwise carried out by a single judge. These include setting the date and time of a trial, giving directions for the conduct of the trial, and making an order for public funding to assist defendants in criminal cases.[275]

In the past justices' clerks were responsible for the general administration of magistrates' courts, in addition to their role as legal advisers. Concerns about this mixing of administrative and legal functions were partly addressed by the Police and Magistrates' Courts Act 1994, which created the new position of justices' chief executive. Many of the clerks' administrative functions were transferred to the holders of this new office,[276] leaving the clerks free to concentrate on their advisory and judicial roles. Each MCC was required to appoint its own chief executive, and his role was to ensure the efficient and effective administration of magistrates' courts in the area. The chief executive was responsible for allocating work between clerks, but the Act expressly provided that clerks should not be subject to his direction when performing their legal functions.[277] The emphasis on separating administrative and legal functions has been continued by the Courts Act 2003, and like its predecessors the Act includes an express guarantee of the clerks' independence.[278] However, now that Her Majesty's Courts Service has taken over the management of magistrates' courts,[279] the office of justices' chief executive has been abolished.[280]

---

[271] See, e.g., Darbyshire, 'For the New Lord Chancellor: Some Causes for Concern about Magistrates' [1997] Crim LR 861 at 872.

[272] Section 27(1) of the Courts Act 2003 makes it possible for a clerk without professional qualifications to remain in post for the time being. However, s 27(6) confers a power to remove this exception at a future date. See also: Assistants to Justices' Clerks Regulations 2006, SI 2006/3405, as amended.

[273] Courts Act 2003, s 28(5); replacing s 45 of the 1997 Act.

[274] *Practice Direction (QBD: Justices: Clerk to Court)* [2000] 4 All ER 895, [2000] 1 WLR 1886.

[275] Crime and Disorder Act 1998, s 49; Justices' Clerks Rules 2005, SI 2005/545, Schedule.

[276] Many of those that remained were transferred by the Access to Justice Act 1999: s 90; Sch 13.

[277] Section 78. Proposals to transfer justices' clerks to a system of fixed-term contracts and performance related pay only added to concerns about judicial independence, and were dropped from the 1994 Bill at an early stage.

[278] Courts Act 2003, s 29.

[279] See p 264.   [280] 2003 Act, s 6.

Jurisdiction

It is common to suppose that the jurisdiction of magistrates' courts is entirely criminal, but they also have a wide and varied civil jurisdiction. In both civil and criminal cases, however, this jurisdiction is limited to relatively minor matters when compared with the cases heard by the High Court, county courts, and Crown Court. Before examining the jurisdiction of the magistrates' courts more closely, it should be noted that when justices of the peace exercise such important functions as the granting of bail and the issuing of summonses and warrants, they are not strictly acting as 'magistrates' courts'.

Criminal jurisdiction

The criminal jurisdiction of magistrates' courts principally concerns summary offences, which are offences triable without a jury. All summary offences are created by statute, and all are of a fairly minor character. Indeed, most summary convictions are for road traffic offences, and so numerous are the convictions for speeding and unauthorized parking that offenders are able to plead guilty by post.[281] Almost 2 million persons each year are found guilty of summary offences in England and Wales.

The maximum penalty that can be imposed for a summary offence at present is six months' imprisonment and a fine limited in amount.[282] However, the Criminal Justice Act 2003 makes provision for the Secretary of State to set a maximum penalty of up to fifty-one weeks' imprisonment for a range of summary offences,[283] and for the sentencing powers of magistrates to be increased accordingly.[284] The Act also provides for a new 'custody plus' sentence, which would, if implemented, replace all short prison sentences (except for intermittent custody) with a short period of imprisonment followed by a period of supervision in the community.[285]

In addition to their jurisdiction over summary offences, magistrates' courts also have jurisdiction over offences 'triable either way',[286] although this is subject to a defendant's right to insist on trial by jury. Where a defendant is convicted of an either-way offence, a magistrates' court may impose penalties similar to those that may be imposed following conviction for a summary offence.

Youth courts and youth justice

Youth courts are magistrates' courts exercising jurisdiction over offences committed by children and young persons.[287] Until 1991 they were known as juvenile courts.[288] A youth court consists of up to three justices selected from a specially trained youth

---

[281] Magistrates' Courts Act 1980, s 12.   [282] See further, p 686.   [283] Section 281(2).

[284] Section 154. Neither provision had been brought into force at the time of writing.

[285] Section 181. Again, this is not yet in force.

[286] See Magistrates' Courts Act 1980, s 17; Sch 1. For details of the procedure for determining the mode of trial of such offences, see p 611.

[287] For these purposes a 'child' is a person aged under 14 years, and a 'young person' is someone aged 14–17: Children and Young Persons Act 1933, s 107.

[288] Criminal Justice Act 1991, s 70.

panel, and must normally include at least one man and one woman.[289] The chair of the court remains constant, although other members serve by rotation. A youth court may also consist of a district judge (magistrates' courts), sitting alone.[290] The proceedings in the youth court are not in public.

Civil jurisdiction

This aspect of the magistrates' courts' jurisdiction is extremely varied. It includes the recovery of certain civil debts such as income tax, National Insurance contributions, Council Tax, and electricity, gas, and water charges. It also includes the licensing of pubs, clubs, and gambling establishments. However, the most important aspect of the magistrates' courts' civil workload is their jurisdiction over family law matters. This is exercised principally under the Family Law Act 1996 and Children Act 1989, in what are known as 'family proceedings courts'.

Family proceedings courts

These courts were created by section 80 of the Domestic Proceedings and Magistrates' Courts Act 1978, and were then known as domestic courts. They were renamed 'family proceedings courts' by the Children Act 1989.[291] They normally consist of two or three justices drawn from a specially trained panel, and as far as practicable they should include a man and a woman.[292] Nominated district judges (magistrates' courts) may sit alongside one or two lay justices, although it is possible for a judge to deal with family proceedings matters when sitting alone.[293] The only persons who may be present during proceedings are officers of the court, the parties, their legal representatives, witnesses, newspaper representatives, and any other persons permitted by the court.[294]

Family proceedings courts have jurisdiction to deal with maintenance applications and to make various orders in respect of children, domestic violence, and the occupation of the family home. They also have a public law jurisdiction to deal with care proceedings brought by local authorities under the Children Act 1989. In fact, their jurisdiction under the Children Act is largely concurrent with that of county courts and the Family Division of the High Court, except that public law actions can only be commenced in a family proceedings court.[295] In view of their overlapping jurisdictions, the Courts Act 2003 established a new Family Procedure Rule Committee with

[289] Children and Young Persons Act 1933, s 45 (as amended); Youth Courts (Constitution of Committees and Right to Preside) Rules 2007, SI 2007/1611, r 10. Exceptionally, a case may be heard by an all-male/all-female panel if, due to unforeseen circumstances, no members of the opposite gender are available and it would not be in the interests of justice to order an adjournment.

[290] 1933 Act, s 45 (as amended); Courts Act 2003, s 66; SI 2007/1611, r 10.   [291] Section 92.

[292] Magistrates' Courts Act 1980, ss 66 and 67 (as amended). See also, Family Proceedings Courts (Constitution of Committees and Right to Preside) Rules 2007, SI 2007/1610.

[293] Magistrates' Courts Act 1980, ss 66 and 67 (as amended).   [294] Ibid, s 69(2).

[295] Children (Allocation of Proceedings) Order 1991, SI 1991/1677, article 3(1). Such cases may be transferred to the county court or to the Family Division if they are sufficiently complex or serious, or where there would otherwise be an unacceptable delay.

the power to make procedural rules governing all three courts.[296] The government is now moving towards the creation of family courts centres, which will bring together the administrative arrangements for county courts and family proceedings courts in particular areas. Where possible, both types of court will be located in the same building.[297] Ultimately, the long-term objective is to create unified family courts.[298]

The Court of Protection

Until recently, applications concerning the property and affairs of persons of unsound mind were dealt with within the Chancery Division, by judges sitting as the Court of Protection. Following implementation of the Mental Capacity Act 2005, the Court of Protection has been given enhanced powers, and it is now a superior court of record in its own right.[299] The President of the Family Division has been appointed as President of the new court, and it is also served by a Vice-President, a Senior Judge, and nominated High Court, circuit and district judges.[300]

Coroners' courts

The office of coroner

This ancient office dates from the twelfth century, when it principally concerned the custody of revenue accruing to the King from fines and forfeiture. In addition, the coroner occasionally exercised the jurisdiction of the sheriff and enquired into treasure trove and unexplained deaths. Some of these functions have since been removed, and the primary role of the modern coroner is to hold inquests into unexplained deaths. The appointment and jurisdiction of coroners is now governed by the Coroners and Justice Act 2009, following a major, and sometimes controversial review of coroners' powers and functions. They may be barristers, solicitors, or registered medical practitioners of not less than five years' standing, and they may be removed from office for misbehaviour or inability to discharge their duties.[301]

Jurisdiction

The role of the coroner is to investigate unexplained deaths and, where necessary, to hold an inquest. To hold an inquest the coroner may, and in some cases must, summon a jury of between seven and eleven members. Witnesses attend and give evidence and

---

[296] Sections 75–81.

[297] DCA, *Response to the Constitutional Affairs Select Committee Report—Family Justice: The Operation of the Family Courts Revisited*, Cm 6971 (HMSO, 2006) at pp 5–6.

[298] DCA, *A Single Civil Court? Responses to the Consultation* (HMSO, 2005) CP(R) 06/05, at p 42.

[299] 2005 Act, s 45—effective from 1 October 2007.   [300] Ibid, s 46.   [301] Ibid, s 3.

the coroner has the power to compel their attendance if necessary. The procedure is inquisitorial, however, and, although interested persons may be represented and may ask questions, it is the coroner who conducts the proceedings and no speeches are made to the jury. The jury's verdict need not be unanimous provided that there are not more than two dissentients.

There is no appeal from an inquest, but the proceedings are subject to judicial review and may be challenged if, for example, there is evidence of bias.[302]

The inquests into the deaths of Diana, Princess of Wales, and Dodi Al Fayed

Issues of bias were among those considered in the case of *R (on the application of Paul)* v *Deputy Coroner of the Queen's Household and Assistant District Coroner for Surrey*.[303] The case concerned the inquests into the deaths of Diana, Princess of Wales, and Dodi Al Fayed. The inquest into the death of the Princess was due to be heard by the coroner of the Queen's household,[304] with the inquiry into Mr Al Fayed's death being transferred to the coroner for Surrey. The inquests were initially adjourned pending Lord Stevens' inquiry into allegations that there had been a conspiracy to murder,[305] but they were resumed when the inquiry concluded that there was no evidence of such a conspiracy. Given the high-profile nature of the case and the heavy workload involved, Baroness Butler-Sloss was simultaneously appointed as Deputy Coroner of the Queen's Household and Assistant Deputy Coroner for Surrey, with the intention being that she should conduct both inquests. She decided to transfer the Al Fayed inquest to the jurisdiction of the Coroner for the Queen's household so that the two inquests could be heard together. She also decided that she should sit without a jury. These rulings were challenged in the Administrative Court on the grounds that: (a) she did not have the authority to transfer jurisdiction over the inquests; (b) it would be inappropriate for the Coroner of the Queen's household to hold the inquests because an informed bystander would perceive a real risk of bias; (c) her support for the publication of Lord Stevens' report had further compromised her independence and impartiality; and (d) the possibility that the deaths were caused in circumstances prejudicial to public safety meant that she should have considered sitting with a jury.

Having considered these arguments, the court concluded that the coroner had acted within the scope of her powers when transferring the Al Fayed inquest from one jurisdiction to another.[306] It was also felt that her support for the publication of Lord Stevens' inquiry would not give rise to a real possibility of bias in the eyes of the fair-minded and informed observer.[307] However, the same could not be said for her decision to hear the case as Coroner for the Queen's household: the appearance that the use

---

[302] For an example, see *R* v *Inner West London Coroner, ex parte Dallaglio* [1994] 4 All ER 139.

[303] [2007] EWHC 408 (Admin), [2007] 3 WLR 503, [2007] 2 All ER 509.

[304] See s 29 of the Coroners Act 1988.

[305] Metropolitan Police, *The Operation Paget Inquiry Report into the Allegation of Conspiracy to Murder Diana, Princess of Wales and Emad El-Din Mohamed Abdel Moneim Fayed* (HMSO, 2006).

[306] [2007] EWHC 408 (Admin), at [29], *per* Smith LJ. See also, s 14 of the 1988 Act.

[307] Ibid, at [65].

of this title might give to members of the public had to be considered, and the decision to sit in this capacity was therefore quashed.[308] The decision to conduct the inquests without a jury was also quashed, since the deaths had occurred in circumstances that might be prejudicial to the safety of a section of the public and the summoning of a jury was mandatory in such circumstances.[309] Baroness Butler-Sloss subsequently stood down from the inquests due to her lack of experience in hearing jury cases, and both inquests were heard by Scott Baker LJ—sitting with a jury—following his appointment to the office of Assistant Deputy Coroner for Inner West London.

The Review of Coroners' Services 2003[310]

In July 2001 the government announced that it was setting up a Review of Coroners' Services, to be chaired by Tom Luce. The Review was completed in April 2003 and it highlighted a number of 'critical defects' in the system. The fact that coroners operate 'in isolation from the mainstreams of medicine and justice administration' was identified as a particular weakness,[311] as was the fact that most coroners are part-time.[312] The Review also criticized the absence of a national structure for leadership and administration,[313] along with the lack of 'a clear and reliable process for clarifying the relationship between the inquest and other formal processes for investigating death'.[314] The reforms recommended by the Review would essentially remodel the coroners' service along the lines of the other major courts:[315]

> The death investigation service—the coroner service—should become a service of predominantly full-time legally qualified professionals, appointed, trained and supported to modern judicial and public service standards.

Specific recommendations included:

(1) making the Lord Chancellor responsible for appointing and supporting the coroners' service, in the same way as for other courts;

(2) requiring coroners to be full-time and to be legally (rather than legally *or medically*) qualified;

(3) appointing a 'statutory medical assessor' (a doctor) to assist each coroner;

(4) establishing a standing Rules Committee to formulate procedural rules for the conduct of inquests;

(5) creating a statutory Coronial Council to oversee the work of the service; and

---

[308] Ibid, at [62].   [309] Ibid, at [39] and [46]. See also, s 8(3)(d) of the 1988 Act.
[310] *Death Certification and Investigation in England, Wales and Northern Ireland: The Report of a Fundamental Review,* Cm 5831 (HMSO, 2003).
[311] Ibid, at para 2.4.e.
[312] The Review found that only twenty-three of the 123 coroners in England and Wales were full-time.
[313] Para 2.4.j.   [314] Para 2.4.k.   [315] Para 3.2.

(6) restructuring the service in England and Wales to create a single jurisdiction headed by a Chief Coroner.[316] The jurisdiction would be split into around sixty districts, based on the existing police areas.

Another issue for the Review group was how to respond to the decision in *Jordan* v *UK*.[317] Article 2 of the ECHR implies a duty on the state to investigate deaths occurring as a result of state action or while the deceased was in state custody. In *Jordan*, the European Court of Human Rights found that the holding of an inquest does not discharge this duty, because it is not a forum for determining the identity and culpability of those responsible for causing death. This decision has since been applied in a number of domestic cases under the Human Rights Act 1998.[318] The matter is further complicated by Article 6. For example, although the ability to compel witnesses to attend an inquest is necessitated by Article 2, the right to a fair trial under Article 6 would seem to require that a witness is not obliged to give evidence that could incriminate him.

The Review recommended that the rule preventing a witness from being compelled to answer incriminating questions should be removed. It proposed instead that there should be a limited immunity, preventing incriminating testimony given by a witness from being used against him in criminal or disciplinary (but not civil) proceedings.[319] More generally, it concluded that the scope of an inquest should be limited only by the proviso that its findings 'do not determine civil or criminal liability',[320] and that the inquest should be the 'default process' for handling the vast majority of Article 2 cases.[321]

The government's initial response to the report was to accept that some reform was needed, but to ask for further research and consultation.[322] A Draft Coroners' Bill was eventually published in June 2006,[323] but this Bill ignored many of the Luce recommendations and was widely criticized for not going far enough.[324] The government then made significant revisions before bringing the Bill before Parliament.

---

[316] A second jurisdiction would cover Northern Ireland.

[317] (2003) 37 EHRR 2; see also *Finucane* v *UK* (2003) 37 EHRR 29.

[318] See *R (on the application of Amin)* v *Secretary of State for the Home Department* [2003] UKHL 51, [2004] 1 AC 653, [2003] 4 All ER 1264 (inquest into the death of a prisoner who had been murdered by his cellmate did not satisfy Article 2). See also *R (on the application of Khan)* v *Secretary of State for Health* [2003] EWCA Civ 1129, [2003] 4 All ER 1239 (Article 2 breached because Mr Khan was unable to obtain legal aid enabling him to be legally represented at his daughter's inquest). These decisions prompted an amendment to the exceptional funding provisions in the Access to Justice Act 1999. Further examples are discussed at p 180.

[319] Para 9.38.   [320] Para 21.33.   [321] Para 10.61.

[322] In November 2003 Tom Luce was asked to link his findings to an inquiry into the failure of various institutions to prevent a GP from murdering his patients. See *The Shipman Inquiry's Third Report: Death Certification and the Investigation of Deaths by Coroners*.

[323] *Coroner Reform: The Government's Draft Bill—Improving Death Investigation in England and Wales*, Cm 6849 (HMSO, 2006).

[324] *Reform of the Coroners' System and Death Certification: Government Response to the Constitutional Affairs Select Committee's Report*, Cm 6943 (HMSO, 2006); DCA, *Coroner Reform: The Government's Draft Bill: Responses to Consultation*, (R) 6849/07 (HMSO, 2007).

The Coroners and Justice Act 2009

The duty of a coroner is to investigate the cause of death in cases in which the body of a deceased is within the coroners' area.[325] In *R v West Yorkshire Coroner, ex parte Smith*,[326] the Court of Appeal held that the phrase 'lying within his jurisdiction' (which was the form of words used prior to the passing of the Coroners Act 1988) applied to a body brought into the district from abroad. This is still the position, and in October 2007 inquests into the deaths of Diana, Princess of Wales, and Dodi Al Fayed, both of whom died in Paris, were opened at the Royal Courts of Justice, concluding some six months later.

There is an obligation to hold an inquest where the coroner has reasonable cause to suspect that a person has died a violent or unnatural death, or has died suddenly from an unknown cause. Deaths in prison or police custody, or state detention and deaths occurring as a result of injury caused by a police officer in the purported execution of his or her duty, also fall within the coroner's jurisdiction.

The presumption is that an inquest is conducted by a coroner without a jury. However, there must be a jury in the circumstances identified by section 7 of the 2009 Act. An inquest is required if the deceased died whilst in custody or otherwise in state detention, where the death is a violent or unnatural death, or where the cause of death is unlawful. So, too, where the death results from an act or omission of a police officer whilst acting in the execution of his duty. The coroner also has a discretion to hold an inquest with a jury where it considered that there is sufficient reason to do so.

Prior to the Criminal Law Act 1977, the jury might return a verdict of murder, manslaughter, or infanticide by a named person, and the coroner could then commit that person for trial. This was abolished and a coroner's inquisition cannot now charge a person with any offence. Although coroners have the power to compel the attendance of witnesses,[327] a witness cannot be obliged to answer questions 'tending to incriminate himself'.[328] Where criminal proceedings are in hand, any inquest relating to the same issues should be adjourned. The coroner has a discretion to resume the inquest on conclusion of the criminal proceedings but, if he does so, any findings as to the cause of death must not be inconsistent with the outcome of the criminal case.[329] A coroner must also adjourn an inquest if he is informed that the circumstances surrounding a death are to be the subject of a public inquiry, unless there is an 'exceptional reason' for not doing so.[330]

KEY ISSUE

The government originally wanted to include a power to permit inquests in private. After considerable parliamentary opposition the current provision was adopted—that in limited circumstances the Lord Chancellor can request the relevant senior coroner to suspend an

---

[325] 1988 Act, s 8.   [326] [1983] QB 335, [1982] 3 All ER 1098.

[327] Coroners and Justice Act 2009. Sch 5.   [328] On this see 2009 Act, s 35 and Sch 8.

[329] Ibid, s 16.   [330] Ibid, s 17A, as inserted by the Access to Justice Act 1999.

investigation on the appointment of a senior judge to chair an inquiry established under Inquiries Act 2005, where it is considered that the cause of death is likely to be adequately investigated by holding an inquiry. The role that inquests play can provide an important element of judging the wisdom or effectiveness of governmental action. The inquests into the death of Diana, Princess of Wales, and into the many soldiers killed in Iraq or Afghanistan, have provide important opportunity for the scrutiny of government action, or lack of it. By contrast the difficulties surrounding the Hutton Inquiry dealing with the cause of death of a government scientist, Dr David Kelly, were very clear when, in 2010, a group of pathologists again raised doubts about the cause of death. This had been investigated by the Hutton Inquiry, but the lack of a formal inquest (replaced by the Inquiry) served only to fuel concerns that the evidence relating to cause of death had not properly been investigated.

❓ Questions

1. What is the purpose of an inquest?
2. Have the changes made to the law and procedure by the 2009 Act made the coroner's role better and fairer?
3. Were the government right in wanting the power for a coroner to conduct an inquest in private?
4. Why do you think this was opposed and finally abandoned?

The Judicial Committee of the Privy Council

Constitution

Prior to the Judicial Committee Act 1833, the jurisdiction of the Privy Council was exercised principally by laymen. The 1833 Act[331] created the Judicial Committee, which, at the time of writing, consists of the Lord President of the Council, the Lord Chancellor, ex-Lord Presidents, the Justices of the Supreme Court, and certain other members who have held high judicial office. From time to time membership has also been extended to persons who have held high judicial office in Commonwealth countries, although such persons may not sit when the Committee is determining 'devolution issues' under the Scotland Act 1998, the Government of Wales Act 1998, and the Northern Ireland Act 1998.

The Justices of the Supreme Court are the members of the Committee who usually sit. Decisions of the Privy Council therefore enjoy great authority, although they are not strictly binding on English courts.[332]

---

[331] As amended by the Judicial Committee Act 1844, the Appellate Jurisdiction Acts 1876–1947 and other Acts. Further amendments will be made by Sch 16 of the Constitutional Reform Act 2005.

[332] See p 79. The Privy Council's decisions on devolution issues are, of course, binding in respect of Wales, Scotland and Northern Ireland.

Appeals are heard at the bar of the Privy Council before not fewer than three—and usually five—members of the Committee.[333] The procedure is similar to that currently followed by the Supreme Court.

Jurisdiction

Although all English courts derive their jurisdiction directly or indirectly from the sovereign, the Judicial Committee of the Privy Council is slightly different, in that its jurisdiction is that of the sovereign in Council. Consequently the Privy Council does not pass judgment; it merely tenders advice to the sovereign, which is then implemented by Order in Council. Only one opinion is usually read and until recently dissents were not even recorded.[334] However, it is now provided by Order in Council that dissenting opinions may be delivered in open court.[335]

The main aspects of the Privy Council's jurisdiction are as follows:[336]

(a) *Appeals from courts outside the United Kingdom*   Since the sovereign is the fountain of justice for all of her dominions, the Privy Council has jurisdiction to hear appeals from the Isle of Man, the Channel Islands, independent Commonwealth countries, and British Colonies and Protectorates. However, since the Statute of Westminster 1931, many Commonwealth states have legislated to exclude appeal to the Privy Council.[337] Leave to appeal in criminal matters is only given in exceptional cases, and mere misdirection will not suffice; there must be some clear departure from the 'requirements of justice', or something that 'deprives the accused of the substance of fair trial and the protection of the law.'[338]

(b) *Admiralty jurisdiction*   Prior to 1875, appeal lay from the High Court of Admiralty to the Privy Council. Since the Judicature Acts most appeals from the High Court now lie to the Court of Appeal, but the Privy Council has retained its jurisdiction to hear appeals from the High Court when sitting as a 'prize court'.[339] A prize court is a court convened to determine issues concerning

---

[333] A greater number has been known: see, e.g., *Pratt v A-G for Jamaica* [1994] 2 AC 1, [1993] 4 All ER 769, where a committee of seven judges declared gross delays in carrying out death sentences in Jamaica to amount to inhuman and degrading treatment.

[334] Compare the Criminal Division of the Court of Appeal, which also delivers only one judgment but for different reasons.

[335] Judicial Committee (General Appellate Jurisdiction) Rules Order 1982, SI 1982/1676, Sch 2, para 16. For a particularly vigorous dissent, see *Abbot v R* [1977] AC 755, [1976] 3 All ER 140.

[336] Until recently the Privy Council had jurisdiction to hear appeals from tribunals governing healthcare professionals, but this jurisdiction has been transferred to the High Court, Queen's Bench Division.

[337] Territories that have ended or ceased to recognize the Privy Council's jurisdiction include: Aden; Australia; Botswana; Burma; Canada; Cyprus; Ghana; Guyana; Hong Kong; India; Kenya; Malaysia; Malta; New Zealand; Nigeria; Pakistan; Sierra Leone; Singapore; Sri Lanka; Tanzania; and Uganda.

[338] *Ibrahim v R* [1914] AC 599 at 614–5, *per* Lord Sumner: see also *Prasad v R* [1981] 1 All ER 319, [1981] 1 WLR 469.

[339] Supreme Court Act 1981, s 16(2). By s 20, the High Court's jurisdiction to sit as a prize court is exercised by the Admiralty Court (part of the Queen's Bench Division); see p 255.

the ownership of ships and cargo, and the validity of their capture by enemy warships.

(c) *Appeals from ecclesiastical courts* The jurisdiction of the ecclesiastical courts was drastically curtailed in 1857,[340] and is now confined to matters affecting the clergy and church buildings. Appeals from the highest ecclesiastical courts lie to the Privy Council.[341] Although archbishops and bishops are not members of the Privy Council, an archbishop (or the Bishop of London) and four other bishops are summoned to sit in an advisory capacity whenever the Council is hearing ecclesiastical appeals.

(d) *Special references* In addition to its appellate jurisdiction, the Privy Council is sometimes required to advise on matters of law at the request of the sovereign.[342] In the past it has advised on such diverse matters as the powers of colonial judges,[343] legislation in Jersey,[344] and the eligibility of a person to sit and vote in the House of Commons.[345]

Courts of particular jurisdiction[346]

Certain courts do not fit within the general hierarchy because they are concerned with matters outside the scope of the ordinary civil and criminal law. The authority of these specialist courts is usually limited to certain members of society who have impliedly agreed to submit to their jurisdiction, although in some instances it extends to all members of the community.

Courts martial[347]

Courts martial exercise jurisdiction over members of the armed forces, and over certain other non-service individuals in the circumstances set out in the Armed Forces Act 2006.[348] They cannot generally exercise jurisdiction over civilians,[349] except where

[340] Court of Probate Act 1857; Matrimonial Causes Act 1857.
[341] Ecclesiastical Jurisdiction Measure 1963, s 1(3)(d); s 8.   [342] Judicial Committee Act 1833, s 4.
[343] *Re Wells* (1840) 3 Moo PCC 216.   [344] *Re Jersey States* (1853) 9 Moo PCC 185.
[345] *Re Macmanaway* [1951] AC 161.
[346] Prior to 1977 there were many courts of local jurisdiction, but the judicial functions of most of them were abolished by the Courts Act 1971, the Local Government Act 1972 and the Administration of Justice Act 1977. The few that remain are listed in the Law Commission report, *Jurisdiction of Certain Ancient Courts* (Law Com No 72).
[347] For background about some of the defects of the law prior to the Armed Forces Act 2006, see: Lyon, 'After *Findlay*: A Consideration of Some Aspects of the Military Justice System' [1998] Crim LR 109; Lyon, 'Two Swords and Two Standards' [2005] Crim LR 850.
[348] See 2006 Act, Sch 15.
[349] The case of *Martin v UK* (2007) 44 EHRR 31 concerned a 17-year-old civilian who was convicted of the murder of another civilian by a court martial in Germany. The courts martial system was used because the defendant was the son of an army corporal, but the procedure was found to be contrary to the right to a fair trial under Article 6, ECHR.

Her Majesty's forces are in armed occupation of hostile territory and a state of martial law has been declared. In addition, civilians who are employed by the forces and are on active service outside the United Kingdom may be tried in what are now known as 'service civilian courts'.[350]

Prior to the coming into force in 2009 of the Armed Forces Act 2006, the disciplinary systems of the three main armed services operated within separate statutory frameworks,[351] although there were many similarities between them. However, the 2006 Act repealed the pre-existing separate pieces of legislation and replaced them with a single, harmonized framework covering all members of the armed forces.

A basic distinction can be drawn between service offences that can be dealt with by summary trial. The accused may be arrested by a superior officer for any offence against military law. If the offence is merely a 'summary' one,[352] he will be tried by his commanding officer, but in other cases he has a choice as to whether to be tried summarily or by court martial[353]. Serious offences are always tried at courts martial, except that murder, manslaughter, treason, and rape committed within the United Kingdom must be tried in the ordinary criminal courts. In all other cases, the jurisdiction of civilian and military courts is concurrent. However, a person who has already been convicted or acquitted by a civilian court cannot subsequently be tried by court martial, and vice versa.[354]

First-instance decisions

Courts martial were convened on an ad hoc basis, and each one consists of a Permanent President of Courts Martial (PPCM), a Judge Advocate from the Judge Advocate General's department,[355] and at least two other officers. The Judge Advocate's role was (and is) to advise on questions of law and to give rulings and directions on matters of practice and procedure. The President and the other officers were (and are) the sole arbiters of fact. The trial itself takes place in open court and is in many ways similar to a trial in the ordinary criminal courts. It is subject to similar rules of evidence and procedure, and the accused is sent for trial on a charge sheet that may be compared with an indictment. The prosecution case is conducted by an officer, either personally or through a civilian counsel, and the accused may appear in person or be represented by counsel, solicitor, or a defending officer. There is no jury, however, and at the conclusion of the evidence the Judge Advocate summarizes the legal and factual issues before leaving the court to arrive at its decision. A majority decision is acceptable. All guilty verdicts and sentences are subject to confirmation by a reviewing authority.[356]

---

[350] See s 51, Armed Forces Act 2006. The Service Civilian Court has jurisdiction to try service offences committed outside the British Islands by civilians who are subject to service law by virtue of Sch 115 of the 2006 Act.

[351] The Army Act 1955, the Air Force Act 1955 and the Naval Discipline Act 1957, all of which are supplemented and amended by the Armed Forces Act 1996.

[352] Defined by 2006 Act, s 53.   [353] 2006 Act s 129.   [354] 2006: Act ss 64 and 66.

[355] The corresponding department in the Navy is the Judge Advocate of the Fleet's department.

[356] Army Act 1955, s 113; Air Force Act 1955, s 113; Naval Discipline Act 1957, s 70.

This body has the power to reduce sentences, quash convictions, and order retrials, but it cannot increase a sentence or interfere with an acquittal. Any person convicted by court martial has a right to appeal against both conviction and sentence to the Court Martial Appeal Court.

The European dimension

The system of courts martial generated much debate and attention by the European Court of Human Rights. In *Findlay* v *UK*, the court-martial procedure was found to be incompatible with the fair trial provisions in Article 6 ECHR, because there were insufficient safeguards to guarantee impartiality.[357] At the time, several aspects of the courts-martial procedure were under the control of a 'convening officer'. This officer had the task of selecting the President and other members of the court, and this usually meant selecting officers who were inferior in rank and perhaps even under his direct command. The convening officer was also responsible for procuring the attendance of witnesses, deciding which charges should be brought against the accused, and sending an abstract of the evidence to the prosecution. All of this gave the impression of a tribunal lacking in impartiality.

The Armed Forces Act 1996 anticipated the decision in *Findlay* and introduced changes designed to safeguard the independence of the system. It abolished the convening officer role and distributed his former functions between the prosecuting authority and the commanding officer, in liaison with the court-martial administration officer and the reviewing authority. However, despite these reforms, the court-martial procedure was the subject of further Article 6 challenges. In *R* v *McKendry*, the Judge Advocate General advised that the office of PPCM was incompatible with the idea of an independent tribunal. He noted that PPCMs were appointed for a limited number of years and did not have any formal security of tenure. He also voiced concern that PPCMs could, as military officers, be subject to periodic review by their superiors.[358] The use of PPCMs was subsequently suspended, but in *R* v *Spear* the Court Martial Appeal Court held that the involvement of PPCMs in a number of earlier hearings had *not* violated Article 6.[359] In each of the appeals before the court, the PPCM had been in his last posting before retirement and was therefore unlikely to have been influenced by the prospect of promotion or preferment. The court noted that PPCMs effectively operated outside the military chain of command, that (in the army at least) they were no longer subject to periodic reviews, and that despite the absence of any written guarantees of tenure, no PPCM had ever actually been removed from his position. On this basis, the Courts Martial Appeal Court was satisfied that each appellant had been tried by an independent and impartial tribunal.

---

[357] (1997) 24 EHRR 221. Procedures at the time were governed by the Armed Forces Act 1981.
[358] *R* v *McKendry* (unreported) 6 March 2000, Aldershot Court-Martial Centre.
[359] *R* v *Spear and others* [2001] EWCA Crim 2, [2001] QB 804, [2001] 2 WLR.

Spear was given leave to appeal to the House of Lords. Before the appeal could be heard, however, the European Court of Human Rights in *Morris* v *UK*[360] decided that despite the improvements made since *Findlay*, the courts-martial system still fell short of what was required by Article 6. The court noted that the roles of the PPCM and the Judge Advocate were important safeguards of independence, but it considered that they were not sufficient to exclude the risk of outside pressure being brought to bear on the other members. In particular, it expressed concern that: (a) these other members received no legal training; (b) there were no statutory or other bars to prevent them from being subjected to external influence; and (c) they remained subject to army discipline and reporting.

Morris was not followed when *R* v *Spear* reached the House of Lords,[361] their Lordships having taken the view that the Strasbourg court had not had sufficient information upon which to base its decision. It was noted that although the ordinary courts-martial members were still subject to army discipline and reporting, their 'judicial' decisions were not evaluated or discussed as part of the reporting process: indeed, officers were prohibited from discussing their deliberations with anyone who was not a member of the court. It was also noted that any attempt to influence a court martial would probably constitute the offence of attempting to pervert the course of justice. Lord Bingham concluded that:[362]

> In my opinion the rules governing the role of junior officers as members of courts-martial are in practice such as effectively to protect the accused against the risk that they might be subject to 'external army influence', as I feel sure the European Court would have appreciated had the position been more fully explained.

Lord Rodger concurred, pointing out that:[363]

> Article 6 does not require that the members of the tribunal should not share the values of the military community to which they belong, any more than it requires that the judge or members of the jury in a civil court should be divorced from the values of the wider community.

In *Cooper* v *UK*,[364] a unanimous Grand Chamber of the Strasbourg court took account of these judgments and departed from its previous case law, declaring itself satisfied that there was, after all, no incompatibility with the Convention. However, the courts in both *Cooper* and *Spear* suggested that the role of the reviewing authorities was anomalous, and while they found no unfairness in the proceedings on the facts, they expressed concern that PPCMs in the RAF were still subject to review by their superior officers.[365]

---

[360] (2002) 34 EHRR 52.

[361] *R* v *Spear and others; R* v *Saunby and others* [2002] UKHL 31, [2003] 1 AC 734, [2002] 3 All ER 1074. For the status of European Court of Human Rights decisions as precedents, see pp 80 and 147.

[362] Ibid at [12].   [363] Ibid at [57].   [364] (2004) 39 EHRR 8.

[365] See also the decision in *Grieves* v *UK* (2004) 39 EHRR 2.

In the more recent case of *Martin* v *UK*, the Court of Human Rights criticized the use of a court martial to try a young civilian accused of murder.[366] The applicant was aged 17 when the offence was committed, and he was living with his family in Germany where his father was serving in the British Army. The applicant contended that his trial by court martial was inherently unfair and oppressive, and the Strasbourg court agreed that the requirements of a fair trial had not been met. The trial had taken place in 1994—before the system was reformed by the 1996 Act—and by the time the case reached Strasbourg many of the issues raised had therefore been addressed. However, the court also raised more general concerns about the use of military courts to try civilians, suggesting that this could only be justified in 'very exceptional circumstances'.[367] In response to this decision, the Ministry of Defence has stated that the rules of the new court martial will require its lay members to be civilians in cases in which civilians are on trial.[368] In its view, this 'civilianization' of the court martial will address any outstanding concerns about the independence of the new system, and will thus ensure that it is Convention-compliant.[369]

The 2006 Act

The government's view was that the existing system worked well, and that changes made since 1996 established a robust, fair, and effective system of law that is Convention-compliant.[370] The main purpose of the 2006 Act was thus to establish a more modern and coherent legal framework, better suited to an era in which the three services increasingly work together. Thus, a Director of Service Prosecutions has been appointed to replace the three pre-existing current authorities,[371] and the offices of Judge Advocate General and Judge Advocate of the Fleet were merged.[372] Instead of being an ad hoc court , henceforth a court martial is a unified standing court with the jurisdiction to sit anywhere in the world,[373] and a service civilian court replaced the separate 'standing civilian courts' .[374] The new court martial will continue to operate under the principle of 'open justice',[375] and its rules on evidence and procedure are be largely unchanged. These rules will, however, be harmonized and will apply to cases involving all three services.[376]

In many respects the system will continue to operate as before, but one notable change concerns the court's composition. In order for the new court to be properly constituted, a Judge Advocate will normally be required to sit with between three and five lay members.[377] The court's findings will be determined by majority vote and, in

---

[366] *Martin* v *UK* (2007) 44 EHRR 31.   [367] Ibid, at [44].

[368] This position was set out in a letter from the MoD to the Joint Committee on Human Rights, dated 22 February 2007.

[369] Ibid.

[370] MoD, *An Overview of the Military Criminal Justice System and the Armed Forces Act 2006* (HMSO, 2006), at pp 3–4.

[371] Armed Forces Act 2006, s 364.   [372] Ibid, s 362; Sch 17.   [373] Ibid, s 154.

[374] Ibid, s 51.   [375] Ibid, s 158.   [376] Ibid, s 163.

[377] Ibid, s 155. Court Martial Rules may provide for the court to sit with up to seven lay members—or without any—in prescribed circumstances.

the event of a decision on the verdict being evenly split, the defendant must be acquitted. The Judge Advocate's role remains: it is to determine legal points, and he does not
have a vote on the verdict itself. However, in the event of an equality of votes on the
sentence, the Judge Advocate will have the casting vote.[378] There will no longer be a
role for the reviewing authority, but those convicted of an offence by the court-martial
have a right of appeal to the Court Martial Appeal Court.[379]

Court Martial Appeal Court[380]

The Court Martial Appeal Court was established by the Courts-Martial (Appeals) Act
1951,[381] and in terms of composition and procedure it closely resembles the Criminal
Division of the Court of Appeal. It comprises the *ex officio* and ordinary members
of the Court of Appeal, nominated[382] judges of the Queen's Bench Division, certain
Scottish and Irish judges, and other persons of legal experience who may be appointed
to sit. Appeals are heard by at least three judges, although only one judgment is delivered. Any subsequent appeal lies to the Supreme Court and can only be made with
leave[383]

Ecclesiastical courts

These courts have a history as old as the common law itself. Although they have been
subject to control by the sovereign since the reign of Henry VIII, and their jurisdiction over laymen has been abolished, there remains a hierarchy of courts within the
Church of England. In addition, the General Synod of the Church of England has
statutory powers[384] to pass Measures concerning any matter affecting the Church of
England, and even concerning Acts of Parliament. These Measures have statutory
force upon receiving the royal assent.

Each diocese has a consistory court with jurisdiction over matters such as parochial libraries, the restoration of churches, and acts relating to land within the diocese.[385] Until recently these courts also had jurisdiction over disciplinary matters,
but a Measure passed in 2003 and given effect in January 2006 establishes separate
disciplinary tribunals for each diocese. These tribunals have jurisdiction over priests
and deacons, and can determine allegations of neglect of duty, conduct unbecoming a
clerk in holy orders, and other forms of misconduct.[386] The Vicar-General's Court for

---

[378] Ibid, s 160.   [379] Ibid, Sch 8.

[380] To be renamed 'the Court Martial Appeal Court' when the Armed Forces Act 2006 comes into effect:
2006 Act, Sch 8.

[381] It is now governed by the Courts-Martial (Appeals) Act 1968. Before 1951 there was no right of appeal
against conviction.

[382] By the Lord Chief Justice.   [383] See p 246.

[384] Under the Church of England Assembly (Powers) Act 1919, as amended by the Synodial Government
Measure 1969, s 2(1).

[385] Ecclesiastical Jurisdiction Measure 1963, ss 1 and 6.

[386] Clergy Discipline Measure 2003, ss 2, 6(1), 7 and 22. It is clear from this Measure that the Church of
England is not immune from the mood of reform that has swept through the legal system in recent years.

each province continues to have jurisdiction over allegations of misconduct involving bishops.[387] Appeals from the above courts lie to the Arches Court of Canterbury or the Chancery Court of York: both of these are presided over by officers who must either be barristers of ten years' standing, or persons who have held high judicial office.[388] Any further appeal lies to the Privy Council.[389]

The Court of Ecclesiastical Causes Reserved has jurisdiction over all members of the clergy in matters of 'doctrine, ritual or ceremonial'. This court is composed of five judges appointed by Her Majesty, and must include two persons who have held high judicial office.[390] Any appeal lies to a Commission of Review, which is currently composed of three Lords of Appeal in Ordinary and two Lords Spiritual.[391]

The ecclesiastical courts can impose a range of penalties, including removal from office. Such a penalty may be imposed when a clergyman is sentenced to imprisonment, or has a decree of divorce or order of separation pronounced against him on one of certain specified grounds.[392]

Further reading

AULD LJ, *Review of the Criminal Courts of England and Wales* (HMSO, 2001)

DEPARTMENT FOR CONSTITUTIONAL AFFAIRS, *A Single Civil Court? The Scope for Unifying the Civil Jurisdictions of the High Court, the County Courts and the Family Proceedings Courts* (HMSO, 2005) CP 06/05

DEPARTMENT FOR CONSTITUTIONAL AFFAIRS, *A Single Civil Court? Responses to the Consultation* (HMSO, 2005) CP(R) 06/05

Its effect will be to transform the ecclesiastical courts into something more recognizable as a judicial system. Amongst other things, it provides for the appointment of a President of Tribunals, the creation of a Disciplinary Commission with an advisory role, and the formulation of a Code of Practice. It also ensures that members of ecclesiastical courts enjoy greater security of tenure and cannot be removed from office without due process.

[387] Ibid, ss 6(2), 7 and 23.　　[388] Ecclesiastical Jurisdiction Measure 1963, ss 1, 3, and 7.

[389] Ibid, s 8.　　[390] Ibid, ss 5 and 10. The others must be bishops.

[391] Ibid, s 7.　　[392] Clergy Discipline Measure 2003, ss 30 and 31.

Tribunals and Inquiries

INTRODUCTION

The focus in this chapter is on the work of tribunals and inquiries. With all of the attention given to courts it is easy to overlook the role of tribunals in the legal system, yet, as revealed in a recent report, they have a workload in the region of a million cases each year. Currently there are dozens of different tribunals, and they differ radically in structure and approach. However, recent legislation makes provision for a radical overhaul of the system, with the aim of producing a unified and integrated framework. This chapter aims to give an overview of the existing system, and to examine the key features of the current programme of reform. Consideration will also be given to the work of different types of inquiry. The specific areas addressed will be:

- the characteristics of tribunals and the differences between tribunals and courts;
- the ways in which tribunals are administered and controlled, including the roles of the Tribunals Service and the Administrative Justice and Tribunals Council;
- the Leggatt Report and the trend towards a more harmonized and integrated system;
- the Tribunals, Courts and Enforcement Act 2007, and the creation of two new tribunals;
- the work of some of the existing tribunals, including the Asylum and Immigration Tribunal and employment tribunals;
- the extent to which tribunals are subject to control and supervision by the courts;
- the work of inquiries and the different forms that inquiries may take.

Tribunals: Overview

In 2001 Sir Andrew Leggatt reported that there were over seventy administrative tribunals operating in England and Wales,[1] in addition to a number of domestic tribunals and other regulatory bodies. The overwhelming majority of these were created during the twentieth century to provide cheap and informal mechanisms for resolving particular types of dispute. Most, although not all, adjudicate on matters

---

[1] *Tribunals for Users: One System, One Service—Report of the Review of Tribunals* (HMSO, 2001), Overview, para 2.

involving the citizen and the state. Over the past half a century, the welfare state has grown rapidly, and virtually every aspect of life—from the economy and industry, to housing and the environment—is increasingly subject to governmental intervention and regulation. The potential for disputes between the citizen and the state has increased phenomenally, and this has been matched by an increase in the jurisdiction and workload of the tribunals. As far back as 1979, tribunals were dealing with almost six times as many cases as the courts.[2] They now handle around a million cases each year:[3]

> That number of cases alone makes their work of great importance to our society, since more of us bring a case before a tribunal than go to any other part of the justice system. Their collective impact is immense.

The characteristics of tribunals

The distinction between tribunals and courts is not a technical one. Although the phrase 'administrative tribunals' is used on occasion, it is important to remember that their role is as part of a process of adjudication. Both courts and tribunals have been described as 'machinery for adjudication',[4] and both have a duty to act judicially. Although the offence of contempt of court[5] can only be committed in relation to a court, some tribunals have been held to be 'courts' for these purposes,[6] and the Employment Appeal Tribunal is actually a superior court of record. So, too, is the new Upper Tribunal. The choice of terminology therefore has no formal significance, and in a general sense, *any* type of court or judicial body can be called a 'tribunal'. In the context of the English legal system, however, the term is usually reserved for bodies that have more specialized areas of jurisdiction than the ordinary courts, and that often comprise both lawyers and expert lay members.

When compared to courts, tribunals are said to be relatively informal, accessible, quick, and inexpensive, but in fact there is enormous variation in the extent to which different tribunals possess these characteristics. Much depends on the nature of the matter being determined. Thus, employment tribunals are rather more formal than the Social Security and Child Support Appeals Chamber, and the Lands Chamber exhibits a degree of formality similar to that of the ordinary courts. There are also differences in the types of decision that individual tribunals are required to make. Some tribunals deal with appeals against the decisions of government departments and public officials,[7] and some even hear appeals against the decisions of other

---

[2] Royal Commission on Legal Services, Cmnd 7648 (HMSO, 1979).
[3] *Tribunals for Users* (HMSO, 2001) at para 1.1.   [4] Royal Commission on Legal Services, para 40.
[5] See p 240.
[6] *Peach Grey & Co* v *Sommers* [1995] 2 All ER 513, [1995] ICR 549 (employment tribunals); applied in *Ewing* v *Security Services* [2003] EWCA Civ 581. *Pickering* v *Liverpool Daily Post and Echo Newspapers plc* [1991] 2 AC 370 [1991] 1 All ER 622 (Mental Health Review Tribunals).
[7] The Social Security and Child Support Appeals Chamber, and the Asylum and Immigration Chamber are just two examples.

tribunals.[8] Others have original jurisdiction to determine matters such as the discharge of patients in compulsory detention,[9] or the legal recognition of the gender of transsexual persons.[10] In addition, a small number of tribunals—notably employment tribunals—have jurisdiction to hear disputes between private citizens.

Although the jurisdiction of most tribunals concerns 'administrative' disputes, it would be a mistake to assume that these disputes are any less important than those coming before the courts. Some tribunals adjudicate on matters affecting fundamental rights, such as asylum decisions, claims of unlawful discrimination, and applications to be discharged from compulsory detention. Others, such as the Lands Tribunal, sometimes deal with claims involving very large sums of money. Historically, tribunals have been subject to the supervisory jurisdiction of the High Court: since the implementation of the Leggatt reforms by the Tribunals Courts and Legal Services Act 2007, there is now an integrated hierarchy of tribunals, review, and appeal. This is explained later.[11]However, with the exception of the EAT,[12] tribunals are generally regarded as inferior to the ordinary courts, and they are subject to the supervisory jurisdiction of the High Court. In some cases they are also subject to the appellate jurisdiction of the High Court or Court of Appeal.[13]

Composition

The composition of most tribunals differs from that of the average court, and usually includes both legally qualified persons and laypeople with relevant expertise. For example, an employment tribunal typically comprises a legally qualified chairman and two 'wing members'. One wing member will be a layman with experience of representing employers' interests; the other will have experience of representing the rights of workers. Similarly, experts in the fields of medicine, disability, and finance sit alongside lawyers in the Social Security and Child Support Appeals Chamber.

It is important that the composition of tribunals be independent, and not appointed from panels of individuals or experts drawn up by government Ministers or departments with responsibility for managing the process in respect of which the tribunal operates. That would negate genuine independence. The arrangements for appointing the lay members of employment tribunals were the subject of a Human Rights Act challenge in *Scanfuture Ltd v Secretary of State for Trade and Industry*.[14] Before 1999 lay members were appointed by the Secretary of State on a short-term basis and they had no real security of tenure. The renewal of their contracts was entirely at the Secretary of State's discretion, and their remuneration was determined by the same Minister. The Employment Appeal Tribunal ruled that 'a fair-minded and informed observer' would justifiably fear that members appointed like this were not

---

[8] See, e.g., the Employment Appeal Tribunal, discussed at p 304.
[9] The Mental Health Review Tribunal.   [10] The Gender Recognition Panel.
[11] See p 294.   [12] Employment Appeal Tribunal: see p 304.
[13] This is discussed further at p 250.   [14] [2001] ICR 1096, [2001] IRLR 416.

independent and impartial. For a tribunal including such members to determine a case involving the Minister was therefore incompatible with the right to a fair trial under Article 6 of the ECHR.[15]

The government had anticipated such a challenge,[16] and the arrangements for appointing the lay members of employment and other tribunals had already been reformed by the time that *Scanfuture* was decided. Under the current arrangements, the wing members of employment tribunals are appointed by the Lord Chancellor in consultation with the Secretary of State for Business, Enterprise and Regulatory Reform.[17] They are appointed for a fixed term that is automatically renewable, and they can only be removed from their posts on specified grounds.[18] The EAT in *Scanfuture* concluded that there is now 'no need or reason, if ever there was, for any lay member to think that... it would help him acquire a renewal of his office by his leaning in favour of the Secretary of State in any hearing'.[19] Thus, in the opinion of the EAT, the current arrangements for appointing lay tribunal members are compatible with Article 6.

A similar issue arose in *Singh v Secretary of State for the Home Department*[20] in the context of a part-time immigration adjudicator. The adjudicator had been appointed for an initial term of one year and, although it was 'normal' for such appointments to be renewed on expiry, his conditions of service made it clear that renewal could not be guaranteed. They also stated that the Lord Chancellor reserved the right to terminate his appointment 'without cause' at one month's notice. The Scottish Court of Session held that these arrangements did not provide security of tenure and were therefore incompatible with both Article 6 and the existing common law test for bias. Again, however, the court noted that a modified appointments system had already been put in place, and it appeared that the new system provided the necessary safeguards.[21]

Sir Andrew Leggatt's review of tribunals[22] also raised concerns about independence, and it recommended that tribunal members should be appointed in the same way as members of the judiciary. Provisions to give effect to this recommendation were included in the Constitutional Reform Act 2005 and the Tribunals, Courts and Enforcement Act 2007. Now, most tribunal members are selected by the Judicial Appointments Commission,[23] and the Lord Chancellor's role in approving or recommending its selections will be largely a formality.

---

[15] Article 6 is discussed further at p 191.

[16] It was clear from the decision in *Starrs v Ruxton* 2000 JC 208, 2000 SLT 42 that the terms upon which many part-time judges and tribunal members held office would have to be reviewed: see p 344.

[17] The equivalent of what used to be the Secretary of State for Trade and Industry.

[18] These grounds are: (a) misbehaviour; (b) incapacity; (c) failure as to training; (d) failure to satisfy the sitting requirements; and (e) sustained failure to observe reasonably expected standards.

[19] *Scanfuture v Secretary of State for Trade and Industry* [2001] ICR 1096 at [41], [2001] IRLR 416 at [41], *per* Lindsay J.

[20] 2004 SLT 1058, (2004) The Times, 23 January, Inner House.

[21] The composition of the Employment Appeal Tribunal was the subject of a different type of Article 6 challenge in *Lawal v Northern Spirit* [2003] UKHL 35, [2004] 1 All ER 187, [2003] ICR 856.

[22] *Tribunals for Users*, at para 2.32.   [23] See p 337.

KEY ISSUE

The question of independence of tribunals has been of fundamental concern since the Donoughmore Report.[24] Tribunals should have same characteristics of independence and impartiality as courts and other forms of dispute adjudication. The changes in appointment and composition are the starting point for ensuring that those qualities are present. The requirements of the Human Rights Act 1998, in making Article 6 standards directly enforceable are, as noted above, important, but reflect the trend towards the creation of fair procedures evident since the Franks Report in 1957.

? Questions

1. How far are appointees to tribunals now genuinely independent?
2. What do you think the difference is between independence and impartiality?

Organization and control

There is a danger that tribunals might be viewed as part of the process of government rather than as part of a legal system providing an independent means of review. Extensive powers of adjudication have been granted to tribunals that were not demonstrably independent of government departments, and for almost a century concerns have been growing[25] about executive encroachment into the legislative and judicial areas. Some of these concerns were addressed by the Donoughmore Committee in 1932.[26] This recommended that:

(a) the supervisory jurisdiction of the High Court over tribunals should be maintained;

(b) tribunals should be compelled by the High Court to observe natural justice;

(c) the reports of statutory inquiries should be published; and

(d) there should be the possibility of an appeal from tribunals on a question of law.

These recommendations were generally given effect,[27] but concerns about independence persisted. Then, in 1957, the Franks Committee carried out a major review of administrative tribunals and inquiries.[28]

The Franks Committee

The Franks Committee Report described tribunals as follows:[29]

[24] See n 26 below.
[25] See, e.g., Lord Hewart CJ's reference to 'administrative lawlessness' in *The New Despotism* (Ernst Benn, 1929).
[26] *Report of the Committee on Ministers' Powers*, Cm 4060 (HMSO, 1932).
[27] The courts' supervisory jurisdiction over tribunals is discussed at p 256.
[28] *Report of the Committee on Administrative Tribunals and Enquiries*, Cmnd 218 (HMSO, 1957).
[29] Ibid, at para 2.45.

[They] are not ordinary courts, but neither are they appendages of Government Departments…tribunals should properly be regarded as machinery provided by Parliament for adjudication rather than as part of the machinery of administration. The essential point is that in all these cases Parliament has deliberately provided for a decision outside and independent of the Department concerned…and the intention of Parliament to provide for the independence of tribunals is clear and unmistakable.

The report highlighted the need for tribunals to have the three key characteristics of openness, impartiality, and fairness. These are in fact the key principles under-pinning the judicial system in England and Wales, and a court in an application for judicial review would consider them to be the basic standards of procedural fairness.[30] The report also noted that tribunals have certain advantages over courts: cheapness, accessibility, informality, expert knowledge of their own areas of operation, and an ability to deal with cases relatively quickly. The volume of work, however, is now very substantial, and this militates against the speedy disposal of applications. By 1999, employment tribunals alone were dealing with in excess of 83,000 cases each year.[31]

The Leggatt Review of Tribunals: *One System, One Service*

In 2000, Sir Andrew Leggatt was asked to chair the first major review of tribunals since the Franks Report. His objective was to recommend a system that would be 'coherent, professional, cost-effective and user-friendly',[32] and which would also be compatible with the requirements for independence under Article 6 of the ECHR.[33] He reviewed the work of more than seventy different tribunals and concluded that they could not really be described as a 'system' at all:[34]

[T]he present collection of tribunals has grown up in an almost entirely haphazard way. Individual tribunals were set up, and usually administered by departments, as they developed new statutory schemes and procedures. The result is a collection of tribunals, mostly administered by departments, with wide variations of practice and approach, and almost no coherence. The current arrangements seem to us to have been developed to meet the needs and conveniences of the departments and other bodies which run tribunals, rather than the needs of the user.

Leggatt expressed concern that most tribunals were still administered by the departments the policies of which they had a duty to consider:[35]

The very fact that a department is responsible for the policy and the legislation, under which cases are brought in the tribunal it sponsors, leads users to suppose that the tribunal is part of the same enterprise as its sponsoring department.

He concluded that greater independence and efficiency could be achieved by establishing a common administrative service with responsibility for *all* tribunals. A more

---

[30] See, e.g., *Doody v Secretary of State for Home Affairs* [1994] 1 AC 531, [1993] 3 All ER 92; *R v Board of Visitors of HM Prison, The Maze, ex parte Hone* [1988] AC 379, [1988] 1 All ER 321. For standards of fairness under Article 6 ECHR, see p 191.

[31] *Tribunals for Users*, chapter on Employment Tribunals at para 3.

[32] Ibid, Overview, para 1.   [33] See p 191.

[34] *Tribunals for Users*, para 1.3.   [35] Ibid, Overview, para 11.

coherent system could be developed by grouping the existing tribunals into nine divisions, with each division relating to a particular subject area. Thus, there should be divisions dealing with education, finance, health and social services, immigration, land and valuation, social security and pensions, transport, regulatory matters, and employment.[36] Each division should have a corresponding appellate or 'second-tier' tribunal, and there should be a right to appeal against first-tier decisions but only on a point of law. Any further appeal should lie to the Court of Appeal.[37] Leggatt also recommended a number of reforms designed to make tribunals more 'understandable, unthreatening and useful to users'.[38] These included training chairmen to provide better assistance to those presenting their own cases, improving tribunal procedures, making relevant information more accessible, and ensuring that voluntary and other advice groups were properly funded.

Transforming public services

The Leggatt Review made a total of 361 separate recommendations and received a fairly cautious welcome from the government. A consultation paper published in August 2001 said that the government had an open mind but wanted to consult more widely.[39] The responses to the consultation revealed very strong support for reform, and in July 2004 the Department for Constitutional Affairs published a White Paper setting out its own vision for the future. This vision was described as 'different from, but compatible with' that of Leggatt:[40]

> We accept Sir Andrew Leggatt's key recommendation that tribunals provided by central government should be brought together into a unified system within what is now the Department for Constitutional Affairs. We believe that this will be more effective and efficient, and will firmly embed the principle of independence. But we see this new body as much more than a federation of existing tribunals. This is a new organisation and a new type of organisation. It will have two central pillars: administrative justice appeals, and employment cases. Its task, together with a transformed Council on Tribunals, will not be just to process cases according to law. Its mission will be to help prevent and resolve disputes, using any appropriate method and working with its partners in and out of government, and to help to improve administrative justice and justice in the workplace, so that the need for disputes is reduced.

Transforming the existing network of tribunals into a unified and coherent system is a major undertaking. In part, the way forward can be seen from the development since 1998 of the Appeals Service, and the creation in 2006 of the Tribunals Service. The passage of the Tribunals Courts and Legal Services Act 2007 provided the fundamental structural change needed for the approach suggested by Leggatt and adopted by the government.

---

[36] Ibid, para 9.   [37] Ibid, para 14.   [38] Ibid, para 6.

[39] Lord Chancellor's Department, *Tribunals for Users: Consultation Paper about the Report of the Review of Tribunals by Sir Andrew Leggatt* (HMSO, 2001).

[40] DCA, *Transforming Public Services: Complaints, Redress and Tribunals*, Cm 6243 (HMSO, 2004), at para 1.14.

The Appeals Service

The Appeals Service was created in 1998 by combining social security appeals tribunals with the disability appeals tribunals, vaccine damage tribunals, medical appeal tribunals, and child support appeal tribunals to form a unified system with a single jurisdiction The resulting Appeals Service—known since 2006 as the Social Security and Child Support Appeals Tribunal—was in some ways a model for the system that has now been put in place. Replacing five jurisdictions with one enabled the Appeals Service to adopt common procedures and allowed greater flexibility in the allocation and deployment of resources. Tribunal members appointed to the single jurisdiction could be allocated to any type of case for which they had suitable expertise. Although Leggatt did not suggest that all tribunals be unified in this way, this is, in effect, the approach adopted under the Tribunals Courts and Enforcement Act 2007, and into which, as part of the Social Entitlement Chamber, the Social Security and Child Support Appeals Tribunal now fits.

The Tribunals Service

The next stage in the reform process was to the continuation of the bringing together of tribunals together. The Leggatt Report identified the advantages to be gained from bringing tribunals together in one coherent structure: the more efficient use of resources, such as judges, panel members, administrative staff, and buildings. Multi-jurisdictional centres can be established and common training, procedures, and rules be adopted where appropriate.

The Tribunals Service, which is an executive agency of the Ministry of Justice, was launched in April 2006. Establishing the Tribunals Service did not require new legislation, but it was a significant development nonetheless, providing the administrative structure within which the system created by the 2007 Act can work.

The following are within the remit of the Tribunals Service. Under the new structure created by the 2007 Act, tribunals are organized into Chambers. These currently are as set out in Figure 8.1.

Tribunals were transferred to the Service in their existing state, but the process of integration and modernization is well under way, including a network of multi-jurisdictional hearing centres[41] and administrative support centres. 'Proportionate dispute resolution procedures' are being introduced with a view to reducing the number of cases proceeding to a full hearing.[42]

> **KEY ISSUE**
>
> A major issue is the extent to which a unified tribunal service can bring benefits to users of the tribunal system. The potential to achieve both service improvements as well as service

---

[41] See, e.g., the opening of Anchorage House, a multi-jurisdictional centre in East London, during 2009.

[42] *Tribunals Service Strategic and Business Plan for 2007–08—Delivering the Future: One System One Service* (HMSO, 2007) at p 6.

Social Entitlement Chamber
Asylum Support
Social Security and Child Support
Criminal Injuries Compensation

Health Education and Social Care
Care Standards
Mental Health
Special Educational Needs &
Disability
Primary Health Lists

War Pensions and Armed Forces Compensation Chamber

Immigration and Asylum Chamber

General Regulatory Chamber
Charity
Claims Management Service
Consumer Credit
Environment
Estate Agents
Gambling Appeals
Immigration Services
Local Government Standards in
England
Transport

Tax Chamber
First-tier Tribunal (Tax)

Fig. 8.1 Chambers of the First-tier Tribunal

efficiencies can be seen from the opening of a multi-jurisdictional centre at Anchorage House in East London. The Tribunal Service Annual Report for 2009–10[43] observes:

> The East London multi-jurisdictional hearing centre...brings together the Employment tribunal and Social Security and Child Support (SSCS) tribunal formerly based [elsewhere]...
>
> These tribunals moved into the new accommodation...Anchorage House is a modern building with excellent transport links across London. It has state of the art facilities such as independent climate control, video conferencing and Wi-Fi. There are 15 hearing rooms, two waiting rooms and four consultation rooms, a fully equipped medical room, and separate rooms for interpreters and presenting officers.

---

[43] At p 19: see **www.tribunals.gov.uk/Tribunals/Publications/publications.htm**

We have received numerous positive comments from our customers. For example: 'I found the service and facilities fantastic' and 'the administrative staff were very helpful, they made the tribunal experience good and eased the stress. Information provided was very helpful, facilities were clear and present'.

The changes permit rationalization, and the removal of replication and administrative inefficiency. This can include common rules and procedures, the development of more multi-jurisdictional centres with thus a better use of physical assets and a more efficient use of judicial time.

 Questions

1. Do you think it was accurate prior to the Leggatt reforms to talk of a 'tribunal system'?
2. Do we now have a tribunal 'system'?

The Tribunals Courts and Enforcement Act 2007

The foundation of the new system of administrative tribunals is the 2007 Act. Section 1 of the Act extends to the tribunal judiciary the same guarantee of judicial independence set out in section 3 of the Constitutional Reform Act 2005. The Lord Chancellor and other Ministers now have a statutory duty to uphold the continued independence of tribunal judges, the Senior President of Tribunals,[44] and certain other tribunal officers, and they are specifically prohibited from seeking to influence particular judicial decisions through any special access to the judiciary. The Lord Chancellor is also required to have regard to the need to *defend* judicial independence, and to ensure that the judiciary have the support necessary to enable them to exercise their functions.[45]

Section 2 of the Act creates the new post of Senior President of Tribunals, and the holder of this office is given a range of functions modelled on those performed by the Lord Chief Justice in relation to courts.[46] For that reason, this office is at the same judicial level as a judge of the Court of Appeal. Many, but not all, of his or her functions are conferred by the 2007 Act. Disciplinary matters in respect of tribunal judiciary remain with the Lord Chief Justice, but delegated to the Senior President.

As to the shape of the new tribunals system, the government rejected as unnecessary Leggatt's proposal for a nine-division structure.[47] Instead, the 2007 Act provides for the creation of two generic tribunals into which most of the existing tribunal jurisdictions will be transferred.[48] Those jurisdictions will, however, be grouped into different 'chambers' within each tribunal, so that similar work can be dealt with by judges and tribunal members with relevant skills and experience.[49]

---

[44] See p 297.   [45] 2005 Act, s 3(6).

[46] See p 249. It would not have been possible for the Lord Chief Justice to perform that role because some tribunal jurisdiction extends to Scotland or to the whole of the United Kingdom.

[47] *Transforming Public Services*, at para 6.38.

[48] Section 3.   [49] Section 7.

The new tribunals

The framework established by the Tribunals, Courts and Enforcement Act 2007 provides for the creation of two new tribunals: the First-tier Tribunal and the Upper Tribunal.[50] The aims of the reforms introduced by the 2007 Act, broadly implementing the Leggatt recommendations, were to ensure: the complete independence of tribunal judiciary and their decision-making from government; the speeding up the delivery of justice; the making of processes easier for the public to understand; and the bringing together of expertise from each tribunal.

The general structure[51] is shown in diagrammatic form in Figure 8.2.

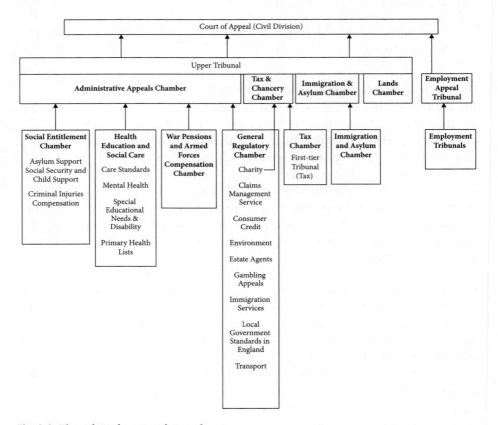

Fig. 8.2 The tribunals system hierarchy

Section 30 empowered the Lord Chancellor to transfer the jurisdictions of tribunals listed in Schedule 6 to either of these new tribunals However, certain jurisdictions

---

[50] Section 3.

[51] In limited cases the general structure may be subject to specific provision to the contrary.

will remain outside the new framework: principally the employment tribunals and Employment Appeal Tribunal because they hear 'party and party' disputes as opposed to appeals against administrative decisions.[52] Tribunals that are currently administered by local government fall outside the scope of the 2007 Act altogether.

The First-tier Tribunal

The First-tier Tribunal has a broad jurisdiction. However, section 7 of the 2007 Act provides for the new tribunal to be divided into distinct Chambers, so that similar types of jurisdiction can be grouped together. The Chamber structure is designed to be flexible, and the Lord Chancellor and Senior President have the power to make changes as and when required.[53]

Each Chamber of the First-tier Tribunal has a President, and each Chamber President must also be a judge of the Upper Tribunal.[54] The tribunal's legally qualified members are titled 'Judge of the First-tier Tribunal', and those who are appointed for their expertise in other areas will be known as 'members'.[55] Section 31(2) provided for the transfer of pre-existing members of tribunals. Others may be appointed by the Lord Chancellor on the basis of their qualifications or experience, following selection by the Judicial Appointments Commission.[56]

The Upper Tribunal

The primary role of the Upper Tribunal is to hear appeals against the decisions of the First-tier Tribunal. The idea is thus to create a common appeals structure for the tribunals system, with any further appeal lying to the Court of Appeal.[57] However, the Upper Tribunal has a first-instance jurisdiction in relation to certain types of case. The test is whether it is thought appropriate for an appeal against the first-instance decision to lie directly to the Court of Appeal.[58]

The Upper Tribunal is a superior court of record,[59] and its decisions are binding on lower tribunals and authoritative on points of law. This leads to the potential development of a coherent system of administrative justice, developing principle and law in a coherent way,[60] with the ordinary courts being involved where points of law of important principle are involved, or there is a breakdown of fundamental procedural standards.[61] Like the First-tier, it is organized into Chambers dealing with particular

---

[52] Others outside the 2007 Act scheme are: Special Immigration Appeals Commission; Reserve Forces Appeals; Proscribed Organisation Appeals Commission; Pathogen Access Appeals Commission; Gender Recognition Panel. However, they are within the remit of the Tribunals Service.

[53] 2007 Act, s 7.   [54] 2007 Act, s 7; Sch 4.   [55] Section 4.

[56] 2007 Act, Sch 2.

[57] Ibid, ss 11–14. The role of the courts in reviewing the decisions of tribunals is discussed further at p 306.

[58] *Transforming Public Services*, at para 203.

[59] 2007 Act, s 3(5). See *R (on application of Cart and others)* v *Special Immigration Appeals Commission, Upper Tribunal and others* [2009] EWHC 3052 (Admin)

[60] See Carnwath, 'Tribunal Justice: A New Start' [2009] PL 48.

[61] See *R (on application of Cart and others)* v *Special Immigration Appeals Commission, Upper Tribunal and others* [2009] EWHC 3052 (Admin).

areas of work.[62] There are now four Chambers, the Immigration and Asylum Chamber having been brought into the structure in 2010.[63] Each Chamber has its own President,[64] and judges and members are appointed in much the same way as for the First-tier Tribunal.[65] Although it can have both judges and other members, its decisions are frequently based on points of law, and this means that non-judicial members are not always required to sit.[66]

Many of the pre-existing tribunals had limited or no rights of appeal, and section 11 of the new Act creates a general right to appeal from the First-tier to the Upper Tribunal on a point of law. This is merely a default position, however, and the right of appeal may be excluded by the Lord Chancellor using delegated legislation. There is also provision for the Upper Tribunal to exercise a judicial review jurisdiction, and it will be able to grant the prerogative remedies already available to the High Court.[67] This is an important change for two reasons: firstly, to permit the development of specialized knowledge and experience in administrative justice cases; secondly, to ease the workload pressure that the Administrative Court has been under.[68] However, this jurisdiction only applies to categories of case specified in directions made by the Lord Chief Justice, and to individual cases transferred by the High Court or Court of Session.[69] A further limitation is that only judges of the High Court, Court of Session and Court of Appeal are able to hear such 'judicial review' cases.[70]

This important innovation has advantages both for the administrative justice process and for the wider court system. Applications for review can be, and sometime are, considered in a matter of days, by a panel with appropriate expertise and experience. The overstretched Administrative Court loses a significant chunk of caseload, potentially easing the pressure on that court.

The Administrative Justice and Tribunals Council

One of the key recommendations of the Franks Report was the creation of a permanent statutory body to supervise and review the working of tribunals within its remit. This recommendation was given effect by the creation of the Council on Tribunals.[71] Its role was advisory and consultative, and its primary function was to keep the workings of tribunals under review and to report on them from time to time. It also gave advice on the appointment and training of tribunal members and on the rules under which they operate. Its influence was limited, however, and one commentator[72] suggested that its reports did 'little more than recite facts and make the occasional grumble'.

---

[62] Ibid, s 7.   [63] *Transforming Public Services*, at para. 179. See Figure 1 at p 294.

[64] 2007 Act, s 7(2).   [65] Ibid, Sch 3.   [66] Ibid, at para 220.

[67] 2007 Act, s 15.   [68] See p 268.

[69] Ibid, ss 18(6), 19 and 20.   [70] Ibid, s 18(8).

[71] Tribunals and Inquiries Act 1958: this was superseded by the Tribunals and Inquiries Act 1992.

[72] Lomas, 'The Twenty-Fifth Annual Report of the Council on Tribunals: An Opportunity Sadly Missed' (1985) 48 MLR 694.

Under the Tribunals, Courts and Enforcement Act 2007, the Council on Tribunals has been transformed into a new body with enhanced powers. The Administrative Justice and Tribunals Council[73] (AJTC) was launched in November 2007, and it is charged with keeping the entire administrative justice system under review.[74] The 'administrative justice system' is defined to mean:

> the overall system by which decisions of an administrative or executive nature are made in relation to particular persons, including: (a) the procedures for making such decisions; (b) the law under which such decisions are made; and (c) the systems for resolving disputes and airing grievances in relation to such decisions.[75]

The Parliamentary Commissioner for Administration is an *ex officio* member of the new body, and he is joined by between ten and fifteen other members appointed by the Lord Chancellor and Scottish and Welsh Ministers.[76] It was intended that the Council will focus first and foremost on the needs of users, and one of its duties is to consider ways of making the administrative justice system more accessible, fair and efficient.[77] Its other functions include: advising the Lord Chancellor and others on proposals for change and other matters;[78] reviewing the work of tribunals and scrutinizing relevant legislation;[79] and reviewing and reporting on the constitution and working of statutory inquiries.[80] The Council must also be consulted with regard to the procedural rules for tribunals within its remit,[81] and it is required to produce annual reports.[82] Ironically, the Council is one of the bodies the future of which is placed in doubt by the terms of the Public Bodies Bill of 2010.[83]

The Senior President of Tribunals

The creation of this post was originally recommended by Leggatt, and section 2 of the Tribunals, Courts and Enforcement Act 2007 gives effect to his recommendation. The holder of the office sits 'at the apex of the tribunals' judiciary, giving a focus and leadership to those tribunals covered by the 2007 Act'.[84] There are two possible ways in which he can be appointed. One option is for the appointment to be made on the recommendation of the Lord Chancellor, following consultation with the Lord Chief Justice and his Scotland and Northern Ireland counterparts.[85] In this case the person selected must be a judge of the Court of Appeal, a judge of the Inner House of the Scottish Court of Session or a Lord Justice of Appeal in Northern Ireland. Alternatively, if the Lord Chancellor and those consulted cannot agree on a suitable candidate, the Judicial Appointments Commission will be asked to make a recommendation instead.[86] If this route is followed, the person recommended must satisfy the judicial-appointment

---

[73] Established under s 44 of the 2007 Act.   [74] 2007 Act, Sch 7, para 13.

[75] Ibid.   [76] Ibid, Sch 7, para 1.   [77] Ibid, Sch 7, para 13.

[78] Ibid.   [79] Ibid, Sch 7, para 14.   [80] Ibid, Sch 7, para 15.

[81] Ibid, Sch 7, para 24.   [82] Ibid, Sch 7, para 21.   [83] See p 9.

[84] Ministry of Justice, *Transforming Tribunals: Implementing Part 1 of the Tribunals, Courts and Enforcement Act 2007* (HMSO, 2007) CP 30/07, at para 138.

[85] The appointment is technically made by the Monarch: see s 2(1) of the 2007 Act.

[86] 2007 Act, Sch 1, para 2(5).

eligibility requirement on a seven-year basis[87] and, as with other judicial appointments, the Lord Chancellor will have only one right of rejection.[88]

The Senior President exercises a range of functions. He or she will have duties relating to the training, guidance, and welfare of tribunal judges and members,[89] and together with the Lord Chancellor will be responsible for determining the structure of tribunal chambers and the allocation of work between them.[90] He or she has the power to issue practice directions,[91] and either the Senior President or his or her nominee chairs a Tribunal Procedure Committee with the power to make Tribunal Procedure Rules.[92] He or she is also responsible for representing the views of tribunal members to Parliament, the Lord Chancellor, and other Ministers.[93] In carrying out his or her functions, he or she is required to have regard to: (a) the need for tribunals to be accessible; (b) the need for tribunal proceedings to be fair and to be handled quickly and efficiently; (c) the need for tribunal members to have expertise in their areas of jurisdiction; and (d) the need to develop innovative methods of dispute resolution.[94]

KEY ISSUE

The test of the reforms in the establishment of the Tribunals Service and the two-tiered approach created by the 2007 Act is how, and to what standard, it creates a more unified and principled system, of administrative justice. The system copes with what are increasing workloads whilst maintaining the standards of fairness, impartiality, and independence that are the fundamental aims sought by and since the Franks Report in 1957. In 2007–08, some 640,000 claims were received by the Tribunals Service; by 2009–10 that had risen to 794,000.[95] Of those some 640,000 had been disposed of during that year, although the Annual Report for 2009–10 indicates that the Tribunals Service had not met its own performance targets for the time taken to dispose of complaints. Although the 2007 Act has rationalized some thirty-six different jurisdictions, the bulk of claims were, in 2009–10, in three major areas: social security and child support (43 per cent); immigration and asylum (20 per cent); and employment (30 per cent), the latter, of course outside the main two-tiered system created by the 2007 Act. The increase in workload is seen by the Tribunal Service as the major reason inhibiting quicker disposal of cases. To overcome this, the Service has appointed more judges and looked to the potential for out-of-normal-hours sittings.

? Questions

1. Why was the Immigration and Asylum Tribunal initially excluded from the new structure?

2. Why are employment tribunals still outside the structure even though they are administered by the Tribunals Service?

[87] Or have an equivalent status within the judiciary of Scotland or Northern Ireland: 2007 Act, Sch 1, para 3. See also p 338.
[88] 2007 Act, Sch 1, para 3. See further, p 339.   [89] 2007 Act, Sch 2, para 8; Sch 3, para 9.
[90] Ibid, s 7.   [91] Ibid, s 23.   [92] Ibid, s 22; Sch 5.
[93] Ibid, Sch 1, para 14.   [94] Ibid, s 2(3).   [95] See Tribunal Service Annual Report 2009–10.

3. What do you think are the advantages of the new system?

4. Do we now have a coherent scheme of administrative justice?

Specific tribunals

The Criminal Injuries Compensation Appeals Panel

In 1964 the government used prerogative powers[96] to create a scheme for compensating the victims of violent crime. Claims were administered by the Criminal Injuries Compensation Board and were assessed on the same basis as common law damages.

The scheme was placed on a statutory footing in 1995[97] and the Board was replaced by the Criminal Injuries Compensation Authority.[98] Awards are now calculated by reference to a tariff, which sets minimum and maximum amounts for each type of injury. A claimant who is dissatisfied with the decision of a claims officer can apply in writing to have it reviewed by someone in a more senior position. If the review is unsuccessful the claimant then has ninety days in which to appeal to the Criminal Injuries Compensation Appeals Panel. The Panel is part of the Social Entitlement Chamber.

The Panel has a chairman and around seventy other members, just under half of whom are legally qualified. Appeals are heard by either two or three members, one of whom must be a lawyer. At the hearing the appellant must prove his or her case on a balance of probabilities. He or she may choose to have a legal adviser or other representative present, and may call, examine, and cross-examine witnesses. The procedure is informal and adjudicators are not bound by strict rules of evidence. The Leggatt Report found that around 60 per cent of claimants were represented at appeal hearings, although it praised the supportive and constructive way in which unrepresented appellants were dealt with.[99] There is no right of appeal against the Panel's decisions but they are subject to the possibility of judicial review, which will be to the Upper Tribunal.[100]

Administrative responsibility for the Panel has rested with the Tribunals Service since its launch in April 2006.

---

[96] See *R v Criminal Injuries Compensation Board, ex parte Lain* [1967] 2 QB 864, [1967] 2 All ER 770.

[97] Criminal Injuries Compensation Act 1995. Provisions to establish a statutory regime were included in the Criminal Justice Act 1988 but were never actually implemented: see *R v Secretary of State for the Home Department, ex parte Fire Brigades Union* [1995] 2 AC 513, [1995] 2 All ER 244. The scheme created under the 1995 Act was later revised and the current version dates from 2001.

[98] The Board was abolished on 1 April 2000.   [99] *Tribunals for Users*, at paras 4 and 9.

[100] See p 295.

The Asylum and Immigration Chamber

Launched in April 2005, the Asylum and Immigration Tribunal has jurisdiction to hear appeals against Home Office decisions in matters relating to immigration and asylum.[101] Decisions such as the refusal of asylum, refusal of entry to the United Kingdom, or refusal of leave to remain, or decisions for the deportation of an individual are all examples of matters in which the Tribunal heard appeals. Its predecessor, the Immigration Appellate Authorities (IAA), comprised two separate bodies: the Immigration Adjudicators and the Immigration Appeal Tribunal (IAT). The Adjudicators handled appeals from decisions made by entry clearance officials, immigration officers, and the Home Secretary, whilst the IAT had jurisdiction to hear second-tier appeals from decisions of the Adjudicators. Before 2002, appeals to the IAT could be based on grounds of both fact and law. This made it almost inevitable that an unsuccessful appeal to the Adjudicators would be the subject of a further challenge in the IAT. In his review of tribunals, Leggatt concluded that these arrangements had a negative effect on the perceived authority of the Adjudicators and contributed to a 'culture of challenge'. He also suggested that the expert contribution of non-lawyers was made too late in the process: all Immigration Adjudicators were legally qualified and usually sat alone, but appeals to the IAT were heard by a legally qualified chairman sitting with one or two lay members. Leggatt recommended that lay members and lawyers should sit together at the Adjudicator stage to determine both the facts and the law: any further appeal to the IAT should only be possible on a point of law and should therefore be determined by a lawyer sitting alone.[102] His recommendations were given partial effect by the Nationality, Immigration and Asylum Act 2002, which restricted the jurisdiction of the IAT to appeals based on points of law.[103] The involvement of lay members remained unchanged, however, with the rather odd result that they were only able to contribute to the appeals process at a stage at which purely legal issues were being determined. Just two years after these reforms were introduced, the entire system was radically overhauled by the Asylum and Immigration (Treatment of Claimants etc.) Act 2004. The system of second-tier appeals was ended, and both the Adjudicators and the IAT were replaced with a single-tier Asylum and Immigration Tribunal.[104] Since 2010 that tribunal has been subsumed into the new scheme as the Immigration and Asylum Chamber.

As with the previous system, the Chamber has no jurisdiction in respect of decisions taken on national security grounds,[105] and it cannot review asylum claims certified by the Home Secretary as being manifestly unfounded or as having originated

---

[101] The key provisions are contained in Part 5 of the Nationality, Immigration and Asylum Act 2002 (as amended by the Asylum and Immigration (Treatment of Claimants etc.) Act 2004).

[102] *Tribunals for Users* (2001), Part III, recommendations 298–301.

[103] 2002 Act, s 101 (now repealed).   [104] Ibid, s 81; as substituted by the 2004 Act, s 26.

[105] On this point see the powers and jurisdiction of the Special Immigration Appeals Commission, as conferred by the Special Immigration Appeals Commission Act 1997, ss 1 and 2.

in a country that is presumed safe.[106] The government had originally intended that the tribunal's decisions should not be subject to judicial review, but its proposed ouster clause was withdrawn from the Asylum Bill in the face of considerable opposition.[107] The compromise eventually reached means that the Chamber's decisions may be judicially reviewed on the grounds of an error of law, but any challenge must be made within five days of the original decision and only written submissions will be examined.[108] Where a Chamber's decision has already been reconsidered, any further challenge on a point of law lies to the Court of Appeal and can only be made with leave.[109]

The Chamber itself comprises both lawyers and persons with suitable non-legal experience, and the Lord Chancellor is required to appoint a President and at least one Deputy President. It is for the President to determine how many members should hear particular cases or classes of case, having regard to their complexity and other circumstances.

Employment tribunals

Employment tribunals are by far the most important example of 'party and party' tribunals—tribunals with jurisdiction to hear disputes between individuals.[110] One of the issues addressed by Leggatt was whether such tribunals should be linked more closely with the courts, but on balance he concluded that this would not be in the interests of the user:[111]

> There are arguments for . . . keeping party and party [tribunals] separate from those dealing with administrative law. They are the parts of the tribunal system closest in essential function to the ordinary courts. The need for a fundamentally adversarial approach to cases has produced similarities in procedure. There is therefore an argument for party and party tribunals either to be merged with the ordinary courts, or to remain a separate body of tribunals but in a closer relationship with the courts . . . [P]arty and party tribunals are falling behind the modern courts in terms of speed, active case management, the effective conduct of hearings, and even informality. A closer relationship might promote modernisation and further the development of the new civil procedures . . .
>
> Against these arguments should be set the distinctive benefits for the user in having cases decided by tribunals: the opportunities if procedures and hearings are simple and informal enough for users reasonably to expect to handle cases themselves, if properly supported; and better decisions if they are taken jointly by lawyers and experts . . . This has led us to conclude that the features which are common to citizen and state tribunals and

---

[106] 2002 Act, s 94 (as amended). The 2004 Act extends the powers of the Secretary of State in this regard, allowing him to certify that all or part of a country is presumed safe for particular classes of person.

[107] See the discussion of cl 11 at p 332.

[108] 2002 Act, s 103A (inserted by the 2004 Act). Those applying from abroad must do so within twenty-eight days.

[109] Ibid, s 103B.

[110] The Lands Tribunal is another example of a tribunal with 'party and party' jurisdiction.

[111] *Tribunals for Users*, paras 3.18–3.19.

party and party tribunals are much more important than those which divide them. Both should therefore form part of the Tribunals System.

The government accepted the recommendation that party and party tribunals should remain part of the system but, in recognition of their distinctive role, employment tribunals remain as separate entities even after the general structural reforms introduced by the 2007 Act.

First created in 1964, and until 1998 known as industrial tribunals,[112] employment tribunals now have jurisdiction to hear more than eighty different types of complaint. Their jurisdiction includes most claims in damages for breach of an employment contract, along with claims relating to unfair dismissal, unlawful discrimination, and equal pay. Until recently they were administered by an agency of the Department of Trade and Industry, but they have now been integrated with the Tribunals Service.[113]

In common with many other tribunals, employment tribunals comprise both lawyers and expert lay members. The lawyers are now known as 'employment judges',[114] and they must be barristers or solicitors of seven years' standing.[115] The lay members are divided into two panels: one comprising those with experience of representing workers; the other consisting of persons experienced in representing employers' interests.[116] Until recently, members of the lay panels were appointed by the Secretary of State for Trade and Industry, prompting concerns that they were not sufficiently independent of the Minister whose policies they often have to consider.[117] These concerns have now been addressed, and under the current arrangements the wing members of employment tribunals are appointed by the Lord Chancellor in consultation with the Secretary of State for Business, Enterprise and Regulatory Reform.[118] Their conditions of service have also been modified to ensure that they have greater security of tenure.[119] In future, all those who sit on employment tribunals will be selected by the Judicial Appointments Commission.

The system is headed by a President of Employment Tribunals,[120] whose functions include determining the number and location of tribunals, selecting employment judges and lay members for hearings, and sitting as a chairman him or herself.[121] Section 4 of the Employment Tribunals Act 1996[122] provides that cases should normally

---

[112] They were renamed by the Employment Rights (Dispute Resolution) Act 1998, s 1.

[113] See p 291.

[114] Employment Tribunals Act 1996, s 3A—as inserted by the Tribunals, Courts and Enforcement Act 2007.

[115] Employment Tribunals (Constitution and Rules of Procedure) Regulations 2004, SI 2004/1861, reg 8.

[116] Ibid.   [117] See p 186.

[118] The equivalent of what used to be the Secretary of State for Trade and Industry.

[119] See p 186; *Scanfuture v Secretary of State for Trade and Industry* [2001] ICR 1096, [2001] IRLR 416.

[120] For England and Wales. A President of the Scottish Employment Tribunals is also appointed.

[121] Employment Tribunals (Constitution and Rules of Procedure) Regulations 2004, SI 2004/1861, regs 4–9.

[122] This was originally called the Industrial Tribunals Act but was renamed by the Employment Rights (Dispute Resolution) Act 1998.

be heard by an employment judge sitting with two lay members. Regulations[123] further stipulate that one lay member should be drawn from each of the two panels, so that both sides of the industry are represented. Decisions are made by majority, and the chairman may therefore be outvoted if the lay members agree with each other as to the appropriate conclusion. Certain types of case can be determined by a chairman sitting alone,[124] including breach of contract cases and cases concerning the minimum wage. In addition, the parties may consent to *any* case being heard by a chairman sitting alone or with one lay member,[125] although the tribunal can override their wishes if a three-member panel is considered more suitable.[126]

Hearings are conducted in much the same way as in the ordinary civil courts, with rules of evidence generally, although not always, being adhered to.[127] An applicant may appear in person or be represented by counsel, a solicitor, a representative of a trade union or employers' association, or any other person whom he or she desires to represent him or her.[128] Many parties do appear in person, but there is concern that it is becoming increasingly difficult for unrepresented parties to contest cases successfully—particularly where aspects of European or anti-discrimination law are involved.[129] Public funding is not currently available for legal representation at employment tribunals, and an obvious way of assisting users would be to lift this restriction. Such a move would be extremely costly, however,[130] and Leggatt suggested that it would be better to concentrate on improving the informality and accessibility of the system.[131] On the other hand, the nature of employment law is such that the Employment Tribunal Taskforce has doubted whether a less formal and complex system can really be achieved.[132]

Appeals against the decisions of employment tribunals lie to the Employment Appeal Tribunal (EAT) on a point of law. The proportion of cases that are the subject of an appeal to the EAT is very low—around 4 per cent[133]—and this is probably due in part to the number of parties who contest employment cases without the benefit of professional advice.

---

[123] SI 2004/1861, reg 9.   [124] These are set out in s 4(3) of the 1996 Act.

[125] Ibid, s 4(1)(b); s 4(3).

[126] *Sogbetun* v *London Borough of Hackney* [1998] IRLR 676, [1998] ICR 1264.

[127] See the 2004 Regulations: SI 2004/1861. See also, MacMillan, 'Employment Tribunals: Philosophies and Practicalities' (1999) 28(1) ILJ 4.

[128] Employment Tribunals Act 1996, s 6. The right to be represented by a person of one's choosing is unqualified and cannot be restricted by the tribunal: *Bache* v *Essex County Council* [2000] 2 All ER 847.

[129] For a recent study of the experiences of tribunal users, see Adler and Gulland, *Tribunal Users' Experiences, Perceptions and Expectations: A Literature Review* (HMSO, 2003). Earlier research by Genn and Genn suggested that the benefits of representation for the tribunal user were significant: *The Effectiveness of Representation at Tribunals* (HMSO, 1989).

[130] In 2006–07, employment tribunals received 132,577 applications: *Employment Tribunal and EAT Statistics (GB): 1 April 2006—31 March 2007.*

[131] *Tribunals for Users*, chapter on employment tribunals, at para 11.

[132] *Report of the Employment Tribunal Taskforce* (HMSO, 2002), at para 8.25.   [133] Ibid, para 8.47.

The Employment Appeal Tribunal

The Employment Appeal Tribunal (EAT) was established in 1976[134] to hear appeals against the decisions of employment tribunals. It is a superior court of record and has all the characteristics of a court.[135] It comprises a number of judges nominated from the High Court and the Court of Appeal, at least one judge from Scotland's Court of Session, and such other lay members as may be appointed.[136] One of the judges is appointed President. The lay members are persons with special knowledge or experience of industrial relations, and they hold the highest judicial office available to a person without legal qualifications. The EAT is duly constituted when sitting with a judge and either two or four lay members.[137] As with employment tribunals, the lay members must be drawn in equal numbers from panels representing both sides of industry.

Senior barristers have sometimes been used as part-time EAT judges, but this practice was called into question when a barrister appeared as an advocate before lay members with whom he had sat in a judicial capacity. The claimant complained that this situation gave rise to a real possibility of bias, and the EAT agreed that his appeal should be heard by a differently constituted tribunal. The issue of principle was eventually referred to the House of Lords,[138] which held that for a judge to appear as an advocate under these circumstances would be contrary to both the common law and the ECHR right to a fair trial:[139]

> Would...an observer consider that it was reasonably possible that the wing member[s] may be subconsciously biased? The observer is likely to approach the matter on the basis that the lay members look to the judge for guidance on the law, and can be expected to develop a fairly close relationship of trust and confidence with the judge.[140]

Their Lordships noted that the chairmen of employment tribunals were not permitted to appear as advocates before other tribunals in the same region, and they recommended that the EAT should adopt the same policy. Following this decision, it was announced that the practice of allowing barristers to sit as part-time EAT judges would be phased out.

The EAT's rules of procedure[141] aim at informality: no one appears robed, there is no bench or witness box, and parties and their advisers sit at tables and address the

---

[134] Employment Protection Act 1975, s 87. Its predecessor, the National Industrial Relations Court, was established under the Industrial Relations Act 1971 and abolished after only three years.

[135] It can only punish for contempt with the consent of one of its judicial members: Employment Tribunals Act 1996, s 36.

[136] Employment Tribunals Act 1996, s 22.

[137] Ibid, s 28. With the consent of the parties, cases may be heard by a judge and either one or three other members.

[138] *Lawal* v *Northern Spirit* [2003] UKHL 35, [2004] 1 All ER 187, [2003] ICR 856.

[139] ECHR, Article 6: see p 191.

[140] [2003] UKHL 35 at [21], [2004] 1 All ER 187 at [21], *per* Lord Steyn.

[141] Employment Appeal Tribunal Rules 1993, SI 1993/2854; Employment Appeal Tribunal (Amendment) Rules 2001, SI 2001/1128; Employment Appeal Tribunal (Amendment) Rules 2004, SI 2004/2526;

court seated. In most other respects, however, EAT hearings are very similar to those found in the ordinary courts. A party may appear in person or may be represented by counsel, a solicitor, a representative of a trade union or employers' association, or any other person whom he or she desires to represent him or her.[142] Although employment tribunals are not covered by the Community Legal Service scheme, eligible persons can apply for public funding for representation at EAT hearings. Any decision of the EAT on a question of fact is final, and as a superior court of record, its decisions are not subject to the High Court's supervisory jurisdiction.[143] Any appeal on a point of law lies to the Court of Appeal.[144] As with employment tribunals, the EAT is administered by the new Tribunals Service.[145]

Domestic tribunals

A number of private and professional associations have set up their own bodies for resolving disputes between their members and enforcing internal discipline. As these bodies are concerned with matters of private rather than public importance, they are often referred to as 'domestic tribunals'. Their jurisdiction is based primarily on contract: by becoming a member of the association or professional body concerned, a person contracts to accept the jurisdiction of its governing tribunal. Nevertheless, in several cases these tribunals exist on a statutory basis with a right of appeal to the courts. Examples of domestic tribunals constituted under statute are the Solicitors Disciplinary Tribunal[146] and the Investigation Committee of the General Medical Council.[147] Examples of tribunals created by private bodies themselves include the Disciplinary Tribunal of the Bar[148] and the Football Association's Disciplinary Committee. The decisions of a non-statutory tribunal cannot be the subject of an appeal to the ordinary courts, and they will not be amenable to judicial review unless the tribunal concerned is a public body performing public functions.[149] It may, however, be possible to mount a legal challenge using some other means: this is considered in more detail below.

Employment Appeal Tribunal (Amendment) Rules 2005, SI 2005/1871; *Practice Direction (EAT: Appeal Procedure)* [2005] IRLR 94.

[142] Employment Tribunals Act 1996, s 29.   [143] See p 256.   [144] 1996 Act, s 37.
[145] See p 291.   [146] Solicitors Act 1974, s 46: see p 398.
[147] Medical Act 1983, s 1(3), as amended.   [148] See p 399.
[149] *Law* v *National Greyhound Racing Club* [1983] 3 All ER 300, [1983] 1 WLR 1302; *R* v *Disciplinary Committee of the Jockey Club, ex parte the Aga Khan* [1993] 2 All ER 853, [1993] 1 WLR 909. The relevant test was established in *R* v *Panel on Take-overs and Mergers, ex parte Datafin plc* [1987] QB 815, [1987] 1 All ER 564. In *R* v *General Council of the Bar, ex parte Percival* [1991] 1 QB 212, [1990] 3 All ER 137, a decision of the Bar Council's Professional Conduct Committee was held to be judicially reviewable.

Control of tribunals by the courts

Appeals from tribunals

There is no right to appeal against the decision of a tribunal at common law, but in some cases a right to appeal on a point of law is provided by statute. The Tribunals and Inquiries Act 1992 establishes a statutory right to appeal to the High Court[150] against the decisions of a number of tribunals. In addition, the EAT is a rare example of a tribunal from which an appeal to the Court of Appeal is currently possible.[151]

The new structure under the 2007 Act has created a coherent appeals system. The Upper Tribunal[152] serves as an appellate body for the rest of the system. There is a general right to appeal from the First-tier to the Upper Tribunal on a point of law, although this right may be excluded by the Lord Chancellor in relation to particular categories of case.[153] Any further appeal lies to the Court of Appeal, and requires the permission of either this court or the Upper Tribunal.[154] Appeals are generally limited to cases that raise important points of principle or practice, or which are justified by other compelling reasons.[155]

Supervisory control

Administrative and 'party and party' tribunals are public bodies performing public functions, and they are amenable to the High Court's supervisory jurisdiction in the same way as the inferior courts. This common law jurisdiction provides a basis for challenging decisions that have been made ultra vires or that are contrary to principles of natural justice. It is usually exercised by issuing one of the prerogative orders[156] in an application for judicial review, although these remedies are not available in respect of bodies whose functions are essentially private in nature.

The supervisory role of the courts over tribunals is, however, slightly more complicated. The prerogative orders[157] have never been applied to control the actions of superior courts. In *R (on the application of Cart and others)* v *Special Immigration Appeal Commission, Upper Tribunals and others*,[158] the Administrative Court considered the argument that the decisions of the Special Immigration Appeal Commission (SIAC), and of the Upper Tribunal, were amenable to challenge by the Administrative Court. Each had been designated as a 'superior court' by the relevant legislation. However, that designation was, said Laws LJ, not determinative of the matter: the characteristics of each body had to be considered to determine whether the protection against

---

[150] Section 11. These appeals are heard by a Divisional Court of the Queen's Bench Division.
[151] Employment Tribunals Act 1996, s 37.   [152] See p 295.
[153] Tribunals, Courts and Enforcement Act 2007, s 11.   [154] Ibid, s 13.
[155] Ibid, s 13(6); *Transforming Public Services* (HMSO, 2004), at para 178.
[156] Mandatory orders, prohibiting orders and quashing orders. Declarations and injunctions are other possible remedies.
[157] Formerly known as prerogative writs.   [158] [2009] EWHC 1352 (Admin).

judicial review traditionally granted to superior courts, extended to these, or other bodies. In relation to the SIAC, its actions were subject to judicial review in so far as it was acting outside its jurisdiction:[159] the fact that it is designated as a 'superior court' and that the presiding judge is of High Court status was not decisive. The question was to be resolved by looking at previous structures, and whether the jurisdiction was limited.

> Some courts are liable to judicial review and some are not, in most cases because some courts possess only a limited jurisdiction and some do not. Unreviewable courts of limited jurisdiction are exceptional. It is true that beneath this apparently simple position there lie some taxing complexities; however the considerations I have here set out are sufficient to refute the defendants' reliance on [statute] excluding the judicial review jurisdiction by force of the legislation's reference to 'superior court of record'. The books demonstrate that despite the usage in some of the cases, this expression cannot be taken to delineate, in principle, those courts which are immune from judicial review writs have not run to superior courts of record and indeed that the expression 'superior courts of record' has consistently been used by judges and commentators to refer to courts not amenable to the writs. Does it follow that the bare designation by Parliament of an institution as such a court... excludes the jurisdiction? I think not.

By contrast the Upper Tribunal was immune from judicial review in most circumstances. Laws LJ stated the reasons for this as follows:

> UT is at the apex of a new and comprehensive judicial structure designed to rationalise and re-organise in a single system the means of adjudication for a multitude of claims previously determined by a variety of disparate tribunals with no common appeal mechanism. Though it is not a court of unlimited jurisdiction, being of course confined to what TCEA gives it, its jurisdiction is very wide. Subject to the fact that some tribunals presently remain outside the fold, it may be said to be an appeal court of general jurisdiction in relation to matters which are consigned to adjudication at first instance by statutory tribunals... In addition [it] possesses a jurisdiction itself to grant judicial review applying the same principles and granting the same relief as the High Court.

This judicial review jurisdiction is created by the Tribunals, Courts and Enforcement Act 2007. It makes provision for the Upper Tribunal to exercise a limited judicial review jurisdiction.[160] However, this jurisdiction will only apply to categories of case specified in directions made by the Lord Chief Justice, and to individual cases transferred by the High Court or Court of Session.[161] A further limitation is that only judges of the High Court, Court of Session, and Court of Appeal are able to hear such 'judicial review' cases.[162]

---

[159] Which includes any fundamental error of law: see *Anisminic v Foreign Compensation Commission* [1969] 2 AC147.
[160] 2007 Act, s 15.   [161] Ibid, ss 18(6), 19 and 20.   [162] Ibid, s 18(8).

KEY ISSUE

The pre-existing arrangements for appeals and review were illogical and incoherent, reflecting the piecemeal historical development of the tribunal system. Appeals routes from first instance tribunals in England and Wales varied between specialized tribunals, the High Court (Administrative Court or Chancery Division), and the Court of Appeal. In some cases there was no statutory right of appeal, but judicial review provided an alternative remedy in the Administrative Court; or judicial review might be required to fill the gaps in a restricted statutory scheme. There were similar variations in the form and nature of the appeal, for example: whether on law only, or on law and fact; whether leave is required; and whether the procedure is primarily oral or written.

The creation of the Upper Tribunal has provided the opportunity not only to rationalize the procedures, but also to establish a strong and dedicated appellate body at the head of the new system. Its authority derives from its specialist skills and its status as a superior court of record, with judicial review powers, presided over by the Senior President.

? Questions

1. What is the significance of the Upper Tribunal having judicial review powers?

2. Do you think the decisions of the Upper Chamber should be judicially reviewable?

3. Why, if Parliament has characterized a body as a 'superior court', does the nature of the jurisdiction matter (as Laws LJ suggested)?

Challenging the decisions of 'private' disciplinary bodies

Few domestic tribunals have public functions, and most derive their authority from a contractual relationship with those under their supervision. The decisions of these private bodies cannot be the subject of a prerogative order,[163] but the courts still have jurisdiction to determine whether they have been made fairly and in accordance with natural justice. The High Court has shown an increased willingness to intervene in the affairs of bodies that can deprive individuals of their livelihoods, and an aggrieved party may be able to challenge a decision by seeking a declaration or injunction.[164] Thus, in *Korda* v *International Tennis Federation*,[165] the court granted a declaration as to the correct interpretation of the Federation's rules. The defendant's disciplinary committee had sanctioned the claimant for a breach of its anti-doping policy, but a dispute arose concerning the circumstances in which the defendant could refer the matter to the Court of Arbitration in Sport. On this occasion the issue was resolved

---

[163] In *R* v *Football Association Ltd, ex parte Football League Ltd* [1993] 2 All ER 833, it was held that the FA was not susceptible to judicial review because it was a private body deriving its authority from a contractual relationship.

[164] In *Nagle* v *Feilden* [1966] 2 QB 633, [1966] 1 All ER 689, the Court of Appeal held that a person had an arguable right not to be arbitrarily excluded from his chosen profession by a governing body. See also: *Bonsor* v *Musicians Union* [1956] AC 104, [1955] 3 All ER 518.

[165] (1999) The Independent, 21 April.

in the defendant's favour: the Court of Appeal found that the rules allowed the Federation to appeal against the decision on the grounds that it was too lenient.

In the absence of an express contractual relationship, the courts may be prepared to find the existence of an *implied* contract between the parties and then to make a ruling as to its terms. In *Modahl v British Athletic Foundation Ltd (No 2)*,[166] the claimant failed a dope test and was banned from competing in events recognized by her sport's governing body. She successfully challenged the ban by using the defendant's own appeals process, but then commenced a civil action for damages. On appeal from the Queen's Bench Division, the Court of Appeal held that the claimant had an implied contract with the defendant, which derived from her participation in the defendant's events and her submission to its disciplinary rules and procedures. The Court of Appeal found that the defendant had not failed in its contractual obligation to provide a fair disciplinary process, and the action was therefore unsuccessful. Nevertheless, this decision demonstrates that that there is at least a theoretical possibility of a civil remedy being awarded in such circumstances.

Inquiries

Inquiries are established for the purpose of investigating specific issues and their role is one of fact-finding rather than adjudication. They are not generally required to adhere to strict rules of evidence[167] and the courts are slow to interfere with their decisions in the absence of a clear breach of natural justice:[168]

> In determining what is relevant to [an] inquiry, regard must be had to its investigatory character. Where broad terms of reference are given to it, as in this case, the [inquiry] is not determining issues between parties but conducting a thorough investigation into the subject matter. It may have to follow leads. It is not bound by rules of evidence. There is no set order in which evidence must be adduced... If [the inquiry] bona fide seeks to establish a relevant connection between certain facts and the subject matter of the inquiry, it should not be regarded as outside its term of reference by doing so...
>
> [A] court... should be very slow to restrain [an inquiry] from pursuing a particular line of questioning and should not do so unless it is satisfied... [that it] is going off on a frolic of its own.

Statutory inquiries

Some statutes require a Minister or public authority to hold an inquiry before a particular type of decision can be taken. These 'statutory inquiries' are covered by the Tribunals and Inquiries Act 1992 and may be the subject of procedural rules made

---

[166] [2001] EWCA Civ 1447, [2002] 1 WLR 1192.

[167] See *Bushell v Secretary of State for the Environment* [1981] AC 75, [1980] 3 WLR 22.

[168] *Ross v Costigan* (1982) 41 ALR 319 at 334–5, *per* Ellicott J; cited with approval by Lord Walker in *Mount Murray Country Club Ltd v MacLeod* [2003] UKPC 53 at [28], The Times, 7 July.

pursuant to section 9 of that Act. Inquiries held at a Minister's discretion will also be subject to the Act if they are designated as statutory inquiries by the Lord Chancellor.[169] Statutory inquiries are an integral part of town and country planning, compulsory purchase, and highways development schemes.[170] They are conducted by inspectors and are usually triggered when objections are lodged against the decisions of public authorities.

The conduct of a statutory inquiry will be governed by the statute under which it is held, although the inspector will often be left with considerable discretion. Any rights of appeal will also be governed by the particular statutory scheme and will usually be restricted to points of law. An aggrieved party may, however, have recourse to judicial review.[171]

Tribunals of inquiry

Some inquiries are instigated by Ministers for the purposes of investigating specific events or issues of public concern. A recent consultation paper described the rationale for such inquiries as follows:[172]

> There has been a long standing practice in the UK of setting up formal and open inquiries, where necessary, to look into matters that have caused public concern. Ministers are not under any statutory duty to set up such inquiries, but have found them to be a useful method of dealing with matters that have warranted formal, independent investigation.

Inquiries of this nature can fall into one of three categories, as follows.

Inquiries instigated by Ministers acting under specific statutory provisions

An example of a provision conferring the power to order such an inquiry is section 49 of the Police Act 1996. This has enabled Home Secretaries to instigate local inquiries into matters connected with the policing of an area.[173] Sir William MacPherson's inquiry into the racially motivated killing of Stephen Lawrence is a striking example of an inquiry ordered under this provision.[174] The police had investigated certain individuals in relation to the killing, but the Crown Prosecution Service had declined to prosecute because of a lack of evidence. A private prosecution brought by the victim's family was thrown out by the judge for the same reason. The scope of the inquiry was limited to an examination of alleged failings in the police investigation. Attempts to question those suspected of the killing in order to establish their guilt were successfully challenged in the Divisional Court, and it was made clear that the inquiry was not a proper forum for conducting a murder trial.[175]

---

[169] Section 16(1).   [170] See, e.g., the Town and Country Planning Act 1990.
[171] See Chapter 7.
[172] DCA, *Effective Inquiries* (HMSO, 2004) CP 12/04 at p 7.
[173] Such inquiries fall within the scope of the Inquiries Act 2005, which repeals section 49.
[174] *Inquiry into the Death of Stephen Lawrence*, 1997–98.
[175] *R v Chairman of Stephen Lawrence Inquiry, ex parte A* (1988) The Times, 25 July.

The inquiry into the Southall rail accident in 1997 is another example of an inquiry set up under subject-specific legislation. The statutory basis for this inquiry was section 14 of the Health and Safety at Work etc. Act 1974.

Inquiries established under the Inquiries Act 2005[176]

The Inquiries Act 2005 provides a framework under which a Minister can establish an inquiry into events that have caused public concern. The procedures adopted by such an inquiry are for the chairman to determine, but the Act confers specific powers to compel the production of documents, to summon witnesses, and to receive evidence on oath.[177] Inquiries that are subject to the Act must generally sit in public and the proceedings may be broadcast or recorded at the chairman's discretion.[178] However, the chairman also has a discretion to restrict publicity if he considers this to be conducive to the inquiry or in the wider public interest.[179]

The predecessor to the 2005 Act—the Tribunals of Inquiry (Evidence) Act 1921—was rarely used,[180] and its procedures were usually reserved for inquires into allegations of misconduct on the part of public authorities. The second Bloody Sunday Inquiry is a notable example: the Saville Report was published in 2010, almost twelve years since the establishment of the inquiry, with a cost estimated to be of the order of £400 million. In 1966 the Royal Commission on Tribunals of Inquiry[181] made a number of recommendations regarding inquiries under the 1921 Act. In particular, it recommended that any person affected by allegations against him should have the right to be legally represented and to cross-examine witnesses, and that any testimony given by such a person should not be admissible as evidence in subsequent criminal or civil proceedings.[182] It also recommended that the facts should be presented to the inquiry panel by independent counsel. To date none of these recommendations have been adopted, and the extent to which cross-examination and legal representation are permitted is still a matter for individual inquiry chairmen.[183]

Non-statutory inquiries

Some inquiries are established on a non-statutory basis, which means that they lack any formal powers of investigation and can only be effective to the extent that those involved are willing to cooperate. Inquiries that could have national security implications or cause political embarrassment are often conducted in this way. They

[176] For a discussion, see: Requa, 'Truth, Transition and the Inquiries Act 2005' [2007] EHRLR 404; Quane, 'Challenging the Report of an Independent Inquiry under the Human Rights Act' [2007] PL 529.
[177] Sections 17 and 21. [178] Section 18. [179] Section 19.
[180] See Winetrobe, 'Inquiries after Scott: The Return of the Tribunal of Inquiry' [1997] PL 18.
[181] Cmnd 3121. The Commission was chaired by Lord Justice Salmon.
[182] Similar recommendations have been made with regard to testimony given in coroners' courts: see p 273.
[183] For an argument that there is already a presumption in favour of allowing legal representation, see Willmott, 'A Presumption of Legal Representation at Judicial Inquiries' (2003) 12(2) Nott LJ 34. Note also that section 40 of the new Act allows chairmen to award payments of 'reasonable amounts' to witnesses, including awards in respect of legal representation.

are usually chaired by senior judges and may sit in private, although their findings are generally made public. A good example of a non-statutory inquiry was the inquiry into the export of arms to Iraq in breach of international embargoes.[184] It was established when several prosecutions collapsed amid allegations that ministers had turned a blind eye to the illegal trade and that the businessmen involved had spied for the security services. The inquiry was chaired by Sir Richard Scott and took four years to complete. Its five-volume report criticized both ministers and officials, and generated a considerable amount of academic literature.[185]

The Hutton inquiry into the circumstances surrounding the death of Dr David Kelly was also conducted on a non-statutory basis.[186] The government had published an intelligence dossier on Iraq shortly before the second Gulf War, and a journalist made a number of highly critical statements about the dossier in an item broadcast on BBC radio. Dr Kelly was a government scientist and he later admitted to officials in the Defence Department that he had been the journalist's 'anonymous' source. He then found himself at the centre of a very public row between the BBC and the government, and he apparently took his own life after his identity was revealed by the media. Lord Hutton's inquiry was highly critical of both the BBC and its journalist, but the government's handling of the incident was largely vindicated. This prompted concerns that the credibility of public inquiries was being undermined, with some suggesting that Lord Hutton had interpreted his terms of reference too narrowly and failed to address the real issues. In the aftermath of the Hutton Report, the government established a further inquiry into the intelligence upon which it based its controversial dossier and its subsequent decision to go to war with Iraq. The inquiry was conducted by Privy Councillors under the chairmanship of Lord Butler and it reported in July 2004.[187]

A common criticism of non-statutory inquiries is that although their main function is to investigate concerns about government action, they can only be instigated by ministers. Moreover, it is for the Minister instigating an inquiry to appoint its chair and determine its terms of reference. As a matter of law, however, there is nothing to prevent a member of the public from setting up his or her own inquiry and finding someone to chair it: the real issue is whether anyone outside the government would be able to fund one and to persuade the relevant people to participate.

KEY ISSUE

The Saville inquiry raises fundamental issues about the purpose of inquiries and whether they are always an appropriate was of proceeding. With the time taken to investigate

---

[184] *Inquiry into the Export of Defence Equipment and Dual-Use Goods to Iraq* (HMSO, 1996).

[185] See, e.g., Blom-Cooper, 'Witnesses and the Scott Inquiry' [1994] PL 1; Howe, 'Procedure at the Scott Inquiry' [1996] PL 445; Leigh and Lustgarten, 'Five Volumes in Search of Accountability: The Scott Report' (1996) 59(5) MLR 695; Scott, 'Procedures at Inquiries: The Duty to be Fair' (1995) 111 LQR 596.

[186] It reported in January 2004: see Blom-Cooper and Munro, 'The Hutton Inquiry' [2004] PL 472; Lord Hutton, 'The Media Reaction to the Hutton Report' [2006] PL 807.

[187] *Review of Intelligence on Weapons of Mass Destruction*, HC Paper 898 (HMSO, 2004).

and report being almost twelve years and costs of the order of £400 million, the question is whether the way in which the inquiry proceeded was appropriate or the right way of proceeding. The report itself addressed the issue of costs:

> Despite the use of information technology, the Inquiry has been lengthy and costly. Many factors have contributed to this. The fact that the scope of the Inquiry could not in our view be limited to the few minutes during which people were killed and wounded on Bloody Sunday and our need to hear almost 1,000 witnesses and read the statements of another 1,500 were two of the factors, to which was added the vast amount of documentary and other material relevant to Bloody Sunday. Other factors included the separate representation of various interest groups where we were persuaded that this was required in the interests of justice; and the requirement to redact countless documents to ensure anonymity. In addition, the Tribunal had to deal with many public interest immunity applications and applications that the Tribunal should not order the disclosure of journalists' sources of information. There were various judicial reviews and some subsequent appeals. The length and cost of the Inquiry was further increased by moving the sittings from Londonderry to London and back to Londonderry, in consequence of an order by the Court of Appeal.

This inquiry was, of course, of a wholly exceptional nature, and held for a variety of reasons, mostly of a political nature. However, it does show the difficulty that an inquiry process can encounter.

❓ Questions

1. Do you think that the holding of statutory or non-statutory inquiries is a useful way of dealing with controversial issues?
2. Does the inquiry process involve the judiciary in matters in which they should not be involved?
3. How should inquiries be streamlined (if at all)?

Further reading

CARNWATH, 'Tribunal Justice: A New Start' [2009] PL 48

DEPARTMENT FOR CONSTITUTIONAL AFFAIRS, *Transforming Public Services: Complaints, Redress and Tribunals*, Cm 6243 (HMSO, 2004)

LEGGATT, *Tribunals for Users: One System, One Service—Report of the Review of Tribunals* (HMSO, 2001)

MINISTRY OF JUSTICE, *Transforming Tribunals: Implementing Part 1 of the Tribunals, Courts and Enforcement Act 2007* (HMSO, 2007) CP 30/07

QUANE, 'Challenging the Report of an Independent Inquiry under the Human Rights Act' [2007] PL 5

WINETROBE, 'Inquiries after Scott: The Return of the Tribunal of Inquiry' [1997] PL 18

9

The Judiciary[1]

INTRODUCTION

The focus in this chapter is on the judiciary and its functions. Judges clearly have a central role in the legal system, being responsible for everything from the determination of disputed points of law to decisions on remedies and punishments. Above all else they have a duty to ensure the fair administration of justice in their courts, and if they are to discharge this duty effectively, they must not only be competent, but also fair, impartial and independent. The underlying theme of this chapter will be to examine how these qualities are ensured, and the following areas will be considered:

- the judicial hierarchy and the different jurisdictions of each judicial rank;
- the role of the Lord Chief Justice and other senior judges, and changes to the law that have removed the judicial functions of the Lord Chancellor;
- the nature of the judicial function in relation to both statute and common law, and the extent to which some judges also have an administrative role;
- the constitutional position of judges and the way in which this is evolving;
- the judicial appointments system and the rules governing eligibility for judicial office;
- diversity within the judiciary;
- the importance of judicial independence and security of tenure.

The judicial hierarchy

The twelve Justices of the Supreme Court are the most senior judges in the United Kingdom. Following the implementation of the Constitutional Reform Act 2005, they superseded the Lords of Appeal in Ordinary who sat in the judicial committee of the House of Lords. Unlike the Law Lords, the Justices of the Supreme Court do not sit in Parliament.

---

[1] See generally: Pannick, *Judges* (OUP, 1987); Griffith, *The Politics of the Judiciary* (Fontana: 5th edn, 1997); Malleson, *The New Judiciary: The Effects of Expansion and Activism* (Ashgate Press, 1999); Stevens, *The English Judges: Their Role in the Changing Constitution* (Hart Publishing, 2002).

Next in order of seniority are the thirty-seven Lord (and Lady) Justices of Appeal.[2] Along with a number of *ex officio* members they are the permanent Court of Appeal judges, and they also sit in the Court Martial Appeal Court and Employment Appeal Tribunal. They can even be asked to hear High Court, Crown Court, and county court cases, although it is very rare in practice to find such a senior judge sitting below High Court level.[3]

Next in line are the 106 full-time High Court judges or 'puisne judges'. All puisne judges have jurisdiction to sit anywhere in the High Court, although in practice each judge is assigned to a particular division.[4] Puisne judges also hear the most serious types of Crown Court case,[5] and frequently sit alongside Lord and Lady Justices in the Court of Appeal—usually in the Criminal Division. Deputy High Court judges are also appointed, and they exercise the same jurisdiction as their full-time counterparts.

Circuit judges and their deputies carry out the majority of Crown Court work,[6] and in 2005 they accounted for 76 per cent of all sitting days in this court. However, they are also responsible for around a quarter of sitting days in the county courts, and a similar proportion of High Court work. They can even sit in the Criminal Division of the Court of Appeal if called upon, and actually did so in approximately 4 per cent of the Division's cases in 2005.[7] Circuit judges are assisted in both their criminal and civil work by deputy circuit judges and recorders, although these judges do not have jurisdiction to sit in the Court of Appeal.

District judges and deputy district judges are responsible for most county court business,[8] in addition to hearing a small number of cases in the High Court. Finally, there are the district judges (magistrates' courts) and their deputies.[9] These judges were formerly known as stipendiary magistrates and, as the name indicates, they have jurisdiction to sit as justices of the peace in magistrates' courts.[10]

Specific judicial offices

The Lord Chancellor

Historically, the highest judicial office in the United Kingdom was that of Lord Chancellor, and the holder of this office was the most senior member of the Appellate Committee of the House of Lords. He was also an *ex officio* member of the Court of

---

[2] See p 249. The title 'Lady Justice' has been officially recognized since January 2004: Supreme Court Act 1981, s 2(3), as amended by the Courts Act 2003, s 63(1). The Court of Appeal's first female judge was originally referred to by the masculine title.

[3] In 2005, Lord and Lady Justices of Appeal collectively sat 250 days in the High Court, accounting for 2 per cent of all High Court sitting days. They did not sit in the Crown Court at all during this period, and they accounted for less than 1 per cent of county court sitting days: *Judicial Statistics 2005*, at pp 133–5.

[4] See p 253. The maximum possible number of such judges is currently 108.   [5] See p 224.

[6] Ibid. Section 151(4) of the Supreme Court Act 1981 provides that unless the context requires otherwise, a reference to a judge of the Supreme Court shall not include a reference to a judge of the Crown Court.

[7] Supreme Court Act 1981, s 9; *Judicial Statistics 2005*, at pp 134–5.

[8] See p 258.   [9] See p 260.

[10] They were renamed by the Access to Justice Act 1999, s 78: see p 265.

Appeal, head of the High Court's Chancery Division, 'speaker' of the House of Lords, and a Cabinet Minister. He was therefore a member of the judicial, legislative, *and* executive branches of the state, giving him a unique position within the constitution. However, his executive role always meant that he did not have the security of tenure enjoyed by other judges and, to this day, he can be replaced at the whim of the Prime Minister in the same way as any other member of government.[11]

In June 2003, the government announced plans to abolish the office of Lord Chancellor in order to achieve a more formal separation of powers.[12] The intention was to transfer the Lord Chancellor's ministerial functions to the new office of Secretary of State for Constitutional Affairs, leaving his judicial functions to be performed by the Lord Chief Justice. Lord Falconer was given the task of implementing the changes, and he was simultaneously appointed as both Lord Chancellor and Secretary of State. There was, however, widespread criticism that the government had not consulted senior judges before making the announcement, and many felt that it had underestimated the implications of its decision.[13] The Lord Chief Justice was among those to express his concerns:[14]

> [T]he announcement of 12 June...clearly indicated an extraordinary lack of appreciation of the significance of what was being proposed. This was followed...without consultation, by the transfer of the Court Service from the Lord Chancellor to the Secretary of State for Constitutional Affairs. This last action could well have been due to oversight but it demonstrates there is a lack of appreciation of the significance of the independence of the judiciary in the corridors of government.

Several weeks *after* announcing its intentions, the government did publish a consultation paper.[15] The Lord Chief Justice was ultimately persuaded of the need for reform and, on behalf of the judiciary, he negotiated a lengthy Concordat with the Secretary of State.[16] This document was intended as a blueprint for the future relationship between the courts and the government, and the subsequent Constitutional Reform Bill broadly reflected its contents. The Lord Chief Justice later said that if the Concordat were accepted in its entirety, it would be 'a highly satisfactory outcome',[17] but not everyone was convinced that change was necessary. Many in the House of Lords felt that abolishing the Lord Chancellor's office would *damage*

---

[11] In June 2003, for example, Lord Falconer was appointed Lord Chancellor when it became clear that his predecessor, Lord Irvine, did not support the government's plans for constitutional reform.

[12] For other aspects of the reform package, see p 246.

[13] See Stevens, 'Reform in Haste and Repent at Leisure: Iolanthe, the Lord High Executioner and *Brave New World*' (2004) 24 LS 1.

[14] Lord Woolf, 'The Rule of Law and a Change in the Constitution' (2004) 63(2) CLJ 317, at 323.

[15] DCA, *Constitutional Reform: Reforming the Office of the Lord Chancellor* (HMSO, 2003) CP 13/03.

[16] DCA, *The Lord Chancellor's Judiciary-Related Functions: Proposals* (HMSO, 2004). The document is widely referred to as 'the Concordat'.

[17] 'The Rule of Law and a Change in the Constitution' (2004) 63(2) CLJ 317 at 325.

judicial independence rather than enhance it, and these sentiments were echoed by the Judges' Council:[18]

> The office has played a critical role in binding together the three arms of the State: the legislature, the executive and the judiciary. The office is a key pillar of the constitution. If it had not been for the office of Lord Chancellor, it is doubtful whether this country would have managed without a formal written constitution. The Lord Chancellor's wide range of responsibilities, including those of a Cabinet Minister with major responsibilities for the administration of justice, has resulted in him being a cohesive force. As Head of the Judiciary he has been able to represent the judiciary at the highest level within govern-ment... [he] has been the constitutional link between The Queen and the judiciary.

In the end, the Judges' Council did not oppose the proposals, but many in the House of Lords did. By the time the Bill reached the House of Commons it had already been significantly amended: instead of abolishing the office of Lord Chancellor, Part 2 of what is now the Constitutional Reform Act 2005 provided for it to continue in a mod-ified form. As a consequence, the Lord Chancellor no longer has any judicial func-tions, but he has retained his role as a member of Parliament and Cabinet Minister. The latter role was effectively expanded with the creation of a Ministry of Justice in May 2007, and the holder of the office of Lord Chancellor now holds the addi-tional title of Secretary of State for Justice.[19] The 2005 Act also paved the way for Lord Chancellors to be appointed from the House of Commons rather than the House of Lords, and in June 2007 Jack Straw became the first Lord Chancellor in history to be appointed from the Commons benches. The Lord Chancellor is still respon-sible for overseeing the administration of most major courts,[20] and for appointing Court Rule Committees,[21] allowing or disallowing Court Rules,[22] overseeing judicial appointments,[23] and overseeing the funding of legal services.[24] He is not, however, eligible to sit in any court.

The Lord Chief Justice and other senior posts

The Lord Chief Justice is President of the Courts of England and Wales,[25] President of the Criminal Division of the Court of Appeal, and, following the decision to end the judicial role of the Lord Chancellor, the country's most senior judge. His office entitles him to sit in any of the ordinary courts in the jurisdiction[26] and it carries with it a number of responsibilities. These include overseeing the arrangements for judi-cial education,[27] supervising the deployment of judges and allocating work within the

---

[18] *Judges' Council Response to the Consultation Papers on Constitutional Reform*, at para 21. The Response is available online at **www.dca.gov.uk/judicial/pdfs/jcresp.pdf**

[19] The post of Secretary of State for Constitutional Affairs was discontinued. See further, p 246.

[20] With the exception of the Appellate Committee of the House of Lords: Courts Act 2003, s 1.

[21] See p 231.   [22] Constitutional Reform Act 2005, s 12; Sch 1.

[23] See p 337.   [24] See p 394.

[25] A post created by the Constitutional Reform Act 2005, s 7(1).

[26] Ibid, s 7(3); (4).   [27] Ibid, s 7(2)(b).

courts,[28] issuing Practice Directions (with the concurrence of the Lord Chancellor),[29] and representing the judiciary's views to Parliament and the government.[30]

The other Heads of Division are the Master of the Rolls (who heads the Civil Division of the Court of Appeal), the Chancellor of the High Court,[31] the President of the Queen's Bench Division, and the President of the Family Division. Other senior posts include those of Head and Deputy Head of Civil Justice,[32] Head and Deputy Head of Criminal Justice, Head and Deputy Head of Family Justice, and President and Deputy President of the Supreme Court.[33] The role of the President of the Upper Tribunal should also be noted.[34]

KEY ISSUE

The changes made to the office of Lord Chancellor were both necessary, in terms of judicial independence, compliance with Article 6 of the European Convention and, probably, desirable changes in their own right enhancing the separation of powers. However, the way in which those changes were announced and carried into effect raises real issues as to how fundamental change can be made with little safeguards against the use of legislative power by a government with a strong parliamentary majority. A case exists for more formal safeguards through constitutional change to ensure the independence of the judicial function against executive encroachment.

❓ Questions

1. What safeguards do you think could, or should, be put in place to prevent executive interference with judicial structures and functions?

2. Do you think the changes made to the office of Lord Chancellor were necessary?

3. The Law Lords (now the Justices of the Supreme Court) no longer sit in the House of Lords in its legislative capacity. Is that a good thing? What might have been lost?

The judicial function

Most of the judges' work is 'judicial', in the sense that they have to adjudicate upon disputes. This means that they must deduce the facts from the evidence presented in court, and apply the law to the facts so that they can give the 'right decision'. Appellate

---

[28] Ibid, s 7(2)(c).   [29] Ibid, s 13; Sch 2.   [30] Ibid, ss 5(1); 7(2)(a).

[31] Formerly known as 'the Vice-Chancellor'. His new title and the formalization of his *de facto* role as Head of the High Court's Chancery Division were brought about by the Constitutional Reform Act 2005: Sch 4, para 115.

[32] Created by the Courts Act 2003, s 62. The current Head of Civil Justice is the Master of the Rolls.

[33] Constitutional Reform Act 2005, ss 8, 9, and 24. The post of Head of Criminal Justice is to be held by the Lord Chief Justice or a person appointed by him: at the time of writing it was held by the President of the Queen's Bench Division. The President of the Family Division is *ex officio* Head of Family Justice.

[34] See p 297.

courts have repeatedly pointed out that the judicial function goes no further than this, and that a court has no duty to seek out some 'independent truth'. Thus:[35] 'If [a] decision has been in accordance with the available evidence and with the law, justice will have been fairly done.' Having found the facts, a judge must apply the existing legal rules to those facts. This function has two elements: (a) the interpretation and construction of statutes; and (b) the application of precedent.

Statutes

Where a case concerns a rule of statute law, the judge's task is to ascertain the intention of the legislature. Different approaches to this task have already been identified,[36] but the traditional view is that judges must interpret statutes in accordance with the literal meaning of the words used.[37] However, strict adherence to this rule is not always possible: the law being considered may be uncertain or ambiguous, and the Act may not provide for the circumstances in question. Judges must create new law in such cases, and this obviously raises questions about the limits of the judicial function. Most would accept that the role of the courts is to decide questions of law, and not to impinge upon the right of the executive to make and apply policy.[38] Yet deciding where this line should be drawn is not easy, particularly in the context of the Human Rights Act and in judicial review cases. In judicial review[39] for example, the courts are often required to determine whether executive bodies have acted within their statutory authority, and this means that they must engage in an interpretative function. Yet where the exercise of discretionary powers is concerned, Parliament's intention may be elusive.[40] Moreover, under section 3 of the Human Rights Act, this intention may have to give way to an interpretation that is compatible with Convention rights.[41] The nature of these rights means that the courts may also have to take a view as to the proportionality of any action or provision interfering with them, and this inevitably requires a measure of policy evaluation.[42]

[35] *Air Canada v Secretary of State for Trade (No 2)* [1983] 2 AC 394 at 438, [1983] 1 All ER 910 at 919, *per* Lord Wilberforce.
[36] See p 36.
[37] See, e.g., the words of Lord Diplock in *Duport Steels Ltd v Sirs* [1980] 1 All ER 529 at 541, [1980] 1 WLR 142, at 157: quoted at p 44.
[38] See *R v Secretary of State for Home Affairs, ex parte Brind* [1991] 1 AC 696, [1991] 1 All ER 720.
[39] See p 256 for the supervisory role of the Administrative Court.
[40] In some cases this intention may be ascertained from the records of parliamentary debates: see *Pepper v Hart* [1993] AC 593, [1993] 1 All ER 42.
[41] See, e.g., *R v A (No 2)* [2001] UKHL 25 at [40], [2002] 1 AC 45 at [40], [2001] 3 All ER 1: discussed at p 47.
[42] See the discussion at p 176.

Common law

Traditional views are also changing in relation to the development of common law principles. In *Jones* v *Secretary of State for Social Services*, Lord Simon stated:[43]

> In this country it was long considered that judges were not makers of law but merely its discoverers and expounders. The theory was that every case was governed by a relevant rule of law, existing somewhere and discoverable somehow, provided sufficient learning and intellectual rigour were brought to bear.... [T]he theory, however unreal, had its value in limiting the sphere of law-making by the judiciary (inevitably at some disadvantage in assessing the potential repercussions of any decision, and increasingly so in a complex modern industrial society), and thus also in emphasising that central feature of our constitution, the sovereignty of Parliament. But the true, even if limited, nature of judicial law-making has been more widely acknowledged of recent years.

Judges do sometimes establish new legal principles, and a good example of this is the judgment of Denning J in *Central London Property Trust Ltd* v *High Trees House Ltd*,[44] which effectively created the doctrine of equitable estoppel. Similarly, the 'neighbour principle' propounded by Lord Atkin in *Donoghue (or M'Alister)* v *Stevenson*[45] is widely acknowledged as the basis of the modern law of negligence. Indeed, it is fair to say that some judges deem the creation of new law to be part of the judicial function, but others believe that any far-reaching change should be left to Parliament. The latter approach is exemplified by the vigorous dissenting speech of Lord Simon in *Miliangos* v *George Frank (Textiles) Ltd*:[46]

> I am sure that an expert committee, including or taking evidence from departmental officials, would apprehend a great number of not immediately apparent repercussions of the decision which my noble and learned friends propose to take. Such a committee might conclude that the repercussions make the decision unacceptable. Or they might suggest some means of mitigating any adverse effect. Or they might advise that the repercussions were on balance acceptable. But at least the crucial decision would be taken in the light of all the consequences involved.
>
> By contrast...judicial advance should be gradual. I am not trained to see the distant scene; 'one step enough for me' should be the motto on the wall opposite the judge's desk. It is, I concede, a less spectacular method of progression than somersaults and cartwheels; but it is the one best suited to the capacity and resources of a judge.

Lord Simon was a lone dissenting voice in this case, and the House of Lords effected a radical reform of the law by holding that English courts have the power to give judgments expressed in foreign currency. However, on other occasions judges have exercised restraint on the basis that the resolution of a problem is best left to Parliament. In *Malone* v *Metropolitan Police Commissioner (No 2)*, for example, Sir Robert Megarry

---

[43] [1972] AC 944 at 1026, [1972] 1 All ER 145 at 198.
[44] [1947] KB 130, [1956] 1 All ER 256n.   [45] [1932] AC 562.
[46] [1976] AC 443 at 481–2, [1975] 3 All ER 801 at 824–5.

considered that the practice of telephone tapping 'cried out' for legislation, but he declined to develop common law rules to fill the vacuum:[47]

> I am not unduly troubled by the absence of English authority: there has to be a first time for everything, and if the principles of English law, and not least analogies from the existing rules, together with the requirements of justice and common sense, pointed firmly to such a right existing, then I think the court should not be deterred from recognising the right. On the other hand, it is no function of the courts to legislate in a new field. The extension of the existing laws and principles is one thing, the creation of an altogether new right is another.

Twenty-five years later, the House of Lords held that although the Human Rights Act had given greater recognition to the right to respect for private life,[48] this did not entitle the courts to create a new tort:[49]

> For the reasons so cogently explained by Sir Robert Megarry in *Malone v Metropolitan Police Comissioner*, this is an area which requires a detailed approach which can be achieved only by legislation rather than the broad brush of common law principle.

The earliest criminal offences were, of course, judge-made, but since the nineteenth century it has been accepted that judges have no power to create new criminal offences.[50] Nevertheless, they have occasionally sought to enforce public morality by declaring that the common law recognizes certain conduct to be criminal. Thus, in *R v Manley*,[51] the defendant falsely alleged that she had been attacked and robbed, and this put the police to considerable trouble and expense. She was convicted of the offence of public mischief and, despite counsel's protestations that no such offence was known to the law, her conviction was upheld on appeal. The decision of the House of Lords in *Shaw v DPP*[52] is equally striking. An agreement to publish the 'Ladies Directory', which advertised the names, addresses, and photographs of prostitutes, was held to constitute the offence of conspiracy to corrupt public morals. The following observation from the speech of Viscount Simonds has been widely quoted:[53]

> In the sphere of criminal law I entertain no doubt that there remains in the courts of law a residual power to enforce the supreme and fundamental purpose of the law, to conserve not only the safety and order but also the moral welfare of the State.

In *Knuller v DPP*,[54] a similar publication aimed at the homosexual market was held to give rise to the same offence, and a majority of the House of Lords suggested that an

---

[47] [1979] Ch 344 at 372, [1979] 2 All ER 620 at 642.   [48] Article 8, ECHR.

[49] *Wainwright v Home Office* [2003] UKHL 53 at [33], [2004] 2 AC 406 at [33], [2003] 4 All ER 969, *per* Lord Hoffmann.

[50] This was virtually the only point upon which all five members of the House of Lords were agreed in *Knuller (Publishing, Printing and Promotions) Ltd v DPP* [1973] AC 435, [1972] 2 All ER 898. Lord Diplock's speech contains a useful account of the historical background: see [1973] AC 435 at 474, [1972] 2 All ER 898 at 918.

[51] [1933] 1 KB 529.   [52] [1962] AC 220, [1961] 2 All ER 446.

[53] [1962] AC 220 at 267–8, [1961] 2 All ER 446 at 452.

[54] [1973] AC 435, [1972] 2 All ER 898. See also *R v Gibson* [1990] 2 QB 619, [1991] 1 All ER 439.

offence of outraging public decency also existed. In the light of these authorities, the principle that judges have no power to create new offences would appear to be illusory. However, in *DPP* v *Withers*,[55] the House of Lords explained that conspiracy to effect a public mischief is not an offence in itself, and that conduct such as that in *R* v *Manley* (above) is criminal only because it amounts to some other established offence.

The approach to such matters is not always consistent, and judicial activism sometimes comes to the fore. Thus, in *R* v *R*, the House of Lords concluded that the rule that a husband could not be criminally liable for raping his wife was no longer part of English law.[56] Other examples of judicial creativity include the recognition of psychological harm as a form of assault,[57] the development of the law of provocation in the context of domestic violence,[58] and the decision that medical treatment may be lawfully withdrawn from a patient in a permanent vegetative state.[59] By contrast, in *C* v *DPP*,[60] the House of Lords declined to abolish the *doli incapax* rule. The rule created a rebuttable presumption that a child under the age of 14 could not possess criminal intent, and at first instance Laws J had said:[61]

> [T]his presumption at the present time is a serious disservice to our law. It means that a child over ten who commits an act of obvious dishonesty, or even grave violence, is to be acquitted unless the prosecution specifically prove...that he understands the obliquity of what he is doing...

In the House of Lords, Lord Lowery set out five general principles:

> (1) If the solution is doubtful the judges should beware of imposing their own remedy; (2) caution should prevail if Parliament has rejected opportunities of clearing up a known difficulty or has legislated while leaving the difficulty untouched; (3) disputed matters of social policy are less suitable areas for judicial intervention than purely legal problems; (4) fundamental legal doctrines should not lightly be set aside; (5) judges should not make a change unless they can achieve finality and certainty.

The application of these principles led him to conclude that the presumption should not be abandoned. It has, however, now been abolished by statute.[62]

Where a case gives rise to a potential Human Rights Act issue, different considerations apply. As discussed previously, the Act does not oblige private bodies to act compatibly with the Convention, and it does not expressly require the courts to give effect to the Convention at common law. It does, however, oblige them to perform their functions in a manner consistent with Convention rights,[63] and, since this is a statutory obligation, it must prevail over any duty to obey established common law principles.

[55] [1975] AC 842, [1974] 3 All ER 984.   [56] [1992] 1 AC 599, [1991] 4 All ER 481.
[57] *R* v *Chan-Fook* [1994] 2 All ER 552, [1994] 1 WLR 689; *R* v *Ireland* [1997] QB 114, [1997] 1 All ER 112; *R* v *Constanza* [1997] 2 Cr App R 492, [1997] Crim LR 576.
[58] *R* v *Thornton* [1992] 1 All ER 306, (1993) 96 Cr App R 112; *R* v *Ahluwalia* [1992] 4 All ER 889, (1993) 96 Cr App R 133.
[59] *Airedale NHS Trust* v *Bland* [1993] AC 789, [1993] 1 All ER 821.
[60] [1996] AC 1, [1995] 2 All ER 43.   [61] [1994] 3 All ER 190 at 196–7.
[62] Crime and Disorder Act 1998, s 34.
[63] Section 6. Convention rights are defined in s 1 of the Act: see p 147 and Chapter 5.

A court may even conclude that it has no option but to depart from a precedent that would otherwise be binding, as when the Court of Appeal made a modest adjustment to the House of Lords' test for bias.[64] The open-textured language of Convention rights also leaves considerable room for interpretation, and on occasions judges have had to determine matters that involve as many moral choices as they do legal ones. In *R (on the application of Pretty) v DPP*,[65] for example, the House of Lords found itself grappling with the difficult question of whether the right to life also gave a terminally ill woman the right to die. Similarly, in *Re A*,[66] a court had to consider whether the same right could prevent surgery to separate conjoined twins, in circumstances in which this would inevitably result in the death of one of them.

Convention rights have undoubtedly had an influence on judicial reasoning but, as indicated above, the courts have thus far stopped short of asserting the authority to create new common law torts. They have, however, sought to give effect to Convention rights—notably the right to respect for private life—by developing established torts such as breach of confidence.[67]

Finally, it should be noted that judges occasionally go beyond the function of dispute resolution by issuing guidelines for future cases. Thus the rates of interest to be awarded on damages in personal injury actions,[68] and the principles to be applied in determining applications for interim injunctions,[69] have both been the subject of House of Lords guidelines. Similarly, the Criminal Division of the Court of Appeal has established a practice of issuing sentencing guidelines to assist Crown Court judges.[70]

Administrative functions

In addition to resolving disputes, judges also exercise certain administrative functions. This is particularly true of justices of the peace, whose functions include licensing and the issuing of summonses and warrants. The judges who sit in the Court of

---

[64] *Director General of Fair Trading* v *Proprietary Association of Great Britain (No 2)* [2001] 1 WLR 700, *sub nom Re Medicaments and Related Classes of Goods (No 2)* [2001] HRLR 17. The approach was subsequently approved by the House of Lords in *Porter* v *Magill* [2001] UKHL 67, [2002] 2 AC 357, [2002] 1 All ER 465.

[65] [2001] UKHL 61, [2002] 1 AC 800, [2002] 1 All ER 1: see p 183.

[66] *Re A (Children) (Conjoined Twins: Surgical Separation)* [2001] Fam 147, [2000] 4 All ER 961.

[67] See, e.g., *A* v *B*; *H* v *Associated Newspapers*, [2002] EWCA Civ 337, [2003] QB 195, [2002] 2 All ER 545; *Douglas* v *Hello! Ltd (No 1)* [2001] QB 967, [2001] 2 All ER 289; *Campbell* v *Mirror Group Newspapers* [2004] UKHL 22, [2004] 2 AC 457, [2004] 2 All ER 995. These and other cases are discussed at pp 167 and 200; cf. *Wainwright* v *Home Office* [2003] UKHL 53, [2004] 2 AC 406, [2003] 4 All ER 969. Note also that in *Peck* v *UK* (2003) 36 EHRR 41, the European Court of Human Rights highlighted significant deficiencies in the ability of domestic law to protect privacy.

[68] See p 546.   [69] See p 530.

[70] This practice seems to have originated in *R* v *Turner* (1975) 61 Cr App R 67 in relation to sentences for robbery and has since been followed in many other sentencing areas. See, e.g., *R* v *Clarke (Linda)* [1982] 3 All ER 232, [1982] 1 WLR 1090 (partially suspended sentences); and *R* v *Armagh* (1982) 76 Cr App R 190 (drugs offences). See now, pp 571–681.

Protection administer the affairs of persons of unsound mind,[71] and in their capacity as 'visitors' of the Inns of Court, High Court judges hear appeals from the Senate of the Inns of Court and the Bar.[72] Courts also deal with various types of non-contentious business, such as the administration of trusts, the winding-up of companies, adoption, and legitimacy. In addition, judges issue Practice Directions, act as presiding judges[73] and Heads of Division, and sit on the various Court Rule Committees that make rules for court practice and procedure.[74]

The constitutional position of judges

Although there is some debate about whether judges are 'servants' of the Crown, there is no doubt that they cannot be controlled in the exercise of their office by either Parliament or the executive, and judicial independence is a fundamental principle of English law. This independence is essential if the courts are to perform their constitutional role of reviewing executive action. The idea is closely linked to the doctrine of the separation of powers, which for many judges is a cornerstone of the constitution:[75]

> It is a feature of the peculiarly British conception of the separation of powers that Parliament, the executive and the courts have each their distinct and largely exclusive domain. Parliament has a legally unchallengeable right to make whatever laws it thinks right. The executive carries on the administration of the country in accordance with the powers conferred on it by law. The courts interpret the laws, and see that they are obeyed.

It is clear, however, that the separation of powers within the United Kingdom is incomplete,[76] and the *balance* of powers between the legislature, executive, and judiciary is unequal. The legislative supremacy of Parliament was described by Wade as 'the ultimate political fact' upon which the system hangs,[77] and the traditional view is that this supremacy is unrestricted.[78] The United Kingdom does not have a written constitution with a superior status to ordinary laws, and as 'the weakest and least dangerous department of government'[79] the judiciary has no authority to strike down

---

[71] This court is discussed at p 270.

[72] For this general jurisdiction, see *R v Visitors to the Inns of Court, ex parte Calder and Persaud* [1994] QB 1, [1993] 2 All ER 876.

[73] Courts and Legal Services Act 1990, s 72.   [74] See p 487.

[75] *R v Secretary of State for the Home Department, ex parte Fire Brigades' Union* [1995] 2 AC 513 at 567, [1995] 2 All ER 244 at 267, *per* Lord Mustill. See also, *Duport Steels v Sirs* [1980] 1 All ER 529 at 541, [1980] 1 WLR 142 at 157, *per* Lord Diplock.

[76] Given that the United Kingdom does not have a written constitution and that it draws its Ministers from the legislature, several academics have questioned whether there is a separation of powers at all: see, e.g., Hood Phillips, 'A Constitutional Myth: Separation of Powers' (1977) 93 LQR 11.

[77] Wade, 'The Basis of Legal Sovereignty' [1955] CLJ 172 at 188.

[78] This view of parliamentary supremacy is closely associated with the work of Dicey; see *Introduction to the Study of the Law of the Constitution* (Macmillan: 10th edn, 1959).

[79] See Lord Steyn: 'The Weakest and Least Dangerous Department of Government' [1997] PL 84.

legislation as unconstitutional or invalid.[80] Yet within this framework there is room for genuine debate about the limits of judicial authority, and about the proper relationship between the courts and the other 'departments of government'.

The changing political climate

Since the 1940s most governments have enjoyed large majorities in the House of Commons, and this has enabled them to control the legislative agenda. The post-war era was characterized by political consensus, but the two main parties became more polarized and ideological during the 1970s, and the political climate since then has been distinctly adversarial. Successive governments have used their large majorities to steer controversial laws through Parliament, prompting Lord Hailsham's famous warning that the United Kingdom was becoming an 'elective dictatorship'.[81] Disputes with a political dimension have frequently come before the courts, and the courts have responded by developing more sophisticated principles of review. Since the 1980s, some Law Lords felt compelled to break the convention against speaking in legislative debates,[82] and the rules preventing judges from commenting on matters of public interest have been abandoned.[83] That choice is, of course, no longer open to them following the abolition of the Judicial Committee of the House of Lords and the creation of the Supreme Court.

Judicial inquiries[84]

Governments often appoint senior judges to head inquiries into matters of public interest. A government with a difficult or sensitive issue to address may rely on the 'borrowed authority'[85] of a judge to conduct an independent review, and to use his forensic ability to examine witnesses and sift evidence. Inevitably, however, the outcome of an inquiry rarely pleases everyone, and judges cannot be expected to produce non-political solutions to political problems. The Denning Report into the Profumo scandal,[86] the Scott inquiry into the sale of arms to Iraq,[87] and the Hutton inquiry into the death of Dr David Kelly,[88] are just three examples of inquiries that have generated intense controversy,[89] and which have arguably had a negative impact on the appearance of judicial impartiality.

---

[80] But see the discussion at pp 18–20.

[81] In 1976: see Lewis, *Lord Hailsham: A Life* (Jonathan Cape, 1997) at p 136. Lord Hailsham ceased to voice such concerns when he was made Lord Chancellor a few years later.

[82] See: Stevens, *op cit*, at pp 93–4.

[83] The so-called 'Kilmuir rules' (named after a former Lord Chancellor) were abandoned in 1989.

[84] See also p 309.

[85] See Griffith, *op cit*, at pp 52–5; Drewery, 'Judicial Inquiries and Public Reassurance' [1996] PL 368.

[86] Cmnd 2152 (HMSO, 1963).

[87] *Inquiry into the Export of Defence Equipment and Dual-Use Goods to Iraq* (HMSO, 1996).

[88] This reported in January 2004: see p 312.

[89] The Inquiries Act 2005 aimed at making their procedures more efficient and effective: see DCA, *Effective Inquiries: A Consultation Paper* (HMSO, 2004) CP 12/04.

Judicial review and judicial activism

Judicial review is the principal mechanism for holding the executive accountable to the law, and it is therefore central to the constitutional role of the courts. Over the last twenty years the courts have developed more sophisticated principles of review, and in *GCHQ*[90] and other cases they have extended the application of these principles to new situations. The courts' powers of review have been further enhanced by the Human Rights Act 1998, and judicial review has thus assumed considerable importance in recent years. This partly explains why the last two decades have witnessed an unprecedented level of conflict between the judiciary and the government. Ministers have increasingly found themselves on the receiving end of adverse judicial comment and, owing to the nature of their responsibilities, and perhaps the personalities involved, Home Secretaries have been particularly susceptible. For example, when Kenneth Baker authorized the deportation of an asylum seeker and ignored a judge's order to return him to the jurisdiction, he became the first Minister in British legal history to be held liable for contempt of court.[91] In the Court of Appeal, Nolan LJ reminded him that:[92]

> [T]he proper constitutional relationship of the executive with the courts is that the courts will respect all acts of the executive within its lawful province, and that the executive will respect all decisions of the courts as to what its lawful province is.

Another Home Secretary, Michael Howard, was defeated in the House of Lords when he purported to use prerogative powers to establish a Criminal Injuries Compensation Scheme instead of implementing the scheme provided for by statute.[93] His attempts to extend the minimum prison term served by the killers of James Bulger were also thwarted by the courts.[94] On each occasion the courts asserted the importance of the separation of powers, but critics accused them of interfering in matters of policy. This was not, however, an argument accepted by Lord Steyn. Writing extrajudicially, he stated that:[95]

> [T]he principle of the separation of powers is an essential constitutional safeguard of judicial independence, and the integrity of the administration of justice. It exists not to eliminate friction between the judiciary and the executive. It exists not to promote efficiency. It exists for one reason only: to prevent the rise of arbitrary executive power.

[90] *Council of Civil Service Unions v Minister for the Civil Service* [1985] AC 374, [1984] 3 All ER 935. In this case it was held that the use of prerogative powers was potentially amenable to judicial review.
[91] *Re M; sub nom M v Home Office* [1994] 1 AC 377, [1993] 3 All ER 537, HL: see p 244.
[92] [1992] QB 270 at 314–15, [1992] 4 All ER 97 at 146.
[93] *R v Secretary of State for Home Affairs, ex parte Fire Brigades Union* [1995] 2 AC 513, [1995] 2 All ER 244. The statute in question was the Criminal Justice Act 1988. Several Law Lords had spoken out against the scheme in Parliament, which effectively meant that they could not sit when this case reached the House of Lords.
[94] *R v Secretary of State for the Home Department, ex parte Venables and Thompson* [1998] AC 407, [1997] 3 All ER 97.
[95] 'The Weakest and Least Dangerous Department of Government' [1997] PL 84, at 87.

Lord Steyn was not the only judge to express his views outside the courtroom. Home Office policies on crime and sentencing were publicly criticized by the Lord Chief Justice,[96] and Laws LJ wrote various articles about the constitution and the role of the courts within it.[97] Some judges even added their voices to campaigns for a written constitution and the incorporation of the European Convention on Human Rights.[98]

The Human Rights Act era

The European Convention on Human Rights was eventually given domestic effect by the Human Rights Act 1998, which requires the courts to balance individual rights against competing public interest claims.[99] It also requires them to engage in creative statutory interpretation, and, wherever possible, to give effect to legislation in a manner that is compatible with Convention rights. Decisions under the Act therefore require a greater level of scrutiny than that previously adopted in judicial review cases, and this has created further opportunities for clashes with the government.

The question of how much judicial 'deference' is appropriate in human rights cases is still unresolved, but it is clear that less deference will be shown where the courts regard the subject matter of a case as falling within their own sphere of expertise.[100] Once again, this has led to conflict between the judiciary and the Home Office. A series of cases, both domestically and in Strasbourg, have effectively wrestled control of sentencing decisions from the Home Secretary.[101] The courts have also modified the interpretation of various statutes, so as to protect the right to a fair trial and to the presumption of innocence.[102] However, it is in the field of asylum and immigration that some of the most significant clashes have occurred. The government's policies in this area have been challenged in several recent cases, and at least one Home Secretary has responded by publicly attacking the courts' decisions. Thus, when Collins J held

---

[96] See Stevens, *op cit*, at pp 50–2.

[97] See, e.g., 'Law and Democracy' [1995] PL 80; 'The Constitution: Morals and Rights' [1996] PL 622.

[98] See, e.g., Bingham, 'The European Convention on Human Rights: Time to Incorporate' [1993] LQR 390; Scarman, *Why Britain Needs a Written Constitution* (Sovereignty Lectures, 1992). Many academics and politicians were opposed to such developments on the basis that they would require the courts to make political judgments: see Griffiths, 'The Political Constitution' (1979) 42 MLR 1; Lyell, 'Whither Strasbourg? Why Britain Should Think Long and Hard Before Incorporating the European Convention on Human Rights' [1997] EHRLR 132.

[99] For a discussion, see p 176.

[100] *R (on the application of Prolife Alliance)* v *BBC* [2003] UKHL 23 at [136], [2004] 1 AC 185 at [136], [2003] 2 All ER 977, *per* Lord Walker; *International Transport Roth GmbH* v *Secretary of State for the Home Department* [2002] EWCA Civ 158, [2003] QB 728, [2002] HRLR 31, *per* Laws LJ. For further discussion, see p 177.

[101] See p 187. See also: Amos, '*R* v *Secretary of State for the Home Department, ex parte Anderson*: Ending the Home Secretary's Sentencing Role' (2004) 67(1) MLR 108.

[102] See, e.g., *R* v *A (No 2)* [2001] UKHL 25, [2002] 1 AC 45, [2001] 3 All ER 1; *R* v *Lambert* [2001] UKHL 37, [2002] 2 AC 545, [2001] 3 All ER 577.

that six asylum seekers had been unlawfully denied state support,[103] the then Home Secretary, David Blunkett, complained that:[104]

> Frankly, I am personally fed up with having to deal with a situation where Parliament debates issues and the judges then overturn them. I don't want any mixed messages going out so I am making it absolutely clear that we don't accept what Justice Collins has said.

The same judge had previously ruled that detaining asylum seekers at 'reception centres' was unlawful.[105] This decision was later overturned on appeal,[106] but not before the Secretary of State had complained that his policies were being thwarted by unaccountable judges.[107] Mr Blunkett was further infuriated when the Special Immigration Appeals Commission—again chaired by Collins J—declared that the detention without trial of suspected foreign terrorists was incompatible with the Human Rights Act.[108] In a landmark decision the Commission's ruling was endorsed by the House of Lords,[109] forcing the government into a major rethink of its anti-terror laws. The internment provisions were subsequently replaced with a new system of control orders,[110] and all of those detained were eventually released. It was not long, however, before the new system fell under the judicial spotlight, and in *Secretary of State for the Home Department* v *JJ*, a majority of the House of Lords quashed six control orders on the grounds that they too were in breach of the Human Rights Act.[111]

Other decisions of note include the ruling that an asylum seeker's benefits could not be withdrawn without notification,[112] and the declaration that penalties applied

---

[103] *R (on the application of Q)* v *Secretary of State for the Home Department* [2003] EWHC 195 (Admin), The Times, 20 February. See also, *R (on the application of Limbuela)* v *Secretary of State for the Home Department* [2004] EWHC 219 (Admin), The Times, 9 February, QBD; [2005] UKHL 66, [2006] 1 AC 396, [2007] 1 All ER 951, HL.

[104] These comments were made in a radio interview and reported by *The Independent*, 20 February 2003: see also Bradley, 'Judicial Independence under Attack' [2003] PL 397. Justice Collins' decision was upheld by the Court of Appeal on slightly modified grounds: [2003] EWCA Civ 364, [2004] QB 36, [2003] 2 All ER 905.

[105] *R (on the application of Saadi)* v *Secretary of State for the Home Department* [2001] EWHC 670 (Admin).

[106] [2002] UKHL 41, [2002] 4 All ER 785, [2002] 1 WLR 3131.

[107] Stevens, *op cit*, at pp 130–1.

[108] *A* v *Secretary of State for the Home Department* [2002] HRLR 45. Collins J later ordered the release of one detainee, having described evidence presented by the Home Office as 'inaccurate' and 'clearly misleading': *Secretary of State* v *M*, unreported, 8 March 2004.

[109] [2004] UKHL 56, [2005] 2 AC 68, [2005] 3 All ER 169. The significance of this case was such that it was heard by nine of the twelve Law Lords. Coincidentally, Mr Blunkett resigned as Home Secretary the day before their Lordships delivered their opinions, and it was left to his successor to plan the government's response.

[110] Prevention of Terrorism Act 2005: the background to this legislation is discussed further at pp 159 and 189.

[111] [2007] UKHL 45, [2007] 3 WLR 642. See further p 159.

[112] *R (on the application of Anufrijeva)* v *Secretary of State for the Home Department* [2003] UKHL 36, [2004] 1 AC 604, [2003] 3 All ER 827.

to hauliers who assisted illegal immigrants were incompatible with Convention rights.[113]

The issues raised by these and other cases have continued to divide lawyers and politicians. Many feel that the courts have been seeking to uphold the rule of law, and they view the government's reaction to certain decisions as an affront to judicial independence. Indeed, when Lord Irvine was Lord Chancellor, he issued a tacit reminder to his own Cabinet colleagues about the need to respect judicial authority:[114]

> In a democracy under the rule of law, it is not mature to cheer the judges when a win is secured and boo them when a loss is suffered…
>
> [The Human Rights Act] was drafted sensitively to the balance of forces within our substantially unwritten constitution. And that means the government can accept adverse court decisions, not as defeats, but as steps on the road to better governance…
>
> In giving greater responsibility to our judges, we are merely confirming that ours is a society governed by the rule of law…We ask our judges to decide many difficult cases. Some are between private citizens. Some are criminal appeals. Others are against ministers; and of these, some are lost and some are won. That is neither avoidable nor unconstitutional. It is simply proof that 'be you ever so high, the law is above you'.

Others, however, would argue that the courts have at times undermined the will of Parliament, and that concerns about judicial independence are misplaced:[115]

> Once appointed, judges of the English High Court and above can be removed only on an address by both Houses of Parliament, which means that they are virtually irremovable. So, against whom does the judiciary need protection? Against the government? Yet, there has never been a time when government decisions have been struck down with greater abandon than now, and even Acts of Parliament have been savaged by the courts…
>
> The real loser is democracy. In a parliamentary democracy like the UK, legislation is intended to give expression to the will of the people. If it fails to do so, the people can turn the government out at the next election. But for unelected judges to make up the law as they go along is contrary not only to the doctrine of the separation of powers, but is also a usurpation of the role of Parliament.

Even Prime Ministers have occasionally succumbed to the urge to criticize the courts, with Tony Blair describing a ruling preventing nine Afghan hijackers from being deported[116] as 'an abuse of common sense'.[117] By the time that this case was decided, the same Prime Minister who had presided over the enactment of the Human Rights Act in 1998 appeared to be having second thoughts, and in a letter to his Home Secretary

[113] *International Transport Roth GmbH* v *Secretary of State for the Home Department* [2002] EWCA Civ 158, [2003] QB 728, [2002] HRLR 31.
[114] 'The Impact of the Human Rights Act: Parliament, the Courts and the Executive' [2003] PL 307, at 323–4.
[115] Arnheim, 'The Rule of Law or the Rule of Lawyers?' (2004) 154 NLJ 776.
[116] *R (on the application of S)* v *Secretary of State for the Home Department* [2006] EWHC 1111 (Admin), (2006) The Times, 14 June. The decision was subsequently affirmed by the Court of Appeal: EWCA Civ 1157, (2006) The Times, 9 October.
[117] Reported in *The Observer*, 14 May 2006.

he suggested that the Act should be reviewed.[118] David Cameron MP, when leader of the opposition, was even more vociferous, repeatedly calling for the Human Rights Act to be replaced with a 'British' bill of rights more 'in tune with British traditions about liberty'.[119] When asked to comment on a ruling that a convicted killer could not be deported at the end of his sentence,[120] he declared that:[121]

> The fact that the Human Rights Act means he cannot be deported flies in the face of common sense. It is a shining example of what is going wrong in our country. He is someone who has been found guilty of murder and should be deported back to his country.

It remains to be seen whether this political view will be reflected by legislative changes now that he heads the current government. Whilst all major political parties may support the call for changes to human rights protection, and a review of the workings of the Human Rights Act 1998 has been instigated, it is perhaps unlikely that the legal status of the Convention of Human Rights will change.

The relationship between the government and the judiciary has undoubtedly been tested over the last two decades, and the Human Rights Act has been at the centre of much of the recent tension. Yet it is not only in the courtroom that clashes have occurred: the enactment of a number of recent statutes has also proved contentious, and two of these are discussed below.

KEY ISSUE

How far should the judges go in making law? This is a question that increases, not diminishes, in importance in the era following the passage of the Human Rights Act 1998. It has already been noted that the operation of the Act gives the courts difficult choices as to how statutes are to be interpreted.[122] The courts have always developed the common law, but the advent of enforceable Convention rights creates new opportunities, and challenges for the courts. The development of concepts of privacy[123] and their responses to laws designed to protect the public from acts of terrorism[124] are two, controversial, examples of where the role of the courts in a law function has been criticized. The separation of powers that seeks to define the proper role of judges within the UK's unwritten constitution requires a careful balance to be struck by the courts: to perform their proper role of enforcing the law and holding the executive to account, and respecting the proper role of government and Parliament in making and enforcing policy choices

? Questions

1. How are judges held accountable?

2. What criteria should judges apply in deciding how far to go in their law-making role?

---

[118] Reported in *The Guardian*, 15 May 2006.   [119] Reported in *The Observer*, 4 November 2007.
[120] *Appellant v Secretary of State for the Home Department*, Appeal Number IA/13107/2006, 17 August 2007, unreported (Asylum and Immigration Tribunal). In fact the disputed decision was based primarily on the application of EU law, with Article 8 of the ECHR being very much a secondary issue.
[121] Reported in *The Guardian*, 22 August 2007.   [122] See p 152.
[123] See p 200.   [124] See p 188.

The Constitutional Reform Act 2005

The original aims of the Constitutional Reform Bill have been considered in detail elsewhere in this book, but they can be broadly summarized as follows:

(a) to abolish the post of Lord Chancellor and transfer his judicial responsibilities to the Lord Chief Justice, leaving his ministerial functions to the Secretary of State for Constitutional Affairs;

(b) to replace the Appellate Committee of the House of Lords with an independent Supreme Court, so that the most senior judges cease to occupy seats in Parliament; and

(c) to establish an independent Judicial Appointments Commission.

On its face, the Bill was intended to achieve a more formal separation of powers, and a judiciary that is more transparently independent of government. One might therefore have expected it to be well received by most judges, but in fact, initial reactions ranged from the mildly sceptical to the deeply suspicious. The government's failure to consult judges before announcing its decision did not help matters, and the Lord Chief Justice could barely conceal his anger that the reforms were thought to be 'capable of being achieved by a press release'.[125] The biggest cause for concern was the proposed abolition of the Lord Chancellor's office.[126] The Judges' Council expressed serious reservations about this proposal, pointing out that the new Secretary of State would be a political figure, who would not be constrained by 'judicial responsibilities and constitutional conventions'.[127] The Law Lords agreed that the Lord Chancellor's role had been a safeguard of judicial independence, and that 'the constitution would be gravely weakened if that safeguard were removed and not replaced'.[128] The judiciary's main concern was whether a Secretary of State, who might not necessarily be a lawyer, could properly defend judicial interests within government. Their unease was exacerbated by the fact that certain politicians appeared not to respect their authority, and they had previously opposed plans to transfer the Court Service to the Home Office for similar reasons:[129]

> It was disturbing that—at that time—it was not appreciated within government that it was inappropriate for the department that most frequently had to defend proceedings for judicial review in the courts and that had to lead responsibility for criminal justice policy to be in charge of what should be seen as an impartial Court Service.

Judges were more ambivalent about the plans for a Supreme Court, but six of the twelve Law Lords publicly opposed the proposals, and eight were in agreement that

[125] Lord Woolf, 'The Rule of Law and a Change in the Constitution' (2004) 63(2) CLJ 317, at 320.

[126] See p 332.

[127] Response to the Consultation Papers on Constitutional Reform; available at **www.dca.gov.uk/ judicial/pdfs/jcresp.pdf**

[128] *The Law Lords' Response to the Government's Consultation Paper on Constitutional Reform: A Supreme Court for the United Kingdom*, CP 11/03 (HMSO, July 2003), at para 5.

[129] Lord Woolf, 'The Rule of Law and a Change in the Constitution' (2004) 63(2) CLJ 317 at 323.

if the reforms *did* go ahead, at least some of the Court's members should continue to sit in the House of Lords.[130] Lord Hobhouse, for example, argued that the Lord Chief Justice and other senior figures should retain their parliamentary seats so that they could continue to speak on behalf of the judiciary.[131] By the time that the Bill was presented to Parliament, many of the judges' preferences had been accommodated, and the Concordat[132] negotiated by the Lord Chief Justice had helped to allay some of their concerns.

The proposed abolition of the Lord Chancellor's office also faced opposition from within Parliament, and the government was 'persuaded' to accept that the office should continue in a modified form. The Constitutional Reform Act 2005 thus removed the Lord Chancellor's judicial functions[133] whilst reminding him of the need to defend judicial independence.[134] It also removed the requirement for him to be either a lawyer or a peer,[135] meaning that he is, in effect, a Secretary of State in all but name. Indeed, the office of Lord Chancellor was combined with the new role of Secretary of State for Justice,[136] now held by Kenneth Clarke QC. The suggestion that certain judges should retain their parliamentary seats was also rejected by the government, and the Act leaves it to the Lord Chief Justice to ensure that their interests are represented by other means.[137]

The 'mother of all ouster clauses'

While the debate about constitutional reform was still ongoing, a second government Bill was generating further controversy. The main purpose of what is now the Asylum and Immigration (Treatment of Claimants) Act 2004 was to create a new, single-tier tribunal to deal with appeals in immigration and asylum cases.[138] In what was described as the 'mother of all ouster clauses',[139] clause 11 of the Bill purported to exclude the tribunal's decisions from any possibility of judicial review. Previous attempts to oust the jurisdiction of the courts have been interpreted narrowly: it has generally been assumed that Parliament would not have intended to prevent the review of a decision made without its authority.[140] Clause 11, however, was clearly drafted with the intention of making it 'judge-proof'.[141] If enacted, it would have expressly precluded the courts from considering claims based on: (i) lack of jurisdiction; (ii) irregularity; (iii) error of law; (vi) breach of natural justice; or (v) any other matter. Senior judges publicly condemned the clause, and the Lord Chief Justice was particularly scathing:[142]

---

[130] The Law Lords' Response (*ante*, n 128), at paras 2 and 21.   [131] Ibid, at para F.2.
[132] See p 331.
[133] Most of these are transferred to the Lord Chief Justice by Schedules 2 and 4.
[134] Section 3(6); s 3(5) prohibits *all* Ministers from seeking to influence judicial decisions.
[135] Section 2: see p 9.   [136] See p 9.   [137] Sections 5(1).
[138] See p 300.   [139] See Jowell, 'Heading for a Constitutional Crisis' (2004) 154 NLJ 401.
[140] *Anisminic* v *Foreign Compensation Commission* [1969] 2 AC 147, [1969] 1 All ER 208: see p 55.
[141] Jowell (2004) 154 NLJ 401.
[142] Lord Woolf, 'The Rule of Law and a Change in the Constitution' (2004) 63(2) CLJ 317, at 328–9.

The provision has to be read to appreciate the lengths to which the government has gone to try and exclude the possibility of intervention by the courts. Extensive consultation took place with myself and other members of the judiciary before the Bill was introduced...our advice was that a clause of the nature now included in the Bill was fundamentally in conflict with the rule of law and should not be contemplated by any government if it had respect for the rule of law.

We advised that the clause was unlikely to be effective and identified why. The result was that clause 11 was extended to close the loopholes we had identified, instead of being abandoned as we had argued...we pointed out that the danger of the proposed ouster clause was that it could bring the judiciary, the executive and the legislature into conflict. Apparently this was of little concern...

I am not over-dramatising the position if I indicate that, if this clause were to become law, it would be so inconsistent with the spirit of mutual respect between the different arms of government that it could be the catalyst for a campaign for a written constitution...The response of the government and the House of Lords to the chorus of criticism of clause 11 will produce the answer to the question of whether our freedoms can be left in their hands under an unwritten constitution.

In the end, the level of opposition to the clause forced the government to withdraw it,[143] and the compromise reached means that the tribunal's decisions can be reviewed on the grounds of an error of law.[144] It remains to be seen, however, whether a constitutional crisis was avoided or merely postponed.

A new balance of powers?

Lord Woolf is one of a small, but growing, number of judges to assert a more powerful role for the courts. Before he was appointed as Lord Chief Justice, he said that if Parliament were to do the unthinkable and attempt to abolish judicial review, he would:[145]

[C]onsider there were advantages in making it clear that ultimately there are even limits on the supremacy of Parliament which it is the courts' inalienable responsibility to identify and uphold.

Similar comments have been made by Laws LJ:[146]

[T]hose who exercise democratic political power must have limits set to what they may do: limits which they are not allowed to overstep...the doctrine of Parliamentary sovereignty cannot be vouched by Parliamentary legislation; a higher order law confers it and must limit it.

---

[143] Lord Falconer, 659 HL Official Report (5th series) col 51, 15 March 2004. For a discussion, see Le Sueur, 'Three Strikes and It's Out? The UK Government's Strategy to Oust Judicial Review from Immigration and Asylum Decision-Making' [2004] PL 225.

[144] Nationality, Immigration and Asylum Act 2002, s 103A: discussed at p 301.

[145] Woolf, '*Droit Public*: English Style' [1995] PL 57 at 69.

[146] Laws, 'Law and Democracy' [1995] PL 80.

Lord Justice Sedley has presented an alternative view, based on:[147]

> [A] bi-polar sovereignty of the Crown in Parliament and the Crown in the courts, to each of which the crown's ministers are answerable—politically to Parliament, legally to the courts.

Not only are these judges asserting their own role within the constitution, but they are also re-examining what is required by the rule of law.[148] Lord Steyn's judgment in *Pierson*, for example, suggests that in addition to requiring some lawful authority for government action, the rule of law might also be capable of tempering Parliament's supremacy:[149]

> Unless there is the clearest provision to the contrary, Parliament must be presumed not to legislate contrary to the rule of law. And the rule of law enforces minimum standards of fairness.

By arguing that Parliament must be *presumed* to legislate in accordance with the rule of law, Lord Steyn avoids making a direct challenge to Parliament's authority. Lord Justice Laws adopted a similar approach in *Thoburn* v *Sunderland City Council*, when he asserted that there are 'constitutional statutes' that can only be repealed by express words.[150] Lord Woolf's approach is more direct, however, and he suggests that the rule of law may impose modest but substantive limits on Parliament's ability to legislate.[151] The ideas expressed by these judges may seem radical, but they are a reminder of Hart's idea that supremacy is 'a rule of recognition',[152] and that its existence depends on Parliament's authority being accepted as legitimate. In other words, if Parliament purports to legislate in an arbitrary or unjust manner, its authority to do so may be called into question.

These views are by no means universally—or even generally—accepted,[153] and outside the field of European law[154] no judge in modern times has attempted to disapply an Act of Parliament. Moreover, even if it could be agreed that there *should* be limits

---

[147] Sedley, 'Human Rights: A Twenty-First Century Agenda' [1995] PL 386.

[148] In a work of this nature it is not possible to give a detailed account of the issues, but see: Allan, 'The Limits of Parliamentary Sovereignty' [1985] PL 614; Allan, 'The Conceptual Foundations of Judicial Review: Conceptual Conundrum or Interpretative Inquiry?' (2002) 61(1) CLJ 87; Craig, 'Public Law, Political Theory and Legal Theory' [2000] PL 211.

[149] *R* v *Secretary of State for the Home Department, ex parte Pierson* [1998] AC 539 at 575, [1997] 3 All ER 577 at 607. The rule of law is explicitly recognized as a 'constitutional principle' by s 1 of the Constitutional Reform Act 2005: the Act does not, however, attempt to define it.

[150] [2002] EWHC 195 (Admin) at [60], [2003] QB 151 at [60], [2002] 4 All ER 156. For a discussion, see p 20.

[151] See the above extracts. Woolf has described the legislative intent approach as 'a harmless fairytale': see '*Droit Public*: English Style' [1995] PL 57.

[152] *The Concept of Law* (OUP, 1961).

[153] See, e.g., Lord Irvine of Lairg, 'Judges and Decision Makers: The Theory and Practice of *Wednesbury* Review' [1996] PL 59.

[154] See pp 20 and 129.

on legislative power, many would dispute whether an unelected and unaccountable judiciary should have the authority to police those limits. Nevertheless, there are signs that the United Kingdom is 'inching towards becoming a constitutional state',[155] and if this trend continues, it is likely to lead to a more influential—and perhaps more equal—role for the judges. At the very least, it could be argued that the recent tensions between the government and the judiciary are a sign of a healthy democracy rather than impending constitutional crisis. David Feldman, for example, has argued that:[156]

> Tension between institutions is...desirable. A functioning constitution requires that the various institutions of the state should provide checks and balances, and checks and balances depend on maintaining a state of tension between institutions and their constitutional positions. Tension between institutions is not pathological; as long as it does not tear the state apart, it is a precondition for a healthy constitution under the rule of law.

Moreover, in enacting the Human Rights Act, Parliament has arguably left the judges with little option but to make controversial—and even 'political'—decisions. Like Feldman, Nicol argues that this is not necessarily bad for democracy:[157]

> [T]he Law Lords have shown ideological unity during the early years of the HRA. It is therefore not entirely fanciful to recast the Law Lords as a political faction. Their particular focus on individual rights may help draw Parliament's attention to a perspective it might otherwise neglect.

However, while Nicol considers it both desirable and inevitable that judges will at times be 'robust' in their condemnation of legislation or government decisions, he sees nothing wrong in politicians being equally robust in their criticism of the courts:[158]

> [W]hen parliamentarians disagree with judicial conceptions of rights they should say so—and say why—forthrightly, and should reiterate the compelling reasons of principle why Parliament, not the courts, remains sovereign. Frank speech...requires abandoning the convention that politicians never express disagreement with court judgments. This inhibition hails from a bygone era when courts were not politically centre-stage, when they were not perceived as 'doing politics'. It certainly should not apply to HRA decisions.

---

[155] Steyn, 'Democracy through Law' [2002] EHRLR 723 at 734. Stevens agrees that 'it is becoming slowly more accurate to describe Britain as a constitutional democracy rather than a parliamentary democracy': *op cit*, at p 148.

[156] Feldman, 'Human Rights, Terrorism and Risk: The Roles of Politicians and Judges' [2006] PL 364, at 383.

[157] Nicol, 'Law and Politics after the Human Rights Act' [2006] PL 722, at 743.

[158] Ibid, at 746.

Judicial appointments and security of tenure

Appointments

The old system

Until 2006 district judges and lay magistrates were appointed directly by the Lord Chancellor, while High Court judges, circuit judges, recorders, and district judges (magistrates' courts) were appointed by the Queen on his advice. In the case of the Law Lords, Court of Appeal judges, and Heads of Division, the Prime Minister was ultimately responsible for 'advising' the Queen on appointments, but in practice the Prime Minister would normally be guided by the Lord Chancellor's recommendations. Thus, the power to determine all judicial appointments rested, in effect, in the hands of senior members of the government.

The idea of judicial independence is of fundamental importance, and many feel strongly that the power to appoint judges should not be in the government's hands. English judges are said to rank highly on any international scale of objectivity[159] and few would seriously contend that they are subject to direct political interference, but they are also predominantly male, white, middle class, and middle-aged. Although the last two decades have witnessed a period of 'unprecedented antagonism between judiciary and government',[160] some argue that the judiciary as an institution has an inherent tendency to support 'conventional, settled and established interests'.[161] In addition, the right to a fair trial before an 'independent and impartial tribunal'[162] requires judges to not only *be* independent but also to be demonstrably so, and once this right was given statutory effect by the Human Rights Act concerns about the judicial appointments system gained momentum.

The reform agenda

In 1999 Sir Leonard Peach carried out an independent scrutiny of the system, and on the basis of his recommendations the government established a Commission for Judicial Appointments.[163] However, the Commission's role was merely advisory and supervisory and it had no direct role in making appointments. In 2003 it carried out an audit of appointments to the High Court bench and concluded that fundamental changes were needed:[164]

---

[159] Stevens, *op cit*, at p 82.

[160] Lord Irvine of Lairg, 'The Impact of the Human Rights Act: Parliament, the Courts and the Executive' [2003] PL 307, at 323. Although Lord Irvine wrote these words as Lord Chancellor and was referring to the period before the Labour government took office, the antagonism between the courts and the executive has actually increased subsequently. For a discussion, see p 327.

[161] Griffith, *op cit*, at p 20.

[162] Article 6, ECHR: see p 193.

[163] *Appointment Processes of Judges and Queen's Counsel in England and Wales.* The Commission was established in 2001. For a discussion, see The Law Society, *Broadening the Bench* (2000), ch 5.

[164] Her Majesty's Commissioners for Judicial Appointments, *Report of the Commissioners' Review of the High Court 2003 Competition* (HMSO, 2004) at para E.10.2.

Our review of the 2003 High Court appointment competition has left us convinced that radical change is needed, to bring the system into line with best practice in other fields. We would be concerned to see any further High Court Judge selection processes take place on the basis of the present system, which we have found to be seriously lacking in transparency and accountability.

By the time that the audit was completed, the government had already published a consultation paper setting out its plans for a more powerful commission:[165]

In a modern democratic society it is no longer acceptable for judicial appointments to be entirely in the hands of a Government Minister. For example the judiciary is often involved in adjudicating on the lawfulness of actions of the Executive. And so the appointments system must be, and must be seen to be, independent of Government. It must be transparent. It must be accountable. And it must inspire public confidence.

More than half of those who responded to the consultation felt that the Commission should be able to make actual appointments, and a further 13 per cent (including the Bar Council, Law Society, and Judges' Council) said that it should at least be able to make appointments to the lower ranks.[166] The government had emphasized the need for accountability, and its preference was for a 'recommending commission' that would leave the final decision to the Minister. However, it was persuaded that the Minister's discretion should be kept to a minimum, and this is reflected in the provisions that were eventually included in the Constitutional Reform Act 2005.

It should be noted, however, that not everyone was convinced of the need to reduce political involvement in the appointments process. Writing in 2002, more than a year before the government's proposals were announced, Robert Stevens argued that:[167]

Judges choosing judges is the antithesis of democracy. In all major common law countries—the US, Canada, Australia and South Africa—the executive chooses the judiciary, although sometimes with advice from a Judicial Appointments Commission. To hand over the appointment of judges to a commission might well ensure bland appointments. The courts do have important political powers and responsibilities...the choice of judges is too important to be left to a quango...At the very least, if there is to be a Constitutional or Supreme Court, its judges must be chosen by elected officials and subject to examination by a democratic body.

The new system: The Judicial Appointments Commission

The Constitutional Reform Act 2005 provides that the Judicial Appointments Commission (JAC) should comprise six lay members, five judges, a solicitor, a barrister, a tribunal member, and one lay justice. One of the lay members must be appointed

[165] DCA, *Constitutional Reform: A New Way of Appointing Judges* (HMSO, 2003) CP 10/03, Foreword.
[166] DCA, *Constitutional Reform: A New Way of Appointing Judges—Summary of Responses to the Consultation* (HMSO, January 2004). See also: Malleson, 'Creating a Judicial Appointments Commission: Which Model Works Best?' [2004] PL 102; The Law Society, *Broadening the Bench* (2000).
[167] Stevens, *op cit*, at p 144.

as Chairman.[168] Twelve of the Commissioners are appointed through a process of open competition, with the other three—those who are senior judges—being selected by the Judges' Council.[169]

Eligibility for judicial office

At one time only experienced barristers were eligible for most judicial appointments, and solicitors could only be appointed at the level of recorder or district judge. The Courts and Legal Services Act 1990 removed some of these barriers by linking the criteria for appointment to its provisions on rights of audience,[170] but a consultation exercise carried out in 2004 suggested that the rules were still perceived as being unduly restrictive.[171]

> The issue of statutory eligibility requirements, both in terms of who could apply [for judicial office] and time served, attracted diverse and strong responses. Some respondents felt that the current arrangements were about right. However, the majority believed that broadening eligibility would widen the pool of potential judges and thus enhance diversity. A number of respondents felt that the current emphasis on rights of audience was too restrictive and that eligibility should be based on wider legal skills and experience (particularly given that advocacy skills are not relevant to judicial office). In addition some thought that 'time served' was not an appropriate judgement of a person's suitability for appointment.

The government's response to these findings was to amend the minimum eligibility requirements for judicial appointments. The new arrangements are set out in Part 2 and Schedule 10 of the Tribunals, Courts and Enforcement Act 2007, and they centre on the concept of the 'judicial-appointment eligibility condition'. Each level of judicial office is now subject to such a condition, and in order to satisfy it a candidate must: (a) have held a relevant qualification for a specified minimum period, and (b) have been gaining experience in law at the same time.[172] What will constitute a 'relevant qualification'[173] is determined by the nature of the post, and this means that certain judicial offices will be open to legal executives and others.[174] For many posts, the minimum period for which a qualification must have been held has also been reduced. However, the additional requirement to have gained *experience* of the law means that a barrister or solicitor who has not actually worked as a lawyer since qualifying will not satisfy the statutory criteria. According to section 52(2) of the Act,

---

[168] See Sch 12, para 1. This composition is more varied than that originally envisaged by the government: its Consultation Paper had proposed (at paras 118–121) that there should be five lay members, five judges, and five lawyers.

[169] Ibid.   [170] See p 382.

[171] DCA, *Increasing Diversity in the Judiciary*: *Summary of Responses to the Consultation* (HMSO, March 2005), at p 6. For the original consultation paper, see DCA, *Increasing Diversity in the Judiciary* (HMSO, 2004) CP 25/04.

[172] 2007 Act, s 50.   [173] Ibid, s 51.

[174] Ibid. Section 51(2) provides that in order to be deemed 'relevant' for these purposes, a qualification must have been awarded either by the Institute of Legal Executives or a body authorized under the Courts and Legal Services Act 1990 to confer rights of audience or rights to conduct litigation. Potentially then, patent agents and trade mark attorneys could be eligible to apply for certain appointments: see further, pp 379 and 381.

a person will be deemed to have gained experience in law by being 'engaged in law-related activities'. Being in practice or employment as a lawyer is just one way of doing this: section 52(4) also refers to things such as teaching or researching law, acting as an arbitrator or mediator, and being engaged in any other activity that the decision-maker considers to be broadly similar to one of those specified.

Once in force, these arrangements will mean that in order to be eligible for appointment as a Lord of Appeal (or Justice of the Supreme Court) a candidate will need to satisfy the judicial-appointment eligibility condition for a minimum of fifteen years.[175] A person seeking appointment as a Lord or Lady Justice will need to satisfy this condition on a seven-year basis or have experience as a High Court judge, and a candidate for the High Court bench will be subject to a seven-year eligibility condition unless he or she has at least two years' experience as a circuit judge.[176] The posts of circuit judge and recorder will also be subject to a seven-year condition, although applicants for the former post will be deemed eligible if they have held one of certain specified posts[177] for a minimum of three years.[178] The eligibility condition applicable to the posts of district judge and district judge (magistrates' courts) will be five years.[179]

Selection procedures

Under the arrangements put in place by the JAC, most judicial positions are widely advertised in both the national press and professional publications, and 'outreach' events are sometimes held to encourage potential applicants to apply. Checks are made as to the eligibility and 'good character' of all applicants, and, in the case of junior appointments, candidates may also be asked to complete a qualifying test or attend a selection day. Shortlisted candidates are then interviewed by a selection panel of Commissioners.

For appointments to the High Court bench and lower judicial ranks, the 2005 Act requires the Commission to recommend a single candidate to the Minister.[180] The Lord Chancellor does have the power to reject the initial selection and to ask the Commission to reconsider or put forward an alternative, but if he does this, he must then appoint either: (a) the next candidate selected; or (b) the Commission's original choice.[181] If at the first stage the Lord Chancellor merely asks the Commission to *reconsider* its selection, he will be entitled to reject the candidate put forward at the second stage (who may or may not be the same person), but he *must* then appoint the next selection. Although the rules are complicated, they mean in essence that the Commission will never be required to put forward more than two or three selections for each post, and that the Lord Chancellor will only ever have one right of rejection. The Act sets

---

[175] Appellate Jurisdiction Act 1876, s 6; Constitutional Reform Act 2005, s 25—as amended by the 2007 Act, s 50; Sch 10.

[176] Supreme Court Act 1981, s 10(3), as amended.

[177] These include coroner, district judge, and certain tribunal offices.

[178] Courts Act 1971, ss 16(3) and 21(2), as amended.

[179] County Courts Act 1984, s 9; Courts Act 2003, ss 22 and 24—as amended.

[180] Section 88.   [181] Section 90.

out similar arrangements for the appointment of the Lord Chief Justice, Heads of Division, Lord and Lady Justices of Appeal, and Senior President of Tribunals,[182] but the Commission is required to convene a special selection panel before making any recommendation. The precise membership of this panel is determined by the nature of the appointment, but it would normally include the Chairman, the Lord Chief Justice, a senior judge and a lay member.[183] At all levels the Commission is required to make its selections on the basis of merit and good character,[184] and to take into account any guidelines issued by the Lord Chancellor.[185]

Now, when a vacancy arises in the new Supreme Court[186] the Lord Chancellor is required to convene a panel comprising the President of the Supreme Court, the Deputy President, and a member of each of the appointments bodies for England and Wales, Scotland, and Northern Ireland.[187] That panel is in turn to be required to consult senior judges and the relevant Minister for each of the United Kingdom jurisdictions.[188] The Lord Chancellor has only one right of rejection,[189] and the actual appointment of these judges will be formally made by the Prime Minister.[190] The Lord Chancellor's role will be to notify him of the selection.

As outlined previously, section 3 of the 2005 Act means that all Ministers have a duty to uphold judicial independence and to refrain from attempting to improperly influence judicial decisions. It further provides that the Lord Chancellor must have regard to the need to *defend* judicial independence and to ensure that judges have the support necessary to enable them to perform their functions. The Act also provides for the appointment of a Judicial Appointments and Conduct Ombudsman, with the power to investigate complaints about appointments and disciplinary matters.[191]

The government is now considering whether its reforms have gone far enough, and it recently invited views as to whether the Lord Chancellor's formal role in the appointments process might be further reduced.[192]

Diversity in the judiciary

At present, members of the judiciary continue to be drawn from a fairly narrow section of society. The first female Law Lord was appointed in January 2004, but there were only two Lady Justices in the Court of Appeal at this time, and fewer than 7 per cent of High Court judges were women. Women were slightly better represented in the lower ranks, accounting for 11 per cent of circuit judges and almost 40 per cent of district judges,[193] but the figures for ethnic minorities were less encouraging. Ethnic minorities comprised just 3 per cent of district judges and 1.5 per cent of circuit

---

[182] This office is discussed further at p 297.

[183] Sections 67–84. Slightly different configurations are adopted when appointing the Lord Chief Justice and Senior President of Tribunals.

[184] Section 63.   [185] Section 65.

[186] See p 246.   [187] Schedule 8, para 1.

[188] Section 27: for England and Wales the Lord Chancellor is the relevant Minister.

[189] Section 29.   [190] Section 26.   [191] Section 62; Sch 13.

[192] Ministry of Justice, *The Governance of Britain: Judicial Appointments*, CP 25/07 (HMSO, October 2007).

[193] DCA, *Statistics: Women in the Judiciary* (HMSO, 2004).

judges, and not a single black or Asian judge was appointed above the level of the circuit bench.[194]

For obvious reasons, the composition of the judiciary has always mirrored that of the Bar, and although the number of female and ethnic minority barristers is increasing, it will be some time before this is reflected in the senior judicial ranks. The Lord Chancellor's 2003 appointments guidelines revealed his personal frustration at the slow rate of progress:[195]

> Appointments must and will be made on merit irrespective of ethnic origin, gender, marital status, political affiliation, sexual orientation, religion or disability. These are not mere words. They are firm principles...I want every vacancy on the Bench to be filled by the best person available, but I can only appoint the judiciary from among those who are ready and willing to do the job. I would like all eligible practitioners to have the confidence to apply.

The implication here is that suitably qualified female and ethnic minority lawyers may be less inclined than their white, male counterparts to apply for judicial office. This perception is borne out by at least some empirical research. Writing in 1991, for example, Hughes suggested that opening up the system to greater competition made it *less* likely that female judges would be appointed, because a sizeable proportion of women lawyers would not put themselves forward without direct encouragement.[196] Similarly, while the Judges' Council broadly supported the creation of the new JAC, it argued that there should still be a place for headhunting:[197] 'The very best candidates frequently do not actively seek appointment. In practice, many judges take an appointment only when encouraged to do so out of a sense of duty.' On the other hand, it would be naive to rely on such headhunting to remedy centuries of inequality and under-representation. Writing extrajudicially, Hale LJ (as she then was) observed that 'women have been entering the [legal] profession in significant numbers for a long time...But [there are]...systemic obstacles to making sufficient progress to be regarded as a serious candidate'.[198] The long-hours culture, the fact that women's lifestyles may make it more difficult to devote time to 'networking', and the fact that High Court judges are still regularly appointed from a handful of elite chambers are all cited as examples of such obstacles. A number of academics have argued that the overwhelmingly white, male culture of the judiciary has a real impact on both the

[194] DCA, *Statistics: Ethnic Minorities in the Judiciary* (HMSO, 2004).
[195] *Judicial Appointments in England and Wales* (HMSO, 2003), at p 1.
[196] *The Circuit Bench: A Women's Place* (1991); cf. Malleson and Banda, *Factors Affecting the Decision to Apply for Silk and Judicial Office* (HMSO, 2000) Lord Chancellor's Department Research Series 02/00; Holland and Spencer, *Without Prejudice? Sex Equality at the Bar and in the Judiciary* (Bar Council, 1992).
[197] *Judges' Council Response to the Consultation Papers on Constitutional Reform*, at para 76: see **www.dca.gov.uk/judicial/pdfs/jcresp.pdf**
[198] Hale, 'Equality and the Judiciary: Why We Should Want More Women Judges' [2001] PL 489 at 492. See also, The Law Society, *Broadening the Bench* (2000).

development of the law and the treatment of those who appear before the courts.[199] For Hale, however, the issue is even more fundamental:[200]

> Judges...are set in authority over others and can sometimes wield enormous power over individuals and businesses. In a democratic society, in which we are all equal citizens, it is wrong in principle for that authority to be wielded by such a very unrepresentative section of the population.

When the government proposed the creation of the new JAC, it also expressed a wider interest in finding new and more inclusive ways of selecting judicial candidates:[201]

> [T]he current judiciary is overwhelmingly white, male, and from a narrow social and educational background. To an extent, this reflects the pool of qualified candidates from which judicial appointments are made: intake to the legal professions has, until recently, been dominated by precisely these social groups.
>
> Of course the fundamental principle in appointing judges is and must remain selection on merit. However, the Government is committed to opening up the system of appointments, to attract suitably qualified candidates both from a wider range of social backgrounds and from a wider range of legal practice.

As this statement suggests, the link between rights of audience and eligibility for judicial office has greatly restricted the pool of potential applicants, and this was one of the main issues raised by the consultation on *Increasing Diversity in the Judiciary*. On the basis of the responses to this consultation, the Department for Constitutional Affairs concluded that:[202]

> The current requirements need to be reviewed, both in terms of the qualification required, and the length of time which must be served before an application for judicial appointment can be made. Examples of the type of people [the Secretary of State] has in mind as potentially having the right sort of skills and experience are legal executives, academics with a legal background; patent and trademark attorneys; and possibly lay magistrates with an appropriate legal qualification.

However, the consultation also revealed widespread support for other measures, such as doing more to attract and support disabled candidates, and allowing more scope for the introduction of flexible sitting arrangements and career breaks.[203] The changes to eligibility criteria being introduced as a result of this consultation will undoubtedly aid efforts to recruit a more diverse judiciary,[204] but the rate of change will also be

---

[199] See, e.g., Kennedy, *Eve Was Framed: Women and British Justice* (Chatto, 1992); Temkin, *Rape and the Legal Process* (Sweet & Maxwell, 1987); Genn, *Paths to Justice* (Hart Publishing, 1997) at p 229; Smart (ed), *Law, Crime and Sexuality: Essays in Feminism* (Sage, 1995).

[200] [2001] PL 489 at 502.

[201] DCA, *Constitutional Reform: A New Way of Appointing Judges* (HMSO, 2003), CP 10/03, Foreword.

[202] DCA, *Increasing Diversity in the Judiciary—Summary of Responses to the Consultation* (HMSO, March 2005), at p 76.

[203] Ibid, at p 8.

[204] See the discussion of the Tribunals, Courts and Enforcement Act 2007, at p 293.

influenced by the government's willingness to address these wider issues, and by the willingness of suitable candidates to put themselves forward.

Tenure

Removal and discipline

Before Stuart times judges could be removed at the will of the King, but this position was altered by the Act of Settlement 1700. The Act provided that, as long as they conducted themselves properly, judges of the superior courts could only be removed on an address by both Houses of Parliament,[205] and this rule still applies to judges of the High Court, Court of Appeal, and House of Lords.[206] No English judge has ever been removed under this procedure, although an Irish judge was removed in 1830 when he was discovered to have misappropriated court funds. Judges of the lower ranks can be removed by the Lord Chancellor without parliamentary approval, but this can only be done on the grounds of incapacity or misbehaviour and with the agreement of the Lord Chief Justice.[207] Judges of all ranks thus enjoy considerable security of tenure.

Serious judicial misconduct is almost unheard of in modern times. In 1983 a circuit judge was removed from office after being convicted of various smuggling offences, but this is an extreme example. On the rare occasions when judges have been disciplined, this has usually taken the form of a reprimand for a lesser 'offence' such as incompetence, neglect, unacceptable delay, or unacceptable personal behaviour.[208] Some judges have responded to allegations of such behaviour by offering their resignation, and others have been asked to do so. Thus, a High Court judge resigned in 1998 after being castigated by the Court of Appeal for taking twenty months to deliver a judgment:[209]

> Conduct like this weakens public confidence in the whole judicial process. Left unchecked, it would be ultimately subversive of the rule of law. Delays on this scale cannot and will not be tolerated.

---

[205] The Lord Chancellor was always an exception: see p 331.

[206] Supreme Court Act 1981, s 11(3) (High Court and Court of Appeal—it is for the Lord Chancellor to formally recommend the exercise of this power to the monarch; s 11(3A); Appellate Jurisdiction Act 1876, s 6 (House of Lords). Special provisions allow the Lord Chancellor to remove a judge who is disabled by permanent infirmity and who does not have the capacity to resign: see the 1981 Act, s 11(8).

[207] Courts Act 1971, s 17(4) (circuit judges); County Courts Act 1984, s 11 (district judges); Courts Act 2003, s 22 (district judges—magistrates' courts). Lay justices have not previously enjoyed the same security of tenure as their professional counterparts, but this position was rectified by s 11 of the Courts Act 2003.

[208] The *Judicial Appointments Annual Report 2002–03* records that two formal reprimands were issued during the relevant period, although the Lord Chancellor received a total of 370 complaints relating to the personal conduct of judges: para 12.2. The Lord Chief Justice now has greater powers in this area: Constitutional Reform Act 2005, s 108.

[209] *Goose* v *Wilson Sandford & Co* (1998) The Times, February 19, *per* Peter Gibson LJ. The judge, Harman J, had regularly featured at the top of a legal journal's 'Worst Judge' poll: see 'Controlling the Judges' (1998) 148 NLJ 234.

Starrs v *Ruxton* and the problem of fixed-term appointments

Unlike other judges, recorders are appointed on a part-time basis and for a specific term of office. Before 2000 the standard length of appointment was three years, and, at the end of this period, the Lord Chancellor had a discretion as to whether a contract should be renewed. These arrangements were called into question by the decision of the Scottish High Court of Justiciary in *Starrs* v *Ruxton*.[210] The court ruled that the use of temporary judges infringed Article 6 of the ECHR, because a judge without security of tenure could not be considered 'independent'. The case was concerned with the use of temporary sheriffs in Scotland, but it had obvious implications for the appointment of recorders and the Lord Chancellor was quick to respond. The terms upon which part-time judges hold office were reviewed, and all are now appointed for a minimum period of five years. They can only be removed on the grounds of misbehaviour, incapacity, failure to comply with sitting requirements, failure to comply with training requirements, or sustained failure to observe reasonably expected standards. In the absence of one of these grounds, contracts will normally be renewed automatically at the end of each five-year term.[211] The Lord Chancellor also took the opportunity to abolish the separate office of 'assistant recorder', and those who already held this title were reappointed as recorders.

Retirement

The standard retirement age for judges is 70,[212] although a judge who has completed twenty years of service can retire with full pension rights at the age of 65.[213] In addition, a judge of the circuit bench or lower ranks may be asked to stay on until he reaches 75,[214] and any retired judge below this age may sit on an ad hoc basis.[215] Lay magistrates also 'retire' at 70, which is when their names are added to the supplemental list and they cease to be able to perform judicial functions.[216] They are, however, unsalaried, and unlike their professional counterparts they do not receive a pension.

Salaries

Judicial salaries are determined by the Lord Chancellor with the consent of the Minister for the Civil Service (the Prime Minister). They are paid from the Consolidated Fund[217] and are not subject to a vote in Parliament. They are deliberately set at a high level so as to provide a further safeguard of independence, the idea being that a well-paid judge will not be vulnerable to bribery and corruption. In fact, however, the high

---

[210] 2000 JC 208, 2000 SLT 42, *sub nom Starrs* v *Procurator Fiscal*. See also: *Scanfuture* v *Secretary of State for Trade and Industry* [2001] ICR 1096, [2001] IRLR 416.

[211] Courts Act 1971, s 21.   [212] Judicial Pensions and Retirement Act 1993, s 26(1); Sch 5.

[213] Judicial Pensions Act 1981. The twenty-year rule means that even if a judge continues until the age of 70, he will be ineligible to receive a full pension unless he was called to the bench by the age of 50.

[214] Judicial Pensions and Retirement Act 1993, s 26(5).   [215] Ibid, s 26(7).

[216] Courts Act 2003, ss 12 and 13 (replacing the Justices of the Peace Act 1997, s 7).

[217] Supreme Court Act 1981, s 12; Administration of Justice Act 1973, s 9.

earning capacity of the most successful practitioners means that accepting a judicial appointment will often involve a reduction in income. As of November 2007, district judges in both the magistrates' and the civil courts received a salary of £98,900, while High Court judges received £165,900 and the Lord Chief Justice got £230,400.[218] By contrast, the most successful barristers can earn over £500,000 per annum, although the *average* income of barristers is much less than this.[219]

KEY ISSUE

For the judiciary to work effectively it must be properly trained. The idea that judges on appointment have sufficient knowledge and expertise has long gone. In 1979 the Judicial Studies Board was established to provide training for both new and experienced judges. The Board is run by judges themselves, and through training courses and refresher courses it seeks to create an awareness of best practice and to equip judges to deal with common problems.[220] It publishes 'Bench Books' to provide model rulings and directions, and runs extensive judicial training courses, developing skills in substantive law as well as skills necessary to deal with different types of case (such as those relating to children or those involving sexual offences), as well as fundamental awareness about sentences and procedure, criminology and penology, racial and equality awareness, and person 'judging' skills.

? Questions

1. What skills do you think judges need?
2. How prescriptive do you think the Judicial Studies Board should be?
3. What do you think is the status of model directions or statements issued by the Judicial Studies Board?

Judicial immunity

The doctrine of judicial immunity is an offshoot of the principle of independence. Historically, the degree of immunity recognized has varied with the status of the judge, and the old cases distinguish between judges of superior and inferior courts. Superior court judges were immune from liability even if acting maliciously, while judges of the inferior courts enjoyed immunity only while acting within their jurisdiction. Thus, a recorder who unlawfully imprisoned a jury for ignoring his direction to convict was held immune from suit,[221] while an unfortunate county court judge was held liable in damages for making an innocent mistake of law.[222]

---

[218] Ministry of Justice, *Judicial Salaries and Fees 2007–2008*.
[219] *Chambers Guide to the Legal Profession 2001–2002*, at p 1247.
[220] For a more detailed discussion, see Partington, 'Training the Judiciary in England and Wales' (1994) 13 CJQ 319; Malleson, *The New Judiciary: The Effects of Expansion and Activism* (Ashgate, 1999), ch 5.
[221] *Hamond* v *Howell* (1677) 2 Mod Rep 218.
[222] *Houlden* v *Smith* (1850) 14 QB 841.

In the modern case of *Sirros* v *Moore*, the Court of Appeal rejected the idea that the degree of immunity should depend upon the status of the court. The claimant was a foreign national who unsuccessfully appealed to the Crown Court against a recommendation that he should be deported. The circuit judge who rejected his appeal was under the mistaken impression that the claimant was in custody and, at the end of the hearing, he ordered a police officer to arrest and detain him. The detention was clearly unlawful, and the claimant brought an action for false imprisonment against both the judge and the police officer. However, the Court of Appeal held that the judge was immune from liability, despite the fact that he was a judge of an inferior court. The police officer was also held to be immune on the basis that he was following the judge's orders. Lord Denning MR even suggested that the principle of immunity should extend to justices of the peace:[223]

> Every judge of the courts of this land from the highest to the lowest should be protected to the same degree, and liable to the same degree. If the reason underlying this immunity is to ensure 'that they may be free in thought and independent in judgment', it applies to every judge, whatever his rank. Each should be protected from liability to damages when he is acting judicially. Each should be able to do his work in complete independence and free from fear. He should not have to turn the pages of his books with trembling fingers, asking himself; 'If I do this, shall I be liable in damages?' So long as he does his work in the honest belief that it is within his jurisdiction, then he is not liable to an action.

In the later case of *McC* v *Mullan*,[224] the House of Lords questioned the assertion that inferior and superior courts are now subject to the same rules. It also confirmed that justices of the peace could be sued if they acted outside their jurisdiction. Nevertheless, *Sirros* v *Moore* remains good law, and justices of the peace now have statutory immunity for acts done in good faith and in the purported execution of their duty.[225] In addition, a judge cannot be compelled to give evidence of matters relating to the performance of his judicial functions, although he is a competent witness to such matters and may testify if he is willing to do so.[226]

The immunity that attaches to judicial proceedings is not personal to the judge. No civil action lies in respect of words spoken in the course of proceedings by parties,[227] witnesses,[228] or advocates;[229] nor can an action be brought in respect of the verdict of a jury.[230] In addition, media reports of judicial proceedings are absolutely privileged in the law of defamation. They must, however, be fair, accurate, and contemporaneous.[231]

---

[223] [1975] QB 118 at 136, [1974] 3 All ER 776 at 785.   [224] [1985] AC 528, [1984] 3 All ER 908.
[225] Courts Act 2003, ss 31 and 32.   [226] *Warren* v *Warren* [1997] QB 488, [1996] 4 All ER 664.
[227] *Astley* v *Younge* (1759) 2 Burr 807.
[228] *Hargreaves* v *Bretherton* [1959] 1 QB 45, [1958] 3 All ER 122.
[229] *Munster* v *Lamb* (1883) 11 QBD 588.   [230] *Bushell's Case* (1670) Vaugh 135.
[231] Defamation Act 1996, s 14.

Further reading

BRADLEY, 'Judicial Independence under Attack' [2003] PL 397

CRAIG, 'Public Law, Political Theory and Legal Theory' [2000] PL 211

LAWS, 'Law and Democracy' [1995] PL 80

NICOL, 'Law and Politics after the Human Rights Act' [2006] PL 722

STEYN, 'The Weakest and Least Dangerous Department of Government' [1997] PL 84

STEYN, 'Democracy through Law' [2002] EHRLR 723

WADE, 'The Basis of Legal Sovereignty' [1955] CLJ 172

WOOLF, '*Droit Public*: English Style' [1995] PL 57

WOOLF, 'The Rule of Law and a Change in the Constitution' (2004) 63(2) CLJ 317

Juries

10

INTRODUCTION

The focus in this chapter will be on the role of the jury in the modern English legal system. In the twenty-first century the majority of criminal cases are tried by magistrates rather than juries and, with the exception of trials for defamation, the use of the jury in civil cases is now almost unheard of. Yet the idea of trial by jury has always been seen as a cornerstone of the English legal system, and it remains the standard mode of trial for dealing with the most serious types of criminal case.

The following aspects of the jury and its role will be addressed in this chapter:

- the origins of the jury system and the use of the jury trial in both criminal and civil cases;
- the way in which juries are selected and empanelled, and the rules governing excusal and disqualification;
- the extent to which the composition of a jury might be challenged by one of the parties to an action, and the powers available to judges when dealing with such challenges;
- the rules governing jury secrecy and their implications for research into jury decisions;
- the extent to which the use of juries is compatible with the idea of 'a fair trial'.

Historical growth of the jury system

The trial of criminals by jury evolved in the thirteenth century to replace trial by ordeal, and by the middle of the fourteenth century the separate roles of the petty jury and grand jury were established.

The grand jury was not a 'trial jury' in the modern sense. Its original function was to present persons for trial at the start of assizes or quarter sessions,[1] but when the system of preliminary investigation by magistrates developed its role was reduced to a mere formality. The grand jury was finally abolished by the Criminal Justice Act 1948.[2]

---

[1] See p 227.
[2] Section 31(3). Grand juries are still used in some US jurisdictions.

The twelve-member petty jury was the equivalent of the modern trial jury, although in its early stages jurors were summoned for their local knowledge and acted as witnesses rather than judges of fact. The petty jury's function changed gradually as the practice of examining independent witnesses grew and by the fifteenth century it had assumed its modern role as arbiter of fact. A landmark decision in 1670[3] established that jurors should decide cases according to their consciences and that they could not be punished for returning a verdict contrary to the evidence or the judge's direction.

In civil cases there was only ever one type of jury: the trial jury of twelve members. This had its origins in the Assize of Clarendon 1166, and by 1304 it was established that all trespass actions in common law courts had to be tried with a jury. As with criminal juries, jurors in civil trials originally acted as witnesses, but a similar transition from witnesses to judges of fact took place. The steady decline of the jury in civil cases began with the Common Law Procedure Act 1854, which allowed common law actions to be tried without a jury if both parties agreed. The use of juries in civil cases is now extremely limited.[4]

The composition of the modern jury

Qualifying for jury duty

Eligibility for jury service used to depend upon the existence of a property qualification, and juries were criticized for being 'predominantly male, middle-aged, middle-minded and middle-class'.[5] Following the recommendations of the Morris Committee[6] the property qualification was abolished and the present system of selecting jurors from the electoral register was introduced.[7] The law was consolidated in the Juries Act 1974 and was most recently amended by the Criminal Justice Act 2003. Section 1 of the 1974 Act now provides that[8] a person will be qualified to serve as a juror and liable to attend for jury service when summoned, if:

(a) he is registered as a parliamentary or local government elector and is not less than 18 nor more than 70[9] years of age;

(b) he has been ordinarily resident in the United Kingdom, the Channel Islands or the Isle of Man for any period of at least five years since attaining the age of 13;

(c) he is not a mentally disordered person; and

(d) he is not disqualified for jury service.

---

[3] *Bushell's case* (1670) Vaugh 135.   [4] See p 364.

[5] Devlin, *Trial by Jury* (Steven & Sons, 1956), at p 20.

[6] *Report of the Departmental Committee on Jury Service*, Cmnd 2627 (HMSO, 1965).

[7] Criminal Justice Act 1972. For the effect of these reforms on the composition of juries, see Baldwin and McConville, *Jury Trials* (Clarendon Press, 1979) at p 94.

[8] As amended by the 2003 Act: with effect from 5 April 2004.

[9] The upper age limit was raised from 65 by the Criminal Justice Act 1988, s 119.

Thus, assuming that the residential and age qualifications are met, anyone listed on the electoral register may be required to serve as a juror unless he or she is *ineligible* by reason of mental disorder[10] or *disqualified* under Schedule 1, Part 2.[11]

Excusal and deferral

The government considers jury service to be 'one of the most important civic duties that anyone can be asked to perform'.[12] Those eligible have a legal obligation to attend if summoned unless they can satisfy the 'appropriate officer'[13] that there is a good reason to excuse or defer them.[14] In a Home Office study of 50,000 people summoned for jury duty,[15] 38 per cent of those in the sample were excused and nearly 17 per cent were granted a deferral.[16] The most common grounds for excusal were childcare responsibilities, illness, and work commitments. Guidelines[17] state that excusals should only be granted to those who can show good reason for not serving at any time within the following twelve months. Religious objections[18] or being out of the country are cited as examples of good reasons for excusal, but deferral is considered more appropriate for those with holiday plans or work commitments.

Before 5 April 2004, members of Parliament, medical professionals, and members of the armed forces were entitled to be excused from jury service as of right, the rationale being that such persons would generally have more pressing duties to perform elsewhere. Those aged over 65 and those belonging to religious societies with beliefs incompatible with jury service[19] could also insist on being excused. In addition, ministers of religion, members of the legal profession, and certain other persons involved in the administration of justice were *ineligible* to serve as jurors by reason of their occupation. The Morris Committee had suggested these occupational exclusions because of concerns that a clergyman or someone with professional knowledge

---

[10] This is defined in Sch 1, Part 1 of the 1974 Act (as amended).

[11] There are three basic categories of disqualification. (1) A person who has been given an extended sentence, or who has been sentenced to a term of imprisonment or detention of five years or more, or to imprisonment or detention for public protection, is effectively disqualified from jury service for life. (2) A person who has served a period of imprisonment, youth custody or detention or who has been the subject of one of the community or rehabilitation orders listed in paragraph 7 of the Schedule is disqualified for ten years after completion of the sentence. (3) A person who is on bail in criminal proceedings is also disqualified.

[12] DCA, *Jury Summoning Guidance*, Consultation Paper (HMSO, 2003), Foreword.

[13] In practice, this task now falls to the Jury Central Summoning Bureau: see p 351.

[14] Juries Act 1974, ss 9 and 9A. Failure to attend is a criminal offence punishable by a fine (s 20), although 'offenders' are rarely pursued: see Darbyshire, Maughan and Stewart, *What can the English Legal System Learn from Jury Research Published up to 2001?—Findings for the Criminal Courts Review* (HMSO, 2001) at p 6.

[15] Airs and Shaw, *Jury Excusal and Deferral*, Home Office Research Findings No 102 (HMSO, 1999), at p 1.

[16] A further 13 per cent were ineligible, disqualified or excused as of right, and 15 per cent had their summonses returned as 'undelivered' or simply did not attend.

[17] Issued in April 2004 under the new s 9AA of the Juries Act 1974: DCA, *Guidance for Summoning Officers when Considering Deferral and Excusal Applications*.

[18] In *R v Crown Court at Guildford, ex parte Siderfin* [1990] 2 QB 683, [1989] 3 All ER 73, it was held that excusal on religious grounds should only be granted where the religious belief would stand in the way of proper performance of the jury function.

[19] Ibid.

of the justice system might exercise undue influence in a jury room. There was also an argument that someone working in the legal system might find it difficult to follow a judge's directions if this meant putting aside his own legal 'knowledge'.

In his *Review of the Criminal Courts*, Auld LJ concluded that despite the reforms of previous decades, juries still lacked diversity and were not sufficiently representative of the communities from which they were drawn. With a view to widening participation, he recommended that 'no-one should be automatically ineligible or excusable from jury service simply because he or she is a member of a certain profession or holds a particular office or job'.[20] This recommendation was given effect by the Criminal Justice Act 2003. The government dismissed concerns that the presence of lawyers in the jury room might be problematic:[21]

> In England and Wales, a large number of people with extensive knowledge of the criminal justice system—legal academics, law students and civil servants working in criminal justice—currently do jury service. There is no evidence to suggest that the involvement of any of these groups in jury service has been a problem. More generally, the diluting effect of the process of random selection, and the group dynamic of the jury, serve to protect the integrity of the deliberative process.

Those who would previously have been ineligible or excused as of right because of their occupations are now subject to the same regime as everyone else: if they wish to be excused from jury service, they must persuade the summoning officer that they have a good reason. Even judges may now be called upon to serve as jurors and the Lord Chief Justice recently wrote to all judges offering advice on what to do if summoned.[22] The only persons automatically entitled to be excused are those who have served (or attended to serve) on a jury within the previous two years.[23] The Department for Constitutional Affairs estimated that a person's chances of doing jury service during his or her lifetime are roughly one in six.[24]

Selecting and summoning jurors

Before 2000, jurors were selected locally by the summoning officers for each court centre, but a Central Summoning Bureau has now been established at Blackfriars Crown Court. The Bureau operates on a national basis and randomly selects names from the electoral register by computer, taking into account the number of prospective jurors needed for each area. It is then responsible for issuing summonses and for dealing with applications for excusal or deferral. Under the old system many local summoning officers developed their own methods for selecting names from the electoral

---

[20] *Review of the Criminal Courts of England and Wales* (HMSO, 2001) at para 5.14.

[21] DCA, *Jury Summoning Guidance*, at p 9.

[22] The text of the letter can be accessed through the Department for Constitutional Affairs website: **www. dca.gov.uk**

[23] Juries Act 1974, s 8. The Auld Review recommended that this timescale should be extended (at para 5.224).

[24] *Jury Summoning Guidance*, at p 6.

lists, and the approach to dealing with excusals and deferrals differed from area to area. The move to a centralized system has gone some way towards improving the randomness and consistency of the selection process, and it should also enable automatic checks to be made to ensure that those disqualified by their criminal convictions do not serve. It does not, however, address the more fundamental criticism that thousands of otherwise eligible people do not qualify for jury service at all because their names do not appear on the electoral register. A particular concern here is that members of certain ethnic groups may be under-represented on jury panels because they are less likely to register to vote than those from other backgrounds. For example, research carried out for the Home Office in 1999 suggested that across the population as a whole the rate of non-registration was around 8 per cent, but for black people this figure was as high as 24 per cent.[25] In reliance on this research, Auld LJ's *Review of the Criminal Courts* recommended that, in racially sensitive cases, there should be a modified selection procedure to ensure that up to three ethnic minority jurors were chosen.[26] However, this recommendation was rejected by the government as being potentially divisive, and a more recent and more comprehensive study commissioned by the Ministry of Justice found no real evidence that ethnic minorities were under-represented on juries:[27]

> [T]he survey revealed that the summoning process reaches BME [black and minority ethnic] groups in remarkable consistency to BME representation in the local population for virtually all Crown Courts. This indicates that the process of computerised random selection from the electoral lists provided by local authorities is successfully summoning ethnically representative groups of potential jurors for Crown Courts in England and Wales.

Challenging the composition of the jury

Once the summonses have been issued, the court officer prepares a 'panel' of prospective jurors and the parties have the right to inspect a list of their names and addresses. The names of those on the list are then put on cards and placed in a box. At the beginning of a trial, cards are drawn from the box by a ballot in open court[28] and those named on them are sworn in as jurors.[29] It is at this point that the parties may exercise their limited rights to challenge those selected.[30] However, as the parties are

---

[25] Airs and Shaw, *Jury Excusal and Deferral*, Home Office Research Findings No 102 (HMSO, 1999), at p 2.

[26] At para 5.60.

[27] Thomas and Balmer, *Diversity and Fairness in the Jury System*, Ministry of Justice Research Series 2/07 (HMSO, 2007), at p 77. For further discussion of the issues surrounding the ethnicity of jurors, see p 335.

[28] Juries Act 1974, s 11. A jury should only be used once except where a second trial commences within twenty-four hours of the jury being constituted: s 11(5)(a). However, individual jurors may be returned to the pool at the conclusion of a trial and may try other cases if their names are drawn in subsequent ballots. The usual period of jury service is two weeks.

[29] For the manner of taking an oath for these purposes, see the Oaths Act 1978, ss 1 and 5.

[30] For a discussion, see Buxton, 'Challenging and Discharging Jurors—Part 1' [1990] Crim LR 225.

given no information about the panel except for a list of names and addresses,[31] they will generally have very little to go on. Characteristics such as gender and race are not legitimate grounds for a challenge,[32] and the parties are not permitted to question jurors to ascertain whether any other grounds exist. In exceptional cases a judge may agree to the use of a questionnaire to determine whether jurors have been influenced by pre-trial publicity,[33] but exposure to pre-trial publicity in itself is not a sufficient basis for a challenge.

The effect of this is that unless a potential juror happens to be personally known to the defendant or one of the witnesses, it is unlikely in practice that the defence will have any basis for a challenge. The prosecution, however, may have a slight advantage over the defence because of the controversial practice known as 'jury vetting'.

Jury vetting

This practice came to light in 1978 when it was discovered that the prosecution in an official secrets trial had 'vetted' the names on the jury panel in order to identify those who might be 'disloyal'. The Attorney-General responded to the criticism that followed by publishing his guidelines on the use of the practice. The current guidelines date from 1988[34] and permit two types of check. The first involves checking the names of potential jurors against police records to ensure that disqualified persons are excluded from the panel.[35] The second type of vetting is more controversial and involves making 'authorized checks' against the records of Special Branch and the security services. Authorized checks can only be made in national security and terrorism cases, and they require the personal consent of the Attorney-General. The aim is to identify potential jurors with extreme political views, on the basis that such persons might find it impossible to assess a case fairly, and might exert improper pressure on other jurors or reveal evidence heard in camera. If the checks reveal information about a juror that is of concern to the Director of Public Prosecutions, the prosecutor in the case may then seek to exclude that person by asking him or her to 'stand by for the Crown'.

---

[31] It is legitimate to withhold the names of jurors from a court if there is a real risk of the jury being 'nobbled'. However, the parties still have the right to challenge for cause and are entitled to insist on inspecting the list of names on the panel: *R v Comerford* [1998] 1 All ER 823, [1998] 1 WLR 191. Note however, that under ss 44 and 46 of the Criminal Justice Act 2003, a jury trial may be dispensed with altogether if there is a 'real and present' danger of jury tampering which cannot be avoided by other measures. The defendant in such a case may be tried by a judge sitting alone.

[32] *R v Ford* [1989] QB 868, [1989] 3 All ER 445.

[33] In *R v Andrews (Tracey)* [1999] Crim LR 156 the Court of Appeal confirmed that this was a possibility, but it upheld the decision of the trial judge to refuse a questionnaire in Miss Andrews's case.

[34] *Practice Note (Juries: Right to Stand by: Jury Checks)* [1988] 3 All ER 1086, (1989) 88 Cr App R 123.

[35] The creation of the Central Summoning Bureau makes it possible for such checks to be made before jurors are even summoned and it is a criminal offence for a person who knows that he is disqualified from jury service to sit.

The legitimacy of jury vetting was challenged in *R* v *Sheffield Crown Court, ex parte Brownlow*, in which Lord Denning MR expressed the view that:[36]

> To my mind it is unconstitutional for the police authorities to engage in jury vetting. So long as a person is eligible for jury service, and is not disqualified, I cannot think it right that, behind his back, the police should go through his record so as to enable him to be asked to 'stand by for the Crown' or to be challenged for the defence. If this sort of thing is to be allowed, what comes of a man's right of privacy?

These comments were merely *obiter* however and, although jury vetting is not specifically sanctioned by the Juries Act, it has been held that the practice is not unlawful.[37]

Standing by for the Crown

The prosecution has always had the right to request that a juror 'stand by for the Crown'. This means, in effect, that he or she will be moved to the back of the queue of potential jurors and will not be called upon for the trial unless and until the entire panel is exhausted. In this way the prosecution is able to prevent the juror from serving, without showing cause, as long as there are enough members of the panel left to form a jury. The most obvious situation in which this form of challenge may be used is in connection with jury vetting. The Attorney-General's guidelines[38] make it clear that jurors should only be stood by in exceptional cases. They also state that where jury vetting has revealed information that strongly suggests that someone on the panel may be biased against the defendant, the prosecution has a duty to make defence counsel aware of the risk.

The right of stand by is controversial because it is not open to the defence. Defence counsel used to have the right to exclude up to three jurors without showing cause in what was known as a peremptory challenge. However, this was abolished by the Criminal Justice Act 1988[39] and the only form of challenge now open to the defence is the right to challenge for cause.

Challenging for cause

Both parties have the right to challenge any or all of the jurors for cause,[40] and this means establishing a good reason why the juror(s) in question should not be involved in the particular case. If prima facie grounds for a challenge can be shown, the issue will be tried by the judge.[41] The fact that a juror is ineligible or disqualified from jury service would clearly be grounds for a challenge,[42] but a juror may also be challenged on the ground of bias.

---

[36] [1980] QB 530 at 542, [1980] 2 All ER 444 at 453.

[37] *R* v *Mason* [1981] QB 881, [1980] 3 All ER 777.

[38] *Practice Note (Juries: Right to Stand by: Jury Checks)* [1988] 3 All ER 1086, (1989) 88 Cr App R 123.

[39] Section 118.   [40] Juries Act 1974, s 12(1)(a); Juries Act 1825, s 29.   [41] Ibid, s 12(2).

[42] Ibid, s 12(4). If a person serves on a jury and is subsequently discovered to have been disqualified or unfit to serve, this will not constitute grounds for reversing the jury's verdict unless an objection was raised at the time: s 18(1).

Bias

Before the implementation of the Human Rights Act 1998, the leading case on the meaning of bias was *R* v *Gough*.[43] The appellant in the case had been indicted on a single count that he had conspired with his brother to commit robbery. His brother's name and address had been disclosed in open court during the trial, and a photograph of both men had been shown to the jury. One of the jurors was a next-door neighbour of the brother, but she did not realize this until he started shouting in court after the appellant was convicted. Gough appealed on the ground that a reasonable and fair-minded person would have had a reasonable suspicion that a fair trial was not possible under these circumstances. The appeal was dismissed, however, and the House of Lords held that no such danger arose on the facts of the case.

When the Human Rights Act came into force, the Court of Appeal[44] made a 'modest adjustment' to the *Gough* test in order to satisfy the requirement that cases should be determined by an 'independent and impartial tribunal'.[45] The modified approach makes the objective nature of the test more explicit and asks whether a 'fair-minded and informed observer' would conclude that there was 'a real possibility of bias'.[46] In *R* v *Pintori (Andrei)*,[47] a conviction was quashed on the grounds that one of the jurors was a civilian police worker who had previously worked with some of the officers called as witnesses at the trial. The Court of Appeal held that in these circumstances a fair-minded and informed observer would conclude that there was a real possibility of the jury being biased. The court had no doubt that the bias test was satisfied as far as the individual juror was concerned, and it followed that there was a real risk of the entire jury's verdict being 'tainted' by her influence.[48]

The issue of race

The principle of random selection lies at the heart of the jury system, and jurors are not generally selected on the basis of gender or ethnic origin. As already noted, the government recently rejected a recommendation that juries in racially sensitive cases should be subject to an ethnic minority quota,[49] and there is still no lawful mechanism for interfering with the composition of a jury in order to achieve a racial balance.[50]

---

[43] [1993] AC 646, [1993] 2 All ER 724.

[44] *Director General of Fair Trading* v *Proprietary Association of Great Britain; sub nom Re Medicaments and Related Classes of Goods (No 2)* [2001] 1 WLR 700, [2001] HRLR 17.

[45] Article 6, ECHR.

[46] The modified test has since been approved by the House of Lords in *Porter* v *Magill* [2001] UKHL 67, [2002] 2 AC 357, [2002] 1 All ER 465.

[47] [2007] EWCA Crim 1700, [2007] Crim LR 997.

[48] The rules governing jury secrecy meant that the court had no way of knowing what role this juror had played in the deliberations, and what influence (if any) she had had over her fellow jurors. For further discussion of the jury secrecy rules, see p 366.

[49] See p 353.

[50] *R* v *Ford* [1989] QB 868, [1989] 3 All ER 445. In the unreported case of *R* v *El Faisal* (20 January 2003), a judge excluded Hindu and Jewish jurors from the trial of a Muslim cleric accused of soliciting the murder of Hindus and Jews. This was, however, a truly exceptional case: see Tausz and Ormerod [2003] Crim LR 633.

In England and Wales there is virtually no mechanism to ensure that juror bias may be removed. Certainly there remains challenge for cause but the defence are given no facts about jurors upon which to base a challenge. Thus, short of a juror having a swastika tattoo in full view of the court, challenge for cause is practically redundant.[51]

The European Court of Human Rights has held that this position is not inherently incompatible with the right to a fair trial. Indeed, in *Gregory* v *UK*,[52] the Strasbourg court held that a black defendant had received a fair trial even though the judge had refused to excuse a member of the jury following complaints of racial bias from another juror. The judge had reminded the jury of the importance of deciding the case according to the evidence, and this was held to be sufficient to satisfy Article 6. The Court of Appeal recently took a similar approach[53] in the case of a black defendant convicted of grievous bodily harm by an all-white jury. The offence had been committed during a violent incident involving the defendant and a group of white men, but the Court of Appeal confirmed that the judge had no discretion to discharge jurors for the purposes of altering the jury's composition. Although the defendant framed his appeal in terms of the right to a fair trial, the court held that fairness was ensured by the principle of random selection.

The present system rests on the assumption that a randomly selected jury with twelve white members is not necessarily incapable of fairly trying a black defendant. Indeed, research done for the Commission for Racial Equality suggested that black defendants are marginally more likely to be acquitted by a jury than white defendants,[54] and another recent study found no evidence that the verdicts of racially mixed juries were influenced by the ethnicity of either the defendant or the victim.[55] The latter study was based on case simulations in which 'juries' were asked to watch recorded footage of a real criminal trial. The juries were made up of real jurors who had just completed their jury service at Blackfriars Crown Court, and the trial footage was carefully edited so that aspects of the trial, including the ethnicity of both the defendant and the victim, could be systematically varied. Although the authors found that the decisions of some jurors did seem to be influenced by ethnicity,[56] with some displaying 'same race

[51] Darbyshire Maughan and Stewart, *What can the English Legal System Learn from Jury Research Published up to 2001?—Findings for the Criminal Courts Review* (HMSO, 2001) at p 18. The authors supported Auld's recommendation that special selection procedures should be used in racially sensitive cases.

[52] (1998) 25 EHRR 577. This decision was distinguished in the later case of *Sander* v *UK* (2001) 31 EHRR 44: see p 369.

[53] *R* v *Smith* [2003] EWCA Crim 283, [2003] 1 WLR 2229.

[54] Bridges, Choongh and McConville, *Ethnic-Minority Defendants and the Right to Elect Jury Trial* (CRE, 2000). It is at least possible that black defendants are more likely than whites to be taken to trial on comparatively weak evidence. See also: Enright, 'Multi-racial Juries' (1991) 41 NLJ 992.

[55] Thomas and Balmer, *Diversity and Fairness in the Jury System*, Ministry of Justice Research Series 2/07 (HMSO, 2007). See now Ministry of Justice, *Are Juries Fair?* (HMSO, 2010), cited at n 138. For a discussion of other aspects of this research, see p 370.

[56] Ibid, at p 164. They found, for example, that jurors were marginally more likely to vote to acquit black and ethnic minority defendants than white ones, and in this respect their findings lend some support to the research commissioned by the CRE. See n 54.

leniency' towards defendants in certain types of case,[57] they also found that ethnicity had no discernible impact on the decisions of juries as a whole.[58] Individual biases were effectively nullified by the process of collective deliberation and by the possibility of majority verdicts. Crucially, however, all of the 'juries' used in this study were racially mixed, and it is by no means clear whether all-white juries would be as effective in nullifying individual biases. As the report's authors acknowledge, demographic factors mean that 'most juries in most Crown Courts in England and Wales are likely to be "all-white juries"',[59] and further research will therefore be needed before we can conclude that ethnicity has no impact on jury decision-making.

Although racism undoubtedly exists,[60] since other forms of prejudice also exist it is questionable whether 'race' should be singled out for special treatment. On this point, Auld argued that:[61]

> [W]hite juries are, or are perceived to be, less fair to black than to white people. It is [the] quality of visible difference and the prejudice that it may engender that singles out race for different treatment from other special interest groups.

Auld's proposal for a modified selection procedure was confined to 'racially sensitive' cases: he did not think that a special procedure should be used simply because a defendant happened to be black. Yet there is surely a 'visible difference' between a white jury and a black defendant in a robbery case, just as there would be if the black defendant was accused of racially motivated violence. Moreover, the absence of a visible difference between the defendant and the jury would not guarantee a bias-free decision in other sensitive cases. It would not, for example, assist a gay man tried before a homophobic jury if the fact of his homosexuality were relevant to the case and revealed during the evidence. Similarly, a religious leader prosecuted for inciting violence towards 'non-believers' would not be able to conceal the fact of his religious difference from members of the jury.[62] Of course, judges already have a discretion to discharge any juror who is incapable of properly performing his or her functions,[63] and an alternative to Auld's proposal might be to allow questionnaires to be used in appropriate cases for the purpose of uncovering possible bias.[64] Such an approach would, however, mark a significant inroad into the principle of random selection.

Challenging the array

At common law it is possible for either party to challenge the entire jury on the ground that the person responsible for summoning the jurors is biased or has acted

---

[57] Those that lacked an explicit 'racial' element: jurors showed no such leniency in cases in which the defendant was accused of a racially aggravated offence: ibid, at p 166.

[58] Ibid, at pp 167–8.   [59] Ibid, at p 190.

[60] In 1995, the victims of nearly 400,000 crimes considered the offences to have been racially motivated: Auld Review, at para 5.56.

[61] Ibid, at para 5.59.   [62] See n 50.   [63] See above.   [64] See p 354.

improperly.[65] This is known as a challenge to the array. Such challenges are now extremely rare, although there was an unsuccessful attempt to challenge an all-white jury on this basis in *R* v *Danvers*.[66]

The judge's discretion to discharge

Where there are doubts about the capacity of a person to act effectively as a juror because of language difficulties[67] or a physical disability,[68] the 1974 Act empowers a judge to discharge that person from jury service. Judges also have a residual discretion to prevent a person from serving in any other circumstances in which it is proper to do so.[69] A judge may, for example, discharge a person who is manifestly unsuited for jury service because of illiteracy, or who might otherwise be the subject of a challenge for cause. It is implicit in section 16 of the Juries Act that a juror may also be discharged once a trial is underway. This may be necessary, for example, if he is taken ill or if it becomes apparent during the course of the trial that he may be biased. A judge may also discharge a juror who experiences professional or personal difficulties during the trial, and a recent practice direction asks judges to be sensitive to the inconvenience that jury service may cause. However, it suggests that where a juror in a longer trial encounters a temporary difficulty such as a childcare problem or an urgent public service commitment, the judge may be able to avoid discharging the juror by allowing a short adjournment instead.[70]

In some circumstances, a failure to discharge a juror may constitute grounds for a subsequent appeal against conviction,[71] and as long as the number of jurors does not fall below nine it is possible for the trial to continue.[72] Exceptionally, the judge may discharge the entire jury if it appears that jury tampering has taken place,[73] or that the jury may be unable to reach a fair verdict because of adverse media reporting.[74]

---

[65] This common law power is expressly preserved by s 12(6) of the Juries Act 1974.

[66] [1982] Crim LR 680.   [67] Section 10.

[68] Section 9B, as inserted by the Criminal Justice and Public Order Act 1994, s 41. In *Re Osman* [1995] 1 WLR 1327, [1996] 1 Cr App R 126, a profoundly deaf person was discharged on the basis that he could only have understood the case with the assistance of an interpreter: as a non-juror, the interpreter could not have been allowed into the jury room. The Lord Chancellor subsequently indicated that he could see no objection to deaf people serving as jurors: Auld Review, at para 5.56.

[69] *Mansell* v *R* (1857) 8 E & B 54; see Buxton, 'Challenging and Discharging Jurors—Part 1' [1990] Crim LR 225.

[70] *Practice Direction (Jury Service: Excusal (Amendment))* [2005] 1 WLR 1361, [2005] 3 All ER 89 (amending *Practice Direction (Criminal Proceedings: Consolidation)* [2002] 1 WLR 2870, [2002] 3 All ER 904).

[71] *R* v *Spencer* [1987] AC 128, [1986] 2 All ER 928.   [72] 1974 Act, s 16(1).

[73] Criminal Justice Act 2003, s 46. The judge must then decide whether to continue the proceedings without a jury (see p 363), or whether to terminate the trial.

[74] In 2001 the judge in the trial of four footballers prosecuted for attacking an Asian student ruled that there was no evidence of a racial motive for the assault. The jury was later discharged when a national newspaper ran a story alleging that the attack *was* racially motivated. Three of the footballers were eventually tried before a second jury but two were cleared of all charges. One was convicted of affray.

KEY ISSUE

The justification for trial by jury is that it represents a judgment by ordinary people on facts put before the court by prosecution or claimant. The jury decides on the evidence put before it.[75] It is regarded as a 'constitutional' protection.[76] Its key quality, apart from the fact that members of a jury are not (generally)[77] legally qualified, is that its composition is random. That does not mean that a jury is, or should be, representative, but nonetheless it should reflect society as a whole. For that reason the widening of the qualification for jury service is to be welcomed, although, for reasons already explained, debates continue as to whether it is desirable to have on a jury individuals with legal qualifications or professional experience.

More challenging are the ongoing debates as to how far proactive steps should be taken to ensure appropriate ethnic, racial, or gender compositions. It is clearly wrong that juries should not be typical of the society as a whole, but any attempt to promote the representation of those currently under-represented in the jury system is likely to diminish the random nature of the composition.

? Questions

1. Should a jury be representative of society as a whole? Or the community in which the defendant lives and works?

2. How far can, or should, a court go in securing a jury of a particular racial or gender composition?

3. How for many people can service on a jury be reconciled with performance of employment or family obligations?

4. Is there a danger that juries will be populated with certain groups that have the time to devote to the role (the unemployed, retired, and so on)? Does it matter?

The use of the jury trial at the present day

Before the present century the jury system was widely pronounced to be one of the chief safeguards against the abuse of prerogative and judicial power. The right to trial by jury was thought to be essential and inviolable, and Blackstone saw the jury in criminal cases as a barrier between the liberties of the people and the prerogative of the Crown.[78] Lord Camden, reflecting the mood of the age, observed: 'Trial by jury is indeed the foundation of our free constitution; take that away, and the whole fabric will soon moulder into dust.'[79] By the middle of the nineteenth century the idea that the jury trial was sacrosanct was disappearing, and the jury began to decline as a factor

[75] See *R* v *Thompson, Crawford, Conulu, Allen, Blake, Kanga* [2010] EWCA (Crim) 1623, and p 363.
[76] See Judge LCJ in *R v J, S, M v R* [2010] EWCA Crim 1755, and p 372.
[77] But see p 351.   [78] 3 Comm 379.
[79] See Jackson, *The Machinery of Justice in England* (Cambridge University Press: 8th edn, 1989), p 391 *et seq.*

in both civil and criminal cases. The rapid growth in the volume of civil cases and the even more rapid growth of summary jurisdiction in criminal cases contributed to this decline, but there was also an increasing awareness that juries were both fallible and unpredictable. Yet although the use of the jury trial has steadily diminished, the debate about its merits continues, and the jury trial is still regarded by many as the hallmark of the English criminal justice system.

Criminal cases

In criminal cases the loss of faith in the jury system has been less marked than in civil cases. Trial by jury is still the standard mode of trial for indictable offences, and where a defendant aged 18 or over[80] is prosecuted for an either-way offence, he or she normally has the right to insist on trial by jury. Nevertheless, the percentage of criminal cases actually tried by jury is surprisingly low. The vast majority of offences committed are triable only summarily, and not all defendants who have the right to insist on trial by jury actually do so.[81] In 2001, some 1.84 million defendants were tried summarily, compared with only 78,000 in the Crown Court.[82] Many of those whose cases are disposed of in the Crown Court plead guilty, and the proportion of defendants whose fate is actually determined by a jury is only around 1 per cent. Thus, although the jury trial still has great symbolic importance in the context of serious offences, in the overall scheme of things it actually plays a fairly minor role.

The right to trial by jury for either-way offences has been under review for a number of years. Critics have pointed out that jury trials cost considerably more than the summary alternative, and that most defendants who opt for trial by jury eventually plead guilty.[83] However, attempts to remove or diminish the right have always met with stiff opposition.[84] The Auld Review[85] recommended that the final decision about mode of trial should rest with the court and not the defendant, but the changes eventually introduced by the Criminal Justice Act 2003 did not go this far. Instead, a variety of procedural changes were made to encourage more defendants to elect summary trial, together with increased sentencing powers for magistrates' courts.

Fraud cases

The Roskill Report in 1986 recommended that serious fraud cases should not be tried by jury at all, but should instead be tried by a judge sitting with two lay assessors. This

[80] There are special provisions for children and young persons; see p 573.
[81] The procedure for the allocation of offences is discussed further at p 611.
[82] *Criminal Statistics 2001*, at p 18.
[83] See, e.g., the *Report of the Royal Commission on Criminal Justice*, Cm 2263 (HMSO, 1993); *The Review of Delay in the Criminal Justice System ('the Narey Report')* (HMSO, 1997).
[84] The Criminal Justice (Mode of Trial) Bill 1999 and the Criminal Justice (Mode of Trial) Bill (No 2) 2000 would both have removed the defendant's right to insist on jury trial for an either-way offence. Both Bills were defeated in the House of Lords.
[85] Auld Review, at para 5.166.

was also advocated by the Auld Review.[86] In addition to allowing trial without jury in cases in which there is a real and present danger of jury tampering,[87] the 2003 Act also makes provision for judge-only trials to be used in complex fraud cases. In order for a jury to be dispensed with in a fraud trial, the judge (with the approval of the Lord Chief Justice or his deputy) would have to be satisfied that it was in the interests of justice to hear the case without a jury.[88] At the time of writing this change had yet to be implemented, but the collapse of the *Jubilee Line Extension* case in March 2005 once again drew attention to the issue. The trial of six defendants on allegations of fraud had lasted for 272 days and had been thwarted by excessive delays and problems with the jury. By the time the trial was abandoned, one juror had already been discharged after becoming pregnant and another had been discharged on the grounds of financial hardship. A third juror had requested a discharge on medical grounds, and the health of one of the defendants was also deteriorating. The trial was discontinued at the prosecution's request, and an inquiry ordered by the Attorney-General.[89] On exactly the same day the Lord Chief Justice issued a Protocol for the Control and Management of Heavy Fraud and other Complex Cases. It provides that serious fraud and other complex trials should not normally be permitted to last longer than three months, although it acknowledges that a small number of exceptional cases may take longer than this. A Practice Direction issued at the same time reminds judges that they may occasionally need to use their discretion to adjourn a trial or discharge members of a jury. Where the length of a trial is expected to be particularly long, it is said to be good practice for the judge to enquire at the outset whether members of the jury panel foresee any difficulties with this.[90]

Jury tampering

As noted above powers to order trial by a judge alone in cases in which there was a danger of jury tampering were introduced by the Criminal Justice Act 2003, and came into force in 2007. Section 44 provides that there must first be evidence of a real and present danger that jury tampering could take place. Second, it must be shown that, despite any steps that could be taken (including the provision of police protection) that might reasonably be taken to prevent jury tampering, there must be a likelihood

---

[86] Ibid, at para 5.192.

[87] Section 44. A clause that would have allowed a defendant charged with an indictable offence to request trial by judge alone was dropped from the Bill, following considerable opposition.

[88] Section 43.

[89] See Wooler, *Review of the Investigation and Criminal Proceedings Relating to the Jubilee Line Case* (HM Crown Prosecution Service Inspectorate, June 2006). The Review included an examination of the experiences and perspectives of the jurors: for a further discussion of this aspect, see Lloyd-Bostock, 'The Jubilee Line Jurors: Does their Experience Strengthen the Argument for Judge-only Trial in Long and Complex Fraud Cases?' [2007] Crim LR 255. The author of this article concludes (at 273) that 'the "problem" with the Jubilee Line case was not the jury's ability to cope, but the unnecessarily excessive length of the case with its consequences for the jurors' lives, together with some aspects of their treatment at court'.

[90] *Practice Direction (Jury Service: Excusal (Amendment))* [2005] 1 WLR 1361, [2005] 3 All ER 89 (amending *Practice Direction (Criminal Proceedings: Consolidation)* [2002] 1 WLR 2870, [2002] 3 All ER 904).

so substantial that tampering would take place such as to render it necessary in the interests of justice for the trial to be conducted without a jury.

The scope of this provision was considered in *J, S and M v R*,[91] in which its use was described by the Lord Chief Justice as one of 'last resort'. There must be a real and present danger of jury tampering. The principle of trial by jury was a 'hallowed principle'. The constitutional responsibilities of the jury were fundamental but were flouted if the integrity of a juror, or jury, was compromised. In the particular case before the court, an order for non-jury trial was made. This was a case involving a high-value, involving £1.75 million in gold bullion. There had already been three jury trials involving the robbery, the last of which had collapsed because of a 'serious attempt at jury tampering'. The estimated cost of the trials already heard was £22 million. The estimated cost of protection for the jury in this case was £1.5 million, with the loss of thirty-two police officers from other duties for a period of up to six months. In these particular circumstances, legal history was made. Lord Judge CJ observed that:

> the principle of trial by jury is precious, but in the end any defendant who is responsible for abusing this principle by attempting to subvert the process has no justified complain that he has been deprived of a right which by his own actions he himself has spurned.

However, note should be taken of the fact that the terms of section 44 do not require the prosecution to show that the threat of jury tampering comes from the defendant or on the defendants' behalf. It should also be noted that nothing in section 44, in the judgment of the Court of Appeal, or in the Criminal Procedure Rules governs in detail the important question of the procedure to be followed by a judge sitting alone, given that traditional procedures in a trial on indictment assume different roles for judge and jury. Thus the judge will be the judge both of law and fact, and may hear evidence that he or she later has to disregard, and deal with a range of other legal or evidential challenges or issues. Thus a trial judge will deal with questions of admissibility of bad character evidence, and admissibility of disputed confessions. Whilst this has been the subject of criticism,[92] this is no different in principle from the role of magistrates or a district judge in summary proceedings.[93]

Trial by jury of sample counts

In a further inroad into the use of jury trials for serious offences, reforms implemented in January 2007 mean that where a defendant is charged with multiple counts on an indictment, the prosecution can request that the trial of some of those counts should be conducted without a jury.[94] As long as certain criteria are satisfied,[95] the judge can then order that a number of sample counts should be tried by jury in the ordinary way, with any remaining counts being tried later by a judge sitting alone.

---

[91] [2010] EWCA Crim 1755.

[92] See, e.g., *Law Society Gazette* 15 April 2010 at **www.lawgazette.co.uk/in-practice/practice-points/practical-consequences-twomey-case-for-non-jury-trials**

[93] See p 262.   [94] Domestic Violence, Crime and Victims Act 2004, s 17.

[95] Ibid. For discussion see p 652.

Trial on the evidence

It should go without saying that the task of the jury is to decide the case on the evidence put before it. Not all factual evidence will be admissible in evidence, and thus there will be factual matters that are not considered by the jury, either for legal reasons or because the evidence is not identified as important by the prosecution or defence. Anything that brings inadmissible evidence before a jury is an irregularity and can lead to the collapse of a jury trial. The problem is exacerbated by the ever-growing availability of news and information through the Internet.

The problem was highlighted by the the Court of Appeal in *R v Thompson, Crawford, Comulu, Allen, Blake and Kasannga*,[96] in which Judge LCJ concluded that 'polite requests' to a jury not to browse the Internet were insufficient. Guidance must be given at the outset of the trial. The jury must be made aware that it is improper to research the case on the Internet, or to discuss it on social networking sites.[97] Web-based research should not be brought into the decision-making process, because that would be unfair. So, too, would be telephone calls or texting in or out of the jury room, discussions between jurors and friends or relatives, and similar use of extraneous sources. The direction to the jury by the judge must make it clear that it is the 'collective responsibility' of the jury to ensure the verdict is fair, and should be in terms that make it clear that this is an order of the judge, not a polite request. Of course, failure to comply with such a direction would potentially create grounds of appeal following a conviction.[98]

Majority verdicts

The standard size of a jury in a criminal case is twelve, but if this figure is reduced because a juror dies or is discharged, it will still be validly constituted as long as the number does not fall below nine.[99] Where a jury has eleven or twelve members, a majority verdict can be accepted if at least ten jurors agree; if a jury has ten members, a majority of nine is acceptable.[100] The verdict of a nine-member jury must be unanimous. The possibility of a majority verdict reduces the likelihood of a jury's decision being affected by bias or tampering, because a single juror will not normally be able to force a retrial. Before a majority verdict can be accepted, however, the jury must have deliberated for a minimum of two hours and the foreman of the jury must state in open court how many jurors agreed with it.[101]

KEY ISSUE

The vast majority of criminal cases are not tried by a jury, but are heard by the magistrates' court, without a jury, where magistrates, or a district judge, decide both matters of fact and law.[102] What justification can there be for permitting trial by jury in the most serious

---

[96] [2010] EWCA (Crim) 1623.

[97] For issues relating to the reporting of cases electronically, through Twitter and other similar applications: see p 240.

[98] See p 691.   [99] Juries Act 1974, s 16(1).   [100] Ibid, s 17.

[101] Ibid, s 17.   [102] See p 609.

cases? Trial by jury is regarded as a fundamental right, of a constitutional status dating back as Magna Carta in 1215. That does not fully explain why the choice of mode of trial is sometimes that of the defendant and not the assessment of a court as to whether the matter is so serious to justify the costs involved.[103] Nonetheless it is the fundamental nature of the right that has led to outcry and difficulty in limiting or abolishing the right. Non-jury trials for serious offences have been used in certain situations—the *Diplock* courts in Northern Ireland during the emergencies involving terrorism in the 1970s and 1980s. The limiting of jury trial in jury-tampering cases—and potentially in fraud trials—is seen by some as the 'thin end of the wedge' to the further limitation (or even abolition) of a mode of trial that means that proceedings can be long, slow, and thus expensive. Juries do not have to state reasons for their decisions—for some that may be one of their strengths, able to reflect values of society as a whole and protect against oppressive use of state prosecutorial power.

❓ Questions

1. Why do we have jury trial?
2. What would be lost if it were further limited or even abolished?
3. Could, or should, juries state reasons for a decision?
4. Are juries an appropriate mechanism for deciding guilt or innocence in fraud cases?

Civil proceedings

It is in civil cases that the decline of the jury has been most marked. Until 1854 most civil actions in the common law courts were tried by jury, but the Common Law Procedure Act 1854 allowed cases to be tried by judge alone if both parties consented. The real turning point was the Administration of Justice (Miscellaneous Provisions) Act 1933, which limited the right to claim trial by jury in a civil action to cases of libel, slander, malicious prosecution, false imprisonment, seduction, breach of promise of marriage, and fraud.[104] So far as the Queen's Bench Division is concerned, the right to a jury trial in these cases is now governed by section 69 of the Supreme Court Act 1981. A jury may only be refused in such a case if the court considers that the trial will involve a scientific or local investigation or a prolonged examination of documents.[105] For all other types of case the grant of a jury is at the discretion of the court. This discretion was once absolute,[106] but in the leading case of *Ward* v *James*[107] the Court of Appeal established that it had to be exercised judicially. It also stated that, unless there were special circumstances, trials in

---

[103] See p 609.

[104] Actions for seduction and breach of promise of marriage were abolished by the Law Reform (Miscellaneous Provisions) Act 1970.

[105] *Beta Construction* v *Channel Four Television* [1990] 2 All ER 1012, [1990] 1 WLR 1042; *Viscount De L'Isle* v *Times Newspapers* [1987] 3 All ER 499, [1988] 1 WLR 49.

[106] *Hope* v *Great Western Rly Co* [1937] 2 KB 130, [1937] 1 All ER 625.

[107] [1966] 1 QB 273, [1965] 1 All ER 563.

personal injury cases should be by judge alone. The court noted the unpredictability of damages awards in jury cases, and suggested that juries tended to make disproportionate awards because they often assumed that the substantive defendant was a deep-pocketed insurance company.

Immediately before *Ward* v *James*, approximately 2 per cent of trials in the Queen's Bench Division took place before a jury. The figure is now minimal. In *H* v *Ministry of Defence*,[108] the court was able to identify only one personal injury case since *Ward* v *James*, in which trial by jury had been ordered, and if the Law Commission's recommendations are implemented, the use of the jury in personal injury cases will disappear entirely.[109] Consequently, in little more than a century, jury trial in civil cases has been virtually superseded by trial by judge alone, the one notable exception being trials for defamation. Jury trials in the county courts are even less common, although it is still possible for a county court to try a case before an eight-person jury,[110] and this occasionally happens in civil actions involving the police. Juries of between seven and eleven persons are also used in coroners' cases.[111]

Coroners' cases aside, the role of juries in civil actions remains controversial, and the extremely large awards of damages made by juries in some defamation cases have attracted considerable criticism. The European Court of Human Rights has suggested that such awards could unlawfully restrict freedom of expression, contrary to Article 10 of the ECHR.[112] In *John* v *Mirror Group Newspapers*, libel damages awarded to the singer Elton John were reduced from £625,000 to £125,000 on appeal, leading the Master of the Rolls to observe that:[113]

> It is in our view offensive to public opinion...that a defamation plaintiff should recover damages for injury to reputation greater, perhaps by a significant factor, than if the same plaintiff had been rendered a helpless cripple.

In *Grobbelaar* v *News Group Newspapers*,[114] the House of Lords famously awarded damages of just £1 to a goalkeeper who sued for defamation when match-fixing allegations were published in a national newspaper. Their Lordships clearly took the view that the claimant was the author of his own misfortunes, and they also ordered him to

---

[108] [1991] 2 QB 103, [1991] 2 All ER 834.

[109] *Damages for Personal Injury: Non-pecuniary Loss*, HC Working Paper no 140, (HMSO, 1995) p 125. For an argument that there should still be a role for jury trials in personal injury cases, see Morris, 'Jury Trials in Personal Injury Claims: Is There a Place for Them?' [2002] 3 *Journal of Personal Injury Law* 310.

[110] County Courts Act 1984, s 66(3). A majority verdict of seven to one is acceptable in such a case: Juries Act 1974, s 17(2).

[111] See p 274.

[112] *Tolstoy Miloslavksy* v *UK* (1995) 20 EHRR 442.

[113] [1997] QB 586 at 614, [1996] 2 All ER 35 at 54, *per* Sir Thomas Bingham MR. See also the comments of Lord Donaldson MR in *Sutcliffe* v *Pressdram Ltd* [1991] 1 QB 153, [1990] 1 All ER 269. Such cases are discussed further at p 560.

[114] [2002] UKHL 40, [2002] 4 All ER 732, [2002] 1 WLR 3024; cf. *Gleaner Co. Ltd* v *Abrahams* [2003] UKPC 55, [2004] 1 AC 628, in which the Privy Council held that the Court of Appeal had not erred in refusing to be guided by awards in personal injury actions when determining the quantum of damages in a defamation case.

pay his own costs. However, they refused to interfere with the jury's finding of liability on the facts, reversing the Court of Appeal's decision in this respect.

More recently, in *Spiller and another* v *Joseph and others*,[115] the Supreme Court had the opportunity of considering the defence of 'fair comment' in an action in defamation. Having surveyed an extremely complex part of the law, Lord Phillips observed:

> Finally, and fundamentally, has not the time come to recognize that defamation is no longer a field in which trial by jury is desirable? The issues are often complex and jury trial simply invites expensive interlocutory battles, such as the one before this court, which attempt to pre-empt issues from going before the jury.

Jury trial may decline still further if the Defamation Bill currently before Parliament is passed. The Bill, in clause 14, reverses the presumption in favour of jury trial in defamation cases. Amongst the factors to be taken account in justifying jury trial are those set out in clause 15: the public importance of the issue; whether any person holds public office; whether a reasoned judgment by a judge is preferable to a verdict of a jury without reasons; whether any complicated question as to the meaning of words arises; whether prolonged consideration of documents is likely to be needed.

KEY ISSUE

Trials for defamation are essentially decisions as to the reputation of an individual and the effect on that reputation of a publication, judged by the views of the ordinary right-thinking person. Some argue that for that reason the diminution of jury trial in defamation cases is a serious erosion of what is a key right. Opposition has been voiced by some, including representatives of the press and broadcasters, to changes that will effectively significantly reduce the incidence of jury trial. However, the law of defamation may have got so technical, and the awards of damages so inconsistent, as to have made change inevitable.

? Questions

1. Should jury trial be limited in this way?
2. What are the justifications for limiting jury trial in defamation cases?

Jury secrecy

A key principle of the jury system is that what takes place in the jury room must not be disclosed, and the secrecy of jurors' deliberations is protected by both common law and statute. Section 8(1) of the Contempt of Court Act 1981 makes it an offence to obtain, disclose, or solicit any particulars of statements made, opinions expressed, arguments advanced, or votes cast by members of a jury in the course of their deliberations. There are only two exceptions to this rule: (a) disclosures for the purpose of

---

[115] [2010] UKSC 53.

enabling the jury to arrive at and deliver its verdict;[116] and (b) disclosures made where an offence is alleged to have been committed in relation to the jury.[117] In *R v Miah*,[118] section 8 was held to apply to 'anything said by one juror to another about the case from the moment the jury is empanelled, at least provided what is said is not over-heard by anyone else who is not a juror'. Breach of this rule amounts to contempt of court, even if the breach is indirect. In *Attorney-General v Associated Newspapers*,[119] a conviction for publishing the views of the jurors in a long and abortive fraud case was upheld, even though the appellants had obtained the information from a researcher and not directly from the jurors.

Evidence of improper conduct by the jury

At common law, the rule is that 'the court will not investigate, or receive evidence about, anything said in the course of the jury's deliberations while they are con-sidering their verdict in their retiring room'.[120] Evidence of the jury's behaviour *outside* the jury room can be admitted, however, and in *R v Young (Stephen)*[121] the Court of Appeal quashed a murder conviction after hearing that the jury had attempted to contact the deceased using a ouija board in a hotel room. The rationale for maintaining the secrecy of jury deliberations was explained by Atkin LJ in an earlier case:[122]

> [O]n the one hand it is in order to secure the finality of decisions arrived at by the jury, and on the other to protect the jurymen themselves and prevent their being exposed to pressure to explain the reasons which actuated them in arriving at their verdict.

It is also assumed that jurors are more likely to express their views honestly and frankly if they feel confident that their deliberations will remain confidential. On the other hand, the law operates with such rigidity that there is a serious risk of miscar-riages of justice going undiscovered and unchallenged.

The scope of both the common law and statutory prohibitions was considered by the House of Lords in *R v Mirza (Shabbir Ali)*.[123] The defendant was a Pakistani man charged with six counts of indecent assault. Because English was not his first lan-guage, he was assisted in court by an interpreter, but the jury sent two separate notes to the judge, indicating that they found the use of the interpreter suspicious. The judge directed the jury that they should draw no adverse inference from the use of the inter-preter, but a letter written by a juror six days after the defendant's conviction indicated

---

[116] Section 8(2)(a). It is lawful, for example, for notes to be passed between the judge and jury for this purpose.

[117] Section 8(2)(b).   [118] [1997] 2 Cr App R 12 at 18, *per* Kennedy LJ.

[119] [1994] 2 AC 238, [1994] 1 All ER 556.

[120] *R v Mirza (Shabbir Ali)* [2004] UKHL 2 at [95], [2004] 1 AC 1118 at [95], [2004] 1 All ER 925, *per* Lord Hope.

[121] [1995] QB 324, [1995] 2 WLR 430.   [122] *Ellis v Deheer* [1922] 2 KB 113 at 121.

[123] [2004] UKHL 2, [2004] 1 AC 1118, [2004] 1 All ER 925.

that they had ignored these instructions and were possibly influenced by racial prejudice. The Court of Appeal dismissed the defendant's appeal against conviction. The issue for the House of Lords was whether a court was prevented, either at common law or under the 1981 Act, from considering evidence of jury deliberations indicating a breach of Article 6. In a partial departure from the previous case law,[124] their Lordships held that section 8 of the 1981 Act was addressed to third parties and did not prevent a court from investigating allegations of injustice. A court had a responsibility to ensure that the defendant received a fair trial and it could not be in contempt of itself. However, a majority of their Lordships also upheld the common law rule against receiving evidence of jury deliberations. Exceptions to this rule could only be made where it was alleged that the jury had been affected by 'extraneous influences' or had declined to deliberate at all.[125]

This approach was applied in *R v Karakaya (Adem)*,[126] in which it was discovered that one of the jurors in a rape trial had done some 'research' on the Internet and taken downloaded documents into the jury room during deliberations. The matter only came to light when the documents were found by the jury bailiff after the trial had concluded. The Court of Appeal had no hesitation in holding that it was entitled to examine the documents, but it did not consider it necessary to question the jurors about the matter: the presence of the extraneous material itself was enough to cast doubt on the safety of the verdict. After some deliberation, the Court also held that it was entitled to look at a handwritten note on the back of one of the documents— apparently written by one of the jurors—in order to form a 'preliminary view' as to whether it might have a bearing on the appeal.[127] In the end it decided that the note did *not* have a bearing on the case because it was merely a summary of the downloaded material. However, it is not clear what the Court would have done if the note had revealed details of the jury's deliberations. Moreover, the recent decision in *R v Marshall (Jay David)*[128] suggests that the discovery of extraneous material in the jury room will not always be grounds for quashing a conviction. Although it was clear in this case that at least one juror had brought downloaded documents with him to the jury's deliberations, the documents in question concerned sentencing tariffs and it was difficult to see how their use could have damaged the verdicts against the two defendants. On this basis the convictions were not unsafe.

---

[124] In *R v Young (Stephen)* [1995] QB 324, [1995] 2 WLR 430, the Court of Appeal held that it was prevented by s 8 from hearing evidence concerning improper conduct in the jury room. See also *R v Qureshi* [2001] EWCA Crim 1807, [2002] 1 WLR 518, [2002] 1 Cr App R 33, in which a juror made allegations of racial bias three days after the verdict. Leave to appeal was refused on the basis that the jury's verdict had been accepted by the trial judge and s 8 of the 1981 Act prevented any investigation into its deliberations.

[125] The 2005 consultation on jury research asks whether clarification of this area of law is needed, although it makes it clear that the government's own preference is to leave such matters to the courts: *Jury Research and Impropriety* CP 04/05, discussed at p 352.

[126] [2005] EWCA Crim 346, [2005] 2 Cr App R 5.

[127] Ibid, at [13], *per* Judge LJ.   [128] [2007] EWCA Crim 35, [2007] Crim LR 562.

The Article 6 dimension

The majority in *Mirza* clearly felt that the existing approach to jury secrecy was not incompatible with the right to a fair trial, but in a strong dissenting judgment, Lord Steyn argued that:[129]

> [T]here is a positive duty on judges, when things have gone seriously wrong in the criminal justice system, to do everything possible to put it right. In the world of today, enlightened public opinion would accept nothing less. It would be contrary to the spirit of these developments to say that in one area, namely the deliberations of the jury, injustice can be tolerated as the price for protecting the jury system.

In *Gregory* v *UK*,[130] the European Court of Human Rights accepted the rules governing the secrecy of jury deliberations as a crucial and legitimate feature of English trial law. Thus, a judge who refused to investigate a juror's allegations that another member of the jury had made racist remarks, and who dealt with the matter by reminding the jury to decide the case according to the evidence, was held to have satisfied Article 6. By contrast, a breach of Article 6 was established on similar facts in *Sander* v *UK*.[131] The judge in this case had responded to the original allegation of racism by asking the jurors to search their consciences, and after receiving a note from the entire jury refuting the allegations, he had declined to do anything further. The distinction between these cases is a fine one, but it would appear that as long as a judge takes reasonable steps to address allegations made during the course of a trial, the court's duty under Article 6 will have been satisfied.

On a related matter, Darbyshire and others have questioned whether the failure of the jury system to provide a defendant with a reasoned verdict is itself a breach of Article 6:[132] 'It is hard to see, in an era when every tribunal and magistrates' court provides a reasoned decision, how the secrecy of jury trials can survive.' Darbyshire concludes that juries should be required to respond to a series of written questions formulated by counsel and the judge, arguing that this would ensure compliance with Article 6 and would also help to reduce the scope for 'perverse verdicts'. The recommendation was endorsed by Auld LJ in his *Review of the Criminal Courts*.[133] In his dissenting opinion in *Mirza*, Lord Steyn suggested that a jury is a judicial tribunal in its own right, and that its obligation to comply with the requirements of Article 6 is independent of any obligation on the judge.[134] This was not, however, a view endorsed by the majority.

---

[129] [2004] UKHL 2 at [4], [2004] 1 AC 1118 at [4], [2004] 1 All ER 925.

[130] (1998) 25 EHRR 577 at 594.

[131] (2001) 31 EHRR 44. See also, *Remli* v *France* (1996) 22 EHRR 253 (breach of Article 6 established when a court failed to investigate allegations of juror bias that came to light after the verdict); Zander, 'The Complaining Juror' (2000) 150 NLJ 723.

[132] Darbyshire, Maughan and Stewart, *What can the English Legal System Learn from Jury Research Published up to 2001? Findings for the Criminal Courts Review* (HMSO, 2001) at p 39. See also, Pritchard, 'A Reform for Jury Trial?' (1998) 148 NLJ 45.

[133] (HMSO, 2001) at para 11.41.

[134] [2004] UKHL 2 at [6], [2004] 1 AC 1118 at [6], [2004] 1 All ER 925.

Jury research

Section 8 of the 1981 Act has been criticized for severely restricting the scope for conducting research into the jury system, and in 1993 the Royal Commission on Criminal Justice proposed an amendment that would make legitimate jury research possible. In 2005 the Department for Constitutional Affairs revealed that such an amendment was finally being considered. The proposal outlined in its consultation paper would have allowed the Secretary of State to authorize specific research projects. These authorized projects would have been subject to strict conditions and governed by a Code of Conduct, while *unauthorized* research into jury deliberations would have remained unlawful.[135] However, following the consultation process, the government concluded that there was scope for doing more research within the existing legal framework, and that the case for amending the 1981 Act had not been made out:[136]

> The Government is not opposed to amending section 8 of the Contempt of Court Act 1981 but does not believe that this should be done until there are specific and detailed questions to be answered that cannot be investigated without altering statute.

In particular, the government supported the idea of conducting more research using mock or shadow juries,[137] the recent study commissioned by the Ministry of Justice[138] being one such example.

The merits of jury trial

Jury trial has been the subject of significant criticism in recent years, with the most contentious issue being what some regard as an unacceptably high acquittal rate in criminal cases.[139] Statistically, jury trials do result in proportionately more acquittals than magistrates' cases,[140] but the proportion of defendants acquitted by juries on all counts is still quite low.[141] Research for the Ministry of Justice published in

---

[135] *Jury Research and Impropriety* (HMSO, 2005) CP 04/05.

[136] DCA, *Jury Research and Impropriety: Response to Consultation* (HMSO, 2005), at p 16.

[137] Ibid.

[138] Thomas and Balmer, *Diversity and Fairness in the Jury System*, Ministry of Justice Research Series 2/07 (HMSO, 2007), discussed at p 356. See also Ministry of Justice, *Are Juries Fair?* (HMSO, 2010), available at **www.justice.gov.uk/publications/docs/are-juries-fair-research.pdf**

[139] See, e.g., Darbyshire, 'For the New Lord Chancellor: Some Causes for Concern about Magistrates' [1997] Crim LR 861.

[140] In 2002 just over 30 per cent of contested cases in the magistrates' courts were dismissed. In the same year, 65 per cent of those pleading not guilty in the Crown Court were either acquitted by the jury or had the case discharged by the judge—*Criminal Statistics 2002*, at p 16.

[141] In 2001, 8.6 per cent of cases committed for trial in the Crown Court resulted in the defendant being acquitted by a jury on all counts. A further 17.3 per cent were acquitted by or on the direction of the judge and 14.8 per cent were convicted on some or all counts after pleading not guilty. The majority of defendants—56.3 per cent—pleaded guilty: *Judicial Statistics 2001*, at pp 68–9. Compare the more recent analysis in the Ministry of Justice study *Are Juries Fair?* cited at n 138.

2010[142] concluded that the majority of verdicts were in fact verdicts of guilty: in the sample groups, juries returned guilty verdicts in 64 per cent of charges on which they deliberated.[143] The 2010 research showed that conviction rates varied according to the nature of the offence, with there being no evidence that conviction rates for rape were higher than for some other serious offences. In particular, non-fatal offences against the person had lower conviction rates (52 per cent). Conviction rates were higher in cases in which direct evidence exist, and lowest when it was the defendant's mental state that was in issue.[144]

In addition, it is difficult to make direct comparisons between trial on indictment and summary trial because the statistics are calculated differently and are influenced by different factors. For example, much of the business of magistrates' courts consists of strict liability offences in which the scope for contesting guilt is reduced and the stakes are lower. The proportion of defendants pleading guilty in summary cases is therefore much higher than for cases in the Crown Court. Similarly, the acquittal rate for either-way cases in the Crown Court may be at least partly explained by the fact that those with a comparatively weak defence are less likely to elect trial by jury because of the risk of receiving a stiffer sentence if convicted.

The reality is that too little is known about how juries work and, as stated previously, research into how juries reach their verdicts is currently prohibited by the Contempt of Court Act 1981. In an attempt to work around this restriction, some research has been carried out using 'shadow juries', where a panel of 'shadow' jurors is asked to follow a real case.[145] Some anecdotal and personal accounts of real jurors have also been published, and in 2001 a group of academics carried out a comprehensive review of jury research published in the United Kingdom and elsewhere.

The merits of the jury system are sometimes stated in terms of the deficiencies of alternative modes of trial. Although the summary process in the magistrates' courts is relatively quick and cheap, it is by no means beyond criticism, and it is often thought that jury trial favours an accused. Other advocates of jury trial rely upon its constitutional importance, and on the safeguards that it is said to provide for defendants.[146] In *Ward* v *James*, Lord Denning MR explained the role of the modern jury as follows:[147]

> Let it not be supposed that this court is in any way opposed to trial by jury. It has been the bulwark of our liberties too long for any of us to seek to alter it. Whenever a man is on trial for serious crime, or when in a civil case a man's honour or integrity is at stake, or when one or other party must be deliberately lying, then trial by jury has no equal.

---

[142] See n 143.   [143] See Thomas, cited at n 138, at Table 3.3, p 46.
[144] Threatening to kill (36 per cent); attempted murder (47 per cent); GBH (48 per cent); rape (55 per cent): see Thomas, cited at n 138.
[145] See McCabe and Purves, *The Shadow Jury at Work* (OUP, 1974); Thomas and Balmer, *Diversity and Fairness in the Jury System*, Ministry of Justice Research Series 2/07 (HMSO, 2007).
[146] On this argument, see: Cornish, *The Jury* (Allen Lane, 1970).
[147] [1966] 1 QB 273 at 295, [1965] 1 All ER 563 at 571.

It was put more graphically by Lord Devlin, who described jury trial as 'the lamp that shows that freedom lives'.[148] Not all commentators are convinced by this romanticism, pointing out that this 'bulwark of our liberties' did not prevent any of the famous miscarriages of justice exposed in the 1990s.[149] Critics have also pointed to the potentially random factors that may affect a jury's deliberations. The fact that juries are laymen who are not required to explain their decisions leaves greater scope for them to be influenced by factors that have nothing to do with the law or the evidence. Thus, they may occasionally reach perverse verdicts because they have acted on the basis of prejudice and stereotypes, or because they have failed to properly understand the legal and evidential issues. Juries may also return verdicts motivated by conscience, and there are many well-known examples of cases in which juries are thought to have acquitted defendants on moral rather than legal grounds. In 1985, for example, a jury found Clive Ponting not guilty of committing official secrets offences, despite clear evidence that he had in fact done what he was accused of. Similarly, in 2000, a multiple sclerosis sufferer was acquitted on charges of possessing cannabis after the jury was told that the defendant used the drug to relieve the symptoms of the disease. For some, the ability of a jury to deliver a moral verdict in such cases is one of the system's great strengths, but for others, these perverse acquittals are an affront to the rule of law.

Academic opinion on the jury system may be divided, but it seems that jurors themselves are strongly in favour of it. A recent Home Office survey, based on interviews with those summoned for jury service in six courts, found that:[150]

> [T]he majority of respondents had a more positive view of the jury trial system after completing their service than they did before. Furthermore, virtually all jurors interviewed considered jury trials to be an important part of the criminal justice system.

Further reading

AULD, RT HON LORD JUSTICE, *Review of the Criminal Courts of England and Wales* (HMSO, 2001), ch 5

BALDWIN and McCONVILLE, *Jury Trials* (Clarendon Press, 1979)

BRIDGES, CHOONGH and McCONVILLE, *Ethnic-Minority Defendants and the Right to Elect Jury Trial* (Commission for Racial Equality, 2000)

BUXTON, 'Challenging and Discharging Jurors: Part 1' [1990] Crim LR 225

CORNISH, *The Jury* (Penguin, 1970)

---

[148] Devlin, *op cit*.

[149] See Darbyshire, 'The Lamp that Shows that Freedom Lives: Is it Worth the Candle?' [1991] Crim LR 740. Ironically, the primacy of jury trial has also been used as a justification for judicial non-interference with verdicts in alleged miscarriage of justice cases: see p 690.

[150] Matthews, Hancock and Briggs: *Jurors' Perceptions, Understanding, Confidence and Satisfaction in the Jury System: A Study in Six Courts* (HMSO, 2004) Home Office Research Study 227, at p 1.

DARBYSHIRE, MAUGHAN and STEWART, *What Can the English Legal System Learn from Jury Research Published up to 2001? Findings for the Criminal Courts Review* (HMSO, 2001)

DEVLIN, *Trial by Jury* (London, Stevens & Sons, 1956)

THOMAS and BALMER, *Diversity and Fairness in the Jury System*, Ministry of Justice Research Series 2/07 (HMSO, 2007)

THORNTON, 'Trial by Jury: 50 Years of Change' [2004] Crim LR 683

Legal Services

11

INTRODUCTION

This chapter will examine the provision of legal services. The availability of high-quality lawyers, and the ability to afford access to their services, is fundamental to the effectiveness of any system of law. It is a fast-changing topic, as government has addressed issues of how legal services should be provided, financed and regulated. Specific areas covered will include:

- how the legal profession is organized;
- what solicitors and barristers do, how they are organized, trained and regulated;
- how complaints against lawyers are resolved;
- how the costs of legal advice and assistance are met;
- the development and evolution of the legal aid schemes;
- the new funding arrangements.

The legal profession: The organizational framework

An overview

A distinctive feature of the English legal system is the division of the legal profession into two separate branches: solicitors and barristers. Such a division is unknown outside Britain and the Commonwealth, and elsewhere all practitioners are simply described as 'lawyers'. The division dates back to around 1340, which is when professional advocacy first evolved:[1] attorneys, who were the forerunners of solicitors, were responsible for carrying out the preparatory stages of an action, but only serjeants and barristers had rights of audience in the common law courts. This basic distinction still exists at a formal level, but the differences between the two professions are rapidly diminishing in practice, with services that used to be the exclusive domain of one side or other of the profession being offered more generally. Thus, while barristers are still thought of primarily as advocates, a very significant amount of advocacy is today performed by solicitors. Some barristers spend a lot of time engaged in 'paperwork' such

---

[1] For details see Baker, *An Introduction to English Legal History* (OUP: 4th edn, 2002).

as the drafting of pleadings, opinions, and other legal paperwork. Employed barristers can conduct litigation[2] and, increasingly, a range of other legal services.[3] Similarly, while solicitors are still responsible for the preparatory stages of litigation, they also deal with a range of non-litigious matters such as conveyancing and the drafting of wills, and all solicitors have rights in audience in at least some courts and tribunals.[4] The Crown Prosecution Service, employing both solicitors and barristers, is the lead in many aspects of prosecution advocacy. And the trend towards the provision of legal services by others who are not solicitors or barristers must be noted.[5]

The structure, function, regulation, and financing of the legal profession has been the subject of ongoing review and change, often of a radical nature. In 1976 a Royal Commission was set up to inquire into the provision of legal services. Its report, published in 1979, suggested that the legal profession was performing its functions well.[6] The report was broadly supportive of the status quo and did not advocate fusing the two branches of the profession.[7] It did, however, prompt further debate and discussion. Over the next ten years the government published White Papers on civil justice,[8] legal services,[9] the legal profession,[10] conveyancing services,[11] and contingency fees.[12] Eventually, in 1990, the Courts and Legal Services Act was passed. The passage of the 1990 Act did not bring to an end the spate of review and reform: far from it. Changes to funding regimes, in complaints mechanisms and in the way in which legal services are provided have all been at the heart of an agenda designed to create efficiency and effectiveness of legal provision. Most recently, the passage of the Criminal Defence Act 2006 and the Legal Services Act 2007 heralds a further sustained period of change, often of a radical nature. Change has been ongoing through a mixture of legislative, administrative, and financial measures. But at the core of the change are several key pieces of legislation.

The Courts and Legal Services Act 1990

The 1990 Act is based on a distinct philosophy, as set out in section 17(1):

> The general objective of this Part is the development of legal services in England and Wales (and in particular the development of advocacy, litigation, conveyancing and probate services) by making provision of new or better ways of providing such services, and a wider choice of persons providing them, while maintaining the proper and efficient administration of justice.

---

[2] See p 381.   [3] See p 386.   [4] See p 382.   [5] See p 379.

[6] *Report of the Royal Commission on Legal Services*, Cmnd 7648 (HMSO, 1979)—'the Benson Report'.

[7] Ibid, paras 17.45–17.46.

[8] *Report of the Review Body on Civil Justice*, Cm 394 (HMSO, 1988).

[9] *Legal Services: A Framework for the Future,* Cm 740 (HMSO, 1989).

[10] *The Workload and Organisation of the Legal Profession*, Cm 570 (HMSO, 1989).

[11] *Conveyancing by Authorised Practitioners*, Cm 572 (HMSO, 1989).

[12] *Contingency Fees*, Cm 571 (HMSO, 1989).

In addition to preserving the existing rights of audience of solicitors and barristers,[13] section 17(3) of the Act[14] established the 'general principle' that rights of audience should be linked to the following criteria:

(i) possession of appropriate qualifications;

(ii) membership of a professional body with effective and enforceable rules of conduct;

(iii) the existence of satisfactory arrangements for ensuring that legal services are not withheld on objectionable grounds; and

(iv) the existence of appropriate rules of conduct.

The Act provided a framework for solicitors to break the monopoly that barristers had enjoyed over advocacy work in the higher courts,[15] and it opened up the possibility that rights of audience might be extended to members of other professions.[16] The rules governing the provision of litigation[17] and probate[18] services were also relaxed, and section 66 of the Act removed the legal obstacles preventing solicitors from forming partnerships with non-solicitors.[19] The Act thus laid the foundations for significant changes to the way in which legal services were provided. It also provided for the appointment of a Legal Services Ombudsman[20] with the power to review complaints handling by the professional regulatory bodies.[21] All of these are now fundamentally affected by the Legal Services Act 2007.

The Access to Justice Act 1999

The Access to Justice Act 1999 made important changes to the funding of legal services: it established two separate schemes to replace what used to be known as 'legal aid', and it relaxed some of the rules governing the remuneration of lawyers through private funds.[22] Part III of the Act continued the theme of the Courts and Legal Services Act, by establishing the general principle that all lawyers with appropriate qualifications should be able to exercise full rights of audience in all proceedings. It also simplified the procedure for approving any further changes to rights of audience and rights to

---

[13] Sections 31–33.   [14] Repealed by Legal Services Act 2007, Sch 23.

[15] See p 382.   [16] Section 27: for more detailed discussion of rights of audience, see p 382.

[17] Section 28: see p 381.

[18] Section 55, which was not implemented until 2004. Due to a lack of demand, provisions that would have further relaxed the rules governing conveyancing services have not been implemented at all: see p 382.

[19] There had been no such legal obstacles relating to barristers, although both solicitors and barristers have in the past been prevented from entering into multidisciplinary partnerships by their own professional rules.

[20] See p 402.   [21] See p 398.

[22] Sections 27–28: see p 408. In the context of funding of criminal cases, the 1999 Act has been significantly amended by the Criminal Defence Services Act 2006.

conduct litigation,[23] in addition to conferring additional powers on the Legal Services Ombudsman.[24]

The Legal Services Act 2007

The 2007 Act makes fundamental changes.[25] It changes the whole regulatory regime of the legal profession by creating a Legal Services Board.[26] The Board is given objectives that the regulatory procedures and mechanisms should seek to achieve, and it is the duty of the Board to promote those objectives. It creates a framework for the conduct of legal activity, and the potential to license bodies to engage in legal activity. It defines what amounts to a 'reserved legal activity', and in section 13 deals with the question of who is entitled to carry on such an activity. It creates a new Office for Legal Complaints and provides in detail a structure for dealing with them. It contains a variety of miscellaneous provisions relating to, or affecting, lawyers.

The new regime for the conduct of legal activity

The provisions of the Legal Services Act 2007 are based largely on the proposals contained in the White Paper *The Future of Legal Services: Putting Consumers First*, published in 2005.[27] That itself was based on the recommendations of the Clementi Report. This review of the regulation of legal services,[28] chaired by Sir David Clementi, had two main terms of reference: (a) 'to consider what regulatory framework would best promote competition, innovation and the public and consumer interest in an efficient, effective and independent legal sector'; and (b) 'to recommend a framework which will be independent in representing the public and consumer interest, comprehensive, accountable, consistent, flexible, transparent, and no more restrictive or burdensome than is clearly justified'. The final report of the review was published in December 2004.[29]

The report made a number of significant recommendations that have a profound effect on the legal landscape. Clementi's concerns fell into three main categories:

- concerns about the complexity and ineffectiveness of the existing regulatory framework;
- concerns about the current approach of the professions to the handling of complaints;
- concerns about the restrictive nature of current business practices.

---

[23] See pp 381.   [24] See p 402.   [25] See p 402.

[26] See p 402.   [27] Cm 6679: available at **www.dca.gov.uk**

[28] *Competition and Regulation in the Legal Services Market: A Report following the Consultation 'In the Public Interest?* (HMSO, 2003).

[29] *Final Report of the Review of the Regulatory Framework for Legal Services in England and Wales* (HMSO, 2004).

The details of these issues will be discussed later.[30] The 2007 provides for a new framework to get rid of what the White Paper described as the 'regulatory maze', but also one that would encourage the creation of 'a legal services market that will enable lawyers and other professionals to work together to provide legal services in new ways'.[31] Clementi had recommended a range of alternative business structures. His key recommendation here was that steps should be taken to enable lawyers from different professional backgrounds to work together to provide legal services to the public. This could be achieved by lifting the restrictions preventing solicitors from entering into partnerships with those from other disciplines, and by the Bar Council changing its own rules to permit barristers to enter into partnerships with others. Such changes would mean, for example, that solicitors and barristers would be able to join together to create 'legal disciplinary practices', in which non-lawyers performing a managerial or administrative role might also be partners. Several well-known companies are already planning the provision of legal services for introduction once the statutory provisions come in to force, in 2011.[32] Clementi recognized, however, that if lawyers and non-lawyers were to be able to enter into partnerships, special safeguards would be needed to ensure the maintenance of ethical standards.[33] The Clementi Report was 'warmly welcomed' by the government, and its recommendations were broadly accepted. Even before it was published, the Lord Chancellor had made it clear that he was keen to explore new way of delivering legal services:[34]

> I want us to adopt the Heineken approach and find legal services which reach parts of the community that no other services have reached...
>
> I want to see a market where everyone, except those with limited means who get free access, can get access to legal services at affordable cost in a modern setting. Shopping centres are the most obvious example of this, where clusters of problems such as employment, housing, debt and family problems can be dealt with together. And this leads to the use of employed solicitors by other businesses... for the legal profession to thrive and survive we must continue to be competitive in the legal market of today and we must not be frightened of innovation and change.

The Legal Services Act 2007 provides the framework to do this.

Section 12 defines 'reserved legal activities'. These are rights of audience, the conduct of litigation, reserved instrument activities, probate activities, notarial activities, and the administration of oaths. A person must be entitled to carry on a reserved activity; he or she commits a criminal offence if he or she does so without being entitled to do so.[35] A person is 'entitled' if he or she is authorized to perform that activity. A lawyer, whether a solicitor or barrister, will be authorized by the relevant regulator for

---

[30] See p 402.

[31] DCA, *Consumers: 21st Century Legal Services* (HMSO, 2006).

[32] See p 379.   [33] Ibid, at paras F11 and F25.

[34] The quote is taken from a speech to the Law Society's Annual Conference, 26 September 2003.

[35] 2007 Act, ss 13, 14.

solicitors or barristers.[36] However, others may be able to perform that activity if they are 'exempt persons' under Schedule 3 to the Act.

The overall effect of this therefore, is that the functions of solicitors and barristers set out below will, when the 2007 Act is fully in force, be performed within the framework of the new Act.

Licensed bodies

It should be evident from what we have just described that the intention is to encourage a wider range of providers of legal services. Part 5 of the 2007 Act is the part of the legislation that creates the framework of powers needed to achieve that. It defines those who are to be regarded as licensing authorities. These are the Legal Services Board or an approved regulator designated to perform a licensing function.[37] Complex provisions exist about the designation of licensing authorities, procedure and the grant, modification, and regulation of licences.[38] The relevant licensing authority will consider applications and the effect of the grant of a licence, with or without conditions, will be, within the terms of the licence, to permit a non-authorized person to perform a relevant reserved activity. Through these means it will be possible for organizations owned or managed by a non-authorized person to provide reserved legal activities.

The Legal Services Board came into effect in 2009. In 2009, provisions in the Act were introduced to permit 'legal disciplinary practices', which allow non-lawyers to enter partnership with lawyers, with up to 25 per cent of a firm's equity owned by non-lawyers. Non-lawyers can therefore join together with solicitors and barristers, with the non-lawyers performing managerial, administrative, or financial roles. The new licensing role of the LSB, through approved licensing authorities such as the Law Society and Bar Council, will also facilitate the creation of 'alternative business structures' (ABSs), perhaps commercial bodies such as the Co-op, Tesco, or the AA, to provide legal services as part of their 'product range', and, as already noted, facilitate the growth of multidisciplinary companies or partnerships. Such ABSs are likely to begin to become operational as from October 2011. Given the impact of organizations of this type in other areas of activity, it would be extremely surprising if the effect on the traditional mode of provision of legal services were not significant. The ABS approach permits full ownership by external bodies and outside investment in the creation and management of legal services. It allows non-legal organizations to dovetail legal services as part of a wider range of non-legal provision. The aim is to increase market competition, providing better value for money, incentives for better practice and innovation, and to be more consumer-friendly.[39]

---

[36] 2007 Act, s 18. For the professional regulators, see p 397.   [37] 2007 Act, s 73.
[38] 2007 Act, ss 73–91.   [39] See **www.legalservicesboard.org.uk**

KEY ISSUE

The structure of the legal profession may still be based on a division between solicitors and barristers, but, as is evident from the the pace and content of legislative and policy change discussed above, little else about the provision of legal services remains unchanged. The trends can be identified as of three types: opening areas of activity to wider groups of individuals and organizations; creating competition to secure efficiency and cost savings; removing restrictive practices. Arguments about whether we should keep a 'divided' profession are, perhaps, superseded by questions about who can best provide particular types of legal service. In its desire to achieve efficiency and choice the government has introduced changes that provide a greater element of 'free market' competition, albeit one within a regulatory framework. What is less clear is what the ultimate effects will be on the provision of the full range of legal services. The opening up of rights of audience may increase the pool of advocates, or might ultimately affect adversely the standards of advocacy provided by an independent and specialized Bar. The opening up of the provision of legal services to commercial non-traditional providers may extend the reach of legal advice and assistance or may, paradoxically, reduce the availability of the range of legal advice by making some private practice unviable. Competition may lead inevitably to fewer and larger providers of legal services.

? Questions

1. What are the factors that persuaded Clementi to recommend the opening-up of the provision of legal services?
2. What benefits might flow from multidisciplinary practices?
3. What impact do you think opening up legal service provision might have?

The work of solicitors and barristers

Solicitors

There are in excess of 100,000 practising solicitors in England and Wales.[40] For most people seeking legal services or advice, a solicitor will be their first point of contact. They practise in various ways: a solicitor may practise in his or her own right, although, in an age of specialization and of block contracts,[41] sole practice has very much declined. Increasingly, solicitors practise in large partnerships, sometimes in the form of limited partnerships that restrict the unlimited liability that is traditionally a characteristic of a partnership arrangement. Size, and limited liability, does not mean that problems do not continue to arise. No matter what their size, solicitors firms are not immune

---

[40] The Law Society *Annual Statistical Report 2005* identified 101,000 practising solicitors. More than half had been in practice for less than ten years. Some 41,807 were female.

[41] See p 414.

to competition and economic realities, as was seen during 2010 when a large regional solicitors' practice collapsed.[42]

In addition to conducting the preparatory stages of litigation, solicitors as a profession provide a wide range of other services. These include conveyancing work, the drafting of wills, the supervision of trusts and settlements, the administration of estates, the provision of advice on matters such as welfare law, immigration, and divorce, and the provision of advice and assistance to persons in custody. In addition, all solicitors enjoy at least some rights of audience before the courts,[43] and advocacy is an increasingly important part of the work of many solicitors, where funding arrangements permit. There is thus considerable variety in the types of work that different solicitors do, but a very clear and growing trend towards specialization. For example, while many high-street firms offer a general range of services, others elect to specialize in certain areas such as conveyancing or personal injury work. The funding arrangements for publicly funded legal work increasingly require cost-efficiencies that can only be achieved through dealing with a large volume of matters of a similar type. The increasing trend for requiring firms to tender for block contracts to be funded at set rates by the Legal Services Commission[44] means that the economic realities of delivering some types of work necessitate specialization and the generation of a sufficient volume of work that enables it to be profitable. Criminal and family law work are two vivid examples of this. At the other end of the scale, many solicitors now work in very large firms (often in the City of London and big provincial centres) that deal only with corporate and commercial law, whilst other solicitors provide legal services at law centres[45] or as employees of local authorities. Indeed, recent changes to professional rules mean that local authorities can offer their 'in-house' legal services to organizations, and possibly individuals, within their local authority area.

The right to conduct litigation

The right to conduct litigation is defined in the Courts and Legal Services Act 1990 as the right:[46]

(a) to issue proceedings before any court; and

(b) to perform any ancillary functions in relation to proceedings (such as entering appearances to actions).

Section 28 of the Act[47] established the principle that any person should be entitled to conduct litigation where the right to do so has been conferred by an appropriate body. At that time, the only body authorized to confer the right was the Law Society, and the Act thus had the effect of preserving the monopoly that solicitors had enjoyed in this area. In 1999 the Bar Council and the Institute of Legal Executives were added to

---

[42] Halliwell Landau, LLP, based in Manchester.   [43] See p 382.   [44] See p 413.
[45] For a survey of recent trends, see the Law Society's *Annual Statistical Report*.
[46] Section 119 (as amended).   [47] Now repealed by the Legal Services Act 2007, Sch 23.

the list of 'authorized bodies' capable of granting litigation rights to their members.[48] However, the Bar Council has so far declined to grant such rights to barristers in independent practice.[49] The Act also established a process by which other organizations could apply to the Lord Chancellor for recognition as authorized bodies.[50] At the time of writing, two organizations had made successful use of this system: the Chartered Institute of Patent Agents and the Institute of Trade Mark Attorneys.[51]

When the 2007 Act is fully in force, authorization to conduct litigation will be granted either by an approved regulator, or by a licensing authority granting a licence.

Other monopolies: Conveyancing and probate

The monopoly of solicitors over conveyancing work was formally ended by the Administration of Justice Act 1985. Part II of that Act introduced a system of licensed conveyancers and established the Council for Licensed Conveyancers to regulate and oversee the new profession. Provisions in the Courts and Legal Services Act 1990[52] were designed to further liberalize the market and to create a new supervisory body, the Authorised Conveyancing Practitioners Board. The implementation of these provisions was postponed indefinitely due to a lack of demand. The Legal Services Act 2007 now provides a framework in which further expansion and diversity can be achieved.

Solicitors have also had a virtual monopoly over the right to perform probate work. Section 55[53] of the 1990 Act provided that any organization that has been 'approved' by the Lord Chancellor may authorize suitably qualified persons to provide probate services for reward. The framework was thus put in place for Licensed Conveyancers, banks, building societies, and insurance companies to offer probate services.

Rights of audience

Solicitors may have slowly lost their monopolies over litigation, conveyancing, and probate work, but they themselves have made significant in-roads into an area that has historically been the preserve of barristers: that of advocacy in the higher courts. Prior to the Courts and Legal Services Act 1990, solicitors had only limited rights of audience: they could appear on behalf of clients in magistrates' courts, county courts, and most tribunals, but barristers had exclusive rights of audience in most Crown Court and High Court cases and in all cases coming before the Court of Appeal and House of Lords.[54] The 1990 Act established the general principle that rights of

---

[48] Access to Justice Act 1999, s 40.

[49] Such rights *have* been granted to employed barristers: see p 388.

[50] Courts and Legal Services Act 1990, s 29; Sch 4 (as amended).

[51] Chartered Institute of Patent Agents Order 1999, SI 1999/3137; Institute of Trade Mark Attorneys Order 2005, SI 2005/240.

[52] Sections 34–53.   [53] Which came into force in December 2004.

[54] These limitations were derived from the practices of the courts themselves. See, e.g., *Practice Direction (Supreme Court: Solicitors: Rights of Audience)* [1986] 2 All ER 226, [1986] 1 WLR 545; *Practice Direction (Crown Court: Solicitors: Rights of Audience)* [1988] 3 All ER 717, [1988] 1 WLR 1427.

audience should be determined on the basis of: (a) qualifications; and (b) membership of a properly regulated profession.[55] The Act did not affect the rights of audience acquired by solicitors and barristers on joining their respective professions, but it did authorize the Law Society and the Bar Council to confer rights of audience on their members. The Law Society's criteria for granting higher court rights of audience to solicitors were approved in 1994.[56]

The Bar Council had argued that their monopoly over higher court advocacy was necessary for the maintenance of high standards and for the preservation of a strong and effective Bar.[57] They had also noted that solicitors had no equivalent of the 'cab-rank' rule,[58] meaning that they had greater freedom than barristers in choosing which cases to accept. The Law Society had responded by pointing out that solicitors were already doing advocacy work in the lower courts, and that the cab-rank rule was often ineffective in practice.[59] In the end the new system appeared to satisfy no one. As Humphries observed in 1998:[60]

> The levels of competence, experience and training required to achieve the qualification have been kept so high that today only 624 out of more than 70,000 solicitors have the right to appear in the higher courts.

The Access to Justice Act 1999 simplified matters by providing that all solicitors who have complied with the Law Society's training requirements should have a full right of audience before every court.[61] By 2004 it was reported that around 2,000 solicitors had obtained higher court advocacy rights.[62]

The principle set out in section 36 applies equally to barristers, and the restrictions on rights of audience that had once been imposed on employed barristers have now been lifted for most purposes.[63] Note also that the Institute of Legal Executives, the Chartered Institute of Patent Agents, and the Institute of Trade Mark Attorneys have been designated as 'authorized bodies' by the Lord Chancellor.[64] This means that they are able to confer limited rights of audience on their members,[65] as will any other authorized regulator designated under the 2007 Act, or granted rights under licence.

---

[55] Section 17(3): see p 396.

[56] These rules required the approval of the Lord Chancellor, the Master of the Rolls, the Lord Chief Justice, and the Vice-Chancellor before they could take effect.

[57] Bar Council, *The Quality of Justice—The Bar's Response* (1989) at pp 128–46.

[58] See p 387.

[59] See *Striking the Balance: The Final Response of the Council of the Law Society on the Green Papers* (1989).

[60] 'Preparing for the New Order in Court', *The Lawyer*, 21 July 1998 at p 14.

[61] Section 36, which substitutes section 31(2)(a) of the Courts and Legal Services Act 1990.

[62] *Final Report of the Review of the Regulatory Framework for Legal Services in England and Wales* (HMSO, 2004) at para 6.

[63] Access to Justice Act 1999, s 37: see p 388.

[64] Courts and Legal Services Act 1990, s 27(9); Sch 4.

[65] Institute of Legal Executives Order 1998, SI 1998/1077; Chartered Institute of Patent Agents Order 1999, SI 1999/3137; Institute of Trade Mark Attorneys Order 2005, SI 2005/240.

The relationship between solicitor and client

A solicitor's authority derives from the retainer given to him by his client, the effect of which is to create a contractual relationship. The precise scope of this relationship will depend on the terms of the retainer, but a solicitor will generally acquire the authority to act as an agent on his client's behalf,[66] and he will be entitled to remuneration on completion of the work agreed. The relationship is not governed solely by the law of contract, however, and it is circumscribed by a variety of statutory rules.[67]

The solicitor–client relationship is also a fiduciary one, which means that a solicitor has an obligation derived from equity to act in good faith in all dealings with his client. But the contractual context should not be overlooked. In *Hilton Barker Booth and Eastwood (a firm)*,[68] Lord Walker observed:

> A solicitor's duty to his client is primarily contractual and its scope depends on the express and implied terms of his retainer...The relationship...is one in which the client reposes trust and confidence in the solicitor...it is a fiduciary relationship...a solicitor's duty of single-minded loyalty to his client's interest, and his duty to respect his client's confidences, do have their roots in the fiduciary nature of the solicitor-client relationship. But they may also have to be moulded and informed by the terms of the contractual relationship.

A solicitor who enters into a transaction with his client must ensure: (a) that he has made a full and honest disclosure of all facts within his knowledge; (b) that the financial terms are fair to the client; and (c) that the transaction was not procured by undue influence. A failure to do any of these things may result in the transaction being set aside.[69] A presumption of undue influence will also arise if a client gives his solicitor an *inter vivos* gift: in *Wright* v *Carter* it was held that this presumption could only be rebutted by evidence that the gift had been made or affirmed after the fiduciary relationship had ended.[70] The presumption of undue influence does not apply to gifts made by will, but where a solicitor prepares a will under which he receives a large benefit a court will require affirmative proof that the testator knew and fully approved of its contents.[71]

Another feature of this fiduciary relationship is the confidential nature of solicitor–client communications. This gives rise to two types of privilege: privilege in the tort of defamation and privilege from disclosure in evidence. This latter privilege is known as legal professional privilege. It is, however, in the future not to be confined to solicitors or barristers. Section 190 of the Legal Services Act 2007 effectively extends the privilege to all authorized bodies providing advocacy, litigation, conveyancing and probate services. Legal professional privilege is to be regarded as fundamental.[72]

---

[66] Enabling the solicitor to legally bind the client.   [67] See the Solicitors Act 1974.

[68] [2005] UKHL 8 [2005] 1 All ER 651, cited with approval in *Conway* v *Patiou* [2005] EWCA Civ 1302, [2006] 1 All ER 571.

[69] *Wright* v *Carter* [1903] 1 Ch 27 at 60, *per* Stirling LJ.

[70] Ibid: evidence that the client had received independent advice from another solicitor did not suffice.

[71] *Wintle* v *Nye* [1959] 1 All ER 552, [1959] 1 WLR 284.

[72] See *R* v *Derby Magistrates' Court, ex parte B* [1996] AC 487, [1995] 4 All ER 526; *Three Rivers District Council* v *Bank of England (Disclosure)* [2004] UKHL 48, [2004] 3 WLR 1274.

Communications between solicitor and client[73] are privileged provided that they were made in confidence and for the purposes of obtaining or giving legal advice about the client's rights, liabilities, obligations, or remedies. In the important case of *Three Rivers District Council* v *Bank of England (Disclosure)*,[74] Lord Scott endorsed the view expressed by Taylor LJ in an earlier case:[75] '[L]egal advice is not confined to telling the client the law; it must include advice as to what should prudently and sensibly be done in the relevant legal context.' The *Three Rivers* case itself concerned advice given to the Bank of England about its submissions to a public inquiry. Despite being largely presentational, the advice was held to be covered by legal professional privilege: the fact that the Bank may have been the subject of criticism by the inquiry gave the advice a legal context. On the other hand, their Lordships made it clear that not all communications between lawyer and client would necessarily be protected in this way. It was observed, for example, that advice relating to investments, finance, and other business matters would often lack a legal context.[76] This decision also confirms that legal professional privilege is absolute, and that once established it can only be waived by the client or overridden by statute.[77] Note finally that privilege also attaches to communications made in connection with current or contemplated litigation, and that in this context it may extend to cover communications with third parties.

Barristers

Inns of Court and entry to the Bar

A person may only practise as a barrister in England if he or she has been 'called to the Bar' of one of the four Inns of Court: Lincoln's Inn; the Inner Temple; the Middle Temple; and Gray's Inn. These Inns are as old as the profession itself and appear to have originated as living quarters for apprentices-at-law. Their jurisdiction derives from the judiciary and is subject to judicial control.[78]

Entry to the Bar has been the responsibility of the General Council of the Bar. The Bar Standards Board has been established and acts as the regulatory arm of the Bar Council.[79] It sets and monitors the standards for training for the Bar, which are currently under review.

A person seeking to qualify as a barrister must join one of the four Inns before he or she can begin the vocational stage of his or her legal training.[80] He or she must also

---

[73] Phrased this way for ease of reference: it will in future apply to all who perform these functions.

[74] [2004] UKHL 48 at [38], [2004] 3 WLR 1274 at [38].

[75] *Balabel* v *Air India* [1988] Ch 317 at 330, [1988] 2 All ER 246 at 254.

[76] [2004] UKHL 48 at [38], [2004] 3 WLR 1274 at [38], *per* Lord Scott.   [77] Ibid at [25].

[78] *R* v *Gray's Inn* (1780) 1 Doug K353, *per* Lord Mansfield; *Lincoln* v *Daniels* [1962] 1 QB 237 at 250, [1961] 3 All ER 740 at 745, *per* Sellers J.

[79] For details of its work see **www.barstandardsboard.org.uk**

[80] The various stages of a barrister's training are discussed further at p 392. For general review of entry to the Bar, see *Entry to the Bar Working Party Final Report* (2007)—'the Neuberger Report': available at **www.barcouncil.org.uk**

keep a number of terms,[81] which means attending some of the dinners, educational days, and residential weekends that are organized by each Inn. The benchers of an Inn, who are judges or senior members of the Bar, have historically had absolute control over the admission of students and the call of barristers. As noted above, these are now matters for the Bar Standards Board. In principle the benchers also have jurisdiction over disciplinary matters, although for most purposes this jurisdiction is in practice delegated to the disciplinary tribunals appointed by the Inns Council. Any appeal against a decision of the benchers lies to the 'Visitors' of the Inns of Court—a domestic tribunal comprising the judges of the High Court.

Such an entrant also has to have appropriate academic qualifications, either a law degree or another non-qualifying degree, and have passed the Graduate Diploma in Law. Having passed the Bar Vocational Course, a pupil barrister must then complete twelve months' pupillage. During the second six months of that pupillage the pupil can spend some of the time on his or her own work.

Practice at the Bar

There are about 11,500 self-employed barristers.[82] Most barristers work in independent practice in sets of chambers, which are associations of barristers sharing common facilities and administrative support. The work of each barrister is organized and arranged by the barrister's clerk, who also plays a key role in reallocating cases when a barrister is unable to appear because of other commitments. The role of the barrister is primarily that of an advocate, and barristers are deemed to have been granted rights of audience before every court in relation to all proceedings.[83] They also deal with matters such as the giving of advice and the drafting of legal documents, although self-employed barristers are currently prevented by Bar Council rules from conducting litigation.[84] The practice of wearing robes continues despite some debate as to its utility,[85] and counsel cannot generally be 'heard' in court unless they are dressed appropriately. The wearing of wigs has now been discontinued in civil cases. They do not wear robes when appearing before courts that are themselves unrobed, magistrates' courts being one example.

Barristers are divided into junior counsel and Queen's Counsel (QCs). The latter are known as 'silks' because they wear silk gowns as opposed to the stuff gowns worn by juniors. Appointments to the office of Queen's Counsel are made by the Crown on the advice of the Lord Chancellor, and are based on ability and experience. Silks are

---

[81] The current requirement is that a student should complete twelve 'qualifying units': a dinner counts as one unit, an educational day counts as two, and a residential weekend counts as three.

[82] Neuberger Report (2007), at para 6, p 14.   [83] Courts and Legal Services Act 1990, s 31(1).

[84] Code of Conduct of the Bar of England and Wales (8th edn, 2004), para 401.

[85] A survey commissioned by the Lord Chancellor's Department found strong support for the reform of court dress from both court users and members of the public. There was no consensus as to what form any change might take, although only 34 per cent of advocates favoured the retention of wigs: ORC International, *Public Perceptions of Working Court Dress in England and Wales* (2002). See also: Lord Chancellor's Department, *Consultation on Court Working Dress in England and Wales* (HMSO, 2003) CP 05/03. At the time of writing it remains unclear whether the practice will survive.

instructed in the most difficult, complex, or important of cases and are able to command much higher fees than their junior counterparts. At one time they were subject to rules preventing them from doing drafting work or giving written opinions on evidence, and they were not permitted to appear in court without a junior. Such formal restrictions no longer exist, although a QC is not obliged to accept instructions to act without a junior if he or she feels that it would not be in the interests of his or her client to do so. The established practice has been for appointments to the office of Queen's Counsel to be made annually, but in 2003 the process was suspended pending the outcome of a consultation exercise.[86] Changes were made to the selection process as a result of this consultation,[87] and the annual round of appointments resumed in 2005. Although the consultation revealed *some* support for the idea that a two-tier system works against the public interest, the overall conclusion was that the title of QC serves as a useful 'kitemark' or indication of quality.[88]

The relationship between barrister and client

Whereas the relationship between solicitor and client is to some extent regulated by statute, a barrister's obligations towards his or her client are largely governed by self-imposed standards.[89] The common law rule that historically prevented self-employed barristers from entering into contracts for the provision of their services was abolished in 1990.[90] However, it was not until 2001 that the Bar Council relaxed its own rules and allowed barristers to accept instructions from solicitors on contractual terms.[91] Further changes in 2004 mean that barristers can now accept instructions directly from lay clients, although they are prohibited from doing so in certain types of case.[92] Barristers may advertise their services by any means permitted by law, although the Bar Council's Code of Conduct[93] prohibits them from publicizing their success rates or making direct comparisons with their competitors.

A barrister has an obligation to preserve the confidences of his or her client, and he or she is deemed to have the authority to conduct proceedings on his or her client's behalf. The scope of this authority is subject to the ordinary principles of agency,[94] and it includes the authority to compromise proceedings and to make admissions on the client's behalf in civil proceedings. Note should also be taken of the 'cab-rank' principle. In theory this obliges barristers to accept any brief in an area in which they practice, provided that they are available and are offered a proper fee. A busy barrister can easily be committed elsewhere, however, and the extent to which the cab-rank

---

[86] DCA, *The Future of Queen's Counsel* (HMSO, 2003) CP 08/03.

[87] QCs are now selected by a panel comprising solicitors, barristers, laymen, and a judge, with the Lord Chancellor having no direct input into the decision.

[88] See Lord Falconer (Lord Chancellor), 661 HL Official Report (5th series) col WS54, 26 May 2004.

[89] See Code of Conduct of the Bar of England and Wales (8th edn, 2004).

[90] Courts and Legal Services Act 1990, s 61(1).

[91] See Annexe G2 of the Code of Conduct: 'The Contractual Terms of Work on which Barristers Offer their Services to Solicitors'.

[92] See Annexe F2 of the Code of Conduct: 'The Public Access Rules'.

[93] At para 710.   [94] See p 384, n 66.

principle operates in practice is questionable.[95] Indeed, in 1973 some twenty-four QCs declined to accept briefs on behalf of the IRA Old Bailey bombers.[96] This is undoubtedly an extreme example and it is impossible to know the reasons given by those who were unable to accept the brief. Nevertheless, it seems unlikely that barristers are regularly forced to undertake work that they would not otherwise have accepted,[97] and in any event the cab-rank rule does not apply to work undertaken on the basis of a contract or conditional fee agreement.[98] In addition, barristers are required by the Bar's Code of Conduct to refuse to accept instructions that might cause 'professional embarrassment' or create a conflict of interests.

Employed barristers

Although most barristers are self-employed and working in independent practice, a sizeable minority supply legal services as salaried employees. There are about 3,500 fully qualified barristers who are employed in the private sector, the Crown Prosecution Service, the Government Legal Service or local government.[99] Some are employed by solicitors' firms, but barristers are also employed in other sectors such as government and commerce. Employed barristers may not supply legal services for reward except in the course of their employment, and in most cases this means that they may only supply legal services to their own employers. However, a barrister in the employment of a solicitor, authorized litigator, legal advice centre, or the Legal Services Commission may also provide legal services for his or her employer's clients.[100]

All employed barristers are permitted by the Bar's Code of Conduct to conduct litigation,[101] provided that they comply with the relevant rules and have completed the necessary training.[102] In addition to performing the other functions normally undertaken by barristers, an employed barrister may also interview witnesses, take statements, and handle his or her employers' funds. However, a barrister who has never practised in chambers may only exercise full rights of audience if he or she practises (or has practised) from the office of an experienced advocate for a period of at least three years.[103]

---

[95] See the survey covered by Walson, 'Advocacy for the Unpopular' (1998) 162 JP 499.

[96] Robertson, *The Justice Game* (Chatto, 1998) at p 379.

[97] See the observations of Lord Steyn in *Arthur JS Hall & Co v Simons* [2002] 1 AC 615 at 678, [2000] 3 All ER 673 at 759.

[98] Barristers have also voted to abandon the rule in certain public-funded cases: see p 420.

[99] Neuberger Report (2007), at para 6, p 14.

[100] Code of Conduct of the Bar of England and Wales, Part V. Employed barristers are not prohibited from supplying legal services to the public free of charge.

[101] At para 504.

[102] Code of Conduct, Annexe I: Employed Barristers (Conduct of Litigation) Rules.

[103] He must also have completed a pupillage: see p 386. A person who has not completed a pupillage may be employed as a barrister without rights of audience if he was called to the Bar before 2002.

KEY ISSUE

The roles of the solicitors' profession and that of the Bar increasingly overlap. To talk today of barristers being advocates and solicitors as primarily engaged in case preparation and non-contentious work is certainly not true, if it ever was. The question remains as to how far that division can still be justified. Significant steps have been taken by the profession to remove restrictive practices and exclusive rights that cannot be justified. Solicitors as well as barristers are eligible for high judicial office. Legal executives, paralegals, licensed conveyancers, and insolvency practitioners already play an important part in legal service provision. An independent, self-employed Bar still exists, available to provide advocacy and other advice work free from the organizational pressures that employed practice may impose, although funding remains an important issue for all.[104]

But questions remain as to whether the division can be justified, or whether it will gradually reduce in importance as the new structure for the provision of legal services takes effect. The merit of the Queens' Counsel distinction at the Bar and the effectiveness of the 'cab-rank' are both issues where further change may be inevitable.

? Questions

1. What were the reasons for a divided legal profession?
2. Does the distinction between solicitors and barristers make any sense today?
3. Is the Bar an independent elite of specialists available to all?
4. How effective or important do you consider the 'cab-rank' principle to be?
5. Should the office of Queen's Counsel be abolished?
6. What purpose does it serve?
7. Do other countries have a divided profession?
8. How could a fused profession work?

The Director of Public Prosecutions and the Crown Prosecution Service

Before 1985 there was no national system for the prosecution of offences, and arrangements varied considerably from one police area to the next. Some forces relied on local authority solicitors or solicitors in private practice, but many had their own prosecuting solicitors departments. The role of the Director of Public Prosecutions (DPP) was supervisory and advisory, and he assumed responsibility for the prosecution of serious offences such as murder. The Royal Commission on Criminal Procedure[105] concluded that an independent system of public prosecutions was essential, and it recommended that once a police force had decided to prosecute, the conduct of that prosecution should be entrusted to a separate authority.[106] The Commission recommended that this new authority should be locally based,[107] but the government opted to create a national prosecution service under the control of the DPP. The government's

[104] See p 410.   [105] Cm 8092 (HMSO, 1981).   [106] Ibid, at para 7.3.   [107] Ibid, at para 7.22.

decision was given effect by the Prosecution of Offences Act 1985, which established the Crown Prosecution Service (CPS).

Section 2 of the Act provides that the DPP must be a barrister or solicitor of not less than ten years' standing, and that he must be appointed by the Attorney-General. His duties are set out in section 3(2) of that Act, and they include the following:

(a) to take over the conduct of all criminal proceedings instituted on behalf of a police force;

(b) to institute and conduct criminal proceedings where the importance or difficulty of the case makes it appropriate that he should do so;

(c) to take over binding over proceedings brought by a police force;

(d) to give advice to police forces on all matters relating to criminal offences; and

(e) to appear in certain appeals.

Any member of the CPS who is a barrister or solicitor may be designated by the DPP as a Crown Prosecutor.[108] Crown Prosecutors have all of the powers of the DPP to institute and conduct proceedings, although they are subject to the direction of the DPP in the exercise of these powers.[109] Crown Prosecutors have the same rights of audience as solicitors, and since 2000 they have been able to appear before the higher courts if qualified to do so.[110] In 2006, the CPS completed its first in-house prosecution of a murder. This trend is regarded as an important strengthening of the prosecution process, assisting in communication with both the police and with victims.[111] The DPP may also confer limited rights of audience on CPS employees who are not Crown Prosecutors, and has done so within prescribed parameters.[112]

The CPS itself is a national organization with offices in regional centres in forty-three CPS areas. It employs 2,879 prosecutors and 4,908 caseworkers.[113] Its role is to prosecute offences; it does not control the process of investigation. Since it was established, however, the context within which it operates has changed significantly: levels of serious crime have risen and a series of high-profile cases have raised concerns about its effectiveness. The Glidewell Report,[114] which reported in May 1998, concluded that the structure of the CPS should be reorganized so as to achieve greater devolution of responsibility. It proposed that each area should be headed by a Chief Crown Prosecutor and supported by an Area Business Manager, with the CPS National Headquarters having responsibility for resourcing and monitoring. The report suggested that each CPS 'area' should be regarded as equivalent to a large legal firm specializing in criminal prosecution, and that it should enjoy a large degree of autonomy

---

[108] 1985 Act, s 1(3).   [109] Ibid, s 1(6).

[110] Courts and Legal Services Act 1990, s 31A (as inserted by the Access to Justice Act 1999).

[111] CPS Annual Report, 2006, p 15.

[112] Prosecution of Offences Act 1985, s 7A (as inserted by then Crime and Disorder Act 1998). See 2006 Annual Report, Annex D. See also Criminal Justice and Immigration Act 2008.

[113] CPS Annual Report, 2006.

[114] *Review of the Crown Prosecution Service*, Cm 3960 (HMSO, 1998).

in carrying out its professional functions. These aims were broadly accepted by the government, and the CPS was the subject of major structural changes in 1999. In particular, the boundaries of CPS areas have been realigned to correspond with police areas,[115] and CPS staff are increasingly being located in or close to police stations. Not only that, but there is also an effective forty-fourth area through CPS Direct, which is a 24-hour telephone service available to advise the police.

Coupled with this structural review, Glidewell also considered the operational performance of the CPS. Statistics showed that more than half of all acquittals in the Crown Court resulted from an order or direction of the judge, and this was viewed with some concern. The report also noted the suspicion that charges were sometimes dropped or downgraded in circumstances in which such action was inappropriate, although it found no firm evidence that this actually occurred.[116] Glidewell took the view that where a case had been reviewed by the CPS, it ought to be strong enough to put to a jury, and it recommended that the preparation of case files in future should be the responsibility of the CPS rather than the police. The idea that the CPS should become involved in the decision-making at an earlier stage was given effect by the Criminal Justice Act 2003. Schedule 2 of the Act amended the Police and Criminal Evidence Act 1984,[117] with the result that the CPS now has much greater involvement in deciding whether a charge should be laid, and what the nature of any charge should be.[118] The approach now is that CPS and police work in partnership to ensure that the right decisions are made at the right time.

The law officers

The 'law officers' are the Attorney-General and the Solicitor-General. They are legal advisers to the Crown and *ex officio* members of the Bar Council, although they may not engage in private practice during their time in office. They are assisted by practising barristers known as Treasury Counsel.

Apart from his political duties, which include advising government departments and answering questions in Parliament, the Attorney-General represents the Crown in certain civil proceedings and in trials for treason and other offences with a political or constitutional element. He also exercises the prerogative power of staying prosecutions on indictment by the entry of a *nolle prosequi*, and certain criminal proceedings can only be commenced with his authority.

The Solicitor-General's position is basically that of the Attorney-General's deputy, and he may exercise any power vested by statute in the Attorney-General (unless the statute in question provides otherwise).[119]

[115] See p 429.   [116] The power to discontinue proceedings is discussed at p 599.
[117] By amending s 37 and inserting new ss 37A, 37B, 37C and 37D.
[118] These reforms are discussed in greater detail at p 595.
[119] Law Officers Act 1997, s 1.

The education and training of lawyers

Solicitors

Section 2 of the Solicitors Act 1974 provided that the Law Society may, with the concurrence of the Lord Chancellor, the Lord Chief Justice, and the Master of the Rolls, make regulations governing the education and training of solicitors. No person could be admitted as a solicitor without a certificate stating that he or she has complied with these training regulations and that the Society is satisfied as to his or her character and suitability.[120] The functions formerly exercised by the Law Society are now exercised by the Solicitors Regulation Authority.[121] This body sets the standards for qualifying as a solicitor, monitors training providers, and administers the roll of solicitors.[122]

The current training regulations stem from changes made in 1990 and they divide the training process into three distinct stages: the academic stage; the vocational stage; and continuing professional development. For many would-be solicitors the academic stage of training is satisfied by graduating with a qualifying law degree.[123] Graduates with a non-qualifying degree can meet the Law Society's requirements by completing a one-year[124] Common Professional Examination course (CPE) or by obtaining a Graduate Diploma in Law (GDL). The only way for non-graduates to complete the academic stage is to follow the ILEX route, which involves working in a legal office and passing the exams needed to qualify as a Member or Fellow of the Institute of Legal Executives. A legal executive who wishes to qualify as a solicitor can then undertake further training and go on to sit the CPE. The ILEX route is described by the Law Society as 'lengthy, demanding and academically challenging',[125] and in practice the overwhelming majority of solicitors enter the profession as graduates. Having completed the academic stage of training, a student can then commence the vocational stage, which means passing a practical-orientated legal practice course and entering into a training contract.[126] The third stage of a solicitor's training—continuing professional development—is undertaken once a solicitor is actually qualified, but it is nevertheless compulsory.

Barristers

As already noted, the Bar Council has the Bar Standards Board as its regulatory arm, which governs entry to the Bar. It deals with the requirements for entry to the

---

[120] Solicitors Act 1974, ss 1, 3.   [121] See, generally: **www.sra.org.uk**

[122] See, further, p 393.

[123] One that covers 'The Foundations of Legal Knowledge': public law, EU law, criminal law, the law of obligations, property law, and equity and the law of trusts. See the Joint Statement on Qualifying Law Degrees issued by the Law Society and the Bar Council (effective 1 September 2001).

[124] Or a longer period for part-time or distance-learning students.

[125] See the Law Society publication, 'Ways to Qualify as a Solicitor'.

[126] ILEX Fellows are exempt from the requirement to enter a training contract.

profession. As far as the academic stage is concerned, the requirements are essentially the same as for a would-be solicitor: they can be satisfied by obtaining either a qualifying law degree[127] or a non-qualifying degree followed by a CPE certificate or Graduate Diploma in Law. There is no equivalent for barristers of the ILEX route. The vocational stage of training comprises the one-year[128] Bar Vocational Course (BVC), which a student cannot commence until he or she has joined one of the Inns of Court.[129] This is followed by a twelve-month pupillage in chambers, the first half of which is spent shadowing a pupil supervisor. Pupils may accept instructions during the last six months of a pupillage, although not without the permission of their supervisors. It is only after each of these requirements has been fulfilled that a person can be called to the Bar and practise as a barrister. Like solicitors, barristers must also undertake continuing professional development activities on a regular basis.[130]

The regulation of legal services

The Law Society

Up until recently, the Law Society was the professional regulatory body governing the work of solicitors. It received its first Royal Charter in 1831 and was originally called 'The Society of Attorneys, Solicitors, Proctors and others not being Barristers, practising in the Courts of Law and Equity of the United Kingdom'. Its name was officially changed to 'the Law Society' by the Supplemental Charter of 1903. It has a President, a Vice-President, and a Deputy Vice-President, and it is governed by a Council of between 100 and 105 members. At present the Council has 105 members, comprising sixty-one solicitors representing regional constituencies, thirty-nine other solicitors, and five lay members.

The Law Society's regulatory powers affected all solicitors, and derived from the Solicitors Act 1974.[131] Their regulatory functions are now performed by the Solicitors Regulation Authority (SRA). The SRA maintains the roll of solicitors. It sets requirements for continuing professional development, and monitors solicitors to ensure that they comply with the relevant professional rules. It has the power to close down solicitor's firms, and to refer complaints to the Solicitors Disciplinary Tribunal.

The Law Society also looks after the welfare of solicitors generally and attempts to maintain good relations with other bodies and with the public. To this end the Council examines the activities of unqualified persons doing the work of solicitors, and in appropriate cases it institutes proceedings. It also performs educative and public relations activities.

---

[127] See n 123.   [128] If full-time; two years, if part-time.   [129] See p 385.

[130] This is a fairly recent innovation: CPD was not a requirement of all barristers until January 2005.

[131] The constitution and general purposes of the Law Society are still governed by its Royal Charter of 1845, which refers to its role in 'promoting professional improvement and facilitating the acquisition of legal knowledge'.

The Bar Council

The General Council of the Bar (usually referred to as the Bar Council) was founded in 1894, although it was reconstituted by the Bar and the Senate of the Inns of Court in 1987. Its membership of 115 barristers includes representatives of the Inns and Specialist Bar Associations, along with *ex officio* members such as the Attorney-General, Solicitor-General, and the Director of Public Prosecutions.

The Bar Council is both a representative and a regulatory body, and it has a wide range of functions. Its regulatory powers do not derive from statute but it is deemed to be an 'authorized body' for the purposes conferring rights of audience and rights to conduct litigation.[132] Other functions include compiling and implementing the Bar's Code of Conduct, maintaining and enhancing professional standards, and representing the interests of the profession to the government and other bodies. It also determines the Bar's policies on education and training and is thus able to regulate entry to the profession.

Review by the courts

Solicitors are officers of the Senior Court of England and Wales,[133] and judges of this court have an inherent jurisdiction to suspend a solicitor for misconduct or to strike his or her name from the Roll of Solicitors. In their capacity as officers of the court, solicitors may be ordered to meet any costs incurred as a result of improper, unreasonable, or negligent conduct,[134] and they may also be liable for any losses that are the natural and probable consequence of such conduct.[135] Barristers are not officers of the Supreme Court and have historically not been subject to this jurisdiction,[136] but since 1990 the major civil and criminal courts have had a statutory jurisdiction to order *any* legal representative to pay the whole or part of any wasted costs.[137] The courts also have an inherent jurisdiction to prevent abuse of their procedures, and in exercising this jurisdiction they could refuse to hear an advocate or restrain his or her participation

---

[132] Courts and Legal Services Act 1990, ss 27(9); 8(5).

[133] The renamed 'Supreme Court'—the renaming was necessary as a result of the creation of the Supreme Court as the final court of appeal: see p 249.

[134] This jurisdiction is preserved by the Solicitors Act 1974, s 50(2). See, e.g., *Holden & Co v Crown Prosecution Service* [1990] 2 QB 261, [1990] 1 All ER 368 (inherent jurisdiction to order defence solicitor to pay prosecution costs following a serious dereliction of duty); *Langley v North West Water Authority* [1991] 3 All ER 610, [1991] 1 WLR 697 (solicitor personally liable for costs resulting from failure to comply with County Court Practice Direction).

[135] *Marsh v Joseph* [1897] 1 Ch 213.

[136] In *Metcalf v Wetherill (Wasted Costs Order)* [2002] UKHL 27, [2003] 1 AC 120, [2002] 3 All ER 721, the House of Lords suggested, *obiter*, that the inherent jurisdiction could be applied to any legal representative. However, it also accepted that the jurisdiction had largely been superseded by statute.

[137] Supreme Court Act 1981, s 51 (civil courts) as amended by the Courts and Legal Services Act 1990; Prosecution of Offences Act 1985, s 19A (criminal courts) as inserted by the 1990 Act. The principles to be applied were considered by the Court of Appeal in *Re A Barrister (Wasted Costs Order (No 1 of 1991))* [1993] QB 293, [1992] 3 All ER 429 and are discussed at p 548.

in a particular trial. In practice, however, a court will only take such a drastic step in the most exceptional of cases.[138]

In addition to the above, a solicitor may incur liability as an officer of the court by giving an undertaking to the court,[139] or by giving an undertaking to an individual when acting in his or her capacity as a solicitor.[140] Such an undertaking will be enforced by the court summarily, not as a contractual obligation but in order to secure the proper conduct of its officers. Finally, both solicitors and barristers may be liable for contempt of court for acts done in a professional capacity.[141]

The Clementi Report and the Legal Services Act 2007: Change to the regulatory framework

The Report and White Paper

We have already noted[142] that the Clementi Report recommended sweeping changes to the regulatory provision in respect of the legal profession, including changes to widen the provision of legal services. The report recommended the creation of a new Legal Services Board with responsibility for overseeing the regulation of all legal service providers.[143] In addition to exercising regulatory powers in respect of the Law Society and Bar Council, the new body would also oversee the Institute of Legal Executives, the Council for Licensed Conveyancers, the Chartered Institute of Patent Agents, the Institute of Trade Mark Attorney, and the Office of the Immigration Services Commissioner. The existing professional bodies would still have front-line responsibility for regulating their own members, but the Legal Services Board would be able to intervene if standards were not being maintained. The Board would also assume a number of powers currently exercised by the Lord Chancellor, including the power to authorize bodies to confer rights of audience and the right to conduct litigation.[144] In addition, Clementi recommended that all front-line regulatory bodies should be required to 'separate out' their own regulatory and representative functions.[145] On the issue of complaints, the report proposed the creation of an Office for Legal Complaints, which would be a single, independent body responsible for handling all consumer complaints. Matters of professional conduct and discipline, however, would continue to be dealt with by the existing professional bodies.[146]

The Clementi Report was welcomed by the government, although it did not consider it went far enough.[147] The reaction of the professions to this news was mixed. The proposal for a new complaints body received a particularly frosty reception

---

[138] *Geveran Trading Co v Skjevesland* [2002] EWCA Civ 1567, [2003] 1 WLR 912, [2003] 1 All ER 1.

[139] *D v A & Co* [1899] D 2136.

[140] *Re A Solicitor, ex parte Hales* [1907] 2 KB 539; *Re A Solicitor* [1966] 3 All ER 52, [1966] 1 WLR 1604.

[141] *Linwood v Andrews and Moore* (1888) 58 LT 612; *Alliance and Leicester Building Society v Ghahremani* [1992] NLJR 313 (1992) The Times, 19 March; *Daw v Eley* (1868) LR 7 Eq 49.

[142] See p 377.   [143] Ibid, at paras B70–B71.

[144] See p 381.   [145] Including the Law Society and the Bar Council: ibid, at para B39.

[146] Ibid, paras C88–C89.   [147] See pp 377–8.

from the Bar Council, which pointed out that its existing complaints system already had a good track record and did not need to be fixed. It also voiced concerns about the possible effect on standards and legal ethics if lawyers were to be allowed to join 'legal disciplinary practices', and it stated that it would continue to oppose the idea of barristers being able to form partnerships with other barristers.[148] For its part, the Law Society was rather more enthusiastic. It had already begun to move towards the separation of regulatory and representative functions envisaged by Clementi, and the prospect of solicitors being able to form alternative business structures was particularly welcomed.[149]

The White Paper, published in 2005,[150] fully endorsed the recommendations of Clementi, and forms the basis for the Legal Services Act 2007.

The Legal Services Board

The 2007 Act creates the Legal Services Board. Figure 11.1[151] shows the role of the Board in the new structure.

The Board is an independent body corporate, which is accountable to the Lord Chancellor, and, through him, to Parliament.[152] It is at the head of the new regulatory regime. Day-to-day regulation is to be provided by front-line regulators, which will be authorized for this purpose by the Board if it is satisfied that they are appropriate bodies who can perform this function. These will include the existing professional bodies, such as the Law Society, Bar Council, Council for Licensed Conveyancers, and the Institute of Legal Executives.

Section 1 of the Legal Services Act 2007 identifies seven regulatory objectives that the Board is under a duty to promote and with which it must comply.[153] These reflect the intention that the provision of legal services should be of high quality and best reflect the interests of consumers. They are:

- protecting and promoting the public interest;
- supporting the constitutional principle of the rule of law;
- improving access to justice;
- protecting and promoting the interests of consumers;
- promoting competition in the provision of legal services;
- encouraging an independent, strong, diverse, and effective legal profession;
- increasing public understanding of the citizen's legal rights and duties.

A Consumer Panel is established.[154] The members of the Panel have experience of consumer affairs. The Panel reports to the Board, and ensures that the views and

---

[148] 'Clementi Must Not Be Used to Compromise the Independence of Lawyers'—press release from the Chairman of the Bar Council, 15 December 2004.
[149] 'The Future of Legal Services'—press release from the President of the Law Society, 22 March 2005.
[150] See p 377.   [151] Taken, with modifications from the White Paper, p 12.
[152] For composition, see Sch 1 to the 2007 Act.   [153] 2007 Act, ss 1, 3.
[154] Ibid, s 8.

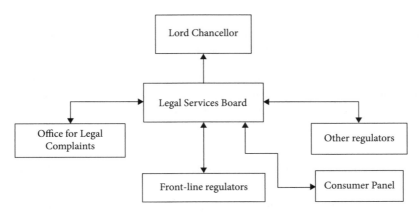

Fig. 11.1 The role of the Legal Services Board

concerns of consumers are heard.[155] An example was seen in May 2010 when the Consumer Panel made recommendations in respect of referral fees, the fees paid by solicitors to promote business and over which there have been ongoing concerns. The Board also relates and interacts with other regulatory boards, such as the Office of Fair Trading.[156]

The powers of the Board enable it to effectively regulate the front-line regulators, although the 2007 Act gives to the Lord Chancellor the power to designate the Board itself as an approved regulator of one or more of the reserved legal activities in limited circumstances in which a designation of a regulator has been cancelled or a new 'reserved legal activity' has been created.[157] The powers conferred by the 2007 Act are wide.[158] It may make rules, set performance targets, issue directions, publicly censure an approved regulator, impose financial penalties, and intervene in respect of an approved regulators' function by the making of directions. Although it is intended that the Board and regulators will work together to improve areas of weakness,[159] it may recommend to the Lord Chancellor that a designation of an approved regulator be cancelled. It must issue a policy statement indicating how these powers are to be exercised.

KEY ISSUE

One key issue is how the process of regulation will extend to managing the new regime created by alternative business structures. The regulatory regimes that sufficed for the regulation of solicitors and barristers will not of themselves be sufficient. The Legal Services Act contains provision that deal with the regulation of such structures. A licensed body must have a head of legal practice and a head of finance and administration, both of whom must

---

[155] White Paper, para 5.3. [156] 2007 Act, s 57. [157] 2007 Act, s 82.
[158] Ibid, Part 4. [159] White Paper, para 5.6.

have been approved by the licensing authority. These individuals will have an obligation to ensure compliance with the terms of the licence and must report failings to the licensing authority. They must be 'fit and proper persons'. There are limitation on the ownership of licensed bodies, again to ensure that individuals are 'fit and proper' persons. There will be special provisions for not-for-profit organizations and trade unions to reflect the distinctive nature of these bodies relative to other providers of legal services.

? Questions

1. Do you think the regulatory regimes introduced by the 2007 Act improve the process of regulation? In what ways?
2. What are the regulatory challenges likely to be faced in respect of the wider range of legal services providers?

Complaints against lawyers

A clear distinction must be drawn between complaints about professional misconduct, and about inadequate professional service. The former are matters that fall within the purview of professional disciplinary processes. The latter may involve allegations of negligence best resolved in the courts, but many complaints can best be dealt through the variety of complaints mechanisms that exist, and that have already been discussed.[160] Complaints in respect of inadequate service have, since 6 October 2010, been within the remit of the Legal Ombudsman, an office established under the Legal Services Act 2007.

Historically both branches of the profession have their own internal mechanisms for dealing with complaints about misconduct and inadequate service. Those existing systems for the redress of complaints were considered inadequate by Clementi[161] and by the White Paper *The Future of Legal Services*.[162] The White Paper reviewed existing provision, and considered that it fell short of what is required. Its recommendations are given effect by the Legal Service Act 2007. We first examine the pre-existing regime, before explaining the new provisions.

The Solicitors Disciplinary Tribunal

Allegations of serious professional misconduct are dealt with by an independent Solicitors Disciplinary Tribunal. The tribunal consists of 'solicitor members', who must be practising solicitors of not less than ten years' standing, and 'lay members', who are neither solicitors nor barristers.[163] It is independent of the Law Society and like other judicial tribunals it may receive evidence on oath and compel the attendance

---

[160] See **www.legalombudsman.org.uk**   [161] See p 377.
[162] At paras 3.3–3.4.   [163] Solicitors Act 1974, s 46.

of witnesses. It is properly constituted when at least three members are present, the majority of whom must be solicitor members. There must also be at least one lay member present.[164]

Most of the tribunal's caseload consists of referrals from the Law Society, although it can also hear applications from solicitors, judges, and members of the public. In addition to dealing with a variety of disciplinary matters, it can hear any application to strike a solicitor's name from the Roll, or to reinstate a solicitor who has previously been struck off or suspended.[165] It can also hear applications concerning the conduct of solicitors' employees.[166] The tribunal can dispose of an application involving a solicitor by making any such order as it thinks fit:[167] in particular, an adverse finding may result in a solicitor being struck off, suspended, reprimanded, fined, or prevented from carrying out work funded by the Legal Services Commission.[168] In the case of an application concerning a solicitor's employee, the tribunal may make an order preventing that person from being employed or remunerated by a solicitor without the Law Society's written permission.[169] Any appeal against a refusal to revoke such an order lies to the Master of the Rolls, and his decision is final.[170] The Master of the Rolls also hears appeals against decisions relating to the reinstatement of a solicitor who has been struck off or suspended.[171] Appeals in all other cases lie to the High Court, and from there (with leave) to the Court of Appeal.[172]

Disciplinary action against barristers

Although barristers have always been subject to the disciplinary jurisdiction of the Inns of Court, the Bar Council did not have a system for dealing with complaints from lay clients until the appointment of a Complaints Commissioner in 1997. The Commissioner is an independent non-lawyer and his function was to examine all complaints received by the Bar Council and to filter out those that are clearly without justification. Complaints that appear to have merit are referred by the Commissioner to the Council's Professional Conduct and Complaints Committee (PCCC). If the PCCC agrees that the complaint may be justified, it will refer the matter to another body for a final determination. Complaints that only raise issues of inadequate professional service are referred to an adjudication panel comprising the Commissioner, a layman, and two barristers: if a complaint is upheld the barrister may be ordered to repay his fees or to pay compensation of up to £5,000. Where a complaint is based wholly or partly on an allegation of professional misconduct[173] the PCCC has three options: (1) to refer the matter to an informal hearing; (2) to refer it to a summary

---

[164] Ibid, s 46(6).   [165] Ibid, s 47(1).   [166] Ibid, s 43.

[167] Ibid, s 47(2).   [168] Ibid, ss 47(2); 47(2A).

[169] Ibid, s 43(2).   [170] Ibid, ss 49(1)(a); 49(6).   [171] Ibid.

[172] Ibid, s 49(1)(b). See, e.g., *Langford* v *Law Society* [2002] EWHC 2802 (Admin); [2003] 153 NLJR 176.

[173] The Code of Conduct of the Bar of England and Wales states that any failure to comply with the Code shall amount to professional misconduct (8th edn, 2004; para 901). It would be unusual however, for very minor breaches to be dealt with as misconduct in practice.

procedure panel; or (3) to refer it to a disciplinary tribunal comprising a judge, two barristers and two laymen. Disciplinary tribunals deal with the most serious cases and can disbar or suspend a barrister if appropriate. A barrister can appeal against the decision of a tribunal or summary procedure panel to the Visitors of the Inns of Court (the High Court Judges).

Complaint handling by the Law Society

In 1996 the Law Society replaced its existing Solicitor's Complaints Bureau with an Office for the Supervision of Solicitors (OSS). The OSS handled complaints about the quality of service provided by solicitors in addition to dealing with allegations of professional misconduct. It was also responsible for overseeing the Solicitors' Compensation Fund. Like its predecessor, the OSS was much criticized for its inefficiency and its perceived lack of independence: despite its semi-autonomous status and the inclusion of a number of lay members, it was directly funded by the Law Society and its membership included several solicitors who sat on the Law Society's Council. The OSS was widely criticized during its short history,[174] and in 2004 the Legal Services Ombudsman reported that the quality of its complaints handling was satisfactory in only 53.3 per cent of cases.[175] Three months before the Ombudsman's report was published, the OSS was replaced by two new bodies: the Consumer Complaints System and the Compliance Directorate. How complaints are handled wass monitored by the Office of the Legal Services Complaints Commissioner, established in 2004, but now abolished.[176]

Complaints that a solicitor has provided an 'inadequate professional service'— for example, by involving the client in unreasonable delays or failing to keep him informed—are handled by the Consumer Complaints Service (CCS). The CCS also offers a free service for checking that solicitors' bills are fair and reasonable, although this is only offered in respect of work that has not involved court proceedings. The emphasis of the CCS is on conciliation, but in appropriate cases it can reduce a solicitor's bill or order a solicitor to pay compensation of up to £5,000. Where some form of professional misconduct is alleged, such as a breach of lawyer–client confidentiality or the mishandling of client funds, the complaint is referred to the Society's Compliance Directorate. No compensation can be awarded in respect of such an allegation unless there is also an element of 'inadequate professional service'.[177] However, the Law Society can take disciplinary action against the solicitor concerned, place conditions on his practising certificate, or intervene in the solicitor's practice. Serious or persistent cases

[174] See, e.g., Moorhead, Sherr and Rogers, 'Willing Blindness? OSS Complaints Handling Procedures (2000); DCA, *Complaints and Regulation in the Legal Services Market: A Scoping Study* (HMSO, 2003).
[175] *In Whose Interest?*—Annual Report of the Legal Services Ombudsman for England and Wales, 2003/2004 at p 13. The role of the Legal Services Ombudsman is discussed further at p 402.
[176] See p 403.
[177] The Solicitors Act 1974 itself makes a distinction between 'conduct' and 'service' issues.

of professional misconduct may be referred to the Solicitors Disciplinary Tribunal.[178] The Law Society also has had an Independent Commissioner with responsibility for overseeing its handling of complaints. The Commissioner had no involvement in dealing with individual complaints but produced an annual report on the Law Society's performance and had the power to make recommendations. His office wass funded by the Law Society and has no statutory basis: his independence derives from the fact that he is appointed by the Master of the Rolls and is not a lawyer. The relationship between the Commissioner and the Law Society has not always been an easy one: in 2006 the Law Society was fined £250,000 for submitting an inadequate complaints-handling plan for 2007.

In dividing responsibility for complaints handling between the CSS and its Compliance Directorate, the Law Society was responding to the Independent Commissioner's recommendation that it should separate its regulatory function from its handling of 'consumer redress'.[179] However,[180] its efforts failed to impress the Legal Services Ombudsman:[181]

> Regardless of the precise motives or details of this latest reorganization, there is no doubt that it represents a high profile change to the Law Society's complaints-handling operations. I was therefore extremely disappointed that the Law Society took such a radical step without any consultation or communication with either my Office … or, as far as I am aware, with any other external stakeholders. This hardly represents the actions of a model regulator prepared to engage openly and transparently with its stakeholders.

The Ombudsman also pointed that 'the most obvious single contribution to improving client satisfaction … would of course be to remove the causes that give rise to complaints in the first place'.[182]

Before the Law Society will consider a complaint about inadequate professional service, it will normally insist that a client has first made use of a solicitor's own 'in-house' complaints procedure. Rule 15 of the Solicitors Practice Rules requires all solicitors to have a complaints-handling procedure in place, and a breach of this rule may itself be a disciplinary matter. Both the Legal Services Ombudsman and the Independent Commissioner indicated that the Law Society had not done enough to enforce this rule in the past, and the Society is now taking steps to address this.[183]

---

[178] See p 398.

[179] See Sir Stephen Lander, Independent Commissioner to the Law Society, *Redress or Rules? Whither the Consumer Redress Scheme?* (2003).

[180] See (2006) 156 NLJ 858, and Annual Report.   [181] See p 51.

[182] Ibid, at p 52.

[183] See *In Whose Interest?*, n 175, at p 53; Annual Report of the Independent Commissioner to the Law Society 2003, Annex III, recommendation 3. See also Moorhead, 'Self-Regulation and the Market for Legal Services'—paper published by the Cardiff Centre for Ethics, Law and Society (Cardiff University, 2004).

The Legal Services Ombudsman

The Ombudsman was an independent non-lawyer appointed for a renewable term of three years.[184] Her role was to investigate allegations made by persons who are dissatisfied at the handling of their complaints by the professional bodies. The focus of any investigation was on the handling of the complaint itself, and the Ombudsman's role was not to review the actions of the lawyer who was originally the subject of that complaint.[185] Depending on the outcome of her investigations, the Ombudsman had the power to require that a complaint be reconsidered and/or that compensation paid by the professional body or the lawyer concerned. The Ombudsman might also make recommendations of a more general nature.[186] In 2003–04 the Ombudsman's Office completed 1,731 investigations and ordered compensation payments totalling £199,840.[187]

The Legal Services Act 2007

Background and overview

We identified above the growing concern about the adequacy of existing complaints resolution mechanisms. The White Paper[188] observed that consumers did not have enough confidence in the current system, and were not convinced of its independence. It stressed the need for timeliness and consistency, and noted that professional bodies still largely set their own standards, but that these did not always represent 'best practice'. It recommended the creation of a single complaints body, the Office for Legal Complaints (OLC). This is established by section 114 of the Legal Services Act 2007.

The OLC is under a duty to comply with the regulatory objectives already described.[189] It is to administer an Ombudsman scheme, which came into operation in 2010. It reports to the Legal Services Board, which, in turn, reports to the Lord Chancellor. The statutory Ombudsman scheme supersedes regulatory regimes of any approved regulator, such as the Law Society or Bar Council, in respect of 'redress'.[190] However, authorized regulators are still expected to have complaints resolution procedures, or participate in procedures established by others, as a condition of its authorization,[191] and the Act makes clear, in section 158, that authorized persons can be required by their regulatory body to have in place a complaints regime as required by section 158. Thus existing requirements in respect of individual solicitors' firms can continue in place, subject to such modifications as may be required from time to time. The offices of the Legal Services Complaints Commissioner and the Legal Services

184 Courts and Legal Services Act 1990, s 21; Sch 3.
185 The Ombudsman's functions are set out in detail in s 22 of the 1990 Act.
186 Ibid, ss 23–24.   187 *In Whose Interest?* at p 13.
188 *Op cit*, paras 3.4–3.5.   189 See p 396.
190 2007 Act, s 157.   191 Ibid, s 112.

Ombudsman are abolished. The Act also envisages the OLC establishing voluntary schemes to supplement the Ombudsman scheme.

The OLC and the Ombudsman

The OLC has the power to appoint a Chief Ombudsman[192] to run the new redress and complaints system. The first Chief Ombudsman was appointed in 2009. The jurisdiction of the Ombudsman is defined by sections 125–128 of the 2007 Act. The Ombudsman may deal with any complaint if the complainant and respondent are within the scheme, and the complaint is not excluded from the scheme. A complaint is excluded if the complainant has not first used the respondent's complaints procedures. The individuals within the scheme[193] must be the recipients of services provided by an authorized person of a reserved legal activity. Another provider of a reserved legal activity, or a public body, is not an eligible complainant. It is not entirely clear why a public authority, such as a local authority, police authority, or the CPS, should not be entitled to rely on the Ombudsman scheme in respect of inadequate legal services.

The Ombudsman scheme rules may exclude specific type of complaint, but may not exclude any complaint on the ground that it relates to a matter that could have been the subject of disciplinary action by the respondent's authorizing complaint. Thus a complaint against a solicitor cannot be excluded by virtue of the fact that disciplinary proceedings have been, or could be, taken.

The details of the scheme are set out in rules regulating in detail the matters identified by section 133. These relate to matters in respect of evidence and procedure, matters to be taken into account by the Ombudsman, costs and dismissal of complaints. Authorized regulators, and, through rules made by them, authorized persons, are under an obligation to provided specified information to the OLC, and there is a duty imposed on authorized persons to cooperate with investigations. The Ombudsman must report any failure to cooperate to the relevant regulatory authority, and may, as a last resort, report to the OLC. Detailed provisions provide for the disclosure of information or documents.[194] The Ombudsman must deal with a complaint in any way that is fair and reasonable in all of the circumstances of the case.[195] This might be an apology, limitation of fees, compliance with a requirement made to give effect to a direction, or the payment of compensation. The maximum limit of compensation ordered to be paid is, initially, £30,000.[196]

Voluntary scheme

The 2007 Act permits the creation of voluntary arrangements being reached by the Legal Services Board to provide assistance in the improving of legal services and promoting legal services. It envisages the establishment of voluntary

[192] Who may delegate to his staff: ibid, s 134.
[193] Section 128(3)(b) envisages that the Lord Chancellor may make persons (other than individuals) eligible by order.
[194] 2007 Act, ss 147–153.   [195] Ibid, s 137.   [196] Ibid, s 138.

complaint-resolution schemes, providing quick and informal resolution of such complaints.[197] These schemes, as and when approved, will be quicker and more informal than the formal procedures of the Ombudsman. The legislation provides the framework. A complaint can only be dealt with under a voluntary scheme if the complainant is an elegible person, which will depend on the voluntary scheme established. He or she must agree. The respondent must be a participant in the scheme. The terms of the scheme will be determined by the OLC when approving the scheme.

Civil liability

Solicitors

Liability to the client

A solicitor's authority derives from the retainer given to him by his client, the effect of which is to create a contractual relationship between the two parties. This relationship is subject to the ordinary law of contract and in particular to that part of contract law concerning agency.[198] Consequently the solicitor has a right to be indemnified by his client for acts done within the scope of his authority, and he is entitled to be put in funds for disbursements. If he is engaged to conduct contentious business he may also require payment of a reasonable sum on account of costs.[199] Beyond this, however, the general rule is that a solicitor undertakes to complete the transaction for which he was retained, and he is not entitled to remuneration until the transaction is completed. In addition to his liability in contract, a solicitor who fails to act with due skill and care may also incur liability in tort. In *Midland Bank Trust Co Ltd* v *Hett, Stubbs and Kemp*,[200] it was held that the relationship between solicitor and client was a 'special relationship' of the kind envisaged in *Hedley Byrne* v *Heller*.[201] A solicitor could thus be liable in tort for negligent advice given in the context of such a relationship. A solicitor may also be liable to his client if incompetent counsel is instructed,[202] or if counsel is not given adequate instructions upon which to act.[203]

Liability to third parties

Where a solicitor contracts on behalf of a client with the knowledge of the other party, the transaction will be subject to the ordinary law of agency: contractual liability to the third party will be assumed by the client rather than the solicitor.[204] This principle applies equally to contracts made by the solicitor with the *ostensible* authority of his

---

[197] Ibid, ss 137, 138.   [198] See the discussion of liability to third parties, above.
[199] Solicitors Act 1974, s 65(2).
[200] [1979] Ch 384, [1978] 3 All ER 571. See also *Ross* v *Caunters* [1980] Ch 297, [1979] 3 All ER 580.
[201] [1964] AC 465, [1963] 2 All ER 575.   [202] *Re A (A Minor)* [1988] Fam Law 339.
[203] *Dauntley* v *Hyde* (1841) 6 Jur 133.
[204] *Wakefield* v *Duckworth & Co* [1915] 1 KB 218 (solicitor not liable for failure to pay a photographer).

client: if the solicitor's actual authority to act is disputed, his liability will be to the client rather than the third party.[205] A solicitor will, however, be contractually liable to a third party if he fails to disclose that he is acting on someone else's behalf.[206] He will also incur liability to a third party if he purports to act with the authority of a client but no such authority exists.[207]

A solicitor may be liable in tort for any tortious act to which he has been a party, whether or not he was acting with the authority of a client. For example, a solicitor who fraudulently induces a third party to buy an estate with a defective title commits the tort of deceit. In some circumstances a solicitor may even be liable to a third party for economic loss caused by his negligence. This occurred in *White* v *Jones*,[208] in which a solicitor's negligence in failing to draft a new will deprived the intended beneficiaries of an inheritance.

Barristers

Liability

As noted previously, barristers were historically prevented from entering into contractual relationships with clients, but this rule has now changed.[209] Since 2004 it has been possible for barristers who comply with certain criteria to undertake 'public access' work, which means that they may accept instructions directly from lay clients. The relationship between barrister and client in such a case will normally be contractual, and the barrister may thus be liable in contract for any failure to perform.

Barristers were historically assumed to be immune from liability in negligence, and in *Rondel* v *Worsley*[210] the House of Lords accepted that this immunity could be justified. Various public policy arguments were cited: it was pointed out, for example, that barristers have an overriding duty to the court that could potentially conflict with a client's wishes, and the fact that barristers are not free to pick and choose their clients was also noted. A particular concern was that disgruntled clients might attempt to sue their barristers as a way of reopening cases that had already been lost. Some of their Lordships also thought that barristers might be inhibited in carrying out their duties if they had to operate under the threat of being sued. Although their Lordships differed in the emphasis that they placed on each of these grounds, they were agreed that barristers should continue to enjoy immunity in respect of their conduct at trial.

In the subsequent case of *Saif Ali* v *Sydney Mitchell & Co*,[211] the House of Lords was once again called upon to consider the scope of barristers' immunity, but this time in relation to work done in chambers in the course of litigation. The effect of

---

[205] A solicitor has ostensible authority to do any act that is within the scope of his retainer, and thus may bind his client to compromise of an action whether or not he has the client's actual authority so to do: *Waugh* v *HB Clifford and Sons Ltd* [1982] Ch 374, [1982] 1 All ER 1095.

[206] *Foster* v *Cranfield* (1911) 46 L Jo 314.   [207] *Yonge* v *Toynbee* [1910] 1 KB 215.

[208] [1993] 3 All ER 481, [1993] 3 WLR 730.   [209] See p 387.

[210] [1969] 1 AC 191, [1967] 3 All ER 993.   [211] [1980] AC 198, [1978] 3 All ER 1033.

this decision was to limit the immunity to matters of pre-trial work that were intimately connected with the conduct of the case in court. Since the barrister's advice and pleadings in the instant case had prevented the claimant's dispute from coming to court at all, it was not within the sphere of a barrister's immunity. Finally, in *Arthur JS Hall & Co v Simons*,[212] the House of Lords departed from *Rondel* v *Worsley*[213] and abolished the controversial immunity altogether. Although their Lordships accepted that some of the justifications for it had merit, they concluded that none of them were sufficient to outweigh the interests of the client in having a remedy for the negligence of his advocate. They pointed out that doctors have no such immunity despite being bound by an ethical code, and they also stressed that a barrister would never be deemed negligent for acting in accordance with his or her duty to court. Concerns that barristers acting in criminal cases might be particularly at risk from unmeritorious claims persuaded a minority of the House that the immunity should only be lifted in respect of civil litigation. The majority, however, shared Lord Hoffmann's view that 'it would ordinarily be an abuse of process for a civil court to be asked to decide that a subsisting conviction was wrong',[214] and as Lord Millett pointed out:[215]

> [To retain the immunity for criminal cases] would mean that a party would have a remedy if the incompetence of his counsel deprived him of compensation for (say) breach of contract or unfair dismissal, but not if it led to his imprisonment for a crime he did not commit and the consequent and uncompensated loss of his job.

The majority thus concluded that the immunity should be removed across the board.

Liability to third parties

In principle, barristers are in the same position as solicitors with regard to their potential liability to third parties. In one case, for example, a barrister who gave negligent advice about the setting up of a trust was successfully sued in tort by its trustees.[216] In practice, however, the nature of the barrister's role means that third-party liability is much less likely to be an issue. One specific point to note is that the standard terms on which a barrister would normally accept a brief from a solicitor do not give rise to any contractual liability. There is, however, nothing to stop barristers from accepting a retainer on contractual terms.[217]

---

[212] [2002] 1 AC 615, [2000] 3 All ER 673.   [213] [1969] 1 AC 191, [1967] 3 All ER 993.

[214] [2002] 1 AC 615 at 706, [2000] 3 All ER 673 at 785.

[215] [2002] 1 AC 615 at 752, [2000] 3 All ER 673 at 829.

[216] *Estill* v *Cowling* [2000] Lloyd's Rep PN 378.

[217] Code of Conduct of the Bar of England and Wales, Annexe G2: The Contractual Terms of Work on which Barristers Offer their Services to Solicitors, 2001.

Fees and costs

One of the aims of the Woolf civil justice reforms[218] has been to reduce cost with a view to improving access to justice.[219] This has become crucial in the light of cutbacks in legal aid, actual and proposed,[220] and the Jackson Review[221] has recommended fundamental changes to costs designed to reduce fees and expenditure. These proposals will affect the operation of conditional fee agreements, and, even more fundamentally affect the question of who bears the costs of litigation. At present the basic rule is that costs follow the event: the losing party to litigation meets the costs of the winning party. Those who engage in litigation have therefore to consider the costs involved not only for themselves but also of the other party. These issues are discussed at Chapter 13.

Many lawyers have sought to address some of these difficulties by not charging for work done on behalf of financially strapped clients, known as pro bono work. In the past it was common for solicitors to tender initial advice free of charge, and the Bar's free representation and pro bono schemes have provided free legal services to many deserving clients. The Legal Services Act 2007 recognizes the importance of this type of work by permitting a court in certain circumstances to order the making of a payment to a 'specified charity'.[222] The work done by bodies such as law centres and Citizens' Advice Bureaux is also important.

Remuneration

The remuneration of solicitors is subject to a variety of statutory and other rules, the application of which depends upon whether the work done by the solicitor is contentious or non-contentious. 'Contentious business' is defined in section 87(1) of the Solicitors Act 1974 as:

> Business done, whether as solicitor or advocate, in or for the purpose of proceedings begun before a court or before an arbitrator appointed under the Arbitration Act [1996], not being business which falls within the definition of non-contentious or common form probate business in the Supreme Court Act 1981, section 128.

The essence of the test is whether proceedings have begun: if they have, then all business relating to those proceedings is contentious. Section 59 of the Solicitors Act authorizes solicitors to enter into agreements with their clients to regulate remuneration in contentious business. In the absence of such an agreement a solicitor may

---

[218] See p 473.   [219] See pp 471 et seq.   [220] See p 421.
[221] Ministry of Justice, *Review of Civil Litigation Costs* (HMSO, January 2010). For proposals for implementation, see *Proposals for Reform of Civil Litigation Funding and Costs in England and Wales*, Ministry of Justice Consultation Paper 13/10, Cm 4947 (HMSO, November 2010).
[222] 2007 Act, s 194. See, further, p 422.

submit either a Bill containing detailed items or one charging a gross sum.[223] The client is entitled to apply to the High Court for a detailed assessment (formerly known as 'taxation') of his bill.[224] If the application is granted the bill will be assessed on an 'indemnity' basis,[225] which means that all costs that have been reasonably incurred and are reasonable in amount will be allowed.[226] Different rules apply where a bill is to be paid from Legal Services Commission funds.

Work done in respect of a dispute that is settled before proceedings are commenced is regarded as 'non-contentious business'. This term also covers a wide range of other matters, such as conveyancing and the drafting of wills and settlements. Save in certain exceptional cases under specific enactments,[227] remuneration for non-contentious business is regulated by an order made under section 56 of the 1974 Act. The basis of remuneration under the current order[228] is that the solicitor's costs must be fair and reasonable, having regard to all of the circumstances of the case. Particular regard must be had to the complexity of the matter, the skill, specialized knowledge and responsibility involved, the number of documents, the time involved, the value of any property or amount of any sum involved, whether any land was registered, and the importance of the matter to the client.[229] As with contentious business the parties are at liberty to make their own agreement as to costs,[230] but any such agreement may still be subject to review by the courts.

Barristers are not covered by the same regulatory regime as solicitors, and they may be remunerated on any basis agreed by the parties as long as it is permitted by law. Again, the principles that apply are often different in respect of work funded by the Legal Services Commission. In addition, counsel's fees may come under scrutiny when costs fall to be considered at the end of a trial and a barrister will not be permitted to charge for work that he has not been instructed to do.[231]

Conditional fee agreements

Conditional fee arrangements are now a fundamentally important way of funding legal services. They shift the burden of financing many types of litigation from the state to the individual person or company.[232] A conditional fee agreement is defined by section 58(2)(a) of the Courts and Legal Services Act 1990 as:

> [A]n agreement with a person providing advocacy or litigation services which provides for his fees and expenses, or any part of them, to be payable only in specified circumstances.

In other words, a lawyer who enters into a conditional fee agreement will only be paid for his services in certain circumstances. The vast majority of such agreements are entered into on what is described as a 'no win, no fee' basis, which means that the

---

[223] Solicitors Act 1974, s 64.   [224] Ibid, s 70.   [225] See p 549.
[226] CPR , Ord 62, r 12(2).   [227] Preserved by s 75 of the 1974 Act.
[228] Solicitors' (Non-Contentious Business) Remuneration Order 1994, SI 1994/2616.
[229] Ibid, article 3.   [230] 1974 Act, s 57.   [231] *Loveday* v *Renton (No 2)* [1992] 3 All ER 184.
[232] See Lord Hoffmann in *Campbell* v *MGN (No 2)* [2005] UKHL 61, [2005] 4 All ER 393, at [17].

solicitor does not receive a fee from his client if he loses the case, but is paid a 'success fee' if he wins. A success fee is an amount that increases the standard fee by a given percentage.[233] Conditional fee agreements were once thought to be contrary to public policy, but the Courts and Legal Services Act 1990 legitimized their use in certain classes of case. These classes are designated by Order and were originally fairly limited, but current legislation permits the use of conditional fees in the vast majority of cases. The only remaining statutory exceptions are: (a) criminal cases; and (b) specified family proceedings cases.[234] For a conditional fee agreement to be enforceable, it must be in writing and its effects must have been made clear to the client. In particular, the agreement must specify the circumstances in which the client may be liable to pay the legal representative's costs, and it must also state what percentage increase (if any) is attributable to a success fee.[235] The maximum percentage increase permitted by the regulations is currently 100 per cent of the normal fee,[236] but the Jackson Review recommendations will affect that significantly and are discussed in Chapter 13.[237]

The existence of a conditional fee agreement places most of the financial risks of litigation with the lawyer, and this justifies an increase in the standard fee. In *Campbell v MGN (No 2)*,[238] the House of Lords observed that success fees were to be regarded as the contribution that unsuccessful litigants make to enable lawyers to take on other cases that might not otherwise be successful but which would provide access to justice for people who could not otherwise afford to sue. It was a proportionate response by the state to secure a valid objective. For that reason, in this libel action a success fee was held not to contravene the right of freedom of expression conferred by Article 10 of the European Convention.[239] This was so even though the claimant was a wealthy celebrity who could well afford to fund her own action, and even though the amount of the success fee went beyond that which might be regarded as fair and reasonable when calculating costs in the normal way.[240]

Even with such an arrangement in place, there will still be some element of risk for the client: the unsuccessful litigant may not have to pay his or her own lawyer but he or she will generally be liable to pay the other side's costs. He or she may also be liable for court fees, the cost of obtaining expert reports, and so on. The current regulations require the lawyer to explain this risk to the client and to advise him or her as to how this risk might be offset. The result is that most litigants who enter into these arrangements are protected by some form of insurance policy covering any potential liability

---

[233] Courts and Legal Services Act 1990, ss 58(2)(b); 58(4)b. See, now, the recommendations of the Jackson Report: see p 480.

[234] Ibid, s 58A.

[235] Ibid, s 58; Conditional Fee Agreement Regulations 2000, SI 2000/692. See also the decision in *Sharratt v London Central Bus Co Ltd (No 1)*; *Hollins v Russell* [2003] EWCA Civ 718, [2003] 1 WLR 2487, [2003] 4 All ER 590, in which the Court of Appeal held that a conditional fee arrangement will normally be enforceable as long as the general purpose of the statutory rules designed for the client's protection has been complied with.

[236] Conditional Fee Agreements Order 2000, SI 2000/823.   [237] See p 480.

[238] [2005] UKHL 61, [2005] 4 All ER 793.   [239] As to which, see p 206.

[240] For the reasonableness of success fees, see p 483.

for costs. In principle, both the lawyer's success fee and the cost of after-the-event insurance are recoverable from the losing party to an action. Ultimately, however, this is a matter for the court's discretion.

Note finally that conditional fee agreements must be carefully distinguished from other types of contingency agreement, such as those common in the USA that involve the lawyer receiving a percentage of any damages awarded. This type of arrangement has historically been unenforceable in England and Wales on public policy grounds.[241] The argument is that a contingency arrangement would give a lawyer an incentive to try to win at all costs and might therefore encourage unscrupulous conduct. In fact, the same argument could be made in respect of conditional fee agreements, and the Middleton Report recommended that the case for contingency fees should be reconsidered.[242] However, the recommendations of the Jackson Committee are likely to result in a greater use of conditional fee agreements, albeit within a modified regime relating to success fees.[243]

Litigation funding agreements

'Litigation funding agreements' are a variation on conditional fee agreements. They are made not with lawyers but with third-party funders such as insurance companies, the idea being that these funders agree to bear the financial risk of litigation, in return for which they can claim a success fee if their clients win. This type of arrangement is provided for in principle by section 28 of the Access to Justice Act 1999, which will insert a new section 58B into the Courts and Legal Services Act 1990. At the time of writing, however, this provision has yet to be implemented.

The funding and cost of legal services

Introduction

The availability of legal services and how they are funded depend fundamentally on what the costs of the law are and who meets them. The best legal services cannot assist if those who need them cannot afford them.

Access to legal advice is a fundamental right under the European Convention on Human Rights, and this right has now been given direct effect in English law.[244] Without access to advice an individual may remain unaware of his or her legal rights and obligations, and he or she may be unable to make effective use of the courts. Yet the cost of exercising this 'right' is high: the Woolf Report[245] found the average cost of litigation in medical negligence cases to be £38,252, while in personal injury cases

---

[241] *Aratra Potato Co Ltd* v *Taylor Jaynson Garrett (A Firm)* [1995] 4 All ER 695.

[242] *Review of Civil Justice and Legal Aid: A Report to the Lord Chancellor* (HMSO, 1997), at para 5.50.

[243] See p 480.   [244] Article 6: given effect by the Human Rights Act 1998.

[245] *Access to Justice: Interim Report*, Annex III, pp 251–6.

it was £20,413. The majority of defendants in criminal cases are in receipt of public funding, but the cost of such cases may still be considerable. In 2003–04, one barrister reportedly earned £800,000 in fees for work done for the Criminal Defence Service[246] and in recent years the Lord Chancellor has 'named and shamed' barristers considered to earn excessive amounts from doing publicly funded work.[247] However, the cost of justice is not solely a matter of lawyers' fees: court fees and other expenses may also be significant, and achieving access to justice in this climate is a real challenge for government.

Legal aid

Introduction

Since the Second World War, and, in particular, following the publication of the Rushcliffe Committee report, legal aid has been the most important mechanism for ensuring affordable access to justice. Pressure on resources has inevitably increased as actions have become more complex and legal costs have risen, and these pressures have forced successive governments to keep the operation of the legal aid system under review. In 1991, the expenditure on legal aid was some £682 million. By 1997, this figure had increased to £1,477 million,[248] and by 2004 the total expenditure on publicly funded legal services was almost £2 billion.[249] The cost pressure has continued, with expenditure now in excess of £2 billion. Of the total legal aid expenditure cost of £2.1 billion in 2008–09, over £1.18 billion was in criminal legal aid.[250] The pressure was such that in November 2010 the Lord Chancellor and Minister of Justice published a consultation paper *Proposals for the Reform of Legal Aid in England and Wales*[251] proposing, in a climate of cuts in many areas of public expenditure, substantial reductions of the order of £350 million to the legal aid budget by 2014–15. Conditional fee agreements, linked with legal expenses insurance, have become a major response to meeting the costs of legal services, making in-roads into the position of legal aid as the major source of funding in a climate of spiralling costs. One government response to these pressures has been to try to recoup money by raising court fees. In 1996 it also sought to repeal certain rules that had exempted persons in receipt of state benefits from paying such fees.[252] However, in *R v Lord Chancellor, ex parte Witham*,[253] its authority to take such action was successfully challenged. Witham was in receipt of income support and wished to bring proceedings for defamation, but since legal aid was unavailable and he was apparently no longer entitled to an exemption, he did

---

[246] 227 Law Society Annual Conference, London (26 September 2003).
[247] See 'Fat Cats': The Facts Behind 'those Figures', *Counsel*, June 1998 at 12.
[248] See Middleton Review, discussed at p 413, *post*.
[249] Legal Services Commission, *Annual Report 2003–04*, preface.
[250] White Paper, 2010, Table 1 at p 29. See n 251 below
[251] (HMSO, 2010), available at **www.justice.gov.uk/publications.htm**
[252] Supreme Court Fees (Amendment) Order 1996, article 3, SI 1996/3191.
[253] [1998] QB 575, [1997] 2 All ER 779.

not have the financial means to issue proceedings. Laws J upheld his claim that the change in the rules was ultra vires, stressing that access to the courts was a constitutional right at common law, and that it could not be abrogated without the clear and specific authority of an Act of Parliament. The Lord Chancellor had claimed that such authority was provided by section 130 of the Courts and Legal Services Act 1990, but Laws J disagreed and found the regulations in question to be invalid. Today, of course, more fundamental solutions are being found.[254]

The development of legal aid

A civil legal aid scheme was introduced in the aftermath of the Second World War as part of the creation of a welfare state.[255] It was not fully implemented, and its impact was limited, but the system expanded in subsequent decades as further legislation was enacted.[256] Criminal legal aid came later,[257] followed by the introduction of the duty solicitor scheme.[258] Eventually, the Legal Aid Act 1988 established a more comprehensive scheme covering both civil and criminal matters.[259] Section 3 of the Act created a Legal Aid Board to administer the new system and ensure the availability of advice, assistance, and representation.[260] The Board was responsible for managing the scheme in its application to civil matters, and also for maintaining a legal aid fund.[261] It could contract with law centres, Citizens Advice Bureaux, and other information agencies, in addition to entering into franchise arrangements with individual firms of solicitors.

The Act incorporated the 'Green Form' scheme, which was originally established under the Legal Advice and Assistance Act 1972. It was applicable to both civil and criminal matters and was designed to secure the availability of legal advice and information to those who would otherwise be unable to afford it. It covered oral or written advice given by a legal representative[262] in relation to any question of English law,[263] and a person who met the criteria for eligibility could obtain assistance equivalent to two hours' worth of work. 'Assistance by way of representation' was also available.[264] In principle, this could cover any steps taken on behalf a person in the institution or conduct of proceedings before a court, tribunal, or statutory inquiry, whether by representing him or her in those proceedings or otherwise. However, the precise application of the scheme was subject to more detailed rules,[265] and not all proceedings were actually covered. The scheme did not, for example, cover representation in defamation cases.[266]

---

[254] See p 480.   [255] Legal Aid and Advice Act 1949.

[256] See the Legal Advice and Assistance Act 1972 and the Legal Aid Acts of 1960, 1964, 1974, and 1979.

[257] Criminal Justice Act 1967.   [258] See p 419.

[259] See *Legal Aid in England and Wales: A New Framework*, Cmnd 118 (HMSO, 1987).

[260] 1988 Act, s 3(2). For the meaning 'advice', 'assistance', and 'representation' see s 2.

[261] Ibid, s 6.   [262] *R v Legal Aid Board, ex parte Bruce* [1992] 1 All ER 133, [1991] 1 WLR 1231.

[263] 1988 Act, s 2(2).   [264] Ibid, ss 2(3); 8(2).

[265] Legal Advice and Assistance (Scope) Regulations 1989, SI 1989/550, reg 9.

[266] 1988 Act, Sch 2, Part II, para 1.

The framework governing legal aid in criminal cases was set out in Part V of the Act, and, as under the previous system, the scheme was administered by the courts.[267] In principle, where legal aid was granted, it could cover representation by a solicitor and counsel, in addition to the provision of advice. In magistrates' courts, however, the cost of representation by counsel would only be covered where a case concerned an unusually grave or difficult indictable offence. In both civil and criminal cases, an assisted person could be ordered by the court to pay such contribution as appeared reasonable, having regard to his or her commitments and resources. Such means-testing did not apply to the duty solicitor scheme, however,[268] which continued to fund the provision of free legal advice in police stations and magistrates' courts.

The Middleton Committee
The Middleton Committee, which reported in 1997,[269] identified a number of weaknesses in the legal aid scheme. In particular, it raised serious concerns about the rapid growth in the cost of the scheme and its inability to target resources on priority areas. The Committee reported that the rise in expenditure on legal aid was some 115 per cent.[270] Some 90 per cent of that expenditure was said to have gone on lawyers' fees. In civil legal aid, expenditure since 1993 had increased by 43 per cent, yet the number of people assisted had gone down by 9 per cent. On the basis of such evidence, the report concluded that significant reforms were needed. It proposed that the Legal Aid Board should use its purchasing power to contract for legal services in a proactive way, setting requirements of quality, access, and value for money. Only contracted suppliers should be able to do legal aid work, and consideration should be given to the possibility of the Board employing its own lawyers to provide legal services. Users of the system should be required to contribute as much as they could afford to the costs of their case, and everyone should be required to pay something. The Middleton Report was followed by publication of the government's own plans for the reform of legal aid.[271] These plans were part of a package of measures that would result in significant changes to the entire civil justice system.[272] In the government's view it was important to reduce the cost of civil justice for all users, so as to ensure greater accessibility and better value for money for both the taxpayer and the individual litigant. The government's proposals drew heavily on the Middleton Report and were given effect by the Access to Justice Act 1999.

The Legal Services Commission
Section 1(1) of the Access to Justice Act 1999 established a new Legal Services Commission (LSC) to replace the Legal Aid Board. The Commission is required by the Act to 'establish, maintain and develop' two separate services: (a) the Community

---

[267] See p 418.   [268] Legal Advice and Assistance (Scope) Regulations 1989, SI 1989/340.
[269] *Review of Civil Justice and Legal Aid: A Report to the Lord Chancellor* (HMSO, 1997).
[270] Ibid, at para 3.3. The rise was from £682m 1991 to £1.477m in 1997
[271] *Modernising Justice* (White Paper), December 1998.
[272] See the discussion at p 424.

Legal Service;[273] and (b) the Criminal Defence Service.[274] It consists of between seven and twelve members,[275] who are appointed for their knowledge and experience in matters such as the provision of legal services, the work of the courts, consumer affairs, social conditions, and management.[276] The Commission has a wide range of powers and responsibilities and it may do anything that it considers necessary or appropriate for the discharge of its functions.[277] It is required to publish an annual plan setting out how it intends to fund its services for the forthcoming year, and at the end of that year it must also publish a report on its performance. Both documents must be submitted to the Lord Chancellor and laid before Parliament.[278]

The aim of the LSC is not only to improve the public's access to advice, but also to ensure that the advice available is of good quality. It has therefore introduced a range of quality marks to recognize high standards in the delivery of different types of service. Three different standards of quality mark are available: (a) information; (b) general help; and (c) specialist help. Within these categories there are specific quality marks for things such as mediation and telephone advice, and there is also a quality mark for the Bar. The 'specialist help' standard is aimed at legal professionals and other specialized agencies, and without this quality mark it is not possible to obtain LSC funding. It will be apparent from this that the other quality mark standards enable the LSC to accredit a range of services that it does not actually fund.

Contracts

Under the old legal aid system the vast majority of funding was provided on a case-by-case basis. Any lawyer could undertake legal aid work and there were no restrictions on the amount that he could do. A new scheme had been introduced in 1994 whereby practitioners could apply for a legal aid franchise in one or more areas of law. Those operating under a franchise had to comply with strict quality and auditing requirements, in return for which they were able to undertake legal aid work on more favourable terms and without seeking prior approval for each case. At this stage the scheme was voluntary, and those who were unwilling (or unable) to obtain a franchise could still do legal aid work on the same terms as before. Since the launch of the Legal Services Commission, however, things have changed significantly.

The position now is that publicly funded legal services can only be provided by those who hold LSC contracts. The terms of these contracts restrict the categories of law in which LSC-funded services can be offered, and they also limit the volume of cases that a provider can undertake. In this way, the LSC is able to exercise much greater control over expenditure than its predecessor: by regulating the types of contract awarded, it can concentrate its funds on the areas in which they are most needed, and by auditing contracted suppliers, it can ensure that proper standards are being maintained. In the government's view, this approach is the key to ensuring a high quality of service for the client and better value for money for the taxpayer. More recently the implementation

---

[273] 1999 Act, ss 1(2)(a); 4(1). See p 415.   [274] Ibid, ss 1(2)(b); 12(1). See p 418.

[275] Ibid, s 1(3).   [276] Ibid, s 1(5).   [277] Ibid, s 3(1).

[278] Ibid, Sch 1, paras 14–15.

of the recommendations of the Carter Review have led to a further limitation of costs through fixed fees.[279]

The Community Legal Service

The Community Legal Service (CLS) was established under section 1(2)(a) of the 1999 Act and is the responsibility of the Legal Services Commission. Its statutory purpose is to promote the availability of a range of services, and to secure access to those services so as to effectively meet individual needs.[280] The services specifically falling within its remit concern: (a) the provision of information about the law and the legal system; (b) the provision of help and advice about the application of the law to particular circumstances; (c) the provision of help in preventing, settling or otherwise resolving disputes about legal rights and duties; (d) the provision of help in enforcing decisions about the resolution of such disputes; and (e) the provision of help in relation to legal proceedings not relating to disputes.[281] The Commission must decide how to prioritize the allocation of its resources, but it must do so within the framework of directions laid down by the Lord Chancellor.[282] Priorities identified thus far include proceedings under the Children Act 1989 and other proceedings concerning child welfare, civil proceedings where the client is at real risk of loss of life or liberty, domestic violence proceedings, and proceedings that allege serious breaches of human rights on the part of public authorities. The Commission is required to maintain a separate fund to support the provision of such services in accordance with the terms of the Act.[283]

What work is covered by CLS contracts?

The Funding Code issued under section 8 of the 1999 Act lists seven levels of service that may be provided by contracted suppliers:

(1) legal help (this covers the provision of advice as to the application of the law and assistance in resolving disputes—in essence it replaces the old Green Form scheme);[284]

(2) help at court (help and advocacy for a client in relation to a particular hearing but falling short of formal legal representation);

(3) approved family help (legal help and some types of representation in family disputes);

(4) legal representation (including litigation and advocacy services and related preparatory work);

(5) support funding (assistance with representation in cases that are otherwise privately funded);

---

[279] See p 420.   [280] Ibid, s 4(1).   [281] Ibid, s 4(2).

[282] Ibid, s 6(1); Community Legal Service Fund Funding Priorities (2000).

[283] Ibid, s 4(5).   [284] See p 412 for a brief explanation of the 'Legal Help scheme'.

(6) family mediation;

(7) such other services as may be authorized by the Lord Chancellor.

Precisely which services are available is determined by the nature of the client's case and the terms of the provider's contract with the LSC. Work done under a Community Legal Service contract may be 'controlled' or 'licensed'. Controlled work is work for which the contract provides full authorization, and for which the supplier does not need to seek approval before accepting each new case. It encompasses all 'legal help' and 'help at court', in addition to covering 'legal representation' before certain tribunals.[285] All other work done under a general contract is known as 'licensed work', and it must be authorized on a case-by-case basis. In 2003–04, 93 per cent of all solicitors holding general civil contracts had been allocated a quota of controlled work.[286] The LSC's total expenditure on controlled work was £383.3 million.[287] In the same year the LSC spent £514.1 million funding licensed work, the majority of which involved legal representation.[288] The Carter Report envisages the potential for longer-term contracts, driven by minimum standards and peer review.[289] The effect of that is to cause some restructuring as 'suppliers of inadequate quality legal services are forced to improve or withdraw from the market'.

Work that falls outside the general contract altogether may be authorized separately under an 'individual case contract', and there are special arrangements for remunerating work done in 'high cost' cases. As with the legal aid scheme, however, there are certain types of work for which community legal service funding is not available at all. These exclusions are listed in Schedule 2 to the 1999 Act, and they comprise: (a) most claims in negligence (except those relating to clinical negligence); (b) conveyancing; (c) boundary disputes; (d) the making of wills; (e) matters of trust law; (f) defamation or malicious falsehood; (g) matters of company or partnership law (h) other business matters; and (i) asylum decisions. Many areas of work *are* covered by CLS funding, including: (a) family; (b) housing; (c) debt; (d) immigration; (e) employment; (f) contract and consumer law; (g) welfare law; (h) community care; (i) clinical negligence; (j) education; (k) mental health; (l) public law; and (m) actions against the police. However, funding for advocacy is only available in relation to certain courts and certain types of proceedings,[290] with the result that representation before most tribunals is not covered by the scheme.

Eligibility for CLS assistance

An individual must satisfy both a merits test and a means test in order to obtain services from the CLS. The merits test derives from section 8 of the Access to Justice Act

---

[285] Mental Health Review Tribunals and the Asylum and Immigration Tribunal: Funding Code, para A3.

[286] Legal Services Commission, *Annual Report 2003–04*, p 21.   [287] Ibid, p 79.

[288] Ibid, p 78.

[289] Carter, *Legal Aid: A Market-Based Approach to Reform* (HMSO, 2006)—'the Carter Report'—at p 3. This report is available at: **www.legalaidprocurementreview.gov.uk/docs/carter-review-p1.pdf**

[290] Access to Justice Act 1999, Sch 2.

and from the Funding Code issued under it. Factors to be considered include: (a) the potential benefit to the client of providing the service in question and the likely cost to the CLS of funding it; (b) the availability and suitability of other sources of funding, such as conditional fee agreements; (c) the prospects of any legal action being successful; (d) the principle that mediation is often better than litigation in family cases; and (e) the public interest. 'High cost' cases and cases in areas such as clinical negligence and judicial review are subject to additional considerations.[291] In many instances, a willingness to engage in mediation may be a precondition to the availability of support.[292]

The rules governing financial eligibility are set out in regulations made under section 7 of the 1999 Act. The current regulations date from 2000,[293] although they have been subject to significant revision. Different types of service used to be subject to different eligibility limits, but standard limits have now been introduced. Those with very low incomes and little capital will be entitled to full CLS assistance,[294] while those who are slightly better-off will be required to pay a contribution towards certain services.[295] The financial limits are reviewed each year and are increased by statutory instrument. More people qualify for assistance under the current regime than were covered by the legal aid system,[296] but the means test is still set at quite a low level—so much so that the Director of the Legal Aid Practitioner's Group has suggested that 'only loan sharks would loan money to someone who is poor enough to qualify for legal aid'.[297]

Not-for-profit organizations and CLS partnerships

It should not be assumed that the CLS is only about the work done by solicitors' firms. Bodies like Shelter and the Citizens' Advice Bureaux can hold general civil contracts and receive LSC funding in much the same way as the private sector. In fact the LSC is increasingly looking to the not-for-profit sector as the number of solicitors doing publicly funded work declines, and in 2003–04 it funded almost a million caseworker hours.[298] Another important feature of the new system is that it requires the LSC to work with other bodies and organizations to find ways of improving access to justice.[299] To this end it has brought solicitors together with law centres, Citizens Advice Bureaux, and local authority advice agencies to establish over 200 community legal service partnerships. A key function of these partnerships is to identify areas

---

[291] See generally, parts 6–13 of the Funding Code.

[292] For proposals to encourage mediation further, see *The Times*, 29 December 2010.

[293] Community Legal Service (Financial) Regulations 2000, SI 2000/516.

[294] Capital is not taken into account if the client is a pensioner or if the capital is the subject matter of the dispute. Those on Income Support and certain other benefits automatically qualify for full assistance.

[295] Services for which no contribution is required include: the provision of general information about the law and legal services; the provision of legal help or help at court; and legal representation in some cases involving children or asylum and immigration disputes—SI 2000/516, article 3 (as amended).

[296] Controversial proposals to treat the equity in a person's home as 'capital' for these purposes were recently abandoned: see LSC, *A New Focus for Civil Legal Aid—Consultation Outcomes* (HMSO, 2005).

[297] Miller, 'Getting the Focus Right for Civil Legal Aid' (2004) NLJ 1673.

[298] Legal Services Commission, *Annual Report 2003–04*, p 78.   [299] 1999 Act, s 4(6).

of 'unmet legal need' and to find ways of addressing them at a local level.[300] These developments are supported by the recommendations of the Carter Report,[301] which stress that there should not be one single model for community legal advice centres, which should be encouraged to develop in a flexible way meeting the needs of local communities.

The Criminal Defence Service

The other service managed by the LSC is the Criminal Defence Service (CDS). This was established under section 1(2)(b) of the Access to Justice Act 1999 and its role is to secure advice, assistance, and representation to persons involved in criminal investigations or proceedings.[302] All solicitors providing services for the CDS[303] must hold a general criminal contract and a specialist quality mark. In this respect the CDS operates in a similar way to the CLS, although work done on behalf of the CDS is not subject to strict quotas.[304] In March 2004, 2,669 solicitors' firms were operating under general criminal contracts.[305] The Carter Report[306] envisaged significant change to criminal legal aid provision and financing. The new contract with the LSC would permit efficient providers of criminal legal aid services to do greater amounts of work, achieving greater efficacy and expertise. This is being accompanied by a greater reliance on a system of fixed fees, and changes to graduated fees for advocacy in the Crown Court, to encourage better preparation of cases at the earlier parts of the trial process.

Three basic levels of service may be provided: (1) advice and assistance; (2) advocacy assistance; and (3) representation. All services funded by the CDS are subject to some form of merits test, although many of them are not means-tested. With regard to initial advice and assistance, the merits test will automatically be satisfied if a suspect or defendant has a statutory right to legal advice,[307] but the provision of any additional assistance must be justified on a case-by-case basis. All criminal legal aid covering legal assistance must meet the 'interests of justice' test: the courts take a number of factors in to account, including the seriousness of the offence, the likelihood of imprisonment or loss of livelihood, the complexity of the case and the capacity of the accused to represent him or herself. A case in the Crown Court is assumed automatically to satisfy the 'interests of justice' test.

One of the most important functions of the CDS is to provide duty solicitor schemes in police stations and magistrates' courts. These schemes cover the provision

---

[300] The Director of JUSTICE has concluded that not-for-profit bodies have benefited considerably from the creation of the CLS: Smith, *Paper for Legal Services Authority Conference on the Future of Community Legal Services: Law for those in Disadvantage* (4 October 2002) at para 44.

[301] *Op cit*, p 8, recommendations 3.5–3.8.

[302] 1999 Act, s 12(1). For these purposes the term 'criminal proceedings' includes proceedings relating to sentencing, appeals, extradition, binding over, and contempt of court: s 12(2).

[303] With the exception of those employed by the Public Defender Service: see p 419.

[304] Compare the concept of 'controlled work' under CLS contracts, discussed at p 414.

[305] Legal Services Commission, *Annual Report 2003–04*, p 6.

[306] Carter Report (2006), p 4.   [307] See p 413.

of 'advice and assistance' to persons who are held in police custody or who are appearing before magistrates in certain types of proceedings.[308] Their services are provided free of charge on a non-means-tested basis, and for the most part they are supplied by solicitors working in private practice. Changes to the general criminal contract mean that advice to those detained in connection with less serious offences will normally be provided by telephone only. Face-to-face assistance will be available if a police interview or identification procedure is to take place, or where the client is a young or vulnerable person, requires the assistance of an interpreter, or has complained of serious mistreatment. It may also be offered if the duty solicitor is already present at the police station. A pilot scheme for telephone advice, CDSDirect, was commenced in October 2005 in certain pilot areas.[309] It involves the provision of telephone advice for some offences, reducing the need for attendance at the police station by the duty solicitor. In 2006 the annual savings to the legal aid fund from the pilot scheme were estimated to be £3.9 million, with 99 per cent of calls answered by CDSDirect within thirty minutes.[310] However, surveys into the pilot have shown some cause for concern in terms of practical operation, in particular with the response rates and times of the police in response to CDSDirect calls, with a significant number of calls from CDSDirect remaining unanswered, and also with aspects of the quality of service provided.[311]

Court duty solicitors may provide 'advocacy assistance' in connection with bail applications and binding-over proceedings, and *any* CDS-contracted solicitor may provide advocacy assistance in relation to antisocial behaviour orders (ASBOs) and certain other court orders, or in cases in which a person risks imprisonment for non-payment of fines. Representation is subject to a merits test and will only be funded where a representation order has been made by a court or the LSC. It is not means-tested at the point of access but the Crown Court has the power to make a recovery of defence costs order at the conclusion of a case. In 2005 the government proposed changes that are now to be found in the Criminal Defence Service Act 2006. These reintroduced means testing in magistrates' courts and require convicted defendants to repay their defence costs if they can afford to do so. In 2010, means testing was adopted in certain Crown Courts.

The Public Defender Service
In addition to delivering services through contracted lawyers in private practice, the CDS is also able to provide legal services through lawyers in its own employment.[312] A public defender service has been launched, which now has offices in Birmingham, Cheltenham, Chester, Darlington, Liverpool, Middlesbrough, Pontypridd, and Swansea. Public defenders participate in local duty solicitor schemes, and provide other CDS services—including representation—directly to their own clients. Public defenders are an established feature of the legal system in the USA and other jurisdictions,

[308] Including bail applications and applications relating to antisocial behaviour and sex offender orders.
[309] Certain parts of Liverpool and Lincolnshire.
[310] See **www.legalservices.gov.uk/criminal/cds_direct.asp**   [311] See (2006) 156 NLJ 205.
[312] 1999 Act, s 13(2)(f) (advice and assistance); s 14(2)(f) (representation).

but they are a radical new development for England and Wales. There are concerns about the extent to which public defenders can be genuinely independent, although the Code of Practice established under section 16 of the Act aims to address some of these concerns. More fundamentally, there are questions concerning the long-term role and remit of the public defender service. In 2007 an evaluation of the pilot scheme was undertaken.[313] It concluded that it was unlikely that the scheme could be seen as a large-scale provider of general criminal defence services, or as a means of competition that would provide a cost benchmark against which private criminal firms could be measured in the context of the Carter reforms.[314] The value of the Public Defender Service as a way of providing services in areas less well serviced by private practice, and by way of developing the quality of criminal defence work undertaken efficiently, was recognized:

> We can envisage a wider role for the PDS as an essential guarantor of quality standards, minimum costs and client choice of representative in a more 'managed market' for such services.[315]

The Public Defender Service is thus an important innovation.

The Carter Review

The task faced by the LSC has been a difficult one. As already noted, the cost of funding legal services has been rising for many years, placing an increasing strain on public finances. Expenditure on legal aid per head of population in England and Wales is greater than anywhere else in the world.[316] Delivering access to justice in this climate is not easy, and defenders of the changes argue that the LSC has made a number of improvements. Changes to the means test have enabled more people to benefit from LSC services than were covered by the old legal aid system, such as the reintroduction of means testing in magistrates courts in 2006 and, now, in Crown Courts.[317] The idea of concentrating funds on early dispute resolution has much to commend it in principle. The increase in funding for not-for-profit organizations has been welcomed, as has the greater emphasis on quality and accountability. There have also been many new initiatives, such as the development of Community Legal Advice (formerly known as Community Legal Service Direct),[318] the introduction of housing possession duty court schemes,[319] and the launch of the public defender service.

---

[313] Bridges, Cape, Fenn, Mitchell, Moorhead and Sherr, *Evaluation of the Public Defender Service in England and Wales* (HMSO, 2007): available at **www.legalservices.gov.uk/docs/pds/Public_Defenders_Report_PDFVersion6.pdf**

[314] As to which, see below.   [315] Bridges et al, *op cit* , ch 8.

[316] Carter Report (2006) at p 3; *Proposals for the Reform of Legal Aid*, 2010, at para 3.42–3.43.

[317] It had been abolished in 2000.

[318] Formerly called 'Just Ask!', this website provides the public with information about how to get advice, and it also includes a national directory of service providers: **www.communitylegaladvice.org.uk/**

[319] Which make housing advisers available in courts; cf. the duty solicitor scheme: see p 419.

Critics, however, argue that, in spite of the LSC's efforts to target funds where they are most needed, access to justice has actually diminished since its launch. The contract system has limited the number of suppliers who are able to provide publicly funded services, and those who do hold contracts are subject to considerable regulatory and administrative burdens. The professional bodies continue to complain that public funded work is poorly remunerated, and all of these factors are having a negative effect on the number of providers willing to work in this sector. A survey by Citizens' Advice found that 68 per cent of their bureaux experienced difficulties in finding Community Legal Service lawyers to do immigration work, with 60 per cent facing similar problems in the field of housing law.[320] Some 39 per cent of bureaux said that they were operating in 'an advice desert',[321] and the overall conclusion of the report was that publicly funded legal services were declining in all parts of the country.[322]

In an effort to tackle rising costs and to make its budget go further, the LSC introduced a mandatory system of fixed fees covering all types of controlled[323] civil work except immigration. By rewarding service providers for 'outputs' rather than for the actual time spent on each case, the new system will be more cost-efficient and will ensure that payments to suppliers reflect market conditions.[324] Fixed fees have since been greatly expanded in their scope. On their introduction for family and criminal work, barristers took the view that they were being denied 'proper remuneration' and they voted to abandon the cab-rank rule for cases that were subject to this system. Protests by publicly funded practitioners were answered robustly. In 2003 the Lord Chancellor, in a speech to the Law Society, observed:[325]

> I know lawyers complain about remuneration rates but may I point out that over the last ten years the average cost per family case in civil representation has gone up by 91 per cent. Inflation in the same period was 30 per cent. I do *not* argue that this is all to the benefit of lawyers. But it does show that arguments about rates are not as straightforward as they first appear.

A growing consensus began to emerge about the need to correct the imbalance between the civil and criminal budgets. It was for that reason, and because of ongoing concerns about the affordability of provision of legal service, and whether they are being provided efficiently, that the Carter Review was established. It reported in 2006.[326] Carter identified the fact that more is spent per head on legal aid in England and Wales than anywhere else in the world. He concluded that the increase in costs was not, of itself, down to wastefulness, but resulted from the way in which legal aid services were

---

[320] *Geography of Advice* (2004) at para 2.15.   [321] Ibid, at para 2.14.
[322] Ibid, at para 5.1.   [323] See p 416.
[324] Legal Services Commission, *Tailored Fixed Fee Scheme Consultation Paper: Civil (Non-Immigration) Controlled Work* (HMSO, 2004). The system became mandatory on 1 April 2005.
[325] Law Society Annual Conference, London (26 September 2003).
[326] Carter Report (2006), *supra* n 271.

procured. He identified potential efficiencies that would save £100 million 'without compromising quality and access to services...' Mindful of an imbalance between civil and criminal legal aid, he considered that his recommendations would reduce spending on criminal legal aid by 20 per cent over four years.

These aims were to be achieved by, in civil work, a wholesale move to fixed fees, with graduations to reflect levels of difficulty and complexity. In the area of criminal legal aid, they were to be achieved by a movement to preferred contractors, based on fixed fees, again subject to increase to reflect complexity and effort, minimum thresholds for the number of cases handled, peer review of quality, and measuring efficiency against performance indicators. Carter envisaged fewer providers, with 'preferred suppliers' of defence representation. In the longer term, providers would be remunerated for work completed, not for the number of hours spent on the work. Market forces should determine the price paid.

The recommendations of Carter were largely accepted by government, which had an aim of moving to best value tendering following implementation of the Carter reforms.[327] Fixed fees have been introduced for most areas of work: police station advice (2008); social welfare, family and immigration work (2007); and mental health (2009). The concept of best value tendering was not, however, achieved, with proposed pilot schemes in Manchester and Avon and Somerset being postponed.

Future changes in legal aid

In November 2010 the government published its Green Paper on legal aid.[328] Having identified the growth of the cost of legal aid, identified above, it outlined proposals designed,

> to encourage people, rather than going to court too readily at the taxpayer's expense, to seek alternative methods of dispute resolution, reserving the courts as a last resort for legal issues where there is a public interest in providing access to public funding.[329]

The proposals for consultation sit alongside other proposals for reform of the criminal justice system, family justice and the wider system of civil justice that are intended, amongst other reasons, to reduce the cost and increase the efficiency of litigation. In respect of criminal legal aid it is proposed that that legal aid should continue to be available for those accused of criminal offences provided that it is in the interests of justice to do so, and subject to the assessment of the means of the individual. This effectively means that there are not likely to be further restrictions on criminal legal aid availability.

By contrast, major changes are proposed to civil legal aid, likely to occur in or after 2012. These changes are mainly driven by the desire to reduce costs, described as 'unsustainable'.[330] The factors that will influence the availability of state financial

---

[327] See White Paper, 2010, at para 3.5
[328] *Proposals for the Reform of Legal Aid in England and Wales* (HMSO, 2010).   [329] Para 1.8.
[330] Para 4.11.

assistance in the future include the importance of the issue to be decided in the litigation: this is defined by the consultation paper objectively, and include cases in which the liberty of the individual is at stake, in which the individual faces intervention by the state in family matters that may result in children being removed from the family, cases in which homelessness may occur, and applications for judicial review. By contrast, cases in which monetary compensation is sought will not ordinarily be regarded as sufficiently important to justify public funding Where the issue arises from the individual's own choice (for example, immigration cases), legal aid is likely to be no longer available. Other relevant factors will be the litigant's ability to present their own case, the availability of alternative sources of funding or other routes for resolution of the dispute. In this respect the proposals on legal aid currently the subject of consultation must be considered in conjunction with proposals for changes in costs and civil procedure currently being considered following the Jackson Report.[331] In particular the gap left by reductions in legal aid may be filled both by the changing rules on conditional fee agreements and by limiting the costs recoverable against unsuccessful litigants.[332]

In addition to changes that will restrict or eliminate funding of a wider range of disputes, proposals will limit further the eligibility of those whose cases fall within the permitted categories of case. The changes will be based on ensuring that those who are able to contribute to some or all of their costs do so. Those who have a certain level of disposable capital, including equity in property, should bring that into account in deciding eligibility. Levels of contribution are also likely to rise.

The result of these proposals, if implemented, would be to take major areas of dispute outside the scope of legal aid. Personal injury cases are already dealt with not by legal aid but by conditional fee agreements.[333] Other claims for compensation, including consumer matters and claims for damages for clinical negligence, are likely to be added to the list of matters that are currently excluded, which include property disputes, wills and defamation. Family matters (other than public family law in respect of public authority involvement in care proceedings of children) are likely to be excluded. No aid for representation before coroners' courts or tribunals is likely to be made available. Legal aid for claims under the criminal injuries compensation scheme will cease. Many claims in tort, for breach of statutory duty negligence or nuisance, will cease to attract funding.

The government accepts that changes to the scheme 'cannot capture the specific circumstances of every litigant bringing a case in relation to particular issues'.[334] For that reason it proposes a new scheme to replace the current scheme of 'exceptional finding'. The new scheme will permit funding for excluded cases in which the government is satisfied that the provision of some level of funding is necessary for the United Kingdom to meet its obligations under the European Convention on Human Rights.

---

[331] See pp 480 and 482.   [332] See pp 408 and 482.
[333] See p 482.   [334] Para 4.33.

It will not extend further than that, and not replicate the wider 'exceptional funding' currently available.

KEY ISSUE

The legal aid changes proposed must be viewed in the light of wider changes to the civil justice system, which is where the main burden of the legal aid cuts will fall. Other forms of funding, such as conditional fee agreements, will become more important, although themselves subject to change.[335]. So too will the use of mediation and other forms of alternative dispute resolution.[336]

At the heart of this issue is the extent to which the government should pay for achieving access to justice. Individual rights are meaningless unless individuals have the financial ability to vindicate them. The gradual growth in state funding since the original conception of legal aid following the report of the Rushcliffe Committee has broadened access to legal services and meant that access to legal advice and the courts is not simply the preserve of the rich or very poor. Cost is fundamental. The proposals themselves seek to limit exposure to cost, whilst other proposals address the separate, but related, question of how costs can be reduced, through the introduction of competition and a restructuring of fees. This may include permitting a proportion of a legally aided claimant's awards made in successful damages claims to be collected and used to supplement the legal aid fund. Other fundamental changes may permit solicitors to act for an individual on the basis of keeping a percentage of the damages recovered.[337]

❓ Questions

1. Do you think that the range of cases being excluded from state funding is reasonable and fair?
2. Why do you think the government proposes a limited exception to comply with requirements of the European Convention on Human Rights?
3. Should funding be refused in any case in which there may be a suitable alternative source of funding?
4. What might the impact of the changes, if implemented, be?
5. Will access to the law be significantly diminished?

Further reading

BRIDGES, CAPE, FENN, MITCHELL, MOORHEAD and SHERR, *Evaluation of the Public Defender Service in England and Wales* (Legal Services, 2007): available at **www.legalservices.gov. uk/docs/pds/Public_Defenders_Report_PDFVersion6.pdf**

CARTER, *Legal Aid: A Market-Based Approach to Reform* (HMSO, 2006) ('the Carter Report')

---

[335] See p 482.   [336] See p 490.   [337] See pp 410 and 480.

CLEMENTI, *Final Report of the Review of the Regulatory Framework for Legal Services in England and Wales* (HMSO, 2004)

DEPARTMENT FOR CONSTITUTIONAL AFFAIRS, *Consumers: 21st Century Legal Services* (HMSO, 2006)

LORD CHANCELLOR'S DEPARTMENT, *The Workload and Organisation of the Legal Profession*, Cm 570 (HMSO, 1989)

LORD CHANCELLOR'S DEPARTMENT, *Contingency Fees*, Cm 571 (HMSO, 1989)

12 The Police and Law Enforcement[1]

INTRODUCTION

This chapter explores the role of the police in the English legal system, in addition to giving a brief overview of the work of civilian officers and other law enforcement agencies. The jurisdiction of England and Wales is currently served by forty-three separate police forces, and the organizational structure of these forces, along with the mechanisms for ensuring their accountability, will be the focus of the first part of this chapter. The latter part will give an overview of some of the most important police powers. The specific areas covered will include:

- the organizational structure of the police, including the roles of central government, local police authorities, chief constables, and individual officers;
- the trend towards greater centralization of certain aspects of policing, and the expansion of the role of civilian officers and non-police employees;
- mechanisms for ensuring police accountability, including rules of evidence, the work of the Independent Police Complaints Commission, and the possibility of civil or criminal proceedings;
- basic concepts such as breach of the peace, reasonable suspicion and reasonable force;
- specific examples of some of the most important police powers, including powers relating to stop and search, arrest, and detention.

The law enforcement function

Law enforcement functions in England and Wales are performed primarily, but not exclusively, by the jurisdiction's forty-three local police forces. These forces are served by over 140,000 full-time police officers, each one of whom exercises the legal powers

---

[1] The literature on the police is extensive. See, e.g., the Report of the Royal Commission on Criminal Procedure, and the research studies listed in Annex D, Cmnd 8092 (HMSO, 1981); Lustgarten, *The Governance of the Police* (Sweet & Maxwell, 1986); Reiner, *The Politics of the Police* (OUP: 3rd edn, 2000); English and Card, *Police Law* (OUP: 10th edn, 2007); Newburn (ed), *Handbook of Policing* (Willan Publishing, 2003); Newburn and Reiner, 'From PC Dixon to Dixon plc: Policing and Policing Powers since 1954' [2004] Crim LR 601.

and privileges of a 'constable'.[2] These salaried officers are assisted by around 14,000 'special constables', who serve on a part-time, unpaid basis. Since 2002, a number of civilian officers have also been designated, although their 'powers and privileges' are less extensive.[3]

In addition to local police forces, several other organizations perform law enforcement functions. The Ministry of Defence Police, the British Transport Police, and the Civil Nuclear Constabulary are examples of specialist police forces, and their officers hold the office of constable within their jurisdictions.[4] The Serious Organised Crime Agency, which was formed in 2006,[5] also operates at a national level, although its future is now in question with proposals to merge it into a new National Crime Agency.[6] In addition, the Director of the Serious Fraud Office has wide-ranging powers to assist in the investigation of complex or serious fraud cases,[7] and bodies such as HM Revenue and Customs (HMRC) and the Health and Safety Executive also have important investigative roles. It is, however, the police who perform the bulk of investigatory and law enforcement work. The creation of a new National Crime Agency would, says the government,[8] 'harness and exploit the intelligence, analytical and enforcement capabilities' of the Serious Organised Crime Agency and the Child Exploitation and Online Protection Centre. The new agency, if created, is also intended to enhance cooperation and liaison between the different agencies.

The role of the individual

All individuals have a duty to preserve the peace, although this is a duty of 'imperfect obligation' and there is generally no sanction for its breach. In *Albert* v *Lavin*,[9] Lord Diplock stated:

> Every citizen in whose presence a breach of the peace is being, or reasonably appears to be about to be, committed has the right to take reasonable steps to make the person who is breaking or threatening to break the peace refrain from doing so; and those reasonable steps in appropriate cases will include detaining him against his will. At common law this is not only the right of every citizen, it is also his duty, although, except in the case of a citizen who is a constable, it is a duty of imperfect obligation.

---

[2] Police Act 1996, s 30.

[3] Police Reform Act 2002, s 38; Sch 4. See p 435.

[4] Ministry of Defence Police Act 1987, s 2; Railways and Transport Safety Act 2003, s 31; Energy Act 2004, s 56.

[5] Serious Organised Crime and Police Act 2005, Part 1: see p 432. Parts of the Immigration Service and Her Majesty's Customs and Excise have also been incorporated into the new Agency.

[6] See Government Consultation Paper, *Policing in the 21st Century: Reconnecting Police and the People* Cm 7925 (HMSO, 2010).

[7] Criminal Justice Act 1987, s 2; see *Smith* v *Director of Serious Fraud Office* [1992] 3 All ER 456.

[8] See statement by Theresa May, MP, Home Secretary, 26 July 2010, reported at **www.bbc.co.uk/news**

[9] [1982] AC 546 at 565, [1981] 3 All ER 878 at 880.

Citizens also have powers of arrest in respect of indictable offences that are being (or have been) committed,[10] and it is these powers that are used by store detectives, doormen, and private security officers.

Beyond this, however, a citizen has no general duty to assist the police. The law proceeds on the basis that individuals have a 'right to silence',[11] and a person is generally under no obligation to answer police questions or to cooperate with any investigation.[12] This common law right is mirrored by the fair trial provisions in Article 6 of the European Convention on Human Rights. There is, however, a duty not to mislead or hinder an investigation: intentional, positive acts that make it more difficult for an officer to do his or her job may constitute the offence of wilfully obstructing a constable in the execution of his or her duty.[13] In *Rice* v *Connolly*, Lord Parker CJ stated that whilst it was not unlawful to refuse to answer police questions, deliberately giving a false story undoubtedly *could* constitute an offence.[14] More recently, the Administrative Court rejected appeals from two men convicted of wilful obstruction after they ran away from officers who wanted to question them about suspicious activity.[15] Although the court conceded that the appellants were under no legal duty to assist the police and would have been entitled to remain silent when questioned, it was held that running off before the officers could apprehend them amounted to an offence of wilful obstruction. The rationale seems to have been that if the suspects had simply refused to assist the police instead of running away, the officers could have considered making an arrest, but this is a controversial decision nonetheless. More straightforward is the decision in *Ingleton* v *Dibble*.[16] In this case a motorist who was about to be breathalysed grabbed a whisky bottle from another man and took a swig from it. His intention was clearly to make it impossible to ascertain whether he had been intoxicated whilst driving, and it was held that his actions amounted to a wilful obstruction of an officer in the execution of his duty. In another case a motorist was convicted of the same offence after ignoring a constable's order to reverse the wrong way down a one-way street to allow an ambulance to pass.[17]

Note, finally, that since 2006 police officers have had the power in certain circumstances to compel persons to answer questions or disclose relevant documents and information. The use of these powers is confined to the investigation of specific serious offences, and the consent of the Attorney-General or Director of Revenue and Customs Prosecutions is required.[18] Similar powers are available to the Serious Fraud Office.

---

[10] Police and Criminal Evidence Act 1984, s 24A: see p 452.   [11] Although see p 679.

[12] *Rice* v *Connolly* [1966] 2 QB 414, [1966] 2 All ER 649.

[13] Police Act 1996, s 89(2): see p 441.   [14] [1966] 2 QB 414 at 420, [1966] 2 All ER 649 at 652.

[15] *Sekfali* v *DPP* [2006] EWHC 894 (Admin), (2006) 170 JP 393.

[16] [1972] 1 QB 480, [1972] 1 All ER 275.

[17] *Johnson* v *Phillips* [1976] 1 WLR 65, [1975] 3 All ER 682.

[18] See Part 2 of the Serious Organised Crime and Police Act 2005. It is not normally possible to use statements made under such compulsion as evidence in any criminal proceedings against their maker: s 65.

The organization of the police

Local accountability

The structures and organization of the police were radically changed by the Police Act 1964, the Police and Criminal Evidence Act 1984, and the Police and Magistrates' Courts Act 1994. The relevant provisions were consolidated by the Police Act 1996, and further changes have since been made by the Police Act 1997, the Police Reform Act 2002, the Police and Justice Act 2006, and the Policing and Crime Act 2009.

Policing is, for the most part, organized on a local basis, and each of the forty-three police areas[19] in England and Wales has its own police authority.[20] Most police authorities outside London have seventeen members, comprising members of local authorities, justices of the peace, and certain other nominated persons.[21] The Metropolitan Police Authority has twenty-three members, but is otherwise similarly constituted.[22] Slightly different arrangements exist for the City of London area, where the Common Council performs the functions of a police authority.[23] The primary duty of a police authority is 'to secure the maintenance of an efficient and effective police force for its area'.[24] To this end, the authority is required to appoint a chief constable[25] and to produce a plan setting out its objectives and its proposed arrangements for policing the area.[26] A police authority must have regard to the public's views on policing policy in its area. [27] In addition, although the appointment of individual police officers is a matter for the chief constable,[28] it is for the police authority to decide how many officers are needed for its area. Despite this apparent local autonomy, there are numerous mechanisms for ensuring the accountability of local police forces to central government, and the last two decades have seen an increasing trend towards centralization. There is also an increasing trend towards collaboration between police forces, a process strengthened by the Police and Crime Act 2009 following the publication of a government Green Paper, *Neighbourhood to the National: Policing our Communities Together*.[29]

There is no direct democratic element in the management of policing, although the coalition government announced in 2010 that it was intending to introduce greater measures of accountability through the election of police chiefs.[30] At present, a democratic input into the governance of the police is achieved through the presence on police authorities of the representatives of local authorities. In addition, section 96 of the Police Act 1996 states that:

(1) Arrangements shall be made for each police area for obtaining—

---

[19] See Sch 1 to the Police Act 1996 for a list of police areas outside London.

[20] Police Act 1996, ss 3; 5B.   [21] Ibid, s 4; Sch 2.

[22] Ibid, s 5C; Sch 2A.   [23] Ibid, s 101.   [24] Ibid, s 6(1)(a).

[25] Ibid, s 11: any appointment requires the Home Secretary's approval. The Metropolitan Police Authority is subject to different arrangements: both the Authority and the Mayor of London have the power to recommend a person for appointment as the Metropolitan Police Commissioner, but the actual appointment is made by the monarch on the advice of the Home Secretary: 1996 Act, s 9B.

[26] Ibid, s 6ZB.   [27] Police Act 1996 as amended by Policing and Crime Act 2009

[28] Ibid, s 13(3).   [29] (2008).   [30] See p 430.

(a) the views of people in that area about matters concerning the policing of the area, and

(b) their co-operation with the police in preventing crime and anti-social behaviour in that area.

Yet the evidence suggests that this is only partially achieved. Police authorities have, in the past, been referred to as 'customers' of their police forces.[31] Only 8 per cent of local authority ward elect members are police authority members.

The current position is not regarded as providing a sufficient degree of local accountability. In July 2010 the government published a White Paper, *Policing in the 21st Century: Reconnecting Police and the People*.[32] It stated:[33]

> To cut crime, policing relies not just on the consent of the people but their active cooperation. But the bond between the police and local people is not strong enough. The police have been encouraged to focus on the issues that national politicians have told them are important rather than the concerns of their local communities. Reports to Ministers and civil servants in Whitehall have taken precedence over information to help the public judge how well the police service is doing.
>
> Targets and standards in policing were driven by Whitehall rather than the public. At best, national targets and standards have not taken account of local needs, and at worst eroded Chief Constables' professional responsibility for taking decisions to meet the particular needs of their local communities. All too often targets have driven perverse incentives. For example the 'Offences Brought to Justice' target incentivised officers to pursue easy to achieve low level detections rather than focusing on more serious offences.
>
> Many individual members of police authorities have made great efforts in recent years to improve police responsiveness and represent local communities. But despite these efforts the public are often unaware of police authorities themselves. A Cabinet Office review in 2007 highlighted that only 7% of the public would know to go to their Police Authority if they had a problem with policing in their local area. The public do not know how to influence local policing, let alone get actively involved. There is no direct way for the public to change or challenge those who govern policing on their behalf.

To remedy these perceived problems the White Paper proposes the introduction of directly elected police and crime commissioners 'who will give the public a voice and strengthen the bond between the public and the police through greater accountability and transparency so that people have more confidence in the police to fight crime and [antisocial behaviour]'. The functions of these new commissioners will include: representing and engaging with all those who live and work in the communities in their force area and identifying their policing needs; setting priorities that meet those needs by agreeing a local strategic plan for the force; holding the chief constable to account for achieving these priorities as efficiently and effectively as possible, and playing a role in wider questions of community safety; and setting the force budget and setting the

[31] *Policing Reform*, Cm2281 (HMSO, 1994).   [32] Cm 7925 (HMSO, 2010).   [33] Paras 1.09–1.11.

precept. The commissioner will also have the power to appoint and remove the chief constable.

The proposals would involve the abolition of police authorities, the removal of 'bureaucratic accountability', the provision of greater communication with the public, and the strengthening of national and regional police cooperation.

KEY ISSUE

Although formal police structures are, historically, of relatively recent origin, dating predominantly from the nineteenth century, local responsibility for law enforcement dates back to the earliest days.[34] A key question is the extent to which in the future policing will remain a locally based function. We discuss below the substantial control, influence, and regulation by central government of the policing process, and the increasing national approach being taken. The potential abolition of police authorities will remove the only formal structure representative of local communities that currently exists. The introduction of elected commissioners may in fact increase accountability at the election stage but potentially reduce local accountability after election. Questions arise as to whether the police will be subject to political pressure or influence, because it is crucial that the operational independence of chief constables is maintained. Election processes by their nature can politicize the task of appointment. And the existence of a strong elected individual heading a police force raises important questions about the relationship of local management of police and central government.

❓ Questions

1. Do you think the election of a commissioner in each police area will strengthen local accountability?
2. Is there a danger that police forces will become influenced by political issues?

Police authorities and central government

A police authority cannot appoint, remove or suspend a chief constable without the approval of the Home Secretary,[35] and the Home Secretary can require a chief constable to retire in the interests of efficiency.[36] The Home Secretary can also direct that a police force be given assistance or reinforced in the interests of justice, safety or public order, and he can do this with or without the agreement of the police authority.[37] Indeed, the Home Secretary has a wide range of powers that can be used to 'promote the efficiency and effectiveness of the police',[38] and it is to him that police authorities must send their plans and reports.[39] The Inspectorate of Constabulary also reports to the Secretary of State,[40] and if the Secretary of State is satisfied that a police authority

[34] See p 228.   [35] Ibid, s 11: see also, n 23, above.
[36] Ibid, s 42(1).   [37] Ibid, s 24.   [38] Ibid, s 36(1).
[39] Ibid, ss 6A and 8. (These provisions will be repealed and policing plans and reports will be governed by new ss 6ZB and 6ZC of the Act when the Police and Justice Act 2006 is brought into force.)
[40] Ibid, s 54.

or its force is failing to discharge its functions effectively he can require the author-ity to take remedial measures.[41] The Secretary of State also determines the size of the central government grant made to each police authority,[42] and the threat to withhold funds can be used as a lever to secure changes in the way in which a force is run.

For his part the Secretary of State has the power to determine 'strategic priorities' for each police area,[43] and he can direct police authorities to establish performance targets.[44] He can also issue codes of practice[45] and make regulations for the use of equipment.[46] In addition to these statutory powers, the royal prerogative allows the Home Secretary to take all reasonably necessary steps to ensure the preservation of the Queen's peace. In *R v Secretary of State for the Home Department, ex parte Northumbria Police Authority*,[47] the Court of Appeal considered the scope of section 41 of the Police Act 1964. At the time, this was the provision authorizing the Home Secretary to pro-vide and maintain services for promoting the efficiency of the police. The court held that this provision entitled the Home Secretary to supply riot-control equipment from central stores, without the approval of the police authority. It also held that even if section 41 could not be construed in this way, the Home Secretary's actions would have been lawful under the prerogative.

Policing at a national level

It would be wrong to view police forces as acting always in isolation. Chief constables can seek mutual aid from other forces,[48] and a number of national policing organ-izations have been created over the years. The Serious Organised Crime Agency is an important recent example. This body was formed by the amalgamation of the National Criminal Intelligence Service, the National Crime Squad, and parts of the Immigration Service and HMRC.[49] Billed as 'an FBI for the UK', it began operating in 2006 and its remit extends throughout the United Kingdom. Its focus is on tack-ling drugs and people trafficking, money laundering, major fraud, and other serious offences. It also has an important role in combating the financing of terrorism and it has a range of new investigative powers at its disposal.[50] The Policing and Crime Act 2009 has introduced new powers to enable collaboration agreements between police forces, and between police authorities.

A further example of the move towards greater centralization is provided by the creation of the National Policing Improvement Agency. Established under section 1 of the Police and Justice Act 2006, the objects of this body include 'the identification, development and promulgation of good practice in policing', the provision of expert advice on operational and other matters, and the provision of support in connection

---

[41] Ibid, ss 40 and 40A.   [42] Ibid, s 46.   [43] Ibid, s 37A.   [44] Ibid, s 38.

[45] Ibid, ss 39 and 39A (codes for police authorities and chief officers); Police and Criminal Evidence Act 1984, ss 60, 60A and 66 (codes for the exercise of police powers and duties); Serious Organised Crime and Police Act 2005, s 10 (codes for SOCA).

[46] Police Reform Act 2002, s 6.   [47] [1989] QB 26, [1988] 1 All ER 556.

[48] Police Act 1996, s 24.   [49] Serious Organised Crime and Police Act 2005, s 1.

[50] See Part 1 of the Act and *One Step Ahead: A 21st Century Strategy to Defeat Organised Crime*, Cm 6167 (HMSO, 2004).

with information technology, training, and the procurement of equipment and servic-es.[51] The Agency has already assumed responsibility for the Police National Computer, the National DNA Database, and the national fingerprint and palm print system (IDENT1). It also provides specialist training and operational advice to assist forces in dealing with major incidents and murder investigations. The Agency is required to submit annual plans and reports to the Secretary of State,[52] who in turn has the power to determine the Agency's strategic objectives.[53]

The creation of the National Reporting Centre during the miners' strike in the mid-1980s provides an example of a less formal centralized body.[54]

KEY ISSUE

The growth of central government influence and power over local police forces is inevita-ble given the nature of modern society, easy communication and travel, and the national and international nature of crimes such as terrorism, financial and international finan-cial, corporate or electronic fraud. Large-scale incidents, such as that involving a gunman engaged in a mass killing in Cumbria in 2010, required inputs from a range of police forces to enable adequate responses to be achieved. There are also the financial realities: central government influence over local policing is bound to be strong whilst central government funds the majority of police costs and expenditure.

 Questions

1. Do we have too many police forces?
2. Would modern policing needs be better served by a national police force?
3. What might the benefits be?
4. What might the disadvantages be?

Police authorities and chief constables

A chief constable is required to produce drafts of policing plans for his police author-ity to finalize,[55] and he must also submit a general report to the authority at the end of each financial year.[56] Beyond this, the police authority's rights are limited, and it has sometimes been said that a chief constable cannot be challenged on operational matters. In reality the position is not so straightforward, but the law does recognize that the chief constable has a wide discretion to determine strategy and other matters. The scope for judicially reviewing a chief constable's decisions is thus extremely lim-ited, and neither the deployment of police resources nor individual policing decisions are normally matters for the courts. In *R* v *Commissioner of Police for the Metropolis*,

---

[51] 2006 Act, Sch 1, para 1.   [52] Ibid, Sch 1, paras 5 and 28.
[53] Ibid, Sch 1, para 6.   [54] See generally, Freeman, 'Law and Order in 1984' [1984] CLP 175.
[55] Police Act 1996, s 8. (This provision will be repealed and policing plans will be governed by a new s 6ZB of the Act when the Police and Justice Act 2006 is brought into force.)
[56] Ibid, s 22.

ex parte Blackburn, the Court of Appeal considered the legality of a policy by which the Commissioner had directed his officers to enforce the Gaming Acts only in certain circumstances. Lord Denning MR stated:[57]

> [It is the duty of the Commissioner], as it is of every Chief Constable, to enforce the law of the land. He must take steps so to post his men that crimes may be detected; and that honest citizens may go about their affairs in peace. He must decide whether or not suspected persons are to be prosecuted... but in all these things he is not the servant of anyone, save of the law itself. No Minister of the Crown can tell him that he must, or must not... prosecute this man or that one. Nor can any police authority tell him so. The responsibility for law enforcement lies on him. He is answerable to the law and to the law alone [but] there are many fields in which [a chief police officer has] a discretion with which the law will not interfere. For instance, it is [for him] to decide in any particular case whether enquiries should be pursued, or whether an arrest should be made... It must be for him to decide on the disposition of his force and the concentration of his resources on any particular crime or area. No court can or should give him direction on such a matter.

The court added that it could intervene if what was at issue was effectively an abdication of duty, but the matter was not put to the test because the policy statement had already been withdrawn. In another case the House of Lords accepted that police discretion could be the subject of judicial review, but it stressed that as long as it was used for a legitimate purpose, the courts would not interfere with the exercise of that discretion.[58] Although these cases do not deal directly with the relationship between the chief constable and his police authority, they clearly illustrate the extent of a chief constable's discretion and the level of autonomy that he has.

Chief constables and individual officers

Constables are office holders under the Crown, although they are not Crown servants or employees of the chief constable. As stated previously, all police officers derive their powers from their status as constables, although certain powers can only be exercised by officers holding a particular rank. An intimate search of a suspect, for example, can only be authorized by an officer of at least the rank of inspector.[59]

The reality of modern policing is that each force has its own policies and command structure, and all officers are subject to rules governing their employment, personal conduct and discipline.[60] However, when exercising the powers of a constable, an officer is legally responsible for his own actions, and he or she cannot be directed to exercise them in a particular way. In *Lindley* v *Rutter*,[61] it was held that a police officer had acted unlawfully in removing an item of underwear from a drunken, arrested

---

[57] [1968] 2 QB 118 at 136, [1968] 1 All ER 763 at 769.
[58] *Holgate-Mohammed* v *Duke* [1984] AC 437, [1984] 1 All ER 1054; cf. *R* v *Chief Constable of Devon & Cornwall, ex parte Central Electricity Generating Board* [1982] QB 458, [1981] 3 All ER 826.
[59] Police and Criminal Evidence Act 1984, s 55.
[60] Police Regulations 2003, SI 2003/527; Police (Conduct) Regulations 2004, SI 2004/645.
[61] [1981] QB 128, [1980] 3 WLR 660.

woman. The officer had wrongly regarded a standing instruction as depriving her of any discretion as to whether such garments should be removed. Although there was a common law power that could have provided the authority for the officer's conduct, she had not considered whether the conditions for exercising this power were satisfied: her actions were therefore unlawful. This does not mean that it will always be improper to rely on a policy or standing instruction; what matters is whether there has been a genuine exercise of discretion.[62]

The extended police family[63]

Civilian officers

The Police Reform Act 2002 allows chief constables to confer limited law enforcement powers on civilians employed by police authorities. The idea is that if civilians are able to perform basic public order and support functions, constables can be given more time to focus on their core policing role. Section 38(2) of the Act provides that a civilian employee may be designated as one or more of the following: (a) a community support officer; (b) an investigating officer; (c) a detention officer; or (d) an escort officer.[64]

The main role of community support officers (CSOs) is to help tackle low-level disorder and antisocial behaviour problems, and they are given a range of specific powers for this purpose.[65] The list of available powers is set out in Schedule 4, Part 1, of the 2002 Act, and initially it was left to individual chief officers to determine which of these powers should be conferred on their CSOs. Perhaps inevitably there was wide variation in the approaches taken by different forces, and this was a source of considerable confusion for members of the public. There was also a concern that CSOs in some areas did not have sufficient powers to be able to contribute effectively to local policing.[66] The 2002 Act was amended in response to these concerns,[67] and the Secretary of State can now confer a standard set of powers on all CSOs. These powers currently include: the power to require a person suspected of antisocial behaviour or a designated offence to give his name and address; powers to deal with alcohol consumption in public places; the power to seize controlled drugs; and the power to issue fixed penalty notices in respect of littering, cycling on the footway, and offences

---

[62] See, e.g., *R v Chief Constable of Avon and Somerset Constabulary, ex parte Robinson* [1989] 2 All ER 15, [1989] 1 WLR 793.

[63] See *Policing in the New Century: A Blueprint for Reform*, Cm 5326 (HMSO, 2001); Morris, 'Extending the Police Family: Issues and Anomalies' [2002] PL 670; Ormerod and Roberts, 'The Police Reform Act 2002: Increasing Centralisation, Maintaining Confidence and Contracting out Crime' [2003] Crim LR 141; Jason-Lloyd, *Quasi-Policing* (Cavendish, 2003).

[64] An amendment made by the Serious Organised Crime and Police Act 2005 will also allow civilians to be appointed as 'staff custody officers', but at the time of writing this amendment has not been brought into force.

[65] Police Reform Act 2002, ss 38 and 38A.

[66] Home Office, *Consultation on the Standard Powers of Community Support Officers* (HMSO, 2005), para 3.

[67] By the Police and Justice Act 2006.

under dog control orders.[68] Chief officers still have discretion as to whether to confer any of the additional powers listed in Schedule 4 of the Act, and perhaps the most controversial of these is the power to use reasonable force to detain persons in certain circumstances.

Investigating officers are essentially civilian scene of crime officers: they have the power to apply for and execute search warrants, and once a suspect has been lawfully arrested they can exercise many of the search and seizure powers available to constables.[69] Detention officers perform various functions with regard to persons in police custody, and they have powers to search, photograph, and fingerprint suspects.[70] Escort officers, on the other hand, are primarily involved in transporting detainees to and from police stations, and their powers are limited accordingly.[71]

Non-police employees

Some police powers can be conferred on civilians who are not employed by police authorities. Thus, where a police force has contracted a private company to provide some of its escort and detention services, the chief constable can designate employees of that company as escort or detention officers.[72] The Act also enables chief constables to establish schemes whereby other non-police employees, such as security guards and traffic wardens, may be accredited to perform community safety functions. Accredited persons cannot exercise the full range of powers available to CSOs, but they can, for example, issue fixed penalty notices for littering and dog-fouling, and in some circumstances they can also require a person to provide his name and address.[73]

Before any powers under the Act can be conferred on a non-police employee, the chief constable must be satisfied that he is a suitable person to exercise those powers, and that he is capable and adequately trained.[74] He must also be satisfied that the person's employer is a 'fit and proper person' to supervise him for these purposes.[75]

Accountability

Private sector employees designated as detention or escort officers are subject to the police complaints regime, as are civilian officers employed by police authorities.[76] There is also little doubt that all those who exercise police powers, including those accredited under community safety schemes, will be liable under the Human Rights Act 1998 if they infringe Convention rights.[77] Nevertheless, the idea of extending police powers to persons who are not trained as constables remains controversial, particularly where

---

[68] Police Reform Act 2002 (Standard Powers and Duties of Community Support Officers) Order 2007, SI 2007/3202.

[69] Police Reform Act 2002, s 38(6); Sch 4, Part 2. [70] Ibid, s 38(6); Sch 4, Part 3.

[71] Ibid, s 38(6); Sch 4, Part 4. [72] Ibid, s 39.

[73] Ibid, ss 40–41; Sch 5. [74] Ibid, ss 39(4) and 41(4). [75] Ibid, ss 39(5) and 41(4).

[76] Police (Complaints and Misconduct) Regulations 2004, SI 2004/643.

[77] See the discussion of s 6 of this Act at p 161.

those persons are not employed by the police authority and are not directly subject to police control. Paradoxically, some critics have also suggested that the new powers do not go far enough. As Jason-Lloyd has noted:[78]

> [I]t is wrong to give civilians limited police powers when they are likely to face unlimited situations on the streets. The present structure of their powers is restricted to certain incidents, but this will not prevent other incidents from occurring within the same scenario where they have not been given specific powers to deal with them.

KEY ISSUE

The growth of the 'police family' is based on the belief that the full range of police skills possessed by an individual with the status and skills of a police constable are not necessary in all circumstances. The danger is that a greater burden of work is placed on CSOs. That in turn raises an important issue about where the boundaries are, or should be, between the role of police constables and other members of the police 'family'. The distinction between them exists in the nature of the office held, and their legal rights and responsibilities have the potential to be blurred.

? Questions

1. What is the difference between police constables and community support officers (CSOs)?
2. Are CSOs simply lower paid and less well-trained police constables?

Police accountability

The accountability of chief constables to police authorities and the Home Secretary has already been discussed, but police accountability is also achieved through a variety of other mechanisms.

Rules of evidence

In general, English courts adhere to the principle that it is no part of their task to punish the police by excluding evidence. Crompton J once observed that, 'it matters not how you get it; if you steal it even, it would be admissible',[79] but the modern reality is that in some circumstances improperly obtained evidence may be excluded by the rules governing admissibility.

---

[78] 'Police Reform: A Better Way?' (2003) 167 JP 805.
[79] *R v Leatham* [1861–73] All ER Rep Ext 1646.

Confession evidence

Confession evidence is only admissible if the prosecution can show beyond reasonable doubt that it was not obtained: (a) by oppression of the person who made it;[80] or (b) in consequence of anything said or done that was likely to render it unreliable.[81] 'Oppression' is defined in section 76(8) of PACE to include 'torture, inhuman or degrading treatment, and the use or threat of violence (whether or not amounting to torture)'. Beyond this, the term carries its ordinary, natural meaning, and in *R v Fulling* the Court of Appeal adopted a definition from the *Oxford English Dictionary*:[82]

> the exercise of authority or power in a burdensome, harsh or wrongful manner; unjust or cruel treatment of subjects, inferiors, etc.; the imposition of unreasonable or unjust burdens.

In *R v Miller*, the Court of Appeal had no doubt that the confession of a defendant 'on the borderline of mental handicap' had been obtained by oppression:[83]

> We are bound to say that on hearing [the interview tape], each member of this Court was horrified. Miller was bullied and hectored. The officers...were not questioning him so much as shouting at him what they wanted him to say. Short of physical violence, it is hard to conceive of a more hostile and intimidating approach by officers to a suspect.

Miller had denied being involved in any offence over 300 times before finally 'confessing' to murder, and the finding that his confession had been obtained by oppression led to his conviction being quashed. It is rare, however, for a court to find that a confession has been obtained by oppression, and where police misconduct does result in confession evidence being excluded it is usually on the grounds of unreliability. Thus, in *R v Trussler*, a drug addict's confession was excluded because he had been denied access to a solicitor and had been interviewed after 18 hours in custody without a rest period.[84] In another case, it was held that confession evidence should have been excluded from the defendant's trial because his interview had not been properly recorded. Although this could not have caused him to make unreliable admissions,[85] it had deprived the court of cogent evidence as to what had happened during the interview, and this made it impossible to be sure that section 76(2)(b) had not been breached. The officers had also offered improper inducements to persuade the defendant to admit his guilt, and this was a further reason for excluding the evidence. By contrast, section 76 did not provide a basis for excluding the confession of a heroin addict who claimed that he would have said anything to get bail and get access to drugs: he

---

[80] PACE, s 76(2)(a). The term 'confession' is defined in s 82(1) to mean a statement wholly or partly adverse to the person who made it.

[81] Ibid, s 76(2)(b).

[82] [1987] QB 426 at 432, [1987] 2 All ER 65 at 69, *per* Lord Lane CJ. On the facts, telling the defendant that her lover had been having an affair was held not to constitute oppression.

[83] (1993) 97 Cr App R 99 at 103, *per* Lord Taylor CJ; cf. *R v Emmerson* (1991) 92 Cr App R 284 (an officer raising his voice and using bad language did not amount to oppression).

[84] [1988] Crim LR 446.   [85] *R v Delaney* (1989) 88 Cr App R 338.

had not been offered any inducements to confess and his admissions were not made 'in consequence of anything said or done'.[86]

Excluding evidence on the grounds of unfairness

Section 78 of PACE is another important provision and is potentially far wider in scope than section 76. It gives the court a discretion to exclude evidence on which the prosecution proposes to rely, where to admit it would create unfairness to the proceedings. It applies to both confession and non-confession evidence and may provide a basis for excluding evidence obtained in breach of PACE and the Codes of Practice. In *R v Samuel*, for example, the Court of Appeal quashed the conviction of a man who confessed after being denied access to a lawyer. The court noted that section 78 requires a judge to take account of how disputed evidence has been obtained, and in this case the police had acted in breach of a 'fundamental' right.[87] Improperly obtained evidence will not always be excluded, however, and the courts have often asserted that their exclusionary powers should not be used as a way of disciplining the police. Thus, in *R v Alladice*, it was not 'unfair' to admit a confession made in breach of the right to legal advice, because the defendant conceded that he had understood his rights and coped well with police interviews.[88] In *R v Mason*, evidence obtained by placing a covert listening device in the defendants' cells was also held to have been properly admitted.[89] The lack of regulation of such surveillance meant that Article 8 of the ECHR had undoubtedly been breached, but the defendants had not been oppressed or tricked into making their admissions and the use of the evidence did not render the proceedings unfair. This approach reflects that adopted in *Khan v UK*, in which the use of a similar device in a suspect's house was found to breach the right to respect for private life, but not the right to a fair trial under Article 6.[90]

Issues of propriety and reliability

It has been argued that, despite statements to the contrary, judges often adopt a disciplinary approach to the exclusion of evidence in practice. In one case a suspect confessed after he and his solicitor were falsely told that his fingerprints had been found on incriminating evidence. In quashing his conviction, the Court of Appeal stated that its decision was not about police discipline; yet it was undoubtedly influenced by the fact that the police had acted in bad faith and had deliberately set out to deceive.[91] In *R v Canale*, it was held that confession evidence should have been excluded because of

---

[86]   *R v Goldenberg* (1989) 88 Cr App R 285.

[87]   *R v Samuel* [1988] QB 615, [1988] 2 All ER 135.

[88]   (1988) 87 Cr App R 380; see also, *R v Dunford* (1990) 91 Cr App R 150.

[89]   *R v Mason (Adrian Craig)* [2002] EWCA Crim 385, [2002] 2 Cr App R 38.

[90]   (2001) 31 EHRR 45.

[91]   *R v Mason (Carl)* [1987] 3 All ER 481, [1988] 1 WLR 139; see Birch, 'The Pace Hots Up: Confessions and Confusions Under the 1984 Act' [1989] Crim LR 95 at 107.

'flagrant … deliberate and cynical' breaches of the recording requirements in PACE;[92] yet in *R v Sanghera (Rashpal)* the defendant's trial was held to have been fair despite the admission of evidence obtained during an improper search.[93] In the latter case the Court of Appeal noted that the police had acted in a bona fide manner, and that at the time of the search they had believed the defendant to be a victim rather than a suspect. As this last case demonstrates, judges are generally reluctant to exclude 'real' evidence on the grounds of impropriety, because there is often little doubt about its reliability. With confession evidence, on the other hand, the issues of propriety and reliability cannot always be so easily separated. It should also be remembered that section 78 is concerned with 'fairness to the proceedings', rather than simply with fairness to the accused: the court in *Sanghera* clearly felt that a greater injustice might be done if the evidence was excluded from the jury.[94] Similarly, evidence that a witness in *R v Forbes* had made an 'unequivocal' identification of the accused was held to have been fairly admitted. This was despite the fact that the police had breached Code of Practice D by failing to hold a formal identification parade.[95]

Abuse of process

Police misconduct may also provide the basis for an application to dismiss a prosecution on the grounds of an abuse of process.[96] The defendant in *DPP v Ara* had made an admission in the absence of a lawyer, and had subsequently made numerous unsuccessful requests to obtain a copy of the interview tape. His solicitor stated that, without the tape, he was unable to advise his client whether to accept a police caution, and the defendant was eventually charged with an offence of assault occasioning actual bodily harm. At a hearing before magistrates it was decided that it would be an abuse of process to proceed with the prosecution.[97] In general, it will also be an abuse of process to proceed with a case in which police entrapment has caused a suspect to commit a crime that would not otherwise have occurred,[98] a stance regarding which English common law has developed independently of the requirements of the European Convention on Human Rights, but which is fully compliant with Article 6.[99]

---

[92] *R v Canale* [1990] 2 All ER 187; see also, *R v Keenan* [1990] 2 QB 54, [1989] 3 All ER 598.

[93] [2001] 1 Cr App R 20, [2000] All ER (D) 1415.

[94] Compare *R v Veneroso* [2002] Crim LR 306: drugs found while officers were on premises illegally were held to be inadmissible on the basis of Article 8, ECHR. The judge indicated, however, that the outcome might have been different if semtex had been found.

[95] [2001] 1 AC 473, [2001] 1 All ER 686.

[96] *R v Horseferry Road Magistrates' Court, ex parte Bennett*; *sub nom Bennett v Horseferry Road Magistrates' Court* [1994] AC 42, [1993] 1 All ER 138.

[97] [2001] EWHC 493 (Admin), [2002] 1 WLR 815. The magistrates were held to have acted lawfully.

[98] *R v Looseley*; *sub nom Attorney-General's Reference (No 3 of 2000)* [2001] UKHL 53, [2001] 4 All ER 897; cf. *Smurthwaite v Gill* [1994] 1 All ER 898, (1994) 98 Cr App R 437 (no grounds for a stay of proceedings or the exclusion of evidence where officers had merely provided a suspect with the opportunity to offend).

[99] See p 582.

Criminal proceedings

Quite apart from its possible effect on the prosecution of a suspect, police misconduct can sometimes amount to a criminal offence in itself. A number of highly publicized miscarriages of justice have involved allegations of police misconduct,[100] and in some cases officers have been prosecuted for perjury or conspiracy to pervert the course of justice. In one recent case the Metropolitan Police were successfully prosecuted under health and safety laws, following the fatal shooting of a man wrongly suspected of being a suicide bomber.[101] More often, the legality of police conduct has been tested in prosecutions brought under section 89 of the Police Act 1996. This section makes it an offence to assault, or to resist or wilfully obstruct, a constable acting in the execution of his duty. The expression 'execution of duty' has a technical meaning for these purposes: an officer who infringes the rights of an individual in the absence of some legal authority will have acted outside the execution of his duty. The effect of such action is that any prosecution under section 89 must fail. Thus, a police officer who is trespassing and who is ejected from the premises using reasonable force will not succeed in a prosecution under section 89.[102] Similarly, a person who is being unlawfully restrained will not be committing a section 89 offence if he uses physical force to secure his release.[103] The key to each of these situations is the concept of unlawful interference with individual rights. If there is no interference with individual rights, or if there is some authority in law for the interference, the constable remains within the execution of duty.

Civil actions

Police misconduct may give rise to a civil action for assault, trespass, or false imprisonment. The legality of police detention may also be tested by applying for a writ of habeas corpus.

A chief constable is liable for any unlawful conduct of an officer acting in the performance of police functions.[104] Police authorities have a duty to indemnify chief constables in such cases, and at their discretion they may also indemnify any member of the police force against whom unlawful conduct is alleged.[105] What is within 'the performance of police functions' was considered in *Makanjuola* v *Commissioner of*

---

[100] Some of these are discussed in Walker and Starmer, *Miscarriages of Justice: A Review of Justice in Error* (OUP, 1999).

[101] See *The Guardian*, 1 November 2007. No individual officer was prosecuted but the force was fined £175,000 after being found guilty of exposing non-employees to health and safety risks, contrary to s 3(1) of the Health and Safety and Work etc. Act 1974.

[102] *Davis* v *Lisle* [1936] 2 KB 434, [1936] 2 All ER 213.

[103] *Kenlin* v *Gardiner* [1967] 2 QB 510, [1966] 3 All ER 931; *Collins* v *Wilcock* [1984] 3 All ER 374, [1984] 1 WLR 1172; cf *Mepstead* v *DPP* [1996] Crim LR 111 (a constable who took a person by the arm to calm him and to emphasize what was being said was acting within the execution of his duty).

[104] Police Act 1996, s 88(1).

[105] Ibid, s 88(2), (4).

Police for the Metropolis,[106] in which an off-duty officer committed a serious sexual assault after using his warrant card to gain entry to premises. The chief constable was held not liable in damages for the assault, because it was not a fraudulent performance of what the constable had the authority to do honestly. Exemplary damages were awarded against the constable. The fact remains, though, that the effectiveness of the civil law remedy may depend upon the liability of the chief constable, since an individual officer may be of modest means and not worth suing.

Unless a police authority is itself in breach of a statutory or common law obligation, it will not be directly liable for the actions of its officers. Moreover, it owes no general duty of care to members of the public in respect of the investigation and prevention of crime.[107] However, a duty of care may be established if a special relationship with a particular member of the public can be identified, and in *Swinney* v *Chief Constable of the Northumbria Police*, it was said to be arguable that a special relationship had arisen between the police and a police informant.[108] Police officers and police authorities also have a duty under the Human Rights Act 1998 to act compatibly with Convention rights, and at least some of these rights may be breached by a failure to respond to a 'real and immediate risk' to an identified individual.[109] In one recent case, for example, the High Court awarded damages to the parents of a witness murdered following inadequate police protection.[110]

Judicial review

It has already been seen that the exercise of police discretion is judicially reviewable.[111] However, the restricted role of the courts in judicial review means that this is not always a satisfactory way of challenging police actions, quite apart from the very substantial cost of mounting judicial review proceedings.

Complaints against the police

The police complaints system provides a non-legal mechanism for dealing with allegations of police misconduct. Pressure for such a system led to the creation of the Police Complaints Board in 1976,[112] but this body was widely regarded as unsatisfactory because the investigation of complaints was handled by the police themselves. In

---

[106] [1992] 3 All ER 617.

[107] *Hill* v *Chief Constable of West Yorkshire* [1989] AC 53, [1988] 2 All ER 238.

[108] [1997] QB 464, [1996] 3 All ER 449: the police were accused of allowing the informant's identity to fall into the public domain.

[109] *Osman* v *UK* (2000) 29 EHRR 245. This case concerned the failure of the police to prevent the death of a man who was murdered by his son's teacher. The teacher was known to have formed an obsessive attachment to the son, and the European Court of Human Rights confirmed that Article 2 may impose a positive duty to protect life. It did not, however, find a breach of Article 2 on the facts.

[110] *Van Colle* v *Chief Constable of Hertfordshire* [2006] EWHC 360 (QB), [2006] 3 All ER 963. The £50,000 awarded was reduced to £25,000 on appeal: [2007] EWCA Civ 325, [2007] 1 WLR 1821, [2007] 3 All ER 122.

[111] See p 534.   [112] Police Act 1976.

an attempt to address this concern, the Police and Criminal Evidence Act 1984 established a new regime under the supervision of the Police Complaints Authority.[113] However, although the creation of this new, independent body was generally welcomed, critics pointed out that its role was largely supervisory and that there was still no independent mechanism by which complaints could actually be investigated. As the Macpherson Inquiry noted in 1999:[114] '[The] investigation of police officers by their own or another Police Service is widely regarded as unjust, and does not inspire public confidence.'

The Independent Police Complaints Commission

In response to criticism in the Macpherson Report and elsewhere, the Police Complaints Authority was replaced by the Independent Police Complaints Commission (IPCC).[115] The IPCC was formally launched in April 2004, and it handles complaints about both officers and civilians who serve with the police. It is also required to record incidents involving criminal conduct on the part of such persons, in addition to recording behaviour justifying disciplinary proceedings.[116] Alongside those who have experienced or witnessed alleged misconduct, any other person who has been adversely affected by it has the right to complain to the Commission.[117] The Commission itself has a chairman and fifteen regional commissioners,[118] and it has the power to temporarily second officers from any police force in the United Kingdom.[119] Chief police officers have a duty to cooperate with any IPCC investigation, and they must ensure that the Commission is provided with access to police premises and relevant evidence.[120] Most complaints continue to be investigated locally by individual police forces, but the IPCC has the power to supervise or manage investigations where appropriate.[121] A report must be submitted to the Commission at the end of any investigation that it has supervised, managed, or conducted, and a copy of this report must also be sent to the relevant police force.[122] The complainant has a right to be informed about the progress and outcome of the investigation,[123] and if evidence of criminal activity or misconduct is found, criminal or disciplinary proceedings will normally follow.

Police powers

Police officers derive their powers from a wide range of sources, both common law and statutory. The detail of such powers is beyond the scope of this book, but a discussion of the general framework is set out below. A crucial issue is whether the system

---

[113] The system was subsequently governed by provisions in the Police Act 1996.
[114] *Report of the Stephen Lawrence Inquiry*, Cm 4262-I (HMSO, 1999) at ch 47, para 58.
[115] Police Reform Act 2002, s 9.   [116] Ibid, s 10.
[117] Ibid, s 12. A complaint may also be made by a representative acting on behalf of such a person.
[118] The minimum requirement is for a Chairman and ten Commissioners: Ibid, s 9(2).
[119] Ibid, Sch 2, para 6.   [120] Ibid, ss 17 and 18.   [121] Ibid, Sch 3, para 15.
[122] Ibid, Sch 3, para 22.   [123] Section 20.

achieves the right balance between protecting the public, on the one hand, and maintaining safeguards for individuals, on the other. The need to secure this balance has been highlighted by several miscarriage of justice cases, and it has assumed particular importance since the rights to liberty and to a fair trial were given explicit recognition by the Human Rights Act 1998.

Historically, police powers were piecemeal and ill-defined, creating problems for both the police and suspects. The Royal Commission on Criminal Procedure, which reported in 1981,[124] carried out a major review of the investigative powers of the police, and the questioning and treatment of suspects. The Report provided the basis for the Police and Criminal Evidence Act 1984 (PACE), although not all of its recommendations were accepted in their entirety.

General considerations

Before looking at the legal framework in more detail, certain matters merit further discussion: (a) the common law concept of breach of the peace; (b) the concepts of 'reasonable suspicion' and 'reasonable belief'; (c) the use of force in the exercise of police powers; and (d) the role of the Codes of Practice.

Breaches of the peace

At common law, a police officer is entitled to take any action necessary to prevent an imminent breach of the peace or to restrain a breach of the peace that is actually occurring.[125] Where a breach of the peace has already happened and there is a likelihood of recurrence, it would appear that an officer may also take reasonable steps to prevent such recurrence. In *Chief Constable of Cleveland* v *McGrogan*,[126] it was held that the police had not acted unlawfully in detaining a man for almost twenty-four hours, because there was a real apprehension that if released sooner he would have committed a further breach of the peace within a short time. Definitions of what constitutes a breach of the peace have varied,[127] but it is now generally accepted that the correct approach is that identified in *R* v *Howell*:[128]

> We cannot accept that there can be a breach of the peace unless there has been an act done or threatened to be done which either actually harms a person, or in his presence his property, or is likely to cause such harm, or which puts somebody in fear of such harm being done.

Once the likelihood of an imminent breach of the peace is established, a police officer has the power to take reasonable steps to prevent it from happening or continuing.

---

[124] Cmnd 8092 (HMSO, 1981).   [125] *Albert* v *Lavin* [1982] AC 546, [1981] 3 All ER 878.

[126] [2002] EWCA Civ 86, [2002] 1 FLR 707.

[127] See, e.g., the approach of Lord Denning in *R* v *Chief Constable of Devon & Cornwall, ex parte Central Electricity Generating Board* [1982] QB 458 at 471, [1981] 3 All ER 826 at 832.

[128] [1982] QB 416 at 426, [1981] 3 All ER 383 at 389, *per* Watkins LJ.

This may involve restraining and temporarily detaining an individual,[129] removing an item from his possession[130] or entering on to private property.[131] It may also mean requiring an individual to carry on his activities elsewhere or in a different way,[132] or requiring him not to travel along a certain route.[133] However, regardless of whether an officer is seeking to make an arrest or to take other preventative action, a breach of the peace must reasonably be believed to be imminent and the steps taken to prevent it must be no more than necessary. Thus, in the recent case of *Laporte*, it was held that when officers searched three coaches carrying anti-war protesters and concluded that a breach of the peace was not imminent, they had no power to prevent the coaches from continuing to the site of a demonstration or to compel the protesters to return to London with a police escort.[134]

Where a breach of the peace *is* reasonably apprehended, a person may be arrested and taken before a magistrates' court, where he may then be bound over to be of good behaviour and to keep the peace.[135] This binding-over power has been criticized by the European Court of Human Rights for its uncertainty,[136] and the Law Commission has recommended its abolition.[137] However, a recent Home Office consultation paper argued that 'it would be better to resolve the underlying issues of certainty and fairness', rather than to remove the power altogether.[138] It also recommended that the sanction for non-compliance should be a fine rather than imprisonment.[139]

It will be apparent that, alongside the extensive body of police powers conferred by Acts of Parliament, the police also have a wide measure of discretionary power that is still governed by the common law. It will be equally apparent that the use of this power can impinge upon conduct that in itself is perfectly lawful. In the Irish case of *Humphries* v *Connor*, for example, an officer was held to have acted lawfully when he removed a political emblem from the lapel of a woman who was attracting a hostile crowd.[140] More recently, however, the courts have emphasized that where a person is

---

[129] *Albert* v *Lavin* [1982] AC 546, [1981] 3 All ER 878.

[130] *Humphries* v *Connor* (1864) 17 ICLR 1.

[131] *McConnell* v *Chief Constable of the Greater Manchester Police* [1990] 1 All ER 423, [1990] 1 WLR 364.

[132] *Duncan* v *Jones* [1936] 1 KB 218, [1935] All ER Rep 710; *Piddington* v *Bates* [1960] 3 All ER 660, [1961] 1 WLR 162.

[133] *Moss* v *McLachlan* (1984) 149 JP 167.

[134] *R (on the application of Laporte)* v *Chief Constable of Gloucester* [2006] UKHL 55, [2007] 2 AC 105, [2007] 2 WLR 46.

[135] For a review of the law, see Law Commission Working Paper 103.

[136] See *Steel* v *UK* (1999) 28 EHRR 603. The Court also ruled that binding over proceedings must be regarded as 'criminal proceedings' for the purposes of the Convention. Note, however, that breach of the peace in itself is not a crime: *Williamson* v *Chief Constable of West Midlands* [2003] EWCA Civ 337, [2004] 1 WLR 14.

[137] *Binding Over* (Law Commission No 222, 1994).

[138] Home Office, *Bind Overs: A Power for the 21st Century* (HMSO, 2003) Consultation Paper, at para 9.4.

[139] Ibid, at para 7.10.7.

[140] (1864) 17 ICLR 1: the emblem in question was an orange lily.

not acting unlawfully and is not himself 'threatening' to breach the peace, the power of arrest should only be used exceptionally.[141]

KEY ISSUE

The use of the breach-of-the-peace power may contravene the Human Rights Act if it interferes with a Convention right in a manner that is not proportionate to a legitimate purpose. For example, detention for longer than is necessary to prevent an imminent breach of the peace or to bring a person before magistrates could amount to an unlawful interference with the right to liberty. Moreover, if through such detention a person is prevented from participating in a demonstration, there may also be an interference with the rights to freedom of expression and freedom of assembly. Whether the detention is unlawful in this respect will depend on whether it can be justified under Articles 10(2) and 11(2) of the ECHR.[142]

The Convention does provide an important limit on what would otherwise be unacceptably wide and unlimited powers.

❓ Questions

1. Do you think the concept of breach of the peace gives the police too much discretionary power?

2. To what extent have the deficiencies of the rules relating to breaches of the peace been remedied by the application of the standards created by the European Convention on Human Rights?

Reasonable suspicion and reasonable belief

Most police powers depend for their rightful exercise on the officer having a particular state of mind at the relevant time. The usual requirement is for a 'reasonable suspicion' of certain facts,[143] and this provides an essential safeguard against the arbitrary use of power. In *Shaaban Bin Hussien* v *Chong Fook Kam*,[144] Lord Devlin observed that 'suspicion in its ordinary meaning is a state of conjecture or surmise where proof is lacking: "I suspect but cannot prove"'. In the later case of *Castorina* v *Chief Constable of Surrey*,[145] the Court of Appeal stated that an honest belief was not a necessary precondition. By contrast, an arrest that is based solely on an honest belief that an offence has been committed may not satisfy the requirements of Article 5 of the ECHR.[146]

---

[141] *R (on the application of Laporte)* v *Chief Constable of Gloucester* [2006] UKHL 55, [2007] 2 AC 105, [2007] 2 WLR 46; *Foulkes* v *Chief Constable for Merseyside* [1998] 3 All ER 705, [1998] 2 FLR 789; *Bibby* v *Chief Constable of Essex* (2000) 164 JP 297.

[142] *R (on the application of Laporte)* v *Chief Constable of Gloucester* [2006] UKHL 55, [2007] 2 AC 105, [2007] 2 WLR 46.

[143] For examples of exceptions, see the powers conferred by the Criminal Justice and Public Order Act 1994, s 60 and the Terrorism Act 2000, s 44.

[144] [1970] AC 942 at 948, [1969] 3 All ER 1626 at 1630.   [145] [1988] NLJR 180.

[146] *Fox, Campbell and Hartley* v *UK* (1991) 13 EHRR 157; cf. *Murray* v *UK* (1995) 19 EHRR 193 (mere suspicion sufficient in circumstances in which officers could demonstrate an objective basis). For further discussion of Article 5, see p 186.

Whether or not a reasonable suspicion exists is a matter to be determined objectively by the court. In order to be reasonable a suspicion must be based on evidence, but this need not be evidence that would be acceptable in a court of law. A suspicion may also be reasonable if based on information from an informant or a fellow officer; it need not be based entirely on the officer's own observations.[147] However, in the context of stop-and-search powers, PACE Code of Practice A makes it clear that a suspicion will not be reasonable if it is based solely on personal factors:[148]

> Reasonable suspicion can never be supported on the basis of personal factors alone without reliable supporting intelligence or information or some specific behaviour by the person concerned. For example, a person's race, age, appearance, or the fact that the person is known to have a previous conviction, cannot be used alone or in combination with each other as the reason for searching that person. Reasonable suspicion cannot be based on generalizations or stereotypical images of certain groups or categories of people as more likely to be involved in criminal activity.

Force
The law allows reasonable force to be used, where necessary, in the exercise of police powers. Section 3 of the Criminal Law Act 1967 provides that a person may use such force as is reasonable in the circumstances, to: (a) prevent crime; or (b) effect or assist in the lawful arrest of an offender, suspected offender, or person unlawfully at large. In addition, section 117 of the Police and Criminal Evidence Act 1984 provides that any power under the Act may be exercised using no more force than is reasonably necessary. Both provisions permit the use of force against property as well as persons. For example, an officer seeking to execute a lawful power of arrest may use reasonable force to gain entry on to premises, as long as he or she can demonstrate the necessity of his or her actions.[149]

Codes of Practice
Section 66 of PACE authorizes the Home Secretary to make Codes of Practice dealing with the different stages of police investigations. Codes have been introduced dealing with the exercise of stop-and-search powers (Code A), the execution of search powers (Code B), the treatment and questioning of suspects (Code C), the identification of suspects (Code D), the tape-recording of police interviews (Code E), the visual recording of interviews (Code F), statutory powers of arrest (Code G), and the detention, treatment and questioning of terror suspects (Code H).[150]

---

[147] *O'Hara* v *Chief Constable of the Royal Ulster Constabulary* [1997] AC 286, [1997] 1 All ER 129; *O'Hara* v *UK* (2002) 34 EHRR 32.

[148] At para 2.2.

[149] *O'Loughlin* v *Chief Constable of Essex* [1998] 1 WLR 374: on the facts of the case the use of force was not lawful, as the officer had not first made it clear that he wanted to enter to make an arrest.

[150] Code F was issued under the authority of s 60A of PACE. The latest version of Codes A–E came into effect on 1 February 2008. The current Codes F and G came into effect on 1 January 2006, and Code H has been in force since 24 July 2006.

The PACE Codes are important to both the practitioner and the police, and, as noted above, if there is a 'significant and substantial' breach of the Codes, evidence obtained as a result of that breach may be excluded from consideration by the courts.[151] A breach of the Codes can also form the basis for disciplinary action against an officer.

Stop-and-search powers

Stop-and-search powers are amongst the most controversial of police powers. On the one hand, they authorize action that some consider necessary for the prevention and detection of crime. On the other, they provide the potential for misuse and for the harassment of minority groups. Before 1984 there existed a wide range of stop-and-search powers, that were exercisable on different criteria, in different circumstances, and by different people. However, the Royal Commission on Criminal Procedure expressed concern at the potential for these powers to be abused,[152] and following its recommendations general powers of stop and search were included in the Police and Criminal Evidence Act 1984.

Section 1 of PACE provides that any person or vehicle may be detained and searched by a constable if he has reasonable grounds to suspect that he will find stolen or prohibited articles.[153] An offensive weapon constitutes a 'prohibited article' for these purposes, and this term covers any article made or adapted for causing injury to a person, or any article intended to cause injury by the person who is carrying it with him.[154] The other articles prohibited by section 1 are articles made, adapted or intended for use in connection with burglary, theft, taking a motor vehicle without authority, obtaining property by deception, or destroying or damaging property.[155] Prohibited fireworks and articles with a blade or point may also be the subject of a stop and search, even if they do not constitute offensive weapons.[156]

The power to stop and search is exercisable in any place to which the public have access,[157] and any stolen or prohibited article found may be seized.[158] There is no specific power to seize any other item discovered, but an officer can make an arrest if he finds anything that he reasonably believes to be evidence of a crime.[159] Care must be taken to ensure that the stop-and-search powers are not abused, and the requirement for reasonable suspicion is thus an important safeguard. In addition, before carrying out a search the officer must inform the person concerned of his name, the name of the police station to which he is attached, the object of the search, and his grounds

---

[151] See p 424, *ante*. See also, *R v Walsh* (1990) 91 Cr App R 161, [1989] Crim LR 822; *R v Aspinall* [1999] 2 Cr App R 115, (1999) 96(7) LSG 35.

[152] Cmnd 8092 (HMSO, 1981), at p 1011.

[153] Section 163 of the Road Traffic Act 1988 provides uniformed constables and traffic officers with a general power to require a person driving a vehicle on a road to stop. It does not in itself authorize the detention or search of the vehicle, although in some circumstances the power to detain may be implied by the courts: see *Lodwick* v *Sanders* [1985] 1 All ER 577, [1985] 1 WLR 382.

[154] Sections 1(7)(a) and 1(9).   [155] Sections 1(7)(b) and 1(8), as amended.

[156] Sections 1(8A) and 1(8B).   [157] Section 1(1).   [158] Section 1(6).

[159] Powers of arrest are discussed at p 452.

for proposing to make it. If he is not in uniform, he must also provide documentary evidence that he is, in fact, a police officer.[160] A further safeguard is the requirement for the officer to make a written record of the search, either at the time or as soon as practicable afterwards.[161]

The person searched is entitled to a copy of this record if he requests one within twelve months. Sir Ronnie Flanagan's recent *Review of Policing* recommended using new technology to streamline these recording requirements. Provisions in the Crime and Security Act 2010 do this in detailed respects,[162] although the government's stated desire to reduce 'police bureaucracy' should not be a justification for reducing necessary safeguards.

Not all stop-and-search powers are so precisely circumscribed. Where a senior officer anticipates violence in a particular locality, he can authorize what amounts to a random power of stop and search for a period not exceeding twenty-four hours.[163] Under such an authorization, a constable may stop and search any person or vehicle for offensive weapons or dangerous instruments. The officer does not need to reasonably suspect the person of being in possession of such an article, and thus for a limited period there is a power to stop and search that is effectively unchallengeable. An even more extensive power may be authorized under section 44 of the Terrorism Act 2000. This power can only be authorized by an officer of at least the rank of assistant chief constable,[164] and only where it is considered expedient for the prevention of acts of terrorism.[165] Once such an authorization is in place, any person or vehicle in the locality may be searched for articles that could be used in connection with terrorism.[166] The authorization can last for up to twenty-eight days and may be renewed at the end of this period. Section 45(1)(b) expressly states that the power may be exercised 'whether or not the constable has grounds for suspecting the presence of articles of that kind', and doubts have been raised about the compatibility of such powers with Article 5 of the ECHR. However, the House of Lords has held that stop-and-search powers will not normally engage Article 5 at all, on the basis that the brief period of detention involved does not amount to a deprivation of liberty.[167]

---

[160] Section 2.   [161] Section 3.

[162] *The Review of Policing: Final Report* (HMSO, 2008), at para. 5.59. The report also recommended scrapping the form used to record 'stop and account' encounters, and replacing it with digital record-keeping and a requirement to issue a simple receipt: see paras 5.60–62.

[163] Criminal Justice and Public Order Act 1994, s 60. In future, senior officers will also be able to authorize searches where it is reasonably believed that: (a) an incident involving serious violence has taken place; and (b) it is expedient to issue an authorization in order to find a dangerous instrument or offensive weapon used in it—see s 60(1)(aa), as inserted by the Serious Crime Act 2007.

[164] Or, in the case of the Metropolitan Police district and the City of London, an officer of at least the rank of commander.

[165] In *R (on the application of Gillan) v Commissioner of Police for the Metropolis* [2006] UKHL 12, [2006] 2 AC 307, [2006] 4 All ER 1041, the House of Lords confirmed that 'expedient' does not mean the same as 'necessary' for these purposes.

[166] Section 45(1)(a).

[167] *R (on the application of Gillan) v Commissioner of Police for the Metropolis* [2006] UKHL 12, [2006] 2 AC 307, [2006] 4 All ER 1041.

The exercise of stop-and-search powers is subject to more detailed guidance in PACE Code of Practice A.[168] This provides that a person searched under section 1 of PACE cannot be required to remove any clothing in public other than an outer coat, jacket, or gloves, although a person searched under the terrorism powers may also be required to remove headgear or footwear. The Code also makes it clear that for searches that require a reasonable suspicion, that suspicion cannot be based on personal factors alone unless there is reliable supporting intelligence or information or some specific behaviour by the person concerned.

PACE does not affect the capacity of an officer to speak to or question a person in the normal course of his duties, as long as there is no attempt to detain and no element of compulsion.[169] Frequently, routine questioning will provide the reasonable suspicion needed to justify detention for the purposes of a search. However, the converse is equally true: the Act allows reasonable suspicion to be eliminated by questioning, and in these circumstances there is no obligation to search. A written record of the encounter should still be made, however, and police officers and staff are also required to record any incident in which a person in a public place is asked to account for himself.[170]

KEY ISSUE

Studies have repeatedly shown that black and Asian people are disproportionately more likely to be stopped and searched than those from other ethnic groups.[171] Moreover, research carried out by one police force showed that a reduction in the use of stop and search had had little effect on levels of crime in the area: the force's detection rate had actually increased during the same period.[172] Throughout the United Kingdom the proportion of searches that result in an arrest is consistently low, and Lustgarten has concluded that 'it is hard to see how a suspicion which misfires so often and so consistently can be credibly described as "reasonable"'.[173] Similar concerns have been expressed in 2010 by government and civil liberties groups about the small number of arrests and charges that have followed the use of stop-and-search powers under the Terrorism Act 2005.

❓ Questions

1. What is the justification for the use of stop-and-search powers?

2. What dangers do they create?

---

[168] The latest version of the Code came into force on 1 February 2008.

[169] For the general principles, see *Rice v Connolly* [1966] 2 QB 414, [1966] 2 All ER 649 (refusal to answer police questions not a wilful obstruction of a constable acting in the execution of duty).

[170] See Code of Practice A, paras 4.7 and 4.12.

[171] *Report of the Stephen Lawrence Inquiry*, Cm. 4262-I (HMSO, 1999) at para. 45.8; Miller, Bland and Quinton, *The Impact of Stops and Searches on Crime and the Community*, Police Research Series Paper No 130 (HMSO, 2000), ch 4; Home Office, *Statistics on Race and the Criminal Justice System* (HMSO, 2000), ch 3.

[172] Lustgarten, 'The Future of Stop and Search' [2002] Crim LR 603, at 614.

[173] Ibid, at 615.

Surveillance

The police sometimes need to use surreptitious means of investigation, and this may involve the use of technical devices such as eavesdropping equipment. Police telephone tapping has been regulated by statute since 1986,[174] but until 1997 there was no statutory regime covering the use of other forms of surveillance. Covert surveillance interfering with property or wireless telegraphy is now regulated by Part IV of the Police Act 1997. Section 93(1) of the Act provides that an 'authorizing officer'[175] may authorize 'the taking of such action as he may specify', if he believes that:

(a) the action is necessary for the purpose of preventing or detecting serious crime;[176] and

(b) the taking of the action is proportionate to what it seeks to achieve.

Authorizations relating to property used mainly as a dwelling, hotel bedroom, or office premises must be approved by a Commissioner appointed under section 91 of the Act. Authorizations that are likely to result in the acquisition of legal, journalistic, or confidential personal information also require approval.[177]

Other forms of covert surveillance are subject to the provisions of the Regulation of Investigatory Powers Act 2000. Surveillance involving interference with postal or communications systems is governed by Part 1 of the Act. Under section 5, the Secretary of State may issue a warrant for the interception of communications if he believes that it is necessary for national security, for the prevention and detection of crime, or for safeguarding the economic well-being of the United Kingdom. A warrant can only be requested by one of the high-ranking officers listed in section 6, and section 17 prevents intercept material from being disclosed or adduced in connection with legal proceedings. The effect of the latter provision is that such surveillance can be used for intelligence purposes but is inadmissible as evidence at any trial. In this respect it can be argued that the Act fails to satisfy the ECHR with regard to both the fair trial requirements in Article 6 and the privacy provisions in Article 8.[178] However, having previously ruled out a change in the law, the government has apparently had a rethink and, following the recommendations of the Chilcot Report,[179] it is now proposing to allow intercept evidence to be used in criminal trials.[180]

---

[174] Interception of Communications Act 1985; since repealed and replaced by the more extensive provisions in the Police Act 1997 and the Regulation of Investigatory Powers Act 2000.

[175] A chief constable or one of the other high-ranking officials listed in s 93(5).

[176] 'Serious crime' is defined for these purposes by s 93(4).   [177] Section 97.

[178] See Ormerod and McKay, 'Telephone Intercepts and their Admissibility' [2004] Crim LR 15. Section 17 has been interpreted as allowing a limited enquiry where it is alleged that communications within a private system have been intercepted with the consent of the owner: *Attorney-General's Reference (No 5 of 2002)* [2004] UKHL 20, [2005] 1 AC 167, [2004] 4 All ER 901.

[179] *Privy Council Review of Intercept as Evidence: Report to the Prime Minister and the Home Secretary*, Cm 7324 (HMSO, 2008).

[180] Gordon Brown MP (Prime Minister), 471 HC Official Report (6th series), col 959, 6 February 2008.

Part II of the 2000 Act regulates the use of covert human intelligence and other forms of surveillance. Intrusive surveillance—that which involves physical intrusion on to residential premises or into a private vehicle—can only be authorized by the Secretary of State or a 'senior authorizing officer'. The person making the authorization must be satisfied that such intrusion is necessary for national security, for the prevention and detection of crime, or for safeguarding the economic well-being of the United Kingdom.[181] Non-intrusive surveillance can be authorized on a much wider range of grounds, and authorization can be granted can by a police superintendent or by certain other senior officials designated by the Secretary of State.[182] Rules for the conduct of covert operations involving human intelligence sources are set out in section 29 of the Act.

Arrest

Arrest is a matter of fact rather than a legal concept, although it does have legal consequences. The essence of arrest is the deprivation of liberty, as explained by Lord Diplock in *Holgate-Mohammed* v *Duke*:[183]

> [A]rrest is a continuing act: it starts with the arrester taking a person into his custody (by action or words restraining him from moving elsewhere beyond the arrester's control) and it continues until the person so restrained is either released from custody, or…is remanded in custody by the magistrate's judicial act.

In that case an officer arrested a person on reasonable suspicion of burglary because he wanted to continue questioning her at the police station. As the power to arrest existed, its use to facilitate further questioning was held to be a legitimate use of police discretion: although the suspect could not simply be 'detained' for the purpose of questioning, there was nothing to prevent the officer from exercising a lawful power of arrest in order to achieve this objective.[184]

In order for an arrest to be lawful, the arresting officer must be able to point to a specific power of arrest, and he or she must comply with any necessary procedural requirements.

Powers of arrest

An arrest may be lawfully made with or without a warrant. In respect of the former, the Magistrates' Courts Act 1980 confers a power on magistrates to issue a warrant of arrest.[185] In relation to arrest without warrant, the Police and Criminal Evidence Act 1984 made radical changes. Section 26 repealed all statutory powers authorizing arrest without a warrant, with the exception of twenty-one specific powers that were

---

[181] Sections 26(3) and 32.

[182] Sections 26(2) and 28; Regulation of Investigatory Powers (Directed Surveillance and Covert Human Intelligence Sources) Order 2003, SI 2003/3171.

[183] [1984] AC 437, [1984] 1 All ER 1054.

[184] But see the discussion of the amended s 24 of PACE at p 453.   [185] Section 1.

expressly preserved by Schedule 2.[186] The common law power to arrest for breach of the peace was also preserved.[187]

Before 2006, section 24 of PACE conferred general powers of arrest in respect of serious or 'arrestable' offences. These powers applied in relation to past, present and future offences, and in some situations were available to both police officers and members of the public. By contrast, an arrest without a warrant for a 'non-arrestable' offence could only be made by a police officer, and only where one or more of the 'general arrest conditions' set out in section 25 of the Act were satisfied.

A constable's powers of arrest under the new regime

In 2006, amendments made by the Serious Organised Crime and Police Act 2005 were implemented. The principal effect of these amendments is to remove the idea of a distinction between arrestable and non-arrestable offences and to make all arrests subject to a test of necessity. The circumstances in which a citizen's arrest can be made have also been narrowed.

In many respects, the powers conferred on constables by the amended section 24 are unchanged. Thus, a constable has the power to arrest without a warrant:

(a) any person who has already committed an offence, or who is suspected on reasonable grounds of having done so;

(b) any person who is (or is reasonably suspected to be) in the act of committing an offence; or

(c) any person who is (or is reasonably suspected to be) about to commit an offence.

A constable can also make an arrest if he reasonably suspects that an offence has been committed and that a particular individual was responsible. As under the previous system, this means that it is possible for an officer to make a lawful arrest in circumstances in which it later transpires that no crime has occurred.

Whereas the original section 24 applied only to 'arrestable' offences, the power set out in the amended provision can be exercised in respect of *any* offence. It is, however, now subject to a test of necessity: in order for an arrest without a warrant to be made, the constable must have reasonable grounds for believing that the arrest is necessary for one of the reasons listed in section 24(5). Most of these reasons replicate the general arrest conditions previously found in section 25. Thus, an arrest may be necessary:

(a) to enable the name or address of the person in question to be ascertained (in cases in which the constable does not know and cannot readily ascertain these details, or has reasonable grounds for doubting whether details provided by the person are genuine);

---

[186]   A number of these powers have been repealed subsequently, and new statutory arrest powers have also been created: s 41 of the Terrorism Act 2000, for example, empowers a constable to arrest a person 'whom he reasonably suspects to be a terrorist'.

[187]   This was the effect of PACE, s 25(6).

(b) to prevent the person in question from causing injury to himself or another, suffering physical injury, causing loss or damage to property, committing an offence against public decency, or causing an unlawful obstruction of the highway; or

(c) to protect a child or other vulnerable person from the person in question.

The other lawful reasons for making an arrest under section 24 had no equivalent under the old system:

(d) to allow the prompt and effective investigation of the offence or the person's conduct; or

(e) to prevent the prosecution of an offence from being hindered by the person's disappearance.

It will be apparent that reason (d) in particular is potentially very wide, and in this respect the new section 24 appears to extend the arrest powers available to police officers. On the other hand, a constable's scope for exercising these powers is now limited by the requirement of necessity, and it could be argued that the overall effect of this is to restrict the discretion outlined in *Holgate-Mohammed* v *Duke*.[188]

> 'Necessary' means that there is no alternative to arrest; that enabling or preventing, as the case may be, one or more of the arrest conditions set out in s 24(5), cannot be achieved by any other means short of arrest. Thus the extremely broad common law discretion, whether or not to arrest, appears to have been replaced by a much narrower statutory discretion, limited by the necessity requirement and the arrest conditions...[189]

Guidance as to the circumstances in which an arrest might be considered necessary is set out in Code of Practice G, but it remains to be seen how the new criteria will be interpreted by the courts.

Citizens' arrests

The arrest powers of the private citizen have always been more limited than those available to police officers, since they only apply where it is reasonably believed that a person has committed or is in the act of committing an offence. Thus, a citizen has no power to arrest a person who is *about* to commit an offence, and he will also be acting unlawfully if he makes an arrest in the *mistaken* belief that an offence has already been committed. In *R* v *Self*,[190] for example, the defendant was charged with assault to escape lawful arrest. The arrest had been made by a citizen assisting a store detective, but the defendant was able to show that he had not in fact stolen the goods in question. Since no offence had been committed by anyone, the arrest was held to be unlawful and the defendant was not guilty of the assault.

---

[188] See p 452.

[189] Austin, 'The New Powers of Arrest: Plus CA Change: More of the Same or Major Change?' [2007] Crim LR 459 at 464.

[190] [1992] 3 All ER 476, [1992] 1 WLR 657. See also: *Walters* v *WH Smith & Son Ltd* [1914] 1 KB 595, [1911–13] All ER Rep 170.

The recent amendments to PACE mean that the scope for making a citizen's arrest has been further restricted. The effect of the new section 24A is that citizens only have a power of arrest in respect of indictable offences, and this power may only be exercised where it is not reasonably practicable for a constable to make the arrest instead. In addition, the person making the arrest must have reasonable grounds for believing that his actions are necessary to prevent injury, to prevent loss of or damage to property, or to prevent the suspect from making off before a constable can assume responsibility for him.

Even before these reforms it was unwise for a citizen to attempt an arrest unless he was absolutely sure of his facts. Now, in addition to being sure that an offence has been (or is being) committed, he also needs to know whether the offence in question is indictable and he must make an assessment as to whether it would be practicable for a police officer to make the arrest instead. As one critic has suggested, these changes 'will deter all but the most foolhardy citizens from exercising the power, and impose upon those citizens who need to exercise it, unacceptable risks of consequent liability'.[191]

The mechanics of arrest

Even where a power of arrest exists, an arrest will only be lawful if the person arrested is told: (a) that he is under arrest;[192] and (b) on what grounds he has been arrested. This information must be given at the time of the arrest or as soon as practicable afterwards.[193] Thus if a suspect manages to escape before a constable is able to explain the grounds for his arrest, the arrest will nevertheless be lawful. Once the suspect is recaptured and the situation is under control, any further delay in explaining the grounds will render the arrest invalid, but only from that moment onwards.[194] Similarly, where an arrest is initially unlawful because of a failure to comply with these requirements, it will become lawful subsequently once the reasons for the arrest are given. In *Lewis and another* v *Chief Constable of the South Wales Constabulary*,[195] the Court of Appeal identified arrest as a continuing act: the claimants' action for damages failed because they had only been unlawfully detained for a short period.

The statement of reasons does not have to specify a particular crime, or give a technical definition of the offence charged. What is needed is sufficient information to enable the arrested person to know why his liberty is being interfered with. In *Abbassy* v *Commissioner of Police*,[196] the plaintiff was told that he was being arrested for 'unlawful possession' of a vehicle. He had been asked four times about ownership of the vehicle, but had responded in a rude and abusive fashion. Police inquiries later showed that he was in fact authorized to drive the vehicle. The claimant was charged with wilfully obstructing a constable in the execution of his duty, contrary to what is now section 89 of the Police Act 1996. The charges were later dropped and

---

[191] Austin [2007] Crim LR 459 at 438.   [192] Section 28(1).

[193] Section 28(3).   [194] *DPP* v *Hawkins* [1988] 3 All ER 673, [1988] 1 WLR 1166.

[195] [1991] 1 All ER 206.

[196] [1990] 1 All ER 193, [1990] 1 WLR 385. The decision confirms that the approach outlined in the pre-PACE case of *Christie* v *Leachinsky* [1947] AC 573, [1947] 1 All ER 567 is still correct.

the claimant sought damages for unlawful arrest and false imprisonment. However, the court ruled that it had been made clear to him that the arrest was for unlawful possession of the vehicle. The fact that the officer had not specifically mentioned the vehicle in his statement of reasons was irrelevant. The judge had therefore misdirected the jury on a matter of law, and a retrial was ordered. The claimant in *Taylor* v *Chief Constable of Thames Valley Police*[197] was a 10-year-old child who was arrested 'on suspicion of violent disorder': he had been throwing stones whilst participating in a demonstration. The child brought an action for false imprisonment and trespass to the person, alleging that he had not been given sufficient information for the arrest to be lawful. The Court of Appeal held that in order for an arrest to comply with section 28 of PACE and Article 5(2) of the ECHR,[198] a person had to be informed of the basis for the arrest in non-technical language that he could understand. The information given to the claimant in this case had been sufficient for these purposes, and the trial judge had been wrong to direct that a reference to throwing stones was needed.

An arrest also has certain physical requirements: it comprises compulsion and submission to that compulsion. There must either be a touching symbolic of seizure of the body or, alternatively, words of compulsion to which there is submission.[199]

The consequences of arrest

By sections 30 and 30A, an arrested person must be taken to a police station or released on bail as soon as practicable after the arrest. However, these steps may be delayed if it is necessary to the investigation for the arrestee to be present elsewhere.[200] By section 32, an arrested person may be searched if the constable has reasonable grounds to believe that: (a) he may present a danger to himself or others; (b) he may have concealed on him an article that may assist him in escaping from lawful custody; or (c) he may have concealed on him an article that is evidence relating to an offence.

If the offence for which the arrest was made is indictable, section 32(2)(b) also confers the power to enter and search the premises where the suspect was arrested, or where he was immediately prior to his arrest. Section 18 confers a similar power in respect of premises occupied or controlled by the arrested person. However, under the former provision the officer can only search for evidence of the offence for which the arrest was made, whereas under section 18 the officer may also search for evidence of 'connected' or 'similar' offences. The exercise of both powers is dependent on a lawful arrest having been made.

---

[197] [2004] EWCA Civ 858, [2004] 1 WLR 3155, [2004] 3 All ER 503.

[198] See p 186 for a discussion of Article 5(2).

[199] *Alderson* v *Booth* [1969] 2 QB 216, [1969] 2 All ER 271.

[200] Section 30(10) and (10A). Section 30A was inserted by the Criminal Justice Act 2003, and it confers a discretion on constables to release an arrested person on what is informally known as 'street bail'—i.e. bail granted elsewhere than at a police station.

Detention

The custody officer performs a key role in relation to the detention, treatment, and questioning of suspects. Each designated police station must have at least one custody officer,[201] and it is to a 'designated station' that an arrested person should normally be taken. Until now, section 36 of PACE has required the person appointed to this role to be a police officer with at least the rank of sergeant. However, amendments made by the Serious Organised Crime and Police Act 2005 pave the way for civilian 'staff custody officers' to be appointed.[202] The main functions of a custody officer are set out in sections 36, 38, 39, and 40 of PACE. They broadly encompass a duty to ensure that the treatment of all detained persons is in accordance with the requirements of the Act, and that the record-keeping required by the Act actually occurs. If these requirements are not complied with, the detention of the suspect is likely to become unlawful. The custody officer also has an important role in ensuring compliance with PACE Code of Practice C, which provides more detailed guidance for the detention, treatment, and questioning of those in police custody.

In order to protect the interests of the suspect, PACE envisages a separation of functions between the custody officer and those investigating the offence. However, whether this concept is sustainable in practice is a moot point. Quite apart from the loyalties and pressures that membership of the same force might create, a custody officer may sometimes find it difficult to cure a natural desire to assist in an investigation himself.[203]

In determining the legality of a suspect's detention and treatment in custody, several points must be considered, as follows.

(a) A person who attends a police station voluntarily is free to leave at any time, unless and until he is arrested.[204]

(b) A custody record must be kept, detailing all actions taken in respect of the arrested person. The custody officer is responsible for the accuracy and completeness of this record, and the timing of each entry must be noted. A solicitor or appropriate adult representing the detainee must be permitted to consult the record at any time.[205]

(c) If an investigating officer concludes that there is sufficient evidence to provide a realistic prospect of conviction, he must refer the case to the custody officer. It is for the custody officer to determine whether the suspect should be charged or released, and whether or not police bail should be granted.[206]

(d) Within six hours of a suspect's detention being authorized, there must be a review to determine whether that detention continues to be necessary. Further

---

[201] *Vince v Chief Constable of the Dorset Police* [1993] 2 All ER 321, [1993] 1 WLR 415.
[202] Sections 120 and 121. See further, p 435.
[203] See, e.g., *R v Absolam* (1989) 88 Cr App Rep 332.　　[204] PACE, s 29.
[205] Code C, para 2. There are references throughout PACE to the various matters that must be recorded.
[206] PACE, s 37; Code C, paras 16.1–16.2.

reviews should be conducted at intervals of nine hours or less for as long as the detainee remains in police custody.[207]

(e) There are strict limits on how long an arrested person can be detained before being either charged or released. The basic rule is that detention shall not last longer than twenty-four hours from the time of arrest, or time of arrival at the police station, whichever is earlier.[208] This twenty-four-hour period may be extended by a further twelve hours (that is, thirty-six hours in total) by an officer of at least the rank of superintendent.[209] The officer must have reasonable grounds to believe that: (i) detention is necessary to secure or preserve evidence relating to the offence for which the arrest was made, or to obtain such evidence by questioning; (ii) that the offence is an indictable offence; and (iii) that the offence is being investigated diligently and expeditiously.

If the police wish to detain a person beyond thirty-six hours, a warrant of further detention must be obtained from a magistrates' court. The period of further detention granted by such a warrant cannot exceed thirty-six hours, although at the end of this period the police can apply to extend the warrant for a further thirty-six hours.[210] Four days (or ninety-six hours) is therefore the maximum permitted period of detention without charge.[211] The grounds for issuing or extending a warrant of further detention are the same as those for authorizing an initial extension of detention by a senior officer.

(f) Once a person has been charged with an offence, the custody officer must order his release unless one of the conditions in section 38 applies. These conditions are that:

(i) the person's name or address cannot be ascertained, or is reasonably believed to be false;

(ii) it is reasonably believed that the person will fail to appear in court to answer bail;

(iii) in the case of a person arrested for an imprisonable offence, it is reasonably believed that detention is necessary to prevent him from committing a further offence;

(iv) detention is necessary to enable a urine or non-intimate sample to be taken for the purposes of a drugs test;

(v) it is reasonably believed that detention is necessary for the protection of, or to prevent physical injury to, any other person or property;

---

[207] PACE, s 40; Code C, para 15. This review should be carried out by the custody officer if the arrestee has been charged; otherwise, the review officer must be an officer of at least the rank of inspector who has not been directly involved in the investigation.

[208] PACE, s 41.   [209] Ibid, s 42(1).   [210] PACE, s 43.

[211] This period is longer for those detained under the Terrorism Act 2000: see Sch 8 of that Act.

(vi) detention is necessary to prevent the arrestee from interfering with the administration of justice or with police investigations of that or other offences; or

(vii) detention is necessary for his own protection.

Treatment of suspects

The Police and Criminal Evidence Act 1984 includes provisions designed to give proper protection to a suspect in the police station. The objective is to ensure not only that suspects are treated in accordance with minimum standards, but also that admissions and other evidence are obtained in such a way that they can safely be relied upon in court. The courts also regard the right of silence as important, and, amongst other things, Code of Practice C seeks to prevent improperly induced self-incrimination.

Search

Section 54 of PACE requires the custody officer to ascertain everything that a detained person has with him when he is brought to the police station. He may cause the person to be searched for this purpose (although such a search is not obligatory), and a search may also be carried out to ascertain whether the detainee is in possession of an item that could be seized under section 54(4).[212] Articles covered by this provision are those that the custody officer believes might be used to: (a) cause physical injury; (b) damage property; (c) interfere with evidence; or (d) assist an escape. The same provision allows the custody officer to seize items in the detainee's possession if he has reasonable grounds for believing them to be evidence of an offence.[213] If necessary, a detained person can also be searched or examined for the purposes of identification.[214] However, the extent of any search must be strictly limited to what is necessary in the circumstances. A detainee should not be strip searched, for example, unless the officer reasonably believes that he might have concealed an article that he would not be allowed to keep.[215]

Intimate searches—those that involve the physical examination of body orifices other than the mouth[216]—are governed by different rules. An intimate search can only be authorized by an officer of at least the rank of inspector, and only where there are reasonable grounds to believe that the detainee may have concealed a Class A drug or an item that he might use to injure himself or others.[217] Intimate searches should normally be carried out by a registered nurse or medical practitioner. Any search

---

[212] Section 54(6A.)

[213] Compare the pre-PACE position as stated in *Lindley* v *Rutter* [1981] QB 128, [1980] 3 WLR 660.

[214] PACE, s54A. Such a search can only be authorized by an officer of at least the rank of inspector.

[215] Code C, Annex A, para B.10.

[216] PACE, s 65(1).This definition was amended to make it easier for the police to deal with suspects who concealed drugs in their mouths. In *R* v *Hughes* [1994] 1 WLR 876, the holding of a suspect's nose and jaw, causing the extrusion of articles in the mouth, was held to be a search, but not an intimate search.

[217] Ibid, s 55.

conducted by a police officer or civilian detention officer, whether intimate or otherwise, must be performed by an officer of the same gender as the detainee.[218]

Information about rights

The arrested person must be informed of the right to have someone notified of his arrest. Section 56 provides that a person held in custody is entitled, at his request, to have a friend, relative, or other person notified of his whereabouts as soon as practicable. If the person named by the detainee is unobtainable, he may nominate two others, and the police may extend the right further if they wish. The right is an important one, to be denied only in limited circumstances in which to grant it would interfere with the investigation. Even if grounds for denying contact with an individual exist, they are unlikely to apply to making contact with a solicitor.[219] The arrested person also has the right to consult the Codes of Practice.[220]

The taking of fingerprints and other samples

Until recently a person who had not been charged with an offence could only be fingerprinted in limited circumstances, but the position now is that any person who has been arrested or charged in respect of a recordable offence may have his fingerprints taken, either by conventional or electronic means.[221]

An 'intimate sample' is defined by section 65 of PACE to mean: (a) a sample of blood, semen or any other tissue fluid, urine, or pubic hair; (b) a dental impression; or (c) a swab taken from a person's genitals or from a body orifice other than the mouth. Before an intimate sample can be taken, an officer must have both the written consent of the detainee and the authorization of a senior officer.[222] Such authorization can only be granted where the officer has reasonable grounds for: (a) suspecting the detainee of involvement in a recordable offence; and (b) believing that the sample will tend to prove or disprove his involvement. An intimate sample may also be taken from a person who is not in police custody, but who has provided at least two non-intimate samples during the course of an investigation that have proved insufficient for the purpose of analysis.[223] Where a detainee refuses, without good cause, to consent to the taking of an intimate sample, adverse inferences may be drawn from this in any subsequent criminal proceedings.[224] By creating a legal framework for such samples to be taken, PACE paved the way for the introduction of a National DNA Database in 1995. By April 2006 this database held over 4 million DNA profiles.[225] However desirable the database may be in terms of assisting in the

---

[218] Ibid, ss 54(9) and 55(7).   [219] *R v Samuel* [1988] QB 615, [1988] 2 All ER 135.

[220] Code C, para 3.1; *DPP v Skinner* [1990] RTR 254.

[221] PACE, s 61, as amended. More recent amendments will, once implemented, allow fingerprints to be taken at a place *away* from a police station where an officer has doubts about the identity of a suspect: Serious Organised Crime and Police Act 2005, s 117. See also Crime and Security Act 2010.

[222] PACE, s 62(1).   [223] Ibid, s 62(1A).   [224] Ibid, s 62(10).

[225] *The National DNA Database Annual Report 2005–2006*, at p 28. The human rights issues arising from the retention of DNA samples were considered in *R (on the application of S) v Chief Constable of South Yorkshire; R (on the application of Marper) v Chief Constable of South Yorkshire* [2004] UKHL 39, [2004] 1

conviction of criminals, it does raise important civil liberties issues. The retention of data from samples taken from juveniles, and those who are acquitted, was found in *Marper v United Kingdom*[226] to be contrary to Article 8 of the ECHR, and, as a result, detailed provisions as to retention and destruction were introduced by the Crime and Security Act 2010.[227]

Hair samples (other than pubic hair), samples taken from the nails, swabs taken from body parts not covered by section 65, saliva, and skin impressions constitute 'non-intimate samples' for the purposes of PACE. Section 63 provides that where a person has been arrested for a recordable offence, a non-intimate sample may be taken without his consent and without the need for authorization from a senior officer. There is also a power to take a non-intimate sample from a person held in police custody on the authority of a court, although in this case the authorization of a senior officer is required.

Conditions of detention

Minimum standards for the conditions of police detention are set out in Parts 8 and 9 of Code of Practice C. They provide that cells should be adequately heated, cleaned, and ventilated, that clean bedding should be supplied, and that access to toilet and washing facilities should be granted. They also stipulate that a replacement must be supplied for any item of clothing taken away for investigation, and that adequate meals must be provided. Brief outdoor exercise should be permitted where practicable, and suspects should be visited at least once an hour (or once every half an hour if a suspect is intoxicated). The custody officer must call for medical treatment if a suspect appears to be suffering from an illness, injury, or mental disorder, or is otherwise in need of clinical attention.

A serious failure to maintain adequate standards could amount to a breach of Article 3 of the ECHR, which prohibits torture and inhuman or degrading treatment. In an extreme case such a failure could also constitute a breach of Article 10 of the Bill of Rights, which prohibits 'cruel and unusual punishments'.

Vulnerable suspects

Special rules apply to vulnerable persons. If the custody officer cannot establish effective communication with a detainee who appears to be deaf, or if there are doubts about the detainee's ability to hear, speak, or understand English, the officer must call for the assistance of an interpreter.[228]

If the person arrested is a juvenile, the 'appropriate adult' must be told of the arrest as soon as possible, and he must be asked to come to the police station.[229] Where the appropriate adult is not the person normally responsible for the juvenile's welfare, the

---

WLR 2196, [2004] 4 All ER 139. See also Roberts and Taylor, 'Privacy and the DNA Database' [2005] EHRLR 373. For amendments to the powers that result from that ruling, see Crime and Justice Act 2010.

[226] (2008).   [227] Section 15.   [228] Code C, para 13.10.
[229] Code C, para 3.15. For the meaning of 'appropriate adult', see para 1.7.

latter party must also be informed of the situation.[230] Similar rules apply to those who are mentally disordered or otherwise mentally vulnerable.

Access to legal advice

In *R v Samuel*,[231] the right of access to legal advice was described as 'fundamental'. The key provision is section 58 of PACE, which states that a person who is in police detention 'shall be entitled, if he so requests, to consult a solicitor privately at any time'. Access to a solicitor can only be delayed in respect of a person arrested for an indictable offence, and such a delay can only be authorized by an officer of at least the rank of superintendent.[232] Before authorizing a delay, an officer must reasonably believe that the exercise of the right will do one of the following: (a) lead to interference with or harm to evidence connected with an indictable offence; (b) lead to interference with or physical injury to other persons; (c) lead to the alerting of other persons suspected of having committed such an offence; (d) hinder the recovery of any property obtained as a result of such an offence; or (e) hinder the recovery of the value of any property obtained by criminal conduct.[233] In the case of a person arrested under the terrorism provisions, the scope for restricting access to legal advice is greater.

These powers of delay have been construed very narrowly by the courts. In *R v Samuel*,[234] the accused was denied access to a solicitor because the police feared that the solicitor might unwittingly alert other suspects. The court held that the police had failed to demonstrate a reasonable belief that the solicitor in question might jeopardize their investigation: even if he had presented such a risk, the appropriate response would have been to ask the suspect to nominate an alternative, or to call the duty solicitor instead. The court also made it clear that legal advice cannot be delayed on the grounds that a solicitor might advise silence or make the investigation harder.[235]

More detailed rules are set out in Part 6 of Code of Practice C. This states that a suspect under arrest at a police station must be informed clearly of his right to consult privately with a solicitor, free of charge, at any time during his period in custody. Posters with this information must be displayed prominently in the charging area of each police station, and at certain stages in the process the suspect must be reminded of the right. There is no obligation on the police to request a solicitor on their own initiative, although if a solicitor attends at the request of the suspect's family, the suspect has the right to see him. The police must not take any action to discourage the exercise of the right, and they must not misrepresent the position.[236]

Once it has been requested, the police must generally wait until legal advice has been tendered before proceeding with an interview. The advice may be given over the telephone or in person, and may come either from a solicitor or from an 'accredited or probationary representative'.[237] Such a representative may be refused access if an

---

[230] Code C, para 3.13.   [231] [1988] QB 615, [1988] 2 All ER 135.
[232] PACE, s 58(6).   [233] Ibid, ss 58(8) and (8A).   [234] [1988] QB 615, [1988] 2 All ER 135.
[235] Ibid. See also *R v Alladice* (1988) 87 Cr App R 380.   [236] See *R v Beycan* [1990] Crim LR 185.
[237] See Code C, para 6.12.

officer of at least the rank of inspector considers that his presence would hinder the investigation;[238] the officer may take into account whether the representative's identity has been properly established, and whether he has a criminal record or is otherwise an unsuitable character. Restricting the presence of a solicitor is a far more serious step, but a solicitor may be asked to leave an interview if his conduct is preventing the police from being able to properly put questions to the suspect.[239]

KEY ISSUE

The courts generally take any denial of the right to legal advice very seriously. The right is a fundamental right, and strictly upheld by the courts. It is also fundamental right under Article 6 of the ECHR.[240]. Breach of the right to any significant respect is likely to render any confession made inadmissible under section 78 of PACE.[241]

The impact of the right under section 58 has been much debated. It seems likely that the mere presence of a lawyer at the police station will reduce the incidence of procedural irregularities, but research suggests that the quality of legal advice received by those in custody is variable.[242] Moreover, whilst the proportion of detainees obtaining legal advice has undoubtedly increased since PACE was introduced, the figure is still quite low. Research by Bucke and Brown found that legal advice was requested by around 40 per cent of detainees in 1997,[243] with most of the other 60 per cent taking the view that they simply did not need a lawyer.[244] The precise reasons for this low uptake are unclear but it seems that a variety of ploys, whether inadvertent or intentional, can dissuade suspects from taking advantage of their rights. For example, many of the detainees in Bucke and Browne's study said that they would wait until later before deciding whether they needed a lawyer; the authors suggest that custody officers may have encouraged this by emphasizing that suspects could change their minds about seeking legal advice at any time.[245] Similarly, Phillips and Brown found that some of the suspects in their study had declined legal advice after being told that they probably would not be charged.[246] The effectiveness of the right to legal advice also depends on the availability of suitably qualified legal advisers, and the duty solicitor scheme funded by the Legal Services Commission has an important role here.[247]

❓ Questions

1. Why is the right to legal advice so fundamental?

2. What do you think the role of the legal adviser is during an interview?

---

[238] Ibid, para 6.12A.   [239] Code C, paras 6.9–6.11.

[240] See p 391.   [241] See p 437.

[242] McConville and Bridges, *Custodial Legal Advice and the Right to Silence* (HMSO, 1993) RCCJ Research Study No 16. See also the Legal Services Commission's Evaluation of the Public Defender Service, which was conducted by Bridges and Sherr. **www.legalservices.gov.uk/criminal/pds/evaluation.asp**

[243] *In Police Custody: Police Powers and Suspects' Rights under the Revised PACE Codes of Practice* (HMSO, 1997) HORS 174, at p 19.

[244] Ibid, at p 22.   [245] Ibid.

[246] *Entry into the Criminal Justice System: A Survey of Police Arrests and their Outcomes* (HMSO, 1998) HORS 185, at p 159.

[247] See p 419.

Interviews

One of the most serious problems identified in recent years is the possibility that confessions made by suspects may not always be reliable. The 1984 Act and Code of Practice C provide a detailed framework for the conduct and recording of interviews, the importance of which was explained in *R v Canale*:[248]

> The object is two-fold: not merely to ensure that the suspect's remarks are accurately recorded and that he has an opportunity when he goes through the contemporaneous record afterwards of checking each answer and initialling each answer, but likewise it is a protection for the police, to ensure, so far as possible, that it cannot be suggested that they induced the suspect to confess by improper approaches or improper promises. If the contemporaneous note is not made then each of those two laudable objects is apt to be stultified.

Initially, there was a danger that the police might seek to circumvent the rules governing interviews by questioning suspects before they were brought to the police station. Amendments to Code C mean that the term 'interview' now covers any questioning of a person regarding his involvement or suspected involvement in a criminal offence or offences.[249] It does not, however, cover routine questioning in the ordinary course of an officer's duties.[250]

The right of silence

The notion of the right of silence is closely linked to the idea of freedom from self-incrimination. A suspect has the right not to be required to self-incriminate, which means that he cannot generally be compelled to answer questions put to him by a police officer[251] or to testify at any subsequent trial. Before 1994, a jury could not be invited to draw any adverse inference from the fact that a defendant had elected to remain silent during police questioning. This has now changed, however, following the enactment of the Criminal Justice and Public Order Act 1994. If a person who is being questioned under caution fails to mention a fact later relied on in his defence, section 34 of this Act provides that a court or jury may draw such inferences from this failure as appear proper. Similar inferences may be drawn from a failure to account for certain matters during questioning,[252] or from the failure of a defendant to testify in his own defence at trial.[253]

---

[248] [1990] 2 All ER 187 at 190, *per* Lord Lane CJ.

[249] For an interpretation of this, see *R v Cox* (1993) 96 Cr App R 464.

[250] Distinguishing between interviews and other forms of questioning is not always easy in practice: see *R v Absolam* (1989) 88 Cr App R 332; *R v Gill (Sewa Singh)* [2003] EWCA Crim 2256, [2004] 1 WLR 469, [2003] 4 All ER 681. **www.legalservices.gov.uk/criminal/pds/evaluation.asp**

[251] There are some limited exceptions to this rule. Section 172 of the Road Traffic Act 1988, for example, imposes a duty to give information about the driver of a vehicle in certain circumstances: see *Brown* v *Stott* [2003] 1 AC 681, [2001] 2 All ER 97.

[252] Sections 36 (failure to account for objects, substances or marks) and 37 (failure to account for presence at a particular place).

[253] Section 35.

Although the right to silence is not expressly mentioned in the European Convention on Human Rights, the watering down of this right does have implications for Article 6 and the right to a fair trial. In *Murray* v *UK*, the court held that the right to silence was not essential to a fair trial: indeed, there was no breach of Article 6 on the facts of the case because the weight of evidence against the accused meant that the drawing of inferences was not unfair.[254] On the other hand, a judge must ensure that appropriate weight is given to any explanation offered by the defendant, and Article 6 would clearly be breached if a defendant was convicted solely on the basis of his silence.[255] Where a suspect has remained silent on the basis of legal advice the effect of this advice must be taken into account, but it will not necessarily preclude the court from drawing adverse inferences. Conversely, the risk of inferences being drawn from silence means that any delay in granting access to lawyer will be regarded as a particularly serious matter.[256] Indeed, section 34(2A) of the 1994 Act provides that if a suspect is questioned before he has had the opportunity to consult a lawyer, no adverse inferences may be drawn from any failure to answer police questions.

Cautions

A caution must be administered before a suspect is questioned with a view to obtaining evidence that may be given in court. A caution must also be administered on arrest. The standard wording of this caution was modified in 1994 to reflect changes in the right to silence. It now states:[257]

> You do not have to say anything. But it may harm your defence if you do not mention when questioned something which you later rely on in court. Anything you do say may be given in evidence.

The conduct of interviews

Interviews must take place at a police station, unless delay would lead to: (a) interference with or harm to evidence connected with an offence; (b) interference with or harm to other people; (c) serious loss of, or damage to, property; (d) the alerting of other persons suspected of committing an offence; or (e) hindrance to the recovery of property obtained in consequence of the commission of an offence.[258]

Code C requires that the suspect should be reminded of his right to free legal advice before any interview is conducted. It also contains specific requirements about breaks from questioning, maximum periods of questioning, and the provision of proper food and refreshments as appropriate. Perhaps more importantly, section 76 of PACE provides that a confession obtained by oppression or in circumstances likely to lead to unreliability must be excluded from evidence at any trial.[259]

---

[254] (1996) 22 EHRR 29.   [255] *Condron* v *UK* (2001) 31 EHRR 1; *Beckles* v *UK* (2003) 36 EHRR 13.
[256] Ibid; *Murray* v *UK* (1996) 22 EHRR 29.   [257] Code C, para 10.5.
[258] Code C, para 11.1.   [259] See p 437.

Records of interviews

Code C requires the police to keep an accurate record of all interviews with suspects, including details of the time, date, location, breaks, and the names of all persons present.[260] Any interview conducted at a police station with a person suspected of an indictable offence must now be tape-recorded in accordance with Code of Practice E.[261] The recording must be carried out openly and two copies must be made. The master copy must be sealed in the suspect's presence,[262] and if the suspect is to be charged or prosecuted, he must be supplied with his own copy as soon as practicable after the conclusion of the interview. Where a suspect objects to being tape-recorded, his objections must be recorded on the tape, but the interviewer may then turn off the tape and record the interview in writing.[263]

Where an interview is recorded in writing, the record must be made contemporaneously with the interview or as soon as possible afterwards.[264] Unless it is impracticable, the suspect should be shown the record for the purposes of verification, and he should be given the opportunity to sign it as correct.[265] If he declines to do so, this must itself be recorded, along with any unsolicited comments made.[266]

The visual recording of interviews is a more recent innovation, which was given a statutory basis in 2001.[267] Visual recording is not yet mandatory,[268] but where it is carried out it must comply with Code of Practice F.

Vulnerable suspects

There is a recognition that certain groups require additional safeguards, and specific rules exist for the protection of juveniles and those who are mentally disordered or otherwise mentally vulnerable. Such persons should not be interviewed or asked to sign an interview record in the absence of an appropriate adult[269] unless the criteria governing urgent interviews are satisfied. Specifically, the police must wait for an appropriate adult unless an officer of at least the rank of superintendent considers that a delay would do one of the following: (a) lead to interference with or harm to evidence connected with an offence; (b) lead to interference with or physical harm to persons or property; (c) lead to the alerting of other persons suspected of having committed an offence; or (d) hinder the recovery of any property obtained as a result of an offence.[270]

---

[260] Code C, para 11.7.

[261] A separate Code of Practice governs the recording of interviews with persons detained under the terrorism provisions.

[262] Code E, para 2.2.   [263] Ibid, para 4.8.   [264] Code C, para 11.8.

[265] Ibid, para 11.11.   [266] Ibid, paras 11.13–11.14.

[267] PACE, s 60A, as amended by the Criminal Justice and Police Act 2001.

[268] A pilot study was conducted between 2002 and 2003, which made visual recording compulsory in certain police areas: Police and Criminal Evidence Act 1984 (Visual Recording of Interviews) (Certain Police Areas) Order 2002, SI 2002/1266.

[269] Code C, para 11.15. See para 1.7 of this Code for the meaning of 'appropriate adult'.

[270] Ibid, para 11.1.

The officer must also be satisfied that the person's physical or mental state will not be significantly harmed by the interview.[271]

Those suffering temporary disability due to drink, drugs or illness should not normally be interviewed until they are fit, although the courts are generally willing to leave this judgment to the police.[272]

Identification

Following a series of wrongful convictions, the Devlin Committee was established to investigate how the law dealt with identification evidence. The Committee recommended[273] that in all but the most exceptional cases, juries should be directed not to convict on the basis of eye-witness testimony unless it was supported by substantial other evidence. No legislation followed, but the Court of Appeal in *R* v *Turnbull* laid down certain guidelines.[274] The guidelines suggest that identification evidence can be split into good and poor quality identification. If, for example, the identification was made in good conditions of light and weather, with ample opportunity to observe, the matter can safely be left to the jury. On the other hand, if the identification is of poor quality, the case should be withdrawn from the jury unless it is supported and confirmed by other evidence. In all cases that depend wholly or substantially on identification evidence, the judge should direct the jury to proceed with special caution. In addition, there is no difference for these purposes between recognition evidence and evidence involving the identification of a stranger: although it might be assumed that the former would be more reliable, the witness in each case is using his particular knowledge of a person to identify him, and the *Turnbull* guidelines therefore apply.

To minimize the risks associated with identification evidence, Code of Practice D sets out specific rules as to how suspects are to be identified. Failure to comply with this Code is likely to result in the evidence being excluded from any trial. If the identity of a suspect is not known, a witness may be shown photographs or taken to a particular locality to observe possible candidates, but certain safeguards must be met.[275] Once the identity of the suspect *is* known, a video identification, group identification or identification parade may be organized. Unless such a procedure would not be practicable or would serve no useful purpose in proving or disproving his involvement in the offence, one of these procedures *must* be offered if a suspect disputes an identification.[276] Such a procedure may also be organized if the officer in

---

[271] Ibid, para 11.18.

[272] *R* v *Lamont* [1989] Crim LR 813; *R* v *Moss* (1990) 91 Cr App R 371.

[273] *Report to the Secretary of State for the Home Department of the Departmental Committee on Evidence of Identification in Criminal Cases* (1976, HC 338).

[274] [1977] QB 224, [1976] 3 All ER 549. Note that the guidelines appear to apply only to the identification of humans, and not to the identification of vehicles and other objects.

[275] Code D, paras 3.2–3.3.

[276] In *R* v *Forbes* [2001] 1 AC 473, [2001] 1 All ER 686 an earlier version of the Code was interpreted to mean that an identification procedure had to be held in all cases, even where the suspect was already well

charge of the investigation considers that it would be useful. The preferred method of identification in either case is video identification. Paragraph 3.14 of the Code states that a suspect should be offered video identification unless one of the other procedures would be a more suitable and practicable alternative. In all cases a suspect must be reminded of his entitlement to free legal advice, and his consent to the procedure must be sought. In the absence of consent the police may use covert or other means of identification, and the suspect's refusal to participate may be given in evidence at any subsequent trial.[277]

Further reading

HOME OFFICE, *Policing in the New Century: A Blueprint for Reform*, Cm 5326 (HMSO, 2001)

HOME OFFICE, *One Step Ahead: A 21st Century Strategy to Defeat Organised Crime*, Cm 6167 (HMSO, 2004)

MORRIS, 'Extending the Police Family: Issues and Anomalies' [2002] PL 670

WALKER and STARMER, *Miscarriages of Justice: A Review of Justice in Error* (Blackstone, 1999)

---

known to the witness. The wording adopted since 2002 ensures that parades need not be held in cases in which they would serve no useful purpose.

[277] Code D, para 3.17.

PART III
Civil Proceedings

The Civil Process

13

INTRODUCTION

This purpose of this chapter is to give an overview of the process of civil litigation. Civil process has undergone radical reform, following the implementation of the reforms recommended by the Woolf Committee. At the same time, growth has occurred in the range and availability of alternative dispute resolution. Specific areas addressed will include:

- the reasons for the recommendations of the Woolf Report;
- its main recommendations;
- how those recommendations have been implemented;
- how the civil justice system is administered;
- alternative forms of dispute resolution, including arbitration and mediation.

The context

Access to justice

Access to justice is a fundamental right. It has even been described as a constitutional right, in so far as such rights exist.[1] For society to operate effectively, there must be means whereby disputes between individuals, and between the state and individuals, can be resolved. The civil justice process provides those means, but must be accessible to those who need such access. Procedural, financial, or other restrictions defeat the whole purpose of the civil justice process, as does unnecessary delay or length.

Civil litigation has, for the most part,[2] traditionally been regarded as adversarial in nature.[3] Within a framework of substantive and procedural law established by the state for the resolution of civil disputes, the main responsibility for the initiation

---

[1] See Laws J in *R v Lord Chancellor, ex parte Witham* [1998] QB 575, [1997] 2 All ER 779. The significance of the constitutional right is that it should only be abrogated by the clear words of an Act of Parliament. For the detail of this case, see p 411.

[2] Proceedings involving children might be regarded as an exception.

[3] *Access to Justice: Interim Report to the Lord Chancellor on the Civil Justice System in England and Wales* (HMSO, June 1995) ('the Woolf Interim Report'), at para 3. See also the Final Report (the 'Woolf Final Report') (HMSO, 1996).

and conduct of proceedings has traditionally rested with the parties to each individual case, with the person bringing the action (the claimant)[4] setting the pace at which the litigation proceeds. The parties to the litigation controlled the commencement of the action, the setting of the legal agenda within which the case was to be decided,[5] the progress of the case, the question of interim relief whilst the case was in progress, the settlement or otherwise of the case, and the acquisition and adducing of evidence. The role of the judge was to adjudicate on issues selected by the parties when they chose to present them to the court. The procedural reforms of the 1990s were made with the intention of changing that role. The two landmark reports by Lord Woolf, the Woolf Interim Report and the Woolf Final Report,[6] were the foundations on which reform of the civil justice system was built, culminating in the new Civil Procedure Rules (CPR).[7] The Woolf reforms have been endorsed by subsequent reports.[8] At the heart of the changes is a continued need to keep in check, and reduce, the costs of civil litigation. In 2010, the Jackson Report[9] was published. At the outset, Jackson concluded that 'in some areas of civil litigation costs are disproportionate and impede access to justice'.[10] The Report contains a multitude of recommendations, focusing primarily on costs and procedures that affect costs.[11]

Cost

The civil justice process has long been criticized for its cost, delay, and complexity.[12] Since the mid-nineteenth century there have been some sixty or so reports on aspects of procedure, including the Civil Justice Review.[13] In 1993 (the year before Lord Woolf's review was commissioned) that civil justice process was condemned by a report published by the Bar Council and Law Society,[14] and was described as 'fragmented and confusing' by the Middleton Report[15] in 1997. The Woolf Interim Report identified a key reason for this as being the absence of effective judicial control. Without this, the adversarial process was likely to encourage an adversarial culture and to degenerate into an environment in which the litigation process was too often seen as a battlefield in which no rules apply. In this environment, questions of expense, delay, compromise, and fairness might have only low priority. The consequence was

---

[4] Formerly known as the 'plaintiff'. For changes in nomenclature, see p 490.

[5] The 'pleadings'.

[6] The Woolf Final Report. For general comment and reference, see Zuckerman and Cranston, *Reform of Civil Procedure: Essays on Access to Justice* (OUP, 1995); Zander, 'The Government's Plans on Civil Justice' (1998) 61 MLR 383; Zander, 'Forwards or Backwards for the New Lord Chancellor' (1997) 16 CJQ 208. Note that not all comment was dismissive of the pre-existing process: see, e.g., Conrad Dehn QC, *Reform of Civil Procedure: Essays on 'Access to Justice'* (OUP, 1995) at pp 149–61.

[7] See p 487.   [8] See p 479.

[9] *Review of Civil Litigation Costs: Final Report* (HMSO, 2010).   [10] Ibid, Foreword.

[11] See, generally, p 475.   [12] Woolf Interim Report, para 8.

[13] *Report of the Review Body on Civil Justice*, Cm 394 (HMSO, 1988).

[14] *Civil Justice on Trial: The Case for Change* (Bar Council, 1993).

[15] *Review of Civil Justice and Legal Aid: Report to the Lord Chancellor by Sir Peter Middleton GCB* ('the Middleton Report') (HMSO, September 1997), at para 1.7.

that expense is often excessive, disproportionate, and unpredictable; and delay is frequently unreasonable.[16]

The question of the cost of civil litigation is not simply dependant on there being efficient process and procedure. The rules relating to recovery of costs[17] by a successful party are also critical. Access to justice is only possible if all parties have adequate funding[18], and if the costs incurred are proportionate.[19] The Jackson Report identified some sixteen general causes that, in differing combinations, give rise to excessive costs, and thus inhibit effective civil process in some types of case.[20] These are dealt with at appropriate parts of this text.

The Woolf analysis

The fact that the Woolf Interim and Final Reports identified fundamental shortcomings in the civil justice process has already been noted above. At the heart of the problems were the adversarial approach of litigation, the expense and complexity of litigation, and the delays with which it was surrounded, although not all such criticisms applied to all proceedings. We have already noted the existence of specialist courts or jurisdictions.[21] For example, the Commercial Court developed specialist procedures and protocols to facilitate the handling of cases within its remit. So, too, with judicial review, where[22] the procedures and processes under Order 53 of the old Rules of the Supreme Court[23] provided speedy (if not necessarily inexpensive) means for the challenge of actions and decisions of public bodies. The question of choice of court also was an important factor contributing to delay, inefficiency, and cost.

Delay and the adversarial nature of civil litigation

The conduct of civil litigation has, historically, been in the hands of the parties, operating within a framework of rules of court, creating the potential for delay. In *Rastin v British Steel plc*,[24] Sir Thomas Bingham pointed out that 'delay has long been recognised as the enemy of justice'. An adversarial process encourages an adversarial culture, and this worked well where all parties were keen to see the case progress, were appropriately represented, and the court had little need to intervene.[25] But the adversarial system in civil litigation has not always in the past delivered that. In one analysis, extrajudicially, Sir Gavin Lightman[26] identified a number of 'disturbing features for those who are more interested in the achievement of justice than playing

---

[16] Woolf Interim Report, para 4.   [17] See p 547.   [18] See p 410.
[19] Jackson, *op cit*, paras 2.5–2.6.   [20] Ibid, para 3.1.   [21] See p 475.
[22] See Chapter 7.   [23] Now Part 54 CPR.   [24] [1994] 2 All ER 641, [1994] 1 WLR 732.
[25] See Andrews, *English Civil Procedure* (OUP, 2003) at paras 2.22–2.23.
[26] High Court judge, in Edward Bramley Memorial Lecture: see (2003) 22 CJQ 235.

the game'.[27] These included the fact that success depends very much on the events at court itself, which in turn turns on the investment made by the respective parties in the litigation—'money talks loud and clear'—and the judge has limited opportunity to redress the balance. The quality of advice varies enormously, from (to quote the metaphor used) 'fine wine' to 'unfit to drink'. The judge has to achieve fairness on the material put before him. Above all, Lightman concluded that the system was expensive and time-consuming: '[Y]ou must purchase your "champions" for the tournament, and champions do not come cheap.' This disenchantment with the adversarial system was heightened by the plethora of judicial pronouncements on matters of substantive law. The Woolf reforms were viewed as advances, but substantial litigation remains 'extravagantly expensive and unpredictable'.

Clearly, whatever the pros and cons of the system, the rules governing preparation for trial often highlighted these problems. The Woolf Interim Report observed that the whole process could be much like a battleground, with the parties waging 'war' often devoid of judicial intervention or control.[28] In 1994, High Court cases on average took 163 weeks in London and 189 weeks elsewhere to progress from commencement of the action to trial. The great majority of this time was between commencement and setting down: 123 weeks in London and 148 weeks elsewhere. The equivalent county court figures were around eighty weeks overall from commencement to trial, with typically around sixty weeks elapsing. In the majority of cases the delay arose from a failure to progress the case efficiently, wasting time on peripheral issues, or from procedural skirmishing to wear down an opponent or to excuse failure to get on with the case.[29] Woolf considered that this approach was too often condoned by the courts, paradoxically for fear of disadvantaging the litigant. Excessive discovery,[30] the use of experts in heavy demand, and the exertion of partisan pressure on experts also each contributed to delay.

Delay, Woolf concluded, was of more benefit to the lawyers than to the parties.[31] It allowed litigators to carry excessive caseloads in which the 'minimum possible action occurs over the maximum possible timescale'. The process of case settlement was addressed at a very late stage, not facilitating speed but, by contrast, creating extra costs. Rules of court were flouted on a vast scale. The timetables they contained were generally ignored and their other requirements complied with when convenient to the interests of one of the parties and not otherwise. Woolf considered that the powers of the courts had fallen behind the more sophisticated and aggressive tactics of some litigators. Orders for costs that resulted[32] were of little

---

[27] His comments were focused on the criminal justice system but may be thought, by some, to have some value in the context of the civil justice system. For the nature of the criminal justice system, see p 578.

[28] Interim Report, paras 29 *et seq*.

[29] For condemnation of the culture, see Lightman, 'Civil Litigation in the 21st Century' (1998) 17 CJQ 383.

[30] The process whereby documents in the hands of one party are made available to other parties in the litigation, and now known as disclosure.

[31] Woolf Interim Report, ch 3, para 31.   [32] See p 547.

value, applied after the damage was done. The delay in being able to obtain effective intervention by the court encouraged rule-breaking and discouraged the party who would be prejudiced from applying for preventive measures. The main procedural tools for conducting litigation efficiently had become subverted from their proper purpose. Pleadings often failed to state the facts as the rules require, leading to a fundamental deficiency: namely the failure to establish the issues in the case at a reasonably early stage, and from which many problems resulted.[33] New procedures had become bogged down in technicalities or excesses, especially in respect to expert evidence and discovery.

The report also focused on equally fundamental issues that result. He wrote:[34]

> Delay is an additional source of distress to parties who have already suffered damage. It postpones the compensation or other remedy to which they may be entitled. It interferes with the normal existence of both individuals and businesses. In personal injury cases, it can exacerbate or prolong the original injury. It can lead to the collapse of relationships and businesses. It makes it more difficult to establish the facts because memories fade and witnesses cannot be traced. It postpones settlement but may lead parties to settle for inadequate compensation because they are worn down by delay or cannot afford to continue.

Many of his recommendations address directly issues of delay.

Expense

Delay and expense are, of course, inextricably linked. If litigation is unaffordable then there is a denial of justice.[35] This problem has not, historically, been fully addressed by the civil legal aid system, which has often catered for the needs of those on the lowest income levels, leaving a range of middle-income earners unable to seek redress in the courts and thus with unmet legal needs. This is a situation addressed by the growth of conditional fee agreements following the gradual phasing out of civil legal aid.[36] Disproportionality was also a problem: a claim that can only be pursued, or defended, at disproportionate cost is one that cannot in reality be brought or defended easily. Woolf noted that the costs in some cases, particularly smaller value cases, were often in excess of the value of what was in dispute. Research undertaken for the Woolf Inquiry showed that in half of the cases examined by the research team, the costs for one party to litigation equalled or exceeded the value of the claim disproportionately.[37] It considered that disproportionate costs permeated many aspects of the civil justice process. In part, this flowed from the cost of legal services, and the level of fees charged by lawyers. It also stemmed from the fact that solicitors generally charge by an hourly rate, thus compounding the effect of cumbersome rules, procedures, or structures that allow the parties to dictate the pace of litigation, and issues to be determined. The question of the awards of costs was also relevant.[38] As noted

---

[33] Woolf Interim Report, para 9.   [34] Ibid, para 30.   [35] Ibid, ch 3, para 13.
[36] See p 422.   [37] Ibid, para 19, citing research of Professor Hazel Genn.
[38] See p 547.

earlier, if no effective rules apply, priority is not always given to the taking of steps to settle the litigation, or to progress it quicker, and therefore more cheaply. Woolf concluded[39] that the expense of litigation is one of the most fundamental problems confronting the civil justice system, a conclusion confirmed more recently by the analysis and recommendations of the Jackson Report.[40] Woolf quoted Sir Thomas Bingham, the Master of the Rolls, as describing it as 'a cancer eating at the heart of the administration of justice'. The problem of cost is fuelled by the combative environment in which litigation is conducted.

Excessive cost deters people from making or defending claims. A number of businesses told the Woolf Inquiry that it is often cheaper to pay up, irrespective of the merits, than to defend an action.[41] This is particularly true at the lower end of the scale of litigation. For individual litigants the unaffordable cost of litigation constitutes a denial of access to justice. This problem of disproportionate cost is most acute in smaller cases in which the costs of litigation, for one side alone, frequently equal or exceed the value of what is at issue. The result is often that it was impossible for ordinary people to take or defend smaller cases unless they are legally aided, have insurance backing, or believe they can be certain of winning their case and their costs. Like the Middleton Report was to do, Woolf also focused on the overall costs to the state, with inexorable rises in the costs of legal aid. This has now, of course, been reversed by the expedient of removing state funding for many classes of litigation. For individual legally aided litigants, the high cost of litigation impacted through the increased contributions that they had to pay throughout the duration of the case and the statutory charge on any compensation they recover. The report concluded that this approach to litigation that then applied usually resulted in total uncertainty for the parties as to what litigation will require, and consequently increased the amount of expenditure in which they may be involved and the timescale of that involvement. This arose from a number of factors:

(a) the rule that costs normally follow the event and the inevitable uncertainty as to the outcome of litigation;

(b) the procedures when management of the case is primarily a matter for the parties and that either side could influence not only its own costs but also its opponent's;

(c) the requirement of the adversarial system that every aspect of a case be fully investigated, which encouraged excessive work and cost on issues that were often recognized from an early stage as peripheral;

(d) the charging system, on a daily or hourly basis, which meant that the more that is done on a case, the more lawyers were paid;

(e) the lack of continuity in the handling of cases, resulting in the additional work necessary to refresh memories.

---

[39] Ibid, ch 1.   [40] See p 480.   [41] Ibid, para 13.

Complexity

Alongside delay and expense is complexity—what one writer has described as 'the unholy trinity of consequences which flow once a lawyer gets hold of a dispute'.[42] Woolf concluded that unnecessary complexity was caused by the then state of the rules of court, the multiplicity of procedures and jurisdictions, the multiplicity of methods of commencing actions, and the multiplicity of Practice Directions. None of the above was helped by 'obscure and uncertain' substantive law.[43] All of these factors created additional problems where, whether for financial or other reasons, there was a growth in the number of unrepresented parties.

Court of trial

Allied to all of the above are issues relating to the structure of the various courts of trial.[44] The question of which court tries an action was at the forefront of the various factors that contribute to current problems about delay, inefficiency, and cost. The jurisdictions of the county court and High Court were separate, but overlapping, with each having similar, but different, regimes of procedure and rules, adding to the complexity and other related problems.

Historically, determination of civil claims has been undertaken by the High Court and the county courts. In some matters, the jurisdiction of the High Court was exclusive, in others concurrent with the county court, in the sense that an action could be commenced in either. The jurisdiction of the county court in respect of which the Queen's Bench Division has jurisdiction had been limited by the financial value of the claim. Prior to 1991, in contract or tort actions, the value of the claim had to be no greater than £5,000. In equity and property matters the figure was £30,000. If the amount of the claim exceeded the jurisdiction of the county court, then the matter had to be dealt with by the High Court, subject to statutory powers of transfer between the two courts. Proceedings in the county court were potentially cheaper, but the procedures followed in the county court were not always either speedy or effective. It was hardly surprising, therefore, that the Review Body on Civil Justice[45] found that much of the work tried at High Court level was not of sufficient importance, complexity, and substance to justify the time and expense involved in High Court proceedings. It identified the types of case that did, in fact, justify proceedings at High Court level. These included:

(a) public law matters, which should be dealt with by way of judicial review;[46]

(b) those matters dealt with in specialist jurisdictions, especially the Commercial Court;[47]

---

[42] Andrews *op cit*, at para 2.6. The author was reflecting on what was identified as a possibly cynical response of a layman.

[43] Woolf Interim Report, ch 3, para 44.   [44] As to which, see p 501. *et seq*.

[45] See Civil Justice Review, p 472.   [46] See p 511.   [47] See p 255.

(c) ordinary cases, which were important, complex, or which involved a substantial claim. The Review Body recommended changes to the jurisdiction of the county court, and improved mechanisms for transfer between the two jurisdictions.

As a result of this review, the Courts and Legal Services Act 1990 altered the whole basis of distribution of work between High Court and county court, although did not adopt in their entirety the recommendations of the Review Body. In 1991 the Lord Chancellor made the High Court and County Court Jurisdiction Order,[48] which adjusted fundamentally the distribution of work between the two courts. By virtue of this order, there was no longer to be any limit to the jurisdiction of the county court in contract or tort. The general principle was that a claimant should be free to choose whichever court is preferred, although in deciding where in fact to commence an action a claimant will usually have regard to the court by which such an action will ultimately be tried. The general principle of freedom of choice expressed above was subject to one important qualification: any action of a value less than £50,000 and involving a claim of damages for personal injuries had to be commenced in the county court. There was also a presumption that a non-personal injuries claim of the value between £25,000 and £50,000 would be started in the county court.

Woolf recognized the value of such changes, but saw the need to go much further, as part of his philosophy that some of the problems identified above stemmed from in the then inability of the court itself to manage the progress and conduct of the case. As noted later,[49] this has led to changes where the jurisdiction of the court is to be determined through a multi-track approach whereby the court of trial, and the procedure followed, will be determined by the nature of the claim, including its financial value.

Recommendations

Woolf did not consider the situation analysed above to be inevitable. The Woolf Report analysed the whole civil process, particularly case management, and the procedures adopted both prior to, and at, trial. In his recommendations he sought to increase the speed proceedings should achieve, to simplify both the language and the process itself, to ensure greater accessibility, to promote settlement and out-of-court resolution of disputes, and to make litigation more efficient and cost-effective. In particular, his approach envisaged that pre-trial process and procedure should be managed and overseen by the court, to ensure that proceedings are conducted at the appropriate speed.

Amongst the detailed recommendations were:

(a) an expanded small claims jurisdiction;

(b) a new fast track for straightforward cases not exceeding £10,000 to be a strictly limited procedure designed to take cases to trial within a short but reasonable timescale;

---

[48] SI 1991/724.   [49] See p 501.

(c) a new multi-track, for cases above £10,000, spanning both High Court and county court cases, and providing appropriate and proportionate case management. Individual hands-on case management was concentrated on those cases that require significant attention and that most benefit from it. Other cases in the multi-track would proceed on standard or individually tailored timetables, according to standard or individual directions;

(d) within the multi-track there would be effective case management, through case management conferences and pre-trial review;

(e) the most complex and important cases were to be heard only by High Court judges and not by deputies. Other cases would be managed and heard by the appropriate level of judge and able to move flexibly within the system to ensure this.

The implementation and effect of the Woolf recommendations are noted at the appropriate part of our discussion about the new system.

The Woolf recommendations were broadly endorsed by the Middleton Report,[50] and accepted generally by the government. To facilitate these fundamental changes, the government took through Parliament what is now the Civil Procedure Act 1997. That Act paved the way for detailed changes. It does so by, in section 1, providing for a new set of procedural rules (the Civil Procedure Rules) that apply to Court of Appeal, High Court, and county court proceedings. The power to make new rules is to be exercised with a view to securing that the civil justice system is accessible, fair, and efficient.[51] Civil Procedure Rules are made by a Civil Procedure Rule Committee. In addition, a Civil Justice Council is established by section 6 of the 1997 Act.

KEY ISSUE

Have the Woolf Reforms worked? The main thrust of his recommendations were implemented through the Civil Procedure Act 1997, the Administration of Justice Act 1999 and the new Civil Procedure Rules.[52] The restricting of where and how cases are dealt with is regarded as a success by many, as is the conscious role of judges in case management, designed to provide greater degrees of expedition and efficiency, thus saving costs. Simplification of language and procedures is to be welcomed.

Woolf found that costs of civil litigation were often disproportionate, resulting in civil justice becoming unaffordable. However, the introduction of conditional fee agreements, although having a positive effect on access to justice,[53] have meant that the question of cost, considered a real problem by Woolf, continues to be a real issue,[54] and one now addressed by the Jackson Review. Lord Woolf himself has said:

Although the general opinion a decade later is that the recommendations I made have benefited civil procedure, it is undoubtedly the fact that one of their objectives has not been achieved: the control of costs. The process...is now far too expensive.[55]

---

[50] See p 487.   [51] 1997 Act, s 1(3).   [52] See p 487.   [53] See p 473.
[54] See p 480.   [55] 25 March 2010, in House of Lords, cited at Consultation Paper, p 10.

The very fact that the issue of cost is one that remains a pivotal issue some twelve years after the Woolf recommendations is perhaps evidence that the Woolf reforms are incomplete.

❓ Questions

1. Why was the Woolf inquiry established?
2. What did Woolf consider to be the main obstacles to obtaining justice in civil matters?
3. What might the benefits of the Woolf reforms have been?
4. Why do you think his concerns about the excessive cost of civil justice remain as valid today as they were at the time he reported?

The Jackson Report

The key importance of costs in creating the opportunities for access to justice has already been noted.[56] In evidence to the Jackson enquiry, one respondent[57] observed that the Woolf reforms aimed to achieve three things: greater speed; greater simplicity; and lower cost. Only the first had been achieved. Jackson identified some sixteen potential causes that give rise to excessive cost. Complex procedural process, the method of lawyers' fee charging (based on hourly rates rather than overall work outputs), the lack of control of pre-action costs, the complexity of some areas of law, the cost-shifting rules whereby the costs of one party are met by another,[58] and, sometimes, a lack of awareness by judges and barristers of what the costs implications of are, are amongst the factors identified by Jackson.

Proportionality of costs

At the outset the report identifies, as Woolf did, the need for costs to be proportionate to the value of the claim. If costs are disproportionate, 'then even a well resourced party may hesitate before pursuing a valid claim or maintaining a valid defence. That party may simply drop a good claim or capitulate to a weak claim'.[59]

Proportionality is a principle recognized in the CPR introduced following the Woolf reforms. The facts of *Lownds* v *Home Office*[60] illustrate the issue, with costs of approximately £17,000 being incurred in respect of a claim compromised at £3,000 damages. Although the appeal failed for transitional reasons in respect of the introduction of the Civil Procedure Rules, the case demonstrates vividly the fact that what is appropriate depends on the whole context of the case. In guidance given in its judgment, the court stated that the question of costs must be assessed (in the context

---

[56] See p 475.
[57] Civil Committee of the Council of Her Majesty's Circuit Judges: see Jackson, *op cit*, at para 3.2.
[58] See p 481.   [59] Report, *op cit*, para 2.5.   [60] [2002] 1 WLR 2450.

of the claimant's costs) in terms of the proportionality of the expenditure to the likely amounts at stake and recoverable. By contrast the proportionality of the defendant's expenditure will be in relation to the amount claimed, for the defendant is entitled to take the claim at face value. If costs appeared to be disproportionate, then it was for the claimant to show that the cost incurred was necessary. This left unclear the difference between expenditure that is proportionate and that which is necessary.[61] Jackson concludes that 'disproportionate costs do not become proportionate because they were necessary'. The continuing ineffectiveness of a proportionality test in controlling costs[62] led the report to recommend that rule changes are needed to ensure that cost benefit analysis has a key role to play. Costs are proportionate if they bear a reasonable relationship to the sums in issue, the value of any non-monetary relief, the complexity of the litigation, any additional work generated by the paying party, and any wider factors such as reputation of public importance.[63]

The incidence of costs

The basic rule is that costs are within the discretion of the court. In most cases the judge will order one side to pay all or a proportion of the costs of his opponent, unless the losing party is legally aided.[64] The basic rule hitherto has been that costs follow the event. A successful litigant had a right to costs at common law, but this right has been virtually removed by legislation so that at the present day the award of costs is discretionary. A court has discretion as to whether costs are payable by one party, the amount to be paid, and when they are to be paid.[65] It is not, of course, an absolute discretion and it is a wrong exercise of the discretion to deprive a party of his costs if he has been completely successful and guilty of no misconduct.[66] However, the exercise of the discretion will take in to account the conduct of the parties in the litigation.[67] The court will have regard to the conduct of the parties. It will need to have regard to the overriding objective, which, following Woolf, applies in civil litigation[68] and the extent, for example, to which pre-action protocols have been followed, with appropriate disclosure, or the extent to which the parties have engaged in alternative dispute resolution.[69] Unless there are special factors present, a successful party may expect his costs from an unsuccessful opponent, paid on an indemnity basis.[70]

---

[61] See Zuckerman, *Civil Procedure: Principles and Procedure* (Thompson, Sweet & Maxwell: 2nd edn, 2006) at paras 26.74–26.87.

[62] See *Willis* v *Nicolson* [2007] EWCA Civ 199; for a vivid example of disproportionate costs, see *Tesco plc* v *Competition Commission* [2009] CAT 26 (£1,391,904 claim for costs reduced to £342,000 in a judicial review claim).

[63] Report, *op cit,* para 5.15.

[64] In some circumstances, costs from a losing legally aided party may be recovered from the Legal Services Commission: see Access to Justice Act 1999, s 11, and Community Legal Service Regulations 2000, para 5.

[65] CPR 44.3(1). This may include costs against an unincorporated association: see *Huntingdon Life Sciences Group plc* v *Cass* [2005] EWHC 2233 (QB), [2005] 4 All ER 899.

[66] *Donald Campbell & Co Ltd* v *Pollack* [1927] AC 732, *per* Viscount Cave at 811–12.

[67] See p 547.   [68] See p 489.   [69] See p 495.   [70] CPR 44.3(2); see p 547.

Clearly, liability to pay not only one's own costs, but also, if unsuccessful, the costs of the successful party, is an inhibitor to access to the courts for civil justice. A number of approaches have been tried to ameliorate the effect of this. One is the growth of the use of conditional fee agreements, which are an important way of ensuring access to justice. We have already noted the development of conditional fee agreements as a means of securing funding for litigation and access to justice.[71] The growth of the use of protective costs orders has also played an important role, particularly in judicial review cases. These are discussed below.[72]

The general approach to costs awards was considered by the Jackson Report. It considered that these cost-shifting rules create 'perverse' incentives to increase costs in two situations. [73] Firstly, a party is running up costs not knowing who will pay the bill. If parties believe that additional expenditure increases the likelihood of success, and thus costs shifting, there is sometimes an incentive to spend. Secondly, where a defendant has admitted liability there is already knowledge as to who pays the costs and thus no incentive to keep them low. As part of a package of recommendations, focused mainly on conditional fee agreements,[74] the report proposed that a scheme of qualified one-way costs shifting should be adopted in some types of case. These would include personal injury and clinical negligence cases, as well as applications for judicial review.[75] A complete cost-shifting approach would mean that the loser would never pay the winner's costs. The proposed qualified shifting scheme will, if implemented, mean that the losing party only pays costs where it is reasonable for him or her to do so. In other words, like legally aided litigants, the loser would not generally be liable for costs unless it were reasonable for him or her not do so. That would be exceptional, and would be, effectively, a reversal of the current presumption that the costs discretion will be exercised in favour of the successful party. By reducing the financial risk there is less chance of a claimant being deterred from litigating against a powerful or wealthy defendant who has the ability to 'bump up' costs. Further, such a scheme will save costs because a claimant would no longer have to take out an after-the-event insurance policy to cover the risks of a costs award against him if he were to lose.[76] Of course, one result might be that unfairness ensues to a non-insured defendant, who would have to meet his own costs himself. The proposed rule would leave a discretion in the hand s of the court to order payment of such costs that it was reasonable to pay having regard to all of the circumstances including financial and the conduct of the litigation.[77]

Conditional fee agreements

We have already seen[78] that such agreements, authorized by the Courts and Legal Services Act 1990 (as amended in 1999 by the Access to Justice Act 1999), have largely superseded legal aid as a means of funding most types of litigation, and allow

[71] See p 408.   [72] See p 485.   [73] Jackson Report, para 3.22, at p 47.
[74] See pp 408 and 485.   [75] See p 511.   [76] See pp 482 and 587.
[77] Jackson Report, para 2.11, p 187.   [78] See p 408.

litigation to be entered into by a claimant on a somewhat inaccurately so-called 'no win, no fee basis'. They achieve this by providing for the client's fees and expenses to be payable only in certain specified circumstances.[79] The agreement specifies a 'success fee' that is chargeable if the case is won, and that provides an uplift to the costs that would normally be charged. The costs and the success fee are, in principle, recoverable from the losing party (subject to the court's discretion already discussed). There is, though, the prospect of lack of success. For that reason, the claimant also incurs the cost of pre-action insurance to cover costs should the claim fail and costs be awarded against the claimant. It is also possible to purchase insurance (after-the-event legal expenses insurance) to cover potential liability for the claimant's own costs. The premium payable will reflect the strength of the case and may be structured so that different sums are payable at different stages.[80] To prove liability for such matters, the claimant will have to produce a copy of the agreement, with non-relevant confidential detail obscured or deleted.[81]

The reasons for this development are well documented, and reflect the modern movement away from state-funded civil litigation through the legal aid scheme. They also potentially widen access to justice.[82] But they also clearly have a significant impact on questions of costs between parties because of the potential liability of a losing defendant for the success fee and the insurance premium. That is one cogent reason for the requirement that details of any conditional fee agreement funding arrangement be given at the commencement of proceedings by the claimant to the defendant.[83]

The principles to be applied in determining costs due in such circumstances have been worked through in a series of cases. One basic issue is the enforceability of the agreement, which must comply with section 58 of the 1990 Act and the Conditional Fee Agreements Regulations of 2000.[84] Insurers have been increasingly concerned to challenge agreements in which breach of the regulations and statutory requirements could be shown. The point was eventually disposed of in *Sharratt* v *London Central Bus Co Ltd (The Accident Group Test Cases)*,[85] in which the court held that only where departure from the requirements had a material adverse effect on either the protection afforded to the client or upon the proper administration of justice would a conditional fee agreement be unenforceable. If the client would have no cause for complaint then the costs basis inherent in the agreement would apply.

Another issue is the level of success fee recoverable from the losing party. The general principle in respect of costs is that they should be reasonable and proportionate. However, the proportionality of the success fee must be considered separately from

---

[79] 1990 Act, s 58(1) (as substituted by Access to Justice Act 1999, s 27). For a good summary of the legislative history, and the development of a principle discussed in *Thai Trading Co (A Firm)* v *Taylor* [1998] 3 All ER 65, see *Sharratt* v *London Central Bus Co Ltd (The Accident Group Test Cases)* [2003] 4 All ER 590 (CA), [2004] 3 All ER 325.

[80] *Rogers* v *Merthyr Tydfil CBC* [2006] EWCA Civ 134.

[81] *Sharratt* v *London Central Bus Co Ltd* [2003] 4 All ER 590 (CA), [2004] 3 All ER 325.

[82] See, e.g., Lord Phillips MR in *R (Factortame Ltd)* v *Secretary of State for the Environment, Transport and the Regions (No 8)* [2002] 3 WLR 104.

[83] See p 408.   [84] SI 2000/692.   [85] [2003] 4 All ER 590.

the normal costs incurred. The court will not simply look at the total sum of costs and success fee, and reach a conclusion as to the proportionality of the total sum. A good example is a defamation case, *Campbell* v *MGN (No 2)*.[86] The success fees in respect of costs attributable to an appeal to the House of Lords were 95 per cent and 100 per cent respectively for solicitor and counsel. The defendant challenged these, arguing that, in a defamation case, such sums were a disproportionate interference with the right to freedom of expression. The claim failed, the levels of success fee having to be considered separately, not as part of the overall level of costs. This conclusion was not accepted by the ECtHR, which has now found the success fees in that case to be disproportionate.

The success fee can be reduced if it is disproportionate. In determining that, regard must be had to the risk that the fee would not be payable, to the legal representative's liability for disbursements, and the availability of other forms of funding.[87] The Court of Appeal in *Callery* v *Gray (No 1)*[88] pointed to a reasonable success fee in a road traffic personal injury claim being no more than 20 per cent, bearing in mind that 99 per cent of such cases succeed. The facts of that case demonstrate the problem. The agreed success fee in the agreement was 60 per cent. An after-the-event insurance policy cost £367. The amount of compensation agreed by way of settlement was approximately £1,500. The costs judge reduced the success fee to 40 per cent, a figure, as noted above, reduced to 20 per cent on appeal. Yet in *Halloran* v *Delaney*[89] it was said that the appropriate success fee in such cases would normally use a figure of 5 per cent as a starting point, unless persuaded otherwise by the particular circumstances of the case, a conclusion supported by the House of Lords in *Callery* v *Gray*[90] in the context of modest and straightforward cases of this type. It also recognized the need, perhaps, for different success fee uplifts for different costs or different parts of the litigation.

There remains the question of the insurance fee. In deciding whether the recovery of such costs is permissible, the court will have regard to the availability of any pre-existing insurance cover, level and extent of the cover provided, whether any part of the premium was debateable in the event of early settlement, and any commission received by the claimant or his agents.[91] The stage at which it is appropriate to take out the insurance cover will be a matter for the court to decide on an individual basis.

It is widely accepted that the introduction of conditional fee agreements has increased access to justice.[92] However, Jackson identified flaws in the system. Conditional fee arrangements are available to all, irrespective of means, provided that there is a solicitor willing to take the case. Those who benefit from such agreements have no direct interest in the level of costs being incurred, because their own costs will usually be

---

[86] See [2005] UKHL 61. But now see the contrary view of the ECtHR in *MGN* v *UK* [2011] ECHR 66.

[87] Practice Direction 44, [11.8].   [88] [2001] 1 WLR 2112.   [89] [2003] 1 WLR 28.

[90] [2002] 3 All ER 652.

[91] Practice Direction 44, [11.100]. See also *Samonini* v *London General Transport Services Ltd* [2005] EWHC 90001 (Costs).

[92] See Ministry of Justice, *Proposals for Reform of Civil Litigation Funding and Costs in England and Wales* (HMSO, November 2010), p 20, para 50.

met either by the after-the-event insurance (if the case is lost) or by the other party if (if the case is won). The costs burden on the losing party is excessive, whilst there is a danger that lawyers will under the conditional fee arrangement will 'cherry pick' cases most likely to be won.[93] Paradoxically, some argue that conditional fee agreements, rather than discouraging weak cases and settlements, encourage taking cases to trial to secure a full success fee, and encourage defendants to make a commercial decision to 'pay off' the claimant as a commercial decision rather than defending the claim at much greater cost.[94]

The solution, Jackson concluded, was to abolish the recoverability of success fees, which would henceforth be borne by the party entering into the conditional fee agreement. That would mean that if the claimant were successful, any damages recovered would be reduced, because the claimant would have to bear the solicitor's success fee. To avoid this conclusion, Jackson recommended that there should be a 10 per cent increase in general damages to assist the claimant in paying the success fee. Together with the proposed regime of qualified one-way costs shifting, this would have the effect of reducing the problems associated with conditional fee agreements whilst protecting the most vulnerable from an award of costs against them.

Protective costs orders

One important development in recent years has been the increasing use of protective costs orders. Originally introduced as a general power vested in a court to order a limit to the amount of costs that could be recovered from a losing party, they have become particularly important in the context of judicial review, where individuals or groups are challenging the power of the state or public authority. Indeed, following an international agreement, a state is under a duty to ensure that individuals have procedures that they can use to challenge decisions by the state that affect the environment.[95] The extension of the use of this power into the judicial review context has facilitated a wide range of judicial review claims, and led to the development of significant case law.[96]

The Jackson Report recommends for the future that the proper approach should be by the principle, explained above, of qualified one-way costs shifting, with a claimant not normally having to bear the costs of the public authority. This would be an approach applicable to all challenges and avoid distinctions between environmental and non-environmental cases that are beginning to develop in the protective costs order case law.

---

[93] Jackson Report, at paras 2.11.   [94] *Reform of Civil Litigation*, at para 60, p 24.

[95] See Aarhus Convention, Article 10a.

[96] See *R (on the application of Corner House Research) v Secretary of State for Trade and Industry* [2005] EWCA Civ 192; *R (on application of Buglife—The Invertebrate Conservation Trust) v Thurrock Thames Gateway Development Corporation* [2008] EWCA Civ 1209; *R (Garner) v Elmbridge Borough Council* [2010] EWCA Civ 1006; *R (Coedbach Action Group) v Secretary of State for Climate Change and Energy* [2010] EWCA 2312.

Wider changes

The report makes widespread and detailed recommendations, much of the detail of which is beyond the scope of this text. These are particularly in the context of conditional fee agreements,[97] the incidence of costs orders,[98] and fixed costs. It makes recommendations of a detailed nature relating to personal injury and other specific types of litigation, recognizing that one size may not fit all types of civil litigation. It makes recommendations relating to pre-action protocols, alternative dispute resolution disclosure, and case management.[99] Through this range of detailed changes, the expectation of the report is that civil litigation will be cheaper and thus both fairer and more effective

KEY ISSUE

The government has accepted the thrust of many of the 109 recommendations made by the Jackson Review.[100] The Green Paper accepts his assessment that costs fall disproportionately on defendants, and that reform of conditional fee agreements would 'significantly reduce' legal costs in civil litigation. A consultation process is under way, which will conclude in spring 2011, and legislation is expected thereafter. The government noted the comments of Lord Woolf that a defect in the system is that it is 'too expensive in that costs often exceed the value of the claim'.[101]

At the heart of the problem is that the conditional fee agreement arrangements, whilst enhancing accessibility to the courts in many cases, and in a great number of cases supplanting legal aid, distorted the balance between the parties, putting the claimant in a better position than the defendant.[102] The changes in the rules relating to the incidence of costs and the recovery of success fees are intended to redress that balance. The potential unfairness to a claimant in restricting recoverability will be met by an enhanced level of damages, many of which will be funded by the defendant or his or her insurer should he or she lose. Thus the approach is not to reduce the costs of damages but to put in place a system where parties may be more aware of the costs of what they do, and the potential impact on themselves.

❓ Questions

1. Will the new rules, if implemented, be fair to all parties?
2. Will the perceived imbalance between claimants and defendants be addressed?
3. What will be the effect of the presumption of the new non-costs-shifting rules?

---

[97] See p 482.   [98] See p 547.
[99] See pp 504, 495 and 489; Ministry of Justice, *op cit*.
[100] See p 480.   [101] Consultation Paper, at p 10.   [102] Consultation Paper, p 11.

Administration of the civil justice system

The growing impetus for change was also driven by the need to achieve efficiency and cost-effectiveness. As the Middleton Report put it:[103]

> The civil justice system as a whole is not managed coherently, nor do its individual parts seem to be managed with efficiency much in mind. There is indeed a view that efficiency might be incompatible with justice: that it is always desirable and necessary to take infinite pains in order to achieve the best possible result in each case. Desirable though this may seem as a principle, it inevitably comes up against the limitation of available resources... I have therefore concentrated on efficiency. I take that to mean getting more out of a given level of resources, or the same amount at lower cost.

Responsibility for administration of civil justice now lies with the Lord Chancellor and the Ministry of Justice. The Woolf Report[104] recommended the establishment of a Civil Justice Council as a body with ongoing responsibility for overseeing and coordinating the proposals for reform contained in that report. Such a Council was established in 1998. Its primary task is to advise the Lord Chancellor on how the civil justice system can be improved. Section 6 of the Civil Procedure Act imposes a duty on the Council to keep the civil justice system under review, to consider how to make the civil justice system more accessible fair and efficient, to advise the Lord Chancellor and the judiciary on the development of the civil justice system, and to refer proposals for change to the Lord Chancellor and the Civil Procedure Rule Committee.

The Council comprised representatives from the judiciary, the legal profession, civil servants with knowledge of the administration of justice, persons with experience and knowledge of consumer affairs, individuals with knowledge and experience of the lay advice sector, and those able to represent the interests of particular kinds of litigant (for example, companies or business).[105]

Rules of court

Civil litigation is conducted by the parties in accordance with rules of court. Prior to the implementation of the Woolf recommendations separate rules existed in respect of the county court (County Court Rules) and the Supreme Court (the Rules of the Supreme Court). The Civil Procedure Rules (CPR) replaced both, and amount to a new procedural code.[106] They are intended to be free-standing, applied individually to the facts of the case, and certainly not limited by pre-CPR case law.[107] That does not mean that the development of principles in pre-CPR case law should be ignored,

---

[103] See p 413.   [104] *Op cit*, para 19.
[105] For general information about the Council, see **www.civiljusticecouncil.gov.uk**
[106] CPR 1.1(1).
[107] *Hamblin* v *Field*, (2000) The Times, 26 April; *Purdy* v *Cambran* [1999] CPLR 843.

still less that the appeal courts should not continue to develop principles as to how the rules should be used.[108]

The rules do not directly affect rules of substantive law.[109] Nor do the rules prevent the courts within their own jurisdiction from innovating where the rules are silent on a point,[110] or deprive the courts of any inherent jurisdiction. In *Grobbelaar* v *News Group Newspapers*,[111] Lord Bingham described this as follows:

> ...the inherent jurisdiction of the court may be defined as the reserve or fund of powers, a residual source of powers, which the court may draw upon as necessary whenever it is just and equitable to do so, and in particular to ensure the observance of the due process of law to prevent improper vexation or oppression, to do justice between the parties and to secure a fair trial between them.

The power of a judge to refuse to hear persons who have no right of audience before the court, or counsel who are improperly dressed, or to sit in camera, or to abort a trial and start a new one where a procedural irregularity has occurred, or to adjourn the proceedings are all inherent powers. The important development of *Mareva* injunctions[112] and *Anton Pillar* orders[113] (under the old regime) derived from the inherent jurisdiction of the court, and there is no reason to doubt that such judicial creativity can continue under the new regime. Likewise, the court has always had inherent power to regulate its own procedure. In *Langley* v *North West Water Authority*,[114] the Court of Appeal held that a Liverpool solicitor was bound to comply with a code of practice issued by the Liverpool county court. This amounted to a local Practice Direction, which the court was entitled to issue under its inherent jurisdiction, except to the extent that it was concurrent with statute law or rules of court.

The power to issue Practice Directions is contained, now, in the Civil Procedure Act 1997,[115] which sets out the process that must be followed. It is not open to a court to ignore that procedure, but the statutory requirements do not take away the

---

[108] See, e.g., *Ford* v *GKR Construction* [2000] 1 All ER 802.

[109] The comments of Henn Collins MR in *Re Coles and Ravenshear* [1907] 1 KB 1, at 4, to the effect that 'the relation of the rules of practice to the work of justice is intended to be that of handmaiden rather than mistress' remain true in concept, but must be viewed in accordance with the overriding objective, as to which see p 489.

[110] See Andrews, *op cit*, at para 1.10 citing as an example *Venables* v *News Group Newspapers Ltd* [2001] 1 All ER 908: perpetual injunction to restrain publication of details of T and V being revealed. T and V had been convicted of the notorious murder of James Bulger, a crime attracting outrage and vigilantism.

[111] [2002] 4 All ER 732, citing Jacob, 'The Inherent Jurisdiction of the Court' (1970) CLP 23.

[112] *Mareva Compania Naviera SA* v *International Bulkcarriers SA* [1980] 1 All ER 213. These are now known as freezing orders: see p 518.

[113] *Anton Pillar KG* v *Manufacturing Processes Ltd* [1976] Ch 55, [1976] 1 All ER 779. These are now known as search orders: see p 515.

[114] [1997] 2 FLR 841. See also Sir John Donaldson in *R* v *Secretary of State for the Home Department, ex parte Swati* [1986] 1 All ER 717, [1986] 1 WLR 477. See now CPR 3.1.

[115] Section 5, as substituted by Constitutional Reform Act 2005.

case-management powers of a court under the Civil Procedure Rules.[116] Nor does this process prevent a court from filling a gap in the rules or in a Practice Direction with its own suggested procedure.[117]

The overriding objective

The CPR commence with the statement of an overriding objective to which any court must seek to give effect when exercising any power given by the rules, or when it interprets any rule (CPR 1.2). At the start, this code defines what dealing with cases 'justly' means. It includes, so far as practicable:

(a) ensuring that the parties are on an equal footing;

(b) saving expense;

(c) dealing with the case in ways that are proportionate to:

    (i) the amount of money involved;

    (ii) the importance of the case;

    (iii) the complexity of the issues;

    (iv) the financial position of each party;

(d) ensuring that it is dealt with fairly and expeditiously;

(e) allotting it to an appropriate share of the court's resources, whilst taking into account the need to allocate resources to other cases.

It is the duty of all parties, and their lawyers, to comply with this objective.[118] It may on occasion guide how a court actually decides a case, or how it deals with questions of costs. One key example of this is the debate that has been ongoing as to whether a court has the right to compel unwilling parties to engage in alternative dispute resolution and whether a failure to do so could, and should, be penalized by a refusal to award costs that otherwise the party would expect to receive.[119]

The CPR contain the relevant rules. They also contain Practice Directions, which amount to guides to the interpretation of the rules themselves,[120] and also pre-action protocols, with which a court will expect a party to comply. A failure to do so may be reflected by a court in the grant, or refusal, of a discretionary remedy or procedure, or may be reflected in any orders for costs (CPR 3.1(4)).

---

[116] See *Bovade* v *Secretary of State for Communities and Local Government* [2009 EWCA Civ 171.

[117] See, e.g., *R (on application of Buglife, The Invertebrate Conservation Trust)* v *Thurrock Thames Gateway Development Corporation* [2008] EWCA Civ 1209

[118] CPR,1.3; Access to Justice Act 1969, s 42.

[119] For discussion of this important issue, see p 491, and see, e.g., *Dunnett* v *Railtrack (Practice Note)* [2002] 1 WLR 2434. For the rules relating to costs, see p 547.

[120] *Godwin* v *Swindon BC* [2001] EWCA Civ 1478 *per* May LJ.

The terminology

As part of the process of seeking to simplify and demystify civil litigation recommended by Woolf, the CPR changed many of the names, terms, and expressions formerly used, and to be found in the pre-CPR case law and texts. Whether the changes achieve their objective, or are simply change for change's sake, is a matter of taste and opinion. Where necessary these are dealt with at the appropriate part of the text, but the following should be noted at the outset:

- plaintiff—now **claimant**;
- guardian *ad litem*—now **litigation friend**;
- writ—now **claim form**;
- leave—now **permission**;
- pleadings—now **statement of case**;
- interlocutory relief—now **interim remedies**;
- *ex parte*—now **without notice**.

Settlement and alternative means of dispute resolution

Introduction

Increasingly, those with disputes have sought alternative means of dispute resolution. As noted above, litigation, particularly in the High Court, is both time-consuming and expensive, and suffers the disadvantage of, generally, being conducted in public. Arbitration has long been seen as an accepted alternative to court procedures, particularly in the sphere of commerce and business, and involves a binding resolution of a dispute by an arbitrator. The principle of arbitration was adopted in respect of small claims in the county court, evolving into the small-claims track introduced as part of the Woolf reforms.[121] In addition, there has begun a tendency to look for other, more informal, forms of mechanism for the resolution of disputes, generally known as alternative dispute resolution (ADR).

Unlike arbitration, the characteristics of such mechanisms are, often, those of conciliation, mediation, and negotiation, which by their nature will not generally involve the imposition of the verdict or conclusion. Such means of avoiding full-scale litigation are particularly helpful to parties to disputes in the commercial or business sectors. As long ago as 1994,[122] the Commercial Court encouraged alternative dispute resolution, particularly where the costs of litigation were likely to be wholly disproportionate to

---

[121] See p 478.
[122] *Practice Note (Commercial Court Alternative Dispute Resolution)* [1994] 1 All ER 34, 1 WLR 14.

the amount at stake, and cost-effective.[123] Woolf envisaged a 'landscape of civil litigation…fundamentally different from what it is now', starting with the premise that litigation should be avoided where possible, but, if it occurred, less adversarial and more cooperative. He urged the use of ADR in the civil justice process, a fact reflected in the provisions of the CPR. 'Active case management' is one of the key principles introduced by the CPR, and that includes a court's 'encouraging parties to use an alternative dispute resolution procedure if it considers that appropriate, and facilitating the use of such a procedure'.[124] ADR is a 'method of resolving disputes otherwise than through the use of such a procedure'.[125] Pre-action protocols[126] emphasize the exchange of information at an early stage and promotion of negotiations leading to settlement. Parties are required to follow a 'reasonable procedure' intended to avoid litigation, and the parties must state whether they are willing to enter into ADR.[127] The effect of decisions elsewhere in the civil justice system also should not be overlooked. Section 4(4)(c) of the Access to Justice Act 1999 requires persons carrying out functions under the Community Legal Service[128] to do so with a view to achieving 'the swift and fair resolution of disputes without unnecessary or unduly protracted proceedings in court'. There are thus financial incentives, which may be increased with changes to the Community Legal Services approach to legal aid.[129] The legal aid scheme has not always encouraged litigation to be seen as a last resort, because of the higher rates lawyers have been paid for representation as opposed to legal help (which provides support for early resolution of disputes), and because most legal aid remuneration has been based on hourly rates (with therefore greater rewards for more adversarial processes).[130]

The Jackson Report[131] also stressed the important of ADR as a means of reducing costs. It concluded that insufficient use was made of ADR, particularly mediation, as a tool. It concluded that an appropriate costs regime would encourage a greater use of ADR.[132.]

Distinctions must be made between the different forms of process mentioned above. Arbitration is an alternative form of dispute adjudication, with the result usually binding on both sides. Mediation, conciliation, and negotiation are, in effect, means of assisted dispute settlement:[133] no settlement can be imposed and the onus is on the parties to come to an agreement. The nature of the process may vary: it can be

---

[123] See, generally, Partington, 'Alternative Dispute Resolution: Recent Developments, Future Challenges' (2004) 23 CJQ 99; Genn, *Court-Based Initiative for Non-Family Civil Disputes: The Commercial Court and the Court of Appeal*, Research Report for LCD (2002).

[124] CPR 4(2)(e).   [125] Glossary, CPR.   [126] See p 504.

[127] *Practice Direction for Pre-Action Protocols*, para 4.2. Some specific pre-action protocols specifically require such consideration: e.g. the clinical negligence protocol.

[128] As to which, see p 415.

[129] See DCA Consultation Paper, *A New Focus for Civil Legal Aid: Encouraging Early Resolution, Discouraging Unnecessary Litigation* (HMSO, 2004).

[130] Consultation Paper, *op cit*, n 57, at p 8.

[131] See p 480.   [132] Report, *op cit*, p 355 at para 1.5.

[133] *Alternative Dispute Resolution: A Discussion Paper* (LCD, November 1999), at para 2.4.

a process 'designed to facilitate agreement'[134] or it can be evaluative by encouraging settlement through evaluation of the parties' rights and case. Different mediators adopt different styles and approaches.[135] And the mediation may not be wholly voluntary: distinctions can be drawn between ADR that forms an alternative to the commencement of proceedings in the first place, and court-ordered ADR once proceedings are under way.[136]

Arbitration

Arbitration is one, long-standing alternative form of dispute resolution used by parties to contracts, particularly contracts involving the construction industry, and favoured as a form of dispute resolution by parties to international commercial contracts.[137] The law hitherto has been governed by statutory provision, principally the Arbitration Acts of 1950 and 1979, as explained and developed by common law. In 1996 a new Arbitration Act was passed, which repealed earlier legislation, and which was designed to provide a statutory statement of the relevant statutory and common law principles, in clear and comprehensible language, complying where appropriate with international rules and principles governing arbitration.[138]

Section 1 of that Act states the general principles governing arbitration:

(a) the object of arbitration is to obtain the fair resolution of disputes by an impartial tribunal without unnecessary delay or expense;

(b) the parties should be free to agree how their disputes are resolved, subject only to such safeguards as are necessary in the public interest;

(c) in matters governed by Part I of the Act (which governs arbitration under an arbitration agreement) the court should not intervene except as the Act provides. The Act applies where the 'seat' of the arbitration is in England and Wales, in other words, that England and Wales is the jurisdiction designated by the parties to the arbitration agreement, or by or in accordance with that agreement.

---

[134] See also DCA Public Service Agreement 3, which aims to reduce the proportion of disputes resolved by resort to the courts.

[135] See the analysis by Prince in *Court-based Mediation: A Preliminary Analysis of the small Claims Mediation Scheme at Exeter Crown Court*, Research Report for the Civil Justice Council (CJC, March 2004), at p 12.

[136] For court-ordered ADR and its implications, see p 497.

[137] The position where there are competing jurisdictions is complex: see *Allianz SPA v Went Tankers Inc, The Fornt Connor* C185/07 [2009] 1 All ER (Comm) 435; *National Navigation Co v Endesa Generacion SA* [2009] EWCA Civ 1397.

[138] See *Report of the Department of Trade and Industry Departmental Advisory Committee on International Commercial Arbitration* (HMSO, 1985) (the Mustill Report). That Committee prepared the draft Bill in 1995.

The jurisdiction of arbitrators usually arises out of contract, although there are numerous statutory provisions that provide for the reference of disputes to arbitration. An agreement to refer disputes to arbitration is a contract and, as such, is subject to the ordinary law of contract.

In *Premium Nafta Products Ltd* v *Fili Shipping Co Ltd*,[139] Lord Hoffmann identified the nature of arbitration. He observed:

> Arbitration is consensual. It depends on the intention of the parties as expressed in their agreement. Only the agreement can tell you what kind of disputes they intended to submit to arbitration. But the meaning which the parties intended to express by the words which they used will be affected by the commercial background and the readers' understanding of the purpose for which the agreement was made.

Such an agreement must be in writing if the provisions of the 1996 Act are to apply.[140] Any provision purporting to oust the jurisdiction of the courts is not effective to do so,[141] and may well infringe Article 6 of the European Convention on Human Rights, although there is no objection to a clause that makes reference to arbitration a condition precedent to a right of action. The effect of such a clause, traditionally known as a *Scott* v *Avery*[142] clause, is that if a party does institute proceedings without referring the dispute to arbitration, the clause may be pleaded as a defence in those proceedings and the other party may, after certain procedural formalities, apply to the court for an order staying the proceedings.[143] The court must grant a stay unless satisfied that the arbitration agreement is null and void, inoperative, or incapable of being performed. Just because it is alleged that the contract the subject of the arbitration is void does not necessarily mean that the arbitration agreement itself is void. That depends on the context and circumstances.

Procedure

Procedure on arbitrations is governed (except, in relation to statutory references, where the statute in question otherwise provides) by the Arbitration Act 1996. The issues arising must (in the absence of contrary agreement) be decided according to the rules of law considered by the court to be applicable, decided in accordance with the principles of conflict of laws.[144] The arbitrator must act fairly and impartially as between the parties, giving each party a reasonable opportunity of putting his case, and for dealing with his opponents' case, and must adopt procedures suitable to the circumstances of the particular case, avoiding unnecessary delay and expense.[145] The arbitrator must decide all procedural and evidential matters, subject to the right of the parties to agree any matter. The arbitrator may thus decide when and where proceedings are to be held, in what language, what documents should be produced and disclosed, what questions should be put to and answered by the parties, whether to apply strict rules of evidence, the extent to which there should be oral or written

[139] [2007] UKHL 40. [140] 1996 Act, s 5(1). [141] Ibid, s 87.
[142] (1856) 5 HL Cas 811. [143] Arbitration Act 1996, s 9. [144] 1996 Act, s 46(3).
[145] Ibid, s 33(1).

submissions, and whether the tribunal should take the initiative in ascertaining the facts and the law.[146] In other words, the arbitrator has complete discretion to depart from traditional procedures, and to act inquisitorially. Arbitrators may appoint experts, legal advisers, or assessors to advise them.[147] Parties to arbitration are entitled to legal representation unless they agree otherwise.[148] They can also obtain a witness summons to secure the attendance of a witness.[149] Section 41 of the 1996 Act entitles an arbitrator to dismiss a claim where:

(a) there has been inordinate and inexcusable delay on the part of the claimant in pursuing the claim; and

(b) the delay:

    (i) will give rise to a substantial risk that it is not possible to have a fair resolution of the issues in that claim; or

    (ii) has caused, or is likely to cause or have caused, serious prejudice to the respondent.

Under section 18 of the 1996 Act the High Court has various powers to appoint arbitrators and umpires in default of appointment by the parties, the Act specifying in detail the various powers that arise so that disputes are resolved without recourse to the court. The High Court also has power to revoke the authority of an arbitrator or umpire on the ground of delay, bias, or improper conduct,[150] and has inherent jurisdiction to stay arbitration proceedings by injunction. There used to be provision whereby an arbitrator might, and, if directed by the court, had to, state in the form of a 'special case' for the opinion of the High Court, either his award or any question of law arising in the reference.[151] The current position is found in section 87 of the 1996 Act. This provides that the parties may enter into an 'exclusion agreement', but only if they do so after the arbitration has commenced. There will then be no power in the High Court to consider a question of law arising in the course of the arbitration; nor will there be any right of appeal. Therefore (subject to the limited power of the High Court to set aside or remit an award for misconduct) the arbitrator's decision will be final. Exclusion agreements entered into before the arbitration is commenced are effective only in a limited class of cases and, in particular, are invalid in the case of a 'domestic arbitration agreement', which is basically, an agreement that does not provide for arbitration outside the United Kingdom and is not one to which no United Kingdom national or resident is a party.[152] The decision of the arbitrator is in the form of an 'award', dealing with all of the issues on which reference was made. The award may contain provision for the payment of money, costs, or an order of specific performance (except of a contract relating to land).[153] As between the parties the award binds the parties in relation to the issues decided, thus extinguishing any cause of action in relation thereto.

---

[146] Ibid, s 34(1).   [147] Ibid, s 37(1).   [148] Ibid, s 36(1).
[149] Ibid, s 43(1), CPR 34.2.   [150] Ibid, s 24.   [151] Arbitration Act 1950, s 21.
[152] 1996 Act, s 85.   [153] Ibid, s 67.

Intervention by the court

The court's powers over arbitrations are governed by the 1996 Act. The court may hear applications, and section 44 gives the court the power to make certain orders during an arbitration, unless the parties otherwise agree. These powers relate to the taking, inspection or preservation of evidence.[154] The court has powers in respect of a completed arbitration, under section 69 of the 1996 Act, including power where there have been serious irregularities or actions outside of jurisdiction by the arbitrator. A right of appeal on a point of law may often exist, unless excluded by agreement.

Mediation and negotiation

Family matters

Conciliation and mediation plays a significant role in divorce proceedings.[155] The trend generally is towards less court intervention in matrimonial matters. Divorce itself is basically a paper exercise, and the majority of financial matters, and matters relating to children, are dealt with by consent. The 1990s saw a general trend towards encouraging, and requiring, mediation in the context of families. The Family Law Act 1996 encourages and requires mediation to occur. The same philosophy applies in the context of cases involving children, and a range of projects aimed to complement the judicial process through ADR in childcare cases, by identifying and exploring the issues to be determined and exploring options on which the parties could agree. Pilot projects have been run in childcare cases involving public law issues: these include a joint Alternative Dispute Resolution Project run by National Family Mediation and the Tavistock Centre, funded by the Department of Health, aiming to provide mediation as an alternative to the court process in child protection, fostering, adoption, or contact cases in which there is a dispute between parents, carers, and local authority social workers.[156] National Family Mediation has also developed policies involving mediation in domestic violence cases. Since section 29 of the Family Law Act 1996 was introduced, the Legal Services Commission requires divorcing or separating couples who are eligible for legal aid and who are in dispute on matters relating to children to attend an interview with a mediator as a precondition to the consideration of an application for legal aid. Mediation services are available at a growing number of major centres. Future changes announced by government may extend this requirement to engage in mediation beyond legally aided litigants to include all litigants in family disputes, even if they are financing their own legal representation, making it clear to all that mediation is a potentially cheaper and less stressful means of dispute resolution.[157]

---

[154] See *Cetelem SA* v *Roust Holdings Ltd* [2005] EWCA Civ 18, [2005] 4 All ER 52, disapproving *Hiscox Underwriting Ltd* v *Dixon, Manchester & Co Ltd* [2004] EWHC 479.

[155] In this and other forms of mediation the quality is important. The Civil Mediation Council in December 2005 introduced an accredited scheme for court mediation: see Fry, 'It's Good to Talk' (2006) 156 NLJ 132.

[156] See Walsh, 'Working in the Family System' [1997] Fam Law at 109–10.

[157] See *The Times*, 29 December 2010.

Changes in legal funding contribute to this process. The Community Legal Service has restructured Legal Help, General Family Help, and Help with Mediation,[158] with a single level of service called Family Help intended to cover all non-adversarial family dispute resolution, coupled with a further reduction in funding for representation in contested proceedings.[159] This is now being piloted and rolled out through the Family Advice and Information Service. The philosophy of diverting from the courts was well summarized as follows:[160]

> [Research] has highlighted parents' awareness of the negative impact of conflict and sub-optimal contact arrangements on their children and their desire to find a better way of sorting these issues out…most do not want to resort to the courts. They are led or feel pressed there. Courts are not possibly the best equipped to deal with the emotional and practical problems being brought before them. The process can be (and is) criticised for being too backward-looking and focused on fact-finding: it is adversarial and may actually increase and prolong conflict…Courts certainly have a place in this—for those cases where safety is an issue or where no amount of help will reduce the conflict—but we estimate that there might be up to 60 per cent of the current court caseload that need not and should not really be there.

Other court-based mediation

Court-based mediation schemes are now normal, and a key way of diverting cases from the long and expensive road to full trial.[161] An example is the Court of Appeal Mediation scheme for non-family appeals, conducted by the Centre of Excellence for Dispute Resolution (CEDR Solve). CEDR deals with some 4,000 mediations each year, excluding small-claims mediations, which number about 2,000 per year.[162] The Civil Mediation Council (CMC) members conducted some 8,204 mediations in 2008, and report a significant upward trend in the numbers.[163] Some areas were identified by the CMC as being somewhat resistant to mediation: personal injury and clinical negligence cases in particular. In addition, all courts now have access to the Small Claims Mediation Service hotline for resolving small claims.

Contractual and regulatory disputes

Some contracts specify a form of dispute resolution that, at any rate initially, requires disputes to be arbitrated or decided by an arbitrator or complaint resolution procedure. Examples of this are many, and include not only standard building agreements, but also more consumer-orientated matters such as some disputes between holiday-maker and travel company. Such agreements do not necessarily oust the jurisdiction

---

[158] As to which, see p 417.

[159] Parental disputes about arrangements for their children amount to some 28 per cent of the civil legal aid budget.

[160] Community Legal Service Consultation Paper, *op cit*, at p 18.

[161] See generally Genn, *op cit*.

[162] Jackson Report, p 356, para 2.2.   [163] Ibid, at para 2.3.

of the courts. In addition, a range of dispute resolution mechanisms may exist, and are on the increase.[164] The Confederation of British Industry has established the Centre for Effective Dispute Resolution (CEDR). The City Disputes Panel was created to deal with disputes in the banking and finance sector.

In the public sector, the government has sought to increase the use of ADR as an alternative to litigation. The Environment Council offers an ADR service for public interest and environmental disputes. The National Health Service has been involved in pilot mediation projects. The Housing Ombudsman refers disputes in relation to public sector housing. The Planning Inspectorate has a pilot project in the context of planning appeals. Indeed Woolf, in his Final Report,[165] identified the fact that applicants for judicial review should be encouraged to settle their disputes without recourse to the courts, through grievance procedures and ombudsman remedies that are increasingly available. Such complaints mechanisms exist increasingly in the sphere of public law: for example, the NHS complaints procedure or the independent Housing Ombudsman noted above.[166]

All of these mechanisms may have consequences for the availability of judicial remedies. For example, section 26 of the Children Act 1989 provided for a mechanism for dealing with complaints. In *R v Birmingham City Council, ex parte A*,[167] the applicant sought judicial review of the actions of the local authority in failing to provide suitable accommodation for a severely disturbed child. The application failed, the court holding that the appropriate response was to utilize the statutory complaints mechanism, not to seek judicial review. Again, and more recently, in *Frank Cowell* v *Plymouth City Council*,[168] Lord Woolf himself criticized the abuse of judicial review in a case involving the rehousing of elderly residents of a care home, describing the process as 'over-judicialized'.

Court-based schemes and court-led ADR requirements

Courts have a key role to play. Judges of the Court of Appeal may recommend mediation when dealing with permission to appeal: in its first year, a settlement rate of 68 per cent of cases referred to it was achieved. The Small Claims Track Mediation Service, provided by the Court Service, achieves a high settlement rate. A further example is the Court Settlement Process (CSP) in the Technology and Construction Court. Since June 2006, specially trained judges offer CSP, where, following a request from the parties, a case-managing judge feels that the parties should be able to achieve an amicable settlement.

It will be clear from the above that some courts have played a role in the development of ADR. Since 1993 the Commercial Court has been identifying cases regarded as appropriate for ADR. In some cases judges have suggested ADR. In others an order

---

[164] See Nesic, 'Mediation: On the Rise in the United Kingdom?', to be found at **www.adr. civiljusticecouncil.gov.uk/updocs/client0/Nesic.doc**

[165] At p 251.   [166] See Nichol, 'Available Dispute Resolution', *Legal Action*, December 1997, p 6.

[167] [1991] 3 All ER 610, [1991] 1 WLR 697.   [168] (2002) The Times, 8 January.

has been made requiring the parties to attempt ADR, a position that needs now to be reviewed in the light of the decision in *Halsey* v *Milton Keynes General NHS Trust*.[169] It stops short of compulsion. It was described as follows in *Halsey*:

> It is the strongest form of encouragement. It requires the parties to exchange lists of neutral individuals who are available to conduct 'ADR procedures', to endeavour in good faith to agree a neutral individual or panel and to 'take such reasonable steps they may be advised to resolve their disputes by ADR procedures before the neutral individual or panel so chosen...' The order also provides that if the case is not settled 'the parties shall inform the court what steps towards ADR have been taken and (without prejudice to matters of privilege) why such steps have failed'.

If, following an ADR order, there has been a failure to settle, the parties must explain what steps were taken towards ADR, and why they failed. By 2000 the number of such orders had reached sixty-eight in a six-month period.[170] Typically, ADR occurred in about 50 per cent of cases in which such an order was made, with a success rate for settlement in those cases of about 52 per cent. The research showed that ADR had some impact in reducing the proportion of cases going to trial, even if the ADR itself had proved unsuccessful. It identified the fact that orders can have a positive effect in opening up communication between the parties and avoiding the fear of one side showing weakness in being the first to suggest settlement.

Many other court-based initiatives can be identified. They include schemes at the Patents Court and the Central London County Court, a scheme in Exeter,[171] and in several other centres.

Given the growth in interest and activity in ADR since the early 1990s, and now the positive obligation to seek to avoid litigation contained in the CPR, key questions remain as to whether the parties can be forced to engage in mediation. Of course, the parties to a contract may have stipulated that a negotiated settlement or mediation is the first step, before litigation may be considered. An agreement to negotiate has been held not to be enforceable, because of the lack of sufficient certainty as to what is means,[172] but, by contrast, the House of Lords in *Channel Tunnel Group Ltd* v *Balfour Beatty Construction Ltd*[173] held that a court has a discretionary power to stay proceedings[174] if there is a dispute mediation clause equivalent to an agreement to arbitrate. Although the matter may not be completely clear,[175] a prior agreement is likely, if it is sufficiently clear and certain, to be binding.[176]

That conclusion is probably inevitable given the attitude of the courts since the introduction of the CPR and its requirement to consider ADR. A contrary conclusion

---

[169] See p 499.   [170] See Genn, *op cit.*
[171] See Prince, *op cit.*   [172] *Walford* v *Miles* [1992] 1 All ER 453.
[173] [1993] AC 334. See also *Scott UK Ltd* v *F E Barber Ltd* [1997] 3 All ER 540.
[174] As to which, see p 524.
[175] See *Halifax Financial Services Ltd* v *Intuitive Systems Ltd* [1999] 1 All ER (Comm) 303.
[176] The key question may be the mandatory nature of the procedure agreed: see *Cable & Wireless* v *IBM* [2002] EWHC 2059 (Comm).

would fly in the face of public policy.[177] Under the CPR parties may seek a stay to attempt ADR[178] and a failure to engage in ADR following a court's direction may be reflected in any costs order sought or made. In *Dunnet v Railtrack plc*,[179] a defendant's application for costs was refused because of a failure to mediate. If parties 'turned down out of hand the chance of alternative dispute resolution when suggested by the court…they may have to face uncomfortable costs consequences'.[180] Another court considered that the right question to ask was: is there, on an objective viewpoint, any real chance of mediation succeeding?[181] On the particular facts the court did not think so, and therefore did not deprive the claimant of his costs.

The authorities generally have proved inconsistent.[182] For that reason the guidance given in two cases in the Court of Appeal, *Halsey* v *Milton Keynes General NHS Trust* and *Steel* v *Joy*,[183] is to be welcomed. In neither case was a party deprived of costs because of a failure to mediate. In *Halsey*, a clinical medical case, the defendant believed that it had a very strong case, that mediation costs would be disproportionately high, and the claimant's requests in pre-action correspondence was highly tactical. In *Steel*, a personal injury case, the claim involved a point of law that it was reasonable to wish to be resolved by the court. The case was probably intrinsically unsuitable for mediation.

The court gave general guidance. It does not have power to order reluctant litigants to mediate. To do so would violate Article 6 of the Convention, because it would be an unacceptable obstruction to right of access to the courts. The court can encourage, not compel. All of those involved in litigation should routinely consider whether the dispute is suitable for ADR. If a party refuses to mediate, the court can displace the normal costs rule and order that party to pay the costs despite winning at trial. This should occur only if that party has acted unreasonably in refusing ADR. The burden of showing that lies with the unsuccessful party. If the case *is* mediated, the parties are entitled to adopt whatever position they want, and the court is not, later, entitled to ask why that position was in fact adopted. This thus preserves the confidentiality of mediation. Above all, although most cases are suitable for ADR there is not a presumption in favour of mediation. In deciding what cases are suitable, regard should be had to the nature of the case, its merits, the extent to which other settlement methods have been attempted, whether the costs of mediation are disproportionately high, and whether delay in arranging mediation would be prejudicial.

None of the above prevents a court from a court imposing an order requiring the parties to consider the suitability of mediate. Refusal will still carry the risk of deprivation of costs.

---

[177] *Cable & Wireless* v *IBM per* Colman J.   [178] CPR 26.4(1).
[179] [2002] CP Rep 35.   [180] Ibid, *per* Brooke LJ.
[181] See *Hurst* v *Leeming* [2002] C P Rep 59; cf. *Leicester Circuits* v *Coates* [2003] EWCA Civ 333.
[182] *Neal* v *Jones; Société Internationale de Télécommunications Aéronautiques* v *Wyatt* [2002] EWHC 2401.
[183] [2004] EWCA (Civ) 576. See also *Burchell* v *Ballard* [2005] EWCA Civ 358.

KEY ISSUE

The Jackson Report concluded that the benefits of ADR were not fully appreciated.[184] Mediation and joint settlement meetings were effective means of dispute resolution, concentrating on what the parties are prepared to accept as opposed to the strict legal position. The belief that the personal injury cases were not suitable for mediation was incorrect. On the other hand, parties should not be compelled to mediate. A court should encourage mediation, and require parties to discuss whether it is an appropriate route, should require explanations from parties who decline mediation (although the court should not receive them until after the resolution of the case). Courts should penalize in costs parties who have unreasonably refused to mediate. To create greater awareness, an authoritative handbook should be prepared, explaining clearly and concisely what ADR is and giving details of all reputable providers of mediation.

? Questions

1. How can ADR or mediation be encouraged?

2. Should a party be penalized in costs if he or she fails to participate in ADR?

3. Should there be a requirement for mandatory ADR?

Further reading

ANDREWS, *English Civil Procedure* (Oxford University Press, 2004)

DHEN et al, *Reform of Civil Procedure: Essays on Access to Justice* (ed. Zuckerman and Cranston) (Clarendon Press, 1995)

GENN, *Judging Civil Justice* (Hamlyn Lectures, 2008)

LIGHTMAN, 'Civil Litigation in the 21st Century' (1998) 17 CJQ 383

WOOLF, *Access to Justice* (Lord Chancellor's Department, 1995) (the 'Woolf Report')

---

[184] Report, *op cit*, p 361, para 3.3.

Pre-trial Process[1]

14

INTRODUCTION

This chapter will examine the important first stage of civil process—the pre-trial process. The right approach before an action is begun, the choice of the right court, and the early procedures are each crucial. Specific areas covered will include:

- the purpose of pre-action protocols and their importance in attempting to avoid proceedings, or in identifying the issues that arise;
- how civil actions are commenced;
- the early procedural issues.

Choice of court

The Woolf Civil Justice Reforms[2] made fundamental changes to the commencement of actions. As already noted,[3] jurisdiction in civil matters has historically been divided between the county court and High Court.[4] The latter has had almost unlimited jurisdiction, unless statute has given jurisdiction exclusively to a county court. The jurisdiction of the county court has been limited historically by value, or by the nature of the subject matter. For example, the county court has not had (and does not have) jurisdiction to deal with claims in libel or slander.[5]

Within that structure, the choice of where to commence the action turned on what was the appropriate court of trial. If the matter was within the exclusive jurisdiction of either the High Court, or of the county court, it was in that court that the action should have been commenced, usually by writ (in the case of the High Court) or summons (in the case of the county court). If the matters fell to be regarded as a small claim, the county court was the appropriate forum for the case. If judicial review[6] was sought, an application had to be made to the Administrative Court (formerly, the Queen's Bench Divisional Court). Increasingly, though, the High Court and county

---

[1] See, generally, Zuckerman, *Civil Procedure* (Sweet & Maxwell, 2003); Andrews, *English Civil Procedure* (OUP, 2002); Loughlin and Gerlis, *Civil Procedure* (Routledge-Cavendish, 2004).

[2] See p 478.   [3] See p 477.   [4] See p 477.

[5] County Courts Act 1984, s 15(2).   [6] See p 511.

court have had concurrent jurisdiction in respect of most matters. The county court can now deal with any matters that are founded on contract or tort whatever the financial value or complexity, jurisdiction over claims in equity and contentious probate where the value involved does not exceed £30,000[7] and unlimited jurisdiction to hear cases for the recovery of land.[8] The county court now has many of the same powers in respect of procedure and remedies as does the High Court. Yet, despite the concurrence of many aspects of jurisdiction the intention has been to keep the High Court for only the most valuable, complex, or important cases. Section 1 of the Courts and Legal Services Act 1990 empowers the Lord Chancellor to make provision for the allocation of business. Article 7 of the High Court and County Court Jurisdiction Order 1991[9] creates a presumption that cases of a value less than £25,000 must be tried in the county court: a claim of less than £15,000 *cannot* be commenced in the High Court. The presumption is that a claim of a value of £50,000 or more *will* be eligible for High Court trial. The position will be otherwise if the application of certain criteria shows that a different court of trial is, in fact, appropriate. These criteria also apply in deciding in which court cases falling between these two financial figures should be tried, with one proviso. Cases involving personal injury claims of an estimated amount less than £50,000 must be commenced in the county court (except in the case of clinical medical negligence claims). The criteria mentioned above are set out in Article 7(5) of the order, which deals primarily with the transfer of cases between the two jurisdictions.[10] However, they are equally relevant to the question of initial choice of jurisdiction. The factors identified are as follows:

(i)   the financial substance of the action, including that of any counterclaim;

(ii)   whether the action is otherwise important, for example by raising issues of general public importance, or where the case will amount to a test case;

(iii) the complexity of the facts, legal issues, remedies, or procedures involved (complex cases are more suitable for High Court trial);

(iv)   whether transfer of the case will lead to more speedy trial, although this alone should not be a determining factor.

To facilitate the greater use of the county court jurisdiction, section 38 of the County Courts Act 1984 gave to the county court, generally speaking, the power to make any order that could be made by the High Court if the proceedings were in that court. That power is subject to any limitation imposed by regulations, and examples of such matters are freezing orders[11] or search orders.[12] In substantial cases in which such orders may be crucial to the obtaining of information or prevention of dissipation of assets, these restrictions may conclusively influence the choice of High Court rather than county court jurisdiction. Some cases, such as professional negligence, claims under

---

[7] County Courts Act 1984, ss 23, 32; County Courts Jurisdiction Order 1981, SI 1981/123.
[8] 1984 Act, s 21.   [9] SI 1991/724.   [10] See CPR 30.3(1), 30.3(2).
[11] See p 518.   [12] See p 515.

the Fatal Accidents Act 1976, claims of fraud or of undue influence, malicious prosecution, and false imprisonment, claims against the police, and contentious probate
may be particularly suitable for High Court trial.[13] All concerned are bound by the
Civil Procedure Rules. A claim should be started in the High Court only if by reason of
its financial value and the amount in dispute and/or the complexity of the facts, legal
issues, or procedures involved, and/or the public importance of the matters involved
the claimant believes the claim should be dealt with by a High Court judge.[14] If a case
does not fall within these criteria, nor is required to be tried in the High Court by
statute or falls within a specialist jurisdiction (such as the Administrative Court),[15]
it will be transferred to the county court.[16] In a case in which the choice of court was
known to be wrong, and intended to intimidate the opponent, or to run up costs, a
court might strike out the case.[17] This should not happen where there has been a bona
fide error or misjudgement, because this would not only be contrary to the spirit of the
'overriding objective'[18] but possibly a breach of the fair trial provisions of Article 6 of
the European Convention that encompasses the right of access to the court. A further
sanction may be a reduction in the costs allowed at the conclusion of the case.[19]

The total effect of these changes is that the vast majority of actions, some 90 per cent,
commence in the county court. The High Court is the forum for the more specialist
and difficult cases.[20] The general powers to transfer between the two levels of court
must be exercised having regard to the matters identified in the Civil Procedure Rules.
These include:[21]

(a) the financial value of the claim, or the amount in dispute;

(b) the convenience or fairness of hearings being held in another court;

(c) the availability of a judge specializing in the type of claims in question;

(d) the complexity of facts, legal issues, remedies, or procedures;

(e) the public importance of the claim;

(f) the facilities available at the court where the claim is being dealt with, in
      particular with regard to the disabilities of a party or witness;

(g) whether any possibility of the making of a declaration of incompatibility.[22]

The court may have regard to matters as diverse as the convenience of the defendant[23]
and the suitability of the court.

---

[13] Practice Direction 29, para 2.6.   [14] Practice Direction 7, para 2.4.

[15] See p 256.

[16] County Court Act 1984, s 40; Practice Direction 29, para 2.6. Similar powers exist to transfer cases from
the county court to the High Court if the latter is the more appropriate venue.

[17] *Restrick* v *Crickmore* [1994] 2 All ER 112.   [18] As to which, see p 489.

[19] Supreme Court Act 1981, s 51(8), (9).

[20] See *Report of the Review Body on Civil Justice*, Cm 394 (HMSO, 1988).

[21] CPR 30.3(2).   [22] As to which, see p 155.   [23] *Pepin* v *Taylor* [2002] EWCA Civ 1522.

Pre-action protocols

We have already seen that pre-action protocols supplement the Civil Procedure Rules.[24] Their purpose was well explained by Brooke LJ in *Carlson* v *Townsend*[25] as 'guides to good litigation and pre-litigation practice, drafted by those who know the difference between good and bad practice'. There is not one general protocol: a government consultation paper that mooted that possibility[26] came in the end to the conclusion that it was better to proceed by way of Practice Direction setting out a general framework within which parties in dispute should act prior to the commencement of formal action.[27] There are ten pre-action protocols dealing with specific types of action: personal injury; clinical disputes; construction and engineering; defamation; professional negligence; judicial review; disease and illness; housing disrepair; rent arrears; and mortgage repossession. The Jackson Report[28] found general professional support for the specific protocols, although not for the general Practice Direction, which, he recommended, should be abolished as serving no useful purpose. It often led to increased and unnecessary costs being incurred. The conduct of litigants could continue to be controlled by imposing costs sanctions for unreasonable behaviour.

The essential elements are that the claimant should set out details of the matter in question, copies of essential documents relied on, and a response within a stated period (a period of one month is identified as a standard). Such a pre-action letter should indicate whether alternative dispute resolution (ADR)[29] is sought. It should also give details of any conditional fee agreement.[30] A response should then follow from the defendant, with an acknowledgement within twenty-one days. This will set out (if that be the case) why the claim is not accepted, again with relevant detail. Clearly, the objective is to avoid litigation if that is possible, and the protocol envisages negotiation to try to avoid litigation prior to the actual commencement of proceedings.[31]

KEY ISSUE

How are parties to be encouraged to settle before commencement of proceedings or to engage in ADR? Specific pre-action protocols have been developed for particular kinds of litigation. These include protocols in respect of personal injury cases, clinical disputes, construction and engineering disputes, defamation cases, professional negligence cases, and judicial review. The common features of clear statements designed to identify what matters are in dispute, what matters are claimed, and the extent to which the parties disagree are

---

[24] See p 487.   [25] [2001] 3 All ER 663.

[26] DCA Consultation Paper, *General Pre-Action Protocol* (HMSO, 2002).

[27] See *Practice Direction—Pre-Action Conduct*, which came into effect on 6 April 2009

[28] *Op cit*, p 345 *et seq*.   [29] See p 490.   [30] See p 482.

[31] Protocol, para 4.7.

all evident. They are intended to assist the process of negotiation and settlement before costly proceedings are begun.

The main sanction for their disregard lies in the area of costs.[32] The Civil Procedure Rules seek to encourage pre-action settlement. Settlement after commencement is encouraged by Part 36 CPR[33]—a process that will be encouraged by further reforms recommended by the Jackson Committee that seek to minimize the cost disincentives to settlement. Throughout, it is cost sanctions that provide the incentive to comply with pre-action protocols.

? Questions

1. Should non-compliance always be penalized in costs?
2. What is the status in law of pre-action protocols?

Commencing a civil action

Prior to the introduction of the Woolf Reforms a complex range of methods of commencement of civil action existed. A county court action was, generally, commenced by summons. An action in the Queen's Bench Division was in most cases commenced by writ of summons, generally referred to as a writ. The last writ was issued on 24 April 1999.[34] Alternative methods of commencement also existed, of which the most important was the originating summons. This was an appropriate method of proceeding in the High Court where the parties' dispute was such that it could be determined without evidence on matters of fact. Woolf recommended that one form should be used for every civil dispute.[35] This in fact has not been completely achieved, but the basis of all procedure is, now, that the *main* way of commencing a civil action, whether in the High Court or county court, is by the issue of a claim form (Part 7 procedure).[36] But not all proceedings are begun by a claim. As noted above, it was possible to commence an action by way of originating summons. This procedure was used, for example, where the matter involved the question of the construction of a statute, or document, or where an application was made to the High Court other than one in pending proceedings and where no other procedure was specified, such as for discovery of documents before commencement of an action.[37] An equivalent procedure was introduced by Part 8 of the Civil Procedure Rules (Part 8 procedure). This is a process used where a decision is sought from the court on a question unlikely to involve a substantial dispute of fact. This could, again, involve the construction of a statute, contract, deed, or will. Part 8 may also be used in other circumstances

---

[32] See, e.g., *Ford* v *GKR Construction Ltd* [2000] 1 All ER 802.   [33] See p 528.
[34] Andrews, *op cit*, para 10.2.
[35] Woolf Final Report, ch 2, para 3; ch 12, para 1.   [36] CPR 7.2.
[37] Under Supreme Court Act 1981, s 33(2). For the equivalent post-Woolf procedure, see p 513.

specified in the CPR, such as the agreement by the court of a settlement agreed on behalf of a child.[38] The choice is not that of the parties alone: the court may overturn the decision of the claimant[39] if the Part 7 procedure is thought more appropriate because of the way in which it identifies complex issues to be determined.

The contents of the claim

A Part 7 claim identifies the claimant and defendant, although, exceptionally, it may be valid despite a failure to name the defendant provided that it identifies those included in the action with sufficient particularity.[40]

The claim instructs the defendant to satisfy the claim, or, alternatively, acknowledge service and state whether the claim will be contested. Without this, the claimant may obtain judgment in default without giving further notice to the defendant. The claim will contain a concise statement of its nature and a description of the remedy sought, although, when it comes to trial, the court may grant such remedy to which the defendant is entitled.[41] The claim will state the amount of any money claimed, or contain a statement of value, which then allows the court to allocate the case to the correct court and track.[42] Importantly, a party who has entered into a conditional fee agreement and who will wish to recover a success fee[43] or an after-the-event insurance premium must file details of those arrangements so that the defendant is aware of the possible financial effects should he or she lose.

A Part 8 claim will set out the nature of the issue or question the claimant wishes the court to resolve, the remedies sought, and the basis on which such remedies might be granted. The evidence supporting the claim, in the form of written statements or affidavits (sworn statements) must accompany the claim. The defence respond in kind. There is, though, no power to strike out an application in default of such a response.[44]

Parties to proceedings

A single claim form may start several claims that can conveniently be disposed of in the same proceedings.[45] This may amount to several claims against a single defendant, or may involve multiple defendants. An action may be representative in nature: where more than one person has the same interest, an action may be conducted by or against the same interest as representative of any other persons who have that same interest.[46] Thus, where several persons have the same interest, whether as claimants or defendants, one or more persons may be authorized to appear on behalf of all persons so interested. However, a representative action is only appropriate where all of the persons to be represented have a common grievance and will all benefit from the relief

[38] CPR Practice Direction 8A, 1.4.   [39] CPR 8.1(3).
[40] *Bloomsbury Publishing Group Ltd* v *News Group Newspapers Ltd* [2003] 3 All ER 736.
[41] CPR 16.2(5).   [42] CPR 16.3.   [43] See p 483.
[44] CPR 8.1(5).   [45] CPR 7.3.   [46] CPR 19.6.

claimed if claimants,[47] or are jointly liable if defendants.[48] Thus where the liability of defendants is several, for example in conspiracy[49] or defamation, they cannot be represented and must be sued in their own names. Nevertheless an action for negligence has been allowed to proceed against representatives of the members of a club on the ground that they were joint occupiers of the club premises.[50] A judgment against representative defendants is binding on them all.

Representative and multi-party actions

Background

Representative actions have been somewhat circumvented by group actions whereby several actions out of a large number of potential claims are litigated to establish liability and the principles for the award of damages. The types of situation suitable for multi-party actions were summarized in 1997[51] as follows.

(a) Major one-off disaster claims (such as the ferry disaster at Zeebrugge and the King's Cross tube station fire disaster) in which causation is generally common to all of the cases and may not be in dispute and in which the class of those affected is clearly defined from the outset. In many cases, the number of individuals in the class will be high.

(b) Product liability claims (especially those involving pharmaceutical products such as Opren and benzodiazepine) in which liability may be difficult to determine and common issues may be difficult to identify. Such claims are frequently complicated by a multiplicity of defendants who all manufactured similar products as well as by a multiplicity of claimants. In a case involving the drug Opren, there were some 1,500 claimants against a drug company, which were litigated on the basis of a 'master' statement of claim, and with certain 'lead cases' to determine different aspects of the overall issue.

(c) Multiple claims relating to industrial diseases deriving from the same cause, such as asbestosis claims, industrial deafness, and vibration white finger claims.

(d) Environmental cases deriving not only from specific incidents, but also from damage occurring over a period of time, such as seepage from an industrial

---

[47] *Smith* v *Cardiff Corporation* [1954] 1 QB 210, [1953] 2 All ER 1373, distinguished in *John* v *Rees* [1970] Ch 345, [1969] 2 All ER 274.

[48] *Mercantile Marine Service Association* v *Toms* [1916] 2 KB 243.

[49] *Hardie & Lane* v *Chilton* [1928] KB 663.

[50] *Campbell* v *Thompson* [1953] QB 445, [1953] 1 All ER 831; see also *Wallersteiner* v *Moir (No 2)* [1975] QB 373, [1975] 1 All ER 849, in which a minority shareholders' action was likened to a representative action on behalf of the company and it was stated by the Court of Appeal that the shareholder, after issuing proceedings, should in effect apply to the court for an order sanctioning the proceedings, the effect of which would be to give the shareholder a right to have the company pay his costs.

[51] *Multi-Party Actions: Consultation Paper from Civil Justice Working Group* (HMSO, 1997).

plant, or a nuclear installation, or prolonged use of chemicals in particular circumstances. These types of claim may involve both personal injury and property damage, as well as, in some cases, loss of amenity.

(e) Claims relating to use or consumption of defective goods or services causing damage to property, or personal injury and/or financial loss. Examples are claims by: tenants of a block of flats or an estate for a landlord's failure to repair; shareholders against a company or its auditors for disseminating misleading information; residents of a neighbourhood against a public authority's decision to build a road or to permit development in their area; a group of package holiday customers against a tour operator; a group of customers who have bought defective goods; or for professional negligence claims. Often, but by no means always, the claims may be individually small, but together quite substantial.

Development of group actions in the United Kingdom has centred on a variety of types of case. There are cases involving 'mass disasters' involving large numbers of individual claims. Instead of having to try separately a whole series of cases arising out of the same 'disaster' it was more efficient for the courts to try the common questions as one action. As a result, the evolution of multi-party actions has largely occurred because of 'an innovative approach by the courts and practitioners to procedure rules, in particular those relating to lead actions, or test cases, and the joining of parties to the action'. Their development was well summarized by Longmore LJ in *Afrika and others v Cape Plc; X, Y and Z and others v Schering Healthcare Ltd; Sayers and others v Merck & Smithkline Beecham plc:*[52]

> Multi-party actions are a comparatively novel feature of English litigation and the courts have attempted over recent years to fashion new types of order to enable viable actions to be brought in situations where a single individual would find it prohibitively expensive to bring proceedings on his or her own. The present appeals arise in three separate multi-party actions: the first is what is known as the MMR/MR litigation in which claims are made for injuries allegedly suffered by children as a result of the administration of vaccine against measles, mumps and rubella (or just measles rubella); the second action is the oral contraception litigation in which claimants seek damages for injuries sustained by the taking of oral contraceptives; the third action is brought by workers in South Africa against the English holding company of the South Africa subsidiary, which employed them, for injuries suffered as a result of exposure to asbestos. Typically defendants are drug manufacturers, health trusts on whose behalf drugs are prescribed, or other large corporations some of whom (or whose insurers) have deep pockets. Claimants are typically individuals who could not contemplate financing litigation themselves, and obtain assistance for that purpose from the Legal Services Commission or, perhaps, under a Conditional Fee Agreements...These actions are difficult, as well as expensive, to run and impose great burdens on the practitioners who conduct them and the judges who try them. They can, however, be a service to many who suffer severe injuries and it is the

---

[52] [2001] EWCA Civ 2017.

policy of the courts to facilitate such actions in appropriate cases and adapt traditional procedures accordingly...

The impact of the actions of the Legal Services Commission contracting representation in this type of case has already been noted.[53]

The Woolf Report and group litigation order

The Woolf Report identified objectives that any new system for multi-party actions should aim to achieve. Firstly, it should provide access to justice where large numbers of people have been affected by another's conduct, but individual loss is so small that it makes an individual action economically unviable. Secondly, it should provide expeditious, effective, and proportionate methods of resolving cases in which individual damages are large enough to justify individual action, but in which the number of claimants and the nature of the issues involved mean that the cases cannot be managed satisfactorily in accordance with normal procedure. Thirdly, the rules should achieve a balance between the normal rights of claimants and defendants, to pursue and defend cases individually, and the interests of a group of parties to litigate the action as a whole in an effective manner. Rules seek to achieve these objectives.

Part 19 of the Civil Procedure Rules makes provision for group litigation pursuant to a group litigation order. Solicitors representing claimants in such a potential case are encouraged to form a solicitor's group, and to appoint one of their number as the lead in seeking a group litigation order.[54] An application is made to the court. When made, such an order provides for the registration of all of the claims in being, and identifies the court that is to manage the case under the case management approach envisaged by Woolf. In the early days of group actions, pre-Woolf, the courts had to be innovative. In *AB v John Wyeth & Brother Ltd*,[55] Steyn LJ observed:

> The procedural powers of a judge in control of a group case are not tied to traditional procedures. Subject to the duty to act fairly, the judge may and often must improvise: sometimes this will involve the adoption of an entirely new procedure.

One problem is the question of who joins the group: litigants have to opt in, and there can often be some disagreement as to how big a class of potential litigants actually is.[56] Some argue that the process would be better if the class were identified, with those falling within it having to opt out.[57]

The rules permit a judge to set a timetable, give directions, and generally manage the case through its often difficult and long processes. The judge will identify the lead solicitor, provide for a cut-off date for joining the group, and identify test claims. The court can order that parties be joined.[58] A judgment given relating to a group litigation

---

[53] See p 414.   [54] Practice Direction 19B.   [55] (1992) 12 BMLR 452.

[56] See *Autologic Holdings plc v Inland Revenue Commissioners* [2005] UKHL 54, [2006] 1 All ER 118; *Hobson v Ashton Martin Slack Solicitors* [2006] EWCA Civ 134 (QB); *Owen v Ministry of Defence* [2006] EWHC 990 (QB); *Davies v Department of Trade and Industry* [2007] 1 WLR 3232, [2006] EWCA Civ 1360.

[57] Mulheran, 'Justice Enhanced: An Opt-Out Class Action for England' (2007) MLR 550.

[58] *Davies and others v Department of Trade and Industry* [2007] 1 All ER 518, [2006] EWCA Civ 1360.

order issue is binding on the parties to all other claims on the group register at the time the judgment or order is made, unless the court orders otherwise.[59] An individual adversely affected may, however, seek permission to appeal.

KEY ISSUE

Multi-party litigation is clearly an important way of achieving justice in some cases. How are issues of costs to be dealt with in multi-party litigation? The Woolf Report observed:[60]

> If the treatment of costs is not examined from the outset, the result is either subsidiary-litigation or protracted problems when the matter comes to [assessment]. My general proposals for information on costs to be made available at every stage when the managing judge is involved are all the more important in relation to multi-party actions, where many claimants will be legally aided and have no direct control over costs and where costs can escalate dramatically. At every stage of the [multi-party situation] the judge should consider, with the help of the parties, the potential impact on costs of the directions that are contemplated and whether they are justified in relation to what is at issue. Parties and their legal representatives, as in other cases on the multi-track, should provide information on cost already incurred and be prepared to estimate the cost of proposed further work....

Rule 48.6A of the Civil Procedure Rules provides for costs where a group litigation order has been made. This provides for cost-sharing orders in respect of common costs, which are divided equally, an approach that was developed further by the court in *Davies* v *Eli Lilly*, applied in *Ward* v *Guinness Mahon plc*.[61]

? Questions

1. What do you think are the benefits of multi-party proceedings?
2. What problems might arise in respect of such proceedings?
3. How can the courts control the costs?

Issue and service of the claim[62]

Once issued, the claim is normally valid for four months beginning with the date of issue.[63] However, it may on application be renewed for a further period not exceeding twelve months if the court is satisfied that it has not been possible to serve it during that period. Such an application is made without giving notice to the other party. An extension will only be granted where the application for extension has been made promptly, and only if the court has been unable to serve the claim form, or the claimant has taken all reasonable steps to serve it, but has been unable to do so.[64] There

---

[59] CPR 19.12(1)(a).   [60] Woolf Final Report, ch 17, para 57.
[61] [1996] 4 All ER 112. See *Afrika and others* v *Cape plc, and other related cases* [2003] 3 All ER 631.
[62] See, generally, *Collier* v *Williams* [2006] EWCA Civ 20.
[63] CPR 7.5(2). See, e.g., *Dickins* v *Solicitors' Indemnity Fund* [2005] EWHC 2754.
[64] CPR 7.6(3).

are provisions in the rules that provide for a series of dates for 'deemed service'. For example, where service is by first-class post, service is deemed to have been effected on the second day[65] after the claim form was posted. These dates are applied rigidly. In *Godwin v Swindon BC*,[66] the court recognized this as a total fiction. Service was deemed to have occurred on Monday 11 September 2000, it having been posted on Thursday 7 September 2000, and thus out of time, even though the letter was in fact received on Friday 8 September, which was within time. This extraordinary result can be justified only on the basis of simplicity and certainty, and raises some issues about whether the individual's right of access to the courts is being limited in an unreasonable and disproportionate way, possibly infringing the fair trial provisions of Article 6 of the European Convention.[67]

The claim is served on the defendant by the court unless the claimant informs the court that he wishes to serve the claim himself, or unless there is a rule, order, or Practice Direction releasing the court from this obligation.[68] The Civil Procedure Rules specify the mode of service.[69] This may be by whatever means are agreed, by personal service, by leaving the claim at an address provided by the defendant for that purpose, leaving the claim at the usual or last-known address of an individual,[70] or through a document exchange system. However, service by post is permitted and is the normal method of service by the court.[71] Electronic service by email or fax is also envisaged in some circumstances in which it has been indicated in writing by an individual that this will be accepted.

The court also has the power to order service by some other means, a process known as 'substituted service'. This might take, for example, the form of service by registered or recorded delivery post to the defendant's last-known address, service on the defendant's solicitor or agent, or service by advertisement in the press. It also has the power to dispense totally with service,[72] but this power should not be used to validate late service.[73]

Public or private law

A second preliminary factor that must be considered is whether the proposed action involves questions of public law. Where in reality an action raises issues of public law, the normal procedure for determination of those questions is by an application for judicial review under Part 54 of the Civil Procedure Rules.[74] A failure to use the Part 54 procedure, with its three-month time limit and the requirement to obtain permission, might in the past have led possibly to an application by the defendant

---

[65] This includes *all* days, and not simply working days: *Anderton v Clwydd CC (No 2)* [1992] 1 WLR 374.
[66] [2002] 1 WLR 997.
[67] See *Andrews, op cit*, at para 10.48. See also *Sealy v Consignia plc* [2002] 3 All ER 801; *Vinos v Marks and Spencer plc* [2001] 3 All ER 784; *Naglegan v Royal Free Hospital NHS Trust* [2002] 1 WLR 1043.
[68] CPR 6.3, 6.13.   [69] See, generally, CPR 6.8–6.9.
[70] Not a property let by him: *O'Hare and another v McDougal* (2005) [2005] EWCA (Civ) 1628.
[71] Practice Direction 6, para 8.1.   [72] CPR 6.9.
[73] *Godwin v Swindon BC* [2001] 4 All ER 641, disapproving *Infantino v Maclean* [2001] 4 All ER 641.
[74] Formerly Ord 53 RSC.

to have the action struck out as an abuse of process of the court; however, the rules governing process are much more relaxed following the wider powers of case management contained in the Civil Procedure Rules and transfer is more likely than striking out.[75]

KEY ISSUE

How are such proceedings to be brought? Proceedings against a public authority in judicial review are an important method of holding public authorities to account. The Part 54 procedure is designed to provide protection for unmeritorious claims by requiring an individual to have a sufficient interest, to make his or her claim within a three-month period following the action or decision being challenged, and to be granted 'leave' (permission) to make the application by a judge of the Administrative Court. As already noted, the rules relating to protective costs orders provide some protection for those who take on a challenge against a public authority.[76]

But the Part 54 procedure is not the only method of challenge. Judicial review proceedings can be dealt within in the Upper Chamber, and also effectively (in some cases) in the Competition Appeals Tribunal.[77]

? Questions

1. Why do you think there is a special jurisdiction for judicial review claims?
2. Why does an applicant for judicial review need permission to apply from the court?

Additional claims

Although additional claims (formerly known as counterclaims, contributions, and indemnities) logically are issues and procedures that arise once the proceedings have been commenced, it is convenient to deal with them here. We have noted the Part 7 and Part 8 procedures for the commencement of actions. Where a party wishes to advance a new claim within existing procedures, Part 20 applies. It permits the making of an additional claim (that is, a claim that the claimant, or the claimant and others, is himself liable to the defendant). Thus if the supplier of goods is suing for the unpaid price, a counterclaim might claim damages of defective goods. But an additional claim can be against a third party, although the permission of the court will be needed to bring in as a further defendant a third party.[78] Thus a purchaser who is defending an action brought by the retailer of a motor vehicle might wish to bring into the action the manufacturer of the car if the defendant wishes to allege gross design or construction

---

[75] *Clark* v *University of Lincoln and Humberside* [2003] 3 All ER 752; *R (on application of Valentines Homes and Construction Ltd)* v *Revenue & Customs Commissioners* [2010] EWCA Civ 345; *R (on application of McIntyre)* v *Gentoo Group* [2010] EWHC 5 (Admin)
[76] See p 485.   [77] See p 295.   [78] CPR 20.5.

faults. Such a claim can be served as of right against the claimant at the same time as the service of the defence, but otherwise permission is required.

A contribution may be sought from someone who is liable to pay part of any damages awarded. Thus a driver potentially liable in damages for injuries caused to a pedestrian may seek a contribution from another driver considered to be partly at fault and responsible for the accident giving rise to the claim. By contrast a defendant may seek an indemnity, usually from an insurance company. Part 20 provides for the procedure to be followed in such cases. This involves the service of a notice setting out the nature and grounds of the claim for a contribution of indemnity. Permission of the court is not required.

Pre-commencement orders and procedures

Questions concerning disclosure and inspection of documents and the inspection, preservation, and the like of property are dealt with during the course of proceedings, usually after the statements of case and defence, and these matters are dealt with below in that context.[79] However, statutory provisions enable parties to obtain orders of this type prior to the commencement of proceedings. There are two distinct procedures of this type, set out below. There are also common law powers.

Disclosure and inspection of documents

A potential litigant often will not know whether a cause of action exists, or a cause of action with realistic prospects of success exists, without knowing the contents of documents held by the potential defendant. For example, the strength of a potential claim in medical negligence against a hospital trust may turn on the contents of medical records held by the hospital. In 1991 a power was introduced by section 33(2) of the Supreme Court Act 1981, which provided that a person who appears to the High Court to be likely to be a party to subsequent proceedings in respect of a claim of personal injuries or death could apply for pre-trial discovery of documents in the possession, custody, or power of a person. The Woolf Report recommended the extension of this power to all categories of case.[80] This was achieved in the Civil Procedure Rules.

For an order to be made, the following conditions must be satisfied.[81]

(a) The person against whom the order is sought must be a likely party to the proceedings; it is not enough that that person is a potential witness.

(b) The document or documents sought would be disclosable under the standard rules of disclosure if the action were in progress.[82]

---

[79] See p 535.   [80] Woolf Final Report.   [81] See, generally, CPR 31.
[82] See p 535.

(c) Pre-action disclosure is desirable in order to dispose fairly of the anticipated proceedings, or to assist the dispute to be resolved without proceedings, or to save costs.

That party may be ordered to disclose whether those documents are in his or her custody, possession, and power and, if so, to produce them to the applicant, unless they are protected from disclosure by the doctrine of privilege. It is immaterial that the likelihood of the claim being made is dependent upon the outcome of the disclosure; the words 'likely' in the rules is to be construed as meaning 'may or may well be made' if, on disclosure, the documents in question indicate that the applicant has a good cause of action.[83] On the other hand a 'thin and fragile case' in *Snowstar Shipping Co Ltd v Graig Shipping Co*[84] was the context when a too widely drawn application was refused.

If the relevant evidence is not in the possession of a person who is likely to be a party, rule 34 applies. If the preconditions are satisfied, the court can order disclosure of documents in the possession of a person or body who is not a party or not likely to be so. The preconditions are that the documents must be likely to support the case of the applicant or adversely affect one of the parties to it.

Inspection, etc. of property

Section 33(1) of the Supreme Court Act 1981 empowers the High Court, in some circumstances, to make an order providing for the inspection, photographing, preservation, custody, or detention of property (including land or chattels) that appears to the court to be property that may become the subject matter of subsequent proceedings in the court, or as to which any question may arise in such proceedings, or for the taking of samples of any such property and the carrying out of any experiment on or with any such property. This is not limited to articles in the possession of a party, a position that may be contrasted with that which exists after commencement of proceedings. The relationship between the power of inspection and that of disclosure was examined in *Huddleston v Control Risks Information Services Ltd*.[85] The court drew a distinction between a party wishing to examine 'the medium' (that is, the document itself) as opposed to being concerned with 'the message' (that is, with the contents of the document). Section 33(1), inspection, applied to the former; section 33(2), discovery, to the latter. Since in this case the claimant's concern was for the contents, which were believed to be defamatory, what was being sought was discovery, for which the relevant conditions, described above, did not apply. The power of inspection could not be used to circumvent these criteria.

---

[83] This was the position under pre-existing law: see *Dunning v United Liverpool Hospital's Board of Governors* [1973] 2 All ER 454, [1973] 1 WLR 586. See, now, *Swain v Hillman* [2001] 1 All ER 91; *Three Rivers DC and others v HM Treasury and Governor and & Co of the Bank of England* [2002] EWCA Civ 1182.

[84] [2003] EWHC 1367.   [85] [1987] 2 All ER 1035, [1987] 1 WLR 701.

The *Norwich Pharmacal* principle

In addition to the powers described above, a court may in some circumstances order disclosure against a third party who has information. If it does so, it is doing so as part of its inherent jurisdiction. Whilst this will often be during litigation, it may be appropriate to obtain such disclosure prior to action, in order to discover whether a basis of action exists, and against whom. The principle, which was first stated by the court in *Norwich Pharmacal Co* v *Commissioners of Customs and Excise*, does not permit disclosure in all circumstances: it is only where the third party is in some way involved in the wrongdoing alleged that the court will order disclosure against that third party.[86] However, the rule has been extended to cases in which a third party has information necessary for locating and recovering missing funds,[87] and to a case in which the defendant (which ran a discussion board on an Internet site), knew the identity of an individual posting allegedly defamatory material in respect of the claimant.[88]

Search orders

The High Court developed what was known as an *Anton Pillar* order, named after the case in which the Court of Appeal first sanctioned the making of such an order.[89] This allowed a court to order a defendant to permit a claimant to enter the defendant's premises in order to inspect, remove, or make copies of documents belonging to the claimant or relating to the claimant's property. The procedure and power is now governed by section 7 of the Civil Procedure Act 1997 and is renamed a search order. An order may be obtained without notice, but will only be made where the claimant shows that there is a grave danger of property being smuggled away or vital evidence destroyed; it is usually applicable to infringement of copyright cases, passing off, or breaches of confidence, or cases of that sort.[90]

A search order may, at first sight, appear to be in the nature of a search warrant issued to a private individual, but in fact it is not; it confers upon the claimant no right to enter the defendant's premises, but rather imposes a duty on a defendant to permit the claimant to enter his premises. Failure on the part of the defendant to comply will, however, be a contempt of court. The use of the power has become extremely popular with claimants and their advisers. By its very nature it may enable a claimant to strike gold in relation to wrongful acts, such as misuse of confidential information or infringement of copyright, which, but for the order, the claimant might possibly never have been in a position to prove (defendants in these matters frequently being less

---

[86] *Harrington* v *North London Polytechnic* [1984] 3 All ER 666; [1984] 1 WLR 1293. In *Ricci* v *Chow* [1987] 3 All ER 534, [1987] 1 WLR 1658, the Court of Appeal decided that disclosure of the identity of the publisher and printer of an alleged defamatory article would not be ordered against the defendant, a person involved in no way in the publication, but who knew the publisher's name.

[87] *Arab Monetary Fund* v *Hashim (No 5)* [1992] 2 All ER 911; *Bankers Trust* v *Shapira* [1980] 3 All ER 353.

[88] *Totalise plc* v *Motley Fool Ltd* [2001] EWCA Civ 1897.

[89] *Anton Pillar KG* v *Manufacturing Processes Ltd* [1976] Ch 55.

[90] See, e.g., *ex parte Island Records Ltd* [1978] Ch 122, [1978] 3 All ER 824.

than frank as to voluntary disclosure); all that the claimant risks is having to pay his opponent's costs of the application and damages if any are caused.

There are three preconditions for the making of a search order. Firstly, there must be a strong prima facie case. Secondly, the damage or potential damage to the applicant must be very serious. Thirdly, there must be clear evidence that the defendants have in their possession incriminating documents or things, and there must be evidence of a real possibility that the defendant may destroy such material before any application on notice can be heard.

In order to minimize speculative and oppressive applications, the courts have formulated several procedural safeguards. Thus the claimant's solicitor should attend when the order is executed; if permission to enter premises is refused, no force should be used; the defendant should have the opportunity to contact his solicitor, and should be advised of his right to obtain legal advice.[91] The requirement to allow entry does not in fact operate immediately, despite the use of the word 'forthwith' in an order, but operates only after there has been a reasonable period of time to obtain legal advice. The applicant must make full disclosure to the court of all matters relevant to his application and if material facts are omitted the order will be discharged. The nature of the search order is exceptional, and creates potential for abuse. In *Universal Thermosensors Ltd* v *Hibben*,[92] Sir Donald Nicholls V-C identified certain key points, that are now reflected in Practice Direction 25.

(1) An order should normally contain a term that, before compliance, the defendant may obtain legal advice, if this is done forthwith. If such a term is to be of use, generally such order should be executed only on working days in office hours, when a solicitor can be expected to be available.

(2) If an order is to be executed on private premises and a woman may be at the house alone, the solicitor serving the order must be, or be accompanied by, a woman.

(3) The order should expressly provide that, unless seriously impracticable, a detailed list of the items being removed should be prepared at the time of removal, with the defendant being given the opportunity to check that list.

(4) Orders sometimes contain a restraining order restraining those on whom they are served from informing others of the existence of the order for a limited period, subject to an exception in respect of communication with a lawyer to gain legal advice. The length of time governed by the restraining order should not be an excessively long period. In the instant case, one week was too long.

(5) An order should not be executed at business premises without a responsible officer or representative being present.

---

[91] Practice Direction 25.   [92] [1992] 3 All ER 257, [1992] 1 WLR 840.

(6) Consideration should be given as to how a competitor of the business subject to the order can be prevented from having unlimited access to the documents of that business.

(7) An order should, where possible, be served by a solicitor other than a member of the firm of solicitors acting for the claimant. That solicitor should also have experience of the search order procedure. The defendant against whom an *ex parte* order has been made may apply to have the order set aside (as can any litigant against whom an *ex parte* order is made); he may even refuse compliance with the order and apply urgently to have it set aside, but he does so at his peril since if his application fails he will be in contempt of court and liable to severe penalties if he has in the interim breached the order, for example by destroying records.

It was held by the House of Lords in *Rank Film Distributors Ltd* v *Video Information Centre*[93] that defendants could resist the making of an order on the ground of privilege against self-incrimination.[94] This was a serious in-road into the scope of what were then known as *Anton Pillar* orders since, in the nature of things, persons against whom such orders are made are frequently engaged in fraudulent activity. To remedy this, section 72 of the Supreme Court Act 1981 withdrew the privilege in relation to High Court proceedings for infringement of rights pertaining to any intellectual property or for passing-off, including proceedings brought to prevent any such infringement anticipated to occur in the future. Other exceptions to the privilege also exist. However, it has become clear that, since the passage of the Human Rights Act 1998,[95] the privilege does not apply in criminal proceedings in relation to independent evidence.[96] This is evidence that came into effect independently of compulsory questioning or disclosure process. It has been held that, for that reason, the rule in civil cases ought to be the same.[97]

The extent to which such orders can be resisted on the grounds of the privilege against self-incrimination was considered by the House of Lords in *AT & T Istel Ltd* v *Tully*.[98] The House was of the opinion that the privilege, which itself in a civil case was an 'archaic and unjustifiable survival from the past', only protected the defendant if compliance with the order would provide evidence against him in a criminal trial. If the defendant could be protected against being exposed to the reasonable risk of the information to be disclosed being used in a criminal prosecution by other means, then the courts were entitled to rely on those other means. In that case the Crown Prosecution Service had agreed not to seek to use in criminal proceedings the documents disclosed.

---

[93] [1982] AC 380, [1981] 2 All ER 76.   [94] As for this, see below.
[95] See p 146.   [96] *Saunders* v *United Kingdom* (1998) 23 EHRR 313.
[97] *C plc* v *P (Secretary of State for the Home Department and another intervening)* [2007] EWCA Civ 493, [2007] 3 All ER 1034.
[98] [1993] AC 45, [1992] 3 All ER 523.

Freezing orders

Jurisdiction

It will be appreciated that the prospective claimant in an action for debt or damages faces two distinct obstacles. The first is to obtain a judgment (or settlement) in his favour; the second is to enforce that judgment. It is of little consolation to most litigants to succeed in the action and yet be unable to enforce the judgment. Regrettably, where a defendant is uninsured against his liability, this is a situation that often arises. Where the defendant is simply insolvent, this is a misfortune that the claimant must bear. However, the courts can and will intervene to prevent a defendant from avoiding his liability to the claimant by disposing of his assets, and in particular removing them outside the jurisdiction of the English courts. An order can be made against a defendant or equally against a third party.[99]

The jurisdiction to issue an injunction to restrain a defendant from removing assets was developed in the *Mareva*[100] case. It is now to be found in the Civil Procedure Rules, and reflects principles developed by case law.[101] The purpose of the order is to prevent the defendant from evading justice by disposing of assets. The claimant must show a good arguable case in relation to the substantive claim.[102] The defendant must have assets, whether inside or outside the jurisdiction. There must also be proved a real risk that, if the court does not grant an order, the defendant will take the opportunity to dissipate those assets or otherwise put them beyond the reach of the court. The standard is a high one: it will be insufficient to show that the defendant is short of money.[103]

The words 'dealing with' encompass disposing of, selling or charging assets. It was at one time thought that one important restriction on the court's power to grant a freezing order lay in the fact that the order is ancillary to a cause of action; it is not a cause of action in itself. Thus, if a claimant's claim is not justiciable in the English courts he cannot obtain an injunction. This view was supported by the Court of Appeal in *The Veracruz I*,[104] in which it was stressed that the powers of the High Court to grant an injunction derived from section 37 of the Supreme Court Act 1981, and were to grant an injunction in all cases in which it was just and convenient to do so. The right to obtain an interim injunction was not a cause of action in itself. However, this conclusion was called into doubt by the decision of the House of Lords in *Channel Tunnel Group Ltd* v *Balfour Beatty Construction Ltd*.[105] In that case Lord Mustill indicated that the fact that proceedings in an English court could be the subject of a stay did not prevent the court from granting interim relief. Lord Browne-Wilkinson doubted whether the authority on which this restriction was based remained good law.

[99] See, e.g., *Revenue and Customs Commissioners* v *Egleton* [2006] EWHC 3213 (Ch); *Fourie* v *Le Roux* [2007] UKHL 1.
[100] *Mareva Compania SA* v *International Bulkcarriers SA* [1975] 2 Lloyds Rep 509.
[101] CPR 25.1.   [102] *Derby* v *Weldon* [1990] Ch 48.
[103] *Midas Merchant Bank plc* v *Bello* [2002] EWCA Civ 274.
[104] [1992] Lloyds Rep 353.   [105] [1993] AC 334, [1993] 1 All ER 664.

Procedure

An applicant for a freezing order is expected to act quickly. To this end, the customary practice is to apply without notice in the first instance, sometimes even before issuing a claim[106] (in which case, the claimant will be required to undertake to issue a claim within a specified period or 'forthwith'). Such an application must be made to the High Court.[107] That court can make an order, which will be made to take effect until the return date on the claim that the claimant will have issued or undertaken to issue. The claimant must swear an affidavit in support of his application. In *Third Chandris Shipping Corporation* v *Unimarine SA*,[108] the Court of Appeal stated guidelines that judges should follow on such applications:

  (i)   the claimant should make full and frank disclosure of all matters in his knowledge that are material for the judge to know;

  (ii) the claimant should give particulars of this claim and the amount thereof and of the defendant's case against it;

  (iii) the claimant should give some grounds for believing that the defendant has assets within the jurisdiction;

  (iv) the claimant should give some grounds (not merely that the defendant is abroad) for believing that there is a risk of the assets of the defendant being removed before the judgment is satisfied;

  (v)   the claimant should give an undertaking in damages, in a suitable case to be supported by a bond or security.

The court has power to order disclosure of documents or to administer interrogatories as to the amount, whereabouts or other details of the defendant's assets, with a view to securing the efficacy of the injunction. Such an order can operate worldwide.[109] Copies of the injunction will generally be served upon the defendant's bank or other body having custody of his assets, so as to fix such body with knowledge of the injunction (since such body would itself be guilty of contempt of court if it were to assist the defendant to act in breach of the injunction, knowing that it is probable that the asset is being disposed of in breach of the injunction). The receipt by a bank of such notice overrides its customer's instructions, for example to honour cheques.

Principles upon which the court acts

By section 37(1) of the Supreme Court Act 1981 the High Court may grant an order 'in all cases in which it appears to the court to be just and convenient to do so'. However, although not subject to statutory fetters, the courts have developed principles on the basis of which to grant or refuse injunctions. The general principles affecting the discretion whether to grant or refuse an interlocutory injunction are those laid down

---

[106] See *Fourie* v *Le Roux and another* [2007] UKHL 1, [2007] 1 All ER 1087.
[107] *Schmidt* v *Wong* [2005] EWCA Civ 1506.   [108] [1979] QB 645.
[109] For enforceability, see *Daqdouria Group Intervention Inc and others* v *Simmons* [2006] EWCA Civ 399.

by the House of Lords in *American Cyanamid Co v Ethicon Ltd*[110] and will be considered in due course. However, there are additional principles that particularly apply to freezing order applications. As a first step, the claimant must satisfy the court: (i) that he has at least a good arguable case; and (ii) that the refusal of an injunction would involve a real risk that a judgment or award in the claimant's favour would remain unsatisfied because of the defendant's removal of assets from the jurisdiction or dissipation of assets within the jurisdiction. An order will not be granted merely for the purpose of providing a claimant with security for a claim, even where it appears likely to succeed and even where the granting of the order will not cause hardship to the defendant. An order will not be granted so as to give the claimant priority over other creditors, nor to prevent the defendant from paying his debts as they fall due or carrying on his legitimate business. It is also common for the order to be expressed so as to exclude periodical payments of reasonable amounts to provide for the living or other expenses of the defendant, including amounts to be paid to his legal advisers to contest the litigation.

Position of third parties

It has been noted that service of a copy of the order upon a third party, such as a bank, operates in effect to freeze the account. This has led to problems and the courts are vigilant to ensure that banks and other third parties do not suffer in consequence of the grant of a freezing order. Thus, a bank is entitled to a variation of the order to enable it to set off against any funds that it holds any right that it has in respect of facilities granted to the client: for example, bank charges, interest, or the balance on another account. Similarly, an order will not be granted, or will be discharged, where the effect would be to interfere substantially with the business of a third party. In *Polly Peck International plc v Nadir (No 2)*,[111] the court indicated that a freezing order ought not to be granted against a bank, except where that bank was likely to act so as to avoid judgment. Where a bank or third party is compelled to enter the proceedings in order to obtain an order, or discharge of an order, the claimant will ordinarily be required to pay its cost on an indemnity basis.

Further reading

ANDREWS, *English Civil Procedure* (Oxford University Press, 2004)

LORD CHANCELLOR'S DEPARTMENT, *Multi-Party Actions: Consultation Paper from Civil Justice Working Group* (HMSO, 1997)

ROBERTS, 'Settlement as Civil Justice' (2000) 63 MLR 739

WARD, 'New Carrots and Sticks: Proposals for Reform of CPR Part 36' (2007) 70 MLR 278

WOOLF, *Access to Justice* (HMSO, 1995) (the 'Woolf Report')

---

[110] See p 531.   [111] [1992] 4 All ER 769.

Civil Trials

15

INTRODUCTION

This chapter will examine the process of trial itself. The landscape has changed in a major way since the Woolf Reforms and the much more case-management approach inherent in the Civil Procedure Rules. The hearing itself is just a part of the process. Specific areas covered will include:

- the three-track approach to allocation of court—*small claims, fast track, multi-track*;
- the settlement and discontinuance of cases;
- how issues to be decided are identified;
- the sharing of relevant information through disclosure;
- the trial itself.

The court of trial

In previous chapters we have examined the nature of the new landscape for civil litigation, introduced following the Woolf Report,[1] and the process that applies in respect of avoiding disputes and in commencing them if that is inevitable. With the Woolf Reforms in place, it is neither possible, nor appropriate, to discuss the civil pre-trial and trial procedure simply, for the complexity of the Civil Procedure Rules, and their applicability in many different ways to different types of action, prevents this within the scope of a general text on the English legal system. This chapter concentrates on key principles, issues, and processes.

The three-track approach

The Woolf Report proposed[2] that cases be allocated to one of three tracks—the *small claims* track, the *fast* track, and the *multi-track*, except where the procedural judge

---

[1] See generally Chapter 14 at p 473.
[2] See *Access to Justice: Judicial Case Management: The Fast Track and Multi Track, A Working Paper* (HMSO, July 1997); see also Middleton, *Review of Civil Justice and Legal Aid: A Report to the Lord Chancellor* (HMSO, 1997), paras 2.24–2.27.

believed that particular characteristics of the individual case made it appropriate for it to be allocated to a different track. This approach reflects the general thrust of the Woolf Report, and of the civil justice reforms, in trying to ensure that the processes undertaken, the requirements made of the parties, and the mode of trial reflect the nature and complexity of what has to be decided, and that procedural requirements (and costs)[3] are proportionate to the dispute with which the law has to deal. In part the pre-existing structures did that by defining specific jurisdictions for the county court and High Court, with powers of transfer between the two. The new procedures under the Civil Procedure Rules address these issues in the context of a common form of commencement of civil process, by reference to criteria that are likely to be good indicators as to the level appropriate to the dispute.

Allocation to the appropriate track is done by a district judge or master, following the completion of an allocation questionnaire. Parties completing an allocation questionnaire can request a stay to pursue settlement, or the court can impose a stay of its own initiative,[4] reflecting the philosophy that where cases can be resolved without course to a hearing, they should be. Decisions about the allocation of some matters are automatic: Part 8 proceedings (the old originating summons procedure)[5] go automatically to the multi-track. So too with proceedings destined for one of specialist lists—the Commercial Court and the Technology and Construction Court, which provide specialist adjudication in their respective areas.[6] The scope of each track is defined by the Rules,[7] but there is no inevitability about that allocation. However, the process in many instances will be almost automatic. The court has to consider the appropriateness of the relevant track, and, in deciding that, must have regard to the following:[8]

(a) the financial value of the claim;
(b) the nature of the remedy sought;
(c) the complexity of facts, law, or evidence;
(d) the number of parties;
(e) the value of any counterclaim, and its complexity;
(f) the likely amount of oral evidence;
(g) the importance of the claim to those who are not parties;
(h) the views expressed by the parties;
(i) the circumstances of the parties.

Special rules apply in respect of multiple claims: they will normally be allocated to the track appropriate to that of highest value, but the parties may agree otherwise.[9]

---

[3] Costs recovery in the small claims and fast tracks are limited: see p 547.
[4] CPR 26.4(2).   [5] See p 505.   [6] See p 505.
[7] CPR 26.6.   [8] CPR 26.8(1).   [9] CPR 26.7(3).

Small claims track

This is the small claims jurisdiction of the county court, and designed to provide a procedurally simple and inexpensive means of disposing of small claims. It is the track to which cases with a financial value of £5,000 or less will normally be allocated, including personal injury claims within which the element of compensation sought for pain and suffering is less than £1,000. Its jurisdiction extends to tenant claims against landlords in relation to defective premises where the cost of repairs does not exceed £1,000. It also has power to deal with cases in which counterclaims exceed £5,000.

The procedure adopted in this track is simplified: no interim relief is available except interim injunctions; disclosure is limited; expert evidence may not be called without the leave of the court. When notified of a hearing date parties are required to exchange all documents on which each intends to rely. Costs are not generally recoverable.[10]

Fast track

This normally apply to all claims above £5,000, but less than £15,000,[11] and claims under that limit that are excluded from the small claims jurisdiction (for example, personal injuries claims where in excess of £1,000 is sought for pain and suffering). The trial must be likely to last no more than one day, and will generally be in the county court. The amount of expert evidence that may be called is limited to one expert, or in some cases two experts per party.[12] The rules provide for directions about the appointment of a joint expert or for experts to try to agree matters. However, where there is a justifiable need for oral expert evidence and the trial is likely to last more than one day, allocation to 'multi-track' may be more appropriate.[13]

When a case is allocated to the fast track, directions relating to disclosure, service of witness statements, expert evidence, and as to date of trial will be given. A timetable will be set with the aim of ensuring trial within thirty weeks. A directions hearing will not generally be held.[14] A pre-trial process will occur to ensure that the timetable imposed and directions made have been complied with,[15] to ensure that parties give notice of any applications that are to be made to the court, and to ensure that an estimate of likely costs is given to the court.

If it becomes evident that the case is no longer suitable for the fast-track procedure because it is of a greater value than anticipated or for any other reason, the court may (although does not have to) reallocate to the multi-track.[16]

---

[10] See p 259.   [11] CPR 26.6(4).   [12] CPR 26.6(5).
[13] *Kearsley* v *Karfield* [2005] EWCA Civ 1510.   [14] CPR 28.2, 28.3.
[15] CPR 28.5.   [16] CPR 26.10.

Multi-track

The multi-track will normally apply to all defended claims valued at more than the fast-track limit, all clinical negligence claims, all claims in categories in respect of High Court jurisdiction, for example judicial review, test cases, cases in which there is a right to a jury trial, or cases in which fraud is alleged against a party. Effective case management, which is inherent in the civil justice reforms,[17] is obviously crucial at the highest level, dealing with a wide variety of the most difficult or complex cases, but the extent to which the court needs to get involved beyond the issuing of standard directions will depend on the nature, complexity, and value of the matter. Directions without a hearing may be given at the allocation stage. The court can require further information from the parties beyond the statement of case, and may give directions relating to disclosure, case management timetables, and expert evidence. A case management conference may be necessary in an appropriate case, and must be held if the court proposes to appoint a joint expert or assessor.[18] At such a conference the court will consider a range of matters, including whether the issues are clear, whether amendments to the claim are needed, what disclosure of documents is necessary, what expert evidence is required, what evidence should be obtained and disclosed, and how matters of law and fact should be tried.[19] Necessary directions will be given, all designed to secure the achievement of minimizing delay and cost and ensuring compliance with the overriding objective. In due course (which may, in cases of real complexity, be after a very long process) a pre-trial checklist is completed, and in some cases a pre-trial review occurs, shortly before trial.

The above snapshot of the different forms of procedure anticipated in the different tracks serves only to demonstrate the key principle: that processes should be appropriate and proportionate to the matter being litigated, within the overall principle of active case management. As noted earlier, effective case management aims to achieve early settlement where that is possible, the diversion of cases to alternative methods for the resolution of disputes, the encouragement of a spirit of cooperation between the parties, the identification of the issues, and progressing a case to trial as quickly and cheaply as possible.

Only the most complex and important cases are heard by High Court judges. Other cases will be managed and heard by the appropriate level of judge and the system permits cases to move flexibly within it to ensure this. As noted earlier, most claims will fall within the jurisdiction of the county court. Case management conferences and other interim hearings may now be conducted by telephone, following successful pilot schemes.[20] The case management role is managed by procedural judges who will generally be Masters or district judges working in teams with High Court and circuit judges. For the heavier cases, requiring full 'hands-on' judicial control, the procedural judge may be a High Court or circuit judge. The procedural judge will:

---

[17] See p 489.   [18] Practice Direction 29, para 4.13.   [19] Practice Direction 29, para 5.3.
[20] In Newcastle, Luton and Bedford.

(a) conduct the initial scrutiny of all cases to allocate them to the appropriate management track;

(b) conduct the case management conference unless it is more appropriate for the trial judge to do so;

(c) generally monitor the progress of the case and investigate if parties are failing to comply with timetables or directions; and

(d) draw the existence of alternative dispute resolution (ADR) to the parties' attention where this is appropriate or desirable.

The trial judge will normally conduct the pre-trial review.

The salient features of the 'fast track' will be a set timetable of twenty to thirty weeks, with a fixed date or 'warned week' set at the outset for trial; limited discovery, short trials (not exceeding one half day); no oral evidence from experts; and limited evidence from non-experts, and a firm timetable for all actions.

Discontinuance and striking out

A party may wish to discontinue an action. The parties and their solicitors, at every stage of the proceedings, will generally be attempting to resolve their dispute without the expense of a trial. In fact very few actions come to trial. If the claimant is satisfied that his or her cause of action was misconceived or has ceased to exist, he or she may at any time consent to judgment being entered against him or her with costs. The result will be to determine finally the issues that he or she has raised in his or her claim. However, the claimant is better advised simply to discontinue his or her action since this course will not prevent him or her from suing again at a more convenient time. This can be done, usually as of right, under Part 38 of the Civil Procedure Rules. However, the permission of the court will be needed to discontinue a claim, or any part of a claim, in respect of which the court has issued an interim injunction, given an undertaking to the court, or has received an interim payment.[21] If the claimant serves notice of discontinuance, the defendant has the power to apply, within twenty-eight days, to have that set aside.[22] The court will then have to decide whether the defendant has suffered any injustice as a result of the discontinuance. This power to strike out a notice of discontinuance will be exercised rarely, and then only in cases in which it effectively amounts to an abuse of process of the court. Such was the case in *Gilham v Browning*,[23] in which the counterclaim that was being discontinued was raised only to circumvent an evidential restriction in that case. A party who discontinues is usually going to be liable in costs.[24]

A court also has the power to strike out a statement of case.[25] This it may do if the case discloses no reasonable grounds to bring or defend the claim, that the statement

---

[21] CPR 38.2.   [22] CPR 38.4.   [23] [1998] 2 All ER 68.
[24] CPR 38.6.   [25] CPR 3.4.

of claim amounts to an abuse of the court's process, or there have been failures to comply with a rule, Practice Direction, or court order. This provision is in addition to the power preserved by section 49(3) of the Supreme Court Act 1981, to stay proceedings as part of its inherent jurisdiction, which may perhaps be exercised where there are concurrent proceedings in another country.[26]

The question of striking out for delay or 'want of prosecution' is a key one especially because one of the objectives of the civil justice reforms was to remove unnecessary delay from civil proceedings, to secure justice within a reasonable time. Questions of default and delay can, under the Civil Procedure Rules, be dealt with by sanctions,[27] from which the parties can seek relief, a power to be exercised in the light of the matters identified in rule 3.9 as those to which the court should have regard. The decision appears to be that which the court considers just in all of the circumstances,[28] but in a way that respects the overriding objective[29] but which also respects the fair trial provisions of Article 6 of the European Convention.[30] One way of achieving compliance is through a peremptory ('or unless') order of the court; in such cases the action is liable to be dismissed on account of the conduct of the party in failing to comply with the court's peremptory order—but the power to strike out a case for delay is an extreme one. Prior to the Civil Procedure Rules, the traditional position of the courts was not generally to use the striking-out power in cases of delay. In *Birkett* v *James*,[31] the House of Lords held that in cases in which the limitation period had not expired (so that if the action were dismissed the plaintiff could simply issue a fresh writ), the court would not, save in rare and exceptional cases, dismiss an action for want of prosecution, unless some factors other than mere delay have prejudiced the defendant. As stated above, such cases are likely to be very rare. Such a position grew increasingly under challenge,[32] In *Arbuthnot Latham Bank Ltd* v *Trafalgar Holdings Ltd*,[33] Lord Woolf MR observed:

> In *Birkett* v *James* the consequences to other litigants and to the courts of inordinate delay was not a consideration which was in issue. From now on it is going to be a consideration of increasing significance. Litigants and their legal advisers must recognise that any delay which occurs from now on will be assessed not only from the point of view of the prejudice caused to the particular litigants whose case it is, but also in relation to the effect it can have on other litigants who are wishing to have their cases heard and the prejudice which is caused to the due administration of justice....

---

[26] *The Abadin Daver* [1984] AC 398, [1984] 1 All ER 470.

[27] See CPR 3.3–3.9.   [28] *Purdy* v *Cambran* [1999] CPLR 843.

[29] See p 489.   [30] Zuckerman, *Civil Procedure* (Sweet & Maxwell, 2003), para 10.97.

[31] [1978] AC 297; [1977] 2 All ER 801. For exceptions at common law, see, e.g., *Spring Grove Services Ltd* v *Deane* (1972) 116 Sol Jo 844, which case was exceptional in that the defence depended essentially on the evidence of two witnesses who were no longer available to the defendant when the second action was brought; cf. *Department of Health and Social Security* v *Ereira* [1973] 3 All ER 421. The matter is one for the discretion of the court: *Arbuthnot Latham Bank Ltd* v *Trafalgar Holdings Ltd* [1998] 2 All ER 181 [1998] 1 WLR 1426.

[32] See, e.g., *Grovit* v *Doctor* [1997] 2 All ER 417.   [33] [1998] 2 All ER 181.

There has thus been a 'change of culture'.[34] The fact that there may be another way of penalizing the delay is not inevitably decisive against a striking out for delay, although, arguably, it is a matter that the court has to bear in mind.[35]

Settlement

The importance of settling any claim without it reaching the stage of a hearing has already been noted.[36] The overriding objective and the pre-action protocols, and indeed the case-management arrangements put in place by the CPR, all lay emphasis at attempting to resolve disputes outside the courtroom. It is usually also in the interests of the parties (or their insurance companies), who are likely to be in constant communication to effect a settlement of the action. This they may do with complete candour since letters that pass between them are privileged from production and any offer or admission of liability made therein is said to be made 'without prejudice'. The nature of a settlement is that it is a contract whereby the parties abandon their previous rights and obligations in return for the creation of new rights and obligations.

The parties may effect a settlement without the consent of the court by giving notice of withdrawal before trial. Where an order of the court is required, which will usually be the case when the action is settled during the trial, the required terms will be drawn up and endorsed on counsels' briefs, or, more usually, the parties will submit to judgment on agreed terms. The settlement of any action on behalf of an infant or patient must be approved by the court.

Summary judgment

A party to proceedings may have little or no prospect of successfully succeeding in his claim or defence. Part 24 of the Civil Procedure Rules permits summary judgment to be given, either on the application of the claimant or of the defendant, or on the court's own initiative. The court has to be satisfied that there is no real prospect of success on the claim or issue, or no real prospect of successfully defending the claim or issue, and, in either situation, there is no other compelling reason why the claim or issue should be disposed of at a trial.[37]

The power is an important one in the context of active case management.[38] A judge should, in an appropriate case, consider of his or her own initiative the merits

---

[34] *Per* Chadwick LJ in *Securum Finance Lyd* v *Ashton* [2001] Ch 291 at 310.

[35] *UCB Corporate Services Ltd (formerly UCB Bank plc)* v *Halifax SW Ltd* [2000] LS Gaz R 24.

[36] See p 490.

[37] CPR 24.2. *Three Rivers District Council and others* v *Governor and Company of the Bank of England (No 3)* [2001] 2 All ER 513; *Celador Production Ltd* v *Melville* [2004] EWHC 2362.

[38] See *Harris* v *Bolt Burdon* (2000) The Times, 8 December; *Swain* v *Hillman & Gay* [2001] 1 All ER 91.

of a case, and if it has no prospects of success, it should not be allowed to continue.[39] The power should, though, be exercised with caution in the context of a litigant in person.[40]

Part 36 offers to settle

The principle

In any action for debt or damages the defendant has in the past been able at any time to pay money into court in satisfaction of any or all of the claims being pursued in the action by the claimant. Prior to the Civil Procedure Rules these were known as 'payments into court', but now the process is governed by Part 36, which permits, and encourages, offers to settle.[41] Offers to settle are not, since 2007, backed by payments.

Part 36 has been described as 'one of the cornerstones of procedure made by the CPR'.[42] This statement serves only to emphasize the key principle, noted throughout, that the promotion of settlement is one of the key aims, which the conduct of litigation should seek to promote, facilitate, and encourage.[43] We have already noted[44] that Part 36 provides for pre-action offers to settle. An offer to settle can be made at any time before proceedings are commenced by either party. Whilst this might seem self-evident, its recognition in Part 36 and in the pre-action protocols is significant: if a party to proceedings unreasonably fails to accept a pre-action Part 36 offer, that is a matter to which the courts can have regard on questions of cost.[45] In *Daniels* v *Commissioner of Police for the Metropolis*,[46] the court stressed that the normal rule is that the unsuccessful party pays costs. It is incumbent on the unsuccessful party to demonstrate that the conduct of the other party in refusing a Part 36 offer was so unreasonable as to justify departure from that rule. In that case the unsuccessful claimant sought to appeal against costs on the basis that the other party should have negotiated. In rejecting that argument, the court concluded that it is not unreasonable to decline to pay a claim that is in fact dismissed. However, uncertainty has been created by *Carver* v *British Airports Authority*,[47] in which the court appeared to adopt an 'is it worth it?' test in respect of the costs of a claimant who had exceeded the amount of the offer to settle by a mere £51. The court concluded that the additional £51 was 'more advantageous' than the offer to settle. The irrecoverable costs of the claimant together with the stress of the proceedings meant that the judgment of the court was

---

[39] *Peter John O'Donnell and others* v *Charly Holdings Inc (A Company Incorporated under the Laws of Burma) and another*, unreported, 14 March 2000.

[40] *Orford* v *Rasmi Electronics and others* [2002] EWCA Civ 1672.

[41] Formerly known as *Calderbank* offers. See, now, CPR 36.5.

[42] *Petrotrade Inc* v *Texaco Ltd* [2001] 4 All ER 853.

[43] Woolf Final Report, ch 10, para 2.   [44] See p 527.

[45] *Ford* v *GKR Construction* [2000] 1 All ER 802.   [46] [2005] EWCA Civ 1312.

[47] [2008] 3 All ER 911.

not, overall, 'more advantageous' to the claimant, who was ordered to pay the costs of the defendant starting from twenty-one days after the date of the defendant's offer. In that context the matter has to be viewed from the perspectives of the parties, not from how, later, it looks to a court.[48]

A party may make a Part 36 offer to settle at any stage in the proceedings. Perhaps surprisingly, a party who rejects an offer may in due course accept it if it has not formally been withdrawn.[49]

Offers to settle are appropriate in respect of proceedings in which non-pecuniary relief is being sought (for example, an injunction). This was made clear in *Amber* v *Stacey*,[50] in which the defendant had made an offer of settlement in the sum of £4,000, followed, later, by a payment into court. When the judge eventually made a judgment for a sum less than that paid into court, he made a costs order in favour of the defendant as from the date of offer of settlement.[51] This was held to be wrong in principle, the court varying the costs order made.

Effects of an offer to settle

Unless the court considers it unjust to do so, the court will order the claimant to pay any costs incurred by the defendant after the latest date on which the offer could have been accepted without needing the permission of the court.[52]

A Part 36 offer will have been made by notice being given to the claimant and other parties. The notice will state various details prescribed by the Rule and Practice Directions. It can be given at any time, but if that is given less than twenty-one days before trial, the offer can only be accepted if the parties agree liability for costs or the court gives permission.[53] Thus, within twenty-one days of the trial, the court permission or agreement of the parties is a key prerequisite. The court has discretion in the matter that is not simply confined to the application of the costs sanction envisaged by Part 36. In *Barclays Bank plc* v *Martin and Mortimer*,[54] the court stressed that it had to consider whether unfairness to the defendant, potentially caused by a change in the circumstances of the litigation, would arise if the claimant were allowed, late, to accept a Part 36 payment.

If an offer is wrongly rejected, the issue of costs arise. Costs will be given to a claimant who, having failed to accept an offer to settle, fails to 'beat' the payment (that is, obtain more by way of monetary sum) or fails to obtain more advantageous terms of judgment than those contained in the offer to settle.[55] Those costs will usually, but not inevitably be on the standard basis.[56] On occasion, if the conduct of the claimant was

---

[48] *LGBLower* v *Reeves* [2010] EWCA Civ 726.
[49] *Gibbon* v *Manchester City Council* [2010] EWCA Civ 726.   [50] [2001] 1 WLR 1225.
[51] For the costs implications, see p 504.
[52] CPR 36.20(2). *Ede Walker Residential Ltd* v *Davis* [2005] EWHC 3483.
[53] CPR 36.5(7).   [54] (2002) The Times, 19 August.
[55] CPR 36.20. See *Daniels* v *Commissioner of Police for the Metropolis* [2005] EWCA 1312.
[56] See p 504.

wholly unjustified, costs might be on an indemnity basis,[57] although such cases are likely to be rare. This costs sanction is not, though, automatic. Whether the defendant gets his or her costs after a failure by the claimant to beat the offer to settle is a matter of judicial discretion.[58] That discretion should, though, normally be exercised in accordance with the general principle that, in this situation, a defendant should receive his costs. Thus, in *Factortame Ltd* v *Secretary of State for the Environment, Transport and the Regions*,[59] the defendant was entitled to his costs after the rejection of a Part 36 offer, even though the defendant had not provided accurate figures as to matters that would have affected the levels of compensation. It was, in each, case a matter for the discretion of the trial judge.

KEY ISSUE

Debate now centres on whether Part 36 fully encourages settlement. The Jackson Report recommended the reversal of the approach in *Carter* v *British Airports Authority*. In relation to monetary offers the term 'more advantageous' should mean that the offer is better in financial terms. This would, it said, provide greater certainty and permit both parties to calculate the risks. The government's consultation paper[60] identified an alternative approach that would involve linking the point at which Part 36 would disqualify the award of full costs to a range of value rather than an exact monetary value (say by a percentage).

The Jackson Report also recommended an additional sanction on a defendant who fails to beat or equal a Part 36 offer made by the claimant. This would be equal to 10 per cent of the total damages awarded by the court, except in cases in which the court considers that it would be unjust to make such an award. The proposal is intended to provide real incentives to settle rather than continue to trial

 Questions

1. What do you consider the advantages of the Part 36 procedure to be?
2. What are the merits of the recommendations made by the Jackson Report?

Interim relief

Interlocutory injunction

An injunction is 'a court order prohibiting a person from doing something or requiring a person to do something'.[61] The power of the High Court to issue injunctions is,

---

[57] *Excelsior Commercial & Industrial Holdings Ltd* v *Salisbury Hammer Asbden & Johnson*, unreported, 12 June 2002. For the indemnity principle, see p 547.

[58] See *Ford* v *GR Construction* [2000] 1 All ER 802.

[59] [2002] 3 WLR 104. For other aspects of the *Factortame* litigation, see p 127.

[60] Ministry of Justice, *Proposals for Reform of Civil Litigation Funding and Costs in England and Wales* (HMSO, November 2010), at p 44.

[61] Glossary to CPR.

of course, inherited from the jurisdiction in equity,[62] but now extends to both High Court and county court by virtue of statutory provisions. In addition to the court's inherent power to grant an injunction by way of final remedy, section 37(1) of the Supreme Court Act 1981[63] empowers the court to grant an injunction by an interlocutory order 'in all cases in which it appears to the court to be just or convenient so to do'.[64] It may be noted that the injunction need not be directed at achieving the same relief as that which is sought by way of final relief in the proceedings. Their purpose was well explained by Lord Oliver in *Attorney-General* v *Times Newspapers*:[65]

> interlocutory injunctions are designed to ensure the effective administration of justice, so that the rights which it is the duty of the courts to protect can fairly be determined and effectively protected and enforced by the courts.

Procedures for obtaining such interim relief are governed by the Civil Procedure Rules, Part 23, and reflect the key principles for the grant of an interim injunction explained in the leading case of *American Cyanamid Co* v *Ethicon Ltd*.[66] Lord Diplock stated that the approach referred to above was incorrect and, in a speech with which the remainder of their Lordships agreed, laid down the following principles.

(1) The claimant must first satisfy the court 'that the claim is not frivolous or vexatious; in other words that there is a serious question to be tried'.

(2) The court should then go on to consider the 'balance of convenience'.

(3) As to that, the court should first consider whether, if the claimant were to succeed at the trial in establishing his right to a permanent injunction, he would be adequately compensated by an award of damages for the loss he would have sustained by refusal of an interlocutory injunction.

(4) If damages would not provide an adequate remedy (for example, because the defendant may be impecunious) the court should consider whether the defendant would be adequately compensated by the claimant's undertaking as to damages (*infra*) in the event of an interlocutory injunction being granted but a permanent injunction being refused at the trial.

(5) Where other matters are equal, it is a 'counsel of prudence to take such measures as are calculated to preserve the status quo'.

(6) Finally, 'if the extent of the uncompensatable disadvantage to each party would not differ widely, it may not be improper to take into account in tipping the balance the relative strength of each party's case as revealed by the affidavit

---

[62] See p 254.   [63] See County Courts Act 1984, s 38.
[64] The position of the Crown was discussed in *Factortame* v *Secretary of State for Transport* [1990] 2 AC 85, [1989] 2 All ER 692.
[65] [1992] 1 AC 191, see also *Attorney-General* v *Punch Ltd* [2002] UKHL 50.
[66] [1975] AC 396, [1975] 1 All ER 504.

evidence'. By this is meant that the court should consider whether the strength of the case of one party is disproportionate to the other.[67]

Lord Diplock made it clear that there may be special factors that operate in 'individual cases' in addition to the principles enumerated above. Nevertheless it is clear that the courts should not embark on anything resembling a trial of the action.

The Court of Appeal initially showed little enthusiasm for these principles. In *Cayne v Global Natural Resources plc*,[68] the Court of Appeal pointed out that where the grant or refusal of an interlocutory injunction will have the practical effect of putting an end to the action, the task of the court is to do its best to avoid injustice, and to balance the risk of doing an injustice to either party. In such cases the *American Cyanamid* guidelines cannot apply, and unless the claimant can show an overwhelming case, he will not be granted an injunction the effect of which would be tantamount to shutting the defendant out from contesting the action. May LJ justified this departure by observing:

> I think that one must be very careful to apply the relevant passages from Lord Diplock's familiar speech in the *Cyanamid* case not as rules but only as guidelines, which is what I am certain Lord Diplock intended them to be.

Special issues arise in the context of publications, and attempts to restrain them by interim injunction. That arises because of the special emphasis that has to be given by a court to the right of freedom of expression, pursuant to section 12 of the Human Rights Act 1998.[69] In *Cream Holdings Ltd v Banerjee*,[70] the Court of Appeal held that, in such a case, it was insufficient that there was a serious issue to be tried. Section 12(3) required the courts to look at the merits, putting the *American Cyanamid* test on one side.

Application for an interim injunction must be made to a judge. In cases of extreme urgency application can be made without leave on affidavit, in which event an injunction will be granted for a very short period until an application by summons or motion can be brought before the court.

As an alternative to injunction the court will usually accept an undertaking from the defendant (which has precisely the same effect). In addition, as a condition of being granted an interim injunction the claimant is customarily required to give his undertaking as to damages: that is, an undertaking to indemnify the defendant in respect of any damages that the latter sustains by reason of the injunction in the event of the action failing. For this reason it is generally improvident for a claimant to apply for an interlocutory injunction unless he has a strong case in circumstances

---

[67] See *Series 5 Software Ltd v Clarke* [1996] 1 All ER 853. A court should not grant interim relief where a new cause of action is relied on: see *Khorasandjian v Bush* [1993] QB 727.

[68] [1984] 1 All ER at 237. The *Cyanamid* principles do not apply to mandatory injunctions: *Locabail International Finance Ltd v Agroexport* [1986] 1 All ER 901, [1986] 1 WLR 657. The factors to be taken into account in the context of mandatory injunctions were set out in *Zockell Group Ltd v Mercury Communications Ltd* [1998] FSR 354. See also *Services Ltd v Merent Psychometric International Ltd* [2002] FSR 8.

[69] As to which, see p 150.   [70] [2003] EWCA Civ 103.

in which the interim will cause the defendant heavy expense, for example by delaying building works.

Interim payment of damages

One long-standing criticism of civil procedure in the English courts was that wholly innocent parties, such as injured passengers in road accidents, had to wait for long periods for their damages while disputes between other parties, such as the car drivers (in fact, their insurers), were being resolved. The *Report of the Committee on Personal Injuries Litigation*[71] recommended that in such litigation courts should have power to make interim payments and effect was given to this recommendation by the Administration of Justice Act 1969. This was replaced by section 32(1) of the Supreme Court Act 1981,[72] which authorizes rules of court enabling the High Court:

> in such circumstances as may be prescribed to make an order requiring a party to the proceedings to make an interim payment of such amount as may be specified in the order, with provision for the payment to be made to such other party to the proceedings as may be so specified or, if the order so provides, by paying it into court.

The power is regulated in detail by rule 25 of the Civil Procedure Rules. An interim payment may only be made if the defendant admits liability in whole or in part, or judgment that damages be assessed has already been obtained, or the court is satisfied that if the matter were to go to trial, the claimant would receive a sum of money substantial in nature. Additional criteria apply in personal injury cases.

Statements of case

Background

Statements of case replace the old pre-Woolf system of pleadings. These were written statements served by each party on his opponent, containing the allegations of fact on which the party pleadings relied. They were supposed to serve various purposes. Principally they enabled each party to determine exactly which facts are alleged against him. This could save a party from preparing evidence to meet allegations that are not being made against him. Also it enabled parties to establish their 'common ground': that is to say, facts on which they are in agreement, thus saving the expense of proving these matters at the trial. Secondly, the action was decided upon the pleadings. Thus the parties and their successors could, by reference to the pleadings, determine in the future exactly what the case decided, so that they may not have to, and indeed may not be allowed to, fight the same issues again. Similarly reference to the pleadings in an action might disclose the *ratio decidendi* of the case for the purpose

---

[71] Cmnd 3691 (1968) (the Pearson Committee).   [72] See also County Courts Act 1984, s 50.

of the doctrine of precedent, since any fact not pleaded would not usually be regarded as a fact upon which a judgment is based.

Whether pleadings always in fact fulfilled these objectives is a matter of doubt. The Woolf Report[73] considered that the use of pleadings by claimants often had the effect not of clarifying the issues, but of merely adding to the adversarial conflict responsible for delay. The system caused extra and unnecessary cost, complications and delays. The report recommended that pleadings should have to spell out the facts relied on so that the parties can identify and define the matters in issue. Their content needed to be verified by the parties, so enabling the court to determine the range and scale of material required to progress the case and the necessary extent of disclosure, witness statements, and the use of experts. In short, this important part of the process should be such as to enable the court adequately to make decisions as to how a case should be managed, in accordance with the overriding objective.[74]

The old 'pleadings' are replaced by the new 'statements of case', a term defined widely to include a claim form,[75] particulars of claim, a defence, a Part 20 claim,[76] a reply to a defence, and any other information supplied either voluntarily or under a court order.[77] They should be characterized by conciseness, and by their capacity to clarify rather an obscure the issues,[78] but obviously have to be sufficiently clear and detailed to achieve that.[79] Where there are allegations of misconduct by an individual, they should be pleaded and put to the individual when testifying at trial.[80]

In *McPhileny v Times Newspapers Ltd*,[81] Lord Woolf MR observed:

> [Statements of case] mark out the parameters of the case that is being advanced by each party [and] identify the issues and the extent of the dispute between the parties. The need for extensive [statements of case] including particulars should be reduced by the requirement that witness statements are now exchanged. In the majority of pleadings identification of the documents upon which a party relies, together with copies of that party's witness statements, will make clear the detail of the nature of the case the other side has to meet obvious.

The new regime for civil procedure from the outset seeks to achieve these aims. The information disclosed pre-action,[82] the contents of the claim form,[83] and duties to exchange documents and information[84] all form part and parcel of this process. Specific types of claim require specific types of information to be supplied. A few examples suffice. A claim under a contract requires a copy of the documents relied on to be attached to, or served with, the particulars of claim.[85] A Fatal Accidents Act 1976 claim should identify details of the dependant. In a personal injury claim, which relies

---

[73] Woolf Final Report, paras 153–164.   [74] See p 489.

[75] See p 505.   [76] See p 512.

[77] CPR 2.3, Part 16. The Part 16 procedure does not apply to Part 8 proceedings (as to which see p 506).

[78] *McPhilemy* v *Times Newspapers Ltd* [1999] 3 All ER 775, *per* Lord Woolf MR.

[79] *The Royal Brompton Hospital NHS Trust* v *Hammond and others* (2001) 76 Con LR 148.

[80] *Abbey Forwarding Ltd (in liquidation)* v *Hore and another* [2010 EWHC 2029 (Ch).

[81] [1999] 3 All ER 775.   [82] See p 504.

[83] See p 506.   [84] See pp 506 and 535.   [85] Practice Direction 16.

on medical evidence, a report from a medical practitioner about the injuries sustained should be attached with the particulars of claim or otherwise served. A defendant who wishes to resist the claim will need to serve details of his defence. This will address every allegation made in the particulars of claim, with admissions or non-admissions (as appropriate). These admissions will identify facts that are agreed or not in dispute, as well as the response on the issues of liability. The basis and detail of any denials or non-admissions must be set out.[86] A claimant is entitled to serve a reply to a defence, but is not obliged to do so.

All statements of case must be accompanied by a statement of truth, a statement that the party putting it forward believes it to be true.[87] A party must also supply relevant details of any conditional fee agreements.[88]

Statements of case may be amended by consent or with permission.[89] Amendments made by agreement will be formally dealt with by means of a consent order, but otherwise the permission of the court will be required. The court has a discretion in the matter, to be exercised in accordance with the overriding objective.[90] Amendments that allow the court to adjudicate on the real issues in the case will generally be allowed, provided that they are not inconsistent with facts that have already been asserted as part of the statement of case.[91] But prejudice might arise if the statement of case is amended in a way that affects the track in which the case is dealt with, or the defendant's response to the case. One example is *Maguire* v *Molin*,[92] in which the amendment sought and refused was to increase the value claimed from £15,000 (the maximum for the fast track) to £80,000. Amendments that introduce effectively new claims after the expiration of any limitation period will not generally be permitted, for otherwise the limitation periods themselves would be circumvented.[93] However, questions of the operation of the Human Rights Act 1998[94] arose in *Goode* v *Martin*,[95] in which, although the court recognized a limitation period as potentially compatible with Article 6 of the Convention, the court used section 3 of the 1998 Act to interpret the requirement so as to allow a new claim beyond the limitation period where it was based on facts that were already in issue.

Disclosure and inspection of documents

Relevant principles and background

Disclosure (formerly known as discovery) is the procedure whereby a party discloses, to the court or to any other party, the relevant documents in the action that he has, or has had, in his possession, custody, or power. Documentary evidence plays

---

[86] CPR 16.5.2.   [87] CPR 22.1(6).   [88] See pp 408 and 482.
[89] CPR 17.1(2).   [90] See p 489.
[91] *Cobbold* v *Greenwich LBC*, unreported, 24 May 2001.   [92] [2002] EWCA Civ 1083.
[93] CPR 17.4(2).   [94] See p 146.   [95] [2001] EWCA Civ 1899.

an important part in nearly all civil cases. Its purpose was explained by Sir John Donaldson as follows:[96]

> In plain language litigation is conducted 'cards face up on the table'. Some people from other lands regard this as incomprehensible. 'Why' they ask 'should I be expected to provide my opponent with the means of defeating me?' The answer, of course, is that litigation is not a war or even a game. It is designed to do real justice between opposing parties and, if the court does not have all the relevant information, it cannot achieve this object.

In an action for breach of contract, for example, the transactions between the parties may be contained entirely in letters that have passed between them. One party's letters may not be intelligible unless read in conjunction with letters in the possession of the other party. Similarly, in an industrial injuries action, the employers are likely to have internal accident reports, machine maintenance records, records of complaints, and the like that it is very much in the claimant's interests to see, while, on the other hand, the claimant may have documents relating to his medical condition, or to his earnings since the accident or state benefits that he has received, all of which may be highly relevant to the quantification of his claim by the defendants.

KEY ISSUE

Full disclosure is an important principle, especially where there are facts to be decided. In judicial review proceedings, where facts are not generally in issue, disclosure is usually unnecessary. However, in *R (on the application of Al-Sweady) v Secretary of State for Defence*,[97] facts were in issue on a judicial review based upon allegations of mistreatment of an individual by British soldiers. Full disclosure was necessary in order for the matter to be resolved fairly and accurately, and in the context of an alleged violation of Convention rights. Following the decision detailed guidance was published[98] governing the duty of the public authority in judicial review proceedings. Nonetheless in one case a public authority, OFSTED, was condemned for 'horrible disclosure failings', delaying the giving of judgment by the court in a case in which evidence had been heard.[99]

? Questions

1. Why is full disclosure important?
2. Do you think it is particularly important in judicial review proceedings? Why, if that is true, should that be?

---

[96] *Davies v Eli Lilly & Co* [1987] 1 All ER 801, [1987] 1 WLR 428.
[97] [2009] EWHC 2387 (Admin).
[98] See *Guidance on Discharging the Duty of Candour and Disclosure in Judicial Review Proceedings* [2010] JR 177.
[99] *R (Shoesmith) v Ofsted* [2010] EWHC 852 (Admin).

A party will want to have his opponent disclose which documents the latter has, or has had, in his possession (disclosure), and, secondly, to inspect and take copies of those documents in his opponent's possession (inspection).[100] Documents in the modern age includes electronic media such as emails, which raises practical issues of real difficulty. As the court observed in *Fiddes v Channel 4 TV Corporation and another,*[101] in an ideal world all relevant documents ought to be disclosed, but 'we do not live in an ideal world'. Accordingly, the court concluded that, in deciding the extent to which it should order the disclosure of deleted emails, it must have regard to their relevance, significance, and to the question of cost.

The questions raised by electronic storage and creation of documents are enormous. The Jackson Report[102] recognized that e-disclosure is inevitable in many cases, with the danger that the data available is so enormous to render it almost unmanageable, an issue that, Jackson concluded, requires significant training for judges and practitioners alike.

Sometimes a party may have documents that are relevant to the litigation, and therefore disclosable, but which he wishes to safeguard against circulation either to third parties, or occasionally to the claimant himself for extraneous reasons. As to this point, the traditional position has been that on disclosure each party impliedly undertakes not to use the documents that are disclosed for any ulterior or improper purpose. The use of such documents in breach of that implied undertaking has been held to be a contempt of court. Thus, in *Home Office v Harman,*[103] a solicitor who passed documents to a journalist to assist in the preparation of an article was held to be in contempt, even though the documents had been read in open court. Nor can a party generally rely upon such documents in other proceedings. Thus where a claimant in proceedings against his employers obtained discovery of a memorandum about him that contained an alleged libel, the court held that he could not found a libel action on that publication since that would be an abuse of the process of the court.[104] In *Crest Homes plc v Marks,*[105] the court indicated that it would release a party from that undertaking if the applicant could demonstrate 'cogent and persuasive reasons' for such a release, and that the release did not cause injustice. If there is a real risk of the claimant using documents for an improper collateral purpose, the court could restrict inspection, for example to a party's legal advisers.

---

[100] 'Inspection' is not limited to ocular inspection but includes examination by any of the senses. Thus, a tape-recording is a document, inspection of which would be effected by playing the same upon a tape-recorder to the inspecting party: *Grant v Southwestern and County Properties Ltd* [1975] Ch 185, [1974] 2 All ER 465; similar considerations apply to untransmitted television film: *Senior v Holdsworth, ex parte Independent Television News Ltd* [1976] QB 23, [1975] 2 All ER 1009.

[101] [2010] EWCA Civ 516.   [102] Jackson Report, at p 365, para 2.1.

[103] [1983] 1 AC 280, [1982] 1 All ER 532. This finding was held to be in breach of the European Convention of Human Rights, Article 10, by the European Court of Human Rights in *Harman v United Kingdom*, in that it infringed the right of freedom of expression and the right to impart and receive information under Article 10.

[104] *Riddick v Thames Board Mills Ltd* [1977] QB 881, [1977] 3 All ER 677.

[105] [1987] AC 829, [1987] 2 All ER 1074.

The position is now governed by the Civil Procedure Rules.[106] A party to whom a document is disclosed may use it only for the purposes of the proceedings and not for any other purpose, except where the document has been read to or by the court, or referred to at a public hearing, the court gives permission, or those who disclosed and received agree. Despite these exceptions the court nonetheless has discretion to restrict or prohibit the use of a document. The presumption will be that a document produced in open court will be disclosable.[107] If, as in the *Lilly Icos* case, the document was of only peripheral importance in the hearing and contained highly sensitive commercial information, there might be a case for restricting disclosure.

The pre-existing system of discovery was roundly condemned by the Woolf Report. One overseas judge observed:

> If there was a hell to which disputatious, uncivil, vituperative lawyers go, let it be one in which the damned are eternally locked in discovery disputes with other lawyers of equally repugnant attributes.

Whatever the element of overstatement, reform was another key objective of the civil justice reforms. The pre-existing law allowed discovery not only of relevant documents, but also of others that might lead to the production of relevant documents.[108] It should be borne in mind that the greater the level of disclosure the greater burden is imposed on parties to identify and produce information. This can potentially add to the length of time litigation takes, and its cost. It is for this reason that the Woolf Report recommended that disclosure should be controlled by the court as part of its case-management function, it being regulated with regard to the size of the case, the cost of disclosure, and the likely cost. For the future it is envisaged that disclosure on the scale that it used to happen will rarely take place.

The rules[109] now define 'standard disclosure' as involving documents on which the party will rely, documents that adversely affect his own case, that adversely affect another parties' case, or that support that case. In addition documents that are required to be disclosed by any Practice Direction must be disclosed. An ongoing duty to disclose exists. The rules governing disclosure apply to fast-track and multi-track litigation, but not claims in the small claims track.

KEY ISSUE

How far should disclosure go? The test of disclosure is narrower than that which existed hitherto, which required parties to disclose everything that was relevant. However, evidence to the Jackson inquiry suggests that many solicitors simply disclose everything, saving costs on their own side but creating a much greater amount of documentation, which of course increases the workload and therefore cost for all. The Jackson Report concluded that, in large commercial cases and in other cases in which the costs of standard disclosure are

---

[106] CPR 31.22.   [107] *Lilly Icos Ltd* v *Pfizer Ltd* [2002] EWCA Civ 2.

[108] See *Compagnie Financire* v *Peruvian Guano Co* (1882) 11 QBD 55. Interesting parallels exist with the development of disclosure in criminal cases.

[109] CPR 31.6.

likely to be disproportionate to the amounts in issue, a 'menu' approach should be adopted, whereby the parties can agree the scope of disclosure, or disclose in broad terms what documents exist, and estimate the costs of standard disclosure to enable case management hearings to determine the extent and detail of such disclosure. However, personal injury and clinical negligence claims should be excluded from this procedure

 Question

What are the advantages of the Jackson recommendation?

Obligations to disclose can arise pre-action. The Court of Appeal in *Black* v *Sumitomo*[110] considered pre-action disclosure to be important, particularly where the claim had not been fully established enabling a potential claimant to decide whether a claim might succeed and on what basis. This was particularly the case in personal injury and medical negligence cases. It was also a necessary prerequisite in some cases in order to obtain funding, to establish what the likelihood of success is in a case potentially the subject of a conditional fee agreement. On the other hand, the court must discourage 'fishing expeditions'. Pre-trial protocols govern what should, ideally, be disclosed voluntarily. But the CPR make provision for an order requiring pre-trial disclosure.[111] This was discussed in Chapter 14.[112]

Disclosure and inspection against other persons

We have already noted the procedure whereby orders for disclosure and inspection of documents against proposed parties may be made before the commencement of proceedings. Under section 34 of the Supreme Court Act 1981, there is, in addition, power, in actions for damages for death or personal injuries, to order a person who is not a party to the proceedings and who appears to be likely to have or have had in his possession, custody, or power any documents that are relevant to an issue arising out of the action to disclose whether these documents are in his possession, custody, or power and to produce those that he has to the applicant. This power is exercisable only after the commencement of proceedings, the application being by summons (which must be served on the person against whom the order is sought and on all parties to the action) supported by affidavit, and now applies to all proceedings.

Action for disclosure

Save for the limited exception, in personal injuries actions, discussed above, there is, as a rule, no procedure for obtaining discovery against persons who are not parties

---

[110] [2002] 1 WLR 1562. The court reviewed earlier case law including *Dunning* v *United Liverpool Hospitals Board of Governors* [1973] 1 WLR 586; *Shaw* v *Vauxhall Motors Ltd* [1974] 2 All ER 1185; *Burns* v *Shuttlehurst* [1999] 1 WLR 1449.
[111] CPR 31.16.   [112] See p 513.

to an action. They can, of course, be compelled to attend the trial and to produce, at that stage, documents in their possession (by means of court order) but there is a rule, sometimes known as the 'mere witness' rule, whereby discovery cannot be obtained against a person against whom no relief is sought but who might be a witness in an action. It follows that if a party wishes to inspect documents in the possession of a person against whom he has no cause of action, he cannot sue that person simply for the purpose of obtaining evidence, by way of disclosure of documents, for use against the party against whom there is a cause of action. This rule appears to have little in the way of logic to commend it but it is, nevertheless, too firmly entrenched to be altered save by way of legislation.

However, it has already been seen that a limited exception to the rule was formulated by the House of Lords in the case of *Norwich Pharmacal Co v Customs and Excise Commissioners*.[113] The facts of the case were unusual. The appellants, who were the owners of a patent covering a chemical compound, learned from information published by the respondents that a number of consignments of the compound had been imported between 1960 and 1970, none of which had been licensed by the appellants. The appellants therefore knew that others were infringing their patent but did not know their identities. The respondents refused to disclose the identities of the importers whereupon the appellants brought an action against the respondents seeking an order for discovery of documents relating to the importations. The House of Lords granted such an order; the reasoning behind the decision was expressed by Lord Reid, as follows:

> if through no fault of his own a person gets mixed up in the tortious acts of others so as to facilitate their wrong-doing he may incur no personal liability but he comes under a duty to assist the person who has been wronged by giving him full information and disclosing the identity of the wrongdoers.

In *Ashworth Hospital Authority v MGN Ltd*,[114] Lord Woolf stressed that the court should start from the proposition that a non-party should not be subjected to the civil process and made to disclose information. He should at least be 'involved', however innocently, in another person's wrongdoing.

Directions

It will be evident from the above that the case-management role of the court throughout the case will give the courts the opportunity to make directions relating to the whole management, conduct, and progress of the case. Amongst those already identified are matters of disclosure, evidence, expert evidence, place, time, and mode of

---

[113] [1974] AC 133, [1973] 2 All ER 943, applied in *Loose v Williamson* [1978] 3 All ER 89, [1978] 1 WLR 639, [1974] AC, at 175, [1973] 2 All ER, at 948; see also, on the *Norwich Pharmacal* principle, *Arab Monetary Fund v Hashim (No 5)* [1992] 2 All ER 911.

[114] [2002] 1 WLR 2033.

trial. Unlike the pre-Woolf system there is not simply one time when these matters will be considered; they are ongoing issues. The involvement of the court will in part depend on the nature and complexity of the matters in issue, and the track the case is on.

Trial

Preparation of evidence

At an early stage of the action the papers will usually have been sent to counsel or solicitor (as appropriate).[115] Counsel will normally settle the statement of case but, in any event, will advise appropriately throughout the various stages of the case. Cases are won and lost in their preparation. Counsel will therefore wish to consider which applications should be made, whether the statement of case requires amendment, and similar matters. The first consideration upon preparing an action for trial is on whom the burden of proof rests. The general rule is that where any allegation of fact is in issue the party who alleges that fact must prove it. The statement of case will disclose where the general burden lies. If an allegation in the statement of case is admitted (expressly or impliedly), it need not be proved at all. If it is denied, then the burden rests on the claimant. If the defendant denies liability because of other facts, the burden of proving them lies on him. Throughout, the standard of proof is the balance of probabilities (the 51 per cent rule), although it must be noted that this is a variable and not absolute standard.[116] However, the burden may shift during the action by the effect of presumptions. If a presumption is raised in favour of a party, the effect is to shift the burden of disproving the matter presumed to his opponent.

Having decided which matters he must prove, counsel will decide how he proposes to prove them. The two principal methods of proof are by witnesses and by documents.

Witnesses

Counsel or solicitor will name the witnesses whom he requires. There is no property in a witness, so that there is no objection to interviewing or calling any witness even if he has been served with a witness summons by an opponent.[117] It is, of course, wrong to call a witness whose testimony is unlikely to support one's case, since a party cannot cross-examine a witness he has called, unless the court gives leave to treat the witness as hostile. Also, to intimidate or otherwise tamper with a witness amounts to a contempt of court.[118] Usually a witness will be prepared to attend voluntarily if he is tendered a reasonable fee. Where he will not, his attendance may be compelled by order. A witness who fails to comply may be committed for contempt of court.

---

[115] For rights of audience, see p 382.   [116] See *Halford* v *Brookes* (1991) The Times, 3 October.

[117] See observations of Lord Denning MR in *Fullam* v *Newcastle Chronicle and Journal Ltd* [1977] 3 All ER 32, [1977] 1 WLR 651; see also *Harmony Shipping Co SA* v *Davis* [1979] 3 All ER 177, [1979] 1 WLR 1380.

[118] *Chapman* v *Honig* [1963] 2 QB 502, [1963] 2 All ER 513.

Evidence

Facts to be proved in a civil case are proved by the testimony of a witness in person and in open court. To that basic rule there are exceptions. Facts can be proved by formal admissions at trial, although a pre-trial admission of liability is not binding.[119] A party need produce no proof of any matter admitted in his favour. Admissions may also be made in answer to interrogatories. A useful means of compelling an opponent to admit a fact is to serve him with a 'notice to admit facts', calling upon him to admit the facts listed in the notice. If he will not admit these facts and they are proved at the trial, unless the court otherwise orders, he will bear the costs of proof. This is, of course, a powerful weapon, but it must not be abused. A party should not be asked to admit the facts in issue or any inference of fact, such as negligence. He should only, in practice, be asked to admit facts of a formal nature or facts that can easily be proved against him if he does not admit them. If admissions are made that clearly establish one party's liability the other party may, without waiting for a trial, apply for judgment based on those admissions.[120] Similar to such a notice is a 'notice to admit documents', calling upon the party served to admit the authenticity of the documents listed, although not the truth of their contents. The effect of failure to admit is, again, that the party who was served with the notice has to pay the costs of proving the documents at the trial, unless the court otherwise orders, which may involve an extra witness, such as a handwriting expert.

Wide powers are conferred on the judge by the Civil Procedure Rules as to the means of proof. Thus he may order evidence to be given at the trial by affidavit or in any other specified manner. For example, he may order the date on which an important event occurred to be proved by production of a newspaper containing a report of the event. In addition he may restrict the number of medical or other expert witnesses who may be called at the trial. In the fast-track procedure there should be a single joint expert.[121] Finally, it should be noted that a court may direct that a written statement be treated as the evidence-in-chief of the witness, including previous inconsistent statements.[122]

Documents

Documentary evidence, especially in contract cases, frequently forms the basis of a party's case. Where he is in possession of the documents himself, he is in no difficulty. However, the documents that are needed by a party may be in the possession of an opponent or of a third party. That problem may be overcome through the revised rules relating to disclosure, which should identify relevant documents in the hands of opponents or third parties.[123] If they are in the possession of a third party, the proper course is to serve him with an order requiring the witness to attend and produce the relevant documents.

---

[119] *Sowerby* v *Charlton* [2005] EWCA Civ 1610.   [120] For summary judgment, see p 527.
[121] CPR 35.7.   [122] *Fifield* v *Denton Hall Legal Services* [2006] EWCA Civ 169.
[123] See p 539.

Notices under the Civil Evidence Act 1995

Where it is desired to put in evidence at the trial statements admissible under the provisions of the Civil Evidence Act 1995, the party desiring to do so must within twenty-one days after setting down serve on every other party a notice containing prescribed particulars of (if the statement is oral) the time, place, and circumstances in which the statement was made, the persons by whom and to whom it was made, and the substance of the statement or, if material, the words used. In the case of written statements admissible by virtue of the Act, the notice must annex a copy of the document in question as well as contain certain prescribed particulars relating to the circumstances of its compilation. If the party giving the notice alleges that the maker cannot be called as a witness at the trial because he is dead, beyond the seas, unfit by reason of his bodily or mental condition to attend as a witness, cannot be found, or cannot reasonably be expected to have any recollection of matters relevant to the accuracy of his statement, the notice must contain a statement to this effect otherwise a party served with a notice may within twenty-one days serve a counter-notice requiring the maker of any statement to be called as a witness by the party who served the original notice, in which event if that person is not called as a witness, his statement is not admissible under the 1995 Act.

When the evidence for each side has been prepared, the parties must await trial. Neither party need serve any notice of the date of trial on his opponent. Accordingly (unless the case has been given a fixed date) all parties must watch the lists carefully. The Week's List is published on Mondays and contains the cases expected to be tried in that week. Each day there is published a Daily Cause List containing the actions to be heard that day and a Warned List consisting of actions likely to be tried in the near future. Thus neither side has any excuse if his case is not ready when the action comes on for trial. If one party fails to appeal, the trial may proceed in his absence. However, if application is made within seven days, a judgment obtained in the absence of a party may be set aside, generally on condition that he pay the costs thrown away. Although adjournment is possible, last-minute postponements are looked upon with disfavour by the judge in charge of the list and may result in the offending firm of solicitors being penalized personally with the extra costs incurred.

Procedure at the trial

Jury trials are now rare in civil proceedings,[124] so a trial is almost certainly by judge and judge alone. It must also be borne in mind that procedures in respect of the small claims track will be very informal and very different from procedures in a complex multi-track case. The following gives some indication of the procedure followed in a High Court or contested county court action in the multi-track, or, to some extent, fast track.

---

[124] See p 364.

Right to begin

If damages are unliquidated or the burden of proving any single issue on the pleadings rests on the claimant, then the claimant begins. Thus the only case in which the defendant has the right to begin is a case in which the claimant claims only liquidated damages and the defendant has not traversed any allegation in the statement of claim. The right to begin and the right to the last word are advantages that are probably exaggerated, especially in the absence of a jury.

Case for the claimant

Counsel for the claimant opens his case stating the facts on which the claimant relies. The court will already have a large amount of information in the case 'bundle' containing skeleton arguments, statement of case, relevant documents, and other appropriate documents. It will be assumed that these have been read and thus the style and content of the advocacy will be very different from that in jury trial. The advocate should not rely upon any fact that he is not permitted to prove, which means, of course, that he cannot allege any fact not pleaded, although he may, even at this late stage, be allowed to amend the statement of case. The claimant's witnesses are then called and sworn. They are examined and may be cross-examined and re-examined. In the course of cross-examining the claimant's witnesses, counsel for the defendant must 'put his case', which includes making clear which part of the claimant's case is challenged and what positive allegations are being made in relation to the evidence of the claimant's witnesses, so that they may have the opportunity of dealing with those allegations. This is important to the efficient conduct of trials because if counsel for the claimant calls a witness whose evidence is not challenged on a particular point, then he is entitled to assume that the point is not in issue and he will not call any other witnesses to deal with it. If the defence lead evidence as to matters that should have been put but were not put to the claimant's witnesses, judicial rebuke is virtually inevitable and, unless counsel was responsible for the oversight (in which event he will, in the interests of his client, immediately accept responsibility for it), the judge is likely to infer, and find, that the evidence in question is a recent invention. His documents, including answers to interrogatories that he wishes to put in, are then put in evidence. Finally, counsel argues the propositions of law upon which he relies, citing to the court all relevant authorities on the point whether they support his own case or that of his opponent. If they tend to support his opponent's case, he must attempt to distinguish them from the present case on their facts. He cannot, however, ignore them, since this would infringe his duty to the court.

Case for the defence

At the close of the claimant's case the defendant has the following courses open to him.

(1) He may submit 'no case to answer'. This is a submission that the claimant has failed to make out a prima facie case, or to establish the elements of a recognized

cause of action. The submission is rare in a civil action since the objection will usually have been taken long before the trial. If it is made, the judge, before deciding, may require the defendant to 'stand on his submission', which means that he can call no evidence if his submission fails. Counsel for the claimant has a right to reply to the submission. If it succeeds, judgment is entered for the defendant. If it fails and the defendant has been put to his election, judgment is entered for the claimant.

(2) He may state that he intends to call no evidence, oral or documentary. Counsel for the claimant will then address the court, followed by defence counsel who thus obtains the right to the last word.

(3) In most cases the defence will be a mixture of law and fact, and the defendant will want to put in some evidence. In this event defence counsel may make an opening speech outlining his defence. His witnesses give their evidence in the same way as those of the claimant followed by the defendant's documents and legal submissions. The claimant may be permitted to adduce evidence in rebuttal where the defence case has raised matters that could not reasonably have been foreseen. Defence counsel then makes a closing speech, following which counsel for the claimant has a right to make a closing speech in reply. Where a party in his closing speech raises any fresh point of law, the other party is entitled to reply but only in relation to that point.

Expert testimony

The whole subject of expert testimony is of importance: if the trial is to be efficient, the situation in which the trial becomes a 'battle of experts' should be avoided, where possible. In the fast track, there will be a single joint expert. Generally neither party should meet the expert witness without the other.[125] Difficulties arise if the experts agree. In *Stallwood v David*,[126] the experts of each party were directed by the court to meet and produce a joint statement. This exercise resulted in the claimant's expert agreeing with that of the defendant, effectively undermining the claimant's case. The court concluded that, in such circumstances, a party would not normally be allowed to call another expert to challenge the first when the reasons for modification of view, or the agreement justify that.

Real difficulties arise where there is disputed expert evidence. It is important that the expert be independent and objective, and keep within his or her area of competence.[127] The issues are common to both civil and criminal procedure.[128]

---

[125] *Peet v Mid-Kent Healthcare Trust (Practice Note)* [2001] EWCA Civ 1703; cf. *Childs v Vernon* [2007] EWCA Civ 305.

[126] [2006] EWHC 2600 (HC).

[127] *National Justice Cia Naviera SA v Prudential Assurance Co Ltd (Ikaria Reefer)*[1993] 2 Lloyds Rep 68; *Re AB (Child Abuse: Expert Witnesses)* [1995] 1 All ER 181.

[128] See p 642.

Verdict and judgment

At the conclusion of all of the evidence and the legal argument for both sides the judge sums up (in the rare case in which there is a jury) or gives judgment, or reserves his judgment if there is not. He must direct the jury (if there is one) as to the issues in the case, stating on whom the burden of proving the individual issues rests, and outlining the evidence in support of those issues. He must also direct upon the standard of proof required from the party on whom the burden rests. He will direct on the law applicable to the issues of fact: for example, whether the words are capable of bearing the defamatory meaning alleged or whether the defendant owes the claimant a duty of care in negligence. He must leave the actual issues of fact and the assessment of damages to the jury, but, now, following a series of cases involving disproportionate damages awards, may give them guidance as to the appropriate level of damages that may be awarded. A modern tendency is for the judge to pose a series of questions to the jury calling for their decision on the facts and, if they find for the claimant on any issue, the amount of damages. Where the claimant has sought an equitable remedy as an alternative or in addition to damages, the grant of this remedy is in the discretion of the judge.

It remains for judgment to be entered in accordance with the verdict. A judge may circulate a draft judgment in confidence where there are complex legal points, although this is more often the case at appellate level. If that happens, a judge can be properly asked to reconsider points of law in the draft.[129]

A judgment crystallizes the rights of the parties in respect of the subject matter of the action. Thus they are estopped from litigating the same issues of fact again. Even if fresh damage becomes apparent, the claimant cannot sue because his right is extinguished. Counsel for the unsuccessful party may apply for a stay of execution pending an appeal. This may be granted on terms. After judgment on the issues of liability and damages the judge may make orders as to interest and costs.

Historically damages have always been expressed in English currency. This has caused hardship in cases in which sterling has been devalued, so a party who bargained for payment in foreign currency has been awarded damages in sterling, the rate of exchange being calculated at the date upon which his entitlement to payment arose (the 'breach date' rule). Accordingly in 1975 the House of Lords changed this rule. Since 1975 the English courts have shown an increasing willingness to give judgment in foreign currency. At first limited to contract actions in which the sum was due under the contract in a foreign currency and the proper law of the contract was the law of that country in the currency of which the obligation was expressed, the power is now exercised in cases in which the claimant's loss would be most truly expressed in a foreign currency, in which case judgment will be given in that currency, and in tort actions, in which damages may be awarded in a currency that the claimant has used to make good the loss that he has suffered. Nevertheless, a judgment can only be enforced in terms of sterling. Accordingly, if enforcement becomes necessary the judgment will

---

[129] See *R (on application of Mohammed) v Secretary of State for the Foreign and Commonwealth Office* [2010] EWCA Civ 158.

be converted into its sterling equivalent at the date when leave is given to enforce the judgment.

Finally, there is, save in personal injuries actions, no procedure for successive awards of damages in the same action. Damages have to be assessed once and for all at the trial. This may cause hardship to either side, since subsequent events may demonstrate the hypotheses upon which the award of damages were based to be false with the result that the damages were too high or too low. This is particularly so in personal injury actions in which, for example, an award of damages for loss of future earnings capacity must necessarily be highly speculative. To remedy this situation, section 32A of the Supreme Court Act contains provision for 'provisional damages' in personal injury actions.

Section 35A of the Supreme Court Act 1981 empowers the court to award simple (but not compound) interest on debts or damages 'at such rate as the court thinks fit or as rules of court may provide'. In commercial cases the usual rate is 1 per cent above United Kingdom clearing banks' base rates over the relevant period. Different rules exist in respect of personal injury actions, in which on most awards the court must grant interest as follows:

(1) the claimant is awarded interest on general damages for pain, suffering and loss of amenities from the date of service of the writ to the date of trial at a conventional rate of 2 per cent per annum;

(2) the claimant is awarded interest on special damages from the date of the accident to the date of trial at half the rates that during that period were payable on money in court placed on special account;

(3) no interest is awarded on future loss of earnings or other prospective financial losses.

Costs

The general power to award costs, and the importance of costs in determining whether access to justice can be achieved, has already been noted. Costs normally follow the event, although the recommendations of the Jackson Report will, if implemented, change that to some degree.[130] A costs order can also be made against a non-party. In *Aiden Shipping Co Ltd* v *Interbulk Ltd*,[131] the House of Lords stressed that section 51 of the Supreme Court Act 1981 permitted the ordering of costs against non-parties, and that 'Courts of first instance are . . . well capable of exercising their discretion under the statute in accordance with reason and justice'. It should, however, be noted that this was a case in which a close relationship existed between the third party (who was in fact a party to a related action) and the parties to the cause in respect of which the costs were awarded.[132] Extensive guidance as to how the power to award costs in such cases

---

[130] See p 486.   [131] [1986] AC 965, [1986] 2 All ER 409.
[132] See [1986] 2 All ER 416; *Steele, Ford and Newton* v *Crown Prosecution Service* [1994] 1 AC 22, [1993] 2 All ER 769; *Shah* v *Karanjia* [1993] 4 All ER 792.

should be used was given by the Court of Appeal in *Symphony Group plc* v *Hodgson*:[133] it was established that it was exceptional for a non-party to be ordered to pay such costs, particularly if the party had a cause of action against the non-party. Fair procedures should be followed to ensure that the non-party had the opportunity to make representations, and to ensure that cross-examination of a non-party is not simply being directed to the issue as to whether the court should make a costs order against that non-party. These procedures are now contained in CPR 48.2.

A good example of the scope and limits of the power can be seen in two recent cases. The first is *Hamilton* v *Al Fayed*,[134] in which the well-known defendant, who had proved successful in a libel action, was unable to recover his costs from the claimant, who was declared bankrupt. The defendant then sought a section 51 order against the group of individuals who had funded the claimant in the litigation. In rejecting the application for a section 51 costs order, the court confirmed that a general principle protects a person who funds litigation from being made the subject of a section 51 order, a principle that extends to any person whose reasons for funding are either familial, out of natural affection, but also where the contribution was motivated to see that a genuine dispute was not lost by default. The right of the defendant to recover his costs had to give way to the public interest in access to the courts. However, in *Phillips* v *Symes*,[135] the court considered whether the potential exists for costs to be awarded against an expert witness. It accepted that a costs order could be made against an expert who, by his or her evidence, causes significant expense to be incurred, although the particular question here in that case was one of potential liability, the question of actual liability being left for a later hearing. The question was whether the witness was in flagrant disregard of his or her duties to the court.

Wasted costs orders

The court may disallow all or any part of costs being claimed, or order a party of his legal representative personally to pay the costs incurred by the other party, if the party or the legal representative is at fault because of failure to comply with a rule, Practice Direction, or court order, or if he has behaved unreasonably or improperly before or during the proceedings.[136] This can include an attempt to inhibit the court from furthering the overriding objective,[137] and is additional to the power to make a wasted costs direction, discussed below.

Section 51(6) of the Supreme Court Act 1981 (as substituted) permits the court to make a 'wasted costs' order against a legal or other representative. It permits the court to disallow costs incurred, or to make an order requiring personal payment, as a result of improper, unreasonable, or negligent acts or omissions by such representatives, or in respect of costs that, in the light of such an act or omission, it would be unreasonable to expect the party on whose behalf they were incurred to pay.

---

[133] [1994] QB 179, [1993] 4 All ER 143.   [134] [2002] EWCA Civ 665.
[135] [2004] EWHC 2330 (Ch), [2005] 4 All ER 519.   [136] CPR 44.14.
[137] See p 489.

This provision was the subject of judicial scrutiny and comment in *Re a Barrister (Wasted Costs Order) (No 1 of 1991).*[138] The court identified a three-stage test, now reflected in a Practice Direction.[139]

(a) Had the legal representative of whom complaint was made acted improperly, unreasonably, or negligently?

(b) If so, did such conduct cause the applicant to incur unnecessary costs?

(c) If so, was it in all of the circumstances just to order the legal representative to compensate the applicant for the whole or part of the relevant costs?

However, in *Ridehalgh* v *Horsefield*,[140] the court stressed that care should be taken not to create a new and costly form of satellite litigation, a point reinforced by the House of Lords in *Metcalfe* v *Wetherill*,[141] in which it was stressed that the discretion to make a wasted costs order should be reserved for those cases in which the unjustifiable conduct can be demonstrated without recourse to disproportionate procedures. It is 'the last resort'.

'Improper conduct' is conduct that would justify disciplinary action; 'unreasonable', means not permitting of reasonable explanation. Sometimes, of course, the legal representative may not be in a position to give a full explanation as to why a particular course of action was undertaken, or not undertaken, because of the doctrine of legal professional privilege. The court should in these circumstances be slow to invoke the wasted costs jurisdiction.[142]

'Negligent' bears the meaning of a failure to act with the competence to be reasonably expected of ordinary members of the profession. It is not improper to pursue a hopeless case, unless that amounts to an abuse of process. Nor is any distinction to be drawn between legally aided and self-financing litigants. A wasted costs order may well be justified where an advocate's conduct of court proceedings is quite plainly unjustifiable. Above all, such applications should not be used as a means of intimidation, and should normally be dealt with at the conclusion of the trial.

Having considered the question of which side must pay costs, the judge must decide what is to be the basis on which the costs are to be assessed, in order to determine how much of an opponent's costs the loser will have to pay. This can be on the standard or the indemnity basis.

Costs on the standard basis is the normal basis of calculation for party and party costs. It requires costs not only to have been incurred necessarily, but also proportionally.[143] The facts of *Lownds* v *Home Office* illustrate the issue, with costs of approximately £17,000 being incurred in respect of a claim compromised at £3,000 damages. Although the appeal failed for transitional reasons in respect of the introduction of the Civil Procedure Rules, the case demonstrates vividly the fact that what is appropriate

---

[138] [1993] QB 293, [1992] 3 All ER 429.   [139] Practice Direction 48, para 53.4.
[140] [1994] Ch 205, [1994] 3 All ER 848.   [141] [2002] UKHL 27.
[142] See *Ridehalgh* v *Horsefield* [1994] 3 All ER 848; *Metcalfe* v *Wetherill*.
[143] *Lownds* v *Home Office* [2002] 1 WLR 2450, [2002] UKHL 27.

depends on the whole context of the case. In guidance given in its judgment, the court stated that the question of costs must be assessed (in the context of the claimant's costs) in terms of the proportionality of the expenditure to the likely amounts at stake and recoverable. By contrast the proportionality of the defendant's expenditure will be in relation to the amount claimed, for the defendant is entitled to take the claim at face value.

But even if the total costs may be proportionate, that of itself will not suffice. The court will look at each item on the statement of costs and determine whether it was reasonably incurred, and of a reasonable amount. On the other hand, if the total bill were disproportionate, the court would allow items that were necessary (as opposed to reasonable) to incur, to the extent that the amount of such items was reasonable.

The Civil Procedure Rules[144] identify the factors to be taken into account in deciding whether expenditure is reasonably or unreasonably incurred:

(a) the conduct of all of the parties, including pre-commencement conduct, and the efforts made to resolve the dispute before and during proceedings;

(b) the amount or value of the money or property involved;

(c) the importance of the matter to all of the parties;

(d) the particular complexity of the matter or the difficulty or novelty of the questions raised;

(e) the skill, effort, specialized knowledge, and responsibility involved;

(f) the time spent on the case;

(g) the place where and the circumstances in which work or any part of it was done. In particular it may be unreasonable to employ more expensive London lawyers if it was unnecessary to do so.[145]

Indemnity costs provide a more generous measure of cost recovery. The courts have a wide discretion as to whether, and in what circumstances, to award costs on an indemnity basis.[146] Despite the fact that the courts have sometimes held that indemnity costs ought only to be awarded if a party has been engaged in culpable misconduct in the conduct of the litigation,[147] there is no need for moral misconduct or lack of probity. Any conduct might be considered by a judge to justify an indemnity costs order, and it was not for the appeal court to limit that discretion. Arguing a case devoid of merit might be one example, or clear breaches of the Civil Procedure Rules another.[148]

---

[144] CPR 44.5(3).

[145] *Sullivan* v *Co-operative Insurance Company Ltd*, (1999) The Times, 19 May; *Wraith* v *Sheffield Forgemasters Ltd* [1998] 1 WLR 132.

[146] *Excelsior Commercial & Industrial Holdings Ltd* v *Salisbury Hammere Aspden & Johnson*, unreported, 12 June 2002.

[147] *See Kiam* v *MGN Ltd (No 2)* [2002] 2 All ER 242.   [148] *Barron* v *Lovell* [1999] CPLR 630.

Indemnity costs are also awarded in certain other situations apart from the court's discretion: these include costs awarded in favour of a trustee or personal representative of an estate, where the parties have entered into an agreement regarding the payment of 'all costs', or a claimant has made an offer to settle the case under the Civil Procedure Rules, Part 36, and it was reasonable for the defendant to have accepted that offer.

Further reading

ACCESS TO JUSTICE, *Judicial Case Management: The Fast-track and Multi-track—A Working Paper* (July 1997)

ANDREWS, *English Civil Procedure* (Oxford University Press, 2004)

Appeals

16

INTRODUCTION

This chapter will explore the final stage of civil process—the right to appeal. It will address:

* when an appeal can be brought;
* the courts that deal with appeals;
* the powers of the Court of Appeal;
* the approach of the Court of Appeal.

The context

The modern appellate process in civil cases has, like all other aspects of civil procedure, undergone significant change.[1] Prior to the implementation of the Woolf Interim and Final Reports,[2] the process was governed by the Supreme Court Act 1981. Now, Part 52 of the Civil Procedure Rules governs appeals both from the High Court and from the county court, as well as in respect of certain other specialist appeals. These include jurisdiction to hear appeals from the Employment Appeal Tribunal,[3] the Lands Tribunal,[4] and various other statutory tribunals.[5]

Prior to the civil justice reforms, the Court of Appeal (Civil Division) was the fulcrum of the civil appellate system, with it dealing with all matters arising from the High Court. The Court of Appeal had jurisdiction to hear appeals from any judgment or order of the High Court, except where appeal went directly to the House of Lords under what was known as the 'leapfrog' procedure.[6] Likewise appeals from the county courts generally, but not always,[7] went to the Court of Appeal.[8]

The new structure creates a hierarchy, with appeals normally going to the next level. Which court will deal with which appeals is dealt with by the Access to Justice

---

[1] See the remarks of Brooke LJ in *Tanfern* v *Cameron-McDonald* [2000] 2 All ER 801.
[2] As to which, see p 478.   [3] See p 304.
[4] See Chapter 8.   [5] See Chapter 8.
[6] Supreme Court Act 1981, s 16. For appeal to the Supreme Court, see p 535.
[7] Appeals from orders in bankruptcy matters lay in the first instance to a Divisional Court of the Chancery Division, and then with leave to the Court of Appeal.
[8] County Courts Act 1984, s 77.

(Destination of Appeals) Order 2000.[9] Thus an appeal from the decision of a county court district judge will normally go to a circuit judge.[10] All appeals from a county court judge are normally dealt with by a High Court judge. Decisions of the High Court master or district judge[11] will, again, normally lie to a High Court judge. As before, decisions of High Court judges lie to the Court of Appeal. The purpose is clear: to ensure that the ever-increasing burden on the Court of Appeal prior to the Woolf reforms[12] was addressed by ensuring that only cases that need to be dealt with by the full Court of Appeal should be. However, such an approach might sometimes exclude from Court of Appeal consideration important points of law or practice. Accordingly, a 'leapfrog' procedure permits some cases to be transferred directly to the Court of Appeal. This is where an appeal would otherwise lie to a circuit judge or High Court judge, but the appeal raises important points of principle or practice, or there is some other compelling reason.[13] The Master of the Rolls also has the power to require a direct first appeal to the Court of Appeal.[14] And despite this hierarchy one important further exception exists: a 'final decision' can proceed to the Court of Appeal. A 'final decision' is one that would finally determine the entire proceedings.[15] This might include points of law, or evidence, such as limitation periods, but does not include striking out the proceedings or a statement of case.[16]

Appeals from the Court of Appeal in limited circumstances lie to the Supreme Court.[17] As noted above, there may, exceptionally, be an appeal directly from the High Court to the Supreme Court.[18]

Rights of appeal

Until the implementation of the civil justice reforms many rights of appeal existed as of right, with permission ('leave') to appeal needed only in a minority of cases.[19] The changed procedures now generally require 'permission'[20] to appeal to be granted.[21] That is not the case if a statutory scheme of appeal exists, because the scheme of appeal permits appeal as of right,[22] nor does it apply in certain situations in which the liberty of the individual is at stake. The cases that fall within this category include orders committing an individual to prison, secure accommodation orders made under section 25

---

[9] SI 2000/1071.   [10] See p 260.   [11] See p 259.

[12] See *Review of the Court of Appeal (Civil Division)* (the Bowman Report). For commentary, see Jacob at (1998) 61 MLR 390.

[13] CPR 52.14(1).   [14] Access to Justice Act 1999, s 57(1)(a).

[15] Destination of Appeals Order 200, SI 2000/1071, article 1(2)(c).

[16] *Tanfern* v *Cameron-McDonald* [2000] 1 WLR 1315.   [17] See p 247.

[18] Administration of Justice Act 1969.

[19] The more important cases included appeals from: Divisional Courts of the High Court; consent orders or orders solely as to costs; interim orders or judgments; decisions of a county court judge where the value of the claim in contract, tort or certain other monetary claims did not exceed £5,000 (£15,000 in equity or probate); a commercial judge on an arbitration appeal.

[20] For the change in terminology made by CPR, see p 490.   [21] CPR 52.3.

[22] *Colley* v *Council for Licensed Conveyancers* [2001] 4 All ER 998.

of the Children Act 1989, or cases in which an application for an order of habeas corpus is refused.[23]

A party wishing to appeal must make an oral application to the court the decision of which he seeks to appeal.[24] That is made to the relevant appeal court, or, if that application is refused, an application for permission can be made to the relevant appeal court provided that the procedures that have been prescribed are followed.[25] These require an appeal notice and an 'appeal bundle' to be prepared. Unless statute provides otherwise, the time period for the lodging of the appeal notice is fourteen days. Leave to extend the time for the filing of an appeal notice may be granted by the court the decision or order of which is being appealed, or by the appeal court provided that the relevant procedure is complied with.[26] The question of extension is one for the court, not for the parties, a position reflecting the obligation of the courts under the Civil Procedure Rules to manage effectively the progress of cases. The decision not to grant an extension is itself a matter that is appealable.[27]

The appeal bundle will include copies of the appeal notice, a skeleton legal argument,[28] a copy of the order being appealed, a copy of the reasons for the decision, any written statements in support of the application,[29] and any other documents reasonably considered to be necessary to enable the appeal court to reach its decision. If there are relevant documents that are not available, for example the judgment giving written reasons for the decision, an explanation must be given. The record of the judgment or ruling being appealed is crucial if the appeal court is to be able to take an informed view of the appeal.[30] More limited documentation is needed if the appeal is one arising from a decision in the small claims track.[31]

The appeal court has various powers in respect of an appeal notice. It may, of course, grant permission. The criteria that the court will apply will be to ask whether the appeal would have a real prospect of success, or whether there is some other compelling reason why the appeal should be heard.[32] Where there has already been an appeal, the criteria are even more strict: the case must raise an important issue of principle, or there must be other compelling reasons why a further appeal should be permitted. This is designed to facilitate the speedier resolution of disputes by making second appeals a rarity.[33]

Permission is unlikely to be granted in respect of case management decisions. In *Thermawear Ltd* v *Linton*,[34] Lord Bingham MR stressed that procedural initiatives would be futile if every decision or initiative could be appealed.

---

[23] As to which, see p 256.   [24] CPR 53.2(3).
[25] See CPR 53.2; Practice Direction 52.   [26] See CPR 52.4.
[27] *Foenander* v *Bond Lewis* & Co [2001] EWCA Civ 759.
[28] Not required from a litigant in person: Practice Direction 52, para 7.7A.   [29] See p 556.
[30] *Plender* v *Hyams* [2001] 2 All ER 179.
[31] See Practice Direction 52. For the small claims track, see p 523.   [32] CPR 52.3(6).
[33] *Tanfer Ltd* v *Cameron-McDonald* [2000] 1 WLR 1311.
[34] (1995) The Times, 20 October.

No right to appeal lies against a refusal of permission to appeal,[35] nor, apparently, are reasons for the refusal of permission needed to be given.[36] Alternatively it may:[37]

(a) strike out the whole or part of an appeal notice;

(b) set aside permission to appeal either in whole or in part;

(c) impose conditions, or vary conditions, upon which an appeal may be brought.

A notice will be struck out only rarely, and usually if the court has been misled or the point at issue is clearly dealt with by statutory provision that had been overlooked.[38] Conditions should only be imposed where there is a 'compelling reason' to do so.[39] These might include security for costs, as in *Aoun* v *Bahri*, in which such a requirement in respect of the costs of the lower court proceedings was held unreasonable. Other examples are an order to pay a judgment debt,[40] or the payment of money into court.[41] The discretion of the court is not in any way limited, subject to questions of reasonableness.

Appeal lies from the civil division of the Court of Appeal to the Supreme Court only with permission of the Court of Appeal or of the Supreme Court.[42] There is no requirement that the appeal be based on a point of law, although almost always appeal to the Supreme Court is based upon a point of law rather than on an issue of fact or an award of damages. Although permission is the only prerequisite for appealing, no appeal lies from the decision of the Court of Appeal where any statute expresses the decision of the Court of Appeal to be final. As noted earlier, the Administration of Justice Act 1969, Part II, provided for a 'leapfrog' appeal direct from the High Court to the Supreme Court subject to the grant of a certificate by the trial judge and of leave by the Supreme Court in any case in which appeal lies to the Court of Appeal (with or without permission). The criteria that apply as preconditions to the grant of such a certificate were stated by the House of Lords in the first 'leapfrog' case under the 1969 Act procedure, *American Cyanamid* v *Upjohn Co.*[43] These are: (1) the consent of all parties must be given; and (2) the case must involve a point of law of general public importance either relating to the construction of an enactment or is a point on which the judge was bound by precedent.

For the purpose of EU law, the Supreme Court is clearly 'a court or tribunal of a Member State, against whose decision there is no judicial remedy under national law', so that where a question arises concerning:

(a) the interpretation of the Treaty;

---

[35] Access to Justice Act 1999, s 54(4).

[36] *North Range Shipping Ltd* v *Seatrans Shipping Corporation* [2002] 1 WLR 2397; *X* v *Federal Republic of Germany* (1981) 25 DR 240; *Nerva* v *United Kingdom* App No 42295/98, 11 July 2000.

[37] CPR 52.9(1).

[38] *Nathan* v *Smilovich* [2002] EWCA Civ 759; *Barings Bank plc (in liquidation)* v *Coopers & Lybrand* EWCA Civ 1155.

[39] *Per* Brooke LJ in *Aoun* v *Bahri* [2002] EWCA Civ 1141.

[40] *Hammond Suddards Solicitors* v *Agrichem International Holdings Ltd* [2001] EWCA Civ 1915.

[41] *Bell Electric Ltd* v *Aweco Appliance Systems GmbH & Co* [2002] EWCA Civ 501.

[42] Administration of Justice (Appeals) Act 1934, s 1.   [43] [1970] 3 All ER 785.

(b) the validity and interpretation of acts of the institutions of the Union; or

(c) the interpretation of the statutes of bodies established by an Act of the Council, where those statutes so provide,

the Supreme Court is bound to refer that question to the European Court of Justice for a preliminary ruling (unless, of course, the High Court or Court of Appeal has already referred the question in the same case) and, having obtained the ruling, is bound to follow it.[44]

Procedure and powers on appeal

The purpose of an appeal is to review the decision of the lower court, and not, generally, a rehearing of the original argument. In *Audergon* v *La Baguette Ltd*,[45] the Court of Appeal held that it was undesirable to formulate criteria to be applied when deciding whether to rehear the case, but the court must have good reason for ordering such a rehearing. In that case the judge hearing the appeal did not have such a good reason, because the master who had conducted the original matter had considered all of the relevant evidence. But good reason might exist if the judge had given inadequate, or no, reasons, because then the process of review would be impossible.[46]

Appeals in the Court of Appeal have traditionally been heard by two or three judges of the court; the court may now consist of a single judge.[47] The court hears full legal argument from both sides and may substitute its own judgment for that of the court below. Even though it is not a complete rehearing, in addition, the appellant is normally confined to the points of law that he raised in the court below. He may in certain circumstances, discussed below, be allowed to take new points on appeal but he cannot, except with leave of the Court of Appeal, rely on any grounds of appeal or apply for any relief not specified in his notice of appeal.[48]

The Court of Appeal has all of the powers, authority, and jurisdiction of the court or tribunal from which the appeal was brought in any matter before it. An appeal court will not generally admit evidence not before the lower court, but does have the power to admit new evidence.[49] This discretion must be exercised in accordance with the overriding objective,[50] in the light of all of the circumstances of the case. The Civil Procedure Rules state[51] that appeal courts will not receive oral evidence or evidence that was not before the lower courts, unless it orders otherwise.

---

[44] See p 136.   [45] [2002] EWCA Civ 10.

[46] *Ansari* v *Puffin Investment Co Ltd* [2002] EWCA 234; cf. *Dyson Ltd* v *Registrar of Trademarks* [2003] EWCHC 1062.

[47] Supreme Court Act 1981, s 54(2)–(4), substituted by Access to Justice Act 1999, s 59.

[48] CPR Part 52.   [49] CPR 52.11.

[50] *Gillingham* v *Gillingham* [2001] EWCA Civ 906. *Hamilton* v *Al-Fayed* (2002), EWCA Civ 605. For the overriding objective, see p 489. For discussion of *Ladd* v *Marshall*, see *Pearce* v *Ove Harup Partnership* [1999] 1 All ER 769; *Shaker* v *Al-Bedrawi* [2002] 4 All ER 835.

[51] CPR 52.11.

The court has power to examine trial witnesses although it rarely does so, being content in most cases to rely upon the judge's note or a transcript of the official short-hand note. It has power to receive further evidence orally, by affidavit or by deposition taken before an examiner but, where there was a trial or hearing on the merits, but, as noted above, the court will not admit further evidence (other than evidence as to matters that have occurred since the trial) except on special grounds. In *Ladd* v *Marshall*,[52] Denning LJ prescribed the following three conditions for the reception of fresh evidence in the Court of Appeal:

> first, it must be shown that the evidence could not have been obtained with reasonable diligence for use at the trial; secondly, the evidence must be such that, if given, it would probably have an important influence on the result of the case, though it need not be decisive; thirdly, the evidence must be such as is presumably to be believed, or, in other words, it must be apparently credible though it need not be incontrovertible.

This statement was approved by the House of Lords in *Skone* v *Skone*,[53] in which the evidence consisted of a bundle of love letters written by the co-respondent in a divorce suit to the wife that tended to prove adultery between them. The trial judge had dismissed the husband's petition and accepted the co-respondent's evidence to the effect that adultery had not taken place. It was argued that these letters (which were in the possession of the wife) could have been obtained by seeking discovery of documents from the wife. The House of Lords rejected this argument on the basis that the husband had no reason to suspect the existence of such letters, that the letters, if genuine, falsified the judge's finding to such an extent that it would be unjust to leave matters where they were, and, furthermore, that there was a strong prima facie case of deception of the court. It must be emphasized that these rigorous conditions need not be satisfied in respect of evidence of matters occurring after the trial. Evidence will be admitted of matters occurring after the trial where the basis on which the trial judge gave his decision has been clearly falsified by subsequent events.

Of course, such authorities pre-date the civil justice reforms, and the approach to the old case law is that it is often no longer relevant or appropriate.[54] But, in *Gillingham* v *Gillingham*,[55] the principles in *Ladd* v *Marshall* were considered to remain good law, not as rules but, rather, as indicators of matters that should be taken into account. In *Gillingham*, the evidence was forgotten correspondence, which had not been disclosed by the other party. Although with reasonable diligence it might have been discovered, the matter could not fairly or satisfactorily be resolved without it, and it was therefore right to allow the appeal and order a new trial.

On appeal the Court has full power to make any order that should have been made in the court below and to substitute its own order as to liability, quantum, or costs for that of the court below. In addition the Court of Appeal is not confined to the points raised in the notice of appeal or respondent's notice. It may, although it rarely does,

---

[52] [1954] 3 All ER 745, applied in *Roe* v *Robert McGregor & Sons Ltd* [1968] 2 All ER 636.
[53] [1971] 2 All ER 582.   [54] See p 487.   [55] See n 50.

take any point of law or fact so far as is necessary to ensure the determination on the merits of the real question in issue between the parties. Should the Court of Appeal wish to decide an issue of fact that has not been raised in the statement of case, an extremely infrequent contingency, it may allow the grounds of appeal to be amended.

The approach to the determination of appeals

Appeal on a point of law

Most appeals are based on a point of law. It has already been stated that, notwithstanding the general power to take a point not raised therein, the Court usually confines itself to the points raised in the notice of appeal or respondent's notice. Furthermore there is a general rule that a party cannot take on appeal a point that he did not take in the court below.[56]

To this rule there are two important exceptions. The first occurs where the point of law was expressly reserved in the court below. This might occur where the court below was not free to consider the point because it was bound by precedent on that point, whereas the Court of Appeal might be free to reconsider the precedent in question. Secondly, an appeal court will allow a point to be taken, and indeed will take the point itself, where not to do so would result in an abuse of the court's process. Thus the illegality of a contract may be raised on appeal even though the point was overlooked in the court below.[57]

Appeal against a finding of fact

An appeal is not, generally, by way of rehearing, and thus an appeal court will be reluctant to interfere with findings of fact made by the judge. However, an appeal court can allow an appeal where the decision being appealed was 'wrong' and make draw such inference of fact that it considers justified on the evidence.[58] This has been held to mean that an appeal court must consider and make up its mind about findings of fact.[59] Whether a judge on appeal will overturn findings of fact, or inferences from fact, will depend on all of the circumstances: did the trial judge reach the conclusion based on assessment or oral testimony, in which circumstance the trial judge will have had the advantage of hearing the evidence? By contrast, inferences from primary facts may be more susceptible to the appeal court taking a different view.[60] Appeal is by way of rehearing; the Court of Appeal has power to substitute its own finding of fact, direct or inferential, for that of the trial judge or jury. However, the appeal court does not have

---

[56] See *Meco Pak AB* v *Electropaint Ltd* [2001] EWCA Civ 1537.
[57] See *Snell* v *Unity Finance Ltd* [1964] 2 QB 203; *Oscroft* v *Benabo* [1967] 2 All ER 548.
[58] CPR 52.11.
[59] See *Todd* v *Adam* [2002] EWCA Civ 509.
[60] *Assicurazioni Generali Spa* v *Arab Insurance Group BSC* [2002] EWCA 1642.

the advantage, which the judge, or, occasionally judge and jury had, of seeing the trial witnesses and observing their demeanour. Consequently the jurisdiction exercised by the Court of Appeal in relation to findings of fact is confined to inferential findings of fact. The court has the power to substitute its own inference from the facts as found for that of the trial judge or jury and will not hesitate to do so. In a pre-CPR case, involving a claim of medical negligence, in which the crucial issue of fact was whether a hospital registrar had pulled 'too long and too hard' on the head of the infant plaintiff in the course of his birth, Lord Bridge explained his willingness to uphold an appeal from the trial judge's finding in the plaintiff's favour in the following words:[61]

> My Lords, I recognise that this is a question of pure fact and that in the realm of fact, as the authorities repeatedly emphasise, the advantages which the judge derives from seeing and hearing the witnesses must always be respected by an appellate court. At the same time the importance of the part played by those advantages in assisting the judge to any particular conclusion of fact varies through a wide spectrum from, at one end, a straight conflict of primary fact between witnesses, where credibility is crucial and the appellate court can hardly ever interfere, to, at the other end, an inference from undisputed primary facts, where the appellate court is in just as good a position as the trial judge to make the decision.

Where a jury has returned a general verdict it is impossible to distinguish direct findings of fact from inferential findings and, indeed, the jury cannot be asked, after they have returned a general verdict, to state what their direct findings of fact were. An appeal court, therefore, can only upset the general verdict of a jury if it cannot be supported by the evidence or is a verdict that no reasonable men could have reached. In *Grobbelaar v News Group Newspapers*,[62] an attempt by the Court of Appeal to overturn a defamation finding because it flew in the face of the evidence as it was read by the Court of Appeal was overturned by the House of Lords. The jury's verdict could not be dismissed as irrational or perverse, although the House of Lords reduced the damages award from £88,000 to a derisory £1.

Appeal against the exercise of a discretion

In many circumstances the judge has a discretion as to whether, and in what manner, to exercise his or her powers. Commonly encountered instances of judicial discretion are the discretion as to costs, the discretion whether to grant or refuse an injunction, and the discretion as to the mode of trial, in particular in relation to the question of whether or not to order jury trial. However, no discretion is absolute and there may be a successful appeal in relation to the exercise of a judicial discretion if the appellant can show that the judge exercised his or her discretion under a mistake of law, or under a misapprehension as to the facts, or that he or she took into account irrelevant matters or gave insufficient weight, or too much weight, to certain factors, or that he

---

[61] *Whitehouse v Jordan* [1981] 1 All ER 267 at 286.
[62] [2002] 1 WLR 3024, HL, overturning [2001] 2 All ER 437.

or she failed to exercise his or her discretion at all.[63] If the judge gives no reasons, or insufficient reasons for the exercise of his or her discretion, the court may infer that he or she has gone wrong in one respect or another, and, indeed, the conclusion may be that there is a breach of the fair trial provisions of Article 6 of the Convention.[64] It is vital for proper reasons to be stated, not only because of the requirements of fairness to the parties but also that the appellate court can perform its function of review.

The burden of proof is on the party who alleges that the discretion was wrongly exercised and, in any event, the Court of Appeal will only allow the appeal if satisfied that the judge's conclusion is one that involves injustice or was clearly wrong. In *Hadmor Productions Ltd* v *Hamilton*, Lord Diplock explained the extent of an appellate court's powers as follows:[65]

> Before adverting to the evidence that was before the judge and the additional evidence that was before the Court of Appeal, it is I think appropriate to remind your Lordships of the limited function of an appellate court in an appeal of this kind. An interlocutory injunction is a discretionary relief and the discretion whether or not to grant it is vested in the High Court judge by whom the application for it is heard. On an appeal from the judge's grant or refusal of an interlocutory injunction the function of an appellate court, whether it be the Court of Appeal or your Lordships' House, is not to exercise an independent discretion of its own. It must defer to the judge's exercise of his discretion and must not interfere with it merely on the ground that the members of the appellate court would have exercised the discretion differently. The function of the appellate court is initially one of review only. It may set aside the judge's exercise of his discretion on the ground that it was based on a misunderstanding of the law or of the evidence before him or on an inference that particular facts existed or did not exist, which, although it was one that might legitimately have been drawn on the evidence that was before the judge, can be demonstrated to be wrong by further evidence that has become available by the time of the appeal, or on the ground that there has been a change of circumstances after the judge made his order that would have justified his acceding to an application to vary it. Since reasons given by judges for granting or refusing interlocutory injunctions may sometimes be sketchy, there may also be occasional cases where even though no erroneous assumption of law or fact can be identified the judge's decision to grant or refuse the injunction is so aberrant that it must be set aside on the ground that no reasonable judge regardful of his duty to act judicially could have reached it. It is only if and after the appellate court has reached the conclusion that the judge's exercise of his discretion must be set aside for one or other of these reasons that it becomes entitled to exercise an original discretion of its own.

Appeal against an award of damages

The approach adopted when determining an appeal against an award of damages differs according to whether the award was made by a jury or by a judge sitting alone.

---

[63] For challenge on judicial review to the exercise of discretionary powers, see *Associated Provincial Picture Houses* v *Wednesbury Corporation* [1948] 1 KB 223.

[64] See pp 191 and 582.   [65] [1983] 1 AC 191 at 220.

Where unliquidated damages are claimed, historically the court has not interfered with the award of a jury unless the damages awarded were so large or, more rarely, so small that no jury could reasonably have given them.[66]

However, a new trial may be ordered if it appears to the court either that the jury took into account irrelevant factors or failed to consider matters that it ought to have considered and in consequence awarded damages that were excessive or inadequate. The case of *Lewis* v *Daily Telegraph Ltd*[67] provides a good example. In that case two national newspapers published, on the same day, paragraphs alleged to be defamatory of the plaintiffs. The jury in the first action awarded the plaintiffs a total of £100,000; in the second action two days later in which there were factors that a jury might be entitled to take into account as aggravating damages, a different jury awarded the plaintiffs a further £117,000. New trials of both actions were ordered on the ground (inter alia) that the damages in each case were excessive. The House of Lords, affirming the decision of the Court of Appeal, stated that, in such a case, pursuant to section 12 of the Defamation Act 1952, each jury should be directed to consider how far the damage suffered can reasonably be attributed solely to the libel with which they are concerned, and how far it ought to be regarded as the joint result of the two libels, bearing in mind that the plaintiff ought not to be compensated twice for the same loss. In *Rantzen* v *Mirror Group Newspapers (1986) Ltd*,[68] the plaintiff, a well-known television presenter, had been awarded £250,000 damages for defamation. The defendant appealed, on the basis that the award was excessive, and sought an order under section 8 of the Courts and Legal Services At 1990, which now provides that where the court has the power to order a new trial on the basis of excessive or inadequate damages, it may be given the power to substitute the proper sum instead of ordering that new trial. The Court of Appeal concluded that this power had to be exercised in the context of Article 10 of the European Convention on Human Rights, which permitted restrictions on freedom of expression only where they were necessary in a democratic society to meet a pressing social need. On this basis large awards of damages were to be subjected to very close scrutiny. The question now to be asked is whether a reasonable jury could have thought the award necessary to compensate the plaintiff. On the facts the award was excessive by any objective standard of reasonable compensation, and an award of £110,000 was substituted for that of the jury. Where the award of damages appealed against was made by a judge sitting alone the Court of Appeal will not hesitate to interfere with the assessment, not only on the ground that the judge applied a wrong principle of law in making the assessment, but also on the ground that the award is out of scale with awards in similar cases.

The matter was considered again by the Court of Appeal in *John* v *MGN Ltd*,[69] in which the court held that, when assessing compensatory damages in a defamation

---

[66] *Johnson* v *Great Western Railway Co* [1904] KB 250; *Cassell & Co Ltd* v *Broome* [1972] AC 1027, [1972] 1 All ER 801.
[67] [1964] AC 234, [1963] 2 All ER 975.   [68] [1994] 2 QB 670, [1993] 4 All ER 975.
[69] [1996] 2 All ER 35.

case, a jury could in future properly be referred by way of comparison to the conventional compensation scales in personal injury cases as well as to previous libel awards made or approved by the Court of Appeal, and there was no reason why the judge, in his directions, or counsel, should not indicate to the jury the level of award that he or she considered appropriate. Those changes of practice would not undermine but rather buttress the constitutional role of the libel jury by rendering their proceedings more rational and so more acceptable to public opinion. The same principle also applies in actions against the police for unlawful conduct.

There is, of course, no prescribed scale of damages in any type of action but, nevertheless, there is a certain degree of parity in awards in respect of similar types of damage, particularly in actions for damages for personal injuries. In such cases the Court of Appeal will not make small adjustments to the sum awarded although it will make a substantial adjustment if that is found necessary. In practice the court will rarely interfere unless an adjustment of at least 20 or 25 per cent is envisaged. It is this diversity of approach to awards of damages made by judges and juries respectively that has led to the virtual disappearance of jury trial in personal injuries actions.

KEY ISSUE

What should the Court of Appeal do? Decide matters itself or order a new trial? This raises issues that are mirrored in the criminal jurisdiction.[70] The Court of Appeal has power under section 17 of the Supreme Court Act 1981 to order a new trial. It may exercise this power on an appeal from a judge and jury or from a judge alone just as it can on a motion for a new trial following a trial with a jury. A new trial may be ordered on any one issue without disturbing the finding of the court below on any other issue. Thus the Court of Appeal may order a new trial on the issue of damages while affirming the decision on the question of liability. Indeed if the only ground of application is the amount of damages, the court should limit the new trial to that issue and leave the findings as to liability undisturbed. If there is a new trial, that trial is completely independent of the first trial. The mode of trial need not be the same, no estoppel arises as a result of the first trial, and the parties may raise new points and may contest issues left uncontested at the first trial. The costs of the first trial are sometimes ordered to await the outcome of the new trial, although, as a rule, the successful applicant ought to be allowed the costs of his or her application.

 Question

What do you think the role of a court of appeal is?

---

[70] See p 700.

Further reading

ANDREWS, *English Civil Procedure* (Oxford University Press, 2004)

BOWMAN, *Review of the Court of Appeal (Civil Division)* (Lord Chancellor's Department, September 1997)

LEGGATT, 'The Future of the Oral Tradition in the Court of Appeal' (1995) 14 CJQ 148

WOOLF, *Access to Justice* (HMSO, 1995) (the 'Woolf Report')

PART IV
Criminal Proceedings

The Criminal Justice System

17

INTRODUCTION

It is only relatively recently that there has been a coherent 'system' of criminal justice. Even now it is characterized by a multiplicity of departments, boards and organizations. This chapter will examine some of the issues arising from this, focusing specifically on:

- how the criminal justice system is managed;
- the adversarial nature of the process;
- the increasing pressure and trend toward case management to ensure fair and efficient determination of charges;
- the concept of a fair trial as required by Article 6 of the European Convention on Human Rights.

Management of the criminal justice process

The 'system'

The use of the word 'system' in the context of the English criminal justice system may be misleading. With a multitude of different government departments, agencies, and others making 'separate and sometimes conflicting'[1] contributions, and in excess of 400,000 staff, the problem of consistent and coherent planning and action is obvious.[2]

In the recent past, several government departments (principally the Home Office and Department of Constitutional Affairs),[3] some forty-two police forces, the Crown Prosecution Service, Magistrates' Courts Committees, the Prison Service, and Courts Service have each had major roles, quite apart from the roles that defence lawyers and defendants themselves play. The Auld Review observed that administrative complexities and muddle of responsibilities had a practical and visible effect on the efficient and effective working of the 'system'.[4] It considered that efficiency and effectiveness are as important as the formal procedural and substantive rules in ensuring

---

[1] See Auld Review, Cm2263 (HMSO, 1993) ch 8, para 1.
[2] For an overview of some of the different agencies involved, see **www.direct.gov.uk**
[3] Formerly the preserve of the Lord Chancellor's Department: see Chapter 2.
[4] Auld Review, ch 8, para 12.

that the aims of the criminal justice system are in fact achieved. This objective is not always easily achieved in the current 'system'.

More recently, emphasis has been placed on the achievement of a more 'joined-up', coordinated, approach. A new National Criminal Justice Committee was established following the Auld Review and publication of the White Paper *Justice for All*.[5] It comprises leading civil servants from relevant government departments, including the Director of Public Prosecutions, the chief executives of relevant criminal justice agencies, a representative of the Association of Chief Police Officers, and a senior judge. The Committee reports to a Cabinet Committee and is responsible for overall criminal justice system delivery. For wider involvement of all those involved in the criminal justice system, a new National Criminal Justice Board comprises representatives not only of the Bar, magistracy, and judiciary, but also the representatives of the Equality and Human Rights Commission, the Law Society, victim and witness organizations, and senior academics. It acts as a consultative and advisory body on the criminal justice system, and gives a voice to a wide range of interests within the criminal justice system, advising on criminal justice reform so that all who work within, or with, the 'system' can have their say and influence decision-making. Some forty-two local Criminal Justice Boards were established during 2002–03.

A variety of other initiatives have, in recent years, been launched. The Youth Justice Board[6] was established in 1998,[7] with its objectives including monitoring the operation of the youth justice system, to publish information about that system, to advise on necessary changes, and to promote good practice. The Courts Act 2003 established a unified court service and management structure,[8] aiming to establish decentralized management and local accountability within a national framework.[9] A National Courts Agency has functions that include setting performance indicators, monitoring performance standards, and managing projects for common systems (such as information technology). All criminal justice agencies should be able to exchange case information electronically, with victims being able to follow the progress of their case online. Through overall coordination and liaison, common IT systems, and better case management, the expectation is that cases should be dealt with quicker, more efficiently, and in a more consistent way. Changes in police structures and organization,[10] the creation of the National Probation Service,[11] and its merger with the Prison Agency into the National Offender Management Service (NOMS) were each a response to the need for a coordinated, efficient and consistent management of process and of punishments.[12] Now, NOMS is responsible for commissioning and delivering offender management services in custody and in the community. Its remit includes helping

---

[5] Ibid, ch 9, para 5. [6] See p 574. [7] Crime and Disorder Act 1998, s 41.

[8] See p 230. [9] *Justice for All, op cit*, para 9.17. [10] See p 429.

[11] Criminal Justice and Courts Services Act 2000, s 2, creates, inter alia, a National Probation Service. Section 2 states that the Home Secretary, local probation boards and probation officers must have regard to: (1) the protection of the public; (2) the reduction of reoffending; and (3) the proper punishment of offenders.

[12] See p 571.

to deliver punishments and reparation, and coordinate rehabilitative, health, educational, employment and housing opportunities for offenders, whether in custody or in the community, as well as overseeing the contracts of privately run prisons, managing probation performance, and creating probation trusts.

So where, then, does actual responsibility lie in this complex structure? Changes over the last few years have created a more logical structure, with a concentration of justice services within the Ministry of Justice. Even so, there are three are three government departments that have responsibility for 'the system', as follows.

The Ministry of Justice

The Ministry of Justice oversees the magistrates' courts, the Crown Court, the Appeal Courts and the Legal Service Commission. It has responsibility for the prisons and the probation service through the National Offender Management Service. A large number of organizations and agencies operate or report through the Ministry.[13]

The Home Office

The Home Office oversees the police.

The Office of the Attorney-General

The Office of the Attorney-General oversees the Crown Prosecution Service, the Serious Fraud Office, and Customs and Excise prosecutors.

The aims of the criminal justice system

The Auld Review identified two main aims that were set by government for the criminal justice system.[14] One was the reduction of crime, and the fear of crime, and its social and economic costs. The other was the dispensing of justice fairly and efficiently, to promote confidence in the law. This second aim had several more specific objectives: to secure just processes and just and effective outcomes; to deal with cases with appropriate speed; to meet the needs of victims, witnesses, and jurors within the system; to respect the rights of defendants and treat them fairly; and to promote confidence in the criminal justice system.

These aims and objectives were accepted by that review as an appropriate starting point, although it counselled against expecting too much of the criminal justice system, and in particular urged that the courts should not be seen as 'a medium for curing the ills of society'.[15] Nonetheless, as noted above, the trend of recent legislation has been to seek greater coordination between the different agencies that deal with the administration of the criminal justice system and those that have some responsibility for policies that may diminish criminal activity, or that might divert persons from the criminal justice system. The Crime and Disorder Act 1998 created a new

---

[13] For a full list, see **www.justice.gov.uk/about/agencies-and-organisations.htm**
[14] Ibid, ch 1, para 7.   [15] Ibid, ch 1, para 9.

framework for the development and management of crime and disorder strategies, requiring police authorities and chief police officers to act in cooperation with each other, and to formulate strategies for the reduction of crime and disorder.[16] It also placed an obligation on local authorities to consider the crime and disorder implications of what they do.

All of these examples demonstrate that there are many interested parties affected by the criminal justice system, and who may view the purpose of what they are doing in different lights. Clearly, ensuring a fair trial for a defendant is fundamental, and a right enshrined in Article 6 of the European Convention.[17] There are, though, other legitimate interests: those of prosecutors, in ensuring that the guilty are in fact convicted; those of victims, in receiving 'justice'; those of government and other public authorities, in reducing the incidence of crime. These competing interests have to be balanced, and this is reflected in the trial and in pre-trial processes. Ensuring that some of these wider aims are achieved may, however, mean adopting approaches such as diverting offenders away from the criminal process to address offending behaviour, through cautioning or youth offender programmes, or using a combination of criminal and civil process to prevent repeat offending behaviour. The White Paper *Justice for All*[18] identified what were seen as weaknesses in critical areas throughout the criminal justice system: the police detected only 23 per cent of the 5.5 million offences recorded during 2000–01; too many defendants offend whilst on bail;[19] the system brings defendants to trial too slowly; too many go unconvicted; and too many are not given the sentence they need. It recommended a more integrated strategy to reduce crime and deliver justice, through a 'virtuous circle'[20] of prevention, detection, prosecution, punishment, and rehabilitation.

KEY ISSUE

The trial process is fundamental, but forms only a part of a wider system designed to meet these diverse interests and objectives. The extent to which the failings identified above can be overcome depends crucially on the success or otherwise of the large number of provisions contained in legislation. Criminal justice legislation is passed by Parliament every year. The extremely complex Criminal Justice Act 2003[21] is an example, with major reforms being introduced but not always implemented. The pace of change to implement these aims, and often to shift the focus of these aims and objectives, is incessant, so much so than in 2009 the Lord Chief Justice complained and urged government to take a pause in the volume of change.[22]

---

[16] Crime and Disorder Act 1998, ss 5–6, based largely on the Report of the Morgan Committee, *Safer Communities: The Local Delivery of Crime Prevention through the Partnership Approach* (HMSO, 1991).
[17] See pp 191 and 582.   [18] Cm 5563 (HMSO, 2002).
[19] Some 25 per cent, rising to 38 per cent of under-18s: ibid, para 1.6.   [20] Ibid, para 1.12.
[21] Containing some 339 sections and thirty-eight schedules. Only some of the provisions had been brought into force as at the date of going to press.
[22] See The Times, 16 December 2009.

Yet despite all of these provisions there continue to be major challenges to achieving a fair, speedy, and effective system for determining all cases. The fact that in 2007 a terrorism trial lasted thirteen months, twice as long as expected, with the jury then deliberating for some twenty-seven days,[23] is a vivid and cogent reminder that there continue to be major challenges that have to be addressed.

? Questions

1. Why do governments produce legislation on criminal justice so often?
2. Why do you think changes introduced in legislation are not always implemented?

Sentencing

The criminal justice system has several purposes, including to detect crime and to try those who are accused of crime. But a third is to deal with those who are found guilty of crime. For that reason the purposes of sentencing are directly relevant to the wider purposes of the criminal justice system

The law governing the sentencing of offenders has undergone frequent, and radical, changes in recent years. In part these changes have been a response to the stated desire of political parties to reduce the incidence of crime, and in part due to the often competing philosophies as to the purpose of custodial sentences. The result has been a plethora of statutes making new provision, or amending existing provision, or even substituting new changes for those that reached the statute book but that were never fully implemented.[24] The position in respect of sentencing legislation reached such a level of complexity that Lord Bingham CJ in *R v Governor of Brockhill Prison, ex parte Evans*[25] was moved to observe (in the context of the date of release of prisoners) as follows:

> The Law Commission has described it as an important feature of any criminal justice system that sentencing provisions should be accessible and comprehensible and has recommended the enactment of a comprehensive statutory consolidation of such provisions... We hope that this may be seen as a task commanding a high degree of priority....

That consolidation occurred in 2000, with the passage of the Powers of Criminal Courts (Sentencing) Act 2000. Any belief that that would provide the desired clarity and ease of access to the statutory provisions was misplaced, with at least one amendment of the 2000 Act before it came into effect,[26] and significant further changes made by the Criminal Justice Act 2003. Those pieces of legislation have served only to create a mass of case law, not easy to apply, and occasionally contradictory.

---

[23] See (2007) The Times, 3 May.

[24] See, e.g., Crime and Disorder Act 1998, ss 69–74, which introduced the new detention and training orders for the never-implemented secure training order provisions in Criminal Justice and Public Order Act 1994, ss 1–18.

[25] [1997] QB 443, [1997] 1 All ER 439.   [26] See Criminal Justice and Courts Services Act 2000.

At the heart of current approaches to the sentencing process are the recommendations of the Halliday Report,[27] the latest in a long line of reports and studies examining
aspects of the sentencing framework. It was born out of a belief that the then existing
sentencing structure suffered from serious deficiencies that reduced its effectiveness to
contribute to crime reduction and public confidence. Amongst those deficiencies were
the lack of any clear message about the effect that repeat offending should have on sentence, the absence of reality as to what sentences in fact mean, and unexplored opportunities for non-custodial sentences, including reparation for victims.[28] The Criminal
Justice Act 1991 had required sentencers to concentrate on the nature of the offences
(the principle of 'just deserts'), and although that approach was diluted by various legislative in-roads (such as the taking into account of previous convictions of offenders
when sentencing, or requirements relating to mandatory or minimum sentences) the
basic approach was proportionality of the sentence to the offence. That did not encourage sentencers to think wider, and address the needs of crime reduction or reparation.
Community sentences were perceived as weak and ineffective.

Those were not the only perceived deficiencies. Despite the work done by the
Sentencing Advisory Panel, in partnership with the Court of Appeal, sentencing law
was confusing and obscure, and was not such as to inspire public confidence. There
needed to be a more accessible framework, and decisions in individual cases needed to
be understood. Community punishments[29] were not considered as sufficiently punitive
or protective. Arrangements for the enforcement of community punishments were,
again, uncertain and unclear. Yet at the same time structural reorganization provided
real opportunities. Management of offenders in custody was the responsibility of the
Prison Service. Management of those offenders serving punishments within the community was the responsibility of the Probation Service. By means of the new National
Offender Management Service, integrating the two,[30] and the development of sophisticated risk assessment techniques and of programmes of treatment accredited by the
Home Office, there were real opportunities to address offending behaviour. Research
considered by Halliday confirmed the potential benefits of such programmes, but an
appropriate sentencing framework was needed to maximize their chances of success.
A change in framework might also help achieve changes in sentencing behaviour,[31]
by placing emphasis on the incapacitation of persistent and dangerous offenders, and
on reparation and reform for others. Resources should be targeted on those most
likely to reoffend and on those who commit offences serious enough to reoffend. This
approach led Halliday to conclude that there should be clear principles of sentencing,

---

[27] *Making Punishments Work: Report of a Review of the Sentencing Framework for England and Wales*
(HMSO, 2001), available at **webarchive.nationalarchives.gov.uk/+/http://www.homeoffice.gov.
uk/documents/halliday-report-sppu**

[28] Ibid, Introduction.

[29] Such as the Community Punishment and Community Rehabilitation Order.

[30] As to which see *Correctional Services Review* (the Carter Review), 11 December 2003, available at
www.homeoffice.gov.uk

[31] Halliday Report, para 1.25.

clear sentencing guidelines, and a mass of important detailed changes in sentencing law. Many of the recent changes dealt with hereafter owe their origin, in whole or in part, to the Halliday Report.

KEY ISSUE

The purpose of the criminal justice process remains a matter of debate. In December 2010 the Minister of Justice, Kenneth Clarke, in launching a consultation paper[32] on sentencing and rehabilitation commented:

> Despite record spending we are not delivering what really matters. Society has the right to expect the criminal justice system to protect them. Prison will always be the place for serious and dangerous offenders.

Of course this punishment is not the sole aim of the criminal justice system but the consultation paper marks another shift in what is seen as the purpose of sentencing. Having moved more towards punishment, with increasing numbers of individuals being imprisoned, the shift is towards a greater use of community sentences and reparation in the community, an approach that has echoes of the changes made in the Criminal Justice Act 1991.

 Question

What do you think is the purpose of the criminal justice system?

Youth justice[33]

Distinct issues arise in the context of juveniles (those aged under 18). Their age, vulnerability and the United Kingdom's obligations under the European Convention of Human Rights all necessitate special treatment in terms of criminal liability, procedure, and sentence. For that reason the structures and rules are very different. So too is the management structure. The Youth Justice Board has a key role.[34].

Youth justice raises very distinct issues that are reflected in the powers, and objectives of the youth court (and of the Crown Court when dealing with children and young persons). Section 44 of the Children and Young Persons Act 1933 requires any court, in fulfilling its duties, to take account of the welfare of the child or young person before it. Considerable debate has occurred as to the role and functions of the youth justice system. In a consultation paper,[35] the government stated that action was needed to bring about greater consistency in the approach to work with young offenders in the community and to ensure that all of the relevant local agencies

---

[32] Ministry of Justice, Breaking the Cycle: Effective Punishment, Rehabilitation, and Sentencing of Offenders (HMSO, 2010).

[33] See, generally, Ward, *Young Offenders* (Jordans: 2001).

[34] See p 574.

[35] *No More Excuses: A New Approach to Tackling Youth Crime in England and Wales*, Cm 3809 (HMSO, 1997).

play a full part. It also believed that the youth justice system should seek to prevent crime. Section 37 of the Crime and Disorder Act 1998 states that:

> It shall be the principal aim of the youth justice system to prevent offending by children and young persons.

By section 37(2) it shall be the duty of all persons and bodies carrying out functions in relation to the youth justice system to have regard to that aim. This is a broad statement of an overall duty that will apply not only to local authorities, health authorities, probation services, voluntary agencies, and the police, but also to the courts in dealing with young offenders after conviction.

The role of local authorities in establishing youth offending teams and creating youth justice strategies should be noted. Each local authority is under a duty to secure that, to such extent as is appropriate for their area, all youth justice services are available there,[36] performed in partnership with other agencies such as the police. Local authorities will operate within the overall guidance given by a new Youth Justice Board.[37] This will comprise ten, eleven, or twelve members, appointed by the Home Secretary, and will include persons with extensive recent experience of the youth justice system. Its functions are set out by section 42(5) of the Crime and Disorder Act 1998, and include:

(a) the monitoring of the operation of the youth justice and the provision of youth justice services;

(b) advising the Home Secretary on the operation of that system and the provision of such services, how the principal aim of that system might most effectively be pursued, the content of any national standards he may see fit to set with respect to the provision of such services, or the accommodation in which children and young persons are kept in custody, and the steps that might be taken to prevent offending by children and young persons;

(c) the monitoring and collection of information about the youth justice system and the provision of services by local authorities;

(d) the identification and promotion of good practice in the context of the operation of the youth justice system and the provision of youth justice services, the prevention of offending by children and young persons, and in respect of working with children and young persons who are or are at risk of becoming offenders.

Youth justice teams are an important element in the strategy to deal with youth offending that was introduced by the Crime and Disorder Act 1998. At least one team exists in each local authority area, and includes at least one probation officer, local authority social worker, police officer, and nominee of a health authority and of the local education authority. These youth justice teams are under a duty to coordinate the provision of youth justice services within the local authority area, and to carry out such

---

[36] 1998 Act, s 38.

[37] Ibid, s 41. For an insight into the workings of the youth justice system, see the Annual Reports of the Youth Justice Board, to be found at **www.yjb.gov.uk**

functions as are assigned to the team in the local authority's youth justice plan made under section 41. Not only is it intended that youth offending teams should coordinate local provision relating to work with young offenders, but they also play a key role in the reprimand and caution system introduced by the 1998 Act, and in respect of several of the orders that may be made by a court when dealing with young offenders. Their primary functions include report-writing for courts, the preparation of reparation or action plans, and the supervision of young offenders within the community, based upon an inter-agency partnership philosophy.[38]

Victims of crime

For the lawyer, the primary emphasis of the criminal justice system has traditionally been on the detection of crime, and the prosecution of those accused of it. The objectives of that process have, of course, always been the prevention of crime, and the punishment of those who engage in it. Yet the victims of criminal conduct have not always been regarded as fundamental players within the criminal justice 'system'. The concern of the criminal justice system has been to determine the issue between the state (the prosecutor) and the defendant. In the past, the victim of the crime has had no direct status or say. Although the power to have regard to the injury or loss suffered by the victim is reflected in the power of the court to make a compensation order,[39] or to receive compensation through the Criminal Injuries Compensation Authority,[40] victims have generally had little role in the criminal justice process, beyond giving evidence. Even in that regard, the process has not always been 'victim-friendly'. The White Paper *Justice for All*[41] observed:

> Justice is not simply about punishment for its own sake. Many victims, when asked, say that they simply want to ensure that no one else has to go through the kind of experience they themselves have. And the best way of ensuring that is to catch, convict and rehabilitate offenders and prevent further crime. Victim's own evidence is crucial in bringing offenders to justice. They must be nurtured and not subject to a host of delays, postponements and barriers... The criminal justice agencies have a particular responsibility to support victims and witnesses... This includes ensuring that they are protected, if vulnerable from intimidation or further crime, and taking into account the impact of the offence on victims when sentencing offenders....

To address this, another White Paper, *A Better Deal for Victims and Witnesses*,[42] reviewed what was working well, and what was not. Amongst the positive developments identified were the development of Victim Support, which, in 2004, helped in excess of a million victims, and the special measures provisions introduced by the

---

[38] Consultation Paper, *op cit*; see also Morgan Report, *Safer Communities: The Local Delivery of Crime Prevention through the Partnership Approach* (HMSO, 1991).

[39] See p 683.   [40] See p 575.

[41] Cm 5074 (HMSO, July 2002) (available at **www.homeoffice.gov.uk**) at paras 2.11–2.12.

[42] (HMSO, 2003).

Youth Justice and Criminal Evidence Act 1999 to help vulnerable witnesses.[43] Yet a range of problems remained: the need to abandon trials because witnesses and victims refuse to testify; the fact that many victims and witnesses felt badly treated by the criminal justice process, in particular by failure to keep them informed of the progress of cases, or informed of significant events such as the release of an offender from prison. Some of these problems have arisen because responsibility for victims and witnesses is distributed too widely across the criminal justice system, causing confusion, inefficiency, and delay. Whatever, victim satisfaction with the police in particular fell from 67 per cent in 1984 to 58 per cent in 2000. The White Paper observed:[44]

> Everyone has the right to justice including those accused of crime. But many victims feel that the rights of defendants take precedence over theirs. Public confidence in [the criminal justice system] is dependent on how people perceive that they, or their family or friends, will be treated as a victim or witness to a crime. Too often the perceptions are that victims and witnesses are the ones on trial rather than the suspect.

A variety of measures—administrative and evidential—have been introduced to address some of the problems that lead to this perception. Greater powers for the police to impose conditions on police bail,[45] greater protection for witnesses,[46] the use of witness statements in some cases to avoid vulnerable witnesses having to go to court,[47] the greater regard for the victim in the sentencing process,[48] and a range of pilot projects and initiatives, often in liaison with the voluntary sector, are examples of the types of measure put in place. Since 2001, the victim personal statement scheme has been in place.[49]

The continued need to promote the issues relating to victims was recognized by the passage of the Domestic Violence, Crime and Victims Act 2004, which requires the Home Secretary to issue a code of practice as to the services to be provided to a victim of criminal conduct by a person who appears to have functions relating to the victims of criminal conduct, or in respect of any aspect of the criminal justice system.[50] These include the Courts Service, the Courts Agency, the Criminal Cases Review Commission, the Criminal Injuries Compensation Authority, the Criminal Injuries Compensation Appeals Panel, Crown Prosecution Service, the police, the Parole Board, the National Association of Victim Support Schemes, and youth offending teams.

Those who have responsibilities under the code are under an obligation to provide services and information to specified classes of victims of crime, particularly victims of offences against the person (including sexual offences) and victims of some offences against property. Special protections will be given to vulnerable victims: a victim falls within this class if he or she is under the age of 17, mentally disordered, has experienced domestic violence, been the subject of harassment or religious or racially aggravated crime, or has been the subject of intimidation. The general nature of the duty was described as follows:[51]

[43] By means of special measures directions: see p 674.
[44] *Op cit*, p 2.   [45] See p 458.   [46] See p 674.
[47] See p 674.   [48] See the Domestic Violence, Crime and Victims Act 2004.
[49] See **www.cps.gov.uk/legal/v_to_z/victim_personal_statements/index.html**
[50] 2004 Act, s 32(1).   [51] *Justice for All*, para 2.43.

Under the [Code] all the services that come into contact with victims...have new responsibilities to ensure that the needs of victims are met...The police...will be responsible for providing information if a suspect is arrested, cautioned or charged; telling them whether the suspect is on bail; protecting them from intimidation; informing them promptly of the date of any court hearing and ensuring that the victim is put in touch with Victim Support Services. The National Probation Service is responsible for keeping victims informed about a prisoner's release and arrangements for their supervision and any licence conditions.

Particular responsibilities were placed on the Crown Prosecution Service,[52] and the police that were to have a wide range of inputs in supporting and keeping informed the victims of crime, including, for example, giving victims an explanation when the prosecution decision is to discontinue a case or to alter the charges substantially. In cases involving certain sex offences or racially aggravated crime, or in serious cases such as those involving a death or child abuse, the CPS may offer to meet the victim or victim's family to explain the basis of the decision.

Amongst the rights conferred upon some (although not all) victims are the right to be informed of key stages and decisions, the right to make representations on certain matters relating to release of offenders on licence,[53] and the right to make complaint to the Parliamentary Commissioner for Administration.[54] Section 48 of and Schedule 8 to the 2004 Act create the office of Commissioner for Victims and Witnesses. The functions of the Commissioner are (under section 49) the promotion of the interests of victims and witnesses, the taking of necessary steps with a view to encouraging good practice in the treatment of victims and witnesses, and the keeping under review of the operation of the code of practice. The first Victims' Commissioner was appointed in March 2010.[55]

KEY ISSUE

The fact remains that there is still much to be done. Further reform was spurred by the campaign of the mother of a murdered child, Sarah Payne, who acted as a victims' champion and in 2009 submitted a report, *Redefining Justice*.[56] The report recommended that victims must be treated as individuals who have individual needs. The government's response was the creation of the National Victims' Service, which, it is intended, will give victims assistance 'from the moment they report a crime until the moment they say they no longer need help'. The appointment of the Commissioner was another response to the report, as was implementation of the 2004 Act changes.

❓ Questions

1. How far do you think the victim has an important role to play in the criminal justice system? What is that role?

2. To what extent should the court act on the wishes of a victim of crime?

---

[52] For the CPS, see p 389.   [53] To the Parole Board.
[54] 2004 Act, s 47, Sch 7, amending the Parliamentary Commissioner Act 1967.
[55] See **www.justice.gov.uk/about/victims-commissioner.htm**   [56] Ibid.

The criminal process

Adversarial nature

Despite the trend towards diverting offenders away from the criminal justice process, the trial remains at the heart of the criminal justice process. It is, essentially, adversarial in nature.[57] The process of investigation and evidence-gathering is conducted by the police or other investigating body, but with the Crown Prosecution Service (CPS)[58] playing an increased role in supervising the investigation and determining what charges, if any, are to be brought.[59] Traditionally, the court plays no significant part in the preparation of the case. The trial itself is not an investigation into events or allegations, but rather a hearing to decide, within complex rules of evidence,[60] whether the prosecution has proved, to the appropriate standard,[61] whether the defendant is guilty of the particular offences with which the prosecution have charged him.[62] By contrast, in many civil law jurisdictions the process is inquisitorial in nature. This term is used to describe systems in which judges or magistrates supervise the pre-trial investigations and preparation of the case, to a greater or lesser extent, and play a significant part in the questioning of the witness at trial, and in the decisions as to what evidence should be considered by the court. Simply put, the trial is much more of an investigation than a contest, although some inquisitorial systems have adversarial characteristics, and over-rigid distinctions should be avoided.

This adversarial characteristic has often been viewed as one of the strengths of the English system. These strengths were identified by the Court of Appeal in *R* v *McIlkenny*:[63]

> Another feature of our law, which goes hand in hand with trial by jury, is the adversarial nature of criminal proceedings. Clearly a jury cannot embark on a judicial investigation. So the material must be placed before the jury. It is sometimes said that the adversarial system leaves too much power in the hands of the police. But that criticism has been met, at least in part, by the creation of the Crown Prosecution Service. The great advantage of the adversarial system is that it enables the defendant to test the prosecution case in open court. Once there is sufficient evidence to commit a defendant for trial, the prosecution has to prove the case against him by calling witnesses to give oral testimony in the presence

---

[57] For assessment generally of the adversarial process, see the various submissions of evidence to the Royal Commission on Criminal Justice, Cm 2263 (HMSO, 1993), and the Royal Commission on Criminal Procedure, Cmnd 8292 (HMSO, 1981), at para 1.8.

[58] See p 389.   [59] See p 593.

[60] Detailed consideration of the rules of evidence is beyond the scope of this book. See, generally, Dennis, *The Law of Evidence* (Sweet & Maxwell: 4nd edn, 2009).

[61] The criminal standard is often described that the court must be satisfied of the defendant's guilt beyond any reasonable doubt.

[62] Whilst a judge has a discretion to call witnesses not called by the prosecution or defence, this power should be used sparingly, and only where necessary in the interests of justice: *R* v *Roberts* (1984) 80 Cr App R 89.

[63] [1992] 2 All ER 417, at 425–6.

of the jury. We doubt whether there is a better example of exposing the weaknesses in the prosecution case, whether the witness be a policeman, a scientist or a bystander, than by cross examination.

Yet, despite these perceived advantages, in recent years focus has turned to whether the criminal trial in fact achieves its purpose, and, more fundamentally, whether the criminal justice system itself delivers what society expects of it. The adversarial approach of the trial, best exemplified by jury trial in the Crown Court,[64] has not seriously been challenged. The Royal Commission on Criminal Procedure,[65] Royal Commission on Criminal Justice,[66] and the Review of the Criminal Courts of England and Wales[67] (the Auld Review) each considered that:

> there is no persuasive case for a general move away from our adversarial process. Not only is it the norm throughout the common law world, it is beginning to find favour in a number of civil law jurisdictions which have become disenchanted with their inquisitorial tradition.[68]

In part, this debate about the nature of the criminal trial and trial process arose because of a series of causes célèbres[69] in which the trial, and indeed pre-trial, process failed to operate in a way to prevent injustice and miscarriage of justice. That was the situation in *R v Ward*.[70] In *R v McIlkenny* itself, the appeal court identified some of the weaknesses of the adversarial process, such as the imbalance in resources between prosecution and defence, and the need for proper disclosure of prosecution evidence to the defence. Above all, the effectiveness of any system depends upon it not being abused by those who work within it. Many, although not all, of the miscarriages of justice that made headline news stemmed not from failures in the trial process itself but, rather, from failures in the investigation process or from failures to apply properly the processes designed to protect the fairness of the trial itself.[71]

Concerns about the workings of the wider criminal justice process, and the balance between its competing aims, have been increasing in recent years. Back in 1993 the Royal Commission on Criminal Justice made some 352 separate recommendations.[72] As already noted, it did not recommend a fundamental change of approach, doubting whether a general move away from the adversarial approach would be desirable. It concluded that a system that keeps separate the roles of the police, prosecutor, and

---

[64] See Chapter 19.   [65] *Op cit*, para 1.8.   [66] *Op cit*, paras 11–14.
[67] The Auld Review (HMSO, 2001).   [68] Ibid, ch 1, para 28.
[69] See, e.g., *R v McIlkenny, ante; R v Maguire* [1992] QB 936, [1992] 2 All ER 433; *R v Silcott, Braithwaite and Raghip* (1991) The Times, 9 December; *R v Kisko* (1992), unreported. See, generally, Walker and Starmer, *Justice in Error* (OUP, 1994). For a host of examples, see the various annual reports of the Criminal Cases Review Commission, at **www.ccrc.gov.uk** and p 693.
[70] [1993] 2 All ER 577; [1993] 1 WLR 619.
[71] Many of the cases in question involved alleged police malpractice: see, e.g., *R v Maguire* [1992] QB 936, [1992] 2 All ER 433.
[72] The Commission did not consider police powers (which had been the subject of change in PACE following the Royal Commission on Criminal Procedure, Cmnd 2263 (HMSO, 1981)), the rules relating to bail or sentencing. The various Research Studies published by the Royal Commission are a valuable source of data relating to, and analysis of, the trial system.

judge offers a basic protection against the risk of 'unnecessarily prolonged detention prior to trial'.[73] Instead, its recommendations were intended to make the pre-existing system 'more capable of serving the interests of justice and efficiency', and intended to deal with matters that seemed to the Commission to turn what ought to be a search for the truth into 'a contest played between opposing players according to a set of rules that the jury does not necessarily accept or even understand'.[74] It recognized that the criminal trial and the criminal justice process had a wider purpose other than simply to protect defendants, although that is a fundamental characteristic of a 'fair trial'. In achieving this balance, the Commission identified certain principles against which detailed rules, and any suggested changes to those rules, had to be judged: 'Are they fair'? 'Are they open?' 'Are they workable?'

Some, although not all, of the recommendations of the Royal Commission formed the basis of subsequent legislation, or informed the deliberations of other committees, commissions or working groups. The 1990s saw a plethora of government and parliamentary activity, with significant quantities of criminal justice legislation,[75] and culminating in the Auld Review in 2000.[76] That report, with its 328 recommendations, has itself informed the most recent legislation, the Criminal Justice Act 2003. This constant flow of legislation addressed not only changes to the adversarial pre-trial, trial, and sentencing powers and processes, but also wider and more fundamental questions about the structure and aims of the criminal justice system.

Case management

This general acceptance of a broadly adversarial approach should not disguise the fact that an increasing degree of case management by the court itself has developed. In the Crown Court, examples of this were the process of pleas and directions hearings and preparatory hearings,[77] the increased duties of disclosure of evidence on both prosecution and defence,[78] the courts' role in protecting witnesses through special measures directions,[79] and in dealing with applications to withhold evidence.[80] In magistrates' courts, following the recommendations of the Narey Report,[81] a scheme of administrative hearings was introduced, giving case-management powers to justices' clerks as well as a greater range of powers to a single justice.[82] These together constitute a significant in-road into the basic principle that the court does not get involved in what

---

[73] Ibid, ch 1, para 14.   [74] Ibid, ch 1, para 11.

[75] See, e.g., Criminal Justice Act 1991; Criminal Justice Act 1993; Criminal Justice and Public Order Act 1994; Criminal Procedure and Investigations Act 1996; Crime (Sentences) Act 1997; Crime and Disorder Act 1998, Youth Justice and Criminal Evidence Act 1999.

[76] See n 67.   [77] See p 655.   [78] See p 634.

[79] See p 674.

[80] A court may allow relevant evidence to be withheld if a claim of public interest immunity is made out. For the procedure to be followed, see in particular, *R v H; R v C* (2004) The Times, 6 February, following the decision of ECHR in *Edwards and Lewis v United Kingdom* (2003) The Times, 29 July.

[81] *Review of Delay in the Criminal Justice System* (1997).

[82] For justices clerks' powers, see Chapter 7. For powers, see Crime and Disorder Act 1998, ss 47–48.

is put before it, and how that is done. In fact, the basic duty on a trial judge to ensure a fair trial, and, now, the wider right to a fair trial under Article 6 of the European Convention on Human Rights,[83] require a judge to perform a key role.[84] In *R* v *Ward*,[85] the appeal court, in quashing a conviction wrongly obtained, stated that it was the responsibility of a trial judge to ensure a fair trial, to reduce the risk of wrongful conviction to a minimum.

The Criminal Procedure Rules

As noted above, a fair trial for the defendant must be the prime objective of the criminal trial. In a note written to the Lord Chancellor, Lord Woolf CJ wrote that 'the presumption of innocence and a robust adversarial process are essential features of English legal tradition and of the defendant's right to a fair trial'. However, the efficient and effective management of cases is crucial if, on the one hand, a defendant is to be tried fairly and expeditiously, and, on the other, the process is to be efficient, and effective in ensuring that those who *are* guilty are convicted and punished. To this end, one important precondition is procedural rules that are clear and concisely expressed, and which can be changed without complex legislative intervention.[86] To achieve this, new Criminal Procedure Rules were introduced, and aim to consolidate the rules and practices that govern the process from beginning to end. These apply both to trial on indictment and summary trial. They were intended to create a culture change, making everybody involved in a case responsible for helping to make the case go ahead efficiently, under the supervision of the court,[87] and are the first step in the creation of a 'comprehensive criminal procedural code'. The Rules are made by a Criminal Procedure Rule Committee.[88] Reference is made in this book to these Rules during detailed consideration of the trial process, where it is necessary to do so. Rule 1.2 imposes a duty on every participant in the case to prepare and conduct the case in accordance with a new overriding objective. This is that 'criminal cases be dealt with justly'.[89] This is, by rule 1.2, to comprise seven elements:

(a) acquitting the innocent and convicting the guilty;

(b) dealing with the prosecution and the defence fairly;

(c) recognizing the rights of a defendant, particularly those arising under Article 6;

(d) respecting the interests of witnesses, victims, and jurors and keeping them informed of the progress of the case;

(e) dealing with the case efficiently and expeditiously;

---

[83] See Chapter 6 and p 191.   [84] See p 580.   [85] [1993] 2 All ER 577.
[86] Auld Review, ch 10.   [87] **www.dca.gov.uk/criminal/crimpr.htm**
[88] For the relevant legislative framework, see Courts Act 2003, ss 69–74.
[89] CPR 2005 1.1. See *Malcolm* v *Director of Public Prosecutions* [2007] EWHC 363; *R* v *Ashton, Draz, O'Reilly* [2006] EWCA Crim 794.

   (f) ensuring that appropriate information is available to the court when bail and sentence are being considered;

   (g) dealing with a case in ways that take into account the gravity of the offence charged, the complexity of the matters in issue, the severity of the consequences for the defendant and others affected, and the needs of other cases.

These may be thought not to be controversial, although (g) above gives to the possible danger of the downgrading of the procedural standards in cases perceived as less serious. The Rules place a duty on all those involved to ensure compliance with their provisions, and to report any 'significant failure', defined as being a failure that might hinder the court in furthering the overriding objective.[90]

Courts should try to avoid deciding cases on the basis of procedural irregularities. The aim, under the Rules, is to decide cases on their merits.[91]

The right to a fair trial

Article 6 ECHR

However we characterize the nature of the process, the right to a fair trial is fundamental, and enshrined in Article 6 of the European Convention on Human Rights.[92] Article 6 states:

   (1) In the determination of his civil rights and obligations or of any criminal charge against him, everyone is entitled to a fair and public hearing within a reasonable time by an independent and impartial tribunal established by law. Judgment shall be pronounced publicly but the press and public may be excluded from all or part of the trial in the interest of morals, public order or national security in a democratic society, where the interests of juveniles or the protection of the private life of the parties so require, or to the extent strictly necessary in the opinion of the court in special circumstances where publicity would prejudice the interests of justice.

   (2) Everyone charged with a criminal offence shall be presumed innocent until proved guilty according to law.

   (3) Everyone charged with a criminal offence has the following minimum rights:

      (a) to be informed properly, in a language which he understands and in detail, of the nature and cause of the accusation against him;

      (b) to have adequate time and facilities for the preparation of his defence;

      (c) to defend himself in person or through legal assistance of his own choosing or, if he has no sufficient means to pay for legal assistance, to be given it free when the interests of justice so require;

---

[90] For the difficulties in respect of sanctions and enforcement, see Denyer, 'Non-Compliance with Case Management Orders and Directions' [2008] Crim LR 784.

[91] *R v Ashton* [2006] EWCA Crim 794.   [92] See also, p 191.

(d) to examine or have examined witnesses against him, and to obtain the attendance and examination of witnesses on his behalf under the same conditions as witnesses against him; to have the free assistance of an interpreter if he cannot understand or speak the language used in court.

It confers protection on those who are subject to a determination of a criminal charge (Article 6(1)). Whether a matter involves a criminal charge will depend on the classification of the proceedings in domestic law, the nature of the offence, and the nature and degree of severity of the penalty that the person concerned risks incurring.[93] Amongst the instances of matters being classified as criminal are the investigation of an allegation of assault with no formal punishment,[94] penalties imposed for breach of military discipline,[95] a regulatory traffic offence,[96] administrative proceedings for customs regulations,[97] and fines imposed by tax authorities.[98] Recent English authorities serve to demonstrate the types of issue that arise. In *R v M; Kerr; H*,[99] it was held that Article 6 does not apply to proceedings under sections 4 and 4A of the Criminal Procedure (Insanity) Act 1964, which relate to the fitness to plead of a defendant. Such proceedings are not criminal, because they do not result in a conviction or a penalty, but merely determine whether the defendant can stand trial. Even if they were criminal, provided that the disadvantages to a defendant under a disability are minimized, the trial could be fair and the defendant's disability would not usually, of itself, found an application for abuse of process.[100] Again, in *Han and another v Commissioners of Customs and Excise*,[101] the issue arose as to whether the imposition of penalties on taxpayers for dishonest evasion of VAT (described as civil penalties) gave rise to criminal charges for the purpose of Article 6 of the Convention. It was held by the VAT and Duties Tribunal that they did, and that the taxpayers were entitled to the minimum rights contained in Article 6(3). On appeal, the Commissioners of Customs and Excise argued that the classification of the penalty was a civil penalty, that civil penalties had been introduced deliberately to decriminalize the VAT system, and there was an absence of any threat of imprisonment. In rejecting this argument, the court noted in particular that alternative regimes existed under the legislation (one of them clearly criminal in nature) and with routes to move from one to another. A further example is the administration of a reprimand or warning under section 65 of the Crime and Disorder Act 1998,[102] which was held in *R (on the Application of U) v Metropolitan Police Commissioner*[103] to be the determination of a criminal charge. Because the offender had not been told that the effect of a reprimand would be registration as a sex offender,[104] there was a breach of Article 6.

---

[93] *Engel v Netherlands (No 1)* (1976) 1 EHRR 647; *AP v Switzerland* (1997) 26 EHRR 541.
[94] *Adolf v Austria* (1982) 4 EHRR 313.   [95] *Engel v Netherlands (No 1)*, ante.
[96] *Ozturk v Germany* (1984) 6 EHRR 409.   [97] *Benedenoun v France* (1994) 18 EHRR 54.
[98] *AP v Switzerland* (1998) 26 EHRR 541.   [99] [2001] All ER (D) 67.
[100] See p 601.   [101] [2001] 4 All ER 687.   [102] See p 591.
[103] [2003] 1 All ER 419.   [104] Under Sexual Offences Act 2003.

Article 6 is not concerned with the fairness of provisions of substantive law. For that reason a challenge in *R v G*[105] to the test of recklessness in respect of the crime of arson failed. The question that Article 6 requires a court to answer is simply: 'is the trial fair?' Nor does Article 6 prescribe rules for the admissibility of evidence.[106] In *Khan (Sultan) v United Kingdom*,[107] the Court of Human Rights found there to be no breach of Article 6 in admitting evidence obtained by interception of conversations obtained by an interference with the property rights of the applicant, even though there might in some circumstances be a breach of the Article 8 rights of the applicant. There was no evidence of unreliability or unfairness. Article 6 does not directly address questions of errors of law or misuse of judicial discretion, unless a wider Convention right is infringed.[108]

Limits to the right?

The right to a fair trial cannot be limited.[109] A court must, though, be mindful that, although it should not accord a margin of appreciation[110] to the national authority, it should give weight to the decisions of a representative legislature and democratic government within the areas of discretionary judgment accorded to them. In deciding what the right to a fair trial involves, a court may ask whether a limit on a right is reasonable, directed by national authorities towards a clear and proper public objective and proportionate to that objective. Thus, in *Brown v Stott (Procurator Fiscal: Dunfermline)*,[111] the Privy Council, on an appeal from Scotland, held that provisions in section 172 of the Road Traffic Act 1988 requiring the registered owner of a motor vehicle to supply information as to the driver of a vehicle at any date and time did not infringe Article 6 rights protection against being required to self-incriminate. There was a clear public interest in dealing with driving that imperils the safety of others.

The concept of applying legal rules to secure a fair trial is, of course, not one that is new, and which only arises under Article 6: English criminal procedure and evidential rules have long proceeded on this basis.[112] Both at common law and under section 78 of the Police and Criminal Evidence Act 1984 (PACE), a trial court must always act to secure a fair trial. It has been described as an 'elementary right of every defendant',[113] and as a 'constitutional right'.[114] One mechanism for achieving this has long been the basic common law discretion, which exists to permit the exclusion of evidence, the probative value of which is low compared with its prejudicial effects.[115] However, Article 6 does raise certain key issues in the context of the criminal process. Amongst

[105] [2002] EWCA 1992.
[106] *Schenk v Switzerland* (1998) 13 EHRR 242; *Doorson v The Netherlands* (1996) 22 EHRR 330; *Trivedi v United Kingdom* [1997] EHRLR 520.
[107] [2000] Crim LR 683.   [108] *Ali v United Kingdom* (1997).
[109] See p 191.   [110] See p 176.   [111] [2001] 2 All ER 97.
[112] In a Scottish case, the same principle (i.e. that fairness does not depend necessarily on Article 6) was confirmed: *Robertson (Stewart) v HM Advocate* [2007] HCJAC 63.
[113] *Per* Lord Hope in *R v Brown (Winston)* [1998] AC 367.
[114] Ibid, *per* Lord Steyn.   [115] *R v Sang* [1980] AC 402.

these are questions as to the presumption of innocence,[116] the principle against self-incrimination,[117] the right to legal advice and representation,[118] and the obligation to employ rules and procedures in a fair way. It also impacts significantly on issues relating to sentence. The detailed issues that it raises are discussed as they arise.

Most fundamental of all, though, is the right to be tried by an independent and impartial tribunal. Justice must not only be done, but be seen to be done. If it can be shown that a court is the subject of actual bias, or, much more likely, gives the appearance of bias or lack of impartiality (judged objectively), then Article 6 rights will be infringed.[119] The question is whether there is a real danger of bias.[120] A court should ascertain the circumstances, and then 'ask itself whether, having regard to those circumstances, a fair-minded and informed observer, having considered the facts, would conclude that there was a reasonable possibility that the tribunal was biased'.[121] The matter must be viewed from the perspective of the 'informed observer'.[122] *R v Gough* is a good example. The brother of the appellant was the next-door neighbour of one member of the jury. The House of Lords concluded that there was not a 'real danger' that the appellant had received a trial that was unfair, the juror having sworn a statement that she was unaware of the connection until after the jury had delivered its verdict. The language of the test adopted in *Gough* was adjusted in subsequent case law[123] to ensure compliance with Article 6 of the Convention that it is the absence of an *appearance* of bias, not simply the absence of the actuality of bias, that is important.

In a criminal case, one aspect of the problem is whether a judge who has made pre-trial rulings or findings can, fairly, preside over the trial itself. There will usually be a legitimate doubt about impartiality if the judge has been involved in the case before trial in a way that involves the formulation of an opinion as to the guilt or innocence of the defendant.[124] There will also be a breach of Article 6 where the prosecuting authority appointed the judge.[125]

Another aspect is potential bias in respect of the jury.[126] Again, the test is to ask: what would a fair-minded observer think? A conviction is likely to be quashed if a reasonable possibility or danger of bias might be thought to exist.[127] This may be an increasing problem now that serving police officers and solicitors are eligible to serve

---

[116] See p 676.   [117] See p 676.   [118] See p 191.

[119] See *Piersack v Belgium* (1982) 5 EHRR 69; *De Cubber v Belgium* (1984) 7 EHRR 236; *Hauschildt v Denmark* (1989) 12 EHRR 416; *Langborger v Sweden* (1989) 12 EHRR 416.

[120] *R v Gough* [1993] AC 646.

[121] *Director General of Fair Trading v Proprietary Association of Great Britain. (Re Medicaments and Related Classes of Goods (No 2)* [2001] 1 WLR 700 *per* Lord Phillips, adopted by Lord Hope in *Porter v Magill* [2001] UKHL 67.

[122] *Locabail (UK) Ltd v Bayfield Properties* [2000] 2 WLR 870; *Porter v Magill* [2001] UKHL 67, [2002] 2 AC 357; *Lawal v Northern Spirit Ltd* [2003] UKHL 35. See also *Director General of Fair Trading v Proprietary Association of Great Britain* [2001] 1 WLR 700.

[123] See authorities cited at n 122 above.   [124] *Brown v United Kingdom* (1985) 8 EHRR 272.

[125] *Findlay v United Kingdom* (1997) 24 EHRR 221; *De Cubber v Belgium* (1984) 7 EHRR 236 (trial judge was previously the investigating judge).

[126] For juries, see p 348.   [127] *R v Evans (Lyn Harris)* [2005] EWCA Crim 766.

on juries.[128] In *R* v *Abdroikov (Nurlon)* and associated appeals,[129] one conviction was quashed because it was not clear that justice was seen to be done when one of the jurors was a full-time, salaried, long-serving employee of the prosecutor. However, the dissenting speeches of Lords Rodger and Carswell serve only to illustrate that the application of this seemingly simple principle is far from easy.

The role of the Attorney-General

The prosecution has a limited role in the sentencing process. It is under a duty to bring to the attention of the sentencing court matters relating to the power of the court, and has the right to correct misstatements of fact that may be made by an accused during the sentencing process. However, the prosecution has no specific right of appeal in an individual case against a sentence perceived as being unduly lenient. It was to permit some higher court review of such sentences that the Criminal Justice Act 1988 introduced powers that entitle the Attorney-General to refer to the Court of Appeal cases in which he considers an over-lenient sentence to have been imposed. Where such a reference is made, the Court of Appeal may quash any sentence imposed and, in its place, impose such sentence as it thinks appropriate, within the powers that were available to the sentencing court. The Court of Appeal will not intervene unless the sentencing judge's sentence was wrong in principle, so that public confidence would be damaged if the sentence were not altered.[130]

KEY ISSUE

The characterization of a trial process as adversarial in nature is often contrasted with an inquisitorial approach perceived to exist in many Continental systems. That is, perhaps, an over-simplification, for Continental systems often have adversarial characteristics. The presumption of innocence in Article 6 of the European Convention supports the principle that there is in one sense always a 'contest' although the procedural rules may vary fundamentally between jurisdictions. The growth of case management functions and increasing duties of disclosure on both prosecution and defence all are examples of a trial process designed not only to be efficient and effective, but also to be conducting a search for the truth.

? Questions

1. What do we mean when we describe our system as 'adversarial'?
2. How far does our system help or hinder a search for the truth?
3. To what extent is our system a search for the 'truth'?

---

[128] See p 350.   [129] [2007] UKHL 37, [2007] 1 WLR 2679.
[130] *Attorney-General's Reference (No 5 of 1989) (R v Hill-Trevor)* (1989) 90 Cr App R 358.

Further reading

Annual Reports of the Criminal Cases Review Commission

ASHWORTH and REDMAYNE, *The Criminal Process* (Oxford University Press: 4th edn, 2010)

AULD, *Review of the Criminal Courts of England & Wales* (**www.criminal-courts-review. org.uk**) (the 'Auld Review')

BELLONI and HODGSON, *Criminal Injustice* (Palgrave, 2000)

Pre-trial Procedure

18

INTRODUCTION

Pre-trial procedure is crucial. It is at this stage that, if the decision to prosecute is taken, the charge or charges will be decided. Selection of the right charges is a key decision and can, if wrong, significantly weaken the chances of successful prosecution. Decisions also have to be made about the mode of trial, and whether bail is to be granted. This chapter will therefore examine:

- the choices that have to be made as to whether to prosecute, and who makes them;
- the role of the Crown Prosecution Service in deciding the charge;
- the classification of offences;
- decisions as to mode of trial;
- the right to grant bail and the grounds on which it may be refused.

The decision to commence proceedings

Discretion and cautioning

The fact that an offence is believed to have been committed does not mean that the commencement of a prosecution is inevitable. Discretion exists at various stages as to whether a prosecution should be commenced, or the suspect cautioned formally or informally. The police and the Crown Prosecution Service (CPS) or other prosecution authority each has discretion at appropriate times. That discretion may be reviewable on normal judicial review principles. It is also the duty of prosecuting authorities to keep under review the decision whether or not to prosecute.

At the policing level, an individual officer has discretion as to what action, if any, he or she should take. He or she can informally caution, make an arrest,[1] or formally report a suspect with a view to prosecution. These decisions will often be made in the light of the overall policies adopted by the police force of which the officer is a part. At a later stage a decision will have to be taken whether an individual should be charged,

---

[1] Arrest for the purposes of cautioning is lawful only if the grounds for arrest in fact exist, and are being used. There is no power to detain for the purposes of cautioning: *Collins* v *Wilcock* [1984] 3 All ER 374.

and, if so, with what offence, or whether a caution should be administered. That practice was originally non-statutory: now the Criminal Justice Act 2003 has introduced a statutory scheme. Whatever, a caution is intended to replace charge and prosecution, although it cannot prevent a private prosecution[2] from being commenced.[3]

The non-statutory background

The practice of formally cautioning, rather than prosecuting, can be traced back to 1929, but until 2003 never had a statutory basis. It was first regulated in 1978,[4] but despite these attempts to achieve greater consistency, cautioning practices varied widely between individual police forces and were confined in the main to elderly offenders, those suffering mental stress, and young first offenders who had committed minor offences.[5] In 1991, some 279,000 offenders were dealt with by way of caution, some 179,000 of these relating to indictable or either-way offences. The Royal Commission on Criminal Justice[6] recommended an extension of cautioning to more petty offenders, but also recognized a need for national guidelines within which cautioning could occur, thus achieving greater consistency. It recommended that consideration should be given to combining cautions with other support, through social services or the probation service, but recognized that a failure to prosecute an individual can itself damage confidence in the criminal justice system.

In 1994, Circular 18/1994 was issued. It encouraged the police to caution formally rather than prosecute in some circumstances. It required there to be clear and reliable evidence of the suspect's guilt relating to the material elements of the offence, sufficient to raise a reasonable prospect of conviction: the suspect must have admitted guilt.[7] The caution amounts to a conviction for the purposes of registration under the provisions of the Sex Offender Notification Requirements.[8] In *R* v *Metropolitan Police Commissioner, ex parte Thompson*,[9] Schiemann LJ stated:

(1) A formal caution is not something to be regarded lightly. Records are kept of the admininistering of cautions…Such a caution while carrying no immediate disagreeable consequence for the recipient, has potential adverse consequences for him should he be accused of offending on a future occasion. He is more likely to be prosecuted for that offence and he will not be able to claim good character before the trial court. If convicted, the existence of a prior formal caution may affect his sentence…

---

[2] As to which, see p 594.

[3] *R* v *Jones & Whally* [2005] EWHC 931, [2006] Crim LR 67.

[4] Home Office Circular 70/1978, replaced by Circular 14/1985.

[5] See Wilkinson and Evans, 'Police Cautioning of Juveniles: The Impact of Circular 14/1985' [1990] Crim LR 165; Westwood, 'The Effects of Home Office Guidelines on the Cautioning of Offenders' [1991] Crim LR 591; Evans, 'Police Cautioning and the Young Offender' [1991] Crim LR 598.

[6] Royal Commission on Criminal Justice, Cm2263 (HMSO, 1993) at ch 5, para 57.

[7] *R (on the application of W)* v *Chief Constable of Hampshire Constabulary* [2006] EWHC 1904 (Admin).

[8] *R (on the application of U)* v *MPC* [2002] 4 All ER 593.

[9] [1997] 1 WLR 1519 at 1521.

The Auld Review observed that some 260,000 cautions were issued in 1999, amounting to some 25 per cent of 'solved' offences.[10] The offences were mainly, but not totally, in respect of less serious offences, with cautioning rates significantly higher in respect of minor thefts and drug offences, but, paradoxically, the cautioning rate for summary-only offences was lower than for either-way offences. The incidence of cautioning was also higher in respect of juveniles. Juveniles are now dealt with under a separate scheme of reprimands and warnings introduced by the Crime and Disorder Act 1998.[11]

This extra-statutory scheme had its drawbacks. There was no sanction in respect of the original offence for an offender who reoffends. The power to caution did not have a power associated with it requiring an offender to engage in activities such as reparation to the victim, to pay compensation, or attend appropriate activities such as a drug or alcohol treatment programme, or sex offender programme. The Auld Review concluded that the cautioning system paid no regard to the feelings of the victim, lacked rigour, and posed a temptation to hard-pressed police forces to use cautions to effect a better clear-up rate. It therefore proposed, for adult offenders, a new system of 'caution-plus', which forms the basis for the conditional caution provisions of the Criminal Justice Act 2003.

Conditional cautions for adult offenders

As noted above, until the passage of the 2003 Act, no statutory power existed governing the cautioning of adult offenders at all, still less one that permitted the imposition of a requirement that the offender should make reparation for his or her offending behaviour, such as the payment of compensation for the damage done by vandalism, or apology to the victim, or a requirement of attendance at particular forms of activity that could address the offending behaviour. This was in stark contrast to the approach taken in respect of young offenders by the Crime and Disorder Act 1998.

Section 22 of the 2003 Act defines a conditional caution as one 'given in respect of an offence and which has conditions attached with which the offender must comply'. Conditions can be imposed only to the extent that they either ensure or facilitate the rehabilitation of the offender or to make sure that he or she makes some reparation. The caution (which amounts to a criminal conviction) is to be administered by the police, or by the CPS, or by any other designated person,[12] thus allowing cautioning in respect of minor offences investigated by non-police bodies, such as the Department of Social Security, or the RSPCA.

There are five prerequisites prescribed by section 23, which must each be satisfied.

---

[10] *Op cit*, ch 10, paras 41–47. The equivalent figures for 2000, excluding motoring offences, was 239,000 offenders: *Cautions Court Proceedings and Sentencing 2000*, Home Office Statistical Bulletin 20/01 (HMSO, November 2001).

[11] See p 591.   [12] 2003 Act, s 22(4).

(1) The cautioner must have evidence that the suspect committed the crime.

(2) The CPS must be satisfied that there is sufficient evidence to charge the suspect with the offence, and that a caution should be given. The CPS thus is the decisive decision-maker, and no doubt will be reluctant to caution in serious cases, or where the suspect has similar convictions, a poor record, or where the offence merits imprisonment.

(3) The suspect must admit the offence to the cautioner.

(4) The nature of the caution, and the consequences of the breach must be made clear to the suspect.[13]

(5) The suspect must sign a document recording the details of the offence and the admission of it by him or her. This in law amounts to a confession,[14] and will be evidence against the offender if he or she is subsequently prosecuted following non-compliance with the conditions attached to the caution.

The Act does not prescribe any limits to the conditions that may be imposed, but a code of practice has been issued, which must be complied with. In *R (Guest) v Director of Public Prosecutions*,[15] a decision to administer a conditional caution in respect of a serious assault ran counter to the code and was quashed as unlawful on judicial review. In addition, any conditions must be compliant with the Article 8 rights of the offender.[16] Clearly, if the conditions impose any restrictions or requirements that affect the Article 8 rights of the offender, those conditions must be necessary and proportionate to ensure Convention-compliance, but, if justified, could include a requirement to clean up graffiti, make financial reparation, or attend treatment or behaviour programmes. If they are broken, the power exists to prosecute the offender for the original offence, a powerful sanction that may well make the conditional caution an effective way of dealing with the lower-level type of offence, whilst at the same time reducing the workload on the courts.

Reprimands and warnings for juveniles

There was always a presumption in favour of cautioning juveniles, where that was at all possible. Unsurprisingly, a statutory scheme for juveniles was introduced several years before that for adults.[17] A reprimand is the required proceeding for less serious offences. Any other offence is dealt with by a final warning. Prosecution follows only for repeat or serious offences.

---

[13] See by analogy, *R v R and R* [2002] Crim LR 349, where there was a failure to explain that acceptance of a caution would result in registration under the sex offender legislation; *R (on application of U) v Metropolitan Police Commissioner* [2002] 4 All ER 593.

[14] Defined by PACE, s 82(3) as a statement wholly or partly adverse to its maker.

[15] [2009] EWHC 594 (Admin); [2009] 2 Cr App R 2009.   [16] See p 197.

[17] See the Crime and Disorder Act 1998.

Judicial scrutiny of the decision to caution

The decision to caution, or to prosecute instead of cautioning, is not beyond judicial scrutiny.[18] In *R v Chief Constable of Kent County Constabulary, ex parte L*,[19] the Divisional Court considered that a decision to prosecute a 12-year-old girl, which was claimed to be in breach of the policy for cautioning of juveniles, was susceptible to judicial review, although on the facts it was found to be a proper exercise of discretion. Watkins LJ considered that the policy of cautioning, instead of prosecuting, was well settled and played a prominent part in the process of decision-making in an individual case. Care should be taken, however, to avoid 'the danger of opening too wide the door of review of the discretion to continue a prosecution', and the Court appeared to draw a distinction between decisions involving adults and those involving juveniles. Another Divisional Court in *R v Inland Revenue Commissioners, ex parte Mead*[20] has stressed that decisions relating to adults are not beyond judicial review, although the situations in which the courts would in fact intervene will be rare.[21]

Police bail

Questions of bail arise at various stages of the criminal process. An arrested person need not, now,[22] always be taken to the police station. Where a suspect's identity and address are known and the offence is minor, there is often no need to go through the time-consuming process of the custody process at the police station. Provisions in PACE[23] permit a constable to release a suspect on 'street bail' before reaching the police station. The change is intended to simplify procedures, reduce administrative burden, save police resources, and speed up the process.[24] The bailed person must be given, or sent, a notice telling him when and where he must answer to his bail, which may be at any time in the future, although it is anticipated that a period of two weeks should be the norm, and should not in any event exceed six weeks.[25] A constable should, in deciding whether to use this power, have regard to the nature of the offence, the ability to progress the case at the police station, the level of confidence in the suspect answering bail, and the level of understanding and awareness of the suspect. The likelihood of further offending, risk to the safety or welfare of the suspect, and the age of the suspect are also relevant.[26]

---

[18] There are distinct limits to judicial review of the decisions of a prosecution authority: see Watkin LJ in *R v General Council of the Bar, ex parte Percival* [1991] 1 QB 212, [1990] 3 All ER 137. See also p 598.

[19] [1993] 1 All ER 756.   [20] [1993] 1 All ER 772.

[21] The fact that there are alternative remedies, e.g., to challenge for abuse of process, does not prevent the exercise of discretion itself from being challenged by way of judicial review.

[22] From 20 January 2004, when Criminal Justice Act 2003, s 4, came into force.

[23] PACE, ss 30A–30D. The Criminal Justice Act 2003, s 4, also amends PACE, ss 30, 34–36, 41, and 47.

[24] *Justice for All*, para 3.10.

[25] Home Office Circular 61/2003, *Bail Elsewhere than at a Police Station*.

[26] Circular 61/2003.

If an arrested person is in fact taken to the police station, a custody officer must order his release from police detention either on bail or without bail, in which case he goes to prison. The powers and duties of the police when dealing with the continued detention of those in custody have already been discussed.[27] The power to order bail is subject to limitations, which apply where the name and address of the arrested person is unknown, if detention is necessary for his protection or for the protection of other persons or property, if the defendant is not likely to answer to his bail, or is likely to interfere with the administration of justice, or, in the case of an imprisonable offence, detention is necessary to prevent his committing further offences.[28]

KEY ISSUE

How far should the cautioning process be used to divert an offender from the court system? The use of cautions, formal and informal, has benefits in that it potentially saves cost and time. However, it can mean that individuals who, in the view of some, ought to be subject to the formal adjudication of a court are not.[29] Care needs to be taken to ensure that cautions are not used for administrative expediency when the seriousness of the matter the subject of the caution ought to be the subject of an appearance in court. In addition the convenience of a caution for an individual, with swift and private disposal, may on occasion encourage acceptance of guilt where that in fact legally may be in doubt.

 Questions

1. What are the advantages and dangers of cautions?

2. What is their purpose?

The decision to prosecute

Introduction

Until the passage of the 2003 Act, the decision to commence proceedings was generally in the hands of the police, although other organizations have law enforcement powers as well. In most cases the police have charged, taken a suspect into custody, or provided the information for the issue of a summons or warrant for arrest. It was, though, the duty of the Director of Public Prosecutions to take over the conduct of all criminal proceedings instituted on behalf of a police force.[30] In reality, the DPP and Crown Prosecution Service played a central role in the decision-making

---

[27] See p 457.   [28] PACE, s 38(1).

[29] See the protests of a court in December 2010 in Nottingham about the cautioning of a police officer for a speeding offence that should have, in the view of the court, come before the court: **www.bbc.co.uk/news/ uk-england-nottinghamshire-11959410** (9 December 2010).

[30] Prosecution of Offences Act 1985, s 3(2)(a). In difficult, important or otherwise appropriate cases, the DPP may institute proceedings: s 3(2)(b). For the office of the DPP, see p 389.

process, as have, in the case of serious or complex fraud, the Serious Fraud Office. The role of the CPS has now changed radically[31] through a new scheme created by the 2003 Act.

Private prosecutions

Persons or bodies other than the police have been entitled to institute proceedings, and that position is not changed by the arrangements discussed below. The Royal Commission on Criminal Procedure[32] in 1981 concluded that it would be both impracticable and undesirable to bring all prosecutions within the ambit of the CPS, although it suggested that a private prosecutor should first be under a duty to notify the Crown Prosecutor, who should then decide whether to take over the prosecution. That latter suggestion was not implemented. The Auld Review[33] likewise considered that the right of private prosecution should remain, even though it is rarely used. Section 6 of the Prosecution of Offences Act 1985 states that nothing in the Act precludes any person from instituting any criminal proceedings to which the Director's duty under the Act does not apply. There are, though, safeguards. By section 42 of the Supreme Court Act 1981, if on an application by the Attorney-General the High Court is satisfied that any person has habitually and persistently and without any reasonable ground instituted vexatious prosecutions (whether against the same or different persons), the court may make a criminal proceedings order. This has the effect that no information shall be laid before a justice of the peace, and no application for leave to prefer a bill of indictment shall be made by that person without the leave of the court. Leave is not to be granted unless the High Court is satisfied that the institution of proceedings does not amount to an abuse of process. In addition, in some cases the consent of the Attorney-General is needed.[34]

The Auld Review rejected any system of pre-charge check or approval. It did, though, endorse the recommendation of the Law Commission[35] that any court before which a private prosecution is initiated should be under a duty forthwith to notify the DPP in writing. The DPP could decide whether to take over the proceedings, or take them over and then discontinue them. That recommendation has not been implemented, but since private prosecutions will in reality usually be known to Crown Prosecutors at some stage, there is nothing to prevent this practice from occurring routinely. However, the fact that an individual has not made a complaint to the police is not of itself a bar to a private prosecution being brought.[36]

---

[31] *Infra.*   [32] *Op cit*, paras 7.40–7.52.   [33] *Op cit*, ch 12, paras 46–51.

[34] See, e.g., offences of incitement to racial hatred (Public Order Act 1986, s 27); offences under the Terrorism Act 2000. Some 150 statutes require the consent of either the Attorney-General or the DPP. The Law Commission, and the Auld Review recommended general abolition of these requirements.

[35] Auld Review, ch 12, para 50, citing Law Commission, *Consents to Prosecution,* Law Comm No 255, paras 7.4–7.8.

[36] *Barry* v *Birmingham Magistrates' Court* [2009] EWHC 2571 (Admin) [2010] 1 Cr App R 13.

The Criminal Justice Act 2003

The 2003 Act gives the CPS much greater involvement in the decision to prosecute and choice of charge. The Auld Review took the view that the CPS 'has still to fill its proper role which . . . should be closer to the more highly regarded Procurator Fiscal in Scotland or the Office of the Director of Public Prosecutions in Northern Ireland'.[37] It recommended that the CPS should, generally, determine the initial charge. Following implementation of changes recommended by the Glidewell Report[38] and the Narey Report,[39] with CPS staff increasingly located in or close to police stations ('co-location'), or on call, greater CPS involvement is, for the first time, a practical proposition. Studies showed, however, that a voluntary approach did not inevitably create closer involvement in the charging process.[40] Given the automatic sending for trial procedure now in place for trial on indictment,[41] the need for speed and efficiency, and the obligation in the Code for Crown Prosecutors not only to consider whether there is sufficient evidence (the 'sufficiency of evidence' test) but also whether it is in the public interest to prosecute (the 'public interest' test),[42] the Auld Review considered that change was essential.

That recommendation has to be viewed in the context of a continuing failure always to get the charge right in the first place. The government White Paper *Justice for All*[43] stated that some 13 per cent of cases had to be discontinued by the CPS, either because there was not enough evidence to convict or because it was not in the public interest to proceed. Some 45 per cent of police files submitted to the CPS were not properly compiled, leading to the collapse of some cases, due to lack of evidence.[44] A failure to get the charge right early also makes the plea before venue procedure[45] less useful that it could be. *Justice for All* reported that pilot co-location projects saved, in cost, some 14 per cent of what would otherwise have been spent in monetary terms, and the number of cases disposed of at first hearing increased by some 20 per cent.

A new section 37B of PACE[46] sets out the duties of the police. Except in minor and road traffic cases, the police must supply the CPS with information specified in guidance. The CPS will then decide whether a charge should be laid, and, if so, whether it should be using the sufficiency of evidence and public interest test. Alternatively,

---

[37] *Op cit*, ch 12, para 12. For the CPS generally, and recent reforms, see p 389.

[38] *A Review of the Crown Prosecution Service* (HMSO, 1998): see p 389.

[39] *Review of Delay in the Criminal Justice System* (HMSO, 1997).

[40] *Reducing Delay in the Criminal Justice System: Evaluation of Pilot Schemes* (Ernst & Young, HMSO, 1999).

[41] See p 627.

[42] See p 397. The police in charging have regard, under Code C, only to the sufficiency of evidence.

[43] *Op cit*, ch 3, p 52. The CPS Inspectorate in its Annual Report 1999–2000 found that some 22 per cent of police charges relating to assault, public order and road traffic were incorrect.

[44] See Ward and Davies, *Practitioners' Guide to the Criminal Justice Act 2003* (Jordans, 2004), para 3.2.

[45] See p 612. and Herbert, 'Mode of Trial and Magistrates' Sentencing Powers: Will Increased Powers Inevitably Lead to a Reduction in the Committal Rate?' [2003] Crim LR 314.

[46] Created by Criminal Justice Act 2003, s 28 and Sch 2. The provisions came into force on 29 January 2004.

the CPS may decide that a conditional caution[47] is appropriate. The decision will be communicated in writing on the police and be binding on them. Co-location should make this process relatively speedy, but no time limit is specified by section 37B, and section 37 of PACE has been amended to allow bail to be granted to a suspect whilst this decision-making process occurs.

The criteria

By section 10 of the Prosecution of Offences Act 1985, the Director of Public Prosecutions is under a duty to issue a Code for Crown Prosecutors. The Code gives guidance on the general principles to be applied by them in determining, in any case, whether proceedings should be instituted, discontinued, or what charges should be made. It is to be found in works such as *Archbold* or *Blackstone's Criminal Practice* or on the CPS website.

The Code is a matter to which the CPS must have regard. Failure to do so opens up the possibility of judicial review,[48] and, on occasion, may also raise Human Rights Act issues. One such case was *R (Purdy)* v *Director of Public Prosecutions*,[49] in which the Supreme Court held that the Code, which gave general guidance as to the principles to be applied, was not to be regarded as forming part of the 'law' for the purpose of the phrase 'in accordance with law', contained in Article 8 of the European Convention on Human Rights. Limitations on the right to private and family life under Article 8[50] had to be prescribed by law. It was thus necessary, said the court, for the Director of Public Prosecutions to promulgate a policy for the enforcement of the criminal offences relating to suicide.[51] Clearly, once issued, it would be the duty of the Director to apply that policy. Another was *R (on the application of McKinnon)* v *Director of Public Prosecutions*,[52] in which the challenge (which was, in the event, unsuccessful) was to a decision by the DPP not to charge the defendant. The defendant, wishing to avoid extradition to the USA, wanted to be prosecuted in the United Kingdom, but failed in his challenge attempting to compel the DPP to charge him.

The first question to be decided is whether there is sufficient evidence. There must be admissible, substantial, and reliable evidence that a criminal offence has been committed by an identified individual. In deciding this, a prima facie case is not enough: the test is whether there is a realistic prospect of conviction. This is an objective test. It means that a jury, or bench of magistrates (or district judge), properly directed in law, is more likely than not to convict the defendant of the charge alleged.[53] In deciding that, a careful study of the available evidence will be undertaken. Relevant factors include the possibility that evidence might be inadmissible in law, or be excluded

[47] See p 590.   [48] See n 18.
[49] [2010] 1 Cr App R 1.   [50] See p 197.
[51] See comment by Roger, 'Prosecutorial Policies, Prosecutorial Systems and the *Purdy* Litigation' [2010] Crim LR 543; Daw and Soloman, 'Assisted Suicide and Identifying the Public Interest in the Decision to Prosecute' [2010] Crim LR 737.
[52] [2009] EWHC 2021.   [53] The so-called '51 per cent' rule.

because of failure to comply with relevant rules, the possibility that a confession may be unreliable, the possibility that a witness may be hostile or likely to be unreliable, or not likely to tell the truth, the impression a witness will make in court, the availability of all necessary witnesses or the likelihood of the court accepting documentary evidence, and the competence of young children. The prosecutor will look at the overall weight of the case, whether dangers of concoction of evidence exists, whether a case can be sustained against more than one defendant (if there is more than one), and whether the public might consider a prosecution to be oppressive. The prosecutor will also consider what the defence case may be.

Having decided whether there is a sufficiency of evidence, the prosecutor is then required to consider the wider public interest, although the interests of the victim also should be borne in mind. The graver the offence the less likelihood there will be that the public interest will permit the case to be dealt with by anything other than prosecution, although the Code does urge prosecutors to strive to ensure that the spirit of cautioning guidelines is observed, where the seriousness of the offence allows. In particular the following factors may provide an indication that prosecution may not be required:

(a) where a court is likely to impose a small or nominal penalty only;

(b) where the offence was committed as a result of a genuine mistake or misunderstanding (balanced against the seriousness of the offence);

(c) where the loss or harm is minor, and results from a single incident (and particularly if it was caused by misjudgement);

(d) where the offences are stale. However, the staleness may have been caused by the offender himself, the offences may only just have come to light, there may have been the need for a long, complex investigation, or the offences may be serious;

(e) prosecution may have a very bad effect on the health of the victim, again bearing in mind the seriousness of the offence;

(f) old age or infirmity;

(g) mental disorder at the time of the commission of the offence. Where the effect of proceedings on the health of the accused is not outweighed by a wider public interest in favour of prosecution, proceedings should not be commenced, or may be discontinued. In this type of case, other relevant factors will be the nature of the mental condition and the likelihood of further offending;

(h) changes in attitude by the complainant, including the making of reparation or putting right loss. However, prosecution cannot be avoided simply by an ability to pay compensation.

In addition to the Code of Practice, the CPS and police have developed charging standards for certain types of offence. These include certain assaults and other offences against the person, driving offences, and public order offences. The intention is to ensure fairness and consistency in the approach to certain types of offence. Certain principles are stated in all of the charging standards. Charges should accurately reflect the extent of the defendant's involvement and responsibility, the choice of charges should accurately reflect the defendant's involvement and responsibility, and the choice of charges should ensure the clear and simple presentation of the case; it is wrong to encourage a defendant to plead guilty to a few charges by selecting more charges than are necessary, and it is wrong to select a more serious charge not supported by the evidence in order to encourage a plea of guilty to a lesser allegation.

Judicial review of the decision to prosecute or discontinue

The court's power to judicially review matters relating to policing and prosecution is limited, although it is clear that the power does exist. An example of this is judicial review of the prosecution process. In *R v Commissioner of Police for the Metropolis, ex parte Blackburn*,[54] the applicant sought an order of mandamus[55] to compel the Commissioner to reverse a policy statement appearing to limit the enforcement of the gaming laws. The Court of Appeal held that mandamus might be appropriate if there was a complete failure to perform a duty imposed by law, but it declined to make an order in the case in question because the policy had already been reversed. In a subsequent case involving the obscene publications laws,[56] the court stressed that the discretion was that of the Commissioner, and that the court could only intervene where there was effectively an abdication of function. By contrast, it will be much easier to justify judicial intervention where a decision affects the ability to exercise legally protected rights. *R v Coventry City Council, ex parte Phoenix Aviation* is an example of such a case.[57] Here, a failure of the police to stop demonstrators from obstructing the applicants' rights to export live animals was held to be reviewable. The application succeeded on the facts.

One area that has evolved in tune with modern approaches to judicial review concerns decisions to institute proceedings. The decisions of the law officers appear generally to be beyond challenge, and in *Gouriet v Union of Post Office Workers*[58] the power to enforce the criminal law through applications for injunctive relief was held to be for the Attorney-General alone. More recently, in *R v Solicitor-General, ex parte Taylor and Taylor*,[59] a Divisional Court held that the decision whether to bring proceedings for contempt of court was not justiciable. However, in the context of judicial review of the decision to prosecute, the courts are more willing to intervene. A distinction has, in the past, been drawn between decisions involving juveniles and those involving adults. In *R v Chief Constable of Kent, ex parte L*,[60] the court stated that, where a policy exists in respect of cautioning juveniles, a decision to commence or discontinue

---

[54] [1968] 2 QB 118, [1968] 1 All ER 763.   [55] See p 256.

[56] *R v Commissioner of Police for the Metropolis, ex parte Blackburn (No 3)* [1973] QB 241, [1973] 1 All ER 324.

[57] [1995] 3 All ER 37.   [58] [1978] AC 435, [1977] 3 All ER 70.

[59] [1996] 1 FCR 206.   [60] [1993] 1 All ER 756.

criminal proceedings will only be reviewable if it can be shown that it was made regardless of, or contrary to, that policy.[61] This approach was applied in *R* v *Commissioner of Police for the Metropolis, ex parte P*,[62] in which it was held that the improper cautioning of a juvenile, in contravention of the Code for Crown Prosecutors, was judicially reviewable. The courts have also been prepared to consider reviewing decisions to prosecute adults. The challenge in *R* v *Inland Revenue Commissioners, ex parte Mead*[63] failed on the facts, because the prosecuting authority had considered the matter fairly and appropriately and had taken all relevant matters into account. More recently, the courts permitted a challenge to a decision not to prosecute police officers following the fatal shooting of an individual wrongly suspected of being a suicide bomber.[64] It had already been established that the Code for Crown Prosecutors was susceptible to judicial review,[65] but the court was satisfied that the DPP had acted within the Code and that his decision had not been unreasonable. The court concluded that there had been no breach of the right to life under Article 2 of the ECHR, and the challenge was therefore unsuccessful.

KEY ISSUE

How far should the courts intervene by judicial review of the exercise of the discretion to prosecute? Clearly, like all executive discretions, it cannot be immune from review, but its exercise often raises policy issues that are not matters for the courts. What is clear from the *Purdy* case is that there must be a clear policy framework in which such decisions are taken and that policy must fairly be applied. What the court must not do is effectively substitute its judgment for that of the prosecuting authorities.

❓ Questions

1. Can the decisions as to when assisting suicide should be prosecuted effectively amount to a change in the law? If not, why not?

2. When should the courts intervene?

Discontinuance

Under section 23 of the Prosecution of Offences Act 1985 notice of discontinuance can be issued, provided that this is done in summary cases before the hearing of the evidence, or, in cases to be tried on indictment, before sending for trial. This can be done by correspondence, and without the expense and inconvenience of a court hearing. It does not replace the power of a prosecutor to go before a court and offer no evidence

---

[61] See *R* v *Havering Justices, ex parte Gould*, unreported (1993).

[62] (1996) 5 Admin LR 6, (1996) 160 JP 369.　　[63] [1993] 1 All ER 772.

[64] *R (on the application of Da Silva)* v *Director of Public Prosecutions* [2006] EWHC 3204 (Admin), (2007) 157 NLJ 31.

[65] *R* v *Director of Public Prosecutions, ex parte Manning* [2001] QB 330, [2001] HRLR 3. For the Code, see p 596.

or withdraw a charge, both of which remain options[66] although the leave of the court is needed.[67] Nor does it interfere with the power of the Attorney-General to prevent proceedings from continuing by the issue of a writ of *nolle prosequi*.

In deciding how to use these powers it is the duty of prosecutors to keep a case under review. In the case of juveniles it may become clear that a reprimand or final warning is a more appropriate way of dealing with the matter. In respect of those suffering illness the effect on health may make it appropriate for the case to be withdrawn.[68]

This power of review has been shown to be important. Since the creation of the Crown Prosecution Service in 1985 the incidence of discontinuance or withdrawal arose from 7 per cent in 1985 to 13 per cent in 2001. In part this is due to the defects in the charging process, now addressed by the 2003 Act. The Narey Report considered[69] that the CPS should not be permitted to discontinue cases on public interest grounds because it considers the offence not to be serious. This recommendation, designed to resolve differences between police and CPS, is unlikely to be implemented given the key role in charging is now given to the CPS itself.

Time limits for prosecution and abuse of process

Requirements of Article 6 ECHR

The right to trial within a reasonable time is part of the Article 6 rights of a defendant, that period being judged from the date on which the defendant is charged or officially notified that he is to be prosecuted,[70] and which continues all the way through the proceedings until a sentence is fixed.[71] Thus, it applies to decisions in respect of the enforcement of compensation orders or fines.[72] The reasonableness of the length of proceedings must be assessed in the light of all of the circumstances of the case, having regard to the complexity of the case, the conduct of the applicant and of the prosecution authorities, and the importance of what is at stake. Where there is a breach of Article 6 there must be such remedy as is just, effective, and proportionate.[73]

Increasing concern has arisen about delays in the criminal justice system.[74] In general there is no time limit on the prosecution of an indictable offence, although by contrast, summary proceedings must be brought within six months from the date

---

[66] *R v Director of Public Prosecutions, ex parte Cooke* (1991) 95 Cr App R 233.

[67] The Royal Commission on Criminal Justice recommended that the CPS should have the power to discontinue a case without the leave of the court at any time prior to the start of the trial: *op cit*, ch 5, para 37.

[68] This power to discontinue remains throughout the trial itself. In *R v Seelig* (1993), the defendant was discharged because he was medically unable to cope with the strains of a long trial in which he was defending himself: see (1993) The Times, 15 February.

[69] *Op cit*, p 580.

[70] *Eckle* v *Germany* (1982) 5 EHRR 1; *Ewing* v *United Kingdom* (1986) 10 EHRR 141.

[71] *Findlay* v *United Kingdom* (1997) 24 EHRR 221; *Phillips* v *United Kingdom* (2001).

[72] *Crowther* v *United Kingdom* [2005] All ER (D) 06 (Feb); *Lloyd* v *Bow Street Magistrates' Court* [2003] EWHC 2294.

[73] *Attorney-General's Reference (No 2 of 2001)* [2004] 1 Cr App R 25.   [74] See p 501.

of commission of the offence.[75] Even in some cases triable on indictment Parliament has, for reasons of policy, imposed a time limit: thus a prosecution for unlawful sexual intercourse with a girl under the age of 16 could not be commenced more than twelve months after the commission of the offence.[76] However, even where no specific time limit exists, the court is not powerless and can intervene to correct abuse of process caused by delay. The elapsing of time may also be a ground leading to a conviction being quashed. In *R v B*,[77] it was held that a residual discretion existed to set aside a conviction considered to be unsafe because of the elapsing of time between offence and prosecution. That decision, though, was exceptional, and distinguished in *R v E (T)*[78] where there was a twelve-year gap between alleged sexual offences against children and their prosecution. The crucial factor in *E (T)* was that there was supporting evidence independent of the allegations by the complainant, and, unlike *B*, it was possible for the defendant to defend himself by cross-examination of the complainant.

Abuse of process

A court can, as part of its inherent power, order a stay to prevent abuse of process.[79] This power is available to a Crown Court, or, in most circumstances, to a magistrates' court.[80] Thus if the prosecution[81] has manipulated or misused the process of the court 'so as to deprive the defendant of a protection provided by the law or if there has been such delay so that prejudice or unfairness to the defendant arises ... ',[82] then the court can order that the prosecution does not proceed. This is a power 'of great constitutional importance',[83] and arises in two classes, which may, of course, overlap. But, whichever class into which the case falls, the crucial factor is the public interest. In *Attorney-General's Reference (No 2 of 2001)*,[84] the majority of the House of Lords held that it was not appropriate to stay proceedings unless: (a) there could no longer be a fair hearing; or (b) it would be otherwise unfair to try the defendant.

To protect fair trial

If the proposed trial would actually be unfair, then there would be an infringement of the fair trial provisions of Article 6. However, where matters of fairness can be dealt with at the trial they should be, rather than the proceedings being stayed for an abuse of process. In *Attorney-General's Reference (No 2 of 2001)*, the court observed that a charge should not be stayed or dismissed if any lesser remedy would be just

---

[75] Or six months from when the matter of complaint arose: see Magistrates' Courts Act 1980, s 127.

[76] See Sexual Offences Act 2003, s 9.   [77] [2003] 2 Cr App R 197.

[78] [2004] 2 Cr App R 36.

[79] *Connolly v Director of Public Prosecutions* [1964] AC 1254, (1964) 48 Cr App R 183.

[80] See *Panday v Virgil (Senior Superintendent of Police)* [2008] UKPC 24, [2008] 2 Cr App R 21.

[81] Including a private prosecutor: see *R (Dacre and another) v Westminster Magistrates' Court* [2009] 1 Cr App R 6.

[82] *R v Derby Magistrates' Court, ex parte Brooks* (1984) 80 Cr App R 164.

[83] *Per* Lord Salmon in *DPP v Humphrys* [1976] 2 All ER 479, at 527.

[84] [2004] 1 Cr App R 25.

and proportionate. This was the case in *R* v *Hopkins*,[85] in which an application to stay proceedings for abuse of process failed. Despite the fact that the prosecution was in respect of complaints of sexual abuse and violence that the police had originally investigated and decided not to proceed with, the subsequent investigation and prosecution did not create unfairness that could not be dealt with at the trial.

Dealing with a case involving delay, Viscount Dilhorne in *Director of Public Prosecutions* v *Humphrys*[86] warned that use of this power should only occur 'in the most exceptional circumstances'. This was an approach echoed by Lord Lane CJ in *A-G's Reference (No 1 of 1990)*,[87] in which he stated that even if delay was unjustifiable the imposition of a stay:[88]

(1) should be the exception rather than the rule. Still more rare should be cases where a stay can properly be imposed in the absence of any fault on the part of the complainant or prosecution.

This remains true despite the provisions of the Human Rights Act 1998, which incorporate the right to a fair trial within a reasonable time.[89] The defendant must show on the balance of probabilities that, owing to the delay, he will suffer serious prejudice to the extent that no fair trial can be held. In deciding this, the ability of the court through the rules of evidence to regulate what is placed before it, and the ability of the judge to warn and to give appropriate directions to the jury, should both be borne in mind. The reasons for delay may also be relevant. Prosecution inefficiency is one factor,[90] as is the nature of the case. A longer period of preparation for the prosecution is only to be expected in complex cases, particularly fraud cases.[91] Delay may also arise because of the nature of the offence alleged, and the reluctance of a victim to come forward.[92] Whatever the reason, long delay is not, inevitably, a justification for a stay. In *R* v *Central Criminal Court, ex parte Randle and Pottle*,[93] a delay of twenty years in a case of assisting the Soviet spy, George Blake, to escape from lawful custody was held, on the facts, not to justify a stay. Again, in *R* v *V*,[94] a twenty-year gap between alleged acts of sexual abuse and the prosecution was held to be no bar to prosecution, the court stressing that staying proceedings for delay should be exceptional. The delay could be explained by the fact that the complainant of the sexual offence was seven years younger than the defendant (his brother) and the defendant had threatened the complainant, had been violent in the past, and the complainant had been reluctant to tell because of the effect on her family.

[85] [2004] All ER (D) 356 (Feb).   [86] [1977] AC 1, [1976] 2 All ER 497.
[87] [1992] QB 630, [1992] 3 All ER 169; *R* v *H* [2003] All ER (D) 403 (Feb).
[88] See 'The Reasonable Time Limit Requirement: An Independent and Meaningful Right' [2005] Crim LR 5.
[89] *R* v *H* [2003] All ER (D) 403. For Article 6, see pp 191 and 600.
[90] *R* v *West London Magistrates' Court, ex parte Anderson* (1984) 80 Cr App R 143.
[91] See Narey Report, *op cit.*
[92] *R* v *LPB* (1990) 91 Cr App R 359; *R* v *Evans (TM)* [2004] EWCA Crim 1441.
[93] (1992) 92 Cr App R 323.
[94] [2004] All ER (D) 207 (Feb); see also *R* v *V* [2004] All ER (D) 207 (Feb).

Statute has created a framework within which prosecutors must work. By section 2 of the Prosecution of Offences Act 1985, and regulations made hereunder, there are time limits regulating how long a defendant may be kept in custody pending the start of summary trial, between the first appearance at court and sending for trial, and between sending for trial and the start of the trial.[95] These are seventy days between first appearance and sending for trial,[96] eighty-six days from date of first appearance to the opening day of the trial, and 112 days from sending for trial until arraignment.[97] Application can be made for extension of those limits, and a right of appeal exists in respect of the decision of a magistrates' court to extend, or a refusal to extend, these time limits. By contrast, no power exists in respect of such an order made by the Crown Court, but since this is not a matter 'relating to trial on indictment' an aggrieved person could seek judicial review of the decision.

Of course, delay may arise not only in respect of the commencement of the proceedings but also in their conduct. The reduction of delays in the criminal justice system is regarded by the government as a matter of high priority. Despite a significant reduction in the number of cases coming before the courts, custody time limits are not always met.[98] This issue is discussed in due course.[99]

Abuse of executive power

The second class of case is where, although the fairness of the trial is not in question, nevertheless it would be unfair to the defendant because of the abuse that has occurred. It will apply where a defendant, but for the abuse, would never have been before the court at all. In short, it is a vindication of the rule of law.

In *R v Croydon Justices, ex parte Dean*,[100] the conviction was quashed, the accused having been assured that he would not be prosecuted. Again, in *R v Horseferry Road MC, ex parte Bennett*,[101] the House of Lords held that the doctrine of abuse of process applied to prevent the trial of an accused who had been brought to the United Kingdom through the collusion of the United Kingdom and South African authorities, in breach of extradition procedures. Despite the fact that the fairness of the trial itself was not in issue, the court considered that the judiciary had a responsibility for the maintenance of the rule of law. A third example is where criminal proceedings are brought vexatiously by a private prosecutor.[102] Nonetheless, the ultimate objective of the discretionary power to stay proceedings is to ensure that there should be a fair trial. It is usually only in cases in which there has been prosecution misconduct that the proceedings will be stayed under this second class, as *ex parte Dean* and *ex*

---

[95] See Prosecution of Offences (Custody Time Limits) Regulations 1987, SI 1987/698.

[96] See p 627.   [97] See p 657.

[98] See Narey Report, *op cit.*   [99] See p 632.

[100] [1993] QB 769, [1993] 3 All ER 129; see also *R v Bow Street Stipendiary Magistrates' ex parte Director of Public Prosecutions* (1989) 91 Cr App R 283; *R v Crown Court at Norwich, ex parte Belsham* [1992] 1 All ER 394, [1992] 1 WLR 54.

[101] [1994] 1 AC 42; see also *R v Beckford* [1996] 1 Cr App R 94; cf. *R v Redmond* [2006] EWCA 1744 [2009] 1 Cr App R 25.

[102] See, e.g., *R v Belmarsh Magistrates' Court, ex parte Watts* [1999] 2 Cr App R 198.

parte Bennett illustrate.[103] The power to stay is sometimes used where there has been entrapment: in other words where the offence would not have been committed but for the intervention of the law enforcement agency and what has occurred is, effectively 'state-created crime'.[104]

Time limits in summary cases

Unless expressly provided to the contrary, a magistrates' court cannot try a summary offence unless the prosecution process (by requisition and charge, formerly by information or summons) was commenced within six months from the time when the offence was committed.[105] However, it may try summarily an either-way offence outside that period, because this statutory time limit is confined to summary offences.[106] Time runs from the time of commission of the offence, not from the time of its discovery; however, it is sufficient if the process is commenced within the six months, even if the trial takes place outside that time. It is in each case a question of construction of the statute whether the offence in question is a continuing offence—that is, committed each day that the act or state of affairs in question continues—or whether it is a 'once and for all' offence—that is, it is committed on one day and one day only. Thus, in *R v Wimbledon Justices, ex parte Derwent*,[107] a statute made it an offence to let or offer to let a house in excess of a certain rent. The Divisional Court held that a person lets a house once and for all when he demises it by means of a lease and that an information laid six months after the date of the demise was out of time. Proceedings could therefore be restrained by prohibition since:

> (1) If in a case brought before justices it can be seen on the face of the proceedings that the offence is alleged to have been committed more than six months before the information was laid, justices have no power to commence dealing with the case at all, because they have no jurisdiction to sit on a court of summary jurisdiction in the case of an offence alleged to have been committed more than six months before the proceedings were instituted.[108]

Even where the offence is continuing it seems that the time limit runs from each day, so that the magistrates cannot hear any charge in respect of an offence as occurring more than six months before the date of the information;[109] in other words, the matter is to be regarded as if the defendant committed the offence once every day. Where an information or charge and requisition is laid in time, it may be amended to charge a

---

[103] See *R (on the application of Ebrahim) v Feltham MC; Muoat v DPP* [2001] 3 All ER 381.
[104] *R v Loosely; Attorney-General's Reference(No 3 of 2002)* [2001] 4 All ER 897.
[105] Magistrates' Courts Act 1980, s 127(1).
[106] Ibid, s 127(2); see also *Kemp v Liebherr (Great Britain) Ltd* [1987] 1 All ER 885, [1987] 1 WLR 607.
[107] [1953] 1 QB 380, [1953] 1 All ER 390.
[108] [1953] 1 QB 380, at 385, [1953] 1 All ER 390, at 391, *per* Lord Goddard CJ.
[109] *R v Chertsey Justices, ex parte Franks* [1961] 2 QB 152, [1961] 1 All ER 825.

different offence, after the expiry of six months from the commission of that offence, provided that this does not cause injustice.[110]

The general need to avoid delay in criminal proceedings has already been noted.[111] So, too, has the doctrine of abuse of process.[112] This doctrine applies to summary proceedings equally as to proceedings on indictment. In *R v Willesden Justices, ex parte Clemmings*,[113] Lord Bingham CJ indicated that magistrates had the power to stop a prosecution where there was an abuse of process, because:

(a) the prosecution has manipulated or misused the process of the court so as to deprive the accused of a protection provided by law or to take unfair advantage of a technicality; or

(b) the accused has been, or would be, prejudiced in the preparation or conduct of his defence by delay on the part of the prosecution, which was unjustifiable.

The principles on which these rules will be exercised are broadly those as apply more generally.[114] The court will consider whether the wrongdoing is deliberate, whether prejudice has been caused or the potential for it arises.[115] One example is *R v Brentford Justices, ex parte Wong*.[116] In that case an information for careless driving was laid two days before the expiration of the statutory six-months time limit. At the time that the information was laid, the prosecution had not decided whether or not to prosecute and did not advise the defendant of the decision to do so until he was informed (by letter) two months later. The summons consequent on the information was not served until five months after the laying of the information, and the trial did not commence until nine months after the laying of the information. On appeal for the refusal of the magistrates' court to stay the proceedings for abuse of process, the Divisional Court held that the police conduct amounted to 'a deliberate attempt to gain further time', and stayed the proceedings.

Bringing the suspect before the court

A suspect could of course have been charged, and thus brought before the court or, alternatively, bailed, and under a duty to surrender to bail. Otherwise proceedings could, prior to the implementation of provisions of the Criminal Justice Act 2003, be commenced by the defendant being brought before the court in one of three ways: firstly, by a summons; secondly, by warrant for arrest; thirdly, by arrest without warrant.

---

[110] *R v Newcastle-upon-Tyne Justices, ex parte John Bryce (Contractors) Ltd* [1976] 2 All ER 611, [1976] 1 WLR 517.

[111] See p 600.   [112] See p 601.

[113] (1987) 87 Cr App R 280.   [114] See p 601.

[115] See generally, *R v Oxford City Justices, ex parte Smith* (1987) 75 Cr App R 200, *R v Canterbury and St Augustine Justices, ex parte Turner* (1983) 147 JP 193; *R v Watford Justices, ex parte Outrim* [1983] RTR 26.

[116] [1981] 1 QB 445.

The Auld Review pointed to the antiquated and inefficient nature of the system described above.[117] Many cases begun by summons were adjourned at the first hearing due to the non-appearance of the accused, which could be compelled only by the issue of a warrant, resulting in a further adjournment. Some cases could in fact be dealt with in the absence of the defendant: they are, however, limited to cases in which the charges are summary-only and carried a maximum punishment of no greater than three months' imprisonment.[118]

Sections 28–31 of the Criminal Justice Act 2003[119] implement the recommendations of the Auld Review, and bring both greater simplicity and efficiency to the commencement of proceedings. A prosecutor issues a *written charge* setting out the allegation and a *requisition* requiring the accused to appear before the magistrates' court at the specified date, and serves both on the court and defendant. This is intended to cut out wasted first and second appearances in motoring, local authority, and breach-of-community-penalty cases.[120] Informations as a means of obtaining a summons are abolished, but remain as an option of obtaining a warrant, and for private prosecutors.

Classification of offences

Some 95 per cent of all criminal cases are tried summarily in the magistrates' or youth court. It is only a small minority of cases that are tried on indictment in the Crown Court.[121] The decision as to whether a charge is tried in the magistrates' court, with its advantages of speed, relative informality, and cost, or on indictment by judge and jury, turns initially on the classification of the offence charged. Prior to the implementation of Part III of the Criminal Law Act 1977, the law relating to the classification of criminal offences and the determination of the appropriate mode of trial—summary or on indictment—was complex. Thus there were provisions for summary offences to be tried on indictment and for indictable offences to be tried summarily, while there was a third class of offences, colloquially (although not by statute) called 'hybrid' offences, which might take on the character of either summary offences or indictable offences according to the election of the parties. These classifications were reviewed by the James Committee in 1975,[122] which had as its twin aims a simplification of the procedure and a possible reduction in the case loads of the Crown Court. Its recommendations were in part controversial, but the majority of them were adopted, and implemented by Part III of the Criminal Law Act 1977.

---

[117] *Op cit*, ch 10, paras 416–422.   [118] Magistrates' Courts Act 1980, s 12.

[119] See also Criminal Procedure Rules 2010, Part 7.

[120] Ward and Davies, *op cit*, para 3.24.

[121] See the admonition by Darbyshire in 'An Essay on the Importance and Neglect of the Magistracy' [1997] Crim LR 639.

[122] *The Distribution of Criminal Business between the Crown Court and Magistrates' Courts*, Cmnd 6323 (HMSO, 1975).

As regards mode of trial, there are now three classes of offence—namely:

(a) offences triable only on indictment;[123]

(b) offences triable only summarily;[124] and

(c) offences triable either way.[125]

Offences triable only on indictment

Because offences can only fall within one of the other two categories if statute so provides, it follows that where there is no express statutory provision, an offence is triable only on indictment. This involves a trial by judge and jury[126] in the Crown Court. The case will not now require committal proceedings and will be sent or transferred for trial.[127]

In practice only the gravest indictable offences are triable only on indictment; these include murder, genocide, manslaughter, infanticide, child destruction, abortion, serious sexual offences, sedition, mutiny, piracy, offences under section 1 of the Official Secrets Act 1911, robbery, wounding or causing grievous bodily harm 'with intent', blackmail, assault with intent to rob, aggravated burglary, and burglary comprising the commission of, or an intention to commit, an offence triable only on indictment. It will, however, be recalled that these are triable only on indictment if committed by an adult. As we shall see, in the case of children and young persons, all indictable offences (other than homicide) may, and in most cases must, be tried summarily.[128]

Offences triable only summarily

The expressions 'summary offence' and 'offence triable only summarily' may be taken as synonymous. A statute creating a summary offence will first define the offence and then state that it is punishable 'on summary conviction' with a particular penalty, thereby indicating that the offence is a summary one. In addition, a number of offences that, prior to the Criminal Law Act 1977, were not summary offences according to the statute creating them became so.[129]

Special rules apply to some offences under the Criminal Damage Act 1971: offences under section 1 of this Act (excluding arson) are triable only summarily if the 'value involved' does not exceed £5,000. Section 22 of the Magistrates' Courts Act 1980 prescribes a procedure for determining whether such offences are to be regarded as

---

[123] This should be distinguished from the phrase 'indictable offences', which means offences that, if committed by an adult, are triable on indictment, either exclusively or because they are 'either-way' offences: Interpretation Act 1978, s 5, Sch 1.

[124] A 'summary offence' means an offence that, if committed by an adult, is triable only summarily.

[125] An offence 'triable either way' means an offence that, if committed by an adult, is triable either on indictment or summarily.

[126] For limited exceptions, see pp 361 and 652.   [127] See p 627.

[128] And tried in the youth courts.   [129] Magistrates' Courts Act 1980, s 17 and Sch 1.

summary or as triable either way (if the value involved exceeds £5,000). The court begins by hearing any representations made by the prosecutor or the accused as to the value involved; if it appears to the court clear that the value involved does not exceed the prescribed sum, it will proceed to summary trial. If it is clear that it does exceed that sum, then it will treat the offence as triable either way (which, of course, it then is).[130] If it is not clear whether or not the value involved does exceed the prescribed sum, then the defendant is given the choice and told that if he consents to summary trial, his liability to imprisonment or to a fine will be limited to the maximum that magistrates have power to impose; the nature of the offence will then be determined in accordance with the accused's decision. If a person is convicted, either by a magistrates' court or by the Crown Court, he cannot appeal on the ground that the magistrates were mistaken as to the value involved.[131]

Offences triable either way

The third class of offence is offences triable either way. In respect of these offences, the court has to determine whether the case is suitable for summary trial, or should be sent to the Crown Court. The defendant must, though, agree to summary trial if the court considers that summary trial is appropriate, and can himself elect jury trial, a right not generally open to a defendant until 1855.[132] The perceived inadequacy of prosecution disclosure, the potential for offence negotiation, the fact that mode of trial is often agreed informally between prosecutor and defendant, and the perception, justified or not, the Crown Court process is superior have all been cited as factors that have encouraged defendants to elect for trial by jury.[133]

The offences that are either way are listed in Schedule 1 to the Magistrates' Courts Act 1980, which consists of thirty-five paragraphs incorporating some sixty-six separate offences; these include unlawful wounding or inflicting grievous bodily harm, with or without a weapon, assault occasioning actual bodily harm, common assault, bigamy, certain forms of perjury and forgery, all indictable offences under the Theft Act 1968 (except robbery, blackmail, assault with intent to rob and certain burglaries), arson, offences under section 1 of the Criminal Damage Act 1971 where the value exceeds £5,000, and indecent assault. In addition many other statutes expressly

---

[130] The court must hear 'representations', meaning submissions, assertions of fact and sometimes production of documents; however, the court is not bound to hear evidence of the value involved: *R v Canterbury and St Augustine Justices, ex parte Klisiak* [1982] QB 398, [1981] 2 All ER 129. Moreover, it is possible in cases of doubt for the prosecution to limit the charge to certain items clearly below the prescribed value, even though in fact other damaged items would take the value above the prescribed value (so as to ensure summary trial). In *R (DPP) v Prestatyn Magistrates' Court* [2002] Law Society Gazette, 1 July 2002, it was held, in the case of genetically modified maize, that it was impossible to ascribe a value, and thus the offence was triable either-way.

[131] Magistrates' Courts Act 1980, s 22(8).   [132] *Op cit*, ch 5, para 123.

[133] See, e.g., Herbert, 'Mode of Trial and Magistrates' Sentencing Powers' [2003] Crim LR 315.

provide for an offence to be triable either summarily or on indictment (the former 'hybrid' offences) and these are now triable either way.[134]

Possible reform

The James Committee[135] recommended the creation of the threefold division outlined above,[136] although noted that the English system was 'unusual' in giving a defendant a right to choose his court of trial.[137] It also considered that it was appropriate to reclassify offences of low-value theft as summary offences, thus restricting the right to jury trial. This proposal met considerable resistance, in the light of the impact any conviction for theft might have on a person's reputation and career. The Royal Commission on Criminal Justice[138] concluded that the distribution of work between magistrates' court and Crown Court was neither rational, nor always amounted to an efficient use of resources recommending that the decision should be by agreement, or, where there was a dispute as to mode of trial, the magistrates' court should determine the matter. This, it anticipated, would lead to fewer mode of trial hearings and fewer cases going to the Crown Court than the 37 per cent of cases the Commission found were electing jury trial. The Commission:

(1) found that those electing trial had one of three or more main objectives: first a wish to put off trial with a view to securing in the meantime the advantages of a more liberal prison regime which would count towards a sentence if convicted and imprisoned; second, a well-founded belief that there was a better chance of acquittal in the Crown Court than before magistrates; and third, a mistaken belief that, if convicted the sentence would be lighter.[139]

A government consultation paper in 1995[140] placed emphasis on the resource implications. It identified a large increase in the proportion of cases involving either-way offences being committed to the Crown Court for trial.[141] In relation to defendants aged 17 or over, the proportion of such cases rose from 15 per cent in 1980 to 23 per cent in 1987, before falling to 17 per cent in 1992. A significant proportion of these cases were committed to the Crown Court because the magistrates themselves declined jurisdiction. In 1987 the relevant percentage was 47 per cent, rising to 64 per cent in 1991 and then falling to 63 per cent in 1992. This increase in committals had an affect not only on the workload of the court itself, but upon the size of the prison population, on the police, the Crown Prosecution Service, and the Legal Aid Fund. The consultation paper considered one option to be a reclassification of the mode of trial of minor thefts and certain other offences. In doing so it mirrored the approach taken by the James Committee. Two other options related not so much to the classifications themselves, but rather to the decision-making process as to where 'either-way' offences should be

---

[134] Ibid, s 17(2).   [135] *Op cit*, Cmnd 6323.
[136] Implemented by the Criminal Law Act 1977.   [137] *Op cit*, para 60.
[138] *Op cit*, ch 6, para 13–19.   [139] *Op cit*, ch 6, paras 6–8.
[140] *Mode of Trial: A Consultation Paper*, Cm 2908 (HMSO, 1995).   [141] Ibid, para 2.

tried. The first option came from the Royal Commission on Criminal Justice. It recommended that a person accused of an either-way offence should no longer be entitled to insist on trial in the Crown Court, but that the mode of trial should be a matter of agreement between the accused and the Crown Prosecution Service, and, in the absence of such agreement, be determined by magistrates. The other option considered was a change in the law relating to the mechanics of the decision-making process, so that magistrates could be aware, at the time of making the choice of mode of trial, of how the accused intends to plead at trial. The consultation paper estimated that a significant number of cases (38,000 in the year ending June 1993) were sent for trial in the Crown Court only for the accused to plead guilty on arraignment, and be given a sentence that the magistrates themselves could have imposed. It identified the fact that a 'significant proportion' of accused falling into that category would in fact be prepared to plead guilty in a magistrates' court to an either-way charge and be dealt with by the magistrates. Such cases were often sent to the Crown Court because magistrates declined jurisdiction. It was this last option that found favour. Amended procedures (plea before venue) were introduced by the Criminal Procedure and Investigations Act 1996.[142]

KEY ISSUE

The debate discussed above remains live. There is no logical reason why the mode of trial adopted should be at the choice of the defendant. The decision as to whether jury trial is necessary logically should lie with a court. However, the idea of a constitutional right to trial by jury continues to exert a powerful influence in justifying the right to elect trial by jury.

The Auld Review[143] considered this question, following hard on the heels of two Mode of Trial Bills that had attempted, in effect, to give the decision-making power as to mode of trial of either-way offences to the magistrates' court, not the defendant.[144] Auld took the view that it was for the court, not the defendant, to determine mode of trial. The review rejected the notion that there was some 'ancient, constitutional, fundamental or even broad right of the citizen to jury trial'.[145] The right to elect in fact began as a right to elect summary trial to avoid the rigour of trial on indictment in a limited number of cases, in the context of a harsh system that provided few protections for defendants. The review considered that the public has 'a legitimate interest in the financial and human cost of the criminal justice system and how best to apply its finite resources and with justice to all'. It is for the court to determine whether the circumstances of the case merit the more elaborate, costly, and time-consuming procedures of the Crown Court. It also concluded that the fact that some defendants perceive juries as more ready to acquit than magistrates is not a sound reason for leaving the power to elect with the defendant. There may be many reasons why

---

[142] See, generally, procedure for mode of trial.   [143] *Op cit*, ch 5, paras 119–172.

[144] Both Bills (Mode of Trial and Mode of Trial (No 2)) were rejected by the House of Lords essentially on the grounds that they diminished the fundamental right to trial by jury for a serious offence, although considerable criticism of their detail was made.

[145] *Op cit*, ch 5, para 166. All references in this discussion are to para 66 *et seq*.

juries are more ready to acquit, although the evidence about acquittal rates is complex.[146] If procedures in the magistrates' courts are unfair, these should be addressed.[147] The review's recommendations, that the court should decide with a limited right of appeal, that committal proceedings for either-way offences and committals for sentence should be abolished, have, however, only been partially implemented. The most recent interventions in this area, contained in the Criminal Justice Act 2003, do not proceed along the same lines as the ill-fated Modes of Trial Bills. Instead they sought to address the issue by modified plea before venue procedures and powers,[148] and by increased powers of sentencing for magistrates.[149]

? Questions

1. Why should the defendant have a right to elect trial by jury?
2. What advantages might trial by jury have for a defendant?
3. Are powers of magistrates' courts adequate?

Procedure for determining the mode of trial

The procedure for determining the mode of trial differs according to whether or not the accused is an adult. If he is, then, as has been noted, he will always be tried on indictment for an offence triable only on indictment and will always be tried summarily for a summary offence; only in the case of an 'either-way' offence are there alternative possibilities (see Figure 18.1). In the case of juveniles the position is quite different. Before considering these procedures it should be noted that if magistrates mistakenly adopt a procedure that is not permitted, for example by 'trying' a case that is triable only on indictment or by sending for trial in the case of an offence triable only summarily, then their 'trial' or 'committal' will be a complete nullity. Even if the defendant has been 'sentenced' he may later be committed for trial and properly tried, if the offence was triable only on indictment.[150]

The choice of charge is that of the prosecution. If the charge preferred is appropriate on the facts given their seriousness, then the defence cannot challenge that charge on the basis that the preferment of another, different charge would have permitted trial on indictment. Problems may also arise where fresh charges are levelled by the prosecutor, which, in reality, amount to attempts to deprive the justices of jurisdiction to try the case themselves. In *R v Brooks (Christopher)*,[151] the appellant appeared before magistrates on a charge under section 20 of the Offences against the Person Act 1861. The appellant was content to be tried summarily, and the justices so ordered. The chief prosecuting solicitor then advised the bringing of a new charge

---

[146] See, Chapter 10.

[147] Citing Ashworth, *The Criminal Process: An Evaluation Study* (OUP, 1998), p 262, and Darbyshire; 'For the New Lord Chancellor: Some Causes for Concern about Magistrates' [1997] Crim LR 869.

[148] See p 513.   [149] See p 686.

[150] See, e.g., *R v West* [1964] 1 QB 15; [1962] 2 All ER 624.   [151] [1985] Crim LR 385.

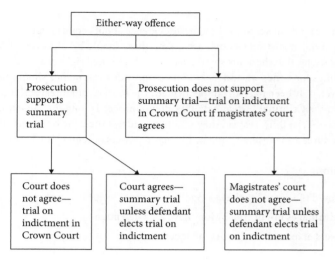

Fig. 18.1 Decisions as to mode of trial

under section 18 of the 1861 Act. In quashing the conviction obtained on such a charge, O'Connor LJ observed that the prosecutor was seeking 'to act as an appellate tribunal from the justices. There is no other explanation for it, and he said as much'. However, in *R v Redbridge Justices, ex parte Whitehouse*,[152] it was made clear that it was the abuse of power that led to the irregularity in *Brooks*. If the facts are capable of supporting a fresh charge, the justices must decide whether it is both proper and appropriate. If they have already decided on summary trial, any further charge that would have the effect of making summary trial impossible should be scrutinized with care, but not totally prohibited. The operation of this principle was seen in *R v Sheffield Justices, ex parte Director of Public Prosecutions*,[153] in which the defendant elected trial on a charge of assault occasioning actual bodily harm. The Crown then substituted a charge of common assault. Upon the magistrates staying the proceedings, the prosecutor successfully applied for judicial review. The substitution was a proper one, despite the fact that it deprived the accused of his right to trial by jury. There was no evidence of manipulation, and the defence had been notified of the proposal at an earlier stage. It was an appropriate charge on the facts.

The plea-before-venue process: Adults

As noted above, the plea-before-venue process is the means by which the decision is taken as to whether an either-way offence is tried by the magistrates' court or sent to the Crown Court for trial by jury. Amended by the Criminal Procedure and Investigations Act 1996 to allow an indication of plea to be given, so that cases in

---

[152] (1991) 94 Cr App R 332.   [153] [1993] Crim LR 136.

which a guilty plea is forthcoming are not sent unnecessarily to the Crown Court, but retained at magistrates' courts level, significant further amendments have been made by the Criminal Justice Act 2003. These amendments are part of a strategy to retain more either-way offences at magistrates' court level. These provisions recognize the inextricable links between mode of trial and sentencing powers, and are designed to achieve fewer cases going to the Crown Court. The Royal Commission on Criminal Justice found[154] that Crown Courts were imposing sentences that were within the powers of the magistrates' court. The amended plea-before-venue system was not working as it should.[155] The early plea provisions introduced in 1996 were not overcoming some of the objections to, or reservations about, summary trial. The 2003 Act will, when fully in force, allow a suspect to seek an indication of likely sentence, so that he can gauge what is his likely fate if he pleads guilty. At the same time the sentencing powers of magistrates are to be extended,[156] committals for sentence largely abolished,[157] and magistrates allowed to take into account previous convictions of the defendant.[158] By this combination of measures it is hoped to achieve a greater number of guilty pleas and significantly reduce the number of cases going to the Crown Court, with a consequent cost saving.

Procedure

Before any evidence is called, a magistrates' court before whom a person aged 17 or over appears charged with an offence triable either way must adopt the following procedure.

(1) If the prosecution is being carried on by the Attorney-General, the Solicitor-General, or the Director of Public Prosecutions and he applies for the offence to be tried on indictment, then it must be tried in that way and the case sent for trial. In any other case the following steps apply.

(2) The court must first cause the charge to be written down, if this has not already been done, and read to the accused.

(3) The court must explain to the defendant in ordinary language that he may indicate whether (if the offence were to proceed to trial) he would plead guilty or not guilty (1980 Act, section 17A).

(4) The defendant must also be warned that if he indicates that he intends to plead guilty, the court will proceed to summary trial.

(5) If the defendant does indicate he would plead guilty, then the court must proceed to summary trial with, of course, the power to commit for sentence

---

[154] *Op cit*, para 6.12, relying on research conducted by Hedderman and Moxon, *Magistrates' Court or Crown Court? Mode of Trial Decisions and Sentencing*, Home Office Research Study No 125 (HMSO, 1992).

[155] See also Herbert, 'Mode of Trial and Magistrates' Courts Powers' [2003] Crim LR 315.

[156] Not yet in force: see p 268.   [157] See p 687.

[158] This is part of a wider theme of the 2003 Act in allowing a greater use of evidence of bad character at trial. See p 680.

that exists under section 3 of the Powers of Criminal Courts (Sentencing) Act 2000,[159] although if the court has given an indication of sentence (see below), this is a power that is unlikely to be used often. This indication of plea does not indicate the formal taking of a plea (1980 Act, section 17A(9)). Thus, if the accused indicates that he intends to plead not guilty, then, if the case is committed for trial, it is necessary for a formal plea to be taken in the Crown Court.

(6) If the accused indicates that his intention is to plead not guilty, then the magistrates' court proceeds to determine mode of trial, in accordance with the procedure set out below (section 18 of the 1980 Act, as amended).

(7) The prosecutor and then the accused are given an opportunity to make representations as to which mode of trial would be more suitable. The prosecutor will be invited to give details of the defendant's previous convictions (1980 Act, section 19(2)).[160]

(8) The court then considers whether the offence appears more suitable for summary trial or for trial on indictment, having regard to the representations referred to in (7) above, to the nature of the case, whether the circumstances make the offence one of a serious character, whether the punishment that a magistrates' court would have power to inflict for it would be adequate, and 'any other circumstances which appear to the court to make it more suitable for the offence to be tried in one way rather than the other'.[161] The court must also have regard to the Allocation Guidelines.[162] These Allocation Guidelines, replacing the pre-existing Mode of Trial Guidelines, are intended to promote consistency in decisions made as to mode of trial.[163]

(9) If, following consideration as above, it appears to the court that the offence is more suitable for trial on indictment, then it must tell the defendant that it has so decided and will then proceed to send the case for trial, the defendant having no power to prevent this course even if neither he nor the prosecution has requested it.

(10) If, on the other hand, it appears to the court that the offence is 'more suitable for summary trial', then the court must explain to the defendant in ordinary language that he can either consent to summary trial or, if he wishes, be tried by a jury. Magistrates' courts have increasingly limited powers to commit to the Crown Court for sentence, if, having dealt with the case summarily, they

---

[159] A new s 3 is substituted for the pre-existing provision, by Sch 3, para 22, Criminal Justice Act 2003. For committal for sentence, see p 687.

[160] As substituted by Criminal Justice Act 2003, Sch 3. This provision amounts to a change from the pre-existing position: see *R v Colchester Justices, ex parte North Essex Building Co Ltd* [1977] 3 All ER 567; *R v Doncaster Magistrates' Court, ex parte Goulding* [1993] 1 All ER 435; *R v South Hackney Juvenile Court, ex parte RB and C* (1983) 4 Cr App R 294.

[161] 1980 Act, s 19(4).   [162] See also p 616.   [163] Criminal Justice Act 2003, s 170(5).

consider their sentencing powers inadequate.[164] The magistrates' court must inform the defendant of that power. Those powers have mostly been abolished by the Criminal Justice Act 2003,[165] the power to commit to be (when the provision is brought into force) under a new section 3A of the Powers of Criminal Court (Sentencing) Act 2000, introduced by the 2003 Act. This will permit committal for sentence only if the defendant is found convicted of a 'specified offence'.[166] The effect of this is that once a magistrates' court accepts jurisdiction it must, in most cases, sentence the defendant, if convicted, within its own sentencing powers, reducing the number of cases that end up at the Crown Court.

(11) After explaining to the defendant his options, the court must ask him whether he consents to be tried summarily or wishes to be tried in the Crown Court. Before making his choice, the defendant may (when a new section 20 of the 1980 Act is fully brought into force)[167] ask the court for an indication of likely sentence. The rationale for this new provision is that if the defendant receives an indication of likely sentence, particularly if it amounts to a statement that the defendant does not face a custodial sentence, he may be more willing to accept summary trial and not exercise his right to elect for jury trial. Again, this is part of the overall strategy of reducing jury trial.

A court is not bound to give such an indication, and some courts may be unwilling in the early stages of operation of the new provisions to do so. An indication is not the taking of a plea,[168] and a defendant may elect trial by jury, or maintain his initial not guilty plea if the indication is one that is not favourable to him.

The defendant may, after the indication of likely sentence, reconsider his initial indication of plea. If he does, he will again be invited to give such an indication (1980 Act, section 20(5), (6)). The court will then deal with the mode of trial issues in the way outlined above.

(12) If the defendant consents to summary trial, the magistrates proceed to try him; if he does not consent, they deal with matters such as bail and send him for trial (see below).

There are provisions in section 25 of the 1980 Act whereby the magistrates may change from summary trial to proceed to decline jurisdiction. Where the court has begun to try an either-way offence summarily, it may, at any time before the conclusion of the evidence for the prosecution, discontinue the summary trial and proceed to send for trial. This will necessitate starting all over again and the court must adjourn the hearing, and is not required to remand the defendant.

---

[164] Powers of Criminal Courts (Sentencing) Act 2000, s 3.
[165] Schedule 3. That provision is not yet in force.
[166] See, further, p 687.   [167] Introduced by Sch 3, Criminal Justice Act 2003.
[168] 1980 Act, s 20A(4), not yet in force.

The defendant must usually be present in court in person during the proceedings at which the mode of trial is determined.[169] However, the court may proceed in the absence of the defendant if it considers that, by reason of his disorderly conduct before it, it is not practicable for the proceedings to be conducted in his presence. In addition, where the defendant is represented by counsel or a solicitor who in his absence signifies to the court the defendant's consent to the proceedings for determining how he is to be tried for the offence being conducted in his absence, and the court is satisfied that there is good reason for proceeding in the absence of the defendant, then the court may proceed in the defendant's absence.[170] In either case the consents required either to summary trial may be given by the defendant's counsel or solicitor.[171]

Factors that influence the mode of trial

It has been noted that, in respect of 'either-way' offences, the mode of trial is determined both by the magistrates' court and by the defendant. Magistrates were given specific guidance as to how these powers should be used by the National Mode of Trial Guidelines, and, now, the Allocation Guidelines.[172] Certain key principles apply:[173]

(a) the court should never make a decision on the ground of convenience or expedition;

(b) the court should assume that the prosecution version of the facts is correct;

(c) the fact that the offences are specimen charges is relevant; by contrast, the fact that the defendant will be asking for other offences to be taken into consideration is not;

(d) where complex questions of fact, or difficult points of law, arise, the court should consider sending for trial;[174]

(e) where two or more defendants are jointly charged with an offence, each has an individual right to elect his mode of trial;

(f) either-way offences should be tried summarily unless the particular case has one of the specified features, and the court considers that its sentencing powers are insufficient;

(g) the court should consider its power to commit for sentence if evidence arises during the course of the hearing that leads the court to conclude that the offence is so serious, or the offender such a risk to the public, that its powers to sentence him are inadequate.[175]

---

[169] 1980 Act, s 18(2).   [170] Ibid, ss 18(3), 23(1).   [171] Ibid, s 23(3), (4).

[172] See p 614.

[173] See Magistrates' Courts Act 1980, s 19, and the various guidelines set out as the mode of trial decisions.

[174] Committals for trial (the phrase used by the Practice Direction) are generally abolished by Criminal Justice Act 2003, Sch 3 (not yet in force). Cases will usually either be sent or transferred for trial.

[175] But note that the power to commit for sentence is heavily restricted by the provisions of Criminal Justice Act 2003 (not yet in force). See pp 288 and 687.

Court bail

The nature of bail

A person is 'granted bail' when he is released from the custody of the law subject to a duty to surrender to custody at some future time. The 'custody' is the custody of a court unless bail was granted by a police officer, in which event it is the custody of the officer. Considerable changes in the law were effected by the Bail Act 1976, which gave effect to many, although not all, of the recommendations of a Home Office Working Party Report[176] that identified the deficiencies of the old law. Previously, bail involved entering into a 'recognizance', which is an acknowledgement of a debt to the Queen payable on default of compliance with the conditions of the recognizance. The 1976 Act abolished personal recognizances from the defendant but preserved them for sureties (where these are required). If granted bail, the defendant is under a duty to surrender to custody when required; if he fails without reasonable cause to do so, he commits an offence under section 6(1) of the 1976 Act, punishable either on summary conviction or as a contempt of court.[177]

Bail may be granted either unconditionally or, in some circumstances, subject to conditions. Before any conditions can be imposed it must appear to the court that such conditions are necessary to prevent a failure to surrender to custody, to prevent the commission of an offence while on bail, to prevent interference with witnesses or an obstruction of the course of justice, or to allow inquiries or reports to be made to assist the court in dealing with him for the offence.[178] A court, in the future, may also impose a condition on a defendant for his own protection or welfare, irrespective of the age of the defendant.[179] These factors are, in fact, similar to those a court may rely upon in refusing bail where the court believes that 'substantial grounds' to believe that any of them apply exist,[180] and in *R* v *Mansfield Justices, ex parte Sharkey*[181] it was argued that 'substantial grounds' likewise had to exist before a court could impose conditions. This argument was rejected by the Court of Appeal. It was enough that a court considered that there was a real and not fanciful risk of an offence being committed whilst the defendant was on bail. In this case, the justices were entitled to impose conditions preventing the defendants from picketing or demonstrating at places other than their own places of work, during a major industrial dispute in the coal industry and where the court knew that disturbances at coal pits had occurred.

Where conditions can be imposed, they may cover a wide variety of matters. They may comprise: the provision of a surety or sureties to secure the person's surrender to custody; the provision of security (if it appears that he is unlikely to remain in Great Britain until the time appointed for him to surrender to custody); and requirements

---

[176] *Bail Procedures in Magistrates' Courts* (HMSO, 1974).
[177] Bail Act 1976, s 3(2).   [178] Ibid, s 3(6).
[179] Bail Act 1976, s 3, as amended by Criminal Justice Act 2003, s 13.
[180] Ibid, Sch 1, para 1.   [181] [1985] QB 613, [1985] 1 All ER 193.

to secure that he surrenders to custody, does not commit any offence while on bail, does not interfere with witnesses or otherwise obstruct the course of justice or make himself available for the purpose of enabling inquiries or a report to be made to assist the court in dealing with him for the offence.[182] A court can also impose a condition requiring a defendant to attend an interview with a legal representative.[183] Failure to obtain legal advice or representation is one of the most common reasons for delay, because the necessary steps to enable the case to proceed have not been taken. What is clear is that any condition must be necessary and proportionate, because the restriction of liberty invokes Convention rights under Article 5 and Article 8, and thus the restrictions must be justifiable.[184] Conditions commonly imposed include conditions of residence, as to surrender of passport, reporting to a police station at prescribed times, not visiting specified premises, and not approaching specified persons. Such conditions can be onerous in their effect. They can be varied by a court on the application of the person bailed, the prosecutor or a constable. In addition, section 16 of the Criminal Justice Act 2003 confers a right of appeal to the Crown Court against certain conditions. These are:

(a) that the person reside away from a particular place or area;

(b) that the person resides at a particular place other than a bail hostel;

(c) for the provision of a surety or the giving of a security;

(d) that the person concerned remains indoors between certain hours;

(e) requirements in respect of electronic monitoring;

(f) that the person makes no contact with another person.

The Crown Court may vary any such condition, a power that previously belonged to the High Court. Presumably, it is open to the Crown Court to vary conditions by deleting a condition entirely, or by adding new, alternative conditions.

Occasions for the grant of bail

The question of when bail may be granted to a person may arise at various stages of his case, from the moment that he is arrested to the final determination of any appeal arising out of his conviction. Bail in cases of treason can only be granted by order of a High Court judge or the Home Secretary.[185] We have also noted the powers of the police regarding bail. In the context of the courts, bail may be granted as follows.

---

[182] Bail Act 1976. These conditions may now be imposed not only by a court but also by a police officer. In murder cases, unless satisfactory reports on the defendant's mental condition have already been obtained, the court must impose as conditions of bail: (a) a requirement that the defendant shall undergo examination by two medical practitioners for the purpose of enabling such reports to be prepared; and (b) a requirement that he shall for that purpose attend such an institution or place as the court directs (ibid, s 3(6A)).

[183] Crime and Disorder Act 1998, s 54(2).   [184] See p 197.

[185] Magistrates' Courts Act 1980, s 41.

By magistrates

Magistrates have power to grant bail at various stages of proceedings, subject to certain restrictions. When a defendant is first brought before a magistrates' court charged with an offence, it quite often happens that the prosecution is not ready to proceed, in which event the proceedings are adjourned and the accused is remanded, either in custody or on bail. This may arise in the course of summary proceedings or where the offence is triable only on indictment (in which event the magistrates will eventually send the case for trial) or where it is triable 'either way'.[186] If magistrates decide to send a defendant to the Crown Court for trial, that sending for trial may be in custody or on bail.[187] Following summary conviction, the magistrates have (now) limited power to commit the defendant to the Crown Court for sentence.[188] If they do so, they may commit in custody or on bail.[189] Finally, following conviction, if the magistrates adjourn for the purpose of considering sentence, they may remand the defendant on bail or in custody[190] and, having imposed a custodial sentence, they may, if a person has given notice of appeal or applied to the magistrates to state a case,[191] grant bail.[192]

If bail is refused on a remand, the maximum period of remand is eight clear days[193] unless the accused is already serving a custodial sentence, in which event it is twenty-eight clear days.[194] There may, of course, be further remands thereafter.[195]

Where magistrates adjourn a summary trial, or the determination of the method of trial of any either-way offence and remand the defendant in custody, they may, if the defendant is an adult, order that he be brought up for any subsequent remands before an alternative magistrates' court nearer to the prison where he is to be confined on remand. If the defendant's presence is required, this may be achievable through a live television link.[196] This is, again, designed to reduce delays—in this instance delays that arise where escorted prisoners arrive late at court.

Although successive applications for bail may be made to a magistrates' court (or to any court having power to grant bail), the Bail Act 1976 restricts the scope for continued applications. If bail has been refused, a second application for bail can be supported with any argument that is desired, whether or not put before the court before. At any subsequent hearings the court need not hear arguments as to fact or law that it has heard previously.[197]

---

[186] See p 608.   [187] Bail Act 1976, s 6(3).   [188] See p 687.

[189] See the terms of ss 3A and 4 of the Powers of Criminal Courts (Sentencing) Act 2000, as amended by Criminal Justice Act 2003.

[190] Magistrates' Courts Act 1980, s 128(1). If the remand is for medical examination and report, it must not be for more than three weeks, if in custody; for four weeks, if on bail; and, if on bail, conditions as to undertaking medical examination must be imposed (ibid, s 30).

[191] See pp 256 and 688.   [192] Magistrates' Courts Act 1980, s 113.

[193] Ibid, s 128(6): 'clear days' means omitting the day of the remand and the day fixed for the appearance. In certain circumstances, this may be exceeded—see 1980 Act, s 128A. The key condition is that a previous remand must have been made.

[194] 1980 Act, s 131(1).   [195] Ibid, s 129(1).

[196] Crime and Disorder Act 1998, s 57.

[197] Even if refused bail on remand, a defendant is entitled to have his right to bail fully reviewed at the stage of sending for trial: *R v Reading Crown Court, ex parte Malik* [1981] QB 451, [1981] 1 All ER 249.

By the Crown Court

The Crown Court may grant bail to any person:[198]

(a) who has been committed in custody for appearance (trial or sentence) before the Crown Court; or

(b) who is in custody pursuant to a sentence imposed by a magistrates' court and has appealed against conviction or sentence; or

(c) who is in the custody of the Crown Court pending the disposal of his case by the Crown Court; or

(d) who, after the decision of the Crown Court in his case, has applied to the Crown Court to state a case for the High Court;[199] or

(e) who has applied to the High Court for an order of certiorari, or for leave to apply, in respect of proceedings in the Crown Court;[200] or

(f) to whom the Crown Court has granted a certificate under the Criminal Appeal Act 1968 (case fit for appeal); or

(g) who has been remanded in custody by a magistrates' court, where he has been refused bail by that court after hearing full argument.

The prosecution also has some rights of appeal against the grant of bail, first introduced in 1993,[201] in respect of an offence punishable by imprisonment for a term of five years or more. That has been changed to extend to any offence punishable with imprisonment,[202] a change designed to overcome the problem of mistaken grant of bail at a time when it can be rectified. For this right to exist the prosecution must have objected to bail at the hearing before the magistrates' court, and has to show that there is a risk to the public of serious harm if the defendant is bailed. The appeal is by way of rehearing.[203] The Crown Court may remand the defendant in custody or on bail subject to such conditions as it thinks fit.

By the High Court

Hitherto, an appeal against a magistrates' court withholding bail, or the imposition of conditions, lay to the High Court. That jurisdiction has largely been abolished.[204]

By the Court of Appeal

The Court of Appeal has power to grant bail pending appeal to that court or pending a retrial ordered by that court following such an appeal[205] or pending appeal from that

---

[198] Supreme Court Act 1981, s 81 (as amended).   [199] See p 688.

[200] This only applies to appellate proceedings in the Crown Court, because whilst it is sitting as a court of first instance it is not amenable to judicial review: see p 256.

[201] Bail (Amendment) Act 1993.   [202] Criminal Justice Act 2003, s 16.

[203] For the relevant procedure, see Supreme Court Act 1981, s 18(2). Where notice of appeal is given orally, the magistrates' court must remand the defendant in custody pending hearing of the appeal.

[204] See Criminal Justice Act 2004, s 17. For the original jurisdiction, see Criminal Justice Act 1967, s 22, as amended by Bail Act 1976, Sch 2.

[205] Criminal Appeal Act 1968, ss 8(2), 19; the power may be exercised by a single judge (ibid, ss 31, 45(2)).

court to the Supreme Court.[206] It is rare for the Court of Appeal to grant bail, but it occasionally does so: for example, where the sentence appealed against is a short one so that it might be served by the time the appeal comes on for hearing, or where there is a strong prima facie likelihood of success.[207]

The right to bail

The marginal note to section 4 of the Bail Act 1976 is 'General right to bail of accused persons and others' (the 'others' being persons who are brought up for breach of the requirements of certain community orders,[208] or persons who have been remanded following conviction for reports). The section created a statutory presumption in favour of granting bail and provides that, except as provided in Schedule 1 to the Act, bail shall be granted to a person who appears before a magistrates' court or the Crown Court in the course of or in connection with proceedings or who applies for bail in connection with proceedings. It does not apply (save in the case of remand for reports) after conviction.

The right to bail was restricted by section 25 of the Criminal Justice and Public Order Act 1994, which originally provided that a person charged with, or convicted of, murder, attempted murder, manslaughter, rape, or attempted rape must not be granted bail. This provision, intended to prevent repeat offences being committed by a person whilst on bail, was introduced despite the lack of clear empirical evidence that it was needed. It is now being modified, to restore an element of discretion in the hands of the court. Section 56 of the Crime and Disorder Act 1998 modified this to permit a grant of bail where 'exceptional circumstances' exist. The Act carefully avoided defining what might be regarded as exceptional circumstances.

Schedule 1 contains detailed provisions relating to circumstances in which bail may justifiably be withheld. The wider Human Rights Act context should not be overlooked. Article 5 of the Convention does indeed permit the deprivation of liberty, but the presumption is in favour of liberty and the state must show that there are 'relevant and sufficient' reasons to justify detention.[209] The period of pre-trial detention must be limited to a reasonable period of time, the public interest in detention must be balanced with the presumption of innocence, and the withholding of bail must be based on individual circumstances and not stereotypes.[210] There is a need to balance the competing interests in preventing interference with the administration of justice, preservation of public order, and the need to protect the defendant. It is in this context that the following grounds permitting refusal of bail, and in some cases

---

[206] Ibid, s 36. By s 37, if the prosecutor is appealing to the Supreme Court and, but for the decision of the Court of Appeal, the appellant would be liable to be detained, the Court of Appeal may make an order providing for his detention or directing that he shall not be released except on bail; there is similar provision on prosecution appeals from the Queen's Bench Divisional Court (Administration of Justice Act 1960, s 5).

[207] *R v Wattam* (1978) 68 Cr App R 293.

[208] See s 4(3), as amended by Criminal Justice Act 1991.

[209] *Letellier* v *France* (1991) 14 EHRR 83.

[210] *Yagci and Sargan* v *Turkey* (1995) 20 EHRR 505; *A* v *France* [1999] 17 EHRR 462.

the presumption against bail, must be judged. These vary according to whether the accused is charged with an 'imprisonable offence' or a 'non-imprisonable offence'— that is, whether or not the offence is punishable with imprisonment (even if the accused himself, for example by reason of his age, would not be liable to be imprisoned for it).

Refusal of bail for non-imprisonable offences

If the offence is non-imprisonable, the only circumstances in which bail may be withheld are:

(1) if the defendant having previously been granted bail, has failed to comply with his obligation to surrender to custody and the court believes that he would so fail again;

(2) if the court is satisfied that the defendant should be kept in custody for his own protection or, if he is a child or young person, for his own welfare;

(3) if he is already in custody pursuant to a court sentence;[211]

(4) if, having been granted bail in the instant proceedings, he has been arrested for absconding or breaking the conditions of his bail.[212]

Refusal of bail for imprisonable offences

If the offence is imprisonable, there is a much wider range of circumstances in which bail may be justifiably withheld, in addition to those listed above.[213] These provisions were significantly amended by the Criminal Justice Act 2003 in the light of research conducted for the White Paper *Justice for All*, which showed that some 18 per cent of adults and 38 per cent of under-18s, and 12 per cent of all those bailed subsequently fail to attend court or offend whilst on bail.[214] The Auld Review[215] reported police disenchantment at the lack of CPS vigour (as it was perceived) in respect of those who abscond, or reoffend, and are later granted bail. The amended Schedule 1 to the Bail Act 1976 addresses some of these issues. A court may refuse bail in the following circumstances:

(5) the court is satisfied that there are substantial grounds for believing that the defendant, if released on bail (whether subject to conditions or not) would:

  (a) fail to surrender to custody; or

  (b) commit an offence while on bail; or

  (c) interfere with witnesses or otherwise obstruct the course of justice;

(6) where it has not been practicable for want of time to obtain sufficient information to enable the court to make its decision;

---

[211] Or a sentence of an authority acting under the Armed Forces Act 1996 (or its predecessors).
[212] Bail Act 1976, Sch 1, Part II.   [213] Ibid, Sch 1, Part I.
[214] *Justice for All*, at ch 3.   [215] *Op cit*, p 429, para 81.

(7) where a case is adjourned for inquiries or report and it appears that it would be impracticable to complete the inquiries or make the report without keeping the defendant in custody.

In considering the grounds referred to under (5) above, the court must have regard to the nature and seriousness of the offence or default, the character, antecedents, associations, and community ties of the defendant, the defendant's record in relation to fulfilling his obligations under previous grants of bail in criminal proceedings, the strength of the evidence against him, and any other considerations that appear to be relevant.[216] A further restriction was introduced into Schedule 1 in 1994[217] in an attempt to reduce the incidence of offending by persons on bail. In 1993, a study conducted by the Metropolitan Police showed that some 40 per cent of suspects arrested in one week were already on bail.[218] Further amendments made by the 2003 Act mean that a court must 'give weight' to the fact that the defendant is already on bail when assessing whether there is a substantial risk that the defendant would commit a further offence if released on bail.[219] This applies in respect of a person accused of any imprisonable offence. It effectively amounts to a presumption against bail. A court should rebail such a defendant only if it is satisfied that there is no significant risk of committing an offence whilst on bail. It is by no means certain that this presumption complies in all circumstances with Article 5 of the Convention. As the Parliamentary Joint Committee observed in 2003:[220]

> . . . the court would be prevented from granting bail in at least some circumstances even though it is not satisfied that there is a sufficient public interest in detaining the defendant pending trial . . . In some cases (for example, where a minor offence has been committed and the defendant poses no real risk to the community) the court would be prevented from granting bail where detaining the defendant in custody would be self-evidently disproportionate to any purpose, and in other cases it might be clear that the public interest in detaining the defendant is outweighed by other considerations . . . [such as] the other Convention rights of the defendant, members of his or her family or other dependants . . .

Further, section 15 of the 2003 Act requires a court to refuse to bail an adult defendant who fails without reasonable cause to answer bail in the same proceedings unless the court is satisfied that there is no significant risk that the defendant would fail to surrender if released on bail. In respect of juveniles there is no such presumption against bail, but the fact of absconding is a relevant fact for the court to consider in deciding whether there is a substantial risk that the juvenile would fail to surrender to bail.

Further restrictions on bail are contained in Schedule 1 to the Bail Act 1976.[221] First, there are a range of measures introduced to address the issue of drug-taking and

---

[216] Schedule 1, para 9.   [217] Criminal Justice and Public Order Act 1994, s 26.
[218] Debates in 1994 Act, Mr Robert McLennan MP, HC Cmttee.
[219] Bail Act 1976, Sch 1, Part I, para 2A, inserted by Criminal Justice Act 2003, s 14.
[220] Cited by Ward and Davies, *op cit*, at para 3.30.
[221] Inserted by Criminal Justice Act 2003, s 19; Criminal Justice and Immigration Act 2008.

drug-related crime. A court may deny bail, unless the court is satisfied that there is no significant risk of reoffending whilst on bail, or the defendant declines to take up the offer of a 'relevant assessment' in respect of his drug-taking, or, having agreed to one, fails to comply with it. In order for this power to exist:

(a) the defendant must be aged 18 or over;

(b) the presence in his body of Class A drugs must have been detected;

(c) either he has been charged with an offence under section 5(2) or 5(3) of the Misuse of Drugs Act 1971, or the court is satisfied that his misuse of Class A drugs caused or contributed to his behaviour, or his offending was wholly or partly motivated by his intended misuse of a Class A drug.

The Act[222] contains detailed provisions for recording the decisions of both courts and police officers in relation to bail and entitling defendants to copies of records of such decisions. Where a court withholds bail or imposes or varies conditions of bail in the case of a person who has a 'right to bail' in criminal proceedings, it must give reasons and these are recorded with the record of the decision.[223]

Secondly, the Criminal Justice and Immigration Act 2008 limits the circumstances in which a person may be refused bail in cases in which there is an imprisonable summary offence. It does so by inserting a new Part 1A of Schedule 1 to the Bail Act 1976 and extends the right of the court to refuse bail where there is a risk of failing to answer to bail, along with three further grounds covering the perceived risk of offending on bail resulting in injury, insufficient information being available to the court to make the bail decision, and exceptions applicable to drug users in certain areas.

Sureties

As already noted, the 1976 Act abolished personal recognizances from defendants (although a person may be required to provide security[224]). Recognizances still exist, however, in relation to sureties; these are persons who are sometimes colloquially said to 'stand bail' for the accused. If a person is granted bail subject to the provision of sureties, the court must fix the amounts of the sureties and must also be satisfied that the proposed sureties are suitable having regard to their financial resources, character, and any previous convictions and proximity (whether in point of kinship, place of residence, or otherwise) to the defendant.[225] In practice courts are usually guided by the police in matters relating to the suitability of proposed sureties.

Before sureties are taken it is the practice to explain the nature of the obligations being undertaken so as to ensure that the proposed surety understands them and

---

[222] Bail Act 1976, s 5.   [223] Ibid, s 5(3), (4).

[224] Hitherto limited to persons unlikely to remain in the United Kingdom, but, now, see Crime and Disorder Act 1998, s 54.

[225] Ibid, s 8(2).

to warn of the consequences of the defendant failing to answer to his bail. These are, prima facie, forfeiture of the amount of the recognizance and possible imprisonment in default. The court has power to order the surety, in the event of default by the defendant, to forfeit the whole of the amount of the recognizance or part thereof.[226] Before exercising its discretion the court must, in some circumstances,[227] give the surety the opportunity to be heard and must take into account circumstances relating either to means or to the surety's culpability for the non-appearance of the defendant that might make it fair and just for the surety not to be ordered to forfeit the whole amount of the recognizance. Although not decisive, the conduct of the surety will be an important factor in the decision of the court as to whether or not to order forfeiture, either in whole or in part. In *R v Southampton Justices, ex parte Green*,[228] Lord Denning MR stated that if the surety was guilty of no want of diligence and used every effort to secure the appearance of the accused, it might be proper to remit the sum entirely. Imprisonment may be ordered in default of payment, of up to twelve months.

It is an offence, punishable on summary conviction or as a contempt of court, to agree to indemnify a surety in criminal proceedings (or, in the case of the surety himself, to be indemnified).[229]

An order of the Crown Court entreating the recognizance of a surety for a defendant who has failed to surrender to his bail to stand trial is not a 'matter relating to trial on indictment' (within section 29(3) of the Supreme Court Act 1981) so that the order is subject to judicial review.[230]

KEY ISSUE

The presumption in favour of bail can sometimes cause problems. The incidence of the commission of offences by a defendant whilst on bail has led to the attempts, discussed above, to limit the powers of courts to grant or refuse bail. This in turn can cause unfairness where the prohibition or restriction on the grant of bail is not appropriate. A key issue is whether the law should restrict the right of a court to grant or refuse bail in any way. Arguably, the matter should be dealt with on an individual basis by the court granting bail.

 Questions

1. What restrictions are there on a court?

2. Are those restrictions fair?

---

[226] Magistrates' Courts Act 1980, s 120(3).
[227] See Crime and Disorder Act 1998: where recognizances not conditioned for the appearance of the defendant, the court is not bound.
[228] [1976] QB 11, [1975] 2 All ER 1073.   [229] Bail Act 1976, s 9.
[230] *Re Smalley* [1985] AC 622; *sub nom Smalley v Crown Court at Warwick* [1985] 1 All ER 769.

Further reading

Ashworth and Redmayne, *The Criminal Process* (Oxford University Press: 4th edn, 2010)

Auld, *Review of the Criminal Courts of England & Wales* (**www.criminal-courts-review. org.uk**) (the 'Auld Review')

Glidewell, *Review of the Crown Prosecution Service* (HMSO, 1988)

James Committee, *The Distribution of Criminal Business between the Crown Court and the Magistrates' Court*, Cmnd 6323 (HMSO, 1988)

Trial

19

INTRODUCTION

Although the proportion of cases that are actually tried by this method is small, trial on indictment indicates the real nature of the criminal trial, and it is the procedure adopted in serious cases tried by judge and jury. This chapter will examine the nature of trial on indictment, looking specifically at:

- how cases are sent for trial by the magistrates' court to the Crown Court;
- the duties of disclosure that the law places on both prosecution and defence, and how disclosure may be resisted;
- the problems that expert evidence creates;
- long trials and the difficulties they cause;
- the procedure to be followed at trial;
- the protections for defendants.

Commital, sending, and transfer for trial

Introduction

The first stage of the trial of an indictable offence has, in recent legal history, been the committal for trial, or, as it was sometimes known, the preliminary inquiry before justices. Increasingly this has been only of a formal nature. Over the years the nature of committal for trial has significantly changed, with numerous legislative attempts to change its nature and purpose: indeed, the whole legislative history might be regarded as a case study into governmental and legislative indecision. Now, cases are sent or committed for trial in accordance with procedures that were significantly changed by the Criminal Justice Act 2003. Committal hearings that consider the evidences, which were routine under the old law, have largely been abolished.[1] . The result is that proccedings are largely formal.

---

[1] Up until the bringing into force of the provisions of Sch 3 to the Criminal Justice Act 2003, either-way offences to be tried in the Crown Court were committed for trial, without consideration of the evidence.

The current procedure is based largely on that introduced by the Crime and Disorder Act 1998 as amended, particularly by the Criminal Justice Act 2003. The 1998 Act abolished committal proceedings in cases in which an adult is charged with an indictable-only offence.[2] Instead a scheme was introduced that basically requires service of the prosecution case in writing, followed by an opportunity for the defendant to make an application to the Crown Court for the case to be dismissed. Such an application may in some circumstances be an oral application. This new procedure now governs cases of serious or complex fraud, or those that involved children, in indictable-only cases, which before had been within the notice of transfer procedures.[3]

As noted above, the Criminal Justice Act 2003 made further changes.[4] The changes were intended to give effect to the recommendations of the Auld Review and the White Paper *Justice for All*, to create greater speed and efficiency in the handling of criminal cases. Their effect is to provide for common offences (that is, those linked together) and linked offenders to be sent to the Crown Court automatically. The court will not have to wait for committal papers to be prepared, although arraignment in the Crown Court will not occur until service of the prosecution's evidence, normally within forty-two days.[5]

The effect of all of these changes has been to achieve a scheme not dissimilar from that recommended by the Royal Commission on Criminal Justice, with three distinct processes:

(a) the automatic transfer to the Crown Court of cases of an adult that include an indictable-only offence;

(b) committal proceedings in respect of most either-way offences; on the coming into force of Schedule 3 of the Criminal Justice Act 2003 the sending for trial procedure described at (a) above will apply to some either-way offences;

(c) the notice of transfer procedures contained in the Criminal Justice Acts of 1987 and 1991, when they apply, in cases other than indictable-only offences.

Procedure

Indictable-only offences

Under the provisions contained in the Crime and Disorder Act 1998, where an adult is charged with an indictable-only offence (other than one to which the transfer for trial provisions apply) he must be sent forthwith to the Crown Court.[6] The person

---

[2] 1998 Act, ss 51–52, and Sch 3.

[3] For the detailed provisions relating to which offences are subject to this procedure, see Criminal Justice Act 1987, s 4 and Criminal Justice Act 1988, s 32(2).

[4] Not yet fully in force

[5] Crime and Disorder Act (Service of Prosecution Evidence) Regulations 2000, SI 2000/3305.

[6] 1998 Act, ss 51–52 and Sch 3. When in force, s 51 will be as substituted by the Criminal Justice Act 2003, Sch 3, para 18. See Criminal Procedure Rules 2010, Part 12 (CPR). For CPR generally, see p 581.

committed will be committed also in respect of any either-way offences or summary offences with which he is also charged that:

(a) appear to the court to be related to the indictable-only offence; and

(b) in the case of summary offences, are punishable with imprisonment or involve obligatory or discretionary disqualification from driving.[7] A summary offence is related to an indictable-only offence if it arises out of circumstances that are the same as, or connected with, those giving rise to the indictable-only offence.[8] In cases in which an adult is jointly charged with an either-way offence that appears to be related to the indictable-only offence he also must be sent for trial. 'Related to' in this context means if the offence could be joined in the same indictment.[9] By contrast if a child or young person is jointly charged with that same indictable-only offence, the court may send for trial, but is not required to do so.

A person who has been sent for trial under the 1998 Act is entitled to receive copies of the documents containing the evidence on which the charge or charges are based.[10] When he has received that evidence, and before arraignment, he may apply either orally (provided that he has given notice of intention to so) or in writing to the Crown Court sitting in the place specified, for the charge, or any of them, to be dismissed.[11] A defendant is only entitled to adduce oral evidence at such a hearing if he is granted leave to do so, and that will only be granted if it appears to the judge, having regard to any matters stated in the application for leave, that the interests of justice require him to do so. The 1998 Act contains detailed provisions that govern the power of the Crown Court to deal with any summary offence.[12] A Crown Court has the power to take a plea of guilty, but not to try such an offence if a plea of not guilty is entered. It can dismiss such a charge if the Crown Prosecution Service does not propose to offer evidence on that charge. A complex procedure applies where, for whatever reason, there ceases to be an indictable-only offence before the court, but an either-way offence remains. In such a case, following an inquiry as to the intended plea, the court has to decide whether trial on indictment or summary trial is more suitable.[13]

When a case is sent for trial the court must specify in a notice the offence or offences that are being sent, and the place at which defendant is to be tried.[14]

Either-way offences

The Criminal Justice Act 2003 substituted new provisions into the Crime and Disorder Act 1998. Cases will be sent for trial where there is an either-way offence that is related to an indictable-only offence. The court, having followed the normal procedure for determining mode of trial, must send the defendant for trial on that charge unless it is

[7] Ibid, s 51(2), (4), (6), (11).
[8] Ibid, s 51(11). When the 2003 Act is in force, the relevant provision is a new s 51E of the 1998 Act.
[9] For joinder of counts in an indictment, see p 647.   [10] Ibid, Sch 3, para 1. See CPR, Part 12.
[11] Ibid, para 2.   [12] Ibid, paras 5–6.   [13] Ibid, para 6.   [14] See p 632.

transferred for trial (see below). The sending for trial procedure is the same as that for indictable-only offences.

Notices of transfer

We have already noted that in certain cases involving serious or complex fraud, or children, the notice of transfer provisions that were contained in the Criminal Justice Act 1987 and Criminal Justice Act 1991 apply. The effect of the coming into force of provisions in the Crime and Disorder Act 1998[15] is that cases involving indictable-only cases of serious or complex that are indictable only are dealt with under the general sending for trial procedures described above. The transfer for trial provisions only now apply in the case of either-way offences that involve serious or complex fraud, or are offences against children.[16]

Voluntary bills of indictment

Historically there has been one way in which a case could reach the Crown Court without committal, sending or transfer for trial. By a procedure known as the voluntary bill procedure, the prosecution can apply to a High Court judge[17] for leave to prefer a bill of indictment against the accused. The judge in his discretion grants or refuses leave,[18] with the result that if leave is granted, the bill is preferred forthwith and there is no need for any proceedings. The defendant loses the advantage of knowing in advance the substance of the case against him. The applicant himself cannot attend unless permitted by the judge to do so, whilst the defendant is not entitled to attend at all. Even where there is a hearing it is not in open court.[19]

The use of this power has always been problematic[20] because it bypassed normal procedures and safeguards. To overcome this, the law now provides safeguards.[21] Except where there is good reason for doing otherwise, a defendant must receive notice of an application to seek a voluntary bill, with supporting documentation, and must have an opportunity to make representations, in writing, and, if desirable, orally. It is, though, exceptional, to be used only when the interests of justice rather than administrative convenience justify it. In one case,[22] the Director of Public Prosecutions had sought a voluntary bill of indictment when he was concerned at the failure of a youth court to commit a young person to the Crown Court

---

[15] Inserted by Criminal Justice Act 2003, Sch 3.

[16] See Criminal Justice Act 1987, s 4 and Criminal Justice Act 1988, s 32(2).

[17] A circuit judge has no power to grant leave to prefer a Bill of indictment: *R v Thompson* [1975] 2 All ER 1028, [1975] 1 WLR 1425.

[18] See, e.g., *Re Roberts* [1967] 1 WLR n474. The issue of a voluntary bill is not susceptible to judicial review: *R v Manchester Crown Court, ex parte Williams* (1990) 154 JP 589.

[19] See, generally, *R v Raymond* [1981] QB 910, [1981] 2 All ER 246, in which an attempt to challenge the validity of the voluntary bill procedure (on the grounds that it infringed standards of procedural fairness) was rejected by the Court of Appeal. Such conclusions might, now, have to be reconsidered in the light of the terms of Article 6 but, for the reasons stated in the body of the text, the issue is unlikely to arise.

[20] See, e.g., *Practice Direction* [1990] 1 WLR 633.

[21] *Consolidated Criminal Practice Direction* [2002] 1 WLR 2870, paras 35.5–35.6.

[22] *R (Director of Public Prosecutions) v Camberwell Youth Court* [2004] EWCA 1805, [2005] 1 Cr App R 6.

for sentence.[23] It was held that proceedings by way of judicial review[24] were more appropriate than seeking to obtain a voluntary bill of indictment.

Publicity

Following a well-publicized murder trial in which pre-trial publicity created a severe risk of prejudice to the trial itself,[25] restrictions on the reporting of committal proceedings were introduced in 1967,[26] and were then contained in the Magistrates' Courts Act 1980. Those provisions are now in turn replaced by those introduced into the Crime and Disorder Act 1998,[27] designed to reflect the regime described above. The effect of these provisions is that it is unlawful to publish anything other than the matters specified in section 52A(7) of the 1998 Act. These provide for the publication only of matters relating to identity

This limitation can be lifted by the court, although if the defendant objects, the court must consider such a course of action to be in the interests of justice.[28] In such cases any wider restrictions on reporting may come into effect.[29] Of course, the changes relating to the process of sending for trial (when fully in force) will reduce still further the need for these provisions.

Sending for trial

When a case is sent for trial, it will be in respect of the offences with which the defendant is charged, in accordance with the principles already discussed. The notice of sending for trial will specify those offences, and the place at which the defendant is to be tried. In the selection of the place of trial the court must have regard to the convenience of the defence, the prosecution, and the witnesses, the desirability of expediting the trial, and any direction given by or on behalf of the Lord Chief Justice in respect of location for trial.[30]

The structure of the Crown Court has already been discussed.[31] It is not a single court but sits in a number of different locations. These are described as first-tier, second-tier, and third-tier centres. First-tier centres deal with both civil and criminal cases and are visited by High Court and circuit judges; second-tier centres deal with criminal cases only but are visited by both High Court and circuit judges; while third-tier centres deal with criminal cases only and are visited only by circuit judges. Each circuit contains a number of each type of centre. Offences in turn are divided into four

---

[23] As to which, see, p 686.   [24] See Chapter 7.

[25] The trial of Dr John Bodkin Adams in 1957. Devlin J stated that it would have been far better if the preliminary proceedings were held in private.

[26] Criminal Justice Act 1967, implementing the recommendations of the Tucker Report, Cmnd 479 (HMSO, 1958).

[27] Crime and Disorder Act 1998, s 52A, introduced by Criminal Justice Act 2003, Sch 3, para 17. See CPR 2010, Part 10.

[28] 1998 Act, s 52A(2).   [29] See Chapter 10.

[30] 1998 Act, s 51D(4), inserted by Criminal Justice Act 2003, Sch 3, para 17. See CPR 2010, Part 12.

[31] See pp 261 and 631.

classes,[32] each containing a number of offences. Offences in Class 1 must normally be tried by a High Court judge although cases of murder may be released by the presiding judge for trial by a circuit judge approved for that purpose by the Lord Chief Justice. Offences in Class 2 must be tried by a High Court judge unless a presiding judge of the circuit releases any particular case for trial by a circuit judge or recorder; examples are manslaughter and rape. Offences in Class 3 may be tried by a High Court judge, or by a circuit judge or recorder; these are all offences triable only on indictment not falling within any other class.

Offences in Class 4 will normally be tried by a circuit judge or recorder, although they may also be tried by a High Court judge; examples are wounding or causing grievous bodily harm with intent, conspiracy, and all offences triable either way.

Therefore, when a magistrates' court sends for trial a person charged with any offence within Classes 1 or 2, it must specify, as the place of trial, the location of the Crown Court where a High Court judge regularly sits. In the case of an offence in Class 4, the magistrates' court must simply specify the most convenient location of the Crown Court. In selecting the most convenient location, the justices must have regard to the location of the Crown Court designated by the presiding judge as the location to which cases should normally be committed from their petty sessions area.[33] The magistrates will also need to have regard to whether live television link facilities exist, if this is likely to be necessary because of a special measures direction or for any other reason.[34]

The magistrates must consider whether to release the defendant on bail, or to send in custody. Factors that must be considered, including the imposition of conditions, have already been explained.[35]

Delay and time limits

Background

It has already been seen that the Prosecution of Offences Act 1985 imposes time limits upon the length of time for which an accused person may be held in custody.[36] The potential for delay to lead to application to stay the proceedings because of abuse of process also exists, although it will only be an exceptional case in which delay is likely to lead to a successful application.[37]

Trial within a reasonable time is one important characteristic of the right to a fair trial under Article 6. This is reflected in the fact that one of the key factors contained in the overriding objective in the Criminal Procedure Rules[38] is the importance of all parties dealing with the case efficiently and expeditiously.

---

[32] By the directions set out in *The Consolidated Practice Direction*.   [33] Ibid, para 3.
[34] See p 674.   [35] See p 621.   [36] See p 600.
[37] See p 601.   [38] Criminal Procedure Rules 2010, r 1.1(e). For the CPR generally, see p 581.

Delay is a particular matter of concern in criminal proceedings, leading to the potential for an unfair trial, because of the time between the event in question and the determination of guilt. It also prolongs the effect of the alleged crime on the victim, witnesses and, indeed, the defendant. It was because of increasing, and unacceptable, delays that the government in 1996 established the Narey Committee to review delays within the criminal justice system. The Narey Report was published in February 1997,[39] and contained some thirty-three different recommendations. These recommendations, discussed at the appropriate parts of this book,[40] ranged over a wide area, including the operation and powers of the CPS, the role of justices' clerks, limitations on trial by jury, abolition of committal proceedings in respect of indictable-only offences, changes to the pleas-and-direction hearing, and major changes to the youth justice system. Many of them, although not all, have been accepted and are the subject of implementation through legislative and administrative changes.[41] Many of the procedural changes made by the Criminal Justice Act 2003, including the revised provisions relating to charging and sending for trial, are based on proposals made by the Auld Review and the White Paper *Justice for All*, intended to create efficiency and reduce delay.

Time limits

One area of importance is the question of time limits under the 1985 Act. The effect of the custody time limits is that, if a defendant is in custody, proceedings need to be commenced within the prescribed limits. If, for whatever reason, delay occurs, the prosecution has to obtain an extension of time from the court under section 22(3) of the 1985 Act. The power to make regulations under section 22 of that Act permits time limits generally to be set and to provide sanctions for non-compliance. Power exists to extend the regulations beyond custody time limits. Section 40 of the Crime and Disorder Act 1998 confers a wider power to make regulations that govern different types of offence, of accused, or different areas of the country. Statutory time limits will be set for all non-custodial cases, both in relation to adults and to juveniles, although with tougher time limits in cases involving persistent young offenders, and young offenders on bail.[42] This latter proposal is part of the general reform of the youth justice system, with the objective of halving the time from arrest to sentence.[43] For adults, it is proposed that statutory time limits be set for the pre-trial stage of all proceedings, both indictable and summary, broken down into three stages: the first listing of the case to start of summary trial; first appearance to committal or transfer; committal or transfer to start of Crown Court trial. It is not intended to set time limits for the period between trial and conviction. To do so would, of course, place the fairness of proceedings in individual cases at risk.

---

[39] *Review of Delay in the Criminal Justice System* (HMSO, 27 February 1997).
[40] See Chapters 19, 20 and 22.   [41] See, in particular, Crime and Disorder Act 1998, ss 43–47.
[42] Ibid, s 41.   [43] See p 573.

Accompanying this extension of time-limit provision are changes in the rules governing enforcement, made by the Crime and Disorder Act 1988 and contained in the Prosecution of Offences Act 1985. Section 22(3) of the 1985 Act now provides that an extension of the time limit may be granted by a court, before the expiration of the time limit, provided that the court is satisfied that the need for the extension is due to:

(i) the illness or absence of the accused, a necessary witness, a judge or magistrate; or

(ii) a postponement that is occasioned by the ordering by the court of separate trials in the case of two or more accused; or

(iii) what is some other good and sufficient cause.

In addition the court will have to be satisfied that the prosecution has acted with all due diligence and expedition, which will be a question of fact for the court to consider in the context of the individual application and its effects. No extension of time limits will be needed in respect of periods during which the accused is unlawfully at large.[44] If, because of prosecution delay, proceedings are stayed, fresh proceedings may in some circumstances be commenced, in cases in which the stay is by a Crown Court, by the preferment of a voluntary Bill or indictment,[45] and in other cases by the laying of a new charge.[46]

Disclosure of evidence

Introduction

The effective working of the adversarial system depends, in part, upon proper disclosure.[47] Unlike in civil proceedings in which production and disclosure of evidence generally is available, the duties of pre-trial disclosure in criminal cases have in the past been limited. The prosecution has always been under a duty to disclose at the stage of committal, or to serve within a certain period in the case of sending for trial,[48] the evidence upon which it proposes to rely, subject only to the right to call additional evidence in some circumstances and subject to certain conditions.[49] Historically, a defendant has been under no general duty to disclose his defence. A defendant, or a suspect, in criminal proceedings, has a 'right of silence'. This 'right of silence'[50] has traditionally permitted the defence at any stage to adduce evidence without notice,

---

[44] Ibid, s 40(5).   [45] See p 630.   [46] See s 40.

[47] See p 578. and note, in particular, *R* v *McIlkenny* [1992] 2 All ER 417.

[48] See Crime and Disorder (Service of Prosecution Evidence) Regulations 2000, SI 2000/3305. The specified period thereunder is forty-two days, although authorities conflict as to whether this is mandatory: see *Gallagher, White Burke and Morris* (2002) Criminal Law Weekly (CLW) 20/05; *R* v *Haynes* (2002) CLW 25/6; *Re Fehily* (2002) CLW 26/9.

[49] Service of the witness statements.

[50] For the various meanings of this term, see Lord Mustill in *R* v *Director of Serious Fraud Office, ex parte Smith* [1993] AC 1, *sub nom Smith* v *Director of Serious Fraud Office* [1992] 3 All ER 456.

and without adverse inferences being drawn in law from that non-disclosure. That rule was modified in 1967 in respect of evidence of alibi,[51] in respect of the adducing of expert evidence,[52] and, more recently, by the provisions that permit inferences from silence in respect of certain matters in particular circumstances.[53] The general right to silence remains, although the practical effect of recent changes in the law may well be to limit or reduce reliance on the right.

The Criminal Procedure and Investigations Act 1996 [54]creates a scheme of disclosure that is basically constructed in three stages. The first is primary prosecution disclosure. The second is the giving of a defence statement, to be followed by the third and final stage, secondary prosecution disclosure. This three-stage process was itself significantly modified by provisions contained in the Criminal Justice Act 2003 mostly brought into force on 4 April 2005. Despite the youth of the 1996 Act provisions, the Auld Review found them to be unsatisfactory in key respects, and not working as Parliament had intended. It also considered that the duties imposed on the defence did not go far enough. These issues are addressed as we deal with the detailed provisions below.

Prosecution disclosure

Section 3(1) originally provided that the prosecutor (that is, the CPS) must disclose to the accused any prosecution material[55] that has not been previously disclosed to the accused, and that, *in the prosecutor's opinion*, might undermine the case for the prosecution against the accused. Alternatively, he must give to the accused a written statement that there is no such material. At the same time, the prosecutor gives to the accused a schedule of non-sensitive material that he has received from the disclosure officer. By these means, the accused should be provided with relevant unused material, together with a schedule of material that is relevant and that has been acquired by the prosecutor, and, through these documents, judge what further documents may, or should, be disclosable in the light of the needs of the defence. Thus, statements by witnesses who contradict the testimony of those who will be called to testify for the prosecution, inconsistent forensic evidence, the previous convictions of prosecution witnesses, matters relating to the credibility of prosecution witnesses, and inconsistent versions of the events in question are all examples of material that fall within the scope of section 3.

This first stage, known originally as primary prosecution disclosure but renamed initial prosecution disclosure by the Criminal Justice Act 2003, made the test at this stage essentially subjective. That, though, was open to criticism, putting the judgment

[51] Criminal Justice Act 1967, s 12.

[52] By Crown Court (Advance Disclosure of Expert Evidence) Rules 1987. See now Criminal Procedure Rules.

[53] Criminal Justice and Public Order Act 1994, ss 34–38.

[54] Supplemented by Civil Procedure Rules 2010, Part 22.

[55] Defined by 1996 Act, s 8. See *DPP* v *Wood, DPP* v *McGillicuddy* [2005] EWHC 2986 (Admin).

of the prosecutor on this matter effectively beyond judicial scrutiny, and is changed by the 2003 Act.[56] The words in section 3 (highlighted above in italics) are repealed, and the duty extended to include evidence that might be considered capable of assisting the defence's case. The decision of the prosecutor is, henceforth, reviewable if any challenge is made by the defence.

Sensitive material

Introduction

A court has the power to refuse to disclose certain types of information in the public interest. The rule of evidence known as public interest immunity permits the withholding of otherwise relevant material from a party to proceedings on the grounds that its disclosure is not in the public interest.[57] For example, it may deal with matters relating to national security, or reveal the identity of a member of the security services thus rendering that person operationally ineffective. One general class of case in which the courts have been prepared to uphold claims of public interest immunity is that relating to information concerning law enforcement. The right of the police to withhold information concerning police informers was recognized in *Marks* v *Beyfus*,[58] and has been extended to the location, and identity of occupants, of police observation posts.[59] Other successful claims of public interest immunity have related to records relating to the welfare of children.[60] The 1996 Act leaves the substantive rules governing disclosure of sensitive material unchanged, but changes the procedure to be followed. Provisions in the 1996 Act[61] permit such material to be withheld where disclosure would be contrary to the public interest.

Definition

The definition of sensitive material goes beyond that protected by public interest immunity, and extends to material that is confidential in nature. What is, or is not, sensitive material will initially be determined by the disclosure officer, but subject to the ultimate decision of the court. Examples of such material given by the Code of Practice issued under the 1996 Act include:[62] material relating to national security; material received from the intelligence and security agencies; material such as telephone subscriber cheques and itemized billing that is supplied to an investigator for intelligence purposes only; material given in confidence; material relating to the identity or activities of informants, or undercover police officers, or other persons

---

[56]　Criminal Justice Act 2003, s 32.

[57]　See, generally, *Conway* v *Rimmer* [1968] AC 910; *Air Canada* v *Secretary of State for Trade* [1983] 1 All ER 96; *Makanjuola* v *Commissioner of Police for the Metropolis* [1992] 3 All ER 617.

[58]　(1890) 25 QBD 494.

[59]　See *R* v *Hackett* [1986] Crim LR 462; *R* v *Hennessy* (1979) 68 Cr App R 419; *R* v *Agar* [1990] Crim LR 183; *R* v *Rankine* [1986] 2 All ER 566.

[60]　*R* v *K (Trevor Douglas)* (1993) 97 Cr App R 342; *Re D (An Infant)* [1970] 1 All ER 1088.

[61]　See ss 3(6), 7(5), 8(5), 9(8).　　　[62]　This list of examples is not exhaustive.

supplying information to the police who may be in danger if their identities are revealed; material revealing the location of premises or other places used for police surveillance or the identity of any person allowing a police officer to use them for surveillance; material revealing, either directly or indirectly, techniques and methods relied on by a police officer in the course of a criminal investigation, for example covert surveillance techniques, or other methods of detecting crime; material the disclosure of which might facilitate the commission of other offences or hinder the prevention and detection of crime.

The disclosure officer in the first instance compiles a list of sensitive material, which is supplied to the prosecutor. It is for the prosecutor to decide whether or not a claim to withhold relevant material is to be made. Clearly, if a document is not relevant and material, it need not be disclosed, and issues of public interest immunity do not arise. Where a claim of immunity is made in respect of documents that are relevant, the court has to balance the respective public interest in maintaining the sensitivity of the document, on the one hand, and in ensuring a fair trial of an accused, on the other. This balancing function, in a criminal case, is not at all easy, and, although the case law[63] suggests that relevant material can be withheld in a criminal case, it is unlikely to be withheld where material may assist the defence. The Scott Report into the Arms for Iraq scandal observed that there was no reported case:

> in which the judge has concluded that documents would be of assistance to the defendant that is none the less declined on public interest immunity grounds to order them to be disclosed. The firm conclusion is, in my opinion justified, that in criminal cases the only question should be whether the documents might be of assistance to the defendant.

KEY ISSUE

Fundamental issues arise, and they do so in a wider context.[64] The common law recognized that the prosecution might have to make an application without the defendant being present, or, exceptionally, without even knowing about the application (known as an *ex parte* application).[65] The 1996 Act sets out a similar procedure for dealing with applications to withhold sensitive material. The question as to how such cases are to be dealt with, consistent with the Article 6 rights of a defendant, was authoritatively dealt with by the House of Lords in *R v H and C*,[66] in dealing with an appeal where the appellant contended that the trial judge was right to require the Attorney-General to appoint special counsel to represent the defendants in an *ex parte* hearing held in their absence and that of their own lawyers.[67] The court considered that derogation from the principle of full disclosure might be justified where there is a risk to an important public interest, but only to the minimum necessary to protect that public interest and never at the expense of the overall fairness of the trial itself.

---

[63] See *R v Chief Constable of the West Midlands Police, ex parte Wiley* [1995] 1 AC 274, [1994] 3 All ER 420. *R v Governor of Brixton Prison, ex parte Osman* [1992] 1 All ER 108, [1991] 1 WLR 281; *R v Clowes* [1992] 3 All ER 440.

[64] See p 191.   [65] *R v Ward* [1993] 2 All ER 577.   [66] [2004] 2 Cr App R 10.

[67] Relying on *Edwards and Lewis v United Kingdom*, App 396457/98 and 40451/98, unreported, 22 July 2003.

If material did not weaken the prosecution case, or strengthen that of the defence, there was no obligation to disclose it. If it were neutral, again no obligation to disclose existed, but it should be brought to the attention of the court. There would be very few cases in which the prosecution could not make some measure of disclosure to the defence, even if that is confined to telling the defendant that an *ex parte* application is being made. If material is of serious help to a defendant, there was a serious question as to whether a defendant could receive a fair trial at all, even if special counsel were, wholly exceptionally, appointed by the Attorney-General to safeguard the interests of the defendant. Special counsel should only be appointed where the trial judge was satisfied that no other course would adequately meet the overriding requirement of fairness to the defendant. On the particular facts, in a drugs case turning on observation evidence and alleged police impropriety, the trial judge had not fully examined the nature of the prosecution evidence and the basis of the claim, and thus the decision to appoint special counsel was premature. However, the special counsel procedures do not of themselves infringe Article 6 of the Convention.[68]

❓ Questions

1. Can it ever be fair to withhold relevant material from a defendant?
2. Can a special counsel procedure adequately protect a defendant's interest?
3. What obligations might Article 6 of the Convention impose?

Defence disclosure

The law has, since 1967, required an accused to give seven days' notice of his intention to adduce evidence in support of an alibi.[69] A failure to do so meant that the evidence could not be adduced without the leave of the court.[70] The purpose of the rule is to enable checks to be made by the prosecution as to the truth or otherwise of the claims of the accused that he was elsewhere at the time of the commission of the offence. Further, in cases of serious or complex fraud in which a preparatory hearing is held,[71] the defence might have been required to disclose the general nature of its defence (although not the names of the witnesses it proposes to call), and the principal areas of disagreement.

Apart from these cases, and the obligation to disclose expert evidence, discussed above, there was no general duty on the defence to disclose in advance the nature and content of the defence upon which it is proposed to rely. This so-called 'right to silence' meant that it was not open to a court to invite a jury to draw adverse inferences from a failure to disclose pre-trial the facts relied upon by the defence.[72] Various calls for change were made. In 1972, the Eleventh Report of the Criminal Law Revision

---

[68] See *R v H & C* [2004] 2 Cr App R 10.

[69] An 'alibi' is an assertion that the accused person was elsewhere at the time of the commission of the offence.

[70] Criminal Justice Act 1967, s 11.   [71] See p 655.

[72] *R v Gilbert* (1977) 66 Cr App R 237.

Committee recommended that a court should be permitted to draw inferences from silence in court, or from a failure to disclose facts subsequently relied upon by the defence.[73] The report was highly controversial,[74] and not acted upon. The question of defence disclosure was one of the most controversial issues considered by the Royal Commission on Criminal Justice. It took the view that no change should be made in respect of the 'right to silence', except in respect of disclosure of the defence proposed to be relied upon. The majority[75] believed that those who intended to contest the charges against them should be obliged to disclose the substance of their defence in advance of trial, or indicate that they would not be calling any evidence but simply argue that the prosecution has failed to prove its case.[76] A failure to do so, or an explanation at trial different from the one given in advance, or the advancing of mutually exclusive alternative defences, should be a matter from which the jury could draw adverse inferences, subject to the discretion of the court to prevent this where good reasons existed. A defendant who did not disclose would not generally be entitled to further disclosure of material from the prosecution.

The rationale for such proposals was a desire to reduce 'trial by ambush' involving springing a defence upon the prosecution without warning. The Royal Commission did not consider the proposals to infringe the right of defendants not to incriminate themselves, but accepted that a problem existed only in a minority of cases.[77] By contrast, the dissenting opinion in essence questioned whether the fundamental right of the defence not to respond until trial, and to require the prosecution to prove its case, should be changed where no real problem exists. It also pointed to the ineffectiveness of the advance disclosure powers in serious fraud cases.[78] These recommendations were, broadly, implemented by the 'right to silence' provisions contained in the Criminal Justice and Public Order Act 1994.

Defence disclosure under the 1996 Act

The scheme of disclosure introduced by the Criminal Procedure and Investigations Act 1996 contained provisions relating to defence disclosure. The Act made a significant change by requiring defence disclosure following primary prosecution disclosure. Under the original section 5, once the prosecutor has complied or purported to comply, with the duty of primary prosecution disclosure, the accused was under a duty to serve on the prosecutor a defence statement. A defence statement was defined as a written statement:

(a) setting out in general terms the nature of the accused's defence;

(b) indicating the matters on which he takes issue with the prosecution;

---

[73] Cmnd 4991 (HMSO, 1972).   [74] See, e.g., MacKenna at [1972] Crim LR 605.
[75] With one dissentient: see RCCJ, pp 221–35.   [76] Ibid, ch 6, paras 56–73.
[77] Chapter 4, para 19, relying on data from the Crown Court survey.
[78] Page 222, para 8, relying on Levi, *The Investigation, Prosecution and Trial of Serious Fraud*, Royal Commission on Criminal Justice Research Study No 14 (HMSO, 1993).

(c) setting out, in the case of each such matter, the reason why he takes issue with the prosecution.

The purpose of this scheme was to avoid so-called 'trial by ambush', with the accused coming up with a defence at a late stage,[79] but also was intended to permit a prosecutor to reassess what has been disclosed, and what further needs to be disclosed, in the light of positive knowledge as to what the defence actually is. Similar provisions applied specifically in the context of alibi evidence.[80] Yet even these provisions were considered inadequate by the Auld Review, which observed:[81]

> I can understand why, as a matter of tactics, a defendant might wish to prefer to keep his cards close to his chest. But that is not a valid reason for preventing a full and fair hearing on the issues canvassed at the trial. A criminal trial is not a game under which a defendant should be presented with a sporting chance. It is a search for the truth.

It concluded that defence statements under pre-existing provisions disclosed very little. Further, despite section 11(3) of the 1996 Act (which allows inferences to be drawn from a failure to make adequate defence disclosure, similar to those in the Criminal Justice Act 1987 concerning cases of serious or complex fraud,[82] and to the provisions in sections 34, 36, and 37 of the Criminal Justice and Public Order Act 1994 governing silence at or before trial),[83] there were few effective sanctions for failure to comply. The results were sometimes aborted trials, poorly prepared prosecution files, wasted witness or victim time through unnecessary attendance at court, and consequential knock-on financial costs to the courts, CPS, and Criminal Defence Service. Changes were thus introduced by the Criminal Justice Act 2003, the effect of which is to widen the requirement for defence disclosure.

A new section 6A of the 1996 Act[84] amends the definition of a defence statement. It must be in writing[85] and:

(a) set out the nature of the accused's defence including any particular defences on which he intends to rely;

(b) indicate the matters of fact on which he takes issue with the prosecution;

(c) set out, in the case of each matter, why he takes issue with the prosecution; and

(d) indicate any point of law (including any point as to the admissibility of evidence) that he wishes to take, and any authority on which he intends to rely for that purpose.

Further, a new section 6C[86] requires a defendant to indicate whether he intends to call any persons (other than himself) as witnesses, unless that detail has already

---

[79] See p 639.   [80] Section 11 of the Criminal Justice Act 1967 is repealed.

[81] Auld Review, ch 10, para 154.   [82] See Criminal Justice Act 1987, s 10.

[83] See p 679.   [84] See Criminal Justice Act 2003, s 33(3).

[85] Such a statement is deemed to be given with the authority of the defendant: see 1996 Act, s 6E, inserted by Criminal Justice Act 2003, s 38.

[86] See Criminal Justice Act 2003, s 34.

been given as part of the details of an alibi. The details to be given include names, addresses, and dates of birth (where known). A failure to give this detail does not prevent the witness being called, but, rather, allows comment to be made and inferences to be drawn from a failure to do so. The purpose of this additional detail is so that investigators can run checks on proposed defence witnesses to look at any criminal record or antecedents, as well as to diminish the effects of 'surprise witnesses'. It facilitates the prosecution examining the veracity of any potential witnesses, although, on the other hand, may deter some potential witnesses from coming forward (not wishing to have details given, in advance, to the police). Because of concerns that witnesses may be, or feel, intimidated, new provisions impose obligations on the Home Secretary to issue a code of practice for police interviews of defence witnesses.[87]

Thus a greater measure or more specific information is required by the new law. The Royal Commission on Criminal Justice had envisaged only brief details as to the offence[88] and the Auld Review itself did not think that changes of this type to defence statement provisions were necessary.[89] The practical difficulties involved in providing this level of detail, within tight time limits, may be substantial. Which facts are in dispute and what points of law are to be taken often will not be clear because of the need to evaluate and investigate the prosecution case, and even changes to legal representation may complicate matters, without always being necessary. Relevant points of law may be obvious on the face of the documentation, or from pleas and directions hearings or preparatory hearings. The provisions as a whole perhaps mark an ongoing trend towards the criminal trial becoming more inquisitorial in nature and less of a 'contest', perhaps a conclusion supported also by the additional provisions on expert evidence.[90]

Further prosecution disclosure

The third stage of the disclosure scheme is further prosecution disclosure. Once the defence has engaged in defence disclosure, it is the duty of the prosecutor to keep the issue of disclosure under review. This duty, formally marked by secondary prosecution disclosure under section 7 of the 1996 Act[91] requires the disclosure of prosecution material that might reasonably be considered capable of undermining the case for the prosecution or assisting the case for the defence (that is, the same test as for initial prosecution disclosure). Material must be disclosed as soon as practicable. This test is objective in nature—that is, it is open to a court to review the judgment made and its reasonableness, but judged by the state of affairs existing at the time.

[87] 1996 Act, s 21A, inserted by Criminal Justice Act 2003, s 40.
[88] Royal Commission, para 68, p 99.　[89] Chapter 10, para 180.
[90] See p 642.　[91] Repealed and replaced by a new s 7A by Criminal Justice Act 2003, s 33.

Expert evidence

Introduction

Section 81 of the Police and Criminal Evidence Act 1984 authorizes the making of rules regarding the disclosure of expert evidence. The Crown Court (Advance Notice of Expert Evidence) Rules 1987 were made under that power, and apply to trials on indictment.[92] Following committal or sending for trial, the party who is seeking to rely on expert evidence, whether of fact or opinion, must furnish to the other party a statement in writing of any finding or opinion upon which he proposes to rely, and, on request in writing, provide a copy of (or access to, if that is more practicable) the records of any observation, test, calculation, or other procedure in respect of which the finding or opinion is based. A failure to disclose means that the evidence cannot be adduced without the leave of the court.

This obligation of disclosure is not the only obligation. In *R v Ward*,[93] the Court of Appeal stressed that there is a common law obligation upon a government forensic scientist to act impartially, and to disclose any scientific evidence that might arguably assist the defence. Failure to comply with this obligation was one of the principal reasons for quashing the convictions of the defendant in that and other cases.[94] Such an obligation to disclose does not meet the criticism of those who argue that the trial process is unfairly tilted in favour of the prosecution because of its command of forensic science and other scientific facilities,[95] and generally the imbalance of resources. Some argue that the court itself should appoint its own expert witnesses, to report impartially to the court.[96] The whole question was examined extensively by the Royal Commission on Criminal Justice.[97]

The Commission considered, but rejected, a proposal to create an independent forensic science agency, as opposed to one being part of a government department or police authority. Instead, it proposed[98] the establishment of a Forensic Science Advisory Council to report to the Home Secretary on the performance, achievements, and efficiency of the forensic science laboratories, in both the private and public sectors. Subject to a rule that the same laboratory should not take on work for both prosecution and defence in the same case, public sector laboratories should look on themselves as equally available to defence and prosecution. This is important in the light of research findings[99] that defence solicitors sometimes encounter difficulty in finding suitable independent experts to interpret prosecution findings.[100] In respect

---

[92] The power to make rules in respect of expert evidence in summary cases has been conferred by the Criminal Procedure and Investigations Act 1996, s 19. See now the Criminal Procedure Rules 2005.

[93] [1993] 2 All ER 577, [1993] 1 WLR 619.

[94] See, e.g., *R v Maguire* [1992] QB 936, [1992] 2 All ER 433.

[95] For a description of the organization of forensic science facilities, see the RCCJ, ch 7, para 6–36.

[96] See *Spencer* [1992] Crim LR.   [97] Report, ch 9.   [98] Chapter 7, para 3.2.

[99] Roberts and Willmore, *The Role of Forensic Science Evidence in Criminal Proceedings*, Royal Commission on Criminal Justice Research Study No 11 (HMSO, 1992); Steventon, *The Ability to Challenge DNA Evidence*, Royal Commission on Criminal Justice Research Study No 9 (HMSO, 1992).

[100] See RCCJ, ch 9, paras 50–53. It should be noted that the National Forensic Science Service is now, in late 2010, under threat, presumably, for cost reasons.

of the general duty of disclosure, the Royal Commission welcomed the approach taken in *R v Ward*.[101] It also recommended streamlining legal aid provision to assist in this respect.

The problems: A more inquisitorial approach?

Of significance is the approach taken by the majority of the Commission towards a more inquisitorial system in respect of forensic science evidence. The Royal Commission found[102] that a sizeable minority of contested Crown Court cases involve scientific evidence. In approximately 25 per cent of such cases there was a defence challenge to such evidence, and in some 800 cases a year not only was such a challenge made but also expert evidence was called on behalf of the defence. In these cases the duty of disclosure applies equally to the defence as to the prosecution. Hitherto, however, the defence has been under no duty to disclose the evidence it has obtained from experts whom it does not intend to call, perhaps because it is unfavourable. Nor was there a duty to disclose expert evidence acquired by the defence for the purposes of discrediting prosecution evidence through cross-examination. The Royal Commission recommended changes that would have had the effect of requiring a greater measure of pre-trial discussion between experts, and imposed a duty to indicate the areas of prosecution expert evidence that are not agreed.[103] It also made recommendations as to the handling of expert evidence at the trial.[104] It emphatically rejected the appointment of a court expert, or an assessor, whose views would not be susceptible to examination or cross-examination.

Changes to the law were not made until the passage of the Criminal Justice Act 2003 following the recommendations of the Auld Review. Section 35 of the 2003 Act inserted into the Criminal Procedure and Investigations Act 1996 a new section 6D, which provides that if the accused instructs a person with a view to his providing an expert opinion for possible use as evidence at the trial of the accused, he must give to the court and the prosecutor a notice specifying that person's name and address unless that has already been specified in the defence statement. This duty is confined to the supply of details as to the name and address of the possible witness. It does not require disclosure of the expert's report, which is likely to be protected from disclosure by the doctrine of legal professional privilege.[105] Curiously, section 11 of the 1996 Act (inferences from failure to supply defence statement) does not apply to the new section 6D, and there is no sanction for non-compliance, which may lead to patchy compliance. Concerns also arise about how this requirement may affect the way in which defence lawyers interact with experts, in particular as to the amount and type of privileged information given to the expert instructed.

---

[101] Ibid, para 47.
[102] Crown Court Survey: see RCCJ, para 57. The estimates ranged from 30 to 40 per cent of cases, in quantity some 10,000 cases per year.
[103] Royal Commission, paras 62–64. [104] Ibid, ch 9, para 4.
[105] As to which, see p 384.

KEY ISSUE

Expert evidence causes real problems. How is the court to proceed? How can a jury adjudicate on different expert opinions put to them?

The real difficulties were vividly illustrated in *R v Harris, Rock, Chery, Faulder*.[106] In relation to the controversial and disputed 'shaken baby syndrome'[107], when four convictions were reviewed, the Court of Appeal heard from no fewer than twenty-five medical expert witnesses. The Court of Appeal reviewed and adopted principles as to how expert evidence should be presented and dealt with. These are of equal validity in criminal and civil cases.

- Expert evidence should be seen to be the independent product of the expert, uninfluenced as to form or content by the case itself.[108]
- The expert should provide an independent assessment by way of objective unbiased opinion in relation to matters only within his expertise.
- The facts and assumptions should be clearly stated.
- If the data on which the evidence is based is inadequate, the expert should say so, and make only a provisional assessment.
- Any change of opinion should be disclosed.
- The basis of any hypothesis on which the opinion is based should be explained, and any controversy about it referred to.[109]

The Criminal Procedure Rules[110] require experts to consult together, to agree points of agreement and disagreement.

❓ Questions

1. Should there be a court-appointed specialist expert?
2. How should conflicts be resolved?
3. What effects might the abolition of the National Forensic Science Service have, if the proposal announced in 2010 was implemented?

KEY ISSUE

The effectiveness of any scheme of prosecution disclosure depends on those whose duty it is to decide such questions being aware of the full extent of evidence available. Research shows that the regime under the 1996 Act may still have problems, with a lack of effective

---

[106] [2006] 1 Cr App R 5.

[107] On this, see, in particular, *R v Clark (Sally)* [2003] EWCA Crim 1020. For other issues regarding expert evidence, see *R v Cannings* [2004] EWCA Crim 1.

[108] For this and other statements, see dicta of Cresswell J in *National Justice Cia Naviera SA v Prudential Assurance Co Ltd (Ikaria Reefer)* [1993] 2 Lloyds Rep 68.

[109] *In re AB (Child Abuse: Expert Witnesses)* [1995] 1 FLR 181.

[110] R 24. See also Guidance given by Attorney-General in February 2006.

judicial enforcement.[111] The findings show that, generally, there is: a lack of resources for both prosecutors and police; a lack of training; police conflicts of interest; reliance on defective schedules; the increasing lack of defence or Crown Court experience of CPS staff; and the lack of adequate remuneration for members of the Bar to read unused material. These findings point to issues other than the disclosure rules themselves as being the key factors if the 1996 Act provisions are to fully achieve their objectives.

 Question

Do you consider the disclosure rules to strike a fair balance between prosecution and defence?

The indictment

Introduction

A bill of indictment is a written or printed accusation of crime made at the suit of the Crown against one or more persons. A bill of indictment may be preferred by any person[112] against any other person before the Crown Court, generally within twenty-eight days of sending for trial or notice of transfer, or within a period to be specified following a person being sent for trial under Schedule 3 of the 1998 Act.[113] However, a bill of indictment is of no legal validity in itself. It only becomes a legal document when it is turned into an indictment proper by being signed by the appropriate officer of the court, who in turn can only sign the draft bill if he is satisfied that the accused is validly before the court.[114] The judge of the court may direct the appropriate officer to sign the bill, either on his own motion or on the application of the prosecution. After it has been signed, the proper officer must on request supply to the defendant a copy free of charge.[115]

Where the bill is preferred following sending for trial it may charge any offence that appears on the statements, in addition to or in place of the offence or offences for which the defendant was committed, subject to the normal rules as to joinder of offences.[116] It is immaterial that the 'added' offences involve a higher penalty than the original charge or charges. Although the accused will necessarily have knowledge of the facts alleged to constitute the offence, if not of the precise charge based on those

---

[111] See Disclosure: A Protocol for the Control and Management of Unused Material in the Crown Court, 2005, available at **www.hmcourts-service.gov.uk**. See Zander, 'Mission Impossible' (2006) 156 NLJ 618. For relevant case law, see R v Harris [2006] 1 Cr App R 5; R v B [2006] EWCA Crim 417, [2006] Crim LR 745.

[112] Except in those cases in which a private person has no right to institute proceedings: see p 594. For detailed provisions regarding indictments, see CPR Part 14.

[113] See p 631.

[114] Through notice of transfer, voluntary Bill, or by direction of the Court of Appeal. An alternative procedure under the Perjury Act 1911, s 9, existed until abolished by the Prosecution of Offences Act 1985, s 28.

[115] Indictment Rules 1971, r 10(1).   [116] See p 647.

facts, there are obvious possibilities of injustice, and the Court of Appeal has said[117] that whenever it is decided to bring such 'fresh' charges, the police ought to see the defendant and warn him of the charges under caution, so that he may make a statement in answer if he wishes.

The whole of the indictment may consist of such 'substitute' charge or charges. If the defendant considers that one or more of such charges does not fairly arise out of the facts in the depositions, he may move to quash the indictment. It is then for the trial judge to rule on the sufficiency of the indictment. Where, however, the defendant was sent for trial in respect of two offences that had been repealed by statute, it was held that he was never lawfully committed at all, and it was immaterial that the third count of the indictment was in respect of an offence that both existed and was disclosed by the depositions.[118]

Form and contents

The rules as to the form of indictments are now contained in the Indictments Act 1915 and Part 14 of the Criminal Procedure Rules 2010. The drafting of the indictment is the responsibility of counsel for the prosecution,[119] the duty of which it is to ensure that it is in proper form for the particular case. In most cases, other than those of complexity or difficulty, the actual drafting is undertaken by, or on behalf of, the Crown Prosecution Service.

An indictment is in three parts: introductory matters; statement of offence; and particulars of offence. The introductory matters are twofold: firstly, the court of trial; and secondly, the name of the defendant, appearing in the form:

THE QUEEN v [Defendant] charged as follows:

As regards the statement of offence and particulars of offence, the rules provide[120] that every indictment must contain, and need not contain more than, a statement of the specific offence with which the defendant is charged, describing the offence shortly, together with such particulars as are necessary to give reasonable information as to the nature of the charge. Where, however, the offence is created by statute, there must be a reference to the statute and to the relevant section, and all of the essential elements of the offence must be disclosed in the particulars, unless the defendant is not prejudiced or embarrassed by failure to describe any such element.[121] The fact that an indictment is defective does not render the trial a nullity. Whether a conviction obtained on an

---

[117] In *R v Dickson* [1969] 1 All ER 729, [1969] 1 WLR 405, where the defendant's solicitors had six days' notice of 'fresh' charges.

[118] *R v Lamb* [1969] 1 All ER 45, [1968] 1 WLR 1946.

[119] *R v Newland* [1988] QB 402; [1988] 2 All ER 891.

[120] CPR, Part 14. There may also be approved forms of indictment for individual offences: ibid.

[121] Ibid. It is not necessary for the indictment to specify or negative any exception, exemption, excuse, proviso, or qualification. There is, again, an analogy with the rules for the content of an information.

indictment that is deficient can stand will turn, ultimately, upon whether injustice or unfairness has been caused to the defendant. Whether these provisions are effective is open to doubt. The Royal Commission on Criminal Justice observed[122] that indictments were largely formal in nature, giving little information. It found widespread evidence of a failure to comply with the duty to give reasonable information as to the nature of the charge, and agreed with the Law Commission when that body observed:

> There are strong reasons of justice and efficiency why the particulars in each count in an indictment should contain sufficiently clear factual allegations to inform the jury of the issues it will have to decide, and more generally, to enable the indictment to operate as a practical agenda for the trial.[123]

Joinder; separate trials

Hitherto we have considered an indictment charging one offence only. However, within certain limits, a single indictment may charge more than one offence, or be drawn in respect of more than one defendant, or both. This is known as joinder.

Joinder of offenders

The basic rule is that where two or more persons join in the commission of an offence, all or any number of them may be jointly indicted for that offence, or each may be indicted separately. If they were in fact indicted separately, there would be no power in any court to order 'consolidation' of the indictments, however desirable this might seem from the point of view of saving time and expense,[124] but, of course, the same result could be achieved through the use of the voluntary bill procedure[125] to supersede existing indictments. However, joinder is now very common. The matter is one of judicial discretion, and what is in the interests of justice. Where the individual offences of the different accused are related to each other by virtue of time or some other link, then it may well be appropriate for them to be tried together.[126] The fact that evidence against one accused is inadmissible against another will be a relevant factor, although not necessarily decisive. Another consideration will be the length of the trial that will ensue should they be tried together. This is returned to later.[127]

Joinder of offences

The basic rule is as follows:

> Charges for any offences may be joined in the same indictment if those charges are found on the same facts or form or are a part of a series of offences of the same or a similar character.

---

[122] Chapter 8, para 5.   [123] Counts in an Indictment (Law Commission, 1992).
[124] *Crane v Director of Public Prosecutions* [1921] 2 AC 299.   [125] See p 630.
[126] *R v Assim* [1966] 2 QB 249, [1966] 2 All ER 881.   [127] See p 649.

It should also be noted that in some limited circumstances summary offences may be tried with offences that are to be tried on indictment.[128]

It is a matter of fact and degree in each case as to whether this rule is satisfied, in accordance with principles set out in the cases. In *Ludlow* v *Metropolitan Police Commissioner*,[129] the House of Lords indicated that in deciding whether offences were of a similar character, regard should be had both to their legal and factual characteristics. To show a 'series of offences', the prosecution must be able to show some nexus between them, a 'feature of similarity which in all the circumstances of the case enables the offences to be tried together'. It is not necessary that the evidence in respect of one charge should be admissible on another, a conclusion left ambiguous and unclear by the House of Lords in *Director of Public Prosecutions* v *P*,[130] in which the tests for the use of evidence relevant to one count to prove another were reviewed and clarified, but appeared to conclude that the tests for admissibility and joinder in a sexual case were the same.[131]

The application of the principle was seen in a non-sexual case in *R* v *Cannan*,[132] in which the Court of Appeal held that a trial judge was entitled in his discretion to order the trial together of six offences involving three separate women. Three counts involved abduction, rape, and buggery against one woman, another alleged attempted kidnapping against a second, and two more counts of alleged abduction and murder of a third. Sexual cases, by contrast, are particularly difficult because of the prejudice that may arise. In *Director of Public Prosecutions* v *Boardman*,[133] Lord Cross seemed to equate the test for joinder of offences with their admissibility as evidence. He stated that if each count were inadmissible in respect of the other offences, then they ought to be tried separately. It is, he said, asking too much of any jury to disregard the other charges when considering each individual charge.

This approach is contrary to the wording of rule 9 itself. Despite the House of Lords not putting the matter beyond doubt in *DPP* v *P*, the wording of rule 9 is clear. In *R* v *Christou*,[134] the House of Lords held that where an accused person was charged with sexual offences against more than one person, where the evidence of one complainant was not admissible on charges concerning other complainants, the trial judge had a discretion to order that the charges be tried together. The judge is not obliged to exercise that discretion in favour of the accused simply because the evidence is not

[128] Criminal Justice Act 1988, s 40. The charge must be founded on the same facts or evidence, or be part of a series of offences.
[129] [1971] AC 29, [1970] 1 All ER 567. The House was considering the appropriate provision of the 1915 Rules, which were materially the same as r 9. See also: *R* v *Kray* [1970] 1 QB 125, [1969] 3 All ER 941.
[130] [1991] 2 AC 447; *sub nom R* v *P* [1991] 3 All ER 337. See *R* v *Tickner* [1992] Crim LR 44.
[131] Evidence can only be considered if it is both relevant and admissible. Admissibility in these circumstances depended on the operation of the so-called similar fact evidence rule. This rule, and others relating to bad character, were significantly altered by Criminal Justice Act 2003, ss 98–114, which came into effect in December 2004.
[132] (1990) 92 Cr App R 16.
[133] [1975] AC 421; *sub nom Boardman* v *Director of Public Prosecutions* [1974] 3 All ER 887.
[134] [1997] AC 117.

admissible on more than one count of the indictment. The key issue is simply: can the issues be resolved fairly? In that case the appellant was charged with sexual offences against his two young female cousins, C and M, with whom he had been living at the time of the alleged offences. The House of Lords concluded that the trial judge had acted properly in requiring that they be tried together, notwithstanding the fact that the evidence of C was not admissible on the counts that related solely to M. Further, in the case of *R* v *West*,[135] the court had to consider the same issue in the context of a non-sexual offence. The appellant had been tried and convicted of ten counts of murder. The evidence on many of these counts was admissible on other counts, under the so-called similar fact evidence rule. The Court of Appeal held, however, that the trial judge had acted properly in declining to sever the indictment and order separate trials in respect of three counts that were unaffected by similar fact evidence. This was a matter for the judge's discretion, which he had not exercised improperly.[136]

Long trials: The number of counts and accused

The reasons for long trials

It has already been seen that the joinder of offenders, and of charges, is permissible. The danger exists that an indictment may become so overloaded that, as a result, the trial becomes too complex in terms of the issues the jury has to comprehend and decide, or unmanageable in terms of time. On many occasions the courts have complained of indictments that are overloaded.

In *R* v *Novac*,[137] in which a large number of counts of sexual offences were laid against four defendants, Bridge LJ observed:

> whatever advantages were expected to accrue from one long trial they were heavily outweighed by the disadvantages. A trial of such dimensions puts an immense burden on both judge and jury. In the course of a four or five day summing up the most careful and conscientious judge may so easily overlook some essential matter. Even if the summing up is faultless, it is by no means cynical to doubt whether the average juror can be expected to take it all in and apply all the directions given. Some criminal prosecutions involve considerations of matters so plainly inextricable and indivisible that a long and complex trial is an ineluctable necessity. But we are convinced that nothing short of the criterion of absolute necessity can justify the imposition of the burden of a very long trial on the court.

The problem has arisen particularly in two different situations. The first concerns the use of conspiracy charges. There may be both evidential and tactical reasons why prosecutors may wish to lay a count of conspiracy in addition to counts alleging specific offences. This practice was disapproved in a Practice Note in 1977.[138] The onus is on the prosecution to justify a joinder of a conspiracy charge with other substantive offences. If it cannot, it must elect to proceed either upon the conspiracy charge

---

[135] [1996] 2 Cr App R 375.

[136] For admissibility of similar fact evidence, see now the Criminal Justice Act 2003, s 101.

[137] (1976) 65 Cr App R 107.   [138] [1977] 2 All ER 540; *sub nom Practice Direction* [1977] 1 WLR 537.

or the substantive offences. Justification might exist where the substantive offences that the prosecution is in a position to prove do not adequately reflect the extent and persistence of the defendants' criminality. Thus, for example, there might be evidence to show that a person had been engaged for some time in the importation of drugs of various kinds, although the prosecution might only be able to prove one specific importation.

Secondly, a number of long complex fraud cases has placed great strain upon the jury trial system.[139] In *R* v *Cohen*,[140] the trial was so long that the judge's summing-up (itself of considerable length) dealt only with one of the issues before the court. In passing sentence following convictions, later quashed on appeal, McKinnon J observed:

> All involved in this case have been called upon to achieve what no-one in our courts should be asked to achieve. That applies to the defendants, to the jury and to me.

Even more startling, a recent fraud case collapsed after over two years, at a cost estimated at over £60 million, having 'lurched from problem to problem, finally [folding] after sickness, jury problems, lengthy delays and disruptions'.[141] Following that fiasco, a Protocol was issued providing detailed guidance as to how such cases should be managed.[142]

But it is not only problems with the subject matter or the indictment. Sometimes it is due to inevitable problems that arise during a trial, and how they are managed. In one recent case a terrorist trial, involving seven defendants, lasted thirteen months, with the jury taking some twenty-seven days—a record—to deliver its verdicts.[143] Reports characterized the trial as plagued by sickness, technical problems, religious holidays, and legal wrangles.

Reform

The Roskill Report on fraud trials[144] advocated the abolition of jury trial in complex fraud cases to be replaced by trial by judge and two specialist assessors. Such recommendations were a response to a recognition that such trials are inevitably long, causing unacceptable disruption to the lives of jurors, and unduly complex, the evidence often being beyond the comprehension of jurors. Such claims are, of course, difficult to gauge in the light of the prohibition on study of how in fact juries reach their verdicts, and upon what evidence.[145] By contrast, others have argued for the simplification of such cases. In its evidence to the Royal Commission, the Law Society[146] argued that such trials should be simplified by not including superfluous counts, and by

---

[139] See, generally, the Roskill Committee and Royal Commission on Criminal Justice Report, ch 7, paras 59–67.

[140] [1992] NLJR 1267. The jury retired on the 184th day of the trial.

[141] (2005) The Times, 23 March.

[142] See Chapter 10. Protocol for the control and management of heavy fraud and other complex cases [2005] 2 All ER 249.

[143] See (2007) The Times, 23 May.   [144] See n 139.

[145] Contempt of Court Act 1981, s 8. For discussion of jury trial generally, see p 359.

[146] *Evidence of the Law Society to the Royal Commission on Criminal Justice* (HMSO, 1992).

keeping prosecution evidence within strict limits, principally by limiting the number of accused in the indictment. The Royal Commission itself considered the restriction of jury trial to be beyond its scope, but echoed the calls set out above for the number of counts or particulars on an indictment to be kept to a minimum.[147] In that regard, its recommendation for a review of the relationship between the criminal law and non-criminal action by financial regulators may be important in reducing the scope of criminal trials in such cases.[148] The Auld Review recommended trial on indictment without a jury.

Non-jury trial on indictment

Long or complex cases

Section 43 of the Criminal Justice Act 2003[149] will, if and when it is brought in to force, permit a prosecutor to apply for a judge-only trial where the subject matter is likely to be complex, the trial long or both long and complex. This change was supported by the Auld Review, which envisaged specialist fraud judge, trial by judge and experts, or trial by judge and lay assessors.[150] A White Paper[151] identified the great strain that long trials imposed on many jurors. Such trials may last for many months, with the juror away from work, perhaps with childcare problems, unable to talk with non-jurors about the case in question, unable to make future plans, or to take time off without adjournments granted by the court. The subject matter may be dry and technical, even tedious.

Examples of failure of high-profile fraud trials are well known. During the period 1988 to 1993, long trials following trials relating to the takeover of the company Guinness led to the conviction of only two of four defendants. In 1995–96, trials of defendants arising out of the dealings of the publisher Robert Maxwell were unsuccessful, costs of up to £30 million having been incurred. And of course the spectacular collapse of the *Jubilee Line* case involving six defendants, after two years and at an estimated cost of £60 million, seemingly makes the case for reform irresistible. Yet, despite these problems, the success rate in cases of serious fraud has been good, in 2002 around 86 per cent.[152] It is a moot question as to whether the system should be judged by the conviction rate alone, but even on that basis the above statistics show that there are many aspects to this problem, particularly as one of the key questions that arises is whether a jury can ever understand a long and complex case. It was, though, the fact that non-jury trial in the Crown Court was seen as wrong in principle by opponents of the change being proposed by the legislation in 2003 that caused this change, and another in section 44, to be so fiercely resisted. Whether in fact it is brought into effect could have been a matter of some doubt in the light of new provisions in

---

[147] Chapter 8, para 79.   [148] Chapter 7, para 64.
[149] The government gave an undertaking to review further the whole question of non-jury trial before s 43 is brought into effect.
[150] Auld Review, ch 5, para 1097.   [151] *Justice for All*, Cm 5563 (HMSO, 2002).
[152] See HC Committee debate on Criminal Justice Bill, HC Cmtte, 4 January 2003, col 321.

Domestic Violence, Crime and Victims Act 2004 relating to non-jury trial of multiple charges,[153] although the latest causes célèbres have reignited the debate.

Section 43 will permit non-jury trial where, because of length or complexity, the trial would be too burdensome for a jury. What that amounts to will be a matter for a judge to decide when an application is made for a non-jury trial at a preparatory hearing.[154] Many shorter cases can involve issues of complexity, and length alone does not signify complexity. They are, though, alternatives. When deciding an application, the judge must look at ways in which the trial could be simplified so that the length or complexity may be reduced. However, no step is to be regarded as reasonable if it would significantly disadvantage the prosecution.[155]

Danger of jury interference

Section 44 of the Criminal Justice Act 2003 addresses the issue of jury 'nobbling', allowing the prosecution to apply for trial by judge alone in cases in which there is, firstly, a real and present danger of interference with the jury, and, secondly, a risk that, despite the fact that steps could be taken to protect from these malign influences, the prospect of jury tampering is so substantial that a non-jury trial is necessary in the interests of justice. This has already been discussed.[156]

Trial of multiple counts without a jury

The provisions in the Domestic Violence, Crime and Victims Act 2004 that permit trial in the Crown Court without a jury in certain circumstances were far less controversial than those discussed above, for several reasons. Firstly, they implement a Law Commission Report[157] designed to overcome practical problems caused by the Court of Appeal decision in *R* v *Kidd*.[158] Secondly, they do not dispense with the role of the jury totally in any one case.

The problem faced by a jury in trying a case with many, multiple, counts (particularly in fraud cases) has already been noted. To overcome those problems, prosecutors have been encouraged to indict on sample counts, counts that are indicative of the nature and type of offending. It was long the practice of courts to try a defendant on sample counts, and then to sentence for the totality of the offending identified by the court. However, in *R* v *Kidd*, it was decided that it was improper for a court to have regard, when sentencing, to offences for which the defendant had not been tried and convicted, or had not admitted. That had the effect in some cases of limiting the power of a sentencing court to reflect in the total sentence the multiple nature of the offending. For example, in a case of multiple benefit fraud, the totality of the offending may

---

[153] As to which, see below.

[154] As to which, see p 655, and Criminal Justice Act 2003, s 45. An order for non-jury trial will require the approval of the Lord Chief Justice.

[155] 2003 Act, s 43(6), (7).   [156] See p 362.

[157] Law Com No 277, October 2002, *The Effective Prosecution of Multiple Offending*.

[158] [1998] 1 WLR 604 (otherwise known as *R* v *Canavan*).

involve many individual procurements of benefit cheques of a total value far in excess of anything that could be adequately reflected by sample counts.[159]

To overcome this problem, section 17 of the 2004 Act permits a prosecutor to apply, at a preparatory hearing,[160] that the trial of some, but not all, counts on an indictment be conducted without a jury. The judge must be satisfied that the number of counts on the indictment is likely to mean that trial by jury on all of them would be impracticable, that sample counts could be identified, and that it is in the interests of justice for an order to be made. The effect is that the sample counts will be tried by judge with a jury in the normal way, and then, at the conclusion of that trial, the judge is able to order trial of the remaining counts (which are reflected by the sample counts) by a judge without a jury. The judge is not to be bound by the verdict of the jury, but clearly it is highly unlikely that trial by judge only would occur in respect of multiple counts where the defendant had been acquitted on the relevant sample counts. On the other hand, the normal rules of evidence will apply: evidence of the multiple offences may well be admissible at the trial before the jury,[161] and convictions in respect of the sample counts will certainly be admissible at the trial without a jury of the multiple examples. The nature of the judge only trial is the same as that identified above.

It remains to be seen what the effect of section 17 is. It may, paradoxically, have the effect of encouraging prosecutors to include more counts in indictments, not fewer as the courts have consistently urged. And it *could* render unnecessary the introduction of the more controversial powers contained in section 43 of the Criminal Justice Act 2003.

Duplicity

Where two or more offences are joined in one indictment, each one must be alleged in a separate count or paragraph of the indictment.[162] If an indictment in fact charges more than one offence in a single count, then it is bad for duplicity. This must be distinguished from the analogous situation that, more accurately, may be described as uncertainty. This arises where a statutory provision contains one offence, which may be committed by a variety of means, or by virtue of different states of mind. Whether a count in an indictment may charge simply by reference to the statutory provision, or must allege the specific ingredients in each count, charging more than one count if necessary, is a question of construction of the relevant statute.

A good example of the problem is contained in section 5 of the Domestic Violence, Crime and Victims Act 2004,[163] which creates an offence of allowing the death of a child or vulnerable adult. The offence can be committed in various ways, and section 5(2) provides that the prosecution does not have to prove which. The question arises

---

[159] The facts of a pre-*Kidd* case, *R* v *Evans* [1992] NLJR 1267. [160] See p 655.

[161] See Criminal Justice Act 2003, s 101.

[162] Indictment Rules 1971, r 4(2), see Criminal Procedure Rules now, 2. Each count is equivalent to a separate indictment. Counts must be numbered consecutively.

[163] Which came into force on 21 March 2005.

as to whether one count in an indictment can allege all or any of the different variants. Of course, a prosecutor can avoid the whole problem in indicting on different counts.

In deciding whether a count is bad for duplicity, regard should be had to the question of whether different maximum punishments exist according to the presence or absence of specific factual ingredients.[164] Where that is so, it is likely that a court will consider the statute to create separate offences, which should therefore be indicated separately. In *Courtie*,[165] Lord Diplock (with whom the other Law Lords concurred) held that where one provision involved the imposition of different penalties depending on whether the prosecution established particular factual ingredients, then Parliament had created two different offences, which should be the subject of separate counts or informations.[166]

Objecting to the indictment: Amendment

If the defendant desires to object to the validity of the indictment, he should do so before he is arraigned. The grounds of objection have already been explained[167] although the power of the court to quash an indictment to prevent abuse of the process of the court should also be noted.

The Court of Appeal does not readily hear objections to the validity of an indictment where the objection was not taken at the trial, although failure to take it is not insuperable. When objection is taken the court may (unless it rules against the objection altogether) either quash the indictment or amend it. The Indictments Act 1915 permits a court to make such order of amendment as it thinks necessary to meet the circumstances of the case, unless amendment cannot be made without injustice.[168]

A new count may be added before the defendant is arraigned, and even after arraignment a count can be added charging a completely new offence;[169] the question is one of degree depending on the facts of the particular case.[170]

Application for amendment may be made by either side and at any time or amendment made by the judge of his own motion. Since counsel for the prosecution has general responsibility for the correctness of the indictment, he should not open his case without being satisfied on the point and should make any necessary application for amendment before the defendant is arraigned, having inspected the indictment for the purpose. Defending counsel should also inspect, in his own client's interests.

---

[164] *R v Courtie* [1984] AC 463, [1984] 1 All ER 740.   [165] See p 647.
[166] See p 647.   [167] See p 647.   [168] Section 5(1).
[169] *R v Radley* (1973) 58 Cr App R 394, where the amendment was made at the conclusion of the prosecution opening; cf. *R v Tirado* (1974) 59 Cr App R 80.
[170] It seems that an amendment on immaterial matter may be made at or after verdict: *R v Dossi* (1918) 87 LJKB 1024.

KEY ISSUE

The discussion about limiting rights to jury trial in long, or complex cases, or in cases involving multiple charges, raises important issues that have to be considered in conjunction with wider issues relating to the role and purpose of jury trial, discussed at Chapter 10.[171] A more practical question is whether a jury is capable of absorbing and assessing the large amounts of often technical material over a long period of time. Conversely, some argue that often the central issue is one of the state of mind of the defendants in the case and that part of the problem lies in how prosecution cases are prepared and presented.

? Questions

1. Do you think a jury should be asked to deal with complex cases involving technical financial or accounting detail?
2. Would judge-only trial be fair to a defendant?

Pre-trial review

Except in cases of serious or complex fraud[172] no formal system for pre-trial review by the court of trial existed until 1996, although informal arrangements operated. Pre-trial reviews in fact operated in Crown Courts across the country, providing a basis for voluntary discussion of matters affecting a forthcoming trial, such as the plea to be entered, length of trial, points of law, or admissibility of evidence.[173] Such reviews appear to have occurred in approximately 25 per cent of cases.[174] The Royal Commission considered one trial project that had involved all cases being listed for a 'pleas and directions' hearing.[175] The majority of the Commission considered such a scheme to be both unnecessary and impracticable. Instead it proposed a scheme based on the automatic completion of forms with details of plea. The disclosure obligations recommended by the Commission[176] would then have been complied with, and both prosecution and defence would then indicate whether a preparatory hearing was needed and for what purpose.[177] Such hearings would occur in a minority of cases, usually those anticipated to last at least five days, although it would be open to the parties to require a hearing in shorter cases.[178] Such hearings would deal with plea, matters of evidence (including issues of admissibility), and expert opinion, matters generally relating to the trial. Such decisions would be binding on the trial judge and

---

[171] See p 360.   [172] See Criminal Justice Act 1987, s 7(1).

[173] The Royal Commission on Criminal Justice (at ch 7, para 10) identified also a scheme based on the exchange of forms, recommended by a Working Party chaired by Watkins LJ. The results obtained in a pilot scheme were disappointing.

[174] Ibid, para 11, relying on the Crown Court Survey.

[175] Working Group on Pre-trial Issues: Recommendation 92 (cited by RCCJ, ch 7, para 12).

[176] See p 634.   [177] RCCJ, para 20.   [178] Ibid, para 17.

counsel. For this reason the Royal Commission was concerned that the practice of returned briefs be minimized as much as possible.[179]

Pleas and directions hearings (PDHs) in Crown Court cases have become in effect mandatory. The advantages of the hearing lie in the ability of the court to engage in effective case management, to the benefit not only of the workload of the court in general but also to the effective handling of individual cases as required by the Criminal Procedure Rules. However, the Narey Report[180] did accept that there may be some merit in the claim that PDHs should not be mandatory in all cases since in straightforward ones they may involve an additional and unnecessary burden.

Following the recommendations of the Royal Commission, the government published in 1995 a consultation paper.[181] This paper recognized the desirability of achieving the objectives identified by the Royal Commission: namely, the achievement of shorter and more efficient trials. However, it did not adopt the Royal Commission's proposals for pre-trial exchange of papers in less complex cases, and considered that the way forward was creation of a system based on a mixture of binding rulings at PDHs, coupled with preparatory hearings to be held in complex or potentially lengthy cases. The government's approach was given statutory effect by Parts III and IV of the Criminal Procedure and Investigations Act of 1996.

By section 40 of the 1996 Act, a judge may, at a pre-trial hearing, make a binding ruling as to:

(a) any question as to the admissibility of evidence;

(b) any other question of law relating to the case concerned.

A 'pre-trial hearing' can be held after sending for trial and before the commencement of the trial itself. In respect of the former, it can be dealt with if necessary by written submissions or limited oral submissions.[182] Pre-trial hearings permit not simply questions of law to be determined, but also whether material should be disclosed, whether counts on an indictment should be quashed, and whether or not orders should be made, for example under section 4 of the Contempt of Court Act 1981.

In addition, by section 29(1) of the 1996 Act, where it appears to a Crown Court judge that an indictment reveals a case of such complexity, or a case the trial of which is likely to be of such length that substantial benefits are likely to accrue from a preparatory hearing, such a hearing may be held. The purpose of the preparatory hearing is defined by section 29(2) as:

(a) identifying issues that are likely to be material to the verdict of the jury;

(b) assisting the comprehension of any such issues;

(c) expediting the proceedings before the jury;

---

[179] Ibid, para 36.   [180] *Op cit*, ch 1, p 2, and ch 8, p 3.

[181] *Improving the Effectiveness of Pre-trial Hearings in the Crown Court*, Cm 2924 (HMSO, 1995).

[182] *R v K* [2006] EWCA Crim 724.

(d) assisting the judge's management of the trial;

(e) determining applications for non-jury trial.[183]

These provisions are not, in principle, new, and are similar to those found in section 7 of the Criminal Justice Act of 1987, dealing with cases of serious or complex fraud. The significance of a preparatory hearing is made clear by section 31(4). Under that subsection, a judge at a preparatory hearing may order the prosecutor:

(1) to give to the court and the accused a written statement of certain matters that include the principal facts of the case for the prosecution, the witnesses who will speak to them, any exhibits relevant to those facts, any proposition of law on which the prosecutor proposes to rely, and the consequences that flow from any of those matters;

(2) to prepare the prosecution evidence and any explanatory material in such a form as required by the court;

(3) to give to the court and the accused written notice of documents the truth of contents of which ought in the prosecutor's view to be admitted, and of any such matters that in his view ought to be agreed;

(4) to make any amendments of any case statement given as appear to the judge to be appropriate.

Arraignment and pleas

Attendance of the accused

On the day fixed the accused will, if he has been detained in custody, be brought from the prison or remand centre where he has been detained and lodged in the cells. If he has been on bail, he must surrender to his bail and will then be placed in the cells to await his trial. It may be that the defendant has been on bail and does not appear, in which case the court of trial may issue a warrant, called a 'bench warrant' for the arrest of the defendant; this is a summary procedure and will not normally be used unless the arrest of the defendant is a matter of urgency.

Still further powers are provided by section 7(3) of the Bail Act 1976 by which a constable may arrest without a warrant any person who has been released on bail in criminal proceedings if, inter alia, he has reasonable grounds for believing that the person is unlikely to appear at the time and place required.

Arraignment

Assuming that the defendant has appeared at, or has been brought to, the court, the first formal step in his trial will be the arraignment, which is the process of calling

---

[183] See p 651.

an accused forward to answer an indictment. The defendant will be brought from the cells into the dock[184] and the proper officer will first ask him his name. Assuming that he is the person named in the indictment, he will then be asked to plead. The indictment will be read to him (omitting only the introductory matters) and he will be asked to plead to it; further, where the indictment contains more than one count, each should be put to the defendant separately and he should be asked to plead separately, for each count is equivalent to a separate indictment.[185]

On arraignment the defendant may, of course, simply say nothing. If this occurs, the first question is whether the defendant is mute of malice—that is, able to speak but refusing to do so—or whether he is mute by 'visitation of God'—that is, temporarily or permanently unable to speak. If there is any doubt, a jury must be sworn to try the issue. Witnesses may be called on either side and counsel may address the jury; the judge will then sum up the case to the jury, who will retire if necessary and then give a verdict.[186] If the finding is that the defendant is mute of malice, the court may then order the proper officer of the court to enter a plea of not guilty on behalf of the defendant (assuming that he still declines to speak);[187] the trial will then proceed as if the defendant had himself pleaded not guilty. If, however, the finding is that the defendant is mute by visitation of God, the defendant may yet be perfectly well able to defend himself, and a plea of not guilty should be entered by the court and the trial should proceed in the ordinary way.

However, there may well be some question of whether the defendant is fit to plead, the test for which is whether he is fit to challenge jurors, instruct counsel, understand the evidence, and give evidence himself.[188] The procedure to be followed is contained in the Criminal Procedure (Insanity) Act 1964, which was substantially amended in 2004.[189] Such matters used to be dealt with by a jury, but are now generally to be dealt with by a judge, research showing that in the vast majority of cases the function of the jury was largely ritualistic, with the clear majority of questions of unfitness not being contested.[190] Evidence may be called by either side and speeches will be made; the judge will direct the jury, who will return a verdict. If the finding is that the defendant is unfit to plead, the trial does not proceed, but the defendant is not free to go; he is liable to be detained in hospital or made subject to various orders.[191] The court has power, in the interests of the accused, to postpone trial of the issue of fitness to

---

[184] The Royal Commission did not recommend that docks be abolished. It considered that they should be situated as near as possible to the accused's legal representatives: ch 8, para 109.

[185] *R v Boyle* [1954] 2 QB 292, [1954] 2 All ER 721.

[186] This may in some circumstances be by a majority: see p 363.

[187] Criminal Law Act 1967, s 6(1)(c).

[188] *R v Berry* (1977) 66 Cr App R 156; not whether he is able to defend himself properly or well: *R v Robertson* [1968] 3 All ER 557, [1968] 1 WLR 1767.

[189] As amended by the Criminal Procedure (Insanity and Unfitness to Plead) Act 1991. See ss 4, 4A, and 5 of the 1964 Act. The provisions were also substantially amended by Domestic Violence, Crime and Victims Act 2004, s 22.

[190] See Mackay and Kearns, 'The Trial of the Issue of Unfitness to Plead' [2000] Crim LR 536.

[191] Criminal Procedure (Insanity and Unfitness to Plead) Act 1991, s 5.

plead until any time up to the opening of the case for the defence. If, before such time, the defendant is acquitted (on a submission of no case to answer), his fitness or otherwise will not be determined.[192] This is to ensure that the case against the person being detained is in fact tested, and to ensure that an innocent person is not subject to detention. If the finding is one of fitness to plead, the defendant will then be called upon to plead to the indictment; if he still declines to answer, a plea of not guilty will be entered on his behalf.

Pleas

Assuming that all questions of fitness to plead have been disposed of adversely to the defendant, in the sense that the trial on the substantive issues must go on, various pleas are open to the defendant. In the vast majority of cases the alternatives are pleas of guilty or not guilty.

The decision to accept a plea to a lesser charge is that of the prosecutor, and does not require the consent of the court unless the decision arises after the prosecution has called its evidence and a case to answer has been found.[193] Such decisions may often assist in avoiding the time and expense of a trial, and are one explanation for the problem of 'cracked trials'. These are cases that are listed for trial but in which, on the day of trial, the defendant pleads guilty.[194] By contrast, the holding of discussions informally with the trial judge to ascertain attitudes to likely sentence is a practice that has been heavily criticized by the Court of Appeal.[195] Out-of-court discussions with the trial judge should not occur unless absolutely essential, and should then be subject to various conditions. The Royal Commission proposed[196] a modification to this rule, so that judges may indicate the highest sentence that they would impose at that point on the basis of the facts put to them.[197] This might occur at pre-hearing, and encourage an accused to plead guilty. There is, of course, a danger that some defendants might plead guilty when they were, in fact, innocent.[198] The Crown Court Survey[199] found some evidence of this, but the significance of the data obtained is open to doubt.[200]

In fact the majority of accused persons at Crown Court plead guilty.[201] Therefore they obtain a 'discount' on the otherwise justified sentence.[202] The Royal Commission proposed a formalized system, of graduated discounts, to encourage early pleas of

---

[192] Ibid, s 4; see, for such a case, *R v Burles* [1970] 2 QB 191, [1970] 1 All ER 642.

[193] *R v Grafton* [1993] QB 101, [1992] 4 All ER 609. The position is different if counsel expressly asks for the approval of the judge: *R v Broad* (1978) 68 Cr App R 281. See, generally, Farquharson Committee Report (1986) LS Gaz 3599.

[194] RCCJ, ch 7, para 13. The Crown Court Study showed that 'cracked' trials were 26 per cent of all cases, creating serious problems (para 45).

[195] *R v Turner* [1970] 2 QB 321, [1970] 2 All ER 281; *R v Coward* (1979) 70 Cr App R 70.

[196] *Op cit.*   [197] Report, ch 7, para 50.

[198] It is for this reason that an accused must plead personally, not through counsel.

[199] See generally Ashworth, 'Plea, Venue and Discontinuance' [1993] Crim LR 830.

[200] RCCJ, ch 7, para 45.   [201] Ibid, ch 6.

[202] See, e.g., *R v Hollington and Emmens* (1985) 82 Cr App R 281.

guilty.[203] In 1994, changes were made to allow credit to be given for an early plea of guilty, and are now to be found in section 144 of the Criminal Justice Act 2003. It does not formally enact that those offenders who fall within its terms must receive a discount on sentence, but that is the effect of sentencing policy and practice.[204] On the other hand, the research shows that approximately 50 per cent of those pleading not guilty are in fact acquitted,[205] with a significant number of 'non-jury' acquittals. These non-jury acquittals merit further mention: the statistical evidence suggests that discharge, usually where the prosecution offers no evidence, is far more common than judges directing a jury to enter a 'not guilty' verdict because of the inadequacy of the evidence before the court.[206]

Plea of guilty

On the assumption that the plea covers the whole indictment, counsel briefed for the prosecution will give a brief outline of the facts and then call a police officer to give the antecedent history of the defendant, in the form of a sheet setting out the defendant's home and educational background, previous jobs, criminal record, and anything else thought to be relevant. He may be cross-examined by defending counsel. The court will then usually consider a pre-sentence report,[207] presented usually on behalf of a probation officer, and, sometimes, a victim impact statement. There is then a plea in mitigation made by counsel for the defence, sometimes supported by witnesses (very rarely the defendant). The defendant will then usually be given the opportunity of saying something himself to the court, after which sentence will be passed. If there are two defendants, one of whom is pleading guilty and the other not guilty, the one pleading guilty will not normally be sentenced until the trial of the other defendant is concluded.[208]

It is customary for the normal rules of evidence to be relaxed at proceedings following a plea of guilty. The rules of evidence do not apply to 'antecedent evidence', which is invariably given by a single police officer on the basis of files concerning the defendant that the officer has in court. Nevertheless, the officer should not make allegations against the defendant that he has reason to think that the latter would deny and that he cannot properly prove.[209] Of course, if matters of importance are disputed, then the court may require them to be formally proved. In addition, where despite the plea of guilty there is a factual dispute that will affect the basis upon which the court

---

[203] Ibid, para 47.

[204] See Reduction in Sentence for Guilty Plea (Sentencing Guidelines Council, 2005).

[205] Vennard, 'The Outcome of Contested Trials' in Moxon (ed) *Managing Criminal Justice* (HMSO, 1985).

[206] Ordered and Directed Acquittals in the Crown Court, RCCJ Research Study No 15 (HMSO, 1993).

[207] Criminal Justice Act 1991, s 3. These were formerly known as Social Inquiry Reports.

[208] *R v Weekes* (1982) 74 Cr App R 161. The position may be different if the accused is going to give evidence for the prosecution against his co-accused.

[209] Compare *R v Robinson* (1969) 53 Cr App R 314, where the officer described the defendant as 'the principal drug pusher' in the Midlands, evidence the reception of which the Court of Appeal described as a 'clear and obvious injustice'. See also *R v Wilkins* (1977) 66 Cr App R 49.

will sentence the accused, the trial judge will hear evidence to determine that question: a so-called *Newton* hearing.[210]

If the defendant pleads guilty to some, but not all, counts or pleads guilty to a lesser offence, the prosecution must decide whether to proceed on the remaining counts or 'accept' the defendant's pleas, in which event the counts to which he has not pleaded guilty will be left 'on the file'. Although the defendant will never have been in peril of conviction on those counts, so that he could theoretically be tried on them, in practice this would not be permitted without leave of the court and, indeed, the counts on the file are sometimes ordered to be marked with words such as 'not to be proceeded with without the leave of this court or of the Court of Appeal'. However, even if the prosecution is content to adopt this course, the judge must, if asked, consent to it and, if he does not, he may order the trial to proceed.[211]

Plea of not guilty

It should be noted that this is not necessarily a positive assertion that the defendant is innocent but merely a request or a challenge to the prosecution to prove the case against him. A defendant may plead guilty to one count in the indictment but not guilty to another, or even admit part of an offence contained in a single count but not the rest of the offence.[212] He may also plead not guilty to the offence charged but guilty to some other offence of which he may lawfully be convicted by way of alternative verdict; thus he may plead not guilty to murder but guilty to manslaughter. The whole question of alternative verdicts is now regulated by section 6(3) of the Criminal Law Act 1967. This enables the jury to acquit of the offence charged, but to convict of another offence that the court has jurisdiction to try and that is expressly or by implication alleged in the indictment.[213]

The point arises, often acutely, when the judge comes to sum up the case to the jury. Where nothing appears on the statements that can be said to reduce the crime charged to the lesser offence of which the defendant wishes to plead guilty, it is the duty of counsel for the Crown to present the offence charged in the indictment, leaving it to the jury 'in the exercise of their undoubted prerogative' to return a verdict of guilty of the lesser offence.[214] Even where there is material on the statements capable of sustaining a lesser charge, the prosecution is entitled to formulate its charges as it thinks fit. However, it is for the discretion of the trial judge whether to direct the jury as to the potential for an alternative verdict.

Secondly, the defendant may change his plea once the trial has started but in this case the appropriate verdict must be returned by the jury that will have been sworn

---

[210] *R v Newton* (1982) 77 Cr App R 13.   [211] *R v Broad* (1978) 68 Cr App R 281.

[212] *Machent v Quinn* [1970] 2 All ER 255.

[213] What is included 'by implication' is often difficult to decide. The test is whether the allegations in the indictment are capable of including the elements of the alternative offence: *Metropolitan Police Commissioner v Wilson* [1984] AC 242; *sub nom R v Wilson* [1983] 3 All ER 448.

[214] *R v Soanes* [1948] 1 All ER 289.

to try the case;[215] it may seem a formality that if the defendant changes his plea, for example, from 'not guilty' to 'guilty', the foreman of the jury should be required to stand up and say that the defendant is guilty, but 'once a prisoner is in charge of a jury he can only be either convicted or discharged by the verdict of the jury'.[216]

Autrefois acquit and *autrefois convict*

These are by far the most important of a number of so-called 'special pleas in bar' that can be raised by the defendant when the indictment is put to him.[217] The substance of the pleas in bar is that there is some reason why the court should not proceed to try the defendant, which should be made the subject of immediate inquiry, so that if the reason is found to be a valid one, the defendant should be released and further proceedings stayed.[218] The general principle of the two pleas of *autrefois acquit* and *autrefois convict* is that the same person should not be put in jeopardy twice for the same offence founded on the same facts, not merely for the same facts. This principle has been subject to important qualification following the passage of retrial provisions contained in the Criminal Justice Act 2003.[219] Nonetheless, the principle remains important.

Autrefois acquit was well explained by a US judge[220] as follows:

> The underlying idea...is that the state with all its resources and power should not be allowed to make repeated attempts to convict an individual for an alleged offence, thereby subjecting him to embarrassment, expense and ordeal and compelling him to live in a continuing state of anxiety and insecurity, as well as enhancing the possibility that even though innocent he may be found guilty.

The principles to be applied are discussed below.

Autrefois acquit and *convict*: The principles

The two pleas were extensively considered by the House of Lords in *Connelly* v *Director of Public Prosecutions*.[221] The following principles emerge from that and subsequent cases.

(1) A man cannot be tried for a crime in respect of which he has previously been convicted or acquitted. The reason for this is that an accused should not be put in peril twice. It is for this reason that the doctrine does not apply where the accused was never in fact in jeopardy. In *R* v *Dabhade*,[222] a charge was formally dismissed, because in law it was defective. The accused was committed for trial

---

[215] *R* v *Heyes* [1951] 1 KB 29, [1950] 2 All ER 587.

[216] Ibid per Lord Goddard CJ [1951] 1 KB at 30, [1950] 2 All ER at 588.

[217] Others are demurrer (that the facts alleged do not constitute the offence charged); plea to the jurisdiction (that the court has no jurisdiction to try); pardon (that a pardon has been granted). These are extremely rare.

[218] See the remarks of Lord Goddard CJ in *R* v *County of London Quarter Sessions, ex parte Downes* [1954] 1 QB 1 at 5–6; [1953] 2 All ER at 750.

[219] See p 699.

[220] Justice Black in *Green* v *United Kingdom* 355 US 184 (1957), 2 Led 2nd 199 at 201.

[221] [1964] AC 1254, [1964] 2 All ER 401.   [222] [1993] QB 329, [1992] 4 All ER 796.

on a substituted charge of theft. In dismissing an appeal against conviction, based upon the principle of *autrefois acquit*, the Court of Appeal indicated that where a charge was dismissed because it was defective, or because the evidence was insufficient to sustain a conviction, or because of a rationalization of the prosecution case, the appellant was never in fact in jeopardy.

(2) The same rule applies where a person could have been convicted of the alleged offence on a previous indictment. In this context the rule as to alternative verdict offences is of importance. As has already been seen,[223] a defendant on being charged with certain crimes may plead, or be found, guilty of certain other crimes and not guilty of the offence charged, without the need for a fresh indictment. Thus on a charge of murder the accused may be convicted of manslaughter. The doctrines of *autrefois acquit* and *autrefois convict* apply to any offence that was an alternative verdict offence to the original offence, and of which the accused was acquitted or convicted. Thus if the defendant is acquitted of murder, the defence of *autrefois acquit* will be open to him if charged with manslaughter or attempted murder arising out of the death of the same person.

(3) The rule applies if the crime in respect of which he is charged is in effect, or substantially the same as, the crime of which he was earlier acquitted or could have been (or was) convicted. This is, in reality, a matter for the common sense of the court.

(4) One test[224] of when the rule applies is to ask whether the evidence necessary to support the second indictment, or whether the facts that constitute the second offence, would have been sufficient to procure a legal conviction on the first indictment either as to the offence charged or of an offence of which the accused could have been found guilty.

(5) The matter is not decided simply by comparing indictments, but on the overall facts. The accused may adduce evidence as to the identity of the persons involved, and as to dates and other facts necessary to show that the doctrine applies.

(6) It is not within the doctrine that the facts under examination, or the witnesses being called in the later proceedings, are the same as those in the earlier proceedings.

(7) Irrespective of the above, a person may be able to show that a matter has in fact been decided already by a court competent to decide it, in the sense of a finding or plea of guilty and a sentence passed pursuant to that finding or plea. The

---

[223] See p 661.

[224] Lords Pearce and Devlin disagreed on this point, identifying this as abuse of process rather than *autrefois acquit*. See, in support, *R v Beedie* [1997] 2 Cr App R 167, adding that both the third and fourth principles amount to an abuse of process, the difference being that *autrefois* is a complete answer to the prosecution case, whereas an abuse of process argument is launched to persuade the judge that it is unfair to try the defendant, the quashing of the indictment being a discretionary remedy not one available.

matter must, though, in fact have been decided. In *Richards* v *R*,[225] the accused pleaded guilty to manslaughter, but had not been sentenced. At a resumed hearing the prosecution was halted, and the appellant subsequently tried and convicted and sentenced to death[226] for murder. In dismissing the appeal against conviction the Privy Council was of the view that the plea of *autrefois convict* did not assist the accused, because the adjudication was not in fact complete.

The Law Commission considered the rule in 1999,[227] and recommended change, which occurred in 2003. Section 75 of the Criminal Justice Act 2003 allows a prosecutor to apply to the Court of Appeal for an order that an individual be retried for a qualifying offence[228] of which he has been acquitted.[229] Clearly, if such an order is made, *autrefois acquit* is no bar, but the terms of section 84 of the 2003 Act apply. The retrial must be on an indictment preferred by direction of the Court of Appeal, and on which the defendant is arraigned within two months of the order of the Court of Appeal. Such a power is not likely to be often used, but provides an important route for dealing with cases in which new evidence arises, or new procedures allow new analysis of existing evidence, such as DNA profiling. Departure from the principle of *autrefois acquit* may appear to offend a long-established principle, but a rule that prevented a person being retried in the face of cogent new evidence might be viewed equally as unjust.[230] However the change is now firmly entrenched and has led to retrial and conviction in 2010 in one well-publicized case.[231]

Motion to quash the indictment

Instead of entering any plea, general or special, the defendant may move to quash the indictment. This may be done on several grounds. If any of the rules, already described,[232] as to the framing of the indictment have not been followed, this may be made the ground for a motion to quash; however, it has already been seen that the court possesses ample power to amend the indictment and it will only be rarely that a motion to quash on this ground will succeed. It could only do so on the ground of some grave defect of substance, such as the insufficiency of the particulars of offence, or duplicity. An indictment may also be quashed on the ground that the offence charged in it is not one known to the law. Yet another ground is that the appropriate officer did not have jurisdiction to sign it; as has already been seen he can sign it only if certain

---

[225] [1993] AC 217, [1992] 4 All ER 807.
[226] It was a Privy Council appeal from Jamaica, where the death penalty still exists.
[227] *Double Jeopardy* (Law Com No 156, 1999).
[228] Defined by Criminal Justice Act 2003, Sch 5, and include serious offences against the person, some sexual offences, serious drugs offences and some criminal damage offences.
[229] See p 699.
[230] See Criminal Justice Act 2003. For examples of where such powers might be used, see, e.g., the ongoing history of the Stephen Lawrence affair, as to which see p 699.
[231] See p 699.   [232] See p 654.

conditions are satisfied. An indictment can also be quashed if it amounts to an abuse of the process of the court.[233]

Preliminary points of law

It sometimes happens that there is a point of law involved in a case the decision of which may effectively dispose of the whole case. Thus, for example, the basic facts alleged by the prosecution may be admitted by the defence, the sole issue being whether those admitted facts amount to the offence charged. In cases of this sort it is obviously a sterile exercise to go through the motions of trial by jury when the outcome of the case will depend entirely upon the judge's decision as to the law. The judge hears argument upon the law (before empanelling a jury); if a ruling is given that, in the view of the accused and his advisers, is fatal to the defence, the accused can then change his plea.[234] The point may, in fact, be dealt with at a preliminary hearing, or through a pre-trial ruling.[235] However, it is necessary for a plea of not guilty to be taken before the point of law is argued.

If points of law are taken successfully at the commencement of the case in this way (or indeed, at any other time) the ruling may prevent the case from continuing. This is known as a terminating ruling. A terminating ruling is any ruling whether on law or evidence that is fatal to the prosecution case, such as: a dismissal for abuse of process; a ruling of *autrefois acquit*; a successful submission of no case to answer; a ruling of public interest immunity adverse to the Crown; and a ruling that the conduct alleged does not form a known criminal offence. The Auld Review[236] and the Law Commission[237] each recommended changes in the law. As the latter put it:

> If a case is to fall on a legal argument it is better for public confidence in the criminal justice system that it should be susceptible to the second opinion of a higher court, that it be appealable.

That is achieved by provisions in the Criminal Justice Act 2003 that confer rights of appeal against terminating rulings.[238]

Empanelling the jury: Challenges

Assuming that there is a plea of not guilty to some part of the indictment, the next stage of the trial will be the swearing of the jury. The Juries Act confers on the Lord Chancellor general responsibility for the summoning of jurors,[239] a function in reality

---

[233] See p 601.

[234] See, e.g., *Director of Public Prosecutions* v *Doot* [1973] AC 807, [1973] 1 All ER 940. An accused who has pleaded guilty in such circumstances can appeal against his conviction on the ground that the preliminary point of law was wrongly decided against him.

[235] See p 655.   [236] *Op cit*, ch 12, paras 47–65.

[237] *Double Jeopardy* (Law Com No 156, 1999).   [238] 2003 Act, ss 57–66. See, further, p 698.

[239] Juries Act 1974, s 2.

performed locally. From all of the jurors summoned, twelve will be chosen by ballot; a jury should be randomly selected[240] and a court has no power to interfere with the selection of a jury except in the rarest of cases, and for cause: for example, relating to the physical or mental fitness of the proposed juror.[241] The selected jurors will take their places in the jury box. Before the jury is sworn the defendant is given the opportunity to challenge members of the jury for cause, either to the whole panel summoned or to an individual juror. The burden is on the party making the challenge to show such a cause, the issue being tried by the trial judge. Prior to 1988 an accused had a right of peremptory challenge of up to three jurors, which meant that, unlike for cause, the defendant did not have to state any reason for challenge. This right was abolished by the Criminal Justice Act 1988. By contrast the right of the Crown to require jurors to 'stand by' still exists.[242] By this procedure, the juror is asked to stand down, but consideration of the cause of challenge (since a challenge by the Crown must be for cause) is postponed. It will usually then happen that there are enough 'spare' jurors for a whole jury to be assembled, however many more challenges are made, so that the trial can proceed and the cause of the Crown's challenge is never made the subject of enquiry. The Crown will usually act on the basis of knowledge of a potential juror's criminal record[243] or, in exceptional cases, of other matters disclosed on an authorized check of police records.[244]

Each member of the jury having been sworn individually, the appropriate officer of the court then tells the jury of the terms of the offences to which the defendant has pleaded not guilty and informs them that it is their duty, having heard the evidence, to say whether he is guilty or not. The trial judge may also explain certain features about a criminal trial to the jury.[245]

Course of the trial

Publicity

English law regards 'open justice' as a fundamental principle,[246] which therefore means that the trial, including the process of arraignment described above, should be open to the public, and may be reported. Despite this, the principle is not unlimited, and may be departed from where necessary—where openness or publicity would harm the interests of justice.[247] Powers exist to postpone the reporting of all or part of a trial,[248]

---

[240] See RCCJ, ch 8, paras 52–64.   [241] See p 352.

[242] See *Attorney General's Guidelines* [1988] 3 All ER 1086.

[243] These may disqualify a juror from service: see Chapter 10.

[244] *Attorney General's Guidelines on Jury Checks* [1988] 3 All ER 1086, and p 353.

[245] Royal Commission on Criminal Procedure, Cmnd 8092 (HMSO, 1981), para 67.

[246] *Scott* v *Scott* [1913] AC 417, [1911–13] All ER Rep 1.   [247] See p 232.

[248] Contempt of Court Act 1981, s 4(2). A right of appeal against such an order exists: Criminal Justice Act 1988, s 159.

to prevent reporting,[249] or in some situations to sit in camera. In addition, a variety of statutory powers exist that limit the principle.[250]

Procedure at the hearing

Speeches

Prosecuting counsel starts by making an opening speech. This will be an outline of the allegations against the defendant and of the evidence that it is proposed to call in support of the allegations. No reference should be made to any item of evidence if counsel has been informed that there is going to be an objection to the admissibility of that evidence. The fact that evidence is relevant[251] is not sufficient: for it to be considered at a trial it must also be admissible, and there are a number of rules of evidence that exclude evidence that might be thought to be relevant. Examples of these include evidence of the character of the accused unless it is directly relevant to the issue before the court and evidence of out-of-court statements.[252] A judge may also exclude from evidence relevant material where the fairness of the trial demands that that be done.[253] Therefore, in opening the case, prosecuting counsel must take care not to refer to evidence that is not admissible, or which is likely to be excluded. Objections to the admissibility of evidence, or for the exclusion of evidence will be tried by the judge, usually (although not always) in the absence of the jury, at the time in the trial when the evidence would otherwise have been called. This procedure is known as a 'voir dire', taking its name from the name of the oath taken by witnesses during that hearing.

The institution of the opening speech has been criticized on the ground that counsel may make allegations that are not borne out by the evidence of his witnesses (even before they are the subject of cross-examination) yet the jury may recollect only the statements of counsel, since they came first. It is a strict rule that prosecuting counsel should limit his observations to what appears in the depositions, or witness statements. The only exception arises in the case of those witnesses in respect of whom a notice of additional evidence has been served. Even this practice is not strictly required by law, but the court has an inherent discretion to prevent oppressive conduct towards the

---

[249] Contempt of Court Act 1981, s 11.   [250] See p 234.

[251] 'Relevance' was defined in *Stephen's Digest* as meaning that '... any two facts to which it is applied are so related to each other that according to the common course of events one either taken by itself or in connection with other facts proves or renders probable the past, present or future existence or non existence of the other.' For the difficulties in determining whether evidence is sufficiently relevant, see *R v Blastland* [1986] AC 41, [1985] 2 All ER 1095; *R v Kearley* [1992] 2 AC 228, [1992] 2 All ER 345.

[252] The use of out-of-court statements as proof of their contents has traditionally been prohibited by the hearsay rule, subject to a number of statutory and common law exceptions. The law relating to hearsay has been significantly changed by Criminal Justice Act 2003, ss 114–131, and is beyond the scope of this book. The effect of the changes may be to allow out-of-court statements in lieu of oral testimony in a greater number of circumstances.

[253] See, in particular PACE, s 78, discussed at p 439.

defendant[254] and it is most unlikely that a judge would allow additional evidence to be called unless a notice of additional evidence, setting out a summary of that witness's evidence, had been served on the defendant.

Witnesses

Prosecution witnesses will then be called[255] and will be subject to examination-in-chief by prosecuting counsel, cross-examination by defending counsel, and re-examination by prosecuting counsel. Examination-in-chief is the first stage in the examination of a witness, and is carried out by the party calling the witness. The purpose of examination-in-chief is to elicit the testimony the witness has to give on the relevant matters. An advocate cannot ask the witness leading questions. A leading question is one that suggests to the witness the answer that is expected or that assumes a fact still to be proved. It is sometimes said that any question that can be answered with a simple 'Yes' or 'No' is a leading question. This is often, although not invariably, true. Leading questions are often permitted on formal matters, such as name, address, and occupation, and it is permissible for a party to lead a witness with the concurrence of the other parties and the court. Nor can an advocate cross-examine his own witness by putting previous inconsistent statements to the witness, unless the court rules that that witness is 'hostile'. A witness is hostile if that witness is 'not desirous of telling the truth at the instance of the party calling him'.[256] Some hostility or animosity is called for: it is not enough that the evidence is unfavourable to the party calling him. If the witness is hostile, then, at common law, he may be asked leading questions by the party calling him, and, under section 3 of the Criminal Procedure Act 1865, previous inconsistent statements may be put to him, which will affect the 'credit' of the witness in the eyes of the jury, and, now, may in some circumstances be evidence of the truth of their contents.[257] More usually, a witness will ask, or be invited, to refresh his memory from an out-of-court statement made when the events were still fresh in the mind.[258]

---

[254] See the remarks of Lord Devlin in *Connelly* v *Director of Public Prosecutions* [1964] AC 1254 at 1346 *et seq.*

[255] It is the duty of the prosecution to take all reasonable steps to secure the attendance at the trial of all witnesses (other than those subject to a conditional witness order) named on the back of the indictment (*R* v *Cavanagh* [1972] 2 All ER 704, [1972] 1 WLR 676). However, the prosecution has a discretion whether to call a particular witness and, having called him, whether to adduce his evidence-in-chief or merely to tender him for cross-examination. Where the witness's evidence is capable of belief, the prosecution should call him even though his evidence is unfavourable to the prosecution case and if it does not do so, the judge may intervene and direct that he be called; on the other hand if the witness's evidence does not appear to be capable of belief, the prosecution need not call him and it will then be for the defence to call him if it wishes to do so; *R* v *Oliva* [1965] 3 All ER 116, [1965] 1 WLR 1028.

[256] *Ewer* v *Ambrose* (1825) 3 B & C 746.   [257] See Criminal Justice Act 2003, s 119.

[258] *R* v *Da Silva* [1990] 1 All ER 29, [1990] 1 WLR 31. If the witness wishes to refresh his memory, and have the document with him, actually whilst testifying, it must be contemporaneous, i.e. made whilst the events were still fresh in the mind of the maker of the statement: *R* v *Richardson* [1971] 2 QB 484. See also *A-G's Reference (No 3 of 1979)* (1979) 69 Cr App R 411 and cf. *R* v *Chisnell* [1992] Crim LR 507 (police officers allowed to refresh memory from notes transcribed many months earlier, but at a time when the events were still fresh in the mind). See, now, Criminal Justice Act 2003, s 120.

The answers of a witness must be accepted by the advocate calling that witness, even if the witness has 'not come up to proof' (that is, not testified as anticipated).

Following examination-in-chief, a witness will be cross-examined by the advocate for the party not calling that witness. The purpose of cross-examination is to weaken the testimony of the witness, either by casting doubt about his testimony, or by eliciting facts favourable to the cross-examiner, or by discrediting the witness in the eyes of the jury. An advocate may, for this purpose, ask leading questions and, indeed, there are few limits on what may be asked in cross-examination: normally, any question relevant to the issues in the case will be allowed.[259] Exceptions to this general rule exist in respect of questions relating to the interception of communications,[260] in respect of matters for which a claim of public interest immunity is successfully made.[261] By contrast, the law imposes limits on questions that may be asked and that affect the credit or credibility of the witness. The basic rule is that the question must, if asked, relate to the likely standing of the witness in the eyes of the court.[262] There are complex and special rules about the questions that may be asked about the bad character of both non-defendants and defendants alike,[263] and in sexual cases section 41 of the Youth Justice and Criminal Evidence Act 1999 imposes strict limits on what may or may not be asked. A complainant may not, subject to limited exceptions, be asked questions relating to his or her sexual experience. Such limitations are designed to give some protection for the witness, and to ensure that rape complainants in particular are not deterred from coming forward by the potential of unnecessary and intrusive questioning. One key authority, R v A (No 2), highlights the restrictive nature of section 41. In a preliminary ruling, the House of Lords ruled that, potentially, section 41 did not prevent questions about the sexual relationship that the appellant and complainant had had, if that was necessary to secure a fair trial. The 'reading down' of section 41 to ensure compliance with Article 6 has already been noted.[264]

Even where questions relating to credit are permitted, the law imposes strict limits as to how far the cross-examiner may adduce other evidence to contradict (that is, rebut) the testimony of that witness. The reason for this is that there is a need to keep the trial to the issues at hand, and to prevent the trial from becoming an exploration of a multiplicity of other matters. This is known as the collateral evidence rule: the answers of a witness in cross-examination to matters that relate to credit are regarded as final, and can only be rebutted if one of the exceptions to the rule exists.[265] There are four such exceptions that potentially arise. The first is if the witness denies a previous conviction: the denial may be rebutted.[266] Secondly, if the witness denies making a previous inconsistent statement, that denial may be rebutted.[267] Thirdly, the

---

[259] *CT Hobbs* v *Tinling & Co* [1929] 2 KB 1; *R v Funderburk* [1990] 2 All ER 482.
[260] Regulation of Investigatory Powers Act 2000, s 17.   [261] See p 636.
[262] See *Hobbs* v *Tinling* [1929] 2 KB 1.   [263] See Criminal Justice Act 2003, s 98, s 100, s 101.
[264] See p 153.   [265] *Harris* v *Tippett* (1810) 2 Camp 637.
[266] Criminal Procedure Act 1865, s 6.   [267] Ibid, s 4.

cross-examiner may rebut a denial of bias.[268] Finally, if the witness denies having a general reputation for untruthfulness, that denial may be rebutted.[269]

Cross-examination is followed, sometimes, by re-examination by the advocate for the party calling the witness. The purpose of re-examination is limited to clarifying matters that have arisen out of the testimony that the witness has given to the court, usually in the hope of bolstering testimony that has been shaken under cross-examination. As in examination-in-chief, leading questions may not be asked. Furthermore, a party cannot use re-examination as an opportunity for raising matters that he omitted to raise in examination-in-chief unless the form of the cross-examination justifies this.

'No case to answer'

When all the witnesses for the prosecution have been examined, prosecuting counsel will close his case by saying 'that is the case for the prosecution' or words to that effect. There may then be a submission by defending counsel that there is no case to answer as regards the whole or some part of the indictment. This may be put in two ways; firstly that there is no evidence that the crime alleged against the accused was committed by him; secondly, that the evidence, taken at its highest, is so tenuous that a jury could not properly convict on it.[270] This is a matter for the judge to determine and, although there is no set rule, it is usually regarded as desirable that the argument on the submission should take place in the absence of the jury. Prosecuting counsel has, of course, a right to reply to defending counsel's submission. If the submission is upheld, the trial will end as regards that part of the indictment at least, although that will be a terminating ruling potentially giving right to a possible right of appeal.[271] The jury should in such a case be instructed to return a formal verdict of not guilty; this is analogous to the case in which the defendant changes his plea to guilty in the course of the trial. Even if no formal verdict is taken, the case, once withdrawn from the jury, is completely 'dead' and cannot be revived by the defendant's own evidence or evidence given by a prosecution witness who is allowed to be recalled.[272] Similarly where two men are jointly charged, and a successful submission is made on behalf of one of them, he is to be regarded as no longer charged during what remains of the trial.[273]

The role of the judge at this stage is crucial. If the prosecution evidence is such that no properly directed jury could convict upon it, then it is the duty of the judge to stop the case.[274] This is particularly so where the prosecution relies wholly on the confession of a person who suffers a significant degree of learning disability, the confession itself being unconvincing. Such a case should be withdrawn from the jury.[275] By contrast,

---

[268] *A-G v Hitchcock* (1847) 1 Exch 91.   [269] *R v Richardson* (1977) 66 Cr App R 6.

[270] *R v Galbraith* [1981] 2 All ER 1060.   [271] Under the Criminal Justice Act 2003.

[272] *R v Plain* [1967] 1 All ER 614, [1967] 1 WLR 565. The corollary of this is that if the submission is wrongly rejected, the accused is entitled to have his subsequent conviction quashed by the Court of Appeal, even though evidence subsequently given would support that conviction; *R v Cockley* [1984] Crim LR 429.

[273] *R v Meek* (1996) 110 Sol J 867.   [274] *R v Galbraith* [1981] 2 All ER 1060.

[275] *R v McKenzie* [1993] 1 WLR 453.

if the case is one in which the strengths or weaknesses of the case depend upon the view to be taken as to the reliability of a witness or other matters properly within the remit of the jury, then the case should be left to the jury to decide. If the submission is simply rejected, the trial will proceed. Even if no submission is made, the judge may, at any time after the close of the prosecution's case, ask the jury whether they think that the prosecution case has been proved and invite them to return a verdict of not guilty if they think that it has not;[276] the more desirable practice is for the judge to take the initiative and direct the jury to return a verdict of not guilty.

Defence case

The defence case will then open, assuming that the trial is proceeding as to part or all of the indictment. Defence counsel has no right to make an opening speech to the jury unless he is calling witnesses as to fact other than the defendant (whether or not he is also calling the defendant); even then the matter is in his discretion.[277] Witnesses for the defence are then called. If the defendant is giving evidence, it is the general rule that he must give evidence before other witnesses; he must be in court, and if he heard the evidence of other witnesses before him,[278] he might be tempted to 'trim' his own evidence. A witness about whose evidence there could be no controversy may, of course, be taken before the defendant. What evidence is called for the defence depends on the nature of the case. An accused person is not a compellable witness in his own defence.[279] However, if he fails to testify in his own defence without good cause, or refuses without good cause to answer any question, the court may draw such inference as it thinks proper.[280] An exception to this is where it appears to the court that the physical or mental condition of the accused makes it undesirable for him to give evidence.

Whether an inference is in fact drawn is a matter for the jury, based on their own perception of common sense.[281] If good cause is argued by the accused, an evidential basis to establish it must exist: it is not enough for the accused simply to assert.[282] Age is not a barrier. Until 1998, no inference could be drawn in respect of an accused aged under 14. This was considered illogical by the government, in the light of the fact that an inference can be drawn from the silence of a suspect aged under 14 at the investigatory stage, and the Crime and Disorder Act 1998 removed the age limitation.

All defence witnesses are subject to examination-in-chief, cross-examination, and re-examination in the normal way. Where there is more than one defendant, cross-examination of prosecution witnesses and speeches will normally be taken in the order in which the defendants' names appear on the indictment, although there is no

---

[276] *R* v *Young* [1964] 2 All ER 480.
[277] The Royal Commission recommended that the right of the defence to make a speech at the commencement of the case should be extended to all cases, in substitution for the right here described.
[278] PACE, s 79.   [279] PACE, s 80.
[280] Criminal Justice and Public Order Act 1994, s 35.
[281] *R* v *Cowan* [1996] QB 373; *Murray* v *DPP* [1999] 1 WLR 1.
[282] See *Practice Direction: Crown Court (Defendants Evidence)* [1995] 2 Cr App R 192.

fixed rule on the matter. Once the case for the defence has been closed the prosecution may be allowed to call rebutting evidence, in the discretion of the judge. The general rule is that rebutting evidence should be allowed only where evidence has been called on behalf of the defendant that could not fairly have been foreseen by the prosecution.[283] In determining this it should be borne in mind that in most cases the defence will have given a defence statement pursuant to section 5 of the Criminal Procedure and Investigations Act 1996.[284] Rebutting evidence may be called at any time up to the conclusion of the summing-up and retirement of the jury, and defending counsel has a right to cross-examine the witnesses called in rebuttal. Further, if evidence is called after the conclusion of the speeches, counsel may deliver supplemental speeches dealing with the new evidence.

The judge has a right to recall witnesses himself or even call witnesses whom neither side has called; he may also question witnesses to clarify matters of doubt or to probe further into matters that he thinks have not been sufficiently investigated. However, a judge must be careful not to overstep the mark. In *R v Grafton*, prosecuting counsel decided during his case to offer no further evidence. The trial judge disagreed with that decision, and called the one remaining prosecution witness. In quashing the resulting conviction, the Court of Appeal stressed that the judge's power to call witnesses should be used sparingly, and only to advance the ends of fairness and justice. Until the case for the Crown is complete it is the Crown's decision as to whether or not the prosecution should proceed.

Closing speeches and the summing-up then follow. These are dealt with later.[285]

Witnesses

The procedure to be followed in the calling of evidence has been noted above. The general rule is that any person who is capable of giving intelligible testimony is a competent witness. A person who is incapable of such testimony because of mental capacity, whether of a permanent or temporary nature,[286] will not be competent and thus will not be heard. Until recently, it was thought that special rules applied to young children, but widespread criticism led to changes in the law. These have the effect of applying the same test of competence to a child as to an adult.[287] Special rules continue to apply to accused persons: an accused is not a competent witness for the prosecution, although he is competent in his own defence.

A witness who is competent is usually compellable. In other words, the witness can be required to attend court to testify, on pain of being punished for contempt of court. The attendance of a witness at the Crown Court is compelled by the issue of a

---

[283] *R v Picher* (1974) 60 Cr App R 1.   [284] See p 639.
[285] See p 680.   [286] *R v Baines* [1987] Crim LR 508.
[287] *DPP v M* [1997] 2 All ER 749; *G v DPP* [1997] 2 All ER 755; *R v McPherson* [2006] 1 Cr App R 30; *R v Powell* [2006] Cr App R 468; *DPP v R* [2007] EWHC 852 (Admin).

witness order or witness summons, issued by the Crown Court.[288] A witness can resist the granting of a witness summons only if he has no relevant evidence to give, or if the witness is entitled to claim public interest immunity to resist the claim that he should testify or produce relevant documents.[289] To the general rule that a witness is compellable there are certain exceptions. An accused person is never compellable in his own defence. The spouse of the accused is only compellable in certain limited situations, contained in section 80(3) of the Police and Criminal Evidence Act 1984. These situations are as follows:

(1) where the offence charged involves an assault on, or injury or threat of injury to, the spouse or a person at the time of the offence under the age of 16 years;

(2) a sexual offence alleged to have been committed against a person under the age of 16 years;

(3) an offence of attempting, conspiring, aiding or abetting, counselling, or inciting such an offence.

Where the spouse is competent but not compellable the trial judge is under a duty to inform the witness of that witness's right not to testify.[290] If the witness then decides to give evidence, that witness can then be treated in the normal way: for example, he or she may be declared hostile.

Various other persons are not compellable witnesses. This includes the sovereign, as well as foreign sovereigns, ambassadors, High Commissioners, and various grades of diplomatic staff. In any legal proceedings to which a bank is not a party, a bank or bank officer cannot be compelled to produce any banker's book the contents of which can be proved by secondary evidence: for example, by the production of documentary evidence.[291]

Where a witness testifies he usually does so orally. The general rule is that all witnesses must give evidence on oath, but a child under the age of 14 always gives unsworn evidence.[292] Any person having authority to hear evidence has the power to administer an oath,[293] but it is usually administered by the clerk to the court. The usual form of oath runs as follows: 'I swear by Almighty God that the evidence I shall give shall be the truth, the whole truth and nothing but the truth.' The witness holds the New Testament, or in the case of Jews the Old Testament, in his uplifted hand.[294] This form of oath is only appropriate to members of the Christian and Jewish faiths. Any person who objects to taking the usual oath may take any other form of oath, according to his religious beliefs, which he declares to be binding on his conscience. As an alternative, a person who objects to being sworn is permitted to 'make his solemn affirmation' instead of taking the oath. This substitutes the words 'I (name) do solemnly

---

[288] Criminal Procedure (Attendance of Witnesses) Act 1965, s 2.   [289] See p 636.

[290] *R v Thompson* (1976) 64 Cr App R 96.   [291] Bankers Book Evidence Act 1879.

[292] Criminal Justice Act 1991, Camberwell Green Youth Court [2005] UKHL 2; [2005] Crim LR 497. See also Crime and Justice Act 2007.

[293] Evidence Act 1851, s 16.   [294] Oaths Act 1978, s 1.

sincerely and truly declare and affirm' for 'I swear by Almighty God...'. A witness is also permitted to affirm if it is not reasonably practicable without inconvenience or delay to administer the form of oath appropriate to the witness's beliefs (for example, because the book on which the witness wishes to swear is not available).[295] An affirmation is not unsworn testimony: it is equivalent to an oath and a false statement on affirmation amounts to perjury.[296]

Once sworn, or having affirmed, a witness gives evidence orally, usually in open court. Exceptions to this are permitted where it is essential for the administration of justice, or where statute specifically authorizes. In 1999, the Youth Justice and Criminal Evidence Act conferred the power to make special measures directions in respect of children or vulnerable witnesses in some circumstances,[297] although not, generally, in respect of a defendant.[298] For example, a witness may give evidence from behind a screen, so that the witness does not have to face the alleged perpetrator of the offence, or through a live television link. The use of video links is particularly important in cases involving children's evidence, especially where it is alleged that the child is the victim of abuse. In such cases the law is increasingly concerned to ensure that the child does not have the damage of the alleged offence compounded by the experience of having to face the alleged perpetrator in open court. This power to take evidence through a live video link also extends to cases in which an adult witness is outside the United Kingdom. In addition, a video-recorded interview with a child may sometimes be admissible as the evidence-in-chief of that child, provided that it was possible for a jury, properly directed, to conclude that it was a credible account.[299] However, the power to permit a video-recorded cross-examination, recommended by the Pigot Report and contained in section 27 of the Youth Justice and Criminal Evidence Act has not been implemented because, amongst other reasons, of the difficulty in making it work appropriately and fairly.[300]

Out-of-court statements

Normally, the evidence given by a witness is oral in nature. Historically, a technical rule of evidence, the hearsay rule, prevents the out-of-court statements of a person being adduced to prove the truth of the assertions contained in those statements. The reasons for this general rule reflect the oral nature of the criminal trial: an out-of-court statement may, if it is made orally, be prone to distortion or inaccuracy. If the maker of the statement is available to testify, his out-of-court statement is self-serving and adds nothing to what he can tell the court. If, by contrast, the maker of the statement is

---

[295] Oaths Act 1978, s 5(2).   [296] Ibid, s 5(4).

[297] See *Home Office Report of the Advisory Group on Video Evidence*, (HMSO, 1989) (the Pigot Report); Birch, 'A Better Deal for Vulnerable Witnesses' [2000] Crim LR 849; Hotano, 'The Child Witness Review: Much Ado About Too Little' [2007] Crim LR 849.

[298] See *R (on application of D) v Camberwell Green Youth Court; R (on Application of DPP) v Cambridge MC* [2005] UKHL 4. See the amendments made in this regard by the Coroners and Justice Act 2009, which introduced a new s 33A and s 33BA to the 1999 Act.

[299] See *R v K (Evidence: Child Video Interview)* [2006] EWCA Crim 472.

[300] See Cooper, 'Pigot Unfulfilled' [2005] Crim LR 456.

unavailable to testify, the witness cannot be cross-examined on what is alleged to have been said in that statement.

Yet it can clearly be seen that the out-of-court statements of an individual may be both relevant and reliable, often made at a time when the events or matters in issue were fresh in the mind of that person. For that reason the hearsay rule has been severely criticized, and is subject to a wide range of exceptions. Changes have been made by the Criminal Justice Act 2003. Section 114 of that Act has recast the rule to preserve some of the common law and statutory exceptions that existed prior to the 2003 Act, and created a new 'safety valve' that can be used to admit evidence of out-of-court statements that infringes the rule but which it is in the interests of justice to receive. These new rules do not, of themselves, infringe Article 6.[301] As a result of this recasting of the rules, the following are the main forms of evidence now potentially admissible in evidence:

(1) statements made by a witness who is unavailable for a variety of reasons. These include death, the fact that the person is physically or mentally unfit to be a witness, the fact that the witness is outside the United Kingdom and it is not reasonably practicable to secure his attendance, or cannot be found, or the witness does testify because of fear;[302]

(2) where statements contained in documents are made or received in the course of a trade, business or profession;[303]

(3) statements in public documents;

(4) spontaneous statements made by individuals where events dominate the mind of the individual (known as *res gestae* statements);[304]

(5) confessions made by a defendant;[305]

(6) statements used to refresh memory;[306]

(7) some previous consistent or inconsistent statements;[307]

(8) statements within the 'safety valve' described above. A good example may be a confession to the crime made by a person other than the defendant, which would technically be hearsay but nonetheless of strong evidential value.[308]

One particular exception to the rule, mentioned above, is the power to consider a video-recording of an interview with a child. In cases involving offences of violence,

---

[301] See *R* v *Labri* [2005] EWCA Crim 3135; *Horncastle* v *R* [2009] UKSC 14.

[302] Criminal Justice Act 2003, s 115. This largely replicates the provisions of Criminal Justice Act 1968, s 23, but extends to both documentary and oral statements.

[303] Criminal Justice Act 2003, s 116. This largely replicates the provisions of Criminal Justice Act 1968, s 24.

[304] For the pre-existing common law, see *R* v *Andrews* [1987] AC 281.

[305] Subject to the requirements of PACE s 76 being satisfied.

[306] Criminal Justice Act 2003, s 139.   [307] 2003 Act, ss 119–120.

[308] For examples of its use (which should be exceptional), see *I* v *McLean* [2007] EWCA Crim 219; *R* v *Y* [2008] EWCA Crim 10; *R* v *O'Hare* [2006] EWCA Crim 2512.

or sexual offences, the video-recording of the interview with a child may, with leave of the court, be adduced. If such a video is shown, what the child says is evidence and can be used to prove the truth of the matters to which the child speaks. Leave will be granted unless:

(a) it appears to the court that the child will not be available for cross-examination;

(b) rules of court governing disclosure of the circumstances in which the recording was made have not been complied with;

(c) the court is of the opinion that, in the interests of justice, the recording ought not to be admitted. In considering whether or not leave should be granted, the court must consider whether any prejudice to the accused that might result is outweighed by the desirability of showing the whole, or substantially the whole, of the video. A Memorandum of Good Practice was adopted intended to govern how such video-recorded interviews should be conducted so as to ensure that the interview can safely be relied on.

The burden of proof and the right of silence

The 'golden thread'

The burden of proof in a criminal case is on the prosecution. The prosecution must prove each element of the crime charged. This includes, subject to certain limited exceptions,[309] disproving any defence that is raised. This fundamental principle was well demonstrated in *Woolmington* v *Director of Public Prosecutions*,[310] in which the accused, charged with murdering his wife, claimed that the killing was an accident. The trial judge in his summing-up directed the jury that if the Crown proved that the accused killed the deceased, the burden rested on the accused to prove provocation or accident. The conviction was quashed in the House of Lords because of this misdirection. In the famous words of Lord Sankey LC:

> …throughout the web of the English criminal law one golden thread is always to be seen, that is the duty of the prosecution to prove the prisoner's guilt, subject to… The defence of insanity and subject also to any statutory exception.[311]

The circumstances in which the law departs from the principle are limited. The burden of proving a special plea in bar is on the accused. Thus, if it is claimed that the accused has been previously acquitted on the same charge, then the doctrine of *autrefois acquit* will apply.[312] The burden of proof on this point will be on the accused. Another example is the defence of insanity: the burden of proving insanity is on the defence where

---

[309] These include the burden of proving a plea in bar (e.g. *autrefois acquit*) of insanity, diminished responsibility, unfitness to plead as well as under certain specific statutory exceptions.

[310] [1935] AC 462; cf. *R* v *Bone* [1968] 2 All ER 644, [1968] 1 WLR 983, in which the defendant's conviction was quashed because of the trial judge's failure to direct that, in relation to the defence of duress, it was for the prosecution to disprove the defence rather than for the defendant to prove it.

[311] Ibid, at p 481.   [312] See p 662.

this issue is raised by the defence, as is the burden of proving diminished responsibility or unfitness to plead.[313] Certain statutory exceptions also exist, which raises important issues in the context of Article 6, discussed below.[314] Whenever a burden of proof is placed on the accused, the standard of proof is not that normally imposed on the prosecution ('beyond reasonable doubt') but the lesser, civil, standard of the balance of probabilities.[315]

Article 6 ECHR

The fact that the burden of proof is on the prosecution is crucially connected with the basic principle that an accused person has the right not to self-incriminate. As already noted,[316] this is a right recognized both by English law and by the European Convention of Human Rights.[317] It is for this reason that an accused person cannot, generally, be required to self-incriminate or be required to testify in his own defence. An accused is a competent, but not compellable, witness in his own defence. Further, if self-incriminatory statements are obtained from an accused person unfairly, or by a trick, or in circumstances in which they should not be relied on because safeguards created by the law have been evaded or ignored,[318] they will be excluded for evidence. In-roads into these principles have in recent years been made by Parliament. The fact that inferences may now be drawn from a failure to mention facts at the investigatory stage, or from a failure to disclose the nature of the defence later relied on, has already been seen, but, as already noted, section 35 of the Criminal Justice and Public Order Act 1994 permits a court to draw such inference as it thinks proper from a failure of an accused to give evidence or his refusal, without good cause, to answer any question. Whether an inference is in fact drawn will depend on all of the circumstances and whether an evidential basis has been established to explain the failure to testify or to answer the relevant question.[319]

This right not to be required to self-incriminate is at the heart of the debate as to whether burdens of proof that raise a presumption of guilt, and place a burden of proof on a defendant are consistent with Article 6. In *Saliabaku* v *France*,[320] the Court of Human Rights observed:

> Presumptions of fact or of law operate in every legal system. Clearly the Convention does not prohibit such presumptions in principle. It does, however, require the Contracting

---

[313] Homicide Act 1957, s 2(2); *R v Dunbar* [1958] 1 QB 1, [1957] 2 All ER 737.

[314] See, e.g., Road Traffic Act 1988, s 5(2); Prevention of Crime Act 1953, s 1. For a general, and important statutory exception, see Magistrates' Courts Act 1980, s 101, which provides that, on summary trial, where an enactment makes the commission of a particular act an offence subject to a proviso, exception, excuse or qualification, the burden of proving that falls on the accused. For the application of s 101, see *R v Hunt* [1987] AC 352, [1987] 1 All ER 1.

[315] *R v Carr-Briant* [1943] KB 607, [1943] 2 All ER 156. Note, though, that the civil standard may not be absolute, and may vary according to the nature of what has to be proved.

[316] See pp 191 and 583.

[317] *Murray* v *United Kingdom* (1966) 22 EHRR 29; *Condron* v *United Kingdom* [2000] Crim LR 679.

[318] *R v Mason* [1987] 3 All ER 481, [1988] 1 WLR 139.

[319] See *R v Cowan* [1996] QB373; [1995] 3WLR 818.   [320] (1988) 13 EHRR 379.

States to remain within certain limits...*art 6(2)* does not regard presumptions of fact or of law provided for in the criminal law with indifference. It requires States to confine them within reasonable limits which take into account the importance of what is at stake and maintain the rights of the defence...

The effect of this, although not very clear,[321] is to require the court in each case to take a view as to whether the legislative interference with the presumption of innocence is justified and proportionate.[322] The constituent rights in Article 6 are not absolutes.[323] In respect of any statutory provision the first step is to determine whether it does in fact impose a burden of proof on the defendant.[324] If it does not, then clearly no issue arises. But if it does, the court must be assessed in the context of Article 6(2). Whilst Article 6 does not inevitably prohibit a burden of proof being placed on a defendant, it will be open to challenge.

Although these principles appear straightforward, they have generated significant debate and disagreement as the courts have sought to implement them in a principled but pragmatic way.[325] In *Lambert*, conflicting opinions were delivered by the House of Lords, when it concluded that section 28 of the Misuse of Drugs Act 1971 was to be read as imposing only an evidential burden on the defendant, leaving on the prosecution the legal burden (that is, of satisfying the court so that it is sure of the guilt of the accused). A five-strong Court of Appeal in *Attorney-General's Reference (No 1 of 12004, R v Edwards and others*[326] examined and explained *Lambert*, but preferred statements made by Lord Nichols made in yet another case, *R v Johnstone*.[327] These differences of emphasis were described by Lord Bingham in *Sheldrake v DPP*[328] as explicable in the light of differences in the subject matter of the two cases. Section 5 of the 1971 Act (*Lambert*) and section 91 of the 1994 Act (*Johnstone*) were directed to serious social and economic problems, but the justifiability and fairness of the respective reverse-onus provisions had to be judged in the particular context of each case. In the latter case the offence was committed by dealers and traders of goods who might be expected to exercise some care about the provenance of goods in which they dealt. The correct approach, concluded the House of Lords in *Sheldrake*, is never to decide whether a reverse burden should be imposed on a defendant, but always to assess whether a burden imposed by Parliament unjustifiably infringes the presumption of innocence. It should not inevitably be assumed that 'Parliament would not have made an exception without good reason': that approach may lead the court to

---

[321] See the comments of Lord Hoffmann in *R v G* [2008] UKHL 37 that this passage was 'meaningless'.

[322] See Lord Steyn in *R v Lambert* [2001] 3 All ER 577 at 590.

[323] See Lord Bingham in *Brown v Stott (Procurator Fiscal, Dunfermline)* [2001] 2 All ER 97.

[324] See *R v Hunt* [1987] 1 All ER 1; Magistrates' Courts Act 1980, s 101.

[325] Amongst the authorities to which regard should be had are the following: *R v Lambert, ante* n 330; *R v DPP, ex parte Kebiline* [1999] 4 All ER 801; *L v DPP* [2002] 1 Cr App R 420; *R v Drummond* [2002] All ER (D) 70; *R v Johnstone* [2003] 3 All ER 884; *R (On application of Grundy & Co Excavations Ltd) v Halton Division Magistrates' Court* (2003) 167 JP; *Attorney-General's Reference (No 1 of 2004), R v Edwards* [2004] All ER (D) 318.

[326] See n 325.   [327] See n 325; Trade Marks Act 1994, s 91(5) held not to infringe Article 6.

[328] [2005] 1 All ER 337.

give too much weight to the enactment under review and too little to the presumption of innocence and the obligation imposed on it by section 3 of the Human Rights Act 1998.[329] Applying these principles, the court in *Shedrake* held that section 5 of the Road Traffic Act 1988[330] imposed a reverse onus, but was plainly directed to a legitimate objective: the prevention of death, injury, and damage on the roads. By contrast, the reverse burden provision in section 12 of the Terrorism Act 2000 was not a proportionate and legitimate response to the problem being addressed. Although a defendant might reasonably be expected to show that an organization of which he was a member was not proscribed for the purpose of the offence under section 11 of the 2000 Act, it would be all but impossible for him to show that he had not taken part in activities of the organization at the time when it was proscribed. It thus was to be read as imposing only an evidential burden.

The clear effect of this mass of case law is to leave cases to be dealt with on their own particular facts, a conclusion that is likely to mean an ongoing stream of case law.[331]

Protection of the defendant

An accused has always had special protections. The right not to be required to self-incriminate has already been noted. It extends not only to the trial itself but also to the pre-trial process. In *Saunders* v *United Kingdom*,[332] the European Court of Human Rights concluded that the principle against self-incrimination extended to the prosecution not being allowed to use evidence obtained through methods of coercion or oppression. That does not mean to say that the use of evidence obtained through self-incrimination by an accused is prohibited. A confession obtained from an accused is admissible provided that it has been obtained fairly and in compliance with the terms of section 76 of PACE.[333] Again, a requirement for information, obtained on pain of penalty, as to the identity of the driver of a motor vehicle was held not to contravene Article 6 in *Brown* v *Stott (Procurator Fiscal, Dunfermline)*[334] because it was a necessary and proportionate limitation of the basic right not to be required to self-incriminate. The provisions in sections 34, 37, and 38 of the Criminal Justice and Public Order Act 1994, which permit inferences to be drawn from a failure, in some circumstances, to supply information are, again, within Article 6 provided that they do not provide the sole or main evidence against the accused.

---

[329] *Per* Lord Bingham in *Sheldrake* v *DPP, ante*, disapproving dicta of the Court of Appeal in *A-G's Reference (No 1 of 2004)*. For the role of the court in applying Human Rights Act 1998, s 3, see p 147.

[330] In respect of excess alcohol in blood, defence to prove no likelihood of driving whilst over prescribed limit.

[331] See Ashworth, 'The Presumption of Innocence in English Law' [1996] Crim LR 30; 'Reverse Onuses and the Presumption of Innocence: In Search of Principle' [2005] Crim LR 901.

[332] (1997) 2 BHRC 358.

[333] Evidence obtained by torture is always inadmissible, even if that torture was not inflicted in the United Kingdom: *A (FC) and others* v *Secretary of State for the Home Department* [2005] UKHL 71.

[334] [2001] 2 All ER 97.

At trial, the right of the accused not to testify has already been noted.[335] It used to be the case that, under section 1(3) of the Criminal Evidence Act 1898, an accused had a unique 'shield' about being asked questions about previous convictions or bad character. This has been significantly changed by the passage of sections 98 and 101 of the Criminal Justice Act 2003, which still give the accused some protections, but place him or her on a much more similar basis to other witnesses. Those rules are complex and outside the scope of this book.

Conclusion of the case

Each side may address the jury, except that where a defendant is unrepresented and either gives no evidence at all or only gives evidence himself the prosecution have no right to sum up their case.[336] In all cases the rule is that prosecuting counsel speaks first and is then followed by counsel for the defendant. The judge will then sum up.

KEY ISSUE

Why does the trial judge 'sum up' the case? The purpose of the summing-up is to instruct the jury as to the burden and standard of proof, the role of judge and jury, and to give directions on points of law where it is necessary to do so. The Judicial Studies Board has prepared model directions on common issues and points of law for the benefit of judges. The judge will also usually give a summary of the facts: indeed, in *R* v *Gregory*,[337] the Court of Appeal suggested that there must be a reminder of the facts in all cases. However, in *R* v *Wilson*,[338] the Court of Appeal upheld a conviction in a case in which a judge considered the trial so short that a summary of the facts was unnecessary. Nor can the judge dictate what verdict the jury should reach, even if he or she considers it to be obvious or inescapable.[339]

Criticism of this part of the judicial function has from time to time been made[340] that summings-up can unwittingly, and occasionally deliberately, influence the jury's view of the facts. Some suggested to the Royal Commission that, as in the USA, no summing-up of the facts should be given. This was rejected, but the Commission did disagree with the approach taken in *R* v *Gregory*, and indicated that it is, in each case, a question of fairness and balance.[341]

❓ Questions

1. Do you think a judge should summarize the evidence?
2. Should the judge express any opinion about the evidence? If so, why?

---

[335] See p 676.

[336] *R* v *Harrison* (1923) 17 Cr App R 156. Where the defendant is represented but calls no evidence, counsel for the prosecution has a right to make a closing speech, but the Court of Appeal has stated that it is a right that it should rarely be necessary to exercise save in long and complex cases: *R* v *Bryant* [1979] QB 108; [1978] 2 All ER 689, an instructive case on the history of the procedure relating to speeches in criminal trials.

[337] [1993] Crim LR 623.   [338] [1991] Crim LR 838.

[339] [2005] UKHL 9, [2005] 2 Cr App R 8.   [340] See RCCJ, ch 8, para 20.

[341] Ibid, para 22.

Verdict

No pressure should be placed on a jury to reach a verdict.[342] The jury generally retire to the jury room to consider their verdict. They are put in charge of officers of the court called jury bailiffs who must take an oath not, without the leave of the court, to allow any person to speak to the jury or to speak to them themselves without such leave, except only to ask them if they are agreed upon their verdict. Once they have retired to consider their verdict, the jury can separate only with leave of the court, which in turn can be given only in cases of 'evident necessity' such as a juror being taken ill in the course of the jury's deliberations. They do not have to stay in the same jury room until they have reached a conclusion, but they must not separate, subject to the very limited exception noted above, and it is desirable, if not essential, for them always to be in the custody of one of the court bailiffs while, for example, staying at a hotel overnight.[343] The jury may, of course, ask for further guidance from the judge upon any point of law or evidence arising in the case, but both the request for information and the answer to it must be given in open court; if the jury have asked for guidance in the form of a note sent to the judge, this note should be read out verbatim and then the answer given.[344]

When the jury have concluded their deliberations they will return to court and one of their number, whom they have appointed foreman, will stand up and, subject to the possibility of a majority verdict, in answer to questions put by the appropriate officer of the court, deliver the verdict of the jury. The Criminal Justice Act 1967 introduced into English law the majority verdict. A verdict need not be unanimous if when there are no fewer than eleven jurors, ten agree on the verdict, and when there are ten, if nine agree. The law cannot accept any majority verdict unless the jury have had not less than two hours of deliberation, or such longer period as the court thinks reasonable having regard to the nature and complexity of the case,[345] nor can the court accept a majority verdict of guilty unless the foreman of the jury states in open court the number of jurors who agreed on, and dissented from, the verdict.[346] A Practice Direction contains procedure whereby it is hoped to conceal the fact that an acquittal

---

[342] *R v McKenna* [1960] 1 QB 411, [1960] 1 All ER 326: judge told jury that they would be kept overnight if they failed to agree a verdict within ten minutes. A guilty verdict was returned after six minutes. The resulting conviction was quashed on appeal. See also: *Bushell's case* (1670) Vaugh 135, 124 ER 1006.

[343] It may be necessary to restrict their reading or television viewing: see *Re Central Independent Television* [1991] 1 All ER 347, [1991] 1 WLR 4.

[344] *R v Neal* [1949] 2 KB 590, [1949] 2 All ER 438. Breach of this rule will almost invariably amount to a material irregularity resulting in a subsequent conviction being quashed; *R v Goodson* [1975] 1 All ER 760, [1975] 1 WLR 549 (where a juror, after retirement, was permitted by the jury bailiff to leave the jury room, following which he was seen making a telephone call); but cf. *R v Alexander* [1974] 1 All ER 539, [1974] 1 WLR 422, in which the irregularity was a trifling one (juror returned to court simply to collect one or more of the exhibits and was observed throughout) and was held to be of insufficient gravity to justify quashing the conviction.

[345] Juries Act 1974, s 17(4).

[346] Ibid, s 17(3). The requirement of this subsection is mandatory so that if, for whatever reason, the foreman does not so state, the conviction will inevitably be quashed: *R v Barry* [1975] 2 All ER 760, [1975] 1 WLR 1190.

was by a majority. In *R v Pigg*,[347] the House of Lords held that the words 'ten agreed' (in answer to the question how many agreed and how many dissented) was sufficient compliance with the statute. If after such discussion as is practicable in the circumstances the jury still cannot reach the necessary measure of agreement, the judge has no option but to discharge them. The defendant will then be remanded in custody or on bail to be tried afresh. Theoretically this can happen several times. Second retrials should be rare, and confined to the small number of cases of extreme gravity in which the evidence against the defendant, viewed objectively, is very powerful.[348]. On a retrial, the fact that there has been a previous trial is usually irrelevant and inadmissible, but it may become necessary to refer to it, for example for the purpose of proving that the defendant or a witness made some particular statement or admission. Thus, in *R v McGregor*,[349] the defendant was charged with receiving. At an earlier, abortive, trial he had admitted possession. A police officer was allowed to give evidence of this admission.

Other circumstances in which the jury may be discharged are:[350]

(1) illness. If during the course of a criminal trial a juror falls ill, he may be discharged by the judge from further service, and depending on the facts, normally will be so discharged. The judge may then discharge the whole jury, but does not have to do so; neither is discharge of the single juror fatal to the continuance of the trial, since statute now provides that when, in the course of a trial, any member of the jury dies or is discharged, the trial may nevertheless continue provided that the number of jurors does not fall below nine. If, however, the charge is murder or any offence punishable by death, the prosecution and every accused must consent in writing to the trial continuing, even if only one juror is discharged or dies;

(2) misconduct of a juror, such as holding improper conversations with a member of the public about the case or absenting himself from his colleagues at the time when the jury were in the course of retiring to consider their verdict; and

(3) improper revelation to the jury of the defendant's past criminal record. In such a case the jury is frequently discharged.

In some circumstances, there is the power for a jury to convict of a lesser, and different offence.[351]

---

[347] [1983] 1 All ER 56, [1983] 1 WLR 6.   [348] *R v Bell* [2010] EWCA Crim 3.

[349] [1968] 1 QB 371, [1967] 2 All ER 267.

[350] Juries Act 1974, s 16. The judge may discharge a juror 'being through illness incapable of continuing to act or for any other reason' (s 16(1)). This is a matter left to the discretion of the trial judge, although the Court of Appeal will interfere if injustice has resulted. In *R v Hambery* [1977] QB 924, [1977] 3 All ER 561, the trial judge discharged a lady juror in order to permit her to go away on holiday, a course that the Court of Appeal saw no reason to criticize.

[351] See *R v Coutts* [2006] UKHL 39; *R v Foster* [2007] EWCA Crim 2869; p 661.

Post-verdict orders and sentence

If the defendant pleads guilty, or is convicted by the jury, questions of sentence arise. Matters of sentence are now so complicated and technical as to be beyond the scope of this text. Unless the judge is required by law to impose a particular sentence, such as the mandatory life sentence for murder, choices have to be made, which are for the judge following conviction on indictment and for the magistrates' or district judge following conviction summarily. Custodial sentences, immediate and suspended, are available for adults if the custody threshold set out in Powers of Criminal Courts (Sentencing) Act 2000 is met. For less serious offences, a range of community punishments can be imposed: community rehabilitation orders; community punishment orders; community punishment and rehabilitation orders; drug treatment and testing orders; drug abstinence orders; supervision orders; attendance centre orders; action plan orders. A special regime operates in the context of youth justice.[352] Financial penalties can be imposed: fines and compensation orders.

But even if the defendant is acquitted, that may not, now, quite be the end of it, because the Domestic Violence, Crime and Victims Act 2004 has given courts the right to impose restraining orders in some circumstances, despite the fact that the defendant has been acquitted.

The sentencing process at the Crown Court

A judge will sentence on the basis of the guilty plea or verdict of the jury. If there is a significant dispute about what factually occurred, then, following a plea of guilty, unless the prosecution accepts the defence version, a hearing is held to decide any dispute.[353] However, if there is a verdict (as opposed to a plea) of guilty, the judge sentences on the basis of the facts as they appear to him, provided that his view is consistent with the verdict of the jury.

Passing sentence

If the defendant has been found guilty on any part of the indictment, the court will then proceed to sentence, in a similar manner to that following a plea of guilty. There is first an inquiry into the defendant's antecedents. A pre-sentence report[354] is then considered. The defendant, through his advocate, makes a speech in mitigation. In the course of this part of the trial it not infrequently happens that the defendant asks for other offences to be taken into consideration. This practice is based on convention and has no statutory foundation; yet at the same time it is extremely convenient both from the point of view of the police and of the defendant. If there are other offences that the

---

[352] See p 573. [353] Known as a *Newton* hearing: *R v Newton* (1982) 77 Cr App R 13.
[354] See p 685.

defendant has committed but that are still untried (or unknown), then the defendant may admit them to the court of trial and ask the judge to take them into consideration when sentencing him for the offence of which he has just been convicted. In practice he will probably tell the police well before the hearing that he wishes certain offences to be taken into consideration or the police may suggest the matter to him and he will then be supplied with an appropriate form of admission; however, there seems to be nothing to prevent a court taking an offence into consideration even if the defendant does not either admit it or ask for it to be taken into consideration until the actual trial. However:

> If justice is to be done it is essential that the practice should not be followed except with the express and unequivocal assent of the offender himself. Accordingly, he should be informed explicitly of each offence which the judge proposes to take into consideration; and should explicitly admit that he committed them and should state his desire that they should be taken into consideration in determining the sentence to be passed on him.[355]

Once the defendant has served his sentence he will not, by long-established custom, be prosecuted in respect of any of the offences that have been taken into consideration, although if he were prosecuted, the defence of *autrefois convict* would not be open to him, there having been no trial, let alone conviction, in respect of those offences.[356] If, however, his conviction were quashed, a prosecution might be brought. The mere fact that the defendant asks for the offence to be taken into consideration does not, of course, compel the court to do so. Certain limitations have been laid down in the cases. Broadly, the offence to be taken into consideration should be of the same character as the offence of which the defendant has been convicted; if the defendant has already been separately committed for trial in respect of the offence to be taken into consideration, the judge should obtain the consent of the prosecution before doing so.[357] Even if the prosecution does consent, the judge ought to consider whether the public interest requires a separate inquiry. Neither ought the court to take into consideration an offence carrying disqualification from driving.[358] The reason is that in very many cases it will be desirable, if not obligatory, to disqualify the defendant, yet there can only be a disqualification on conviction, and taking other offences into consideration does not amount to a conviction in respect of them.

A sentence takes effect from the beginning of the day on which it is imposed, unless the court otherwise directs. The court should make clear whether any terms of imprisonment are concurrent or consecutive. Any sentence imposed, or other order made, by the Crown Court may, under section 47(2) of the Supreme Court Act 1981, be varied or rescinded by the Crown Court within the period of twenty-eight days from the date of such sentence or order.

---

[355] *Anderson v Director of Public Prosecutions* [1978] AC 964 at 977; *sub nom Director of Public Prosecutions v Anderson* [1978] 2 All ER 512, at 515–16, *per* Lord Diplock.

[356] *R v Nicholson* [1947] 2 All ER 535.   [357] *R v McLean* [1911] 1 KB 332.

[358] *R v Williams* [1962] 3 All ER 639, [1962] 1 WLR 1268.

Deferment of sentence

As an alternative to passing sentence immediately upon an offender, the judge has power to defer sentence for the purpose of enabling the court or any other court to which it falls to deal with him to have regard, in dealing with him, to his conduct after conviction (including, where appropriate, the making by him of reparation for his offence) or to any change in his circumstances.[359] The deferment can only be made if the offender consents and the court is satisfied, having regard to the nature of the offence and the character and circumstances of the offender, that it would be in the interests of justice to do so. The offender must also agree to comply with such requirements as to his conduct during the period of deferment that the court considers it appropriate to impose. There are no statutory limits as to what requirements may be imposed, although a court will need to ensure that any such requirements are necessary, proportionate, and reasonable in order to prevent arguments as to whether they infringe Article 8 of the Convention.[360] A court will monitor the offender's progress against those requirements. Progress will continue to act as a mitigating factor in respect of the final sentence, and might, for example, persuade a court that a community sentence rather than a custodial term is appropriate.

The power to defer sentence is intended for cases such as those in which a persistent offender has at last shown an inclination to settle down and work or those in which persons have, under domestic or financial pressure, stolen from their employers sums that they say they propose to repay. Accordingly, it will not be appropriate to defer sentence where the offence is so minor that it would not merit a sentence of imprisonment in any event; nor is it appropriate to do so where the offence is so serious that it must inevitably result in a substantial custodial sentence. This is because it would not be appropriate to impose a custodial sentence if the information before the court about the offender's conduct during the period of deferment is favourable to him. The period of deferment may be anything up to six months and there must not be a further deferment on the specified date.[361] Furthermore, where sentence is deferred, all aspects of the sentence should be deferred; the sentence must not be 'split' by, for example, imposing an immediate disqualification from driving, but deferring the remainder of the sentence.

Pre-sentence reports and other reports

A court must generally consider a pre-sentence report (PSR)[362] before sentencing an offender to a custodial sentence. Such a report will also be a precondition to the

---

[359] See Powers of Criminal Courts (Sentencing) Act 2000, ss 1, 1A–1F, 2, as amended and substituted by Criminal Justice Act 2003, s 278 and Sch 23.

[360] See p 197.

[361] *R v Fairhead* [1975] 2 All ER 737. However, a restitution order may be made under the Theft Act 1968, even if the passing of the sentence is in other respects deferred: Theft Act 1968, s 28(1) (as amended by the Criminal Law Act 1977, Sch 12).

[362] For the relevant statutory provisions, see Criminal Justice Act 2003, ss 156–159 re-enacting, with amendments, Powers of Criminal Courts (Sentencing) Act 2000, s 156.

imposition of certain community orders, or requirements in them.[363] A PSR is a written report usually prepared by the probation service, although it may well be prepared by a social worker or other member of the youth offending team[364] if the offender is under the age of 18. Failure to consider such a report does not invalidate a sentence passed, but in the event of an appeal the court must obtain one. The report, prepared in accordance with national standards, will contain an assessment of the offence and its seriousness, of any factors that relate to the offender that may affect the assessment of seriousness, and especially of any risk that the offender poses. It should address the attitudes of the offender and other matters that may be relevant to the sentence ultimately imposed. It is not the practice of probation to prepare PSR in respect of those accused who indicate an intention to deny the offence. In such a case there will need to be an adjournment in order for a report to be prepared, causing delay. It was for this reason that the requirement to obtain a PSR was modified in 1994,[365] to permit a court to sentence without one where such a report is considered unnecessary. This exception does not apply in respect of offenders aged under 18, unless the offence for which the offender is being sentenced is triable only on indictment, and it is considered that sufficient information is available.

In addition to a PSR a court may wish, or be required, to consider other reports. Thus, a court may require a specialist report indicating the risk to the community that a sex offender poses. Other orders may require a report from a doctor or psychologist setting out details of a particular condition or addiction as a prerequisite to the making of a particular order. Thus, for example, before a court can impose a community rehabilitation order with a requirement for medical treatment, it must first consider a report from a qualified medical practitioner. Where a PSR has been obtained, a copy is given to the offender or his solicitor, and the prosecutor, although statute limits the use to which the report may be put. The court has the power to require a financial circumstances statement,[366] which it will use where it is contemplating the imposition of a fine and wishes to find out the means of the offender.

The sentencing process in the magistrates' court

The sentencing process itself does not, in principle, differ in cases tried summarily rather than on indictment, although the particular role of the youth court in dealing with young defendants should be borne in mind.[367] But the sentencing powers of the magistrates' courts are limited by statute. Those limitations, upon the maximum term of imprisonment or maximum fine, are important not only in respect of how

---

[363] Where additional requirements are being considered: see s 156(2) of the 2003 Act.
[364] See p 573.   [365] Criminal Justice and Public Order Act 1994, Sch 9, paras 40–42.
[366] Criminal Justice Act 2003, s 162, re-enacting with amendments Powers of Criminal Courts (Sentencing) Act 2000, s 126.
[367] See p 268.

the defendant is dealt with, but in wider issues about the proportion of cases that are sent for trial by the magistrates' courts.

Currently, magistrates' courts do not have the power to impose a term of imprisonment of more than six months in respect of any one offence and twelve months in total for multiple offences. Powers of committal for sentence exist, where the sentencing powers of the magistrates' court are considered to be inadequate. Those limits are set to change when section 154 of the Criminal Justice Act 2003 is implemented. When that happens, magistrates' courts will have the power to impose a sentence of no more than fifty-one weeks[368] in respect of any one offence and a total, in the case of multiple offences, of sixty-five weeks. The rationale for this significant change is inextricably bound up with decisions relating to mode of trial.[369] The government wished to see fewer cases going for trial to the Crown Court. Whether inadequate sentencing powers is a primary reason for the numbers of cases being sent to trial at the Crown Court is arguable, with some evidence existing to show that significant cases that are committed attract sentences that the magistrates' court itself could in fact have imposed.[370]

As a consequential but necessary change, if the magistrates' court is to retain a greater number of cases for sentence, the powers of the magistrates' court to commit for sentence are restricted.

Further reading

ASHWORTH and BLAKE, 'The Presumption of Innocence in English Law' [1996] Crim LR 849

ASHWORTH and REDMAYNE, *The Criminal Process* (Oxford University Press: 4th edn, 2010)

AULD, *Review of the Criminal Courts of England & Wales* (**www.criminal-courts-review. org.uk**) (the 'Auld Review')

DENNIS, 'Reverse Onuses and the Presumption of Innocence' [2005] Crim LR 901

HOME OFFICE, *Report of the Advisory Group on Video Evidence* (HMSO, 1989)

ROSKILL COMMITTEE, *The Roskill Report on Fraud Trials* (HMSO, 1987)

---

[368] The fifty-one-week maximum is explained by the fact that this is also the maximum length of a 'custody-plus' sentence. (The total length of a custody-plus sentence for any one offence must be between twenty-eight and fifty-one weeks, comprising a custodial period of between two and thirteen weeks followed by a further period on licence.)

[369] See p 606.

[370] See Herbert, 'Mode of Trial and Magistrates' Sentencing Powers' [2003] Crim LR 315; RCCJ, para 6.12, citing research conducted by Hedderman and Moxon, *Magistrates' Court or Crown Court: Mode of Trial Decisions and Sentencing*, Research Study No 125 (HMSO, 1992).

20 Appeals and Miscarriages of Justice

INTRODUCTION

In some ways the appellate system is the most important element of the entire judicial system: however good a trial process may be, there will rarely be complete certainty as to matters of 'fact', and because of the inevitable risk of human error, the potential for miscarriages of justice arises. Over the years the criminal justice system has been dogged by a series of miscarriages of justice—some well known, but others not so. The existence of strong processes for investigating and dealing with suspected wrongful convictions is therefore crucial. This chapter will examine:

- the role of the Court of Appeal (Criminal Division);
- the powers of the Court of Appeal (Criminal Division);
- the role and powers of the Criminal Cases Review Commission.

Appeals

If a defendant is convicted on indictment at the Crown Court, his appeal lies, if at all, to the Court of Appeal (Criminal Division). Appeals from the decisions of the magistrates' court acting summarily, and from the Crown Court acting in its appellate capacity, lie to the Divisional Court of the Queen's Bench Division. In limited circumstances, a further appeal lies to the Supreme Court. The appeal structure is set out below.

Court of Appeal (Criminal Division)

The role and powers of the Court of Appeal (Criminal Division) have been the subject of a great deal of debate in recent years,[1] largely generated by a series of cases in which convictions have had to be overturned, often some years after conviction

---

[1] See O'Connor, 'The Court of Appeal: Re-Trials and Tribulations' [1990] Crim LR 615; JUSTICE, *Report on Miscarriages of Justice* (1989). See also, and generally, Spencer, 'Does our Present Court of Appeal System Make Sense?' [2006] Crim LR 677.

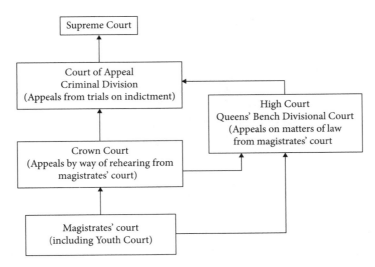

Fig. 20.1 Criminal court hierarchy

and subsequent appeal.[2] In particular, the questions of when the court should be able to overturn a conviction, how it should treat fresh evidence, whether it should have greater powers to order retrials following an appeal, and whether the Court of Appeal should have the right to order a retrial of a defendant who has, in fact, been acquitted have each been raised, and the subject of consideration, by the Royal Commission on Criminal Justice[3] and the Auld Review.[4]

The development of the Court of Appeal (Criminal Division)

It is important to remember that controversy about the criminal appellate system is not new. Until 1907 there was, in fact, no right of appeal at all. Where points of law arose on trial on indictment the trial judge could, but was not obliged to, refer such points for consideration by a court known as the Court for Crown Cases Reserved. Not until the passage of the Criminal Appeal Act 1907 was a formal appellate system introduced, and that Act was passed largely in response to a miscarriage of justice caused by the mistaken identification of an accused.[5] The 1907 Act created the Court of Criminal Appeal, which was given powers to allow appeals against conviction if that conviction was unreasonable or could not be supported having regard to the evidence, or if there was a wrong decision on a question of law. No power to order a retrial existed at that time. The Criminal Appeal Act 1964 created a power to order a new trial, although only on the ground of 'fresh evidence',[6] a restriction that was not

---

[2] See, e.g., *R v Maguire* [1992] QB 936, [1992] 2 All ER 433; *R v McIlkenny* [1992] 2 All ER 417.
[3] Cm 2263 (HMSO, 1993).   [4] *Op cit*, ch 9.   [5] The *Adolph Beck* case.
[6] Section 1, re-enacted in Criminal Appeal Act 1968, s 7.

removed until the passing of the Criminal Justice Act 1988.[7] By the Criminal Appeal Act 1966, the jurisdiction of the Court of Criminal Appeal was transferred to the Court of Appeal (Criminal Division).[8]

The whole of the pre-existing legislation was consolidated in the Criminal Appeal Act 1968 and then, following consideration by the Royal Commission on Criminal Justice, by the Criminal Appeal Act 1995. The 1995 Act, as subsequently amended, forms the basis for the powers of the Court of Appeal (Criminal Division).

Before looking at the substance of the powers themselves, three general points need to be remembered, as follows.

(a) The right of appeal has traditionally been that of the defendant, except in cases referred to the court by the Criminal Cases Review Commission.[9] Until recently, the prosecution has had no right of appeal against acquittal, or against unfavourable legal rulings. Significant exceptions to that principle now exist.[10]

(b) The court's powers derive solely from statute. The court has no inherent or residual power that entitles it to fill gaps in the statutory provisions. Criticism can fairly be made of the statutory provisions, not only in the obvious cases in which the court's role has been limited, but also in other areas in which gaps in the appellate system exist.

(c) The recent controversies about the actions of the court must be viewed in the light of the overall function and role of the court. This is dealt with below.

The role of the Court of Appeal

The court has been at pains to stress the limits of its powers. In *R* v *McIlkenny*,[11] Lloyd, Mustill, and Farquharson LJJ in a joint judgment observed:

> Under jury trial juries not only find the facts; they also apply the law. Since they are not experts in the law, they are directed as to the relevant law by the judge. But the task of applying the law to the facts, and so reaching a verdict, belongs to the jury and the jury alone. The primacy of the jury in the English criminal justice system explains why, historically, the Court of Appeal had so limited a function Since justice is as much concerned with the conviction of the guilty as the acquittal of the innocent, and the task of convicting the guilty belongs constitutionally to the jury, not to us, the role [of the Court] is necessarily limited. Hence it is true to say that whereas the Civil Division of the Court of Appeal has appellate jurisdiction in the full sense, the Criminal Division is perhaps more accurately described as a court of review.

The point has also cogently been made that not only is the court subordinate to the jury; also the jury's role is itself limited.[12] It is not the task of the jury within the adversarial system to pronounce innocence or guilt, but rather whether it has been

---

[7] See p 704.   [8] Being one of two divisions of the Court of Appeal: Supreme Court Act 1981, s 3(1).
[9] See p 693.   [10] See p 698.
[11] [1992] 2 All ER 417.   [12] See p 691.

proved, according to law, that the accused is guilty as charged. For these reasons the Court of Appeal has considered itself constrained in dealing with appeals, particularly those based upon new evidence. The extent to which these constraints are justifiable, or in the public interest, is a matter for debate. The Royal Commission on Criminal Justice concluded that such considerations as to the role of the jury have too heavily influenced the court, and that the Court of Appeal should be 'readier to overturn jury verdicts than it has shown itself in the past'.[13] In particular it should be more prepared to consider arguments that a jury has made a mistake, and to admit evidence that might favour a defendant even if it was, or could have been, available at the trial. It is debatable as to how far the various legislative changes will, in fact, result in a greater willingness by the Court of Appeal to follow a more liberal approach.

KEY ISSUES

The role of the Court of Appeal raises fundamental questions. What is it for? Answering that question is not as simple as might first appear, and raises issues about the purpose of the criminal process itself—is it a search for the truth? The Court of Appeal's role is not to decide the same question as the jury. The jury has its own independent role, as the court in *McIllkenny* demonstrates. Should the Court of Appeal always respect a jury verdict? Part of the task of the court is to ensure that a conviction is safe. It is because of some of these contradictions that the Court of Appeal has sometimes struggled with how it should use its powers and deal with questions of fresh evidence.

 Questions

1. What is the role of the Court of Appeal?
2. How far should the court respect the verdict of a jury?

The grounds of appeal

Appeal against conviction

By section 1 of the Criminal Appeal Act 1968, a person convicted on indictment may appeal to the Court of Appeal:

(a) against his conviction, on any ground that involves a question of law alone;

(b) with the leave of the Court of Appeal, against his conviction on any ground that involves a question of fact alone, or a question of mixed law and fact, or any other ground that appears to the court to be a sufficient ground of appeal.

Where leave to appeal is required, it may be granted in the first instance by a single judge of the court; if he refuses, the applicant may have his case considered by

---

[13] Report, ch 10.

the court itself.[14] This process excludes a large proportion of cases, although the proportion of cases in which leave is granted is increasing, with, in 2004, leave being
granted in some 34 per cent of cases.[15] The Royal Commission found that the chances
of success are distinctly higher where the defendant is represented. In this regard the
Commission found uneven and unsatisfactory provision for the giving of legal advice
on appeal, which is part of the professional duty of solicitor and counsel. Initial advice
after the case on appeal is within the scope of criminal legal aid (99 per cent of cases
within the Crown Court). The research also found misunderstandings about the powers of the court regarding length of sentence. The Commission concluded that interpreter facilities should be made available by the Prison Service to facilitate the giving
of advice to those who do not understand English. The present requirement to obtain
leave should be kept, and legal aid extended to cover advice as to whether an application should be renewed.

The trial judge may also grant a certificate that the case is fit for appeal, on a question of fact or mixed law and fact. This should only be done where the trial judge is
satisfied that there is a substantial point, and one worthy of consideration by the Court
of Appeal.[16]

Nothing in the Act prevents an appeal against conviction in a case in which the
accused in fact pleaded guilty at his trial. However, an appeal in such circumstances
will only succeed if: (i) the defendant did not appreciate the nature of the charge; or
(ii) he did not intend to admit that he was guilty of it; or (iii) on the admitted facts,
he could not in law have been guilty of the offence to which he pleaded guilty. Such
cases are rare, but not unknown.[17] In *R* v *Boal*,[18] the court was prepared to entertain
an appeal where the defendant had pleaded guilty as a result of advice based upon a
misunderstanding of the law by his barrister.

Appeal against sentence

The defendant may appeal against the sentence passed on him after conviction unless
the sentence is one fixed by law. Such an appeal requires the leave of a single judge,
or, if refused, of the full court.[19] The appeal can be not only against the sentence,
but also against any order that forms part of the sentence, such as a compensation
order,[20] disqualification from driving, a binding-over order,[21] or recommendation for
deportation.[22] There is no right of appeal against a recommendation that a defendant convicted of murder should serve a certain number of years, because this is not a

---

[14] Criminal Appeal Act 1968, s 31(3).

[15] See, generally, Spencer, 'Does the Present Criminal Appeal System Make Sense?' [2006] Crim LR 677.

[16] *R* v *Eyles* (1963) 47 Cr App R 260; cf. *R* v *Smith* [1974] QB 354, [1974] 1 All ER 6.32.

[17] *R* v *Forde* [1923] 2 KB 400, at 403; *R* v *Gould* [1968] 2 QB 65 [1968] 1 All ER 849; cf. *R* v *Vickers* [1975] 2
All ER 945, [1975] 1 WLR 811.

[18] [1992] QB 591; [1992] 3 All ER 177.   [19] Criminal Appeal Act 1968, s 1.

[20] Se p 683.   [21] *R* v *Williams* [1982] 3 All ER 1092, [1982] 1 WLR 1398.

[22] See the Criminal Appeal Act 1968, s 50(1), defining sentence to include 'any order made by a court when
dealing with an offender'.

recommendation binding on the Home Secretary.[23] By contrast, if a judge makes an order, in respect of a discretionary life sentence, specifying what part of the sentence must expire before the offender is able to have his case referred to the Parole Board, this has legal consequences and would appear to be a matter that can be subject to an appeal.[24]

The prosecution also has the right to have the sentence of a court reviewed.[25] If it appears to the Attorney-General that the sentencing of a person in a proceeding in the Crown Court has been unduly lenient, in respect of an offence triable only on indictment (or such other offence as the Secretary of State may order), then, with leave of the Court of Appeal, the case may be referred to it for the sentence to be reviewed.[26] The application must be made within twenty-eight days of the sentence being passed.[27]

Concern was expressed at the time this power was introduced that a defendant is in jeopardy twice.[28] The power to review granted by the Act is in respect of a sentence perceived to be unduly lenient, not simply in respect of a sentence with which the court disagrees. The power is used where the judge has erred as a matter of sentencing principle, and thus is a means of achieving consistent application of sentencing policy.[29]

The Criminal Cases Review Commission

Background

Once the avenues of appeal outlined above have been exhausted, then, unless a final appeal to the House of Lords is permitted, the one remaining formal option open to an accused is the making of an application to the Criminal Cases Review Commission. The Commission was established by the 1995 Act following consistent, and justified, criticism of the pre-existing system under section 17 of the 1968 Act whereby a convicted person might apply to the Home Secretary for his case to be referred back to the Court of Appeal, or whereby the Home Secretary might of his own motion refer back a case, on a point arising in a case.[30] This is what occurred in *R v Berry (No 2)*,[31] in which a finding on a point of law by the Court of Appeal led to that court quashing a conviction, the court not determining another ground of appeal that was before the court. On appeal to the House of Lords by the prosecution, the decision of the Court of Appeal was reversed. The Court of Appeal now being without jurisdiction to deal with this further point, the only way in which it could now be dealt with by the court

---

[23] *R v Aitken* [1966] 2 All ER 453n, [1966] 1 WLR 1076.

[24] See the terms of Criminal Justice Act 1991, s 34(2).

[25] Introduced by Criminal Justice Act 1988, s 36.

[26] See Criminal Justice Act 1988 (Review of Sentencing) Order 2006, SI 2006/1116.

[27] Criminal Justice Act 1988, Sch 3.   [28] See p 662.

[29] For wider issues in this context, see p 571.   [30] 1968 Act, s 17(1)(a).

[31] [1991] 2 All ER 789, [1991] 1 WLR 125; for the resulting decision, see *R v Berry*, unreported, 3 April 1992.

was for the Home Secretary to make a reference under section 17, which is in fact what occurred. Yet the approach of the Home Office was on the whole slow and cautious, showing 'too great a constitutional deference' to the Court of Appeal.[32]

The reasons for change

The operation of section 17, and, generally the role of the Home Office, was considered by the Royal Commission on Criminal Justice.[33] It noted that the royal prerogative of mercy in respect of trials on indictment was 'seldom exercised',[34] and it noted also that section 17 references were made in only a small proportion of the cases of those brought to the attention of the Home Office by the parties, or by campaigning groups such as JUSTICE.[35] The restrictive nature of the test[36] used by the Home Secretary to decide whether a reference should be made had been identified by the May Committee,[37] which also criticized the Home Office for not being proactive in miscarriage cases. References back were only made in cases in which fresh evidence had emerged since the trial and appeal. The view of the May Committee that there was a need for change was supported by the Royal Commission. It recommended that the Home Secretary's power to make references under section 17 should be abolished. Instead, the role now performed by the Home Office should be given to an independent body, a new Criminal Cases Review Authority. This authority, to comprise both lawyers and lay persons, would oversee any further investigations needed into cases referred to it by complainants, although it would not appear to have powers to instigate investigations on its own motion.

The Commission

The recommendation of the May Committee was accepted in principle. The result was the creation, by the 1995 Act, of the Criminal Cases Review Commission. At least one-third of the members of the Commission must be lawyers,[38] and two-thirds persons who have knowledge or expertise of any part of the criminal justice system.[39] There are eleven Commissioners, appointed by the Crown on the advice of the Prime Minister.[40] They hold office for an initial term of five years, renewable only once. The Commissioners are aided by caseworkers, and have a general power to undertake, or to arrange the undertaking by others, of inquiries.[41] The number and type of cases

---

[32] See Nobles and Schiff, 'The Criminal Cases Review Commission: Establishing a Workable Relationship with the Court of Appeal' [2005] Crim LR 173; 'The Criminal Cases Review Commission & The Court of Appeal: The Commissions' Perspective' [2005] Crim LR 937.

[33] *Op cit*, ch 11.   [34] Ibid, para 3.

[35] A campaigning organization with a primary aim of investigation of, and campaigning against, miscarriages of justice. See, in particular, JUSTICE, *op cit*.

[36] Royal Commission Report, ch 1.

[37] Established to report on the miscarriage of justice in the Guildford and Woolwich pub bombings cases.

[38] Criminal Appeal Act 1995, s 8(5).   [39] Ibid, s 8(6).

[40] Ibid s 8(4).   [41] Ibid, s 21.

can be discovered by looking at the annual reports for the Commission, and the Commission's website.[42]

For the effective working of the Commission's role, the availability of legal advice and assistance is crucial, for the issues involved are usually complex. *Pro bono* work[43] by publicly spirited lawyers may be available. Public funding may be available under the legal advice and assistance schemes from a firm holding a general criminal contract[44] provided that the convicted individual satisfies the restricted financial criteria for public funding.

The use of the powers

By mid-2010[45] the Commission had received 12,745 applications.[46] Of these, some 12,078 had been dealt with, some 265 applications waiting to be dealt with and some 402 applications under review. Of those 12,078, 422 had been referred to the Court of Appeal, with 299 of those referrals resulting in a conviction being quashed. Some 123 convictions were upheld.

The nature of the cases referred spans the range of serious crime, including many cases of murder, rape, or other serious assault.[47] However, the CCRC case library reveals reviews in respect of offences as diverse as illegal importation of drugs, obtaining by deception or allowing a dog to be in a public place without a muzzle.

Referral of murder cases shows the greatest proportion of appeals that are dismissed.[48] Where convictions are overturned, the most common reason was fresh evidence casting doubt on the reliability of prosecution witnesses.[49] Flawed or doubtful expert evidence is also an issue, as demonstrated vividly in a series of cases relating to deaths of babies.[50] The Commission observed:[51]

> The reasons for referral have been diverse but a strong underlying theme can be identified. In most cases there has been fresh evidence casting doubt on the reliability of prosecution witnesses. Concerns were identified about the way in which original exhibits had been handled in a rape case. Doubt was raised about the original medical evidence in a shaken baby case.
>
> Psychological evidence suggests that a confession was unreliable...In other cases, referral resulted from the identification of defects in the investigative or trial process...In four cases the applicant had pleaded guilty and in three of those cases there had been no previous appeal but the Commission decided there were exceptional grounds to justify referral. This illustrates the fact that even though there may be no new evidence, careful analysis of the facts and circumstances at the time of trial can provide compelling reasons for referral on the basis of new argument.

---

[42] See **www.ccrc.gov.uk**   [43] See Chapter 11, p 407.

[44] See p 414.   [45] Statistics are to 30 June 2010—see **www.ccrc.gov.uk**

[46] Including 279 transferred from the Home Office on inception

[47] See generally **www.ccrc.gov.uk/case.htm**   [48] CCRC Annual Report 2003–04, p 14.

[49] See *R* v *Mills and Poole* (1978) 68 Cr App R 154; *R* v *Cooper and McMahon* [1969] 1 QB 267.

[50] *R* v *Cannings* [2004] 2 Cr App R 7, *R* v *Clark* [2000] EWCA Crim 54.

[51] CCCRC, Annual Report, p 18.

Although the Commission has the power to undertake inquiries, this is likely to be exceptional. Rather, the intention is that inquiries be carried out by the police under the supervision and instruction of the Commission, a position regarded as inevitable by the Royal Commission on Criminal Justice. The Review Commission has the power to require the original investigatory body to appoint an investigating officer to report back to the Commission,[52] or to appoint an investigator from another police force.[53]

The criteria

The Commission takes over the powers formerly exercised by the Home Secretary under section 17 of the 1968 Act. The powers to refer cases (which now include convictions on summary trial) are contained in section 13 of the 1995 Act. Firstly, there must be a real possibility that a conviction would not be upheld if a reference were made. Secondly, the reason for this must be that an argument or evidence was not raised at trial or on appeal. Finally, an appeal must have been heard or leave to appeal refused. The second and third criteria are not absolutes: the Commission can, despite them, refer a case in which exceptional circumstances exist.[54]

The judgment therefore required of the Commission is a difficult one, and it is its alone.[55] It involves a prediction of the view the Court of Appeal may take, which may in turn require the Commission to assess what attitude the court will take on a fresh evidence application.[56] The key words are therefore '*real possibility*', because it is at best a judgment. The Commission has to make this judgment even though the criteria applied by the court include a power to hear evidence when it is necessary or expedient in the interests of justice to do so.[57] One good example of the interrelationship between Commission and Court of Appeal is *R* v *Mills and Poole*.[58] In that case the Commission had decided not to refer a case following a libel case in which a detective whose testimony was crucial was disbelieved. The Commission did so because it considered that the facts, which had been thoroughly examined at trial and on appeal, had not changed. On judicial review of the Commission's refusal the Divisional Court accepted the propriety of the Commission's decision but nonetheless invited a reference. That was duly made, and the Court of Appeal did not regard the situation as unfair, but quashed the conviction for a previously undiscovered legal error.

Another problem for the Commission is how it should deal with cases in which there has been a change in the law or practice of the Court of Appeal. The Divisional Court in *R (on the application of the Director of Public Prosecutions)* v *Criminal Cases Review Commission*[59] suggested that the Commission should ignore any aspect of the

---

[52] Ibid, s 19.   [53] Ibid, s 2.

[54] Ibid, s 13(2). Perhaps a good example is the referral of the case of *Mills* (1978) 68 Cr App R 154.

[55] See *R* v *Criminal Cases Review Commission, ex parte Pierson* (1999).

[56] For the powers of the Court of Appeal, see p 700.

[57] See, generally, powers of the Court.

[58] See [1998] 1 Cr App R 43, [2001] EWCA Crim 753, [2004] 1 Cr App R 7.

[59] [2007] 1 Cr App R 30.

law or practice applied by the court. That view was rejected by the Court of Appeal,[60] which concluded that, except in exceptional circumstances, a conviction should not normally be referred to the Court of Appeal on the basis of a change in the law. Any other conclusion would lead to conflict with the approach of the Court of Appeal itself, and between the court and the Commission. The Criminal Justice and Immigration Act 2008 reinforces this approach, by permitting the Court of Appeal to disregard the development of the law since the date of conviction.[61] However, that still leaves the Commission with the difficult judgment, in an exceptional case, to determine whether to uphold a conviction would cause 'substantial injustice'.

If the Commission decides to make a reference, then the case returns to the Court of Appeal to be dealt with in the normal way. The appeal may not be on any ground other than one related to reasons given by the Commission for making the reference.[62] There are no legal obstacles to old cases being referred. Cases have been referred that go back many years,[63] although the utility of referring old cases has been criticized, both judicially and extrajudicially.

The court has the power itself to refer a case to the Commission for investigation and report.[64] Eleven such referrals have been made since the establishment of the Commission,[65] and the work of the Commission is likely to increase now that court referrals may be made at the stage of application of leave to appeal, rather than simply at the appeal itself.[66] For that reason, the changes made by the 1995 Act to the powers of the court are just as important as the creation of the Commission itself. If the Commission decides not to make a reference, it is required to state the reasons why it has so decided.[67]

Reference following acquittal[68]

The prosecution does not have any right to appeal against acquittal, unlike the position in cases of summary trial. However, the Criminal Justice Act 1972[69] gives to the prosecution a limited right to have points of law that arose during a trial resulting in an acquittal reconsidered by the Court of Appeal. The nature of the procedure is that of a reference of a point of law, rather than an appeal, for the outcome of the reference has no effect on the acquittal in the case.

---

[60] See [2008] Crim LR 50.   [61] 2008 Act, s 42.

[62] Criminal Appeal Act 1965, s 14(4A) inserted by Criminal Justice Act 2003, s 315. This followed a case where the appeal went far beyond the reference: see *R v Day* [2003] EWCA Crim 1060.

[63] See, e.g., *R v Mattan*, (1998) The Times, 5 March; *R v Hanratty* [2002] 2 Cr App R 30; *Ellis* [2003] EWCA Crim 3556; *Knighton* [2002] EWCA Crim 2227 (a seventy-five-year-old conviction).

[64] Ibid, s 15.   [65] CCRC Annual Report, 2003–04, p 46.

[66] See Criminal Justice Act 2003, s 315.

[67] Ibid, s 14(6). See, generally, *R v Secretary of State for the Home Department, ex parte Hickey (No 2)* [1995] 1 All ER 490, [1995] 1 WLR 734.

[68] See Ormerod, Waterman and Fortson 'Prosecution Appeals: Too Much of Good Thing?' [2010] Crim LR 169.

[69] 1972 Act, s 36(1).

The Act and the rules made hereunder go to great lengths to protect the acquitted person. Not only is his acquittal unaffected, but he may also appear to present argument in the Court of Appeal, is entitled to be represented by counsel, and have his costs paid out of central funds. His identity must not be disclosed during the proceedings in the Court of Appeal except by his consent.

The purpose of the power is to enable clarification of points of law that are important, and before wrong interpretations of law become entrenched at trial court level. The court may, of its own motion or on application, refer the point to the House of Lords.

Prosecution rights of appeal

Although defendants have many rights of appeal, the prosecutor has had only the extremely limited rights noted above. The position differed somewhat in the case of summary trial, in which there has always been the power to apply to the High Court by way of case stated,[70] a right exercisable both by defence and the prosecution. That lack of a general means whereby the prosecution could seek recourse to appeal courts to correct legal error has been the subject of increasing concern. The Law Commission in 2001 observed:[71]

> If a case falls on legal argument it is better for public confidence in the criminal justice system that it should be susceptible to the second opinion of a higher court, than it be unappealable.

The Auld Review likewise regarded the position as unsatisfactory.[72] It recommended that the prosecution should have three new rights: appeals from preparatory hearings against potentially terminating rulings; then a right to appeal against an acquittal resulting from a terminating ruling up to the end of the prosecution case; and a right of appeal against a finding of no case to answer. Those recommendations form for the basis of provisions in Part 9 of the Criminal Justice Act 2003. They apply to trials on indictment.

The general right of prosecution appeal in respect of rulings, subject to the leave of the trial judge or the Court of Appeal, are contained in section 58 of the 2003 Act. Section 58 does not use the expression 'terminating rulings', but it is such matters that section 58 is intended to address, although also a phrase best avoided. The Solicitor-General in debate, put the matter graphically by observing:[73]

> A terminating ruling is like an elephant. One can recognize it when it comes lumbering through the doors of the court. If it looks like a terminal ruling it is appealable.

---

[70] Magistrates' Courts Act 1980, s 111. This is not technically an appeal but a review on certain grounds.
[71] *Double Jeopardy and Prosecution Appeals* (Law Com No 267, 2001).
[72] Auld Review, ch 12, paras 47–65.
[73] HC Committee, 25 February 2003. For guidance, see *R v Clarke* [2007] EWCA Crim 2532; *R v Y* [2008] EWCA Crim 10.

The type of matters that are likely to 'lumber through the door' are matters that are so fatal to the prosecution case, and mean that it cannot, effectively, succeed. This might include: stays for abuse of process;[74] a successful argument of *autrefois acquit* or *autrefois convict*;[75] a successful submission of no case to answer;[76] an adverse public interest immunity ruling;[77] or a ruling that the facts alleged disclose no offence known to English law. The effect of this power may be that a trial has to adjourn whilst the appeal is dealt with, presumably as a matter of some urgency.

A second prosecution right of appeal is in respect of evidentiary rulings, defined by section 62(2) as such rulings that significantly weaken the prosecution case. These need not be rulings that effectively are 'terminating' and thus fall within section 58.

Finally, although not technically a right of appeal, we have already noted that in limited circumstances the prosecution may apply to the Court of Appeal for leave to permit the prosecution to proceed to a second prosecution of a defendant who has already been acquitted.[78] This is an exceptional course of action and runs counter to the general principle that an individual should not be tried again for an offence of which he has been acquitted.

Where a trial on indictment has ended in acquittal, the Attorney-General has the power to refer points of law arising from the case to the Court of Appeal.[79] However, the purpose of such a reference is simply to clarify the law for future cases, and the Court of Appeal's opinion on the matter does not affect the outcome for the defendant. Indeed, before the Criminal Justice Act 2003, a jury's decision to acquit a defendant was final and could not be challenged by the prosecution. However, the 2003 Act gives prosecutors new powers to appeal against the outcome of a trial on indictment. They can ask the Court of Appeal to quash an acquittal and order a retrial, where a person has been tried for a qualifying offence and certain conditions are met.[80] The first such application was made in the case of *R* v *D*.[81] While serving a prison sentence for an unrelated offence, the defendant had admitted to prison officers that he had committed a murder for which he had previously been tried and acquitted. An application to quash his acquittal was granted, and the defendant subsequently pleaded guilty to murder. Prosecutors can also appeal against a judge's decision to terminate a prosecution or to make an evidentiary ruling that significantly weakens their case.[82]

---

[74] See p 601.   [75] See p 662.
[76] In such a situation, the procedure to be adopted is dealt with by 2003 Act, s 58(7).
[77] See p 636.   [78] See p 698.
[79] Criminal Justice Act 1972, s 36; see p 697.
[80] 2003 Act, s 76(1): see p 252. 'Qualifying offences' are listed in Sch 5, para 1. For a more detailed analysis see Ward and Davies, *Criminal Justice Act 2003: A Practitioner's Guide* (Jordans, 2004).
[81] [2006] EWCA Crim 1354, [2007] 1 WLR 1657, [2007] 1 All ER 593. See further, p 654.
[82] Sections 58 and 62.

Powers of the court

Power to quash a conviction

The powers to quash a conviction are contained in section 2 of the 1968 Act. In its *original* form, section 2 set out three grounds. These were:

(a)   under all of the circumstances of the case the conviction[83] is unsafe and unsatisfactory;

(b)   there was a wrong decision on a point of law;

(c)   there was a material irregularity in the course of the trial.

In addition, section 2 contained a proviso. The Court of Appeal might, on an appeal against conviction, dismiss the appeal, even though of the opinion that the point raised might be decided in favour of the appellant, if it were considered that no miscarriage of justice has actually occurred. The test was whether a reasonable jury, after a proper summing-up, could have failed to convict the appellant:[84] in other words, the court was putting itself in the place of the jury. It was often applied where there had been misdirection on a matter of law.

The relationship between the proviso and the powers contained in section 2(1) of the 1968 Act discussed was complex.[85] For this reason it was argued that there was really only one test that the court should apply in deciding the use of section 2(1): has there been a miscarriage of justice?[86]

The majority of the Royal Commission took the view that:[87]

(1)   if a conviction was safe despite an error, then the appeal should be dismissed;

(2)   if an error was made that rendered the conviction unsafe, then the conviction should be quashed;

(3)   if an error may render a conviction unsafe, then the conviction should be quashed and a retrial ordered. This would render the proviso redundant.

The majority also took the view that this should be the case even where appeals are based upon pre-trial malpractice or procedural irregularity. It is not the purpose

---

[83]   'Conviction' was substituted for 'verdict of the jury' by the Criminal Law Act 1977, s 44. The previous wording appeared to preclude an appeal if the accused pleaded guilty, unless the count to which the accused pleaded guilty disclosed no offence known to the law or (perhaps) on the admitted facts he could not, in point of law, have been guilty of the offence; this, presumably erroneous, drafting in the 1968 Act went judicially unnoticed until *Director of Public Prosecutions* v *Shannon* [1975] AC 717; *sub nom R* v *Shannon* [1974] 2 All ER 1009, in which case Lord Salmon drew attention to the need for some amendment to s 2(1) of the 1968 Act.

[84]   *Stirland* v *Director of Public Prosecutions* [1944] AC 315, [1944] 2 All ER 13; see also (among many cases) *R* v *Haddy* [1944] KB 442, [1944] 1 All ER 319. For the proper attitude to application of the proviso in a murder case, see *Anderson* v *R* [1972] AC 100, [1971] 3 All ER 768.

[85]   See *R* v *Maguire* [1992] QB 936, [1992] 2 All ER 433.

[86]   See O'Connor [1990] Crim LR 615.   [87]   Report, ch 10, para 38.

of the appellate process to discipline the police or prosecution; the judge will have excluded tainted evidence anyway.

In 1995 the Criminal Appeal Act changed the law, by introducing a single test. The proviso was abolished. Under the new section 2, the test is this: the court must allow an appeal against conviction if it thinks that the conviction is 'unsafe'. This formulation should be compared with the recommendation of the Royal Commission that the single ground be 'the conviction is or may be unsafe'.[88] The difference in wording is of little consequence, in the light of the tests adopted by the court to the question as to whether a conviction is unsafe, and in the light of parliamentary intent.

The key issue is how the words in section 2 are interpreted and used by the Court of Appeal. The wording of the original section 2 ('unsafe or unsatisfactory') was considered by the House of Lords in *Stafford* v *Director of Public Prosecutions*,[89] in which Viscount Dilhorne cited with approval a passage from the judgment of the court in *R* v *Cooper*:[90]

> The court must in the end ask itself a subjective question, whether we are content to let the matter stand as it is, or whether there is not some lurking doubt in our minds which makes us wonder whether an injustice has been done. This is a reaction which may not be based strictly on the evidence as such; it is a reaction that can be produced by the general feeling of the case as the court experiences it to be.

The Royal Commission received conflicting evidence about the application of this 'lurking doubt' approach. Research indicated that, between 1968 and 1989, only six cases applied the test, and in 1989 one out of 114 appeals. Yet the more recent research for the period 1991–92 showed a greater use of this power (fourteen out of 102).[91] However, the language of lurking doubt was not always used by the court. For the court to conclude that a verdict was unsatisfactory because of an injustice in the case and in the verdict was no different from an application of the 'lurking doubt' test. Nevertheless, the court in *R* v *Maguire*[92] stressed that it is the words of the Act that have to be applied, not some other reformulation of the question. Despite the fact that the word 'or' was used, the weight of authority suggests that 'unsafe' and 'unsatisfactory' in fact were regarded as bearing the same meaning.[93] This was a view supported by the Royal Commission. On this basis, the change in wording in section 2 does not change or limit the scope of the role of the court.[94] Not only will the court be able to interfere where the verdict of the jury is unsatisfactory on the evidence, but also on the various other grounds relating to errors of law, misdirections, and the like that underpinned the majority of successful appeals. Errors in the summing-up, misdirection on matters of law, and a failure in appropriate cases to withdraw the case from the jury are all instances in which section 2(1)(a) operate and will continue to do so.

---

[88] Ibid, para 46.　　[89] 1974] AC 878, [1973] 3 All ER 762.

[90] [1969] 1 QB 267, at 271, [1969] 1 All ER 32, at 34, *per* Widgery LJ (as he then was).

[91] Report, ch 10, para 43.　　[92] *R* v *Maguire* [1992] QB 936, [1992] 2 All ER 433.

[93] See O'Connor[1990] Crim LR 615; cf. Smith, 'The Criminal Appeal Act 1995' [1995] Crim LR 920.

[94] See Smith [1995] Crim LR 920 at 924, as to parliamentary intent.

The unsafeness of the conviction may have arisen because of the way the case was conducted. In respect of appeals based upon error by lawyers, the test identified in *R v Ensor*[95] was whether injustice had been suffered as a result of flagrantly incompetent advocacy. This was, in the view of the Royal Commission,[96] too narrow:

> It cannot possibly be right that there should be defendants serving prison sentences for no other reason than that their lawyers made a decision which later turns out to have been mistaken. What matters is not the degree to which the lawyers were at fault, but whether the particular decision, whether reasonable or unreasonable, caused a miscarriage of justice.

A wide variety of errors, usually of a procedural nature, may cause a conviction to be unsafe. These might include unfair conduct or undue interruption by the judge, improper disclosure to the jury of the defendant's character, tampering with a juror, misconduct on the part of a juror, and failure to inform an undefended person of his right to call witnesses. In *R v Maguire*,[97] it was held that a failure to comply with the requirements concerning disclosure of unused material amounted to a 'material irregularity'. However, the central question should be: what is the impact on the safety of the conviction of the procedural error? Does it render the conviction 'unsafe'?[98] The balance of authority suggests that a conviction is not rendered unsafe simply because the court is dissatisfied at what went on at trial.[99] In *R v Mullen*,[100] a conviction obtained as a result of a trial that should not have taken place, because of illegality in bringing the appellant to the United Kingdom to face trial, was unsafe. A broad approach to the meaning of 'unsafe' should be adopted. This difference from the approach in *Chalkey* is supported by more recent cases. In *R v Randall*,[101] Lord Bingham said:

> it is not every departure from good practice which renders a trial unfair. But the right of a defendant to a fair trial is absolute. There will come a point when the departure from good practice is so gross, or so persistent, or so prejudicial, or so irremediable that an appellant court will have no choice but to condemn a trial as unfair and quash a conviction as unsafe, however strong the grounds for believing the defendant to be guilty.

This position is regarded as unsatisfactory by the government, concerned about 'guilty' persons being acquitted.[102] The government is introducing provisions into what will be the Criminal Justice and Immigration Act 2008, to reverse this approach, and to reinstate the approach adopted in *Chalkey*.

Another area of uncertainty that remains are cases in which a conviction for an offence, other than that for which the accused was tried, is upheld on appeal by virtue

---

[95] [1989] 2 All ER 586, [1989] 1 WLR 497.   [96] Report, para 59.

[97] [1992] QB 936, [1992] 2 All ER 433.   [98] *R v Renda* [2005] EWCA Crim 2827.

[99] *R v Chalkey* [1997] EWCA Crim 3416. See also *R v Rajcoomar* [1999] EWCA Crim 447; *R v Thomas* [1999] EWCA Crim 1266.

[100] [1999] EWCA Crim 278. See also *R v Smith* [1999] 2 Cr App R 238.

[101] [2002] 1 WLR 2237; see also *R v Abdroikov* [2005] EWCA 470; *R v O'Hare* [2006] EWCA Crim 471; *R v Russell* [2006] EWCA Crim 470.

[102] *Quashing Convictions: Report of a Review by the Lord Chancellor, the Home Secretary and the Attorney-General* (HMSO, 2007).

of the proviso. One such case was *R v Pickford*,[103] in which the accused had pleaded guilty to an offence that, in law, he could not have committed as charged. The Court of Appeal upheld the conviction, applying the proviso, on the grounds that although the appellant had not in law committed the offence charged (incitement of a boy to commit incest with the boy's mother), he had in fact incited the mother to commit the incest (which was in law an offence). It is unclear as to whether this type of case is no longer good law on the grounds that the proviso has been abolished, or whether such a conviction would be regarded as 'safe'. The fact that the court felt constrained to use the proviso provides clear evidence that such a conviction cannot be regarded as 'safe'.

It might also be noted that the conclusion that a conviction is 'unsafe' does not necessarily reflect on the trial process itself. In *R v B*,[104] a conviction for sexual assault was overturned even though the trial had been conducted perfectly properly, because it had taken thirty years for the complainant to make the allegation.

Power to substitute an alternative verdict

Where the defendant has been convicted of an offence and (1) the jury could on the same indictment have found him guilty of some other offence, and (2) it appears to the Court of Appeal that the jury must have been satisfied of the facts proving him guilty of that other offence, the court may, instead of allowing or dismissing the appeal against conviction, substitute a verdict of guilty of that other offence and pass sentence on the defendant for it.[105] The sentence must not be greater than that passed on the defendant at the trial, and must not, of course, exceed the maximum permitted by law for the substituted offence.[106] The court exercises this power with care, particularly in the light of (2) above, which involves some consideration of a verdict of a jury for which no reasons are given. Further, it is a material, although not decisive, point against exercising the power if the jury were not given any direction as to the alternative offence.[107] Where the indictment contains counts for two offences (such as theft and handling) that are in the circumstances alternative to each other, and the jury convict of one but acquit of the other, the court cannot substitute a verdict of guilty of the latter, even if that seems the correct verdict, since the jury expressly acquitted. The proper course, if there is a conviction on one, is for the jury to be discharged from giving a verdict on the other, whereupon the Court of Appeal may substitute a verdict of guilty.[108] This may also be important from the point of view of a retrial.

---

[103] [1995] 1 Cr App R 420. For other authorities in similar vein, see *R v Boal* [1992] QB 591; *R v Ayres* (1984) 78 Cr App R 232; *R v McHugh* (1976) 64 Cr App R 92.
[104] [2003] EWCA Crim 319.   [105] Criminal Appeal Act 1968, s 3(1).
[106] Ibid, s 3(2).
[107] See, generally, *R v Caslin* [1961] 1 All ER 246, [1961] 1 WLR 59. This case was decided under the corresponding provisions of the Criminal Appeal Act 1907, but appears still to be good law.
[108] *R v Melvin and Eden* [1953] 1 QB 481, [1953] 1 All ER 294.

Power to receive fresh evidence and to order a new trial

The power to receive fresh evidence was contained in the 1907 Act, and is now to be found in section 23 of the 1968 Act, as now amended by the Criminal Appeal Act 1995. This section contains both a duty and discretion. Originally worded in a restrictive way, which set too high a threshold,[109] section 23 was amended by the 1995 Act. Section 23(2) creates *a right* to admit fresh evidence (that is, evidence not adduced at the trial) if they think it necessary or expedient in the interests of justice. It imposes a *duty* to do so if:

(a) the evidence is likely to be credible, and would have been admissible at the trial; and

(b) there is a reasonable explanation for the evidence not being adduced at trial.

Thus the intent of the change is that the court now, when considering the exercise of the duty, has to consider whether such evidence is capable of being believed without having to take a view as to whether, on the facts, it is likely to be so. The court may decline to receive such evidence if it is satisfied that the evidence, if received, would not afford any ground for allowing the appeal.[110]

As noted, by section 23(1) the court has a discretion to admit the evidence of any witness or document if it thinks it necessary or expedient in the interests of justice to do so. It may be thought curious to have a discretion that in fact allows the court to by-pass the more detailed criteria in section 23(2). That, though, simply reflects the basic role of the Court of Appeal in the criminal justice system: namely, to ensure fairness and justice. It does, however, make the role of the Criminal Cases Review Commission more difficult in trying to predict how the Court of Appeal will deal with any particular case.[111] In this situation the evidence does not have to satisfy the criteria in section 23(2) of not being tendered at the trial. An example of the use of this discretion was seen in *R* v *Lattimore*,[112] in which some of the evidence was in fact given at the trial, and all of it was in fact available. It was allowed to be heard because it cast doubt upon the confession evidence upon which the prosecution case largely depended. The court will only exceptionally allow the discretion to be used as a means of different defences being put forward at the appellate stage. In *R* v *Ahluwalia*,[113] the court, exceptionally, allowed fresh medical evidence to be adduced to support a defence of diminished responsibility to the charge of murder of the appellant's husband, a defence that had not been raised at trial, an approach that did not reflect the balance of earlier authority[114] but which demonstrates the concern of the court to ensure that any conviction is in fact safe. Although the court warned against running defences on appeal

---

[109] And which required the evidence to be 'likely to be credible'.

[110] Criminal Appeal Act 1968, s 23(2).   [111] See 696.

[112] (1975) 62 Cr App R 53.   [113] [1992] 4 All ER 889.

[114] See *R* v *Dodd*, unreported, 1971; *R* v *Melville* [1976] 1 WLR 181; *R* v *Straw* [1995] 1 All ER 187 (decided in 1987, but not reported until 1995).

that had not been advanced at trial, the particular facts were such as to justify the course in fact taken.

Appeals on the grounds of fresh evidence used to be relatively rare, but are of increasing importance given the role of the Criminal Cases Review Commission, and the nature of the cases it handles.[115] The case law has continued to demonstrate the real problems the courts face in this area in deciding whether to admit the evidence, how to evaluate it, what judgments to make, whether to quash a conviction, and whether or not to order a retrial. The power to order a new trial was first introduced in 1964.[116] The court may order a new trial if it considers that the interests of justice so require.[117] This power to order retrial is not now confined to fresh evidence cases.[118] The power to order retrials is at the heart of the debate as to how cases in which fresh evidence comes to light should be dealt with. It was argued by Lord Devlin[119] that a conviction should always be quashed where fresh evidence has been received, since a conviction is bound to be unsafe or unsatisfactory if not based on all of the evidence. That, though, is not the approach of the courts. In *Stafford* v *Director of Public Prosecutions*,[120] the House of Lords considered that the verdict should be quashed if the court itself considers the verdict to be unsafe or unsatisfactory, thus requiring the court to take a view of the effect of the fresh evidence tendered. Viscount Dilhorne stated that:

> While…the Court of Appeal and this House may find it a convenient approach to consider what a jury might have done if they had heard the fresh evidence, the ultimate responsibility rests with them and them alone for dealing with the question…[121]

This approach was criticized as restricting the use of the retrial powers,[122] but was considered and affirmed in the definitive restatement of the law by the House of Lords in *R* v *Pendleton*.[123]

In *R* v *McIlkenny*,[124] the Court of Appeal had described its approach as follows:

> Nor is there any difficulty in fresh evidence cases, where the fresh evidence is discovered soon after the trial. If the evidence is incredible, or inadmissible, or would not afford a ground for allowing the appeal, we decline to receive it. If the fresh evidence surmounts that preliminary hurdle, we first quash the conviction, if we think it unsafe or unsatisfactory, and then order a retrial if the interests of justice so require. Where new evidence is conclusive, we quash the conviction without ordering a retrial. The difficulty becomes acute when there is no contest. For then we have to make up our minds whether the convictions are unsafe or unsatisfactory without having the benefit of having the evidence

---

[115] See p 695.   [116] Criminal Appeal Act 1964, s 1.

[117] Criminal Appeal Act 1968 ss 7–8.

[118] See 1968 Act, s 7, amended by Criminal Justice Act 1988.

[119] See RCCJ Report, ch 10, para 62.

[120] [1974] AC 898, [1973] 3 All ER 762.

[121] Applied in *R* v *Hakala* [2002] EWCA Crim 730; *R* v *Hanratty (decd)* [2002] 3 All ER 534; *R* v *Ishtiaq Ahmed* [2002] EWCA Crim 2781. Approved in *Dial and another* v *State of Trinidad & Tobago* [2005] UKPC 4, [2005] 1 WLR 1660. See also *R* v *Cannings* [2004] 2 Cr App R 7.

[122] See RCCJ, at para 66.   [123] [2002] 1 All ER 72.

[124] [1992] 2 All ER 417.

tested by cross-examination. Where a retrial is still possible, the quashing of the conviction is only the first half of a two stage process. Where a retrial is no longer possible, it is the end of the road.

Some ten years later the approach of the House of Lords in *Pendleton* was very much the same. If the court is sure of innocence, it should quash the conviction. If it is sure of guilt, it should uphold the conviction. In less clear-cut cases, it should ask itself the question: what might have been the effect of this evidence on the jury? The Court of Appeal should be aware that the primary decision-maker is the jury, and that it may have an incomplete understanding of the full process that led the jury to convict. The Court of Appeal can make its own assessment, but it would usually be wise to test that assessment against the question: if the evidence had been tendered at trial, might it reasonably be thought that the conclusion would have been affected?

What is clear is that the courts, now, take the view that its discretion cannot be fettered by inflexible mechanistic rules.[125] The court is also more likely to be generous in cases of expert medical evidence.[126]

Venire de novo

The appeal court has always had the power to order a *venire de novo* where proceedings in the court of trial were so defective as to amount to a nullity. To the defendant this no doubt seems very like ordering a new trial, but strictly the court is ordering not a new trial but a proper one. It has not, unfortunately, been established what degree of irregularity suffices to render proceedings a nullity; there are only particular examples in the cases of proceedings that have been held to be a nullity. This has been held to be so where the judge at the trial was not properly qualified,[127] where the defendant specifically asked for but was denied his right of peremptory challenges,[128] or where a plea of not guilty was misheard and dealt with as a plea of guilty.[129]

Hospital orders

The court has certain powers to consider whether a hospital order was rightly made, and in some circumstances can substitute a verdict of guilty for an offence that was charged at the trial, of which the defendant could have been convicted, for the special verdict of not guilty by reason of insanity or against a finding of unfitness to plead reached at the trial.[130]

---

[125] See *R v Mackerney and Pinfold* [2003] EWCA Crim 3643; *R v Gee*, (2006) The Times, 22 April.
[126] *R v O'Brian*, 2000, unreported.   [127] *R v Cronin* [1940] 1 All ER 618.
[128] But no such right now exists: see p 352.   [129] *R v Scothern* [1961] Crim LR 326.
[130] See p 658.

Appeals against sentence

On an appeal against sentence the court may reduce the sentence, or may vary it, by substituting one form of detention for another. The court will interfere with a sentence where it is 'wrong in principle', an approach that applies also to references made by the Attorney-General. Where the sentence is against conviction only there is no power to interfere with the sentence in any way; nor, except on an Attorney-General's reference, has the court the power to increase sentence—a power that once existed but was rarely used.

Procedure

Under section 9(d) and (e) of the Criminal Appeal Act 1907 the court had the power to appoint a special commissioner to conduct an inquiry into documents and to appoint assessors where their special expert knowledge was likely to be required for the determination of a case. These powers were little, if ever used, and not re-enacted by the 1968 Act. The Royal Commission considered that the Court of Appeal is not well constituted to supervise or direct police or other investigations. Nor should the same body exercise judicial and investigatory functions.[131]

As noted above, some appeals to the court may be brought without leave, but in most cases there must be an application to the court itself for leave. The time limit for giving notice of appeal, or application for leave to appeal, is twenty-eight days from the date of conviction or sentence. This time may be extended by the court. Such application is made in the first instance to a single judge of the court, who considers it in private. A single judge has most of the powers of a court of three judges (besides, of course, the power to grant leave); exceptionally he does not have any of the powers relating to fresh evidence. An application may of course be abandoned, and notice of abandonment cannot be withdrawn, although it may be treated as a nullity if the abandonment was not the result of a deliberate and informed decision in the sense that 'the mind of the appellant did not go with his act of abandonment'.[132] For example, where an application for leave to appeal was granted but, because of a postal strike, was not communicated to the applicant before he gave notice of abandonment, he was permitted to withdraw his notice.[133] If the single judge refuses leave to appeal (or to exercise any other of his powers), the applicant may be considered by a court of two judges. Both the single judge and the court may grant legal aid and bail. Bail, for obvious reasons, is very rarely granted; indeed almost the only cases in which it will be granted are those in which the defendant has obtained (or does not need) leave to appeal and has a very good chance of succeeding on appeal, or in which the defendant has been given a

---

[131] Report, ch 11, para 11. [132] *R v Medway* [1976] QB 799.
[133] *R v Noble* [1971] 3 All ER 361.

comparatively short sentence after a long and complex trial. In the latter case he might otherwise have served much of his sentence before the appeal was heard.

Appeal to the Supreme Court

A further appeal lies by either prosecution or defence from the Court of Appeal (Criminal Division) to the Supreme Court if:

(1) the Court of Appeal certifies that a point of law of general public importance is involved in the decision; and

(2) either the Court of Appeal or the Supreme Court gives leave to appeal on the ground that the point is one that ought to be considered by the Supreme Court.

The certificate was considered a necessary condition, to avoid the House of Lords (as it then was) being inundated with hopeless applications. This justification was not accepted by the Royal Commission, which recommended its abolition.[134] If the Court of Appeal is satisfied that there is a point of law of general public importance involved, it will give the certificate, as it were, automatically. There will always, nevertheless, be an element of discretion as to whether an appeal is allowed to proceed, since even if the point were of general public importance, it might still not be worthy of consideration by the Supreme Court in the particular case: for example, it might already be the subject of clear and satisfactory decisions of lower courts. This element of discretion is preserved by the requirement that there can be no further proceedings. On the other hand, the Court of Appeal may give a certificate and yet refuse leave, in which case a petition may be made to the Supreme Court for leave to appeal, the petition being heard by the Appeals Committee of the Supreme Court.

It is proper and convenient that the certificate should state what the point of law of general public importance is;[135] however, it seems likely that other points may be raised by either side once the case is before the Supreme Court on the point certified.[136] But the grant of a certificate on some point affecting the validity of the conviction does not enable the appellant to argue that the sentence is invalid. The Supreme Court may exercise similar powers to those of the court below.

The procedure described above does not apply following the hearing of an Attorney-General's reference after acquittal. In these cases the Court of Appeal may, of its own motion or in pursuance of an application, refer the point of law in the case to the Supreme Court 'if they appear to the court that the point ought to be considered by that [Supreme Court]' and there is, accordingly, no need for a certificate that a point of law of general public importance is involved. Indeed the point of law need not be

---

[134] Report, ch 10, para 79.
[135] *Jones v Director of Public Prosecutions* [1962] AC 635, [1962] 1 All ER 569.
[136] *A-G for Northern Ireland v Gallagher* [1963] AC 349, [1961] 3 All ER 299.

a point of general public importance, although no doubt the Court of Appeal would only refer such a point to the Supreme Court as a matter of practice.

Further reading

ASHWORTH and REDMAYNE, *The Criminal Process* (Oxford University Press: 4th edn, 2010)

AULD, *Review of the Criminal Courts of England & Wales* (**www.criminal-courts-review. org.uk**) (the 'Auld Review')

JUSTICE, *Report on Miscarriages of Justice* (Justice, 1989)

SPENCER, 'Does the Present Criminal Appeal System Make Sense?' [2006] Crim LR 677

Index